D1526713

THE
LITURGY OF THE HOURS

THE DIVINE OFFICE

revised by decree of the Second Vatican Ecumenical
Council and published by authority of Pope Paul VI

THE

LITURGY OF THE HOURS

According to the Roman Rite

Approved by the Episcopal Conferences
of The Antilles, Bangladesh, Burma, Canada,
of the Pacific CEPAC (Fiji Islands, Rarotonga,
Samoa and Tokelau, Tonga), Ghana, India, New Zealand,
Pakistan, Papua New Guinea and The Solomons,
The Philippines, Rhodesia, South Africa, Sri Lanka,
Tanzania, Uganda, and the United States of America
for use in their dioceses
and Confirmed by the Apostolic See

I

ADVENT SEASON

•

CHRISTMAS SEASON

English Translation Prepared by the
International Commission on English in the Liturgy

CATHOLIC BOOK PUBLISHING CO.
NEW YORK
1975

Concordat Cum Originali:

✠James P. Mahoney, D.D.
Vicar General, Archdiocese of New York

English translation of the Liturgy of the Hours:
General Instruction, Antiphons, Invitatories, Responsories, Intercessions, Psalm 95, the Canticle
of the Lamb, Psalm Prayers, Non-Biblical Readings, and Hagiographical Introductions; original
texts of the Opening Prayers and Alternative
Opening Prayers from the Roman Missal, and
the Roman Calendar.

For hymns and poetry see acknowledgments on
page 1714.

(T-401)

CONTENTS

SACRED CONGREGATION
FOR DIVINE WORSHIP

Prot. no. 1000/71

DECREE

From ancient times the Church has had the custom of celebrating each day the liturgy of the hours. In this way the Church fulfills the Lord's precept to pray without ceasing, at once offering its praise to God the Father and interceding for the salvation of the world.

The Second Vatican Council showed the importance of the traditional discipline of the Church and desired to renew that discipline. It was, therefore, very concerned to bring about a suitable restoration of this liturgy of prayer so that priests and other members of the Church in today's circumstances might celebrate it better and more effectively (see Constitution on the Sacred Liturgy, *Sacrosanctum Concilium*, number 84).

Now that this work of restoration has been approved by Pope Paul VI in the apostolic constitution *Laudis canticum* of November 1, 1970, this Sacred Congregation for Divine Worship has published the Latin book for the celebration of the liturgy of the hours in accordance with the Roman Rite, and it declares that the present edition is the typical edition.

Anything to the contrary notwithstanding.

From the Office of the Sacred Congregation for Divine Worship, Easter Sunday, April 11, 1971.

Arturo Cardinal Tabera

Prefect

Annibale Bugnini

Secretary

APOSTOLIC CONSTITUTION
PROMULGATION

THE DIVINE OFFICE
REVISED BY DECREE OF THE
SECOND VATICAN ECUMENICAL COUNCIL

PAUL, BISHOP
SERVANT OF THE SERVANTS OF GOD
FOR AN EVERLASTING MEMORIAL

The hymn of praise that is sung through all the ages in the heavenly places and was brought by the high priest, Christ Jesus, into this land of exile has been continued by the Church with constant fidelity over many centuries, in a rich variety of forms.

The Liturgy of the Hours gradually developed into the prayer of the local church, a prayer offered at regular intervals and in appointed places under the presidency of a priest. It was seen as a kind of necessary complement to the fullness of divine worship that is contained in the eucharistic sacrifice, by means of which that worship might overflow to reach all the hours of daily life.

The book of the Divine Office, gradually enlarged by many additions in the course of time, became a suitable instrument for the sacred action for which it was designed. However, over the generations quite a number of changes were introduced in the form of celebration, including the practice of individual recitation. It is not strange, therefore, that the Breviary, as it was sometimes called, underwent many transformations, sometimes affecting the principles of its arrangements.

The Council of Trent, unable, because of shortness of time, to complete the reform of the Breviary, left this matter to the Apostolic See. The Roman Breviary, promulgated by our predecessor Saint Pius V in 1568, achieved above all what was earnestly requested, the introduction of uniformity in the canonical prayer of the Latin Church, after this uniformity had lapsed.

In subsequent centuries many revisions were made by Sixtus V, Clement VIII, Urban VIII, Clement XI, and other popes.

Saint Pius X promulgated a new Breviary, prepared at his command. The ancient custom was restored of reciting the 150 psalms each week, and the arrangement of the psalter was entirely revised, to remove all repetitions, and to harmonize the weekday psalter and the cycle of biblical readings with the office of the saints. In addition, the office of Sunday was raised in rank and dignity, to take general precedence over feasts of saints.

The whole work of liturgical revision was undertaken again by Pius XII. For both private and public recitation of the office he permitted the use of the new translation of the psalter prepared by the Pontifical Biblical Institute, and established in 1947 a special commission with the responsibility of studying the question of the breviary. In 1955 all the bishops throughout the world were questioned about this matter. The fruits of this process of consultation were first seen in the decree on the simplification of the rubrics, published March 23, 1955, and in the regulations for the breviary which were issued by John XXIII in the Codex of Rubrics of 1960.

Though he sanctioned only part of the liturgical revision, Pope John XXIII was aware that the fundamental principles on which the liturgy rests required further study. He entrusted this task to the Second Vatican Ecumenical Council, which in the meantime he had summoned. The result was that the Council treated the liturgy as a whole, and the Hours in particular, with such thoroughness and skill, such spirituality and power, that there is scarcely a parallel to it in the entire history of the Church.

While the Vatican Council was still in session, it was our concern that after the promulgation of the constitution on the Sacred Liturgy, its decrees should be put immediately into effect. For this purpose we established a special commission within the Consilium for the Implementation of the Constitution on the Liturgy. With the help of scholars and specialists in the liturgical, theological, spiritual, and pastoral disciplines, the Consilium worked with the greatest zeal and diligence over a period of seven years to produce the new Liturgy of the Hours.

The principles underlying it, its whole arrangement as well as its individual parts, were approved by the Consilium and also by the Synod of Bishops of 1967, after consultation with the bishops of the whole Church and a very large number of pastors, religious and laity.

It will be helpful to set out the principles embodied in the new Liturgy of the Hours, together with its detailed structure.

1. As required by the constitution *Sacrosanctum Concilium*, account was taken of the circumstances in which priests engaged in apostolic works find themselves today.

The Office has been drawn up and arranged in such a way that not only clergy but also religious and indeed laity may participate in it, since it is the prayer of the whole people of God. People of different callings and circumstances, with their individual needs, were kept in mind, and a variety of ways of celebrating the office has been provided, by means of which the prayer can be adapted to suit the way of life and vocation of different groups using the Liturgy of the Hours.

2. Since the Liturgy of the Hours is the means of sanctifying the day, the order of this prayer was revised so that the canonical hours could be more easily related to the chronological hours of the day in the circumstances of contemporary life.

For this reason the hour of Prime was suppressed; Morning Prayer and Evening Prayer, as hinges of the entire office, were assigned the most important role and now have the character of true morning and evening prayer; the Office of Readings retains its character as a night office for those who celebrate it during the night, but is suitable for any hour of the day; the Daytime Prayer, Midmorning, Midday, or Midafternoon, is so arranged that those who choose to say only one Hour may say the one most suitable to the actual time of day, without losing any part of the four-week psalter.

3. To ensure that in celebrating the Office mind and voice may be more easily united, and the Liturgy of the Hours become in reality "a source of devotion and nourishment for personal prayer,"[1] in the new book of Hours, the quantity of daily prayer has been considerably reduced, variety in the texts has been notably increased, various aids to meditation on the psalms are provided, for example, titles, antiphons, psalm-prayers, while optional periods of silence are suggested.

[1] Second Vatican Council, constitution *Sacrosanctum Concilium,* no. 90: *AAS* 56 (1964) 122.

4. In accordance with the ruling by the Council,[2] the weekly cycle of the Psalter has been replaced by an arrangement of the psalms over a period of four weeks, in the new version prepared by the Commission for the New Edition of the Vulgate Bible which we ourselves established. In this new arrangement of the psalms some few of the psalms and verses which are somewhat harsh in tone have been omitted, especially because of the difficulties that were foreseen from their use in vernacular celebration. In addition, some new canticles from the Old Testament have been added to Morning Prayer to increase its spiritual richness, and canticles from the New Testament now increase the beauty of Evening Prayer.

5. In the new cycle of readings from holy Scripture there is a more ample selection from the treasury of God's word, intended to harmonize with the cycle of readings at Mass.

The passages provide in general a certain unity of theme and have been chosen to present, in the course of the year, the principal stages of history of salvation.

6. In accordance with the norms laid down by the Ecumenical Council, the daily reading from the works of the Fathers and Church writers has been revised in such a way that the best of the writings of Christian authors, especially of the Fathers, is included. Besides this, an optional lectionary will be prepared with a fuller selection of the spiritual riches of these writers, from which more abundant fruits may be achieved.

7. Anything that is not in harmony with historical truth has been removed from the text of the Liturgy of the Hours. Moreover, the readings, especially those in

[2]*Ibid.*, no. 91:122–123.

honor of the saints, have been revised in such a way that, first and foremost, the spiritual image of the saint and his significance for the life of the Church emerge and are placed in their true context.

8. Intercessions (*preces*) have been added to Morning Prayer to proclaim the consecration of the day and to offer prayer for the day's work about to begin. There is also a short act of supplication at Evening Prayer, drawn up in the form of general intercessions.

The Lord's Prayer has been restored to its position at the end of these prayers. Since the Lord's Prayer is also said at Mass, this change represents a return in our time to early Christian usage, namely, of saying this prayer three times in the day.

Now that the prayer of Holy Church has been renewed and entirely revised in accordance with its very ancient tradition and in the light of the needs of our day, it is supremely to be hoped that the Liturgy of the Hours may pervade and penetrate the whole of Christian prayer, giving it life, direction and expression and effectively nourishing the spiritual life of the people of God.

We have, therefore, every confidence that an appreciation of that "unceasing" prayer[3] which our Lord Jesus Christ entrusted to his Church will take on new life, since the Liturgy of the Hours, distributed as it is over suitable intervals of time, continually strengthens and supports that prayer. The very celebration of the Liturgy of the Hours, especially when a community is assembled for this purpose, expresses the genuine nature of the praying Church and is seen as a wonderful sign of that Church.

[3]See Luke 18:1; 21:36; 1 Thessalonians 5:17; Ephesians 6:18.

Christian prayer is above all the prayer of the whole human community, which Christ joins to himself.[4] Everyone shares in this prayer, which is proper to the one body as it offers prayers that give expression to the voice of the beloved spouse of Christ, to the hopes and desires of the whole Christian people, to supplications and petitions for the needs of all mankind.

This prayer takes its unity from the heart of Christ, for our Redeemer desired "that the life he had entered upon in his mortal body with supplications and with his sacrifice should continue without interruption through the ages in his mystical body, which is the Church."[5] Because of this, the prayer of the Church is at the same time "the prayer of Christ and his body to the Father."[6] We must recognize, therefore, as we celebrate the Office, our own voices echoing in Christ, his voice echoing in ours.[7]

To manifest this quality of our prayer more clearly, "the warm and living love for holy Scripture"[8] which is the atmosphere of the Liturgy of the Hours must come to life in all of us, so that Scripture may indeed become the chief source of all Christian prayer. In particular, the praying of the psalms, which continually ponders and proclaims the action of God in the history of salvation, must be embraced with new warmth by the people of God. This will be achieved more easily if a deeper understanding of the psalms, in the meaning in which they are used in the liturgy, is more diligently promoted among the clergy and communicated to all the faithful by means

[4] See *Sacrosanctum Concilium,* no. 83: *AAS* 56 (1964) 121.
[5] See Pius XII, encyclical letter *Mediator Dei,* November 20, 1942, no. 2: *AAS* 39 (1947) 522.
[6] *Sacrosanctum Concilium,* no. 85: *AAS* 56 (1964) 121.
[7] See Saint Augustine, *Enarrationes in psalmis* 85, no. 1.
[8] *Sacrosanctum Concilium,* no. 24: *AAS* 56 (1964) 106–107.

of appropriate catechesis. The wider range of Scripture readings provided, not only in the Mass but also in the new Liturgy of the Hours, will enable the history of salvation to be constantly recalled and its continuation in the life of mankind effectively proclaimed

Because the life of Christ in his mystical body also perfects and elevates for each member of the faithful his own personal life, any conflict between the prayer of the Church and personal prayer must be entirely rejected, and the relationship between them strengthened and enlarged. Mental prayer should draw unlimited nourishment from readings, psalms, and the other parts of the Liturgy of the Hours. The recitation of the Office should be adapted, as far as possible, to the needs of living and personal prayer, so that as the General Instruction provides, rhythms and melodies are used, and forms of celebration chosen, that are more suited to the spiritual needs of those who pray it. If the prayer of the Divine Office becomes genuine personal prayer, the relation between the liturgy and the whole Christian life also becomes clearer. The whole life of the faithful, hour by hour during day and night, is a kind of *leitourgia* or public service, in which the faithful give themselves over to the ministry of love toward God and men, identifying themselves with the action of Christ, who by his life and self-offering sanctified the life of all mankind.

The Liturgy of the Hours clearly expresses and effectively strengthens this most profound truth, embodied in the Christian life.

For this reason the Hours are recommended to all Christ's faithful members, including those who are not bound by law to their recitation.

Those who have received from the Church a mandate to celebrate the Liturgy of the Hours are to complete its entire course dutifully each day, keeping as far as possible to the appropriate time of the day; first and foremost, they are to give due importance to Morning and Evening Prayer.

Those who are in holy orders, and are marked in a special way with the sign of Christ the Priest, as well as those consecrated in a particular way to the service of God and of the Church by the vows of religious profession, should not only be moved to celebrate the Hours through obedience to law, but should also feel themselves drawn to them because of their intrinsic excellence and their pastoral and ascetical value. It is extremely desirable that the public prayer of the Church should be offered by all from hearts renewed, in acknowledgment of the intimate relationship within the whole body of the Church, which, like its head, cannot be described except in terms of a Church that prays.

May the praise of God reecho in the Church of our day with greater grandeur and beauty by means of the new Liturgy of the Hours, which now by Apostolic authority we sanction, approve, and promulgate. May it join the praise sung by saints and angels in the court of heaven. May it go from strength to strength in the days of this earthly exile and soon attain that fullness of praise which will be given throughout eternity "to the One who sits upon the throne, and to the Lamb."[9]

We decree that this new Liturgy of the Hours may be brought into use as soon as it is published. Meanwhile, the episcopal conferences should see to the preparation of editions of this liturgical work in the vernacular and,

[9]See Revelation 5:13.

after approval and confirmation by the Apostolic See, should fix the date when vernacular versions may or must be used, either in whole or in part. Beginning on the day when these vernacular versions are to be used for vernacular celebrations, only the revised form of the Liturgy of the Hours is to be followed by those who continue to use Latin.

It is lawful, however, for those who because of advanced age or for special reasons experience serious difficulties in observing the new rite, to continue to use the former Roman Breviary, in whole or in part, with the consent of their Ordinary, and exclusively in individual recitation.

We wish that these decrees and prescriptions be firm and effective now and in the future, notwithstanding, to the extent necessary, Apostolic Constitutions and Ordinances issued by our predecessors, and other prescriptions, even those deserving particular mention and derogation.

Given at Rome, at Saint Peter's, on the feast of All Saints, November 1, 1970, the eighth year of our pontificate.

PAUL VI, POPE

GENERAL INSTRUCTION
OF THE
LITURGY OF THE HOURS

CHAPTER I

THE IMPORTANCE OF THE LITURGY OF THE HOURS OR THE DIVINE OFFICE IN THE LIFE OF THE CHURCH

1. Public and common prayer by the people of God is rightly considered to be among the primary duties of the Church. From the very beginning those who were baptized "devoted themselves to the teaching of the apostles and to the community, to the breaking of the bread and to the prayers" (Acts 2:42). The Acts of the Apostles give frequent testimony to the fact that the Christian community prayed with one accord.[1]

The witness of the early Church teaches us that individual Christians devoted themselves to prayer at fixed times. Then, in different places, the custom soon grew of assigning special times to common prayer, for example, the last hour of the day, when evening draws on and the lamp is lighted, or the first hour, when night draws to a close with the rising of the daystar.

In the course of time other hours came to be sanctified by common prayer. These were seen by the Fathers as foreshadowed in the Acts of the Apostles. There we read of the disciples gathered together at the third hour.[2] The prince of the apostles "went up on the housetop to pray, about the sixth hour" (10:9); "Peter and John were going up to the temple at the hour of prayer, the ninth hour" (3:1); "about midnight Paul and Silas were praying and singing hymns to God" (16:25).

[1] See Acts 1:14; 4:24; 12:5, 12; see Ephesians 5:19-21.
[2] See Acts 2:1-15.

2.   This kind of common prayer gradually took shape in the form of an ordered round of Hours. This Liturgy of the Hours or Divine Office, enriched by readings, is principally a prayer of praise and petition. In fact, it is the prayer of the Church with Christ and to Christ.

I.   THE PRAYER OF CHRIST

Christ the Intercessor with the Father

3.   When he came to give men and women a share in God's life, the Word proceeding from the Father as the splendor of his glory, "Christ Jesus, the high priest of the new and eternal Covenant, took our human nature and introduced into the world of our exile that hymn of praise which is sung in the heavenly places throughout all ages."[3] From then on the praise of God wells up from the heart of Christ in human words of adoration, propitiation and intercession, presented to the Father by the head of the new humanity, the mediator between God and mankind, in the name of all and for the good of all.

4.   In his goodness the Son of God, who is one with his Father (see John 10:30), and who said on entering the world: "Here I am! I come, God, to do your will" (Hebrews 10:9; see John 6:38), has left us testimony to his own prayer. The gospels very frequently show us Christ at prayer: when his mission is revealed by the Father,[4] before he calls the apostles,[5] when he blesses God at the multiplication of the loaves,[6] when he is transfigured on the mountain,[7] when he heals the deaf mute,[8] when he raises Lazarus,[9] before he asks for Peter's confession of

---

[3]Second Vatican Council, constitution *Sacrosanctum Concilium*, no. 83.

[4]Luke 3:21-22.

[5]Luke 6:12.

[6]Matthew 14:19; 15:36; Mark 6:41; 8:7; Luke 9:16; John 6:11.

[7]Luke 9:28-29.

[8]Mark 7:34.   [9]John 11:41ff.

faith,[10] when he teaches the disciples how to pray,[11] when the disciples return from their mission,[12] when he blesses the little children,[13] when he prays for Peter.[14]

The work of each day was closely bound up with his prayer, indeed flowed out from it. He would retire into the desert or into the hills to pray,[15] rising very early[16] or spending the night as far as the fourth watch[17] in prayer to God.[18]

We are right in believing that he took part in public prayers, in the synagogues, which he entered on the Sabbath "as his custom was,"[19] and in the temple, which he called a house of prayer,[20] as well as in the private prayers which devout Israelites would recite regularly every day. He used the traditional blessings of God at meals. This is expressly mentioned in connection with the multiplication of the loaves,[21] the Last Supper,[22] the meal at Emmaus;[23] he also joined with the disciples in a hymn of praise.[24]

To the very end of his life, as his Passion was approaching,[25] at the Last Supper,[26] in the agony in the

[10]Luke 9:18.
[11]Luke 11:1.
[12]Matthew 11:25ff; Luke 10:21ff.
[13]Matthew 19:13.
[14]Luke 22:32.
[15]Mark 1:35; 6:46; Luke 5:16; see Matthew 4:1 and parallels; Matthew 14:23.
[16]Mark 1:35.
[17]Matthew 14:23, 25; Mark 6:46, 48.
[18]Luke 6:12.
[19]Luke 4:16.
[20]Matthew 21:13 and parallels.
[21]Matthew 14:19 and parallels; Matthew 15:36 and parallels.
[22]Matthew 26:26 and parallels.
[23]Luke 24:30.
[24]Matthew 26:30 and parallels.
[25]John 12:27ff.
[26]John 17:1-26.

garden,[27] and on the cross,[28] the divine teacher showed that prayer was the soul of his messianic ministry and paschal death. "In the days of his life on earth he offered up prayers and entreaties with loud cries and tears to the one who could deliver him out of death, and because of his reverent attitude his prayer was heard" (Hebrews 5: 7). By a single offering on the altar of the cross, "he has made perfect for ever those who are being sanctified" (Hebrews 10:14). Raised from the dead, he is alive for ever and makes intercession for us.[29]

II. THE PRAYER OF THE CHURCH

The Commandment To Pray

5. Jesus has commanded us to do as he did. On many occasions he said: "Pray," "ask," "seek,"[30] "in my name."[31] He gave us a formula of prayer in what is known as the Lord's Prayer.[32] He taught us that prayer is necessary,[33] that it should be humble,[34] vigilant,[35] persevering, confident in the Father's goodness,[36] single-minded and in conformity with God's nature.[37]

The apostles have handed on to us, scattered throughout their letters, many prayers, especially of praise and thanksgiving. They warn us that we must be urgent and

[27]Matthew 26:36-44 and parallels.
[28]Luke 23:34, 46; Matthew 27:46; Mark 15:34.
[29]See Hebrews 7:25.
[30]Matthew 5:44; 7:7; 26:41; Mark 13:33; 14:38; Luke 6:28; 10:2; 11:9; 22:40, 46.
[31]John 14:13ff; 15:16; 16:23ff, 26.
[32]Matthew 6:9-13; Luke 11:2-4.
[33]Luke 18:1.
[34]Luke 18:9-14.
[35]Luke 21:36; Mark 13:33.
[36]Luke 11:5-13; 18:1-8; John 14:13; 16:23.
[37]Matthew 6:5-8; 23:14; Luke 20:47; John 4:23.

persevering[41] in prayer offered to God[40] in the Holy Spirit[38] through Christ.[39] They tell us of its sure power in sanctifying[42] and speak of the prayer of praise,[43] of thanksgiving,[44] of petition[45] and of intercession on behalf of all.[46]

Christ's Prayer Continued by the Church

6. Since man depends wholly on God, he must recognize and express this sovereignty of the Creator, as the devout people of every age have done by means of prayer.

Prayer directed to God must be linked with Christ, the Lord of all, the one mediator[47] through whom alone we have access to God.[48] He unites to himself the whole community of mankind[49] in such a way that there is an intimate bond between the prayer of Christ and the prayer of the whole human race. In Christ and in Christ alone the religious activity of mankind receives its redemptive value and attains its goal.

7. There is a special, and very close, bond between Christ and those whom he makes members of his body, the Church, through the sacrament of rebirth. Thus, from the head all the riches that belong to the Son flow

[38]Romans 8:15, 26; 1 Corinthians 12:3; Galatians 4:6; Jude 20.
[39]2 Corinthians 1:20; Colossians 3:17.
[40]Hebrews 13:15.
[41]Romans 12:12; 1 Corinthians 7:5; Ephesians 6:18; Colossians 4:2; 1 Thessalonians 5:17; 1 Timothy 5:5; 1 Peter 4:7.
[42]1 Timothy 4:5; James 5:15ff; 1 John 3:22; 5:14ff.
[43]Ephesians 5:19ff; Hebrews 13:15; Revelation 19:5.
[44]Colossians 3:17; Philippians 4:6; 1 Thessalonians 5:17; 1 Timothy 2:1.
[45]Romans 8:26; Philippians 4:6.
[46]Romans 15:30; 1 Timothy 2:1ff; Ephesians 6:18; 1 Thessalonians 5:25; James 5:14, 16.
[47]1 Timothy 2:5; Hebrews 8:6; 9:15; 12:24.
[48]Romans 5:2; Ephesians 2:18; 3:12.
[49]See Second Vatican Council, constitution *Sacrosanctum Concilium*, no. 83.

throughout the whole body: the fellowship of the Spirit, the truth, the life and the sharing of his divine sonship, manifested in all his prayer when he dwelt among us.

The priesthood of Christ is also shared by the whole body of the Church, so that the baptized are consecrated as a spiritual temple and holy priesthood through the rebirth of baptism and the anointing by the Holy Spirit,[50] and become able to offer the worship of the New Covenant, a worship that derives, not from our own powers but from the merit and gift of Christ.

"God could give no greater gift to mankind than to give them as their head the Word through whom he created all things, and to unite them to him as his members, so that he might be Son of God and Son of man, one God with the Father, one man with men. So, when we speak to God in prayer we do not separate the Son from God, and when the body of the Son prays it does not separate its head from itself, but it is the one savior of his body, our Lord Jesus Christ, the Son of God, who himself prays for us, and prays in us, and is the object of our prayer. He prays for us as our priest, he prays in us as our head, he is the object of our prayer as our God. Let us then hear our voices in his voice, and his voice in ours."[51]

The excellence of Christian prayer lies in this, that it shares in the very love of the only-begotten Son for the Father and in that prayer which the Son put into words in his earthly life and which still continues unceasingly in the name of the whole human race and for its salvation, throughout the universal Church and in all its members.

---

[50]Second Vatican Council, dogmatic constitution *Lumen gentium*, no. 10.
[51]Saint Augustine, Discourse on psalm 85, 1: *CCL* 39, 1176.

The Action of the Holy Spirit

8. The unity of the Church at prayer is brought about by the Holy Spirit, who is the same in Christ,[52] in the whole Church, and in every baptized person. It is this Spirit who "helps us in our weakness" and "intercedes for us with longings too deep for words" (Romans 8: 26). As the Spirit of the Son, he gives us "the spirit of adopted sonship, by which we cry out: Abba, Father" (Romans 8:15; see Galatians 4:6; 1 Corinthians 12:3; Ephesians 5:18; Jude 20). There can be no Christian prayer without the action of the Holy Spirit who unites the whole Church and leads it through the Son to the Father.

Prayer as Community Prayer

9. It follows that the example and precept of our Lord and the apostles in regard to constant and persevering prayer are not to be seen as a purely legal regulation. They belong to the very essence of the Church itself. The Church is a community, and it must express its nature as a community in its prayer as well as in other ways. Hence, when the community of the faithful is first mentioned in the Acts of the Apostles, it is seen as a community gathered together at prayer "with the women and Mary, the Mother of Jesus, and his brothers" (Acts 1:14). "There was one heart and soul in the company of those who believed" (Acts 4:32). Their oneness in spirit was founded on the word of God, on the brotherly communion, on the prayer and on the Eucharist.[53]

Though prayer in one's room behind closed doors[54] is always necessary and to be encouraged[55] and is perform-

---

[52]See Luke 10:21.   [53]See Acts 2:42 (Greek).
[54]See Matthew 6:6.
[55]See Second Vatican Council, constitution *Sacrosanctum Concilium*, no. 12.

ed by the members of the Church through Christ in the Holy Spirit, yet there is a special excellence in the prayer of the community. Christ himself has said: "Where two or three are gathered together in my name, I am there in their midst" (Matthew 18:20).

III. THE LITURGY OF THE HOURS

The Consecration of Time

10. Christ has taught us the necessity of praying at all times without losing heart (Luke 18:1). The Church has been faithful in obeying this instruction; it never ceases to offer prayer, and makes this exhortation its own: "Through him (Jesus) let us offer to God an unceasing sacrifice of praise" (Hebrews 15:15). The Church satisfies this requirement not only by the celebration of the Eucharist but in other ways also, especially through the Liturgy of the Hours, which is distinguished from other liturgical actions by the fact that it consecrates to God the whole cycle of day and night, as it has done from early Christian times.[56]

11. Since the purpose of the Liturgy of the Hours includes the sanctification of the day and of the whole range of human activity, its structure has been revised in such a way that, as far as possible, each Hour might be celebrated once more at the proper time and account taken of the circumstances of life today.[57]

Hence, "in order that the day may be truly sanctified and the Hours themselves recited with spiritual profit, it is preferable that they should be recited at the hour nearest to the one indicated by each canonical Hour."[58]

[56]See *ibid.*, no. 83-84.
[57]See *ibid.*, no. 88.
[58]*Ibid.*, no. 94.

The Liturgy of the Hours and the Eucharist

12. The Liturgy of the Hours extends[59] to the different hours of the day the praise and thanksgiving, the commemoration of the mysteries of salvation, the petitions and the foretaste of heavenly glory, that are present in the eucharistic mystery, "the center and apex of the whole life of the Christian community."[60]

The Liturgy of the Hours is an excellent preparation for the celebration of the Eucharist itself, for it inspires and deepens in a fitting way the dispositions necessary for the fruitful celebration of the Eucharist: faith, hope, love, devotion and the spirit of self-denial.

The Priesthood of Christ in the Liturgy of the Hours

13. In the Holy Spirit Christ carries out through the Church "the work of man's redemption and God's perfect glorification,"[61] not only when the Eucharist is celebrated and the sacraments administered but also in other ways, and especially when the Liturgy of the Hours is celebrated.[62] In it Christ himself is present, in the assembled community, in the proclamation of God's word, "in the prayer and song of the Church."[63]

Man's Sanctification

14. Man's sanctification is accomplished,[64] and worship offered to God, in the Liturgy of the Hours in an exchange or dialogue between God and man in which "God speaks to his people . . . and his people reply to him in song and prayer."[65]

---

[59]See Second Vatican Council, decree *Presbyterorum ordinis*, no. 5.
[60]Second Vatican Council, decree *Christus Dominus*, no. 30.
[61]Second Vatican Council, constitution *Sacrosanctum Concilium*, no. 5.
[62]See *ibid.*, nos. 83 and 98.   [64]See *ibid.*, no. 10.
[63]*Ibid.*, no. 7.   [65]*Ibid.*, no. 33.

Those taking part in the Liturgy of the Hours have access to holiness of the richest kind through the life-giving word of God, to which it gives such great importance. The readings are drawn from Sacred Scripture, God's words in the psalms are sung in his presence, and the intercessions, prayers and hymns are steeped in the inspired language of Scripture.[66]

Hence, it is not only when those things are read "that are written for our instruction" (Romans 15:4), but also when the Church prays or sings, that faith is deepened for those who take part, and their minds are lifted up to God, so that they may offer him spiritual worship and receive grace·from him in greater abundance.[67]

Praising God with the Church in Heaven

15. In the Liturgy of the Hours the Church exercises the priestly office of its head and offers to God "unceasingly"[68] a sacrifice of praise, that is, a tribute of lips acknowledging his name.[69] This prayer is "the voice of the bride herself as she addresses the bridegroom; indeed, it is also the prayer of Christ and his body to the Father."[70] "All therefore who offer this prayer are fulfilling a duty of the Church, and also sharing in the highest honor given to Christ's bride, because as they render praise to God they are standing before God's throne in the name of Mother Church."[71]

16. When the Church offers praise to God in the Liturgy of the Hours it unites itself with that hymn of praise which is sung in the heavenly places throughout all ages;[72] it also receives a foretaste of the song of praise in

---

[66]See ibid., no. 24.
[67]See ibid., no. 33.
[68]1 Thessalonians 5:17.
[69]See Hebrews 13:15.
[70]See Second Vatican Council, constitution Sacrosanctum Concilium, no. 84.
[71]Ibid., no. 85.
[72]See ibid., no. 83.

heaven, described by John in the Book of Revelation, the song that is sung without ceasing before the throne of God and of the Lamb. Our close union with the Church in heaven is given effective voice when "we rejoice together and celebrate the praise of God's glory, when all who have been redeemed in the blood of Christ from every tribe and tongue and people and nation (see Revelation 5:9) and have been gathered into the one Church glorify the one and triune God in one canticle of praise"[73]

This liturgy of heaven was commonly foreseen by the prophets as a victory of day without night, of light without darkness: "The sun will no more be your light by day, and the brightness of the moon will not shine upon you, but the Lord will be your everlasting light" (Isaiah 60:19; see Revelation 21:23, 25). "There will be a single day, known to the Lord, not day and night, and at evening there will be light" (Zechariah 14:7). Already "the end of the ages has come upon us" (see 1 Corinthians 10:11), and the renewal of the world has been irrevocably established and in a true sense is being anticipated in this world."[74] We are taught by faith the meaning of our temporal life also, so that we look forward with all creation to the revealing of God's sons.[75] In the Liturgy of the Hours we proclaim this faith, we express and nourish this hope, we share in some degree the joy of everlasting praise and of that day which knows no setting.

Petition and Intercession

17. Besides the praise of God, the Church in the Liturgy of the Hours expresses the prayers and desires of all the

---

[73]Second Vatican Council, dogmatic constitution *Lumen gentium,* no. 50; see constitution *Sacrosanctum Concilium,* nos. 8 and 104.

[74]Second Vatican Council, dogmatic constitution *Lumen gentium,* no. 48.   [75]See Romans 8:19.

Christian faithful; indeed, it prays to Christ, and through him to the Father, for the salvation of the whole world.[76] The voice of the Church is not just its own; it is also the voice of Christ, since its prayers are offered in the name of Christ, that is, "through our Lord Jesus Christ," and so the Church continues to offer the prayer and petition which Christ poured out in the days of his earthly life[77] and which have therefore a unique effectiveness. The ecclesial community thus exercises a true maternal function in bringing souls to Christ, not only by charity, good example and works of penance but also by prayer.[78]

This work of prayer belongs especially to all who have been called by a special mandate to carry out the Liturgy of the Hours: to bishops and priests as they pray in virtue of their office for their own people and for the whole people of God,[79] to other sacred ministers and also to religious.[80]

The Apex and Source of Pastoral Activity

18. Those then who take part in the Liturgy of the Hours bring growth to God's people in a hidden but fruitful apostolate,[81] for the work of the apostolate is directed to this end, "that all who are made sons of God through faith and baptism may come together in unity, praise God in the midst of the Church, share in the sacrifice and eat the supper of the Lord."[82]

[76]See Second Vatican Council, constitution *Sacrosanctum Concilium*, no. 83.

[77]See Hebrews 5:7.

[78]See Second Vatican Council, decree *Presbyterorum ordinis*, no. 6.

[79]See Second Vatican Council, dogmatic constitution *Lumen gentium*, no. 41.

[80]See below, no. 24.

[81]See Second Vatican Council, decree *Perfectae caritatis*, no. 7.

[82]Second Vatican Council, constitution *Sacrosanctum Concilium*, no. 10.

Thus by their lives the faithful show forth and reveal to others "the mystery of Christ and the genuine nature of the true Church. Its characteristic is to be . . . visible, yet endowed with invisible realities, fervent in action, yet devoted to contemplation, present in the world, yet a pilgrim and a stranger."[83]

In their turn the readings and prayers of the Liturgy of the Hours form a wellspring of the Christian life, which is nourished at the table of Sacred Scripture and the writings of the saints, and receives strength from the prayers. Only the Lord, without whom we can do nothing,[84] can give, in response to our request, power and increase to what we do,[85] so that we may be built up each day in the Spirit into the temple of God,[86] to the full stature of Christ,[87] and also receive greater strength to bring the good news of Christ to those outside.[88]

Harmony of Mind and Voice

19. Mind and voice must be in harmony in a celebration that is worthy, attentive and devout if this prayer is to be made their own by those taking part in it, and be a source of devotion, a means of gaining God's manifold grace, a deepening of personal prayer and an incentive to the work of the apostolate.[89] All should be zealous in cooperating with God's grace, so as not to receive it fruitlessly. They should seek Christ, penetrating ever more deeply into the mystery of Christ through prayer,[90] and

---

[83]*Ibid.*, no. 2.   [84]See John 15:5.

[85]See Second Vatican Council, constitution *Sacrosanctum Concilium*, no. 86.

[86]See Ephesians 2:21-22.

[87]See Ephesians 4:13.

[88]See Second Vatican Council, constitution *Sacrosanctum Concilium*, no. 2.

[89]See *ibid.*, no. 90; Saint Benedict, *Rule*, Chapter 19.

[90]See Second Vatican Council, decree *Presbyterorum ordinis*, no. 14; decree *Optatam totius*, no. 8.

so offer praise and petition to God with the same mind and heart as the divine Redeemer when he prayed to God.

IV. THE PARTICIPANTS IN THE LITURGY OF THE HOURS

a) Celebration in Common

20. The Liturgy of the Hours, like other liturgical actions, is not something private but belongs to the whole body of the Church, which it manifests and influences.[91] Its relation to the Church is most clearly seen when it is celebrated by a local Church in the presence of its bishop in the company of his priests and ministers,[92] for in the local Church "the one, holy, catholic and apostolic Church of Christ is truly present and active."[93] Such a celebration is therefore most highly recommended. When the Liturgy of the Hours is celebrated, in the absence of the bishop, by the chapter of canons or other priests, it should always follow the proper times for the Hours, and as far as possible the people should take part. The same is to be said of collegiate chapters.

21. Where possible, the principal Hours should be celebrated communally in church by other groups of the faithful. The most important of these groups are the local parishes—the cells of the diocese—established under a pastor acting for the bishop. These "represent in some degree the visible Church established throughout the world."[94]

22. Hence, when the faithful are invited to the Liturgy

[91] See Second Vatican Council, constitution *Sacrosanctum Concilium*, no. 26.   [92] See *ibid.*, no. 41.
[93] Second Vatican Council, decree *Christus Dominus*, no. 11.
[94] Second Vatican Council, constitution *Sacrosanctum Concilium*, no. 42; see decree *Apostolicam actuositatem*, no. 10.

of the Hours and come together in unity of heart and voice, they show forth the Church in its celebration of the mystery of Christ.[95]

23. Those in holy orders or with a special canonical mission[96] have the responsibility of initiating and directing the prayer of the community; "they must work hard to ensure that all entrusted to their care may be united in prayer."[97] They must therefore see to it that the faithful are invited—and prepared by suitable instruction—to celebrate the principal Hours in common, especially on Sundays and feast days.[98] They should teach them how to make the celebration a sincere prayer;[99] they should therefore give them suitable guidance in the Christian understanding of the psalms, so that they may be led by degrees to a greater appreciation and more frequent use of the prayer of the Church.[100]

24. Communities of canons, monks, nuns and other religious which celebrate the Liturgy of the Hours by rule or according to their constitutions, whether in the common rite or in a particular rite, in whole or in part, represent in a special way the Church at prayer. They are a fuller sign of the Church as it continuously praises God with one voice, and they fulfill the duty of "working," above all by prayer, "to build up and increase the whole mystical Body of Christ, and for the good of the local Churches."[101] This is especially true of those who follow the contemplative life.

[95]See Second Vatican Council, constitution *Sacrosanctum Concilium*, nos. 26 and 84.
[96]See Second Vatican Council, decree *Ad gentes*, no. 17.
[97]Second Vatican Council, decree *Christus Dominus*, no. 15.
[98]See Second Vatican Council, constitution *Sacrosanctum Concilium*, no. 100.
[99]See Second Vatican Council, decree *Presbyterorum ordinis*, no. 5.
[100]See below, nos. 100-109.
[101]Second Vatican Council, decree *Christus Dominus*, no. 33; see decree *Perfectae caritatis*, nos. 6 and 7, 15; decree *Ad gentes*, no. 15.

25. Sacred ministers, and all clerics (not otherwise bound to a common celebration) living in community or assembling together, should arrange to say at least some part of the Liturgy of the Hours in common, particularly Morning and Evening Prayer.[102]

26. It is strongly recommended that religious of either sex, not bound to a common celebration, as well as members of any institute of perfection, should gather together, by themselves or with the faithful, to celebrate the Liturgy of the Hours or part of it.

27. Gatherings of the laity—for prayer, apostolic work or any other reason—are encouraged to fulfill the Church's office[103] by celebrating part of the Liturgy of the Hours. The laity must learn, especially in liturgical actions, how to adore God the Father in spirit and in truth,[104] and be reminded that through public worship and prayer they are in touch with all mankind and can contribute in no small degree to the salvation of the whole world.[105]

Finally, it is desirable that the family, the domestic sanctuary of the Church, should not only pray together to God but should also celebrate some parts of the Liturgy of the Hours as occasion offers, so as to enter more deeply into the life of the Church.[106]

b) The Mandate of the Liturgy of the Hours

28. The Liturgy of the Hours is entrusted to sacred ministers in such a special way that even when the faithful are not present it should be recited by individuals

---

[102]See Second Vatican Council, constitution *Sacrosanctum concilium*, no. 99.

[103]See *ibid.*, no. 100.

[104]See John 4:23.

[105]See Second Vatican Council, declaration *Gravissimum educationis*, no. 2; decree *Apostolicam actuositatem*, no. 16.

[106]See Second Vatican Council, decree *Apostolicam actuositatem*, no. 11.

with the adaptations necessary under these circumstances. The Church commissions them to celebrate the Liturgy of the Hours in order that, at least in their persons, the duty of the whole community may be carried out regularly and reliably, and the prayer of Christ continue unceasingly in the Church.[107]

The bishop represents Christ in an eminent and visible way and is the high priest of his flock; the life in Christ of his faithful people may be said to derive from him and depend on him.[108] He should then be the first of all the members of his Church in offering prayer. In the recitation of the Liturgy of the Hours his prayer is always in the name of the Church and on behalf of the Church entrusted to him.[109]

Priests, united as they are with the bishop and the whole presbyterium, are themselves representative in a special way of Christ the priest,[110] and so share the same responsibility of praying to God for the people entrusted to them, and indeed for the whole world.[111]

All fulfill the ministry of the good Shepherd who prays for his sheep, that they may have life and so be brought into perfect unity.[112] In the Liturgy of the Hours, which the Church sets before them, they are not only to find a source of devotion and a strengthening of personal prayer[113] but must also nourish and foster pastoral and missionary action by abundant contemplation, and so bring joy to the whole Church of God.[114]

[107]See Second Vatican Council, decree *Presbyterorum ordinis,* no. 13.

[108]See Second Vatican Council, constitution *Sacrosanctum Concilium,* no, 41; dogmatic constitution *Lumen gentium,* no. 21.

[109]See Second Vatican Council, dogmatic constitution *Lumen gentium,* no. 26; decree *Christus Dominus,* no. 15.

[110]See Second Vatican Council, decree *Presbyterorum ordinis,* no. 13.

[111]See *ibid.,* no. 5.   [112]See John 10:11; 17:20, 23.

[113]See Second Vatican Council, constitution *Sacrosanctum Concilium,* no. 90.

[114]See Second Vatican Council, dogmatic constitution *Lumen gentium,* no. 41.

29. Hence, bishops and priests and other sacred ministers, who have received from the Church the mandate of celebrating the Liturgy of the Hours (see no. 17), should recite the full sequence of Hours each day, as far as possible at the appropriate times.

They should, first and foremost, attach due importance to those Hours that are, as it were, the hinge of the Liturgy of the Hours, that is, Morning and Evening Prayer, which should not be omitted except for a serious reason.

They should faithfully recite the Office of Readings, which is above all a liturgical celebration of the word of God. In this way they fulfill daily a duty that is particularly their own, that is, of receiving the word of God into their lives, so that they may become more perfect as disciples of the Lord and experience more deeply the unfathomable riches of Christ.[115]

In order to sanctify the whole day more perfectly, they will have also at heart the recitation of the Daytime Hour and Night Prayer, to round off the whole "Work of God" and to commend themselves to God before retiring.

30. It is most fitting that permanent deacons should recite daily at least some part of the Liturgy of the Hours, to be determined by the conference of bishops.[116]

31. (a) Cathedral and collegiate chapters should celebrate in choir those parts of the Liturgy of the Hours that are prescribed for them by common or particular law.

---

[115]See Second Vatican Council, dogmatic constitution *Dei verbum*, no. 25; decree *Presbyterorum ordinis*, no. 13.

[116]Paul VI, Motu proprio, *Sacrum Diaconatus ordinem*, June 18, 1967, no. 27: *AAS* 59 (1967) 703.

In private recitation individual members of these chapters should include those Hours that are recited in their chapter, besides the Hours prescribed for all sacred ministers.[117]

(b) Religious communities, bound to the recitation of the Liturgy of the Hours, and their individual members, should celebrate the Hours in accordance with their own particular law, but observing the prescription of no. 29 in regard to those in holy Orders.

Communities bound to choir should celebrate the whole sequence of the Hours daily in choir;[118] when absent from choir their members should recite the Hours in accordance with their own particular law, but observing always the prescriptions given in no. 29.

32. Other religious communities, and their individual members, are advised to celebrate some parts of the Liturgy of the Hours, in accordance with circumstances, for it is the prayer of the Church and makes the whole Church, scattered throughout the world, one in heart and soul.[119]

This exhortation applies also to lay people.[120]

(c) The Structure of the Celebration

33. The Liturgy of the Hours, while it combines those elements that are found in other Christian celebrations, is arranged according to its own laws. It is so constructed that, after a hymn, there is always psalmody, then a long or a short reading of Sacred Scripture, and finally intercessions.

---

[117]See Congregation of Rites, instruction *Inter Oecumenici*, September 26, 1964, no. 78b: *AAS* 56 (1964) 895.

[118]See Second Vatican Council, constitution *Sacrosanctum Concilium*, no. 95.

[119]See Acts 4:32.

[120]See Second Vatican Council, constitution *Sacrosanctum Concilium*, no. 100.

In a celebration in common or in individual recitation the essential structure of this liturgy remains the same, that is, it is a conversation between God and man. Celebration in common reveals more clearly the ecclesial nature of the Liturgy of the Hours; it makes for the active participation of all, each in his own role, by means of acclamations, dialogue, alternating psalmody and similar elements, and allows greater scope to variety of expression.[121] Hence, whenever it is possible to have a celebration in common, with the faithful present and actively sharing in it, this kind of celebration is to be preferred to one that is individual and as it were private.[122] It is also preferable to sing the Office in choir and in community as opportunity offers, in accordance with the nature and function of its individual parts.

In this way the apostle's exhortation is obeyed: "Let the word of Christ dwell in you in all its richness, as you teach and advise each other in all wisdom by psalms, hymns and spiritual canticles, singing thankfully in your hearts to God" (Colossians 3:16; see Ephesians 5:19-20).

[121] See *ibid.*, nos. 26, 28-30.
[122] See *ibid.*, no. 27.

CHAPTER II

THE SANCTIFICATION OF THE DAY: THE DIFFERENT LITURGICAL HOURS

I. THE INTRODUCTION TO THE WHOLE OFFICE

34. The whole Office regularly begins with an invitatory. This consists in the verse Lord, open my lips. And my mouth will proclaim your praise, and psalm 95. This psalm invites the faithful each day to sing God's praise and to listen to his voice and draws them to hope for "the Lord's rest."[1]

In place of psalm 95, psalm 100, psalm 67 or psalm 24 may be used.

It is preferable to recite the invitatory psalm responsorially (as indicated in the appropriate place), that is, the antiphon is recited at the beginning and then repeated, and repeated again after each strophe.

35. The invitatory is placed at the beginning of the whole sequence of the day's prayer, that is, it precedes either Morning Prayer or the Office of Readings, whichever of these liturgical actions begins the day. The psalm with its antiphon may, however, be omitted when it should precede Morning Prayer.

36. The variations of the antiphon at the invitatory, to suit the different liturgical days, are indicated in the appropriate place.

II. MORNING AND EVENING PRAYER

37. "In keeping with the ancient tradition of the universal Church, Morning and Evening Prayer form a double hinge of the daily Office and are therefore to be considered the principal Hours and celebrated as such."[2]

[1] See Hebrews 3:7—4:16.
[2] Second Vatican Council, constitution *Sacrosanctum Concilium*, no. 89a; see *ibid.*, no. 100.

38. Morning Prayer, as is clear from many of the elements that make it up, is intended and arranged for the sanctification of the morning. Saint Basil the Great gives an excellent description of its character in these words:

It is said in the morning in order that the first stirrings of our mind and will may be consecrated to God, and that we may take nothing in hand until we have been gladdened by the thought of God, as it is written: "I was mindful of God and was glad" (Psalm 77:4), or set our bodies to any task before we do what has been said: "I will pray to you, Lord, you will hear my voice in the morning; I will stand before you in the morning and gaze on you" (Psalm 5:4-5).[3]

This Hour, celebrated as it is as the light of a new day is dawning, also recalls the resurrection of the Lord Jesus, the true light enlightening all mankind (see John 1:9) and "the Sun of justice" (Malachi 4:2), "rising from on high" (Luke 1:78). Hence, we can well understand the advice of Saint Cyprian: "There should be prayer in the morning, so that the resurrection of the Lord may be celebrated by morning prayer."[4]

39. When evening approaches and the day is already far spent, Evening Prayer is celebrated in order that "we may give thanks for what has been given us, or what we have done well, during the day."[5] We also recall the redemption through the prayer which we send up "like incense in the Lord's sight," and in which "the raising up of our hands" becomes "an evening sacrifice."[6] This

---

[3]Saint Basil the Great, *Regulae fusius tractatae*, Resp. 37, 3: PG 31, 1014.
[4]Saint Cyprian, *The Lord's Prayer*, 35: PL 4, 561.
[5]Saint Basil the Great, *op. cit.*: PG 31, 1015.   [6]See psalm 140:2.

"may be understood also in a deeper spiritual sense of that true evening sacrifice which, as is handed down to us, was offered in the evening by the Lord and Savior, at supper with the apostles, when he instituted the most holy mysteries of the Church, or of the evening sacrifice, that is, the sacrifice at the end of the ages, in which on the next day he was offered to the Father as he raised up his hands for the salvation of the whole world."[7] Again, in order to fix our hope on the light that knows no setting, "we pray and make petition for the light to come down on us anew and ask Christ to give us the grace of eternal light."[8] Finally, at this hour we join with the Churches of the East in calling upon the "joy-giving light of holy glory, born of the immortal, heavenly Father, holy and blessed, Jesus Christ; now that we have come to the setting of the sun and seen the evening star, we sing in praise of the Father and the Son and the Holy Spirit as God. . . ."

40. Morning and Evening Prayer are therefore to be reckoned as of the highest importance, as the prayer of the Christian community. Their public or communal celebration should be encouraged, especially in the case of those who live in community. Indeed, the recitation of these Hours should be recommended also to individual members of the faithful unable to take part in a celebration in common.

41. Morning and Evening Prayer begin with the introductory verse God, come to my assistance. Lord, make haste to help me. There follows the Glory to the Father, with As it was in the beginning and Alleluia (the Alleluia is omitted during Lent). This introduction is omitted at

[7]Cassian, *De institutione coenob.*, book 3, chapter 3: PL 49, 124, 125.
[8]Saint Cyprian, *op cit.*: PL 4, 560.

Morning Prayer when the Invitatory immediately precedes it.

42. Immediately after, an appropriate hymn is sung. The purpose of the hymn is to provide a setting for the Hour or the feast, and, especially in celebrations with a congregation, to form a simple and pleasant introduction to prayer.

43. After the hymn there follows the psalmody, in accordance with the rules laid down in nos. 121-125. The psalmody of Morning Prayer consists of one morning psalm, then a canticle from the Old Testament, and finally a second psalm of praise, following the tradition of the Church.

The psalmody of Evening Prayer consists of two psalms (or two parts of a longer psalm) suitable for the Hour and for celebration with the people, and a canticle from the letters of the apostles or from the Book of Revelation.

44. After the psalmody there is a reading, either a short reading or a longer one.

45. The short reading varies with the day, the season and the feast. It is to be read and received as a true proclamation of God's word, setting out some passage of Sacred Scripture in a striking way, or highlighting some shorter sentences that may receive less attention in the continuous cycle of Scripture readings.

The short readings are different for each day of the psalter cycle.

46. There is freedom to choose—especially in a celebration with the people—a longer Scripture reading, either from the Office of Readings or the *Lectionary for Mass*, particularly texts which for some reason have not been

used. In addition, there is nothing to prevent the use from time to time of a more suitable reading, in accordance with the rules laid down in nos. 248-249 and 251.

47. In a celebration with the people a short homily may follow the reading to explain its meaning.

48. After the reading or homily a period of silence may be observed.

49. As a response to the word of God a responsorial chant or short responsory is given; this may be omitted. Other chants with the same purpose and character may be substituted in its place, provided that these have been duly approved by the conference of bishops.

50. There follows the solemn recitation of the Gospel canticle with its antiphon, that is, the Canticle of Zechariah at Morning Prayer and the Canticle of Mary at Evening Prayer. These canticles, sanctioned by age-old popular usage in the Roman Church, are expressions of praise and thanksgiving for our redemption. The antiphon for each canticle is given to suit the day, the season or the feast.

51. After the canticle, there follow at Morning Prayer petitions for the consecration of the day and its work to God, and at Evening Prayer intercessions (see nos. 179-193).

52. After the petitions or intercessions the Lord's Prayer is said by all.

53. Immediately after the Lord's Prayer there follows the concluding prayer, which for weekdays in Ordinary Time is found in the Psalter, and for other days in the Proper.

54. Then, if a priest or deacon is presiding he dismisses the people with the greeting The Lord be with you, and

the blessing as at Mass. He adds the invitation Go in
peace. Thanks be to God. In the absence of a priest or
deacon the celebration concludes with May the Lord
bless us, etc.

III. THE OFFICE OF READINGS

55. The Office of Readings seeks to provide God's people, and in particular those consecrated to God in a special way, with an ampler selection of passages from Sacred Scripture for meditation, together with the finest
extracts from spiritual writers. Though the cycle of
scriptural readings at daily Mass is now richer, the treasures of revelation and tradition to be found in the Office
of Readings will contribute greatly to the spiritual life.
Bishops and priests in particular should seek out these
riches, so that they may hand on to others the word of
God they have themselves received and make their
teaching "nourishment for God's people."[9]

56. Prayer should accompany "the reading of Sacred
Scripture so that there may be a conversation between
God and man: 'we talk with God when we pray, we
listen to him when we read God's words.'"[10] For this
reason the Office of Readings consists also of psalms, a
hymn, prayer and other texts, giving it the character of
true prayer.

57. The Constitution on the Sacred Liturgy directs
that the Office of Readings, "though it should retain its
character as a night office of praise when celebrated in
choir, should be suitable for recitation at any hour of the
day and consist of fewer psalms and longer readings."[11]

[9]Roman Pontifical, *The Ordination of Priests,* no. 14.
[10]Saint Ambrose, *De officiis ministrorum* I, 20, 88: PL 16, 50; Second
Vatican Council, dogmatic constitution *Dei verbum,* no. 25.
[11]Second Vatican Council, constitution *Sacrosanctum Concilium,*
no. 89 c.

58. Those obliged by their own particular law, and others laudably desiring to retain the character of this Office as a night office of praise, either by saying it at night or very early in the morning and before Morning Prayer, during Ordinary Time choose the hymn from the selection given for this purpose. For Sundays, solemnities and certain feasts, what is said in nos. 70-73 on vigils should be borne in mind.

59. Without prejudice to the regulations given above, the Office of Readings may be recited at any hour of the day, even during the night hours of the previous day, after Evening Prayer has been said.

60. If the Office of Readings is said before Morning Prayer, the invitatory precedes it, as noted above (nos. 34-36). Otherwise, it begins with the verse God, come to my assistance with the Glory to the Father, As it was in the beginning and (outside Lent) the Alleluia.

61. Then the hymn is sung. In Ordinary Time this is chosen, from the selection given, to suit the time when it is sung, either at night (as in no. 58) or during the day.

62. The psalmody follows. This consists of three psalms (or parts of psalms if the psalms are longer psalms). During the Easter triduum, on days within the octaves of Easter and Christmas, on solemnities and feasts, the psalms are proper, with proper antiphons.

On Sundays and weekdays, however, the psalms and antiphons are taken from the current week and day of the psalter. On memorials of the saints they are similarly taken from the current week and day of the psalter, unless there are proper psalms or antiphons (see nos. 218ff.).

63. Between the psalmody and the readings there is regularly a verse, forming a transition of prayer from psalmody to listening.

64. There are two readings: the first is from the Scriptures, the second is from the writings of the Fathers or Church writers, or else a reading connected with the saints.

65. After each reading there is a responsory (see nos. 169-172).

66. The scriptural reading is normally to be taken from the Proper of Seasons, in accordance with the rules given below (nos. 140-155). On solemnities and feasts, however, it is taken from the Proper or the Common.

67. The second reading with its responsory is taken either from the Liturgy of the Hours or from the optional Lectionary described in no. 161 below. It is normally taken from the Proper of Seasons.

On solemnities and feasts of saints a proper second reading is used; if there is none, the second reading is taken from the appropriate Common. On memorials of saints where the celebration is not impeded, the reading in connection with the saint replaces the current second reading (see nos. 166 and 235).

68. On Sundays outside Lent, on days within the octaves of Easter and Christmas, on solemnities and feasts, after the second reading with its responsory the Te Deum is said. This is omitted on memorials and weekdays. The last part of this hymn, that is, from the verse Save your people, Lord to the end, may be omitted.

69. The Office of Readings normally concludes with the prayer proper to the day, and, at least in recitation in common, with the acclamation Let us praise the Lord. And give him thanks.

IV. VIGILS

70. The Easter vigil is celebrated by the whole Church, in the rites given in the relevant liturgical books. "The vigil of this night," as Saint Augustine said, "is of such importance that it could claim exclusively for itself the name of 'vigil,' common though it is to all other vigils."[12] "We keep vigil on that night when the Lord rose again and inaugurated for us in his humanity that life . . . in which there is neither death nor sleep. . . . Hence, the one whose resurrection we celebrate by keeping watch a little longer will see to it that we reign with him by living a life without end."[13]

71. As with the Easter vigil, it was customary to begin certain solemnities (different in different Churches) with a vigil. Among these solemnities Christmas and Pentecost are pre-eminent. This custom should be maintained and fostered, according to the particular usage of each Church. Where it seems good to celebrate other solemnities or occasions of pilgrimage with a vigil, the general norms for celebrations of the word should be observed.

72. The Fathers and spiritual writers have frequently encouraged the faithful, especially those who practice the contemplative life, to pray at night. Such prayer gives expression and stimulus to our hope in the Lord's return: "At midnight the cry went up: See, the bridegroom is coming, go out to meet him" (Matthew 25:6); "Keep watch, then, for you do not know when the master of the house is coming, whether late or at midnight or at cockcrow or in the morning, so that if he comes unexpectedly he may not find you sleeping" (Mark 13:35-36). Praise is therefore due to all who

---

[12]*Sermo Guelferbytanus* 5: PLS 2, 550.   [13]*Ibid.*: PLS 2, 552.

maintain the character of the Office of Readings as a night office.

73. Again, since in the Roman rite the Office of Readings is always of a uniform brevity, especially for the sake of those engaged in apostolic work, those who desire to extend the celebration of the vigils of Sundays, solemnities and feasts in accordance with tradition should do as follows.

First, the Office of Readings is to be celebrated as in the Liturgy of the Hours up to the end of the readings. After the two readings, and before the Te Deum, canticles should be added from the special appendix in the Liturgy of the Hours. Then the Gospel should be read; a homily on the Gospel may be added. After this the Te Deum is sung, and then the prayer.

On solemnities and feasts the gospel should be taken from the *Lectionary for Mass;* on Sundays it should be taken from the series of gospels on the paschal mystery, in the appendix to the Liturgy of the Hours.

V. The Daytime Hours

74. Following a very ancient tradition Christians have been accustomed to pray out of private devotion at various times of the day, even in the course of their work, in order to imitate the apostolic Church. In the course of time this tradition has been embodied in liturgical celebrations of various kinds.

75. Liturgical custom in both East and West has retained Midmorning, Midday and Midafternoon Prayer, principally because these Hours were linked to a commemoration of the events of the Lord's Passion and of the first preaching of the Gospel.

76. The Second Vatican Council decreed that these lesser Hours should be maintained in choir.[14]

The liturgical custom of saying these three Hours is to be retained, without prejudice to a particular law, by those who practice the contemplative life. It is recommended also for all, especially those who take part in spiritual retreats or pastoral gatherings.

77. Outside choir, without prejudice to a particular law, it is permitted to choose from the three Hours the one most appropriate to the time of day, so that the tradition of prayer in the course of the day's work may be maintained.

78. Daytime Prayer is so arranged as to take into account both those who recite only one Hour and those who are obliged, or desire, to say all three Hours.

79. The daytime Hours begin with the introductory verse God, come to my assistance, with the Glory to the Father, As it was in the beginning and the Alleluia (omitted in Lent). Then a hymn is sung, one appropriate to the Hour. Afterward there follows the psalmody, then the reading followed by the verse. The Hour concludes with the prayer, and, at least in recitation in common, with the acclamation Let us praise the Lord. And give him thanks.

80. Different hymns and prayers are given for each of the Hours so that they may, in keeping with tradition, correspond to the time of day and thus sanctify it in a more appropriate way. Those who recite only one Hour should therefore choose the texts that correspond to it.

In addition, the readings and prayers vary in keeping with the day, the season or the feast.

[14]See Second Vatican Council, Constitution *Sacrosanctum Concilium*, no. 89 e.

81. Two psalmodies are provided: the current psalmody and the complementary psalmody. Those who say one Hour should use the current psalmody. Those who say more than one Hour should use the current psalmody at one, and the complementary psalmody at the other two.

82. The current psalmody consists of three psalms (or parts of psalms in the case of longer psalms) from the psalter, with their antiphons, unless directions are given to the contrary.

On solemnities, the Easter triduum and days within the octave of Easter, proper antiphons are said with three psalms chosen from the complementary psalmody, unless special psalms are to be used or the celebration falls on a Sunday when the psalms are those from the Sunday of the first week of the psalter.

83. The complementary psalter consists of three sets of three psalms, normally chosen from the "gradual" psalms.

VI. Night Prayer

84. Night Prayer is the last prayer of the day, said before retiring at night, even after midnight.

85. Night Prayer begins, like the other Hours, with the verse God, come to my assistance, with the Glory to the Father, As it was in the beginning and the Alleluia (omitted in Lent).

86. An examination of conscience may suitably follow; in a celebration in common this takes place in silence or as part of a penitential rite using the formulas of the Roman Missal.

87. An appropriate hymn follows.

88. After Evening Prayer I of Sunday the psalmody consists of psalm 4 and psalm 134; after Evening Prayer II of Sunday it consists of psalm 91.

On the other days psalms are chosen which are full of confidence in the Lord; it is permissible to use the Sunday psalms instead, for the convenience especially of those who may wish to say Night Prayer from memory.

89. After the psalmody there is a reading, followed by the responsory Into your hands. Then, as a climax to the whole Hour, the Canticle of Simeon Lord, now you let your servant go in peace is said, with its antiphon.

90. The concluding prayer is then said.

91. After the prayer the blessing May the all-powerful Lord is said, even in private recitation.

92. Finally, one of the antiphons in honor of the Blessed Virgin Mary is said. In the Easter season this will be the Regina caeli. In addition to the antiphons given in the Liturgy of the Hours others may be approved by the conference of bishops.[15]

VII. COMBINING THE HOURS WITH MASS
OR WITH EACH OTHER

93. In particular cases, if circumstances require it, it is possible to link an Hour more closely with Mass when there is a celebration of the Liturgy of the Hours in public or in common, according to the following norms, provided that the Mass and the Hour belong to one and the same Office. Care must be taken, however, that this does not result in harm to pastoral work, especially on Sundays.

94. When Morning Prayer, celebrated in choir or in common, comes immediately before Mass, the whole

[15]See *ibid.*, no. 38.

celebration may begin either with the introductory verse and hymn of Morning Prayer, especially on weekdays, or with the entrance song, procession and celebrant's greeting (especially on feast days), one or other of the introductory rites being thus omitted.

The psalmody of Morning Prayer follows as usual, up to, but excluding, the reading. After the psalmody the penitential rite is omitted and at choice the Kyrie; then the Glory to God in the highest is said, if required by the rubrics, and the celebrant says the opening prayer of the Mass. The liturgy of the word follows as usual.

The general intercessions are made in the place and form customary at Mass. On weekdays, at Mass in the morning, the intercessions of Morning Prayer may replace the daily form of intercessions at Mass.

After the communion with its communion song the Canticle of Zechariah Blessed be the Lord with its antiphon, from Morning Prayer, is sung. Then follows the prayer after communion; the rest is as usual.

95. If one of the daytime Hours, celebrated in public at the appropriate time of day, is immediately followed by Mass, the whole celebration may begin in the same way, either with the introductory verse and hymn from the Hour, especially on weekdays, or with the entrance song, procession and celebrant's greeting, especially on feast days, one or other of the introductory rites being thus omitted.

The psalmody of the Hour follows as usual, up to, but excluding, the reading. After the psalmody the penitential rite is omitted and at choice the Kyrie; then the Glory to God in the highest is said, if required by the rubrics, and the celebrant says the opening prayer of the Mass.

96. Evening Prayer, celebrated immediately before Mass, is joined to it in the same way as Morning Prayer. Evening Prayer I of solemnities, Sundays or feasts of the Lord falling on Sundays may not be celebrated until after Mass of the preceding day or Saturday.

97. When a daytime Hour or Evening Prayer follows Mass, the Mass is celebrated in the usual way up to, and including, the prayer after communion.

When the prayer after communion has been said, the psalmody of the Hour begins without introduction. At a daytime Hour, after the psalmody the prayer is said (omitting the reading), and the dismissal takes place as at Mass. At Evening Prayer, after the psalmody and omitting the reading, the Canticle of Mary with its antiphon follows immediately. The intercessions and the Lord's Prayer are omitted, the concluding prayer is said and the blessing given to the people.

98. Except for the night of Christmas the combining of Mass with the Office of Readings is normally excluded, since the Mass already has its own cycle of readings, to be kept distinct from any other. If, however, by way of exception, it should be necessary to join the two, then immediately after the second reading from the Office, with its responsory, the rest is omitted, and the Mass begins with the hymn Glory to God in the highest, if it is to be said; otherwise, the Mass begins with the opening prayer.

99. If the Office of Readings is said immediately before another Hour of the Office, then the appropriate hymn for that Hour may be sung at the beginning of the Office of Readings. At the end of the Office of Readings the prayer and conclusion are omitted, and in the Hour following the introductory verse with the Glory to the Father is omitted.

Chapter III

THE DIFFERENT ELEMENTS
IN THE LITURGY OF THE HOURS

I. The Psalms and Christian Prayer

100. In the Liturgy of the Hours the prayer of the Church is in large measure in the words of those great hymns composed under the inspiration of the Holy Spirit by sacred writers of the Old Testament. Their origin gives them great power to raise minds to God, to inspire devotion, to evoke gratitude in favorable times and to bring consolation and fortitude in times of trial.

101. The psalms are, however, only a foreshadowing of the fullness of time that came to be in Christ the Lord, from which the prayer of the Church derives its power. Hence, while the faithful are all agreed on the supreme value to be placed on the psalms, they can sometimes experience difficulty in making these inspired hymns their own prayer.

102. Yet the Holy Spirit, under whose inspiration the psalms were written, is always present by his grace to those who use them with faith and good will. More, however, is necessary: they must "acquire a richer scriptural formation, especially in regard to the psalms,"[1] according to each one's capacity, so that they may understand how, and by what method, they may pray them properly.

103. The psalms are not readings or prose prayers. They can on occasion be recited as readings, but they are properly called *tehillim* ("songs of praise") in Hebrew and *psalmoi* ("songs to be sung to the lyre") in Greek. In fact, all the psalms have a musical quality which de-

[1]Second Vatican Council, constitution *Sacrosanctum Concilium*, no. 90.

termines the correct way of delivering them. When a psalm is recited and not sung, its delivery must still be governed by its musical character. A psalm presents a text to the minds of the faithful, but it aims rather at moving the hearts of those singing it or listening to it, and also of those accompanying it "on the lyre and harp."

104. To sing the psalms "with understanding" we must meditate on them verse by verse, our hearts always ready to respond in the way the Holy Spirit desires. The Holy Spirit, as the one who inspired the psalmist, will also be present to those who in faith and love are ready to receive his grace. For this reason the singing of psalms, though it demands the reverence due to God's majesty, should be the expression of a joyful spirit and a loving heart, in keeping with their character as sacred poetry and inspired song, and above all with the freedom of the children of God.

105. Often the words of a psalm help us to pray with greater ease and fervor, whether in thanksgiving and joyful praise of God or in prayer for help in the depths of suffering. But difficulties may arise, especially when the psalm is not addressed directly to God. The psalmist is a poet, and he often addresses the people as he recalls Israel's history; sometimes he addresses others, even the brute creation. He even introduces dialogue between God and men, even (as in psalm 2) between God and his enemies. This shows that a psalm is a different kind of prayer from a prayer or collect composed by the Church. Besides, it is in keeping with the poetic and musical character of the psalms that they do not necessarily address God but are sung in God's presence. Saint Benedict warns us: "We must consider what it means to

be in the sight of God and his angels, and stand to sing so that our mind may be in harmony with our voice."[2]

106. In praying the psalms we should open our hearts to the different attitudes they express, varying with the class of writing to which each belongs (psalms of grief, trust, gratitude, etc.), and which Scripture scholars rightly emphasize.

107. In keeping to the meaning of the words the person who prays the psalms is looking for the human value of the text for the life of faith.

It is clear that each psalm was written in its own individual circumstances, which the titles given at the head of each psalm in the Hebrew psalter are meant to indicate. But whatever its historical origin each psalm has its own meaning, which we cannot overlook even in our own day. Though the psalms originated very many centuries ago in the East they express accurately the pain and hope, the unhappiness and trust, of people of every age and country, and celebrate especially faith in God, revelation and redemption.

108. The person who prays the psalms in the Liturgy of the Hours prays not so much in his own person as in the name of the Church, and, in fact, in the person of Christ himself. If one bears this in mind difficulties disappear when one notices in prayer that the feelings of the heart in prayer are different from the emotions expressed in the psalm, for example, when a psalm of joy confronts a person who is sad and overcome with grief, or a psalm of sorrow confronts a person full of joy. This kind of situation is easily avoided in purely private prayer, when it is permissible to choose a psalm matching one's mood. But

---

[2]*Regula monasteriorum*, chapter 19.

in the divine Office the public cycle of the psalms is gone through, not as a private exercise but in the name of the Church, even by someone saying an Hour by himself. The person who prays the psalms in the name of the Church can always find a reason for joy or sadness, for the saying of the Apostle applies in this case also: "Rejoice with the joyful and weep with those who weep" (Romans 12:15). In this way human frailty, wounded by self-love, is healed in that degree of love in which the mind and voice of one praying the psalms are in harmony.[3]

109. The person who prays the psalms in the name of the Church should be aware of their total meaning (*sensus plenus*), especially their messianic meaning, which was the reason for the Church's introduction of the psalter into its prayer. This messianic meaning was fully revealed in the New Testament and indeed was publicly acknowledged by Christ the Lord in person when he said to the apostles: "All that is written about me in the law of Moses and the prophets and the psalms must be fulfilled" (Luke 24:44). The best known example of this messianic meaning is the dialogue in Matthew's gospel on the Messiah as Son of David and David's Lord:[4] there, psalm 110 is interpreted as messianic.

Following this line of thought, the Fathers of the Church saw the whole psalter as a prophecy of Christ and the Church and explained it in this sense; for the same reason the psalms have been chosen for use in the sacred liturgy. Though somewhat tortuous interpretations were at times proposed, yet, in general, the Fathers, and the liturgy itself, could legitimately hear in the sing-

[3] See Saint Benedict, *Regula monasteriorum*, chapter 19.
[4] Matthew 22:44ff.

ing of the psalms the voice of Christ crying out to the
Father, or of the Father conversing with the Son; indeed, they also recognized in the psalms the voice of the
Church, the apostles and the martyrs. This method of
interpretation also flourished in the middle ages; in many
manuscripts of the period the Christological meaning of
each psalm is set out at its head. A Christological meaning is by no means confined to the recognized messianic
psalms but is given also to many others. Some of these
interpretations are doubtless Christological only in an
accommodated sense, but they have the traditional approval of the Church.

On feast days especially, the choice of psalms is often
based on their Christological meaning, and antiphons
taken from these psalms are frequently used to throw
light on this meaning.

II. The Antiphons and Other Aids to Praying the Psalms

110. In the Latin tradition of psalmody three elements
have greatly contributed to an understanding of the
psalms and their use as Christian prayer: the titles, the
psalm-prayers and in particular the antiphons.

111. In the psalter of the Liturgy of the Hours a title
is added at the head of each psalm to explain its meaning
and its human value for the life of faith. These titles are
intended only as an aid to prayer. A sentence from the
New Testament or the Fathers of the Church is added
to foster prayer in the light of Christ's new revelation;
it invites one to pray the psalms in their Christological
meaning.

112. Psalm-prayers for each psalm are given in the
supplement to the Liturgy of the Hours, to help in
understanding them in a predominantly Christian way.

They may be used in the ancient traditional way: after the psalm a period of silence is observed, then the prayer gathers up and rounds off the thoughts and aspirations of those taking part.

113. Even when the Liturgy of the Hours is recited, not sung, each psalm retains its own antiphon, which is to be said even in private recitation. The antiphons help to bring out the character of the psalm; they highlight a sentence which may otherwise not attract the attention it deserves; they suggest an individual quality in a psalm, varying with different contexts; indeed, as long as extravagant accommodated meanings are avoided, they are of great value in helping toward an understanding of the typological meaning, or the meaning appropriate to the feast; they can also add pleasure and variety to the recitation of the psalms.

114. The antiphons in the psalter have been designed to lend themselves to vernacular translation; they are also constructed for repetition after each strophe, in accordance with no. 125. When the office of Ordinary Time is recited, not sung, the sentences attached to the psalms may be used in place of these antiphons (see no. 111).

115. When a psalm may be divided, because of its length, into several sections within one and the same Hour, an antiphon is given for each section. This is to provide variety, especially when the Hour is recited, not sung, and also to help toward a better understanding of the riches of the psalm. It is permissible to say or sing the whole psalm without interruption, using only the first antiphon.

116. Proper antiphons are given for each of the psalms of Morning and Evening Prayer during the Easter tri-

duum, on the days within the octaves of Easter and Christmas, on the Sundays of Advent, Christmas, Lent and Easter, on the weekdays of Holy Week and the Easter season, and from the 17th to the 24th of December.

117. On solemnities proper antiphons are given for the Office of Readings, Morning Prayer, the daytime Hours and Evening Prayer; if not, the antiphons are taken from the Common. On feasts the same applies to the Office of Readings, and Morning and Evening Prayer.

118. Any memorials of the saints which have proper antiphons retain them (see no. 235).

119. The antiphons for the Canticles of Zechariah and of Mary are taken, during Ordinary Time, from the Proper of Seasons if they are given there; if not, they are taken from the current week and day of the psalter. On solemnities and feasts they are taken from the Proper if they are given there; if not, they are taken from the Common. On memorials without proper antiphons the antiphon may be taken either from the Common or from the current week and day of the psalter.

120. During the Easter season Alleluia is added to all antiphons unless it would be out of keeping with the meaning of a particular antiphon.

III. Methods of Singing the Psalms

121. Different psalms may be sung in different ways, to bring out their spiritual unction and beauty. The choice of ways is dictated by the character or length of each psalm, by the language used, whether Latin or the vernacular, and especially by the kind of celebration, whether individually or with a group or with a congregation. The use of the psalms is not simply to provide a set amount of prayer; consideration has also been given to

139.   Both psalmody and readings are arranged in keeping with the traditional rule that the Old Testament is read first, then the writings of the apostles, and finally the gospel.

VI. THE READINGS FROM SACRED SCRIPTURE

a) The Reading of Sacred Scripture in General

140. The reading of Sacred Scripture, which, following an ancient tradition, takes place publicly in the liturgy, is to be held in the highest respect by all Christians, not only in the celebration of the Eucharist but also in the Divine Office. This reading is not the result of individual choice or devotion but is the planned decision of the Church itself, in order that in the course of the year the bride of Christ may unfold the mystery of Christ "from incarnation and nativity to ascension, Pentecost and expectation of the blessed hope and coming of the Lord."[6] In addition, in liturgical celebration the reading of Sacred Scripture is always accompanied by prayer in order that the reading may yield greater fruit, and prayer—especially prayer of the psalms—may in its turn gain fuller understanding and become more fervent and devout.

141. In the Liturgy of the Hours there is a longer reading of Sacred Scripture and a shorter reading.

142. The longer reading, optional at Morning and Evening Prayer, is described above in no. 46.

b) The Cycle of Scripture Readings in the Office of Readings

143. In the cycle of readings from Sacred Scripture in the Office of Readings, account has been taken of those

sacred seasons during which by an ancient tradition particular books are to be read, as well as of the cycle of readings at Mass. The Liturgy of the Hours has therefore been related to the Mass in this way, that the scriptural readings in the Office are complementary to the readings at Mass, and so provide a conspectus of the whole history of salvation.

144. Without prejudice to the exception noted in no. 73, there are no readings from the gospels in the Liturgy of the Hours, since they are read as a whole each year at Mass.

145. There are two cycles of biblical readings. The first is a one year cycle and is incorporated in the Liturgy of the Hours; the second is a two year cycle, like the cycle of readings at weekday Masses in Ordinary Time, and is given for optional use in a supplement.

146. The two year cycle of readings for the Liturgy of the Hours is so arranged that each year nearly all the books of Sacred Scripture may be read, in addition to longer and more difficult texts only rarely suitable for use at Mass. The New Testament as a whole is read each year, partly at Mass, partly in the Liturgy of the Hours; but a selection has been made of those parts of the Old Testament that are of greater importance for the understanding of the history of salvation and for deepening devotion.

The principle of complementarity between the readings in the Liturgy of the Hours and at Mass, far from assigning the same texts to the same days or the same books indiscriminately to the same seasons (for this would leave the Liturgy of the Hours with the less important passages, and disturb the continuity of the texts), demands only that the same book should be used at Mass and in the Liturgy of the Hours in alternate years, or at least after an interval if it is read in the same year.

147. During Advent, following an ancient tradition, passages are read from Isaiah in semi-continuous sequence, alternating in a two year cycle. In addition, the Book of Ruth and certain prophecies from Micah are read. Since there are special readings from the 17th to the 24th of December (both dates included), readings for the third week of Advent which fall on these dates are omitted.

148. From the 29th of December until the 5th of January the readings for the first year are taken from the Letter to the Colossians (which considers the incarnation of the Lord within the context of the whole history of salvation), and the readings for the second year are taken from the Song of Songs (which foreshadows the union of God and man in Christ: "God the Father prepared a wedding feast for God his Son when he united him with human nature in the womb of the Virgin, when before the ages God willed that his Son should become man at the end of the ages").[7]

149. From the 7th of January until the Saturday after the Epiphany eschatological texts, from Isaiah 60—66 and Baruch, are read. Readings remaining unused are omitted for that year.

150. During Lent, the readings for the first year are passages from Deuteronomy and the Letter to the Hebrews. Those for the second year provide a conspectus of the history of salvation from Exodus, Leviticus and Numbers. The Letter to the Hebrews interprets the Old Covenant in the light of the paschal mystery of Christ.

[7] Saint Gregory the Great, *Homilia 34 in Evangelia:* PL 76, 1282.

A passage from the same letter, on Christ's sacrifice (9: 11-28), is read on Good Friday; another, on the Lord's rest (4:1-16), is read on Holy Saturday. On the other days of Holy Week the readings for the first year are the third and fourth Songs of the Servant of the Lord and extracts from the Lamentations; in the second year the prophet Jeremiah is read, as a type of Christ in his Passion.

151. During the Easter season, apart from the First and Second Sundays of Easter and the solemnities of the Ascension and Pentecost, there are the traditional readings from the First Letter of Peter, the Book of Revelation and the Letters of John (for the first year), and from the Acts of the Apostles (for the second year).

152. From the Monday after the feast of the Baptism of the Lord until Lent, and from the Monday after Pentecost until Advent, there is a continuous series of thirty-four weeks in Ordinary Time.

This series is interrupted from Ash Wednesday until Pentecost. On the Monday after Pentecost Sunday the cycle of readings in Ordinary Time is resumed, beginning with the week after the one interrupted because of Lent, and omitting the reading assigned to the Sunday.

In years with only thirty-three weeks in Ordinary Time, the week immediately following Pentecost is dropped, so that the readings of the last weeks, which are eschatological in character, may not be omitted.

The books of the Old Testament are arranged so as to follow the history of salvation. God reveals himself in the history of his people as he leads and enlightens them in progressive stages. The prophets are therefore read along with the historical books, taking into account the times in which they lived and taught. Hence, the cycle of readings from the Old Testament contains, in the first year, the historical books and prophetic utterances from the book of Joshua as far as, and including, the time of the exile. In the second year, after the readings from Genesis (read before Lent) the history of salvation is resumed after the exile up to the time of the Maccabees. The same year includes the later prophets, the wisdom literature and the narrative books of Esther, Tobit and Judith.

Those letters of the apostles that are not read at special times are arranged in a way that takes account of the readings at Mass and of the chronological order in which these letters were written.

153. The one year cycle is a shortened selection of passages from Sacred Scripture, taking account of the two year cycle of readings at Mass, to which it is intended to be complementary.

154. On solemnities and feasts proper readings are given; otherwise, the readings are taken from the appropriate Common.

155. Individual readings maintain, as far as possible, a certain unity; to strike a balance in length (otherwise difficult to achieve in view of the different literary syles represented) some verses are occasionally omitted, though omissions are always noted. One may laudably read them in full from an approved text.

c) The Short Readings

156. The short readings or "chapters" (*capitula*) are referred to in no. 45, which describes their role in the Liturgy of the Hours. They are chosen to give brief and precise expression to a reflection or exhortation. Care has also been taken to provide variety.

157. Accordingly, the psalter provides four one week cycles of short readings in Ordinary Time, so that there may be variety for each day of the four weeks. In addition, there are one week cycles for the seasons of Advent, Christmas, Lent and Easter. There are also proper short readings for solemnities and feasts, and for certain memorials, as well as a one week cycle for Night Prayer.

158. The choice of short readings is based on these principles:

(a) the gospels have been excluded in accordance with tradition;

(b) the special character of Sunday, of Friday and of the individual Hours, has as far as possible been respected;

(c) the readings at Evening Prayer, following as they do a New Testament Canticle, have been chosen from the New Testament only.

VII. THE READINGS FROM THE FATHERS AND CHURCH WRITERS

159. In accordance with the tradition of the Roman Church the Office of Readings provides, after the biblical reading, a reading from the Fathers or Church writers, with a responsory unless there is to be a reading relating to a saint (see nos. 228-239).

160. Texts for this reading are given from the writings of the Fathers and doctors of the Church, and from other Church writers of the Eastern and Western Church. Pride of place is given to the Fathers of the Church who enjoy special authority in the Church.

161. Besides the readings assigned to each day in the Liturgy of the Hours there is an optional lectionary with a larger selection of readings, in order that the treasures

of the Church's tradition may be more widely available to those who pray the Liturgy of the Hours. Everyone has permission to take the second reading either from the Liturgy of the Hours or from the optional lectionary.

162. In addition, conferences of bishops may prepare additional texts, adapted to the traditions and mentality of their own region,[8] for inclusion in the optional lectionary as a supplement. These texts should be taken from the works of Catholic writers, outstanding for their teaching and holiness of life.

163. The purpose of the second reading is principally to provide a meditation on the word of God as received by the Church in its tradition. The Church has always been convinced of the necessity of teaching the word of God authentically to the faithful, so that "the line of interpretation in regard to the prophets and apostles may follow the norm of ecclesiastical and catholic understanding."[9]

164. By constant use of the writings handed down by the universal tradition of the Church those who read them are led to a deeper reflection on Sacred Scripture, and a relish and love for it. The writings of the Fathers are an outstanding witness to the contemplation of the word of God over the centuries by the bride of the incarnate Word: the Church, "cherishing within her the counsel and spirit of her bridegroom and God,"[10] is always seeking to attain a more profound understanding of the Sacred Scriptures.

---

[8]See Second Vatican Council, constitution *Sacrosanctum Concilium*, no. 38.

[9]Saint Vincent Lerins, *Commonitorium*, 2: PL 50, 640.

[10]Saint Bernard, *Sermo 3 in vigilia Nativitatis 1*: PL 183 (edit. 1879) 94.

165.   The reading of the Fathers leads Christians to an understanding also of the liturgical seasons and feasts. In addition, it gives them access to the priceless spiritual treasures which form the unique patrimony of the Church and provide a firm foundation for the spiritual life and a rich diet for devotion. Preachers of God's word have thus at hand a daily course of the finest examples of sacred preaching.

VIII.   THE READINGS IN HONOR OF SAINTS

166.   The "hagiographical" readings or readings in honor of saints are either texts from a Father of the Church or other Church writer which refer specifically to the saint who is being commemorated or are rightly applied to him or her, or texts from his or her own writings or an account of his or her life.

167.   In preparing individual Propers for saints care must be taken to insure historical accuracy[11] as well as genuine spiritual benefit for those who will read or hear the readings in their honor. Anything that merely feeds the imagination should be carefully avoided. Emphasis should be given to the individual spiritual characteristics of the saints, in a way suited to modern conditions; stress should also be laid on their contribution to the life and spirituality of the Church.

168.   A short biographical note, giving merely historical facts and a brief sketch of the saint's life, is provided at the head of the reading. This is for information only and is not for reading aloud.

IX.   THE RESPONSORIES

169.   The biblical reading in the Office of Readings is followed by its own responsory. The text of this respon-

[11]See Second Vatican Council, constitution *Sacrosanctum Concilium*, no. 92 c.

sory, drawn from traditional sources or freshly composed, is intended to throw new light on the passage just read, to put it in the context of the history of salvation, to lead from the Old Testament to the New, to turn what has been read into prayer and contemplation, or to provide pleasant variety by its poetic beauty.

170. In a similar way the second reading is followed by a responsory, less closely connected with the text of the reading and allowing therefore a greater freedom in regard to meditation.

171. The responsories, therefore, with their individual parts, which should be said even in private recitation, retain their value. The part that is usually repeated may be omitted if it is not sung, unless the meaning requires it.

172. In a similar but simpler way, the responsory at Morning, Evening and Night Prayer (see nos. 49 and 89 above), and the verse at Daytime Prayer, are linked to the short reading as a kind of acclamation, enabling God's word to sink deeper into the mind and heart.

X. The Hymns and Other Non-Biblical Songs

173. Hymns have formed part of the Office from very early times and still retain their place in it.[12] As their name implies, they are designed for God's praise because of their musical and poetic character; they also provide participation for the people. Indeed, they generally have an immediate effect in creating the particular quality of the Hour or individual feast, more so than other parts of the Office, and are able to move mind and heart to devotion, a power frequently enhanced by their beauty of style. In the Office the hymns are the chief poetic element contributed by the Church.

[12]See ibid., no. 93.

174.   A hymn follows the traditional rule by ending with a doxology, usually addressed to the same divine person as the hymn itself.

175.   In the Office for Ordinary Time, in the interests of variety, a twofold cycle of hymns is given for each Hour, for use in alternate weeks.

176.   In addition, a twofold cycle of hymns has been introduced into the Office of Readings for Ordinary Time, one for use at night, the other for use during the day.

177.   New hymns can be sung to traditional melodies of the same rhythm and meter.

178.   For vernacular celebrations, conferences of bishops may adapt the Latin hymns to suit the character of their own language and introduce fresh compositions,[13] provided that these are in complete harmony with the spirit of the Hour, season or feast. Great care must be taken not to allow popular "songs" which have no artistic merit and are not in true conformity with the dignity of the liturgy.

XI.   THE INTERCESSIONS, THE LORD'S PRAYER AND THE CONCLUDING PRAYER

a) The Prayers or Intercessions at Morning and Evening Prayer

179.   The Liturgy of the Hours is a celebration in praise of God. Jewish and Christian tradition does not separate prayer of petition from praise of God; often enough, praise turns somehow to petition. The apostle Paul exhorts us to offer "prayers, petitions, intercessions and thanksgiving for all men: for kings and all in authority, so that we may be able to live quiet and peaceful lives in the full practice of religion and of morality, for this is

[13]See *ibid.*, no. 38.

good and acceptable before God our Savior, who wishes all to be saved and to come to the knowledge of the truth" (1 Timothy 2:1-4). The Fathers of the Church frequently explained this as an exhortation to offer prayer in the morning and in the evening.[14]

180. The intercessions, restored in the Mass of the Roman rite, have their place also at Evening Prayer, though in a different form, as will be explained below.

181. Since there is also a tradition of morning prayer that commends the whole day to God, there are invocations at Morning Prayer for the purpose of commending or consecrating the day to God.

182. The word *preces* covers both the intercessions at Evening Prayer and the invocations for dedicating the day to God at Morning Prayer.

183. In the interests of variety, and especially to give fuller expression to the many needs of the Church and of mankind in relation to different states, groups, persons, circumstances and seasons, different formulas are given for each day of the four week psalter in Ordinary Time and for the sacred seasons of the liturgical year, as well as for certain feasts.

184. In addition, conferences of bishops have the right to adapt the formulas given in the Liturgy of the Hours and also to approve new formulas,[15] in accordance with the norms that follow.

185. As in the Lord's Prayer, petitions should be linked with praise of God and acknowledgment of his glory or with a reference to the history of salvation.

---

[14]For example, Saint John Chrysostom, *In Epist. ad Tim. I, Homilia 6: PG* 62, 530.

[15]See Second Vatican Council, constitution *Sacrosanctum Concilium*, no. 38.

186. In the intercessions at Evening Prayer the last intention is always for the dead.

187. Since the Liturgy of the Hours is above all the prayer of the whole Church for the whole Church, indeed for the salvation of the whole world,[16] universal intentions should take precedence over all others: the Church and its ministers; secular authorities; the poor, the sick and the sorrowful; the needs of the whole world, that is, peace and other intentions of this kind.

188. It is, however, permissible to include particular intentions at both Morning and Evening Prayer.

189. The intercessions in the Office are so arranged that they can be adapted for celebration with a congregation or in a small community or for private recitation.

190. Thus, the intercessions in a celebration with a congregation or in common are introduced by a brief invitation, given by the priest or minister and including the response to be made by the congregation after each petition.

191. Further, the intentions are addressed directly to God, so as to be suitable for both common celebration and private recitation.

192. Each intention consists of two parts; the second may be used as an alternative response.

193. Different methods can therefore be used for the intercessions. The priest or minister may say both parts of the intention and the congregation respond with a uniform response or a silent pause, or the priest or minister may say only the first part of the intention and the congregation respond with the second part.

---

[16]See *ibid.*, nos. 83 and 89.

b) The Lord's Prayer

194. Following an ancient tradition, the Lord's Prayer is given a place in keeping with its dignity at the more frequented Hours of Morning and Evening Prayer, after the intercessions.

195. In future, therefore, the Lord's Prayer will be said with solemnity on three occasions during the day: at Mass, and at Morning and Evening Prayer.

196. The Lord's Prayer is said by all, after a brief introduction if this seems opportune.

c) The Concluding Prayer

197. At the end of the whole Hour the concluding prayer is said to round it off. In a celebration in public and with the people, it belongs to a priest or deacon, in accordance with tradition, to say this prayer.[17]

198. In the Office of Readings this prayer is normally the prayer proper to the day. At Night Prayer the prayer is always the prayer given in that Hour.

199. At Morning and Evening Prayer the concluding prayer is taken from the Proper on Sundays, on the weekdays of Advent, Christmas, Lent and Easter, and on solemnities, feasts and memorials. On weekdays in Ordinary Time the prayer is the one given in the four week psalter to express the character of the appropriate Hour.

200. At Daytime Prayer the concluding prayer is taken from the Proper on Sundays, on the weekdays of Advent, Christmas, Lent and Easter, and on solemnities and feasts. On other days the prayers are those that express the character of each Hour. These are given in the four week psalter.

[17]See below, no. 256.

XII.   SACRED SILENCE

201.   It is a general principle that care should be taken in liturgical actions to see that "a sacred silence is observed at its proper time."[18] An opportunity for silence should therefore be provided in the celebration of the Liturgy of the Hours.

202.   In order to receive in our hearts the full resonance of the voice of the Holy Spirit and to unite our personal prayer more closely with the word of God and the public voice of the Church, it is permissible, as occasion offers and prudence suggests, to have an interval of silence, either after the repetition of the antiphon at the end of the psalm, in the traditional way, especially if the psalm-prayer (see no. 112) is to be said after the pause, or after the short or longer readings, before or after the responsory.

Care must be taken to avoid the kind of silence that would disturb the structure of the Office, or embarrass and weary those taking part.

203.   In individual recitation there is greater freedom to pause in meditation on some text that moves the spirit, and the Office does not on this account lose its public character.

[18]Second Vatican Council, constitution *Sacrosanctum Concilium*, no. 30.

CHAPTER IV

VARIOUS CELEBRATIONS THROUGHOUT THE YEAR

I. THE MYSTERIES OF THE LORD

a) Sunday

204. The Office of Sunday begins with Evening Prayer I. It is taken entirely from the four week psalter, except those parts that are marked as proper.

205. When a feast of the Lord is celebrated on Sunday, it has a proper Evening Prayer I.

206. The celebration of Sunday vigils, where desired, is discused in no. 73 above.

207. It is fitting to celebrate at least Evening Prayer with the faithful, where this is possible, in accordance with a very ancient custom.[1]

b) The Easter Triduum

208. In the Easter Triduum the Office is celebrated in the way described in the Proper of Seasons.

209. Those who take part in the evening Mass of the Lord's Supper, or the celebration of the Lord's Passion on Good Friday, do not say Evening Prayer on Thursday or Friday respectively.

210. On Good Friday and Holy Saturday a public celebration of the Office of Readings with the people should take place before Morning Prayer, as far as this is possible.

---

[1]See Second Vatican Council, constitution *Sacrosanctum Concilium*, no. 100.

211. Night Prayer for Holy Saturday is said only by those who are not present at the Easter Vigil.

212. The Easter Vigil takes the place of the Office of Readings. Those not present at the solemn celebration of the Vigil should therefore choose from it at least four readings with the chants and prayers. It is desirable that these readings should be from Exodus, from Ezekiel, from Saint Paul and from the gospel. The Te Deum follows, with the prayer of the day.

213. Morning Prayer for Easter Sunday is said by all. It is fitting that Evening Prayer should be celebrated in a more solemn way, to mark the ending of so holy a day and to commemorate the occasions when the Lord showed himself to his disciples. Great care should be taken to maintain, where it exists, the particular tradition on Easter Sunday of celebrating Evening Prayer in honor of baptism, when there is a procession to the font as the as the psalms are being sung.

c) Easter Season

214. The Liturgy of the Hours takes on a paschal character from the acclamation Alleluia, added to most antiphons (see no. 120); from the hymns, antiphons and special intercessions and from the proper readings for each Hour.

d) Christmas Season

215. On Christmas night it is fitting that a solemn vigil, using the Office of Readings, should be celebrated before Mass. Night Prayer is not said by those who are present at this vigil.

216. Morning Prayer on Christmas Day is normally said before the Mass at Dawn.

e) Other Solemnities and Feasts of the Lord

217. In arranging the Office for solemnities and feasts of the Lord, what is said in nos. 225-233 below should be observed, with any necessary changes.

II. THE SAINTS

218. The celebrations in honor of the saints are so arranged that they do not take precedence over feast days or sacred seasons commemorating the mysteries of salvation,[2] or continually interrupt the sequence of psalms and biblical readings, or give rise to undue repetitions. At the same time, the legitimate honor paid to each saint is fostered and given suitable opportunity for expression. These are the principles which form the basis for the reform of the Calendar, carried out by order of the Second Vatican Council, and for the regulations governing celebrations in honor of the saints, described in the following paragraphs.

219. Celebrations in honor of the saints are either solemnities, feasts or memorials.

220. Memorials are either obligatory or, if unspecified, optional. In deciding whether to celebrate an optional memorial in an Office celebrated with the people or in common, account should be taken of the common good or the genuine devotion of the congregation, not simply that of the person presiding.

221. If more than one optional memorial falls on the same day, only one may be celebrated; the rest are omitted.

222. Solemnities alone are transferred, in accordance with the rubrics.

[2] See *ibid.*, no. 111.

223.   The norms which follow apply in the case of saints mentioned in the General Roman Calendar and of those with a place in particular calendars.

224.   Where proper parts are not given, they are supplied from the appropriate Common.

1) The Office for Solemnities

225.   Solemnities begin with Evening Prayer I on the day before.

226.   At Evening Prayer I and II, the hymn, the antiphons, the reading with its responsory, and the concluding prayer are proper. Where anything proper is missing, it is supplied from the Common.

At Evening Prayer I both psalms are normally taken from the *Laudate* psalms (psalms 113, 117, 135, 146, 147A, 147B), following an ancient tradition. The New Testament canticle is given in its appropriate place. At Evening Prayer II the psalms and canticles are proper; the intercessions are either proper or from the Common.

227.   At Morning Prayer, the hymn, the antiphons, the reading with its responsory, and the concluding prayer are proper. Where anything proper is missing, it is supplied from the Common. The psalms are to be taken from the Sunday of the first week of the four week psalter; the intercessions are either proper or from the Common.

228.   In the Office of Readings, everything is proper: the hymn, the antiphons and psalms, the readings and responsories. The first reading is from Scripture, the second is in honor of the saint. In the case of a saint with a purely local cult and without special texts even in the local Proper, everything is taken from the Common.

At the end of the Office of Readings the Te Deum is said, followed by the prayer from the Proper.

229. At Daytime Prayer the hymn of the weekday is used, unless other directions are given. The psalms are from the gradual psalms, with a proper antiphon. On Sundays the psalms are taken from the Sunday of the first week of the four week psalter, and the reading and concluding prayer are proper. On certain solemnities of the Lord there are special psalms.

230. At Night Prayer everything is said as on Sundays after Evening Prayer I and II respectively.

2) The Office for Feasts

231. Feasts have no Evening Prayer I, except those feasts of the Lord which fall on a Sunday. At the Office of Readings and Morning and Evening Prayer, all is done as on solemnities.

232. At Daytime Prayer the hymn of the weekday is used, unless other directions are given. The weekday psalms with their antiphons are said, unless a special reason or tradition requires a proper antiphon; this will be indicated at the appropriate place. The reading and concluding prayer are proper.

233. Night Prayer is said as on ordinary days.

3) The Office for Memorials

234. There is no difference in the arrangement of the Office for obligatory and optional memorials except in the case of optional memorials falling during privileged seasons.

a) Memorials during Ordinary Time

235. In the Office of Readings and at Morning and Evening Prayer:

a) the psalms and their antiphons are taken from the current week and day, unless there are proper antiphons or proper psalms, as indicated for each such occasion;

b) the antiphon at the invitatory, the hymn, the reading, the antiphons at the Canticles of Zechariah and of Mary, and the intercessions are those of the saint if these are given in the Proper; otherwise, they are taken either from the Common or from the current week and day;

c) the concluding prayer is from the Office of the saint;

d) in the Office of Readings the Scripture reading with its responsory is from the current cycle. The second reading is the one in honor of the saint, with a proper responsory or one taken from the Common; if there is no proper reading, the current patristic reading is used.

The Te Deum is not said.

236. At Daytime Payer and Night Prayer all is from the weekday, and nothing is from the Office of the saint.

b) Memorials during Privileged Seasons

237. On Sundays, solemnities and feasts, on Ash Wednesday, during Holy Week and during the octave of Easter no regard is taken of any memorials that may fall on these days.

238. On the weekdays from the 17th to the 24th of December, during the octave of Christmas and on the weekdays of Lent, obligatory memorials are not celebrated, even those in particular calendars. If any happen to fall during Lent in a given year, they are treated as optional memorials.

239. During these seasons, if it is desired to celebrate the Office of a saint on a day assigned to his memorial:

a) in the Office of Readings, after the patristic reading (with its responsory) from the Proper of Seasons, a proper reading in honor of the saint (with its responsory) may follow, with the concluding prayer of the saint;

   b) at Morning and Evening Prayer, the ending of the concluding prayer may be omitted, and the saint's antiphon (from the Proper or Common) and prayer added.

c) Memorial of the Blessed Virgin Mary on Saturday

240. On Saturdays in Ordinary Time, when optional memorials are permitted, an optional memorial of the Blessed Virgin Mary may be celebrated in the same way as other memorials, with a proper reading.

III. THE CALENDAR AND CHOICE OF OFFICE OR PART OF AN OFFICE

a) The Calendar To Be Followed

241. The Office in choir and in common is to be celebrated according to the proper calendar: of the diocese, of the religious institute or of the individual church.[3] Members of religious institutes join with the community of the local Church in celebrating the dedication of the cathedral and the feasts of the principal patrons of the place, and of the wider region, in which they live.[4]

242. When any cleric or religious, bound on any title to say the Divine Office, joins in an Office celebrated in common according to a calendar or rite different from his own, he fulfills his obligation in respect of the part of the Office at which he is present.

243. In individual celebration, the calendar of the place or one's own calendar may be followed except on proper solemnities and feasts.[5]

---

[3]See General Norms for the Liturgical Year and the Calendar, no. 52.
[4]See *ibid.*, no. 52 c.
[5]See Table of Liturgical Days, nos. 4 and 8.

b) Choice of Office

244. On weekdays when an optional memorial is permitted, for a good reason the Office of a saint named on that day in the Roman Martyrology, or in an approved Appendix to it, may be celebrated in the same way as other memorials (see nos. 234-239).

245. For a public reason or out of devotion, except on solemnities, the Sundays of Advent, Lent and Easter, Ash Wednesday, Holy Week, the octave of Easter and the 2nd of November, a votive Office may be celebrated, in whole or in part, for example, on the occasion of a pilgrimage, a local feast or the external solemnity of a saint.

c) Choice of Texts

246. In particular cases, one may choose for the Office texts different from those given for the day, provided that the general arrangement of the Office is not disturbed and the following rules are observed.

247. In the Office for Sundays, solemnities, feasts of the Lord given in the General Calendar, the weekdays of Lent and Holy Week, the days within the octaves of Easter and Christmas, and the weekdays from the 17th to the 24th of December inclusively, it is never permissible to change the texts that are proper or appropriate to the celebration, such as antiphons, hymns, readings, responsories, prayers and very often psalms as well.

In place of the Sunday psalms of the current week one may substitute the Sunday psalms of a different week, and even, in the case of an Office celebrated with the people, other psalms especially chosen to lead them step by step to an understanding of the psalms.

248. In the Office of Readings, the current cycle of Sacred Scripture must always be held in honor. The desire of the Church "that, within a fixed cycle of years,

the more important parts of the Sacred Scriptures may be read to the people"[6] applies also to the Office.

Because of this, the cycle of readings from Scripture that is provided in the Office must not be abandoned during the seasons of Advent, Christmas, Lent and Easter. During Ordinary Time, however, on a particular day or for a few days in succession, one may, for a good reason, choose readings from those provided on other days, or even other biblical readings, for example, on the occasion of retreats or pastoral gatherings or prayers for Christian unity or other such events.

249. When the continuous reading is interrupted because of a solemnity or feast or special celebration, it is permissible during the same week, taking into account the readings for the whole week, either to combine the parts omitted with others or to decide which of the texts are to be preferred.

250. In the Office of Readings one may also, for a good reason, choose another reading from the same season, from the Liturgy of the Hours or the optional Lectionary (no. 161), in preference to the second reading appointed for the day. In addition, on weekdays in Ordinary Time and, if it seems opportune, even in the seasons of Advent, Christmas, Lent and Easter, one may choose for quasi-continuous reading the work of a Father of the Church, in harmony with the biblical and liturgical context.

251. The readings, prayers, songs and intercessions appointed for the weekdays of a particular season may be used on other weekdays of the same season.

[6]Second Vatican Council, constitution *Sacrosanctum Concilium*, no. 51.

252. **Although** the observance of the complete cycle of the four week psalter should be dear to each one's heart,[7] one may, for spiritual or pastoral reasons, replace the psalms appointed for a particular day with others from the same Hour of a different day. There are also circumstances occasionally arising when it is permissible to choose suitable psalms or other texts as for a votive Office.

CHAPTER V

THE RITES FOR CELEBRATION IN COMMON

I. THE VARIOUS ROLES

253. In the celebration of the Liturgy of the Hours, as in all other liturgical actions, "the person, whether minister or member of the faithful, who exercises a role, should perform everything that belongs to him by the nature of his role and the rules governing the liturgy, and nothing else."[1]

254. If a bishop presides, especially in the cathedral, he should be attended by his priests and by ministers, with full and active participation by the people. A priest or deacon should normally preside at every celebration with the people, and ministers should also be present.

255. The priest or deacon who presides at a celebration may wear a stole over the alb or surplice; a priest may also wear a cope. On a greater solemnities there is nothing to prevent several priests from wearing copes or several deacons from wearing dalmatics.

256. It is for the presiding priest or deacon, from the chair, to open the celebration with the introductory verse, to begin the Lord's Prayer, to say the concluding prayer, to greet the people, bless them and dismiss them.

257. Either the priest or a minister may give out the intercessions.

258. In the absence of a priest or deacon, the one who presides at the Office is only one among equals; he does not enter the sanctuary, or greet and bless the people.

---

[1]Second Vatican Council, constitution *Sacrosanctum Concilium*, no. 28.

259. Those who act as readers stand in a suitable place to read either the long readings or the short readings.

260. The antiphons, psalms and other chants should be begun by a cantor or cantors. With regard to the psalmody, the directions of nos. 121-125 should be observed.

261. During the Gospel Canticle at Morning and Evening Prayer the altar, then the priest and the people, may be incensed.

262. The obligation of choir applies to the community, not to the place of celebration, which need not be a church, especially in the case of those Hours that are performed without solemnity.

263. All taking part stand:

(a) during the introduction to the Office and the introductory verses of each Hour;

(b) during the hymn;

(c) during the Gospel Canticle;

(d) during the intercessions, the Lord's Prayer and the concluding prayer.

264. All should sit to listen to the readings, except at the Gospel.

265. While the psalms and other canticles (with their antiphons) are being said, the assembly either sits or stands, according to custom.

266. All make the sign of the cross, from forehead to breast and from left shoulder to right:

(a) at the beginning of the Hours, when God, come to my assistance is being said;

(b) at the beginning of the Gospel Canticles of Zechariah, of Mary and of Simeon.

The sign of the cross is made on the mouth at the beginning of the invitatory, at the words Lord, open my lips.

II. SINGING IN THE OFFICE

267. In the rubrics and norms of this Instruction, the words "say," "recite," etc., are to be understood to refer to singing or recitation, in the light of the principles given below.

268. "Sung celebration of the Office, because it is more in keeping with the nature of this prayer and is a mark of greater solemnity, and the expression of a deeper union of hearts, in offering praise to God, is earnestly commended to those who perform the Divine Office in choir or in common."[2]

269. The declarations of the Second Vatican Council on liturgical singing apply to all liturgical actions but in a special way to the Liturgy of the Hours.[3] Though every part of it has been revised in such a way that all may be fruitfully recited even by individuals, many of these parts are lyrical in form and do not yield their fuller meaning unless they are sung: above all, the psalms, canticles, hymns and responsories.

270. Hence, in celebrating the liturgy singing is not to be regarded as an extrinsic embellishment to prayer; rather, it wells up from the depths of a soul intent on prayer and the praise of God and reveals in a full and perfect way the community nature of Christian worship.

[2]Congregation of Rites, instruction *Musicam sacram*, March 5, 1967, no. 37: AAS 59 (1967) 310; see Second Vatican Council, constitution *Sacrosanctum Concilium*, no. 99.
[3]See Second Vatican Council, constitution *Sacrosanctum Concilium*, no. 113.

Christian communities of all kinds seeking to use this form of prayer as frequently as possible deserve our praise. Clerics and religious, as well as members of the faithful, must be trained by suitable instruction and practice to join together in singing the Hours in a spirit of joy, especially on feast days. Since, however, it is no easy task to sing the whole Office, and since too the Church's praise is not to be considered the exclusive possession of clerics and monks either in its origin or by its nature, but belongs to the whole Christian community, several principles must be borne in mind if the sung celebration of the Liturgy of the Hours is to be correctly performed and seen in its true nature and beauty.

271. It is particularly appropriate that there should be singing at least on Sundays and feast days, and through its use the different degrees of solemnity come to be recognized.

272. In the same way, since not all the Hours are of equal importance, it is desirable that those Hours which are the true hinges of the Office, that is, Morning and Evening Prayer, should receive greater honor by the use of singing.

273. A celebration performed entirely with singing is commendable, provided that it has artistic and spiritual excellence; but it may be useful on occasion to apply the principle of "progressive solemnity." There are practical reasons for this; there is also the fact that the various elements of liturgical celebration are not then treated indiscriminately, but each of them can be restored to its original meaning and genuine function. The Liturgy of the Hours is then seen, not as an artistic relic of the past, arousing our admiration only if it is preserved without change, but on the contrary as capable of living and

growing in a new environment, and of becoming once again an unmistakable testimony to a community full of vigorous life.

Thus, the principle of "progressive solemnity" is one that recognizes several intermediate stages between the full sung Office and the simple recitation of all its parts. Its application offers the possibility of a rich and pleasing variety; its criteria are the particular day or Hour being celebrated, the character of the individual elements comprising the Office, the size and composition of the community, as well as the number of singers available in the circumstances.

With this increased scope for variation, it will be possible for the public praise of the Church to be sung more frequently and be adapted in a variety of ways to different circumstances. There is great hope that new ways and expressions of public worship may be found for our own age, as has always happened in the life of the Church.

274. For liturgical celebrations sung in Latin, Gregorian Chant, as the music proper to the Roman Liturgy, should have pride of place, in normal circumstances, *ceteris paribus*.[4] Nevertheless, "the Church does not exclude from liturgical actions any type of music provided that it corresponds to the spirit of the liturgical action itself and the nature of the individual parts, and that it does not prevent the people from taking their due and active part."[5] At a sung Office, if a melody is not available for the given antiphon, another antiphon should be taken from those in the repertoire, provided that it is suitable in terms of nos. 113 and 121-125.

---

[4] See *ibid.*, no. 116.
[5] Congregation of Rites, instruction *Musicam sacram*, March 5, 1967, no. 9: AAS 59 (1967) 303; see Second Vatican Council, constitution *Sacrosanctum Concilium*, no. 116.

275. Since the Liturgy of the Hours may be celebrated in the vernacular, "due care should be taken to provide melodies for use in singing the Divine Office in the vernacular."[6]

276. There is, however, nothing to prevent different parts from being sung in different languages at one and the same celebration.[7]

277. The choice of parts particularly suited for singing follows from the correct arrangement of a liturgical celebration. This demands that the significance and function of each part and of singing should be carefully respected. Some parts by their nature are for singing:[8] in particular, acclamations, responses to the greeting of priest and minister, responses in litanies, responses within a psalm, hymns and canticles.[9]

278. It is an established fact that the psalms (see nos. 103-120) are closely linked with music, as Jewish and Christian tradition both confirm. Indeed, it is no small contribution to the full appreciation of the psalms if they are sung, or at least are always seen in the perspective of poetry and music. If it is feasible, the sung form is to be preferred, at least on more important days and at the principal Hours, and with respect for the inborn character of the psalms.

279. The different methods of reciting the psalms are described above in nos. 121-123. The choice of method should depend not so much on external circumstances as on the different character of the psalms to be recited in the same celebration. Thus, it may be better to read

---

[6]Congregation of Rites, instruction *Musicam sacram*, March 5, 1967, no. 41; see nos. 54-61: *AAS* 59 (1967), pp. 312, 316-317.

[7]*Ibid.*, no. 51: p. 315.

[8]See *ibid.*, no. 6: p. 302.

[9]See *ibid.*, nos. 16a, 38: pp. 305, 311.

sapiential and historical psalms, whereas psalms of praise and thanksgiving are of their nature designed for singing in common. The overriding consideration is to ensure that the celebration is not too inflexible or over-elaborate or concerned only with merely formal observance but matches the reality of what is celebrated. One must strive above all to inspire hearts with a desire for genuine prayer and to show that the celebration of God's praise is a thing of joy (see psalm 147).

280. Even when the Hours are recited, hymns can nourish prayer, provided that they have doctrinal and artistic excellence; but of their nature they are designed for singing, and so, as far as possible, should be sung at a celebration in common.

281. The responsory after the reading at Morning and Evening Prayer (see no. 49) is of its nature designed for singing, and indeed for singing by the people.

282. The responsories following the readings in the Office of Readings by their very nature and function also demand to be sung. In the Office they are composed in such a way that they can retain their power even in individual and private recitation. Responsories with simpler and easier melodies will be able to be sung more frequently than those which have come down from liturgical sources.

283. The longer readings, and the short readings, are not of themselves designed for singing. When they are recited, great care should be taken that they are read in a fitting manner, and with clarity and distinctness, so as to be properly heard and correctly understood by all. The only acceptable melody is therefore one that enables the words to be more easily heard and the meaning better understood.

284. Texts that are said only by the person presiding, as the concluding prayer, can be sung gracefully and appropriately, especially in Latin. This will be more difficult in some languages, unless singing enables the words to be heard more clearly by all.

TABLE OF LITURGICAL DAYS

from the General Norms for the Liturgical Year and the New General Roman Calendar, nos. 59-61

The order of precedence for liturgical days is governed solely by the following table.

I

1. Easter triduum of the Lord's passion and resurrection
2. Christmas, Epiphany, Ascension, and Pentecost, Sundays of Advent, Lent, and the season of Easter

   Ash Wednesday

   Weekdays of Holy Week, Monday to Thursday inclusive

   Days within the octave of Easter
3. Solemnities of the Lord, the Blessed Virgin Mary, and saints listed in the general calendar, All Souls' Day
4. Proper solemnities, namely:

a) Solemnity of the principal patron of the place, city, or state

b) Solemnity of the dedication and anniversary of the dedication of a particular church

c) Solemnity of the titular saint of a particular church

d) Solemnity of the titular saint, founder, or principal patron of an order or congregation

II

5. Feasts of the Lord in the general calendar
6. Sundays of the Christmas season and Sundays in ordinary time
7. Feasts of the Blessed Virgin Mary and of the saints in the general calendar
8. Proper feasts, namely:

a) Feast of the principal patron of the diocese

b) Feast of the anniversary of the dedication of the cathedral

c) Feast of the principal patron of the territory, province, country, or more extensive territory

d) Feast of the titular saint, founder, or principal patron of an order, congregation, or religious province, observing the directives in no. 4

e) Other feasts proper to an individual church

f) Other feasts listed in the calendar of the diocese, order, or congregation

9. Weekdays of Advent from December 17 to December 24 inclusive

Days within the octave of Christmas

Weekdays of Lent

III

10. Obligatory memorials in the general calendar

11. Proper obligatory memorials, namely:

a) Memorial of a secondary patron of the place, diocese, region or province, country, or more extensive territory; or of an order, congregation, or religious province

b) Obligatory memorials proper to an individual church

c) Obligatory memorials listed in the calendar of a diocese, order, or congregation

12. Optional memorials, as described in the instructions indicated for the Mass and office, may be observed even on the days in no. 9

In the same manner obligatory memorials may be celebrated as optional memorials if they happen to fall on the Lenten weekdays

13. Weekdays of Advent up to December 16 inclusive

Weekdays of the Christmas season from January 2 until the Saturday after Epiphany

Weekdays of the Easter season from Monday after the

octave of Easter until the Saturday before Pentecost inclusive

Weekdays in ordinary time

CELEBRATIONS ON THE SAME DAY

If several celebrations fall on the same day, the one that holds the higher rank according to the above table is observed. A solemnity, however, which is impeded by a liturgical day that takes precedence over it should be transferred to the closest day which is not a day listed in nos. 1-8 in the table of precedence, the rule of no. 5 remaining in effect. Other celebrations are omitted that year.

If on the same day vespers of the current office and first vespers of the following day are to be celebrated, the vespers of the day holding the higher rank in the table of liturgical days takes precedence; if both days are of the same rank, vespers of the current day takes precedence.

PRINCIPAL CELEBRATIONS OF THE LITURGICAL YEAR

Year	Ash Wednesday	Easter	Ascension	Pentecost
1974	27 February	14 April	23 May	2 June
1975	12 February	30 March	8 May	18 May
1976	3 March	18 April	27 May	6 June
1977	23 February	10 April	19 May	29 May
1978	8 February	26 March	4 May	14 May
1979	28 February	15 April	24 May	3 June
1980	20 February	6 April	15 May	25 May
1981	4 March	19 April	28 May	7 June
1982	24 February	11 April	20 May	30 May
1983	16 February	3 April	12 May	22 May
1984	7 March	22 April	31 May	10 June
1985	20 February	7 April	16 May	26 May
1986	12 February	30 March	8 May	18 May
1987	4 March	19 April	28 May	7 June
1988	17 February	3 April	12 May	22 May
1989	8 February	26 March	4 May	14 May
1990	28 February	15 April	24 May	3 June
1991	13 February	31 March	9 May	19 May
1992	4 March	19 April	28 May	7 June
1993	24 February	11 April	20 May	30 May
1994	16 February	3 April	12 May	22 May
1995	1 March	16 April	25 May	4 June
1996	21 February	7 April	16 May	26 May
1997	12 February	30 March	8 May	18 May
1998	25 February	12 April	21 May	31 May
1999	17 February	4 April	13 May	23 May

PRINCIPAL CELEBRATIONS OF THE LITURGICAL YEAR

| | Weeks in Ordinary Time | | | | |
| | before Lent | | after Easter Season | | |
Corpus Christi	Number of weeks	Ending	Beginning	Number of weeks	First Sunday of **Advent**
13 June	7	26 February	3 June	9	1 December
29 May	5	11 February	19 May	7	30 November
17 June	8	2 March	7 June	10	28 November
9 June	7	22 February	30 May	9	27 November
25 May	5	7 February	15 May	6	3 December
14 June	8	27 February	4 June	9	2 December
5 June	6	19 February	26 May	8	30 November
18 June	8	3 March	8 June	10	29 November
10 June	7	23 February	31 May	9	28 November
2 June	6	15 February	23 May	8	27 November
21 June	9	6 March	11 June	10	2 December
6 June	6	19 February	27 May	8	1 December
29 May	5	11 February	19 May	7	30 November
18 June	8	3 March	8 June	10	29 November
2 June	6	16 February	23 May	8	27 November
25 May	5	7 February	15 May	6	3 December
14 June	8	27 February	4 June	9	2 December
30 May	5	12 February	20 May	7	1 December
18 June	8	3 March	8 June	10	29 November
10 June	7	23 February	31 May	9	28 November
2 June	6	15 February	23 May	8	27 November
15 June	8	28 February	5 June	9	3 December
6 June	7	20 February	27 May	8	1 December
29 May	5	11 February	19 May	7	30 November
11 June	7	24 February	1 June	9	29 November
3 June	6	16 February	24 May	8	28 November

GENERAL ROMAN CALENDAR

JANUARY

1. Octave of Christmas
   SOLEMNITY OF MARY, MOTHER OF GOD
   Solemnity
2. Basil the Great and Gregory Nazianzen,
   bishops and doctors Memorial
3.
4.
5.
6. **EPIPHANY** Solemnity
7. *Raymond of Penyafort, priest**
8.
9.
10.
11.
12.
13. *Hilary, bishop and doctor*
14.
15.
16.
17. Anthony, abbot Memorial
18.
19.
20. *Fabian, pope and martyr*
    Sebastian, martyr
21. Agnes, virgin and martyr Memorial
22. *Vincent, deacon and martyr*
23.
24. Francis de Sales, bishop and doctor Memorial
25. CONVERSION OF PAUL, APOSTLE Feast
26. Timothy and Titus, bishops Memorial
27. *Angela Merici, virgin*
28. Thomas Aquinas, priest and doctor Memorial
29.
30.
31. John Bosco, priest Memorial

Sunday after January 6: BAPTISM OF THE LORD Feast

*When no rank is given, it is an optional memorial.

FEBRUARY

1.
2. **PRESENTATION OF THE LORD**   Feast
3. *Blase, bishop and martyr*
   Ansgar, bishop
4.
5. Agatha, virgin and martyr   Memorial
6. Paul Miki and companions, martyrs   Memorial
7.
8. *Jerome Emiliani*
9.
10. Scholastica, virgin   Memorial
11. *Our Lady of Lourdes*
12.
13.
14.   Cyril, monk, and Methodius, bishop   Memorial
15.
16.
17. *Seven Founders of the Order of Servites*
18.
19.
20.
21. *Peter Damian, bishop and doctor*
22. **CHAIR OF PETER, APOSTLE**   Feast
23. Polycarp, bishop and martyr   Memorial
24.
25.
26.
27.
28.

MARCH

1.
2.
3.
4. *Casimir*
5.
6.
7. Perpetua and Felicity, martyrs   Memorial
8. *John of God, religious*
9. *Frances of Rome, religious*
10.
11.
12.
13.
14.
15.
16.
17. *Patrick, bishop*
18. *Cyril of Jerusalem, bishop and doctor*
19. JOSEPH, HUSBAND OF MARY   Solemnity
20.
21.
22.
23. *Turibius de Mongrovejo, bishop*
24.
25. ANNUNCIATION   Solemnity
26.
27.
28.
29.
30.
31.

APRIL

1.
2. *Francis of Paola, hermit*
3.
4. *Isidore, bishop and doctor*
5. *Vincent Ferrer, priest*
6.
7. John Baptist de la Salle, priest   Memorial
8.
9.
10.
11. *Stanislaus, bishop and martyr*
12.
13. *Martin I, pope and martyr*
14.
15.
16.
17.
18.
19.
20.
21. *Anselm, bishop and doctor*
22.
23. *George, martyr*
24. *Fidelis of Sigmaringen, priest and martyr*
25. MARK, EVANGELIST   Feast
26.
27.
28. *Peter Chanel, priest and martyr*
29. Catherine of Siena, virgin and doctor   Memorial
30. *Pius V, pope*

MAY

1. *Joseph the Worker*
2. Athanasius, bishop and doctor   Memorial
3. PHILIP AND JAMES, APOSTLES   Feast
4.
5.
6.
7.
8.
9.
10.
11.
12. *Nereus and Achilleus, martyrs*
    Pancras, martyr
13.
14. MATTHIAS, APOSTLE   Feast
15.
16.
17.
18. *John I, pope and martyr*
19.
20. *Bernardine of Siena, priest*
21.
22.
23.
24.
25. *Venerable Bede, priest and doctor*
    Gregory VII, pope
    Mary Magdalene de Pazzi, virgin
26. Philip Neri, priest   Memorial
27. *Augustine of Canterbury, bishop*
28.
29.
30.
31. VISITATION   Feast

First Sunday after Pentecost: **HOLY TRINITY**   Solemnity
Thursday after Holy Trinity: **CORPUS CHRISTI**   Solemnity
Friday following Second Sunday after Pentecost:
    SACRED HEART   Solemnity
Saturday following Second Sunday after Pentecost:
    Immaculate Heart of Mary

JUNE

1. Justin, martyr   Memorial
2. *Marcellinus and Peter, martyrs*
3. Charles Lwanga and companions, martyrs   Memorial
4.
5. Boniface, bishop and martyr   Memorial
6. *Norbert, bishop*
7.
8.
9. *Ephrem, deacon and doctor*
10.
11. Barnabas, apostle   Memorial
12.
13. Anthony of Padua, priest and doctor   Memorial
14.
15.
16.
17.
18.
19. *Romuald, abbot*
20.
21. Aloysius Gonzaga, religious   Memorial
22. *Paulinus of Nola, bishop*
   John Fisher, bishop and martyr, and
       Thomas More, martyr
23.
24. BIRTH OF JOHN THE BAPTIST   Solemnity
25.
26.
27. *Cyril of Alexandria, bishop and doctor*
28. Irenaeus, bishop and martyr   Memorial
29. PETER AND PAUL, APOSTLES   Solemnity
30. *First Martyrs of the Church of Rome*

JULY

1.
2.
3. THOMAS, APOSTLE   Feast
4. *Elizabeth of Portugal*
5. *Anthony Zaccaria, priest*
6. *Maria Goretti, virgin and martyr*
7.
8.
9.
10.
11. Benedict, abbot   Memorial
12.
13. *Henry*
14. *Camillus de Lellis, priest*
15. Bonaventure, bishop and doctor   Memorial
16. *Our Lady of Mount Carmel*
17.
18.
19.
20.
21. *Lawrence of Brindisi, priest and doctor*
22. Mary Magdalene   Memorial
23. *Bridget, religious*
24.
25. JAMES, APOSTLE   Feast
26. Joachim and Ann, parents of Mary   Memorial
27.
28.
29. Martha   Memorial
30. *Peter Chrysologus, bishop and doctor*
31. Ignatius of Loyola, priest   Memorial

AUGUST

1. Alphonsus Liguori, bishop and doctor — Memorial
2. *Eusebius of Vercelli, bishop*
3.
4. John Vianney, priest — Memorial
5. *Dedication of St. Mary Major*
6. TRANSFIGURATION — Feast
7. *Sixtus II, pope and martyr, and companions, martyrs*
   Cajetan, priest
8. Dominic, priest — Memorial
9.
10. LAWRENCE, DEACON AND MARTYR — Feast
11. Clare, virgin — Memorial
12.
13. *Pontian, pope and martyr, and Hippolytus,*
    priest and martyr
14.
15. ASSUMPTION — Solemnity
16. *Stephen of Hungary*
17.
18.
19. *John Eudes, priest*
20. Bernard, abbot and doctor — Memorial
21. Pius X, pope — Memorial
22. Queenship of Mary — Memorial
23. *Rose of Lima, virgin*
24. BARTHOLOMEW, APOSTLE — Feast
25. *Louis*
    Joseph Calasanz, priest
26.
27. Monica — Memorial
28. Augustine, bishop and doctor — Memorial
29. Beheading of John the Baptist, martyr — Memorial
30.
31.

SEPTEMBER

1.
2.
3. Gregory the Great, pope and doctor   Memorial
4.
5.
6.
7.
8. BIRTH OF MARY   Feast
9.
10.
11.
12.
13. John Chrysostom, bishop and doctor   Memorial
14. TRIUMPH OF THE CROSS   Feast
15. Our Lady of Sorrows   Memorial
16. Cornelius, pope and martyr, and
    Cyprian, bishop and martyr   Memorial
17. *Robert Bellarmine, bishop and doctor*
18.
19. *Januarius, bishop and martyr*
20.
21. MATTHEW, APOSTLE AND EVANGELIST   Feast
22.
23.
24.
25.
26. *Cosmas and Damian, martyrs*
27. Vincent de Paul, priest   Memorial
28. *Wenceslaus, martyr*
29. MICHAEL, GABRIEL, AND RAPHAEL,
    ARCHANGELS   Feast
30. Jerome, priest and doctor   Memorial

OCTOBER

1. Theresa of the Child Jesus, virgin   Memorial
2. Guardian Angels   Memorial
3.
4. Francis of Assisi   Memorial
5.
6. *Bruno, priest*
7. Our Lady of the Rosary   Memorial
8.
9. *Denis, bishop and martyr, and companions, martyrs*
   John Leonardi, priest
10.
11.
12.
13.
14. *Callistus I, pope and martyr*
15. Teresa of Avila, virgin and doctor   Memorial
16. *Hedwig, religious*
   Margaret Mary Alacoque, virgin
17. Ignatius of Antioch, bishop and martyr   Memorial
18. LUKE, EVANGELIST   Feast
19. *Isaac Jogues and John de Brebeuf, priests and*
   martyrs, and companions, martyrs
   Paul of the Cross, priest
20.
21.
22.
23. *John of Capistrano, priest*
24. *Anthony Claret, bishop*
25.
26.
27.
28. SIMON AND JUDE, APOSTLES   Feast
29.
30.
31.

NOVEMBER

1.	ALL SAINTS	Solemnity
2.	ALL SOULS	
3.	*Martin de Porres, religious*	
4.	Charles Borromeo, bishop	Memorial
5.		
6.		
7.		
8.		
9.	DEDICATION OF ST. JOHN LATERAN	Feast
10.	Leo the Great, pope and doctor	Memorial
11.	Martin of Tours, bishop	Memorial
12.	Josaphat, bishop and martyr	Memorial
13.		
14.		
15.	*Albert the Great, bishop and doctor*	
16.	*Margaret of Scotland*	
	Gertrude, virgin	
17.	Elizabeth of Hungary, religious	Memorial
18.	*Dedication of the churches of Peter and Paul, apostles*	
19.		
20.		
21.	Presentation of Mary	Memorial
22.	Cecilia, virgin and martyr	Memorial
23.	*Clement I, pope and martyr*	
	Columban, abbot	
24.		
25.		
26.		
27.		
28.		
29.		
30.	ANDREW, APOSTLE	Feast

Last Sunday in Ordinary Time:
CHRIST THE KING   Solemnity

DECEMBER

1.
2.
3. Francis Xavier, priest   Memorial
4. *John Damascene, priest and doctor*
5.
6. *Nicholas, bishop*
7. Ambrose, bishop and doctor   Memorial
8. IMMACULATE CONCEPTION   Solemnity
9.
10.
11. *Damasus I, pope*
12. *Jane Frances de Chantal, religious*
13. Lucy, virgin and martyr   Memorial
14. John of the Cross, priest and doctor   Memorial
15.
16.
17.
18.
19.
20.
21. *Peter Canisius, priest and doctor*
22.
23. *John of Kanty, priest*
24.
25. CHRISTMAS   Solemnity
26. STEPHEN, FIRST MARTYR   Feast
27. JOHN, APOSTLE AND EVANGELIST   Feast
28. HOLY INNOCENTS, MARTYRS   Feast
29. *Thomas Becket, bishop and martyr*
30.
31. *Sylvester I, pope*

Sunday within the octave of Christmas or if there is
no Sunday within the octave, December 30:
HOLY FAMILY   Feast

PROPER CALENDAR FOR THE DIOCESES OF THE UNITED STATES OF AMERICA

JANUARY

4.	Elizabeth Ann Seton	Memorial
5.	Blessed John Neumann, bishop	Memorial

MAY

15. *Isidore*

JULY

4. *Independence Day*

SEPTEMBER

9. Peter Claver, priest Memorial

19. Isaac Jogues and John de Brebeuf, priests
and martyrs, and companions, martyrs Memorial

NOVEMBER

13. Frances Xavier Cabrini, virgin Memorial
Fourth Thursday *Thanksgiving Day*

DECEMBER

12. Our Lady of Guadalupe Memorial

PROPER OF SEASONS

ADVENT SEASON

The following hymns may be sung during the Advent Season before December 17.

Office of Readings

HYMN

S T Th Sa

On Jordan's bank the Baptist's cry
Announces that the Lord is nigh;
Awake and hearken, for he brings
Glad tidings of the King of kings.

Then cleansed be ev'ry heart from sin,
Make straight the way of God within;
O let us all our hearts prepare
For Christ to come and enter there.

For you are man's salvation, Lord,
Our refuge and our great reward;
Once more upon your people shine,
And fill the world with love divine.

To God the Son all glory be,
Whose advent set all nations free,
Whom with the Father we adore,
And Holy Spirit ever more.

Melody: Winchester New L.M.   Music: *Musikalisches*
                                                  Handbuch,
                                          Hamburg, 1690
                    Text: *Iordanis Ora Praevia*, Charles Coffin,
                                                       1736
Or: Translator: John Chandler, 1837, alt.

Antiphon: MWF

Maranatha! Come, O Christ the Lord!

I am the Root of Jesse and David's Son,
The radiant Star of morning and God's own Light.

Antiphon

121

The Spirit and the Bride say: "Come!" Let him who
hears their voices say:
"Come!"

Antiphon

He who has thirst, let him come,
and he who has desire, let him drink
the waters of everlasting life.

Antiphon

"Yes, I come very soon!"
Amen!
Come, O Lord Jesus!

Antiphon

Melody: Maranatha   Music: Lucien Deiss, C.S.Sp., 1965
                               Text: Lucien Deiss, C.S. Sp., 1965

Morning Prayer

HYMN   S F

Come, thou long expected Jesus,
Born to set thy people free;
From our fears and sins release us,
Let us find our rest in thee.

Israel's strength and consolation,
Hope of all the earth thou art;
Dear desire of every nation,
Joy of every longing heart.

Born thy people to deliver,
Born a child, and yet a king,
Born to reign in us for ever,
Now thy gracious kingdom bring.

By thine own eternal Spirit
Rule in all our hearts alone;
By thine all-sufficient merit
Raise us to thy glorious throne.

Melody: Stuttgart 87-87   Music: adapted from C. F. Witt.
                                                  1660-1716
                               Text: Charles Wesley, 1707-1788

Or: M 5a

Refrain:
Be consoled, my people;
take courage, O fair Jerusalem,
for your slav'ry has come to an end.

Speak to the heart of Jerusalem
and call to her that her slav'ry has ended,
her sin is forgiven and her punishment over and
    done.

               Refrain

A voice cries "Prepare in the wilderness
a way for our God and make a straight highway
for the Lord 'cause he's comin'
to rescue our desert land."

               Refrain

Let every valley be filled in,
every mountain made low
and let ev'ry cliff become a plain,
let nothing hinder our God.

               Refrain

Then the glory of Yahweh shall be revealed
and all mankind shall see it;
it is I your God who have spoken.

Melody: Be Consoled, My People   Music: Tom Parker, 1968
                                        Text: Tom Parker, 1968
Or:
                                      T
Hear the herald voice resounding:
"Christ is near," it seems to say,
Cast away the dreams of darkness,
Welcome Christ, the light of day!"

Wakened by this solemn warning,
Let the earthbound soul arise;

Christ her sun, all sloth dispelling,
Shines upon the morning skies.

See the Lamb so long expected,
Comes with pardon down from heav'n;
Hasten now, with tears of sorrow,
One and all to be forgiv'n.

So when next he comes with glory,
Shrouding all the earth in fear,
May he then as our defender
On the clouds of heav'n appear.

Honor, glory, virtue, merit,
To the Father and the Son,
With the co-eternal Spirit,
While eternal ages run.

Melody: Merton 87.87   Music: W. H. Monk, 1823-1889
Text: *Vox clara ecce intonat*, 6th century
Translator: E. Caswall, 1814-1878,
adapted by Anthony G. Petti

Or:

Refrain:

The King of glory comes, the nation rejoices;
Open the gates before him, lift up your voices.
In all of Galilee, in city or village,
He goes among his people curing their illness.

Who is the king of glory;
how shall we call him?
He is Emmanuel, the promised of ages.

Refrain

Sing then of David's Son,
our Savior and brother;
In all of Galilee was never another.

Refrain

He gave his life for us,
the lamb of salvation,
He took upon himself the sins of the nation.

Refrain

He conquered sin and death,
he truly has risen,
And he will share with us his heavenly vision.

Refrain

Melody: Israeli Folksong

Music: Israeli Folksong
Text W.F. Jabusch, 1967

Or:

Wake, awake, the night is dying,
And prophets from of old are crying:
Awake, ye children of the light!
Lo, the Dawn shall banish sadness,
The Rising Sun shall bring us gladness,
And all the blind shall see aright.

Refrain:

Rejoice, the King is near,
Our praises he will hear,
Alleluia!
But we must be
Prepared to see
The Brightness of eternity.

We shall heed the prophets' warning,
And rise to greet the Prince of Morning:
His gentle rule shall bring us peace.
Love and mercy are his treasure,
The seas and skies obey his pleasure:
His mighty rule shall never cease.

Refrain

Let the shadows be forsaken:
The time has come for us to waken,
And to the Day our lives entrust.
Search the sky for heaven's portal:
The clouds shall rain the Light Immortal,
And earth will soon bud forth the Just.

Refrain

Melody: Wachet Auf 898.898.664.448   Music: Philip Nicolai, 1599
Text: Melvin Farrell, S.S.

Evening Prayer

HYMN

Creator of the stars of night,
Your people's everlasting light,
Jesus, Redeemer, save us all,
And hear your servants when they call.

Now, grieving that the ancient curse
Should doom to death a universe,
You heal all men who need your grace
To save and heal a ruined race.

At whose great name, majestic now,
All knees must bend, all hearts must bow;
All things in heaven and earth adore,
And own thee King for evermore.

To God the Father, God the Son,
And God the Spirit, Three in One,
Praise, honor, might, and glory be
From age to age eternally.

Melody: Conditor Alme Siderum L.M.   Music: Sarum plainsong
Mode IV,
c. 9th century
Text: Anon., 7th century
Translator: J. M. Neale and others, alt.

Or:

Refrain:
You heavens, open from above, that clouds may rain
the Just One.

Do not be angry, Lord our God,
No longer be mindful that we have sinned before
you.
See how Zion, your city, now is left abandoned.
Zion is left unguarded now, Jerusalem now is deso-
late:
City that claimed your loving blessing and worked
for your glory,
City where our fathers sang your praises.

Refrain

We know our sin, and we are burdened as with
some loathsome thing,
And have fallen down just like leaves in the blast
of winter:
And the sins we have committed just like winds
have blown us all about.
You have taken from us your brightness and comfort,
And you have broken us by laying the debt of our
sins upon us.

Refrain

Lord, now turn to us and see your chosen people's
affliction
And send down him who is to come,
The One promised, Lamb and yet Lord of all lands,
From the rock in the desert to the mount of Zion,
your daughter,
That he may bring pardon, freeing us captives of
our burden.

Refrain

Be you comforted, be you comforted, hear me, my
people:
Soon shall come to you Christ, your Savior.
Why do you give way to sorrowing:
Has this grieving ended your sadness?
Your Savior comes, do not be fearful, for it is I,
your God and your mighty Ruler,
Zion's Holy One and your Redeemer.

Refrain

Melody: Rorate Coeli

Music: P. Bourget (?)
Text: Paris, 1634
Translator: Melvin Farrell, S.S., 1966

Or:

Refrain:
Rorate coeli desuper, et nubes pluant iustum.

Ne irascaris, Domine, ne ultra memineris iniquitatis:
Ecce civitas sancti facta est deserta:
Sion deserta facta est: Ierusalem desolata est:
Domus sanctificationis tuae et gloriae tuae,
Ubi laudaverunt te patres nostri.

Refrain

Peccavimus, et facti sumus tamquam immundus
nos,
Et cicidimus quasi folium universi:
Et iniquitatis nostrae quasi ventus abstulerunt nos:
Abscondisti faciem tuam a nobis,
Et allisisti nos in manu iniquitatis nostrae.

Refrain

Vide, Domine, afflictionem populi tui,
Et mitte quam missurus es:
Emitte Agnum dominatorem terrae,
De petra deserti ad montem filiae Sion:
Ut auferat ipse iugum captivitatis nostrae.

Refrain

Consolamini, consolamini, popule meus:
Cito veniet salus tua:
Quare moerore consumeris, quia innovavit dolor?
Salvabo te, noli timere, ego enim sum Dominus
   Deus tuus,
Sanctus Israel, Redemptor tuus.

Refrain

Melody: Rorate Coeli   Music: P. Bourget(?), 1634
                                         Text: Paris, 1634

Or:

O come, O come, Emmanuel,
And ransom captive Israel,
That mourns in lonely exile here
Until the Son of God appear.

Refrain:
Rejoice! Rejoice! O Israel
To thee shall come Emmanuel!

O come, thou wisdom, from on high,
And order all things far and nigh;
To us the path of knowledge show,
And teach us in her ways to go.

Refrain

O come, O come, thou Lord of might,
Who to thy tribes on Sinai's height
In ancient times did give the law,
In cloud, and majesty, and awe.

Refrain

O come, thou rod of Jesse's stem,
From ev'ry foe deliver them
That trust thy mighty power to save,
And give them vict'ry o'er the grave.

Refrain

O come, thou key of David, come,
And open wide our heav'nly home,
Make safe the way that leads on high,
That we no more have cause to sigh.

Refrain

O come, thou Dayspring from on high,
And cheer us by thy drawing nigh;
Disperse the gloomy clouds of night
And death's dark shadow put to flight.

Refrain

O come, Desire of nations, bind
In one the hearts of all mankind;
Bid every strife and quarrel cease
And fill the world with heaven's peace.

Refrain

Melody: Veni, Veni
Emmanuel

Music: Thomas Helmore, 1811-1890,
Adapted from a first Mode Responsory in
in a 15th century French *Processional*
Text: *Veni, Veni Emmanuel*, a paraphrase
of the Latin, 12th-13th century "Great O"
antiphons in *Psalteriolum Cantionum Catholicarum*
Translators: Thomas Helmore, 1811-1890,
J. M. Neale, 1818-1866, and others

Or:

Veni, veni, Emmanuel,
Captivum solve Israel,
Qui gemit in exilio,
Privatus Dei Filio.

Refrain:

Gaude! Gaude! Emmanuel,
Nascetur pro te, Israel!

Veni, O Sapientia,
Quae hic disponis omnia,
Veni, viam prudentiae
Ut doceas et gloriae.

Refrain

Veni, veni, Adonai,
Qui populo in Sinai
Legem dedisti vertice
In maiestate gloriae.

Refrain

Veni, O Iesse virgula,
Ex hostis tuos ungula,
De specu tuos tartari
Educ et antro barathri.

Refrain

Veni, Clavis Davidica,
Regna reclude caelica,
Fac iter tutum superum,
Et claude vias inferum.

Refrain

Veni, veni, O Oriens,
Solari nos adveniens,
Noctis depelle nebulas,
Dirasque mortis tenebras.

Refrain

Veni, veni, Rex Gentium,
Veni, Redemptor omnium,
Ut salvas tuos famulos
Peccati sibi conscios.

Refrain

The following hymns may be sung during the Advent Season after December 17.

Office of Readings

HYMN

The coming of our God
To fill our world with peace
Should make us raise our voices high
In songs that never cease.

As Judge, on clouds of light,
Again will he descend
And all his members then unite
In joys that ever end.

And now to us today
His saving acts he brings.
In Eucharistic mystery
Come quickly, King of kings!

Melody: Williams S.M.   Music: Aaron Williams, 1763
Text: *Instantis Adventum Dei*,
Charles Coffin, 1736;
Stanza 3, Roger Nachtwey, 1965
Translator: Roger Nachtwey, 1965

Morning Prayer

HYMN

Behold a Virgin bearing him
Who comes to save us from our sin;
The prophets cry: prepare his way!
Make straight his paths to Christmas Day.

Behold our Hope and Life and Light,
The promise of the holy night;
We lift our prayer and bend our knee
To his great love and majesty.

Melody: Behold a Virgin   Music: Rheinfels *Gesangbuch*, 1666
Bearing Him L.M.   Text: Michael Gannon, 1955

Or:

Antiphon: *M WF*

The night now is ending,
the day is drawing near!

People who live in darkness,
soon will know who their savior is,
who unexpected comes from far
the son of man, the morning star.

Antiphon

Signs in the star, in sun and moon,
say that the day is coming soon.
Hear the Lord speak: rise up be free,
for your salvation's soon to be.

Antiphon

When the sea roars and floods the land,
striking your life out of your hand,
Know in your fear and dying pain
that you will rise and live again.

Antiphon

Melody: Song of Salvation   Music: Bernard Huijbers, 1970
                             Text: Huub Oosterhuis, 1970

HYMN   **Evening Prayer**   *S W Sa*

Behold, a rose of Judah
From tender branch has sprung,
From Jesse's lineage coming,
As men of old have sung.
It came a flower bright
Amid the cold of winter,
When half spent was the night.

Isaiah has foretold it
In words of promise sure,
And Mary's arms enfold it,

A virgin meek and pure.
Through God's eternal will
She bore for men a savior
At midnight calm and still.

Melody: Es ist ein' Ros 7.6.7.6.7.6   Music: Traditional Melody from
Alte Catholische Geistliche Kirchengesang, Cologne, 1599
Text: *Es ist ein' Ros entsprungen*, 15th century
Translator: Composite

Or:

O come, O come, Emmanuel,
And ransom captive Israel,
That mourns in lonely exile here
Until the Son of God appear.

Refrain:

Rejoice! Rejoice! O Israel
To thee shall come Emmanuel!

O come, thou Wisdom, from on high,
And order all things far and nigh;
To us the path of knowledge show,
And teach us in her ways to go.

Refrain

O come, O come, thou Lord of might,
Who to thy tribes on Sinai's height
In ancient times did give the law,
In cloud, and majesty, and awe.

Refrain

O come, thou rod of Jesse's stem,
From ev'ry foe deliver them
That trust thy mighty power to save,
And give them vict'ry o'er the grave.

Refrain

O come, thou key of David, come,
And open wide our heav'nly home;

Make safe the way that leads on high,
That we no more have cause to sigh.

Refrain

O come, thou Dayspring from on high,
And cheer us by thy drawing nigh;
Disperse the gloomy clouds of night
and death's dark shadow put to flight.

Refrain

O come, Desire of nations, bind
In one the hearts of all mankind;
Bid every strife and quarrel cease
And fill the world with heaven's peace.

Refrain

Melody: Veni, Veni Emmanuel   Music: Thomas Helmore, 1811-1890, Adapted from a first Mode Responsory in in a 15th century French *Processional*
Text: *Veni, Veni Emmanuel,* a paraphrase of the Latin, 12th-13th century "Great O" antiphons in *Psalteriolum Cantionum Catholicarum*
Translators: Thomas Helmore, 1811-1890, J. M. Neale, 1818-1866, and others

Or:

Veni, veni, Emmanuel,
Captivum solve Israel,
Qui gemit in exilio,
Privatus Dei Filio.

Refrain:

Gaude! Gaude! Emmanuel,
Nascetur pro te, Israel!

Veni, O Sapientia,
Quae hic disponis omnia,
Veni, viam prudentiae
Ut doceas et gloriae.

Refrain

Veni, veni, Adonai,
Qui populo in Sinai
Legem dedisti vertice
In maiestate gloriae.

Refrain

Veni, O Iesse virgula,
Ex hostis tuos ungula,
De specu tuos tartari
Educ et antro barathri.

Refrain

Veni, Clavis Davidica,
Regna reclude caelica,
Fac iter tutum superum,
Et claude vias inferum.

Refrain

Veni, veni, O Oriens,
Solari nos adveniens,
Noctis depelle nebulas,
Dirasque mortis tenebras.

Refrain

Veni, veni, Rex Gentium,
Veni, Redemptor omnium,
Ut salvas tuos famulos
Peccati sibi conscios.

Refrain

FIRST SUNDAY OF ADVENT

Evening Prayer I

HYMN, 126.

Ant. 1 Proclaim the good news among the nations: Our God will come to save us.

Psalms and canticle from Sunday, Week I, 678.

Ant. 2 Know that the Lord is coming and with him all his saints; that day will dawn with a wonderful light, alleluia.

Ant. 3 The Lord will come with mighty power; all mortal eyes shall see him.

READING   1 Thessalonians 5:23-24

May the God of peace make you perfect in holiness. May he preserve you whole and entire, spirit, soul, and body, irreproachable at the coming of the Lord Jesus Christ. He who calls us is trustworthy, therefore he will do it.

RESPONSORY

Lord, show us your mercy and love.
—Lord, show us your mercy and love.

And grant us your salvation,
—your mercy and love.

Glory to the Father . . .
—Lord, show us . . .

CANTICLE OF MARY

Ant. See the Lord coming from afar; his splendor fills the earth.

137

INTERCESSIONS

Jesus Christ is the joy and happiness of all who look
   forward to his coming. Let us call upon him and say:
   Come, Lord, and do not delay!
In joy, we wait for your coming,
—come, Lord Jesus.
Before time began, you shared life with the Father,
—come now and save us.
You created the world and all who live in it,
—come to redeem the work of your hands.
You did not hesitate to become man, subject to death,
—come to free us from the power of death.
You came to give us life to the full,
—come and give us your unending life.
You desire all people to live in love in your kingdom,
—come and bring together those who long to see you face
   to face.

Our Father . . .

Prayer

All-powerful God,
increase our strength of will for doing good
that Christ may find an eager welcome at his coming
and call us to his side in the kingdom of heaven,
where he lives and reigns with you and the Holy Spirit,
one God, for ever and ever.

Alternative Prayer

Father in heaven,
our hearts desire the warmth of your love
and our minds are searching for the light of your Word.
Increase our longing for Christ our Savior
and give us the strength to grow in love,
that the dawn of his coming

may find us rejoicing in his presence
and welcoming the light of his truth.
We ask this in the name of Jesus the Lord.

Invitatory

Ant.   Come, let us worship the Lord, the King who is to
come.

Invitatory psalm, as in the Ordinary, 648.

Office of Readings

HYMN, 121.

Ant. 1   This is our heavenly King; he comes with
power and might to save the nations, alleluia.

Psalms and canticle from Sunday, Week I, 683.

Ant. 2   Daughter of Jerusalem, rejoice and be glad;
your King will come to you. Zion, do not fear,
your Savior hastens on his way.

Ant. 3   Let us cleanse our hearts for the coming of our
great King, that we may be ready to welcome
him; he is coming and will not delay.

Lift up your heads and see.
—Your redemption is now at hand.

FIRST READING

From the beginning of the book of the
prophet Isaiah   1:1-18

The reproof of the people

The vision which Isaiah, son of Amoz, had concerning
Judah and Jerusalem in the days of Uzziah, Jotham,
Ahaz and Hezekiah, kings of Judah.

Hear, O heavens, and listen, O earth,
   for the Lord speaks:
Sons have I raised and reared,
   but they have disowned me!
An ox knows its owner,
   and an ass, its master's manger;
But Israel does not know,
   my people has not understood.

Ah! sinful nation, people laden with wickedness,
   evil race, corrupt children!
They have forsaken the Lord,
   spurned the Holy One of Israel, apostatized.

Where would you yet be struck,
   you that rebel again and again?
The whole head is sick,
   the whole heart faint.
From the sole of the foot to the head
   there is no sound spot:
Wound and welt and gaping gash,
   not drained, or bandaged,
   or eased with salve.

Your country is waste,
   your cities burnt with fire;
Your land before your eyes
   strangers devour
   [a waste, like Sodom overthrown]—

And daughter Zion is left
   like a hut in a vineyard,
Like a shed in a melon patch,
   like a city blockaded.
Unless the Lord of hosts
   had left us a scanty remnant,

We had become as Sodom,
  we should be like Gomorrah.

Hear the word of the Lord,
  princes of Sodom!
Listen to the instruction of our God,
  people of Gomorrah!

What care I for the number of your sacrifices?
  says the Lord.
I have had enough of whole-burnt rams
  and fat of fatlings;
In the blood of calves, lambs and goats
  I find no pleasure.
When you come in to visit me,
  who asks these things of you?
Trample my courts no more!
  Bring no more worthless offerings;
  your incense is loathsome to me.
New moon and sabbath, calling of assemblies,
  octaves with wickedness: these I cannot bear.
Your new moons and festivals I detest;
  they weigh me down, I tire of the load.
When you spread out your hands,
  I close my eyes to you;
Though you pray the more,
  I will not listen.

Your hands are full of blood!
  Wash yourselves clean!
Put away your misdeeds from before my eyes;
  cease doing evil; learn to do good.
Make justice your aim: redress the wronged,
  hear the orphan's plea, defend the widow.

Come now, let us set things right,
  says the Lord:

Though your sins be like scarlet,
   they may become white as snow;
Though they be crimson red,
   they may become white as wool.

RESPONSORY   Isaiah 1:16, 18, 17

Wash yourselves, be clean.
Banish evil from your hearts,
away from my sight.
—Though your sins be scarlet,
they shall be made white as snow.

Cease to do evil and learn to do good,
seek always what is just.
—Though your sins . . .

SECOND READING

From a catechetical instruction by Saint Cyril of
Jerusalem, bishop

(Cat. 15, 1-3: PG 33, 870-874)

On the twofold coming of Christ

We do not preach only one coming of Christ, but a
second as well, much more glorious than the first. The
first coming was marked by patience; the second will
bring the crown of a divine kingdom.

In general, what relates to our Lord Jesus Christ has
two aspects. There is a birth from God before the ages,
and a birth from a virgin at the fullness of time. There is
a hidden coming, like that of rain on fleece, and a coming
before all eyes, still in the future.

At the first coming he was wrapped in swaddling
clothes in a manger. At his second coming he will be
clothed in light as in a garment. In the first coming he
endured the cross, despising the shame; in the second

coming he will be in glory, escorted by an army of angels. We look then beyond the first coming and await the second. At the first coming we said: *Blessed is he who comes in the name of the Lord.* At the second we shall say it again; we shall go out with the angels to meet the Lord and cry out in adoration: *Blessed is he who comes in the name of the Lord.*

The Savior will not come to be judged again, but to judge those by whom he was judged. At his own judgment he was silent; then he will address those who committed the outrages against him when they crucified him and will remind them: *You did these things, and I was silent.*

His first coming was to fulfill his plan of love, to teach men by gentle persuasion. This time, whether men like it or not, they will be subjects of his kingdom by necessity. Malachi the prophet speaks of the two comings. *And the Lord whom you seek will come suddenly to his temple:* that is one coming.

Again he says of another coming: *Look, the Lord almighty will come, and who will endure the day of his entry, or who will stand in his sight? Because he comes like a refiner's fire, a fuller's herb, and he will sit refining and cleansing.*

These two comings are also referred to by Paul in writing to Titus: *The grace of God the Savior has appeared to all men, instructing us to put aside impiety and worldly desires and live temperately, uprightly, and religiously in this present age, waiting for the joyful hope, the appearance of the glory of our great God and Savior, Jesus Christ.* Notice how he speaks of a first coming for which he gives thanks, and a second, the one we still await.

That is why the faith we profess has been handed on to you in these words: *He ascended into heaven, and is seated at the right hand of the Father, and he will come again in glory to judge the living and the dead, and his kingdom will have no end.*

Our Lord Jesus Christ will therefore come from heaven. He will come at the end of the world, in glory, at the last day. For there will be an end to this world, and the created world will be made new.

RESPONSORY

Watching from afar, I see the power of God advancing,
and the whole earth enveloped in a cloud.
Go out to meet him crying:
—Tell us if you are the One who is to reign over the
  people of Israel.

All peoples of the earth,
all children of men,
—rich and poor alike, go out to meet him crying:

Shepherd of Israel, hear us,
you who lead Joseph's race like a flock,
—tell us if you are the One.

Throw wide the gates, you princes,
let the King of glory enter,
—who is to reign over the people of Israel.

Watching from afar to people of Israel.

HYMN, Te Deum, 651.

Prayer, as in Morning Prayer.

Morning Prayer

HYMN, 122.

Ant. 1   On that day sweet wine will flow from the
          mountains, milk and honey from the hills,
          alleluia.

Psalms and canticle from Sunday, Week I, 688.

Ant. 2 The mountains and hills will sing praise to God;
        all the trees of the forest will clap their hands,
        for he is coming, the Lord of a kingdom that
        lasts for ever, alleluia.

Ant. 3 A great prophet will come to Jerusalem; of that
        people he will make a new creation.

READING   Romans 13:11-12

It is now the hour for you to wake from sleep, for our
salvation is closer than when we first accepted the faith.
The night is far spent; the day draws near. Let us cast off
deeds of darkness and put on the armor of light.

RESPONSORY

Christ, Son of the living God, have mercy on us.
—Christ, Son of the living God, have mercy on us.

You are the one who is to come,
—have mercy on us.

Glory to the Father . . .
—Christ, Son of . . .

CANTICLE OF ZECHARIAH

Ant. The Holy Spirit will come upon you, Mary; you
      have no need to be afraid. You will carry in your
      womb the Son of God, alleluia.

INTERCESSIONS

To God our Father, who has given us the grace to wait in
    joyful hope for the revelation of our Lord Jesus Christ,
    let us make our prayer:
    Show us your mercy, Lord.
Sanctify us in mind and body,
—keep us without sin until the coming of your Son.

Make us walk this day in holiness,
__and live upright and devout lives in this world.
May we be clothed in our Lord Jesus Christ,
__and filled with the Holy Spirit.
Lord, help us to stand watchful and ready,
__until your Son is revealed in all his glory.

Our Father . . .

Prayer

All-powerful God,
increase our strength of will for doing good
that Christ may find an eager welcome at his coming
and call us to his side in the kingdom of heaven,
where he lives and reigns with you and the Holy Spirit,
one God, for ever and ever.

Alternative Prayer

Father in heaven,
our hearts desire the warmth of your love
and our minds are searching for the light of your Word.
Increase our longing for Christ our Savior
and give us the strength to grow in love,
that the dawn of his coming
may find us rejoicing in his presence
and welcoming the light of his truth.
We ask this in the name of Jesus the Lord.

Daytime Prayer

Hymn, 658.
Midmorning

Ant.   This is the good news the prophets foretold: The
Savior will be born of the Virgin Mary.

READING   Romans 13:13-14a

Let us live honorably as in daylight; not in carousing
and drunkenness, not in sexual excess and lust, not in
quarreling and jealousy. Rather, put on the Lord Jesus
Christ.

The nations will revere your name, O Lord.
—And the great ones of the earth will acknowledge your
glory.

Midday

Ant.   The angel Gabriel said to Mary in greeting: Hail,
full of grace, the Lord is with you; blessed are you
among women.

READING   1 Thessalonians 3:12-13

May the Lord make you overflow with love for one
another and for all, even as our love does for you. May he
strengthen your hearts, making them blameless and holy
before our God and Father at the coming of our Lord
Jesus with all his holy ones.

Remember us, Lord, because of the love you have for
your people.
—Come and bring us your salvation.

Midafternoon

Ant.   Mary said: My soul is deeply troubled; what can
this greeting mean? Am I to give birth to my King
and yet remain a virgin for ever?

READING   See 2 Thessalonians 1:6, 7, 10

Strict justice would require that God will provide relief
to you who are sorely tried, as well as to us, when the
Lord Jesus is revealed from heaven with his mighty
angels; when he comes to be glorified with his holy ones
and adored by all who have believed.

Come, Lord, do not delay.
—Free your people from their sinfulness.

Prayer, as in Morning Prayer.

Evening Prayer II

Hymn, 126.

Ant. 1　Rejoice, daughter of Zion; shout for joy, daughter of Jerusalem, alleluia.

Psalms and canticle from Sunday, Week I, 695.

Ant. 2　Christ our King will come to us: the Lamb of God foretold by John.

Ant. 3　I am coming soon, says the Lord; I will give to everyone the reward his deeds deserve.

READING　　　　　　　　　　　　　　　Philippians 4:4-5

Rejoice in the Lord always! I say it again. Rejoice! Everyone should see how unselfish you are. The Lord is near.

RESPONSORY

Lord, show us your mercy and love.
—Lord, show us your mercy and love.

And grant us your salvation,
—your mercy and love.

Glory to the Father . . .
—Lord, show us . . .

CANTICLE OF MARY

Ant.　Do not be afraid, Mary, you have found favor with God; you will conceive and give birth to a Son, alleluia.

INTERCESSIONS

To Jesus Christ, our Redeemer, the way, the truth, and
the life, let us make our humble prayer:
Come and stay with us, Lord.

Son of the Most High, your coming was announced to
the Virgin Mary by Gabriel,
—come and rule over your people for ever.

Holy One of God, in your presence John the Baptist leapt
in Elizabeth's womb,
—bring the joy of salvation to all the earth.

Jesus the Savior, the angel revealed your name to Joseph
the just man,
—come and save your people from their sins.

Light of the world, for whom Simeon and all the just
waited,
—come and comfort us.

O Rising Sun that never sets, Zechariah foretold that you
would visit us from above,
—come and shine on those who dwell in darkness and the
shadow of death.

Our Father . . .

Prayer

All-powerful God,
increase our strength of will for doing good
that Christ may find an eager welcome at his coming
and call us to his side in the kingdom of heaven,
where he lives and reigns with you and the Holy Spirit,
one God, for ever and ever.

Alternative Prayer

Father in heaven,
our hearts desire the warmth of your love
and our minds are searching for the light of your Word.

Increase our longing for Christ our Savior
and give us the strength to grow in love,
that the dawn of his coming
may find us rejoicing in his presence
and welcoming the light of his truth.

We ask this in the name of Jesus the Lord.

MONDAY

Office of Readings

Lord, show us your mercy and love.
—And grant us your salvation.

FIRST READING

From the book of the prophet Isaiah   1:21-27; 2:1-5

The judgment and deliverance of Zion. The gathering of the nations

How has she turned adulteress,
    the faithful city, so upright!
Justice used to lodge within her,
    but now, murderers.
Your silver is turned to dross,
    your wine is mixed with water.
Your princes are rebels
    and comrades of thieves;
Each one of them loves a bribe
    and looks for gifts.
The fatherless they defend not,
    and the widow's plea does not reach them.

Now, therefore, says the Lord,
    the Lord of hosts, the Mighty One of Israel:

Ah! I will take vengeance on my foes
    and fully repay my enemies!
I will turn my hand against you,
    and refine your dross in the furnace,
    removing all your alloy.
I will restore your judges as at first,
    and your counselors as in the beginning;
After that you shall be called
    city of justice, faithful city.
Zion shall be redeemed by judgment,
    and her repentant ones by justice.

This is what Isaiah, son of Amoz, saw concerning Judah and Jerusalem.

    In days to come,
The mountain of the Lord's house
    shall be established as the highest mountain
    and raised above the hills.
All nations shall stream toward it;
    many peoples shall come and say:

"Come, let us climb the Lord's mountain,
    to the house of the God of Jacob,
That he may instruct us in his ways,
    and we may walk in his paths."
For from Zion shall go forth instruction,
    and the word of the Lord from Jerusalem.

He shall judge between the nations,
    and impose terms on many peoples.
They shall beat their swords into plowshares
    and their spears into pruning hooks;
One nation shall not raise the sword against another,
    nor shall they train for war again.

O house of Jacob, come,
    let us walk in the light of the Lord!

RESPONSORY   Micah 4:2; John 4:25

Come, let us go up to the mountain of the Lord,
to the house of the God of Jacob.
—He will teach us his ways,
and we will walk in his paths.

The Messiah, who is called the Christ, is coming.
When he comes, he will teach us everything.
—He will teach . . .

SECOND READING

From a pastoral letter by Saint Charles Borromeo, bishop

(Acta Ecclesiae Mediolanensis, t. 2, Lugduni, 1683, 916-917)

The season of Advent

Beloved, now is the acceptable time spoken of by the Spirit, the day of salvation, peace and reconciliation: the great season of Advent. This is the time eagerly awaited by the patriarchs and prophets, the time that holy Simeon rejoiced at last to see. This is the season that the Church has always celebrated with special solemnity. We too should always observe it with faith and love, offering praise and thanksgiving to the Father for the mercy and love he has shown us in this mystery. In his infinite love for us, though we were sinners, he sent his only Son to free us from the tyranny of Satan, to summon us to heaven, to welcome us into its innermost recesses, to show us truth itself, to train us in right conduct, to plant within us the seeds of virtue, to enrich us with the treasures of his grace, and to make us children of God and heirs of eternal life.

Each year, as the Church recalls this mystery, she urges us to renew the memory of the great love God has shown us. This holy season teaches us that Christ's coming was not only for the benefit of his contemporaries; his power has still to be communicated to us all. We shall share his power, if, through holy faith and the sacraments, we willingly accept the grace Christ earned for us, and live by that grace and in obedience to Christ.

The Church asks us to understand that Christ, who came once in the flesh, is prepared to come again. When we remove all obstacles to his presence he will come, at any hour and moment, to dwell spiritually in our hearts, bringing with him the riches of his grace.

In her concern for our salvation, our loving mother the Church uses this holy season to teach us through hymns, canticles and other forms of expression, of voice or ritual, used by the Holy Spirit. She shows us how grateful we should be for so great a blessing, and how to gain its benefit: our hearts should be as much prepared for the coming of Christ as if he were still to come into this world. The same lesson is given us for our imitation by the words and example of the holy men of the Old Testament.

RESPONSORY   See Jl 2:15; Is 62:11; Jer 4:5

Sound the trumpets in Zion, summon the nations;
call the people together and tell them the good news:
—Our God and our Savior is coming.

Proclaim the good news, let it be heard;
tell it to everyone, shout it aloud.
—Our God and . . .

Prayer, as in Morning Prayer

Morning Prayer

READING   Isaiah 2:3

Come, let us climb the Lord's mountain,
    to the house of the God of Jacob,

That he may instruct us in his ways,
  and we may walk in his paths.
For from Zion shall go forth instruction,
  and the word of the Lord from Jerusalem.

RESPONSORY

Your light will come, Jerusalem;
the Lord will dawn on you in radiant beauty.
  —Your light will come, Jerusalem;
the Lord will dawn on you in radiant beauty.

You will see his glory within you;
  —the Lord will dawn on you in radiant beauty.

Glory to the Father . . .
  —Your light will . . .

CANTICLE OF ZECHARIAH

Ant.   Lift up your eyes, Jerusalem, and see the great
       power of your King; your Savior comes to set you
       free.

INTERCESSIONS

Christ the Lord, Son of the living God, light from light,
   leads us into the light and reveals his holiness. With
   confidence let us make our prayer:
   Come, Lord Jesus.
Light that never fades, dispel the mists about us,
   —awaken our faith from sleep.
Guard us from all harm today,
   —may your glory fill us with joy.
Give us unfailing gentleness at all times,
   —toward everyone we meet.
Come to create a new earth for us,
   —where there will be justice and peace.

Our Father . . .

Prayer

Lord our God,
help us to prepare
for the coming of Christ your Son.
May he find us waiting,
eager in joyful prayer.

We ask this through our Lord Jesus Christ, your Son,
who lives and reigns with you and the Holy Spirit,
one God, for ever and ever.

Daytime Prayer

Midmorning

Ant.   This is the good news the prophets foretold: The
       Savior will be born of the Virgin Mary.

READING   See Isaiah 10:20-21

       On that day
The remnant of Israel,
   the survivors of the house of Jacob,
Will lean upon the Lord,
   the Holy One of Israel, in truth.
A remnant will return, the remnant of Jacob,
   to the mighty God.

The nations will revere your name, O Lord.
—And the great ones of the earth will acknowledge your
   glory.

Midday

Ant.   The angel Gabriel said to Mary in greeting: Hail,
       full of grace, the Lord is with you; blessed are you
       among women.

READING   See Isaiah 10:24a, 27

Thus says the Lord, the God of hosts:
O my people, who dwell in Zion,
    do not fear.
        On that day,
The burden shall be taken from your shoulder,
    and the yoke shattered from your neck.

Remember us, Lord, because of the love you have for
    your people.
—Come and bring us your salvation.

Midafternoon

Ant.   Mary said: My soul is deeply troubled; what can
        this greeting mean? Am I to give birth to my King
        and yet remain a virgin for ever?

READING   See Isaiah 13:22b—14:1a

Her time is near at hand
    and her days shall not be prolonged.
The Lord has pity on Jacob
    and again chooses Israel.

Come, Lord, do not delay.
—Free your people from their sinfulness.

Prayer, as in Morning Prayer.

Evening Prayer

READING   Philippians 3:20b-21

We eagerly await the coming of our Savior, the Lord
Jesus Christ. He will give a new form to this lowly body
of ours and remake it according to the pattern of his

glorified body, by his power to subject everything to himself.

Come and set us free, Lord God of power and might.
—Come and set us free, Lord God of power and might.

Let your face shine upon us and we shall be saved,
—Lord God of power and might.

Glory to the Father . . .
—Come and set . . .

CANTICLE OF MARY

Ant.   The angel of the Lord brought God's message to Mary, and she conceived by the power of the Holy Spirit, alleluia.

INTERCESSIONS

We cry to the Lord, who will come to bring us salvation:
   Come, Lord, and save us.
Lord Jesus Christ, our God, Savior of all,
—come swiftly and save us.
Lord, by your coming into this world,
—free us from the sin of the world.
You came from the Father,
—show us the path that leads to him.
You were conceived by the Holy Spirit,
—by your word renew the same Spirit in our hearts.
You became incarnate from the Virgin Mary,
—free our bodies from corruption.
Lord, be mindful of all men,
—who from the beginning of time have placed their trust in you.

Our Father . . .

Prayer

Lord our God,
help us to prepare
for the coming of Christ your Son.
May he find us waiting,
eager in joyful prayer.

We ask this through our Lord Jesus Christ, your Son,
who lives and reigns with you and the Holy Spirit,
one God, for ever and ever.

TUESDAY

Office of Readings

A voice is heard, crying in the wilderness: Prepare the
way of the Lord.
—Make straight the path of our God.

FIRST READING

From the book of the prophet Isaiah   2:6-22; 4:2-6

The judgment of God

O Lord, you have abandoned your people,
    the house of Jacob,
Because they are filled with fortunetellers
    and soothsayers, like the Philistines;
    they covenant with strangers.
Their land is full of silver and gold,
    and there is no end to their treasures;
Their land is full of horses,
    and there is no end to their chariots.

Their land is full of idols;
>   they worship the works of their hands,
>   that which their fingers have made.

But man is abased,
>   each one brought low.
>   [Do not pardon them!]
Get behind the rocks,
>   hide in the dust,
From the terror of the Lord
>   and the splendor of his majesty!

The haughty eyes of man will be lowered,
>   the arrogance of men will be abased,
>   and the Lord alone will be exalted, on that day.
For the Lord of hosts will have his day
>   against all that is proud and arrogant,
>   all that is high, and it will be brought low;
Yes, against all the cedars of Lebanon
>   and all the oaks of Bashan,
Against all the lofty mountains
>   and all the high hills,
Against every lofty tower
>   and every fortified wall,
Against all the ships of Tarshish
>   and all stately vessels.

Human pride will be abased,
>   the arrogance of men brought low,
And the Lord alone will be exalted, on that day.
>   The idols will perish forever.
Men will go into caves in the rocks
>   and into holes in the earth,
From the terror of the Lord
>   and the splendor of his majesty,
>   when he arises to overawe the earth.

On that day men will throw to the moles and the bats
the idols of silver and gold which they made for worship.

They go into caverns in the rocks
    and into crevices in the cliffs,
From the terror of the Lord
    and the splendor of his majesty,
    when he arises to overawe the earth.

As for you, let man alone,
    in whose nostrils is but a breath;
    for what is he worth?

        On that day,
The branch of the Lord will be luster and glory,
    and the fruit of the earth will be honor and splendor
    for the survivors of Israel.
He who remains in Zion
    and he that is left in Jerusalem
Will be called holy:
    every one marked down for life in Jerusalem.

When the Lord washes away
    the filth of the daughters of Zion,
And purges Jerusalem's blood from her midst
    with a blast of searing judgment,
Then will the Lord create,
    over the whole site of Mount Zion
    and over her place of assembly,
A smoking cloud by day
    and a light of flaming fire by night.
For over all, his glory will be shelter and protection:
    shade from the parching heat of day,
    refuge and cover from storm and rain.

RESPONSORY   Isaiah 2: 11; Matthew 24:30

The proud man will lower his eyes,
the arrogant man will be humbled;
—the Lord alone shall be exalted on that day.

They will see the Son of Man
coming in the clouds of heaven
with great power and majesty.
—The Lord alone . . .

SECOND READING

From a sermon by Saint Gregory Nazianzen, bishop

(Oratio 45, 9, 22. 26. 28: PG 36, 634-635. 654. 658-659. 662)

The marvel of the Incarnation

The very Son of God, older than the ages, the invisible, the incomprehensible, the incorporeal, the beginning of beginning, the light of light, the fountain of life and immortality, the image of the archetype, the immovable seal, the perfect likeness, the definition and word of the Father: he it is who comes to his own image and takes our nature for the good of our nature, and unites himself to an intelligent soul for the good of my soul, to purify like by like. He takes to himself all that is human, except for sin. He was conceived by the Virgin Mary, who had been first prepared in soul and body by the Spirit; his coming to birth had to be treated with honor, virginity had to receive new honor. He comes forth as God, in the human nature he has taken, one being, made of two contrary elements, flesh and spirit. Spirit gave divinity, flesh received it.

He who makes rich is made poor; he takes on the poverty of my flesh, that I may gain the riches of his divinity. He who is full is made empty; he is emptied for a brief space of his glory, that I may share in his fullness.

What is this wealth of goodness? What is this mystery that surrounds me? I received the likeness of God, but failed to keep it. He takes on my flesh, to bring salvation to the image, immortality to the flesh. He enters into a second union with us, a union far more wonderful than the first.

Holiness had to be brought to man by the humanity assumed by one who was God, so that God might overcome the tyrant by force and so deliver us and lead us back to himself through the mediation of his Son. The Son arranged this for the honor of the Father, to whom the Son is clearly obedient in all things.

The Good Shepherd, who lays down his life for the sheep, came in search of the straying sheep to the mountains and hills on which you used to offer sacrifice. When he found it, he took it on the shoulders that bore the wood of the cross, and led it back to the life of heaven.

Christ, the light of all lights, follows John, the lamp that goes before him. The Word of God follows the voice in the wilderness; the bridegroom follows the bridegroom's friend, who prepares a worthy people for the Lord by cleansing them by water in preparation for the Spirit.

We need God to take our flesh and die, that we might live. We have died with him, that we may be purified. We have risen again with him, because we have died with him. We have been glorified with him, because we have risen again with him.

RESPONSORY   See Gal. 4:4-5; Eph. 2:4; Rom. 8:3

When at last the appointed time had come,
God sent his Son into the world,
born of a virgin, subject to the law,
—to redeem those who were subject to the law.

Because of his great love for us,
God sent his Son in the likeness of our sinful human
    nature.
—To redeem those . . .

Prayer, as in Morning Prayer.

Morning Prayer

READING   Genesis 49: 10

The scepter shall never depart from Judah,
    or the mace from between his legs,
While tribute is brought to him,
    and he receives the people's homage.

RESPONSORY

Your light will come, Jerusalem;
the Lord will dawn on you in radiant beauty.
—Your light will come, Jerusalem;
the Lord will dawn on you in radiant beauty.

You will see his glory within you;
—the Lord will dawn on you in radiant beauty.
Glory to the Father . . .
—Your light will . . .

CANTICLE OF ZECHARIAH

Ant.   From the root of Jesse a flower will blossom, the
        glory of the Lord will fill the earth, and all crea-
        tion shall see the saving power of God.

INTERCESSIONS

God the almighty Father stretches forth his hand again to
    take possession of the remnant of his people. Let us
    make our prayer to him:
    Lord, may your kingdom come.

Lord, grant that our works of penance may please you,
—and that we may be ready for your kingdom which is so
near.
Prepare a path in our hearts for the coming of your
Word,
—and let his glory be revealed among us.
Bring low the mountains of our pride,
—and fill up the valleys of our weakness.
Break down the wall of hatred that divides the nations,
—and make level for mankind the paths to peace.
Our Father . . .

Prayer

God of mercy and consolation,
help us in our weakness and free us from sin.
Hear our prayers
that we may rejoice at the coming of your Son,
who lives and reigns with you and the Holy Spirit,
one God, for ever and ever.

Daytime Prayer

Midmorning

Ant.   This is the good news the prophets foretold: The
Savior will be born of the Virgin Mary.

READING   Jeremiah 23:5

Behold, the days are coming, says the Lord,
    when I will raise up a righteous shoot to David;
As king he shall reign and govern wisely,
    he shall do what is just and right in the land.

The nations will revere your name, O Lord.
—And the great ones of the earth will acknowledge your glory.

Midday

Ant. The angel Gabriel said to Mary in greeting: Hail, full of grace, the Lord is with you; blessed are you among women.

READING   Jeremiah 23:6

In his days Judah shall be saved,
    Israel shall dwell in security.
This is the name they give him:
    "The Lord our justice."

Remember us, Lord, because of the love you have for your people.
—Come and bring us your salvation.

Midafternoon

Ant. Mary said: My soul is deeply troubled; what can this greeting mean? Am I to give birth to my King and yet remain a virgin for ever?

READING   Ezekiel 34:15-16

I myself will pasture my sheep; I myself will give them rest, says the Lord God. The lost I will seek out, the strayed I will bring back, the injured I will bind up, the sick I will heal, shepherding them rightly.

Come, Lord, do not delay.
—Free your people from their sinfulness.

Prayer, as in Morning Prayer.

Evening Prayer

READING   See 1 Corinthians 1:7b-9

We await the revelation of our Lord Jesus Christ, who
will strengthen us to the end, so that we will be blameless
on the day of our Lord Jesus Christ. God is faithful, and
it was he who called us to fellowship with his Son.

RESPONSORY

Come and set us free, Lord God of power and might.
—Come and set us free, Lord God of power and might.

Let your face shine upon us and we shall be saved,
—Lord God of power and might.

Glory to the Father . . .
—Come and set . . .

CANTICLE OF MARY

Ant.   Seek the Lord while he may be found; call on him
        while he is near, alleluia.

INTERCESSIONS

To the eternal Word who became man to reveal to us the
    new and living way, let us make our humble prayer:

    Come, Lord, and save us.

God, in whom we live and move and have our being,
—come and teach us that you have made us your own.
You are not far from each of us,
—show yourself to all who search for you.
Father of the poor and consoler of the afflicted,
—set captives free, give joy to those who mourn.
You hate death and love life,
—free all mankind from eternal death.

Our Father . . .

Prayer

God of mercy and consolation,
help us in our weakness and free us from sin.
Hear our prayers
that we may rejoice at the coming of your Son,
who lives and reigns with you and the Holy Spirit,
one God, for ever and ever.

WEDNESDAY

Office of Readings

Turn back to us, O Lord, our God.
—Show us your face and we shall be saved.

First Reading

From the book of the prophet Isaiah   5:1-7

Against the vineyard of the Lord

Let me now sing of my friend,
    my friend's song concerning his vineyard.

My friend had a vineyard
    on a fertile hillside;
He spaded it, cleared it of stones,
    and planted the choicest vines;
Within it he built a watchtower,
    and hewed out a wine press.
Then he looked for the crop of grapes,
    but what it yielded was wild grapes.

Now, inhabitants of Jerusalem and men of Judah,
    judge between me and my vineyard:

What more was there to do for my vineyard
    that I had not done?
Why, when I looked for the crop of grapes,
    did it bring forth wild grapes?

Now, I will let you know
    what I mean to do to my vineyard:
Take away its hedge, give it to grazing,
    break through its wall, let it be trampled!
Yes, I will make it a ruin:
    it shall not be pruned or hoed,
    but overgrown with thorns and briers;
I will command the clouds
    not to send rain upon it.

The vineyard of the Lord of hosts is the house of Israel,
    and the men of Judah are his cherished plant;
He looked for judgment, but see, bloodshed!
    for justice, but hark, the outcry!

RESPONSORY   Psalm 80:14, 15, 3, 16, 15

A boar from the forest has torn down the vine you
    planted;
the beasts of the field have devoured it.
See, Lord, and arise in your mighty power;
—let not the work of your hands be destroyed.

Lord God of power and might, look down from heaven,
see this vine and come to protect it.
—Let not the . . .

SECOND READING

From a sermon by Saint Bernard, abbot

(Sermo 5, In Adventu Domini, 1-3: Opera omnia, Edit. cisterc. 4
[1966], 188-190)

God's Word will come to us

We know that there are three comings of the Lord.
The third lies between the other two. It is invisible, while
the other two are visible. In the first coming he was seen
on earth, dwelling among men; he himself testifies that
they saw him and hated him. In the final coming *all flesh
will see the salvation of our God,* and *they will look on him
whom they pierced.* The intermediate coming is a hidden
one; in it only the elect see the Lord within their own
selves, and they are saved. In his first coming our Lord
came in our flesh and in our weakness; in this middle
coming he comes in spirit and in power; in the final coming he will be seen in glory and majesty.

Because this coming lies between the other two, it is
like a road on which we travel from the first coming to
the last. In the first, Christ was our redemption; in the
last, he will appear as our life; in this middle coming, he
is our rest and consolation.

In case someone should think that what we say about
this middle coming is sheer invention, listen to what our
Lord himself says: *If anyone loves me, he will keep my
word, and my Father will love him, and we will come to
him.* There is another passage of Scripture which reads:
He who fears God will do good, but something further has
been said about the one who loves, that is, that he will
keep God's word. Where is God's word to be kept?
Obviously in the heart, as the prophet says: *I have hidden
your words in my heart, so that I may not sin against you.*

Keep God's word in this way. Let it enter into your
very being, let it take possession of your desires and your
whole way of life. Feed on goodness, and your soul will
delight in its richness. Remember to eat your bread, or
your heart will wither away. Fill your soul with richness
and strength.

If you keep the word of God in this way, it will also keep you. The Son with the Father will come to you. The great Prophet who will build the new Jerusalem will come, the one who makes all things new. This coming will fulfill what is written: *As we have borne the likeness of the earthly man, we shall also bear the likeness of the heavenly man.* Just as Adam's sin spread through all mankind and took hold of all, so Christ, who created and redeemed all, will glorify all, once he takes possession of all.

RESPONSORY   See Psalm 29:11; Isaiah 40:10

The Lord will come down to us,
radiant in his splendor, awesome in his power.
—He will bring his people peace
and give them everlasting life.

Our God will come, awesome in his power.
—He will bring . . .

Prayer, as in Morning Prayer.

Morning Prayer

READING   Isaiah 7:14b-15

The virgin shall be with child, and bear a son, and shall name him Immanuel. He shall be living on curds and honey by the time he learns to reject the bad and choose the good.

RESPONSORY

Your light will come, Jerusalem;
the Lord will dawn on you in radiant beauty.
—Your light will come, Jerusalem;
the Lord will dawn on you in radiant beauty.

You will see his glory within you;
—the Lord will dawn on you in radiant beauty.

Glory to the Father . . .
—Your light will . . .

CANTICLE OF ZECHARIAH

Ant.   The One who is coming after me is greater than I;
I am not worthy to untie the strap of his sandals.

INTERCESSIONS

The Word of God humbled himself to dwell with us so
that we might see his glory. Rejoicing in hope, let us
call upon him:
Emmanuel, be with us.
Ruler, just and righteous,
—bring justice to the poor and the oppressed.
King of peace, you beat swords into plowshares and
spears into pruning hooks,
—turn hatred into love and our grievances into
forgiveness.
You do not judge by appearances,
—recognize those who are your own.
When you come with power and might upon the clouds,
—grant that we may come before you without shame.

Our Father . . .

Prayer

Lord our God,
grant that we may be ready
to receive Christ when he comes in glory
and to share in the banquet of heaven,
where he lives and reigns with you and the Holy Spirit,
one God, for ever and ever.

Daytime Prayer

Midmorning

Ant.　This is the good news the prophets foretold: The
　　　Savior will be born of the Virgin Mary.

READING　　　　　　　　　　　　　See Isaiah 2:11-12

The haughty eyes of man will be lowered,
　the arrogance of men will be abased,
　　and the Lord alone will be exalted, on that day.

The nations will revere your name, O Lord.
—And the great ones of the earth will acknowledge your
　glory.

Midday

Ant.　The angel Gabriel said to Mary in greeting: Hail,
　　　full of grace, the Lord is with you; blessed are you
　　　among women.

READING　　　　　　　　　　　　　　　　Isaiah 12:2

God indeed is my savior;
　I am confident and unafraid.
My strength and courage is the Lord,
　and he has been my savior.

Remember us, Lord, because of the love you have for
　your people.
—Come and bring us your salvation.

Midafternoon

Ant.　Mary said: My soul is deeply troubled; what can
　　　this greeting mean? Am I to give birth to my King
　　　and yet remain a virgin for ever?

READING Daniel 9:19

O Lord, hear! O Lord, pardon! O Lord, be attentive and act without delay, for your own sake, O my God, because this city and your people bear your name!

Come, Lord, do not delay.
—Free your people from their sinfulness.

Prayer, as in Morning Prayer.

Evening Prayer

READING 1 Corinthians 4:5

Stop passing judgment before the time of the Lord's return. He will bring to light what is hidden in darkness and manifest the intentions of hearts. At that time, everyone will receive his praise from God.

RESPONSORY

Come and set us free, Lord God of power and might.
—Come and set us free, Lord God of power and might.

Let your face shine upon us and we shall be saved,
—Lord God of power and might.

Glory to the Father . . .
—Come and set . . .

CANTICLE OF MARY

Ant. The law will go forth from Zion; the word of the Lord from Jerusalem.

INTERCESSIONS

Let us pray to God the Father, who sent his Son to bring us endless peace:
  Lord, your kingdom come.

Father most holy, look kindly on your Church,
—come and visit this vine which your own right hand has
   planted.
Be mindful, Lord, of all the sons of Abraham,
—fulfill the promises you made to their fathers.
Merciful God, look kindly upon men and women of every race,
—may they honor you for your goodness.
Eternal Shepherd, visit the sheep of your flock,
—and gather them together into one fold.
Remember those who have gone forth from this world in
   your peace,
—lead them into glory with your Son.

Our Father . . .

Prayer

Lord our God,
grant that we may be ready
to receive Christ when he comes in glory
and to share in the banquet of heaven,
where he lives and reigns with you and the Holy Spirit,
one God, for ever and ever.

THURSDAY

Office of Readings

Hear the word of the Lord, all you nations.
—Proclaim it to the ends of the earth.

FIRST READING

From the book of the prophet Isaiah   16:1-5; 17:4-8

Zion, refuge of the Moabites. The conversion of Ephraim

Send them forth, hugging the earth like reptiles,
    from Sela across the desert,
      to the mount of daughter Zion.
Like flushed birds,
    like startled nestlings,
Are the daughters of Moab
    at the fords of the Arnon.

Offer counsel, take their part;
    at high noon let your shadow be like the night,
To hide the outcasts,
    to conceal the fugitives.
Let the outcasts of Moab live with you,
    be their shelter from the destroyer.

When the struggle is ended, the ruin complete,
    and they have done with trampling the land,
A throne shall be set up in mercy,
    and on it shall sit in fidelity
    [in David's tent]
A judge upholding right
    and prompt to do justice.

    On that day
The glory of Jacob shall fade,
    and his full body grow thin,

Like the reaper's mere armful of stalks
　　when he gathers the standing grain;
Or as when one gleans the ears
　　in the Valley of Rephaim.
Only a scattering of grapes shall be left!
　　As when an olive tree has been beaten,
Two or three olives remain at the very top,
　　four or five on its fruitful branches,
　　says the Lord, the God of Israel.

On that day man shall look to his maker,
　　his eyes turned toward the Holy One of Israel.
He shall not look to the altars, his handiwork,
　　nor shall he regard what his fingers have made:
　　the sacred poles or the incense stands.

RESPONSORY　　　　　　Jeremiah 33:15, 16; Isaiah 16:5

I shall raise up an heir for David,
one who is just;
he will make fair judgment prevail on earth,
—and this is the name they will give him:
the Lord is our righteousness.

A throne of mercy will be set up;
there a true judge will sit,
one who seeks justice and is swift to do right.
—And this is . . .

SECOND READING

From a commentary on the Diatessaron by Saint
Ephrem, deacon

(Cap. 18, 15-17: SC 121, 325-328)

Keep watch; he is to come again

To prevent his disciples from asking the time of his
coming, Christ said: *About that hour no one knows, neither
the angels nor the Son. It is not for you to know times or*

moments. He has kept those things hidden so that we may keep watch, each of us thinking that he will come in our own day. If he had revealed the time of his coming, his coming would have lost its savor: it would no longer be an object of yearning for the nations and the age in which it will be revealed. He promised that he would come but did not say when he would come, and so all generations and ages await him eagerly.

Though the Lord has established the signs of his coming, the time of their fulfillment has not been plainly revealed. These signs have come and gone with a multiplicity of change; more than that, they are still present. His final coming is like his first. As holy men and prophets waited for him, thinking that he would reveal himself in their own day, so today each of the faithful longs to welcome him in his own day, because Christ has not made plain the day of his coming.

He has not made it plain for this reason especially, that no one may think that he whose power and dominion rule all numbers and times is ruled by fate and time. He described the signs of his coming; how could what he has himself decided be hidden from him? Therefore, he used these words to increase respect for the signs of his coming, so that from that day forward all generations and ages might think that he would come again in their own day.

Keep watch; when the body is asleep nature takes control of us, and what is done is not done by our will but by force, by the impulse of nature. When deep listlessness takes possession of the soul, for example, faintheartedness or melancholy, the enemy overpowers it and makes it do what it does not will. The force of nature, the enemy of the soul, is in control.

When the Lord commanded us to be vigilant, he meant vigilance in both parts of man: in the body, against the tendency to sleep; in the soul, against lethargy and timidity. As Scripture says: *Wake up, you just,* and *I have risen, and am still with you;* and again, *Do not lose heart. Therefore, having this ministry, we do not lose heart.*

RESPONSORY   Isaiah 55:3-4; Acts 28:28

I shall make with you an everlasting covenant,
I shall send the promise given in mercy to David.
—I have set him as a witness to the peoples,
as leader and teacher of all nations.

This saving act of God is for all nations,
and they will heed it.
—I have set . . .

Prayer, as in Morning Prayer.

Morning Prayer

READING   Isaiah 45:8

Let justice descend, O heavens, like dew from above,
   like gentle rain let the skies drop it down.
Let the earth open and salvation bud forth;
   let justice also spring up!

RESPONSORY

Your light will come, Jerusalem;
the Lord will dawn on you in radiant beauty.
—Your light will come, Jerusalem;
the Lord will dawn on you in radiant beauty.

You will see his glory within you;
—the Lord will dawn on you in radiant beauty.

Glory to the Father . . .
—Your light will . . .

CANTICLE OF ZECHARIAH

Ant.   I shall wait for my Lord and Savior and point him
       out when he is near, alleluia.

INTERCESSIONS

Christ is the wisdom and power of God, and his delight is
    to be with the children of men. With confidence let us
    pray:
        Draw near to us, Lord.
Lord Jesus Christ, you have called us to your glorious
    kingdom,
—make us walk worthily, pleasing God in all we do.
You who stand unknown among us,
—reveal yourself to men and women.
You are nearer to us than we to ourselves,
—strengthen our faith and our hope of salvation.
You are the source of holiness,
—keep us holy and without sin now and until the day of
    your coming.

Our Father . . .

Prayer

Father,
we need your help.
Free us from sin and bring us to life.
Support us by your power.

Grant this through our Lord Jesus Christ, your Son,
who lives and reigns with you and the Holy Spirit,
one God, for ever and ever.

Daytime Prayer

Midmorning

Ant.   This is the good news the prophets foretold: The
       Savior will be born of the Virgin Mary.

READING   Micah 5:4-5a

The ruler in Israel shall stand firm and shepherd his flock
    by the strength of the Lord,
    in the majestic name of the Lord, his God;
And they shall remain, for now his greatness
    shall reach to the ends of the earth;
    he shall be peace.

The nations will revere your name, O Lord.
—And the great ones of the earth will acknowledge your
    glory.

Midday

Ant.   The angel Gabriel said to Mary in greeting: Hail,
       full of grace, the Lord is with you; blessed are you
       among women.

READING   Haggai 2:6, 9

One moment yet, a little while,
    and I will shake the heavens and the earth,
    the sea and the dry land.
Greater will be the future glory of this house
    than the former;
And in this place I will give peace,
    says the Lord of hosts!

Remember us, Lord, because of the love you have for
    your people.
—Come and bring us your salvation.

Midafternoon

Ant.   Mary said: My soul is deeply troubled; what can
       this greeting mean? Am I to give birth to my King
       and yet remain a virgin for ever?

READING   Malachi 4:2

For you who fear my name, there will arise
   the sun of justice with its healing rays;
And you will gambol like calves out of the stall,
   says the Lord of hosts.

Come, Lord, do not delay.
—Free your people from their sinfulness.

Prayer, as in Morning Prayer.

Evening Prayer

READING   James 5:7-8, 9b

   Be patient, my brothers, until the coming of the Lord.
See how the farmer awaits the precious yield of the soil.
He looks forward to it patiently while the soil receives the
winter and the spring rains. You, too, must be patient.
Steady your hearts, because the coming of the Lord is at
hand. See! The judge stands at the gate.

RESPONSORY

Come and set us free, Lord God of power and might.
—Come and set us free, Lord God of power and might.
Let your face shine upon us and we shall be saved,
—Lord God of power and might.

Glory to the Father . . .
—Come and set . . .

CANTICLE OF MARY

Ant. Blessed are you among women, and blessed is the fruit of your womb.

INTERCESSIONS

To Christ, the great light promised by the prophets to those who live in the shadow of death, let us raise our voices in prayer:
Come, Lord Jesus.
Word of God, in the beginning you created all things and in the fullness of time assumed our nature,
—come and deliver us from death.
True light, shining on mankind,
—come and dispel our darkness.
Only-begotten Son, dwelling in the Father's heart,
—come and tell us of God's loving kindness.
Christ Jesus, you come among us as the Son of Man,
—transform those who know you into the sons of God.
You welcome all who call upon you in need,
—bring into your wedding feast those who beg at the door.

Our Father . . .

Prayer

Father,
we need your help.
Free us from sin and bring us to life.
Support us by your power.

Grant this through our Lord Jesus Christ, your Son,
who lives and reigns with you and the Holy Spirit,
one God, for ever and ever.

FRIDAY

Office of Readings

Let your compassion come upon me, Lord.
—Your salvation, true to your promise.

FIRST READING

From the book of the prophet Isaiah 19:16-25

The future conversion of Egypt and Assyria

On that day the Egyptians shall be like women, trembling with fear, because of the Lord of hosts shaking his fist at them. And the land of Judah shall be a terror to the Egyptians. Every time they remember Judah, they shall stand in dread because of the plan which the Lord of hosts has in mind for them.

On that day there shall be five cities in the land of Egypt speaking the language of Canaan and swearing by the Lord of hosts; one shall be called "City of the Sun."

On that day there shall be an altar to the Lord in the land of Egypt, and a sacred pillar to the Lord near the boundary. It shall be a sign and a witness to the Lord of hosts in the land of Egypt, when they cry out to the Lord against their oppressors, and he sends them a savior to defend and deliver them. The Lord shall make himself known to Egypt, and the Egyptians shall know the Lord in that day; they shall offer sacrifices and oblations, and fulfill the vows they make to the Lord. Although the Lord shall smite Egypt severely, he shall heal them; they shall turn to the Lord and he shall be won over and heal them.

On that day there shall be a highway from Egypt to Assyria; the Assyrians shall enter Egypt, and the Egyptians enter Assyria, and Egypt shall serve Assyria.

On that day Israel shall be a third party with Egypt and
Assyria, a blessing in the midst of the land, when the
Lord of hosts blesses it: "Blessed be my people Egypt,
and the work of my hands Assyria, and my inheritance,
Israel."

<small>RESPONSORY</small>   Isaiah 19:21; Luke 13:29

On that day the Egyptians will acknowledge the Lord;
—with offerings and gifts they will worship him.
They will come from east and west, from north and
    south,
to be seated at the feast in the kingdom of God.
—With offerings and . . .

<small>SECOND READING</small>

From the Proslogion by Saint Anselm, bishop

(Cap. 1: Opera omnia, Edit. Schmitt, Secovii, 1938, 1, 97-100)

Desire for the vision of God

Insignificant man, escape from your everyday business
for a short while, hide for a moment from your restless
thoughts. Break off from your cares and troubles and be
less concerned about your tasks and labors. Make a little
time for God and rest a while in him.

Enter into your mind's inner chamber. Shut out
everything but God and whatever helps you to seek him;
and when you have shut the door, look for him. Speak
now to God and say with your whole heart: *I seek your
face; your face, Lord, I desire.*

Lord, my God, teach my heart where and how to seek
you, where and how to find you. Lord, if you are not here
where shall I look for you in your absence? Yet if you are
everywhere, why do I not see you when you are present?
But surely you dwell in "light inaccessible." And where
is light inaccessible? How shall I approach light

inaccessible? Or who will lead me and bring me into it that I may see you there? And then, by what signs and under what forms shall I seek you? I have never seen you, Lord my God; I do not know your face.

Lord most high, what shall this exile do, so far from you? What shall your servant do, tormented by love of you and cast so far from your face? He yearns to see you, and your face is too far from him. He desires to approach you, and your dwelling is unapproachable. He longs to find you, and does not know your dwelling place. He strives to look for you, and does not know your face.

Lord, you are my God and you are my Lord, and I have never seen you. You have made me and remade me, and you have given me all the good things I possess, and still I do not know you. I was made in order to see you, and I have not yet done that for which I was made.

Lord, how long will it be? How long, Lord, will you forget us? How long will you turn your face away from us? When will you look upon us and hear us? When will you enlighten our eyes and show us your face? When will you give yourself back to us?

Look upon us, Lord, hear us and enlighten us, show us your very self. Restore yourself to us that it may go well with us whose life is so evil without you. Take pity on our efforts and our striving toward you, for we have no strength apart from you.

Teach me to seek you, and when I seek you show yourself to me, for I cannot seek you unless you teach me, nor can I find you unless you show yourself to me. Let me seek you in desiring you and desire you in seeking you, find you in loving you and love you in finding you.

RESPONSORY   Psalm 80:19, 20; 106:4

Never will we leave you, Lord;
you will fill us with life,

and we will call on your name.
—Show us your face and we shall be saved.

Remember us, Lord, because of the love you have for
 your people.
Come and bring us your salvation.
—Show us your . . .

Prayer, as in Morning Prayer.

Morning Prayer

READING   Jeremiah 30:21, 22

   Thus says the Lord:
His leader shall be from Jacob
   and his ruler shall come from his kin.
When I summon him,
   he shall approach me.
You shall be my people,
   and I will be your God.

RESPONSORY

Your light will come, Jerusalem;
the Lord will dawn on you in radiant beauty.
—Your light will come, Jerusalem;
the Lord will dawn on you in radiant beauty.

You will see his glory within you;
—the Lord will dawn on you in radiant beauty.

Glory to the Father . . .
—Your light will . . .

CANTICLE OF ZECHARIAH

Ant.   Our God comes, born as man of David's line,
        enthroned as king for ever, alleluia.

INTERCESSIONS

Through his Son, God the Father revealed his glory to
    men and women. Therefore, let our joyful cry re-
    sound:
    Lord, may your name be glorified.
Teach us, Lord, to love each other,
— as Christ loved us for God's glory.
Fill us with all joy and peace in faith,
—that we may walk in the hope and strength of the Holy
    Spirit.
Help all mankind, Lord, in your loving mercy,
—be near to those who seek you without knowing it.
You call and sanctify the elect,
—though we are sinners, crown us with eternal
    happiness.

Our Father . . .

Prayer

Jesus, our Lord,
save us from our sins.
Come, protect us from all dangers
and lead us to salvation,
for you live and reign with the Father and the Holy
    Spirit,
one God, for ever and ever.

Daytime Prayer

Midmorning

Ant.   This is the good news the prophets foretold: The
        Savior will be born of the Virgin Mary.

READING   Jeremiah 29:11, 13

I know well the plans I have in mind for you, says the
Lord, plans for your welfare, not for woe! plans to give

you a future full of hope. When you look for me, you will find me: when you seek me with all your heart.

The nations will revere your name, O Lord.
—And the great ones of the earth will acknowledge your glory.

Midday

Ant.   The angel Gabriel said to Mary in greeting: Hail, full of grace, the Lord is with you; blessed are you among women.

READING   Jeremiah 30:18

Thus says the Lord:
See! I will restore the tents of Jacob,
  his dwellings I will pity.

Remember us, Lord, because of the love you have for your people.
—Come and bring us your salvation.

Midafternoon

Ant.   Mary said: My soul is deeply troubled; what can this greeting mean? Am I to give birth to my King and yet remain a virgin for ever?

READING   Baruch 3:5–6a

Remember at this time not the misdeeds of our fathers, but your own hand and name: for you are the Lord our God.

Come, Lord, do not delay.
—Free your people from their sinfulness.

Prayer, as in Morning Prayer

Evening Prayer

READING   2 Peter 3:8b-9

In the Lord's eyes, one day is as a thousand years and a thousand years are as a day. The Lord does not delay in keeping his promise—though some consider it "delay." Rather, he shows you generous patience, since he wants none to perish but all to come to repentance.

RESPONSORY

Come and set us free, Lord God of power and might.
—Come and set us free, Lord God of power and might.

Let your face shine upon us and we shall be saved,
—Lord God of power and might.

Glory to the Father . . .
—Come and set . . .

CANTICLE OF MARY

Ant.   Out of Egypt I have called my Son; he will come to save his people.

INTERCESSIONS

With confidence let us call upon Christ, the shepherd and guardian of our souls:
   Lord, have mercy on us.
Good shepherd of God's flock,
—gather all into your Church.
Lord Jesus, help the shepherds of your pilgrim people,
—until you come again may they zealously feed your flock.
Choose from among us heralds of your word,
—to proclaim your Gospel to the ends of the earth.
Take pity on all who struggle and fall along the way,
—may they find a friend to help them.

Show your glory in heaven,
—to those who listen to your voice on earth.

Our Father . . .

Prayer

Jesus, our Lord,
save us from our sins.
Come, protect us from all dangers
and lead us to salvation,
for you live and reign with the Father and the Holy
    Spirit,
one God, for ever and ever.

SATURDAY

Office of Readings

The Lord proclaims his word to Jacob,
—His laws and decrees to Israel.

FIRST READING

From the book of the prophet Isaiah   21:6–12

The watchman announces the ruin of Babylon

    Thus says my Lord to me:
Go, station a watchman,
    let him tell what he sees.
If he sees a chariot,
    a pair of horses,
Someone riding an ass,
    someone riding a camel,

Then let him pay heed,
   very close heed.

    Then the watchman cried,
"On the watchtower, O my Lord,
   I stand constantly by day;
And I stay at my post
   through all the watches of the night.

"Here he comes now:
   a single chariot,
   a pair of horses;
He calls out and says,
   'Fallen, fallen is Babylon,
And all the images of her gods
   are smashed to the ground.'"

O my people who have been threshed,
   beaten on my threshing floor!
What I have heard
   from the Lord of hosts,
The God of Israel,
   I have announced to you.

    Oracle on Edom:
They call to me from Seir,
   "Watchman, how much longer the night?
Watchman, how much longer the night?"
    The watchman replies,
"Morning has come, and again night.
   If you will ask, ask; come back again."

RESPONSORY   Revelation 18:2, 4, 5

An angel cried in a voice like thunder:
Babylon the great is fallen!
Then I heard another voice from heaven:

—Come out, my people, come out from her;
  you must not take part in her sins.

High as heaven her iniquities pile up;
the Lord has the record in hand.
—Come out, my . . .

From a treatise On the Value of Patience by Saint
Cyprian, bishop and martyr

(Nn. 13 et 15: CSEL 3, 406-408)

We hope for what we do not see

Patience is a precept for salvation given us by our
Lord, our teacher: *Whoever endures to the end will be
saved.* And again: *If you persevere in my word, you will
truly be my disciples; you will know the truth, and the truth
will set you free.*

Dear brethren, we must endure and persevere if we are
to attain the truth and freedom we have been allowed to
hope for; faith and hope are the very meaning of our
being Christians, but if faith and hope are to bear their
fruit, patience is necessary.

We do not seek glory now, in the present, but we look
for future glory, as Saint Paul instructs us when he says:
*By hope we were saved. Now hope which is seen is not hope;
how can a man hope for what he sees? But if we hope for
what we do not see, we wait for it in patience.* Patient
waiting is necessary if we are to be perfected in what we
have begun to be, and if we are to receive from God what
we hope for and believe.

In another place the same Apostle instructs and
teaches the just, and those active in good works, and
those who store up for themselves treasures in heaven
through the reward God gives them. They are to be

patient also, for he says: *Therefore while we have time, let us do good to all, but especially to those who are of the household of the faith. But let us not grow weary in doing good, for we shall reap our reward in due season.*

Paul warns us not to grow weary in good works through impatience, not to be distracted or overcome by temptations and so give up in the midst of our pilgrimage of praise and glory, and allow our past good deeds to count for nothing because what was begun falls short of completion.

Finally the Apostle, speaking of charity, unites it with endurance and patience. *Charity,* he says, *is always patient and kind; it is not jealous, is not boastful, is not given to anger, does not think evil, loves all things, believes all things, hopes all things, endures all things.* He shows that charity can be steadfast and persevering because it has learned how to endure all things.

And in another place he says: *Bear with one another lovingly, striving to keep the unity of the Spirit in the bond of peace.* He shows that neither unity nor peace can be maintained unless the brethren cherish each other with mutual forbearance and preserve the bond of harmony by means of patience.

RESPONSORY   Habakkuk 2:3; Hebrews 10:37

He will appear at last: he is true to his word;
—keep watching for him, he will surely come without
   delay.

A little while longer, a very little while,
and the promised one will come.
—Keep watching for . . .

Prayer, as in Morning Prayer.

Morning Prayer

READING   Isaiah 11:1–2

A shoot shall sprout from the stump of Jesse,
    and from his roots a bud shall blossom.
The spirit of the Lord shall rest upon him:
    a spirit of wisdom and of understanding,
A spirit of counsel and of strength,
    a spirit of knowledge and of fear of the Lord,
    and his delight shall be the fear of the Lord.

RESPONSORY

Your light will come, Jerusalem;
the Lord will dawn on you in radiant beauty.
—Your light will come, Jerusalem;
the Lord will dawn on you in radiant beauty.

You will see his glory within you;
—the Lord will dawn on you in radiant beauty.

Glory to the Father . . .
—Your light will . . .

CANTICLE OF ZECHARIAH

Ant.   Banish your fears, O people of Zion; God, your
        own God, is coming to you, alleluia.

INTERCESSIONS

Let us pray to God our Father, who from of old has
    called his people to salvation:
        Lord, protect your people.
You promised to plant the seed of justice among your
    people,
—protect the holiness of your Church.
Lord, teach all men and women to listen to your word,
—and help believers to persevere in holiness.

Keep us in the love of your Spirit,
—that we may receive the mercy of your Son who is to
    come.
Father most merciful, strengthen us to the last,
—until the day of the coming of Jesus Christ our Lord.

Our Father . . .

Prayer

God our Father,
you loved the world so much
you gave your only Son to free us
from the ancient power of sin and death.
Help us who wait for his coming,
and lead us to true liberty.

We ask this through our Lord Jesus Christ, your Son,
who lives and reigns with you and the Holy Spirit,
one God, for ever and ever.

Daytime Prayer

Midmorning

Ant.   This is the good news the prophets foretold: The
        Savior will be born of the Virgin Mary.

READING   Isaiah 4:2

    On that day,
The branch of the Lord will be luster and glory,
    and the fruit of the earth will be honor and splendor
    for the survivors of Israel.

The nations will revere your name, O Lord.
—And the great ones of the earth will acknowledge your
    glory.

Midday

Ant.   The angel Gabriel said to Mary in greeting: Hail, full of grace, the Lord is with you; blessed are you among women.

READING   Isaiah 4:3

He who remains in Zion
   and he that is left in Jerusalem
Will be called holy:
   every one marked down for life in Jerusalem.

Remember us, Lord, because of the love you have for your people.
—Come and bring us your salvation.

Midafternoon

Ant.   Mary said: My soul is deeply troubled; what can this greeting mean? Am I to give birth to my King and yet remain a virgin for ever?

READING   Isaiah 61:11

As the earth brings forth its plants,
   and a garden makes its growth spring up,
So will the Lord God make justice and praise
   spring up before all the nations.

Come, Lord, do not delay.
—Free your people from their sinfulness.

Prayer, as in Morning Prayer.

SECOND SUNDAY OF ADVENT

Evening Prayer I

HYMN, 126.

Ant. 1   New city of Zion, let your heart sing for joy; see how humbly your King comes to save you.

Psalms and canticle from Sunday, Week II, 794.

Ant. 2   Have courage, all of you, lost and fearful; take heart and say: Our God will come to save us, alleluia.

Ant. 3   The law was given to Moses, but grace and truth come through Jesus Christ.

READING   1 Thessalonians 5:23–24

May the God of peace make you perfect in holiness. May he preserve you whole and entire, spirit, soul, and body, irreproachable at the coming of our Lord Jesus Christ. He who calls us is trustworthy, therefore he will do it.

RESPONSORY

Lord, show us your mercy and love.
—Lord, show us your mercy and love.
And grant us your salvation,
—your mercy and love.
Glory to the Father . .
—Lord, show us . . .

CANTICLE OF MARY

Ant.   Come to us, Lord, and may your presence be our
        peace; with hearts made perfect we shall rejoice in
        your companionship for ever.

INTERCESSIONS

Jesus is Lord, born of the Virgin Mary. Let us pray to
    him with joyful hearts:
        Come, Lord Jesus!
Son of God, you will come again as the true messenger of
    the covenant,
—help the world to recognize and accept you.
Born in your Father's heart, you became man in the
    womb of the Virgin Mary,
— free us from the tyranny of change and decay.
In your life on earth, you came to die as a man,
—save us from everlasting death.
When you come to judge, show us your loving mercy,
—and forgive us our weaknesses.
Lord Jesus, by your death you have given hope to those
    who have died,
—be merciful to those for whom we now pray.

Our Father . . .

Prayer

God of power and mercy,
open our hearts in welcome.
Remove the things that hinder us from receiving Christ
    with joy,
so that we may share his wisdom
and become one with him
when he comes in glory,
for he lives and reigns with you and the Holy Spirit,
one God, for ever and ever.

Alternative Prayer

Father in heaven,
the day draws near when the glory of your Son
will make radiant the night of the waiting world.
May the lure of greed not impede us from the joy
which moves the hearts of those who seek him.
May the darkness not blind us
to the vision of wisdom
which fills the minds of those who find him.
We ask this through Christ our Lord.

Invitatory

Ant.   Come, let us worship the Lord, the King who is to
come.

Invitatory psalm, as in the Ordinary, 648.

Office of Readings

HYMN, 126.

Ant. 1   This is our heavenly King; he comes with
power and might to save the nations, alleluia.

Psalms from Sunday, Week II, 799.

Ant. 2   Daughter of Jerusalem, rejoice and be glad;
your King will come to you. Zion, do not fear;
your Savior hastens on his way.

Ant. 3   Let us cleanse our hearts for the coming of our
great King, that we may be ready to welcome
him; he is coming and will not delay.

Lift up your heads and see.
—Your redemption is now at hand.

FIRST READING

From the book of the prophet Isaiah   22:8b–23

Against the pride of Jerusalem and Shebna

On that day you looked to the weapons in the House of the Forest; you saw that the breaches in the City of David were many; you collected the water of the lower pool. You numbered the houses of Jerusalem, tearing some down to strengthen the wall; you made a reservoir between the two walls for the water of the old pool. But you did not look to the city's Maker, nor did you consider him who built it long ago.

On that day the Lord,
   the God of hosts, called on you
To weep and mourn,
   to shave your head and put on sackcloth.
But look! you feast and celebrate,
   you slaughter oxen and butcher sheep,
You eat meat and drink wine:
   "Eat and drink, for tomorrow we die!"
This reaches the ears of the Lord of hosts—
   You shall not be pardoned this wickedness till you die,
   says the Lord, the God of hosts.

Thus says the Lord, the God of hosts:
   Up, go to that official,
   Shebna, master of the palace,
Who has hewn for himself a sepulcher on a height
   and carved his tomb in the rock:
"What are you doing here, and what people have you here,
   that here you have hewn for yourself a tomb?"
The Lord shall hurl you down headlong, mortal man!
   He shall grip you firmly

And roll you up and toss you like a ball
   into an open land
To perish there, you and the chariots you glory in,
   you disgrace to your master's house!

I will thrust you from your office
   and pull you down from your station.
On that day I will summon my servant
   Eliakim, son of Hilkiah;
I will clothe him with your robe,
   and gird him with your sash,
   and give over to him your authority.
He shall be a father to the inhabitants of Jerusalem,
   and to the house of Judah.

I will place the key of the House of David on his
     shoulder;
   when he opens, no one shall shut,
   when he shuts, no one shall open.
I will fix him like a peg in a sure spot,
   to be a place of honor for his family.

Responsory   Revelation 3:7, 8

This is the message of the holy and the true one,
who holds the key of David:
—Behold I have put before you an open door
which no one is able to close.

You have kept my word
and have not denied my name.
—Behold I have . . .

Second Reading

From a commentary on Isaiah by Eusebius of Caesarea, bishop

(Cap. 40: PG 24, 366-367)

The voice in the wilderness

The voice of one crying in the wilderness: Prepare the way of the Lord, make straight the paths of our God. The prophecy makes clear that it is to be fulfilled, not in Jerusalem but in the wilderness: it is there that the glory of the Lord is to appear, and God's salvation is to be made known to all mankind.

It was in the wilderness that God's saving presence was proclaimed by John the Baptist, and there that God's salvation was seen. The words of this prophecy were fulfilled when Christ and his glory were made manifest to all: after his baptism the heavens opened, and the Holy Spirit in the form of a dove rested on him, and the Father's voice was heard, bearing witness to the Son: *This is my beloved Son, listen to him.*

The prophecy meant that God was to come to a deserted place, inaccessible from the beginning. None of the pagans had any knowledge of God, since his holy servants and prophets were kept from approaching them. The voice commands that a way be prepared for the Word of God: the rough and trackless ground is to be made level, so that our God may find a highway when he comes. *Prepare the way of the Lord:* the way is the preaching of the Gospel, the new message of consolation, ready to bring to all mankind the knowledge of God's saving power.

Climb on a high mountain, bearer of good news to Zion. Lift up your voice in strength, bearer of good news to Jerusalem. These words harmonize very well with the meaning of what has gone before. They refer opportunely to the evangelists and proclaim the coming of God to men, after speaking of the voice crying in the wilderness. Mention of the evangelists suitably follows the prophecy on John the Baptist.

What does Zion mean if not the city previously called Jersualem? This is the mountain referred to in that passage from Scripture: *Here is mount Zion, where you dwelt.* The Apostle says: *You have come to mount Zion.* Does not this refer to the company of the apostles, chosen from the former people of the circumcision?

This is the Zion, the Jerusalem, that received God's salvation. It stands aloft on the mountain of God, that is, it is raised high on the only-begotten Word of God. It is commanded to climb the high mountain and announce the word of salvation. Who is the bearer of the good news but the company of the evangelists? What does it mean to bear the good news but to preach to all nations, but first of all to the cities of Judah, the coming of Christ on earth?

RESPONSORY   See Matthew 11:11, 9

The herald of the Lord approaches,
of whom the Lord says:
— No one born of woman
is greater than John the Baptist.

Truly this is a great prophet,
and more than a prophet,
of whom the Lord says:
— No one born . . .

HYMN, **Te Deum,** 651.

Prayer, as in Morning Prayer.

Morning Prayer

HYMN, **121.**

Ant. 1   Zion is our mighty citadel, our saving Lord its wall and its defense; throw open the gates, for our God is here among us, alleluia.

Psalms and canticle from Sunday, Week II, **804.**

Ant. 2 Come to the waters, all you who thirst; seek the
        Lord while he can be found, alleluia.

Ant. 3 Our God will come with great power to
        enlighten the eyes of his servants, alleluia.

READING   Romans 13:11-12

It is now the hour for you to wake from sleep, for our
salvation is closer than when we first accepted the faith.
The night is far spent; the day draws near. Let us cast off
deeds of darkness and put on the armor of light.

RESPONSORY

Christ, Son of the living God, have mercy on us.
—Christ, Son of the living God, have mercy on us.

You are the one who is to come,
—have mercy on us.

Glory to the Father . . .
—Christ, Son of . . .

CANTICLE OF ZECHARIAH

Ant. I am sending my angel before me to prepare the
      way for my coming.

INTERCESSIONS

To the Lord Jesus Christ, judge of the living and the
    dead, let us pray:
    Come, Lord Jesus!
Lord Jesus, you came to save sinners,
—protect us in times of temptation.

You will come in glory to be our judge,
—show in us your power to save.

Help us to keep the precepts of your law with the
     strength of the Spirit,
—and to look forward in love to your coming.
You are praised throughout the ages; in your mercy help
     us to live devoutly and temperately in this life,
—as we wait in joyful hope for the revelation of your
     glory.

Our Father . . .

Prayer

God of power and mercy,
open our hearts in welcome.
Remove the things that hinder us from receiving Christ
     with joy,
so that we may share his wisdom
and become one with him
when he comes in glory,
for he lives and reigns with you and the Holy Spirit,
one God, for ever and ever.

Alternative Prayer

Father in heaven,
the day draws near when the glory of your Son
will make radiant the night of the waiting world.
May the lure of greed not impede us from the joy
which moves the hearts of those who seek him.
May the darkness not blind us
to the vision of wisdom
which fills the minds of those who find him.
We ask this through Christ our Lord.

Daytime Prayer

HYMN, 658.

Midmorning

Ant.   This is the good news the prophets foretold: The Savior will be born of the Virgin Mary.

READING   Romans 13:13-14a

Let us live honorably as in daylight; not in carousing and drunkenness, not in sexual excess and lust, not in quarreling and jealousy. Rather, put on the Lord Jesus Christ.

The nations will revere your name, O Lord.
—And the great ones of the earth will acknowledge your glory.

Midday

Ant.   The angel Gabriel said to Mary in greeting: Hail, full of grace, the Lord is with you; blessed are you among women.

READING   1 Thessalonians 3:12-13

May the Lord make you overflow with love for one another and for all, even as our love does for you. May he strengthen your hearts, making them blameless and holy before our God and Father at the coming of our Lord Jesus with all his holy ones.

Remember us, Lord, because of the love you have for your people.
—Come and bring us your salvation.

Midafternoon

Ant.   Mary said: My soul is deeply troubled; what can this greeting mean? Am I to give birth to my King and yet remain a virgin for ever?

See 2 Thessalonians 1:6, 7, 10

Strict justice would require that God will provide relief
to you who are sorely tried, as well as to us, when the
Lord Jesus is revealed from heaven with his mighty angels; when he comes to be glorified with his holy ones and
adored by all who have believed.

Come, Lord, do not delay.
—Free your people from their sinfulness.

Prayer, as in Morning Prayer.

Evening Prayer II

HYMN, 126.

Ant. 1   The Lord will come on the clouds of heaven
with great power and might, alleluia.

Psalms and canticle from Sunday, Week II, 811.

Ant. 2   The Lord will come; he is true to his word. If
he seems to delay, keep watch for him, for he
will surely come, alleluia.

Ant. 3   The Lord our king and lawgiver will come to
save us.

READING   Philippians 4: 4-5

Rejoice in the Lord always! I say it again. Rejoice!
Everyone should see how unselfish you are. The Lord is
near.

RESPONSORY

Lord, show us your mercy and love.
—Lord, show us your mercy and love.

And grant us your salvation,
—your mercy and love.

Glory to the Father . . .
  —Lord, show us . . . .

CANTICLE OF MARY

Ant.   Blessed are you, O Virgin Mary, for your great
        faith; all that the Lord promised you will come to
        pass through you, alleluia.

INTERCESSIONS

To Christ the Lord, who was born of the Virgin Mary, let
    us pray with joyful hearts:
    Come, Lord Jesus!
Lord Jesus, in the mystery of your incarnation, you
    revealed your glory to the world,
—give us new life by your coming.
You have taken our weakness upon yourself,
—grant us your mercy.
You redeemed the world from sin by your first coming in
    humility,
—free us from all guilt when you come again in glory.
You live and rule over all,
—in your goodness bring us to our eternal inheritance.
You sit at the right hand of the Father,
—gladden the souls of the dead with your light.

Our Father . .

Prayer

God of power and mercy,
open our hearts in welcome.
Remove the things that hinder us from receiving Christ
    with joy,
so that we may share his wisdom
and become one with him
when he comes in glory,

for he lives and reigns with you and the Holy Spirit,
one God, for ever and ever.

Alternative Prayer

Father in heaven,
the day draws near when the glory of your Son
will make radiant the night of the waiting world.
May the lure of greed not impede us from the joy
which moves the hearts of those who seek him.
May the darkness not blind us
to the vision of wisdom
which fills the minds of those who find him.
We ask this through Christ our Lord.

MONDAY

Office of Readings

Lord, show us your mercy and love.
—And grant us your salvation.

FIRST READING

From the book of the prophet Isaiah   24:1-18

The coming of the Lord on that day

Lo, the Lord empties the land and lays it waste;
   he turns it upside down,
     scattering its inhabitants:
Layman and priest alike,
   servant and master,

The maid as her mistress,
   the buyer as the seller,
The lender as the borrower,
   the creditor as the debtor.
The earth is utterly laid waste, utterly stripped,
   for the Lord has decreed this thing.

The earth mourns and fades,
   the world languishes and fades;
   both heaven and earth languish.
The earth is polluted because of its inhabitants,
   who have transgressed laws, violated statutes,
   broken the ancient covenant.
Therefore a curse devours the earth,
   and its inhabitants pay for their guilt;
Therefore they who dwell on earth turn pale,
   and few men are left.

The wine mourns, the vine languishes,
   all the merry-hearted groan.
Stilled are the cheerful timbrels,
   ended the shouts of the jubilant,
   stilled is the cheerful harp.
They cannot sing and drink wine;
   strong drink is bitter to those who partake of it.

Broken down is the city of chaos,
   shut against entry, every house.
In the streets they cry out for lack of wine;
   all joy has disappeared
   and cheer has left the land.
In the city nothing remains but ruin;
   its gates are battered and desolate.
Thus it is within the land,
   and among the peoples,

As with an olive tree after it is beaten,
   as with a gleaning when the vintage is done.

These lift up their voice in acclaim;
   from the sea they proclaim the majesty of the Lord:
"For this, in the coastlands,
   give glory to the Lord!
In the coastlands of the sea,
   to the name of the Lord, the God of Israel!"
From the end of the earth we hear songs:
   "Splendor to the Just One!"

But I said, "I am wasted, wasted away.
   Woe is me! The traitors betray:
   with treachery have the traitors betrayed!
Terror, pit, and trap
   are upon you, inhabitant of the earth;
He who flees at the sound of terror
   will fall into the pit;
He who climbs out of the pit
   will be caught in the trap.
For the windows on high will be opened
   and the foundations of the earth will shake.

RESPONSORY   Isaiah 24:14, 15; Psalm 96:1
Singing in praise they lift their voices:
__ Let the Lord be glorified in your teachings.

Sing to the Lord a new song;
__ let all the earth sing to the Lord.

SECOND READING
From a treatise on The Ascent of Mount Carmel by Saint
John of the Cross, priest

(Lib. 2, cap. 22)

In Christ God has spoken to us

Under the ancient law prophets and priests sought from God revelations and visions which indeed they needed, for faith had as yet no firm foundation and the gospel law had not yet been established. Their seeking and God's responses were necessary. He spoke to them at one time through words and visions and revelations, at another in signs and symbols. But however he responded and what he said and revealed were mysteries of our holy faith, either partial glimpses of the whole or sure movements toward it.

But now that faith is rooted in Christ, and the law of the gospel has been proclaimed in this time of grace, there is no need to seek him in the former manner, nor for him so to respond. By giving us, as he did, his Son, his only Word, he has in that one Word said everything. There is no need for any further revelation.

This is the true meaning of Paul's words to the Hebrews when he urged them to abandon their earlier ways of conversing with God, as laid down in the law of Moses, and to set their eyes on Christ alone: *In the past God spoke to our fathers through the prophets in various ways and manners; but now in our times, the last days, he has spoken to us in his Son.* In effect, Paul is saying that God has spoken so completely through his own Word that he chooses to add nothing. Although he had spoken but partially through the prophets he has now said everything in Christ. He has given us everything, his own Son.

Therefore, anyone who wished to question God or to seek some new vision or revelation from him would commit an offense, for instead of focusing his eyes entirely on Christ he would be desiring something other than Christ, or beyond him.

God could then answer: *This is my beloved Son in whom I am well pleased; hear him.* In my Word I have already said everything. Fix your eyes on him alone for in him I have revealed all and in him you will find more than you could ever ask for or desire.

I, with my Holy Spirit, came down upon him on Mount Tabor and declared: *This is my beloved Son in whom I am well pleased; hear him.* You do not need new teachings or ways of learning from me, for when I spoke before it was of Christ who was to come, and when they sought anything of me they were but seeking and hoping for the Christ in whom is every good, as the whole teaching of the evangelists and apostles clearly testifies.

RESPONSORY   Micah 4:2; John 4:25

Many nations will come and say:
Let us go up to the mountain of the Lord,
to the home of the God of Jacob.
—He will teach us his ways,
and we will walk in his paths.

The Messiah, who is called the Christ, is coming.
When he comes, he will teach us everything.
—He will teach . . .

Prayer, as in Morning Prayer.

Morning Prayer

READING   Isaiah 2:3b

Come, let us climb the Lord's mountain,
    to the house of the God of Jacob,
That he may instruct us in his ways,
    and we may walk in his paths.
For from Zion shall go forth instructions,
    and the word of the Lord from Jerusalem.

RESPONSORY

Your light will come, Jerusalem;
the Lord will dawn on you in radiant beauty.
—Your light will come, Jerusalem;
the Lord will dawn on you in radiant beauty.

You will see his glory within you;
—the Lord will dawn on you in radiant beauty.

Glory to the Father . . .
—Your light will . . .

CANTICLE OF ZECHARIAH

Ant.   The Lord proclaims: Repent, the kingdom of God
is upon you, alleluia.

INTERCESSIONS

To Christ our Redeemer, who will come again to free
from the power of death all those who return to him,
let us humbly pray:
Come, Lord Jesus!
As we proclaim your coming, Lord,
—cleanse our hearts of every vain desire.
Lord, may the Church which you founded,
—proclaim your greatness to all peoples.
Your law is a light to our eyes,
—let it protect those who trust in you.
You allow the joys of your coming to be foretold to us by
your Church,
—may we receive you with eager devotion.

Our Father . . .

Prayer

Lord,
free us from our sins and make us whole.

Hear our prayer,
and prepare us to celebrate the incarnation of your Son,
who lives and reigns with you and the Holy Spirit,
one God, for ever and ever.

Daytime Prayer

Midmorning

Ant.   This is the good news the prophets foretold: The
Savior will be born of the Virgin Mary.

READING   See Isaiah 10:20-21

On that day
The remnant of Israel,
    the survivors of the house of Jacob,
Will lean upon the Lord,
    the Holy One of Israel, in truth.
A remnant will return, the remnant of Jacob,
    to the mighty God.

The nations will revere your name, O Lord.
—And the great ones of the earth will acknowledge your
    glory.

Midday

Ant.   The angel Gabriel said to Mary in greeting: Hail,
full of grace, the Lord is with you; blessed are you
among women.

READING   See Isaiah 10:24, 27

Thus says the Lord, the God of hosts:
O my people, who dwell in Zion,
    do not fear.

On that day,
The burden shall be taken from your shoulder,
 and the yoke shattered from your neck.

Remember us, Lord, because of the love you have for
 your people.
—Come and bring us your salvation.

Midafternoon

Ant.   Mary said: My soul is deeply troubled; what can
        this greeting mean? Am I to give birth to my King
        and yet remain a virgin for ever?

READING   See Isaiah 14:1

Her time is near at hand
 and her days shall not be prolonged.
The Lord has pity on Jacob
 and again chooses Israel.

Come, Lord, do not delay.
—Free your people from their sinfulness.

Prayer, as in Morning Prayer.

Evening Prayer

READING   Philippians 3:20b-21

We eagerly await the coming of our Savior, the Lord
Jesus Christ. He will give a new form to this lowly body
of ours and remake it according to the pattern of his
glorified body, by his power to subject everything to
himself.

RESPONSORY

Come and set us free, Lord God of power and might.
—Come and set us free, Lord God of power and might.

Let your face shine upon us and we shall be saved,
—Lord God of power and might.

Glory to the Father . . .
—Come and set . . .

CANTICLE OF MARY

Ant.   See, your King comes, the master of the earth; he
         will shatter the yoke of our slavery.

INTERCESSIONS

To Christ our Lord, judge of the living and the dead, let
    us cry out with faith:
    Come, Lord Jesus!
Lord, may the world know your justice which the
    heavens proclaim,
—may your glory fill the earth.
For us you took upon yourself the weakness of man,
—protect us with the strength of your own divine life.
Come to those imprisoned in the darkness of ignorance,
—show them the radiance of your own divine light.
In your humility as a man, you took away our sin,
—now in your glory grant us true happiness.
When you come in glory to judge us,
—gather the dead into your kingdom.

Our Father . . .

Prayer

Lord,
free us from our sins and make us whole.
Hear our prayer,
and prepare us to celebrate the incarnation of your Son,
who lives and reigns with you and the Holy Spirit,
one God, for ever and ever.

TUESDAY

Office of Readings

A voice is heard, crying in the wilderness: Prepare the
    way of the Lord.
—Make straight the path of our God.

First Reading

From the book of the prophet Isaiah   24:19—25:5

The kingdom of God. Thanksgiving

On that day the earth will burst asunder,
    the earth will be shaken apart,
    the earth will be convulsed.
The earth will reel like a drunkard,
    and it will sway like a hut;
Its rebellion will weigh it down,
    until it falls, never to rise again.

On that day the Lord will punish
    the host of the heavens in the heavens,
    and the kings of the earth on the earth.
They will be gathered together
    like prisoners into a pit;
They will be shut up in a dungeon,
    and after many days they will be punished.
Then the moon will blush
    and the sun grow pale,
For the Lord of hosts will reign
    on Mount Zion and in Jerusalem,
    glorious in the sight of his elders.

O Lord, you are my God,
    I will extol you and praise your name;
For you have fulfilled your wonderful plans of old,
    faithful and true.

For you have made the city a heap,
  the fortified city a ruin;
The castle of the insolent is a city no more,
  nor ever to be rebuilt.

Therefore, a strong people will honor you,
  fierce nations will fear you.
For you are a refuge to the poor,
  a refuge to the needy in distress;
Shelter from the rain,
  shade from the heat.
As with the cold rain,
  as with the desert heat,
  even so you quell the uproar of the wanton.

RESPONSORY   Isaiah 25:1, 4

O Lord, you are my God;
I will extol you and praise your name,
—because you fulfilled your wondrous plans.

For you are a refuge for the poor man,
and a shelter for the needy man in his distress.
—Because you fulfilled . . .

SECOND READING

From the dogmatic constitution on the Church of the
Second Vatican Council.
(Lumen Gentium, n. 48)

The eschatological character of the pilgrim Church

The Church, to which we are all called in Christ Jesus
and in which we acquire holiness through the grace of
God, will reach its perfection only in the glory of heaven,
when the time comes for the renewal of all things, and
the whole world, which is intimately bound up with man

and reaches its perfection through him, will, along with the human race, be perfectly restored in Christ.

Lifted above the earth, Christ drew all things to himself. Rising from the dead, he sent his life-giving Spirit upon his disciples, and through the Spirit established his Body, which is the Church, as the universal sacrament of salvation. Seated at the right hand of the Father, he works unceasingly in the world, to draw men into the Church and through it to join them more closely to himself, nourishing them with his own body and blood, and so making them share in his life of glory.

The promised renewal that we look for has already begun in Christ. It is continued in the mission of the Holy Spirit. Through the Spirit it goes on developing in the Church: there we are taught by faith about the meaning also of our life on earth as we bring to fulfillment—with hope in the blessings that are to come—the work that has been entrusted to us in the world by the Father, and so work out our salvation.

The end of the ages is already with us. The renewal of the world has been established, and cannot be revoked. In our era it is in a true sense anticipated: the Church on earth is already sealed by genuine, if imperfect, holiness. Yet, until a new heaven and a new earth are built as the dwelling place of justice, the pilgrim Church, in its sacraments and institutions belonging to this world of time, bears the likeness of this passing world. It lives in the midst of a creation still groaning and in travail as it waits for the sons of God to be revealed in glory.

RESPONSORY　　　　　　　　　　　　　Philippians 3:20-21

We eagerly await the coming of our Savior, the Lord
　　Jesus Christ;
—he will renew our lowly bodies
and make them like his own glorified body.

Sober, just, and godly we live in this world,
as we wait in blessed hope for the glorious coming of the
    almighty God.
—He will renew . . .

Prayer, as in Morning Prayer.

Morning Prayer

READING   Genesis 49:10

The scepter shall never depart from Judah,
    or the mace from between his legs,
While tribute is brought to him,
    and he receives the people's homage.

RESPONSORY

Your light will come, Jerusalem;
the Lord will dawn on you in radiant beauty.
—Your light will come, Jerusalem;
the Lord will dawn on you in radiant beauty.

You will see his glory within you;
—the Lord will dawn on you in radiant beauty.

Glory to the Father . . .
—Your light will . . .

CANTICLE OF ZECHARIAH

Ant.   Rejoice and be glad, O daughter of Zion; I will
        come and make my dwelling in you, says the
        Lord.

INTERCESSIONS

To Christ our Lord, the light of the world, let us cry out
    with joy:
    Come, Lord Jesus!

Dispel our darkness with the light of your presence,
__and make us worthy of your gifts.
Save us, Lord our God,
__that we may praise your holy name this day.
Enkindle in our hearts the flame of your love,
__and make us long to be united with you.
You bore our infirmity,
__aid the sick and those who are to die this day.

Our Father . . .

Prayer

Almighty God,
help us to look forward
to the glory of the birth of Christ our Savior:
his coming is proclaimed joyfully
to the ends of the earth,
for he lives and reigns with you and the Holy Spirit,
one God, for ever and ever.

Daytime Prayer

Midmorning

Ant.   This is the good news the prophets foretold: The
       Savior will be born of the Virgin Mary.

READING   Jeremiah 23:5
Behold, the days are coming, says the Lord,
  when I will raise up a righteous shoot to David;
As king he shall reign and govern wisely,
  he shall do what is just and right in the land.

The nations will revere your name, O Lord.
__ And the great ones of the earth will acknowledge your
  glory.

Midday

Ant.   The angel Gabriel said to Mary in greeting: Hail,
full of grace, the Lord is with you; blessed are you
among women.

READING   Jeremiah 23:6

In his days Judah shall be saved,
  Israel shall dwell in security.
This is the name they give him:
  "The Lord our justice."

Remember us, Lord, because of the love you have for
  your people.
—Come and bring us your salvation.

Midafternoon

Ant.   Mary said: My soul is deeply troubled; what can
this greeting mean? Am I to give birth to my King
and yet remain a virgin for ever?

READING   Ezekiel 34:15-16

I myself will pasture my sheep; I myself will give them
rest, says the Lord God. The lost I will seek out, the
strayed I will bring back, the injured I will bind up, the
sick I will heal, shepherding them rightly.

Come, Lord, do not delay.
—Free your people from their sinfulness.

Prayer, as in Morning Prayer.

Evening Prayer

READING   See 1 Corinthians 1:7b-9

We await the revelation of our Lord Jesus Christ, who
will strengthen us to the end, so that we will be blameless

on the day of our Lord Jesus Christ. God is faithful, and it was he who called us to fellowship with his Son.

RESPONSORY

Come and set us free, Lord God of power and might.
—Come and set us free, Lord God of power and might.

Let your face shine upon us and we shall be saved,
—Lord God of power and might.

Glory to the Father . . .
—Come and set . . .

CANTICLE OF MARY

Ant.   A voice is heard crying in the wilderness: Prepare the way of the Lord; make straight the path of our God.

INTERCESSIONS

To Christ, our Lord and Redeemer, who will appear openly on the last day, let us joyfully pray:
    Come, Lord Jesus!
Our Redeemer and Lord, by your birth as a man you freed us from the yoke of the law,
—complete in us the works of your loving kindness.
From us you took whatever served your divinity,
—give us whatever we need to serve you.
Grant the desire we ask of you today,
—inflame our hearts with the fire of your love.
On earth we live with you by faith,
—in glory may we rejoice with you.
Steep the souls of the faithful departed,
—in the dew of your loving kindness.

Our Father . . .

Prayer

Almighty God,
help us to look forward
to the glory of the birth of Christ our Savior:
his coming is proclaimed joyfully
to the ends of the earth,
for he lives and reigns with you and the Holy Spirit,
one God, for ever and ever.

WEDNESDAY

Office of Readings

Turn back to us, O Lord, our God.
—Show us your face and we shall be saved.

First Reading

From the book of the prophet Isaiah   25:6—26:6

The banquet of God. The song of the redeemed

On this mountain the Lord of hosts
    will provide for all peoples
A feast of rich food and choice wines,
    juicy, rich food and pure, choice wines.
On this mountain he will destroy
    the veil that veils all peoples,
The web that is woven over all nations;
    he will destroy death forever.
The Lord God will wipe away
    the tears from all faces;
The reproach of his people he will remove
    from the whole earth; for the Lord has spoken.

On that day it will be said:
"Behold our God, to whom we looked to save us!
　　This is the Lord for whom we looked;
　　　let us rejoice and be glad that he has saved us!"
For the hand of the Lord will rest on this mountain,
　　but Moab will be trodden down
　　as a straw is trodden down in the mire.
He will stretch forth his hands in Moab
　　as a swimmer extends his hands to swim;
He will bring low their pride
　　as his hands sweep over them.
The high-walled fortress he will raze,
　　and strike it down level with the earth, with the very
　　　dust.
On that day they will sing this song in the land of Judah:
"A strong city have we;
　　he sets up walls and ramparts to protect us.
Open up the gates
　　to let in a nation that is just,
　　one that keeps faith.
A nation of firm purpose you keep in peace;
　　in peace, for its trust in you."

Trust in the Lord forever!
　　For the Lord is an eternal Rock.
He humbles those in high places,
　　and the lofty city he brings down;
He tumbles it to the ground,
　　levels it with the dust.
It is trampled underfoot by the needy,
　　by the footsteps of the poor.

RESPONSORY   Revelation 21:3; Isaiah 25:8

I heard a voice proclaiming from the throne:
Now God has a dwelling place among men

and he will live with them;
__they will be his people
and he, their God, will be with them.
The Lord will cast down death for ever
and wipe the tears from every face.
__They will be. . . .

SECOND READING

From a discourse on the psalms by Saint Augustine,
bishop

(In ps. 109, 1-3: CCL 40, 1601-1603)

God's promises are held out to us by his Son

God established a time for his promises and a time for
their fulfillment.

The time for promises was in the time of the prophets,
until John the Baptist; from John until the end is the
time of fulfillment.

God, who is faithful, put himself in our debt, not by
receiving anything but by promising so much. A promise
was not sufficient for him; he chose to commit himself in
writing as well, as it were making a contract of his
promises. He wanted us to be able to see the way in
which his promises were redeemed when he began to
discharge them. And so the time of the prophets was, as
we have often said, the foretelling of the promises.

He promised eternal salvation, everlasting happiness
with the angels, an immortal inheritance, endless glory,
the joyful vision of his face, his holy dwelling in heaven,
and after resurrection from the dead no further fear of
dying. This is as it were his final promise, the goal of all
our striving. When we reach it, we shall ask for nothing
more. But as to the way in which we are to arrive at our
final goal, he has revealed this also, by promise and
prophecy.

He has promised men divinity, mortals immortality, sinners justification, the poor a rising to glory.

But, brethren, because God's promises seemed impossible to men—equality with the angels in exchange for mortality, corruption, poverty, weakness, dust and ashes—God not only made a written contract with men, to win their belief but also established a mediator of his good faith, not a prince or angel or archangel, but his only Son. He wanted, through his Son, to show us and give us the way he would lead us to the goal he has promised.

It was not enough for God to make his Son our guide to the way; he made him the way itself, that you might travel with him as leader, and by him as the way.

Therefore, the only Son of God was to come among men, to take the nature of men, and in this nature to be born as a man. He was to die, to rise again, to ascend into heaven, to sit at the right hand of the Father, and to fulfill his promises among the nations, and after that to come again, to exact now what he had asked for before, to separate those deserving his anger from those deserving his mercy, to execute his threats against the wicked, and to reward the just as he had promised.

All this had therefore to be prophesied, foretold, and impressed on us as an event in the future, in order that we might wait for it in faith, not find it a sudden and dreadful reality.

RESPONSORY   Micah 7:19; Acts 10:43

Our God will again have compassion on us;
—he will put aside our wickedness,
and bury our sins in the depth of the sea.

All the prophets testify to him, saying:

Everyone who believes in him has forgiveness of sins
    through his name.
—He will put . . .

Prayer, as in Morning Prayer.

Morning Prayer

READING   Isaiah 7:14b–15

The virgin shall be with child, and bear a son, and
shall name him Immanuel. He shall be living on curds
and honey by the time he learns to reject the bad and
choose the good.

RESPONSORY

Your light will come, Jerusalem;
the Lord will dawn on you in radiant beauty.
—Your light will come, Jerusalem;
the Lord will dawn on you in radiant beauty.

You will see his glory within you;
—the Lord will dawn on you in radiant beauty.

Glory to the Father . . .
—Your light will . . .

CANTICLE OF ZECHARIAH

Ant.   He will be enthroned in David's place to be king
        for ever, alleluia.

INTERCESSIONS

To Jesus Christ our Lord, who came among us in his
    mercy, let us constantly cry out with joy:
    Come, Lord Jesus!
You came from the Father to take on our human nature,
—now set free what was harmed in us by sin.

One day you will come again in glory to your chosen
    people,
—come to us today and help us sinners to recognize your
    mercy and tender love.
We glory in praising you, Lord Jesus,
—come and bring us your salvation.
Through faith you lead us into light,
—may we reveal your justice through our deeds.

Our Father . . .

Prayer

All-powerful Father,
we await the healing power of Christ your Son.
Let us not be discouraged by our weaknesses
as we prepare for his coming.
Keep us steadfast in your love.

We ask this through our Lord Jesus Christ, your Son,
who lives and reigns with you and the Holy Spirit,
one God, for ever and ever.

Daytime Prayer

Midmorning

Ant.   This is the good news the prophets foretold: The
        Savior will be born of the Virgin Mary.

READING   See Isaiah 2:11–12

The haughty eyes of man will be lowered,
    the arrogance of men will be abased,
    and the Lord alone will be exalted, on that day.

The nations will revere your name, O Lord.
—And the great ones of the earth will acknowledge your
    glory.

Midday

Ant. The angel Gabriel said to Mary in greeting: Hail,
full of grace, the Lord is with you; blessed are you
among women.

READING   Isaiah 12:2

God indeed is my savior;
  I am confident and unafraid.
My strength and my courage is the Lord,
  and he has been my savior.

Remember us, Lord, because of the love you have for
  your people.
—Come and bring us your salvation.

Midafternoon

Ant. Mary said: My soul is deeply troubled; what can
this greeting mean? Am I to give birth to my King
and yet remain a virgin for ever?

READING   Daniel 9:19

O Lord, hear! O Lord, pardon! O Lord, be attentive
and act without delay, for your own sake, O my God,
because your people bear your name!

Come, Lord, do not delay.
—Free your people from their sinfulness.

Prayer, as in Morning Prayer.

Evening Prayer

READING   1 Corinthians 4:5

Stop passing judgment before the time of the Lord's
return. He will bring to light what is hidden in darkness
and manifest the intentions of hearts. At that time,
everyone will receive his praise from God.

RESPONSORY

Come and set us free, Lord God of power and might.
—Come and set us free, Lord God of power and might.

Let your face shine upon us and we shall be saved,
—Lord God of power and might.

Glory to the Father . . .
—Come and set . . .

CANTICLE OF MARY

Ant.   Zion, you will be renewed, and you will see the
Just One who is coming to you.

INTERCESSIONS

We humbly pray to Jesus Christ, who rescues us from the
darkness of sin, and in faith we cry out:
Come, Lord Jesus!
Lord, gather together all the people of the earth,
—and establish with them your everlasting covenant.
Lamb of God, you came of old to take away the sin of the
world,
—purge us from the dregs of our guilt.
You came to recover what was lost,
—come once again in your mercy lest you punish what
you have recovered.
Our faith seeks you out,
—let us find everlasting joy with you when you come.
You will judge the living and the dead,
—graciously gather the dead into the ranks of the
blessed.

Our Father . . .

Prayer

All-powerful Father,
we await the healing power of Christ your Son.

Let us not be discouraged by our weaknesses
as we prepare for his coming.
Keep us steadfast in your love.

We ask this through our Lord Jesus Christ, your Son,
who lives and reigns with you and the Holy Spirit,
one God, for ever and ever.

THURSDAY

Office of Readings

Hear the word of the Lord, all you nations.
—Proclaim it to the ends of the earth.

<small>FIRST READING</small>

From the book of the prophet Isaiah   26:7–21

The song of the just. The promise of new life

The way of the just is smooth;
   the path of the just you make level.
Yes, for your way and your judgments, O Lord,
   we look to you;
Your name and your title
   are the desire of our souls,

My soul yearns for you in the night,
   yes, my spirit within me keeps vigil for you;
When your judgment dawns upon the earth,
   the world's inhabitants learn justice.

The wicked man, spared, does not learn justice;
   in an upright land he acts perversely,
   and sees not the majesty of the Lord.

O Lord, your hand is uplifted,
 but they behold it not;
Let them be shamed when they see your zeal for your
  people:
 let the fire prepared for your enemies consume them.

O Lord, you mete out peace to us,
 for it is you who have accomplished all we have done.
O Lord, our God, other lords than you have ruled us;
 it is from you only that we can call upon your name.

Dead they are, they have no life,
 shades that cannot rise;
For you have punished and destroyed them,
 and wiped out all memory of them.

You have increased the nation, O Lord,
 increased the nation to your own glory,
 and extended far all the borders of the land.

O Lord, oppressed by your punishment,
 we cried out in anguish under your chastising.
As a woman about to give birth
 writhes and cries out in her pains,
 so were we in your presence, O Lord.

We conceived and writhed in pain,
 giving birth to wind;
Salvation we have not achieved for the earth,
 the inhabitants of the world cannot bring it forth.

But your dead shall live, their corpses shall rise;
 awake and sing, you who lie in the dust.
For your dew is a dew of light,
 and the land of shades gives birth.

Go, my people, enter your chambers,
 and close your doors behind you;

Hide yourselves for a brief moment,
  until the wrath is past.

See, the Lord goes forth from his place,
  to punish the wickedness of the earth's inhabitants;
The earth will reveal the blood upon her,
  and no longer conceal her slain.

RESPONSORY   Isaiah 26:19; Daniel 12:2

Awake and sing, you who sleep in the earth,
—for the dew of the Lord is a dew of light.

Many of those who sleep in the dust of the earth will
  awaken.
—For the dew . . .

SECOND READING

From a sermon by Saint Peter Chrysologus, bishop
(Sermo 147: PL 52, 594-595)

Love desires to see God

When God saw the world falling to ruin because of fear, he immediately acted to call it back to himself with love. He invited it by his grace, preserved it by his love, and embraced it with compassion. When the earth had become hardened in evil, God sent the flood both to punish and to release it. He called Noah to be the father of a new era, urged him with kind words, and showed that he trusted him; he gave him fatherly instruction about the present calamity, and through his grace consoled him with hope for the future. But God did not merely issue commands; rather with Noah sharing the work, he filled the ark with the future seed of the whole world. The sense of loving fellowship thus engendered removed servile fear, and a mutual love could continue to preserve what shared labor had effected.

God called Abraham out of the heathen world, symbolically lengthened his name, and made him the father of all believers. God walked with him on his journeys, protected him in foreign lands, enriched him with earthly possessions, and honored him with victories. He made a covenant with him, saved him from harm, accepted his hospitality, and astonished him by giving him the offspring he had despaired of. Favored with so many graces and drawn by such great sweetness of divine love, Abraham was to learn to love God rather than fear him, and love rather than fear was to inspire his worship.

God comforted Jacob by a dream during his flight, roused him to combat upon his return, and encircled him with a wrestler's embrace to teach him not to be afraid of the author of the conflict, but to love him. God called Moses as a father would, and with fatherly affection invited him to become the liberator of his people.

In all the events we have recalled, the flame of divine love enkindled human hearts and its intoxication overflowed into men's senses. Wounded by love, they longed to look upon God with their bodily eyes. Yet how could our narrow human vision apprehend God, whom the whole world cannot contain? But the law of love is not concerned with what will be, what ought to be, what can be. Love does not reflect; it is unreasonable and knows no moderation. Love refuses to be consoled when its goal proves impossible, despises all hindrances to the attainment of its object. Love destroys the lover if he cannot obtain what he loves; love follows its own promptings, and does not think of right and wrong. Love inflames desire which impels it toward things that are forbidden. But why continue?

It is intolerable for love not to see the object of its longing. That is why whatever reward they merited was nothing to the saints if they could not see the Lord. A love that desires to see God may not have reasonableness on its side, but it is the evidence of filial love. It gave Moses the temerity to say: *If I have found favor in your eyes, show me your face.* It inspired the psalmist to make the same prayer: *Show me your face.* Even the pagans made their images for this purpose: they wanted actually to see what they mistakenly revered.

RESPONSORY See Is. 66:13; 1 Kgs. 11:36; Is. 66:14; 46:13

As a mother comforts her sons,
so will I comfort you, says the Lord;
help will come to you from the city of Jerusalem
which I have chosen.
—You shall see this, and your heart will rejoice.

I will give salvation in Zion
and my glory in Jerusalem.
—You shall see . . .

Prayer, as in Morning Prayer.

Morning Prayer

READING   Isaiah 45:8

Let justice descend, O heavens, like dew from above,
    like gentle rain let the skies drop it down.
Let the earth open and salvation bud forth;
    let justice also spring up!

RESPONSORY

Your light will come, Jerusalem;
the Lord will dawn on you in radiant beauty.
—Your light will come, Jerusalem;
the Lord will dawn on you in radiant beauty.

You will see his glory within you;
__the Lord will dawn on you in radiant beauty.

Glory to the Father . . .
__Your light will . . .

CANTICLE OF ZECHARIAH

Ant.   I will help you, says the Lord. I am your Savior, the Holy One of Israel.

INTERCESSIONS

Let us pray to God our Father who sent his Son to save mankind:

Show us your mercy, Lord!

Father most merciful, we confess our faith in your Christ with our words,
__keep us from denying him in our actions.

You have sent your Son to rescue us,
__remove every sorrow from the face of the earth and from our country.

Our land looks forward with delight to the approach of your Son,
__let it experience the fullness of your joy.

Through your mercy make us live holy and chaste lives in this world,
__eagerly awaiting the blessed hope and coming of Christ in glory.

Our Father . . .

Prayer

Almighty Father,
give us the joy of your love
to prepare the way for Christ our Lord.
Help us to serve you and one another.

We ask this through our Lord Jesus Christ, your Son,

who lives and reigns with you and the Holy Spirit,
one God, for ever and ever.

Daytime Prayer

Midmorning

Ant.   This is the good news the prophets foretold: The
Savior will be born of the Virgin Mary.

READING   Micah 5:4–5a

The ruler in Israel shall stand firm and shepherd his flock
    by the strength of the Lord,
    in the majestic name of the Lord, his God;
And they shall remain, for now his greatness
    shall reach to the ends of the earth;
    he shall be peace.

The nations will revere your name, O Lord.
—And the great ones of the earth will acknowledge your
    glory.

Midday

Ant.   The angel Gabriel said to Mary in greeting: Hail,
full of grace, the Lord is with you; blessed are you
among women.

READING   Haggai 2:6, 9

One moment yet, a little while,
    and I will shake the heavens and the earth,
    the sea and the dry land.
Greater will be the future glory of this house
    than the former;
And in this house I will give peace,
    says the Lord of hosts!

Remember us, Lord, because of the love you have for
    your people.
—Come and bring us your salvation.

Midafternoon

Ant.   Mary said: My soul is deeply troubled; what can
           this greeting mean? Am I to give birth to my King
           and yet remain a virgin for ever?

READING   See Malachi 4:2

For you who fear my name, there will arise
    the sun of justice with its healing rays;
And you will gambol like calves out of the stall,
    says the Lord of hosts.

Come, Lord, do not delay.
—Free your people from their sinfulness.

Prayer, as in Morning Prayer.

Evening Prayer

READING   James 5:7-8, 9b

    Be patient, my brothers, until the coming of the Lord.
See how the farmer awaits the precious yield of the soil.
He looks forward to it patiently while the soil receives the
winter and the spring rains. You, too, must be patient.
Steady your hearts, because the coming of the Lord is at
hand. See! The judge stands at the gate.

RESPONSORY

Come and set us free, Lord God of power and might.
—Come and set us free, Lord God of power and might.

Let your face shine upon us and we shall be saved,
—Lord God of power and might.

Glory to the Father . .

—Come and set . . .

CANTICLE OF MARY

Ant.   The one who is coming after me existed before
       me; I am not worthy to untie his sandals.

INTERCESSIONS

To Christ our Lord, who humbled himself for our sake,
   we joyfully say:
   Come, Lord Jesus!
Lord Jesus, by your coming you rescued the world from
   sin,
—cleanse our souls and bodies from guilt.
By the mystery of your incarnation we are made your
   brothers and sisters,
—do not let us become estranged from you.
Do not judge harshly,
—those you redeemed with such great cost.
No age, O Christ, is without your goodness and holy
   riches,
—enable us to merit the unfading crown of glory.
Lord, to you we commend the souls of your departed
   servants,
—having died to the world, may they be alive in you for
   ever.

Our Father . . .

Prayer

Almighty Father,
give us the joy of your love
to prepare the way for Christ our Lord.
Help us to serve you and one another.

We ask this through our Lord Jesus Christ, your Son,
who lives and reigns with you and the Holy Spirit,
one God, for ever and ever.

FRIDAY

Office of Readings

Let your compassion come upon me, Lord.
—Your salvation, true to your promise.

FIRST READING

From the book of the prophet Isaiah   27:1–13

The Lord cares for his vineyard once again

On that day,
The Lord will punish with his sword
    that is cruel, great, and strong,
Leviathan the fleeing serpent,
    Leviathan the coiled serpent;
    and he will slay the dragon that is in the sea.

On that day—
The pleasant vineyard, sing about it!
    I, the Lord, am its keeper,
    I water it every moment;
Lest anyone harm it,
    night and day I guard it.

I am not angry,
    but if I were to find briers and thorns,
In battle I should march against them;
    I should burn them all.
Expunging and expelling, I should strive against them,
    carrying them off with my cruel wind in time of storm.

In days to come Jacob shall take root,
    Israel shall sprout and blossom,
    covering all the world with fruit.
Is he to be smitten as his smiter was smitten?
    or slain as his slayer was slain?

Or shall he cling to me for refuge?
>   He must make peace with me;
>   peace shall he make with me!

This, then, shall be the expiation of Jacob's guilt,
>   this the whole fruit of the removal of his sin:
He shall pulverize all the stones of the altars
>   like pieces of chalk;
>   no sacred poles or incense altars shall stand.
For the fortified city shall be desolate,
>   an abandoned pasture, a forsaken wilderness,
>   where calves shall browse and lie.
Its boughs shall be destroyed,
>   its branches shall wither and be broken off,
>   and women shall come to build a fire with them.
This is not an understanding people;
>   therefore their maker shall not spare them,
>   nor shall he who formed them have mercy on them.

>   On that day,
The Lord shall beat out the grain
>   between the Euphrates and the Wadi of Egypt,
>   and you shall be gleaned one by one, O sons of Israel.

>   On that day,
A great trumpet shall blow,
>   and the lost in the land of Assyria
>   and the outcasts in the land of Egypt
Shall come and worship the Lord
>   on the holy mountain, in Jerusalem.

RESPONSORY   See Matthew 24:31; Isaiah 27:13

The Lord will send forth his angels with a mighty
>   trumpet blast;
—they will gather his chosen ones from the four winds,
from one end of the heavens to the other.

They shall come and worship the Lord on his holy
    mountain in Jerusalem.
—They will gather his chosen ones from the four winds,
from one end of the heavens to the other.

SECOND READING

From a treatise *Against Heresies* by Saint Irenaeus,
bishop
(Lib. 5, 19, 1; 20, 2; 21, 1: SC 153, 248-250. 260-264)

Eve and Mary

The Lord, coming into his own creation in visible
form, was sustained by his own creation which he himself
sustains in being. His obedience on the tree of the cross
reversed the disobedience at the tree in Eden; the good
news of the truth announced by an angel to Mary, a virgin subject to a husband, undid the evil lie that seduced
Eve, a virgin espoused to a husband.

As Eve was seduced by the word of an angel and so fled
from God after disobeying his word, Mary in her turn
was given the good news by the word of an angel, and
bore God in obedience to his word. As Eve was seduced
into disobedience to God, so Mary was persuaded into
obedience to God; thus the Virgin Mary became the advocate of the virgin Eve.

Christ gathered all things into one, by gathering them
into himself. He declared war against our enemy,
crushed him who at the beginning had taken us captive in
Adam, and trampled on his head, in accordance with
God's words to the serpent in Genesis: *I will put enmity*
between you and the woman, and between your seed and her
seed; he shall lie in wait for your head, and you shall lie in
wait for his heel.

The one lying in wait for the serpent's head is the one
who was born in the likeness of Adam from the woman,
the Virgin. This is the seed spoken of by Paul in the letter

to the Galatians: *The law of works was in force until the seed should come to whom the promise was made.* He shows this even more clearly in the same letter when he says: *When the fullness of time had come, God sent his Son, born of a woman.* The enemy would not have been defeated fairly if his vanquisher had not been born of a woman, because it was through a woman that he had gained mastery over man in the beginning, and set himself up as man's adversary.

That is why the Lord proclaims himself the Son of Man, the one who renews in himself that first man from whom the race born of woman was formed; as by a man's defeat our race fell into the bondage of death, so by a man's victory we were to rise again to life.

RESPONSORY   See Luke 1:26, 27, 30, 31, 32

The angel Gabriel was sent to the Virgin Mary who was
     betrothed to Joseph.
The light filled her with fear,
but the angel said to her:
Do not be afraid, Mary; you have found favor with God.
—Behold you shall conceive and bear a son,
and he will be called the Son of the Most High.

The Lord God will give him the throne of David, his
     father,
and he will rule over the house of Jacob for ever.
—Behold you shall . . .

Prayer, as in Morning Prayer.

Morning Prayer

READING   Jeremiah 30:21-22

     Thus says the Lord:
His leader shall be from Jacob,
     and his ruler shall come from his kin.

When I summon him,
   he shall approach me.
You shall be my people,
   and I will be your God.

RESPONSORY

Your light will come, Jerusalem;
the Lord will dawn on you in radiant beauty.
—Your light will come, Jerusalem;
the Lord will dawn on you in radiant beauty.

You will see his glory within you;
—the Lord will dawn on you in radiant beauty.

Glory to the Father . . .
—Your light will . . .

CANTICLE OF ZECHARIAH

Ant.   Say to the fainthearted: Take courage! The Lord
       our God is coming to save us.

INTERCESSIONS

To Christ our Redeemer, who comes to save us from our
   sins, let us cry out with joy:
   Come, Lord Jesus!
The prophets of old foretold your birth among us,
—now make virtue come to life in us.
We proclaim your saving work,
—now grant us your salvation.
You came to heal the contrite,
—heal the weaknesses of your people.
You came and saw fit to reconcile the world,
—when you come again in judgment, free us from the
   torments of punishment.

Our Father . . .

Prayer

All-powerful God,
help us to look forward in hope
to the coming of our Savior.
May we live as he has taught,
ready to welcome him with burning love and faith.

We ask this through our Lord Jesus Christ, your Son,
who lives and reigns with you and the Holy Spirit,
one God, for ever and ever.

Daytime Prayer

Midmorning

Ant.　This is the good news the prophets foretold: The
Savior will be born of the Virgin Mary.

READING　　　　　　　　　　　　　　　Jeremiah 29:11,13

I know well the plans I have in mind for you, says the
Lord, plans for your welfare, not for woe! plans to give
you a future full of hope. When you look for me, you will
find me, yes, when you see me with all your heart.

The nations will revere your name, O Lord.
—And the great ones of the earth will acknowledge your
glory.

Midday

Ant.　The angel Gabriel said to Mary in greeting: Hail,
full of grace, the Lord is with you; blessed are you
among women.

READING　　　　　　　　　　　　　　　Jeremiah 30:18

Thus says the Lord:
See! I will restore the tents of Jacob.
his dwellings I will pity.

Remember us, Lord, because of the love you have for
  your people.
—Come and bring us your salvation.

Midafternoon

Ant.   Mary said: My soul is deeply troubled; what can
        this greeting mean? Am I to give birth to my King
        and yet remain a virgin for ever?

<small>READING</small>   Baruch 3:5–6a

Remember at this time not the misdeeds of our fathers,
but your own hand and name; for you are the Lord our
God.

Come, Lord, do not delay.
—Free your people from their sinfulness.

Prayer, as in Morning Prayer.

Evening Prayer

<small>READING</small>   2 Peter 3:8b–9

In the Lord's eyes, one day is as a thousand years and a
thousand years are as a day. The Lord does not delay in
keeping his promise—though some consider it "delay."
Rather, he shows you generous patience, since he wants
none to perish but all to come to repentance.

<small>RESPONSORY</small>

Come and set us free, Lord God of power and might.
—Come and set us free, Lord God of power and might.

Let your face shine upon us and we shall be saved,
—Lord God of power and might.

Glory to the Father . . .
—Come and set . . .

CANTICLE OF MARY

Ant.   Rejoicing you shall draw water from the well-
        springs of the Savior.

INTERCESSIONS

To our Redeemer who came to bring good news to the
    poor, let us earnestly pray:
    Let all men see your glory!
Show yourself to those who have never known you,
—let them see your saving work.
Let your name be preached to the ends of the earth,
—that all may find the way to you.
You first came to save the world,
—now come again and save those who believe in you.
You brought freedom to us by saving us,
—continue to save us and make us free.
You came once as a man; you will return in judgment,
—bring eternal reward to those who have died.

Our Father . . .

Prayer

All-powerful God,
help us to look forward in hope
to the coming of our Savior.
May we live as he has taught,
ready to welcome him with burning love and faith.

We ask this through our Lord Jesus Christ, your Son,
who lives and reigns with you and the Holy Spirit,
one God, for ever and ever.

SATURDAY

Office of Readings

The Lord proclaims his word to Jacob.
—His laws and decrees to Israel.

FIRST READING

From the book of the prophet Isaiah   29:1-8

God's judgment on Jerusalem

Woe to Ariel, Ariel,
     the city where David encamped!
Add year to year,
     let the feasts come round.
But I will bring distress upon Ariel,
     with mourning and grief.
You shall be to me like Ariel,
     I will encamp like David against you;
I will encircle you with outposts
     and set up siege works against you.

Prostrate you shall speak from the earth,
     and from the base dust your words shall come.
Your voice shall be like a ghost's from the earth,
     and your words like chirping from the dust.
The horde of your arrogant shall be like fine dust,
     the horde of the tyrants like flying chaff.
Then suddenly, in an instant,
     you shall be visited by the Lord of hosts,
With thunder, earthquake, and great noise,
     whirlwind, storm, and the flame of consuming fire.
Then like a dream,
     a vision in the night,
Shall be the horde of all the nations
     who war against Ariel
     with all the earthworks of her besiegers.

As when a hungry man dreams he is eating
   and awakens with an empty stomach,
Or when a thirsty man dreams he is drinking
   and awakens faint and dry,
So shall the horde of all the nations be,
   who make war against Zion.

<small>RESPONSORY</small>   Isaiah 54:4; 29:5, 6, 7

Jerusalem, fear not; you shall not be put to shame;
—for the Lord of hosts will come to visit you.

The passing multitudes of all nations, which have
   struggled against you,
will be like flying dust.
—For the Lord . . .

<small>SECOND READING</small>

From a sermon by Blessed Isaac of Stella, abbot

(Sermo 51: PL 194, 1862-1863, 1865)

Mary and the Church

   The Son of God is the firstborn of many brothers. Although by nature he is the only-begotten, by grace he has joined many to himself and made them one with him. For to those who receive him *he has given the power to become the sons of God.*

   He became the Son of man and made many men sons of God, uniting them to himself by his love and power, so that they became as one. In themselves they are many by reason of their human descent, but in him they are one by divine rebirth.

   The whole Christ and the unique Christ—the body and the head—are one: one because born of the same God in heaven, and of the same mother on earth. They are many sons, yet one son. Head and members are one son, yet many sons; in the same way, Mary and the Church are one mother, yet more than one mother; one virgin, yet more than one virgin.

Both are mothers, both are virgins. Each conceives of the same Spirit, without concupiscence. Each gives birth to a child of God the Father, without sin. Without any sin, Mary gave birth to Christ the head for the sake of his body. By the forgiveness of every sin, the Church gave birth to the body, for the sake of its head. Each is Christ's mother, but neither gives birth to the whole Christ without the cooperation of the other.

In the inspired Scriptures, what is said in a universal sense of the virgin mother, the Church, is understood in an individual sense of the Virgin Mary, and what is said in a particular sense of the virgin mother Mary is rightly understood in a general sense of the virgin mother, the Church. When either is spoken of, the meaning can be understood of both, almost without qualification.

In a way, every Christian is also believed to be a bride of God's Word, a mother of Christ, his daughter and sister, at once virginal and fruitful. These words are used in a universal sense of the Church, in a special sense of Mary, in a particular sense of the individual Christian. They are used by God's Wisdom in person, the Word of the Father.

This is why Scripture says: *I will dwell in the inheritance of the Lord.* The Lord's inheritance is, in a general sense, the Church; in a special sense, Mary; in an individual sense, the Christian. Christ dwelt for nine months in the tabernacle of Mary's womb. He dwells until the end of the ages in the tabernacle of the Church's faith. He will dwell for ever in the knowledge and love of each faithful soul.

RESPONSORY   Lv. 26:11-12; 2 Cor. 6:16

I shall establish my dwelling place among you
and shall not reject you;
—I shall walk among you;
I shall be your God and you will be my people.

You are the temple of the living God,
as God himself has said.
—I shall walk . . .

Prayer, as in Morning Prayer.

Morning Prayer

READING   Isaiah 11:1-3a

A shoot shall sprout from the stump of Jesse,
   and from his roots a bud shall blossom.
The spirit of the Lord shall rest upon him:
   a spirit of wisdom and of understanding,
A spirit of counsel and of strength,
   a spirit of knowledge and of fear of the Lord,
   and his delight shall be the fear of the Lord.

RESPONSORY

Your light will come, Jerusalem;
the Lord will dawn on you in radiant beauty.
—Your light will come, Jerusalem;
the Lord will dawn on you in radiant beauty.

You will see his glory within you;
—the Lord will dawn on you in radiant beauty.

Glory to the Father . . .
—Your light will . . .

CANTICLE OF ZECHARIAH

Ant.   The Lord will set up his standard in the sight of
      all the nations, and gather to himself the dispersed
      of Israel.

INTERCESSIONS

To Jesus Christ, our Redeemer, who will come again in glory with great power, let us make our humble prayer:

Come, Lord Jesus!

Lord Jesus, you will come with great power,

—look on our lowliness and make us worthy of your gifts.

You came to be the good news for mankind,

—may we always proclaim your saving work.

You are worthy of praise, for you have life and rule all things,

—help us to wait in joyful hope for the coming of your glory.

We long for the grace of your coming,

—console us with the gift of your own divine life.

Our Father . . .

Prayer

Lord,
let your glory dawn to take away our darkness.
May we be revealed as the children of light
at the coming of your Son,
who lives and reigns with you and the Holy Spirit,
one God, for ever and ever.

Daytime Prayer

Midmorning

Ant.   This is the good news the prophets foretold: The Savior will be born of the Virgin Mary.

READING   Isaiah 4:2

On that day,
The branch of the Lord will be luster and glory,

and the fruit of the earth will be honor and splendor
for the survivors of Israel.

The nations will revere your name, O Lord.
—And the great ones of the earth will acknowledge your
glory.

Midday

Ant.   The angel Gabriel said to Mary in greeting: Hail,
full of grace, the Lord is with you; blessed are you
among women.

READING   Isaiah 4:3

He who remains in Zion
and he that is left in Jerusalem
Will be called holy:
every one marked down for life in Jerusalem.

Remember us, Lord, because of the love you have for
your people.
—Come and bring us your salvation.

Midafternoon

Ant.   Mary said: My soul is deeply troubled; what can
this greeting mean? Am I to give birth to my King
and yet remain a virgin for ever?

READING   Isaiah 61:11

As the earth brings forth its plants,
and a garden makes its growth spring up,
So will the Lord God make justice and praise
spring up before all the nations.

Come, Lord, do not delay.
—Free your people from their sinfulness.

Prayer, as in Morning Prayer.

THIRD SUNDAY OF ADVENT

When this Sunday occurs on December 17, the hymns are taken from those given on 132-136. The readings, antiphons for the canticles of Zechariah and Mary, and the intercessions, 318-325, assigned for each day, are used. Those for the Third Sunday are then omitted.

Evening Prayer I

HYMN, 126 or 133.

Ant. 1   Rejoice, Jerusalem, let your joy overflow; your Savior will come to you, alleluia.

Psalms and canticle from Sunday, Week III, 921.

Ant. 2   I, the Lord, am coming to save you; already I am near; soon I will free you from your sins.

Ant. 3   Lord, send the Lamb, the ruler of the earth, from the rock in the desert to the mountain of the daughter of Zion.

READING   1 Thessalonians 5:23-24

May the God of peace make you perfect in holiness. May he preserve you whole and entire, spirit, soul, and body, irreproachable at the coming of our Lord Jesus Christ. He who calls us is trustworthy, therefore he will do it.

RESPONSORY

Lord, show us your mercy and love.
    —Lord, show us your mercy and love.
And grant us your salvation,
    —your mercy and love.
Glory to the Father . . .
    —Lord, show us . . .

CANTICLE OF MARY

Ant.   There was no god before me and after me there
        will be none; every knee shall bend in worship,
        and every tongue shall praise me.

INTERCESSIONS

Jesus Christ is the joy and happiness of all who look
    forward to his coming. Let us call upon him and say:
    Come, Lord, and do not delay!
In joy, we wait for your coming,
—come, Lord Jesus.
Before time began, you shared life with the Father,
—come now and save us.
You created the world and all who live in it,
—come to redeem the work of your hands.
You did not hesitate to become man, subject to death,
—come to free us from the power of death.
You came to give us life to the full,
—come and give us your unending life.
You desire all people to live in love in your kingdom,
—come and bring together those who long to see you face
    to face.

Our Father . . .

Prayer

Lord God,
may we, your people,
who look forward to the birthday of Christ
experience the joy of salvation
and celebrate that feast with love and thanksgiving.

We ask this through our Lord Jesus Christ, your Son,
who lives and reigns with you and the Holy Spirit,
one God, for ever and ever.

Alternative Prayer

Father of our Lord Jesus Christ,
ever faithful to your promises
and ever close to your Church:
the earth rejoices in hope of the Savior's coming
and looks forward with longing
to his return at the end of time.
Prepare our hearts and remove the sadness
that hinders us from feeling the joy
which his presence will bestow,
for he is Lord for ever and ever.

Invitatory

Before December 17

Ant.   Come, let us worship the Lord, the King who is to
come.

December 17,

Ant.   The Lord is close at hand; come, let us worship
him.

Invitatory psalm, as in the Ordinary, 648.

Office of Readings

HYMN, 121 or 132.

Ant. 1   This is our heavenly King; he comes with
power and might to save the nations, alleluia.

Psalms from Sunday, Week III, 926.

Ant. 2   Daughter of Jerusalem, rejoice and be glad;
your King will come to you. Zion, do not fear;
your Savior hastens on his way.

Ant. 3   Let us cleanse our hearts for the coming of our
great King, that we may be ready to welcome
him; he is coming and will not delay.

On December 17, the verse, readings, and responsories are found on **318**.

Before December 17, they are said as follows:

Lift up your heads and see.
—Your redemption is now at hand.

FIRST READING

From the book of the prophet Isaiah   29:13-24

The judgment of the Lord is announced

The Lord God said:
Since this people draws near with words only
    and honors me with their lips alone,
    though their hearts are far from me,
And their reverence for me has become
    routine observance of the precepts of men,
Therefore I will again deal with this people
    in surprising and wondrous fashion:
The wisdom of its wise men shall perish
    and the understanding of its prudent men be hid.

Woe to those who would hide their plans
    too deep for the Lord!
Who work in the dark, saying,
    "Who sees us, or who knows us?"

Your perversity is as though the potter
    were taken to be the clay:
As though what is made should say of its maker,
    "He made me not!"
Or the vessel should say of the potter,
    "He does not understand."

But a very little while,
    and Lebanon shall be changed into an orchard,
    and the orchard be regarded as a forest!

On that day the deaf shall hear
    the words of a book;
And out of gloom and darkness,
    the eyes of the blind shall see.

The lowly will ever find joy in the Lord,
    and the poor rejoice in the Holy One of Israel.
For the tyrant will be no more
    and the arrogant will have gone;
All who are alert to do evil will be cut off,
    those whose mere word condemns a man,
Who ensnare his defender at the gate,
    and leave the just man with an empty claim.

Therefore thus says the Lord,
    the God of the house of Jacob,
    who redeemed Abraham:
Now Jacob shall have nothing to be ashamed of,
    nor shall his face grow pale.
When his children see
    the work of my hands in his midst,
They shall keep my name holy;
    they shall reverence the Holy One of Jacob,
    and be in awe of the God of Israel.
Those who err in spirit shall acquire understanding
    and those who find fault shall receive instruction.

RESPONSORY   Is. 29:18, 19; see Mt. 11:4, 5

On that day the deaf shall hear the words of a book,
and out of darkness and fog the eyes of the blind shall
    see.
—And the poor will rejoice in the Holy One of Israel.

Go back and tell John what you have heard and seen:
the blind see, cripples walk, the deaf hear,
and the poor have the good news preached to them.
—And the poor . . .

SECOND READING

From a sermon by Saint Augustine, bishop
(Sermo 293,3: PL 1328-1329)

The voice is John, the Word is Christ

John is the voice, but the Lord *is the Word who was in the beginning.* John is the voice that lasts for a time; from the beginning Christ is the Word who lives for ever.

Take away the word, the meaning, and what is the voice? Where there is no understanding, there is only a meaningless sound. The voice without the word strikes the ear but does not build up the heart.

However, let us observe what happens when we first seek to build up our hearts. When I think about what I am going to say, the word or message is already in my heart. When I want to speak to you, I look for a way to share with your heart what is already in mine.

In my search for a way to let this message reach you, so that the word already in my heart may find place also in yours, I use my voice to speak to you. The sound of my voice brings the meaning of the word to you and then passes away. The word which the sound has brought to you is now in your heart, and yet it is still also in mine.

When the word has been conveyed to you, does not the sound seem to say: *The word ought to grow, and I should diminish?* The sound of the voice has made itself heard in the service of the word, and has gone away, as though it were saying: *My joy is complete.* Let us hold on to the word; we must not lose the word conceived inwardly in our hearts.

Do you need proof that the voice passes away but the divine Word remains? Where is John's baptism today? It served its purpose, and it went away. Now it is Christ's baptism that we celebrate. It is in Christ that we all believe; we hope for salvation in him. This is the messsage the voice cried out.

Because it is hard to distinguish word from voice, even John himself was thought to be the Christ. The voice was thought to be the word. But the voice acknowledged what it was, anxious not to give offense to the word. *I am not the Christ,* he said, *nor Elijah, nor the prophet.* And the question came: *Who are you, then?* He replied: *I am the voice of one crying in the wilderness: Prepare the way for the Lord.*

The voice of one crying in the wilderness is the voice of one breaking the silence. *Prepare the way for the Lord,* he says, as though he were saying: "I speak out in order to lead him into your hearts, but he does not choose to come where I lead him unless you prepare the way for him."

To prepare the way means to pray well; it means thinking humbly of oneself. We should take our lesson from John the Baptist. He is thought to be the Christ; he declares he is not what they think. He does not take advantage of their mistake to further his own glory.

If he had said, "I am the Christ," you can imagine how readily he would have been believed, since they believed he was the Christ even before he spoke. But he did not say it; he acknowledged what he was. He pointed out clearly who he was; he humbled himself.

He saw where his salvation lay. He understood that he was a lamp, and his fear was that it might be blown out by the wind of pride.

RESPONSORY   John 3:30; 1:27; Mark 1:8

I must decrease, but he must increase;
the one who comes after me existed before me;
—and I am not worthy to untie the strap of his sandal.

I have baptized you with water,
but he will baptize you with the Holy Spirit.
—And I am . . .

HYMN, **Te Deum**, 651.

Prayer, as in Morning Prayer.

Morning Prayer

HYMN, 122 or 132.

Ant. 1   The Lord is coming without delay. He will
          reveal things kept hidden and show himself to
          all mankind, alleluia.

Psalms and canticle from Sunday, Week III, 929.

Ant. 2   Mountains and hills shall be level, crooked
          paths straight, rough ways smooth. Come,
          Lord, do not delay, alleluia.

Ant. 3   I shall enfold Zion with my salvation and shed
          my glory around Jerusalem, alleluia.

READING   Romans 13:11-12

It is now the hour for you to wake from sleep, for our
salvation is closer than when we first accepted the faith.
The night is far spent; the day draws near. Let us cast off
deeds of darkness and put on the armor of light.

RESPONSORY

Christ, Son of the living God, have mercy on us.
—Christ, Son of the living God, have mercy on us.

You are the one who is to come,
—have mercy on us.

Glory to the Father . . .
—Christ, Son of . . .

CANTICLE OF ZECHARIAH

Ant. **When John, in prison, heard of the works of Christ, he sent two of his disciples with this question: Are you the One whose coming was foretold, or should we look for another?**

If this Sunday occurs on December 17, the ant. **Believe me,** and the intercessions, **322,** are said.

INTERCESSIONS

To God our Father, who has given us the grace to wait in joyful hope for the revelation of our Lord Jesus Christ, let us make our prayer:
> *Show us your mercy, Lord.*

Sanctify us, in mind and body,
—keep us without reproach until the coming of your Son.

Make us walk this day in holiness,
—and live upright and devout lives in this world.

May we be clothed in our Lord Jesus Christ,
—and filled with the Holy Spirit.

Lord, help us to stand watchful and ready,
—until your Son is revealed in all his glory.

Our Father . . .

Prayer

Lord God,
may we, your people,
who look forward to the birthday of Christ
experience the joy of salvation
and celebrate that feast with love and thanksgiving.

We ask this through our Lord Jesus Christ, your Son,
who lives and reigns with you and the Holy Spirit,
one God, for ever and ever.

Alternative Prayer

Father of our Lord Jesus Christ,
ever faithful to your promises
and ever close to your Church:
the earth rejoices in hope of the Savior's coming
and looks forward with longing
to his return at the end of time.
Prepare our hearts and remove the sadness
that hinders us from feeling the joy
which his presence will bestow,
for he is Lord for ever and ever.

Daytime Prayer

HYMN, 658.

Midmorning

Ant.   This is the good news the prophets foretold: The
       Savior will be born of the Virgin Mary.

READING   Romans 13:13-14a

Let us live honorably as in daylight; not in carousing
and drunkenness, not in sexual excess and lust, not in
quarreling and jealousy. Rather, put on the Lord Jesus
Christ.

The nations will revere your name, O Lord.
—And the great ones of the earth will acknowledge your
   glory.

Midday

Ant.   The angel Gabriel said to Mary in greeting: Hail,
       full of grace, the Lord is with you; blessed are you
       among women.

READING   1 Thessalonians 3:12-13

May the Lord make you overflow with love for one another and for all, even as our love does for you. May he strengthen your hearts, making them blameless and holy before our God and Father at the coming of our Lord Jesus with all his holy ones.

Remember us, Lord, because of the love you have for your people.
—Come and bring us your salvation.

Midafternoon

Ant.   Mary said: My soul is deeply troubled; what can this greeting mean? Am I to give birth to my King and yet remain a virgin for ever?

READING   See 2 Thessalonians 1:6, 7, 10a

Strict justice requires that God will provide relief to you who are sorely tried, as well as to us, when the Lord Jesus is revealed from heaven with his mighty angels, on the Day when he comes, to be glorified in his holy ones and adored by all who have believed.

Come, Lord, do not delay.
—Free your people from their sinfulness.

Prayer, as in Morning Prayer.

Evening Prayer II

HYMN, 126 or 133.

Ant. 1   Our Lord will come to claim his glorious throne in the assembly of the princes.

Psalms and canticle from Sunday, Week III, 937.

Ant. 2   Let the mountains break out with joy and the hills with answering gladness, for the world's true light, the Lord, comes with power and might.

Ant. 3   Let us live in holiness and love as we patiently await our blessed hope, the coming of our Savior.

READING   Philippians 4:4-5

Rejoice in the Lord always! I say it again. Rejoice! Everyone should see how unselfish you are. The Lord is near.

RESPONSORY

Lord, show us your mercy and love.
—Lord, show us your mercy and love.
And grant us your salvation,
—your mercy and love.
Glory to the Father . . .
—Lord, show us . . .

CANTICLE OF MARY

Ant.   Are you the One whose coming was foretold, or should we look for another? Tell John what you see: the blind have their sight restored, the dead are raised to life, the poor have the good news preached to them, alleluia.

If this Sunday occurs on December 17, the ant. O Wisdom and the intercessions, 325, are said.

INTERCESSIONS

To Jesus Christ, our Redeemer, the way, the truth, and the life, let us make our humble prayer:
   Come and stay with us, Lord.

Son of the Most High, your coming was announced to
   the Virgin Mary by Gabriel,
—come and rule over your people for ever.

Holy One of God, in your presence John the Baptist leapt
   in Elizabeth's womb,
—bring the joy of salvation to all the earth.

Jesus the Savior, the angel revealed your name to Joseph
   the just man,
—come and save your people from their sins.

Light of the world, for whom Simeon and all the just
   waited,
—come and comfort us.

O Rising Sun that never sets, Zechariah foretold that you
   would visit us from above,
—come and shine on those who dwell in darkness and the
   shadow of death.

Our Father . .

Prayer

Lord God,
may we, your people,
who look forward to the birthday of Christ
experience the joy of salvation
and celebrate that feast with love and thanksgiving.

We ask this through our Lord Jesus Christ, your Son,
who lives and reigns with you and the Holy Spirit,
one God, for ever and ever.

Alternative Prayer

Father of our Lord Jesus Christ,
ever faithful to your promises
and ever close to your Church:
the earth rejoices in hope of the Savior's coming
and looks forward with longing
to his return at the end of time.

Prepare our hearts and remove the sadness
that hinders us from feeling the joy
which his presence will bestow,
for he is Lord for ever and ever.

On the weekdays from December 17 to December 23 inclusive,
everything designated for Week III is omitted; invitatory,
hymns, readings, responsories, verses, prayers, and the
intercessions for Morning and Evening Prayer are said, **318ff.**

MONDAY

Office of Readings

Lord, show us your mercy and love.
—And grant us your salvation.

<small>First Reading</small>

From the book of the prophet Isaiah   30:18-26

The promise of future happiness

The Lord is waiting to show you favor,
     and he rises to pity you;
For the Lord is a God of justice:
     blessed are all who wait for him!

O people of Zion, who dwell in Jerusalem,
     no more will you weep;
He will be gracious to you when you cry out,
     as soon as he hears he will answer you.

The Lord will give you the bread you need
     and the water for which you thirst.
No longer will your Teacher hide himself,
     but with your own eyes you shall see your Teacher,
While from behind, a voice shall sound in your ears:
     "This is the way; walk in it,"
     when you would turn to the right or to the left.

And you shall consider unclean your silver-plated idols
   and your gold-covered images;
You shall throw them away like filthy rags
   to which you say, "Begone!"

He will give rain for the seed
   that you sow in the ground,
And the wheat that the soil produces
   will be rich and abundant.
On that day your cattle will graze
   in spacious meadows;
The oxen and the asses that till the ground
   will eat silage tossed to them
   with shovel and pitchfork.

Upon every high mountain and lofty hill
   there will be streams of running water.

On the day of the great slaughter,
   when the towers fall,
The light of the moon will be like that of the sun
   and the light of the sun will be seven times greater
   [like the light of seven days].
On the day the Lord binds up the wounds of his people,
   he will heal the bruises left by his blows.

RESPONSORY   Isaiah 30:26, 18; Psalm 27:14

On that day the Lord will bind up the wounds of his
   people,
and God will heal the bruises left by the stroke of his
   judgment.
—Happy are all who await him.

Wait for the Lord, act courageously;
let your heart be strong and uphold the Lord.
—Happy are all . . .

SECOND READING

From a discourse On the Contemplation of God by
William of Saint Thierry, abbot

(Nn. 9-11: SC 61, 90-96)

He loved us first

Truly you alone are the Lord. Your dominion is our
salvation, for to serve you is nothing else but to be saved
by you! O Lord, salvation is your gift and your blessing is
upon your people; what else is your salvation but
receiving from you the gift of loving you or being loved
by you? That, Lord, is why you willed that the Son at
your right hand, the man whom you made strong for
yourself, should be called Jesus, that is to say, Savior, *for
he will save his people from their sins, and there is no other in
whom there is salvation.* He taught us to love him by first
loving us, *even to death on the cross.* By loving us and
holding us so dear, he stirred us to love him who had first
loved us to the end.

And this is clearly the reason: you first loved us so that
we might love you—not because you needed our love,
but because we could not be what you created us to be,
except by loving you.

In many ways and on various occasions you spoke to
our fathers through the prophets. Now in these last days
you have spoken to us in the Son, your Word; by him the
heavens were established and all their powers came to be
by the breath of his mouth.

For you to speak thus in your Son was to bring out in
the light of day how much and in what way you loved us,
for you did not spare your own Son but delivered him up
for us all. He also *loved us and gave himself up for us.*

This, Lord, is your Word to us, this is your
all-powerful message: while all things were in midnight

silence (that is, were in the depths of error), he came from his royal throne, the stern conqueror of error and the gentle apostle of love.

Everything he did and everything he said on earth, even enduring the insults, the spitting, the buffeting— the cross and the grave—all of this was actually you speaking to us in your Son, appealing to us by your love and stirring up our love for you.

You know that this disposition could not be forced on men's hearts, my God, since you created them; it must rather be elicited. And this, for the further reason that there is no freedom where there is compulsion, and where freedom is lacking, so too is righteousness.

You wanted us to love you, then, we who could not with justice have been saved had we not loved you, nor could we have loved you except by your gift. So, Lord, as the apostle of your love tells us, and as we have already said, *you first loved us:* you are first to love all those who love you.

Thus we hold you dear by the affection you have implanted in us. You are the one supremely good and ultimate goodness. Your love is your goodness, the Holy Spirit proceeding from the Father and the Son! From the beginning of creation it was he who hovered over the waters—that is, over the wavering minds of men, offering himself to all, drawing all things to himself. By his inspiration and holy breath, by keeping us from harm and providing for our needs, he unites God to us and us to God.

RESPONSORY   Isaiah 54:10

My mercy will not leave you,
and the covenant of my peace will not be changed;
—I shall make all your sons learned in the Lord,
and they shall enjoy a lasting peace.

I am the Lord your God who teaches you what is good
and guides you in the path you should walk.
—I shall make . . .

Prayer, as in Morning Prayer.

Morning Prayer

READING   Isaiah 2:3b

Come, let us climb the Lord's mountain,
   to the house of the God of Jacob,
That he may instruct us in his ways,
   and we may walk in his paths.
For from Zion shall go forth instruction,
   and the word of the Lord from Jerusalem.

RESPONSORY

Your light will come, Jerusalem;
the Lord will dawn on you in radiant beauty.
—Your light will come, Jerusalem;
the Lord will dawn on you in radiant beauty.

You will see his glory within you;
   —the Lord will dawn on you in radiant beauty.

Glory to the Father . . .
—Your light will . . .

CANTICLE OF ZECHARIAH

Ant.   From heaven he comes, the Lord and Ruler; in
       his hand are honor and royal authority.

INTERCESSIONS

Christ the Lord, Son of the living God, light from light,
   leads us into the light and reveals his holiness. With
   confidence let us make our prayer:
   Come, Lord Jesus!

Light that never fades, rise to dispel the mists about us,
—awaken our faith from sleep.
Guard us from all harm today,
—may your glory fill us with joy.
Give us unfailing gentleness at all times,
—toward everyone we meet.
Come to create a new earth for us,
—where there will be justice and peace.

Our Father . . .

Prayer

Lord,
hear our voices raised in prayer.
Let the light of the coming of your Son
free us from the darkness of sin.
We ask this through our Lord Jesus Christ, your Son,
who lives and reigns with you and the Holy Spirit,
one God, for ever and ever.

Daytime Prayer
Midmorning

Ant.   This is the good news the prophets foretold: The
Savior will be born of the Virgin Mary.

READING   See Isaiah 10:20-21

On that day
The remnant of Israel,
    the survivors of the house of Jacob,
Will lean upon the Lord,
    the Holy One of Israel, in truth.
A remnant will return, the remnant of Jacob,
    to the mighty God.

The nations will revere your name, O Lord.
—And the great ones of the earth will acknowledge your
    glory.

Midday

Ant.   The angel Gabriel said to Mary in greeting: Hail, full of grace, the Lord is with you; blessed are you among women.

READING   Isaiah 10:24a, 27

Thus says the Lord, the God of hosts:

O my people, who dwell in Zion,
    do not fear.
        On that day,
The burden shall be taken from your shoulder,
    and the yoke shattered from your neck.

Remember us, Lord, because of the love you have for your people.
—Come and bring us your salvation.

Midafternoon

Ant.   Mary said: My soul is deeply troubled; what can this greeting mean? Am I to give birth to my King and yet remain a virgin for ever?

READING   Isaiah 13:22b—14:1a

Her time is near at hand
    and her days shall not be prolonged.
The Lord has pity on Jacob
    and again chooses Israel.

Come, Lord, do not delay.
—Free your people from their sinfulness.

Prayer, as in Morning Prayer.

Evening Prayer

READING   Philippians 3:20b-21

We eagerly await the coming of our Savior, the Lord Jesus Christ. He will give a new form to this lowly body of ours and remake it according to the pattern of his glorified body, by his power to subject everything to himself.

RESPONSORY

Come and set us free, Lord God of power and might.
—Come and set us free, Lord God of power and might.

Let your face shine upon us and we shall be saved,
—Lord God of power and might.

Glory to the Father . . .
—Come and set . .

CANTICLE OF MARY

Ant.   All generations will call me blessed: the Lord has looked with favor on his lowly servant.

INTERCESSIONS

We cry to the Lord, who will come to bring us salvation:
    Come, Lord, and save us.

Lord Jesus Christ, our God, Savior of all,
—come swiftly and save us.

Lord, by your coming into this world,
—free us from the sin of the world.

You came from the Father,
—show us the path that leads to him.

You were conceived by the Holy Spirit,
—by your word renew the same Spirit in our hearts.

You became incarnate from the Virgin Mary,
—free our bodies from corruption.

Lord, be mindful of all men,
—who from the beginning of time have placed their trust in you.

Our Father . . .

Prayer

Lord,
hear our voices raised in prayer.
Let the light of the coming of your Son
free us from the darkness of sin.

We ask this through our Lord Jesus Christ, your Son,
who lives and reigns with you and the Holy Spirit,
one God, for ever and ever.

TUESDAY

If Tuesday occurs after December 16, everything is taken from
the corresponding day, **318ff.**

Office of Readings

A voice is heard, crying in the wilderness: Prepare the
way of the Lord.
—Make straight the path of our God.

FIRST READING

From the book of the prophet Isaiah   30:27-33; 31:4-9

Jerusalem is delivered from the power of Assyria

See the name of the Lord coming from afar
   in burning wrath, with lowering clouds!
His lips are filled with fury,
   his tongue is like a consuming fire;
His breath, like a flood in a ravine
   that reaches suddenly to the neck,
Will winnow the nations with a destructive winnowing,
   and with repeated winnowings will he battle against
      them
   [and a bridle on the jaws of the peoples to send them
      astray].

The Lord will make his glorious voice heard,
    and let it be seen how his arm descends
In raging fury and flame of consuming fire,
    in driving storm and hail.

When the Lord speaks, Assyria will be shattered,
    as he strikes with the rod;
While at every sweep of the rod
    which the Lord will bring down on him in pun-
        ishment,

You will sing
    as on a night when a feast is observed,
And be merry of heart,
    as one marching along with a flute
Toward the mountain of the Lord,
    toward the Rock of Israel,
        accompanied by the timbrels and lyres.
For the pyre has long been ready,
    prepared for the king;
Broad and deep it is piled
    with dry grass and wood in abundance,
And the breath of the Lord, like a stream of sulphur,
    will set it afire.

        Thus says the Lord to me:
As a lion or a lion cub
    growling over its prey,
with a band of shepherds
    assembled against it,
Is neither frightened by their shouts
    nor disturbed by their noise,
So shall the Lord of hosts come down
    to wage war upon the mountain and hill of Zion.
Like hovering birds, so the Lord of hosts
    shall shield Jerusalem,

To protect and deliver,
   to spare and rescue it.

Return, O children of Israel, to him whom you have utterly deserted. On that day each one of you shall spurn his sinful idols of silver and gold, which he made with his hands.

Assyria shall fall by a sword not wielded by man,
   no mortal sword shall devour him;
He shall flee before the sword,
   and his young men shall be impressed as laborers.
He shall rush past his crag in panic,
   and his princes shall flee in terror from his standard,
Says the Lord who has a fire in Zion
   and a furnace in Jerusalem.

RESPONSORY   Isaiah 31:4, 5; 30:29

The Lord of Hosts will come down upon Mount Zion;
— like birds on the wing, so will the Lord protect Jerusalem, covering and rescuing it.

Your song will befit a night of profound holiness, and your heart will be full of joy.
— Like birds on . . .

SECOND READING

From The Imitation of Christ

(Lib. II, cap. 2-3)
                        On humility and peace

Do not care much who is with you and who is against you; but make it your greatest care that God is with you in everything you do.

Have a good conscience, and God will defend you securely; no one can hurt you if God wishes to help you.

If you know how to suffer in silence, you will surely receive God's help. Since he knows best the time and the way to set you free, resign yourself to him, for God helps you and frees you from all confusion.

It is often good for us, and helps us to remain humble, if others know our weaknesses and confront us with them.

When a man humbles himself for his faults, he more easily pleases others and mollifies those he has angered.

God protects and frees a humble man; he loves and consoles a humble man; he favors a humble man; he showers him with graces; then, after his suffering, God raises him up to glory.

He reveals his secrets to a humble man and in his kindness invitingly draws that man to himself. When a humble man is brought to confusion, he experiences peace, because he stands firm in God and not in this world. Do not think that you have made any progress unless you feel that you are the lowest of all men.

Above all things, keep peace within yourself, then you will be able to create peace among others. It is better to be peaceful than learned.

The passionate man often thinks evil of a good man and easily believes the worst; a good and peaceful man turns all things to good.

A man who lives at peace suspects no one. But a man who is tense and agitated by evil is troubled with all kinds of suspicions; he is never at peace with himself, nor does he permit others to be at peace.

He often speaks when he should be silent, and he fails to say what would be truly useful. He is well aware of the obligations of others but neglects his own.

So be zealous first of all with yourself, and then you will be more justified in expressing zeal for your neighbor.

You are good at excusing and justifying your own deeds, and yet you will not listen to the excuses of others.

It would be more just to accuse yourself and to excuse your brother.

If you wish others to put up with you, first put up with them.

RESPONSORY   Psalm 25:9-10; Zechariah 7:9

The Lord leads the humble to justice;
he teaches the meek his ways.
—Mercy and truth are the Lord's ways,
his witness to all who seek him.

Judge with true judgment,
and let each one be merciful and forgiving to his brother.
—Mercy and truth . . .

Prayer, as in Morning Prayer.

Morning Prayer

READING   Genesis 49:10

The scepter shall never depart from Judah,
   or the mace from between his legs,
While tribute is brought to him,
   and he receives the people's homage.

RESPONSORY

Your light will come, Jerusalem;
the Lord will dawn on you in radiant beauty.
—Your light will come, Jerusalem;
the Lord will dawn on you in radiant beauty.

You will see his glory within you;
—the Lord will dawn on you in radiant beauty.

Glory to the Father . . .
—Your light will . . .

CANTICLE OF ZECHARIAH

Ant.　Arise, arise! Wake from your slumber, Jerusalem; shake the chain from your neck, captive daughter Zion.

INTERCESSIONS

God the almighty Father stretches forth his hand again to take possession of the remnant of his people. Let us make our prayer to him:

Lord, may your kingdom come.

Lord, grant that our works of penance may please you,
—and that we may be ready for your kingdom which is so near.

Prepare a path in our hearts for the coming of your Word,
—and let his glory be revealed among us.

Bring low the mountains of our pride,
—and fill up the valleys of our weakness.

Break down the walls of hatred that divide the nations,
—and make level for mankind the paths to peace.

Our Father . . .

Prayer

Father of love,
you made a new creation
through Jesus Christ your Son.
May his coming free us from sin
and renew his life within us,
for he lives and reigns with you and the Holy Spirit,
one God, for ever and ever.

Daytime Prayer

Midmorning

Ant.　This is the good news the prophets foretold: The Savior will be born of the Virgin Mary.

READING   Jeremiah 23:5

Behold, the days are coming, says the Lord,
  when I will raise up a righteous shoot to David;
As king he shall reign and govern wisely,
  he shall do what is just and right in the land.

The nations will revere your name, O Lord.
—And the great ones of the earth will acknowledge your
  glory.

Midday

Ant.   The angel Gabriel said to Mary in greeting: Hail,
       full of grace, the Lord is with you; blessed are you
       among women.

READING   Jeremiah 23:6

In his days Judah shall be saved,
  Israel shall dwell in security.
This is the name they give him:
  "The Lord our justice."

Remember us, Lord, because of the love you have for
  your people.
—Come and bring us your salvation.

Midafternoon

Ant.   Mary said: My soul is deeply troubled; what can
       this greeting mean? Am I to give birth to my King
       and yet remain a virgin for ever?

READING   Ezekiel 34:15-16

I myself will pasture my sheep; I myself will give them
rest, says the Lord God. The lost I will seek out, the
strayed I will bring back, the injured I will bind up, the
sick I will heal, shepherding them rightly.

Come, Lord, do not delay.
—Free your people from their sinfulness.

Prayer, as in Morning Prayer

Evening Prayer

READING   See 1 Corinthians 1:7b-9

We await the revelation of our Lord Jesus Christ, who will strengthen us to the end, so that we will be blameless on the day of our Lord Jesus Christ. God is faithful, and it was he who called us to fellowship with his Son.

RESPONSORY

Come and set us free, Lord God of power and might.
—Come and set us free, Lord God of power and might.

Let your face shine upon us and we shall be saved,
—Lord God of power and might.

Glory to the Father . . .
—Come and set . . .

CANTICLE OF MARY

Ant.   Before Mary and Joseph had come together, they learned that Mary was with child by the power of the Holy Spirit, alleluia.

INTERCESSIONS

To the eternal Word who became man to reveal to us the new and living way, let us make our humble prayer:
Come, Lord, and save us.
God, in whom we live and move and have our being,
—come and teach us that you have made us your own.
You are not far from each of us,
—show yourself to all who search for you.
Father of the poor and consoler of the afflicted,
—set captives free, give joy to those who mourn.

You hate death and love life,
—free all mankind from eternal death.

Our Father . . .

Prayer

Father of love,
you made a new creation
through Jesus Christ your Son.
May his coming free us from sin
and renew his life within us,
for he lives and reigns with you and the Holy Spirit
one God, for ever and ever.

WEDNESDAY

If Wednesday occurs after December 16, everything is taken
from the corresponding day, 318ff.

Office of Readings

Turn back to us, O Lord, our God.
—Show us your face and we shall be saved.

First Reading

From the book of the prophet Isaiah   31:1-3; 32:1-8

The reign of perfect justice

Woe to those who go down to Egypt for help,
    who depend upon horses;
Who put their trust in chariots because of their number,
    and in horsemen because of their combined power,
But look not to the Holy One of Israel
    nor seek the Lord!

Yet he too is wise and will bring disaster;
     he will not turn from what he has threatened to do.
He will rise up against the house of the wicked
     and against those who help evildoers.

The Egyptians are men, not God,
     their horses are flesh, not spirit;
When the Lord stretches forth his hand,
     the helper shall stumble, the one helped shall fall,
     and both of them shall perish together.

See, a king will reign justly
     and princes will rule rightly.
Each of them will be a shelter from the wind,
     a retreat from the rain.
They will be like streams of water in a dry country,
     like the shade of a great rock in a parched land.

The eyes of those who see will not be closed;
     the ears of those who hear will be attentive.
The flighty will become wise and capable,
     and the stutterers will speak fluently and clearly.
No more will the fool be called noble,
     nor the trickster be considered honorable.

For the fool speaks foolishly,
     planning evil in his heart:
How to do wickedness,
     to speak perversely against the Lord,
To let the hungry go empty
     and the thirsty be without drink.

And the trickster uses wicked trickery,
     planning crimes:
How to ruin the poor with lies,
     and the needy when they plead their case.
But the noble man plans noble things,
     and by noble things he stands.

RESPONSORY   Isaiah 32:3, 4; Jeremiah 23:5
The eyes of those who see shall not be clouded,
and the ears of those who hear shall listen attentively;
—the heart of the foolish shall be open to knowledge.

I will raise up to David a righteous branch,
as king he shall rule and be wise.
—The heart of . . .

SECOND READING

From a treatise *Against Heresies* by Saint Irenaeus, bishop

(Lib. 4, 20, 4-5: SC 100, 634-640)

When Christ comes, God will be seen by men

There is one God, who by his word and wisdom created all things and set them in order. His Word is our Lord Jesus Christ, who in this last age became man among men to unite end and beginning, that is, man and God.

The prophets, receiving the gift of prophecy from this same Word, foretold his coming in the flesh, which brought about the union and communion between God and man ordained by the Father. From the beginning the word of God prophesied that God would be seen by men and would live among them on earth; he would speak with his own creation and be present to it, bringing it salvation and being visible to it. He would *free us from the hands of all who hate us,* that is, from the universal spirit of sin, and enable us *to serve him in holiness and justice all our days.* Man was to receive the Spirit of God and so attain to the glory of the Father.

The prophets, then, foretold that God would be seen by men. As the Lord himself says: *Blessed are the clean of heart, for they shall see God.* In his greatness and inexpressible glory *no one can see God and live,* for the

Father is beyond our comprehension. But in his love and generosity and omnipotence he allows even this to those who love him, that is, even to see God, as the prophets foretold. *For what is impossible to men is possible to God.*

By his own powers man cannot see God, yet God will be seen by men because he wills it. He will be seen by those he chooses, at the time he chooses, and in the way he chooses, for God can do all things. He was seen of old through the Spirit in prophecy; he is seen through the Son by our adoption as his children, and he will be seen in the kingdom of heaven in his own being as the Father. The Spirit prepares man to receive the Son of God, the Son leads him to the Father, and the Father, freeing him from change and decay, bestows the eternal life that comes to everyone from seeing God.

As those who see light are in the light sharing its brilliance, so those who see God are in God sharing his glory, and that glory gives them life. To see God is to share in life.

RESPONSORY   Dt. 18:18; Lk. 20:9; Jn. 6:14

I will raise up for them a prophet,
and I will place my words in his mouth.
—He will tell them all that I command.

I am sending my own beloved Son.
He is truly the prophet who is to come into the world.
—He will tell . . .

Prayer, as in Morning Prayer.

Morning Prayer
READING   Isaiah 7:14b-15

The virgin shall be with child, and bear a son, and shall name him Immanuel. He shall be living on curds and honey by the time he learns to reject the bad and choose the good.

RESPONSORY

Your light will come, Jerusalem;
the Lord will dawn on you in radiant beauty.
—Your light will come, Jerusalem;
the Lord will dawn on you in radiant beauty.

You will see his glory within you;
—the Lord will dawn on you in radiant beauty.

Glory to the Father . . .
—Your light will . . .

CANTICLE OF ZECHARIAH

Ant.   Be comforted, my people; be comforted, says the
Lord your God.

INTERCESSIONS

The Word of God humbled himself to dwell with us so
that we may see his glory. Rejoicing in hope, let us call
upon him:
Emmanuel, be with us.
Ruler, just and righteous,
—bring justice to the poor and the oppressed.
King of peace, you beat swords into plowshares and
spears into pruning hooks,
—turn hatred into love and our grievances into
forgiveness.
You do not judge by appearances,
—recognize those who are your own.
When you come with power and might upon the clouds,
—grant that we may come before you without shame.

Our Father . . .

Prayer

Father,
may the coming celebration of the birth of your Son

bring us your saving help
and prepare us for eternal life.

Grant this through our Lord Jesus Christ, your Son,
who lives and reigns with you and the Holy Spirit,
one God, for ever and ever.

Daytime Prayer

Midmorning

Ant.   This is the good news the prophets foretold: The
Savior will be born of the Virgin Mary.

READING   See Isaiah 2:11-12

The haughty eyes of man will be lowered,
     the arrogance of men will be abased,
     and the Lord alone will be exalted, on that day.

The nations will revere your name, O Lord.
—And the great ones of the earth will acknowledge your
     glory.

Midday

Ant.   The angel Gabriel said to Mary in greeting: Hail,
full of grace, the Lord is with you; blessed are you
among women.

READING   Isaiah 12:2

God indeed is my savior;
     I am confident and unafraid.
My strength and my courage is the Lord,
     and he has been my savior.

Remember us, Lord, because of the love you have for
     your people.
—Come and bring us your salvation.

Midafternoon

Ant.   Mary said: My soul is deeply troubled; what can
this greeting mean? Am I to give birth to my King
and yet remain a virgin for ever?

READING   Daniel 9:19

O Lord, hear! O Lord, pardon! O Lord, be attentive
and act without delay, for your own sake, O my God,
because your people bear your name!

Come, Lord, do not delay.
—Free your people from their sinfulness.

Prayer, as in Morning Prayer.

Evening Prayer

READING   1 Corinthians 4:5

Stop passing judgment before the time of the Lord's
return. He will bring to light what is hidden in darkness
and manifest the intentions of hearts. At that time,
everyone will receive his praise from God.

RESPONSORY

Come and set us free, Lord God of power and might.
—Come and set us free, Lord God of power and might.

Let your face shine upon us and we shall be saved,
—Lord God of power and might.

Glory to the Father . . .
—Come and set . . .

CANTICLE OF MARY

Ant.   You, O Lord, are the One whose coming was foretold; we long for you to come and set your people
free.

INTERCESSIONS

Let us pray to God the Father, who sent his Son to bring
us endless peace:

Lord, your kingdom come.

Father most holy, look kindly on your Church,
—come and visit this vine which your own right hand has
planted.

Be mindful, Lord, of all the sons of Abraham,
—fulfill the promises you made to their fathers.

Merciful God, look kindly upon men and women of every race,
—may they honor you for your goodness.

Eternal Shepherd, visit the sheep of your flock,
—and gather them together in one fold.

Remember those who have gone forth from this world in
your peace,
—lead them into glory with your Son.

Our Father . . .

Prayer

Father,
may the coming celebration of the birth of your Son
bring us your saving help
and prepare us for eternal life.

Grant this through our Lord Jesus Christ, your Son,
who lives and reigns with you and the Holy Spirit,
one God, for ever and ever.

THURSDAY

If Thursday occurs after December 16, everything is taken from the corresponding day, 318ff.

Office of Readings

Hear the word of the Lord, all you nations.
— Proclaim it to the ends of the earth.

First Reading

From the book of the prophet Isaiah   32:15—33:6

The promise of deliverance. The hope of the faithful

In those days the spirit from on high
    will be poured out on us.
Then will the desert become an orchard
    and the orchard be regarded as a forest.
Right will dwell in the desert
    and justice abide in the orchard.
Justice will bring about peace;
    right will produce calm and security.

My people will live in peaceful country,
    in secure dwellings and quiet resting places.
Happy are you who sow beside every stream,
    and let the ox and the ass go freely!

Woe, O destroyer never destroyed,
    O traitor never betrayed!
When you finish destroying, you will be destroyed;
    when wearied with betraying, you will be betrayed

O Lord, have pity on us, for you we wait.
    Be our strength every morning,
    our salvation in time of trouble!
At the roaring sound, peoples flee;
    when you rise in your majesty, nations are scattered.

Men gather spoil as caterpillars are gathered up;
>they rush upon it like the onrush of locusts.

The Lord is exalted, enthroned on high;
>he fills Zion with right and justice.
That which makes her seasons lasting,
>the riches that save her, are wisdom and knowledge;
>the fear of the Lord is her treasure.

RESPONSORY   Isaiah 32:18, 17; John 14:27

My people will be enthroned amidst the beauty of peace
>and in the tents of security;
—and peace will be the fruit of justice.

My peace I give you;
do not let your hearts be disturbed or terrified.
—And peace will . . .

SECOND READING

From the dogmatic constitution on Divine Revelation of the Second Vatican Council

(Dei Verbum, nn. 3-4)

Christ brings all revelation to perfection

God, who through the Word creates all things and keeps them in being, provides men with unfailing testimony to himself in creation. With the intention of opening up the way of salvation from above, he also revealed himself to our first parents from the very beginning.

After their fall, he lifted them up to hope for salvation by the promise of redemption, and watched over mankind with unceasing care, in order that he might give eternal life to all who in persevering in good works seek out salvation.

In his own good time God called Abraham, to make of him a mighty nation. After the patriarchs, he taught this nation through Moses and the prophets to acknowledge himself alone as the living and true God, a provident father and just judge, and to look forward to the promised Savior. So, through the ages, he prepared a way for the Gospel. After speaking *at various times and in different ways through the prophets, God has finally spoken to us in these days through the Son.*

He sent his Son, the eternal Word who enlightens all men, to dwell among men and make known to them the innermost things of God. Jesus Christ, the Word made flesh, sent as *a man to men, speaks the words of God,* and brings to perfection the saving work that the Father gave him to do.

To see him is to see the Father also. By his whole presence and self-revelation, by words and actions, by signs and miracles, especially by his death and glorious resurrection from the dead, and finally by sending the Spirit of truth, he completes revelation and brings it to perfection, sealing by divine testimony its message that God is with us to free us from the darkness of sin and death, and to raise us up to eternal life.

The Christian dispensation, because it is the new and definitive covenant, will never pass away, and no new public revelation is any longer to be looked for before the manifestation in glory of our Lord Jesus Christ.

RESPONSORY   Isaiah 30:20-21; Deuteronomy 18:15
Your eyes shall look upon your teacher;
—your ears shall hear the admonition:
    This is the path, follow it.

The Lord your God will raise up a prophet
from among your tribe and from among your brothers.
—Your ears shall . . .

Prayer, as in Morning Prayer.

Morning Prayer

READING   Isaiah 45:8

Let justice descend, O heavens, like dew from above,
    like gentle rain let the skies drop it down.
Let the earth open and salvation bud forth;
    let justice also spring up.

RESPONSORY

Your light will come, Jerusalem;
the Lord will dawn on you in radiant beauty.
—Your light will come, Jerusalem;
the Lord will dawn on you in radiant beauty.

You will see his glory within you;
—the Lord will dawn on you in radiant beauty.

Glory to the Father . . .
—Your light will . . .

CANTICLE OF ZECHARIAH

Ant.   Arise, arise, Lord; show us your power and
       might.

INTERCESSIONS

Christ is the wisdom and power of God, and his delight is
    to be with the children of men. With confidence let us
    pray:
       Draw near to us, Lord.
Lord Jesus Christ, you have called us to your glorious
    kingdom,
__make us walk worthily, pleasing God in all we do.
You who stand unknown among us,
__reveal yourself to men and women.
You are nearer to us than we to ourselves,
__strengthen our faith and our hope of salvation.
You are the source of holiness,

—keep us holy and without sin now and until the day of
  your coming.

Our Father . . .

Prayer

Lord,
our sins bring us unhappiness.
Hear our prayer for courage and strength.
May the coming of your Son
bring us the joy of salvation.
We ask this through our Lord Jesus Christ, your Son,
who lives and reigns with you and the Holy Spirit,
one God, for ever and ever.

Daytime Prayer

Midmorning

Ant.   This is the good news the prophets foretold: The
       Savior will be born of the Virgin Mary.

READING   Micah 5:3-4a

The ruler in Israel shall stand firm and shepherd his flock
  by the strength of the Lord,
    in the majestic name of the Lord, his God;
And they shall remain, for now his greatness
  shall reach to the ends of the earth;
    he shall be peace.

The nations will revere your name, O Lord.
—And the great ones of the earth will acknowledge your
  glory.

Midday

Ant.   The angel Gabriel said to Mary in greeeting: Hail,
       full of grace, the Lord is with you; blessed are you
       among women.

READING   Haggai 2:6, 9

One moment yet, a little while,
   and I will shake the heavens and the earth,
   the sea and the dry land.
Greater will be the future glory of this house
   than the former;
And in this house I will give peace,
   says the Lord of hosts!

Remember us, Lord, because of the love you have for
   your people.
—Come and bring us your salvation.

Midafternoon

Ant.   Mary said: My soul is deeply troubled; what can
      this greeting mean? Am I to give birth to my King
      and yet remain a virgin for ever?

READING   Malachi 3:20

For you who fear my name, there will arise
   the sun of justice with its healing rays;
And you will gambol like calves out of the stall,
   says the Lord of hosts.

Come, Lord, do not delay.
—Free your people from their sinfulness.

Prayer, as in Morning Prayer.

Evening Prayer

READING   James 5:7-8, 9b

Be patient, my brothers, until the coming of the Lord.
See how the farmer awaits the precious yield of the soil.
He looks forward to it patiently while the soil receives the
winter and the spring rains. You, too, must be patient.

Steady your hearts, because the coming of the Lord is at hand. See! The judge stands at the gate.

RESPONSORY

Come and set us free, Lord God of power and might.
—Come and set us free, Lord God of power and might.

Let your face shine upon us and we shall be saved,
—Lord God of power and might.

Glory to the Father . . .
—Come and set . . .

CANTICLE OF MARY

Ant.   All you who love Jerusalem, rejoice with her for ever.

INTERCESSIONS

To Christ, the great light promised by the prophets to those who live in the shadow of death, let us raise our voices in prayer:
    Come, Lord Jesus!
Word of God, in the beginning you created all things and in the fullness of time assumed our nature,
—come and deliver us from death.
True light, shining on mankind,
—come and dispel our darkness.
Only-begotten Son, dwelling in the Father's heart,
—come and tell us of God's loving kindness.
Christ Jesus, you come among us as the Son of Man,
—transform those who know you into the sons of God.
You welcome all who call upon you in need,
—bring into your wedding feast those who beg at the door.

Our Father . . .

Prayer

Lord,
our sins bring us unhappiness.
Hear our prayer for courage and strength.
May the coming of your Son
bring us the joy of salvation.
We ask this through our Lord Jesus Christ, your Son,
who lives and reigns with you and the Holy Spirit,
one God, for ever and ever.

FRIDAY

If Friday occurs after December 16 everything is taken from
the corresponding day, **318ff.**

Office of Readings

Let your compassion come upon me, Lord.
—Your salvation, true to your promise.

FIRST READING

From the book of the prophet Isaiah   33:7-24

The future salvation

See, the men of Ariel cry out in the streets,
   the messengers of Shalem weep bitterly.
The highways are desolate,
   travelers have quit the paths,
Covenants are broken, their terms are spurned;
   yet no man gives it a thought.
The country languishes in mourning,
   Lebanon withers with shame;
Sharon is like the steppe,
   Bashan and Carmel are stripped bare.

Now will I rise up, says the Lord,
   now will I be exalted, now be lifted up.
You conceive dry grass, bring forth stubble;
   my spirit shall consume you like fire.
The peoples shall be as in a limekiln,
   like brushwood cut down for burning in the fire.
Hear, you who are far off, what I have done;
   you who are near, acknowledge my might.

On Zion sinners are in dread,
   trembling grips the impious:
"Who of us can live with the consuming fire?
   who of us can live with the everlasting flames?"

He who practices virtue and speaks honestly,
   who spurns what is gained by oppression,
Brushing his hands free of contact with a bribe,
   stopping his ears lest he hear of bloodshed,
   closing his eyes lest he look on evil—
He shall dwell on the heights,
   his stronghold shall be the rocky fastness,
   his food and drink in steady supply.

Your eyes will see a king in his splendor,
   they will look upon a vast land.
Your mind will dwell on the terror:
   "Where is he who counted, where is he who weighed?
   Where is he who counted the towers?"
To the people of alien tongue you will look no more,
   the people of obscure speech,
   stammering in a language not understood.

Look to Zion, the city of our festivals;
   let your eyes see Jerusalem
   as a quiet abode, a tent not to be struck,
Whose pegs will never be pulled up,
   nor any of its ropes severed.

Indeed the Lord will be there with us, majestic;
    yes, the Lord our judge, the Lord our lawgiver,
    the Lord our king, he it is who will save us.

In a place of rivers and wide streams
    on which no boat is rowed,
    where no majestic ship passes,
The rigging hangs slack;
    it cannot hold the mast in place,
    nor keep the sail spread out.
Then the blind will divide great spoils
    and the lame will carry off the loot.
No one who dwells there will say, "I am sick";
    the people who live there will be forgiven their guilt.

RESPONSORY   See Isaiah 33:22; Psalm 97:1

The Lord is our judge,
the Lord is our lawgiver,
the Lord is our king.
—He himself will come to save us.

The Lord has taken command, let the earth rejoice;
let the many islands be glad.
—He himself will . . .

SECOND READING

From a discourse on the psalms by Saint Augustine, bishop

(In ps. 37, 13-14: CCL 38, 391-392)

The desire of your heart constitutes your prayer

In the anguish of my heart I groaned aloud. There is a hidden anguish which is inaudible to men. Yet when a man's heart is so taken up with some particular concern that the hurt inside finds vocal expression, one looks for the reason. And one will say to oneself: perhaps this is what causes his anguish, or perhaps such and such has happened to him. But who can be certain of the cause except God, who hears and sees his anguish? Therefore the psalmist says: *In the anguish of my heart I groaned aloud.* For if men hear at all, they usually hear only bodily groaning and know nothing of the anguish of the heart from which it issues.

Who then knows the cause of man's groaning? *All my desire is before you.* No, it is not open before other men, for they cannot understand the heart; *but before you is all my desire.* If your desire lies open to him who is your Father and who sees in secret, he will answer you.

For the desire of your heart is itself your prayer. And if the desire is constant, so is your prayer. The Apostle Paul had a purpose in saying: *Pray without ceasing.* Are we then ceaselessly to bend our knees, to lie prostrate, or to lift up our hands? Is this what is meant in saying: *Pray without ceasing?* Even if we admit that we pray in this fashion, I do not believe that we can do so all the time.

Yet there is another, interior kind of prayer without ceasing, namely, the desire of the heart. Whatever else you may be doing, if you but fix your desire on God's Sabbath rest, your prayer will be ceaseless. Therefore, if you wish to pray without ceasing, do not cease to desire.

The constancy of your desire will itself be the ceaseless voice of your prayer. And that voice of your prayer will be silent only when your love ceases. For who are silent? Those of whom it is said: *Because evil has abounded, the love of many will grow cold.*

The chilling of love means that the heart is silent; while burning love is the outcry of the heart. If your love is without ceasing, you are crying out always; if you always cry out, you are always desiring; and if you desire, you are calling to mind your eternal rest in the Lord.

And all my desire is before you. What if the desire of our heart is before him, but not our groaning? But how is that possible, since the groaning is the voice of our desire? And therefore it is said: *My groaning is not concealed from you*. It may be concealed from men, but it is not concealed from you. Sometimes God's servant seems to be saying in his humility: *My anguish is not concealed from you*. At other times he seems to be laughing. Does that mean that the desire of his heart has died within him? If the desire is there, then the groaning is there as well. Even if men fail to hear it, it never ceases to sound in the hearing of God.

RESPONSORY

We are Christ's pilgrim people,
journeying until we reach our homeland,
singing on the way as we eagerly expect the fulfillment of
    our hope.
—For if one hopes, even though his tongue is still, he is
    singing always in his heart.

But the man who has no hope,
no matter what clamors and shouts he makes to be heard
    by men,
is speechless in the presence of God.
—For if one . . .

Prayer, as in Morning Prayer.

Morning Prayer

READING   Jeremiah 30:21, 22

    Thus says the Lord:
His leader shall be from Jacob,
    and his ruler shall come from his kin.
When I summon him,
    he shall approach me.
You shall be my people,
    and I will be your God.

RESPONSORY

Your light will come, Jerusalem;
the Lord will dawn on you in radiant beauty.
—Your light will come, Jerusalem;
the Lord will dawn on you in radiant beauty.

You will see his glory within you;
—the Lord will dawn on you in radiant beauty.

Glory to the Father . . .
—Your light will . . .

CANTICLE OF ZECHARIAH

Ant. Guard what is good and cherish what is true, for
our salvation is at hand.

INTERCESSIONS

Through his Son, God the Father revealed his glory to
men and women. Therefore, let our joyful cry resound:
Lord, may your name be glorified.
Teach us, Lord, to love each other,
—as Christ loved us for God's glory.
Fill us with all joy and peace in faith,
—that we may walk in the hope and strength of the Holy
Spirit.
Help all mankind, Lord, in your loving mercy,
—be near to those who seek you without knowing it.
You call and sanctify the elect,
—though we are sinners, crown us with eternal
happiness.

Our Father . . .

Prayer

All-powerful Father,
guide us with your love
as we await the coming of your Son.

Keep us faithful
that we may be helped through life
and brought to salvation.

We ask this through our Lord Jesus Christ, your Son,
who lives and reigns with you and the Holy Spirit,
one God, for ever and ever.

Daytime Prayer

Midmorning

Ant.　This is the good news the prophets foretold: The
Savior will be born of the Virgin Mary.

READING　　　　　　　　　　　　　　Jeremiah 29:11, 13

I know well the plans I have in mind for you, says the
Lord, plans for your welfare, not for woe! plans to give
you a future full of hope. When you look for me, you will
find me, yes, when you seek me with all your heart.

The nations will revere your name, O Lord.
—And the great ones of the earth will acknowledge your
glory.

Midday

Ant.　The angel Gabriel said to Mary in greeting: Hail,
full of grace, the Lord is with you; blessed are you
among women.

READING　　　　　　　　　　　　　　　Jeremiah 30:18

Thus says the Lord:
See! I will restore the tents of Jacob,
his dwellings I will pity.

Remember us, Lord, because of the love you have for
your people.
—Come and bring us your salvation.

Midafternoon

Ant. Mary said: My soul is deeply troubled; what can
this greeting mean? Am I to give birth to my King
and yet remain a virgin for ever?

READING   Baruch 3:5-6a

Remember at this time not the misdeeds of our fathers,
but your own hand and name; for you are the Lord our
God.

Come, Lord, do not delay.
—Free your people from their sinfulness.

Prayer, as in Morning Prayer.

Evening Prayer

READING   2 Peter 3:8b–9

In the Lord's eyes, one day is as a thousand years and a
thousand years are as a day. The Lord does not delay in
keeping his promise—though some consider it "delay."
Rather, he shows you generous patience, since he wants
none to perish but all to come to repentance.

RESPONSORY

Come and set us free, Lord God of power and might.
—Come and set us free, Lord God of power and might.

Let your face shine upon us and we shall be saved,
—Lord God of power and might.

Glory to the Father . . .
—Come and set . . .

CANTICLE OF MARY

Ant. This was the witness of John the Baptist: The One
who comes after me existed before me.

INTERCESSIONS

With confidence let us call upon Christ, the shepherd and
    guardian of our souls:
    Lord, have mercy on us.

Good shepherd of God's flock,
—gather all into your Church.

Lord Jesus, help the shepherds of your pilgrim people,
—until you come again may they zealously feed your
    flock.

Choose from among us heralds of your word,
—to proclaim your Gospel to the ends of the earth.

Take pity on all who struggle and fall along the way,
—may they find a friend to help them.

Show your glory in heaven,
—to those who listen to your voice on earth.

Our Father . . .

Prayer

All-powerful Father,
guide us with your love
as we await the coming of your Son.
Keep us faithful
that we may be helped through life
and brought to salvation.

We ask this through our Lord Jesus Christ, your Son,
who lives and reigns with you and the Holy Spirit,
one God, for ever and ever.

On Saturday, everything is taken from the corresponding day,
318ff.

FOURTH SUNDAY OF ADVENT

Evening Prayer I

HYMN, 133.

Ant. 1   He comes, the desire of all human hearts; his dwelling place shall be resplendent with glory, alleluia.

Psalms and canticle from Sunday, Week IV, 1043.

Ant. 2   Come, Lord, do not delay; free your people from their sinfulness.

Ant. 3   The fullness of time has come upon us at last; God sends his Son into the world.

READING   1 Thessalonians 5:23-24

May the God of peace make you perfect in holiness. May he preserve you whole and entire, spirit, soul, and body, irreproachable at the coming of our Lord Jesus Christ. He who calls us is trustworthy, therefore he will do it.

RESPONSORY

Lord, show us your mercy and love.
—Lord, show us your mercy and love.

And grant us your salvation,
—your mercy and love.

Glory to the Father . . .
—Lord, show us . . .

For the Canticle of Mary, the antiphon is taken from the office of the day, 325ff.

INTERCESSIONS

Jesus is Lord, born of the Virgin Mary. Let us pray to
    him with joyful hearts:
    Come, Lord Jesus!

Son of God, you will come again as the true messenger of
    the covenant,
—help the world to recognize and accept you.

Born in your Father's heart, you became man in the
    womb of the Virgin Mary,
—free us from the tyranny of change and decay.

In your life on earth, you came to die as a man,
—save us from everlasting death.

When you come to judge, show us your loving mercy,
—and forgive us our weaknesses.

Lord Jesus, by your death you have given hope to those
    who have died,
—be merciful to those for whom we now pray.

Our Father . . .

Prayer

Lord,
fill our hearts with your love,
and as you revealed to us by an angel
the coming of your Son as man,
so lead us through his suffering and death
to the glory of his resurrection,
for he lives and reigns with you and the Holy Spirit,
one God, for ever and ever.

Alternative Prayer

Father, all-powerful God,
your eternal Word took flesh on our earth
when the Virgin Mary placed her life
at the service of your plan.

Lift our minds in watchful hope
to hear the voice which announces his glory
and open our minds to receive the Spirit
who prepares us for his coming.

We ask this through Christ our Lord.

Invitatory

If this Sunday occurs on December 24, everything is taken from the corresponding day, 376.

Ant.   The Lord is close at hand; come, let us worship him.

Invitatory psalm, as in the Ordinary, 648.

Office of Readings

HYMN, 132.

Ant. 1   This is our heavenly King, he comes with power and might to save the nations, alleluia.

Psalms, from Sunday, Week IV, 1048.

Ant. 2   Daughter of Jerusalem, rejoice and be glad; your King will come to you. Zion, do not fear; your Savior hastens on his way.

Ant. 3   Let us cleanse our hearts for the coming of our great King, that we may be ready to welcome him; he is coming and will not delay.

Verse, readings and responsories are taken from the office of the day, 318ff.

HYMN, Te Deum, 651.

Prayer, as in Morning Prayer.

Morning Prayer

HYMN, 132.

If this Sunday occurs on December 24, everything is taken from the corresponding day, 381. Otherwise:

Ant. 1   Sound the trumpet in Zion, the day of the Lord is near; he comes to save us, alleluia.

Psalms and canticle from Sunday, Week IV, 1053.

Ant. 2   The Lord is here; go out to meet him, saying: Great his birth, eternal his kingdom, strong God, Ruler of all, Prince of peace, alleluia.

Ant. 3   Your all-powerful Word, O Lord, will come to earth from his throne of glory, alleluia.

READING   Romans 13:11-12

It is now the hour for you to wake from sleep, for our salvation is closer than when we first accepted the faith. The night is far spent; the day draws near. Let us cast off deeds of darkness and put on the armor of light.

RESPONSORY

Christ, Son of the living God, have mercy on us.
—Christ, Son of the living God, have mercy on us.

You are the one who is to come,
—have mercy on us.

Glory to the Father . . .
—Christ, Son of . . .

For the Canticle of Zechariah, the antiphon is taken from the office of the day, 322ff.

INTERCESSIONS

To the Lord Jesus Christ, judge of the living and the
    dead, let us pray:
    Come, Lord Jesus!

Lord Jesus, you came to save sinners,
—protect us in times of temptation.

You will come in glory to be our judge,
—show in us your power to save.

Help us to keep the precepts of your law with the
    strength of the Spirit,
—and to look forward in love to your coming.

You are praised throughout the ages; in your mercy help
    us to live devoutly and temperately in this life,
—as we wait in joyful hope for the revelation of your
    glory.

Our Father . . .

Prayer

Lord,
fill our hearts with your love,
and as you revealed to us by an angel
the coming of your Son as man,
so lead us through his suffering and death
to the glory of his resurrection,
for he lives and reigns with you and the Holy Spirit,
one God, for ever and ever.

Alternative Prayer

Father, all-powerful God,
your eternal Word took flesh on our earth
when the Virgin Mary placed her life
at the service of your plan.
Lift our minds in watchful hope
to hear the voice which announces his glory

and open our minds to receive the Spirit
who prepares us for his coming.
We ask this through Christ our Lord.

Daytime Prayer

If this Sunday occurs on December 24, everything is taken
from the corresponding day, **383**.

HYMN, **658**.

Midmorning

Ant.   This is the good news the prophets foretold: The
         Savior will be born of the Virgin Mary.

READING   Romans 13:13-14a

Let us live honorably as in daylight; not in carousing
and drunkenness, not in sexual excess and lust, not in
quarreling and jealousy. Rather, put on the Lord Jesus
Christ.

The nations will revere your name, O Lord.
—And the great ones of the earth will acknowledge your
   glory.

Midday

Ant.   The angel Gabriel said to Mary in greeting: Hail,
         full of grace, the Lord is with you; blessed are you
         among women.

READING   1 Thessalonians 3:12-13

May the Lord make you overflow with love for one
another and for all, even as our love does for you. May he
strengthen your hearts, making them blameless and holy

before our God and Father at the coming of our Lord
Jesus with all his holy ones.

Remember us, Lord, because of the love you have for
   your people.
—Come and bring us your salvation.

Midafternoon

Ant.   Mary said: My soul is deeply troubled; what can
       this greeting mean? Am I to give birth to my King
       and yet remain a virgin for ever?

READING   See 2 Thessalonians 1:6, 7, 10a

   Strict justice requires that God will provide relief to
you who are sorely tried, as well as to us, when the Lord
Jesus is revealed from heaven with his mighty angels, on
the Day when he comes, to be glorified in his holy ones
and adored by all who have believed.

Come, Lord, do not delay.
—Free your people from their sinfulness.

Prayer, as in Morning Prayer.

Evening Prayer II

HYMN, 133.

Ant. 1   See how glorious he is, coming forth as Savior
         of all peoples!

Psalms and canticle from Sunday, Week IV, 1060.

Ant. 2   Crooked paths will be straightened, and rough
         ways made smooth. Come, O Lord, do not
         delay, alleluia.

Ant. 3   Ever wider will his kingdom spread, eternally at
         peace, alleluia.

READING   Philippians 4:4-5

Rejoice in the Lord always! I say it again. Rejoice! Everyone should see how unselfish you are. The Lord is near.

RESPONSORY

Lord, show us your mercy and love.
—Lord, show us your mercy and love.

And grant us your salvation,
—your mercy and love.

Glory to the Father . . .
—Lord, show us . . .

For the Canticle of Mary, the antiphon is taken from the office of the day, 325ff.

INTERCESSIONS

To Christ the Lord, who was born of the Virgin Mary, let us pray with joyful hearts:
   Come, Lord Jesus!
Lord Jesus, in the mystery of your incarnation, you revealed your glory to the world,
—give us new life by your coming.
You have taken our weakness upon yourself,
—grant us your mercy.
You redeemed the world from sin by your first coming in humility,
—free us from all guilt when you come again in glory.
You live and rule over all,
—in your goodness bring us to our eternal inheritance.
You sit at the right hand of the Father,
—gladden the souls of the dead with your light.

Our Father . . .

Prayer

Lord,
fill our hearts with your love,
and as you revealed to us by an angel
the coming of your Son as man,
so lead us through his suffering and death
to the glory of his resurrection,
for he lives and reigns with you and the Holy Spirit,
one God, for ever and ever.

Alternative Prayer

Father, all-powerful God,
your eternal Word took flesh on our earth
when the Virgin Mary placed her life
at the service of your plan.
Lift our minds in watchful hope
to hear the voice which announces his glory
and open our minds to receive the Spirit
who prepares us for his coming.
We ask this through Christ our Lord.

DECEMBER 17

Office of Readings

The Lord proclaims his word to Jacob.
—His laws and decrees to Israel.

FIRST READING

From the book of the prophet Isaiah   45:1-13

The salvation of Israel through Cyrus

Thus says the Lord to his anointed, Cyrus,
   whose right hand I grasp,
Subduing nations before him,
   and making kings run in his service,
Opening doors before him
   and leaving the gates unbarred:

I will go before you
   and level the mountains;
Bronze doors I will shatter,
   and iron bars I will snap.
I will give you treasures out of the darkness,
   and riches that have been hidden away,
That you may know that I am the Lord,
   the God of Israel, who calls you by your name.

For the sake of Jacob, my servant,
   of Israel my chosen one,
I have called you by your name,
   giving you a title, though you knew me not.
I am the Lord and there is no other,
   there is no God besides me.
It is I who arm you, though you know me not,
   so that toward the rising and the setting of the sun
   men may know that there is none besides me.

I am the Lord, there is no other;
  I form the light, and create the darkness,
I make well-being and create woe;
  I, the Lord, do all these things.

Let justice descend, O heavens, like dew from above,
  like gentle rain let the skies drop it down.
Let the earth open and salvation bud forth;
  let justice also spring up!
  I, the Lord, have created this.

Woe to him who contends with his Maker;
  a potsherd among potsherds of the earth!
Dare the clay say to its modeler, "What are you doing?"
  or, "What you are making has no hands"?
Woe to him who asks a father, "What are you
    begetting?"
  or a woman, "What are you giving birth to?"

Thus says the Lord,
  the Holy One of Israel, his maker:
You question me about my children,
  or prescribe the work of my hands for me!
It was I who made the earth
  and created mankind upon it;
It was my hands that stretched out the heavens;
  I gave the order to all their host.
It was I who stirred up one for the triumph of justice;
  all his ways I make level.
He shall rebuild my city
  and let my exiles go free
Without price or ransom,
  says the Lord of hosts.

RESPONSORY   Isaiah 45:8; see 16:1

Let the heavens drop down gentle showers,
let the clouds rain down the Just One,
—and let the earth bring forth a Savior.

Lord, send the Lamb, the ruler of the earth, from the
   Rock in the desert to the mountain of the daughter of
   Zion.
—And let the . . .

SECOND READING

From a letter by Saint Leo the Great, pope

(Ep. 31, 2-3: PL 54, 791-793)

The mystery of our reconciliation with God

To speak of our Lord, the son of the blessed Virgin
Mary, as true and perfect man is of no value to us if we do
not believe that he is descended from the line of ancestors
set out in the Gospel. Matthew's gospel begins by setting
out *the genealogy of Jesus Christ, son of David, son of
Abraham,* and then traces his human descent by bringing
his ancestral line down to his mother's husband, Joseph.
On the other hand, Luke traces his parentage backward
step by step to the actual father of mankind, to show that
both the first and the last Adam share the same nature.

No doubt the Son of God in his omnipotence could
have taught and sanctified men by appearing to them in a
semblance of human form as he did to the patriarchs and
prophets, when for instance he engaged in a wrestling
contest or entered into conversation with them, or when
he accepted their hospitality and even ate the food they
set before him. But these appearances were only types,
signs that mysteriously foretold the coming of one who
would take a true human nature from the stock of the
patriarchs who had gone before him. No mere figure,
then, fulfilled the mystery of our reconciliation with God,

ordained from all eternity. The Holy Spirit had not yet come upon the Virgin nor had the power of the Most High overshadowed her, so that within her spotless womb Wisdom might build itself a house and the Word become flesh. The divine nature and the nature of a servant were to be united in one person so that the Creator of time might be born in time, and he through whom all things were made might be brought forth in their midst.

For unless the new man, by being made *in the likeness of sinful humanity,* had taken on himself the nature of our first parents, unless he had stooped to be one in substance with his mother while sharing the Father's substance and, being alone free from sin, united our nature to his, the whole human race would still be held captive under the dominion of Satan. The Conqueror's victory would have profited us nothing if the battle had been fought outside our human condition. But through this wonderful blending the mystery of new birth shone upon us, so that through the same Spirit by whom Christ was conceived and brought forth we too might be born again in a spiritual birth; and in consequence the evangelist declares the faithful to *have been born not of blood, nor of the desire of the flesh, nor of the will of man, but of God.*

RESPONSORY   See Isaiah 11:10; Luke 1:32

Behold the root of Jesse will come down to save the people,
the nations will entreat him;
—and his name will be held in reverence.

The Lord God will give him the throne of David, his father,
and he will rule over the house of Jacob for ever.
—And his name . . .

Prayer, as in Morning Prayer.

Morning Prayer

The antiphons are given in the proper place in the Psalter.

READING   Isaiah 11:1-3a

A shoot shall sprout from the stump of Jesse,
  and from his roots a bud shall blossom.
The spirit of the Lord shall rest upon him:
  a spirit of wisdom and of understanding,
A spirit of counsel and of strength,
  a spirit of knowledge and of fear of the Lord,
  and his delight shall be the fear of the Lord.

RESPONSORY

Your light will come, Jerusalem;
the Lord will dawn on you in radiant beauty.
—Your light will come, Jerusalem;
the Lord will dawn on you in radiant beauty.

You will see his glory within you;
—the Lord will dawn on you in radiant beauty.

Glory to the Father . . .
—Your light will . . .

CANTICLE OF ZECHARIAH

Ant.   Believe me, the kingdom of God is at hand; I tell
       you solemnly, your Savior will not delay his
       coming.

INTERCESSIONS

Let us pray to God our Father, who from of old has
    called his people to salvation:
    Lord, protect your people.
You promised to plant the seed of justice among your
    people,
—protect the holiness of your Church.

Lord, teach all men and women to listen to your word,
—and help believers to persevere in holiness.
Keep us in the love of your Spirit,
—that we may know the mercy of your Son who is to
  come.
Father most merciful, strengthen us to the last,
—until the day of the coming of Jesus Christ our Lord.

Our Father . . .

Prayer

Father,
creator and redeemer of mankind,
you decreed, and your Word became man,
born of the Virgin Mary.
May we come to share the divinity of Christ,
who humbled himself to share our human nature,
for he lives and reigns with you and the Holy Spirit,
one God, for ever and ever.

Daytime Prayer

Midmorning

Ant.   This is the good news the prophets foretold: The
       Savior will be born of the Virgin Mary.

READING   Isaiah 4:2

     On that day,
The branch of the Lord will be luster and glory,
   and the fruit of the earth will be honor and splendor
   for the survivors of Israel.

The nations will revere your name, O Lord.
—And the great ones of the earth will acknowledge your
  glory.

Midday

Ant.   The angel Gabriel said to Mary in greeting: Hail,
full of grace, the Lord is with you; blessed are you
among women.

READING   Isaiah 4:3

He who remains in Zion
   and he that is left in Jerusalem
Will be called holy:
   every one marked down for life in Jerusalem.

Remember us, Lord, because of the love you have for
   your people.
—Come and bring us your salvation.

Midafternoon

Ant.   Mary said: My soul is deeply troubled; what can
this greeting mean? Am I to give birth to my
King   and yet remain a virgin for ever?

READING   Isaiah 61:11

As the earth brings forth its plants,
   and a garden makes its growth spring up,
So will the Lord God make justice and praise
   spring up before all the nations.

Come, Lord, do not delay.
—Free your people from their sinfulness.

Prayer, as in Morning Prayer.

Evening Prayer

The antiphons are given in the proper place in the Psalter.

READING   1 Thessalonians 5:23-24

May the God of peace make you perfect in holiness.
May he preserve you whole and entire, spirit, soul, and

body, irreproachable at the coming of our Lord Jesus Christ. He who calls us is trustworthy, therefore he will do it.

RESPONSORY

Lord, show us your mercy and love.
—Lord, show us your mercy and love.

And grant us your salvation,
—your mercy and love.

Glory to the Father . . .
—Lord, show us . . .

CANTICLE OF MARY

Ant.   Wisdom, O holy Word of God, you govern all creation with your strong yet tender care. Come and show your people the way to salvation.

INTERCESSIONS

Jesus Christ is the joy and happiness of all who look forward to his coming. Let us call upon him and say:
Come, Lord, and do not delay!
In joy, we wait for your coming,
—come, Lord Jesus.
Before time began, you shared life with the Father,
—come now and save us.
You created the world and all who live in it,
—come to redeem the work of your hands.
You did not hesitate to become man, subject to death,
—come to free us from the power of death.
You came to give us life to the full,
—come and give us your unending life.
You desire all people to live in love in your kingdom,
—come and bring together those who long to see you face to face.

Our Father . . .

Prayer

Father,
creator and redeemer of mankind,
you decreed, and your Word became man,
born of the Virgin Mary.
May we come to share the divinity of Christ,
who humbled himself to share our human nature,
for he lives and reigns with you and the Holy Spirit,
one God, for ever and ever.

DECEMBER 18

Office of Readings

Lift up your heads and see.
—Your redemption is now at hand.

FIRST READING

From the book of the prophet Isaiah   46:1-13

The Lord opposes the idols of Babylon

Bel bows down, Nebo stoops,
    their idols are upon beasts and cattle;
They must be borne up on shoulders,
    carried as burdens by the weary.
They stoop and bow down together;
    unable to save those who bear them,
    they too go into captivity.

Hear me, O house of Jacob,
    all who remain of the house of Israel,

My burden since your birth,
    whom I have carried from your infancy.
Even to your old age I am the same,
    even when your hair is gray I will bear you;
It is I who have done this, I who will continue,
    and I who will carry you to safety.

Whom would you compare me with, as an equal,
    or match me against, as though we were alike?
There are those who pour out gold from a purse
    and weigh out silver on the scales;
Then they hire a goldsmith to make it into a god
    before which they fall down in worship.
They lift it to their shoulders to carry;
    when they set it in place again, it stays,
    and does not move from the spot.
Although they cry out to it, it cannot answer;
    it delivers no one from distress.

Remember this and be firm,
    bear it well in mind, you rebels;
    remember the former things, those long ago:
I am God, there is no other;
    I am God, there is none like me

At the beginning I foretell the outcome;
    in advance, things not yet done.
I say that my plan shall stand,
    I accomplish my every purpose.
I call from the east a bird of prey
    from a distant land, one to carry out my plan.
Yes, I have spoken, I will accomplish it;
    I have planned it, and I will do it.

Listen to me, you fainthearted,
    you who seem far from the victory of justice:

I am bringing on my justice, it is not far off,
   my salvation shall not tarry;
I will put salvation within Zion,
   and give to Israel my glory.

Isaiah 46:12, 13
Listen to me, you fainthearted, who are far from justice.
—I will grant salvation in Zion, and give my glory to
   Israel.

I am bringing my justice near at hand;
it shall not be delayed,
nor shall my salvation tarry.
—I will grant . . .

SECOND READING
From a letter to Diognetus

(Cap. 8, 5—9,6: Funk 1, 325-327)

God has revealed his love through the Son

No man has ever seen God or known him, but God has
revealed himself to us through faith, by which alone it is
possible to see him. God, the Lord and maker of all
things, who created the world and set it in order, not only
loved man but was also patient with him. So he has
always been, and is, and will be: kind, good, free from
anger, truthful; indeed, he and he alone is good.

He devised a plan, a great and wonderful plan, and
shared it only with his Son. As long as he preserved this
secrecy and kept his own wise counsel he seemed to be
neglecting us, to have no concern for us. But when
through his beloved Son he revealed and made public
what he had prepared from the very beginning, he gave
us all at once gifts such as we could never have dreamt of,
even sight and knowledge of himself.

When God had made all his plans in consultation with
his Son, he waited until a later time, allowing us to follow

our own whim, to be swept along by unruly passions, to be led astray by pleasure and desire. Not that he was pleased by our sins: he only tolerated them. Not that he approved of that time of sin: he was planning this era of holiness. When we had been shown to be undeserving of life, his goodness was to make us worthy of it. When we had made it clear that we could not enter God's kingdom by our own power, we were to be enabled to do so by the power of God.

When our wickedness had reached its culmination, it became clear that retribution was at hand in the shape of suffering and death. The time came then for God to make known his kindness and power (how immeasurable is God's generosity and love!). He did not show hatred for us or reject us or take vengeance; instead, he was patient with us, bore with us, and in compassion took our sins upon himself; he gave his own Son as the price of our redemption, the holy one to redeem the wicked, the sinless one to redeem sinners, the just one to redeem the unjust, the incorruptible one to redeem the corruptible, the immortal one to redeem mortals. For what else could have covered our sins but his sinlessness? Where else could we—wicked and sinful as we were—have found the means of holiness except in the Son of God alone?

How wonderful a transformation, how mysterious a design, how inconceivable a blessing! The wickedness of the many is covered up in the holy One, and the holiness of One sanctifies many sinners.

RESPONSORY   Acts 4:12; Isaiah 9:6

There is no salvation in any other person or place;
—nor is there any other name under heaven given to
    men,
by which we should be saved.

His name shall be Wonder-counselor, God of strength,
  Father of future ages, Prince of peace.
—Nor is there . . .

Prayer, as in Morning Prayer.

Morning Prayer

The antiphons are given in the proper place in the Psalter.

READING   Romans 13:11-12

It is now the hour for you to wake from sleep, for our
salvation is closer than when we first accepted the faith.
The night is far spent; the day draws near. Let us cast off
deeds of darkness and put on the armor of light.

RESPONSORY

Your light will come, Jerusalem;
the Lord will dawn on you in radiant beauty.
—Your light will come, Jerusalem;
the Lord will dawn on you in radiant beauty.

You will see his glory within you;
  —the Lord will dawn on you in radiant beauty.

Glory to the Father . . .
—Your light will . . .

CANTICLE OF ZECHARIAH

Ant.   Let everything within you watch and wait, for the
       Lord our God draws near.

INTERCESSIONS

To the Lord Jesus Christ, judge of the living and the
  dead, let us pray:
    Come, Lord Jesus!
Lord Jesus, you came to save sinners,
—protect us in times of temptation.

You will come in glory to be our judge,
—show in us your power to save.
Help us to keep the precepts of your law with the
   strength of the Spirit,
—and to look forward in love to your coming.
You are praised throughout the ages; in your mercy help
   us to live devoutly and temperately in this life,
—as we wait in joyful hope for the revelation of your
   glory.

Our Father . . .

Prayer

All-powerful God,
renew us by the coming feast of your Son
and free us from our slavery to sin.

Grant this through our Lord Jesus Christ, your Son,
who lives and reigns with you and the Holy Spirit,
one God, for ever and ever.

Daytime Prayer

Midmorning

Ant.   This is the good news the prophets foretold: The
       Savior will be born of the Virgin Mary.

READING   Romans 13:13-14

Let us live honorably as in daylight; not in carousing
and drunkenness, not in sexual excess and lust, not in
quarreling and jealousy. Rather, put on the Lord Jesus
Christ.

The nations will revere your name, O Lord.
—And the great ones of the earth will acknowledge your
   glory.

Midday

Ant.   The angel Gabriel said to Mary in greeting: Hail,
        full of grace, the Lord is with you; blessed are you
        among women.

READING   1 Thessalonians 3:12-13

May the Lord make you overflow with love for one
another and for all, even as our love does for you. May he
strengthen your hearts, making them blameless and holy
before our God and Father at the coming of our Lord
Jesus with all his holy ones.

Remember us, Lord, because of the love you have for
    your people.
—Come and bring us your salvation.

Midafternoon

Ant.   Mary said: My soul is deeply troubled; what can
        this greeting mean? Am I to give birth to my King
        and yet remain a virgin for ever?

READING   See 2 Thessalonians 1:6, 7, 10

Strict justice requires that God will provide relief to
you who are sorely tried, as well as to us, when the Lord
Jesus is revealed from heaven with his mighty angels, on
the Day when he comes, to be glorified in his holy ones
and adored by all who have believed.

Come, Lord, do not delay.
—Free your people from their sinfulness.

Prayer, as in Morning Prayer.

Evening Prayer

The antiphons are given in the proper place in the Psalter.

READING   Philippians 4:4-5

Rejoice in the Lord always! I say it again. Rejoice!
Everyone should see how unselfish you are. The Lord is
near.

RESPONSORY

Lord, show us your mercy and love.
—Lord, show us your mercy and love.

And grant us your salvation,
—your mercy and love.

Glory to the Father . . .
—Lord, show us . . .

CANTICLE OF MARY

Ant.   O sacred Lord of ancient Israel, who showed
       yourself to Moses in the burning bush, who gave
       him the holy law on Sinai mountain: come, stretch
       out your mighty hand to set us free.

INTERCESSIONS

To Christ the Lord, who was born of the Virgin Mary, let
    us pray with joyful hearts:
    Come, Lord Jesus!
Lord Jesus, in the mystery of your incarnation, you
    revealed your glory to the world,
—give us new life by your coming.
You have taken our weaknesses upon yourself,
—grant us your mercy.
You redeemed the world from sin by your first coming in
    humility,
—free us from all guilt when you come again in glory.

You live and rule over all,
—in your goodness bring us to our eternal inheritance.
You sit at the right hand of the Father,
—gladden the souls of the dead with your light.

Our Father . . .

Prayer

All-powerful God,
renew us by the coming feast of your Son
and free us from our slavery to sin.

Grant this through our Lord Jesus Christ, your Son,
who lives and reigns with you and the Holy Spirit,
one God, for ever and ever.

DECEMBER 19

Office of Readings

Lord, show us your mercy and love.
—And grant us your salvation.

FIRST READING

From the book of the prophet Isaiah　　　　47:1, 3b-15

Lament for Babylon

Come down, sit in the dust,
　　O virgin daughter Babylon;
Sit on the ground, dethroned,
　　O daughter of the Chaldeans.
No longer shall you be called
　　dainty and delicate.
I will take vengeance,
　　I will yield to no entreaty,
　　says our redeemer,

Whose name is the Lord of hosts,
   the Holy One of Israel.

Go into darkness and sit in silence,
   O daughter of the Chaldeans,
No longer shall you be called
   sovereign mistress of kingdoms.

Angry at my people,
   I profaned my inheritance,
And I gave them into your hand;
   but you showed them no mercy,
And upon old men
   you laid a very heavy yoke.
You said, "I shall remain always,
   a sovereign mistress forever!"
But you did not lay these things to heart,
   you disregarded their outcome.

Now hear this, voluptuous one,
   enthroned securely,
Saying to yourself,
   "I, and no one else!
I shall never be a widow,
   or suffer the loss of my children"—
Both these things shall come to you
   suddenly, in a single day:
Complete bereavement and widowhood
   shall come upon you
For your many sorceries
   and the great number of your spells;
Because you felt secure in your wickedness,
   and said, "No one sees me."

Your wisdom and your knowledge
   led you astray,

And you said to yourself,
  "I, and no one else!"
But upon you shall come evil
  you will not know how to predict;
Disaster shall befall you
  which you cannot allay.
Suddenly there shall come upon you
  ruin which you will not expect.

Keep up, now, your spells
  and your many sorceries;
Perhaps you can make them avail,
  perhaps you can strike terror!
You wearied yourself with many consultations,
  at which you toiled from your youth;
Let the astrologers stand forth to save you,
  the stargazers who forecast at each new moon
  what would happen to you.

Lo, they are like stubble,
  fire consumes them;
They cannot save themselves
  from the spreading flames.
This is no warming ember,
  no fire to sit before.
Thus do your wizards serve you
  with whom you have toiled from your youth;
Each wanders his own way,
  with none to save you.

RESPONSORY   Isaiah 49:13; 47:4

Rejoice, you heavens, and celebrate, O earth;
cry out with praise, you mountains;
—for the Lord will have compassion on his poor.

Our Redeemer, the Lord God of power and might is his
  name, the Holy One of Israel.

—For the Lord . . .

SECOND READING

From a treatise *Against Heresies* by Saint Irenaeus, bishop

(Lib. 3, 20, 2-3: SC 34, 342-344)

The plan of redemption through the Incarnation

God is man's glory. Man is the vessel which receives God's action and all his wisdom and power.

Just as a doctor is judged in his care for the sick, so God is revealed in his conduct with men. That is Paul's reason for saying: *God has made the whole world prisoner of unbelief that he may have mercy on all.* He was speaking of man, who was disobedient to God, and cast off from immortality, and then found mercy, receiving through the Son of God the adoption he brings.

If man, without being puffed up or boastful, has a right belief regarding created things and their divine Creator, who, having given them being, holds them all in his power, and if man perseveres in God's love, and in obedience and gratitude to him, he will receive greater glory from him. It will be a glory which will grow ever brighter until he takes on the likeness of the one who died for him.

He it was who took on the likeness of sinful flesh, to condemn sin and rid the flesh of sin, as now condemned. He wanted to invite man to take on his likeness, appointing man an imitator of God, establishing man in a way of life in obedience to the Father that would lead to the vision of God, and endowing man with power to receive the Father. He is the Word of God who dwelt with man and became the Son of Man to open the way for man to receive God, for God to dwell with man, according to the will of the Father.

For this reason *the Lord himself gave* as the sign of our salvation, the one who was born of *the Virgin, Emmanuel.* It was *the Lord himself who saved them,* for of themselves they had no power to be saved. For this reason Paul speaks of the weakness of man, and says: *I know that no good dwells in my flesh.* He means that the blessing of our salvation comes not from us but from God. Again, he says: *I am a wretched man; who will free me from this body doomed to die?* Then he speaks of a liberator, thanks to Jesus Christ our Lord.

Isaiah says the same: *Hands that are feeble, grow strong! Knees that are weak, take courage! Hearts that are faint, grow strong! Fear not—see, our God is judgment and he will repay. He himself will come and save us.* He means that we could not be saved of ourselves but only with God's help.

RESPONSORY   See Jeremiah 31:10; 4:5

Listen to the word of the Lord, you peoples,
and proclaim it to the ends of the earth;
— say to the far-off islands: Our Savior is coming.

Proclaim the good news, let it be heard;
tell it to everyone, shout it aloud.
— Say to the . . .

Prayer, as in Morning Prayer.

Morning Prayer

The antiphons are given in the proper place in the Psalter.

READING   Isaiah 2:3b

Come, let us climb the Lord's mountain,
   to the house of the God of Jacob,
That he may instruct us in his ways,
   and we may walk in his paths.
For from Zion shall go forth instruction,
   and the word of the Lord from Jerusalem.

RESPONSORY

Your light will come, Jerusalem;
the Lord will dawn on you in radiant beauty.
—Your light will come, Jerusalem;
the Lord will dawn on you in radiant beauty.

You will see his glory within you;
—the Lord will dawn on you in radiant beauty.

Glory to the Father . . .
—Your light will . . .

CANTICLE OF ZECHARIAH

Ant.   Like the sun in the morning sky, the Savior of
the world will dawn; like rain on the meadows he
will descend to rest in the womb of the Virgin,
alleluia.

INTERCESSIONS

To Christ our Redeemer, who will come again to free
from the power of death all those who return to him,
let us humbly pray:
Come, Lord Jesus!
As we proclaim your coming, Lord,
—cleanse our hearts of every vain desire.
Lord, may the Church which you founded,
—proclaim your greatness to all peoples.
Your law is a light to my eyes,
—let it protect those who trust in you.
You allow the joys of your coming to be foretold to us by
your Church,
—may we receive you with eager devotion.

Our Father . . .

Prayer

Father,
you show the world the splendor of your glory
in the coming of Christ, born of the Virgin.
Give to us true faith and love
to celebrate the mystery of God made man.

We ask this through our Lord Jesus Christ, your Son,
who lives and reigns with you and the Holy Spirit,
one God, for ever and ever.

Daytime Prayer

Midmorning

Ant.   This is the good news the prophets foretold: The
       Savior will be born of the Virgin Mary.

READING   See Isaiah 10:20-21

On that day
The remnant of Israel,
   the survivors of the house of Jacob,
Will lean upon the Lord,
   the Holy One of Israel in truth.
A remnant will return, the remnant of Jacob,
   to the mighty God.

The nations will revere your name, O Lord.
—And the great ones of the earth will acknowledge your
   glory.

Midday

Ant.   The angel Gabriel said to Mary in greeting: Hail,
       full of grace, the Lord is with you; blessed are you
       among women.

READING   See Isaiah 10:24a, 27

Thus says the Lord, the God of hosts:
O my people, who dwell in Zion,
    do not fear.
        On that day,
The burden shall be taken from your shoulder,
    and the yoke shattered from your neck.

Remember us, Lord, because of the love you have for
    your people.
—Come and bring us your salvation.

Midafternoon

Ant. Mary said: My soul is deeply troubled; what can
      this greeting mean? Am I to give birth to my King
      and yet remain a virgin for ever?

READING   See Isaiah 13:22b-14:1

Her time is near at hand
    and her days shall not be prolonged.
The Lord has pity on Jacob
    and again chooses Israel.

Come, Lord, do not delay.
—Free your people from their sinfulness.

Prayer, as in Morning Prayer.

Evening Prayer

The antiphons are given in the proper place in the Psalter.

READING   Philippians 3:20b-21

We eagerly await the coming of our Savior, the Lord
Jesus Christ. He will give a new form to this lowly body
of ours and remake it according to the pattern of his
glorified body, by his power to subject everything to
himself.

RESPONSORY

Come and set us free, Lord God of power and might.
—Come and set us free, Lord God of power and might.

Let your face shine upon us and we shall be saved,
—Lord God of power and might.

Glory to the Father . . .
—Come and set . . .

CANTICLE OF MARY

Ant.   O Flower of Jesse's stem, you have been raised up
as a sign for all peoples; kings stand silent in your
presence; the nations bow down in worship before
you. Come, let nothing keep you from coming to
our aid.

INTERCESSIONS

To Christ our Lord, judge of the living and the dead, let
us cry out with faith:
Come, Lord Jesus!
Lord, may the world know your justice which the
heavens proclaim,
—may your glory fill the earth.
For us you took upon yourself the weakness of man,
—protect us with the strength of your own divine life.
Come to those imprisoned in the darkness of ignorance,
—show them the radiance of your own divine light.
In your humility as a man, you took away our sin,
—now in your glory grant us true happiness.
When you come in glory to judge us,
—gather the dead into your kingdom.

Our Father . . .

Prayer

Father,
you show the world the splendor of your glory
in the coming of Christ, born of the Virgin.
Give to us true faith and love
to celebrate the mystery of God made man.

We ask this through our Lord Jesus Christ, your Son,
who lives and reigns with you and the Holy Spirit,
one God, for ever and ever.

DECEMBER 20

Office of Readings

A voice is heard, crying in the wilderness: Prepare the
    way of the Lord.
—Make straight the path of our God.

FIRST READING

From the book of the prophet Isaiah   48:1-11

God alone is Lord of the future

Hear this, O house of Jacob
    called by the name Israel,
    sprung from the stock of Judah,
You who swear by the name of the Lord
    and invoke the God of Israel
    without sincerity or justice,
Though you are named after the holy city
    and rely on the God of Israel,
    whose name is the Lord of hosts.

Things of the past I foretold long ago,
    they went forth from my mouth, I let you hear of
        them;

Because I know that you are stubborn
   and that your neck is an iron sinew
   and your forehead bronze,
I foretold them to you of old;
   before they took place I let you hear of them,
That you might not say, "My idol did them,
   my statue, my molten image commanded them."
Now that you have heard, look at all this;
   must you not admit it?

From now on I announce new things to you,
   hidden events of which you knew not.
Now, not long ago, they are brought into being,
   and beforetime you did not hear of them,
   so that you cannot claim to have known them;
You neither heard nor knew,
   they did not reach your ears beforehand.
Yes, I know you are utterly treacherous,
   a rebel you were called from birth.

For the sake of my name I restrain my anger,
   for the sake of my renown I hold it back from you,
   lest I should destroy you.
See, I have refined you like silver,
   tested you in the furnace of affliction.
For my sake, for my own sake, I do this;
   why should I suffer profanation?
   My glory I will not give to another.

RESPONSORY   Isaiah 48:10, 11; 54:8
I have tried you in the furnace of distress.
For me, for my own sake, I do this, that I be not
   blasphemed.
—I will not give my glory to another.

In a moment of indignation I hid my face from you for a
   little while,
then suddenly I took action and they came to be;

but in my everlasting mercy I had compassion on you.
—I will not . . .

SECOND READING

From a homily In Praise of the Virgin Mother by Saint Bernard, abbot

(Hom. 4, 8–9: Opera omnia, Edit. Cisterc. 4 [1966], 53–54)

The whole world awaits Mary's reply

You have heard, O Virgin, that you will conceive and bear a son; you have heard that it will not be by man but by the Holy Spirit. The angel awaits an answer; it is time for him to return to God who sent him. We too are waiting, O Lady, for your word of compassion; the sentence of condemnation weighs heavily upon us.

The price of our salvation is offered to you. We shall be set free at once if you consent. In the eternal Word of God we all came to be, and behold, we die. In your brief response we are to be remade in order to be recalled to life.

Tearful Adam with his sorrowing family begs this of you, O loving Virgin, in their exile from Paradise. Abraham begs it, David begs it. All the other holy patriarchs, your ancestors, ask it of you, as they dwell in the country of the shadow of death. This is what the whole earth waits for, prostrate at your feet. It is right in doing so, for on your word depends comfort for the wretched, ransom for the captive, freedom for the condemned, indeed, salvation for all the sons of Adam, the whole of your race.

Answer quickly, O Virgin. Reply in haste to the angel, or rather through the angel to the Lord. Answer with a word, receive the Word of God. Speak your own word, conceive the divine Word. Breathe a passing word, embrace the eternal Word.

Why do you delay, why are you afraid? Believe, give praise, and receive. Let humility be bold, let modesty be confident. This is no time for virginal simplicity to forget prudence. In this matter alone, O prudent Virgin, do not fear to be presumptuous. Though modest silence is pleasing, dutiful speech is now more necessary. Open your heart to faith, O blessed Virgin, your lips to praise, your womb to the Creator. See, the desired of all nations is at your door, knocking to enter. If he should pass by because of your delay, in sorrow you would begin to seek him afresh, the One whom your soul loves. Arise, hasten, open. Arise in faith, hasten in devotion, open in praise and thanksgiving. *Behold, the handmaid of the Lord,* she says, *be it done to me according to your word.*

RESPONSORY   See Luke 1:31, 42

Receive, O Virgin Mary, the word
which the Lord has made known to you by the message
    of the angel:
You will conceive and give birth to a son, both God and
    man,
—and you will be called blessed among women.

A virgin, you will indeed bear a son;
ever chaste and holy, you will be the mother of our
    Savior.
—And you will . . .

Prayer, as in Morning Prayer.

Morning Prayer

The antiphons are given in the proper place in the Psalter.

READING   Genesis 49:10

The scepter shall never depart from Judah,
    or the mace from between his legs,

While tribute is brought to him,
and he receives the people's homage.

Your light will come, Jerusalem;
the Lord will dawn on you in radiant beauty.
—Your light will come, Jerusalem;
the Lord will dawn on you in radiant beauty.

You will see his glory within you;
—the Lord will dawn on you in radiant beauty.

Glory to the Father . . .
—Your light will . . .

CANTICLE OF ZECHARIAH

Ant.   The angel Gabriel was sent to the Virgin Mary,
who was engaged to be married to Joseph.

INTERCESSIONS

To Christ our Lord, the light of the world, let us cry out
with joy:
Come, Lord Jesus!
Dispel our darkness with the light of your presence,
—and make us worthy of your gifts.
Save us, Lord our God,
—that we may praise your holy name this day.
Enkindle in our hearts the flame of your love,
—and make us long to be united with you.
You bore our infirmity,
—aid the sick and those who are to die this day.

Our Father . . .

Prayer

God of love and mercy,
help us to follow the example of Mary,
always ready to do your will.

At the message of an angel
she welcomed your eternal Son
and, filled with the light of your Spirit,
she became the temple of your Word,
who lives and reigns with you and the Holy Spirit,
one God, for ever and ever.

Daytime Prayer

Midmorning

Ant. This is the good news the prophets foretold: The
Savior will be born of the Virgin Mary.

READING Jeremiah 23:5

Behold, the days are coming, says the Lord,
when I will raise up a righteous shoot to David;
As king he shall reign and govern wisely,
he shall do what is just and right in the land.

The nations will revere your name, O Lord.
—And the great ones of the earth will acknowledge your
glory.

Midday

Ant. The angel Gabriel said to Mary in greeting: Hail,
full of grace, the Lord is with you; blessed are you
among women.

READING Jeremiah 23:6

In his days Judah shall be saved,
Israel shall dwell in security.
This is the name they give him:
"The Lord our justice."

Remember us, Lord, because of the love you have for
your people.
—Come and bring us your salvation.

Midafternoon

Ant. Mary said: My soul is deeply troubled; what can this greeting mean? Am I to give birth to my King and yet remain a virgin for ever?

READING   Ezekiel 34:15-16

I myself will pasture my sheep; I myself will give them rest, says the Lord God. The lost I will seek out, the strayed I will bring back, the injured I will bind up, the sick I will heal, shepherding them rightly.

Come, Lord, do not delay.
—Free your people from their sinfulness.

Prayer, as in Morning Prayer.

Evening Prayer

The antiphons are given in the proper place in the Psalter.

READING   See 1 Corinthians 1:7b-9

We await the revelation of our Lord Jesus Christ, who will strengthen us to the end, so that we will be blameless on the day of our Lord Jesus Christ. God is faithful, and it was he who called us to fellowship with his Son.

RESPONSORY

Come and set us free, Lord God of power and might.
—Come and set us free, Lord God of power and might.

Let your face shine upon us and we shall be saved,
—Lord God of power and might.

Glory to the Father . . .
—Come and set . . .

CANTICLE OF MARY

Ant. O Key of David, O royal Power of Israel
      controlling at your will the gate of heaven: come,
      break down the prison walls of death for those
      who dwell in darkness and the shadow of death;
      and lead your captive people into freedom.

INTERCESSIONS

To Christ our Lord and Redeemer, who will appear
    openly on the last day, let us joyfully pray:
    Come, Lord Jesus!
Our Redeemer and Lord, by your birth as a man you freed
    us from the heavy yoke of the law,
—complete in us the works of your loving kindness.
From us you took whatever served your divinity,
—give us whatever we need to serve you.
Grant the desire we ask of you today,
—inflame our hearts with the fire of your love.
On earth we live with you by faith,
—in glory may we rejoice with you.
Steep the souls of the faithful departed,
—in the dew of your loving kindness.

Our Father . . .

Prayer

God of love and mercy,
help us to follow the example of Mary,
always ready to do your will.
At the message of an angel
she welcomed your eternal Son
and, filled with the light of your Spirit,
she became the temple of your Word,
who lives and reigns with you and the Holy Spirit,
one God, for ever and ever.

DECEMBER 21

Office of Readings

Turn back to us, O Lord, our God.
—Show us your face and we shall be saved.

FIRST READING

From the book
of the prophet Isaiah   48:12-21; 49:9b-13

The new Exodus

Thus says the Lord:
Listen to me, Jacob,
    Israel, whom I named!
I, it is I who am the first,
    and also the last am I.
Yes, my hand laid the foundations of the earth;
    my right hand spread out the heavens.
When I call them,
    they stand forth at once.

All of you assemble and listen:
    Who among you foretold these things?
The Lord's friend shall do his will
    against Babylon and the progeny of Chaldea.

I myself have spoken, I have called him,
    I have brought him, and his way succeeds!
Come near to me and hear this!
    Not from the beginning did I speak it in secret;
At the time it comes to pass, I am present:
    "Now the Lord God has sent me, and his spirit."

Thus says the Lord, your redeemer,
    the Holy One of Israel:

I, the Lord, your God,
   teach you what is for your good,
   and lead you on the way you should go.

If you would hearken to my commandments,
   your prosperity would be like a river,
   and your vindication like the waves of the sea;
Your descendants would be like the sand,
   and those born of your stock like its grains,
Their name never cut off
   or blotted out from my presence.

Go forth from Babylon, flee from Chaldea!
   With shouts of joy proclaim this, make it known;
Publish it to the ends of the earth, and say,
   "The Lord has redeemed his servant Jacob.
They did not thirst
   when he led them through dry lands;
Water from the rock he set flowing for them;
   he cleft the rock, and waters welled forth."

Along the ways they shall find pasture,
   on every bare height shall their pastures be.
They shall not hunger or thirst,
   nor shall the scorching wind or the sun strike them;
For he who pities them leads them
   and guides them beside springs of water.
I will cut a road through all my mountains,
   and make my highways level.

See, some shall come from afar,
   others from the north and the west,
   and some from the land of Syene.
Sing out, O heavens, and rejoice, O earth,
   break forth into song, you mountains.
For the Lord comforts his people
   and shows mercy to his afflicted.

RESPONSORY   Psalm 96:11; Isaiah 49:13; Psalm 72:7

Rejoice, you heavens, and celebrate, O earth;
cry out with praise, you mountains,
for the Lord is coming.
—He will have compassion on his poor.

In his days justice will flourish and peace will abound.
—He will have . . .

SECOND READING

From a commentary on Luke by Saint Ambrose,
bishop

(Lib. 2, 19. 22–23. 26–27: CCL 14, 39–42)

Mary visits Elizabeth

When the angel revealed his message to the Virgin
Mary he gave her a sign to win her trust. He told her of
the motherhood of an old and barren woman to show
that God is able to do all that he wills.

When she hears this Mary sets out for the hill country.
She does not disbelieve God's word; she feels no
uncertainty over the message or doubt about the sign.
She goes eager in purpose, dutiful in conscience,
hastening for joy.

Filled with God, where would she hasten but to the
heights? The Holy Spirit does not proceed by slow,
laborious efforts. Quickly, too, the blessings of her coming and the Lord's presence are made clear: as soon as
Elizabeth heard Mary's greeting the child leapt in her womb,
and she was filled with the Holy Spirit.

Notice the contrast and the choice of words. Elizabeth
is the first to hear Mary's voice, but John is the first to be
aware of grace. She hears with the ears of the body, but
he leaps for joy at the meaning of the mystery. She is

aware of Mary's presence, but he is aware of the Lord's: a woman aware of a woman's presence, the forerunner aware of the pledge of our salvation. The women speak of the grace they have received while the children are active in secret, unfolding the mystery of love with the help of their mothers, who prophesy by the spirit of their sons.

The child leaps in the womb; the mother is filled with the Holy Spirit, but not before her son. Once the son has been filled with the Holy Spirit, he fills his mother with the same Spirit. John leaps for joy, and the spirit of Mary rejoices in her turn. When John leaps for joy Elizabeth is filled with the Holy Spirit, but we know that though Mary's spirit rejoices she does not need to be filled with the Holy Spirit. Her son, who is beyond our understanding, is active in his mother in a way beyond our understanding. Elizabeth is filled with the Holy Spirit after conceiving John, while Mary is filled with the Holy Spirit before conceiving the Lord. Elizabeth says: *Blessed are you because you have believed.*

You also are blessed because you have heard and believed. A soul that believes both conceives and brings forth the Word of God and acknowledges his works.

Let Mary's soul be in each of you to proclaim the greatness of the Lord. Let her spirit be in each to rejoice in the Lord. Christ has only one mother in the flesh, but we all bring forth Christ in faith. Every soul receives the Word of God if only it keeps chaste, remaining pure and free from sin, its modesty undefiled. The soul that succeeds in this proclaims the greatness of the Lord, just as Mary's soul magnified the Lord and her spirit rejoiced in God her Savior. In another place we read: *Magnify the Lord with me.* The Lord is magnified, not because the human voice can add anything to God but because he is magnified within us. Christ is the image of God, and if the soul does what is right and holy, it magnifies that image of God, in whose likeness it was created and, in magnifying the image of God, the soul has a share in its greatness and is exalted.

RESPONSORY   Luke 1:45, 46; Psalm 66:16

Happy are you who have believed,
because the Lord's promises will be accomplished in you.
And Mary said:
—My soul proclaims the greatness of the Lord.

Come, and listen,
and I will tell what great things God has accomplished for
    me.
—My soul proclaims . . .

Prayer, as in Morning Prayer.

Morning Prayer

The antiphons are given in the proper place in the Psalter.

READING   Isaiah 7:14b-15

The virgin shall be with child, and bear a son, and shall name him Immanuel. He shall be living on curds and honey by the time he learns to reject the bad and choose the good.

RESPONSORY

Your light will come, Jerusalem;
the Lord will dawn on you in radiant beauty.
—Your light will come, Jerusalem;
the Lord will dawn on you in radiant beauty.

You will see his glory within you;
—the Lord will dawn on you in radiant beauty.

Glory to the Father . . .
—Your light will . . .

CANTICLE OF ZECHARIAH

Ant.   There is no need to be afraid; in five days our Lord will come to us.

INTERCESSIONS

To Jesus Christ our Lord, who came among us in his mercy, let us constantly cry out with joy:

Come, Lord Jesus!

You came from the Father to take on our human nature,

—now set free what was harmed in us by sin.

One day you will come again in glory to your chosen people,

—come to us today and help us sinners to recognize your mercy and tender love.

We glory in praising you, Lord Jesus,

—come and bring us your salvation.

Through faith you lead us into light,

—may we reveal your justice through our deeds.

Our Father . . .

Prayer

Lord,
hear the prayers of your people.
May we who celebrate the birth of your Son as man
rejoice in the gift of eternal life when he comes in glory,
for he lives and reigns with you and the Holy Spirit,
one God, for ever and ever.

Daytime Prayer

Midmorning

Ant.   This is the good news the prophets foretold: The Savior will be born of the Virgin Mary.

READING   Isaiah 2:11-12

The haughty eyes of man will be lowered,
   the arrogance of men will be abased,
      and the Lord alone will be exalted, on that day.

The nations will revere your name, O Lord.
—And the great ones of the earth will acknowledge your
   glory.

Midday

Ant.   The angel Gabriel said to Mary in greeting: Hail,
       full of grace, the Lord is with you; blessed are you
       among women.

READING   Isaiah 12:2

God indeed is my savior;
   I am confident and unafraid.
My strength and my courage is the Lord,
   and he has been my savior.

Remember us, Lord, because of the love you have for
   your people.
—Come and bring us your salvation.

Midafternoon

Ant.   Mary said: My soul is deeply troubled; what can
       this greeting mean? Am I to give birth to my King
       and yet remain a virgin for ever?

READING   Daniel 9:19

   O Lord, hear! O Lord, pardon! O Lord, be attentive
and act without delay, for your own sake, O my God,
because your people bear your name!

Come, Lord, do not delay.
—Free your people from their sinfulness.

Prayer, as in Morning Prayer.

Evening Prayer

The antiphons are given in the proper place in the Psalter.

READING   1 Corinthians 4:5

Stop passing judgment before the time of the Lord's return. He will bring to light what is hidden in darkness and manifest the intentions of hearts. At that time, everyone will receive his praise from God.

RESPONSORY

Come and set us free, Lord God of power and might.
—Come and set us free, Lord God of power and might.

Let your face shine upon us and we shall be saved,
—Lord God of power and might.

Glory to the Father . . .
—Come and set . . .

CANTICLE OF MARY

Ant.   O Radiant Dawn, splendor of eternal light, sun of justice: come, shine on those who dwell in darkness and the shadow of death.

INTERCESSIONS

We humbly pray to Jesus Christ, who rescues us from the darkness of sin, and in faith we cry out:
    Come, Lord Jesus!
Lord, gather together all the people of the earth,
—and establish your everlasting covenant with them.
Lamb of God, you came of old to take away the sin of the world,
—purge us from all the dregs of our guilt.
You came to recover what was lost,
—come once again in your mercy lest you punish what you have recovered.

Our faith seeks you out,
—let us find everlasting joy with you when you come.
You will judge the living and the dead,
—graciously gather the dead into the ranks of the
   blessed.

Our Father . . .

Prayer

Lord,
hear the prayers of your people.
May we who celebrate the birth of your Son as man
rejoice in the gift of eternal life when he comes in glory,
for he lives and reigns with you and the Holy Spirit,
one God, for ever and ever.

DECEMBER 22

Office of Readings

Hear the word of the Lord, all you nations.
—Proclaim it to the ends of the earth.

FIRST READING

From the book of the prophet Isaiah   49:14—50:1

The restoration of Zion

Zion said, "The Lord has forsaken me;
   my Lord has forgotten me."
Can a mother forget her infant,
   be without tenderness for the child of her womb?
Even should she forget,
   I will never forget you.

See, upon the palms of my hands I have written your
    name;
  your walls are ever before me.
Your rebuilders make haste,
  as those who tore you down and laid you waste
  go forth from you;

Look about and see,
  they are all gathering and coming to you.
As I live, says the Lord,
  you shall be arrayed with them all as with adornments,
  like a bride you shall fasten them on you.
Though you were waste and desolate,
  a land of ruins,
Now you shall be too small for your inhabitants,
  while those who swallowed you up will be far away.
The children whom you had lost
  shall yet say to you,
"This place is too small for me,
  make room for me to live in."
You shall ask yourself:
  "Who has borne me these?
I was bereft and barren
  [exiled and repudiated];
  who has reared them?
I was left all alone;
  where then do these come from?"

    Thus says the Lord God:
See, I will lift up my hand to the nations,
  and raise my signal to the peoples;
They shall bring your sons in their arms,
  and your daughters shall be carried on their shoulders.
Kings shall be your foster fathers,
  their princesses your nurses;

Bowing to the ground, they shall worship you
 and lick the dust at your feet.
Then you shall know that I am the Lord,
 and those who hope in me shall never be disappointed.

Thus says the Lord:
Can booty be taken from a warrior?
 or captives be rescued from a tyrant?
Yes, captives can be taken from a warrior,
 and booty be rescued from a tyrant;
Those who oppose you I will oppose,
 and your sons I will save.

I will make your oppressors eat their own flesh,
 and they shall be drunk with their own blood
 as with the juice of the grape.
All mankind shall know
 that I, the Lord, am your savior,
 your redeemer, the mighty one of Jacob.

Thus says the Lord:
Where is the bill of divorce
 with which I dismissed your mother?
Or to which of my creditors
 have I sold you?
It was for your sins that you were sold,
 for your crimes that your mother was dismissed.

RESPONSORY   Isaiah 49:15; see Psalm 27:10

Could a mother ever forget her infant,
and not take compassion on the child of her womb?
—Even if a mother should forget,
I would never forget you, says the Lord.

My father and my mother have neglected me,
but you, Lord, have lifted me up.
—Even if a . . .

SECOND READING

From a commentary on Luke by Venerable Bede, priest

(Lib. 1, 46-55: CCL 120, 37-39)

The Magnificat

Mary said: My soul proclaims the greatness of the Lord, my spirit rejoices in God my Savior.

The Lord has exalted me by a gift so great, so unheard of, that language is useless to describe it, and the depths of love in my heart can scarcely grasp it. I offer then all the powers of my soul in praise and thanksgiving. As I contemplate his greatness, which knows no limits, I joyfully surrender my whole life, my senses, my judgment, for my spirit rejoices in the eternal Godhead of that Jesus, that Savior, whom I have conceived in this world of time.

The Almighty has done great things for me, and holy is his name.

Mary looks back to the beginning of her song, where she said: *My soul proclaims the greatness of the Lord.* Only that soul for whom the Lord in his love does great things can proclaim his greatness with fitting praise and encourage those who share her desire and purpose, saying: *Join with me in proclaiming the greatness of the Lord; let us extol his name together.*

Those who know the Lord, yet refuse to proclaim his greatness and sanctify his name to the limit of their power, *will be called least in the kingdom of heaven.* His name is called holy because in the sublimity of his unique power he surpasses every creature and is far removed from all that he has made.

He has come to the help of his servant Israel for he has remembered his promise of mercy.

In a beautiful phrase Mary calls Israel the servant of the Lord. The Lord came to his aid to save him. Israel is an obedient and humble servant, in the words of Hosea: *Israel was a servant, and I loved him.*

Those who refuse to be humble cannot be saved. They cannot say with the prophet: *See, God comes to my aid; the Lord is the helper of my soul.* But *anyone who makes himself humble like a little child is greater in the kingdom of heaven.*

The promise he made to our fathers, to Abraham and his children for ever.

This does not refer to the physical descendants of Abraham, but to his spiritual children. These are his descendants, sprung not from the flesh only, but who, whether circumcised or not, have followed him in faith. Circumcised as he was, Abraham believed, and this was credited to him as an act of righteousness.

The coming of the Savior was promised to Abraham and to his descendants for ever. These are the children of promise, to whom it is said: *If you belong to Christ, then you are descendants of Abraham, heirs in accordance with the promise.*

RESPONSORY   Luke 1:48-50

From this day all generations will call me blessed.
—The Almighty has done great things for me,
holy is his Name.

He has mercy on those who fear him
in every generation.
—The Almighty has . . .

Prayer, as in Morning Prayer.

Morning Prayer

The antiphons are given in the proper place in the Psalter.

READING Isaiah 45:8

Let justice descend, O heavens, like dew from above,
  like gentle rain let the skies drop it down.
Let the earth open and salvation bud forth;
  let justice also spring up.

RESPONSORY

Your light will come, Jerusalem;
the Lord will dawn on you in radiant beauty.
—Your light will come, Jerusalem;
the Lord will dawn on you in radiant beauty.

You will see his glory within you;
—the Lord will dawn on you in radiant beauty.

Glory to the Father . . .
—Your light will . . .

CANTICLE OF ZECHARIAH

Ant.   The moment that your greeting reached my ears,
       the child within my womb leapt for joy.

INTERCESSIONS

To Christ our Redeemer, who comes to save us from our
  sins, let us cry out with joy:
    Come, Lord Jesus!
The prophets of old foretold your birth among us,
—now make virtue come to life in us.
We proclaim your saving work,
—now grant us your salvation.
You came to heal the contrite of heart,
—heal the weaknesses of your people.
You came and saw fit to reconcile the world,

—when you come again in judgment, free us from the
  torments of punishment.

Our Father . . .

Prayer

God our Father,
you sent your Son
to free mankind from the power of death.
May we who celebrate the coming of Christ as man
share more fully in his divine life,
for he lives and reigns with you and the Holy Spirit,
one God, for ever and ever.

Daytime Prayer

Midmorning

Ant.   This is the good news the prophets foretold: The
        Savior will be born of the Virgin Mary.

READING   Micah 5:3-4a'

The ruler in Israel shall stand firm and shepherd his flock
    by the strength of the Lord,
    in the majestic name of the Lord, his God;
And they shall remain, for now his greatness
    shall reach to the ends of the earth;
    he shall be peace.

The nations will revere your name, O Lord.
—And the great ones of the earth will acknowledge your
  glory.

Midday

Ant.   The angel Gabriel said to Mary in greeting: Hail,
        full of grace, the Lord is with you; blessed are you
        among women.

READING   Haggai 2:6b, 9

One moment yet, a little while,
  and I will shake the heavens and the earth,
  the sea and the dry land.
Greater will be the future glory of this house
  than the former;
And in this house I will give peace,
  says the Lord of hosts!

Remember us, Lord, because of the love you have for
  your people.
—Come and bring us your salvation.

Midafternoon

Ant.   Mary said: My soul is deeply troubled; what can
        this greeting mean? Am I to give birth to my King
        and yet remain a virgin for ever?

READING   Malachi 3:20

For you who fear my name, there will arise
  the sun of justice with its healing rays;
And you will gambol like calves out of the stall,
  says the Lord of hosts.

Come, Lord, do not delay.
—Free your people from their sinfulness.

Prayer, as in Morning Prayer.

Evening Prayer

The antiphons are given in the proper place in the Psalter.

READING   James 5:7-8, 9b

Be patient, my brothers, until the coming of the Lord.
See how the farmer awaits the precious yield of the soil.
He looks forward to it patiently while the soil receives the

winter and the spring rains. You, too, must be patient. Steady your hearts, because the coming of the Lord is at hand. See! The judge stands at the gate.

RESPONSORY

Come and set us free, Lord God of power and might.
—Come and set us free, Lord God of power and might.

Let your face shine upon us and we shall be saved,
—Lord God of power and might.

Glory to the Father . . .
—Come and set . . .

CANTICLE OF MARY

Ant. O King of all the nations, the only joy of every human heart; O Keystone of the mighty arch of man, come and save the creature you fashioned from the dust.

INTERCESSIONS

To Christ our Lord, who humbled himself for our sake, we joyfully say:
Come, Lord Jesus!
Lord Jesus, by your coming you rescued the world from sin,
—cleanse our souls and bodies from guilt.
By the mystery of your incarnation we are made your brothers and sisters,
—do not let us become estranged from you.
Do not judge harshly,
—those you redeemed with such great cost.
No age, O Christ, is without your goodness and holy riches,
—enable us to merit the enduring crown of your glory.

Lord, to you we commend the souls of your departed
    servants,
—having died to the world, may they be alive in you for
    ever.

Our Father . . .

Prayer

God our Father,
you sent your Son
to free mankind from the power of death.
May we who celebrate the coming of Christ as man
share more fully in his divine life,
for he lives and reigns with you and the Holy Spirit,
one God, for ever and ever.

DECEMBER 23

Office of Readings

Let your compassion come upon me, Lord.
—Your salvation, true to your promise.

FIRST READING

From the book of the prophet Isaiah   51:1-11

The salvation promised to the children of Abraham

Listen to me, you who pursue justice,
    who seek the Lord;
Look to the rock from which you were hewn,
    to the pit from which you were quarried;
Look to Abraham, your father,
    and to Sarah, who gave you birth;
When he was but one I called him,
    I blessed him and made him many.

Yes, the Lord shall comfort Zion
    and have pity on all her ruins;
Her deserts he shall make like Eden,
    her wasteland like the garden of the Lord;
Joy and gladness shall be found in her,
    thanksgiving and the sound of song.

Be attentive to me, my people;
    my folk, give ear to me.
For law shall go forth from my presence,
    and my judgment, as the light of the peoples.
I will make my justice come speedily;
    my salvation shall go forth
    [and my arm shall judge the nations];
In me shall the coastlands hope,
    and my arm they shall await.

Raise your eyes to the heavens,
    and look at the earth below;
Though the heavens grow thin like smoke,
    the earth wears out like a garment
    and its inhabitants die like flies,
My salvation shall remain forever
    and my justice shall never be dismayed.

Hear me, you who know justice,
    you people who have my teaching at heart:
Fear not the reproach of men,
    be not dismayed at their revilings.
They shall be like a garment eaten by moths,
    like wool consumed by grubs;
But my justice shall remain forever
    and my salvation, for all generations.

Awake, awake, put on strength,
    O arm of the Lord!

Awake as in the days of old,
   in ages long ago!
Was it not you who crushed Rahab,
   you who pierced the dragon?
Was it not you who dried up the sea,
   the waters of the great deep,
Who made the depths of the sea into a way
   for the redeemed to pass over?

Those whom the Lord has ransomed will return
   and enter Zion singing,
   crowned with everlasting joy;
They will meet with joy and gladness,
   sorrow and mourning will flee.

RESPONSORY   See Isaiah 51:4, 5; 35:10

My people, listen to me;
hear me, all you who belong to my race;
—close at hand is my Just One, my Savior draws near.

Now those redeemed by the Lord will come back and
   enter Zion with songs of praise.
—Close at hand . . .

SECOND READING

From a treatise against the heresy of Noetus by Saint Hippolytus, priest

(Cap. 9-12: PG 10, 815-819)

The manifestation of the hidden mystery

There is only one God, brethren, and we learn about him only from sacred Scripture. It is therefore our duty to become acquainted with what Scripture proclaims and to investigate its teachings thoroughly. We should believe them in the sense that the Father wills, thinking of the Son in the way the Father wills, and accepting the

teaching he wills to give us with regard to the Holy
Spirit. Sacred Scripture is God's gift to us and it should
be understood in the way that he intends: we should not
do violence to it by interpreting it according to our own
preconceived ideas.

God was all alone and nothing existed but himself when
he determined to create the world. He thought of it, willed
it, spoke the word and so made it. It came into being in-
stantaneously, exactly as he had willed. It is enough then
for us to be aware of a single fact: nothing is coeternal
with God. Apart from God there was simply nothing else.
Yet although he was alone, he was manifold because he
lacked neither reason, wisdom, power nor counsel. All
things were in him and he himself was all. At a moment
of his own choosing and in a manner determined by himself, God manifested his Word, and through him he
made the whole universe.

When the Word was hidden within God himself he was
invisible to the created world, but God made him visible.
First God gave utterance to his voice, engendering light
from light, and then he sent his own mind into the world
as its Lord. Visible before to God alone and not to the
world, God made him visible so that the world could be
saved by seeing him. This mind that entered our world
was made known as the Son of God. All things came into
being through him; but he alone is begotten by the
Father.

The Son gave us the law and the prophets, and he filled
the prophets with the Holy Spirit to compel them to
speak out. Inspired by the Father's power, they were to
proclaim the Father's purpose and his will.

So the Word was made manifest, as Saint John
declares when, summing up all the sayings of the
prophets, he announces that this is the Word through
whom the whole universe was made. He says: *In the*

beginning was the Word, and the Word was with God, and the Word was God. Through him all things came into being; not one thing was created without him. And further on he adds: The world was made through him, and yet the world did not know him. He entered his own creation, and his own did not receive him.

RESPONSORY   See Isaiah 9:6, 7; John 1:4

A little child is born to us,
and he shall be called the mighty God.
—He himself will sit upon the throne of David his father
   to rule; the authority of David rests on his shoulders.

In him was life, and the life was the light of men.
—He himself will . . .

Prayer, as in Morning Prayer.

Morning Prayer

The antiphons are given in the proper place in the Psalter.

READING   Jeremiah 30:21, 22

   Thus says the Lord:
His leader shall be from Jacob,
   and his rulers shall come from his kin.
When I summon him,
   he shall approach me.
You shall be my people,
   and I will be your God.

RESPONSORY

Your light will come, Jerusalem;
the Lord will dawn on you in radiant beauty.
—Your light will come, Jerusalem;
the Lord will dawn on you in radiant beauty.

You will see his glory within you;
—the Lord will dawn on you in radiant beauty.

Glory to the Father . . .
—Your light will . . .

CANTICLE OF ZECHARIAH

Ant.   All that God promised to the virgin through the
message of the angel has been accomplished.

INTERCESSIONS

Let us pray to God our Father who sent his Son to save
mankind:
Show us your mercy, Lord.
Father most merciful, we confess our faith in your Christ
with our words,
—keep us from denying him in our actions.
You have sent your Son to rescue us,
—remove every sorrow from the face of the earth and
from our country.
Our land looks forward with delight at the approach of
your Son,
—let it experience the fullness of your joy.
Through your mercy make us live holy and chaste lives in
this world,
—eagerly awaiting the blessed hope and coming of Christ
in glory.

Our Father . . .

Prayer

Father,
we contemplate the birth of your Son.
He was born of the Virgin Mary
and came to live among us.
May we receive forgiveness and mercy
through our Lord Jesus Christ, your Son,
who lives and reigns with you and the Holy Spirit,
one God, for ever and ever.

Daytime Prayer

Midmorning

Ant.   This is the good news the prophets foretold: The Savior will be born of the Virgin Mary.

READING   Jeremiah 29:11, 13

I know well the plans I have in mind for you, says the Lord, plans for your welfare, not for woe! plans to give you a future full of hope. When you look for me, you will find me, yes, when you seek me with all your heart.

The nations will revere your name, O Lord.
—And the great ones of the earth will acknowledge your glory.

Midday

Ant.   The angel Gabriel said to Mary in greeting: Hail, full of grace, the Lord is with you; blessed are you among women.

READING   Jeremiah 30:18a

Thus says the Lord:
See! I will restore the tents of Jacob,
    his dwellings I will pity.

Remember us, Lord, because of the love you have for your people.
—Come and bring us your salvation.

Midafternoon

Ant.   Mary said: My soul is deeply troubled; what can this greeting mean? Am I to give birth to my King and yet remain a virgin for ever?

READING   Baruch 3:5-6a

Remember at this time not the misdeeds of our fathers, but your own hand and name; for you are the Lord our God.

Come, Lord, do not delay.
—Free your people from their sinfulness.

Prayer, as in Morning Prayer.

Evening Prayer

The antiphons are given in the proper place in the Psalter.

READING   2 Peter 3:8b-9

In the Lord's eyes, one day is as a thousand years and a thousand years are as a day. The Lord does not delay in keeping his promise—though some consider it "delay." Rather, he shows you generous patience, since he wants none to perish but all to come to repentance.

RESPONSORY

Come and set us free, Lord God of power and might.
—Come and set us free, Lord God of power and might.

Let your face shine upon us and we shall be saved,
—Lord God of power and might.

Glory to the Father . . .
—Come and set . . .

CANTICLE OF MARY

Ant.   O Emmanuel, king and lawgiver, desire of the nations, Savior of all people, come and set us free, Lord our God.

INTERCESSIONS

To our Redeemer who came to bring good news to the
  poor, let us earnestly pray:
  Let all men see your glory.
Show yourself to those who have never known you,
  —let them see your saving work.
Let your name be preached to the ends of the earth,
  —that all may find the way to you.
You came first to save the world,
  —now come again and save those who believe in you.
You brought freedom to us by saving us,
  —continue to save us and make us free.
You came once as a man; you will return in judgment,
  —bring eternal reward to those who have died.

Our Father . . .

Prayer

Father,
we contemplate the birth of your Son.
He was born of the Virgin Mary
and came to live among us.
May we receive forgiveness and mercy
through our Lord Jesus Christ, your Son,
who lives and reigns with you and the Holy Spirit,
one God, for ever and ever.

DECEMBER 24

Invitatory

Ant.   Today you will know the Lord is coming, and in
       the morning you will see his glory.

Invitatory psalm, as in the Ordinary, 648.

Office of Readings

HYMN, 132.

Psalms and antiphons from the current weekday.

The Lord proclaims his word to Jacob.
—His law and decrees to Israel.

FIRST READING

From the book
of the prophet Isaiah   51:17—52:2, 7-10

The good news is brought to Jerusalem

Awake, awake!
    Arise, O Jerusalem,
You who drank at the Lord's hand
    the cup of his wrath;
Who drained to the dregs
    the bowl of staggering!
She has no one to guide her
    of all the sons she bore;
She has no one to grasp her by the hand,
    of all the sons she reared!—

Your misfortunes are double;
    who is there to condole with you?
Desolation and destruction, famine and sword!
    Who is there to comfort you?
Your sons lie helpless
    at every street corner
    like antelopes in a net.
They are filled with the wrath of the Lord,
    the rebuke of your God.

But now, hear this, O afflicted one,
    drunk, but not with wine,

Thus says the Lord, your Master,
    your God, who defends his people:

See, I am taking from your hand
    the cup of staggering;
The bowl of my wrath
    you shall no longer drink.
I will put it into the hands of your tormentors,
    those who ordered you
        to bow down, that they might walk over you,
While you offered your back like the ground,
    like the street for them to walk on.

Awake, awake!
    Put on your strength, O Zion;
Put on your glorious garments,
    O Jerusalem, holy city.
No longer shall the uncircumcised
    or the unclean enter you.

Shake off the dust,
    ascend to the throne, Jerusalem;
Loose the bonds from your neck,
    O captive daughter Zion!

How beautiful upon the mountains
    are the feet of him who brings glad tidings,
Announcing peace, bearing good news,
    announcing salvation, and saying to Zion,
    "Your God is King!"
Hark! Your watchmen raise a cry,
    together they shout for joy,
For they see directly, before their eyes,
    the Lord restoring Zion.

Break out together in song,
    O ruins of Jerusalem!

For the Lord comforts his people,
  he redeems Jerusalem.
The Lord has bared his holy arm
  in the sight of all the nations;
All the ends of the earth will behold
  the salvation of our God.

RESPONSORY   See Ex. 19:10, 11; Dt. 7:15; see Dn. 9:24

Cleanse yourselves, sons of Israel, says the Lord;
for tomorrow your Lord will come down,
—and he will take away from you all weaknesses.

Tomorrow the wickedness of the earth will be destroyed,
and the Savior of the world will rule over us.
—And he will . . .

SECOND READING

From a sermon by Saint Augustine, bishop

(Sermo 185: PL 38, 997-999)

*Truth has arisen from the earth, and justice looked down
from heaven*

Awake, mankind! For your sake God has become man.
*Awake, you who sleep, rise up from the dead, and Christ
will enlighten you.* I tell you again: for your sake, God
became man.

You would have suffered eternal death, had he not
been born in time. Never would you have been freed
from sinful flesh, had he not taken on himself the
likeness of sinful flesh. You would have suffered
everlasting unhappiness, had it not been for this mercy.
You would never have returned to life, had he not shared
your death. You would have been lost if he had not
hastened to your aid. You would have perished, had he
not come.

Let us then joyfully celebrate the coming of our salvation and redemption. Let us celebrate the festive day on which he who is the great and eternal day came from the great and endless day of eternity into our own short day of time.

He has become our justice, our sanctification, our redemption, so that, as it is written: Let him who glories glory in the Lord.

Truth, then, has arisen from the earth: Christ who said, *I am the Truth*, was born of a virgin. *And justice looked down from heaven:* because believing in this new-born child, man is justified not by himself but by God.

Truth has arisen from the earth: because *the Word was made flesh. And justice looked down from heaven:* because *every good gift and every perfect gift is from above.*

Truth has arisen from the earth: flesh from Mary. *And justice looked down from heaven:* for *man can receive nothing unless it has been given him from heaven.*

Justified by faith, let us be at peace with God: for *justice and peace have embraced one another. Through our Lord Jesus Christ:* for *Truth has arisen from the earth. Through whom we have access to that grace in which we stand, and our boast is in our hope of God's glory.* He does not say: "of our glory," but *of God's glory:* for *justice* has not proceeded from us but has *looked down from heaven.* Therefore *he who glories, let him glory,* not in himself, but *in the Lord.*

For this reason, when our Lord was born of the Virgin, the message of the angelic voices was: *Glory to God in the highest, and peace to his people on earth.*

For how could there be peace on earth unless *Truth has arisen from the earth,* that is, unless Christ were born of our flesh? And *he is our peace who made the two into one:* that we might be men of good will, sweetly linked by the bond of unity.

Let us then rejoice in this grace, so that our glorying may bear witness to our good conscience by which we glory, not in ourselves, but in the Lord. That is why Scripture says: *He is my glory, the one who lifts up my head.* For what greater grace could God have made to dawn on us than to make his only Son become the son of man, so that a son of man might in his turn become son of God?

Ask if this were merited; ask for its reason, for its justification, and see whether you will find any other answer but sheer grace.

<small>RESPONSORY</small>   Isaiah 11:1, 5, 2

A shoot shall grow from the root of Jesse,
and there a flower shall blossom.
—Justice will be the girdle around his loins,
and faithfulness the belt around his waist.

The Spirit of the Lord will rest upon him:
a spirit of wisdom and understanding, a spirit of counsel
    and fortitude
—Justice will be . . .

If December 24 occurs on Sunday, the Te Deum, 651, is said.

Prayer, as in Morning Prayer.

Morning Prayer

<small>HYMN,</small> 132.

Ant. 1   Bethlehem in Judah's land, how glorious your
future! The king who will rule my people comes
from you.

Psalms and canticle from the current weekday.

Ant. 2   Lift up your heads and see; your redemption is
now at hand.

Ant. 3 The day has come at last when Mary will bring
forth her firstborn Son.

READING Isaiah 11:1-3a

A shoot shall sprout from the stump of Jesse,
    and from his roots a bud shall blossom.
The spirit of the Lord shall rest upon him:
    a spirit of wisdom and of understanding,
A spirit of counsel and of strength,
    a spirit of knowledge and of fear of the Lord,
    and his delight shall be the fear of the Lord.

RESPONSORY

Tomorrow will be the day of your salvation,
the sinfulness of earth will be destroyed.
—Tomorrow will be the day of your salvation,
the sinfulness of earth will be destroyed.

The Savior of the world will be our king;
—the sinfulness of earth will be destroyed.

Glory to the Father . . .
—Tomorrow will be . . .

CANTICLE OF ZECHARIAH

Ant The time has come for Mary to give birth to her
firstborn Son.

INTERCESSIONS

To Jesus Christ, our Redeemer, who will come again in
    glory with great power, let us make our humble
    prayer:
    Come, Lord Jesus!
Lord Jesus, you will come with great power,
—look on our lowliness and make us worthy of your
    gifts.

You came to be the good news for mankind,
—may we always proclaim your saving work.
You are worthy of praise, for you have life and rule all
    things,
—help us to wait in joyful hope for the coming of your
    glory.
We long for the grace of your coming,
—console us with the gift of your own divine life.

Our Father . . .

Prayer

Come, Lord Jesus,
do not delay;
give new courage to your people who trust in your love.
By your coming, raise us to the joy of your kingdom,
where you live and reign with the Father and the Holy
    Spirit,
one God, for ever and ever.

Daytime Prayer
Midmorning

Ant.   This is the good news the prophets foretold: The
        Savior will be born of the Virgin Mary.

READING   Isaiah 4:2

    On that day,
The branch of the Lord will be luster and glory,
    and the fruit of the earth will be honor and splendor
    for the survivors of Israel.

The nations will revere your name, O Lord.
—And the great ones of the earth will acknowledge your
    glory.

Midday

Ant.   The angel Gabriel said to Mary in greeting: Hail,
       full of grace, the Lord is with you; blessed are you
       among women.

READING   Isaiah 4:3

He who remains in Zion
    and he that is left in Jerusalem
Will be called holy:
    every one marked down for life in Jerusalem.

Remember us, Lord, because of the love you have for
    your people.
—Come and bring us your salvation.

Midafternoon

Ant.   Mary said: My soul is deeply troubled; what can
       this greeting mean? Am I to give birth to my King
       and yet remain a virgin for ever?

READING   Isaiah 61:11

As the earth brings forth its plants,
    and a garden makes its growth spring up,
So will the Lord God make justice and praise
    spring up before all the nations.

Come, Lord, do not delay.
—Free your people from their sinfulness.

Prayer, as in Morning Prayer.

CHRISTMAS SEASON

One of the following hymns may be used:

Antiphon:

Unto us a Child is born, unto us a Son is given.
Eternal is his sway.

The people who walk in darkness have seen a great
light;
For men abiding in the land of death, a new splendor
has appeared;
To them you have brought abundant joy; before you
they rejoice,
As with the joy at harvest, as men rejoice when
dividing spoils.

Antiphon

For the yoke of his burden and the bar on his
shoulder,
And the rod of the oppressor you have broken, as on
the day of Madian;
For ev'ry boot that tramped in battle, for every
cloak that rolled in blood,
Will be set aside, will go to feed the blazing fire.

Antiphon

For to us a Child is born, to our race a Son is given;
His shoulders will bear the scepter of his reign, and
his name shall be called:
Counselor of marvelous deeds, Mighty Warrior of
God, everlasting Father of
nations, and royal Prince of Peace.

Antiphon

Ever wider shall his dominion be over his kingdom;
Upon the throne of David, in a peace that never
ends.

He has established it and made it firm, based on
   justice and on right;
Both now and forever the Lord of hosts will do these
   mighty deeds.

Antiphon

Melody: A Child is Born   Music: Lucien Deiss, C.S.Sp., 1965
                                  Text: Lucien Deiss, C.S.Sp., 1965
Or:

From heaven high I come to you,
I bring you tidings good and new;
Good tidings of great joy I bring;
Thereof will I both say and sing:

For you a little child is born
Of God's own chosen maid this morn,
A fair and tender baby bright,
To be your joy and your delight.

Lo, he is Christ, the Lord indeed,
Our God to guide you in your need,
And he will be your Savior, strong
To cleanse you from all sin and wrong.

Melody: Vom Himmel Hoch L.M.   Music: *Geistliche Lieder*,
                                            Leipzig, 1539
                                  Text: Vom Himmel Hoch,
                                     Martin Luther, 1483-1546
                           Translator: Winfred Douglas, 1867-1944
Or:

Refrain:

Go tell it on the mountain
Over the hills and everywhere,
Go tell it on the mountain,
Our Jesus Christ is born.

When I was a learner,
I sought both night and day;
I asked the Lord to help me,
And he showed me the way.

While shepherds kept their watching
O'er wand'ring flocks at night;
Behold from out the heavens
There came a holy light.

Lo, when they had seen it,
They all bowed down and prayed;
They traveled on together
To where the babe was laid.

Melody: Go Tell It On The Mountain   Music: Negro Spiritual
Or: Text: Anon.

Candor aeternae Deitatis alme,
Christe, tu lumen venis atque vita,
advenis morbis hominum medela,
    porta salutis.

Intonat terrae chorus angelorum
caelicum carmen, nova saecla dicens,
gloriam Patri, generique nostro
    gaudia pacis.

Qui iaces parvus dominans et orbi,
Virginis fructus sine labe sanctae,
Christe, iam mundo potiaris omni,
    semper amandus.

Nasceris caelos patriam daturus,
unus e nobis, caro nostra factus;
innova mentes, trahe caritatis
    pectora vinclis.

Coetus exsultans canit ecce noster,
angelis laeto sociatus ore,
et Patri tecum parilique Amori
    cantica laudis. Amen.

Or:

O come, all ye faithful, joyful and triumphant,
O come ye, O come ye to Bethlehem;
Come and behold him, born the King of angels;

Refrain:

O come, let us adore him,
O come, let us adore him,
O come, let us adore him,
Christ the Lord.

Sing, choirs of angels, sing in exultation,
Sing, all ye citizens of heaven above;
Glory to God, in the highest glory:

Refrain

Savior, we greet thee, born this happy morning,
Jesus, to thee be all glory giv'n;
Word of the Father, now in flesh appearing:

Refrain

Melody: Adeste Fideles   Music: J.F. Wade, 1751
                                         Text: Latin, 18th century
                              Translator: Frederick Oakeley, 1841 et al.

Or:

Adeste fideles, laeti triumphantes:
Venite, venite in Bethlehem:
Natum videte Regem Angelorum:

Refrain:

Venite, adoremus,
Venite, adoremus,
Venite adoremus Dominum.

En grege relicto, humiles ad cunas
Vocati pastores approparant:
Et nos ovanti gradu festinemus:

Refrain

Aeterni Parentis splendorem aeternum
Velatum sub carne videbimus:
Deum infantem, pannis involutum:

Refrain

Pro nobis egenum et foeno cubantem
Piis foveamus amplexibus:
Sic nos amentem quis non redamaret?

Refrain

Melody: Adeste Fideles   Music: J. F. Wade, 1711-1786
                                Text: Latin: 18th century

Or:

Songs of praise the angels sang,
Heav'n with alleluias rang,
When creation was begun,
When God spoke and it was done.

Songs of praise awoke the morn
When the Prince of Peace was born;
Songs of praise arose when he
Captive led captivity.

Heav'n and earth must pass away,
Songs of praise shall crown that day;
God will make new heav'n and earth,
Songs of praise shall hail their birth.

And will voice of man be dumb
Till that glorious kingdom come?
No, the Church delights to raise
Psalms and hymns and songs of praise.

Saints below, with hearts and voice,
Still in songs of praise rejoice,
Learning here, by faith and love,
Songs of praise to sing above.

Borne upon their final breath,
Songs of praise shall conquer death;
Then, amidst eternal joy,
Songs of praise their powers employ.

Melody: Lauds 77.77

Music: John Wilson
Text: James Montgomery
1771-1854, adapted
by Anthony G. Petti

Or:

Virgin born, we bow before you;
Blessed was the womb that bore you;
Mary, Mother meek and mild,
Blessed was she in her Child.
Blessed was the maid that fed you;
Blessed was the hand that led you;
Blessed was the parent's eye
That watched your slumbering infancy.

Blessed she by all creation,
Who brought forth the world's salvation;
And blessed they forever blest,
Who love you most and serve you best.
Virgin born, we bow before you:
Blessed was the womb that bore you;
Mary, Mother meek and mild,
Blessed was she in her Child.

Melody: Mon Dieu, Prete Moi   Music: *Genevan Psalter*, 1543
L'Oreille 88-77.D   Text: R. Heber, 1783-1826, alt.
(Genevan Psalm 86)

Or:

What child is this, who, laid to rest,
On Mary's lap is sleeping?
Whom angels greet with anthems sweet,
While shepherds watch are keeping?
This, this is Christ the King,
Whom shepherds guard and angels sing;

Haste, haste to bring him laud,
The Babe, the Son of Mary.

Why lies he in such mean estate,
Where ox and ass are feeding?
Good Christian, fear, for sinners here
The silent Word is pleading.
Nails, spear, shall pierce him through,
The cross be borne for me, for you:
Hail, hail, the Word made flesh,
The Babe, the Son of Mary!

So bring him incense, gold and myrrh,
Come, peasant, king, to own him;
The King of Kings salvation brings,
Let loving hearts enthrone him.
Raise, raise the song on high,
The virgin sings her lullaby:
Joy, joy, for Christ is born,
The Babe, the Son of Mary!

Melody: Greensleeves   Music: 16th century English Melody
87.87.68.67   Text: William Chatterton Dix, 1837-1898

Or:

A Child is born in Bethlehem, alleluia;
O come, rejoice Jerusalem, alleluia, alleluia.

Refrain:

Let grateful hearts now sing,
A song of joy and holy praise
To Christ the new-born King.

Though found within a manger poor, alleluia,
His Kingdom shall for e'er endure, alleluia, alleluia.

Refrain

As brother in the flesh he came, alleluia,
Our King whose name we now proclaim, alleluia, al-
    leluia.

Refrain

Melody: Gregorian, Mode I   Music: Traditional, Gregorian
Text: *Puer Natus in Bethlehem*
Translator: J. W. Hewett, 1859, alt.

Or:

Christe, redemptor omnium,
ex Patre, Patris Unice,
solus ante principium
natus ineffabiliter,

Tu lumen, tu splendor Patris,
tu spes perennis omnium,
intende quas fundunt preces
tui per orbem servuli.

Salutis auctor, recole
quod nostri quondam corporis,
ex illibata Virgine
nascendo, formam sumpseris.

Hic praesens testatur dies,
currens per anni circulum,
quod solus a sede Patris
mundi salus adveneris;

Hunc caelum, terra, hunc mare,
hunc omne quod in eis est,
auctorem adventus tui
laudat exsultans cantico.

Nos quoque, qui sancto tuo
redempti sumus sanguine,
ob diem natalis tui
hymnum novum concinimus.

Iesu, tibi sit gloria,
qui natus es de Virgine,
cum Patre et almo Spiritu,
in sempiterna saecula. Amen.

Or:

A solis ortus cardine
adusque terrae limitem
Christum canamus principem,
natum Maria Virgine.

Beatus auctor saeculi
servile corpus induit,
ut carne carnem liberans
non perderet quod condidit.

Clausae parentis viscera
caelestis intrat gratia;
venter puellae baiulat
secreta quae non noverat.

Domus pudici pectoris
templum repente fit Dei;
intacta nesciens virum
verbo concepit Filium.

Enixa est puerpera
quem Gabriel praedixerat,
quem matris alvo gestiens
clausus Ioannes senserat.

Feno iacere pertulit,
praesepe non abhorruit,
parvoque lacte pastus est
per quem nec ales esurit.

Gaudet chorus caelestium
et angeli canunt Deum,
palamque fit pastoribus
pastor, creator omnium.

Iesu, tibi sit gloria,
qui natus es de Virgine,
cum Patre et almo Spiritu,
in sempiterna saecula. Amen.

December 25

CHRISTMAS

Evening Prayer I

HYMN

Unto us a Child is given,
Christ our Savior bring release;
Counselor, Eternal Father,
God made man, and Prince of Peace.

Born of Mary, gentle virgin,
By the Spirit of the Lord;
From eternal ages spoken:
This the mighty Father's Word.

Love and truth in him shall flower,
From his strength their vigor take.
Branches that are bare shall blossom;
Joy that slept begins to wake.

Praise the everlasting Father,
And the Word, his only Son;
Praise them with the holy Spirit,
Perfect Trinity in One.

Melody: Drakes Boughton 87.87   Music: S. P. Waddington
                                  Text: Stanbrook Abbey

PSALMODY

Ant. 1 He comes in splendor, the King who is our
        peace; the whole world longs to see him.

Psalm 113

Praise, O servants of the Lord,
praise the name of the Lord!

394

May the name of the Lord be blessed
both now and for evermore!
From the rising of the sun to its setting
praised be the name of the Lord!

High above all nations is the Lord,
above the heavens his glory.
Who is like the Lord, our God,
who has risen on high to his throne
yet stoops from the heights to look down,
to look down upon heaven and earth?

From the dust he lifts up the lowly,
from his misery he raises the poor
to set him in the company of princes,
yes, with the princes of his people.
To the childless wife he gives a home
and gladdens her heart with children.

Ant.   He comes in splendor, the King who is our peace;
        the whole world longs to see him.

Ant. 2 He sends forth his word to the earth, and his
        command spreads swiftly through the land.

Psalm 147: 12-20

O praise the Lord, Jerusalem!
Zion, praise your God!

He has strengthened the bars of your gates,
he has blessed the children within you.
He established peace on your borders,
he feeds you with finest wheat.

He sends out his word to the earth
and swiftly runs his command.
He showers down snow white as wool,
he scatters hoar-frost like ashes.

He hurls down hailstones like crumbs.
The waters are frozen at his touch;
he sends forth his word and it melts them:
at the breath of his mouth the waters flow.

He makes his word known to Jacob,
to Israel his laws and decrees.
He has not dealt thus with other nations,
he has not taught them his decrees.

Ant. He sends forth his word to the earth, and his command spreads swiftly through the land.

Ant. 3 The eternal Word, born of the Father before time began, today emptied himself for our sake and became man.

Canticle   Philippians 2:6-11

Though he was in the form of God,
Jesus did not deem equality with God
something to be grasped at.

Rather, he emptied himself
and took the form of a slave,
being born in the likeness of men.

He was known to be of human estate,
and it was thus that he humbled himself,
obediently accepting even death,
death on a cross!

Because of this,
God highly exalted him
and bestowed on him the name
above every other name,

So that at Jesus' name
every knee must bend
in the heavens, on the earth,

and under the earth,
and every tongue proclaim
to the glory of God the Father:
JESUS CHRIST IS LORD!

Ant.   The eternal Word, born of the Father before time
began, today emptied himself for our sake and
became man.

READING   Galatians 4:4-5

When the designated time had come, God sent forth
his Son born of a woman, born under the law, to deliver
from the law those who were subjected to it, so that we
might receive our status as adopted sons.

RESPONSORY

Today you will know the Lord is coming.
—Today you will know the Lord is coming.

And in the morning you will see his glory.
—The Lord is coming.

Glory to the Father . . .
—Today you will . . .

CANTICLE OF MARY

Ant.   When the sun rises in the morning sky, you will
see the King of kings coming forth from the Father like a radiant bridegroom from the bridal
chamber.

INTERCESSIONS

Christ Jesus emptied himself and took the form of a
slave. He was tested like us in all things and did not
sin. Now let us worship him and pray to him with
deep faith:
By the power of your birth, comfort those who are saved.

You came into the world heralding the new age foretold
   by the prophets,
—give your holy people the gift of renewal in every
   generation.
You once took on the weakness of our human condition,
—be light now for those who do not see, strength for the
   wavering and comfort for the troubled of heart.
You were born into poverty and lowliness,
—look with favor on the poor and comfort them.
By your birth bring joy to all peoples with the promise of
   unending life,
—give joy to the dying through the hope of heavenly
   birth.
You came to earth to lead everyone into the kingdom,
—share your life of glory with those who have died.

Our Father . . .

Prayer

God our Father,
every year we rejoice
as we look forward to this feast of our salvation.
May we welcome Christ as our Redeemer,
and meet him with confidence when he comes to be our
   judge,
who lives and reigns with you and the Holy Spirit,
one God, for ever and ever.

Alternative Prayer

God of endless ages, Father of all goodness,
we keep vigil for the dawn of salvation
and the birth of your Son.
With gratitude we recall his humanity,
the life he shared with the sons of men.
May the power of his divinity
help us answer his call to forgiveness and life.
We ask this through Christ our Lord.

Night prayer is said by those who do not participate in the
Office of Readings and in the Mass at midnight.

Invitatory

Ant.   Christ is born for us; come, let us adore him.

Invitatory psalm, as in the Ordinary, 648.

Office of Readings

HYMN

What child is this, who, laid to rest,
On Mary's lap is sleeping?
Whom angels greet with anthems sweet,
While shepherds watch are keeping?
This, this is Christ the King,
Whom shepherds guard and angels sing;
Haste, haste to bring him laud,
The Babe the Son of Mary.

Why lies he in such mean estate,
Where ox and ass are feeding?
Good Christian, fear, for sinners here
The silent Word is pleading.
Nails, spear, shall pierce him through,
The cross be borne for me, for you:
Hail, hail, the Word made flesh,
The Babe, the Son of Mary!

So bring him incense, gold and myrrh,
Come, peasant, king, to own him;
The King of kings salvation brings,
Let loving hearts enthrone him.
Raise, raise the song on high,
The virgin sings her lullaby:
Joy, joy, for Christ is born,
The Babe, the Son of Mary!

Melody: Greensleeves   Music: 16th century English Melody
87.87.68.67   Text: William Chatterton Dix, 1837-1898

Ant. 1   The Lord said to me: You are my Son, today I have begotten you.

Psalm 2

Why this tumult among nations,
among peoples this useless murmuring?
They arise, the kings of the earth,
princes plot against the Lord and his Anointed.
"Come, let us break their fetters,
come, let us cast off their yoke."

He who sits in the heavens laughs;
the Lord is laughing them to scorn.
Then he will speak in his anger,
his rage will strike them with terror.
"It is I who have set up my king
on Zion, my holy mountain."

I will announce the decree of the Lord:
The Lord said to me:"You are my Son.
It is I who have begotten you this day.
Ask and I shall bequeath you the nations,
put the ends of the earth in your possession.
With a rod of iron you will break them,
shatter them like a potter's jar."

Now, O kings, understand,
take warning, rulers of the earth,
serve the Lord with awe
and trembling, pay him your homage
lest he be angry and you perish;
for suddenly his anger will blaze.

Blessed are they who put their trust in God.

Ant.   The Lord said to me: You are my Son, today I have begotten you.

Ant. 2   The Lord comes forth, the bridegroom from his
          bridal chamber.

Psalm 19 A

The heavens proclaim the glory of God
and the firmament shows forth the work of his
    hands.
Day unto day takes up the story
and night unto night makes known the message.

No speech, no word, no voice is heard
yet their span extends through all the earth,
their words to the utmost bounds of the world.

There he has placed a tent for the sun;
it comes forth like a bridegroom coming from his
    tent,
rejoices like a champion to run its course.

At the end of the sky is the rising of the sun;
to the furthest end of the sky is its course.
There is nothing concealed from its burning heat.

Ant.   The Lord comes forth, the bridegroom from his
          bridal chamber.

Ant. 3   Your words are filled with grace, because God
          has blessed you for ever.

Psalm 45

My heart overflows with noble words.
To the king I must speak the song I have made;
my tongue as nimble as the pen of a scribe.

You are the fairest of the children of men
and graciousness is poured upon your lips:
because God has blessed you for evermore.

O mighty one, gird your sword upon your thigh;
in splendor and state, ride on in triumph
for the cause of truth and goodness and right.

Take aim with your bow in your dread right hand.
Your arrows are sharp: peoples fall beneath you.
The foes of the king fall down and lose heart.

Your throne, O God, shall endure for ever.
A scepter of justice is the scepter of your kingdom.
Your love is for justice; your hatred for evil.

Therefore God, your God, has anointed you
with the oil of gladness above other kings:
your robes are fragrant with aloes and myrrh.

From the ivory palace you are greeted with music.
The daughters of kings are among your loved ones.
On your right stands the queen in gold of Ophir.

Listen, O daughter, give ear to my words:
forget your own people and your father's house.
So will the king desire your beauty:
he is your lord, pay homage to him.

And the people of Tyre shall come with gifts,
the richest of the people shall seek your favor.
The daughter of the king is clothed with splendor,
her robes embroidered with pearls set in gold.

She is led to the king with her maiden companions.
They are escorted amid gladness and joy;
they pass within the palace of the king.

Sons shall be yours in place of your fathers:
you will make them princes over all the earth.
May this song make your name for ever remem-
    bered.
May the peoples praise you from age to age.

Ant.   Your words are filled with grace, because God has
            blessed you for ever.

The Word was made man, alleluia.
—He lived among us, alleluia.

From the book of the prophet Isaiah   11:1-10

The root of Jesse

Thus says the Lord God:
A shoot shall sprout from the stump of Jesse,
    and from his roots a bud shall blossom.
The spirit of the Lord shall rest upon him:
    a spirit of wisdom and of understanding,
A spirit of counsel and of strength,
    a spirit of knowledge and of fear of the Lord,
    and his delight shall be the fear of the Lord.

Not by appearance shall he judge,
    nor by hearsay shall he decide,
But he shall judge the poor with justice,
    and decide aright for the land's afflicted.
He shall strike the ruthless with the rod of his mouth,
    and with the breath of his lips he shall slay the wicked.
Justice shall be the band around his waist,
    and faithfulness a belt upon his hips.

Then the wolf shall be a guest of the lamb,
    and the leopard shall lie down with the kid;
The calf and the young lion shall browse together,
    with a little child to guide them.
The cow and the bear shall be neighbors,
    together their young shall rest;
    the lion shall eat hay like the ox.
The baby shall play by the cobra's den,
    and the child lay his hand on the adder's lair.

There shall be no harm or ruin on all my holy mountain;
   for the earth shall be filled with knowledge of the Lord
   as water covers the sea.

    On that day,
The root of Jesse,
   set up as a signal for the nations,
The Gentiles shall seek out,
   for his dwelling shall be glorious.

RESPONSORY

Today, for our sake, the King of heaven chose to be born
   of his virgin mother,
to reclaim lost men for the heavenly kingdom.
—All the angels cry aloud with joy,
for God has come himself to save mankind.

Glory to God in the highest,
and peace to his people on earth.
—All the angels . . .

SECOND READING

From a sermon by Saint Leo the Great, pope
(Sermo 1 in Nativitate Domini, 1-3; PL 54, 190-193)

Christian, remember your dignity

Dearly beloved, today our Savior is born; let us
rejoice. Sadness should have no place on the birthday of
life. The fear of death has been swallowed up; life brings
us joy with the promise of eternal happiness.

No one is shut out from this joy; all share the same
reason for rejoicing. Our Lord, victor over sin and death,
finding no man free from sin, came to free us all. Let the
saint rejoice as he sees the palm of victory at hand. Let
the sinner be glad as he receives the offer of forgiveness.
Let the pagan take courage as he is summoned to life.

In the fullness of time, chosen in the unfathomable depths of God's wisdom, the Son of God took for himself our common humanity in order to reconcile it with its creator. He came to overthrow the devil, the origin of death, in that very nature by which he had overthrown mankind.

And so at the birth of our Lord the angels sing in joy: *Glory to God in the highest,* and they proclaim *peace to his people on earth* as they see the heavenly Jerusalem being built from all the nations of the world. When the angels on high are so exultant at this marvelous work of God's goodness, what joy should it not bring to the lowly hearts of men?

Beloved, let us give thanks to God the Father, through his Son, in the Holy Spirit, because in his great love for us he took pity on us, *and when we were dead in our sins he brought us to life with Christ,* so that in him we might be a new creation. Let us throw off our old nature and all its ways and, as we have come to birth in Christ, let us renounce the works of the flesh.

Christian, remember your dignity, and now that you share in God's own nature, do not return by sin to your former base condition. Bear in mind who is your head and of whose body you are a member. Do not forget that you have been rescued from the power of darkness and brought into the light of God's kingdom.

Through the sacrament of baptism you have become a temple of the Holy Spirit. Do not drive away so great a guest by evil conduct and become again a slave to the devil, for your liberty was bought by the blood of Christ.

RESPONSORY

Today true peace came down to us from heaven.
—Today the whole earth was filled with heaven's sweetness.

Today a new day dawns,
the day of our redemption, prepared by God from ages
    past,
the beginning of our never ending gladness.
—Today the whole . . .

For the vigil a canticle is added, as in Appendix I, 1622, and
the gospel of the Vigil Mass.

After the gospel or, if the vigil is not used, after the responsory,
the **Te Deum** is said, 651.

If the Mass at midnight does not immediately follow the celebration of the Office of Readings, the following is said:

Prayer

Lord God,
we praise you for creating man,
and still more for restoring him in Christ.
Your Son shared our weakness:
may we share his glory,
for he lives and reigns with you and the Holy Spirit,
one God, for ever and ever.

Alternative Prayer

God of love, Father of all,
the darkness that covered the earth
has given way to the bright dawn of your Word
made flesh.

Make us a people of this light.
Make us faithful to your Word,
that we may bring your life to the waiting world.

Grant this through Christ our Lord.

If Mass follows, the **Gloria** is said in place of the **Te Deum**. The
introductory rites are omitted; the opening prayer and the
readings immediately follow.

The plan of the hours demands that Morning Prayer not be
celebrated immediately after the Mass at midnight, but in the
morning.

Morning Prayer

HYMN

O come, all ye faithful, joyful and triumphant,
O come ye, O come ye to Bethlehem;
Come and behold him, born the King of angels;

Refrain:

O come, let us adore him,
O come, let us adore him,
O come, let us adore him,
Christ the Lord.

Sing, choirs of angels, sing in exultation,
Sing, all ye citizens of heav'n above;
Glory to God, in the highest glory:

Refrain

Savior, we greet thee, born this happy morning,
Jesus, to thee be all glory giv'n;
Word of the Father, now in flesh appearing:

Refrain

Melody: Adeste Fideles

Music: J. F. Wade, 1751
Text: Latin, 18th century
Translator: Fredcrick Oakeley, 1841 et al.

Ant. 1 Tell us, shepherds, what have you seen? Who
has appeared on earth? We have seen a
newborn infant and a choir of angels praising
the Lord, alleluia.

Psalms and canticle from Sunday, Week 1, **688.**

Ant. 2 The angel said to the shepherds: I proclaim to
you a great joy; today the Savior of the world is
born for you, alleluia.

Ant. 3 A little child is born for us today; little and yet
called the mighty God, alleluia.

READING   Hebrews 1:1-2

In times past, God spoke in fragmentary and varied ways to our fathers through the prophets; in this, the final age, he has spoken to us through his Son, whom he has made heir of all things and through whom he first created the universe.

RESPONSORY

The Lord has made known, alleluia, alleluia.
—The Lord has made known, alleluia, alleluia.

His saving power.
—Alleluia, alleluia.

Glory to the Father . . .
—The Lord has . . .

CANTICLE OF ZECHARIAH

Ant.   Glory to God in the highest, and peace to his people on earth, alleluia.

INTERCESSIONS

The Word of God existed before the creation of the universe yet was born among us in time. We praise and worship him as we cry out in joy:
    Let the earth ring out with joy for you have come.
You are the eternal Word of God who flooded the world with joy at your birth,
—fill us with joy by the continuous gift of your life.
You saved us and by your birth revealed to us the covenant faithfulness of the Lord,
—help us to be faithful to the promises of our baptism.
You are the King of heaven and earth who sent messengers to announce peace to all,

—let our lives be filled with your peace.
You are the true vine that brings forth the fruit of life,
—make us branches of the vine, bearing much fruit.

Our Father . . .

Prayer

Father,
we are filled with the new light
by the coming of your Word among us.
May the light of faith
shine in our words and actions.

Grant this through our Lord Jesus Christ, your Son,
who lives and reigns with you and the Holy Spirit,
one God, for ever and ever

Alternative Prayer

Almighty God and Father of light,
a child is born for us and a son is given to us.
Your eternal Word leaped down from heaven
in the silent watches of the night,
and now your Church is filled with wonder
at the nearness of her God.
Open our hearts to receive his life
and increase our vision with the rising of dawn,
that our lives may be filled with his glory and his peace,
who lives and reigns for ever and ever.

Daytime Prayer

PSALMODY

Antiphons

Midmorning

Joseph and Mary, the mother of Jesus, were filled with
wonder at all that was said of the child.

Midday

Mary treasured all these words and pondered them in her heart.

Midafternoon

My own eyes have seen the salvation which you have prepared in the sight of every people.

Psalm 19 B

The law of the Lord is perfect,
it revives the soul.
The rule of the Lord is to be trusted,
it gives wisdom to the simple.

The precepts of the Lord are right,
they gladden the heart.
The command of the Lord is clear,
it gives light to the eyes.

The fear of the Lord is holy,
abiding for ever.
The decrees of the Lord are truth
and all of them just.

They are more to be desired than gold,
than the purest of gold
and sweeter are they than honey,
than honey from the comb.

So in them your servant finds instruction;
great reward is in their keeping.
But who can detect all his errors?
From hidden faults acquit me.

From presumption restrain your servant
and let it not rule me.
Then shall I be blameless,
clean from grave sin.

May the spoken words of my mouth,
the thoughts of my heart,
win favor in your sight, O Lord,
my rescuer, my rock!

Psalm 47

All peoples, clap your hands,
cry to God with shouts of joy!
For the Lord, the Most High, we must fear,
great king over all the earth.

He subdues peoples under us
and nations under our feet.
Our inheritance, our glory, is from him,
given to Jacob out of love.

God goes up with shouts of joy;
the Lord goes up with trumpet blast.
Sing praise for God, sing praise,
sing praise to our king, sing praise.

God is king of all the earth.
Sing praise with all your skill.
God is king over the nations;
God reigns on his holy throne.

The princes of the peoples are assembled
with the people of Abraham's God.
The rulers of the earth belong to God,
to God who reigns over all.

Psalm 48

The Lord is great and worthy to be praised
in the city of our God.
His holy mountain rises in beauty,
the joy of all the earth.

Mount Zion, true pole of the earth,
the Great King's city!
God, in the midst of its citadels,
has shown himself its stronghold.

For the kings assembled together,
together they advanced.
They saw; at once they were astounded;
dismayed, they fled in fear.

A trembling seized them there,
like the pangs of birth.
By the east wind you have destroyed
the ships of Tarshish.

As we have heard, so we have seen
in the city of our God,
in the city of the Lord of hosts
which God upholds for ever.

O God, we ponder your love
within your temple.
Your praise, O God, like your name
reaches the ends of the earth.

With justice your right hand is filled.
Mount Zion rejoices;
the people of Judah rejoice
at the sight of your judgments.

Walk through Zion, walk all round it;
count the number of its towers.
Review all its ramparts,
examine its castles,

that you may tell the next generation
that such is our God,
our God for ever and always.
It is he who leads us.

At the other hours the complementary psalmody is used, 1191.

Midmorning

Ant.   Joseph and Mary, the mother of Jesus, were filled
with wonder at all that was said of the child.

READING   Titus 2:11–12

The grace of God has appeared, offering salvation to all
men. It trains us to reject godless ways and worldly
desires, and live temperately, justly, and devoutly in this
age.

The Lord has remembered his gracious promise, alleluia.
—He has kept faith with his people Israel, alleluia.

Prayer

Lord God,
we praise you for creating man,
and still more for restoring him in Christ.
Your Son shared our weakness:
may we share his glory,
for he lives and reigns with you and the Holy Spirit,
one God, for ever and ever.

Alternative Prayer

God of love, Father of all,
the darkness that covered the earth
has given way to the bright dawn of your Word made
flesh.
Make us a people of this light.
Make us faithful to your Word,
that we may bring your life to the waiting world.
Grant this through Christ our Lord.

Midday

Ant. Mary treasured all these words and pondered
      them in her heart.

READING   1 John 4:9

God's love was revealed in our midst in this way:
he sent his only Son to the world
that we might have life through him.

All the ends of the earth, alleluia.
—Have seen the saving power of God, alleluia.

Prayer, as in Midmorning Prayer.

Midafternoon

Ant. My own eyes have seen the salvation which
      you have prepared in the sight of every people.

READING   Acts 10:36

   This is the message God has sent to the sons of Israel,
the good news of peace proclaimed through Jesus Christ
who is Lord of all.

Mercy and truth have come together, alleluia.
—Justice and peace have kissed, alleluia.

Prayer, as in Midmorning Prayer.

Evening Prayer II

HYMN

   A Child is born in Bethlehem, alleluia;
   O come, rejoice Jerusalem, alleluia, alleluia.
   Refrain:
   Let grateful hearts now sing,
   A song of joy and holy praise
   To Christ the new-born King.

Though found within a manger poor, alleluia,
His Kingdom shall for e'er endure, alleluia, alleluia.

Refrain

As brother in the flesh he came, alleluia,
Our King whose name we now proclaim, alleluia, alleluia.

Refrain

Melody: Gregorian, Mode 1   Music: Traditional, Gregorian
                                       Text: *Puer Natus in Bethlehem*
                                       Translator: J. W. Hewett, 1959, alt.

PSALMODY

Ant. 1   You have been endowed from your birth with
         princely gifts; in eternal splendor, before the
         dawn of light on earth, I have begotten you.

Psalm 110:1-5, 7

The Lord's revelation to my Master:
"Sit on my right:
your foes I will put beneath your feet."

The Lord will wield from Zion
your scepter of power:
rule in the midst of all your foes.

A prince from the day of your birth
on the holy mountains;
from the womb before the dawn I begot you.

The Lord has sworn an oath he will not change.
" You are a priest for ever,
a priest like Melchizedek of old!"

The Master standing at your right hand
will shatter kings in the day of his great wrath.
He shall drink from the stream by the wayside
and therefore he shall lift up his head.

Ant. You have been endowed from your birth with
princely gifts; in eternal splendor, before the
dawn of light on earth, I have begotten you.

Ant. 2 With the Lord is unfailing love; great is his
power to save.

Psalm 130

Out of the depths I cry to you, O Lord,
Lord, hear my voice!
O let your ears be attentive
to the voice of my pleading.

If you, O Lord, should mark our guilt,
Lord, who would survive?
But with you is found forgiveness:
for this we revere you.

My soul is waiting for the Lord,
I count on his word.
My soul is longing for the Lord
more than watchman for daybreak.
Let the watchman count on daybreak
and Israel on the Lord.

Because with the Lord there is mercy
and fullness of redemption,
Israel indeed he will redeem
from all its iniquity.

Ant. With the Lord is unfailing love; great is his power
to save.

Ant. 3 In the beginning, before time began, the Word
was God; today he is born, the Savior of the
world.

Canticle   Colossians 1:12-20

Let us give thanks to the Father
for having made you worthy
to share the lot of the saints
in light.

He rescued us
from the power of darkness
and brought us
into the kingdom of his beloved Son.
Through him we have redemption,
the forgiveness of our sins.

He is the image of the invisible God,
the first-born of all creatures.
In him everything in heaven and on earth was
     created,
things visible and invisible.

All were created through him;
all were created for him.
He is before all else that is.
In him everything continues in being.

It is he who is head of the body, the church!
he who is the beginning,
the first-born of the dead,
so that primacy may be his in everything.

It pleased God to make absolute fulness reside in him
and, by means of him, to reconcile everything in his
     person,
both on earth and in the heavens,
making peace through the blood of his cross.

Ant. In the beginning, before time began, the Word
      was God; today he is born, the Savior of the
      world.

READING

This is what we proclaim to you:
what was from the beginning,
what we have heard,
what we have seen with our eyes,
what we have looked upon
and our hands have touched—
we speak of the word of life.
(This life became visible;
we have seen and bear witness to it,
and we proclaim to you the eternal life
that was present to the Father
and became visible to us.)
What we have seen and heard
we proclaim in turn to you
so that you may share life with us.
This fellowship of ours is with the Father
and with his Son, Jesus Christ.

RESPONSORY

The Word was made man, alleluia, alleluia.
—The Word was made man, alleluia, alleluia.

He lived among us.
—Alleluia, alleluia.

Glory to the Father . . .
—The Word was . . .

CANTICLE OF MARY

Ant. Christ the Lord is born today; today, the Savior
has appeared. Earth echoes songs of angel choirs,
archangels' joyful praise. Today on earth his
friends exult: Glory to God in the highest, alleluia.

INTERCESSIONS

At the birth of Jesus, angels proclaimed peace to the
world. We worship him now with joy, and we pray
with hearts full of faith:
May your birth bring peace to all.

Lord, fill your holy people with whatever good they
need,

—let the mystery of your birth be the source of our
peace.

You came as chief shepherd and guardian of our lives,

—let the pope and bishops be faithful channels of your
many gifts of grace.

King from all eternity, you desired to be born within
time and to experience the day-to-day life of men and
women,

—share your gift of unending life with us, weak people,
doomed to death.

Awaited from the beginning of the world, you came only
in the fullness of time,

—now reveal your presence to those who are still
expecting you.

You became man and gave new life to our human
condition in the grip of death,

—now give the fullness of life to all who have died.

Our Father . . .

Prayer

Lord God,
we praise you for creating man,
and still more for restoring him in Christ.
Your Son shared our weakness:
may we share his glory,
for he lives and reigns with you and the Holy Spirit,
one God, for ever and ever.

Alternative Prayer

God of love, Father of all,
the darkness that covered the earth
has given way to the bright dawn of your Word made
   flesh.
Make us a people of this light.
Make us faithful to your Word,
that we may bring your life to the waiting world.
Grant this through Christ our Lord.

During the octave of Christmas, with the exception of the
solemnities and the Sunday celebration in honor of the Holy
Family, Evening Prayer is taken each day from within the
octave, as below, even though at the other hours the office is
taken from the feast.

Each day either form of Night Prayer from Sunday, 1164 or
1172, is said.

Sunday in the Octave of Christmas

HOLY FAMILY

Feast

When Christmas occurs on Sunday, the feast of the Holy Family is celebrated on December 30 and there is no Evening Prayer I.

Evening Prayer I

HYMN

Sing of Mary, pure and lowly,
Virgin mother undefiled,
Sing of God's own Son most holy
Who became her little child.
Fairest child of fairest mother,
God the Lord, who came to earth,
Word made flesh, our very brother,
Takes our nature by his birth.

Sing of Jesus, son of Mary,
In the home at Nazareth.
Toil and labor cannot weary
Love enduring unto death.
Constant was the love he gave her,
Though he went forth from her side,
Forth to preach and heal and suffer,
Till on Calvary he died.

Glory be to God the Father,
Glory be to God the Son:
Glory be to God the Spirit,
Glory to the Three in One.
From the heart of blessed Mary,
From all saints the song ascends,
And the Church the strain re-echoes
Unto earth's remotest ends.

Melody: Pleading
Saviour 87.87.D

Music: The Christian Lyre, 1831
Text: Anon., 1914

Ant. 1 Jacob was the father of Joseph, the husband of
        Mary; Mary gave birth to Jesus who is called
        the Christ.

Psalms and canticle from the common of the Blessed Virgin
Mary, 1321.

Ant. 2 Joseph, son of David, do not be afraid to take
        Mary as your wife; the child in her womb is
        conceived by the Holy Spirit.

Ant. 3 The shepherds went in haste and found Mary
        and Joseph, with the child cradled in a manger.

READING   2 Corinthians 8:9

You are well acquainted with the favor shown you by
our Lord Jesus Christ: how for your sake he made
himself poor though he was rich, so that you might
become rich by his poverty.

RESPONSORY

The Word was made man; he lived among us.
—The Word was made man; he lived among us.

From his fullness we have all received.
—He lived among us.

Glory to the Father . . .
—The Word was . . .

CANTICLE OF MARY

Ant. The child Jesus remained in Jerusalem, and his
      parents did not know it. They thought he was in
      the group of travelers and looked for him among
      their relatives and friends.

INTERCESSIONS

Let us adore the Son of the living God who humbled
    himself to become a son of a human family, and let us
    proclaim:
    Lord, you are the model and Savior of all.
Christ, by the mystery of your subjection to Mary and
    Joseph,
—teach all people reverence and obedience to lawful
    authority.
You loved your parents and were loved by them,
—establish our families in mutual love and peace.
You were eager to be about your Father's business,
—may he be honored in every home.
Christ, after three days your anxious parents found you
    in your Father's house,
—teach all to seek first the kingdom of God.
Christ, you have made Mary and Joseph sharers in
    heavenly glory,
—admit the dead into the family of the blessed.

Our Father . . .

Prayer

Father,
help us to live as the holy family,
united in respect and love.
Bring us to the joy and peace of your eternal home.

Grant this through our Lord Jesus Christ, your Son,
who lives and reigns with you and the Holy Spirit,
one God, for ever and ever.

Alternative Prayer

Father in heaven, creator of all,
you ordered the earth to bring forth life
and crowned its goodness by creating the family of man.

In history's moment when all was ready,
you sent your Son to dwell in time,
obedient to the laws of life in our world.
Teach us the sanctity of human love,
show us the value of family life,
and help us to live in peace with all men
that we may share in your life for ever.
We ask this through Christ our Lord.

Invitatory

Ant.   Come, let us worship Christ, the Son of God, who
was obedient to Mary and Joseph.

Invitatory psalm, as in the Ordinary, 648.

Office of Readings

Hymn

Joseph of Nazareth, you are the man
Last in the line that rose from David, King,
Down through the royal generations ran,
And ends with Jesus Christ.

Gabriel from heaven came to Mary's side,
Came with the joyful promise of a King,
Came to you also, Joseph, to confide
That God conceived this Child.

Guardian and foster-father of the Christ,
Honor to you, so chosen by our God!
Husband of Virgin Mary, you are first
To show us Christian love.

Melody: Joseph of Nazareth   Music: Stephen Somerville, 1971
                                Text: Stephen Somerville, 1972

Ant. 1   When his parents brought the Child Jesus into
the temple, Simeon took him in his arms and
praised God.

Psalms from the common of the Blessed Virgin Mary, 1328.

Ant. 2   The Magi entered the house and found the
         child with Mary, his mother.

Ant. 3   Joseph rose in the night and took the child and
         his mother into Egypt.

Your children will be taught by the Lord himself.
—He will bless them with fullness of peace.

FIRST READING

From the letter of the apostle Paul
to the Ephesians   5:21—6:4

Christian life in the family and in society

Defer to one another out of reverence for Christ.

Wives should be submissive to their husbands as if to
the Lord because the husband is head of his wife just as
Christ is head of his body the church, as well as its savior.
As the church submits to Christ, so wives should submit
to their husbands in everything.

Husbands, love your wives, as Christ loved the
church. He gave himself up for her to make her holy,
purifying her in the bath of water by the power of the
word, to present to himself a glorious church, holy and
immaculate, without stain or wrinkle or anything of that
sort. Husbands should love their wives as they do their
own bodies. He who loves his wife loves himself.

Observe that no one ever hates his own flesh; no, he
nourishes it and takes care of it as Christ cares for the
church—for we are members of his body.

    "For this reason a man shall leave his father and
        mother,
        and shall cling to his wife,
        and the two shall be made into one."

This is a great foreshadowing; I mean that it refers to Christ and the church. In any case, each one should love his wife as he loves himself, the wife for her part showing respect for her husband.

Children, obey your parents in the Lord, for that is what is expected of you. "Honor your father and mother" is the first commandment to carry a promise with it—"that it may go well with you, and that you may have long life on the earth."

Fathers, do not anger your children. Bring them up with the training and instruction befitting the Lord.

RESPONSORY   Ephesians 6:1-2; Luke 2:51

Children, obey your parents in the Lord,
for that is your duty;
—honor your father and your mother.

Jesus returned with Mary and Joseph to Nazareth;
there he lived and was obedient to them.
—Honor your father . . .

SECOND READING

From an address by Pope Paul VI

(Nazareth, January 5, 1964)

Nazareth, a model

Nazareth is a kind of school where we may begin to discover what Christ's life was like and even to understand his Gospel. Here we can observe and ponder the simple appeal of the way God's Son came to be known, profound yet full of hidden meaning. And gradually we may even learn to imitate him.

Here we can learn to realize who Christ really is. And here we can sense and take account of the conditions and circumstances that surrounded and affected his life on earth: the places, the tenor of the times, the culture, the language, religious customs, in brief everything which Jesus used to make himself known to the world. Here everything speaks to us, everything has meaning. Here we can learn the importance of spiritual discipline for all who wish to follow Christ and to live by the teachings of his Gospel.

How I would like to return to my childhood and attend the simple yet profound school that is Nazareth! How wonderful to be close to Mary, learning again the lesson of the true meaning of life, learning again God's truths. But here we are only on pilgrimage. Time presses and I must set aside my desire to stay and carry on my education in the Gospel, for that education is never finished. But I cannot leave without recalling, briefly and in passing, some thoughts I take with me from Nazareth.

First, we learn from its silence. If only we could once again appreciate its great value. We need this wonderful state of mind, beset as we are by the cacophony of strident protests and conflicting claims so characteristic of these turbulent times. The silence of Nazareth should teach us how to meditate in peace and quiet, to reflect on the deeply spiritual, and to be open to the voice of God's inner wisdom and the counsel of his true teachers. Nazareth can teach us the value of study and preparation, of meditation, of a well-ordered personal spiritual life, and of silent prayer that is known only to God.

Second, we learn about family life. May Nazareth serve as a model of what the family should be. May it show us the family's holy and enduring character and exemplifying its basic function in society: a community of love and sharing, beautiful for the problems it poses and the rewards it brings; in sum, the perfect setting for rearing children—and for this there is no substitute.

Finally, in Nazareth, the home of a craftsman's son, we learn about work and the discipline it entails. I would especially like to recognize its value—demanding yet redeeming—and to give it proper respect. I would remind everyone that work has its own dignity. On the other hand, it is not an end in itself. Its value and free character, however, derive not only from its place in the economic system, as they say, but rather from the purpose it serves.

In closing, may I express my deep regard for people everywhere who work for a living. To them I would point out their great model, Christ their brother, our Lord and God, who is their prophet in every cause that promotes their well being.

RESPONSORY   2 Cor 13:11; Eph 5:9; Col 3:23

Have a rejoicing heart, try to grow holy,
help one another, keep united, live in peace.
—Sing and make music to the Lord in your hearts.

What ever you do, put your whole self into it,
as if for the Lord and not for men.
—Sing and make . . .

HYMN, TE DEUM, 651.

Prayer, as in Morning Prayer.

Morning Prayer

HYMN

Joseph of Nazareth, you are the man
Last in the line that rose from David, King,
Down through the royal generations ran,
And ends with Jesus Christ.

Gabriel from heaven came to Mary's side,
Came with the joyful promise of a King,

Came to you also, Joseph, to confide
That God conceived this Child.

Guardian and foster-father of the Christ,
Honor to you, so chosen by our God!
Husband of Virgin Mary, you are first
To show us Christian love.

Melody: Joseph of Nazareth   Music: Stephen Somerville, 1971
                               Text: Stephen Somerville, 1972

Ant. 1   The parents of Jesus went each year to
         Jerusalem for the solemn feast of Passover.

Psalms and canticle from Sunday, Week I, 688.

Ant. 2   The child grew in wisdom and strength, and the
         favor of God was upon him.

Ant. 3   His father and mother were full of wonder at
         what was said about their child.

READING   Deuteronomy 5:16

Honor your father and your mother, as the Lord, your
God, has commanded you, that you may have a long life
and prosperity in the land which the Lord, your God, is
giving you.

RESPONSORY

Christ, Son of the living God, have mercy on us.
—Christ, Son of the living God, have mercy on us.

You were obedient to Mary and Joseph,
—have mercy on us.

Glory to the Father . . .
—Christ, Son of . . .

CANTICLE OF ZECHARIAH

Ant.   Lord, give us light through the example of your
        family and guide our feet into the way of peace.

INTERCESSIONS

Let us adore the Son of the living God who humbled
    himself to become a son of a human family, and let us
    beseech him:
    Jesus, you became obedient; sanctify us.

Jesus, eternal Word of the Father, you made yourself
    subject to Mary and Joseph,
—teach us humility.

You are our teacher, and your own mother pondered in
    her heart every one of your words and deeds,
—make us attentive to your word, and let us ponder it in
    hearts that are pure and good.

Christ, by your work the world was made, but you were
    willing to be called a worker's son,
—teach us to work diligently.

Jesus, in the family at Nazareth you grew in wisdom,
    age, and grace before God and men,
—help us to grow in all things toward you, our Head.

Our Father . . .

Prayer

Father,
help us to live as the holy family,
united in respect and love.
Bring us to the joy and peace of your eternal home.

Grant this through our Lord Jesus Christ, your Son,
who lives and reigns with you and the Holy Spirit,
one God, for ever and ever.

Alternative Prayer

Father in heaven, creator of all,
you ordered the earth to bring forth life

and crowned its goodness by creating the family of man.
In history's moment when all was ready,
you sent your Son to dwell in time,
obedient to the laws of life in our world.
Teach us the sanctity of human love,
show us the value of family life,
and help us to live in peace with all men
that we may share in your life for ever

We ask this through Christ our Lord.

Daytime Prayer

Psalms from Sunday, Week I, **692**. When this feast is not celebrated on Sunday, psalms are taken from the current weekday,
773. For the gradual psalms, in place of psalm 122, psalm 129,
1129, is said, and in place of 127, psalm 131 may be said, **972**.

Midmorning

Ant.   Mary, the mother of Jesus, and Joseph were filled
with wonder at all that was said of the child.

READING   Colossians 3:12-13

Because you are God's chosen ones, holy and beloved,
clothe yourselves with heartfelt mercy, with kindness,
humility, meekness, and patience. Bear with one
another; forgive whatever grievances you have against
one another. Forgive as the Lord has forgiven you.

The Lord will teach us his way.
—And we will follow in his footsteps.

Midday

Ant.   Mary treasured all these words and pondered
them in her heart.

READING   Colossians 3:14-15

Over all these virtues put on love, which binds the rest together and makes them perfect. Christ's peace must reign in your hearts, since as members of the one body you have been called to that peace. Dedicate yourselves to thankfulness.

I am a poor man. I have worked since my youth.
—I was raised up only to be brought low and left bewildered.

Midafternoon

Ant.   My own eyes have seen the salvation which you have prepared in the sight of every people.

READING   Colossians 3:17

Whatever you do, whether in speech or in action, do it in the name of the Lord Jesus. Give thanks to God the Father through him.

Your children will be taught by the Lord himself.
—He will bless them with fullness of peace.

Prayer, as in Morning Prayer.

Evening Prayer II

HYMN

Sing of Mary, pure and lowly,
Virgin mother undefiled,
Sing of God's own Son most holy
Who became her little child.
Fairest child of fairest mother,
God the Lord, who came to earth,
Word made flesh, our very brother,
Takes our nature by his birth.

Sing of Jesus, son of Mary,
In the home at Nazareth.
Toil and labor cannot weary
Love enduring unto death.
Constant was the love he gave her,
Though he went forth from her side,
Forth to preach and heal and suffer,
Till on Calvary he died.

Glory be to God the Father,
Glory be to God the Son:
Glory be to God the Spirit,
Glory to the Three in One.
From the heart of blessed Mary,
From all saints the song ascends,
And the Church the strain re-echoes
Unto earth's remotest ends.

Melody: Pleading Saviour   Music: The Christian Lyre, 1831
87.87.D   Text: Anon., c. 1914

Ant. 1   After three days, Jesus was found in the temple,
          seated in the midst of the doctors, listening to
          them and asking them questions.

Psalms and canticle from the common of the Blessed Virgin
Mary, 1345.

Ant. 2   Jesus returned with Mary and Joseph to
          Nazareth; there he lived and was obedient to
          them.

Ant. 3   Jesus grew in wisdom with the years and was
          pleasing to God and men.

READING   Philippians 2:6-7

Though he was in the form of God, Christ Jesus did
not deem equality with God something to be grasped at.

Rather, he emptied himself and took the form of a slave, being born in the likeness of men. He was known to be of human estate.

RESPONSORY

He had to become like his brothers in every way to show the fullness of his mercy.
—He had to become like his brothers in every way to show the fullness of his mercy.

He was seen on earth and lived among men and women,
—to show the fullness of his mercy.

Glory to the Father . . .
—He had to . . .

CANTICLE OF MARY

Ant. Son, why have you done this to us? Think what anguish your father and I have endured looking for you. But why did you look for me? Did you not know that I had to be in my Father's house?

INTERCESSIONS

Let us adore the Son of the living God who humbled himself to become a son of a human family, and let us proclaim:
Lord, you are the model and Savior of all.
Christ, by the mystery of your subjection to Mary and Joseph,
—teach all people reverence and obedience to lawful authority.
You loved your parents and were loved by them,
—establish our families in mutual love and peace.
You were eager to be about your Father's business,
—may he be honored in every home.

Christ, after three days your anxious parents found you
    in your Father's house,
—teach all to seek first the kingdom of God.
Christ, you have made Mary and Joseph sharers in
    heavenly glory,
—admit the dead into the family of the blessed.

Our Father . . .

Prayer

Father,
help us to live as the holy family,
united in respect and love.
Bring us to the joy and peace of your eternal home.

Grant this through our Lord Jesus Christ, your Son,
who lives and reigns with you and the Holy Spirit,
one God, for ever and ever.

Alternative Prayer

Father in heaven, creator of all,
you ordered the earth to bring forth life
and crowned its goodness by creating the family of man.
In history's moment when all was ready,
you sent your Son to dwell in time,
obedient to the laws of life in our world.
Teach us the sanctity of human love,
show us the value of family life,
and help us to live in peace with all men
that we may share in your life for ever.

We ask this through Christ our Lord.

DECEMBER 26

At the Office of Readings, Morning Prayer, and Daytime Prayer, everything is taken from the feast of St. Stephen, First Martyr, 1253.

Evening Prayer

Hymn, antiphons, psalms, and canticle, as in Evening Prayer II of Christmas, 414.

READING   1 John 1:5b, 7

God is light;
in him there is no darkness.
If we walk in light,
as he is in the light,
we have fellowship with one another,
and the blood of his Son Jesus cleanses us from all sin.

RESPONSORY

The Word was made man, alleluia, alleluia.
—The Word was made man, alleluia, alleluia.

He lived among us.
—Alleluia, alleluia.

Glory to the Father . . .
—The Word was . . .

CANTICLE OF MARY

Ant.   While earth was rapt in silence and night only half
       through its course, your almighty Word, O Lord,
       came down from his royal throne, alleluia.

INTERCESSIONS

The Word of God, by coming to dwell with us, has
    opened the path to eternal salvation. Let us pray to
    him with sincere humility:
    Lord, deliver us from evil.

Through the mystery of your incarnation, through your
   birth and infancy,
—through your whole life, dedicated to the Father:
   Lord, deliver us from evil.
Through your labor, your preaching and your journeys,
—through your continual encounters with sinners:
   Lord, deliver us from evil.
Through your agony and passion, your cross and
   desolation,
—through your sufferings, your death and burial:
   Lord, deliver us from evil.
Through your resurrection and ascension, through your
   gift of the Holy Spirit, through your joys and
   everlasting glory,
—free our departed brothers and sisters, O Lord.
   Lord, deliver us from evil.

Our Father . . .

Prayer

All-powerful God,
may the human birth of your Son
free us from our former slavery to sin
and bring us new life.

We ask this through our Lord Jesus Christ, your Son,
who lives and reigns with you and the Holy Spirit,
one God, for ever and ever.

DECEMBER 27

At the Office of Readings, Morning Prayer, and Daytime Prayer, everything is taken from the feast of St. John, Apostle and Evangelist, 1261.

Evening Prayer

Hymn, antiphons, psalms and canticle, as in Evening Prayer II, of Christmas, 414.

READING   Romans 8:3-4

God sent his Son in the likeness of sinful flesh as a sin offering, thereby condemning sin in the flesh, so that the just demands of the law might be fulfilled in us who live, not according to the flesh, but according to the spirit.

RESPONSORY

The Word was made man, alleluia, alleluia.
—The Word was made man, alleluia, alleluia.

He lived among us.
—Alleluia, alleluia.

Glory to the Father . . .
—The Word was . . .

CANTICLE OF MARY

Ant.   Virgin Mary, all that the prophets foretold of Christ has been fulfilled through you: as a virgin, you conceived, and after you gave birth, a virgin you remained.

INTERCESSIONS

Dear friends, let us humbly pray to God the Father who so loved us that he sent us his Son:
    May the favor of your Son be with us, Lord.
God of love, Father of our Lord Jesus Christ, you had mercy on those walking in darkness,

—receive the prayers we offer for the salvation of all
  people.

Lord, remember your Church spread over all the world,

—bless your Christian people and give them peace.

You are the Father of all people; graciously grant peace
  to all, direct the eyes of all to your Son,

—and pour forth the spirit of peace on those who rule
  them.

You announced peace on earth at the coming of your
  Son,

—give eternal peace to those who have died.

Our Father . . .

Prayer

Father,
we are filled with the new light
by the coming of your Word among us.
May the light of faith
shine in our words and actions.

Grant this through our Lord Jesus Christ, your Son,
who lives and reigns with you and the Holy Spirit,
one God, for ever and ever.

DECEMBER 28

At the Office of Readings, Morning Prayer, and Daytime Prayer, everything is taken from the feast of the Holy Innocents, 1272.

Evening Prayer

Hymn, antiphons, psalms and canticle, as in Evening Prayer II of Christmas, 414.

READING — Ephesians 2:3b-5

By nature we deserved God's wrath like the rest. But God is rich in mercy; because of his great love for us he brought us to life with Christ when we were dead in sin. By this favor you were saved.

RESPONSORY

The Word was made man, alleluia, alleluia.
—The Word was made man, alleluia, alleluia.

He lived among us.
—Alleluia, alleluia.

Glory to the Father . . .
—The Word was . . .

CANTICLE OF MARY

Ant.   The holy Virgin gave birth to God who became for us the frail, tender baby she nursed at her breast. Let us worship the Lord who comes to save us.

INTERCESSIONS

God sent his Son, fashioned from a woman, made subject to the law, to redeem those under the law. Trusting in this hope, let us pray with confidence:
May the favor of your Son be with us, O Lord.
God of love and peace, renew the faith of all Christians in the incarnation of your Son,

—that they may give thanks at all times.

Increase the hope of the weak, the poor and the aged,
—give relief to the oppressed, confidence to those who
    despair, consolation to those who mourn.

Be mindful of all those in prison,
—and of those driven from their homeland.

You let the angels be heard praising you at the birth of
    your Son,
—let the departed praise you for ever with this heavenly
    host.

Our Father . . .

Prayer

Lord God,
we praise you for creating man,
and still more for restoring him in Christ.
Your Son shared our weakness:
may we share his glory,
for he lives and reigns with you and the Holy Spirit,
one God, for ever and ever.

December 29

FIFTH DAY IN THE OCTAVE OF CHRISTMAS

Invitatory

Ant.   Christ is born for us; come, let us adore him.

Invitatory psalm, as in the ordinary, 648.

Office of Readings

HYMN, 385.

PSALMODY

Ant. 1   The Lord of power and might is with us; the God of Jacob is our stronghold.

Psalm 46

God is for us a refuge and strength,
a helper close at hand, in time of distress:
so we shall not fear though the earth should rock,
though the mountains fall into the depths of the sea,
even though its waters rage and foam,
even though the mountains be shaken by its waves.

The Lord of hosts is with us:
the God of Jacob is our stronghold.

The waters of a river give joy to God's city,
the holy place where the Most High dwells.
God is within, it cannot be shaken;
God will help it at the dawning of the day.
Nations are in tumult, kingdoms are shaken:
he lifts his voice, the earth shrinks away.

The Lord of hosts is with us:
the God of Jacob is our stronghold.

Come, consider the works of the Lord,
the redoubtable deeds he has done on the earth.

He puts an end to wars over all the earth;
the bow he breaks, the spear he snaps.
He burns the shields with fire.
"Be still and know that I am God,
supreme among the nations, supreme on the earth!"

The Lord of hosts is with us:
the God of Jacob is our stronghold.

Ant.   The Lord of power and might is with us; the God
of Jacob is our stronghold.

Ant. 2 Fullness of peace will dawn on the day of the
Lord, and he will be our King.

Psalm 72

I

O God, give your judgment to the king,
to a king's son your justice,
that he may judge your people in justice
and your poor in right judgment.

May the mountains bring forth peace for the people
and the hills, justice.
May he defend the poor of the people
and save the children of the needy
and crush the oppressor.

He shall endure like the sun and the moon
from age to age.
He shall descend like rain on the meadow,
like raindrops on the earth.

In his days justice shall flourish
and peace till the moon fails.
He shall rule from sea to sea,
from the Great River to earth's bounds.

Before him his enemies shall fall,
his foes lick the dust.
The kings of Tarshish and the sea coasts
shall pay him tribute.

The kings of Sheba and Seba
shall bring him gifts.
Before him all kings shall fall prostrate,
all nations shall serve him.

Ant.   Fullness of peace will dawn on the day of the
       Lord, and he will be our King.

Ant. 3   The Lord himself will come to save the poor.

II

For he shall save the poor when they cry
and the needy who are helpless.
He will have pity on the weak
and save the lives of the poor.

From oppression he will rescue their lives,
to him their blood is dear.
Long may he live,
may the gold of Sheba be given him.
They shall pray for him without ceasing
and bless him all the day.

May corn be abundant in the land
to the peaks of the mountains.
May its fruit rustle like Lebanon;
may men flourish in the cities
like grass on the earth.

May his name be blessed for ever
and endure like the sun.
Every tribe shall be blessed in him,
all nations bless his name.

Blessed be the Lord, God of Israel,
who alone works wonders,
ever blessed his glorious name.
Let his glory fill the earth.

Amen! Amen!

Ant. The Lord himself will come to save the poor.

When the shepherds saw the child.
—They understood what the angel had said of him.

FIRST READING

The beginning of the letter of the apostle Paul
to the Colossians   1:1–14

Thanksgiving and intercession

Paul, an apostle of Christ Jesus by the will of God, and
Timothy our brother, to the holy ones at Colossae,
faithful brothers in Christ. May God our Father give you
grace and peace.

We always give thanks to God, the Father of our Lord
Jesus Christ, in our prayers for you because we have
heard of your faith in Christ Jesus and the love you bear
toward all the saints—moved as you are by the hope held
in store for you in heaven. You heard of this hope
through the message of truth, the gospel, which has come
to you, has borne fruit, and has continued to grow in
your midst, as it has everywhere in the world. This has
been the case from the day you first heard it and
comprehended God's gracious intention through the
instructions of Epaphras, our dear fellow slave, who
represents us as a faithful minister of Christ. He it was
who told us of your love in the Spirit.

Ever since we heard this we have been praying for you
unceasingly and asking that you may attain full
knowledge of his will through perfect wisdom and

spiritual insight. Then you will lead a life worthy of the Lord and pleasing to him in every way. You will multiply good works of every sort and grow in the knowledge of God. By the might of his glory you will be endowed with the strength needed to stand fast, even to endure joyfully whatever may come, giving thanks to the Father for having made you worthy to share the lot of the saints in light. He rescued us from the power of darkness and brought us into the kingdom of his beloved Son. Through him we have redemption, the forgiveness of our sins.

RESPONSORY   Colossians 1:12, 13; James 1:17

Let us give thanks to God our Father,
—because he has rescued us from the power of darkness and brought us into the kingdom of his beloved Son.

Every good and perfect gift comes down to us from above,
from the Father of light.
—Because he has . . .

SECOND READING

From a sermon by Saint Bernard, abbot

(Sermo 1, in Epiphania Domini, 1–2: PL 133, 141–143)

In the fullness of time the fullness of divinity appeared

The goodness and humanity of God our Savior have appeared in our midst. We thank God for the many consolations he has given us during this sad exile of our pilgrimage here on earth. Before the Son of God became man his goodness was hidden, for God's mercy is eternal, but how could such goodness be recognized? It was promised, but it was not experienced, and as a result few believed in it. *Often and in many ways the Lord used to*

speak through the prophets. Among other things, God said:
I think thoughts of peace and not of affliction. But what did
men respond, thinking thoughts of affliction and
knowing nothing of peace? They said: *Peace, peace, there
is no peace.* This response made the *angels of peace weep
bitterly,* saying: *Lord, who has believed our message?* But
now men believe because they see with their own eyes,
and because *God's testimony has now become even more
credible.* He has gone so far as to *pitch his tent in the sun* so
even the dimmest eyes see him.

Notice that peace is not promised but sent to us; it is
no longer deferred, it is given; peace is not prophesied
but achieved. It is as if God the Father sent upon the
earth a purse full of his mercy. This purse was burst open
during the Lord's passion to pour forth its hidden
contents—the price of our redemption. It was only a
small purse, but it was very full. As the Scriptures tell us:
*A little child has been given to us, but in him dwells all the
fullness of the divine nature.* The fullness of time brought
with it the fullness of divinity. God's Son came in the
flesh so that mortal men could see and recognize God's
kindness. When God reveals his humanity, his goodness
cannot possibly remain hidden. To show his kindness
what more could he do beyond taking my human form?
My humanity, I say, not Adam's—that is, not such as he
had before his fall.

How could he have shown his mercy more clearly than
by taking on himself our condition? For our sake the
Word of God became as grass. What better proof could
he have given of his love? Scripture says: *Lord, what is
man that you are mindful of him; why does your heart go out
to him?* The incarnation teaches us how much God cares
for us and what he thinks and feels about us. We should
stop thinking of our own sufferings and remember what
he has suffered. Let us think of all the Lord has done for

us, and then we shall realize how his goodness appears
through his humanity. The lesser he became through his
human nature the greater was his goodness; the more he
lowered himself for me, the dearer he is to me. *The
goodness and humanity of God our Savior have appeared*,
says the Apostle.

Truly great and manifest are the goodness and
humanity of God. He has given us a most wonderful
proof of his goodness by adding humanity to his own
divine nature.

RESPONSORY   Ephesians 1:5, Romans 8:29

From all eternity, God destined us in Jesus Christ to be
    his children by adoption,
—for it was his loving purpose to show in us the glory of
    his grace.

Long ago he knew us and chose to make us in the
    likeness of his own Son.
—For it was . . .

HYMN, TE DEUM, 651.

Prayer, as in Morning Prayer.

Morning Prayer

Hymn, antiphons, psalms and canticle, as in Morning Prayer of
Christmas, 407.

READING   Hebrews 1:1-2

In times past, God spoke in fragmentary and varied
ways to our fathers through the prophets; in this, the
final age, he has spoken to us through his Son, whom he
has made heir of all things and through whom he first
created the universe.

RESPONSORY

The Lord has made known, alleluia, alleluia.
—The Lord has made known, alleluia, alleluia.

His saving power.
—Alleluia, alleluia.

Glory to the Father . . .
—The Lord has . . .

CANTICLE OF ZECHARIAH

Ant. The shepherds said to one another: Let us make our way to Bethlehem and see for ourselves this thing which the Lord has revealed to us.

INTERCESSIONS

Because God has been merciful to us and sent his Son, the Prince of peace, let us cry out with confidence:
Peace to his people on earth.

Almighty God, Father of our Lord Jesus Christ, the Church now celebrates your saving love,
—graciously receive our praise.

From the very beginning you promised mankind your victory through Christ our Savior,
—let all be enlightened by the good news.

In praise of your Son whose coming was joyously foreseen by Abraham, hoped for by the patriarchs, announced by the prophets and yearned for by the Gentiles,
—save the whole people of Israel.

You wished the birth of your Son to be proclaimed by angels and to be praised by the apostles, martyrs and faithful of all ages,
—grant the world that peace which the angels proclaimed.

Our Father . . .

Prayer

All-powerful and unseen God,
the coming of your light into our world
has made the darkness vanish.
Teach us to proclaim the birth of your Son Jesus Christ,
who lives and reigns with you and the Holy Spirit,
one God, for ever and ever.

Daytime Prayer

Psalms from the current weekday.

Midmorning

Ant. Mary, the mother of Jesus, and Joseph were filled
with wonder at all that was said of the child.

READING   Titus 2:11-12

The grace of God has appeared, offering salvation to all
men. It trains us to reject godless ways and worldly
desires, and live temperately, justly, and devoutly in this
age.

The Lord has remembered his gracious promise, alleluia.
—He has kept faith with his people Israel, alleluia.

Midday

Ant. Mary treasured all these words and pondered
them in her heart.

READING   1 John 4:9

God's love was revealed in our midst in this way:
he sent his only Son to the world
that we might have life through him.

All the ends of the earth, alleluia.
—Have seen the saving power of God, alleluia.

Midafternoon

Ant. My own eyes have seen the salvation which you
have prepared in the sight of every people.

READING   Acts 10:36

This is the message God has sent to the sons of Israel,
the good news of peace proclaimed through Jesus Christ
who is Lord of all.

Mercy and truth have come together, alleluia.
— Justice and peace have kissed, alleluia.

Prayer, as in Morning Prayer.

Evening Prayer

Hymn, antiphons, psalms and canticle as in Evening Prayer II
of Christmas, 414.

READING   1 John 1:1-3

This is what we proclaim to you:
what was from the beginning,
what we have heard,
what we have seen with our eyes,
what we have looked upon
and our hands have touched—
we speak of the word of life.
(This life became visible;
we have seen and bear witness to it,
and we proclaim to you the eternal life
that was present to the Father
and became visible to us.)
What we have seen and heard
we proclaim in turn to you
so that you may share life with us.
This fellowship of ours is with the Father
and with his Son, Jesus Christ.

RESPONSORY

The Word was made man, alleluia, alleluia.
—The Word was made man, alleluia, alleluia.

He lived among us.
—Alleluia, alleluia.

Glory to the Father . . .
—The Word was . . .

CANTICLE OF MARY

Ant.   The King of heaven humbled himself to be born
of a virgin, that he might restore man to the
kingdom he had lost.

INTERCESSIONS

Let us ask the Father of mercies who anointed his Son
with the Holy Spirit and sent him to preach the good
news to the poor:
God of mercy, have mercy on us.
Merciful, ever-living God, you desire all to be saved and
to come to the knowledge of your truth. We thank you
for giving your only-begotten Son to the world,
—let the whole world rejoice in his birth.
You sent him to proclaim the good news to the poor, to
announce release to captives and proclaim a time of
favor,
—grant freedom and peace to mankind.
You directed the wise men to adore your Son,
—receive the homage of our faith and prayer.
After the wise men you called all people out of the darkness and into your wonderful light, so that at Jesus'
name every knee should bend,
—make us go forth as witnesses of the good news.
You made Christ, born in Bethlehem, a light to the
nations,

—reveal your glory to our brothers and sisters who have died.

Our Father . . .

Prayer

All-powerful and unseen God,
the coming of your light into our world
has made the darkness vanish.
Teach us to proclaim the birth of your Son Jesus Christ,
who lives and reigns with you and the Holy Spirit,
one God, for ever and ever.

December 30

SIXTH DAY IN THE OCTAVE OF CHRISTMAS

When there is no Sunday within the Octave of Christmas, the feast of the Holy Family is celebrated today, 421. Evening prayer I is omitted.

Invitatory

Ant.   Christ is born for us; come, let us adore him.

Invitatory psalm, as in the Ordinary, 648.

Office of Readings

HYMN, 385.

PSALMODY

Ant. 1   Truth has arisen from the earth, and justice has looked down from the heavens.

Psalm 85

O Lord, you once favored your land
and revived the fortunes of Jacob,
you forgave the guilt of your people
and covered all their sins.
You averted all your rage,
you calmed the heat of your anger.

Revive us now, God, our helper!
Put an end to your grievance against us.
Will you be angry with us for ever,
will your anger never cease?

Will you not restore again our life
that your people may rejoice in you?
Let us see, O Lord, your mercy
and give us your saving help.

I will hear what the Lord God has to say,
a voice that speaks of peace,
peace for his people and his friends

and those who turn to him in their hearts.
His help is near for those who fear him
and his glory will dwell in our land.

Mercy and faithfulness have met;
justice and peace have embraced.
Faithfulness shall spring from the earth
and justice look down from heaven.

The Lord will make us prosper
and our earth shall yield its fruit.
Justice shall march before him
and peace shall follow his steps.

Ant.   Truth has arisen from the earth, and justice has
       looked down from the heavens.

Ant. 2 Wherever you are, Lord, there is mercy, there
        is truth.

Psalm 89:2–38

I

I will sing for ever of your love, O Lord;
through all ages my mouth will proclaim your truth.
Of this I am sure, that your love lasts for ever,
that your truth is firmly established as the heavens.

"With my chosen one I have made a covenant;
I have sworn to David my servant:
I will establish your dynasty for ever
and set up your throne through all ages."

The heavens proclaim your wonders, O Lord;
the assembly of your holy ones proclaims your truth.
For who in the skies can compare with the Lord
or who is like the Lord among the sons of God?

A God to be feared in the council of the holy ones,
great and dreadful to all around him.

O Lord God of hosts, who is your equal?
You are mighty, O Lord, and truth is your garment.

It is you who rule the sea in its pride;
it is you who still the surging of its waves.
You crushed the monster Rahab and killed it,
scattering your foes with your mighty arm.

The heavens are yours, the world is yours.
It is you who founded the earth and all it holds;
it is you who created the North and the South.
Tabor and Hermon shout with joy at your name.

Yours is a mighty arm, O Lord;
your hand is strong, your right hand ready.
Justice and right are the pillars of your throne,
love and truth walk in your presence.

Happy the people who acclaim such a king,
who walk, O Lord, in the light of your face,
who find their joy every day in your name,
who make your justice the source of their bliss.

For you, O Lord, are the glory of their strength;
by your favor it is that our might is exalted:
for our ruler is in the keeping of the Lord;
our king in the keeping of the Holy One of Israel.

Ant.   Wherever you are, Lord, there is mercy, there is
        truth.

Ant. 3 He himself will call out to me: You are my
        Father, alleluia.

II

Of old you spoke in a vision.
To your friends the prophets you said:
"I have set the crown on a warrior,
I have exalted one chosen from the people.

I have found David my servant
and with my holy oil anointed him.
My hand shall always be with him
and my arm shall make him strong.

The enemy shall never outwit him
nor the evil man oppress him.
I will beat down his foes before him
and smite those who hate him.

My truth and my love shall be with him;
by my name his might shall be exalted.
I will stretch out his hand to the Sea
and his right hand as far as the River.

He will say to me: 'You are my father,
my God, the rock who saves me.'
And I will make him my first-born,
the highest of the kings of the earth.

I will keep my love for him always;
with him my covenant shall last.
I will establish his dynasty for ever,
make his throne endure as the heavens."

Ant.   He himself will call out to me: You are my Father,
        alleluia.

The Lord has made known, alleluia.
—His saving power, alleluia.

FIRST READING

From the letter to the Colossians   1:15—2:3

*Christ, the head of the Church; Paul the servant of the
Church*

   Christ Jesus is the image of the invisible God, the
first-born of all creatures. In him everything in heaven
and on earth was created, things visible and invisible,

whether thrones or dominations, principalities or powers; all were created through him, and for him. He is before all else that is. In him everything continues in being.

It is he who is head of the body, the church; he who is the beginning, the first-born of the dead, so that primacy may be his in everything. It pleased God to make absolute fullness reside in him and, by means of him, to reconcile everything in his person, both on earth and in the heavens, making peace through the blood of his cross.

You yourselves were once alienated from him; you nourished hostility in your hearts because of your evil deeds. But now Christ has achieved reconciliation for you in his mortal body by dying, so as to present you to God holy, free of reproach and blame. But you must hold fast to faith, be firmly grounded and steadfast in it, unshaken in the hope promised you by the gospel you have heard. It is the gospel which has been announced to every creature under heaven, and I, Paul, am its servant.

Even now I find my joy in the suffering I endure for you. In my own flesh I fill up what is lacking in the sufferings of Christ for the sake of his body, the church. I became a minister of this church through the commission God gave me to preach among you his word in its fullness, that mystery hidden from ages and generations past but now revealed to his holy ones. God has willed to make known to them the glory beyond price which this mystery brings to the Gentiles—the mystery of Christ in you, your hope of glory. This is the Christ we proclaim while we admonish all men and teach them in the full measure of wisdom, hoping to make every man complete in Christ. For this I work and struggle, impelled by that energy of his which is so powerful a force within me.

I want you to know how hard I am struggling for you and for the Laodiceans and the many others who have never seen me in the flesh. I wish their hearts to be strengthened and themselves to be closely united in love, enriched with full assurance by their knowledge of the mystery of God—namely Christ—in whom every treasure of wisdom and knowledge is hidden.

RESPONSORY   Colossians 1:18, 17

Christ is the head, and the Church is his body;
he is the firstborn of the dead,
—so that in every way the primacy is his.

Before anything came into being, he existed:
he holds all things in unity.
—So that in . . .

SECOND READING

From a treatise On the Refutation of All Heresies by Saint Hippolytus, priest

(Cap. 10, 33–34: PG 16, 3452–3453)

The Word made flesh makes man divine

Our faith is not founded upon empty words; nor are we carried away by mere caprice or beguiled by specious arguments. On the contrary, we put our faith in words spoken by the power of God, spoken by the Word himself at God's command. God wished to win men back from disobedience, not by using force to reduce him to slavery but by addressing to his free will a call to liberty.

The Word spoke first of all through the prophets, but because the message was couched in such obscure language that it could be only dimly apprehended, in the last days the Father sent the Word in person, commanding him to show himself openly so that the world could see him and be saved.

We know that by taking a body from the Virgin he refashioned our fallen nature. We know that his manhood was of the same clay as our own; if this were not so, he would hardly have been a teacher who could expect to be imitated. If he were of a different substance from me, he would surely not have ordered me to do as he did, when by my very nature I am so weak. Such a demand could not be reconciled with his goodness and justice.

No. He wanted us to consider him as no different from ourselves, and so he worked, he was hungry and thirsty, he slept. Without protest he endured his passion, he submitted to death and revealed his resurrection. In all these ways he offered his own manhood as the firstfruits of our race to keep us from losing heart when suffering comes our way, and to make us look forward to receiving the same reward as he did, since we know that we possess the same humanity.

When we have come to know the true God, both our bodies and our souls will be immortal and incorruptible. We shall enter the kingdom of heaven, because while we lived on earth we acknowleged heaven's King. Friends of God and coheirs with Christ, we shall be subject to no evil desires or inclinations, or to any affliction of body or soul, for we shall have become divine. It was because of our human condition that God allowed us to endure these things, but when we have been deified and made immortal, God has promised us a share in his own attributes.

The saying "Know yourself" means therefore that we should recognize and acknowledge in ourselves the God who made us in his own image, for if we do this, we in turn will be recognized and acknowledged by our Maker. So let us not be at enmity with ourselves, but change our way of life without delay. *For Christ who is God, exalted above all creation*, has taken away man's sin and has refashioned our fallen nature. In the beginning God made man in his image and so gave proof of his love for us. If we obey his holy commands and learn to imitate his goodness, we shall be like him and he will honor us. God is not beggarly, and for the sake of his own glory he has given us a share in his divinity.

RESPONSORY   John 1:14; Baruch 3:38

The Word was made man, and lived among us.
—We have seen his glory,
the glory of the Father's only Son, full of grace and truth.

He was seen on earth and lived among men.
—We have seen . . .

HYMN, TE DEUM, 651.

Prayer, as in Morning Prayer.

Morning Prayer

Hymn, antiphons, psalms and canticle, as in Morning Prayer of Christmas, 407.

READING   Isaiah 9:6

A child is born to us, a son is given us;
    upon his shoulder dominion rests.
They name him Wonder-Counselor, God-Hero,
    Father-Forever, Prince of Peace.

RESPONSORY

The Lord has made known, alleluia, alleluia.
—The Lord has made known, alleluia, alleluia.

His saving power.
—Alleluia, alleluia.

Glory to the Father . . .
—The Lord has . . .

CANTICLE OF ZECHARIAH

Ant.   At the Lord's birth the choirs of angels sang:
Blessed be our God enthroned as King and
blessed be the Lamb.

INTERCESSIONS

Let us pray to Christ, in whom the Father willed to make
all things new:
Beloved Son of God, hear us.

Son of God, you were with the Father in the beginning,
and in the fullness of time you became a man,
— give us a brother's love for all people.

You became poor to make us rich; you emptied yourself
that we might be lifted up by your lowliness and share
in your glory,
— make us faithful ministers of your Gospel.

You shone on those who dwelt in darkness and the
shadow of death,
— give us holiness, justice and peace.

Give us a heart that is upright and sincere, so that we may
listen to your word,
— and bring it to perfection in ourselves and in the world
for the sake of your glory.

Our Father . . .

Prayer

All-powerful God,
may the human birth of your Son
free us from our former slavery to sin
and bring us new life.

We ask this through our Lord Jesus Christ, your Son,
who lives and reigns with you and the Holy Spirit,
one God, for ever and ever.

Daytime Prayer

Psalms from the current weekday.

Midmorning

Ant.   Mary, the mother of Jesus, and Joseph were filled
       with wonder at all that was said of the child.

READING   Deuteronomy 4:7

What great nation is there that has gods so close to it as
the Lord, our God, is to us whenever we call upon him?

The Lord has remembered his gracious promise, alleluia.
—He has kept faith with his people Israel, alleluia.

Midday

Ant.   Mary treasured all these words and pondered
       them in her heart.

READING   Isaiah 12:5-6

Sing praise to the Lord for his glorious achievement;
    let this be known throughout all the earth.
Shout with exultation, O city of Zion,
    for great in your midst
    is the Holy One of Israel!

All the ends of the earth, alleluia.
—Have seen the saving power of God, alleluia.

Midafternoon

Ant.   My own eyes have seen the salvation which you
       have prepared in the sight of every people.

READING   Tobit 14:6-7

All the nations shall abandon their idols and come to
Jerusalem to dwell, and all the kings of the earth shall
rejoice in her, worshiping the king of Israel.

Mercy and truth have come together, alleluia.
—Justice and peace have kissed, alleluia.

Prayer, as in Morning Prayer.

Evening Prayer

Hymn, antiphons, psalms and canticle, as in Evening Prayer II
of Christmas, 414.

READING   See 2 Peter 1:3-4

The divine power of Christ has freely bestowed on us
everything necessary for a life of genuine piety, through
knowledge of him who called us by his own glory and
power. By virtue of them he has bestowed on us the great
and precious things he promised, so that through these
you who have fled a world corrupted by lust might
become sharers of the divine nature.

RESPONSORY

The Word was made man, alleluia, alleluia.
—The Word was made man, alleluia, alleluia.

He lived among us.
—Alleluia, alleluia.

Glory to the Father . . .
—The Word was . . .

CANTICLE OF MARY

Ant.   We sing your praises, holy Mother of God: you
        gave birth to our Savior, Jesus Christ; watch over
        all who honor you.

INTERCESSIONS

Let us joyfully acclaim Christ, born at Bethlehem in
    Judea, for he gives nourishment and guidance to his
    holy people:

Let your favor rest upon us, Lord.

Christ the Savior, desired of the nations, spread your
   Gospel to places still deprived of the Word of life,
—draw every person to yourself.

Christ the Lord, let your Church grow and extend the
   boundaries of its homeland,
—until it embraces men and women of every language
   and race.

King of kings, direct the hearts and minds of rulers,
—to seek justice, peace and freedom for all nations.

Almighty ruler, strength of the weak, support those in
   temptation, lift up the fallen, protect those living in
   danger,
—console those who have been deceived, comfort the
   incurably ill, strengthen the faith of the anxious.

Consoler of the sorrowful, comfort the dying,
—and lead them to the fountains of living water.

Our Father . . .

Prayer

All-powerful God,
may the human birth of your Son
free us from our former slavery to sin
and bring us new life.
We ask this through our Lord Jesus Christ, your Son,
who lives and reigns with you and the Holy Spirit,
one God, for ever and ever.

December 31

SEVENTH DAY IN THE OCTAVE OF CHRISTMAS

Invitatory

Ant.   Christ is born for us; come, let us adore him.

Invitatory psalm, as in the Ordinary, 648.

Office of Readings

HYMN, 385.

PSALMODY

Ant. 1   Let the heavens rejoice and the earth be glad in the presence of the Lord, for he has come.

Psalm 96

O sing a new song to the Lord,
sing to the Lord, all the earth.
O sing to the Lord, bless his name.

Proclaim his help day by day,
tell among the nations his glory
and his wonders among all the peoples.

The Lord is great and worthy of praise,
to be feared above all gods;
the gods of the heathens are naught.

It was the Lord who made the heavens,
his are majesty and state and power
and splendor in his holy place.

Give the Lord, you families of peoples,
give the Lord glory and power,
give the Lord the glory of his name.

Bring an offering and enter his courts,
worship the Lord in his temple.
O earth, tremble before him.

Proclaim to the nations: "God is king."
The world he made firm in its place;
he will judge the peoples in fairness.

Let the heavens rejoice and earth be glad,
let the sea and all within it thunder praise,
let the land and all it bears rejoice,
all the trees of the wood shout for joy

at the presence of the Lord for he comes,
he comes to rule the earth.
With justice he will rule the world,
he will judge the peoples with his truth.

Ant.   Let the heavens rejoice and the earth be glad in
the presence of the Lord, for he has come.

Ant. 2   A light has dawned for the just; joy has come to
the upright of heart, alleluia.

Psalm 97

The Lord is king, let earth rejoice,
let all the coastlands be glad.
Cloud and darkness are his raiment;
his throne, justice and right.

A fire prepares his path;
it burns up his foes on every side.
His lightnings light up the world,
the earth trembles at the sight.

The mountains melt like wax
before the Lord of all the earth.
The skies proclaim his justice;
all peoples see his glory.

Let those who serve idols be ashamed,
those who boast of their worthless gods.
All you spirits, worship him.

Zion hears and is glad;
the people of Judah rejoice
because of your judgments, O Lord.

For you indeed are the Lord,
most high above all the earth,
exalted far above all spirits.

The Lord loves those who hate evil:
he guards the souls of his saints;
he sets them free from the wicked.

Light shines forth for the just
and joy for the upright of heart.
Rejoice, you just, in the Lord;
give glory to his holy name.

Ant.   A light has dawned for the just; joy has come to
the upright of heart, alleluia.

Ant. 3   The Lord has made known his saving power,
alleluia.

Psalm 98

Sing a new song to the Lord
for he has worked wonders.
His right hand and his holy arm
have brought salvation.

The Lord has made known his salvation;
has shown his justice to the nations.
He has remembered his truth and love
for the house of Israel.

All the ends of the earth have seen
the salvation of our God.
Shout to the Lord all the earth,
ring out your joy.

Sing psalms to the Lord with the harp,
with the sound of music.
With trumpets and the sound of the horn
acclaim the King, the Lord.

Let the sea and all within it thunder;
the world, and all its peoples.
Let the rivers clap their hands
and the hills ring out their joy

Rejoice at the presence of the Lord,
for he comes to rule the earth.
He will rule the world with justice
and the peoples with fairness.

Ant.   The Lord had made known his saving power,
alleluia.

In these last days God has spoken to us through his Son.
—The Word through whom he made all things.

First Reading

From the letter to the Colossians   2:4-15

Our faith in Christ

I tell you all this so that no one may delude you with
specious arguments. I may be absent in body but I am
with you in spirit, happy to see good order among you
and the firmness of your faith in Christ.

Continue, therefore, to live in Christ Jesus the Lord,
in the spirit in which you received him. Be rooted in him
and built up in him, growing ever stronger in faith, as
you were taught, and overflowing with gratitude.

See to it that no one deceives you through any empty,
seductive philosophy that follows mere human traditions, a philosophy based on cosmic powers rather than
on Christ.

In Christ the fullness of deity resides in bodily form. Yours is a share of this fullness, in him who is the head of every principality and power.

You were also circumcised in him, not with the circumcision administered by hand but with Christ's circumcision which strips off the carnal body completely. In baptism you were not only buried with him but also raised to life with him because you believed in the power of God who raised him from the dead. Even when you were dead in sin and your flesh was uncircumcised, God gave you new life in company with Christ. He pardoned all our sins.

He canceled the bond that stood against us with all its claims, snatching it up and nailing it to the cross. Thus did God disarm the principalities and powers. He made a public show of them and, leading them off captive, triumphed in the person of Christ.

RESPONSORY   Colossians 2:9, 10, 12

The fullness of divinity lives in Christ's humanity;
—he is the head over every power and authority.

In baptism we were buried with Christ,
and in baptism we have risen to a new life with him
through our faith in the power of God.
—He is the . . .

SECOND READING

From a sermon by Saint Leo the Great, pope

(Sermo 6 in Nativitate Domini, 2–3, 5: PL 54, 213–216)

The birthday of the Lord is the birthday of peace!

Although the state of infancy, which the majesty of the Son of God did not disdain to assume, developed with the passage of time into the maturity of manhood, and although after the triumph of the passion and the resurrection all his lowly acts undertaken on our behalf belong to the past, nevertheless today's feast of Christmas renews for us the sacred beginning of Jesus' life, his birth from the Virgin Mary. In the very act in which we are reverencing the birth of our Savior, we are also celebrating our own new birth. For the birth of Christ is the origin of the Christian people; and the birthday of the head is also the birthday of the body.

Though each and every individual occupies a definite place in this body to which he has been called, and though all the progeny of the church is differentiated and marked with the passage of time, nevertheless as the whole community of the faithful, once begotten in the baptismal font, was crucified with Christ in the passion, raised up with him in the resurrection and at the ascension placed at the right hand of the Father, so too it is born with him in this Nativity, which we are celebrating today.

For every believer regenerated in Christ, no matter in what part of the whole world he may be, breaks with that ancient way of life that derives from original sin, and by rebirth is transformed into a new man. Henceforth he is reckoned to be of the stock, not of his earthly father, but of Christ, who became Son of Man precisely that men could become sons of God; for unless in humility he had come down to us, none of us by our own merits could ever go up to him.

Therefore the greatness of the gift which he has bestowed on us demands an appreciation proportioned to its excellence; for blessed Paul the Apostle truly teaches: *We have received not the spirit of this world, but the Spirit which is from God, that we might understand the gifts bestowed on us by God.* The only way that he can be

worthily honored by us is by the presentation to him of
that which he has already given to us.

But what can we find in the treasure of the Lord's
bounty more in keeping with the glory of this feast than
that peace which was first announced by the angelic choir
on the day of his birth? For that peace, from which the
sons of God spring, sustains love and mothers unity; it
refreshes the blessed and shelters eternity; its characteristic function and special blessing is to join to God those
whom it separates from this world.

Therefore, may those *who were born, not of blood nor of
the will of the flesh nor of the will of man, but of God,* offer
to the Father their harmony as sons united in peace; and
may all those whom he has adopted as his members meet
in the firstborn of the new creation who came not to do
his own will but the will of the one who sent him; for the
grace of the Father has adopted as heirs neither the
contentious nor the dissident, but those who are one in
thought and love. The hearts and minds of those who
have been reformed according to one and the same image
should be in harmony with one another.

The birthday of the Lord is the birthday of peace, as
Paul the Apostle says: *For he is our peace, who has made us
both one;* for whether we be Jew or Gentile, *through him
we have access in one Spirit to the Father.*

RESPONSORY   Ephesians 2:13-14, 17

You were once far away from God,
but now you have been brought very near through the
    blood of Christ.
—He himself is our peace who has made us all one.

Christ came to proclaim the good news to us:
peace to you who were far away,
and peace to those who were near.
—He himself is . . .

HYMN, TE DEUM, 651.
Prayer as in Morning Prayer.

Morning Prayer

Hymn, antiphons, psalms and canticle from Morning Prayer of
Christmas, 407.

READING   Isaiah 4:2-3

On that day,
The branch of the Lord will be luster and glory,
  and the fruit of the earth will be honor and splendor
  for the survivors of Israel.
He who remains in Zion
  and he that is left in Jerusalem
Will be called holy,
  every one marked down for life in Jerusalem.

RESPONSORY

The Lord has made known, alleluia, alleluia.
—The Lord has made known, alleluia, alleluia.

His saving power.
—Alleluia, alleluia.

Glory to the Father . . .
—The Lord has . . .

CANTICLE OF ZECHARIAH

Ant.   Suddenly there was with the angel a great compa-
       ny of the heavenly hosts, praising God and sing-
       ing: Glory to God in the highest and peace to his
       people on earth, alleluia.

INTERCESSIONS

Humbly yet confidently, let us invoke Christ the Lord
  whose favor has been shown to all people:
    Lord, have mercy.

Christ, born of the Father before the ages, splendor of his
    glory, image of his being, your word holds all creation
    in being,
—we ask you to give new life to our world through your
    Gospel.
Christ, you were born into the world at the fullness of
    time to save mankind and to give freedom to every
    creature,
—we ask you to extend the liberty of our sonship in you
    to all people.
Christ, consubstantial Son of the Father, begotten before
    the dawn of day, and born in Bethlehem in fulfillment
    of the Scriptures,
—we ask you to make your Church a notable example of
    poverty and simplicity.
Christ, God and man, Lord of David and Son of David,
    fulfillment of all prophecies,
—we pray that Israel may recognize you as its Messiah.

Our Father . . .

Prayer

Ever-living God,
in the birth of your Son
our religion has its origin and its perfect fulfillment.
Help us to share in the life of Christ
for he is the salvation of mankind,
who lives and reigns with you and the Holy Spirit,
one God, for ever and ever.

Daytime Prayer

Psalms from the current weekday.

Midmorning

Ant.   Mary, the mother of Jesus, and Joseph were filled
       with wonder at all that was said of the child.

READING   Isaiah 45:13

It was I who stirred up one for the triumph of justice;
    all his ways I make level.
He shall rebuild my city
    and let my exiles go free
Without price or ransom,
    says the Lord of hosts.

The Lord has remembered his gracious promise, alleluia.
—He has kept faith with his people Israel, alleluia.

Midday

Ant.   Mary treasured all these words and pondered
        them in her heart.

READING   Isaiah 48:20

With shouts of joy proclaim this,
    make it known;
Publish it to the ends of the earth, and say,
    "The Lord has redeemed his servant Jacob."

All the ends of the earth, alleluia.
—Have seen the saving power of God, alleluia.

Midafternoon

Ant.   My own eyes have seen the salvation which you
        have prepared in the sight of every people.

READING   Isaiah 65:1

I was ready to respond to those who asked me not,
    to be found by those who sought me not.
I said: Here I am! Here I am!
    to a nation that did not call upon my name.

Mercy and truth have come together, alleluia.
—Justice and peace have kissed, alleluia.

Prayer, as in Morning Prayer.

Octave of Christmas

MARY, MOTHER OF GOD

Solemnity

Evening Prayer I

HYMN

Antiphon:
Joy to you, O Virgin Mary, Mother of the Lord!

Humble maiden of Nazareth town,
Betrothed to the carpenter Joseph,
You became the mother of God.

Antiphon

You are the handmaid of God;
You found favor with him;
Full of grace, the Lord is with you.

Antiphon

Lovely Mother of Abraham's Son,
Praised Mother of David's Son,
Holy Mother of Jesus, the Lord:

Antiphon

You are blessed among all women;
Blessed is the fruit of your womb;
You are praised by all generations.

Antiphon

Your Son you bore in a manger,
Angels sang: "Glory to God,
On earth, peace to men of good will!"

Antiphon

You showed your child to the wise men,
You brought him up to the temple,
You brought joy to Simeon's old age.

Antiphon

Chosen Mother of the Messiah,
Virgin and daughter of Zion,
Joy and glory of God's holy people.

Antiphon

Melody: Joy to You   Music: Lucien Deiss, C.S.Sp., 1970
                            Text: Lucien Deiss, C.S.Sp., 1970

Ant. 1 O marvelous exchange! Man's Creator has
        become man, born of a virgin. We have been
        made sharers in the divinity of Christ who
        humbled himself to share in our humanity.

Psalms and canticle from the common of the Blessed Virgin
Mary, 1321.

Ant. 2 By your miraculous birth of the Virgin you have
        fulfilled the Scriptures: like a gentle rain falling
        upon the earth you have come down to save
        your people. O God, we praise you.

Ant. 3 Your blessed and fruitful virginity is like the
        bush, flaming yet unburned, which Moses saw
        on Sinai. Pray for us, Mother of God.

READING   Galatians 4:4-5

When the designated time had come, God sent forth
his Son born of a woman, born under the law, to deliver
from the law those who were subjected to it, so that we
might receive our status as adopted sons.

RESPONSORY

The Word was made man, alleluia, alleluia.
—The Word was made man, alleluia, alleluia.

He lived among us.
—Alleluia, alleluia.

Glory to the Father . . .

—The Word was . . .

CANTICLE OF MARY

Ant.   In his great love for us, God sent his Son in the
        likeness of our sinful nature, born of a woman and
        subject to the law, alleluia.

INTERCESSIONS

Blessed be the Lord Jesus, our Peace, who came to unite
    man with God. Let us pray to him in humility:
    Lord, grant your peace to all.

When you were born you showed your kindness and
    gentleness,

—help us always to be grateful for all your blessings.

You made Mary, your Mother, full of grace,

—give all people the fullness of grace.

You came to announce God's good news to the world,

—increase the number of preachers and hearers of your
    word.

You desired to become our brother by being born of the
    Virgin Mary,

—teach men and women to love each other in mutual
    brotherhood.

You came as the Sun rising over the earth,

—show the light of your countenance to those who have
    died.

Our Father . . .

Prayer

God our Father,

may we always profit by the prayers

of the Virgin Mother Mary,

for you bring us life and salvation

through Jesus Christ her Son

who lives and reigns with you and the Holy Spirit,

one God, for ever and ever.

Alternative Prayer

Father,
source of light in every age,
the virgin conceived and bore your Son
who is called Wonderful God, Prince of Peace.
May her prayer, the gift of a mother's love,
be your people's joy through all ages.
May her response, born of a humble heart,
draw your Spirit to rest on your people.
Grant this through Christ our Lord.

Invitatory

Ant.   Let us celebrate the motherhood of the Virgin
Mary; let us worship her Son, Christ the Lord.

Invitatory psalm, as in the Ordinary, 648.

Office of Readings

HYMN

Virgin born, we bow before you;
Blessed was the womb that bore you;
Mary, Mother meek and mild,
Blessed was she in her Child.
Blessed was the maid that fed you;
Blessed was the hand that led you;
Blessed was the parent's eye
That watched your slumbering infancy.

Blessed she by all creation,
Who brought forth the world's salvation;
And blessed they forever blest,
Who love you most and serve you best.
Virgin born, we bow before you:
Blessed was the womb that bore you;

Mary, Mother meek and mild,
Blessed was she in her Child.

Melody: Geneva

Music: Genevan Psalter, 1543
Text: R. Heber, 1783–1826, alt.

PSALMODY

Ant. 1　Lift high the ancient portals. The King of glory
　　　　enters.

Psalm 24

The Lord's is the earth and its fullness,
the world and all its peoples.
It is he who set it on the seas;
on the waters he made it firm.

Who shall climb the mountain of the Lord?
Who shall stand in his holy place?
The man with clean hands and pure heart,
who desires not worthless things,
who has not sworn so as to deceive his neighbor.

He shall receive blessings from the Lord
and reward from the God who saves him.
Such are the men who seek him,
seek the face of the God of Jacob.

O gates, lift high your heads;
grow higher, ancient doors.
Let him enter, the king of glory!

Who is the king of glory?
The Lord, the mighty, the valiant,
the Lord, the valiant in war.

O gates, lift high your heads;
grow higher, ancient doors.
Let him enter, the king of glory!

Who is he, the king of glory?
He, the Lord of armies,
he is the king of glory.

Ant.   Lift high the ancient portals. The King of glory
enters.

Ant. 2   The Lord Most High has founded a city, and all
people will be called its children.

Psalm 87

On the holy mountain is his city
cherished by the Lord.
The Lord prefers the gates of Zion
to all Jacob's dwellings.
Of you are told glorious things,
O city of God!

"Babylon and Egypt I will count
among those who know me;
Philistia, Tyre, Ethiopia,
these will be her children
and Zion shall be called 'Mother'
for all shall be her children."

It is he, the Lord Most High,
who gives each his place.
In his register of peoples he writes:
"These are her children,"
and while they dance they will sing:
"In you all find their home."

Ant.   The Lord Most High has founded a city, and all
people will be called its children.

Ant. 3   Begotten of the Father, before the daystar
shone or time began, the Lord and Savior has
humbled himself to be born for us today.

Psalm 99

The Lord is king; the peoples tremble.
He is throned on the cherubim; the earth quakes.
The Lord is great in Zion.

He is supreme over all the peoples.
Let them praise his name, so terrible and great.
He is holy, full of power.

You are a king who loves what is right;
you have established equity, justice and right;
you have established them in Jacob.

Exalt the Lord our God;
bow down before Zion, his footstool.
He the Lord is holy.

Among his priests were Aaron and Moses,
among those who invoked his name was Samuel.
They invoked the Lord and he answered.

To them he spoke in the pillar of cloud.
They did his will; they kept the law,
which he, the Lord, had given.

O Lord our God, you answered them.
For them you were a God who forgives;
yet you punished all their offenses.

Exalt the Lord our God;
bow down before his holy mountain
for the Lord our God is holy.

Ant.   Begotten of the Father, before the daystar shone
       or time began, the Lord and Savior has humbled
       himself to be born for us today.

The Word was made man, alleluia.
—And lived among us, alleluia.

FIRST READING

From the letter to the Hebrews   2:9-17

Christ is like his brothers in every way

We see Jesus crowned with glory and honor because he suffered death: Jesus, who was made for a little while lower than the angels, that through God's gracious will he might taste death for the sake of all men.

Indeed, it was fitting that when bringing many sons to glory, God, for whom and through whom all things exist, should make their leader in the work of salvation perfect through suffering. He who consecrates and those who are consecrated have one and the same Father. Therefore, he is not ashamed to call them brothers, saying,

"I will announce your name to my brothers,
I will sing your praise in the midst of the assembly";
and,
"I will put my trust in him";
and again,
"Here am I, and the children God has given me!"

Now since the children are men of blood and flesh, Jesus likewise had a full share in ours, that by his death he might rob the devil, the prince of death, of his power, and free those who through fear of death had been slaves their whole life long. Surely he did not come to help angels, but rather the children of Abraham; therefore he had to become like his brothers in every way, that he might be a merciful and faithful high priest before God on their behalf, to expiate the sins of the people.

RESPONSORY   Luke 1:28

How blessed are you, Virgin Mary,
for you carried within you the Lord, the Creator of the
    world.

—Mother of your Maker, you remain a virgin for ever.

Hail Mary, full of grace, the Lord is with you.
—Mother of your . . .

SECOND READING

From a letter by Saint Athanasius, bishop

(Epist. Ad Epictetum, 5-9: PG 26, 1058. 1062-1066)

The Word took our nature from Mary

The Apostle tells us: *The Word took to himself the sons of Abraham, and so had to be like his brothers in all things.* He had then to take a body like ours. This explains the fact of Mary's presence: she is to provide him with a body of his own, to be offered for our sake. Scripture records her giving birth, and says: *She wrapped him in swaddling clothes.* Her breasts, which fed him, were called blessed. Sacrifice was offered because the child was her firstborn. Gabriel used careful and prudent language when he announced his birth. He did not speak of "what will be born *in you*" to avoid the impression that a body would be introduced into her womb from outside; he spoke of "what will be born *from you,*" so that we might know by faith that her child originated within her and from her.

By taking our nature and offering it in sacrifice, the Word was to destroy it completely and then invest it with his own nature, and so prompt the Apostle to say: *This corruptible body must put on incorruption; this mortal body must put on immortality.*

This was not done in outward show only, as some have imagined. This is not so. Our Savior truly became man, and from this has followed the salvation of man as a whole. Our salvation is in no way fictitious, nor does it apply only to the body. The salvation of the whole man, that is, of soul and body, has really been achieved in the Word himself.

What was born of Mary was therefore human by nature, in accordance with the inspired Scriptures, and the body of the Lord was a true body: It was a true body because it was the same as ours. Mary, you see, is our sister, for we are all born from Adam.

The words of Saint John: *The Word was made flesh,* bear the same meaning, as we may see from a similar turn of phrase in Saint Paul: *Christ was made a curse for our sake.* Man's body has acquired something great through its communion and union with the Word. From being mortal it has been made immortal; though it was a living body it has become a spiritual one; though it was made from the earth it has passed through the gates of heaven.

Even when the Word takes a body from Mary, the Trinity remains a Trinity, with neither increase nor decrease. It is for ever perfect. In the Trinity we acknowledge one Godhead, and thus one God, the Father of the Word, is proclaimed in the Church.

RESPONSORY

O pure and holy Virgin,
how can I find words to praise your beauty?
—The highest heavens cannot contain God whom you
   carried in your womb.

Blessed are you among women,
and blessed is the fruit of your womb.
—The highest heavens. . .

HYMN, Te Deum, 651.

Prayer, as in Morning Prayer

Morning Prayer

HYMN

> O Mary, of all women,
> You are the chosen one,
> Who, ancient prophets promised,
> Would bear God's only Son;
> All Hebrew generations
> Prepared the way to thee,
> That in your womb the God-man
> Might come to set man free.
>
> O Mary, you embody
> All God taught to our race,
> For you are first and foremost
> In fullness of his grace;
> We praise this wondrous honor
> That you gave birth to him
> Who from you took his manhood
> And saved us from our sin.

Melody: Au fort de ma detresse 76.76D   Music: 17th century
Flemish Melody
Text: Michael Gannon

Ant. 1   The Virgin has given birth to the Savior: a
flower has sprung from Jesse's stock and a star
has risen from Jacob. O God, we praise you.

Psalms and canticle from Sunday, Week I, 688.

Ant. 2   Mary has given birth to our Savior. John the
Baptist saw him and cried out: This is the
Lamb of God, who takes away the sins of the
world, alleluia.

Ant. 3   Mary has given birth to a King whose name is
everlasting; hers the joy of motherhood, hers
the virgin's glory. Never was the like seen
before, never shall it be seen again, alleluia.

READING   Micah 5:2, 3, 4a

The ruler in Israel will give them up, until the time
    when she who is to give birth has borne,
And the rest of his brethren shall return
    to the children of Israel.
He shall stand firm and shepherd his flock
    by the strength of the Lord,
    in the majestic name of the Lord, his God.
He shall be peace.

RESPONSORY

The Lord has made known, alleluia, alleluia.
  —The Lord has made known, alleluia, alleluia.

His saving power.
  —Alleluia, alleluia.

Glory to the Father . . .
  —The Lord has . . .

CANTICLE OF ZECHARIAH

Ant. Marvelous is the mystery proclaimed today: man's
       nature is made new as God becomes man; he
       remains what he was and becomes what he was
       not. Yet each nature stays distinct and for ever
       undivided.

INTERCESSIONS

Let us give glory to Christ who was born of the Virgin
    Mary by the power of the Holy Spirit, and let us pray
    to him in these words:
    Son of the Virgin Mary, have mercy on us.
Christ, born of the Virgin Mary, you are Wonder-
    Counselor and Prince of Peace,

—give your peace to the world.

Our King and our God, you have raised us up by your coming,

—help us to honor you all the days of our lives by our faith and our deeds.

You made yourself like us,

—in your mercy grant that we may become more like you.

You made yourself a citizen of our earthly city,

—grant that we may become citizens of our true homeland, your kingdom in heaven.

Our Father . . .

Prayer

God our Father,
may we always profit by the prayers
of the Virgin Mother Mary,
for you bring us life and salvation
through Jesus Christ her Son
who lives and reigns with you and the Holy Spirit,
one God, for ever and ever.

Alternative Prayer

Father,
source of light in every age,
the virgin conceived and bore your Son
who is called Wonderful God, Prince of Peace.
May her prayer, the gift of a mother's love,
be your people's joy through all ages.
May her response, born of a humble heart,
draw your Spirit to rest on your people.
Grant this through Christ our Lord.

Daytime Prayer

Complementary psalmody, 1191, unless January 1 occurs on Sunday. In place of 122, psalm 129 is said, 1129, and in place of psalm 127, psalm 131, 972, may be said.

Midmorning

Ant.   Mary, the mother of Jesus, and Joseph were filled with wonder at all that was said of the child.

READING   Zephaniah 3:14, 15b

Shout for joy, O daughter Zion!
   sing joyfully, O Israel!
Be glad and exult with all your heart,
   O daughter Jerusalem!
The King of Israel, the Lord,
   is in your midst.

The Lord has remembered his gracious promise, alleluia.
—He has kept faith with his people Israel, alleluia.

Midday

Ant.   Mary treasured all these words and pondered them in her heart.

READING   Zechariah 9:9a

Rejoice heartily, O daughter Zion,
   shout for joy, O daughter Jerusalem.
See, your king shall come to you;
   a just savior is he.

All the ends of the earth, alleluia.
—Have seen the saving power of God, alleluia.

Midafternoon

Ant.   My own eyes have seen the salvation which you have prepared in the sight of every people.

READING   Baruch 5:3-4

God will show all the earth your splendor:
    you will be named by God forever
    the peace of justice, the glory of God's worship.

Mercy and truth have come together, alleluia.
—Justice and peace have kissed, alleluia.

Prayer, as in Morning Prayer

Evening Prayer II

HYMN

Antiphon:
Joy to you, O Virgin Mary, Mother of the Lord!

Humble maiden of Nazareth town,
Betrothed to the carpenter Joseph,
You became the mother of God.

Antiphon

You are blessed among all women;
Blessed is the fruit of your womb;
You are praised by all generations.

Antiphon

Your Son you bore in a manger,
Angels sang: "Glory to God,
On earth, peace to men of good will!"

Antiphon

You showed your child to the wise men,
You brought him up to the temple,
You brought joy to Simeon's old age.

Antiphon

Chosen Mother of the Messiah,
Virgin and daughter of Zion,
Joy and glory of God's holy people;

Antiphon

Suffering Mother under the cross,
Glorious Mother of the Apostles,
Queen and mother of all generations.

Antiphon

Melody: Joy to You   Music: Lucien Deiss, C.S.Sp., 1970
                            Text: Lucien Deiss, C.S. Sp., 1970

Ant.   O marvelous exchange! Man's Creator has become
       man, born of a virgin. We have been made sharers
       in the divinity of Christ who humbled himself to
       share in our humanity.

Psalms and canticle from the common of the Blessed Virgin
Mary, 1345.

Ant. 2 By your miraculous birth from the virgin you
        have fulfilled the Scriptures: like a gentle rain
        falling upon the earth you have come down to
        save your people. O God, we praise you.

Ant. 3 Your blessed and fruitful virginity is like the
        bush, flaming yet unburned, which Moses saw
        on Sinai. Pray for us, Mother of God.

READING   Galatians 4:4-5

   When the designated time had come, God sent forth
his Son born of a woman, born under the law, to deliver
from the law those who were subjected to it, so that we
might receive our status as adopted sons.

RESPONSORY

The Word was made man, alleluia, alleluia.
—The Word was made man, alleluia, alleluia.

He lived among us.
—Alleluia, alleluia.

Glory to the Father . . .
—The Word was . . .

CANTICLE OF MARY

Ant.   Blessed is the womb which bore you, O Christ,
        and the breast that nursed you, Lord and Savior
        of the world, alleluia.

INTERCESSIONS

To Christ, Emmanuel, whom the Virgin conceived and
    brought forth, let us give praise and pray to him:
    Son of the Virgin Mary, hear us.
You gave Mary the joy of motherhood,
—give all parents true joy in their children.
King of peace, your kingdom is one of justice and peace,
—help us to seek the paths of peace.
You came to make the human race the holy people of
    God,
—bring all nations to acknowledge the unifying bond of
    your love.
By your birth you strengthened family ties,
—help families to come to a greater love for one another.
You desired to be born into the days of time,
—grant that our departed brothers and sisters may be
    born into the day of eternity.

Our Father . . .

Prayer

God our Father,
may we always profit by the prayers
of the Virgin Mother Mary,
for you bring us life and salvation
through Jesus Christ her Son
who lives and reigns with you and the Holy Spirit,
one God, for ever and ever.

Alternative Prayer

Father,
source of light in every age,

the virgin conceived and bore your Son
who is called Wonderful God, Prince of Peace.
May her prayer, the gift of a mother's love,
be your people's joy through all ages.
May her response, born of a humble heart,
draw your Spirit to rest on your people.

Grant this through Christ our Lord.

Where the solemnity of the Epiphany is celebrated on the Sunday between January 2 and January 8, the office of the Second Sunday after Christmas is not used. After the Epiphany is celebrated, the office is as given on 385–393, with the proper parts on 575ff, unless Sunday occurs on January 7 or 8, in which case Ordinary Time begins on the following day, the feast of the Baptism of the Lord being omitted.

SECOND SUNDAY AFTER CHRISTMAS

Sunday between January 2 and 5
when Epiphany is celebrated on January 6

Psalter, Week II

Evening Prayer I

HYMN, 385.

Ant. 1 Trusting in the Lord's promise, the Virgin Mary conceived a child, and remaining a virgin she gave birth to the King of kings.

Psalms and canticle from Sunday, Week II, 794.

Ant. 2 Sing for joy with Jerusalem; the Lord has refreshed her like a river of peace.

Ant. 3 He who was from the beginning, God from God, Light from Light, is born for us.

READING   1 John 5:20

We know that the Son of God has come and has given us discernment to recognize the One who is true, for we are in his Son Jesus Christ. He is the true God and eternal life.

RESPONSORY

The Word was made man, alleluia, alleluia.
—The Word was made man, alleluia, alleluia.

He lived among us.
—Alleluia, alleluia.

Glory to the Father . . .
—The Word was . . .

Ant. By the power of the Holy Spirit the Virgin Mary has conceived a child; she carries in her womb this mystery which she cannot comprehend.

INTERCESSIONS

Christ Jesus emptied himself and took the form of a
  slave. He was tested like us in all things and did not
  sin. Now let us worship him and pray to him with
  deep faith:
  By the power of your birth, comfort those who are saved.

You came into the world heralding the new age foretold
  by the prophets,
—give your holy people the gift of renewal in every
  generation.

You once took on the weakness of our human condition,
—be light now for those who do not see, strength for the
  wavering, and comfort for the troubled of heart.

You were born into poverty and lowliness,
—look with favor on the poor and comfort them.

By your birth bring joy to all peoples with the promise of
  unending life,
—give joy to the dying through the hope of heavenly
  birth.

You came to earth to lead everyone into the kingdom,
—share your life of glory with those who have died.

Our Father . . .

Prayer

God of power and life,
glory of all who believe in you,
fill the world with your splendor
and show the nations the light of your truth.

We ask this through our Lord Jesus Christ, your Son,
who lives and reigns with you and the Holy Spirit,
one God, for ever and ever.

Alternative Prayer

Father of our Lord Jesus Christ,
our glory is to stand before the world

as your own sons and daughters.
May the simple beauty of Jesus' birth
summon us always to love what is most deeply human,
and to see your Word made flesh
reflected in those whose lives we touch.
We ask this through Christ our Lord.

Invitatory

Ant.   Christ is born for us; come, let us adore him.

Invitatory Psalm, as in the Ordinary, 648.

Office of Readings

HYMN, 385.

Antiphons and psalms from Sunday, Week II, 798. Verse, readings and responsories from the current weekday, 502ff.

HYMN, Te Deum, 651.

Prayer, as in Morning Prayer.

Morning Prayer

HYMN, 385.

Ant. 1   A light has dawned for the just man: the Savior of the world is born, alleluia.

Psalms and canticle from Sunday, Week II, 822.

Ant. 2   Let us sing with joy to the Lord our God.

Ant. 3   The people who lived in darkness have seen a great light.

READING   Hebrews 1:1-2

In times past, God spoke in fragmentary and varied ways to our fathers through the prophets; in this, the final age, he has spoken to us through his Son, whom he has made heir of all things and through whom he first created the universe.

RESPONSORY

Christ, Son of the living God, have mercy on us.
—Christ, Son of the living God, have mercy on us.
You were born of the Virgin Mary.
—Have mercy on us.
Glory to the Father . . .
—Christ, Son of . . .

CANTICLE OF ZECHARIAH

Ant.   The Virgin believed in the Lord's promise: as a
        virgin she gave birth to the Word made man, and
        yet she remained a virgin. Let us praise her and
        say: Blessed are you among women.

INTERCESSIONS

The Word of God existed before the creation of the
    universe yet was born among us in time. We praise
    and worship him as we cry out in joy:
    Let the earth ring out with joy for you have come.
You are the unending Word of God who flooded the
    world with joy at your birth,
—fill us with joy by the continuous gift of your life.
You saved us and by your birth revealed to us the
    covenant faithfulness of the Lord,
—help us to be faithful to the promises of our baptism.
You are the King of heaven and earth who sent
    messengers to announce peace to all,
—let our lives be filled with your peace.
You are the true vine that brings forth the fruit of life,
—make us branches of the vine, bearing much fruit.

Our Father . . .

Prayer

God of power and life,
glory of all who believe in you,
fill the world with your splendor
and show the nations the light of your truth.

We ask this through our Lord Jesus Christ, your Son,
who lives and reigns with you and the Holy Spirit,
one God, for ever and ever.

Alternative Prayer

Father of our Lord Jesus Christ,
our glory is to stand before the world
as your own sons and daughters.
May the simple beauty of Jesus' birth
summon us always to love what is most deeply human,
and to see your Word made flesh
reflected in those whose lives we touch.

We ask this through Christ our Lord.

Daytime Prayer

Midmorning

Ant.   Mary, the mother of Jesus, and Joseph were filled
        with wonder at all that was said of the child.

READING   Titus 2:11-12

The grace of God has appeared, offering salvation to all
men. It trains us to reject godless ways and worldly
desires, and live temperately, justly, and devoutly in this
age.

The Lord has remembered his gracious promise, alleluia.
—He has kept faith with his people Israel, alleluia.

Midday

Ant.   Mary treasured all these words and pondered
       them in her heart.

READING   1 John 4:9

God's love was revealed in our midst in this way:
he sent his only Son to the world
that we might have life through him.

All the ends of the earth, alleluia.
—Have seen the saving power of God, alleluia.

Midafternoon

Ant.   My own eyes have seen the salvation which you
       have prepared in the sight of every people.

READING   Acts 10:36

    This is the message God has sent to the sons of Israel,
the good news of peace proclaimed through Jesus Christ
who is Lord of all.

Mercy and truth have come together, alleluia.
—Justice and peace have kissed, alleluia.

Prayer, as in Morning Prayer.

Evening Prayer II

HYMN, 385.

Ant. 1   This pledge of new redemption and promise of
         eternal joy, prepared through ages past, has
         dawned for us today.

Psalms and canticle from Sunday, Week II, 811.

Ant. 2   The Lord has made manifest his steadfast love
         for us.

Ant. 3   The Lord, the King of kings, is born for us; the
          day of the world's salvation has come; the
          promise of our redemption is fulfilled, alleluia.

READING   1 John 1:1-3

This is what we proclaim to you:
what was from the beginning,
what we have heard,
what we have seen with our eyes,
what we have looked upon
and our hands have touched—
we speak of the word of life.
(This life became visible;
we have seen and bear witness to it,
and we proclaim to you the eternal life
that was present to the Father
and became visible to us).
What we have seen and heard
we proclaim in turn to you
so that you may share life with us.
This fellowship of ours is with the Father
and with his Son, Jesus Christ.

RESPONSORY

The Word was made man, alleluia, alleluia.
—The Word was made man, alleluia, alleluia.

He lived among us.
—Alleluia, alleluia.
Glory to the Father . . .
—The Word was . . .

CANTICLE OF MARY

Ant.   Blessed is the womb that bore the Son of the
       Eternal Father, and blessed are the breasts that
       nursed Christ the Lord.

INTERCESSIONS

At the birth of Jesus, angels proclaimed peace to the
    world. We worship him now with joy, and we pray
    with hearts full of faith:
    May your birth bring peace to all.
Lord, fill your holy people with whatever good they
    need,
—let the mystery of your birth be the source of our
    peace.
You came as chief shepherd and guardian of our lives,
—let the pope and bishops be faithful channels of your
    many gifts of grace.
King from all eternity, you desired to be born within
    time and to experience the day-to-day life of men and
    women,
—share your gift of unending life with us, weak people,
    doomed to death.
Awaited from the beginning of the world, you came only
    in the fullness of time,
—now reveal your presence to those who are still
    expecting you.
You became man and gave new life to our human
    condition in the grip of death,
—now give the fullness of life to all who have died.

Our Father . . .

Prayer

God of power and life,
glory of all who believe in you,
fill the world with your splendor
and show the nations the light of your truth.

We ask this through our Lord Jesus Christ, your Son,
who lives and reigns with you and the Holy Spirit,
one God, for ever and ever.

Alternative Prayer

Father of our Lord Jesus Christ,
our glory is to stand before the world
as your own sons and daughters.
May the simple beauty of Jesus' birth
summon us always to love what is most deeply human,
and to see your Word made flesh
reflected in those whose lives we touch.
We ask this through Christ our Lord

from January 2 to Epiphany

MONDAY

Office of Readings

Sing to the Lord and bless his name.
—Proclaim his saving love day after day.

FIRST READING

From the letter to the Colossians   2:16—3:4

New life in Christ

No one is free to pass judgment on you in terms of
what you eat or drink or what you do on yearly or
monthly feasts, or on the sabbath. All these were but a
shadow of things to come; the reality is the body of
Christ. Let no one rob you of your prize by insisting on
servility in the worship of angels. Such a one takes his
stand on his own experience; he is inflated with empty
pride by his human reflections when he should be in close
touch with the head. The whole body, mutually
supported and upheld by joints and sinews, achieves a
growth from this source which comes from God.

If with Christ you have died to cosmic forces, why should you be bound by rules that say, "Do not handle! Do not taste! Do not touch!" as though you were still living a life bounded by this world? Such prescriptions deal with things that perish in their use. They are based on merely human precepts and doctrines. While these make a certain show of wisdom in their affected piety, humility, and bodily austerity, their chief effect is that they indulge men's pride.

Since you have been raised up in company with Christ, set your heart on what pertains to higher realms where Christ is seated at God's right hand. Be intent on things above rather than on things of earth. After all, you have died! Your life is hidden now with Christ in God. When Christ our life appears, then you shall appear with him in glory.

RESPONSORY   Colossians 3:1-2; Luke 12:34

Since you share with Christ his risen life,
set your hearts on the things of heaven where Christ is
    seated
at the right hand of the Father.
— Let your thoughts be on heavenly things and not on
    the things of earth.

Where your treasure is, there is your heart.
— Let your thoughts . . .

SECOND READING

From the book On the Holy Spirit by Saint Basil the Great, bishop

(Cap. 26, Nn. 61, 64: PG 32, 179-182. 186)

The Lord gives life to his body in the spirit

A spiritual man is one who no longer lives by the flesh but is led by the Spirit of God, one called a son of God, remade in the likeness of God's Son. As the power of sight is active in a healthy eye, so the Holy Spirit is active in a purified soul.

We may form a word either as a thought in the heart or as a sound on the lips. So the Holy Spirit, bearing witness to our spirit, cries out in our hearts, saying: *Abba, Father,* or speaks in our place, as Scripture says: *It is not you who speak; it is the Spirit of the Father who speaks in you.*

In the gifts that he distributes we can see the Spirit as a whole in relation to its parts. We are all members of one another, but with different gifts according to the grace God gives us. So *the eye cannot say to the hand, I do not need you, nor can the head say to the feet, I have no need of you.* All the members together make up the body of Christ in the unity of the Spirit, and render each other a necessary service through their gifts. God has arranged the various parts of the body according to his own will, but there exists among them all a spiritual fellowship which makes it natural for them to share one another's feelings and to be concerned for one another. *If one member suffers, all suffer with it; if one member is honored, all rejoice together.* Moreover, as parts are present in a single whole, so each of us is in the Spirit since all who make up the one body have been baptized into the one Spirit.

As the Father is seen in the Son, so the Son is seen in the Spirit. To worship in the Spirit, then, is to have our minds open to the light, as we may learn from our Lord's words to the Samaritan woman. Misled by the tradition of her country, she imagined that it was necessary to worship in a certain place, but our Lord gave her a different teaching. He told her that one must worship in Spirit and in truth, and clearly by the truth he meant himself.

As we speak of worship in the Son because the Son is the image of God the Father, so we speak of worship in the Spirit because the Spirit is the manifestation of the divinity of the Lord. Through the light of the Spirit we behold the Son, the splendor of God's glory, and through the Son, the very stamp of the Father, we are led to him who is the source both of his stamp, who is the Son, and of its seal, who is the Holy Spirit.

RESPONSORY   1 Corinthians 2:12, 10; Ephesians 3:5

It is not the spirit of the world we have received,
but the Spirit of God himself that we may know the gifts
    of God,
—for the Spirit penetrates the depths of everything,
even the deep mysteries of God.

What no other men have known,
God has now revealed in the Spirit to his holy apostles
    and prophets.
—For the Spirit . . .

If this day occurs on Sunday, the Te Deum is said, 651.

Prayer, as in Morning Prayer.

Morning Prayer

READING   Isaiah 49:8-9

In a time of favor I answer you,
    on the day of salvation I help you,
To restore the land
    and allot the desolate heritages,
Saying to the prisoners: Come out!
    to those in darkness: Show yourselves!

RESPONSORY

The Lord has made known, alleluia alleluia.
—The Lord has made known, alleluia, alleluia.

His saving power.
—Alleluia, alleluia.

Glory to the Father . . .
—The Lord has . . .

CANTICLE OF ZECHARIAH

Ant.   Helpless, he lay in a manger; glorious, he shone in
the heavens. Humbled, he lived among men;
eternal, he dwelt with the Father.

INTERCESSIONS

Let us direct our prayers to Christ, the heavenly man and
the new Adam, who became a life-giving spirit:
Lord, have mercy.
Christ, Sun of Justice, you revealed your glory in our
human nature in order to bring to perfection the old
covenant,
—we ask you to pour out your light upon us.
Christ, you were glorified by the angels, announced by
the shepherds, confessed and proclaimed by Simeon
and Anna,
—let your Gospel be accepted by the people of the
promise.
Christ, when you were born, angels sang glory to God in
the highest and peace on earth,
—we ask you to spread your peace throughout the world.
Christ, as the new Adam you gave new life to the old
man, and prepared for us a dwelling place in your
kingdom,
—may those overwhelmed by evil be encouraged by
hope in you.

Our Father . . .

Prayer

Lord,
keep us true in the faith,
proclaiming that Christ your Son,
who is one with you in eternal glory,
became man and was born of a virgin mother.
Free us from all evil
and lead us to the joy of eternal life.

We ask this through our Lord Jesus Christ, your Son,
who lives and reigns with you and the Holy Spirit,
one God, for ever and ever.

Daytime Prayer

Midmorning

Ant.   Mary, the mother of Jesus, and Joseph were filled
with wonder at all that was said of the child.

READING   1 Timothy 1:15

You can depend on this as worthy of full acceptance:
that Christ Jesus came into the world to save sinners.

The Lord has remembered his gracious promise, alleluia.
—He has kept faith with his people Israel, alleluia.

Midday

Ant.   Mary treasured all these words and pondered
them in her heart.

READING   Revelation 21:23-24

The city had no need of sun or moon, for the glory of
God gave it light, and its lamp was the Lamb. The
nations shall walk by its light; to it the kings of the earth
shall bring their treasures.

All the ends of the earth, alleluia.
—Have seen the saving power of God, alleluia.

Midafternoon

Ant.   My own eyes have seen the salvation which you
        have prepared in the sight of every people.

READING   1 John 1:5

Here is the message
we have heard from him
and announce to you:
that God is light;
in him there is no darkness.

Mercy and truth have come together, alleluia.
—Justice and peace have kissed, alleluia.

Prayer, as in Morning Prayer.

Evening Prayer

READING   Colossians 1:13-15

God rescued us from the power of darkness and
brought us into the kingdom of his beloved Son.
Through him we have redemption, the forgiveness of our
sins. He is the image of the invisible God, the first-born
of all creatures.

RESPONSORY

The Word was made man, alleluia, alleluia.
—The Word was made man, alleluia, alleluia.

He lived among us.
—Alleluia, alleluia.

Glory to the Father . . .
—The Word was . . .

CANTICLE of MARY

Ant. O radiant child! You brought healing to human
      life as you came forth from the womb of Mary,
      your mother, like the bridegroom from his
      marriage chamber.

INTERCESSIONS

God spoke to us in many different ways through his
    prophets and last of all he spoke to us through his Son.
    Let us invoke his compassion:
    Kyrie, eleison.

For your holy Church,
—that your children may profess the name of the Savior
    with faith and with courage:
    Kyrie eleison.

For those spreading the good news of salvation,
—that the workers sent by you may preach the name of
    the Savior with full confidence:
    Kyrie, eleison.

For our sick brothers and sisters,
—that they may regain their health by calling upon the
    name of the Savior:
    Kyrie, eleison.

For Christians subject to persecution,
—that they may endure the injustice done them for the
    name of the Savior:
    Kyrie, eleison.

For our brothers and sisters who have died through the
    sin of man,
—that through your compassion they may have life:
    Kyrie, eleison.

Our Father . . .

Prayer

Lord,
keep us true in the faith,
proclaiming that Christ your Son,
who is one with you in eternal glory,
became man and was born of a virgin mother.
Free us from all evil
and lead us to the joy of eternal life.

We ask this through our Lord Jesus Christ, your Son,
who lives and reigns with you and the Holy Spirit,
one God, for ever and ever.

from January 2 to Epiphany

TUESDAY

Office of Readings

The Son of God has come to give us understanding.
—That we might know the true God.

FIRST READING

From the letter to the Colossians   3:5-16

Life of a new man

Put to death whatever in your nature is rooted in earth: fornication, uncleanness, passion, evil desires, and that lust which is idolatry. These are the sins which provoke God's wrath. Your own conduct was once of this sort, when these sins were your very life. You must put that aside now: all the anger and quick temper, the malice, the insults, the foul language.

Stop lying to one another. What you have done is put aside your old self with its past deeds and put on a new man, one who grows in knowledge as he is formed anew in the image of his Creator. There is no Greek or Jew here, circumcised or uncircumcised, foreigner, Scythian, slave, or freeman. Rather, Christ is everything in all of you.

Because you are God's chosen ones, holy and beloved, clothe yourselves with heartfelt mercy, with kindness, humility, meekness, and patience. Bear with one another; forgive whatever grievances you have against one another. Forgive as the Lord has forgiven you.

Over all these virtues put on love, which binds the rest together and makes them perfect. Christ's peace must reign in your hearts, since as members of the one body you have been called to that peace. Dedicate yourselves to thankfulness. Let the word of Christ, rich as it is, dwell in you. In wisdom made perfect, instruct and admonish one another. Sing gratefully to God from your hearts in psalms, hymns, and inspired songs.

RESPONSORY   See Galatians 3:27-28

All of you who have been baptized in Christ
have put on Christ.
—Now all of us are one in Christ Jesus our Lord.

No longer are we divided into Jew and Greek,
slave or free, man and woman.
—Now all of . . .

SECOND READING

From a treatise on John by Saint Augustine, bishop

(Tract. 17, 7–9: CCL 36, 174–175)

The double commandment of love

The Lord, the teacher of love, full of love, came in person *with summary judgment on the world,* as had been foretold of him, and showed that the law and the prophets are summed up in two commandments of love.

Call to mind, brethren, what these two commandments are. They ought to be very familiar to you; they should not only spring to mind when I mention them, but ought never to be absent from your hearts. Keep always in mind that we must love God and our neighbor: *Love God with your whole heart, your whole soul, and your whole mind, and your neighbor as yourself.*

These two commandments must be always in your thoughts and in your hearts, treasured, acted on, fulfilled. Love of God is the first to be commanded, but love of neighbor is the first to be put into practice. In giving two commandments of love Christ would not commend to you first your neighbor and then God but first God and then your neighbor.

Since you do not yet see God, you merit the vision of God by loving your neighbor. By loving your neighbor you prepare your eye to see God: Saint John says clearly: *If you do not love your brother whom you see, how will you love God whom you do not see!*

Consider what is said to you: Love God. If you say to me: Show me whom I am to love, what shall I say if not what Saint John says: *No one has ever seen God!* But in case you should think that you are completely cut off from the sight of God, he says: *God is love, and he who remains in love remains in God.* Love your neighbor, then, and see within yourself the power by which you love your neighbor; there you will see God, as far as you are able.

Begin, then, to love your neighbor. *Break your bread to feed the hungry, and bring into your home the homeless poor; if you see someone naked, clothe him, and do not look down on your own flesh and blood.*

What will you gain by doing this? *Your light will then burst forth like the dawn.* Your light is your God; he is your *dawn,* for he will come to you when the night of time is over. He does not rise or set but remains for ever.

In loving your neighbor and caring for him you are on a journey. Where are you traveling if not to the Lord God, to him whom we should love with our whole heart, our whole soul, our whole mind? We have not yet reached his presence, but we have our neighbor at our side. Support, then, this companion of your pilgrimage if you want to come into the presence of the one with whom you desire to remain for ever.

RESPONSORY   1 John 4:10-11, 16

God loved us first, and sent his own Son to be the
    sacrifice that takes away our sin.
—Since God has loved us so much, surely we too should
    love one another.

We have come to know and to believe the love God has
    for us.
—Since God has . . .

If this day occurs on Sunday, the **Te Deum** is said, 651.
Prayer, as in Morning Prayer.

Morning Prayer

READING   Isaiah 62:11-12

Say to daughter Zion,
    your savior comes!
Here is his reward with him,
    his recompense before him.
They shall be called the holy people,
    the redeemed of the Lord.

RESPONSORY

The Lord has made known, alleluia, alleluia.
—The Lord has made known, alleluia, alleluia.

His saving power.
—Alleluia, alleluia.

Glory to the Father . . .
—The Lord has . . .

CANTICLE OF ZECHARIAH

Ant.   The Word was made man; full of grace and truth,
he lived among us. From his fullness we all have
received gift upon gift of his love, alleluia.

INTERCESSIONS

Let us joyfully invoke the Son of God, our Redeemer,
who became man in order to restore man:
Be with us, Emmanuel.

Jesus, Son of the living God, King of glory, and Son of
the Virgin Mary,
—brighten this day with the glory of your incarnation.

Jesus, Wonder-Counselor, Mighty-God, Father of the
future, Prince of peace,
—direct our lives according to the holiness of your
human nature.

Jesus, all-powerful, patient, obedient, meek and humble
of heart,
—show the power of your gentleness to all.

Jesus, Father of the poor, immeasurable goodness, our
way and our life,
—grant your Church the spirit of poverty.

Our Father . . .

Prayer

God our Father,
when your Son was born of the Virgin Mary
he became like us in all things but sin.
May we who have been reborn in him
be free from our sinful ways.
We ask this through our Lord Jesus Christ, your Son,

who lives and reigns with you and the Holy Spirit
one God, for ever and ever.

Daytime Prayer

Midmorning

Ant.   Mary, the mother of Jesus, and Joseph were filled
with wonder at all that was said of the child.

READING   Isaiah 2:3-4

From Zion shall go forth instruction,
  and the word of the Lord from Jerusalem.
He shall judge between the nations,
  and impose terms on many peoples.
They shall beat their swords into ploughshares
  and their spears into pruning hooks.
One nation shall not raise the sword against another,
  nor shall they train for war again.

The Lord has remembered his gracious promise, alleluia.
— He has kept faith with his people Israel, alleluia.

Midday

Ant.   Mary treasured all these words and pondered
them in her heart.

READING   Isaiah 9:1

The people who walked in darkness
  have seen a great light;
Upon those who dwelt in the land of gloom
  a light has shone.

All the ends of the earth, alleluia.
— Have seen the saving power of God, alleluia.

Midafternoon

Ant.   My own eyes have seen the salvation which you
have prepared in the sight of every people.

READING   Isaiah 60:4-5

Your sons, O Jerusalem, come from afar,
   and your daughters in the arms of their nurses.
Then you shall be radiant at what you see,
   your heart shall throb and overflow,
For the riches of the sea shall be emptied out before you,
   the wealth of nations shall be brought to you.

Mercy and truth have come together, alleluia.
—Justice and peace have kissed, alleluia.

Prayer, as in Morning Prayer.

Evening Prayer

READING   1 John 1:5b, 7

God is light;
in him there is no darkness.
If we walk in light,
as he is in the light,
we have fellowship with one another,
and the blood of his Son Jesus cleanses us from all sin.

RESPONSORY

The Word was made man, alleluia, alleluia.
—The Word was made man, alleluia, alleluia.

He lived among us.
—Alleluia, alleluia.

Glory to the Father . . .
—The Word was . . .

CANTICLE OF MARY

Ant.   Let us dance with delight in the Lord and let our
       hearts be filled with rejoicing, for eternal salvation
       has appeared on the earth, alleluia.

INTERCESSIONS

At the coming of Christ, God's holy people were made
    sharers in new life. With joy and gratitude let us say to
    our Savior:
    May your birth bring joy to the world.
Christ, our life, you came to be the head of your Church,
—grant your body growth rooted in charity.
Fully human, fully divine, you deserve our adoration,
—mold our humanity in your divine image.
You became our mediator through your incarnation,
—unite your servants in the Church more closely to your
    work through the holiness of their lives.
When you came you inaugurated a new era,
—lead all nations to your salvation.
By your birth you destroyed the chains of death,
—free the dead from all their chains.

Our Father . . .

Prayer

God our Father,
when your Son was born of the Virgin Mary
he became like us in all things but sin.
May we who have been reborn in him
be free from our sinful ways.
We ask this through our Lord Jesus Christ, your Son,
who lives and reigns with you and the Holy Spirit,
one God, for ever and ever.

from January 2 to Epiphany

WEDNESDAY

Office of Readings

In Christ was life.
—And that life was the light of mankind.

FIRST READING

From the letter to the Colossians   3:17—4:1

The life of the Christian family

Whatever you do, whether in speech or in action, do it in the name of the Lord Jesus. Give thanks to God the Father through him.

You who are wives, be submissive to your husbands. This is your duty in the Lord. Husbands, love your wives. Avoid any bitterness toward them.

You children, obey your parents in everything as the acceptable way in the Lord.

And fathers, do not nag your children lest they lose heart.

To slaves I say, obey your human masters perfectly, not with the purpose of attracting attention and pleasing men but in all sincerity and out of reverence for the Lord. Whatever you do, work at it with your whole being. Do it for the Lord rather than for men, since you know full well you will receive an inheritance from him as your reward. Be slaves of Christ the Lord. Whoever acts unjustly will be repaid for the wrong he has done. No favoritism will be shown.

You slaveowners, deal justly and fairly with your slaves, realizing that you too have a master in heaven.

RESPONSORY   Colossians 3:17

Whatever you do in word and deed,
—do all in the name of the Lord Jesus.

Give thanks to our God and Father through his Son.
—Do all in . . .

SECOND READING

From the Five Hundred Chapters by Saint Maximus the
Confessor, abbot

(Centuria 1, 8–13: PG 90, 1182–1186)

A mystery ever new

The Word of God, born once in the flesh (such is his
kindness and his goodness), is always willing to be born
spiritually in those who desire him. In them he is born as
an infant as he fashions himself in them by means of their
virtues. He reveals himself to the extent that he knows
someone is capable of receiving him. He diminishes the
revelation of his glory not out of selfishness but because
he recognizes the capacity and resources of those who
desire to see him. Yet, in the transcendence of mystery,
he always remains invisible to all.

For this reason the apostle Paul, reflecting on the
power of the mystery, said: *Jesus Christ, yesterday and
today: he remains the same for ever.* For he understands
the mystery as ever new, never growing old through our
understanding of it.

Christ is God, for he had given all things their being
out of nothing. Yet he is born as man by taking to himself
our nature, flesh endowed with intelligent spirit. A star
glitters by day in the East and leads the wise men to the
place where the incarnate Word lies, to show that the
Word, contained in the Law and the Prophets, surpasses

in a mystical way knowledge derived from the senses, and to lead the Gentiles to the full light of knowledge.

For surely the word of the Law and the Prophets when it is understood with faith is like a star which leads those who are called by the power of grace in accordance with his decree to recognize the Word incarnate.

Here is the reason why God became a perfect man, changing nothing of human nature, except to take away sin (which was never natural anyway). His flesh was set before that voracious, gaping dragon as bait to provoke him: flesh that would be deadly for the dragon, for it would utterly destroy him by the power of the Godhead hidden within it. For human nature, however, his flesh was to be a remedy since the power of the Godhead in it would restore human nature to its original grace.

Just as the devil had poisoned the tree of knowledge and spoiled our nature by its taste, so too, in presuming to devour the Lord's flesh he himself is corrupted and is completely destroyed by the power of the Godhead hidden in it.

The great mystery of the divine incarnation remains a mystery for ever. How can the Word made flesh be essentially the same person that is wholly with the Father? How can he who is by nature God become by nature wholly man without lacking either nature, neither the divine by which he is God nor the human by which he became man?

Faith alone grasps these mysteries. Faith alone is truly the substance and foundation of all that exceeds knowledge and understanding.

RESPONSORY   John 1:14, 1
The Word was made flesh and lived among us.
—We have seen his glory,
the glory of the Father's only Son, full of grace and truth.

In the beginning was the Word,
and the Word was with God,
and the Word was God.
—We have seen . . .

If this day occurs on Sunday, the **Te Deum** is said, 651.
Prayer, as in Morning Prayer.

Morning Prayer

READING   Isaiah 45:22-23

Turn to me and be safe,
   all you ends of the earth,
      for I am God; there is no other!
By myself I swear,
   uttering my just decree
   and my unalterable word:
To me every knee shall bend;
   by me every tongue shall swear.

RESPONSORY

The Lord has made known, alleluia, alleluia.
—The Lord has made known, alleluia, alleluia.

His saving power.
—Alleluia, alleluia.

Glory to the Father . . .
—The Lord has . . .

CANTICLE OF ZECHARIAH

Ant.   Christ our God, in whom the fullness of the
       Godhead dwells, took upon himself our wounded
       nature and became the first new man, alleluia.

INTERCESSIONS

Let us glorify the Word of God who was revealed in the
   flesh, appeared to the angels, and was proclaimed to
   the nations. Let us faithfully acknowledge him:

We adore you, only-begotten Son of the Father.

Liberator of mankind, through the Virgin Mary you
   came to renew us,
—through her intercession keep us from our old ways.

You made your uncreated justice radiate from heaven to
   earth,
—direct our days and our nights in the brightness of this
   Sun.

Son of God, you have shown us the Father's love,
— help us to show him to one another by our love.

You chose to dwell with us,
—make us worthy of your companionship.

Our Father . . .

Prayer

All-powerful Father,
you sent your Son Jesus Christ
to bring the new light of salvation to the world.
May he enlighten us with his radiance,
who lives and reigns with you and the Holy Spirit,
one God, for ever and ever.

Daytime Prayer

Midmorning

Ant.   Mary, the mother of Jesus, and Joseph were filled
         with wonder at all that was said of the child.

READING   Jeremiah 31:7-8
Shout with joy for Jacob,
   exult at the head of the nations;
   proclaim your praise and say:
The Lord has delivered his people,
   the remnant of Israel.
Behold, I will bring them back
   from the land of the north;

I will gather them from the ends of the world.

The Lord has remembered his gracious promise, alleluia.
—He has kept faith with his people, alleluia.

Midday

Ant.   Mary treasured all these words and pondered
       them in her heart.

READING   Jeremiah 31:11-12
The Lord shall ransom Jacob,
   he shall redeem him from the hand of his conqueror.
Shouting, they shall mount the heights of Zion,
   they shall come streaming to the Lord's blessings.

All the ends of the earth, alleluia.
—Have seen the saving power of God, alleluia.

Midafternoon

Ant.   My own eyes have seen the salvation which you
       have prepared in the sight of every people.

READING   Zechariah 8:7-8
   Lo, I will rescue my people from the land of the rising
sun, and from the land of the setting sun. I will bring
them back to dwell within Jerusalem. They shall be my
people, and I will be their God, with faithfulness and
justice.

Mercy and truth have come together, alleluia.
—Justice and peace have kissed, alleluia.

Prayer, as in Morning Prayer.

Evening Prayer

READING   Romans 8:3-4
   God sent his Son in the likeness of sinful flesh as a
sin-offering, thereby condemning sin in the flesh, so that
the just demands of the law might be fulfilled in us who
live, not according to the flesh, but according to the
spirit.

RESPONSORY

The Word was made man, alleluia, alleluia
—The Word was made man, alleluia, alleluia.

He lived among us.
—Alleluia, alleluia.

Glory to the Father . . .
—The Word was . .

CANTICLE OF MARY

Ant.   I have come forth from God into the world; I have
not come of myself, but the Father sent me.

INTERCESSIONS

Christ came and gave himself up to purify his people, to
make of them an acceptable offering, a band of
disciples to continue his good work. With fervent
devotion let us call upon him:
Lord, have mercy.
For your holy Church,
—that all her children may be born again into a new life:
Lord, have mercy.
For the poor, for prisoners and for refugees,
—may they find you, the incarnate Son of God, in our
love:
Lord, have mercy.
That our joy may be full,
—and that we may marvel at the Father's gift, which he
has given us in you:
Lord, have mercy.
That your servants who have died with the knowledge of
your birth may see your face,
—and that night may fall upon them no more:
Lord, have mercy.

Our Father . . .

Prayer

All-powerful Father,
you sent your Son Jesus Christ
to bring the new light of salvation to the world.
May he enlighten us with his radiance,
who lives and reigns with you and the Holy Spirit,
one God, for ever and ever.

from January 2 to Epiphany

THURSDAY

Office of Readings

Christ is the true light.
—He gives light to all people.

First Reading

From the letter to the Colossians   4:2-18

The conclusion of the letter

Pray perseveringly, be attentive to prayer, and pray in a spirit of thanksgiving. Pray for us, too, that God may provide us with an opening to proclaim the mystery of Christ, for which I am a prisoner. Pray that I may speak it clearly, as I must.

Be prudent in dealing with outsiders; make the most of every opportunity. Let your speech be always gracious and in good taste, and strive to respond properly to all who address you.

Tychicus, our dear brother, our faithful minister and fellow slave in the Lord, will give you all the news about me. I am sending him to you for this purpose, and to comfort your hearts. With him is Onesimus, our dear and faithful brother, who is one of you. They will tell you all that has happened here.

Aristarchus, who is a prisoner along with me, sends you greetings. So does Mark, the cousin of Barnabas. You have received instructions about him: if he comes to you, make him welcome. Jesus known also as Justus sends greetings. These are the only circumcised ones among those who are working with me for the kingdom of God. They have been a great comfort to me.

Epaphras, who is one of you, sends greetings. He is a servant of Christ Jesus who is always pleading earnestly in prayer that you stand firm, that you be perfect and have full conviction about whatever pertains to God's will. I can certainly testify how solicitous he is for you and for those at Laodicea and Hierapolis. Luke, our dear physician, sends you greetings. So does Demas.

Give our best wishes to the brothers at Laodicea and to Nymphas and the assembly that meets at his house. Once this letter has been read to you, see that it is read in the assembly of the Laodiceans as well, and that you yourselves read the letter that is coming from Laodicea. To Archippus say, "Take care to discharge the ministry you have received in the Lord."

This greeting is from Paul—in my own hand! Remember my chains. Grace be with you.

RESPONSORY   Colossians 4:3; see Psalm 51:17

Let us pray for one another,
that God may give us an opportunity
—to proclaim the mystery of Christ.
May the Lord open our lips that we may declare God's praises.
—To proclaim the . . .

SECOND READING

From a sermon by Saint Augustine, bishop

(Sermo 194, 3–4: PL 38, 1016–1017)

The vision of the Word will fulfill all our desires

What man knows all the treasures of wisdom and knowledge hidden in Christ, concealed in the poverty of his flesh? Scripture says: *Although he was rich he became poor for our sake to enrich us by his poverty.* He showed himself poor when he assumed our mortal nature and destroyed death, yet he promised us riches, for he had not been robbed of his wealth but was keeping it in reserve.

How great are the blessings of his goodness which he reserves for those who fear him and shows to those who hope in him! Until he gives them to us in their plenitude, we can have only the faintest conception of them; but to enable us to receive these blessings, he who in his divine nature is the equal of the Father assumed the condition of a slave and became like us, and so restored to us our likeness to God. The only Son of God became a son of man to make many men sons of God. He instructed slaves by showing himself in the form of a slave, and now he enables free men to see him in the form of God.

For *we are the sons of God, and although what we shall be has not yet been revealed, we know that when he appears we shall be like him for we shall see him as he is.* For what are those treasures of wisdom and knowledge, what those divine riches, if not the one thing that can fulfill our longing? What are the great blessings of his goodness, if not the one thing that will content us? Therefore: *Show us the Father, and all our desires will be satisfied.*

Christ speaks both in us and for us when, in one of the psalms, he says to the Father: *I shall be satisfied when your glory is revealed.* For he and the Father are one, and whoever sees him sees the Father also. *The Lord of hosts is himself the king of glory.* He will transform us and show us his face, and we shall be saved; all our longing will be fulfilled, all our desires will be satisfied.

But this has not yet been accomplished; he has not yet given us the vision that will satisfy every desire; we have not yet drunk our fill of the fountain of life. So while all this remains in the future and we still walk by faith, absent from the Lord, while we still hunger and thirst for justice and with inexpressible longing yearn for God's beauty, let us reverently celebrate the day he was born into our own servile condition.

Since we can as yet form no conception of his generation by the Father before the daystar, let us keep the festival of his birth of a virgin in the hours of the night. Since it is still beyond our understanding that *his name endures for ever and existed before the sun*, let us at least recognize *his dwelling* that he has placed *beneath the sun.* We cannot yet behold him as the only Son, abiding for ever in his Father, so let us recall *his coming forth like a bridegroom from his chamber.* We are not yet ready for the banquet of our Father, so let us contemplate the manger of Jesus Christ our Lord.

RESPONSORY   1 John 1:2; 5:20

This life was made visible;
we have seen it and we proclaim to you the eternal life
—which was with the Father and has appeared to us.

We know that the Son of God has come and given us
    understanding,
that we might know the true God,
for we are in his Son, Jesus Christ.
He is the true God and eternal life.
—Which was with . . .

If this day occurs on Sunday, the **Te Deum** is said, 651.

Prayer, as in Morning Prayer.

Morning Prayer

READING   Wisdom 7:26–27

Wisdom is the refulgence of eternal light,
  the spotless mirror of the power of God,
  the image of his goodness,
And she, who is one, can do all things,
  and renews everything while herself perduring;
And passing into holy souls from age to age,
  she produces friends of God and prophets.

RESPONSORY

The Lord has made known, alleluia, alleluia.
—The Lord has made known, alleluia, alleluia.

His saving power.
—Alleluia, alleluia.

Glory to the Father . . .
—The Lord has . . .

CANTICLE OF ZECHARIAH

Ant. The Lord God has come to his people and set
      them free.

INTERCESSIONS

Christ embodied the wisdom of God, his justice, his
    holiness and his saving power. Let us praise him and
    call upon him confidently:
    Lord, save us by your birth.
King of the world, the shepherds found you wrapped in
    swaddling clothes,
—make us willing participants in your poverty and
    simplicity.

Lord of heaven, from your royal throne you came down
    to the world,
—teach us to respect our less fortunate brothers and sis-
    ters.

Christ, light eternal, when you assumed our nature you
    did not take on its stain,
—help your faithful people to use the good things of the
    earth for your honor and glory.

You are the divine spouse of your Church; you stand in
    its midst as an impregnable tower,
—help the faithful to persevere in your Church toward
    salvation.

Our Father . . .

Prayer

Father,
you make known the salvation of mankind
at the birth of your Son.
Make us strong in faith
and bring us to the glory you promise.

We ask this through our Lord Jesus Christ, your Son,
who lives and reigns with you and the Holy Spirit,
one God, for ever and ever.

Daytime Prayer

Midmorning

Ant.   Mary, the mother of Jesus, and Joseph were filled
    with wonder at all that was said of the child.

READING   Ezekiel 20:41-42a

As a pleasing odor I will accept you, when I have
brought you from among the nations and gathered you
out of the countries over which you were scattered; and
by means of you I will manifest my holiness in the sight
of the nations. Thus you shall know that I am the Lord.

The Lord has remembered his gracious promise, alleluia.
—He has kept faith with his people Israel, alleluia.

Midday

Ant.   Mary treasured all these words and pondered
        them in her heart.

READING   Ezekiel 34:11-12

I myself will look after and tend my sheep. As a
shepherd tends his flock when he finds himself among his
scattered sheep, so will I tend my sheep. I will rescue
them from every place where they were scattered when it
was cloudy and dark.

All the ends of the earth, alleluia.
—Have seen the saving power of God, alleluia.

Midafternoon

Ant.   My own eyes have seen the salvation which you
        have prepared in the sight of every people.

READING   Micah 2:12

I will gather you, O Jacob, each and every one,
    I will assemble all the remnant of Israel;
I will group them like a flock in the fold,
    like a herd in the midst of its corral.

Mercy and truth have come together, alleluia.
—Justice and peace have kissed, alleluia.

Prayer, as in Morning Prayer

Evening Prayer

Where the Epiphany is celebrated on Sunday between January
2 and January 8:

READING   1 John 5:20

We know that the Son of God has come and has given
us discernment to recognize the One who is true. And we
are in the One who is true, for we are in his Son Jesus
Christ. He is the true God and eternal life.

RESPONSORY

The Word was made man, alleluia, alleluia.
—The Word was made man, alleluia, alleluia.
He lived among us.
—Alleluia, alleluia.
Glory to the Father . . .
—The Word was . .

CANTICLE OF MARY

Ant.   We have found Jesus of Nazareth, the son of Jo-
        seph. He is the one of whom Moses and the
        prophets wrote.

INTERCESSIONS

To Christ, Emmanuel, whom the Virgin conceived and
    brought forth, let us give praise and pray to him:
        Son of the Virgin Mary, hear us.
You gave Mary the joy of motherhood,
—give all parents true joy in their children.
You made yourself a child,
—grant children wisdom and grace.
You came to make the human race the holy people of
    God,
—bring all nations to acknowledge the unifying bond of
    your love.
By your birth you strengthened family ties,
—help families to come to a greater love for one another.
You desired to be born into the days of time,

—grant that our departed brothers and sisters may be
 born into the day of eternity.

Our Father . . .

Prayer

Father,
you make known the salvation of mankind
at the birth of your Son.
Make us strong in faith
and bring us to the glory you promise.
We ask this through our Lord Jesus Christ, your Son,
who lives and reigns with you and the Holy Spirit,
one God, for ever and ever.

from January 2 to Epiphany
FRIDAY

Office of Readings

Sing to the Lord and bless his name.
—Proclaim his saving love day after day.

FIRST READING

From the book of the prophet Isaiah   42:1-8

The gentle servant of God

Here is my servant whom I uphold,
    my chosen one with whom I am pleased,
Upon whom I have put my spirit;
    he shall bring forth justice to the nations,
Not crying out, not shouting,
    not making his voice heard in the street.

A bruised reed he shall not break,
    and a smoldering wick he shall not quench,
Until he establishes justice on the earth;
    the coastlands will wait for his teaching.

Thus says God, the Lord,
    who created the heavens and stretched them out,
    who spreads out the earth with its crops,
Who gives breath to its people
    and spirit to those who walk on it:
I, the Lord, have called you for the victory of justice,
    I have grasped you by the hand;
I formed you, and set you
    as a covenant of the people,
    a light for the nations,
To open the eyes of the blind,
    to bring out prisoners from confinement,
    and from the dungeon, those who live in darkness.

I am the Lord, this is my name;
    my glory I give to no other,
    nor my praise to idols.

RESPONSORY   Matthew 12:18, 21 (Isaiah 42:1)

This is my servant whom I have chosen; my beloved in
    whom I take delight.
—All nations will hope in his name.

My Spirit will rest upon him,
and he will teach the nations the meaning of justice.
—All the nations . . .

SECOND READING

This reading with its responsory is taken from Sunday of the
Baptism of the Lord, **634**.

Prayer, as in Morning Prayer.

Morning Prayer

READING   Isaiah 61:1-2a

The spirit of the Lord God is upon me,
  because the Lord has anointed me;
He has sent me to bring glad tidings to the lowly,
  to heal the brokenhearted,
To proclaim liberty to the captives
  and release to the prisoners,
To announce a year of favor from the Lord.

RESPONSORY

The Lord has made known, alleluia, alleluia.
—The Lord has made known, alleluia, alleluia.

His saving power.
—Alleluia, alleluia.

Glory to the Father . . .
—The Lord has . . .

CANTICLE OF ZECHARIAH

Ant.   He came through blood and water, Jesus Christ
       our Lord.

INTERCESSIONS

The Word of God existed before the creation of the
    universe yet was born among us in time. We praise
    and worship him as we cry out in joy:
    Let the earth ring out with joy for you have come.
You are the unending Word of God who flooded the
    world with joy at your birth,
—fill us with joy by the continuous gift of your life.

You saved us and by your birth revealed to us the
   covenant faithfulness of the Lord,
—help us to be faithful to the promises of our baptism.
You are King of heaven and earth who sent messengers
   to announce peace to all,
—let our lives be filled with your peace.
You are the true vine that brings forth the fruit of life,
—make us branches of the vine, bearing much fruit.

Our Father . . .

Prayer

Lord,
fill our hearts with your light.
May we always acknowledge Christ as our Savior
and be more faithful to his gospel,
for he lives and reigns with you and the Holy Spirit,
one God, for ever and ever.

Daytime Prayer

Midmorning

Ant.   Mary, the mother of Jesus, and Joseph were filled
       with wonder at all that was said of the child.

READING   Isaiah 11:1-3a

A shoot shall sprout from the stump of Jesse,
   and from his roots a bud shall blossom.
The spirit of the Lord shall rest upon him:
   a spirit of wisdom and of understanding,
A spirit of counsel and of strength,
   a spirit of knowledge and of fear of the Lord,
   and his delight shall be the fear of the Lord.

The Lord has remembered his gracious promise, alleluia.
—He has kept faith with his people Israel, alleluia.

Midday

Ant. Mary treasured all these words and pondered them in her heart.

READING   Isaiah 42:1

Here is my servant whom I uphold,
  my chosen one with whom I am pleased,
Upon whom I have put my spirit;
  he shall bring forth justice to the nations.

All the ends of the earth, alleluia.
—Have seen the saving power of God, alleluia.

Midafternoon

Ant. My own eyes have seen the salvation which you have prepared in the sight of every nation.

READING   Isaiah 49:6

    The Lord said to me:
It is too little for you to be my servant,
  to raise up the tribes of Jacob,
  and restore the survivors of Israel;
I will make you a light to the nations,
  that my salvation may reach to the ends of the earth.

Mercy and truth have come together, alleluia.
—Justice and peace have kissed, alleluia.

Prayer, as in Morning Prayer.

Evening Prayer

READING   Acts 10:37-38

    I take it you know what has been reported all over Judea about Jesus of Nazareth, beginning in Galilee with the baptism John preached; of the way God anointed him with the Holy Spirit and power. He went about doing good works and healing all who were in the grip of the devil, and God was with him.

RESPONSORY

The Word was made man, alleluia, alleluia.
—The Word was made man, alleluia, alleluia.

He lived among us.
—Alleluia, alleluia.

Glory to the Father . . .
—The Word was . . .

CANTICLE OF MARY

Ant.   From heaven the Father's voice proclaimed: You are my Son, my beloved, in whom I take delight.

INTERCESSIONS

At the birth of Jesus, angels proclaimed peace to the world. We worship him now with joy, and we pray with hearts full of faith:
May your birth bring peace to all.
Lord, fill your holy people with whatever good they need,
—let the mystery of your birth be the source of our peace.
You came as chief shepherd and guardian of our lives,
—let the pope and bishops be faithful channels of your many gifts of grace.
King from all eternity, you desired to be born within time and to experience the day-to-day life of men and women,
—share your gift of unending life with us, weak people, doomed to death.
Awaited from the beginning of the world, you came only in the fullness of time,

—now reveal your presence to those who are still
    expecting you.
You became man and gave new life to our human
    condition in the grip of death,
—now give the fullness of life to all who have died.

Our Father . . .

Prayer

Lord,
fill our hearts with your light.
May we always acknowledge Christ as our Savior
and be more faithful to his gospel,
for he lives and reigns with you and the Holy Spirit,
one God, for ever and ever.

from January 2 to Epiphany

SATURDAY

Office of Readings

In these last days God has spoken to us through his Son.
—The Word through whom he made all things.

FIRST READING

From the book of the prophet Isaiah   61:1-11

The Spirit of the Lord is upon his servant

The spirit of the Lord God is upon me,
    because the Lord has anointed me;
He has sent me to bring glad tidings to the lowly,
    to heal the brokenhearted,

To proclaim liberty to the captives
    and release to the prisoners,
To announce a year of favor from the Lord
    and a day of vindication by our God,
    to comfort all who mourn;
To place on those who mourn in Zion
    a diadem instead of ashes,
To give them oil of gladness in place of mourning,
    a glorious mantle instead of a listless spirit.
They will be called oaks of justice,
    planted by the Lord to show his glory.

They shall rebuild the ancient ruins,
    the former wastes they shall raise up
And restore the ruined cities,
    desolate now for generations.

Strangers shall stand ready to pasture your flocks,
    foreigners shall be your farmers and vinedressers.
You yourselves shall be named priests of the Lord,
    ministers of our God you shall be called.
You shall eat the wealth of the nations
    and boast of riches from them.

Since their shame was double
    and disgrace and spittle were their portion,
They shall have a double inheritance in their land,
    everlasting joy shall be theirs.

For I, the Lord, love what is right,
    I hate robbery and injustice;
I will give them their recompense faithfully,
    a lasting covenant I will make with them.

Their descendants shall be renowned among the nations,
    and their offspring among the peoples;
All who see them shall acknowledge them
    as a race the Lord has blessed.

I rejoice heartily in the Lord,
   in my God is the joy of my soul;
For he has clothed me with a robe of salvation,
   and wrapped me in a mantle of justice,
Like a bridegroom adorned with a diadem,
   like a bride bedecked with her jewels.

As the earth brings forth its plants,
   and a garden makes its growth spring up,
So will the Lord God make justice and praise
   spring up before all the nations.

RESPONSORY   Isaiah 61:1; John 8:42

The Spirit of God rests upon me,
for the Lord has anointed me;
and he has sent me to bring good news to the poor,
  —to heal the broken-hearted,
to proclaim that captivity is now ended and prisoners are
   set free.

I have come forth from God and have come into the
   world.
I did not come of myself; the Father has sent me.
  —To heal the . . .

SECOND READING

From a sermon by Saint Augustine, bishop

(Sermo 13 de Tempore: PL 39, 1097–1098)

   God became man so that man might become God

   Beloved, our Lord Jesus Christ, the eternal creator of
all things, today became our Savior by being born of a
mother. Of his own will he was born for us today, in
time, so that he could lead us to his Father's eternity.
God became man so that man might become God. The

Lord of the angels became man today so that man could eat the bread of angels.

Today, the prophecy is fulfilled that said: *Pour down, heavens, from above, and let the clouds rain the just one: let the earth be opened and bring forth a savior.* The Lord who had created all things is himself now created, so that he who was lost would be found. Thus man, in the words of the psalmist, confesses: *Before I was humbled, I sinned.* Man sinned and became guilty; God is born a man to free man from his guilt. Man fell, but God descended; man fell miserably, but God descended mercifully; man fell through pride, God descended with his grace.

My brethren, what miracles! What prodigies! The laws of nature are changed in the case of man. God is born. A virgin becomes pregnant with man. The Word of God marries the woman who knows no man. She is now at the same time both mother and virgin. She becomes a mother, yet she remains a virgin. The virgin bears a son, yet she does not know man; she remains untouched, yet she is not barren. He alone was born without sin, for she bore him without the embrace of a man, not by the concupiscence of the flesh but by the obedience of the mind.

RESPONSORY   1 John 4:14; 1:9

We have seen with our own eyes and we bear witness:
—the Father sent his own Son to be the Savior of the world.

He has come to take away the burden of our sins
and to cleanse us of every stain of evil.
—The Father sent . . .

Prayer, as in Morning Prayer.

Morning Prayer

READING   Isaiah 9:5

A child is born to us, a son is given us;
     upon his shoulder dominion rests.
They name him Wonder-Counselor, God-Hero,
     Father-Forever, Prince of Peace.

RESPONSORY

The Lord has made known, alleluia, alleluia.
—The Lord has made known, alleluia, alleluia.

His saving power.
—Alleluia, alleluia.

Glory to the Father . . .
—The Lord has . . .

CANTICLE OF ZECHARIAH

Ant.   He is the one of whom it has been written: Christ
       is born in Israel; his kingdom will last for ever.

INTERCESSIONS

All the ends of the earth have seen Jesus Christ, the
     saving power of God. Let us praise him and cry out in
     joy:
     Glory be to you, Lord Jesus Christ.
Redeemer of all, you came to tear down the walls separa-
     ting Jew from Gentile,
—root out the prejudices which erode the depths of our
     humanity.
Through your incarnation and your birth you established
     your presence among us,

—teach us to recognize the many forms of your presence
   in the Church and in one another.
You are the fullest revelation of God to men and women,
—show us how we can assent to your word with integrity
   of faith and action.
You are God-with-us, wondrously transforming all
   creation,
—let every heart, every voice, every deed throughout the
   universe now be transformed.

Our Father . . .

Prayer

All-powerful and ever-living God,
you give us a new vision of your glory
in the coming of Christ your Son.
He was born of the Virgin Mary
and came to share our life.
May we come to share his eternal life
in the glory of your kingdom,
where he lives and reigns with you and the Holy Spirit,
one God, for ever and ever,

Daytime Prayer

Midmorning

Ant.   Mary, the mother of Jesus, and Joseph were filled
         with wonder at all that was said of the child.

READING   Deuteronomy 4:7

   What great nation is there that has gods so close to it as
the Lord, our God, is to us whenever we call upon him?

The Lord has remembered his gracious promise, alleluia.
—He has kept faith with his people Israel, alleluia.

Midday

Ant.   Mary treasured all these words and pondered
       them in her heart.

READING   Isaiah 12:5-6

Sing praise to the Lord for his glorious achievement;
    let this be known throughout all the earth.
Shout with exultation, O city of Zion,
    for great in your midst is the Holy One of Israel.

All the ends of the earth, alleluia .
—Have seen the saving power of God, alleluia.

Midafternoon

Ant.   My own eyes have seen the salvation which you
       have prepared in the sight of every nation.

READING   See Tobit 14:6-7

All the nations shall abandon their idols and come to
Jerusalem to dwell. And all the kings of the earth shall
rejoice in her, worshiping the king of Israel.

Mercy and truth have come together, alleluia.
—Justice and peace have kissed, alleluia.

Prayer, as in Morning Prayer.

January 6 or the Sunday between January 2 and January 8

EPIPHANY

Solemnity

Evening Prayer I

HYMN

As with gladness men of old,
Did the guiding star behold,
As with joy they hailed its light,
Leading onwards, beaming bright,
So, most gracious God, may we
Evermore be led to thee.

As with joyful steps they sped
To that lowly manger-bed,
There to bend the knee before
Him whom heaven and earth adore,
So may we with willing feet
Ever seek thy mercy-seat.

As they offered gifts most rare
At that manger rude and bare,
So may we with holy joy,
Pure, and free from sin's alloy,
All our costliest treasures bring,
Christ, to thee our heavenly king.

Holy Jesus, every day
Keep us in the narrow way;
And, when earthly things are past,
Bring our ransomed souls at last
Where they need no star to guide,
Where no clouds thy glory hide.

In the heavenly country bright
Need they no created light;
Thou its light, its joy, its crown,
Thou its sun which goes not down:
There for ever may we sing
Alleluias to our king.

Melody: Dix 77.77.77   Music: Adapted by W. H. Monk,
1823–1889, from a chorale by
Conrad Kocher, 1786–1872
Text: W. Chatterton Dix, 1837–1898

PSALMODY

Ant. 1   Begotten of the Father before the daystar shone
or time began, the Lord our Savior has
appeared on earth today.

Psalm 135
I

Praise the name of the Lord,
praise him, servants of the Lord,
who stand in the house of the Lord
in the courts of the house of our God.

Praise the Lord for the Lord is good.
Sing a psalm to his name for he is loving.
For the Lord has chosen Jacob for himself
and Israel for his own possession.

For I know the Lord is great,
that our Lord is high above all gods.
The Lord does whatever he wills,
in heaven, on earth, in the seas.

He summons clouds from the ends of the earth;
makes lightning produce the rain;
from his treasuries he sends forth the wind.

The first-born of the Egyptians he smote,
of man and beast alike.
Signs and wonders he worked
in the midst of your land, O Egypt,
against Pharaoh and all his servants.

Nations in their greatness he struck
and kings in their splendor he slew.
Sihon, king of the Amorites,
Og, the king of Bashan,
and all the kingdoms of Canaan.
He let Israel inherit their land;
on his people their land he bestowed.

Ant. Begotten of the Father before the daystar shone or time began, the Lord our Savior has appeared on earth today.

Ant. 2 Great is the Lord, our God, transcending all other gods.

II

Lord, your name stands for ever,
unforgotten from age to age:
for the Lord does justice for his people;
the Lord takes pity on his servants.

Pagan idols are silver and gold,
the work of human hands.
They have mouths but they cannot speak;
they have eyes but they cannot see.

They have ears but they cannot hear;
there is never a breath on their lips.
Their makers will come to be like them
and so will all who trust in them!

Sons of Israel, bless the Lord!
Sons of Aaron, bless the Lord!

Sons of Levi, bless the Lord!
You who fear him, bless the Lord!

From Zion may the Lord be blessed,
he who dwells in Jerusalem!

Ant.   Great is the Lord, our God, transcending all other gods.

Ant. 3   The star burned like a flame, pointing the way to God, the King of kings; the wise men saw the sign and brought their gifts in homage to their great King.

Canticle   See 1 Timothy 3:16

The mystery and glory of Christ

R. Praise the Lord, all you nations.

Christ manifested in the flesh,
Christ justified in the Spirit.

R. Praise the Lord, all you nations.

Christ contemplated by the angels,
Christ proclaimed by the pagans.

R. Praise the Lord, all you nations.

Christ who is believed in the world,
Christ exalted in glory.

R. Praise the Lord, all you nations.

Ant.   The star burned like a flame, pointing the way to God, the King of kings; the wise men saw the sign and brought their gifts in homage to their great King.

READING   2 Timothy 1:9-10

God has saved us and has called us to a holy life, not because of any merit of ours but according to his own design—the grace held out to us in Christ Jesus before the world began but now made manifest through the appearance of our Savior. He has robbed death of its power and has brought life and immortality into clear light through the gospel.

RESPONSORY

All peoples will be blessed in him, men and women of every race.
—All peoples will be blessed in him, men and women of every race.
All nations will acclaim his glory.
—Men and women of every race.
Glory to the Father . . .
—All peoples will . . .

CANTICLE OF MARY

Ant. Seeing the star, the wise men said: This must signify the birth of some great king. Let us search for him and lay our treasures at his feet: gold, frankincense and myrrh.

INTERCESSIONS

Today our Savior was adored by the Magi. Let us also worship him with joy as we pray:
Save the poor, O Lord.
King of the nations, you called the Magi to adore you as the first representatives of the nations,
—give us a willing spirit of adoration and service.
King of glory, you judge your people with justice,
—grant mankind an abundant measure of peace.
King of ages, you endure from age to age,
—send your word as fresh spring rain falling on our hearts.
King of justice, you desire to free the poor who have no advocate,

—be compassionate to the suffering and the afflicted.
Lord, your name is blessed for all ages,
—show the wonders of your saving power to our
    deceased brothers and sisters.

Our Father . . .

Prayer

Father,
you revealed your Son to the nations
by the guidance of a star.
Lead us to your glory in heaven
by the light of faith.

We ask this through our Lord Jesus Christ, your Son,
who lives and reigns with you and the Holy Spirit,
one God, for ever and ever.

Alternative Prayer

Father of light, unchanging God,
today you reveal to men of faith
the resplendent fact of the Word made flesh.
Your light is strong,
your love is near;
draw us beyond the limits which this world imposes,
to the life where your Spirit makes all life complete.
We ask this through Christ our Lord.

Invitatory

Ant.   Christ has appeared to us; come, let us adore him.

Invitatory psalm, as in the Ordinary, 648.

Office of Readings

HYMN

Antiphon:
    Sion, sing, break into song!
    For within you is the Lord
    with his saving power.

Rise and shine forth, for your light has come,
And upon you breaks the glory of the Lord;
For the darkness covers the earth,
And the thick clouds, the people.

Antiphon

But upon you the Lord shall dawn,
And in you his splendor shall be revealed;
Your light shall guide the Gentiles on their path,
And kings shall walk in your brightness.

Antiphon

Wonder and thanksgiving shall fill your heart,
As the wealth of nations enriches you;
You shall be called the City of the Lord,
Dear to the Holy One of Israel.

Antiphon

You who were desolate and alone,
A place unvisited by men,
Shall be the pride of ages untold,
And everlasting joy to the nations.

Antiphon

No more shall the sun be your light by day,
Nor the moon's beam enlighten you by night;
The Lord shall be your everlasting light,
And your God shall be your glory.

Antiphon

No more for you the setting of suns,
No more the waning of moons;
The Lord shall be your everlasting light,
And the days of your mourning shall come to an end.

Antiphon

Melody: Sion, Sing   Music: Lucien Deiss, C.S.Sp., 1965
                            Text: Lucien Deiss, C.S.Sp., 1965

Psalmody

Ant. 1   From Tarshish and from the islands, kings have
         come to offer gifts to the Lord our King.

Psalm 72

O God, give your judgment to the king,
to a king's son your justice,
that he may judge your people in justice
and your poor in right judgment.

May the mountains bring forth peace for the people
and the hills, justice.
May he defend the poor of the people
and save the children of the needy
and crush the oppressor.

He shall endure like the sun and the moon
from age to age.
He shall descend like rain on the meadow,
like raindrops on the earth.

In his days justice shall flourish
and peace till the moon fails.
He shall rule from sea to sea,
from the Great River to earth's bounds.

Before him his enemies shall fall,
his foes lick the dust.
The kings of Tarshish and the sea coasts
shall pay him tribute.

The kings of Sheba and Seba
shall bring him gifts.
Before him all kings shall fall prostrate,
all nations shall serve him.

For he shall save the poor when they cry
and the needy who are helpless.

He will have pity on the weak
and save the lives of the poor.

From oppression he will rescue their lives,
to him their blood is dear.
Long may he live,
may the gold of Sheba be given him.
They shall pray for him without ceasing
and bless him all the day.

May corn be abundant in the land
to the peaks of the mountains.
May its fruit rustle like Lebanon;
may men flourish in the cities
like grass on the earth.

May his name be blessed for ever
and endure like the sun.
Every tribe shall be blessed in him,
all nations bless his name.

Blessed be the Lord, God of Israel,
who alone works wonders,
ever blessed his glorious name.
Let his glory fill the earth.

Amen! Amen!

Ant.   From Tarshish and from the islands, kings have
come to offer gifts to the Lord our King.

Ant. 2   Adore the Lord in his holy court, alleluia.

Psalm 96

O sing a new song to the Lord,
sing to the Lord, all the earth.
O sing to the Lord, bless his name.

Proclaim his help day by day,
tell among the nations his glory
and his wonders among all the peoples.

The Lord is great and worthy of praise,
to be feared above all gods;
the gods of the heathens are naught.

It was the Lord who made the heavens,
his are majesty and state and power
and splendor in his holy place.

Give the Lord, you families of peoples,
give the Lord glory and power,
give the Lord the glory of his name.

Bring an offering and enter his courts,
worship the Lord in his temple.
O earth, tremble before him.

Proclaim to the nations: "God is king."
The world he made firm in its place;
he will judge the peoples in fairness.

Let the heavens rejoice and earth be glad,
let the sea and all within it thunder praise,
let the land and all it bears rejoice,
all the trees of the wood shout for joy

at the presence of the Lord for he comes,
he comes to rule the earth.
With justice he will rule the world,
he will judge the peoples with his truth.

Ant.   Adore the Lord in his holy court, alleluia.

Ant. 3   Worship the Lord, all you his angels, alleluia.

Psalm 97

The Lord is king, let earth rejoice,
the many coastlands be glad.

Cloud and darkness are his raiment;
his throne, justice and right.

A fire prepares his path;
it burns up his foes on every side.
His lightnings light up the world,
the earth trembles at the sight.

The mountains melt like wax
before the Lord of all the earth.
The skies proclaim his justice;
all peoples see his glory.

Let those who serve idols be ashamed,
those who boast of their worthless gods.
All you spirits, worship him.

Zion hears and is glad;
the people of Judah rejoice
because of your judgments, O Lord.

For you indeed are the Lord,
most high above all the earth,
exalted far above all spirits.

The Lord loves those who hate evil:
he guards the souls of his saints;
he sets them free from the wicked.

Light shines forth for the just
and joy for the upright of heart.
Rejoice, you just, in the Lord;
give glory to his holy name.

Ant.   Worship the Lord, all you his angels, alleluia.

The heavens proclaim the justice of God.
—All nations shall see his glory.

FIRST READING

From the book of the prophet Isaiah   60:1-22

The revelation of God's glory over Jerusalem

Rise up in splendor, O Jerusalem! Your light has come,
   the glory of the Lord shines upon you.

See, darkness covers the earth,
   and thick clouds cover the peoples;
But upon you the Lord shines,
   and over you appears his glory.
Nations shall walk by your light,
   and kings by your shining radiance.

Raise your eyes and look about;
   they all gather and come to you:
Your sons come from afar,
   and your daughters in the arms of their nurses.

Then you shall be radiant at what you see,
   your heart shall throb and overflow,
For the riches of the sea shall be emptied out before you,
   the wealth of nations shall be brought to you.

Caravans of camels shall fill you,
   dromedaries from Midian and Ephah;
All from Sheba shall come
   bearing gold and frankincense,
   and proclaiming the praises of the Lord.

All the flocks of Kedar shall be gathered for you,
   the rams of Nebaioth shall be your sacrifices;
They will be acceptable offerings on my altar,
   and I will enhance the splendor of my house.

What are these that fly along like clouds,
   like doves to their cotes?
All the vessels of the sea are assembled,
   with the ships of Tarshish in the lead,

To bring your children from afar
    with their silver and gold,
In the name of the Lord, your God,
    the Holy One of Israel, who has glorified you.

Foreigners shall rebuild your walls,
    and their kings shall be your attendants;
Though I struck you in my wrath,
    yet in my good will I have shown you mercy.

Your gates shall stand open constantly;
    day and night they shall not be closed
But shall admit to you the wealth of nations,
    and their kings, in the vanguard.
For the people or kingdom shall perish
    that does not serve you;
    those nations shall be utterly destroyed.

The glory of Lebanon shall come to you:
    the cypress, the plane and the pine,
To bring beauty to my sanctuary,
    and glory to the place where I set my feet.

The children of your oppressors shall come,
    bowing low before you;
All those who despised you
    shall fall prostrate at your feet.
They shall call you "City of the Lord,"
    "Zion of the Holy One of Israel."

Once you were forsaken,
    hated and unvisited.
Now I will make you the pride of the ages,
    a joy to generation after generation.

You shall suck the milk of nations,
    and be nursed at royal breasts;
You shall know that I, the Lord, am your savior,
    your redeemer, the mighty one of Jacob.

In place of bronze I will bring gold,
    instead of iron, silver;
In place of wood, bronze,
    instead of stones, iron;
I will appoint peace your governor,
    and justice your ruler.

No longer shall violence be heard of in your land,
    or plunder and ruin within your boundaries.
You shall call your walls "Salvation"
    and your gates "Praise."

No longer shall the sun
    be your light by day,
Nor the brightness of the moon
    shine upon you at night;
The Lord shall be your light forever,
    your God shall be your glory.

No longer shall your sun go down,
    or your moon withdraw,
For the Lord will be your light forever,
    and the days of your mourning shall be at an end.

Your people shall all be just,
    they shall always possess the land,
They, the bud of my planting,
    my handiwork to show my glory.

The smallest shall become a thousand,
    the youngest, a mighty nation;
I, the Lord, will swiftly accomplish these things
    when their time comes.

RESPONSORY   Isaiah 60:1, 3

Arise, shine forth, Jerusalem, for now your light has
  come:
—the glory of your God has risen upon you.

All nations will walk in your brightness,
and kings in the splendor of your dawn.
—The glory of your God has risen upon you.

SECOND READING

From a sermon by Saint Leo the Great, pope

(Sermo 3 in Epiphania Domini, 1-3. 5:PL 54, 240–244)

The Lord has made his salvation known to the whole world

The loving providence of God determined that in the last days he would aid the world, set on its course to destruction. He decreed that all nations should be saved in Christ.

A promise had been made to the holy patriarch Abraham in regard to these nations. He was to have a countless progeny, born not from his body but from the seed of faith. His descendants are therefore compared with the array of the stars. The father of all nations was to hope not in an earthly progeny but in a progeny from above.

Let the full number of the nations now take their place in the family of the patriarchs. Let the children of the promise now receive the blessing in the seed of Abraham, the blessing renounced by the children of his flesh. In the persons of the Magi let all people adore the Creator of the universe; let God be known, not in Judea only, but in the whole world, so that *his name may be great in all Israel.*

Dear friends, now that we have received instruction in this revelation of God's grace, let us celebrate with spiritual joy the day of our first harvesting, of the first calling of the Gentiles. Let us give thanks to the merciful God, *who has made us worthy,* in the words of the Apostle, *to share the position of the saints in light; who has rescued us from the power of darkness, and brought us into the kingdom of his beloved Son.* As Isaiah prophesied: *The people of the Gentiles, who sat in darkness, have seen a great light, and for those who dwelt in the region of the shadow of death a light has dawned.* He spoke of them to the Lord: *The Gentiles, who do not know you, will invoke you, and the peoples, who knew you not, will take refuge in you.*

This is *the day that Abraham saw, and rejoiced to see,* when he knew that the sons born of his faith would be blessed in his seed, that is, in Christ. Believing that he would be the father of the nations, he looked into the future, *giving glory to God, in full awareness that God is able to do what he has promised.*

This is the day that David prophesied in the psalms, when he said: *All the nations that you have brought into being will come and fall down in adoration in your presence, Lord, and glorify your name.* Again, *the Lord has made known his salvation; in the sight of the nations he has revealed his justice.*

This came to be fulfilled, as we know, from the time when the star beckoned the three wise men out of their distant country and led them to recognize and adore the King of heaven and earth. The obedience of the star calls us to imitate its humble service: to be servants, as best we can, of the grace that invites all men to find Christ.

Dear friends, you must have the same zeal to be of help to one another; then, in the kingdom of God, to which faith and good works are the way, you will shine as children of the light: through our Lord Jesus Christ, who lives and reigns with God the Father and the Holy Spirit for ever and ever. Amen.

RESPONSORY

This is the glorious day on which Christ himself, the
    savior of the world, appeared;
the prophets foretold him, the angels worshiped him;

—the Magi saw his star and rejoiced to lay their treasures
  at his feet.

God's holy day has dawned for us at last;
come, all you peoples, and adore the Lord.
—The Magi saw . . .

Hymn, Te Deum, 651.

Prayer, as in Morning Prayer.

Morning Prayer

HYMN

  Antiphon:

    All you nations, sing out your joy to the Lord:
    Alleluia, alleluia!

    Joyfully shout, all you on earth,
    give praise to the glory of God;
    And with a hymn, sing out his glorious praise:
    Alleluia!

           Antiphon

    Let all the earth kneel in his sight,
    extolling his marvelous fame;
    Honor his name, in highest heaven give praise:
    Alleluia!

           Antiphon

    Come forth and see all the great works
    that God has brought forth by his might;
    Fall on your knees before his glorious throne:
    Alleluia!

           Antiphon

    Glory and thanks be to the Father;
    honor and praise to the Son;

And to the Spirit, source of life and of love:
Alleluia!

Antiphon

Melody: All You Nations   Music: Lucien Deiss, C.S.Sp., 1965
                              Text: Lucien Deiss, C.S.Sp., 1965

Ant. 1 The wise men opened their treasures and
offered to the Lord gifts of gold, frankincense
and myrrh, alleluia.

Psalms and canticle from Sunday, Week I, 688.

Ant. 2 Mighty seas and rivers, bless the Lord; springs
of water, sing his praises, alleluia.

Ant. 3 Jerusalem, your light has come; the glory of the
Lord dawns upon you. Men of every race shall
walk in the splendor of your sunrise, alleluia.

READING   Isaiah 52:7-10

How beautiful upon the mountains
    are the feet of him who brings glad tidings,
Announcing peace, bearing good news,
    announcing salvation, and saying to Zion,
    "Your God is King!"
Hark! Your watchmen raise a cry,
    together they shout for joy,
For they see directly, before their eyes,
    the Lord restoring Zion.
Break out together in song,
    O ruins of Jerusalem!
For the Lord comforts his people,
    he redeems Jerusalem.
The Lord has bared his holy arm
    in the sight of all the nations;
All the ends of the earth will behold
    the salvation of our God.

RESPONSORY

All the kings of the earth will bow down in worship.
—All the kings of the earth will bow down in worship.

Men and women of every nation will serve him.
—They will bow down in worship.

Glory to the Father . . .
—All the kings . . .

CANTICLE OF ZECHARIAH

Ant. Today the Bridegroom claims his bride, the Church, since Christ has washed her sins away in Jordan's waters; the Magi hasten with their gifts to the royal wedding; and the wedding guests rejoice, for Christ has changed water into wine, alleluia.

INTERCESSIONS

Today our Savior was adored by the Magi. Let us also worship him with joy as we pray:
   Light from Light, shine on us this day.
Christ, you revealed yourself in the flesh,
—sanctify us through prayer and the word of God.
Christ, your witness was the Spirit,
—free our lives from the spirit of doubt.
Christ, you revealed yourself to the angels,
—help us to feel the joy of heaven on earth.
Christ, you were proclaimed to the nations,
—by the power of the Holy Spirit open the hearts of all.
Christ, you generated faith in the world,
—renew the faith of all believers.
Christ, you were taken up in glory,
—enkindle in us a longing for your kingdom.

Our Father . . .

Prayer

Father,
you revealed your Son to the nations
by the guidance of a star.
Lead us to your glory in heaven
by the light of faith.

We ask this through our Lord Jesus Christ, your Son,
who lives and reigns with you and the Holy Spirit,
one God, for ever and ever.

Alternative Prayer

Father of light, unchanging God,
today you reveal to men of faith
the resplendent fact of the Word made flesh.
Your light is strong,
your love is near;
draw us beyond the limits which this world imposes,
to the life where your Spirit makes all life complete.

We ask this through Christ our Lord.

Daytime Prayer

PSALMODY

Antiphons

Midmorning

Ant.   This mystery, which has been hidden through all
ages and from all generations, is revealed to us
today.

Midday

Ant.   Christ Jesus has come, bringing the joyful news:
peace to those who were far off; peace to those
who are near.

Midafternoon

Ant. I have raised you up as a light for all the nations;
through you my salvation will be proclaimed to
the ends of the earth.

Psalm 47

All peoples, clap your hands,
cry to God with shouts of joy!
For the Lord, the Most High, we must fear,
great king over all the earth.

He subdues peoples under us
and nations under our feet.
Our inheritance, our glory, is from him,
given to Jacob out of love.

God goes up with shouts of joy;
the Lord goes up with trumpet blast.
Sing praise for God, sing praise,
sing praise to our king, sing praise.

God is king of all the earth.
Sing praise with all your skill.
God is king over the nations;
God reigns on his holy throne.

The princes of the peoples are assembled
with the people of Abraham's God.
The rulers of the earth belong to God,
to God who reigns over all.

Psalm 86:1-10

Turn your ear, O Lord, and give answer
for I am poor and needy.
Preserve my life, for I am faithful:
save the servant who trusts in you.

You are my God, have mercy on me, Lord,
for I cry to you all the day long.
Give joy to your servant, O Lord,
for to you I lift up my soul.

O Lord, you are good and forgiving,
full of love to all who call.
Give heed, O Lord, to my prayer
and attend to the sound of my voice.

In the day of distress I will call
and surely you will reply.
Among the gods there is none like you, O Lord;
nor work to compare with yours.

All the nations shall come to adore you
and glorify your name, O Lord:
for you are great and do marvellous deeds,
you who alone are God.

Psalm 98

Sing a new song to the Lord
for he has worked wonders.
His right hand and his holy arm
have brought salvation.

The Lord has made known his salvation;
has shown his justice to the nations.
He has remembered his truth and love
for the house of Israel.

All the ends of the earth have seen
the salvation of our God.
Shout to the Lord all the earth,
ring out your joy.

Sing psalms to the Lord with the harp
with the sound of music.

With trumpets and the sound of the horn
acclaim the King, the Lord.

Let the sea and all within it thunder;
the world, and all its peoples.
Let the rivers clap their hands
and the hills ring out their joy

Rejoice at the presence of the Lord,
for he comes to rule the earth.
He will rule the world with justice
and the peoples with fairness.

At the other hours the complementary psalmody is used, 1191.

Midmorning

Ant. This mystery, which has been hidden through all
      ages and from all generations, is revealed to us
      today.

READING   Revelation 15:4

Who would dare refuse you honor,
    or the glory due your name, O Lord?
Since you alone are holy,
    all nations shall come
    and worship in your presence.

He was seen on the earth.
—He was a man among men.

Midday

Ant. Christ Jesus has come, bringing the joyful news:
      peace to those who were far off; peace to those
      who are near.

Isaiah 49:6

> The Lord said to me:
> It is too little for you to be my servant,
>   to raise up the tribes of Jacob,
>   and restore the survivors of Israel;
> I will make you a light to the nations,
>   that my salvation may reach to the ends of the earth.

All nations will see the glory of your holy One.
—All the kings of the earth will acknowledge your
    majesty.

Midafternoon

Ant.   I have raised you up as a light for all the nations;
       through you my salvation will be proclaimed to
       the ends of the earth.

READING   Zechariah 2:11

Many nations shall join themselves to the Lord on that
day, and they shall be his people, and he will dwell
among you, and you shall know that the Lord of hosts
has sent me to you.

All you peoples, praise our God.
—Sing to the glory of his name.

Prayer, as in Morning Prayer.

Evening Prayer II

HYMN

> As with gladness men of old,
> Did the guiding star behold,
> As with joy they hailed its light,
> Leading onwards, beaming bright,
> So, most gracious God, may we
> Evermore be led to thee.

As with joyful steps they sped
To that lowly manger-bed,
There to bend the knee before
Him whom heaven and earth adore,
So may we with willing feet
Ever seek thy mercy-seat.

As they offered gifts most rare
At that manger rude and bare,
So may we with holy joy,
Pure, and free from sin's alloy,
All our costliest treasures bring,
Christ, to thee our heavenly king.

Holy Jesus, every day
Keep us in the narrow way;
And, when earthly things are past,
Bring our ransomed souls at last
Where they need no star to guide,
Where no clouds thy glory hide.

In the heavenly country bright
Need they no created light;
Thou its light, its joy, its crown,
Thou its sun which goes not down:
There for ever may we sing
Alleluias to our king.

Melody: Dix 77.77.77

Music: Adapted by W.H. Monk,
1823–1889, from a chorale by
Conrad Kocher, 1786-1872
Text: W. Chatterton Dix, 1837-1898

PSALMODY

Ant. 1   He comes in splendor, the King who is our
peace; he is supreme over all the kings of the
earth.

Psalm 110:1-5, 7

The Lord's revelation to my Master:
"Sit on my right:
your foes I will put beneath your feet."

The Lord will wield from Zion
your scepter of power:
rule in the midst of all your foes.

A prince from the day of your birth
on the holy mountains;
from the womb before the dawn I begot you.

The Lord has sworn an oath he will not change.
"You are a priest for ever,
a priest like Melchizedek of old."

The Master standing at your right hand
will shatter kings in the day of his great wrath.

He shall drink from the stream by the wayside
and therefore he shall lift up his head.

Ant.   He comes in splendor, the King who is our peace;
he is supreme over all the kings of the earth.

Ant. 2 A light has shone through the darkness for the
upright of heart; the Lord is gracious, merciful
and just.

Psalm 112

Happy the man who fears the Lord,
who takes delight in all his commands.
His sons will be powerful on earth;
the children of the upright are blessed.

Riches and wealth are in his house;
his justice stands firm for ever.
He is a light in the darkness for the upright:
he is generous, merciful and just.

The good man takes pity and lends,
he conducts his affairs with honor.
The just man will never waver:
he will be remembered for ever.

He has no fear of evil news;
with a firm heart he trusts in the Lord.
With a steadfast heart he will not fear;
he will see the downfall of his foes.

Open-handed, he gives to the poor;
his justice stands firm for ever.
His head will be raised in glory.

The wicked man sees and is angry,
grinds his teeth and fades away;
the desire of the wicked leads to doom.

Ant.   A light has shone through the darkness for the
upright of heart; the Lord is gracious, merciful
and just.

Ant. 3   All the people, whom you have made, will come
and worship before you, Lord.

Canticle   Revelation 15:3-4

Mighty and wonderful are your works,
Lord God Almighty!
Righteous and true are your ways,
O King of the nations!

Who would dare refuse you honor,
or the glory due your name, O Lord?

Since you alone are holy,
all nations shall come
and worship in your presence.
Your mighty deeds are clearly seen.

Ant.   All the people, whom you have made, will come
        and worship before you, Lord.

READING   Titus 3:4-5

When the kindness and love of God our Savior
appeared, he saved us; not because of any righteous
deeds we had done, but because of his mercy. He saved
us through the baptism of new birth and renewal by the
Holy Spirit.

RESPONSORY

All peoples will be blessed in him, men and women of
    every race.
—All peoples will be blessed in him, men and women
    of every race.

All nations will acclaim his glory.
—Men and women of every race.

Glory to the Father . . .
—All peoples will . . .

CANTICLE OF MARY

Ant.   Three mysteries mark this holy day: today the star
        leads the Magi to the infant Christ; today water is
        changed into wine for the wedding feast; today
        Christ wills to be baptized by John in the river
        Jordan to bring us salvation.

INTERCESSIONS

On this day our Savior was adored by the Magi. Let us
    also worship him with joy as we pray to him:
        Save the poor, O Lord.
King of the nations, you called the Magi to adore you as
    the first representatives of the nations,
—give us a willing spirit of adoration and service.
King of glory, you judge your people with justice,
—grant mankind an abundant measure of peace.

King of ages, you endure from age to age,
—send your word as fresh spring rain falling on our
hearts.
King of justice, you desire to free the poor who have no
advocate,
—be compassionate to the suffering and the afflicted.
Lord, your name is blessed for all ages,
—show the wonders of your saving power to our
deceased brothers and sisters.

Our Father . . .

Prayer

Father,
you revealed your Son to the nations
by the guidance of a star.
Lead us to your glory in heaven
by the light of faith.

We ask this through our Lord Jesus Christ, your Son,
who lives and reigns with you and the Holy Spirit,
one God, for ever and ever.

Alternative Prayer

Father of light, unchanging God,
today you reveal to men of faith
the resplendent fact of the Word made flesh.
Your light is strong,
your love is near;
draw us beyond the limits which this world imposes,
to the life where your Spirit makes all life complete.

We ask this through Christ our Lord.

On the days following, until the Sunday celebration of the
Baptism of the Lord, the proper parts are taken from below,
575. Ordinary Time begins after the Sunday celebration of the
Baptism of the Lord.

Where the solemnity of Epiphany is celebrated on the Sunday between January 2 and January 8, on the days following the Epiphany, the proper parts are taken from below, unless January 7 or 8 occurs on Sunday in which case Ordinary Time begins on the following day, the feast of the Baptism of the Lord being omitted.

after Epiphany to the Baptism of the Lord

MONDAY

Psalter, Week II

Office of Readings

The heavens proclaim the justice of God.
—All nations shall see his glory.

FIRST READING

From the book of the prophet Isaiah   61:1-11

The Spirit of the Lord is upon his servant

The spirit of the Lord God is upon me,
    because the Lord has anointed me;
He has sent me to bring glad tidings to the lowly,
    to heal the brokenhearted,
To proclaim liberty to the captives
    and release to the prisoners,
To announce a year of favor from the Lord
    and a day of vindication by our God,
    to comfort all who mourn;
To place on those who mourn in Zion
    a diadem instead of ashes,
To give them oil of gladness in place of mourning,
    a glorious mantle instead of a listless spirit.

They will be called oaks of justice,
   planted by the Lord to show his glory.

They shall rebuild the ancient ruins,
   the former wastes they shall raise up
And restore the ruined cities,
   desolate now for generations.

Strangers shall stand ready to pasture your flocks,
   foreigners shall be your farmers and vinedressers.
You yourselves shall be named priests of the Lord,
   ministers of our God you shall be called.
You shall eat the wealth of the nations
   and boast of riches from them.

Since their shame was double
   and disgrace and spittle were their portion,
They shall have a double inheritance in their land,
   everlasting joy shall be theirs.

For I, the Lord, love what is right,
   I hate robbery and injustice;
I will give them their recompense faithfully,
   a lasting covenant I will make with them.

Their descendants shall be renowned among the nations,
   and their offspring among the peoples;
All who see them shall acknowledge them
   as a race the Lord has blessed.

I rejoice heartily in the Lord,
   in my God is the joy of my soul;
For he has clothed me with a robe of salvation,
   and wrapped me in a mantle of justice,
Like a bridegroom adorned with a diadem,
   like a bride bedecked with her jewels.

As the earth brings forth its plants,
   and a garden makes growth spring up,

So will the Lord God make justice and praise
    spring up before all the nations.

Isaiah 61-1: John 8:42

The Spirit of God rests upon me,
for the Lord has anointed me;
he has sent me to bring good news to the poor,
—to heal the broken-hearted,
to proclaim that captivity is now ended and prisoners are
    set free.

I have come forth from God and have come into the
    world.
I have not come of myself; the Father has sent me.
—To heal the . . .

SECOND READING

From a sermon by Saint Peter Chrysologus, bishop
(Sermo 160: PL 52, 620-622)

In choosing to be born for us, God chose to be known by us

In the mystery of our Lord's incarnation there were
clear indications of his eternal Godhead. Yet the great
events we celebrate today disclose and reveal in different
ways the fact that God himself took a human body.
Mortal man, enshrouded always in darkness, must not be
left in ignorance, and so be deprived of what he can
understand and retain only by grace.

In choosing to be born for us, God chose to be known
by us. He therefore reveals himself in this way, in order
that this great sacrament of his love may not be an
occasion for us of great misunderstanding.

Today the Magi find, crying in a manger, the one they
have followed as he shone in the sky. Today the Magi see
clearly, in swaddling clothes, the one they have long
awaited as he lay hidden among the stars.

Today the Magi gaze in deep wonder at what they see: heaven on earth, earth in heaven, man in God, God in man, one whom the whole universe cannot contain now enclosed in a tiny body. As they look, they believe and do not question, as their symbolic gifts bear witness: incense for God, gold for a king, myrrh for one who is to die.

So the Gentiles, who were the last, become the first: the faith of the Magi is the first fruits of the belief of the Gentiles.

Today Christ enters the Jordan to wash away the sin of the world. John himself testifies that this is why he has come: *Behold the Lamb of God, behold him who takes away the sins of the world.* Today a servant lays his hand on the Lord, a man lays his hand on God, John lays his hand on Christ, not to forgive but to receive forgiveness.

Today, as the psalmist prophesied: *The voice of the Lord is heard above the waters.* What does the voice say? *This is my beloved Son, in whom I am well pleased.*

Today the Holy Spirit hovers over the waters in the likeness of a dove. A dove announced to Noah that the flood had disappeared from the earth; so now a dove is to reveal that the world's shipwreck is at an end for ever. The sign is no longer an olive-shoot of the old stock: instead, the Spirit pours out on Christ's head the full richness of a new anointing by the Father, to fulfill what the psalmist had prophesied: *Therefore God, your God, has anointed you with the oil of gladness above your fellows.*

Today Christ works the first of his signs from heaven by turning water into wine. But water [mixed with wine] has still to be changed into the sacrament of his blood, so that Christ may offer spiritual drink from the chalice of his body, to fulfill the psalmist's prophecy: *How excellent is my chalice, warming my spirit.*

RESPONSORY

The wise men offered three precious gifts to the Lord on
    that day,
and each of these gifts has a divine significance:
—gold signifies the power of a king;
frankincense, the office of high priest;
and myrrh, the Lord's burial.

The wise men came to the stable to worship the author of
    our salvation,
and from their treasures they offered these symbolic
    gifts.
—Gold signifies the . . .

Prayer, as in Morning Prayer.

Morning Prayer

READING   Isaiah 9:5

A child is born to us, a son is given us;
    upon his shoulder dominion rests.
They name him Wonder-Counselor, God-Hero,
    Father-Forever, Prince of Peace.

RESPONSORY

All the kings of the earth will bow down in worship.
—All the kings of the earth will bow down in worship.

Men and women of every nation will serve him.
—They will bow down in worship.

Glory to the Father . . .
—All the kings . . .

CANTICLE OF ZECHARIAH

Ant.   The wise men came from the East to adore the
        Lord in Bethlehem. Opening their treasures, they

offered him three precious gifts: gold for the great King, frankincense for the true God, and myrrh for his burial, alleluia.

INTERCESSIONS

All the ends of the earth have seen Jesus Christ, the saving power of God. Let us praise him and cry out in joy:

Glory be to you, Lord Jesus Christ.

Redeemer of all, you came to tear down the walls separating Jew from Gentile,

—root out the prejudices which erode the depths of our humanity.

Through your incarnation and your birth you established your presence among us,

—teach us to recognize the many forms of your presence in the Church and in one another.

You are the fullest revelation of God to men and women,

—show us how we can assent to your word with integrity of faith and action.

You are God-with-us, wondrously transforming all creation,

—let every heart, every voice, every deed throughout the universe now be transformed.

Our Father. . .

Prayer

Lord,
let the light of your glory shine within us,
and lead us through the darkness of this world
to the radiant joy of our eternal home.

We ask this through our Lord Jesus Christ, your Son,
who lives and reigns with you and the Holy Spirit,
one God, for ever and ever.

Daytime Prayer

Midmorning

Ant. This mystery, which has been hidden through all
ages and from all generations, is revealed now to
us.

READING   Deuteronomy 4:7

What great nation is there that has gods so close to it as
the Lord, our God, is to us whenever we call upon him?

He was seen on the earth.
—He was a man among men.

Midday

Ant. Christ Jesus has come, bringing the joyful news:
peace to those who were far off; peace to those
who are near.

READING   Isaiah 12:5-6

Sing praise to the Lord for his glorious achievement;
let this be known throughout all the earth.
Shout with exultation, O city of Zion,
for great in your midst is the Holy One of Israel!

All nations will see the glory of your holy One.
—All the kings of the earth will acknowledge your
majesty.

Midafternoon

Ant. I have raised you up as a light for all the nations;
through you my salvation will be proclaimed to
the ends of the earth.

READING   See Tobit 14:6-7

All the nations shall abandon their idols and come to Jerusalem to dwell. And all the kings of the earth shall rejoice in her, worshiping the king of Israel.

All you peoples, praise our God.
—Sing to the glory of his name.

Prayer, as in Morning Prayer.

Evening Prayer

READING   2 Peter 1:3-4

The divine power of Christ has freely bestowed on us everything necessary for a life of genuine piety, through knowledge of him who called us by his own glory and power. By virtue of them he has bestowed on us the great and precious things he promised, so that through these you who have fled a world corrupted by lust might become sharers of the divine nature.

RESPONSORY

All peoples will be blessed in him, men and women of every race.
—All peoples will be blessed in him, men and women of every race.
All nations will acclaim his glory.
—Men and women of every race.
Glory to the Father . . .
—All peoples will . . .

CANTICLE OF MARY

Ant.   When they saw the star the Magi were filled with great joy; entering the house, they offered their gifts to the Lord: gold, frankincense and myrrh.

INTERCESSIONS

Blessed be Jesus Christ, the Lord, who has come to bring
   light to those sitting in darkness and in the shadow of
   death. With deep faith we beg him:
   Christ, Rising Sun, give us your light.

Lord Jesus, at your coming you brought to birth your
   body, the Church,
—let her be rooted in love and gifted with growth.

You hold heaven and earth in your hands,
—let all peoples and their leaders recognize your royal
   power.

Through your incarnation you became eternal high
   priest,
—let all priests be genuine ministers of your saving work.

In the womb of the Virgin Mary, you brought about a
   mystical union of divinity and humanity,
—bless the virgins consecrated to you, their heavenly
   Spouse.

You did not create the power of death but you destroyed
   it by becoming man,
—graciously transform the mortality of our deceased
   brothers and sisters into eternal life.

Our Father . . .

Prayer

Lord,
let the light of your glory shine within us,
and lead us through the darkness of this world
to the radiant joy of our eternal home.

We ask this through our Lord Jesus Christ, your Son,
who lives and reigns with you and the Holy Spirit,
one God, for ever and ever.

after Epiphany to the Baptism of the Lord

TUESDAY

Office of Readings

Praise the Lord, Jerusalem.
—He sends forth his word to give life to the earth.

FIRST READING

From the book of the prophet Isaiah   62:1-12

The approach of redemption

For Zion's sake I will not be silent,
  for Jerusalem's sake I will not be quiet,
Until her vindication shines forth like the dawn
  and her victory like a burning torch.

Nations shall behold your vindication,
  and all kings your glory;
You shall be called by a new name
  pronounced by the mouth of the Lord.
You shall be a glorious crown in the hand of the Lord,
  a royal diadem held by your God.

No more shall men call you "Forsaken,"
  or your land "Desolate,"
But you shall be called "My Delight,"
  and your land "Espoused."
For the Lord delights in you,
  and makes your land his spouse.

As a young man marries a virgin,
  your Builder shall marry you;
And as a bridegroom rejoices in his bride
  so shall your God rejoice in you.

Upon your walls, O Jerusalem,
    I have stationed watchmen;
Never, by day or by night,
    shall they be silent.

O you who are to remind the Lord,
    take no rest
And give no rest to him,
    until he re-establishes Jerusalem
And makes of it
    the pride of the earth.

The Lord has sworn by his right hand
    and by his mighty arm:
No more will I give your grain
    as food to your enemies;
Nor shall foreigners drink your wine,
    for which you toiled.
But you who harvest the grain shall eat it,
    and you shall praise the Lord;
You who gather the grapes shall drink the wine
    in the courts of my sanctuary.

Pass through, pass through the gates,
    prepare the way for the people;
Build up, build up the highway,
    clear it of stones,
    raise up a standard over the nations.

See, the Lord proclaims
    to the ends of the earth:
Say to daughter Zion,
    your savior comes!
Here is his reward with him,
    his recompense before him.
They shall be called the holy people,
    the redeemed of the Lord,

And you shall be called "Frequented,"
  a city that is not forsaken.

Isaiah 62:2-3

The nations shall see your justice,
all kings shall witness your glory;
—and the Lord himself will give you a new name by
  which you shall be called.

You will be a crown of glory in the hand of the Lord,
and a kingly diadem in the hand of your God.
—And the Lord . . .

SECOND READING

From a sermon on the Epiphany attributed to Saint
Hippolytus, priest

(Nn. 2. 6–8. 10: PG 10, 854. 858–859. 862)

Water and the Spirit

That Jesus should come and be baptized by John is
surely cause for amazement. To think of the infinite river
that gladdens the city of God being bathed in a poor little
stream of the eternal; the unfathomable fountainhead
that gives life to all men being immersed in the shallow
waters of this transient world! He who fills all creation,
leaving no place devoid of his presence, he who is
incomprehensible to the angels and hidden from the sight
of man, came to be baptized because it was his will. And
*behold, the heavens opened and a voice said: "This is my
beloved Son in whom I am well pleased."*

The beloved Father begets love, and spiritual light
generates light inaccessible. In his divine nature he is my
only Son, though he was known as the son of Joseph.
This is my beloved Son. Though hungry himself, he feeds
thousands; though weary, he refreshes those who labor.
He has no place to lay his head yet holds all creation in

his hand. By his passion [inflicted on him by others], he frees us from the passions [unleashed by our disobedience]; by receiving a blow on the cheek he gives the world its liberty; by being pierced in the side he heals the wound of Adam.

I ask you now to pay close attention, for I want to return to that fountain of life and contemplate its healing waters at their source.

The Father of immortality sent his immortal Son and Word into the world; he came to us men to cleanse us with water and the Spirit. To give us a new birth that would make our bodies and souls immortal, he breathed into us the spirit of life and armed us with incorruptibility. Now if we become immortal, we shall also be divine; and if we become divine after rebirth in baptism through water and the Holy Spirit, we shall also be coheirs with Christ after the resurrection of the dead.

Therefore, in a herald's voice I cry: Let peoples of every nation come and receive the immortality that flows from baptism. This is the water that is linked to the Spirit, the water that irrigates Paradise, makes the earth fertile, gives growth to plants, and brings forth living creatures. In short, this is the water by which a man receives new birth and life, the water in which even Christ was baptized, the water into which the Holy Spirit descended in the form of a dove.

Whoever goes down into these waters of rebirth with faith renounces the devil and pledges himself to Christ. He repudiates the enemy and confesses that Christ is God, throws off his servitude, and is raised to filial status. He comes up from baptism resplendent as the sun, radiant in his purity, but above all, he comes as a son of God and a coheir with Christ. To him and to his most holy and life-giving Spirit be glory and power now and for ever. Amen.

RESPONSORY   John 1:32, 34, 33

I saw the Spirit coming down from heaven like a dove,
    resting upon him.
—I have seen and given witness that he is the Son of God.

He who sent me to baptize with water said to me:
The one on whom you see the Spirit come down and rest,
this is he who will baptize with the Holy Spirit.
—I have seen . . .

Prayer, as in Morning Prayer.

Morning Prayer

READING   Isaiah 4:2-3

    On that day,
The branch of the Lord will be luster and glory,
    and the fruit of the earth will be honor and splendor
    for the survivors of Israel.
He who remains in Zion
    and he that is left in Jerusalem
Will be called holy:
    everyone marked down for life in Jerusalem.

RESPONSORY

All the kings of the earth will bow down in worship.
—All the kings of the earth will bow down in worship.

Men and women of every nation will serve him.
—They will bow down in worship.

Glory to the Father . . .
—All the kings . . .

CANTICLE OF ZECHARIAH

Ant. The wise men offered gifts of gold, frankincense,
      and myrrh to the Lord, the Son of God and King
      most high, alleluia.

INTERCESSIONS

Let us rejoice in the compassion of Christ, who came to
free mankind from the slavery of corruption and to
give us the freedom of the sons of God. Trusting in
this divine compassion, we plead:
By your birth, deliver us from evil.

Lord, you existed before the ages, yet you entered into a
new life,
—renew us continually through the mystery of your
birth.

Without surrendering your divinity, you wondrously
took on our humanity,
—grant that our lives may press on to a fuller
participation in your divinity.

You came to be a light to the nations, the teacher of
holiness,
—let your words be a light along our way.

Word of God made flesh in the womb of the Virgin Mary,
you entered this world,
—live in our hearts always through faith.

Our Father . . .

Prayer

Father,
your Son became like us
when he revealed himself in our nature:
help us to become more like him,
who lives and reigns with you and the Holy Spirit,
one God, for ever and ever.

Daytime Prayer

Midmorning

Ant.   This mystery, which has been hidden through all
ages and from all generations, is now revealed to
us.

READING   Isaiah 45:13

It was I who stirred up one for the triumph of justice;
   all his ways I make level.
He shall rebuild my city
   and let my exiles go free
Without price or ransom,
   says the Lord of hosts.

He was seen on the earth.
—He was a man among men.

Midday

Ant.   Christ Jesus has come, bringing the joyful news:
      peace to those who were far off; peace to those
      who are near.

READING   Isaiah 48:20

With shouts of joy proclaim this,
   make it known;
Publish it to the ends of the earth, and say,
   "The Lord has redeemed his servant Jacob."

All nations will see the glory of your holy One.
—All the kings of the earth will acknowledge your
   majesty.

Midafternoon

Ant.   I have raised you up as a light for all the nations;
      through you my salvation will be proclaimed to
      the ends of the earth.

READING   Isaiah 65:1

I was ready to respond to those who asked me not,
   to be found by those who sought me not.
I said: Here I am! Here I am!
   to a nation that did not call upon my name.

All you peoples, praise our God.
—Sing to the glory of his name.

Prayer, as in Morning Prayer.

Evening Prayer

READING   Ephesians 2:3b-5

By nature we deserved God's wrath like the rest. But God is rich in mercy; because of his great love for us he brought us to life with Christ when we were dead in sin. By this favor you were saved.

RESPONSORY

All peoples will be blessed in him, men and women of every race.
—All peoples will be blessed in him, men and women of every race.

All nations will acclaim his glory.
—Men and women of every race.

Glory to the Father . . .
—All peoples will . . .

CANTICLE OF MARY

Ant. Christ, you are Light from Light; when you appeared on the earth, the wise men offered their gifts to you, alleluia.

INTERCESSIONS

United with all Christians in prayer and praise, we entreat the Lord:
Father, hear your children.
Help those who know not God but seek your presence in the shadows and projections of the human mind,
—make them new persons in the light of Christ.

Look with favor on all who adore you as the one true God
   and who await your coming in judgment on the last
   day,
—may they recognize your constant love for us.
Remember all those on whom you bestow life, light and
   all good things,
—let them never be far from you.
Watch over all travelers with angelic protection,
—and keep them from sudden and unforeseen death.
You revealed your truth to the dead while they were on
   earth,
—lead them to contemplate the beauty of your
   countenance.

Our Father . . .

Prayer

Father,
your Son became like us
when he revealed himself in our nature:
help us to become more like him,
who lives and reigns with you and the Holy Spirit,
one God, for ever and ever.

after Epiphany to the Baptism of the Lord

WEDNESDAY

Office of Readings

The Lord will teach us his ways.
—And we will follow in his footsteps.

FIRST READING

From the book of the prophet Isaiah 63:7-19

The mercy of the Lord is remembered by a people forsaken

The favors of the Lord I will recall,
  the glorious deeds of the Lord,
Because of all he has done for us;
  for he is good to the house of Israel,
He has favored us according to his mercy
  and his great kindness.

He said: They are indeed my people,
  children who are not disloyal;
So he became their savior
  in their every affliction.
It was not a messenger or an angel,
  but he himself who saved them.
Because of his love and pity
  he redeemed them himself,
Lifting them and carrying them
  all the days of old.

But they rebelled, and grieved
  his holy spirit;
So he turned on them like an enemy,
  and fought against them.

Then they remembered the days of old
  and Moses, his servant;
Where is he who brought up out of the sea
  the shepherd of his flock?
Where is he who put his holy spirit
  in their midst;
Whose glorious arm
  was the guide at Moses' right;

Who divided the waters before them,
    winning for himself eternal renown;
Who led them without stumbling through the depths
    like horses in the open country,
Like cattle going down into the plain,
    the spirit of the Lord guiding them?
Thus you led your people,
    bringing glory to your name.

Look down from heaven and regard us
    from your holy and glorious palace!
Where is your zealous care and your might,
    your surge of pity and your mercy?

O Lord, hold not back,
    for you are our father.
Were Abraham not to know us,
    nor Israel to acknowledge us,
You, Lord, are our father,
    our redeemer you are named forever.

Why do you let us wander, O Lord, from your ways,
    and harden our hearts so that we fear you not?
Return for the sake of your servants,
    the tribes of your heritage.
Why have the wicked invaded your holy place,
    why have our enemies trampled your sanctuary?
Too long have we been like those you do not rule,
    who do not bear your name.

Oh, that you would rend the heavens and come down,
    with the mountains quaking before you!

RESPONSORY   Isaiah 63:19; 59:11

Lord, we are like those over whom you do not rule,
like those who do not hear your name.
—O, that you would rend the heavens and come down!

We have yearned for justice and there is none;
for salvation and it is kept far off from us.
—O, that you . . .

SECOND READING

From a sermon by Saint Proclus of Constantinople, bishop

(Sermo 7 in sancta Theophania, 1-3: PG 65, 758-759)

The waters are made holy

Christ appeared in the world, and, bringing beauty out of disarray, gave it luster and joy. He bore the world's sin and crushed the world's enemy. He sanctified the fountains of waters and enlightened the minds of men. Into the fabric of miracles he interwove ever greater miracles.

For on this day land and sea share between them the grace of the Savior, and the whole world is filled with joy. Today's feast of the Epiphany manifests even more wonders than the feast of Christmas.

On the feast of the Savior's birth, the earth rejoiced because it bore the Lord in a manger; but on today's feast of the Epiphany it is the sea that is glad and leaps for joy; the sea is glad because it receives the blessing of holiness in the river Jordan.

At Christmas we saw a weak baby, giving proof of our weakness. In today's feast, we see a perfect man, hinting at the perfect Son who proceeds from the all-perfect Father. At Christmas the King puts on the royal robe of his body; at Epiphany the very source enfolds and, as it were, clothes the river.

Come then and see new and astounding miracles: the Sun of righteousness washing in the Jordan, fire immersed in water, God sanctified by the ministry of man.

Today every creature shouts in resounding song: *Blessed is he who comes in the name of the Lord*. Blessed is he who comes in every age, for this is not his first coming.

And who is he? Tell us more clearly, I beg you, blessed David: *The Lord is God and has shone upon us*. David is not alone in prophesying this; the apostle Paul adds his own witness, saying: *The grace of God has appeared bringing salvation for all men, and instructing us*. Not for some men, but *for all*. To Jews and Greeks alike God bestows salvation through baptism, offering baptism as a common grace for all.

Come, consider this new and wonderful deluge, greater and more important than the flood of Noah's day. Then the water of the flood destroyed the human race, but now the water of baptism has recalled the dead to life by the power of the one who was baptized. In the days of the flood the dove with an olive branch in its beak foreshadowed the fragrance of the good odor of Christ the Lord; now the Holy Spirit, coming in the likeness of a dove reveals the Lord of mercy.

RESPONSORY

Today, Jesus, Light from Light, whom John baptized in
     the Jordan has appeared to us:
—we believe that he was born of the Virgin Mary.

The heavens opened above him,
and the voice of the Father was heard.
—We believe that . . .

Prayer, as in Morning Prayer.

Morning Prayer

READING   Isaiah 49:8-9

In a time of favor I answer you,
  on the day of salvation I help you,
To restore the land
  and allot the desolate heritage,
Saying to the prisoners: Come out!
  to those in darkness: Show yourselves!

RESPONSORY

All the kings of the earth will bow down in worship.
—All the kings of the earth will bow down in worship.

Men and women of every nation will serve him.
—They will bow down in worship.

Glory to the Father . . .
—All the kings . . .

CANTICLE OF ZECHARIAH

Ant.   We have seen his star in the East and have come
        with gifts to worship the Lord.

INTERCESSIONS

In the fullness of time, the eternal Word was begotten of
    the Father. He is the child who is born for us, the son
    who is given to us. To him we lift our voices in joy:
    Praise be to you, Lord.
Son of the living God, you existed before the world was
    made and you came on earth to save all,
—enable us to be witnesses to your Gospel.
Sun of Justice, whose brightness shone forth from the
    bosom of the Father and flooded the entire world,
—be light for all who dwell in darkness and the shadow
    of death.

You became a little child and lay in a manger,
—renew in us the simplicity of little children.
For our sake you became the living bread of eternal life,
—fill us with joy through the sacrament of your altar.

Our Father . . .

Prayer

God, light of all nations,
give us the joy of lasting peace,
and fill us with your radiance
as you filled the hearts of our fathers.

We ask this through our Lord Jesus Christ, your Son,
who lives and reigns with you and the Holy Spirit,
one God, for ever and ever.

Daytime Prayer

Midmorning

Ant.   This mystery, which has been hidden through all
ages and from all generations, is now revealed to
us.

READING   1 Timothy 1:15

You can depend on this as worthy of full acceptance:
that Christ Jesus came into the world to save sinners.

He was seen on the earth.
—He was a man among men.

Midday

Ant.   Christ Jesus has come, bringing the joyful news:
peace to those who were far off; peace to those
who are near.

READING   Revelation 21:23-24

The holy city of Jerusalem had no need of sun or moon, for the glory of God gave it light, and its lamp was the Lamb. The nations shall walk by its light; to it the kings of the earth shall bring their treasures.

All nations will see the glory of your holy One.
—All the kings of the earth will acknowledge your majesty.

Midafternoon

Ant. I have raised you up as a light for all the nations; through you my salvation will be proclaimed to the ends of the earth.

READING   1 John 1:5

Here is the message
we have heard from him
and announce to you:
that God is light;
in him there is no darkness.

All you peoples, praise our God.
—Sing to the glory of his name.

Prayer, as in Morning Prayer.

Evening Prayer

READING   Colossians 1:13-15

God rescued us from the power of darkness and brought us into the kingdom of his beloved Son. Through him we have redemption, the forgiveness of our sins. He is the image of the invisible God, the first-born of all creatures.

RESPONSORY

All peoples will be blessed in him, men and women of every race.
—All peoples will be blessed in him, men and women of every race.
All nations will acclaim his glory.
—Men and women of every race.
Glory to the Father . . .
—All peoples will . . .

CANTICLE OF MARY

Ant.   Herod questioned the Magi: What is this sign of which you speak, this sign of a newborn king? We saw a brilliant star in the heavens; its splendor filled the world.

INTERCESSIONS

Let us praise the Word of God, for he has come to cast our sins into the sea. Strengthened by this knowledge, let us pray to him:
Lord, show us your compassion.
As eternal high priest you entered the world and established the fullest expression of worship,
—through your Church let all men and women share in this sacred liturgy.
As physician of bodies and spirits you came to visit all who were sick,
—heal and strengthen those who are ill.
You were a source of joy for all at your birth,
—give hope to those in torment and to those in sin that they may be able to rejoice in you.
Mighty King, you cut the bonds of our former slavery,
—release those who are captives and show your care for those in prison.
You came as the door leading into heaven,

—let the dead pass through that door into the heavenly
 kingdom.

Our Father . . .

Prayer

God, light of all nations,
give us the joy of lasting peace,
and fill us with your radiance
as you filled the hearts of our fathers.

We ask this through our Lord Jesus Christ, your Son,
who lives and reigns with you and the Holy Spirit,
one God, for ever and ever.

after Epiphany to the Baptism of the Lord

THURSDAY

Office of Readings

The Son of God has come to give us understanding.
—That we might know the true God.

FIRST READING

From the book of the prophet Isaiah   63:19b—64:11

God's people plead for his coming

Oh, that you would rend the heavens and come down,
 with the mountains quaking before you,
As when brushwood is set ablaze,
 or fire makes the water boil!

Thus your name would be made known to your enemies
  and the nations would tremble before you,
While you wrought awesome deeds we could not hope
    for,
  such as they had not heard of from of old.

No ear has ever heard, no eye ever seen,
  any God but you
  doing such deeds for those who wait for him.

Would that you might meet us doing right,
  that we were mindful of you in our ways!
Behold, you are angry, and we are sinful:
  all of us have become like unclean men,
  all our good deeds are like polluted rags;
We have all withered like leaves,
  and our guilt carries us away like the wind.
There is none who calls upon your name,
  who rouses himself to cling to you;
For you have hidden your face from us
  and have delivered us up to our guilt.

Yet, O Lord, you are our father;
  we are the clay and you the potter:
  we are all the work of your hands.
Be not so very angry, Lord,
  keep not our guilt forever in mind;
  look upon us, who are all your people.
Your holy cities have become a desert,
  Zion is a desert, Jerusalem a waste.

Our holy and glorious temple
  in which our fathers praised you
Has been burned with fire;
  all that was dear to us is laid waste.
Can you hold back, O Lord, after all this?
  Can you remain silent, and afflict us so severely?

RESPONSORY   See Isaiah 56:1; Micah 4:9; Isaiah 43:3

Jerusalem, your salvation comes quickly:
why are you consumed by sorrow?
Has your pain returned since you have no counselors?
—I will save and deliver you, have no fear.

For I am the Lord your God, the Holy One of Israel,
   your Redeemer.
—I will save . . .

SECOND READING

From a commentary on the Gospel of John by Saint
Cyril of Alexandria, bishop

(Lib. 5, Cap. 2: PG 73, 751–754)

The gift of the Holy Spirit to all mankind

In a plan of surpassing beauty the Creator of the
universe decreed the renewal of all things in Christ. In
his design for restoring human nature to its original
condition, he gave a promise that he would pour out on it
the Holy Spirit along with his other gifts, for otherwise
our nature could not enter once more into the peaceful
and secure possession of those gifts.

He therefore appointed a time for the Holy Spirit to
come upon us : this was the time of Christ's coming. He
gave this promise when he said: *In those days,* that is, the
days of the Savior, *I will pour out a share of my Spirit on all
mankind.*

When the time came for this great act of unforced
generosity, which revealed in our midst the only-begotten Son, clothed with flesh on this earth, a man born of
woman, in accordance with Holy Scripture, God the
Father gave the Spirit once again. Christ, as the
firstfruits of our restored nature, was the first to receive
the Spirit. John the Baptist bore witness to this when he

said: *I saw the Spirit coming down from heaven, and it rested on him.*

Christ "received the Spirit" in so far as he was man, and in so far as man could receive the Spirit. He did so in such a way that, though he is the Son of God the Father, begotten of his substance, even before the incarnation, indeed before all ages, yet he was not offended at hearing the Father say to him after he had become man: *You are my Son; today I have begotten you.*

The Father says of Christ, who was God, begotten of him before the ages, that he has been "begotten today," for the Father is to accept us in Christ as his adopted children. The whole of our nature is present in Christ, in so far as he is man. So the Father can be said to give the Spirit again to the Son, though the Son possesses the Spirit as his own, in order that we may receive the Spirit in Christ. The Son therefore took to himself the seed of Abraham, as Scripture says, and became like his brothers in all things.

The only-begotten Son receives the Spirit, but not for his own advantage, for the Spirit is his, and is given in him and through him, as we have already said. He receives it to renew our nature in its entirety and to make it whole again, for in becoming man he took our entire nature to himself. If we reason correctly, and use also the testimony of Scripture, we can see that Christ did not receive the Spirit for himself, but rather for us in him; for it is also through Christ that all gifts come down to us.

RESPONSORY   Ezekiel 37:27-28; Hebrews 8:8

I will be their God and they shall be my people.
—The nations shall know that I am the Lord, the Sanctifier of Israel,
when my holiness will be established in their midst for all eternity.

I shall bring to fulfillment my new covenant
with the house of Israel and with the house of Judah.
—The nations shall . . .

Prayer, as in Morning Prayer.

Morning Prayer

READING   Isaiah 62:11-12

Say to daughter Zion,
  your savior comes!
Here is his reward with him,
  his recompense before him.
They shall be called the holy people,
  the redeemed of the Lord.

RESPONSORY

All peoples will be blessed in him, men and women of every race.
—All peoples will be blessed in him, men and women of every race.

All nations will acclaim his glory.
—Men and women of every race.

Glory to the Father . . .
—All peoples will . . .

CANTICLE OF ZECHARIAH

Ant.   All peoples, bearing gifts, will come from afar, alleluia.

INTERCESSIONS

Rejoice in the wonderful works of the Lord for he has given us hope through the birth of his Son. Let us all cry out with great joy:
  Glory to God in the highest.
With the angels and patriarchs and prophets,
—we praise you, Lord.

With Mary, the Virgin Mother of God,
—our whole being proclaims your greatness, Lord.
With the apostles and evangelists,
—we give you thanks, Lord.
With all the holy martyrs,
—we offer our bodies to you as consecrated victims.
With all your holy witnesses in the Church,
—we dedicate our lives to you in deepest faith.

Our Father . . .

Prayer

God our Father,
through Christ your Son
the hope of eternal life dawned on our world.
Give to us the light of faith
that we may always acknowledge him as our Redeemer
and come to the glory of his kingdom,
where he lives and reigns with you and the Holy Spirit,
one God, for ever and ever.

Daytime Prayer

Midmorning

Ant.   This mystery, which has been hidden through all
ages and from all generations, is now revealed to
us.

READING   Isaiah 2:3-4

From Zion shall go forth instruction,
    and the word of the Lord from Jerusalem.
He shall judge between the nations,
    and impose terms on many peoples.
They shall beat their swords into ploughshares
    and their spears into pruning hooks.

One nation shall not raise the sword against another,
nor shall they train for war again.

He was seen on the earth.
—He was a man among men.

Midday

Ant. Christ Jesus has come, bringing the joyful news:
peace to those who were far off; peace to those
who are near.

READING Isaiah 9:1

The people who walked in darkness
have seen a great light;
Upon those who dwelt in the land of gloom
a light has shone.

All nations will see the glory of your holy One.
—All the kings of the earth will acknowledge your
majesty.

Midafternoon

Ant. I have raised you up as a light for all the nations;
through you my salvation will be proclaimed to
the ends of the earth.

READING Isaiah 60:4-5

Your sons, O Jerusalem, come from afar,
and your daughters in the arms of their nurses.
Then you shall be radiant at what you see,
your heart shall throb and overflow,
For the riches of the sea shall be emptied out before you,
the wealth of nations shall be brought to you.

All you peoples, praise our God.
—Sing to the glory of his name.

Prayer, as in Morning Prayer.

Evening Prayer

READING   1 John 1:5b, 7

God is light;
in him there is no darkness.
If we walk in light,
as he is in the light,
we have fellowship with one another,
and the blood of his Son Jesus cleanses us from all sin.

RESPONSORY

All peoples will be blessed in him, men and women of every race.
—All peoples will be blessed in him, men and women of every race.

All nations will acclaim his glory.
—Men and women of every race.

Glory to the Father . . .
—All peoples will . . .

CANTICLE OF MARY

Ant. The people of Saba shall come bringing gold, frankincense and myrrh, alleluia.

INTERCESSIONS

United in prayer with all of our brothers and sisters, we bless God and invoke his name:
    Lord, show us your compassion.
Holy Father, we pray for those who know you only by the light of human reason,
—may they be enriched by the light of the Gospel as well.
Look with favor on all who live outside the Church as they seek liberation from the harsh constraints of human existence,
—may they discover Christ as the way, the truth and the life.

Help all who practice their faith in sincerity,
—may they attain to the marvelous light of your anointed
     one.
Keep pure the hearts of believers,
—may they see you more clearly at every moment.
Let your compassion be visible to those who have died,
—clothe them in the glory of your chosen people.

Our Father . . .

Prayer

God our Father,
through Christ your Son
the hope of eternal life dawned on our world.
Give to us the light of faith
that we may always acknowledge him as our Redeemer
and come to the glory of his kingdom,
where he lives and reigns with you and the Holy Spirit,
one God, for ever and ever.

after Epiphany to the Baptism of the Lord

FRIDAY

Office of Readings

In Christ was life.
—And that life was the light of mankind.

FIRST READING

From the book of the prophet Isaiah   65:13-25

A new heaven and a new earth

     Thus says the Lord God:
Lo, my servants shall eat,
     but you shall go hungry;

My servants shall drink,
   but you shall be thirsty;
My servants shall rejoice,
   but you shall be put to shame;
My servants shall shout
   for joy of heart,
But you shall cry out for grief of heart
   and howl for anguish of spirit.

The Lord God shall slay you,
   and the name you leave
Shall be used by my chosen ones for cursing;
   but my servants shall be called by another name
By which he will be blessed
   on whom a blessing is invoked in the land;
He who takes an oath in the land
   shall swear by the God of truth;
For the hardships of the past shall be forgotten,
   and hidden from my eyes.

Lo, I am about to create new heavens
   and a new earth;
The things of the past shall not be remembered
   or come to mind.
Instead, there shall always be rejoicing and happiness
   in what I create;
For I create Jerusalem to be a joy
   and its people to be a delight;
I will rejoice in Jerusalem
   and exult in my people.
No longer shall the sound of weeping be heard there,
   or the sound of crying;
No longer shall there be in it
   an infant who lives but a few days,
   or an old man who does not round out his full lifetime;

He dies a mere youth who reaches but a hundred years,
  and he who fails of a hundred shall be thought
    accursed.

They shall live in the houses they build,
  and eat the fruit of the vineyards they plant;
They shall not build houses for others to live in,
  or plant for others to eat.
As the years of a tree, so the years of my people;
  and my chosen ones shall long enjoy
    the produce of their hands.

They shall not toil in vain,
  nor beget children for sudden destruction;
For a race blessed by the Lord
  are they and their offspring.
Before they call, I will answer;
  while they are yet speaking, I will hearken to them.

The wolf and the lamb shall graze alike,
  and the lion shall eat hay like the ox
    [but the serpent's food shall be dust].
None shall hurt or destroy
  on all my holy mountain, says the Lord.

RESPONSORY   Revelation 21:1, 3, 4

I saw the new heaven and the new earth;
and I heard a loud voice from heaven, saying:
— This is God's dwelling place among men.
He shall live with them.

The Lord will wipe away every tear from their eyes;
death will no longer hold sway over them,
for all that used to be has passed away.
—This is God's . . .

SECOND READING

From a sermon by Saint Maximus of Turin, bishop

(Sermo 100, de sancta Epiphania 1, 3: CCL 23, 398–400)

The mystery of the Lord's baptism

The Gospel tells us that the Lord went to the Jordan River to be baptized and that he wished to consecrate himself in the river by signs from heaven.

Reason demands that this feast of the Lord's baptism, which I think could be called the feast of his birthday, should follow soon after the Lord's birthday, during the same season, even though many years intervened between the two events.

At Christmas he was born a man; today he is reborn sacramentally. Then he was born from the Virgin; today he is born in mystery. When he was born a man, his mother Mary held him close to her heart; when he is born in mystery, God the Father embraces him with his voice when he says: *This is my beloved Son in whom I am well pleased: listen to him.* The mother caresses the tender baby on her lap; the Father serves his Son by his loving testimony. The mother holds the child for the Magi to adore; the Father reveals that his Son is to be worshiped by all the nations.

That is why the Lord Jesus went to the river for baptism, that is why he wanted his holy body to be washed with Jordan's water.

Someone might ask, "Why would a holy man desire baptism?" Listen to the answer: Christ is baptized, not to be made holy by the water, but to make the water holy, and by his cleansing to purify the waters which he touched. For the consecration of Christ involves a more significant consecration of the water.

For when the Savior is washed all water for our baptism is made clean, purified at its source for the dispensing of baptismal grace to the people of future ages. Christ is the first to be baptized, then, so that Christians will follow after him with confidence.

I understand the mystery as this. The column of fire went before the sons of Israel through the Red Sea so they could follow on their brave journey; the column went first through the waters to prepare a path for those who followed. As the apostle Paul said, what was accomplished then was the mystery of baptism. Clearly it was baptism in a certain sense when the cloud was covering the people and bringing them through the water.

But Christ the Lord does all these things: in the column of fire he went through the sea before the sons of Israel; so now, in the column of his body, he goes through baptism before the Christian people. At the time of the Exodus the column provided light for the people who followed; now it gives light to the hearts of believers. Then it made a firm pathway through the waters; now it strengthens the footsteps of faith in the bath of baptism.

RESPONSORY   John 1:29; Isaiah 53:11

John saw Jesus coming to him and said:
Behold the Lamb of God;
—behold him who takes away the sins of the world.

He will justify many and he himself will bear our sins.
—Behold him who . . .

Prayer, as in Morning Prayer.

Morning Prayer

READING   Isaiah 45:22-23

Turn to me and be safe,
   all you ends of the earth,
    for I am God; there is no other!
By myself I swear,
   uttering my just decree
   and my unalterable word:
To me every knee shall bend;
   by me every tongue shall swear.

RESPONSORY

All peoples will be blessed in him, men and women of every race.
—All peoples will be blessed in him, men and women of
   every race.

All nations will acclaim his glory.
—Men and women of every race.

Glory to the Father . . .
—All peoples will . . .

CANTICLE OF ZECHARIAH

Ant. All who once reviled you will come and bow down
     in worship before your very footprints.

INTERCESSIONS

Give honor and glory to Jesus Christ who comes to create
   a new heart and a new spirit in man. We call on him as
   we say:
   By the power of your birth, make us new persons.
You took on our life and offered us in return the mystery
   of God's life,
—help us to recognize you in the mysteries of your word
   and your eucharist which you entrusted to your
   Church.

Founder of the human race, through the spotless Virgin
  you became a man among men,
—through her intercession, may we touch your divinity
  and be healed.
Our Redeemer, you descended upon the earth as the rain
  which fell upon the sheepskin of Gideon,
—now drench our lives in the living water that springs up
  to provide eternal life.
As we celebrate the beginning of your life on this earth,
—let us imitate that perfect manhood which you revealed
  in your life among us.

Our Father . . .

Prayer

All-powerful Father,
you have made known the birth of the Savior
by the light of a star.
May he continue to guide us with his light,
for he lives and reigns with you and the Holy Spirit,
one God, for ever and ever.

Daytime Prayer

Midmorning

Ant.   This mystery, which has been hidden through all
       ages and for all generations, is now revealed to us.

READING   Jeremiah 31:7-8

Shout with joy for Jacob,
  exult at the head of the nations;
  proclaim your praise and say:
The Lord has delivered his people,
  the remnant of Israel.
Behold, I will bring them back
  from the land of the north;
I will gather them from the ends of the world.

He was seen on the earth.
—He was a man among men.

Midday

Ant.   Christ Jesus has come, bringing the joyful news: peace to those who were far off; peace to those who are near.

READING   Jeremiah 31:11-12

The Lord shall ransom Jacob,
  he shall redeem him from the hand of his conqueror.
Shouting, they shall mount the heights of Zion,
  they shall come streaming to the Lord's blessings.

All nations will see the glory of your holy One.
—All the kings of the earth will acknowledge your majesty.

Midafternoon

Ant.   I have raised you up as a light for all the nations; through you my salvation will be proclaimed to the ends of the earth.

READING   Zechariah 8:7-8

Lo, I will rescue my people from the land of the rising sun, and from the land of the setting sun. I will bring them back to dwell within Jerusalem. They shall be my people, and I will be their God, with faithfulness and justice.

All you peoples, praise our God.
—Sing to the glory of his name.

Prayer, as in Morning Prayer.

Evening Prayer

READING   Romans 8:3-4

God sent his Son in the likeness of sinful flesh as a
sin-offering, thereby condemning sin in the flesh, so that
the just demands of the law might be fulfilled in us who
live, not according to the flesh, but according to the
spirit.

RESPONSORY

All peoples will be blessed in him, men and women of ev-
    ery race.
—All peoples will be blessed in him, men and women of
    every race.

All nations will acclaim his glory.
—Men and women of every race.

Glory to the Father . . .
—All peoples will . . .

CANTICLE OF MARY

Ant.   An angel warned the wise men in a dream to
        return to their own country by a different route.

INTERCESSIONS

We pray now to the Father who has appointed Christ a
    light to the nations:
        Father, hear our prayer.
Give increase to your Church,
—and spread the glory of your Son.
Eternal Father, you led the wise men from the East to
    your Son,
—reveal him to all who seek the truth.
Draw all nations into your marvelous light,
—so that at the name of Jesus every knee will bend.

Send laborers into your vineyard,
—let them preach the Gospel to the poor and announce a
   time of grace.
Grant to the dead the fullness of redemption,
—that they may rejoice in the victory of Christ, your
   Son.

Our Father . . .

Prayer

All-powerful Father,
you have made known the birth of the Savior
by the light of a star.
May he continue to guide us with his light,
for he lives and reigns with you and the Holy Spirit,
one God, for ever and ever.

after Epiphany to the Baptism of the Lord

SATURDAY

Office of Readings

Christ is the true light.
—He gives light to all people.

FIRST READING

From the book of the prophet Isaiah   66:10-14, 18-23

Salvation for all people

Rejoice with Jerusalem and be glad because of her,
   all you who love her;
Exult, exult with her,
   all you who were mourning over her!
Oh, that you may suck fully
   of the milk of her comfort,

That you may nurse with delight
   at her abundant breasts!

     For thus says the Lord:
Lo, I will spread prosperity over her like a river,
   and the wealth of the nations like an overflowing
     torrent.
As nurslings, you shall be carried in her arms,
   and fondled in her lap;
As a mother comforts her son,
   so will I comfort you;
   in Jerusalem you shall find your comfort.
When you see this, your heart shall rejoice,
   and your bodies flourish like the grass;
The Lord's power shall be known to his servants,
   but to his enemies, his wrath.

   I come to gather nations of every language; they shall
come and see my glory. I will set a sign among them;
from them I will send fugitives to the nations; to
Tarshish, Put and Lud, Mosoch, Tubal and Javan, to the
distant coastlands that have never heard of my fame, or
seen my glory; and they shall proclaim my glory among
the nations. They shall bring all your brethren from all
the nations as an offering to the Lord, on horses and in
chariots, in carts, upon mules and dromedaries, to
Jerusalem, my holy mountain, says the Lord, just as the
Israelites bring their offering to the house of the Lord in
clean vessels. Some of these I will take as priests and
Levites, says the Lord.

As the new heavens and the new earth
   which I will make
Shall endure before me, says the Lord,
   so shall your race and your name endure.

From one new moon to another,
   and from one sabbath to another,
All mankind shall come to worship
   before me, says the Lord.

Behold I come to bring together all nations and tongues.
—They shall come and see my glory and proclaim it to
   the far-off lands.

I have revealed your name to those you have given to me
   out of the world.
As you have sent me, so now I send them.
—They shall come . . .

SECOND READING

From a sermon by Faustus of Riez, bishop
(Sermo 5, de Epiphania 2: PLS 3, 560—562)

The marriage of Christ and the Church

On the third day there was a wedding. What wedding
can this be but the joyful marriage of man's salvation, a
marriage celebrated by confessing the Trinity or by faith
in the resurrection. That is why the marriage took place
"on the third day," a reference to the sacred mysteries
which this number symbolizes.

Hence, too, we read elsewhere in the Gospel that the
return of the younger son, that is, the conversion of the
pagans, is marked by song, and music and wedding
garments.

Like a bridegroom coming from his marriage chamber our
God descended to earth in his incarnation, in order to be
united to his Church which was to be formed of the

pagan nations. To her he gave a pledge and a dowry: a pledge when God was united to man; a dowry when he was sacrificed for man's salvation. The pledge is our present redemption; the dowry, eternal life.

To those who see only with the outward eye, all these events at Cana are strange and wonderful; to those who understand, they are also signs. For, if we look closely, the very water tells us of our rebirth in baptism. One thing is turned into another from within, and in a hidden way a lesser creature is changed into a greater. All this points to the hidden reality of our second birth. There water was suddenly changed; later it will cause a change in man.

By Christ's action in Galilee, then, wine is made, that is, the law withdraws and grace takes its place; the shadows fade and truth becomes present; fleshly realities are coupled with spiritual, and the old covenant with its outward discipline is transformed into the new. For, as the Apostle says: *The old order has passed away; now all is new!* The water in the jars is not less than it was before, but now begins to be what it had not been; so too the law is not destroyed by Christ's coming, but is made better than it was.

When the wine fails, new wine is served: the wine of the old covenant was good, but the wine of the new is better. The old covenant, which Jews follow, is exhausted by its letter; the new covenant, which belongs to us, has the savor of life and is filled with grace.

The *good wine*, that is, good precepts, refers to the law; thus we read: *You shall love your neighbor but hate your enemy.* But the Gospel is a better and a stronger wine: *My command to you is: love your enemies, pray for your persecutors.*

RESPONSORY   Tobit 13:11, 13-14; Luke 13:29

City of God, you will shine with wondrous light;
all the ends of the earth will see your light and adore the
    Lord.
The nations will come to you from afar.
—They will come bearing gifts to worship the Lord.

They shall come from the east and the west, from the
    north and the south.
—They will come . . .

Prayer as in Morning Prayer.

Morning Prayer

READING   Wisdom 7:26-27

Wisdom is the refulgence of eternal light,
    the spotless mirror of the power of God,
    the image of his goodness.
And she, who is one, can do all things,
    and renews everything while herself perduring;
And passing into holy souls from age to age,
    she produces friends of God and prophets.

RESPONSORY

All the kings of the earth will bow down in worship.
—All the kings of the earth will bow down in worship.

Men and women of every nation will serve him.
—They will bow down in worship.

Glory to the Father . . .
—All the kings . . .

CANTICLE OF ZECHARIAH

Ant.   At Cana in Galilee Jesus worked the first of the
       signs which revealed his glory.

INTERCESSIONS

Let us give glory to Christ, the image of God, as we call
upon him in faith:
Christ, Son of God, hear us.

Son of God, you showed us the Father's love,
—reveal him to men and women through the love we
show toward one another.

You revealed yourself as Lord of life,
—now grant us the fullness of your life.

Let our bodies be signs of your life,
—as we bear your dying in our flesh.

Illuminate our hearts,
—with the brilliant knowledge of God's light.

Our Father . . .

Prayer

God our Father,
through your Son you made us a new creation.
He shared our nature and became one of us;
with his help, may we become more like him,
who lives and reigns with you and the Holy Spirit,
one God, for ever and ever.

Daytime Prayer

Midmorning

Ant.   This mystery, which has been hidden through all
ages and from all generations, is now revealed to
us.

READING   Ezekiel 10:41-42a

As a pleasing odor I will accept you, when I have
brought you from among the nations and gathered you
out of the countries over which you were scattered; and

by means of you I will manifest my holiness in the sight of the nations. Thus you shall know that I am the Lord.

He was seen on the earth.
—He was a man among men.

Midday

Ant.   Christ Jesus has come, bringing the joyful news: peace to those who were far off; peace to those who are near.

READING   Ezekiel 34:11-12

I myself will look after and tend my sheep. As a shepherd tends his flock when he finds himself among his scattered sheep, so will I tend my sheep. I will rescue them from every place where they were scattered when it was cloudy and dark.

All nations will see the glory of your holy One.
—All the kings of the earth will acknowledge your majesty.

Midafternoon

Ant.   I have raised you up as a light for all the nations; through you my salvation will be proclaimed to the ends of the earth.

READING   Micah 2:12

I will gather you, O Jacob, each and every one,
    I will assemble all the remnant of Israel;
I will group them like a flock in the fold,
    like a herd in the midst of its corral.

All you peoples, praise our God.
—Sing to the glory of his name.

Prayer, as in Morning Prayer.

BAPTISM OF THE LORD

Feast

Evening Prayer I

Sing praise to our Creator,
O sons of Adam's race;
God's children by adoption,
Baptized into his grace.

Refrain:

Praise the holy Trinity,
Undivided Unity;
Holy God, Mighty God,
God Immortal, be adored.

To Jesus Christ give glory,
God's coeternal Son;
As members of his Body
We live in him as one.

Refrain

Now praise the Holy Spirit
Poured forth upon the earth
Who sanctifies and guides us,
Confirmed in our rebirth.

Refrain

Melody: Mainz 76.76 with Refrain   Music: Mainz Melody
                                    Text: Omer Westendorf, 1961

Ant. 1 John was in the wilderness baptizing and
proclaiming a baptism of penance for the
forgiveness of sins.

Psalms and canticle as in Evening Prayer I of Epiphany, **547**.

Ant. 2   I baptize you with water, but the one who is coming will baptize with the Holy Spirit and with fire.

Ant. 3   As soon as Jesus was baptized, he came out of the water, and the heavens opened before him.

READING   Acts 10:37-38

I take it you know what has been reported all over Judea about Jesus of Nazareth, beginning in Galilee with the baptism John preached; of the way God anointed him with the Holy Spirit and power. He went about doing good works and healing all who were in the grip of the devil, and God was with him.

RESPONSORY

O Lord our God, hear the cry of your people.
—O Lord our God, hear the cry of your people.

Open for them the spring of living water.
—Hear the cry of your people.

Glory to the Father . . .
—O Lord our . . .

CANTICLE OF MARY

Ant.   Our Savior came to be baptized, so that through the cleansing waters of baptism he might restore the old man to new life, heal our sinful nature, and clothe us with unfailing holiness.

INTERCESSIONS

Our Redeemer desired to be baptized in the Jordan by John; let us make our petition to him:
    Lord, send forth your Spirit upon us.

Christ, Servant of God, the Father acknowledged you as
   his own Son with whom he was pleased,
—send forth your Spirit upon us.

Christ, Chosen One of God, you did not break the
   crushed reed or extinguish the wavering flame,
—have mercy on all who are seeking you in good faith.

Christ, Son of God, the Father called you to be a light to
   the nations in the new covenant,
—open the eyes of the blind by the waters of baptism.

Christ, Savior of mankind, the Father anointed you with
   the Holy Spirit for the ministry of salvation,
—lead all mankind to see you and to believe in you, that
   they may have eternal life.

Christ, our hope, you lead those in darkness to the light
   of salvation,
—receive our departed brothers and sisters into your
   kingdom.

Our Father . . .

Prayer

Almighty, eternal God,
when the Spirit descended upon Jesus
at his baptism in the Jordan,
you revealed him as your own beloved Son.
Keep us, your children born of water and the Spirit,
faithful to our calling.

We ask this through our Lord Jesus Christ, your Son,
who lives and reigns with you and the Holy Spirit,
one God, for ever and ever.

Alternative Prayer

Father in heaven,
you revealed Christ as your Son
by the voice that spoke over the waters of the Jordan.

May all who share in the sonship of Christ
follow in his path of service to man,
and reflect the glory of his kingdom
even to the ends of the earth,
for he is Lord for ever and ever.

Invitatory

Ant.   Come, let us worship Christ, the beloved Son in
whom the Father was well pleased.

Invitatory Psalm, as in the Ordinary, 648.

Office of Readings

Hymn

When Jesus comes to be baptized,
He leaves the hidden years behind,
The years of safety and of peace,
To bear the sins of all mankind.

The Spirit of the Lord comes down,
Anoints the Christ to suffering,
To preach the word, to free the bound,
And to the mourner, comfort bring.

He will not quench the dying flame,
And what is bruised he will not break,
But heal the wound injustice dealt,
And out of death his triumph make.

Our everlasting Father, praise,
With Christ, his well-beloved Son,
Who with the Spirit reigns serene,
Untroubled Trinity in One.

Melody: Saint Venantius   Music: (Saint Venantius)
or Winchester New L.M.   Rouen Church Melody
or (Winchester New) *Musicalisches
Handbuch,* Hamburg, 1690
Text: Stanbrook Abbey, 1971

PSALMODY

Ant. 1   The voice of the Lord, the God of majesty,
echoes over the waters.

Psalm 29

O give the Lord, you sons of God,
give the Lord glory and power;
give the Lord the glory of his name.
Adore the Lord in his holy court.

The Lord's voice resounding on the waters,
the Lord on the immensity of waters;
the voice of the Lord, full of power,
the voice of the Lord, full of splendor.

The Lord's voice shattering the cedars,
the Lord shatters the cedars of Lebanon;
he makes Lebanon leap like a calf
and Sirion like a young wild-ox.

The Lord's voice flashes flames of fire.

The Lord's voice shaking the wilderness,
the Lord shakes the wilderness of Kadesh;
the Lord's voice rending the oak tree
and stripping the forest bare.

The God of glory thunders.
In his temple they all cry: "Glory!"
The Lord sat enthroned over the flood;
the Lord sits as king for ever.

The Lord will give strength to his people,
the Lord will bless his people with peace.

Ant.   The voice of the Lord, the God of majesty, echoes
over the waters.

Ant. 2   Let all the earth adore you, Lord, and let it be
joyful; for a new light has dawned upon the
ages.

Psalm 66

I

Cry out with joy to God all the earth,
O sing to the glory of his name.
O render him glorious praise.
Say to God: "How tremendous your deeds!

Because of the greatness of your strength
your enemies cringe before you.
Before you all the earth shall bow;
shall sing to you, sing to your name!"

Come and see the works of God,
tremendous his deeds among men.
He turned the sea into dry land,
they passed through the river dry-shod.

Let our joy then be in him;
he rules for ever by his might.
His eyes keep watch over the nations:
let rebels not rise against him.

O peoples, bless our God,
let the voice of his praise resound,
of the God who gave life to our souls
and kept our feet from stumbling.

For you, O God, have tested us,
you have tried us as silver is tried:
you led us, God, into the snare;
you laid a heavy burden on our backs.

You let men ride over our heads;
we went through fire and through water
but then you brought us relief.

Ant. Let all the earth adore you, Lord, and let it be
joyful; for a new light has dawned upon the ages.

Ant. 3   Blessed be God, for he has willed that my soul
         should live; he has led me to a place of refuge.

II

Burnt offering I bring to your house;
to you I will pay my vows,
the vows which my lips have uttered,
which my mouth spoke in my distress.

I will offer burnt offerings of fatlings
with the smoke of burning rams.
I will offer bullocks and goats.

Come and hear, all who fear God.
I will tell what he did for my soul:
to him I cried aloud,
with high praise ready on my tongue.

If there had been evil in my heart,
the Lord would not have listened.
But truly God has listened;
he has heeded the voice of my prayer.

Blessed be God who did not reject my prayer
nor withhold his love from me.

Ant.   Blessed be God, for he has willed that my soul
        should live; he has led me to a place of refuge.

This is my beloved Son.
—Listen to him.

FIRST READING

From the book of the prophet Isaiah   42:1-9; 49:1-9

The gentle servant of the Lord is a light to the nations

Here is my servant whom I uphold,
    my chosen one with whom I am pleased,

Upon whom I have put my spirit;
    he shall bring forth justice to the nations,
Not crying out, not shouting,
    not making his voice heard in the street.
A bruised reed he shall not break,
    and a smoldering wick he shall not quench,
Until he establishes justice on the earth;
    the coastlands will wait for his teaching.

Thus says God, the Lord,
    who created the heavens and stretched them out,
    who spreads out the earth with its crops,
Who gives breath to its people
    and spirit to those who walk on it:

I, the Lord, have called you for the victory of justice,
    I have grasped you by the hand;
I formed you, and set you
    as a covenant of the people,
    a light for the nations,
To open the eyes of the blind,
    to bring out prisoners from confinement,
    and from the dungeon, those who live in darkness.

I am the Lord, this is my name;
    my glory I give to no other,
    nor my praise to idols.
See, the earlier things have come to pass,
    new ones I now foretell;
Before they spring into being,
    I announce them to you.

Hear me, O coastlands,
    listen, O distant peoples.
The Lord called me from birth,
    from my mother's womb he gave me my name.

He made of me a sharp-edged sword
    and concealed me in the shadow of his arm.
He made me a polished arrow,
    in his quiver he hid me.

You are my servant, he said to me,
    Israel, through whom I show my glory.
Though I thought I had toiled in vain,
    and for nothing, uselessly, spent my strength,
Yet my reward is with the Lord,
    my recompense is with my God.

For now the Lord has spoken
    who formed me as his servant from the womb,
That Jacob may be brought back to him
    and Israel gathered to him
And I am made glorious in the sight of the Lord,
    and my God is now my strength!

It is too little, he says, for you to be my servant,
    to raise up the tribes of Jacob,
    and restore the survivors of Israel;
I will make you a light to the nations,
    that my salvation may reach to the ends of the earth.

Thus says the Lord,
    the redeemer and the Holy One of Israel,
To the one despised, whom the nations abhor,
    the slave of rulers;
When kings see you, they shall stand up,
    and princes shall prostrate themselves
Because of the Lord who is faithful,
    the Holy One of Israel who has chosen you.

    Thus says the Lord:
In a time of favor I answer you,
    on the day of salvation I help you,

To restore the land
and allot the desolate heritages,
Saying to the prisoners: Come out!
To those in darkness: Show yourselves!
Along the ways they shall find pasture,
on every bare height shall their pastures be.

RESPONSORY   Matthew 3:16, 17; Luke 3:22

Today in the Jordan as the Lord was baptized,
the heavens opened and the Spirit in the form of a dove
rested upon him;
the voice of the Father was heard:
—This is my beloved Son in whom I am well pleased.

The Spirit descended in visible form as a dove,
and a voice from heaven was heard:
—This is my . . .

SECOND READING

From a Sermon by Saint Gregory of Nazianzus, bishop
(Oratio 39 in Sancta Lumina, 14-16, 20: PG 36, 350–351, 354, 358–359)

The baptism of Christ

Christ is bathed in light; let us also be bathed in light.
Christ is baptized; let us also go down with him, and rise
with him.

John is baptizing when Jesus draws near. Perhaps he
comes to sanctify his baptizer; certainly he comes to bury
sinful humanity in the waters. He comes to sanctify the
Jordan for our sake and in readiness for us; he who is
spirit and flesh comes to begin a new creation through
the Spirit and water.

The Baptist protests; Jesus insists. Then John says: *I ought to be baptized by you.* He is the lamp in the presence of the sun, the voice in the presence of the Word, the friend in the presence of the Bridegroom, the greatest of all born of woman in the presence of the firstborn of all creation, the one who leapt in his mother's womb in the presence of him who was adored in the womb, the forerunner and future forerunner in the presence of him who has already come and is to come again. *I ought to be baptized by you;* we should also add: *and for you,* for John is to be baptized in blood, washed clean like Peter, not only by the washing of his feet.

Jesus rises from the waters; the world rises with him. The heavens like Paradise with its flaming sword, closed by Adam for himself and his descendants, are rent open. The Spirit comes to him as to an equal, bearing witness to his Godhead. A voice bears witness to him from heaven, his place of origin. The Spirit descends in bodily form like the dove that so long ago announced the ending of the flood and so gives honor to the body that is one with God.

Today let us do honor to Christ's baptism and celebrate this feast in holiness. Be cleansed entirely and continue to be cleansed. Nothing gives such pleasure to God as the conversion and salvation of men, for whom his every word and every revelation exist. He wants you to become a living force for all mankind, lights shining in the world. You are to be radiant lights as you stand beside Christ, the great light, bathed in the glory of him who is the light of heaven. You are to enjoy more and more the pure and dazzling light of the Trinity, as now you have received—though not in its fullness—a ray of its splendor, proceeding from the one God, in Christ Jesus our Lord, to whom be glory and power for ever and ever. Amen.

RESPONSORY   Psalm 114:5

Today the heavens opened and the waters of the sea
    became sweet and fragrant;
the earth rejoiced, the mountains and hills exulted,
—because Christ was baptized by John in the Jordan.

What has happened that the sea has been put to flight,
and the Jordan has turned back upon itself?
—Because Christ was baptized . . .

HYMN, Te Deum, 651.

Prayer, as in Morning Prayer.

Morning Prayer

HYMN

> Songs of thankfulness and praise,
> Jesus, Lord, to thee we raise,
> Manifested by the star
> To the wise men from afar;
> Branch of royal David's stem
> In thy birth at Bethlehem;
> Praises be to thee addressed,
> God in man made manifest.
>
> Manifest at Jordan's stream,
> Prophet, Priest, and King supreme;
> And at Cana wedding guest,
> In thy Godhead manifest;
> Manifest in power divine,
> Changing water into wine;
> Praises be to thee addressed,
> God in man made manifest.
>
> Grant us grace to see thee, Lord,
> Mirrored in thy holy Word;
> May we imitate thee now,

And be pure, as pure art thou;
That we like to thee may be
At thy great Epiphany;
And may praise thee, ever blessed,
God in man made manifest.

Melody: Salzburg 77.77.D   Music: J. Hintze, 1678
                    Text: Christopher Wordsworth, 1862

Ant. 1   The soldier baptizes his king, the servant his
         Lord, John his Savior; the waters of the Jordan
         tremble, a dove hovers as a sign of witness, and
         the voice of the Father is heard: This is my Son.

Psalms and canticle from Sunday, Week I, 688.

Ant. 2   Springs of water were made holy as Christ
         revealed his glory to the world. Draw water
         from the fountain of the Savior, for Christ our
         God has hallowed all creation.

Ant. 3   You burned away man's guilt by fire and the
         Holy Spirit. We give praise to you, our God and
         Redeemer.

READING   Isaiah 61:1-2a

The spirit of the Lord God is upon me,
   because the Lord has anointed me;
He has sent me to bring glad tidings to the lowly,
   to heal the broken hearted,
To proclaim liberty to the captives
   and release to the prisoners,
To announce a year of favor from the Lord.

RESPONSORY

Christ, Son of the living God, have mercy on us.
—Christ, Son of the living God, have mercy on us.

Today you revealed yourself to us.
—Have mercy on us.

Glory to the Father . . .
—Christ, Son of . . .

CANTICLE OF ZECHARIAH

Ant.   Christ is baptized, the world is made holy; he has
         taken away our sins. We shall be purified by water
         and the Holy Spirit.

INTERCESSIONS

Our Redeemer desired to be baptized in the Jordan by
    John; let us make this prayer to him:
    Lord, have mercy.
Christ, you made your light shine on us by revealing
    yourself,
—grant us the spirit of humble service to all people.
Christ, you humbled yourself and received baptism from
    your servant to show us the way of humility,
—grant us the spirit of humble service to our fellow men.
Christ, through your baptism you cleansed us of every
    blemish and made us children of your Father,
—bestow your spirit of adoption on all who seek you.
Christ, through baptism you have consecrated creation
    and opened the door of repentance to all who prepare
    for baptism,
—make us servants of your Gospel in the world.
Christ, through your baptism you revealed to us the Holy
    Trinity when the Father called you his beloved Son
    and the Holy Spirit came down upon you,
—renew the spirit of adoption among the royal
    priesthood of the baptized.

Our Father . . .

Prayer

Almighty, eternal God,
when the Spirit descended upon Jesus
at his baptism in the Jordan,
you revealed him as your own beloved Son.
Keep us, your children born of water and the Spirit,
faithful to our calling.

We ask this through our Lord Jesus Christ, your Son,
who lives and reigns with you and the Holy Spirit,
one God, for ever and ever.

Alternative Prayer

Father in heaven,
you revealed Christ as your Son
by the voice that spoke over the waters of the Jordan.
May all who share in the sonship of Christ
follow in his path of service to man,
and reflect the glory of his kingdom
even to the ends of the earth,
for he is Lord for ever and ever.

Daytime Prayer

Psalms from Sunday, Week III, **934**, unless this feast occurs on
January 7 in which case the psalms are taken from Sunday,
Week II, **808**.

Midmorning

Ant.   John tried to prevent Jesus and said: I should be
        baptized by you, and do you come to me?

READING   Isaiah 11:1-3

A shoot shall sprout from the stump of Jesse,
    and from his roots a bud shall blossom.

The spirit of the Lord shall rest upon him:
   a spirit of wisdom and of understanding,
A spirit of counsel and of strength,
   a spirit of knowledge and of fear of the Lord,
   and his delight shall be the fear of the Lord.

He must grow greater.
—I must grow less.

Midday

Ant.   Jesus answered John: For the moment, this is
       what must be; we do well to fulfill all that God
       commands.

READING   Isaiah 42:1

Here is my servant whom I uphold,
   my chosen one with whom I am pleased,
Upon whom I have put my spirit;
   he shall bring forth justice to the nations.

This is my servant whom I love.
—My chosen one in whom I delight.

Midafternoon

Ant.   This was John's witness: I saw the Spirit coming
       down from heaven like a dove and resting upon
       him.

READING   Isaiah 49:6

   The Lord said to me:
It is too little for you to be my servant,
   to raise up the tribes of Jacob,
   and restore the survivors of Israel;
I will make you a light to the nations,
   that my salvation may reach to the ends of the earth.

Upon him my spirit will rest.
—And he will show all nations the holiness of God.

Prayer, as in Morning Prayer.

Evening Prayer II

HYMN

> Sing praise to our Creator,
> O sons of Adam's race;
> God's children by adoption,
> Baptized into his grace.

> Refrain:
> Praise the holy Trinity,
> Undivided Unity;
> Holy God, Mighty God,
> God Immortal, be adored.

> To Jesus Christ give glory,
> God's coeternal Son;
> As members of his Body
> We live in him as one.

> Refrain

> Now praise the Holy Spirit
> Poured forth upon the earth;
> Who sanctifies and guides us,
> Confirmed in our rebirth.

> Refrain

Melody: Mainz 76.76 with Refrain   Music: Mainz Melody
                                    Text: Omer Westendorf, 1961

PSALMODY

Ant. 1   The Father's voice resounded from the heav-
          ens: This is my Son in whom I delight, listen to
          what he says to you.

Psalms and canticle from Evening Prayer II of the Epiphany, 571.

Ant. 2   In the Jordan river our Savior crushed the serpent's head and wrested us free from his grasp.

Ant. 3   A wondrous mystery is declared to us today: the Creator of the universe has washed away our sins in the waters of the Jordan.

READING   Acts 10:37-38

I take it you know what has been reported all over Judea about Jesus of Nazareth, beginning in Galilee with the baptism John preached; of the way God anointed him with the Holy Spirit and power. He went about doing good works and healing all who were in the grip of the devil, and God was with him.

RESPONSORY

Christ comes to us. He comes in water and in blood.
—Christ comes to us. He comes in water and in blood.

Jesus Christ our Lord.
—Comes in water and in blood.

Glory to the Father . . .
—Christ comes to . . .

CANTICLE OF MARY

Ant.   Christ Jesus loved us, poured out his blood to wash away our sins, and made us a kingdom and priests for God our Father. To him be glory and honor for ever.

INTERCESSIONS

Our Redeemer desired to be baptized in the Jordan by John; let us make our petition to him:

Lord, send forth your Spirit upon us.

Christ, Servant of God, the Father acknowledged you as
his own Son with whom he was pleased,

—send forth your Spirit upon us.

Christ, Chosen One of God, you did not break the
crushed reed or extinguish the wavering flame,

—have mercy on all who are seeking you in good faith.

Christ, Son of God, the Father called you to be a light to
the nations in the new covenant,

—open the eyes of the blind by the waters of baptism.

Christ, Savior of mankind, the Father anointed you with
the Holy Spirit for the ministry of salvation,

—lead all to see you and to believe in you, that they
may have eternal life.

Christ, our hope, you lead those in darkness to the light
of salvation,

—receive our departed brothers and sisters into your
kingdom.

Our Father . . .

Prayer

Almighty, eternal God,
when the Spirit descended upon Jesus
at his baptism in the Jordan,
you revealed him as your own beloved Son.
Keep us, your children born of water and the Spirit,
faithful to our calling.

We ask this through our Lord Jesus Christ, your Son,
who lives and reigns with you and the Holy Spirit,
one God, for ever and ever.

Alternative Prayer

Father in heaven,
you revealed Christ as your Son

by the voice that spoke over the waters of the Jordan.
May all who share in the sonship of Christ
follow in his path of service to man,
and reflect the glory of his kingdom
even to the ends of the earth,
for he is Lord for ever and ever.

After the feast of the Baptism of the Lord, Ordinary Time
begins.

THE ORDINARY
OF THE LITURGY OF THE HOURS
FROM THE FIRST SUNDAY OF
ADVENT TO THE FEAST OF THE
BAPTISM OF THE LORD

Invitatory

The invitatory belongs at the very beginning of each day's prayer. It precedes either the Office of Readings or Morning Prayer; the liturgical day may begin with either hour.

Lord, open my lips.
—And my mouth will proclaim your praise.

Afterward psalm 95 is said with its antiphon. The antiphon is said before the psalm, then immediately repeated; it is repeated after each strophe of the psalm.

In individual recitation, the antiphon may be said only at the beginning of the psalm; it need not be repeated after each strophe.

For Sundays and weekdays during Advent the antiphon for the invitatory is:

From the First Sunday of Advent until December 16:

Come, let us worship the Lord, the King who is to come.

From December 17 to December 23:

The Lord is close at hand; come, let us worship him.

December 24:

Today you will know the Lord is coming, and in the morning you will see his glory.

For the Sunday and weekday offices during Christmas until the Epiphany:

Christ is born for us; come, let us adore him.

From the Epiphany until the feast of the Baptism of the Lord:

Christ has appeared to us; come, let us adore him.

For solemnities and feasts, the antiphon for the invitatory is found in either the Proper of Seasons or the Common of Saints.

For the memorials of saints, the antiphon, unless it is proper, may be taken from either the Commons or the weekday.

Ordinary

STh

Psalm 95

A call to praise God

Encourage each other daily while it is still today
(Hebrews 3:13)

(The antiphon is recited and then repeated)

Come, let us sing to the Lord
and shout with joy to the Rock who saves us.
Let us approach him with praise and thanksgiving
and sing joyful songs to the Lord.

(Antiphon repeated)

The Lord is God, the mighty God,
the great king over all the gods.
He holds in his hands the depths of the earth
and the highest mountains as well.
He made the sea; it belongs to him,
the dry land, too, for it was formed by his hands.

(Antiphon repeated)

Come, then, let us bow down and worship,
bending the knee before the Lord, our maker.
For he is our God and we are his people,
the flock he shepherds.

(Antiphon repeated)

Today, listen to the voice of the Lord:
Do not grow stubborn, as your fathers did
in the wilderness,
when at Meriba and Massah
they challenged me and provoked me,
Although they had seen all of my works.

(Antiphon repeated)

Forty years I endured that generation.

I said, "They are a people whose hearts go astray
   and they do not know my ways."
So I swore in my anger,
   "They shall not enter into my rest."

(Antiphon repeated)

Glory to the Father, and to the Son, and to the Holy
   Spirit:
as it was in the beginning, is now, and will be for ever.
   Amen.

(Antiphon repeated)

For psalm 95 one may substitute psalm 100 (p.772), 67 (p.
869), or 24 (p. 720). If any of these psalms should occur in the
office, psalm 95 is then said in place of it.

The psalm with its antiphon may be omitted when the
invitatory precedes Morning Prayer.

Office of Readings

God,[1] come to my assistance.
—Lord, make haste to help me.

Glory to the Father, and to the Son, and to the Holy
   Spirit:
as it was in the beginning, is now, and will be for ever.
   Amen.

If the office begins with the invitatory, all the above is omitted.

HYMN

Then the appropriate hymn is said.

For the Sunday and weekday offices, the hymn is given at the
beginning of each season.

For solemnities and feasts, the hymn is found in the Proper of
Saints or in the Common of Saints.

---

[1] For musical purposes the invocation **"God"** may be expanded, for
example, **"God our Father," "Lord God," "O God,"** etc.

For the memorials of saints, the hymn, unless it is proper, may be taken from either the Commons or the weekday.

PSALMODY

The psalmody follows the hymn and consists of three psalms or sections of psalms, together with the appropriate antiphons.

For solemnities and feasts and during the octave of Christmas, the psalms and antiphons are proper.

For the Sunday and weekday offices, the psalms and antiphons are taken from the current week of the Psalter. The Sundays of Advent have proper antiphons.

For the memorials of saints, the psalms and antiphons are taken from the current week of the Psalter, unless there are proper psalms and antiphons.

VERSES

The verse is said before the readings, to mark the transition from the psalmody to the hearing of the word of God. This verse is given before the first reading.

READINGS

There are two readings. The first is a biblical reading with its responsory, taken from the Proper of Seasons, except for solemnities and feasts when it is taken from the Proper of Saints or Commons.

The second reading is hagiographical on the celebration of saints: solemnities, feasts or memorials.

Otherwise the second reading is from the Church Fathers or other ecclesiastical writers and is taken from the Liturgy of the Hours, where it follows the biblical reading, or from the optional Lectionary. The appropriate responsory follows the second reading.

Hymn, Te Deum

For Sundays, the octave of Christmas, solemnities and feasts, the hymn **Te Deum** follows the second reading and its responsory.

You are God: we praise you;
You are the Lord: we acclaim you;
You are the eternal Father:
All creation worships you.

To you all angels, all the powers of heaven,
Cherubim and Seraphim, sing in endless praise:
    Holy, holy, holy, Lord, God of power and might,
    heaven and earth are full of your glory.

The glorious company of apostles praise you.
The noble fellowship of prophets praise you.
The white-robed army of martyrs praise you.

Throughout the world the holy Church acclaims you:
    Father, of majesty unbounded,
    your true and only Son, worthy of all worship,
    and the Holy Spirit, advocate and guide.

You, Christ, are the King of glory,
the eternal Son of the Father.

When you became man to set us free
you did not spurn the Virgin's womb.

You overcame the sting of death,
and opened the kingdom of heaven to all believers.

You are seated at God's right hand in glory.
We believe that you will come, and be our judge.

Come then, Lord, and help your people,
bought with the price of your own blood,
and bring us with your saints
to glory everlasting.

V. Save your people, Lord, and bless your inheritance.
R. Govern and uphold them now and always.
V. Day by day we bless you.
R. We praise your name for ever.
V. Keep us today, Lord, from all sin.
R. Have mercy on us, Lord, have mercy.
V. Lord, show us your love and mercy;
R. for we put our trust in you.
V. In you, Lord, is our hope:
R. and we shall never hope in vain.

The concluding part of the hymn may be omitted.

CONCLUDING PRAYER

After the **Te Deum** or, if it is not said, after the second responsory, the concluding prayer is said. It is taken from the Proper of Seasons or from the Proper of Saints or Commons, depending on the office of the day.

The prayer is preceded by the invitation **Let us pray**; it is concluded as follows:

If the prayer is directed to the Father:

We ask this (Grant this) through our Lord Jesus Christ,
    your Son,
who lives and reigns with you and the Holy Spirit,
one God, for ever and ever.

If it is directed to the Father after which a mention of the Son is made:

who lives and reigns with you and the Holy Spirit,
one God, for ever and ever.

If it is directed to the Son:

You live and reign with the Father and the Holy Spirit,
one God, for ever and ever.

Response at the conclusion of the prayer:

Amen.

The following acclamation is added, at least in the communal celebration of the office:

Let us praise the Lord.
—And give him thanks.

In an extended vigil celebration of a Sunday or solemnity, canticles may be sung and the gospel read before the **Te Deum,** as indicated in Appendix I, 1613.

If the Office of Readings is celebrated immediately before another hour, the hymn designated for the latter may replace the hymn at the beginning of the Office of Readings. When another hour follows immediately, the prayer and acclamation at the end of the Office of Readings are omitted. The introductory verse with the **Glory to the Father** is omitted as the next hour begins.

Morning Prayer

God, come to my assistance.
—Lord, make haste to help me.

Glory to the Father, and to the Son, and to the Holy Spirit:
as it was in the beginning, is now, and will be for ever. Amen. Alleluia.

This verse and response are omitted when the hour begins with the invitatory.

Hymn

Then the appropriate hymn is said.

For the Sunday and weekday offices and for the days within the octave of Christmas, the hymn is given at the beginning of each season.

For solemnities and feasts, the hymn is found in the Proper of Saints or in the Commons.

For the memorials of saints, the hymn, unless it is proper, may be taken from either the Commons or the weekday.

Psalmody

The psalmody follows the hymn and consists of one morning psalm, an Old Testament canticle and another psalm of praise, together with the appropriate antiphons.

For the Sunday and weekday offices, the psalms, canticle, and antiphons are taken from the current week of the Psalter. The Sundays of Advent and Christmas and the weekdays from December 17-24 have proper antiphons.

For solemnities, days within the octave of Christmas, and feasts, the psalms and canticle are taken from the first Sunday of the Psalter, the antiphons from the Proper of Saints or Commons.

For the memorials of saints, the psalms, canticle, and antiphons are taken from the current week of the Psalter, unless there are proper psalms and antiphons.

After the psalmody the reading follows.

Reading

For the Sunday and weekday offices, the reading is given in the Proper of Seasons.

For solemnities and feasts, the reading is found in the Proper of Saints or the Commons.

For the memorials of saints, the reading, unless it is proper, may be from either the Commons or the weekday.

A longer reading may be selected, especially in celebrations with the people, in accord with number 46 of the General Instruction; a short homily on the reading may also be added.

Response to the Word of God

A period of silence may be observed after the reading or homily.

Next a responsorial song or the responsory after the reading follows.

Other suitable songs may be substituted provided they have been approved by the conference of bishops.

Gospel Canticle Luke 1:68-79

The following gospel canticle with the appropriate antiphon is then said.

The antiphon is taken from the Proper of Seasons.

In the celebrations of saints, unless there is a proper antiphon, the antiphon is taken from the Commons; for the memorials, the antiphon is taken from the current weekday.

The Messiah and his forerunner

Blessed be the Lord, the God of Israel;
he has come to his people and set them free.

He has raised up for us a mighty savior,
born of the house of his servant David.

Through his holy prophets he promised of old
that he would save us from our enemies,
from the hands of all who hate us.

He promised to show mercy to our fathers
and to remember his holy covenant.

This was the oath he swore to our father Abraham:
to set us free from the hands of our enemies,
free to worship him without fear,
holy and righteous in his sight
all the days of our life.

You, my child, shall be called the prophet of the Most High,
for you will go before the Lord to prepare his way,
to give his people knowledge of salvation
by the forgiveness of their sins.

In the tender compassion of our God
the dawn from on high shall break upon us,
to shine on those who dwell in darkness and the shadow of death,
and to guide our feet into the way of peace.

The **Glory to the Father** is said at the end of the canticles, unless otherwise noted.

The antiphon is repeated as usual.

INTERCESSIONS

The intercessions follow the canticle.

For the Sunday and weekday offices, the intercessions are found in the Proper of Seasons.

For solemnities and feasts, the intercessions are found in the Proper of Saints or the Commons.

For the memorials of saints, the intercessions, unless they are proper, may be taken from either the Commons or from the weekday.

All then say the **Lord's Prayer.** It may be preceded by a brief invitation:

Now let us offer together the prayer our Lord Jesus Christ taught us:

Now let us pray as Christ the Lord has taught us:

With longing for the coming of God's kingdom let us offer our prayer to the Father:

Gathering our prayers and praises into one, let us offer the prayer Christ himself taught us:

Let us make our prayers and praise complete by offering the Lord's prayer:

Let us conclude our prayers with the Lord's prayer:

Let us again offer our praise to God and pray in the words of Christ:

To Christ:

Remember us, Lord, when you come to your kingdom and teach us how to pray:

And now let us pray with confidence as Christ our Lord asked:

And now let us pray as the Lord told us:

We pattern our prayer on the prayer of Christ our Lord, and say:

Now let us offer the prayer Christ has given us as the model for all prayer:

The Lord's Prayer

Our Father . . .

The concluding prayer, without the invitation **Let us pray,** is added immediately after the **Lord's Prayer.**

The concluding prayer is taken from the Proper. This prayer is concluded in the way described above (652).

DISMISSAL

If a priest or deacon presides, he dismisses the people:

The Lord be with you.
—And also with you.

May almighty God bless you,
the Father, and the Son, and the Holy Spirit.
—Amen.

Another form of the blessing may be used, as at Mass.

Then he adds:

Go in peace.
—Thanks be to God.

In the absence of a priest or deacon and in individual recitation, Morning Prayer concludes:

May the Lord bless us,
protect us from all evil
and bring us to everlasting life.
—Amen.

Daytime Prayer

God, come to my assistance.
—Lord, make haste to help me.

Glory to the Father, and to the Son, and to the Holy
    Spirit:
as it was in the beginning, is now, and will be for ever.
    Amen. Alleluia.

Then the appropriate hymn follows. The memorials of saints
are not celebrated at these hours.

HYMN

Midmorning

Breathe on me, breath of God,
Fill me with life anew,
That I may love the things you love,
And do what you would do.

Breathe on me, breath of God,
Until my heart is pure,
Until with you I have one will,
To live and to endure.

Breathe on me, breath of God,
My soul with grace refine,
Until this earthly part of me
Glows with your fire divine.

Breathe on me, breath of God,
So I shall never die,
But live with you the perfect life
In your eternity.

Melody: Yattendon 46   Music: H. E. Wooldridge, 1845–1917
                                    Text: Edwin Hatch, 1835–1889,
                                  adapted by Anthony G. Petti

Or:

    From all that dwell below the skies
    Let the Creator's praise arise:
    Let the Redeemer's name be sung
    Through every land, by every tongue,
          Hallelujah!

    Eternal are thy mercies, Lord;
    Eternal truth attends thy word:
    Thy praise shall sound from shore to shore,
    Till suns shall rise and set no more:
          Hallelujah!

Melody: Erschienen ist der herrliche   Music: Nikolaus Hermann,
Tag or Eisenach (without   1560 or Johann H. Schein, 1583–1630
hallelujahs) L.M.   Text: Isaac Watts, 1719

Or:

    Father, Lord of earth and heaven,
    King to whom all gifts belong,
    Give your greatest Gift, your Spirit,
    God the holy, God the strong.

    Son of God, enthroned in Glory,
    Send your promised Gift of grace,
    Make your Church your holy Temple,
    God the Spirit's dwelling-place.

    Spirit, come, in peace descending
    As at Jordan, heav'nly Dove,
    Seal your Church as God's anointed,
    Set our hearts on fire with love.

    Stay among us, God the Father,
    Stay among us, God the Son,
    Stay among us, Holy Spirit:
    Dwell within us, make us one.

Melody: Drakes Boughton 87.87   Music: S. P. Waddington
    Text: James Quinn, S.J.

Or:

Holy Spirit, come, confirm us
In the truth that Christ makes known;
We have faith and understanding
Through your helping gifts alone.

Holy Spirit, come, console us,
Come as Advocate to plead,
Loving Spirit from the Father,
Grant in Christ the help we need.

Holy Spirit, come, renew us,
Come yourself to make us live:
Holy through your loving presence,
Holy through the gifts you give.

Holy Spirit, come, possess us,
You the Love of Three in One,
Holy Spirit of the Father,
Holy Spirit of the Son.

Melody: Laus Deo 87.87   Music: Richard Redhead, 1820–1901
                                              Text: Brian Foley

Or:

Come, Holy Ghost, who ever one
Art with the Father and the Son,
Come, Holy Ghost, our souls possess
With thy full flood of holiness.

In will and deed, in heart and tongue
With all the powers, thy praise be sung;
And love light up our mortal frame
Till others catch the living flame.

Almighty Father, hear our cry
Through Jesus Christ, our Lord most high,
Who with the Holy Ghost and thee
Doth live and reign eternally.

Melody: Saint Venantius L.M.   Music: Clausener Gesangbuch, 1653
                                              Text: St. Ambrose (?)
                        Translator: J. H. Newman, 1801–1890

Midday

Help us, O Lord, to learn
The truths thy Word imparts:
To study that thy laws may be
Inscribed upon our hearts.

Help us, O Lord, to live
The faith which we proclaim,
That all our thoughts and words and deeds
May glorify your name.

Help us, O Lord, to teach
The beauty of your ways,
That yearning souls may find the Christ,
And sing aloud his praise.

Melody: Franconia S.M.   Music: J. B. Konig, 1691–1758, adapted
by W. H. Havergal, 1793–1870
Text: W. W. Reid, 1923–

Or:

Lord of all hopefulness, Lord of all joy,
Whose trust, ever childlike, no cares could destroy,
Be there at our waking, and give us, we pray,
Your bliss in our hearts, Lord, at the break of the
day.

Lord of all eagerness, Lord of all faith,
Whose strong hands were skilled at the plane and the
lathe,
Be there at our labors, and give us, we pray,
Your strength in our hearts, Lord, at the noon of the
day.

Lord of all kindliness, Lord of all grace,
Your hand swift to welcome, your arms to embrace,
Be there at our homing, and give us, we pray,
Your love in our hearts, Lord, at the eve of the day.

Lord of all gentleness, Lord of all calm,
Whose voice is contentment, whose presence is balm,
Be there at our sleeping, and give us, we pray,
Your peace in our hearts, Lord, at the end of the day.

Melody: Slane 10.11.11.12   Music: Irish Traditional Melody
Text: Jan Struther, 1901–1953

Or:

Lord of all being, throned afar,
Your glory flames from sun and star;
Center and soul of every sphere,
And yet to loving hearts how near.

Sun of our life, your living ray
Sheds on our path the glow of the day;
Star of our hope, your gentle light
Shall ever cheer the longest night.

Lord of all life, below, above,
Whose light is truth, whose warmth is love;
Before the brilliance of your throne
We ask no luster of our own.

Give us your grace to make us true,
And kindling hearts that burn for you,
Till all your living altars claim
One holy light, one heavenly flame.

Melody: Uffingham L.M.   Music: Jeremiah Clarke, 1659–1707
Text: Oliver Wendell Holmes, 1809–1894

Or:

Almighty Ruler, God of truth
Who guide and master all,
The rays with which you gild the dawn
With noonday heat now fall.

O quench the fires of hatred, Lord,
Of anger and of strife;
Bring health to every mind and heart
That peace may enter life.

Most holy Father, grant our prayer
Through Christ your only Son,
That in your Spirit we may live
And praise you ever one.

Melody: Ballerma C.M.   Music: F. Barthelemon, 1741–1808
Text: Ralph Wright, O.S.B.

Midafternoon

Firmly I believe and truly
God is three and God is one;
And I next acknowledge duly
Manhood taken by the Son.

And I trust and hope most fully
In that manhood crucified;
And I love supremely, solely
Christ who for my sins has died.

And I hold in veneration,
For the love of him alone,
Holy Church as his creation,
And her teachings as his own.

Praise and thanks be ever given
With and through the angel host,
To the God of earth and heaven,
Father, Son and Holy Ghost.

Melody: Halton Holgate 87.87   Music: William Boyce, 1710–1779
Text: John Henry Newman, 1801–1890,
adapted by Anthony G. Petti

Or:

Lord God and Maker of all things,
Creation is upheld by you.
While all must change and know decay,
You are unchanging, always new.

You are man's solace and his shield,
His rock secure on which to build,
You are the spirit's tranquil home,
In you alone is hope fulfilled.

To God the Father and the Son
And Holy Spirit render praise,
Blest Trinity, from age to age
The strength of all our living days.

Melody: Auctoritate Saeculi L.M.   Music: Poitiers Antiphoner,
                                                1746
                                    Text: Stanbrook Abbey

Or:

Most ancient of all mysteries,
Before your throne we lie;
Have mercy now, most merciful,
Most holy Trinity.

When heaven and earth were still unmade,
When time was yet unknown,
You in your radiant majesty
Did live and love alone.

You were not born, there was no source
From which your Being flowed;
There is no end which you can reach,
For you are simply God.

How wonderful creation is,
The work which you did bless,
What then must you be like, dear God,
Eternal loveliness!

Most ancient of all mysteries,
Before your throne we lie;
Have mercy now and evermore,
Most holy Trinity.

Melody: Saint Flavian C.M.   Music: Adapted from Psalm 132,
                                            Day's Psalter, 1562
                         Text: Frederick William Faber, 1814–1863

Or:

Faith of our fathers! faith and prayer
Shall win all nations unto thee;
And through the truth that comes from God,
Mankind shall then indeed be free.

Refrain:
Faith of our fathers, holy faith!
We will be true to thee till death.

Faith of our fathers! we will love
Both friend and foe in all our strife:
And preach thee too, as love knows how,
By kindly deeds and virtuous life.

Refrain

Melody: Saint Catherine L.M.   Music: Henry F. Hemy,
with Refrain   1818–1888, and
                                      James G. Walton, 1821–1905
                         Text: Frederick W. Faber, 1814–1863

PSALMODY

The psalms and antiphons are said after the hymn.

Two psalmodies are given in the Psalter: the one is current; the
other is complementary.

The current psalmody is comprised of three psalms or three
selections from psalms taken from the cycle of the Psalter.

The complementary psalmody is made up of invariable psalms,
chosen from those which are called gradual psalms, p. 1191.

Those who say only one of the three hours use the current psalmody even on feasts.

Those who say several hours use the current psalmody for one hour; in the other hours they use the complementary psalmody.

For solemnities the psalms are taken from the complementary psalmody for each of the three hours. If, however, a solemnity occurs on Sunday, the psalms are taken from Sunday, Week I, p. **692**.

For solemnities the antiphons are proper.

Outside of solemnities, the antiphons, unless they are proper, are taken from the appropriate Season.

READING

A reading follows the psalmody.

For the Sunday and weekday offices, the reading is taken from the Proper of Seasons.

For solemnities and feasts, the reading is found in the Proper of Saints or the Commons.

A period of silence may be observed after the reading. After the reading a very brief verse is proposed.

CONCLUDING PRAYER

Afterward the concluding prayer, with the invitation **Let us pray** and the appropriate conclusion, is said:

If the prayer is directed to the Father:

We ask this (Grant this) through Christ our Lord, or **We ask this in the name of Jesus the Lord.**

If the prayer is directed to the Father after which a mention of the Son is made:

Who lives and reigns with you for ever and ever.

If it is directed to the Son:

You live and reign for ever and ever.

Response at the conclusion of the prayer:

Amen.

In the communal celebration of the office, the acclamation is added:

Let us praise the Lord.
—And give him thanks.

Evening Prayer

God, come to my assistance.
—Lord, make haste to help me.

Glory to the Father, and to the Son, and to the Holy Spirit:
as it was in the beginning, is now, and will be for ever. Amen.

HYMN

Then the appropriate hymn is said.

For the Sunday and weekday offices and for the days within the octave of Christmas, the hymn is given at the beginning of each season.

For solemnities and feasts, the hymn is found in the Proper of Saints or in the Commons.

For the memorials of saints, the hymn, unless it is proper, may be taken from either the Commons or the weekday.

PSALMODY

The psalmody follows the hymn and consists of two psalms or parts of psalms, and a New Testament canticle, together with the appropriate antiphons.

For the Sunday and weekday offices, the psalms, canticle and antiphons are taken from the current week of the Psalter. The Sundays of Advent and Christmas and the weekdays from December 17–24 have proper antiphons.

For solemnities, days within the octave of Christmas, and feasts, the psalms and canticle are taken from the first Sunday of the Psalter, the antiphons from the Proper of Saints or Commons.

For the memorials of saints, the psalms, canticle, and antiphons are taken from the current week of the Psalter, unless there are proper psalms and antiphons.

After the psalmody the reading follows.

READING

For the Sunday and weekday offices, the reading is given in the Proper of Seasons.

For solemnities and feasts, the reading is found in the Proper of Saints or the Commons.

For the memorials of saints, the reading, unless it is proper, may be from either the Commons or the weekday.

A longer reading may be selected, especially in celebrations with the people, in accord with number 46 of the General Instruction; a short homily on the reading may also be added.

RESPONSE TO THE WORD OF GOD

A period of silence may be observed after the reading or homily.

Next a responsorial song or the responsory after the reading follows.

Other suitable songs may be substituted provided they have been approved by the conference of bishops.

GOSPEL CANTICLE   Luke 1:46-55

The following gospel canticle with the appropriate antiphon is
then said.

The antiphon is taken from the Proper of Seasons.

In the celebrations of saints, unless there is a proper antiphon,
the antiphon is taken from the Commons; for the memorials,
the antiphon is taken from the current weekday.

The soul rejoices in the Lord

My soul proclaims the greatness of the Lord,
my spirit rejoices in God my Savior
for he has looked with favor on his lowly servant.

From this day all generations will call me blessed:
the Almighty has done great things for me,
and holy is his Name.

He has mercy on those who fear him
in every generation.

He has shown the strength of his arm,
he has scattered the proud in their conceit.

He has cast down the mighty from their thrones,
and has lifted up the lowly.

He has filled the hungry with good things,
and the rich he has sent away empty.

He has come to the help of his servant Israel
for he has remembered his promise of mercy,
the promise he made to our fathers,
to Abraham and his children for ever.

The antiphon is repeated as usual.

INTERCESSIONS

The intercessions follow the canticle.
For the Sunday and weekday offices, the intercessions are
found in the Proper of Seasons.

For solemnities and feasts, the intercessions are found in the Proper of Saints or the Commons.

For the memorials of saints, the intercessions, unless they are proper, may be taken from either the Commons or from the weekday.

All then say the **Lord's Prayer.** It may be preceded by a brief invitation:

Now let us offer together the prayer our Lord Jesus Christ taught us:

Now let us pray as Christ the Lord has taught us:

With longing for the coming of God's kingdom let us offer our prayer to the Father:

Gathering our prayers and praises into one, let us offer the prayer Christ himself taught us:

Let us make our prayers and praise complete by offering the Lord's prayer:

Let us conclude our prayers with the Lord's prayer:

Let us again offer our praise to God and pray in the words of Christ:

To Christ:

Remember us, Lord, when you come to your kingdom and teach us how to pray:

And now let us pray with confidence as Christ our Lord asked:

And now let us pray as the Lord told us:

We pattern our prayer on the prayer of Christ our Lord, and say:

Now let us offer the prayer Christ has given us as the model for all prayer:

The Lord's Prayer

Our Father . . .

The concluding prayer, without the invitation **Let us pray,** is added immediately after the **Lord's Prayer**.

The concluding prayer is taken from the Proper. This prayer is concluded in the way described above (**652**).

DISMISSAL

If a priest or deacon presides, he dismisses the people:

The Lord be with you.
—And also with you.

May almighty God bless you,
the Father, and the Son, and the Holy Spirit.
—Amen.

Another form of the blessing may be used, as at Mass.

Then he adds:

Go in peace.
—Thanks be to God.

In the absence of a priest or deacon and in individual recitation, Evening Prayer concludes:

May the Lord bless us,
protect us from all evil
and bring us to everlasting life.
—Amen.

Night Prayer

God, come to my assistance.
—Lord, make haste to help me.

Glory to the Father, and to the Son, and to the Holy
    Spirit:
as it was in the beginning, is now, and will be for ever.
    Amen. Alleluia.

A brief examination of conscience may be made. In the communal celebration of the office, a penitential rite using the formulas of the Mass may be inserted here.

HYMN, as in the Psalter, pp. **1164-1168.**

PSALMODY

After Evening Prayer I of Sundays and of solemnities, psalms 4 and 134 are said, p. **1169;** after Evening Prayer II, psalm 91, p. **1172,** is said. Both forms of Night Prayer for Sunday may be used with the octave of Christmas.

On all other days, the psalms and antiphons are found in the Psalter. One may, however, use Night Prayer from Sunday during the week.

READING

A brief reading, and a responsory, found in the Psalter, follow the psalmody.

RESPONSORY

Into your hands, Lord, I commend my spirit.
—Into your hands, Lord, I commend my spirit.

You have redeemed us, Lord God of truth.
—I commend my spirit.

Glory to the Father . . .
—Into your hands . . .

GOSPEL CANTICLE   Luke 2:29-32

Ant.   Protect us, Lord, as we stay awake; watch over us as we sleep; that awake, we may keep watch with Christ, and asleep, rest in his peace.

Christ is the light of the nations and the glory of Israel

Lord, now you let your servant go in peace;
your word has been fulfilled:

my own eyes have seen the salvation
which you have prepared in the sight of every people:

a light to reveal you to the nations
and the glory of your people Israel.

Glory to the Father, and to the Son, and to the Holy
Spirit:
as it was in the beginning, is now, and will be for ever.
Amen.

The antiphon is repeated as usual.

CONCLUDING PRAYER

Afterward the prayer, with the invitation **Let us pray,** as given
in the Psalter is said. The response at the conclusion of the
prayer:

Amen.

The blessing is said, even in individual recitation:

May the all-powerful Lord grant us a restful night and a
peaceful death.
—Amen.

Antiphons in Honor of the Blessed Virgin

Then one of the antiphons in honor of Mary is said (see Psalter,
1188. Other hymns approved by the conference of bishops may
be used.

THE FOUR-WEEK PSALTER

The four-week cycle of the Psalter is so arranged in conjunction with the liturgical year that the first week of the cycle coincides with the First Sunday of Advent. It then continues until the feast of the Baptism of the Lord, exclusive.

THE FOUR-WEEK PSALTER

SUNDAY

Evening Prayer I

God, come to my assistance. Glory to the Father. As it
was in in the beginning. Alleluia.

Hymn, 126.

Or:

Now thank we all our God
With heart and hands and voices,
Who wondrous things has done,
In whom his world rejoices;
Who from our mothers' arms
Has blessed us on our way
With countless gifts of love,
And still is ours today.

O may this gracious God
Through all our life be near us,
With ever joyful hearts,
And blessed peace to cheer us;
Preserve us in his grace,
And guide us in distress,
And free us from all sin,
Till heaven we possess.

All praise and thanks to God
The Father now be given,
The Son and Spirit blest,
Who reigns in highest heaven;
Eternal, Triune God,
Whom earth and heaven adore;
For thus it was, is now,
And shall be ever more.

Melody: Nun Danket 67.67.66.66.　　　Music: Johann Cruger,
1598–1662
Text: Martin Rinkart, 1586–1649
Translator: Catherine Winkworth, 1829–1878

PSALMODY

Antiphon 1

Advent:　　**Proclaim the good news among the nations:
Our God will come to save us.**

Psalm 141:1–9

A prayer when in danger

*An angel stood before the face of God, thurible in hand. The
fragrant incense soaring aloft was the prayer of God's people
on earth* (Revelation 8:4).

I have called to you, Lord; hasten to help me!
Hear my voice when I cry to you.
Let my prayer arise before you like incense,
the raising of my hands like an evening oblation.

Set, O Lord, a guard over my mouth;
keep watch at the door of my lips!
Do not turn my heart to things that are wrong,
to evil deeds with men who are sinners.

Never allow me to share in their feasting.
If a good man strikes or reproves me it is kindness;
but let the oil of the wicked not anoint my head.
Let my prayer be ever against their malice.

Their princes were thrown down by the side of the
rock:
then they understood that my words were kind.
As a millstone is shattered to pieces on the ground,
so their bones were strewn at the mouth of the grave.

To you, Lord God, my eyes are turned:
in you I take refuge; spare my soul!

From the trap they have laid for me keep me safe:
keep me from the snares of those who do evil.

Glory to the Father, and to the Son, and to the
 Holy Spirit:
as it was in the beginning, is now, and will be for
 ever. Amen.

All psalms and canticles are concluded with the **Glory to the
Father** unless otherwise indicated.

Psalm-prayer

Lord, from the rising of the sun to its setting your
name is worthy of all praise. Let our prayer come like
incense before you. May the lifting up of our hands be as
an evening sacrifice acceptable to you, Lord our God.

Advent: Proclaim the good news among the nations:
   Our God will come to save us.

Antiphon 2

Advent: Know that the Lord is coming and with him
   all his saints; that day will dawn with a
   wonderful light, alleluia.

Psalm 142

You, Lord, are my refuge

*What is written in this psalm was fulfilled in our Lord's
passion* (Saint Hilary).

With all my voice I cry to the Lord,
with all my voice I entreat the Lord.
I pour out my trouble before him;
I tell him all my distress
while my spirit faints within me.
But you, O Lord, know my path.

On the way where I shall walk
they have hidden a snare to entrap me.
Look on my right and see:
there is not one who takes my part.
I have no means of escape,
not one who cares for my soul.

I cry to you, O Lord.
I have said: "You are my refuge,
all I have left in the land of the living."
Listen then to my cry
for I am in the depths of distress.

Rescue me from those who pursue me
for they are stronger than I.
Bring my soul out of this prison
and then I shall praise your name.
Around me the just will assemble
because of your goodness to me.

Psalm-prayer

Lord, we humbly ask for your goodness. May you help
us to hope in you, and give us a share with your chosen
ones in the land of the living.

Advent: Know that the Lord is coming and with him
             all his saints; that day will dawn with a
             wonderful light, alleluia.

Antiphon 3

Advent: The Lord will come with mighty power; all
             mortal eyes shall see him.

Canticle   Philippians 2:6-11

Christ, God's holy servant

Though he was in the form of God,
Jesus did not deem equality with God
something to be grasped at.

Rather, he emptied himself
and took the form of a slave,
being born in the likeness of men.

He was known to be of human estate,
and it was thus that he humbled himself,
obediently accepting even death,
death on a cross!

Because of this,
God highly exalted him
and bestowed on him the name
above every other name,

So that at Jesus' name
every knee must bend
in the heavens, on the earth,
and under the earth,
and every tongue proclaim
to the glory of God the Father:
JESUS CHRIST IS LORD!

Advent: The Lord will come with mighty power; all
mortal eyes shall see him.

Reading, responsory, antiphon for the canticle of Mary,
intercessions and prayer, as in the Proper of Seasons.

Conclusion, as in the Ordinary.

Invitatory
Lord, open my lips.

Advent: Come, let us worship the Lord, the King who
is to come.

Invitatory Psalm, 648.

Office of Readings
God, come to my assistance. Glory to the Father. As it
was in the beginning. Alleluia.

This verse and response are omitted when the hour begins with the invitatory.

HYMN, 121.

Or:

Antiphon:

All you nations, sing out your joy to the Lord:
Alleluia, alleluia!

Joyfully shout, all you on earth,
give praise to the glory of God;
And with a hymn, sing out his glorious praise:
Alleluia!

Antiphon

Let all the earth kneel in his sight,
extolling his marvelous fame;
Honor his name, in highest heaven give praise:
Alleluia!

Antiphon

Come forth and see all the great works
that God has brought forth by his might;
Fall on your knees before his glorious throne:
Alleluia!

Antiphon

Glory and thanks be to the Father;
honor and praise to the Son;
And to the Spirit, source of life and of love:
Alleluia!

Antiphon

Melody: All You Nations   Music: Lucien Deiss, C.S.Sp., 1965
                                   Text: Lucien Deiss, C.S.Sp., 1965

Antiphon 1

Advent: This is our heavenly King; he comes with power and might to save the nations, alleluia.

Psalm 1

There are two ways a man may take

They are happy who, putting all their trust in the cross, have plunged into the water of life (from an author of the second century).

> Happy indeed is the man
> who follows not the counsel of the wicked;
> nor lingers in the way of sinners
> nor sits in the company of scorners,
> but whose delight is the law of the Lord
> and who ponders his law day and night.
>
> He is like a tree that is planted
> beside the flowing waters,
> that yields its fruit in due season
> and whose leaves shall never fade;
> and all that he does shall prosper.
> Not so are the wicked, not so!
>
> For they like winnowed chaff
> shall be driven away by the wind.
> When the wicked are judged they shall not stand,
> nor find room among those who are just;
> for the Lord guards the way of the just
> but the way of the wicked leads to doom.

Psalm-prayer

Lord, you are the fullness of life, of holiness and of joy. Fill our days and nights with the love of your

wisdom, that we may bear fruit in the beauty of holiness,
like a tree watered by running streams.

Advent: This is our heavenly King; he comes with
           power and might to save the nations, alleluia.

Antiphon 2

Advent: Daughter of Jerusalem, rejoice and be glad;
           your King will come to you. Zion, do not fear;
           your Savior hastens on his way.

Psalm 2

The Messiah, king and conqueror

*The rulers of the earth joined forces to overthrow Jesus, your
anointed Son* (Acts 4:27).

Why this tumult among nations,
among peoples this useless murmuring?
They arise, the kings of the earth,
princes plot against the Lord and his Anointed.
"Come, let us break their fetters,
come, let us cast off their yoke."

He who sits in the heavens laughs;
the Lord is laughing them to scorn.
Then he will speak in his anger,
his rage will strike them with terror.
"It is I who have set up my king
on Zion, my holy mountain."

I will announce the decree of the Lord:

The Lord said to me: "You are my Son.
It is I who have begotten you this day.
Ask and I shall bequeath you the nations,
put the ends of the earth in your possession.
With a rod of iron you will break them,
shatter them like a potter's jar."

Now, O kings, understand,
take warning, rulers of the earth;
serve the Lord with awe
and trembling, pay him your homage
lest he be angry and you perish;
for suddenly his anger will blaze.

Blessed are they who put their trust in God.

Psalm-prayer

Lord God, you gave the peoples of the world as the
inheritance of your only Son; you crowned him as King
of Zion, your holy city, and gave him your Church to be
his Bride. As he proclaims the law of your eternal
kingdom, may we serve him faithfully, and so share his
royal power for ever.

Advent: Daughter of Jerusalem, rejoice and be glad;
          your King will come to you. Zion, do not fear;
          your Savior hastens on his way.

Antiphon 3

Advent: Let us cleanse our hearts for the coming of our
          great King, that we may be ready to welcome
          him; he is coming and will not delay.

Psalm 3

I am safe in the Lord's keeping

*Christ fell asleep in death, but he rose from the dead, for God
was his deliverer* (Saint Irenaeus).

How many are my foes, O Lord!
How many are rising up against me!
How many are saying about me:
"There is no help for him in God."

But you, Lord, are a shield about me,
my glory, who lift up my head.
I cry aloud to the Lord.
He answers from his holy mountain.

I lie down to rest and I sleep.
I wake, for the Lord upholds me.
I will not fear even thousands of people
who are ranged on every side against me.

Arise, Lord; save me, my God,
you who strike all my foes on the mouth,
you who break the teeth of the wicked!
O Lord of salvation, bless your people!

Psalm-prayer

Lord God, you heard the cry of your Son when he was
oppressed and saved him from the sleep of death. Arise,
Lord, help your Church. Be its shield so that it may hold
up its head and radiate the glory of the resurrection.

Advent: Let us cleanse our hearts for the coming of our
           great King, that we may be ready to welcome
           him; he is coming and will not delay.

Verse, reading and prayer, as in the Proper of Seasons.

Morning Prayer

God, come to my assistance. Glory to the Father. As it
was in the beginning. Alleluia.

This verse and response are omitted when the hour begins with
the invitatory.

HYMN, 122.

Or:

On this day, the first of days,
God the Father's name we praise;
Who, creation's Lord and spring,
Did the world from darkness bring.

On this day the eternal Son
Over death his triumph won;
On this day the Spirit came
With his gifts of living flame.

Father, who didst fashion man
Godlike in thy loving plan,
Fill us with that love divine,
And conform our wills to thine.

Word made flesh, all hail to thee!
Thou from sin hast set us free;
And with thee we die and rise
Unto God in sacrifice.

Holy Spirit, you impart
Gifts of love to every heart;
Give us light and grace, we pray,
Fill our hearts this holy day.

God, the blessed Three in One,
May thy holy will be done;
In thy word our souls are free.
And we rest this day with thee.

Melody: Gott Sei Dank 77.77   Music: Freylinghausen's
                                                      Gesangbuch, 1704
                                        Text: *Le Mans Breviary*, 1748
                                  Translator: Henry W. Baker, 1821–1877

PSALMODY

Antiphon 1

Advent: On that day sweet wine will flow from the
mountains, milk and honey from the hills,
alleluia.

Psalm 63:2-9
A soul thirsting for God

Whoever has left the darkness of sin yearns for God.

O God, you are my God, for you I long;
for you my soul is thirsting.
My body pines for you
like a dry, weary land without water.
So I gaze on you in the sanctuary
to see your strength and your glory.

For your love is better than life,
my lips will speak your praise.
So I will bless you all my life,
in your name I will lift up my hands.
My soul shall be filled as with a banquet,
my mouth shall praise you with joy.

On my bed I remember you.
On you I muse through the night
for you have been my help;
in the shadow of your wings I rejoice.
My soul clings to you;
your right hand holds me fast.

Psalm-prayer

Father, creator of unfailing light, give that same light
to those who call to you. May our lips praise you; our
lives proclaim your goodness; our work give you honor,
and our voices celebrate you for ever.

Advent: On that day sweet wine will flow from the
mountains, milk and honey from the hills,
alleluia.

Antiphon 2

Advent: The mountains and hills will sing praise to
God; all the trees of the forest will clap their

hands, for he is coming, the Lord of a
kingdom that lasts for ever, alleluia.

Canticle   Daniel 3:57-88, 56

Let all creatures praise the Lord

All you servants of the Lord, sing praise to him (Revelation
19:5).

Bless the Lord, all you works of the Lord.
Praise and exalt him above all forever.
Angels of the Lord, bless the Lord.
You heavens, bless the Lord.
All you waters above the heavens, bless the Lord.
All you hosts of the Lord, bless the Lord.
Sun and moon, bless the Lord.
Stars of heaven, bless the Lord.

Every shower and dew, bless the Lord.
All you winds, bless the Lord.
Fire and heat, bless the Lord.
Cold and chill, bless the Lord.
Dew and rain, bless the Lord.
Frost and chill, bless the Lord.
Ice and snow, bless the Lord.
Nights and days, bless the Lord.
Light and darkness, bless the Lord.
Lightnings and clouds, bless the Lord.

Let the earth bless the Lord.
Praise and exalt him above all forever.
Mountains and hills, bless the Lord.
Everything growing from the earth, bless the Lord.
You springs, bless the Lord.
Seas and rivers, bless the Lord.
You dolphins and all water creatures, bless the Lord.
All you birds of the air, bless the Lord,

All you beasts, wild and tame, bless the Lord.
You sons of men, bless the Lord.

O Israel, bless the Lord.
Praise and exalt him above all forever.
Priests of the Lord, bless the Lord.
Servants of the Lord, bless the Lord.
Spirits and souls of the just, bless the Lord.
Holy men of humble heart, bless the Lord.
Hananiah, Azariah, Mishael, bless the Lord.
Praise and exalt him above all forever.

Let us bless the Father, and the Son, and the Holy
    Spirit.
Let us praise and exalt him above all forever.
Blessed are you, Lord, in the firmament of heaven.
Praiseworthy and glorious and exalted above all
    forever.

At the end of the canticle the Glory to the Father is not said.

Advent: The mountains and hills will sing praise to
           God; all the trees of the forest will clap their
           hands, for he is coming, the Lord of a
           kingdom that lasts for ever, alleluia.

Antiphon 3

Advent: A great prophet will come to Jerusalem; of
           that people he will make a new creation.

Psalm 149

The joy of God's holy people

*Let the sons of the Church, the children of the new people,
rejoice in Christ, their King* (Hesychius).

Sing a new song to the Lord,
    his praise in the assembly of the faithful.
Let Israel rejoice in its Maker,

let Zion's sons exult in their king.
Let them praise his name with dancing
and make music with timbrel and harp.

For the Lord takes delight in his people.
He crowns the poor with salvation.
Let the faithful rejoice in their glory.
shout for joy and take their rest.
Let the praise of God be on their lips
and a two-edged sword in their hand,

to deal out vengeance to the nations
and punishment on all the peoples;
to bind their kings in chains
and their nobles in fetters of iron;
to carry out the sentence pre-ordained:
this honor is for all his faithful.

Psalm-prayer

Let Israel rejoice in you, Lord, and acknowledge you
as creator and redeemer. We put our trust in your
faithfulness and proclaim the wonderful truths of
salvation. May your loving kindness embrace us now and
for ever.

Advent: A great prophet will come to Jerusalem; of
           that people he will make a new creation.

Reading, responsory, antiphon for the canticle of Zechariah,
intercessions and prayer, as in the Proper of Seasons.

Conclusion, as in the Ordinary.

Daytime Prayer

God, come to my assistance. Glory to the Father. As it
was in the beginning. Alleluia.

HYMN, as in the Ordinary, 658.

PSALMODY

Antiphon, as in the Proper of Seasons.

Psalm 118

Song of joy for salvation

This Jesus is the stone which, rejected by you builders, has become the chief stone supporting all the rest (Acts 4:11).

I

Give thanks to the Lord for he is good,
for his love endures for ever.

Let the sons of Israel say:
"His love endures for ever."
Let the sons of Aaron say:
"His love endures for ever."
Let those who fear the Lord say:
"His love endures for ever."

I called to the Lord in my distress;
he answered and freed me.
The Lord is at my side; I do not fear.
What can man do against me?
The Lord is at my side as my helper:
I shall look down on my foes.

It is better to take refuge in the Lord
than to trust in men:
it is better to take refuge in the Lord
than to trust in princes.

II

The nations all encompassed me;
in the Lord's name I crushed them.
They compassed me, compassed me about;
in the Lord's name I crushed them.

They compassed me about like bees;
they blazed like a fire among thorns.
In the Lord's name I crushed them.

I was hard-pressed and was falling
but the Lord came to help me.
The Lord is my strength and my song;
he is my savior.
There are shouts of joy and victory
in the tents of the just.

The Lord's right hand has triumphed;
his right hand raised me up.
The Lord's right hand has triumphed;
I shall not die, I shall live
and recount his deeds.
I was punished, I was punished by the Lord,
but not doomed to die.

III

Open to me the gates of holiness:
I will enter and give thanks.
This is the Lord's own gate
where the just may enter.
I will thank you for you have answered
and you are my savior.

The stone which the builders rejected
has become the corner stone.
This is the work of the Lord,
a marvel in our eyes.
This day was made by the Lord;
we rejoice and are glad.

O Lord, grant us salvation;
O Lord, grant success.
Blessed in the name of the Lord
is he who comes.

We bless you from the house of the Lord;
the Lord God is our light.

Go forward in procession with branches
even to the altar.
You are my God, I thank you.
My God, I praise you.
Give thanks to the Lord for he is good;
for his love endures for ever.

Psalm-prayer

Lord God, you have given us the great day of rejoicing:
Jesus Christ, the stone rejected by the builders, has
become the cornerstone of the Church, our spiritual
home. Shed upon your Church the rays of your glory,
that it may be seen as the gate of salvation open to all
nations. Let cries of joy and exultation ring out from its
tents, to celebrate the wonder of Christ's resurrection.

At the other hours, the complementary psalmody is used, 1191.

Reading, verse and prayer, as in the Proper of Seasons.

Conclusion, as in the Ordinary.

Evening Prayer II

God, come to my assistance. Glory to the Father. As it
was in the beginning. Alleluia.

HYMN, 126.

Or:

O Christ, you are the light and day
Which drives away the night,
The ever shining Sun of God
And pledge of future light.

As now the ev'ning shadows fall
Please grant us, Lord, we pray,
A quiet night to rest in you
Until the break of day.

Remember us, poor mortal men,
We humbly ask, O Lord,
And may your presence in our souls
Be now our great reward.

Melody: Saint Anne C.M.   Music: William Croft, 1708
                                          Text: *Christe qui Lux es et Dies*
                                   Translator: Rev. M. Quinn, O.P. et al.

PSALMODY

Antiphon 1

Advent: Rejoice, daughter of Zion; shout for joy,
           daughter of Jerusalem, alleluia.

Psalm 110:1-5, 7

The Messiah, king and priest

*Christ's reign will last until all his enemies are made subject
to him* (1 Corinthians 15:25).

The Lord's revelation to my Master:
"Sit on my right:
your foes I will put beneath your feet."

The Lord will wield from Zion
your scepter of power:
rule in the midst of all your foes.

A prince from the day of your birth
on the holy mountains;
from the womb before the dawn I begot you.

The Lord has sworn an oath he will not change.
"You are a priest for ever,
a priest like Melchizedek of old."

The Master standing at your right hand
will shatter kings in the day of his great wrath.

He shall drink from the stream by the wayside
and therefore he shall lift up his head.

Psalm-prayer

Father, we ask you to give us victory and peace. In
Jesus Christ, our Lord and King, we are already seated at
your right hand. We look forward to praising you in the
fellowship of all your saints in our heavenly homeland.

Advent: Rejoice, daughter of Zion; shout for joy,
            daughter of Jerusalem, alleluia.

Antiphon 2

Advent: Christ our King will come to us, the Lamb of
            God foretold by John.

Psalm 114

The Israelites are delivered from the bondage of Egypt

*You too left Egypt when, at baptism, you renounced that
world which is at enmity with God* (Saint Augustine).

When Israel came forth from Egypt,
Jacob's sons from an alien people,
Judah became the Lord's temple,
Israel became his kingdom.

The sea fled at the sight:
the Jordan turned back on its course,
the mountains leapt like rams
and the hills like yearling sheep.

Why was it, sea, that you fled,
that you turned back, Jordan, on your course?
Mountains, that you leapt like rams,
hills, like yearling sheep?

Tremble, O earth, before the Lord,
in the presence of the God of Jacob,
who turns the rock into a pool
and flint into a spring of water.

Psalm-prayer

Almighty God, ever-living mystery of unity and
Trinity, you gave life to the new Israel by birth from
water and the Spirit, and made it a chosen race, a royal
priesthood, a people set apart as your eternal possession.
May all those you have called to walk in the splendor of
the new light render you fitting service and adoration.

Advent: Christ our King will come to us, the Lamb of
            God foretold by John.

Antiphon 3

Advent: I am coming soon, says the Lord; I will give to
            everyone the reward his deeds deserve.

The following canticle is said with the **Alleluia** when Evening
Prayer is sung; when the office is recited, the **Alleluia** may be
said at the beginning and end of each strophe.

Canticle   See Revelation 19:1-7

The wedding of the Lamb

Alleluia.
Salvation, glory, and power to our God:
(R. Alleluia.)
his judgments are honest and true.
R. Alleluia (alleluia).

Alleluia.
Sing praise to our God, all you his servants;
(R. Alleluia.)
all who worship him reverently, great and small.
R. Alleluia (alleluia).

Alleluia.
The Lord our all-powerful God is King,
(R. Alleluia.)
let us rejoice, sing praise, and give him glory.
R. Alleluia (alleluia).

Alleluia.
The wedding feast of the Lamb has begun,
(R. Alleluia.)
and his bride is prepared to welcome him.
R. Alleluia (alleluia).

Advent: I am coming soon, says the Lord; I will give to
everyone the reward his deeds deserve.

Reading, responsory, antiphon for the canticle of Mary,
intercessions and prayer, as in the Proper of Seasons.

Conclusion, as in the Ordinary.

MONDAY, WEEK I

Invitatory

Lord, open my lips.

Antiphon, as in the Ordinary, 647.

Invitatory Psalm, 648.

Office of Readings

God, come to my assistance. Glory to the Father. As it was in the beginning. Alleluia.

This verse and response are omitted when the hour begins with the invitatory.

HYMN

O God of truth, prepare our minds
To hear and heed your holy word;
Fill every heart that longs for you
With your mysterious presence, Lord.

Almighty Father, with your Son
And blessed Spirit, hear our prayer;
Teach us to love eternal truth
And seek its freedom everywhere.

Melody: Warrington L. M.   Music: R. Harrison, 1748–1810
                                                      Text: Stanbrook Abbey

PSALMODY

Ant. 1   Show me your mercy, Lord, and keep me safe.

Psalm 6

A suffering man cries to God for mercy

I am filled with dismay . . . Father, save me from this hour (John 12:27).

Lord, do not reprove me in your anger;
punish me not in your rage.

Have mercy on me, Lord, I have no strength;
Lord, heal me, my body is racked;
my soul is racked with pain.

But you, O Lord . . . how long?
Return, Lord, rescue my soul.
Save me in your merciful love,
for in death no one remembers you;
from the grave, who can give you praise?

I am exhausted with my groaning;
every night I drench my pillow with tears;
I bedew my bed with weeping.
My eye wastes away with grief;
I have grown old surrounded by my foes.

Leave me, all you who do evil;
for the Lord has heard my weeping.
The Lord has heard my plea;
the Lord will accept my prayer.
All my foes will retire in confusion,
foiled and suddenly confounded.

Psalm-prayer

Lord God, you love mercy and tenderness; you give
life and overcome death. Look upon the many wounds of
your Church; restore it to health by your risen Son, so
that it may sing a new song in your praise.

Ant.   Show me your mercy, Lord, and keep me safe.

Ant. 2   The poor are not alone in their distress; God is
here to help them.

Psalm 9A

Thanksgiving for victory

You will come again to judge the living and the dead.

I

I will praise you, Lord, with all my heart;
I will recount all your wonders.
I will rejoice in you and be glad,
and sing psalms to your name, O Most High.

See how my enemies turn back,
how they stumble and perish before you.
You upheld the justice of my cause;
you sat enthroned, judging with justice.

You have checked the nations, destroyed the wicked;
you have wiped out their name for ever and ever.
The foe is destroyed, eternally ruined.
You uprooted their cities: their memory has
    perished.

But the Lord sits enthroned for ever.
He has set up his throne for judgment;
he will judge the world with justice,
he will judge the peoples with his truth.

For the oppressed let the Lord be a stronghold,
a stronghold in times of distress.
Those who know your name will trust you:
you will never forsake those who seek you.

Ant.   The poor are not alone in their distress; God is
        here to help them.

Ant. 3 I will be the herald of your praises, Lord, where
        the people of Zion gather.

II

Sing psalms to the Lord who dwells in Zion.
Proclaim his mighty works among the peoples;
for the Avenger of blood has remembered them,
has not forgotten the cry of the poor.

Have pity on me, Lord, see my sufferings,
you who save me from the gates of death;
that I may recount all your praise
at the gates of the city of Zion
and rejoice in your saving help.

The nations have fallen in the pit which they made,
their feet caught in the snare they laid.
The Lord has revealed himself, and given judgment.
The wicked are snared in the work of their own
hands.

Let the wicked go down among the dead,
all the nations forgetful of God.
For the needy shall not always be forgotten
nor the hopes of the poor be in vain.

Arise, Lord, let men not prevail!
Let the nations be judged before you.
Lord, strike them with terror,
let the nations know they are but men.

Psalm-prayer

Lord God, when you judge, do not be deaf to the
shouts of the poor; bring havoc to the madness of
oppressors. Look at our wounds and save us from the
gates of death, so that we may always rejoice in your help
and speak your praise in the gates of Zion.

Ant. I will be the herald of your praises, Lord, where
the people of Zion gather.

Verse, reading and prayer, as in the Proper of Seasons.

Morning Prayer

God, come to my assistance. Glory to the Father. As it
was in the beginning. Alleluia.

This verse and response are omitted when the hour begins with the invitatory.

HYMN

Brightness of the Father's glory
Springing from eternal light,
Source of light by light engendered,
Day enlightening every day,

In your ever-lasting radiance
Shine upon us, Christ, true sun,
Bringing life to mind and body
Through the Holy Spirit's pow'r.

Father of unfading glory
Rich in grace and strong to save,
Hear our prayers and come to save us,
Keep us far from sinful ways.

Dawn is drawing ever nearer,
Dawn that brings us all we seek,
Son who dwells within the Father,
Father uttering one Word.

Glory be to God the Father,
Glory to his Only Son,
Glory now and through all ages
To the Spirit Advocate.

Melody: Halton Holgate   Music: William Boyce, c. 1710-1779
87.87   Text: Mount Saint Bernard Abbey

PSALMODY

Ant. 1 I lift up my heart to you, O Lord, and you will
        hear my morning prayer.

Psalm 5: 2-10, 12-13

A morning prayer asking for help

Those who welcome the Word as the guest of their hearts will have abiding joy.

To my words give ear, O Lord,
give heed to my groaning.
Attend to the sound of my cries,
my King and my God.

It is you whom I invoke, O Lord.
In the morning you hear me;
in the morning I offer you my prayer,
watching and waiting.

You are no God who loves evil;
no sinner is your guest.
The boastful shall not stand their ground
before your face.

You hate all who do evil:
you destroy all who lie.
The deceitful and bloodthirsty man
the Lord detests.

But I through the greatness of your love
have access to your house.
I bow down before your holy temple,
filled with awe.

Lead me, Lord, in your justice,
because of those who lie in wait;
make clear your way before me.

No truth can be found in their mouths,
their heart is all mischief,
their throat a wide-open grave,
all honey their speech.

All those you protect shall be glad
and ring out their joy.
You shelter them; in you they rejoice,
those who love your name.

It is you who bless the just man, Lord:
you surround him with favor as with a shield.

Psalm-prayer

Lord, all justice and all goodness come from you; you
hate evil and abhor lies. Lead us, your servants, in the
path of your justice, so that all who hope in you may
rejoice with the Church and in Christ.

Ant. I lift up my heart to you, O Lord, and you will
hear my morning prayer.

Ant. 2 We praise your glorious name, O Lord, our
God.

Canticle 1 Chronicles 29:10-13

Glory and honor are due to God alone

Blessed be the God and Father of our Lord Jesus Christ
(Ephesians 1:3).

Blessed may you be, O Lord,
God of Israel our father,
from eternity to eternity.

Yours, O Lord, are grandeur and power,
majesty, splendor, and glory.

For all in heaven and on earth is yours;
yours, O Lord, is the sovereignty:
you are exalted as head over all.

Riches and honor are from you,
and you have dominion over all.
In your hand are power and might;
it is yours to give grandeur and strength to all.

401-12-O

Therefore, our God, we give you thanks
and we praise the majesty of your name.

Ant.   We praise your glorious name, O Lord, our God.

Ant. 3   Adore the Lord in his holy court.

Psalm 29
A tribute of praise to the Word of God

The Father's voice proclaimed: "This is my beloved Son"
(Matthew 3:17).

O give the Lord, you sons of God,
give the Lord glory and power;
give the Lord the glory of his name.
Adore the Lord in his holy court.

The Lord's voice resounding on the waters,
the Lord on the immensity of waters;
the voice of the Lord, full of power,
the voice of the Lord, full of splendor.

The Lord's voice shattering the cedars,
the Lord shatters the cedars of Lebanon;
he makes Lebanon leap like a calf
and Sirion like a young wild-ox.

The Lord's voice flashes flames of fire.

The Lord's voice shaking the wilderness,
the Lord shakes the wilderness of Kadesh;
the Lord's voice rending the oak tree
and stripping the forest bare.

The God of glory thunders.
In his temple they all cry: "Glory!"
The Lord sat enthroned over the flood;
the Lord sits as king for ever.

The Lord will give strength to his people,
the Lord will bless his people with peace.

Psalm-prayer

You live for ever, Lord and King. All things of the earth justly sing your glory and honor. Strengthen your people against evil that we may rejoice in your peace and trust in your eternal promise.

Ant.   Adore the Lord in his holy court.

Reading, responsory, antiphon for the canticle of Zechariah, intercessions and prayer, as in the Proper of Seasons.

Conclusion, as in the Ordinary.

Daytime Prayer

God, come to my assistance. Glory to the Father. As it was in the beginning. Alleluia.

Hymn, as in the Ordinary, 658.

Psalmody

Antiphon, as in the Proper of Seasons.

Psalm 19B

Praise of God who gave us the law of love

You must be perfect as your heavenly Father is perfect (Matthew 5:48).

The law of the Lord is perfect,
it revives the soul.
The rule of the Lord is to be trusted,
it gives wisdom to the simple.

The precepts of the Lord are right,
they gladden the heart.
The command of the Lord is clear,
it gives light to the eyes.

The fear of the Lord is holy,
abiding for ever.

The decrees of the Lord are truth
and all of them just.

They are more to be desired than gold,
than the purest of gold
and sweeter are they than honey,
than honey from the comb.

So in them your servant finds instruction;
great reward is in their keeping.
But who can detect all his errors?
From hidden faults acquit me.

From presumption restrain your servant
and let it not rule me.
Then shall I be blameless,
clean from grave sin.

May the spoken words of my mouth,
the thoughts of my heart,
win favor in your sight, O Lord,
my rescuer, my rock!

Psalm-prayer

May our words in praise of your commandments find
favor with you, Lord. May our faith prove we are not
slaves, but sons, not so much subjected to your law as
sharing your power.

Psalm 7

Prayer of a God-fearing man who is being calumniated

Here stands the judge, at our very door (James 5:9).

I

Lord God, I take refuge in you.
From my pursuer save me and rescue me,
lest he tear me to pieces like a lion
and drag me off with no one to rescue me.

Lord God, if my hands have done wrong,
if I have paid back evil for good,
I who saved my unjust oppressor:
then let my foe pursue me and seize me,
let him trample my life to the ground
and lay my soul in the dust.

Lord, rise up in your anger,
rise against the fury of my foes;
my God, awake! You will give judgment.
Let the company of nations gather round you,
taking your seat above them on high.
The Lord is judge of the peoples.

Give judgment for me, Lord; I am just
and innocent of heart.
Put an end to the evil of the wicked!
Make the just stand firm,
you who test mind and heart,
O just God!

Psalm-prayer

Father, you weigh what is in our hearts. Free us from
oppressors, and, as we wait for your day of judgment, set
a firm guard on our thoughts, so that while we return
good for evil, we may still praise your kind of justice.

II

God is the shield that protects me,
who saves the upright of heart.
God is a just judge
slow to anger;
but he threatens the wicked every day,
men who will not repent.

God will sharpen his sword;
he has braced his bow and taken aim.

For them he has prepared deadly weapons;
he barbs his arrows with fire.
Here is one who is pregnant with malice,
conceives evil and brings forth lies.

He digs a pitfall, digs it deep;
and in the trap he has made he will fall.
His malice will recoil on himself;
on his own head his violence will fall.

I will thank the Lord for his justice:
I will sing to the Lord, the Most High.

Psalm-prayer

You know our hearts, Lord, but you are slow to anger
and merciful in judging. Come, examine your Church,
wash her clean of sin and great crowds will surround you
with songs of praise.

At the other hours, the complementary psalmody is used, 1191.
Reading, verse and prayer, as in the Proper of Seasons.
Conclusion, as in the Ordinary.

Evening Prayer

God, come to my assistance. Glory to the Father. As it
was in the beginning. Alleluia.

HYMN

Lord Jesus Christ, abide with us,
Now that the sun has run its course;
Let hope not be obscured by night,
But may faith's darkness be as light.

Lord Jesus Christ, grant us your peace,
And when the trials of earth shall cease;
Grant us the morning light of grace,
The radiant splendor of your face.

Immortal, Holy, Threefold Light,
Yours be the kingdom, pow'r, and might;

All glory be eternally
To you, life giving Trinity!

Melody: Old 100th L.M.   Music: Louis Bourgeois, 1551
                              Text: Saint Joseph's Abbey, 1967, 1968

PSALMODY

Ant. 1   The Lord looks tenderly on those who are poor.

Psalm 11
God is the unfailing support of the just

Blessed are those who hunger and thirst for justice; they shall be satisfied (Matthew 5:6).

In the Lord I have taken my refuge.
How can you say to my soul:
"Fly like a bird to its mountain.

See the wicked bracing their bow;
they are fixing their arrows on the string
to shoot upright men in the dark.
Foundations once destroyed, what can the just do?"

The Lord is in his holy temple,
the Lord, whose throne is in heaven.
His eyes look down on the world;
his gaze tests mortal men.

The Lord tests the just and the wicked:
the lover of violence he hates.
He sends fire and brimstone on the wicked;
he sends a scorching wind as their lot.

The Lord is just and loves justice:
the upright shall see his face.

Psalm-prayer

Lord God, you search the hearts of all, both the good and the wicked. May those who are in danger for love of you, find security in you now, and, in the day of judgment, may they rejoice in seeing you face to face.

Ant. The Lord looks tenderly on those who are poor.

Ant. 2 Blessed are the pure of heart, for they shall see God.

Psalm 15

Who is worthy to stand in God's presence?

You have come to Mount Zion, to the city of the living God (Hebrews 12:22).

Lord, who shall be admitted to your tent
and dwell on your holy mountain?

He who walks without fault;
he who acts with justice
and speaks the truth from his heart;
he who does not slander with his tongue;

he who does no wrong to his brother,
who casts no slur on his neighbor,
who holds the godless in disdain,
but honors those who fear the Lord;

he who keeps his pledge, come what may;
who takes no interest on a loan
and accepts no bribes against the innocent.
Such a man will stand firm for ever.

Psalm-prayer

Make our lives blameless, Lord. Help us to do what is right and to speak what is true that we may dwell in your tent and find rest on your holy mountain.

Ant. Blessed are the pure of heart, for they shall see God.

Ant. 3 God chose us in his Son to be his adopted children.

Canticle   Ephesians 1:3-10

God our Savior

Praised be the God and Father
of our Lord Jesus Christ,
who has bestowed on us in Christ
every spiritual blessing in the heavens.

God chose us in him
before the world began
to be holy
and blameless in his sight.

He predestined us
to be his adopted sons through Jesus Christ,
such was his will and pleasure,
that all might praise the glorious favor
he has bestowed on us in his beloved.

In him and through his blood, we have been
    redeemed,
and our sins forgiven,
so immeasurably generous
is God's favor to us.

God has given us the wisdom
to understand fully the mystery,
the plan he was pleased
to decree in Christ.

A plan to be carried out
in Christ, in the fullness of time,
to bring all things into one in him,
in the heavens and on earth.

Ant. God chose us in his Son to be his adopted
      children.

Reading, responsory, antiphon for the canticle of Mary,
intercessions and prayer, as in the Proper of Seasons.

Conclusion, as in the Ordinary.

TUESDAY, WEEK I

Invitatory

Lord, open my lips.

Antiphon, as in the Ordinary, 647.

Invitatory psalm, 648.

Office of Readings

God, come to my assistance. Glory to the Father. As it was in the beginning. Alleluia.

This verse and response are omitted when the hour begins with the invitatory.

HYMN

Lord, your word abiding,
And our footsteps guiding,
Gives us joy for ever,
Shall desert us never.

Who can tell the pleasure,
Who recount the treasure,
By your word imparted
To the simplehearted?

Word of mercy giving
Succor to the living;
Word of life supplying
Comfort to the dying.

O that we, discerning
Its most holy learning,
Lord, may love and fear you,
Evermore be near you.

Melody: Ravenshaw 66.66

Music: *Ave Hierarchia*, M. Weisse,
1480-1534,
adapted by W. H. Monk, 1823-1889
Text: Henry Williams Baker, 1821-
1877, adapted by Anthony G. Petti

Or:

Lord Jesus, once you spoke to men
Upon the mountain, in the plain;
O help us listen now, as then,
And wonder at your words again.

We all have secret fears to face,
Our minds and motives to amend;
We seek your truth, we need your grace,
Our living Lord and present Friend.

The Gospel speaks, and we receive
Your light, your love, your own command,
O help us live what we believe
In daily work of heart and hand.

Melody: O Jesu, mi dulcissime
L.M.

Music: *Clausener Gesangbuch,* 1653
Text: H. C. A. Gaunt, 1902-

PSALMODY

Ant. 1 **The Lord is just; he will defend the poor.**

Psalm 10

Prayer of thanksgiving

Blessed are the poor; the kingdom of heaven is theirs (Luke 6:20).

I

Lord, why do you stand afar off
and hide yourself in times of distress?
The poor man is devoured by the pride of the wicked:
he is caught in the schemes that others have made.

For the wicked man boasts of his heart's desires;
the covetous blasphemes and spurns the Lord.
In his pride the wicked says: "He will not punish.
There is no God." Such are his thoughts.

His path is ever untroubled;
your judgment is far from his mind.
His enemies he regards with contempt.
He thinks: "Never shall I falter:
misfortune shall never be my lot."

His mouth is full of cursing, guile, oppression,
mischief and deceit under his tongue.
He lies in wait among the reeds;
the innocent he murders in secret.

His eyes are on the watch for the helpless man.
He lurks in hiding like a lion in his lair;
he lurks in hiding to seize the poor;
he seizes the poor man and drags him away.

He crouches, preparing to spring,
and the helpless fall beneath his strength.
He thinks in his heart: "God forgets,
he hides his face, he does not see."

Ant.   The Lord is just; he will defend the poor.

Ant. 2   Lord, you know the burden of my sorrow.

II

Arise then, Lord, lift up your hand!
O God, do not forget the poor!
Why should the wicked spurn the Lord
and think in his heart: "He will not punish"?

But you have seen the trouble and sorrow,
you note it, you take it in hand.
The helpless trusts himself to you;
for you are the helper of the orphan.

Break the power of the wicked and the sinner!
Punish his wickedness till nothing remains!
The Lord is king for ever and ever.
The heathen shall perish from the land he rules.

Lord, you hear the prayer of the poor;
you strengthen their hearts; you turn your ear
to protect the rights of the orphan and oppressed:
so that mortal man may strike terror no more.

Psalm-prayer

Rise up, Lord, in defense of your people, do not hide
your face from our troubles. Father of orphans, wealth of
the poor, we rejoice in making you known; may we find
comfort and security in times of pain and anxiety.

Ant.   Lord, you know the burden of my sorrow.

Ant. 3   The words of the Lord are true, like silver from
         the furnace.

Psalm 12

A cry for God's help against powerful oppressors

The Father sent his Son into the World to defend the poor
(Saint Augustine).

Help, O Lord, for good men have vanished:
truth has gone from the sons of men.
Falsehood they speak one to another,
with lying lips, with a false heart.

May the Lord destroy all lying lips,
the tongue that speaks high-sounding words,
those who say:"Our tongue is our strength;
our lips are our own, who is our master?"

"For the poor who are oppressed and the needy who
    groan
I myself will arise," says the Lord.
"I will grant them the salvation for which they
    thirst."

The words of the Lord are words without alloy,
silver from the furnace, seven times refined.

It is you, O Lord, who will take us in your care
and protect us for ever from this generation.
See how the wicked prowl on every side,
while the worthless are prized highly by the sons of
    men.

Psalm-prayer

Your light is true light, Lord, and your truth shines
like the day. Direct us to salvation through your
life-giving words. May we be saved by always embracing
your word.

Ant.   The words of the Lord are true, like silver from
       the furnace.

Verse, reading and prayer, as in the Proper of Seasons.

Morning Prayer

God, come to my assistance. Glory to the Father. As it
was in the beginning. Alleluia.

This verse and response are omitted when the hour begins with
the invitatory.

HYMN

Antiphon:
Sion, sing, break into song!
For within you is the Lord
With his saving power.

Rise and shine forth, for your light has come,
And upon you breaks the glory of the Lord;
For the darkness covers the earth,
And the thick clouds, the people.

Antiphon

But upon you the Lord shall dawn,
And in you his splendor shall be revealed;
Your light shall guide the Gentiles on their path,
And kings shall walk in your brightness.

Antiphon

Wonder and thanksgiving shall fill your heart,
As the wealth of nations enriches you;
You shall be called the City of the Lord,
Dear to the Holy One of Israel.

Antiphon

You who were desolate and alone,
A place unvisited by men,
Shall be the pride of ages untold,
And everlasting joy to the nations.

Antiphon

No more shall the sun be your light by day,
Nor the moon's beam enlighten you by night;
The Lord shall be your everlasting light,
And your God shall be your glory.

Antiphon

No more for you the setting of suns,
No more the waning of moons;
The Lord shall be your everlasting light,
And the days of your mourning shall come to an end.

Antiphon

Melody: Sion, Sing   Music: Lucien Deiss, C.S.Sp., 1965
                            Text: Lucien Deiss, C.S.Sp., 1965

PSALMODY

Ant. 1   **The man whose deeds are blameless and whose
         heart is pure will climb the mountain of the
         Lord.**

When psalm 24 is the invitatory psalm, psalm 95, **648,** is used
as the first psalm of Morning Prayer.

Psalm 24

The Lord's entry into his temple

Christ opened heaven for us in the manhood he assumed
(Saint Irenaeus).

The Lord's is the earth and its fullness,
the world and all its peoples.
It is he who set it on the seas;
on the waters he made it firm.

Who shall climb the mountain of the Lord?
Who shall stand in his holy place?
The man with clean hands and pure heart,
who desires not worthless things,
who has not sworn so as to deceive his neighbor.

He shall receive blessings from the Lord
and reward from the God who saves him.
Such are the men who seek him,
seek the face of the God of Jacob.

O gates, lift high your heads;
grow higher, ancient doors.
Let him enter, the king of glory!

Who is the king of glory?
The Lord, the mighty, the valiant,
the Lord, the valiant in war.

O gates, lift high your heads;
grow higher, ancient doors.
Let him enter, the king of glory!

Who is he, the king of glory?
He, the Lord of armies,
he is the king of glory.

Psalm-prayer

King of glory, Lord of power and might, cleanse our
hearts from all sin, preserve the innocence of our hands,
and keep our minds from vanity, so that we may deserve
your blessing in your holy place.

Ant.   The man whose deeds are blameless and whose
        heart is pure will climb the mountain of the Lord.

Ant. 2 Praise the eternal King in all your deeds.

401-12-I

Canticle   Tobit 13:1-8

God afflicts but only to heal

Blessed be the God and Father of our Lord Jesus Christ, who in his great love for us has brought us to a new birth (1 Peter 1:3).

Blessed be God who lives forever,
because his kingdom lasts for all ages.

For he scourges and then has mercy;
he casts down to the depths of the nether world,
and he brings up from the great abyss.
No one can escape his hand.

Praise him, you Israelites, before the Gentiles,
for though he has scattered you among them,
he has shown you his greatness even there.

Exalt him before every living being,
because he is the Lord our God,
our Father and God forever.

He scourged you for your iniquities,
but will again have mercy on you all.
He will gather you from all the Gentiles
among whom you have been scattered.

When you turn back to him with all your heart,
to do what is right before him,
then he will turn back to you,
and no longer hide his face from you.

So now consider what he has done for you,
and praise him with full voice.
Bless the Lord of righteousness,
and exalt the King of the ages.

In the land of my exile I praise him,
and show his power and majesty to a sinful nation.

"Turn back, you sinners! do the right before him:
perhaps he may look with favor upon you
and show you mercy.

"As for me, I exalt my God,
and my spirit rejoices in the King of heaven.
Let all men speak of his majesty,
and sing his praises in Jerusalem."

Ant.   Praise the eternal King in all your deeds.

Ant. 3   The loyal heart must praise the Lord.

Psalm 33

Song of praise for God's continual care

Through the Word all things were made (John 1:3).

Ring out your joy to the Lord, O you just;
for praise is fitting for loyal hearts.

Give thanks to the Lord upon the harp,
with a ten-stringed lute sing him songs.
O sing him a song that is new,
play loudly, with all your skill.

For the word of the Lord is faithful
and all his works to be trusted.
The Lord loves justice and right
and fills the earth with his love.

By his word the heavens were made,
by the breath of his mouth all the stars.
He collects the waves of the ocean;
he stores up the depths of the sea.

Let all the earth fear the Lord,
all who live in the world revere him.
He spoke; and it came to be.
He commanded; it sprang into being.

He frustrates the designs of the nations,
he defeats the plans of the peoples.
His own designs shall stand for ever,
the plans of his heart from age to age.

They are happy, whose God is the Lord,
the people he has chosen as his own.
From the heavens the Lord looks forth,
he sees all the children of men.

From the place where he dwells he gazes
on all the dwellers on the earth,
he who shapes the hearts of them all
and considers all their deeds.

A king is not saved by his army,
nor a warrior preserved by his strength.
A vain hope for safety is the horse;
despite its power it cannot save.

The Lord looks on those who revere him,
on those who hope in his love,
to rescue their souls from death,
to keep them alive in famine.

Our soul is waiting for the Lord.
The Lord is our help and our shield.
In him do our hearts find joy.
We trust in his holy name.

May your love be upon us, O Lord,
as we place all our hope in you.

Psalm-prayer

Nourish your people, Lord, for we hunger for your
word. Rescue us from the death of sin and fill us with
your mercy, that we may share your presence and the
joys of all the saints.

Ant.   The loyal heart must praise the Lord.

Reading, responsory, antiphon for the canticle of Zechariah intercessions and prayer, as in the Proper of Seasons.

Conclusion, as in the Ordinary.

Daytime Prayer

God, come to my assistance. Glory to the Father. As it was in the beginning. Alleluia.

HYMN, as in the Ordinary, 658.

PSALMODY

Antiphon, as in the Proper of Seasons.

Psalm 119:1-8

I (Aleph)

A meditation on God's law

Loving God means keeping his commandments (1 John 5:3).

They are happy whose life is blameless,
who follow God's law!
They are happy who do his will,
seeking him with all their hearts,
who never do anything evil
but walk in his ways.

You have laid down your precepts
to be obeyed with care.
May my footsteps be firm
to obey your statutes.
Then I shall not be put to shame
as I heed your commands.

I will thank you with an upright heart
as I learn your decrees.
I will obey your statutes:
do not forsake me.

Psalm-prayer

Lord God, you proclaim victorious those whose lives
are blameless and give your law to those who seek it.
Make us seek your righteous ways in our hearts.

Psalm 13

The lament of the just man who does not lose hope in
God

May the God of hope fill you with every joy (Romans
15:13).

How long, O Lord, will you forget me?
How long will you hide your face?
How long must I bear grief in my soul,
this sorrow in my heart day and night?
How long shall my enemy prevail?

Look at me, answer me, Lord my God!
Give light to my eyes lest I fall asleep in death,
lest my enemy say: "I have overcome him";
lest my foes rejoice to see my fall.

As for me, I trust in your merciful love.
Let my heart rejoice in your saving help:
Let me sing to the Lord for his goodness to me,
singing psalms to the name of the Lord, the Most
High.

Psalm-prayer

Saving God, by the resurrection of your Son, you have
given light to our eyes, and they shall not sleep in death
for ever. Look upon the sufferings of your Church so that
our hearts may rejoice in your saving help and sing you
songs of praise.

Psalm 14

The foolishness of sinners

Sin has increased but grace has far surpassed it (Romans 5:20).

The fool has said in his heart:
"There is no God above."
Their deeds are corrupt, depraved;
not a good man is left.

From heaven the Lord looks down
on the sons of men
to see if any are wise,
if any seek God.

All have left the right path,
depraved, every one:
there is not a good man left,
no, not even one.

Will the evil-doers not understand?
They eat up my people
as though they were eating bread:
they never pray to the Lord.

See how they tremble with fear
without cause for fear:
for God is with the just.
You may mock the poor man's hope,
but his refuge is the Lord.

O that Israel's salvation might come from Zion!
When the Lord delivers his people from bondage,
then Jacob will be glad and Israel rejoice.

Psalm-prayer

God of wisdom and truth, without you neither truth
nor holiness can survive. Safeguard the Church you have
gathered into one and make us glad in proclaiming you.

At the other hours, the complementary psalmody is used, **1191**.

Reading, verse and prayer, as in the Proper of Seasons.

Conclusion, as in the Ordinary.

Evening Prayer

God, come to my assistance. Glory to the Father. As it
was in the beginning. Alleluia.

HYMN

> The setting sun now dies away,
> And darkness comes at close of day;
> Your brightest beams, dear Lord, impart,
> And let them shine within our heart.
>
> We praise your name with joy this night:
> Please watch and guide us till the light;
> Joining the music of the blest,
> O Lord, we sing ourselves to rest.
>
> To God the Father, God the Son,
> And Holy Spirit, Three in One,
> Trinity blest, whom we adore,
> Be praise and glory evermore.

Melody: Angelus L.M.   Music: Georg Joseph, 1657
                                        Text : *Jam sol recedit igneus*
                        Translator: Geoffrey Laycock; translation
                                    based on version in *Primer*, 1706

PSALMODY

Ant. 1   God has crowned his Christ with victory.

Psalm 20

A prayer for the king's victory

Whoever calls upon the name of the Lord will be saved (Acts 2:21).

May the Lord answer in time of trial;
may the name of Jacob's God protect you.

May he send you help from his shrine
and give you support from Zion.
May he remember all your offerings
and receive your sacrifice with favor.

May he give you your heart's desire
and fulfill every one of your plans.
May we ring out our joy at your victory
and rejoice in the name of our God.
May the Lord grant all your prayers.

I am sure now that the Lord
will give victory to his anointed,
will reply from his holy heaven
with the mighty victory of his hand.

Some trust in chariots or horses,
but we in the name of the Lord.
They will collapse and fall,
but we shall hold and stand firm.

Give victory to the king, O Lord,
give answer on the day we call.

Psalm-prayer

Lord, you accepted the perfect sacrifice of your Son upon the cross. Hear us during times of trouble and protect us by the power of his name, that we who share his struggle on earth may merit a share in his victory.

Ant.   God has crowned his Christ with victory.

Ant. 2   We celebrate your mighty works with songs of
         praise, O Lord.

Psalm 21:2-8, 14

Thanksgiving for the king's victory

He accepted life that he might rise and live for ever (Saint
Hilary).

O Lord, your strength gives joy to the king;
how your saving help makes him glad!
You have granted him his heart's desire;
you have not refused the prayer of his lips.

You came to meet him with the blessings of success,
you have set on his head a crown of pure gold.
He asked you for life and this you have given,
days that will last from age to age.

Your saving help has given him glory.
You have laid upon him majesty and splendor,
you have granted your blessings to him for ever.
You have made him rejoice with the joy of your
     presence.

The king has put his trust in the Lord:
through the mercy of the Most High he shall stand
     firm.
O Lord, arise in your strength,
we shall sing and praise your power.

Psalm-prayer

Father, you have given us life on this earth and have
met us with the grace of redemption. Bestow your
greatest blessing on us, the fullness of eternal life.

Ant.   We celebrate your mighty works with songs of
         praise, O Lord.

Ant. 3 Lord, you have made us a kingdom and priests for God our Father.

Canticle Revelation 4:11; 5:9, 10, 12

Redemption hymn

O Lord our God, you are worthy
to receive glory and honor and power.

For you have created all things;
by your will they came to be and were made.

Worthy are you, O Lord,
to receive the scroll and break open its seals.

For you were slain;
with your blood you purchased for God
men of every race and tongue,
of every people and nation.

You made of them a kingdom,
and priests to serve our God,
and they shall reign on the earth.

Worthy is the Lamb that was slain
to receive power and riches,
wisdom and strength,
honor and glory and praise.

Ant. Lord, you have made us a kingdom and priests for God our Father.

Reading, responsory, antiphon for the canticle of Mary, intercessions and prayer, as in the Proper of Seasons.

Conclusion, as in the Ordinary.

WEDNESDAY, WEEK I

Invitatory

Lord, open my lips.

Antiphon, as in the Ordinary, 647.

Invitatory psalm, 648.

Office of Readings

God, come to my assistance. Glory to the Father. As it was in the beginning. Alleluia.

This verse and response are omitted when the hour begins with the invitatory.

HYMN

> God, whose almighty word
> Chaos and darkness heard
> And took their flight:
> Hear us, we humbly pray,
> And where the Gospel day
> Sheds not its glorious ray
> Let there be light.
>
> Savior, who came to bring
> On your redeeming wing
> Healing and sight—
> Health to the sick in mind,
> Sight to the inly blind—
> O now to all mankind
> Let there be light.
>
> Spirit of truth and love,
> Lifegiving, holy dove,
> Speed forth your flight;
> Move on our planet's face,

Bearing the lamp of grace,
And in earth's darkest place
Let there be light.

Holy and blessed Three,
Glorious Trinity,
Wisdom, Love, Might,
Boundless as ocean-tide
Rolling in fullest pride,
Through the world, far and wide
Let there be light.

Melody: Moscow 664.6664   Music: Felice De Giardini,
                                              1716–1796
                                  Text: John Marriott, 1780–1835,
                                    adapted by Anthony G. Petti

PSALMODY

Ant. 1   I love you, Lord; you are my strength.

Psalm 18:2-30

Thanksgiving for salvation and victory

At that time there was a violent earthquake (Revelation 11:15).

I

I love you, Lord, my strength,
my rock, my fortress, my savior.
My God is the rock where I take refuge;
my shield, my mighty help, my stronghold.

The Lord is worthy of all praise:
when I call I am saved from my foes.

The waves of death rose about me;
the torrents of destruction assailed me;
the snares of the grave entangled me;

the traps of death confronted me.

In my anguish I called to the Lord;
I cried to my God for help.
From his temple he heard my voice;
my cry came to his ears.

Ant.   I love you, Lord; you are my strength.

Ant. 2   The Lord has saved me; he wanted me for his
own.

II

Then the earth reeled and rocked;
the mountains were shaken to their base:
they reeled at his terrible anger.
Smoke came forth from his nostrils
and scorching fire from his mouth:
coals were set ablaze by its heat.

He lowered the heavens and came down,
a black cloud under his feet.
He came enthroned on the cherubim,
he flew on the wings of the wind.

He made the darkness his covering,
the dark waters of the clouds, his tent.
A brightness shone out before him
with hailstones and flashes of fire.

The Lord thundered in the heavens;
the Most High let his voice be heard.
He shot his arrows, scattered the foe,
flashed his lightnings, and put them to flight.

The bed of the ocean was revealed;
the foundations of the world were laid bare
at the thunder of your threat, O Lord,
at the blast of the breath of your anger.

From on high he reached down and seized me;
he drew me forth from the mighty waters.
He snatched me from my powerful foe,
from my enemies whose strength I could not match.

They assailed me in the day of my misfortune,
but the Lord was my support.
He brought me forth into freedom,
he saved me because he loved me.

Ant. The Lord has saved me; he wanted me for his own.

Ant. 2 Lord, kindle a light for my guidance and scatter my darkness.

III

He rewarded me because I was just,
repaid me, for my hands were clean,
for I have kept the way of the Lord
and have not fallen away from my God.

For his judgments are all before me:
I have never neglected his commands.
I have always been upright before him;
I have kept myself from guilt.

He repaid me because I was just
and my hands were clean in his eyes.
You are loving with those who love you:
you show yourself perfect with the perfect.

With the sincere you show yourself sincere,
but the cunning you outdo in cunning.
For you save a humble people
but humble the eyes that are proud.

You, O Lord, are my lamp,
my God who lightens my darkness.

With you I can break through any barrier.
with my God I can scale any wall.

Psalm-prayer

Lord God, our strength and salvation, put in us the flame of your love and make our love for you grow to a perfect love which reaches to our neighbor.

Ant. Lord, kindle a light for my guidance and scatter my darkness.

Verse, reading and prayer, as in the Proper of Seasons.

Morning Prayer

God, come to my assistance. Glory to the Father. As it was in the beginning. Alleluia.

This verse and response are omitted when the hour begins with the invitatory.

HYMN

Morning has broken
Like the first morning,
Blackbird has spoken
Like the first bird.
Praise for the singing!
Praise for the morning!
Praise for them, springing
Fresh from the Word!

Sweet the rains new fall
Sunlit from heaven,
Like the first dew fall
On the first grass.
Praise for the sweetness

Of the wet garden,
Sprung in completeness
Where his feet pass.

Mine is the sunlight!
Mine is the morning,
Born of the one light
Eden saw play!
Praise with elation,
Praise every morning,
God's re-creation
Of the new day!

Melody: Bunessan 55.54.D

Music: Old Gaelic Melody
Text: Eleanor Farjeon, 1881–1965

Or:

Darkness has faded, night gives way to morning;
Sleep has refreshed us, now we thank our Maker,
Singing his praises, lifting up to heaven
    Hearts, minds and voices.

Father of mercies, bless the hours before us;
While there is daylight may we work to please you,
Building a city fit to be your dwelling,
    Home for all nations.

Daystar of heaven, Dawn that ends our darkness,
Sun of salvation, Lord enthroned in splendor,
Stay with us, Jesus; let your Easter glory
    Fill all creation.

Flame of the Spirit, fire with love's devotion
Hearts love created, make us true apostles;
Give us a vision wide as heav'n's horizon,
    Bright with your promise.

Father in heaven, guide your children homewards;
Jesus, our Brother, walk beside us always;

Joy-giving Spirit, make the world one people,
Sign of God's Kingdom.

Melody: Christe Sanctorum 11.11.11.5   Music: Paris *Antiphoner*,
1681
Text: James Quinn, S.J.

PSALMODY

Ant. 1   O Lord, in your light we see light itself.

Psalm 36

The malice of sinners and God's goodness

*No follower of mine wanders in the dark; he shall have the
light of life* (John 8:12).

Sin speaks to the sinner
in the depths of his heart.
There is no fear of God
before his eyes.

He so flatters himself in his mind
that he knows not his guilt.
In his mouth are mischief and deceit.
All wisdom is gone.

He plots the defeat of goodness
as he lies on his bed.
He has set his foot on evil ways,
he clings to what is evil.

Your love, Lord, reaches to heaven;
your truth to the skies.
Your justice is like God's mountain,
your judgments like the deep.

To both man and beast you give protection.
O Lord, how precious is your love.
My God, the sons of men
find refuge in the shelter of your wings.

They feast on the riches of your house;
they drink from the stream of your delight.
In you is the source of life
and in your light we see light.

Keep on loving those who know you,
doing justice for upright hearts.
Let the foot of the proud not crush me
nor the hand of the wicked cast me out.

See how the evil-doers fall!
Flung down, they shall never arise.

Psalm-prayer

Lord, you are the source of unfailing light. Give us
true knowledge of your mercy so that we may renounce
our pride and be filled with the riches of your house.

Ant.   O Lord, in your light we see light itself.

Ant. 2   O God, you are great and glorious; we marvel at
your power.

Canticle   Judith 16:2-3a, 13-15

God who created the world takes care of his people

They were singing a new song (Revelation 5:9).

Strike up the instruments,
a song to my God with timbrels,
chant to the Lord with cymbals.
Sing to him a new song,
exalt and acclaim his name.

A new hymn I will sing to my God.
O Lord, great are you and glorious,
wonderful in power and unsurpassable.

Let your every creature serve you;
for you spoke, and they were made.
You sent forth your spirit, and they were created;
no one can resist your word.

The mountains to their bases, and the seas, are
    shaken;
the rocks, like wax, melt before your glance.
But to those who fear you,
you are very merciful.

Ant.   O God, you are great and glorious; we marvel at
       your power.

Ant. 3   Exult in God's presence with hymns of praise.

Psalm 47
The Lord Jesus is King of all

*He is seated at the right hand of the Father, and his kingdom
will have no end.*

All peoples, clap your hands,
cry to God with shouts of joy!
For the Lord, the Most High, we must fear,
great king over all the earth.

He subdues peoples under us
and nations under our feet.
Our inheritance, our glory, is from him,
given to Jacob out of love.

God goes up with shouts of joy;
the Lord goes up with trumpet blast.
Sing praise for God, sing praise,
sing praise to our king, sing praise.

God is king of all the earth.
Sing praise with all your skill.
God is king over the nations;
God reigns on his holy throne.

The princes of the peoples are assembled
with the people of Abraham's God.
The rulers of the earth belong to God,
to God who reigns over all.

Psalm-prayer

God, King of all peoples and all ages, it is your victory
we celebrate as we sing with all the skill at our command.
Help us always to overcome evil by good, that we may
rejoice in your triumph for ever.

Ant.   Exult in God's presence with hymns of praise.

Reading, responsory, antiphon for the canticle of Zechariah,
intercessions and prayer, as in the Proper of Seasons.

Conclusion, as in the Ordinary.

Daytime Prayer

God, come to my assistance. Glory to the Father. As it
was in the beginning. Alleluia.

HYMN, as in the Ordinary, 658.

PSALMODY

Antiphon, as in the Proper of Seasons.

Psalm 119:9-16

II (Beth)

How shall the young remain sinless?
By obeying your word.
I have sought you with all my heart:
let me not stray from your commands.

I treasure your promise in my heart
lest I sin against you.
Blessed are you, O Lord;
teach me your statutes.

With my tongue I have recounted
the decrees of your lips.
I rejoiced to do your will
as though all riches were mine.

I will ponder all your precepts
and consider your paths.
I take delight in your statutes;
I will not forget your word.

Psalm-prayer

Lord, may we treasure your commandments as the
greatest of all riches; never let us fear that anything will
be wanting to us while you are at our side.

Psalm 17

Save me, Lord, from those who hate you

*During his life on earth . . . Jesus prayed to his Father
and was heard* (Hebrews 5:7).

I

Lord, hear a cause that is just,
pay heed to my cry.
Turn your ear to my prayer:
no deceit is on my lips.

From you may my judgment come forth.
Your eyes discern the truth.

You search my heart, you visit me by night.
You test me and you find in me no wrong.
My words are not sinful as are men's words.

I kept from violence because of your word,
I kept my feet in your paths;
there was no faltering in my steps.

I am here and I call, you will hear me, O God.
Turn your ear to me; hear my words.
Display your great love, you whose right hand saves
your friends from those who rebel against them.

Guard me as the apple of your eye.
Hide me in the shadow of your wings
from the violent attack of the wicked.

II

My foes encircle me with deadly intent.
Their hearts tight shut, their mouths speak proudly.
They advance against me, and now they surround
me.

Their eyes are watching to strike me to the ground
as though they were lions ready to claw
or like some young lion crouched in hiding.

Lord, arise, confront them, strike them down!
Let your sword rescue my soul from the wicked;
let your hand, O Lord, rescue me from men,
from men whose reward is in this present life.

You give them their fill of your treasures;
they rejoice in abundance of offspring
and leave their wealth to their children.

As for me, in my justice I shall see your face
and be filled, when I awake, with the sight of your
glory.

Psalm-prayer

Turn our eyes to see the truth of your judgments,
Lord, that, when our spirits are tried by fire, the

anticipation of seeing you may make us rejoice in your justice.

At the other hours, the complementary psalmody is used, 1191.

Reading, verse and prayer, as in the Proper of Seasons.

Conclusion, as in the Ordinary.

Evening Prayer

God, come to my assistance. Glory to the Father. As it was in the beginning. Alleluia.

Hymn

> O Father, whose creating hand
> Brings harvest from the fruitful land,
> Your providence we gladly own,
> And bring our hymns before your throne
> To praise you for the living bread
> On which our lives are daily fed.
>
> O Lord, who in the desert fed
> The hungry thousands in their need,
> Where want and famine still abound
> Let your relieving love be found,
> And in your name may we supply
> Your hungry children when they cry.
>
> O Spirit, your revealing light
> Has led our questing souls aright;
> Source of our science, you have taught
> The marvels human minds have wrought,
> So that the barren deserts yield
> The bounty by your love revealed.

Melody: Wych Cross   Music: (Wych Cross) Erik Routley, 1917-
or Melita 88.88.88   or (Melita) John B. Dykes, 1823-1876
                          Text: Donald Hughes, 1911-1967

PSALMODY

Ant. 1   The Lord is my light and my help; whom shall I
          fear?

Psalm 27

God stands by us in dangers

God now truly dwells with men (Revelation 21:3:).

I

The Lord is my light and my help;
whom shall I fear?
The Lord is the stronghold of my life;
before whom shall I shrink?

When evil-doers draw near
to devour my flesh,
it is they, my enemies and foes,
who stumble and fall.

Though an army encamp against me
my heart would not fear.
Though war break out against me
even then would I trust.

There is one thing I ask of the Lord,
for this I long,
to live in the house of the Lord,
all the days of my life,
to savor the sweetness of the Lord,
to behold his temple.

For there he keeps me safe in his tent
in the day of evil.
He hides me in the shelter of his tent,
on a rock he sets me safe.

And now my head shall be raised
above my foes who surround me
and I shall offer within his tent
a sacrifice of joy.
I will sing and make music for the Lord.

Ant.   The Lord is my light and my help; whom shall I
        fear?

Ant. 2 I long to look on you, O Lord; do not turn your
        face from me.

II

Some rose to present lies and false evidence against Jesus
(Mark 14:57).

O Lord, hear my voice when I call;
have mercy and answer.
Of you my heart has spoken:
"Seek his face."

It is your face, O Lord, that I seek;
hide not your face.
Dismiss not your servant in anger;
you have been my help.

Do not abandon or forsake me,
O God my help!
Though father and mother forsake me,
the Lord will receive me.

Instruct me, Lord, in your way;
on an even path lead me.

When they lie in ambush protect me
from my enemy's greed.
False witnesses rise against me,
breathing out fury.

I am sure I shall see the Lord's goodness
in the land of the living.
Hope in him, hold firm and take heart.
Hope in the Lord!

Psalm-prayer

Father, you protect and strengthen those who hope in
you; you heard the cry of your Son and kept him safe in
your tent in the day of evil. Grant that your servants who
seek your face in times of trouble may see your goodness
in the land of the living.

Ant.   I long to look on you, O Lord; do not turn your
face from me.

Ant. 3   He is the first-born of all creation; in every way
the primacy is his.

Canticle   Colossians 1:12-20

Christ the first-born of all creation and the first-born
from the dead

Let us give thanks to the Father
for having made you worthy
to share the lot of the saints
in light.

He rescued us
from the power of darkness
and brought us
into the kingdom of his beloved Son.
Through him we have redemption,
the forgiveness of our sins.

He is the image of the invisible God,
the first-born of all creatures.
In him everything in heaven and on earth was
created,
things visible and invisible.

All were created through him;
all were created for him.
He is before all else that is.
In him everything continues in being.

It is he who is head of the body, the church!
he who is the beginning,
the first-born of the dead,
so that primacy may be his in everything.

It pleased God to make absolute fulness reside in him
and, by means of him, to reconcile everything in his
    person,
both on earth and in the heavens,
making peace through the blood of his cross.

Ant.   He is the first-born of all creation; in every way
       the primacy is his.

Reading, responsory, antiphon for the canticle of Mary,
intercessions and prayer, as in the Proper of Seasons.

Conclusion, as in the Ordinary.

THURSDAY, WEEK I

Invitatory

Lord, open my lips.

Antiphon, as in the Ordinary, 647.

Invitatory psalm, 648.

Office of Readings

God, come to my assistance. Glory to the Father. As it was in the beginning. Alleluia.

This verse and response are omitted when the hour begins with the invitatory.

HYMN

Eternal Father, through your Word
You gave new life to Adam's race,
Transformed them into sons of light,
New creatures by your saving grace.

To you who stooped to sinful man
We render homage and all praise:
To Father, Son and Spirit blest
Whose gift to man is endless days.

Melody: Erhalt uns, Herr L.M.   Music: *Geistliche Lieder,*
                                                Wittenberg, 1543
                                      Text: Stanbrook Abbey

PSALMODY

Ant. 1   The word of the Lord is a strong shield for all who put their trust in him.

Psalm 18:31-51

Hymn of thanksgiving

If God is on our side who can be against us? (Romans 8:31).

749

IV

As for God, his ways are perfect;
the word of the Lord, purest gold.
He indeed is the shield
of all who make him their refuge.

For who is God but the Lord?
Who is a rock but our God?
The God who girds me with strength
and makes the path safe before me.

My feet you made swift as the deer's;
you have made me stand firm on the heights.
You have trained my hands for battle
and my arms to bend the heavy bow.

Ant.   The word of the Lord is a strong shield for all who
        put their trust in him.

Ant. 2   Your strong right hand has upheld me, Lord.

V

You gave me your saving shield;
you upheld me, trained me with care.
You gave me freedom for my steps;
my feet have never slipped.

I pursued and overtook my foes,
never turning back till they were slain.
I smote them so they could not rise;
they fell beneath my feet.

You girded me with strength for battle;
you made my enemies fall beneath me,
you made my foes take flight;
those who hated me I destroyed.

They cried, but there was no one to save them;
they cried to the Lord, but in vain.

I crushed them fine as dust before the wind;
trod them down like dirt in the streets.

You saved me from the feuds of the people
and put me at the head of the nations.
People unknown to me served me:
when they heard of me they obeyed me.

Foreign nations came to me cringing:
foreign nations faded away.
They came trembling out of their strongholds.

Ant.   Your strong right hand has upheld me, Lord.

Ant. 3   May the living God, my Savior, be praised for
ever.

VI

Long life to the Lord, my rock!
Praised be the God who saves me,
the God who gives me redress
and subdues people under me.

You saved me from my furious foes.
You set me above my assailants.
You saved me from violent men,
so I will praise you, Lord, among the nations:
I will sing a psalm to your name.

He has given great victories to his king
and shown his love for his anointed,
for David and his sons forever.

Psalm-prayer

Lord God, our strength and salvation, put in us the
flame of your love and make our love for you grow to a
perfect love which reaches to our neighbor.

Ant.   May the living God, my Savior, be praised for
ever.

Verse, reading and prayer, as in the Proper of Seasons.

Morning Prayer

God, come to my assistance. Glory to the Father. As it was in the beginning. Alleluia.

This verse and response are omitted when the hour begins with the invitatory.

HYMN

When morning fills the sky,
Our hearts awaking cry:
May Jesus Christ be praised.
In all our works and prayer
His Sacrifice we share:
May Jesus Christ be praised.
The night becomes as day,
When from our hearts we say:
May Jesus Christ be praised.
The powers of darkness fear
When this glad song they hear:
May Jesus Christ be praised.

In heav'n our joy will be
To sing eternally:
May Jesus Christ be praised.
Let earth and sea and sky
From depth to height reply:
May Jesus Christ be praised.
Let all the earth now sing
To our eternal King:
May Jesus Christ be praised.
By this the eternal song,
Through ages all along:
May Jesus Christ be praised.

Melody: O Seigneur   Music: Louis Bourgeois, 1500-1561
667.667.D   Text: E. Caswall, 1814-1878, alt.

PSALMODY

Ant. 1   Awake, lyre and harp, with praise let us wake
          the dawn.

Psalm 57

Morning prayer in affliction

This psalm tells of our Lord's passion (Saint Augustine).

Have mercy on me, God, have mercy
for in you my soul has taken refuge.
In the shadow of your wings I take refuge
till the storms of destruction pass by.

I call to God the Most High,
to God who has always been my help.
May he send from heaven and save me
and shame those who assail me.

May God send his truth and his love.

My soul lies down among lions,
who would devour the sons of men.
Their teeth are spears and arrows,
their tongue a sharpened sword.

O God, arise above the heavens;
may your glory shine on earth!

They laid a snare for my steps,
my soul was bowed down.
They dug a pit in my path
but fell in it themselves.

My heart is ready, O God,
my heart is ready.
I will sing, I will sing your praise.
Awake, my soul,
awake, lyre and harp,
I will awake the dawn.

I will thank you, Lord, among the peoples,
among the nations I will praise you,
for your love reaches to the heavens
and your truth to the skies.

O God, arise above the heavens;
may your glory shine on earth!

Psalm-prayer

Lord, send your mercy and your truth to rescue us
from the snares of the devil, and we will praise you
among the peoples and proclaim you to the nations,
happy to be known as companions of your Son.

Ant.   Awake, lyre and harp, with praise let us wake the
        dawn.

Ant. 2 My people, says the Lord, will be filled with my
        blessings.

                    Canticle   Jeremiah 31:10-14

The happiness of a people who have been redeemed

*Jesus was to die . . . to gather God's scattered children into
one fold* (John 11:51, 52).

Hear the word of the Lord, O nations,
proclaim it on distant coasts and say:
He who scattered Israel, now gathers them together,
he guards them as a shepherd his flock.

The Lord shall ransom Jacob,
he shall redeem him from the hand of his conqueror.

Shouting, they shall mount the heights of Zion,
they shall come streaming to the Lord's blessings:
The grain, the wine, and the oil,
the sheep and the oxen;
They themselves shall be like watered gardens,
never again shall they languish.

Then the virgins shall make merry and dance,
and young men and old as well.
I will turn their mourning into joy,
I will console and gladden them after their sorrows.
I will lavish choice portions upon the priests,
and my people shall be filled with my blessings,
says the Lord.

Ant. My people, says the Lord, will be filled with my
      blessings.

Ant. 3 The Lord is great and worthy to be praised in
        the city of our God.

Psalm 48

Thanksgiving for the people's deliverance

*He took me up a high mountain and showed me Jerusalem,
God's holy city* (Revelation 21:10).

The Lord is great and worthy to be praised
in the city of our God.
His holy mountain rises in beauty,
the joy of all the earth.

Mount Zion, true pole of the earth,
the Great King's city!
God, in the midst of its citadels,
has shown himself its stronghold.

For the kings assembled together,
together they advanced.
They saw; at once they were astounded;
dismayed, they fled in fear.

A trembling seized them there,
like the pangs of birth.
By the east wind you have destroyed
the ships of Tarshish.

As we have heard, so we have seen
in the city of our God,
in the city of the Lord of hosts
which God upholds for ever.

O God, we ponder your love
within your temple.
Your praise, O God, like your name
reaches the ends of the earth.

With justice your right hand is filled.
Mount Zion rejoices;
the people of Judah rejoice
at the sight of your judgments.

Walk through Zion, walk all round it;
count the number of its towers.
Review all its ramparts,
examine its castles,

that you may tell the next generation
that such is our God,
our God for ever and always.
It is he who leads us.

Psalm-prayer

Father, the body of your risen Son is the temple not
made by human hands and the defending wall of the new
Jerusalem. May this holy city, built of living stones,
shine with spiritual radiance and witness to your
greatness in the sight of all nations.

Ant.   The Lord is great and worthy to be praised in the
       city of our God.

Reading, responsory, antiphon for the canticle of Zechariah,
intercessions and prayer, as in the Proper of Seasons.

Conclusion, as in the Ordinary.

Daytime Prayer

God, come to my assistance. Glory to the Father. As it was in the beginning. Alleluia.

HYMN, as in the Ordinary, 658.

PSALMODY
Antiphon, as in the Proper of Seasons.

Psalm 119:17-24

III (Ghimel)

Bless your servant and I shall live
and obey your word.
Open my eyes that I may see
the wonders of your law.

I am a pilgrim on the earth;
show me your commands.
My soul is ever consumed
as I long for your decrees.

You threaten the proud, the accursed,
who turn from your commands.
Relieve me from scorn and contempt
for I do your will.

Though princes sit plotting against me
I ponder on your rulings.
Your will is my delight;
your statutes are my counsellors.

Psalm-prayer

Father, giver of all good gifts, do not let us go astray from your commands but help us to seek you with all our hearts.

Psalm 25

Prayer for God's favor and protection

Our hope will never be disappointed (Romans 5:5).

I

To you, O Lord, I lift up my soul.
I trust you, let me not be disappointed;
do not let my enemies triumph.
Those who hope in you shall not be disappointed,
but only those who wantonly break faith.

Lord, make me know your ways.
Lord, teach me your paths.
Make me walk in your truth, and teach me:
for you are God my savior.

In you I hope all day long
because of your goodness, O Lord.
Remember your mercy, Lord,
and the love you have shown from of old.
Do not remember the sins of my youth.
In your love remember me.

The Lord is good and upright.
He shows the path to those who stray,
he guides the humble in the right path;
he teaches his way to the poor.

His ways are faithfulness and love
for those who keep his covenant and law.
Lord, for the sake of your name
forgive my guilt; for it is great.

Psalm-prayer

To you, Lord, we lift up our souls; rescue us, do not let
us be put to shame for calling out to you. Do not remember the sins of our youth and stupidity, but remember us
with your love.

II

If anyone fears the Lord,
he will show him the path he should choose.

His soul shall live in happiness
and his children shall possess the land.
The Lord's friendship is for those who revere him;
to them he reveals his covenant.

My eyes are always on the Lord;
for he rescues my feet from the snare.
Turn to me and have mercy
for I am lonely and poor.

Relieve the anguish of my heart
and set me free from my distress.
See my affliction and my toil
and take all my sins away.

See how many are my foes;
how violent their hatred for me.
Preserve my life and rescue me.
Do not disappoint me, you are my refuge.
May innocence and uprightness protect me:
for my hope is in you, O Lord.

Redeem Israel, O God, from all its distress.

Psalm-prayer

Through your Son, Lord, you spared sinners to show
us your mercy and love. Do not remember our sins, but
show us your ways; relieve our distress, and satisfy the
longing of your people, so that all our hopes for eternal
peace may reach fulfillment.

At the other hours, the complementary psalmody is used, 1191.

Reading, verse and prayer, as in the Proper of Seasons.

Conclusion, as in the Ordinary.

Evening Prayer

God, come to my assistance. Glory to the Father. As it
was in the beginning. Alleluia.

Hymn

> For the fruits of his creation,
>   Thanks be to God;
> For the gifts to every nation,
>   Thanks be to God;
> For the ploughing, sowing, reaping,
> Silent growth while men are sleeping,
> Future needs in earth's safe keeping,
>   Thanks be to God.

> In the just reward of labor,
>   God's will is done;
> In the help we give our neighbor,
>   God's will is done;
> In our world-wide task of caring
> For the hungry and despairing,
> In the harvests men are sharing,
>   God's will is done;

> For the harvests of his spirit,
>   Thanks be to God;
> For the good all men inherit,
>   Thanks be to God;
> For the wonders that astound us,
> For the truths that still confound us,
> Most of all, that love has found us
>   Thanks be to God.

Melody: East Acklam 84.84.88.84
Music: Francis Jackson
Text: F. Pratt Green

PSALMODY

Ant. 1   I cried to you, Lord, and you healed me; I will
          praise you for ever.

Psalm 30

Thanksgiving for deliverance from death

Christ, risen in glory, gives continual thanks to his Father
(Cassian).

> I will praise you, Lord, you have rescued me
> and have not let my enemies rejoice over me.
>
> O Lord, I cried to you for help
> and you, my God, have healed me.
> O Lord, you have raised my soul from the dead,
> restored me to life from those who sink into the
> grave.
>
> Sing psalms to the Lord, you who love him,
> give thanks to his holy name.
> His anger lasts but a moment; his favor through life.
> At night there are tears, but joy comes with dawn.
>
> I said to myself in my good fortune:
> "Nothing will ever disturb me."
> Your favor had set me on a mountain fastness,
> then you hid your face and I was put to confusion.
>
> To you, Lord, I cried,
> to my God I made appeal:
> "What profit would my death be, my going to the
> grave?
> Can dust give you praise or proclaim your truth?"
>
> The Lord listened and had pity.
> The Lord came to my help.
> For me you have changed my mourning into
> dancing,

you removed my sackcloth and clothed me with joy.
So my soul sings psalms to you unceasingly.
O Lord my God, I will thank you for ever.

Psalm-prayer

God our Father, glorious in giving life, and even more
glorious in restoring it, when his last night on earth
came, your Son shed tears of blood, but dawn brought
incomparable gladness. Do not turn away from us, or we
shall fall back into dust, but rather turn our mourning
into joy by raising us up with Christ.

Ant.   I cried to you, Lord, and you healed me; I will
        praise you for ever.

Ant. 2 The one who is sinless in the eyes of God is
        blessed indeed.

Psalm 32

They are happy whose sins are forgiven

*David speaks of the happiness of the man who is holy in
God's eyes not because of his own worth, but because God has
justified him* (Romans 4:6).

Happy the man whose offense is forgiven,
whose sin is remitted.
O happy the man to whom the Lord
imputes no guilt,
in whose spirit is no guile.

I kept it secret and my frame was wasted.
I groaned all the day long
for night and day your hand
was heavy upon me.
Indeed, my strength was dried up
as by the summer's heat.

But now I have acknowledged my sins;
my guilt I did not hide.

I said: "I will confess
my offense to the Lord."
And you, Lord, have forgiven
the guilt of my sin.

So let every good man pray to you
in the time of need.
The floods of water may reach high
but him they shall not reach.
You are my hiding place, O Lord;
you save me from distress.
You surround me with cries of deliverance.

I will instruct you and teach you
the way you should go;
I will give you counsel
with my eye upon you.

Be not like horse and mule, unintelligent,
needing bridle and bit,
else they will not approach you.
Many sorrows has the wicked
but he who trusts in the Lord,
loving mercy surrounds him.

Rejoice, rejoice in the Lord,
exult, you just!
O come, ring out your joy,
all you upright of heart.

Psalm-prayer

You desired, Lord, to keep from us your indignation
and so did not spare Jesus Christ, who was wounded for
our sins. We are your prodigal children, but confessing
our sins we come back to you. Embrace us that we may
rejoice in your mercy together with Christ your beloved
Son.

Ant.   The one who is sinless in the eyes of God is
        blessed indeed.

Ant. 3 The Father has given Christ all power, honor
        and kingship; all people will obey him.

Canticle   Revelation 11:17-18; 12:10b-12a

The judgment of God

We praise you, the Lord God Almighty,
who is and who was.
You have assumed your great power,
you have begun your reign.

The nations have raged in anger,
but then came your day of wrath
and the moment to judge the dead:
The time to reward your servants the prophets
and the holy ones who revere you,
the great and the small alike.

Now have salvation and power come,
the reign of our God and the authority
of his Anointed One.
For the accuser of our brothers is cast out,
who night and day accused them before God.

They defeated him by the blood of the Lamb
and by the word of their testimony;
love for life did not deter them from death.
So rejoice, you heavens,
and you that dwell therein!

Ant.   The Father has given Christ all power, honor and
        kingship; all people will obey him.

Reading, responsory, antiphon for the canticle of Mary,
intercessions and prayer, as in the Proper of Seasons.

Conclusion, as in the Ordinary.

Invitatory

Lord, open my lips.

Antiphon, as in the Ordinary, 647.

Invitatory psalm, 648.

Office of Readings

God, come to my assistance. Glory to the Father. As it was in the beginning. Alleluia.

This verse and response are omitted when the hour begins with the invitatory.

HYMN

In ancient times God spoke to man
Through prophets, and in varied ways,
But now he speaks through Christ his Son,
His radiance through eternal days.

To God the Father of the world,
His Son through whom he made all things,
And holy Spirit, bond of love,
All glad creation glory sings.

Melody: Herr Jesu Christ, mein
Lebens Licht L.M.

Music: *As Hymnodus Sacer,*
Leipzig, 1625
Text: Stanbrook Abbey

PSALMODY

Ant. 1   Rise up, Lord, and come to my aid.

Psalm 35:1-2, 3c, 9-19, 22-23, 27-28

The Lord as Savior in time of persecution

They came together . . . and laid their plans to capture Jesus by treachery and put him to death (Matthew 26:3-4).

I

O Lord, plead my cause against my foes;
fight those who fight me.
Take up your buckler and shield;
arise to help me.

O Lord, say to my soul:
"I am your salvation."

But my soul shall be joyful in the Lord
and rejoice in his salvation.
My whole being will say:
"Lord, who is like you
who rescue the weak from the strong
and the poor from the oppressor?"

Lying witnesses arise
and accuse me unjustly.
They repay me evil for good:
my soul is forlorn.

Ant. Rise up, Lord, and come to my aid.

Ant. 2 All-powerful Lord, stand by me and defend
me.

II

When they were sick I went into mourning,
afflicted with fasting.
My prayer was ever on my lips,
as for a brother, a friend.
I went as though mourning a mother,
bowed down with grief.

Now that I am in trouble they gather,
they gather and mock me.
They take me by surprise and strike me
and tear me to pieces.
They provoke me with mockery on mockery
and gnash their teeth.

Ant.   All-powerful Lord, stand by me and defend me.

Ant. 3   My tongue will speak of your goodness all the day long.

III

O Lord, how long will you look on?
Come to my rescue!
Save my life from these raging beasts,
my soul from these lions.
I will thank you in the great assembly,
amid the throng I will praise you.

Do not let my lying foes
rejoice over me.
Do not let those who hate me unjustly
wink eyes at each other.

O Lord, you have seen, do not be silent,
do not stand afar off!
Awake, stir to my defense,
to my cause, O God!

Let there be joy for those who love my cause.
Let them say without end:
"Great is the Lord who delights
in the peace of his servant."
Then my tongue shall speak of your justice,
all day long of your praise.

Psalm-prayer

Lord, you rescue the poor from their oppressors, and you rose to the aid of your beloved Son against those who unjustly sought his life. Look on your Church as we journey to you, that the poor and weak may recognize the help you provide and proclaim your saving acts.

Ant.   My tongue will speak of your goodness all the day long.

Verse, reading and prayer, as in the Proper of Seasons.

Morning Prayer

God, come to my assistance. Glory to the Father. As it was in the beginning. Alleluia.

This verse and response are omitted when the hour begins with the invitatory.

HYMN

Lord, whose love in humble service
Bore the weight of human need,
Who did on the Cross, forsaken,
Show us mercy's perfect deed:
We, your servants, bring the worship
Not of voice alone, but heart;
Consecrating to your purpose
Every gift which you impart.

As we worship, grant us vision,
Till your love's revealing light,
Till the height and depth and greatness
Dawns upon our human sight;
Making known the needs and burdens
Your compassion bids us bear,
Stirring us to faithful service,
Your abundant life to share.

Called from worship into service
Forth in your great name we go,
To the child, the youth, the aged,
Love in living deeds to show.
Hope and health, goodwill and comfort,
Counsel, aid, and peace we give,
That your children, Lord, in freedom,
May your mercy know, and live.

Melody: In Babilone 87.87.D   Music: Traditional Dutch Melody
Text: Albert Bayly, 1901–

PSALMODY

Ant. 1 Lord, you will accept the true sacrifice offered on your altar.

Psalm 51

O God, have mercy on me

Your inmost being must be renewed, and you must put on the new man (Ephesians 4:23-24).

Have mercy on me, God, in your kindness.
In your compassion blot out my offense.
O wash me more and more from my guilt
and cleanse me from my sin.

My offenses truly I know them;
my sin is always before me.
Against you, you alone, have I sinned;
what is evil in your sight I have done.

That you may be justified when you give sentence
and be without reproach when you judge.
O see, in guilt I was born,
a sinner was I conceived.

Indeed you love truth in the heart;
then in the secret of my heart teach me wisdom.
O purify me, then I shall be clean;
O wash me, I shall be whiter than snow.

Make me hear rejoicing and gladness,
that the bones you have crushed may revive.
From my sins turn away your face
and blot out all my guilt.

A pure heart create for me, O God,
put a steadfast spirit within me.
Do not cast me away from your presence,
nor deprive me of your holy spirit.

401-13-O

Give me again the joy of your help;
with a spirit of fervor sustain me,
that I may teach transgressors your ways
and sinners may return to you.

O rescue me, God, my helper,
and my tongue shall ring out your goodness.
O Lord, open my lips
and my mouth shall declare your praise.

For in sacrifice you take no delight,
burnt offering from me you would refuse,
my sacrifice, a contrite spirit.
A humbled, contrite heart you will not spurn.

In your goodness, show favor to Zion:
rebuild the walls of Jerusalem.
Then you will be pleased with lawful sacrifice,
holocausts offered on your altar.

Psalm-prayer

Father, he who knew no sin was made sin for us, to save us and restore us to your friendship. Look upon our contrite heart and afflicted spirit and heal our troubled conscience, so that in the joy and strength of the Holy Spirit we may proclaim your praise and glory before all the nations.

Ant.   Lord, you will accept the true sacrifice offered on your altar.

Ant. 2 All the descendants of Israel will glory in the Lord's gift of victory.

Canticle   Isaiah 45:15-25

People of all nations will become disciples of the Lord

Every knee shall bend at the name of Jesus (Philippians 2:10).

Truly with you God is hidden,
the God of Israel, the savior!
Those are put to shame and disgrace
who vent their anger against him.
Those go in disgrace
who carve images.

Israel, you are saved by the Lord,
saved forever!
You shall never be put to shame or disgrace
in future ages.

For thus says the Lord,
the creator of the heavens,
who is God,
the designer and maker of the earth
who established it,
not creating it to be a waste,
but designing it to be lived in:

I am the Lord, and there is no other.
I have not spoken from hiding
nor from some dark place of the earth.
And I have not said to the descendants of Jacob,
"Look for me in an empty waste."
I, the Lord, promise justice,
I foretell what is right.

Come and assemble, gather together,
you fugitives from among the gentiles!
They are without knowledge who bear wooden idols
and pray to gods that cannot save.

Come here and declare
in counsel together:
Who announced this from the beginning
and foretold it from of old?
Was it not I, the Lord,

besides whom there is no other God?
There is no just and saving God but me.

Turn to me and be safe,
all you ends of the earth,
for I am God; there is no other!

By myself I swear,
uttering my just decree
and my unalterable word:

To me every knee shall bend;
by me every tongue shall swear,
saying, "Only in the Lord
are just deeds and power.

"Before him in shame shall come
all who vent their anger against him.
In the Lord shall be the vindication and the glory
of all the descendants of Israel."

Ant. All the descendants of Israel will glory in the
      Lord's gift of victory.

Ant. 3 Let us go into God's presence singing for joy.

When psalm 100 is the invitatory psalm, psalm 95, **648**, is used
as the third psalm at Morning Prayer.

Psalm 100
The joyful song of those entering God's temple

The Lord calls his ransomed people to sing songs of victory
(Saint Athanasius).

Cry out with joy to the Lord, all the earth.
Serve the Lord with gladness.
Come before him, singing for joy.

Know that he, the Lord, is God.
He made us, we belong to him,
we are his people, the sheep of his flock.

Go within his gates, giving thanks.
Enter his courts with songs of praise.
Give thanks to him and bless his name.

Indeed, how good is the Lord,
eternal his merciful love.
He is faithful from age to age.

Psalm-prayer

With joy and gladness we cry out to you, Lord, and
ask you: open our hearts to sing your praises and
announce your goodness and truth.

Ant.   Let us go into God's presence singing for joy.

Reading, responsory, antiphon for the canticle of Zechariah,
intercessions and prayer, as in the Proper of Seasons.

Conclusion, as in the Ordinary.

Daytime Prayer

God, come to my assistance. Glory to the Father. As it
was in the beginning. Alleluia.

HYMN, as in the Ordinary, 658.

PSALMODY

Antiphon, as in the Proper of Seasons.

Psalm 119:25-32

IV (Daleth)

My soul lies in the dust;
by your word revive me.
I declared my ways and you answered:
teach me your statutes.

Make me grasp the way of your precepts
and I will muse on your wonders.
My soul pines away with grief;
by your word raise me up.

Keep me from the way of error
and teach me your law.
I have chosen the way of truth
with your decrees before me.

I bind myself to do your will;
Lord, do not disappoint me.
I will run the way of your commands;
you give freedom to my heart.

Psalm-prayer

Lord, we are citizens of this earth and ask to be made
citizens of heaven by your free gift. Help us to run in the
way of your commandments and to set our hearts on you
alone.

Psalm 26

Trusting prayer of an innocent man

God chose us in Christ to be holy and sinless (Ephesians 1:4).

Give judgment for me, O Lord:
for I walk the path of perfection.
I trust in the Lord; I have not wavered.

Examine me, Lord, and try me;
O test my heart and my mind,
for your love is before my eyes
and I walk according to your truth.

I never take my place with liars
and with hypocrites I shall not go.
I hate the evil-doer's company:
I will not take my place with the wicked.

To prove my innocence I wash my hands
and take my place around your altar,
singing a song of thanksgiving,
proclaiming all your wonders.

O Lord, I love the house where you dwell,
the place where your glory abides.

Do not sweep me away with sinners,
nor my life with bloodthirsty men
in whose hands are evil plots,
whose right hands are filled with gold.

As for me, I walk the path of perfection.
Redeem me and show me your mercy.
My foot stands on level ground:
I will bless the Lord in the assembly.

Psalm-prayer

Send the fire of your Holy Spirit deep within us, Lord,
so that we can serve you with chaste bodies and please
you with pure minds.

Psalm 28:1-3, 6-9

Entreaty and thanksgiving

Father, I thank you, for you have heard me (John 11:41).

To you, O Lord, I call,
my rock, hear me.
If you do not heed I shall become
like those in the grave.

Hear the voice of my pleading
as I call for help,
as I lift up my hands in prayer
to your holy place.

Do not drag me away with the wicked,
with the evil-doers,
who speak words of peace to their neighbors
but with evil in their hearts.

Blessed be the Lord for he has heard
my cry, my appeal.
The Lord is my strength and my shield;
in him my heart trusts.

I was helped, my heart rejoices
and I praise him with my song.

The Lord is the strength of his people,
a fortress where his anointed find salvation.
Save your people; bless Israel your heritage.
Be their shepherd and carry them for ever.

Psalm-prayer

You are the strength of the people, Father. Save us
from the pit of death and unite us as one in your holy
temple, so that we may attain in our hearts the peace our
tongues proclaim.

At the other hours, the complementary psalmody is used, 1191.

Reading, verse and prayer, as in the Proper of Seasons.

Conclusion, as in the Ordinary.

Evening Prayer

God, come to my assistance. Glory to the Father. As it
was in the beginning. Alleluia.

HYMN

When, in his own image,
God created man,
He included freedom
In creation's plan.
For he loved us even
From before our birth;
By his grace he made us
Freemen of this earth.

God to man entrusted
Life as gift and aim.
Sin became our prison,
Turning hope to shame.

Man against his brother
Lifted hand and sword,
And the Father's pleading
Went unseen, unheard.

Then in time, our maker
Chose to intervene,
Set his love in person
In the human scene.
Jesus broke the circle
Of repeated sin,
So that man's devotion
Newly might begin.

Choose we now in freedom
Where we should belong,
Let us turn to Jesus,
Let our choice be strong.
May the great obedience
Which in Christ we see
Perfect all our service:
Then we shall be free!

Melody: King's Weston 65.65.D   Music: R. Vaughan Williams,
1872–1958
Text: Fred Kaan, 1929-

PSALMODY

Ant. 1   Lord, lay your healing hand upon me, for I
have sinned.

Psalm 41

Prayer of a sick person

One of you will betray me, yes, one who eats with me (Mark
14:18).

Happy the man who considers the poor and the
weak.

The Lord will save him in the day of evil,
will guard him, give him life, make him happy in the
    land
and will not give him up to the will of his foes.
The Lord will help him on his bed of pain,
he will bring him back from sickness to health.

As for me, I said: "Lord, have mercy on me,
heal my soul for I have sinned against you."
My foes are speaking evil against me.
"How long before he dies and his name be
    forgotten?"
They come to visit me and speak empty words,
their hearts full of malice, they spread it abroad.

My enemies whisper together against me.
They all weigh up the evil which is on me:
"Some deadly thing has fastened upon him,
he will not rise again from where he lies."
Thus even my friend, in whom I trusted,
who ate my bread, has turned against me.

But you, O Lord, have mercy on me.
Let me rise once more and I will repay them.
By this I shall know that you are my friend,
if my foes do not shout in triumph over me.
If you uphold me I shall be unharmed
and set in your presence for evermore.

Blessed be the Lord, the God of Israel
from age to age. Amen. Amen.

Psalm-prayer

Lord Jesus, healer of soul and body, you said: Blessed
are the merciful, they will obtain mercy. Teach us to
come to the aid of the needy in a spirit of brotherly love,
that we in turn may be received and strengthened by you.

Ant. Lord, lay your healing hand upon me, for I have
      sinned.

Ant. 2 The mighty Lord is with us; the God of Jacob is
        our stronghold.

Psalm 46

God our refuge and strength

He shall be called Emmanuel, which means: God-with-us
(Matthew 1:23).

God is for us a refuge and strength,
a helper close at hand, in time of distress:
so we shall not fear though the earth should rock,
though the mountains fall into the depths of the sea,
even though its waters rage and foam,
even though the mountains be shaken by its waves.

The Lord of hosts is with us:
the God of Jacob is our stronghold.

The waters of a river give joy to God's city,
the holy place where the Most High dwells.
God is within, it cannot be shaken;
God will help it at the dawning of the day.
Nations are in tumult, kingdoms are shaken:
he lifts his voice, the earth shrinks away.

The Lord of hosts is with us:
the God of Jacob is our stronghold.

Come, consider the works of the Lord,
the redoubtable deeds he has done on the earth.
He puts an end to wars over all the earth;
the bow he breaks, the spear he snaps.
He burns the shields with fire.
"Be still and know that I am God,
supreme among the nations, supreme on the earth!"

The Lord of hosts is with us:
the God of Jacob is our stronghold.

Psalm-prayer

All-powerful Father, the refuge and strength of your
people, you protect in adversity and defend in prosperity
those who put their trust in you. May they persevere in
seeking your will and find their way to you through
obedience.

Ant.   The mighty Lord is with us; the God of Jacob is
       our stronghold.

Ant. 3 All nations will come and worship before you,
        O Lord.

                              Canticle   Revelation 15:3-4
                    Hymn of adoration

       Mighty and wonderful are your works,
       Lord God Almighty!
       Righteous and true are your ways,
       O King of the nations!

       Who would dare refuse you honor,
       or the glory due your name, O Lord?

       Since you alone are holy,
       all nations shall come
       and worship in your presence.
       Your mighty deeds are clearly seen.

Ant.   All nations will come and worship before you, O
       Lord.

Reading, responsory, antiphon for the canticle of Mary,
intercessions and prayer, as in the Proper of Seasons.

Conclusion, as in the Ordinary.

Invitatory

Lord, open my lips.

Antiphon, as in the Ordinary, 647.

Invitatory psalm, 648.

Office of Readings

God, come to my assistance. Glory to the Father. As it was in the beginning. Alleluia.

This verse and response are omitted when the hour begins with the invitatory.

HYMN

Lord Jesus, once you spoke to men
Upon the mountain, in the plain;
O help us listen now, as then,
And wonder at your words again.

We all have secret fears to face,
Our minds and motives to amend;
We seek your truth, we need your grace,
Our living Lord and present Friend.

The Gospel speaks, and we receive
Your light, your love, your own command.
O help us live what we believe
In daily work of heart and hand.

Melody: O Jesu, mi dulcissime L.M.

Music: *Clausener
Gesangbuch*, 1653
Text: H.C.A. Gaunt, 1902

Ant. 1 Sing praise to the Lord; remember the wonders
he has wrought.

Psalm 105

The Lord is faithful to his promises

*The apostles proclaim to the nations the wonders which God
wrought when he came among us* (Saint Athanasius).

I

Give thanks to the Lord, tell his name,
make known his deeds among the peoples.

O sing to him, sing his praise;
tell all his wonderful works!
Be proud of his holy name,
let the hearts that seek the Lord rejoice.

Consider the Lord and his strength;
constantly seek his face.
Remember the wonders he has done,
his miracles, the judgments he spoke.

O children of Abraham, his servant,
O sons of the Jacob he chose.
He, the Lord, is our God:
his judgments prevail in all the earth.

He remembers his covenant for ever,
his promise for a thousand generations,
the covenant he made with Abraham,
the oath he swore to Isaac.

He confirmed it for Jacob as a law,
for Israel as a covenant for ever.
He said: "I am giving you a land,
Canaan, your appointed heritage."

When they were few in number,
a handful of strangers in the land,
when they wandered from country to country
and from one kingdom and nation to another,

he allowed no one to oppress them;
he admonished kings on their account:
"Do not touch those I have anointed;
do no harm to any of my prophets."

Ant. Sing praise to the Lord; remember the wonders he
has wrought.

Ant. 2 The Lord did not abandon the good man who
was sold into slavery, but freed him from the
power of sinners.

II

But he called down a famine on the land;
he broke the staff that supported them.
He had sent a man before them,
Joseph, sold as a slave.

His feet were put in chains,
his neck was bound with iron,
until what he said came to pass
and the word of the Lord proved him true.

Then the king sent and released him;
the ruler of the peoples set him free,
making him master of his house
and ruler of all he possessed,

to instruct his princes as he pleased
and to teach his elders wisdom.

Ant. The Lord did not abandon the good man who was
sold into slavery, but freed him from the power of
sinners.

Ant. 3   The Lord was true to his sacred promise; he led
his people to freedom and joy.

III

So Israel came into Egypt,
Jacob lived in the country of Ham.

He gave his people increase;
he made them stronger than their foes‸
whose hearts he turned to hate his people
and to deal deceitfully with his servants.

Then he sent Moses his servant
and Aaron the man he had chosen.
Through them he showed his marvels.
and his wonders in the country of Ham.

He sent darkness, and dark was made
but Egypt resisted his words.
He turned the waters into blood
and caused their fish to die.

Their land was alive with frogs,
even in the halls of their kings.
He spoke; the dog-fly came
and gnats covered the land.

He sent hail-stones in place of the rain
and flashing fire in their land.
He struck their vines and fig-trees;
he shattered the trees through their land.

He spoke; the locusts came,
young locusts, too many to be counted.
They ate up every blade in the land;
they ate up all the fruit of their fields.

He struck all the first-born in their land,
the finest flower of their sons.

He led out Israel with silver and gold.
In his tribes were none who fell behind.

Egypt rejoiced when they left
for dread had fallen upon them.
He spread a cloud as a screen
and fire to give light in the darkness.

When they asked for food he sent quails;
he filled them with bread from heaven.
He pierced the rock to give them water;
it gushed forth in the desert like a river.

For he remembered his holy word,
which he gave to Abraham his servant.
So he brought out his people with joy,
his chosen ones with shouts of rejoicing.

And he gave them the land of the nations.
They took the fruit of other men's toil,
that thus they might keep his precepts,
that thus they might observe his laws.

Psalm-prayer

Abraham, Joseph and Moses prefigured your plan,
Father, to redeem mankind from slavery and to lead
them into the land of promise. Through the death and
resurrection of your Son, your Church fulfills these
promises. Grant us living water from the rock and bread
from heaven, that we may survive our desert pilgrimage
and thank you eternally for your kindness.

Ant. The Lord was true to his sacred promise; he led
      his people to freedom and joy.

Verse, reading and prayer, as in the Proper of Seasons.

Morning Prayer

God, come to my assistance. Glory to the Father. As it was in the beginning. Alleluia.

This verse and response are omitted when the hour begins with the invitatory.

HYMN

Praise, my soul, the King of heaven;
To his feet your tribute bring;
Ransomed, healed, restored, forgiven,
Evermore his praises sing:
Alleluia! Alleluia!
Praise the everlasting King.

Praise him for his grace and favor
To his children in distress;
Praise him still the same as ever,
Slow to chide and swift to bless:
Alleluia! Alleluia!
Glorious in his faithfulness.

Father-like he tends and spares us;
Well our feeble frame he knows;
In his hand he gently bears us,
Rescues us from all our foes.
Alleluia! Alleluia!
Widely yet his mercy flows.

Angels, help us to adore him;
You behold him face to face;
Sun and moon, bow down before him,
Join the praises of our race:
Alleluia! Alleluia!
Praise with us the God of grace.

Melody: Lauda Anima 87.87.87

Music: John Goss , 1869
Text: H.F. Lyte, 1834, alt.

PSALMODY

Ant. 1   Dawn finds me ready to welcome you, my God.

Psalm 119:145-152
XIX (Koph)

I call with all my heart; Lord, hear me,
I will keep your commands;
I call upon you, save me
and I will do your will.

I rise before dawn and cry for help,
I hope in your word.
My eyes watch through the night
to ponder your promise.

In your love hear my voice, O Lord;
give me life by your decrees.
Those who harm me unjustly draw near:
they are far from your law.

But you, O Lord, are close:
your commands are truth.
Long have I known that your will
is established for ever.

Psalm-prayer

Save us by the power of your hand, Father, for our
enemies have ignored your words. May the fire of your
word consume our sins and its brightness illumine our
hearts.

Ant.   Dawn finds me ready to welcome you, my God.

Ant. 2   The Lord is my strength, and I shall sing his
praise, for he has become my Savior.

Canticle   Exodus 15:1-4a, 8-13, 17-18

Hymn of victory after the crossing of the Red Sea

Those who had conquered the beast were singing the song of Moses, God's servant (see Revelation 15:2-3).

I will sing to the Lord, for he is gloriously
   triumphant;
horse and chariot he has cast into the sea.

My strength and my courage is the Lord,
and he has been my savior.
He is my God, I praise him;
the God of my father, I extol him.

The Lord is a warrior,
Lord is his name!
Pharaoh's chariots and army he hurled into the sea.
At a breath of your anger the waters piled up,
the flowing waters stood like a mound,
   the flood waters congealed in the midst of the sea.

The enemy boasted, "I will pursue and overtake
   them;
I will divide the spoils and have my fill of them;
I will draw my sword; my hand shall despoil them!"
When your wind blew, the sea covered them;
like lead they sank in the mighty waters.

Who is like to you among the gods, O Lord?
Who is like to you, magnificent in holiness?
O terrible in renown, worker of wonders,
   when you stretched out your right hand, the earth
   swallowed them!

In your mercy you led the people you redeemed;
in your strength you guided them to your holy
   dwelling.

And you brought them in and planted them on the
    mountain of your inheritance—
the place where you made your seat, O Lord,
the sanctuary, O Lord, which your hands estab-
    lished.
The Lord shall reign forever and ever.

Ant.   The Lord is my strength, and I shall sing his
    praise, for he has become my Savior.

Ant. 3   O praise the Lord, all you nations.

Psalm 117

Praise for God's loving compassion

*I affirm that . . . the Gentile peoples are to praise God
because of his mercy* (Romans 15: 8-9).

O praise the Lord, all you nations,
acclaim him, all you peoples!

Strong is his love for us;
he is faithful for ever.

Psalm-prayer

God our Father, may all nations and peoples praise
you. May Jesus, who is called faithful and true and who
lives with you eternally, possess our hearts for ever.

Ant.   O praise the Lord, all you nations.

Reading, responsory, antiphon for the canticle of Zechariah,
intercessions and prayer, as in the Proper of Seasons.

Conclusion, as in the Ordinary.

Daytime Prayer

God, come to my assistance. Glory to the Father. As it
was in the beginning. Alleluia.

HYMN, as in the Ordinary, 658.

PSALMODY

Antiphon, as in the Proper of Seasons.

Psalm 119:33-40

V (He)

Teach me the demands of your precepts
and I will keep them to the end.
Train me to observe your law,
to keep it with my heart.

Guide me in the path of your commands;
for there is my delight.
Bend my heart to your will
and not to love of gain.

Keep my eyes from what is false:
by your word, give me life.
Keep the promise you have made
to the servant who fears you.

Keep me from the scorn I dread,
for your decrees are good.
See, I long for your precepts:
then in your justice, give me life.

Psalm-prayer

In your justice give us life, Father. Do not allow greed
to possess us but incline our hearts to your commands.
Give us understanding to know your law and direct us
according to your will.

Psalm 34

God the savior of the just

You have tasted the sweetness of the Lord (1 Peter 2:3)

I

I will bless the Lord at all times,
his praise always on my lips;

in the Lord my soul shall make its boast.
The humble shall hear and be glad.

Glorify the Lord with me.
Together let us praise his name.
I sought the Lord and he answered me;
from all my terrors he set me free.

Look towards him and be radiant;
let your faces not be abashed.
This poor man called; the Lord heard him
and rescued him from all distress.

The angel of the Lord is encamped
around those who revere him, to rescue them.
Taste and see that the Lord is good.
He is happy who seeks refuge in him.

Revere the Lord, you his saints.
They lack nothing, those who revere him.
Strong lions suffer want and go hungry
but those who seek the Lord lack no blessing.

II

Come, children, and hear me
that I may teach you the fear of the Lord.
Who is he who longs for life
and many days, to enjoy his prosperity?

Then keep your tongue from evil
and your lips from speaking deceit.
Turn aside from evil and do good;
seek and strive after peace.

The Lord turns his face against the wicked
to destroy their remembrance from the earth.
The Lord turns his eyes to the just
and his ears to their appeal.

They call and the Lord hears
and rescues them in all their distress.
The Lord is close to the broken-hearted;
those whose spirit is crushed he will save.

Many are the trials of the just man
but from them all the Lord will rescue him.
He will keep guard over all his bones,
not one of his bones shall be broken.

Evil brings death to the wicked;
those who hate the good are doomed.
The Lord ransoms the souls of his servants.
Those who hide in him shall not be condemned.

Psalm-prayer

Graciously hear us, Lord, for we seek only you. You
are near to those whose heart is right. Open yourself to
accept our sorrowful spirit; calm our bodies and minds
with the peace which surpasses understanding.

At the other hours, the complementary psalmody is used, 1191.

Reading, verse and prayer, as in the Proper of Seasons.

Conclusion, as in the Ordinary.

SUNDAY

Evening Prayer I

God, come to my assistance. Glory to the Father. As it was in the beginning. Alleluia.

HYMN, 126
Or:

At the name of Jesus
Ev'ry knee shall bow,
Ev'ry tongue confess him
King of glory now;
'Tis the Father's pleasure,
We should call him Lord,
Who from the beginning
Was the mighty Word.

Humbled for a reason,
To receive a name
From the lips of sinners,
Unto whom he came,
Faithfully he bore it,
Spotless to the last,
Brought it back victorious,
When from death he passed.

Bore it up triumphant,
With its human light,
Through all ranks of creatures,
To the central height,
To the throne of Godhead,
To the Father's breast;
Filled it with the glory
Of that perfect rest.

In your hearts enthrone him;
There, let him subdue
All that is not holy
All that is not true;
May your voice entreat him
In temptation's hour;
Let his will enfold you
In its light and power.

Brothers, this Lord Jesus
Shall return again,
With his Father's glory,
O'er the earth to reign;
He is God the Savior,
He is Christ the Lord,
Ever to be worshiped,
Always blest, adored.

Melody: King's Weston 65.65.D   Music: R. Vaughan Williams,
                                            d. 1958
                                 Text: C. Noel, d. 1877, alt.

Antiphon 1

Advent: New city of Zion, let your heart sing for joy;
          see how humbly your King comes to save you.

Psalm 119:105-112
XIV (Nun)

This is my commandment: that you should love one another
(John 15:12).

Your word is a lamp for my steps
and a light for my path.
I have sworn and have made up my mind
to obey your decrees.

Lord, I am deeply afflicted:
by your word give me life.

Accept, Lord, the homage of my lips
and teach me your decrees.

Though I carry my life in my hands,
I remember your law.
Though the wicked try to ensnare me
I do not stray from your precepts.

Your will is my heritage for ever,
the joy of my heart.
I set myself to carry out your will
in fullness, for ever.

Psalm-prayer

Let your Word, Father, be a lamp for our feet and a
light to our path, so that we may understand what you
wish to teach us and follow the path your light marks
out for us.

Advent: New city of Zion, let your heart sing for joy;
            see how humbly your King comes to save you.

Antiphon 2

Advent: Have courage, all of you, lost and fearful; take
            heart and say: Our God will come to save us,
            alleluia.

Psalm 16

The Lord himself is my heritage

The Father raised up Jesus, freeing him from the grip of
death (Acts 2:24).

Preserve me, God, I take refuge in you.
I say to the Lord: "You are my God.
My happiness lies in you alone."

He has put into my heart a marvellous love
for the faithful ones who dwell in his land.

Those who choose other gods increase their sorrows.
Never will I offer their offerings of blood.
Never will I take their name upon my lips.

O Lord, it is you who are my portion and cup;
it is you yourself who are my prize.
The lot marked out for me is my delight:
welcome indeed the heritage that falls to me!

I will bless the Lord who gives me counsel,
who even at night directs my heart.
I keep the Lord ever in my sight:
since he is at my right hand, I shall stand firm.

And so my heart rejoices, my soul is glad;
even my body shall rest in safety.
For you will not leave my soul among the dead,
nor let your beloved know decay.

You will show me the path of life,
the fullness of joy in your presence,
at your right hand happiness for ever.

Psalm-prayer

Lord Jesus, uphold those who hope in you and give us your counsel, so that we may know the joy of your resurrection and deserve to be among the saints at your right hand.

Advent: Have courage, all of you, lost and fearful; take heart and say: Our God will come to save us, alleluia.

Antiphon 3

Advent: The law was given to Moses, but grace and truth come through Jesus Christ.

Canticle   Philippians 2:6-11

Christ, God's holy servant

Though he was in the form of God,
Jesus did not deem equality with God
something to be grasped at.

Rather, he emptied himself
and took the form of a slave,
being born in the likeness of men.

He was known to be of human estate,
and it was thus that he humbled himself,
obediently accepting even death,
death on a cross!

Because of this,
God highly exalted him
and bestowed on him the name
above every other name,

So that at Jesus' name
every knee must bend
in the heavens, on the earth,
and under the earth,
and every tongue proclaim
to the glory of God the Father:
JESUS CHRIST IS LORD!

Advent: The law was given to Moses, but grace and
            truth come through Jesus Christ.

Reading, responsory, antiphon for the canticle of Mary,
intercessions and prayer, as in the Proper of Seasons.

Conclusion, as in the Ordinary.

Invitatory

Lord, open my lips.

Advent: Come, let us worship the Lord, the King who
           is to come.

Invitatory psalm, 648.

Office of Readings

God, come to my assistance. Glory to the Father. As it
was in the beginning. Alleluia.

This verse and response are omitted when the hour begins with
the invitatory.

HYMN, 121.
Or:
  Holy, holy, holy! Lord God Almighty!
  Early in the morning our song shall rise to thee:
  Holy, holy, holy! Merciful and mighty,
  God in three persons, blessed Trinity.

  Holy, holy, holy! All the saints adore thee,
  Though the eye of sinful man thy glory may not see;
  Only thou art holy; there is none beside thee,
  Which were, and are, and ever more shall be.

  Holy, Holy, Holy! Lord God Almighty!
  All thy works shall praise thy name,
  in earth, and sky and sea;
  Holy, Holy, Holy! Merciful and mighty,
  God in three persons, blessed Trinity. Amen.

Melody: Nicaea 11.12.12.10 Music: John B. Dykes, 1823-1876
          Text: Reginald Heber, 1783-1826

Antiphon 1

Advent: This is our heavenly King; he comes with
           power and might to save the nations, alleluia.

Psalm 104

Hymn to God the Creator

*To be in Christ means being a completely new creature.
Everything of the old is gone, now everything is made anew*
(2 Corinthians 5:17).

I

Bless the Lord, my soul!
Lord God, how great you are,
clothed in majesty and glory,
wrapped in light as in a robe!

You stretch out the heavens like a tent.
Above the rains you build your dwelling.
You make the clouds your chariot,
you walk on the wings of the wind,
you make the winds your messengers
and flashing fire your servants.

You founded the earth on its base,
to stand firm from age to age.
You wrapped it with the ocean like a cloak:
the waters stood higher than the mountains.

At your threat they took to flight;
at the voice of your thunder they fled.
They rose over the mountains and flowed down
to the place which you had appointed.
You set limits they might not pass
lest they return to cover the earth.

You make springs gush forth in the valleys:
they flow in between the hills.
They give drink to all the beasts of the field;
the wild-asses quench their thirst.
On their banks dwell the birds of heaven;
from the branches they sing their song.

Advent: This is our heavenly King; he comes with
           power and might to save the nations, alleluia.

Antiphon 2

Advent: Daughter of Jerusalem, rejoice and be glad;
           your King will come to you. Zion, do not fear;
           your Savior hastens on his way.

II

From your dwelling you water the hills;
earth drinks its fill of your gift.
You make the grass grow for the cattle
and the plants to serve man's needs,

that he may bring forth bread from the earth
and wine to cheer man's heart;
oil, to make him glad
and bread to strengthen man's heart.

The trees of the Lord drink their fill,
the cedars he planted on Lebanon;
there the birds build their nests:
on the tree-top the stork has her home.
The goats find a home on the mountains
and rabbits hide in the rocks.

You made the moon to mark the months;
the sun knows the time for its setting.
When you spread the darkness it is night
and all the beasts of the forest creep forth.
The young lions roar for their prey
and ask their food from God.

At the rising of the sun they steal away
and go to rest in their dens.
Man goes forth to his work,
to labor till evening falls.

Advent: Daughter of Jerusalem, rejoice and be glad;
your King will come to you. Zion, do not fear;
your Savior hastens on his way.

Antiphon 3

Advent: Let us cleanse our hearts for the coming of our
great King, that we may be ready to welcome
him; he is coming and will not delay.

III

How many are your works, O Lord!
In wisdom you have made them all.
The earth is full of your riches.

There is the sea, vast and wide,
with its moving swarms past counting,
living things great and small.
The ships are moving there
and the monsters you made to play with.

All of these look to you
to give them their food in due season.
You give it, they gather it up:
you open your hand, they have their fill.

You hide your face, they are dismayed;
you take back your spirit, they die,
returning to the dust from which they came.
You send forth your spirit, they are created;
and you renew the face of the earth.

May the glory of the Lord last for ever!
May the Lord rejoice in his works!
He looks on the earth and it trembles;
the mountains send forth smoke at his touch.

I will sing to the Lord all my life,
make music to my God while I live.

May my thoughts be pleasing to him.
I find my joy in the Lord.
Let sinners vanish from the earth
and the wicked exist no more.

Bless the Lord, my soul.

Psalm-prayer

Father, as you made springs in valleys to form streams
between mountains, so you made living streams of grace
flow from the apostles that their teaching may bring
salvation to all nations. May we have a practical
knowledge of their doctrine, be obedient to their
commands, obtain remission of sins through their
prayers, and finally receive the reward of eternal
happiness.

Advent: Let us cleanse our hearts for the coming of our
           great King, that we may be ready to welcome
           him; he is coming and will not delay.

Verse, reading and prayer, as in the Proper of Seasons.

Morning Prayer

God, come to my assistance. Glory to the Father. As it
was in the beginning. Alleluia.

This verse and response are omitted when the hour begins with
the invitatory.

HYMN, 122.

Or:

Sing with all the sons of glory,
Sing the resurrection song!
Death and sorrow, earth's dark story,
To the former days belong.

All around the clouds are breaking,
Soon the storms of time shall cease;
In God's likeness man awaking,
Knows the everlasting peace.

O what glory, far exceeding
All that eye has yet perceived!
Holiest hearts for ages pleading,
Never that full joy conceived.
God has promised, Christ prepares it,
There on high our welcome waits;
Every humble spirit shares it,
Christ has passed the eternal gates.

Life eternal! heaven rejoices:
Jesus lives who once was dead;
Join, O man, the deathless voices;
Child of God, lift up thy head!
Patriarchs from the distant ages,
Saints all longing for their heaven,
Prophets, psalmists, seers, and sages,
All await the glory given.

Life eternal! O what wonders
Crowd on faith; what joy unknown,
When, amidst earth's closing thunders,
Saints shall stand before the throne!
O to enter that bright portal,
See that glowing firmament,
Know, with thee, O God immortal,
"Jesus Christ whom thou hast sent!"

Melody: Hymn to Joy   Music: Arr. from Ludwig van Beethoven,
87.87.D   1770-1827, by Edward Hodges, 1796-1867
                             Text: William J. Irons, 1812-1883

PSALMODY

Antiphon 1

Advent: Zion is our mighty citadel, our saving Lord its
wall and its defense; throw open the gates, for
our God is here among us, alleluia.

Psalm 118

Song of joy for salvation

*This Jesus is the stone which, rejected by you builders, has
become the chief stone supporting all the rest* (Acts 4:11).

Give thanks to the Lord for he is good,
for his love endures for ever.

Let the sons of Israel say:
"His love endures for ever."
Let the sons of Aaron say:
"His love endures for ever."
Let those who fear the Lord say:
"His love endures for ever."

I called to the Lord in my distress;
he answered and freed me.
The Lord is at my side; I do not fear.
What can man do against me?
The Lord is at my side as my helper:
I shall look down on my foes.

It is better to take refuge in the Lord
than to trust in men:
it is better to take refuge in the Lord
than to trust in princes.

The nations all encompassed me;
in the Lord's name I crushed them.
They compassed me, compassed me about;
in the Lord's name I crushed them.

They compassed me about like bees;
they blazed like a fire among thorns.
In the Lord's name I crushed them.

I was hard-pressed and was falling
but the Lord came to help me.
The Lord is my strength and my song;
he is my savior.
There are shouts of joy and victory
in the tents of the just.

The Lord's right hand has triumphed;
his right hand raised me up.
The Lord's right hand has triumphed;
I shall not die, I shall live
and recount his deeds.
I was punished, I was punished by the Lord,
but not doomed to die.

Open to me the gates of holiness:
I will enter and give thanks.
This is the Lord's own gate
where the just may enter.
I will thank you for you have answered
and you are my savior.

The stone which the builders rejected
has become the corner stone.
This is the work of of the Lord,
a marvel in our eyes.
This day was made by the Lord;
we rejoice and are glad.

O Lord, grant us salvation;
O Lord, grant success.
Blessed in the name of the Lord
is he who comes.

We bless you from the house of the Lord;
the Lord God is our light.

Go forward in procession with branches
even to the altar.
You are my God, I thank you.
My God, I praise you.
Give thanks to the Lord for he is good;
for his love endures for ever.

Psalm-prayer

Lord God, you have given us the great day of rejoicing:
Jesus Christ, the stone rejected by the builders, has
become the cornerstone of the Church, our spiritual
home. Shed upon your Church the rays of your glory,
that it may be seen as the gate of salvation open to all
nations. Let cries of joy and exultation ring out from its
tents, to celebrate the wonder of Christ's resurrection.

Advent:　　Zion is our mighty citadel, our saving Lord its
　　　　　　wall and its defense; throw open the gates, for
　　　　　　our God is here among us, alleluia.

Antiphon 2

Advent:　　Come to the waters, all you who thirst; seek
　　　　　　the Lord while he can be found, alleluia.

Canticle　　　　　　Daniel 3:52-57

Let all creatures praise the Lord

The Creator . . . is blessed for ever (Romans 1:25).

Blessed are you, O Lord, the God of our fathers,
praiseworthy and exalted above all forever.

And blessed is your holy and glorious name,
praiseworthy and exalted above all for all ages.

Blessed are you in the temple of your holy glory,
praiseworthy and glorious above all forever.

Blessed are you on the throne of your kingdom,
praiseworthy and exalted above all forever.

Blessed are you who look into the depths
from your throne upon the cherubim,
praiseworthy and exalted above all forever.

Blessed are you in the firmament of heaven,
praiseworthy and glorious forever.

Bless the Lord, all you works of the Lord,
praise and exalt him above all forever.

Advent: Come to the waters, all you who thirst; seek
the Lord while he can be found, alleluia.

Antiphon 3

Advent: Our God will come with great power to
enlighten the eyes of his servants, alleluia.

Psalm 150

Praise the Lord

*Let mind and heart be in your song: this is to glorify God
with your whole self* (Hesychius).

Praise God in his holy place,
praise him in his mighty heavens.
Praise him for his powerful deeds,
praise his surpassing greatness.

O praise him with sound of trumpet,
praise him with lute and harp.
Praise him with timbrel and dance,
praise him with strings and pipes.

O praise him with resounding cymbals,
praise him with clashing of cymbals.

Let everything that lives and that breathes
give praise to the Lord.

Psalm-prayer

Lord God, maker of heaven and earth and of all
created things, you make your just ones holy and you
justify sinners who confess your name. Hear us as we
humbly pray to you: give us eternal joy with your saints.

Advent: Our God will come with great power to
           enlighten the eyes of his servants, alleluia.

Reading, responsory, antiphon for the canticle of Zechariah,
intercessions and prayer, as in the Proper of Seasons.

Conclusion, as in the Ordinary.

Daytime Prayer

God, come to my assistance, Glory to the Father. As it
was in the beginning. Alleluia.

HYMN, as in the Ordinary, 658.

PSALMODY

Antiphon, as in the Proper of Seasons.

Psalm 23

The Good Shepherd

*The Lamb himself will be their shepherd and will lead them
to the springs of living water* (Revelation 7:17).

The Lord is my shepherd;
there is nothing I shall want.
Fresh and green are the pastures
where he gives me repose.
Near restful waters he leads me,
to revive my drooping spirit.

He guides me along the right path;
he is true to his name.
If I should walk in the valley of darkness
no evil would I fear.
You are there with your crook and your staff;
with these you give me comfort.

You have prepared a banquet for me
in the sight of my foes.
My head you have anointed with oil;
my cup is overflowing.

Surely goodness and kindness shall follow me
all the days of my life.
In the Lord's own house shall I dwell
for ever and ever.

Psalm-prayer

Lord Jesus Christ, shepherd of your Church, you give
us new birth in the waters of baptism, anoint us with
saving oil, and call us to salvation at your table. Dispel the terrors of death and the darkness of error. Lead
your people along safe paths, that they may rest securely
in you and live for ever in your Father's house.

Psalm 76

Thanksgiving for victory

They will see the Son of Man coming on the clouds of heaven
(Matthew 24:30).

I

God is made known in Judah;
in Israel his name is great.
He set up his tent in Jerusalem
and his dwelling place in Zion.
It was there he broke the flashing arrows,
the shield, the sword, the armor.

You, O Lord, are resplendent,
more majestic than the everlasting mountains.
The warriors, despoiled, slept in death;
the hands of the soldiers were powerless.
At your threat, O God of Jacob,
horse and rider lay stunned.

II

You, you alone, strike terror.
Who shall stand when your anger is roused?
You uttered your sentence from the heavens;
the earth in terror was still
when God arose to judge,
to save the humble of the earth.

Men's anger will serve to praise you;
its survivors surround you in joy.
Make vows to your God and fulfill them.
Let all pay tribute to him who strikes terror,
who cuts short the breath of princes,
who strikes terror in the kings of the earth.

Psalm-prayer

Your power is awesome, Father, and wonderful is your
holiness. In your presence the earth both trembles and
stands still, for you shattered death's power by the cross.
Rise to help your people: give your light, and grant
salvation to the meek of the earth, that they may praise
your name in heaven.

At the other hours, the complementary psalmody is used, 1191.

Reading, verse and prayer, as in the Proper of Seasons.

Conclusion, as in the Ordinary.

Evening Prayer II

God, come to my assistance. Glory to the Father. As it was in the beginning. Alleluia.

HYMN, 126.

Or:

> Love divine, all loves excelling,
> Joy of heaven to earth come down,
> And impart to us, here dwelling,
> Grace and mercy all around.
> Jesus, source of all compassion,
> Pure, unbounded love you share;
> Grant us many choicest blessings,
> Keep us in your loving care.
>
> Come, oh source of inspiration,
> Pure and spotless let us be:
> Let us see your true salvation,
> Perfect in accord with thee.
> Praising Father for all glory
> With the Spirit and the Son;
> Everlasting thanks we give thee,
> Undivided, love, in one.

Melody: Hyfrydol 87.87.D   Music: Rowland H. Prichard
1811-1887
Text: Charles Wesley, 1707-1788, adapted by C. T. Andrews,1968

PSALMODY

Antiphon 1

Advent: **The Lord will come on the clouds of heaven
with great power and might, alleluia.**

Psalm 110:1-5,7

The Messiah, king and priest

*Christ's reign will last until all his enemies are made subject
to him* (1 Corinthians 15:25).

The Lord's revelation to my Master:
"Sit on my right:
your foes I will put beneath your feet."

The Lord will wield from Zion
your scepter of power:
rule in the midst of all your foes.

A prince from the day of your birth
on the holy mountains;
from the womb before the dawn I begot you.

The Lord has sworn an oath he will not change.
"You are a priest for ever,
a priest like Melchizedek of old."

The Master standing at your right hand
will shatter kings in the day of his great wrath.

He shall drink from the stream by the wayside
and therefore he shall lift up his head.

Psalm-prayer

Almighty God, bring the kingdom of Christ, your anointed one, to its fullness. May the perfect offering of your Son, eternal priest of the new Jerusalem, be offered in every place to your name and make all nations a holy people for you.

Advent: The Lord will come on the clouds of heaven with great power and might, alleluia.

Antiphon 2

Advent: The Lord will come; he is true to his word. If he seems to delay, keep watch for him, for he will surely come, alleluia.

Psalm 115

Praise of the true God

You have renounced idol worship to serve the living and true God (1 Thessalonians 1:9).

Not to us, Lord, not to us,
but to your name give the glory
for the sake of your love and your truth,
lest the heathen say:"Where is their God?"

But our God is in the heavens;
he does whatever he wills.
Their idols are silver and gold,
the work of human hands.

They have mouths but they cannot speak;
they have eyes but they cannot see;
they have ears but they cannot hear;
they have nostrils but they cannot smell.

With their hands they cannot feel;
with their feet they cannot walk.
No sound comes from their throats.
Their makers will come to be like them
and so will all who trust in them.

Sons of Israel, trust in the Lord;
he is their help and their shield.
Sons of Aaron, trust in the Lord;
he is their help and their shield.

You who fear him, trust in the Lord;
he is their help and their shield.
He remembers us, and he will bless us;
he will bless the sons of Israel.
He will bless the sons of Aaron.

The Lord will bless those who fear him,
the little no less than the great:
to you may the Lord grant increase,
to you and all your children.

May you be blessed by the Lord,
the maker of heaven and earth.
The heavens belong to the Lord
but the earth has given to men.

The dead shall not praise the Lord,
nor those who go down into the silence.
But we who live bless the Lord
now and for ever. Amen.

Psalm-prayer

Father, creator and ruler of heaven and earth, you made man in your likeness to subdue the earth and master it, and to recognize the work of your hands in created beauty. Grant that your children, thus surrounded on all sides by signs of your presence, may live continually in Christ, praising you through him and with him.

Advent: The Lord will come; he is true to his word. If he seems to delay, keep watch for him, for he will surely come, alleluia.

Antiphon 3

Advent: The Lord our king and lawgiver will come to save us.

The following canticle is said with the **Alleluia** when Evening Prayer is sung; when the office is recited, the **Alleluia** may be said at the beginning and end of each strophe.

Canticle   See Revelation 19:1-7

The wedding of the Lamb

Alleluia.
Salvation, glory, and power to our God:
(R. Alleluia.)
his judgments are honest and true.
R. Alleluia (alleluia).

Alleluia.
Sing praise to our God, all you his servants,
(R. Alleluia.)
all who worship him reverently, great and small.
R. Alleluia (alleluia).

Alleluia.
The Lord our all-powerful God is King,
(R. Alleluia.)
let us rejoice, sing praise, and give him glory.
R. Alleluia (alleluia).

Alleluia.
The wedding feast of the Lamb has begun,
(R. Alleluia.)
and his bride is prepared to welcome him.
R. Alleluia (alleluia).

Advent: The Lord our king and lawgiver will come to
           save us.

Reading, responsory, antiphon for the canticle of Mary,
intercessions and prayer, as in the Proper of Seasons.

Conclusion, as in the Ordinary.

MONDAY, WEEK II

Invitatory

Lord, open my lips.

Antiphon, as in the Ordinary, 647.

Invitatory psalm, 648.

Office of Readings

God, come to my assistance. Glory to the Father. As it was in the beginning. Alleluia.

This verse and response are omitted when the hour begins with the invitatory.

HYMN

Sing praise to God who reigns above,
The God of all creation,
The God of power, the God of love,
The God of our salvation;
With healing balm my soul he fills,
And every faithless murmur stills:
To God all praise and glory.

What God's almighty power hath made,
His gracious mercy keepeth;
By morning glow or evening shade
His watchful eye never sleepeth;
Within the kingdom of his might,
Lo! all is just and all is right:
To God all praise and glory.

Then all my gladsome way along,
I sing aloud thy praises,
That men may hear the grateful song
My voice unwearied raises;
Be joyful in the Lord, my heart,

Both soul and body, bear your part:
To God all praise and glory.

O ye who name Christ's holy name,
Give God all praise and glory;
All ye who own his power, proclaim
Aloud the wondrous story!
Cast each false idol from his throne.
The Lord is God, and he alone:
To God all praise and glory.

Melody: Mit Freuden Zart 87.87.887   Music: *Bohemian
Brethren's Hymnbook*, 1566
Text: Johann J. Schutz, 1640-1690
Translator: Frances E. Cox, 1812–1897

PSALMODY

Ant. 1   Bow down and hear me, Lord; come to my
rescue.

Psalm 31:1-17, 20-25

A troubled person's confident appeal to God

Father, into your hands, I commend my spirit (Luke 23:46).

I

In you, O Lord, I take refuge
Let me never be put to shame.
In your justice, set me free,
hear me and speedily rescue me.

Be a rock of refuge for me,
a mighty stronghold to save me,
for you are my rock, my stronghold.
For your name's sake, lead me and guide me.

Release me from the snares they have hidden
for you are my refuge, Lord.
Into your hands I commend my spirit.
It is you who will redeem me, Lord.

O God of truth, you detest
those who worship false and empty gods.
As for me, I trust in the Lord:
let me be glad and rejoice in your love.

You who have seen my affliction
and taken heed of my soul's distress,
have not handed me over to the enemy,
but set my feet at large.

Ant. Bow down and hear me, Lord; come to my
rescue.

Ant. 2 Lord, let the light of your countenance shine on
your servant.

II

Have mercy on me, O Lord,
for I am in distress.
Tears have wasted my eyes,
my throat and my heart.

For my life is spent with sorrow
and my years with sighs.
Affliction has broken down my strength
and my bones waste away.

In the face of all my foes
I am a reproach,
an object of scorn to my neighbors
and of fear to my friends.

Those who see me in the street
run far away from me.
I am like a dead man, forgotten
like a thing thrown away.

I have heard the slander of the crowd,
fear is all around me,
as they plot together against me,
as they plan to take my life.

But as for me, I trust in you, Lord,
I say: "You are my God.
My life is in your hands, deliver me.
from the hands of those who hate me.

Let your face shine on your servant.
Save me in your love."

Ant.   Lord, let the light of your countenance shine on
       your servant.

Ant. 3   Blessed be the Lord, for he has poured out his
         mercy upon me.

III

How great is the goodness, Lord,
that you keep for those who fear you,
that you show to those who trust you
in the sight of men.

You hide them in the shelter of your presence
from the plotting of men:
you keep them safe within your tent.
from disputing tongues.

Blessed be the Lord who has shown me
the wonders of his love
in a fortified city.

"I am far removed from your sight,"
I said in my alarm.
Yet you heard the voice of my plea
when I cried for help.

Love the Lord, all you saints.
He guards his faithful
but the Lord will repay to the full
those who act with pride.

Be strong, let your heart take courage,
all who hope in the Lord.

Psalm-prayer

God of kindness and truth, you saved your Chosen
One, Jesus Christ, and you gave your martyrs strength.
Watch over your people who come to you here and
strengthen the hearts of those who hope in you, that they
may proclaim your saving acts of kindness in the eternal
city.

Ant.   Blessed be the Lord, for he has poured out his
       mercy upon me.

Verse, reading and prayer, as in the Proper of Seasons.

Morning Prayer

God, come to my assistance. Glory to the Father. As it
was in the beginning. Alleluia.

This verse and response are omitted when the hour begins with
the invitatory.

HYMN

I sing the mighty power of God,
That made the mountains rise;
That spread the flowing seas abroad,
And built the lofty skies.
I sing the wisdom that ordained
The sun to rule the day;
The moon shines full at his command,
And all the stars obey.

I sing the goodness of the Lord,
That filled the earth with food;
He formed the creatures with his word,
And then pronounced them good.
Lord, how your wonders are displayed,
Where e'er I turn my eye:
If I survey the ground I tread,
Or gaze upon the sky!

There's not a plant or flower below,
But makes your glories known;
And clouds arise, and tempests blow,
By order from your throne;
While all that borrows life from you
Is ever in your care,
And everywhere that man can be,
You, God, are present there.

Melody: Ellacombe C.M.D.　　Music: *Wurtemburg Gesangbuch*,
　　　　　1784, adapted in the *Mainz Gesangbuch*, 1833,
　　　and further adapted in the *St. Gall Gesangbuch*, 1863
Or:　　　　　　　　　　　Text: Isaac Watts, 1715

Antiphon:

All you nations, sing out your joy to the Lord:
Alleluia, alleluia!

Joyfully shout, all you on earth,
give praise to the glory of God;
And with a hymn, sing out his glorious praise:
Alleluia!
Antiphon

Let all the earth kneel in his sight,
extolling his marvelous fame;
Honor his name, in highest heaven give praise:
Alleluia!
Antiphon

Come forth and see all the great works
that God has brought forth by his might;
Fall on your knees before his glorious throne:
Alleluia!
Antiphon

Glory and thanks be to the Father;
honor and praise to the Son;
And to the Spirit, source of life and of love:
Alleluia!
Antiphon

Melody: All You Nations　　Music: Lucien Deiss, C.S.Sp., 1965
　　　　　　　　　　　　Text: Lucien Deiss, C.S.Sp., 1965

PSALMODY

Ant. 1   **When will I come to the end of my pilgrimage
and enter the presence of God?**

Psalm 42

Longing for the Lord's presence in his Temple

*Let all who thirst come; let all who desire it, drink from the
life-giving water* (Revelation 22:17).

Like the deer that yearns
for running streams,
so my soul is yearning
for you, my God.

My soul is thirsting for God,
the God of my life;
when can I enter and see
the face of God?

My tears have become my bread,
by night, by day,
as I hear it said all the day long:
"Where is your God?"

These things will I remember
as I pour out my soul:
how I would lead the rejoicing crowd
into the house of God,
amid cries of gladness and thanksgiving,
the throng wild with joy.

Why are you cast down, my soul,
why groan within me?
Hope in God; I will praise him still,
my savior and my God.

My soul is cast down within me
as I think of you,

from the country of Jordan and Mount Hermon,
from the Hill of Mizar.

Deep is calling on deep,
in the roar of waters:
your torrents and all your waves
swept over me.

By day the Lord will send
his loving kindness;
by night I will sing to him,
praise the God of my life.

I will say to God, my rock:
"Why have you forgotten me?
Why do I go mourning
oppressed by the foe?"

With cries that pierce me to the heart,
my enemies revile me,
saying to me all the day long:
"Where is your God?"

Why are you cast down, my soul,
why groan within me?
Hope in God; I will praise him still,
my savior and my God.

Psalm-prayer

Father in heaven, when your strength takes possession
of us we no longer say: Why are you cast down, my soul?
So now that the surging waves of your indignation have
passed over us, let us feel the healing calm of your
forgiveness. Inspire us to yearn for you always, like the
deer for running streams, until you satisfy every longing
in heaven.

Ant. When will I come to the end of my pilgrimage and
      enter the presence of God?

Ant. 2 Lord, show us the radiance of your mercy.

Canticle Sirach 36:1-5, 10-13

Prayer of entreaty for the holy city, Jerusalem

This is eternal life: to know you, the one true God, and Jesus Christ whom you have sent (John 17:3).

> Come to our aid, O God of the universe,
> and put all the nations in dread of you!
> Raise your hand against the heathen,
> that they may realize your power.

> As you have used us to show them your holiness,
> so now use them to show us your glory.
> Thus they will know, as we know,
> that there is no God but you.

> Give new signs and work new wonders;
> show forth the splendor of your right hand and arm.

> Gather all the tribes of Jacob,
> that they may inherit the land as of old.
> Show mercy to the people called by your name;
> Israel, whom you named your first-born.

> Take pity on your holy city,
> Jerusalem, your dwelling place.
> Fill Zion with your majesty,
> your temple with your glory.

Ant. Lord, show us the radiance of your mercy.

Ant. 3 The vaults of heaven ring with your praise, O Lord.

Psalm 19A

Praise of the Lord, Creator of all

The dawn from on high shall break on us . . . to guide our feet into the way of peace (Luke 1:78, 79).

The heavens proclaim the glory of God
and the firmament shows forth the work of his
    hands.
Day unto day takes up the story
and night unto night makes known the message.

No speech, no word, no voice is heard
yet their span extends through all the earth,
their words to the utmost bounds of the world.

There he has placed a tent for the sun;
it comes forth like a bridegroom coming from his
    tent,
rejoices like a champion to run its course.

At the end of the sky is the rising of the sun;
to the furthest end of the sky is its course.
There is nothing concealed from its burning heat.

Psalm-prayer

To enlighten the world, Father, you sent to us your
Word as the sun of truth and justice shining upon
mankind. Illumine our eyes that we may discern your
glory in the many works of your hand.

Ant. The vaults of heaven ring with your praise, O
    Lord.

Reading, responsory, antiphon for the canticle of Zechariah,
intercessions and prayer, as in the Proper of Seasons.

Conclusion, as in the Ordinary.

Daytime Prayer

God, come to my assistance. Glory to the Father. As it
was in the beginning. Alleluia.

Hymn, as in the Ordinary, 658.

Psalmody

Antiphon, as in the Proper of Seasons.

Psalm 119:41-48
VI (Vau)

Lord, let your love come upon me,
the saving help of your promise.
And I shall answer those who taunt me
for I trust in your word.

Do not take the word of truth from my mouth
for I trust in your decrees.
I shall always keep your law
for ever and ever.

I shall walk in the path of freedom
for I seek your precepts.
I will speak of your will before kings
and not be abashed.

Your commands have been my delight;
these I have loved.
I will worship your commands and love them
and ponder your will.

Psalm-prayer

Father, let your salvation come to us as you have
promised, that we may keep your law always and, taught
by the Word of truth, find strength in his salvation.

Psalm 40:2-14, 17-18
Thanksgiving and plea for help

*It was not sacrifice and oblation you wanted, but you have
prepared a body for me* (Hebrews 10:5).

I

I waited, I waited for the Lord
and he stooped down to me;
he heard my cry.

He drew me from the deadly pit,
from the miry clay.
He set my feet upon a rock
and made my footsteps firm.

He put a new song into my mouth,
praise of our God.
Many shall see and fear
and shall trust in the Lord.

Happy the man who has placed
his trust in the Lord
and has not gone over to the rebels
who follow false gods.

How many, O Lord my God,
are the wonders and designs
that you have worked for us;
you have no equal.
Should I proclaim and speak of them,
they are more than I can tell!

You do not ask for sacrifice and offerings,
but an open ear.
You do not ask for holocaust and victim.
Instead, here am I.

In the scroll of the book it stands written
that I should do your will.
My God, I delight in your law
in the depth of my heart.

II

Your justice I have proclaimed
in the great assembly.
My lips I have not sealed;
you know it, O Lord.

I have not hidden your justice in my heart
but declared your faithful help.

I have not hidden your love and your truth
from the great assembly.

O Lord, you will not withhold
your compassion from me.
Your merciful love and your truth
will always guard me.

For I am beset with evils
too many to be counted.
My sins have fallen upon me
and my sight fails me.
They are more than the hairs of my head
and my heart sinks.

O Lord, come to my rescue,
Lord, come to my aid.

O let there be rejoicing and gladness
for all who seek you.
Let them ever say: "The Lord is great,"
who love your saving help.

As for me, wretched and poor,
the Lord thinks of me.
You are my rescuer, my help,
O God, do not delay.

Psalm-prayer

Lord Jesus Christ, you were made obedient unto death
and your name was exalted above all others. Teach us
always to do the Father's will, so that, made holy by
obedience which unites us to the sacrifice of your body,
we can expect your great love in times of sorrow and sing
a new song to our God.

At the other hours, the complementary psalmody is used, 1191.

Reading, verse and prayer, as in the Proper of Seasons.

Conclusion, as in the Ordinary.

Evening Prayer

God, come to my assistance. Glory to the Father. As it
was in the beginning. Alleluia.

HYMN

Now fades all earthly splendor,
The shades of night descend;
The dying of the daylight
Foretells creation's end.
Though noon gives place to sunset,
Yet dark gives place to light:
The promise of tomorrow
With dawn's new hope is bright.

The silver notes of morning
Will greet the rising sun,
As once the Easter glory
Shone round the Risen One.
So will the night of dying
Give place to heaven's day,
And hope of heaven's vision,
Will light our pilgrim way.

So will the new creation
Rise from the old reborn
To splendor in Christ's glory
And everlasting morn.
All darkness will be ended
As faith gives place to sight
Of Father, Son and Spirit,
One God, in heaven's light.

Melody: Ewing 76.76.D   Music: Alexander Ewing, 1830–1895
                                Text: James Quinn, S.J., 1968

PSALMODY

Ant. 1 Yours is more than mortal beauty; every word
        you speak is full of grace.

Psalm 45

The marriage of the king

The Bridegroom is here; go out and welcome him (Matthew
25:6).

I

My heart overflows with noble words.
To the king I must speak the song I have made;
my tongue as nimble as the pen of a scribe.

You are the fairest of the children of men
and graciousness is poured upon your lips:
because God has blessed you for evermore.

O mighty one, gird your sword upon your thigh;
in splendor and state, ride on in triumph
for the cause of truth and goodness and right.

Take aim with your bow in your dread right hand.
Your arrows are sharp: peoples fall beneath you.
The foes of the king fall down and lose heart.

Your throne, O God, shall endure for ever.
A scepter of justice is the scepter of your kingdom.
Your love is for justice; your hatred for evil.

Therefore God, your God, has anointed you
with the oil of gladness above other kings:
your robes are fragrant with aloes and myrrh.

From the ivory palace you are greeted with music.
The daughters of kings are among your loved ones.
On your right stands the queen in gold of Ophir.

Ant.   Yours is more than mortal beauty; every word you
        speak is full of grace.

Ant. 2 The Bridegroom is here; go out and welcome
        him.

II

Listen, O daughter, give ear to my words:
forget your own people and your father's house.
So will the king desire your beauty:
he is your lord, pay homage to him.

And the people of Tyre shall come with gifts,
the richest of the people shall seek your favor.
The daughter of the king is clothed with splendor,
her robes embroidered with pearls set in gold.

She is led to the king with her maiden companions.
They are escorted amid gladness and joy;
they pass within the palace of the king.

Sons shall be yours in place of your fathers:
you will make them princes over all the earth.
May this song make your name for ever remembered.
May the peoples praise you from age to age.

Psalm-prayer

When you took on flesh, Lord Jesus, you made a
marriage of mankind with God. Help us to be faithful to
your word and endure our exile bravely, until we are
called to the heavenly marriage feast, to which the Virgin
Mary, exemplar of your Church, has preceded us.

Ant.   The Bridegroom is here; go out and welcome him.

Ant. 3   God planned in the fullness of time to restore all
things in Christ.

Canticle   Ephesians 1:3-10

God our Savior

Praised be the God and Father
of our Lord Jesus Christ,

who has bestowed on us in Christ
every spiritual blessing in the heavens.

God chose us in him
before the world began
to be holy
and blameless in his sight.

He predestined us
to be his adopted sons through Jesus Christ,
such was his will and pleasure,
that all might praise the glorious favor
he has bestowed on us in his beloved.

In him and through his blood, we have been
   redeemed,
and our sins forgiven,
so immeasurably generous
is God's favor to us.

God has given us the wisdom
to understand fully the mystery,
the plan he was pleased
to decree in Christ.

A plan to be carried out
in Christ, in the fullness of time,
to bring all things into one in him,
in the heavens and on earth.

Ant.   God planned in the fullness of time to restore all
        things in Christ.

Reading, responsory, antiphon for the canticle of Mary,
intercessions and prayer, as in the Proper of Seasons.

Conclusion, as in the Ordinary.

TUESDAY, WEEK II

Invitatory

Lord, open my lips.

Antiphon, as in the Ordinary, 647.

Invitatory psalm, 648.

Office of Readings

God, come to my assistance. Glory to the Father. As it was in the beginning. Alleluia.

This verse and response are omitted when the hour begins with the invitatory.

HYMN

> With hearts renewed by living faith,
> We lift our thoughts in grateful prayer
> To God our gracious Father,
> Whose plan it was to make us sons
> Through his own Son's redemptive death,
> That rescued us from darkness.
> Lord, God, Savior,
> Give us strength to mold our hearts in your true
>   likeness.
> Sons and servants of our Father.
>
> So rich God's grace in Jesus Christ,
> That we are called as sons of light
> To bear the pledge of glory.
> Through him in whom all fullness dwells,
> We offer God our gift of self
> In union with the Spirit.
> Lord, God, Savior,

Give us strength to mold our hearts in your true
  likeness.
Sons and servants of our Father.

Melody: Frankfort 887.887.48.48   Music: Philip Nicolai, 1599,
                                        arr. by J.S. Bach, 1730
                                    Text: Jack May, S.J.

PSALMODY

Ant. 1   Surrender to God, and he will do everything for
         you.

Psalm 37

The lot of the wicked and the good

Blessed are the meek, for they shall inherit the earth
(Matthew 5:5).

I

Do not fret because of the wicked;
do not envy those who do evil:
for they wither quickly like grass
and fade like the green of the fields.

If you trust in the Lord and do good,
then you will live in the land and be secure.
If you find your delight in the Lord,
he will grant your heart's desire.

Commit your life to the Lord,
trust in him and he will act,
so that your justice breaks forth like the light,
your cause like the noon-day sun.

Be still before the Lord and wait in patience;
do not fret at the man who prospers;
a man who makes evil plots
to bring down the needy and the poor.

Calm your anger and forget your rage;
do not fret, it only leads to evil.

For those who do evil shall perish;
the patient shall inherit the land.

A little longer—and the wicked shall have gone.
Look at his place, he is not there.
But the humble shall own the land
and enjoy the fullness of peace.

Ant.   Surrender to God, and he will do everything for
you.

Ant. 2   Turn away from evil, learn to do God's will; the
Lord will strengthen you if you obey him.

II

The wicked man plots against the just
and gnashes his teeth against him;
but the Lord laughs at the wicked
for he sees that his day is at hand.

The sword of the wicked is drawn,
his bow is bent to slaughter the upright.
Their sword shall pierce their own hearts
and their bows shall be broken to pieces.

The just man's few possessions
are better than the wicked man's wealth;
for the power of the wicked shall be broken
and the Lord will support the just.

He protects the lives of the upright,
their heritage will last for ever.
They shall not be put to shame in evil days,
in time of famine their food shall not fail.

But all the wicked shall perish
and all the enemies of the Lord.
They are like the beauty of the meadows,
they shall vanish, they shall vanish like smoke.

The wicked man borrows without repaying,
but the just man is generous and gives.
Those blessed by the Lord shall own the land,
but those he has cursed shall be destroyed.

The Lord guides the steps of a man
and makes safe the path of one he loves.
Though he stumble he shall never fall
for the Lord holds him by the hand.

I was young and now I am old,
but I have never seen the just man forsaken
nor his children begging for bread.
All the day he is generous and lends
and his children become a blessing.

Then turn away from evil and do good
and you shall have a home for ever;
for the Lord loves justice
and will never forsake his friends.

The unjust shall be wiped out for ever
and the children of the wicked destroyed.
The just shall inherit the land;
there they shall live for ever.

Ant.   Turn away from evil, learn to do God's will; the
       Lord will strengthen you if you obey him.

Ant. 3   Wait for the Lord to lead, then follow in his
       way.

III

The just man's mouth utters wisdom
and his lips speak what is right;
the law of his God is in his heart,
his steps shall be saved from stumbling.

The wicked man watches for the just
and seeks occasion to kill him.

The Lord will not leave him in his power
nor let him be condemned when he is judged.

Then wait for the Lord, keep to his way.
It is he who will free you from the wicked,
raise you up to possess the land
and see the wicked destroyed.

I have seen the wicked triumphant,
towering like a cedar of Lebanon.
I passed by again; he was gone.
I searched; he was nowhere to be found.

See the just man, mark the upright,
for the peaceful man a future lies in store,
but sinners shall all be destroyed.
No future lies in store for the wicked.

The salvation of the just comes from the Lord,
their stronghold in time of distress.
The Lord helps them and delivers them
and saves them: for their refuge is in him.

Psalm-prayer

You proclaimed the poor to be blessed, Lord Jesus, for the kingdom of heaven is given them. Fill us generously with your gifts. Teach us to put our trust in the Father and to seek his kingdom first of all rather than imitate the powerful and envy the rich.

Ant.   Wait for the Lord to lead, then follow in his way.

Verse, reading and prayer, as in the Proper of Seasons.

Morning Prayer

God, come to my assistance. Glory to the Father. As it was in the beginning. Alleluia.

This verse and response are omitted when the hour begins with
the invitatory.

HYMN

This day God gives me
Strength of high heaven,
Sun and moon shining,
         Flame in my hearth,
Flashing of lightning,
Wind in its swiftness,
Deeps of the ocean,
         Firmness of earth.

This day God sends me
Strength as my steersman,
Might to uphold me,
         Wisdom as guide.
Your eyes are watchful,
Your ears are listening,
Your lips are speaking,
         Friend at my side.

God's way is my way,
God's shield is round me,
God's host defends me,
         Saving from ill.
Angels of heaven,
Drive from me always
All that would harm me,
         Stand by me still.

Rising, I thank you,
Mighty and strong one,
King of creation,
         Giver of rest,

Firmly confessing
Threeness of persons,
Oneness of Godhead,
      Trinity blest.

Melody: Bunessan 55.54.D   Music: Old Gaelic Melody
                      Text: James Quinn, S.J.

Or:

God Father, praise and glory
Your children come to sing.
Good will and peace to mankind,
The gifts your kingdom brings.

Refrain:

O most Holy Trinity,
Undivided Unity;
Holy God, Mighty God,
God Immortal, be adored.

And you, Lord Coeternal,
God's sole begotten Son;
O Jesus, King anointed,
You have redemption won.

                    Refrain

O Holy Ghost, Creator,
The Gift of God most high;
Life, love and holy wisdom,
Our weakness now supply.

                    Refrain

Melody: Mainz 76.76 with Refrain   Music: Mainz Melody
                                Text: Anon.
Translator: John Rathensteiner,
                                 1936, alt.

PSALMODY

Ant. 1 **Lord, send forth your light and your truth.**

Psalm 43

Longing for the temple

I have come into the world to be its light (John 12:46).

Defend me, O God, and plead my cause
against a godless nation.
From deceitful and cunning men
rescue me, O God.

Since you, O God, are my stronghold,
why have you rejected me?
Why do I go mourning,
oppressed by the foe?

O send forth your light and your truth;
let these be my guide.
Let them bring me to your holy mountain,
to the place where you dwell.

And I will come to the altar of God,
the God of my joy.
My redeemer, I will thank you on the harp,
O God, my God.

Why are you cast down, my soul,
why groan within me?
Hope in God; I will praise him still,
my savior and my God.

Psalm-prayer

Almighty Father, source of everlasting light, send
forth your truth into our hearts and pour over us the
brightness of your light.

Ant. Lord, send forth your light and your truth.

Ant. 2 Lord, keep us safe all the days of our life.

Canticle   Isaiah 38:10-14, 17-20

Anguish of a dying man and joy in his restoration

I am living, I was dead . . . and I hold the keys of death
(Revelation 1:17-18).

Once I said,
"In the noontime of life I must depart!
To the gates of the nether world I shall be consigned
for the rest of my years."

I said, "I shall see the Lord no more
in the land of the living.
No longer shall I behold my fellow men
among those who dwell in the world."

My dwelling, like a shepherd's tent,
is struck down and borne away from me;
you have folded up my life, like a weaver
who severs the last thread.

Day and night you give me over to torment;
I cry out until the dawn.
Like a lion he breaks all my bones;
day and night you give me over to torment.

Like a swallow I utter shrill cries;
I moan like a dove.
My eyes grow weak, gazing heaven-ward:
O Lord, I am in straits; be my surety!

You have preserved my life
from the pit of destruction,
when you cast behind your back
all my sins.

For it is not the nether world that gives you thanks,
nor death that praises you;
Neither do those who go down into the pit
await your kindness.

The living, the living give you thanks,
as I do today.
Fathers declare to their sons,
O God, your faithfulness.

The Lord is our savior;
we shall sing to stringed instruments
in the house of the Lord
all the days of our life.

Ant.   Lord, keep us safe all the days of our life.

Ant. 3   To you, O God, our praise is due in Zion.

Psalm 65

Solemn thanksgiving

Zion represents heaven (Origen).

To you our praise is due
in Zion, O God.
To you we pay our vows,
you who hear our prayer.

To you all flesh will come
with its burden of sin.
Too heavy for us, our offenses,
but you wipe them away.

Blessed is he whom you choose and call
to dwell in your courts.
We are filled with the blessings of your house,
of your holy temple.

You keep your pledge with wonders,
O God our savior,
the hope of all the earth
and of far distant isles.

You uphold the mountains with your strength,
you are girded with power.

You still the roaring of the seas,
the roaring of their waves
and the tumult of the peoples.

The ends of the earth stand in awe
at the sight of your wonders.
The lands of sunrise and sunset
you fill with your joy.

You care for the earth, give it water,
you fill it with riches.
Your river in heaven brims over
to provide its grain.

And thus you provide for the earth;
you drench its furrows,
you level it, soften it with showers,
you bless its growth.

You crown the year with your goodness.
Abundance flows in your steps,
in the pastures of the wilderness it flows.

The hills are girded with joy,
the meadows covered with flocks,
the valleys are decked with wheat.
They shout for joy, yes, they sing.

Psalm-prayer

Lord God, hope of all the earth, hear the humble
prayer of your children as we sing your praises. Pour out
your Spirit on us so that our lives may bear fruit
abundantly.

Ant.   To you, O God, our praise is due in Zion.

Reading, responsory, antiphon for the canticle of Zechariah,
intercessions and prayer, as in the Proper of Seasons.

Conclusion, as in the Ordinary.

Daytime Prayer

God, come to my assistance. Glory to the Father. As it
was in the beginning. Alleluia.

HYMN, as in the Ordinary, 658.

PSALMODY

Antiphon, as in the Proper of Seasons.

Psalm 119:49-56

VII (Zain)

Remember your word to your servant
by which you gave me hope.
This is my comfort in sorrow
that your promise gives me life.

Though the proud may utterly deride me
I keep to your law.
I remember your decrees of old
and these, Lord, console me.

I am seized with indignation at the wicked
who forsake your law.
Your commands have become my song
in the land of exile.

I think of your name in the night-time
and I keep your law.
This has been my blessing,
the keeping of your precepts.

Psalm-prayer

Lord, you raise us up from our lowliness by giving us
the hope of eternal life. May we always serve you in this
our pilgrimage and come to enjoy the happiness of our
home with you.

Psalm 53

The foolishness of sinners

We all have sinned and are deprived of God's glory (Romans 3:23).

> The fool has said in his heart:
> "There is no God above."
> Their deeds are corrupt, depraved;
> not a good man is left.
>
> God looks down from heaven
> on the sons of men,
> to see if any are wise,
> if any seek God.
>
> All have left the right path;
> depraved, every one.
> There is not a good man left,
> no, not even one.
>
> Will the evil-doers not understand?
> They eat up my people
> as though they were eating bread;
> they never pray to God.
>
> See how they tremble with fear
> without cause for fear:
> for God scatters the bones of the wicked.
> They are shamed, God rejects them.
>
> O that Israel's salvation might come from Zion!
> When God delivers his people from bondage,
> then Jacob will be glad and Israel rejoice.

Psalm-prayer

Almighty Father, apart from you there is nothing true, nothing holy on earth. Dismiss our sins, and give us strength in our weakness so that all who believe in your Son may rejoice in his glory.

Psalm 54:1-6, 8-9

Plea for help

The prophet prays that God will deliver him from the malice of his enemies (Cassian).

O God, save me by your name;
by your power, uphold my cause.
O God, hear my prayer;
listen to the words of my mouth.

For proud men have risen against me,
ruthless men seek my life.
They have no regard for God.
But I have God for my help.
The Lord upholds my life.

I will sacrifice to you with willing heart
and praise your name for it is good:
for you have rescued me from all my distress
and my eyes have seen the downfall of my foes.

Psalm-prayer

We humbly ask you, Father, to save us from every evil
and trial on earth that we may seek with our hearts and
deeds our Lord and helper, Jesus Christ, whom we look
to in the heavens.

At the other hours, the complementary psalmody is used, **1191.**

Reading, verse and prayer, as in the Proper of Seasons.

Conclusion, as in the Ordinary.

Evening Prayer

God, come to my assistance. Glory to the Father. As it
was in the beginning. Alleluia.

HYMN

Day is done, but love unfailing
  Dwells ever here;
Shadows fall, but hope, prevailing,
  Calms every fear.
Loving Father, none forsaking,
Take our hearts, of Love's own making,
Watch our sleeping, guard our waking,
  Be always near.

Dark descends, but Light unending
  Shines through our night;
You are with us, ever lending
  New strength to sight;
One in love, your truth confessing,
One in hope of heaven's blessing,
May we see, in love's possessing,
  Love's endless light!

Eyes will close, but you, unsleeping,
  Watch by our side;
Death may come: in Love's safe keeping
  Still we abide.
God of love, all evil quelling,
Sin forgiving, fear dispelling,
Stay with us, our hearts indwelling;
  This eventide.

Melody: Ar Hyd Y Nos   Music: *Welsh Traditional Melody*
84.84.88.84   Text: James Quinn, S.J., 1968

PSALMODY

Ant. 1   **You cannot serve both God and mammon.**

Psalm 49
Emptiness of riches
It is difficult for a rich man to enter the kingdom of heaven
(Matthew 19:23).

I

Hear this, all you peoples,
give heed, all who dwell in the world,
men both low and high,
rich and poor alike!

My lips will speak words of wisdom.
My heart is full of insight.
I will turn my mind to a parable,
with the harp I will solve my problem.

Why should I fear in evil days
the malice of the foes who surround me,
men who trust in their wealth,
and boast of the vastness of their riches?

For no man can buy his own ransom,
or pay a price to God for his life.
The ransom of his soul is beyond him.
He cannot buy life without end,
nor avoid coming to the grave.

He knows that wise men and fools must both perish
and leave their wealth to others.
Their graves are their homes for ever,
their dwelling place from age to age,
though their names spread wide through the land.

In his riches, man lacks wisdom:
he is like the beasts that are destroyed.

Psalm-prayer

Make our mouths speak your wisdom, Lord Jesus, and
help us to remember that you became man and redeemed
us from death that we might merit the beauty of your
light.

Ant.   You cannot serve both God and mammon.

Ant. 2   Store up for yourselves treasure in heaven, says
the Lord.

II

This is the lot of those who trust in themselves,
who have others at their beck and call.
Like sheep they are driven to the grave,
where death shall be their shepherd
and the just shall become their rulers.

With the morning their outward show vanishes
and the grave becomes their home.
But God will ransom me from death
and take my soul to himself.

Then do not fear when a man grows rich,
when the glory of his house increases.
He takes nothing with him when he dies,
his glory does not follow him below.

Though he flattered himself while he lived:
"Men will praise me for all my success,"
yet he will go to join his fathers,
who will never see the light any more.

In his riches, man lacks wisdom:
he is like the beasts that are destroyed.

Psalm-prayer

You condemned the rich, Lord Jesus, because they
have already received their reward, and you proclaimed
the poor blessed because the kingdom of heaven is theirs.
Teach us to seek for imperishable goods and to have
confidence in your blood, poured out as the price of our
redemption.

Ant.   Store up for yourselves treasure in heaven, says
the Lord.

Ant. 3 Adoration and glory belong by right to the Lamb who was slain.

Canticle   Revelation 4:11; 5:9, 10, 12

Redemption hymn

O Lord our God, you are worthy
to receive glory and honor and power.

For you have created all things;
by your will they came to be and were made.

Worthy are you, O Lord,
to receive the scroll and break open its seals.

For you were slain;
with your blood you purchased for God
men of every race and tongue,
of every people and nation.

You made of them a kingdom,
and priests to serve our God,
and they shall reign on the earth.

Worthy is the Lamb that was slain
to receive power and riches,
wisdom and strength,
honor and glory and praise.

Ant. Adoration and glory belong by right to the Lamb who was slain.

Reading, responsory, antiphon for the canticle of Mary, intercessions and prayer, as in the Proper of Seasons.

Conclusion, as in the Ordinary.

WEDNESDAY, WEEK II

Invitatory

Lord, open my lips.

Antiphon, as in the Ordinary, 647.

Invitatory psalm, 648.

Office of Readings

God, come to my assistance. Glory to the Father. As it was in the beginning. Alleluia.

This verse and response are omitted when the hour begins with the invitatory.

HYMN

Lord Jesus Christ, be present now,
And let your Holy Spirit bow
All hearts in love and truth today
To hear your word and keep your way.

Give us the grace to grasp your word,
That we may do what we have heard.
Instruct us thru the scriptures, Lord,
As we draw near, O God adored.

May your glad tidings always bring
Good news to men, that they may sing
Of how you came to save all men.
Instruct us till you come again.

To God the Father and the Son
And Holy Spirit, three in one;
To you, O blessed Trinity,
Be praise thruout eternity.

Melody: Herr Jesu   Music: *Cantionale Germanicum*, Dresden, 1628.
Christ Dich L.M.   Text: Herr Jesu Christ Dich, Anon.
Translator: Catherine Winkworth, 1863, alt.
Stanza 2, Dennis Fitzpatrick

Or:

Praise to the Lord, the Almighty, the King of
    creation:
O my soul, praise him, for he is thy health and
    salvation.
All ye who hear,
Now to this altar draw near,
Joining in glad adoration.

Praise to the Lord, who doth prosper thy work and
    defend thee;
Surely his goodness and mercy shall daily attend
    thee.
Ponder anew
What the Almighty can do,
Who with his love doth befriend thee.

Praise to the Lord, O let all that is in me adore him!
All that has life and breath come now in praises
    before him!
Let the Amen
Sound from his people again:
Now as we worship before him.

Melody: Lobe Den Herren   Music: *Straslund Gesangbuch*, 1665
14.14.478   Text: J. Neander, 1650-1680
                            Translator: Catherine Winkworth, 1829-1878

PSALMODY

Ant. 1 We groan in pain as we await the redemption of
        our bodies.

Psalm 39

Urgent prayer of a sick person

*Creation is made subject to futility . . . by him who
subjected it, but it is not without hope* (Romans 8:20).

I

I said: "I will be watchful of my ways
for fear I should sin with my tongue.
I will put a curb on my lips
when the wicked man stands before me."
I was dumb, silent and still.
His prosperity stirred my grief.

My heart was burning within me.
At the thought of it, the fire blazed up
and my tongue burst into speech:
"O Lord, you have shown me my end,
how short is the length of my days.
Now I know how fleeting is my life.

You have given me a short span of days;
my life is as nothing in your sight.
A mere breath, the man who stood so firm,
a mere shadow, the man passing by,
a mere breath, the riches he hoards,
not knowing who will have them."

Ant.   We groan in pain as we await the redemption of
      our bodies.

Ant. 2   Hear and answer my prayer, O Lord; let me not
       weep in vain.

II

And now, Lord, what is there to wait for?
In you rests all my hope.
Set me free from all my sins,
do not make me the taunt of the fool.
I was silent, not opening my lips,
because this was all your doing.

Take away your scourge from me.
I am crushed by the blows of your hand.

You punish man's sins and correct him;
like the moth you devour all he treasures.
Mortal man is no more than a breath;
O Lord, hear my prayer.

O Lord, turn your ear to my cry.
Do not be deaf to my tears.
In your house I am a passing guest,
a pilgrim, like all my fathers.
Look away that I may breathe again
before I depart to be no more.

Psalm-prayer

Through your Son you taught us, Father, not to be
fearful of tomorrow but to commit our lives to your care.
Do not withhold your Spirit from us but help us find a
life of peace after these days of trouble.

Ant.   Hear and answer my prayer, O Lord; let me not
       weep in vain.

Ant. 3   I have put all my trust in God's never-failing
         mercy.

Psalm 52
Against a calumniator

If anyone would boast, let him boast in the Lord (1
Corinthians 1:31).

Why do you boast of your wickedness,
you champion of evil,
planning ruin all day long,
your tongue like a sharpened razor,
you master of deceit?

You love evil more than good;
lies more than truth.
You love the destructive word,
you tongue of deceit.

For this God will destroy you
and remove you for ever.
He will snatch you from your tent and uproot you
from the land of the living.

The just shall see and fear.
They shall laugh and say:
"So this is the man who refused
to take God as his stronghold,
but trusted in the greatness of his wealth
and grew powerful by his crimes."

But I am like a growing olive tree
in the house of God.
I trust in the goodness of God
for ever and ever.

I will thank you for evermore;
for this your doing.
I will proclaim that your name is good,
in the presence of your friends.

Psalm-prayer

Father, you cut down the unfruitful branch for burning and prune the fertile to make it bear more fruit. Make us grow like laden olive trees in your domain firmly rooted in the power and mercy of your Son, so that you may gather from us fruit worthy of eternal life.

Ant.   I have put all my trust in God's never-failing mercy.

Verse, reading and prayer, as in the Proper of Seasons.

Morning Prayer

God, come to my assistance. Glory to the Father. As it was in the beginning. Alleluia.

This verse and response are omitted when the hour begins with the invitatory.

Hymn

All creatures of our God and King,
Lift up your voice and with us sing
   Alleluia, alleluia!
Thou burning sun with golden beam,
Thou silver moon with softer gleam:

Refrain:

O praise him, O praise him, Alleluia, alleluia,
alleluia!

Thou rushing winds that are so strong,
Ye clouds that sail in heaven along,
   O praise him, alleluia!
Thou rising morn, in praise rejoice,
Ye lights of evening, find a voice:

Refrain

Melody: Vigiles et Sancti   Music: Cologne *Gesangbuch*, 1623
88.44.88.44.44.444   Text: St. Francis of Assisi, 1182-1226
             Translator: William H. Draper, 1855-1933, alt.

Or:

We plough the fields and scatter
The good seed on the land,
But it is fed and watered
By God's almighty hand;
He sends the snow in winter,
The warmth to swell the grain,
The breezes and the sunshine,
And soft refreshing rain:

Refrain:

All good gifts around us
Are sent from heav'n above,
Then thank the Lord,
O thank the Lord for all his love.

He only is the maker
Of all things near and far;

He paints the wayside flower,
He lights the ev'ning star.
The winds and waves obey him,
By him the birds are fed:
Much more to us his children,
He gives our daily bread:

Refrain

We thank you then, dear Father,
For all things bright and good:
The seedtime and the harvest,
Our life, our health, our food.
And all that we can offer
Your boundless love imparts,
The gifts to you most pleasing
Are humble, thankful hearts:

Refrain

Melody: Wir Pflugen 76.76.D   Music: Johann A. P. Schultz,
with Refrain   1747–1800
                                   Text: *Wir pflugen und wir streuen,*
                                        M. Claudius, 1740–1815
                                   Translator: Jane N. Campbell

PSALMODY

Ant. 1   O God, all your ways are holy; what god can
         compare with our God!

Psalm 77

Recalling God's works

We suffer all kinds of afflictions and yet are not overcome (2
Corinthians 4:8).

I cry aloud to God,
cry aloud to God that he may hear me.

In the day of my distress I sought the Lord.
My hands were raised at night without ceasing;
my soul refused to be consoled.
I remembered my God and I groaned.
I pondered and my spirit fainted.

You withheld sleep from my eyes.
I was troubled, I could not speak.
I thought of the days of long ago
and remembered the years long past.
At night I mused within my heart.
I pondered and my spirit questioned.

"Will the Lord reject us for ever?
Will he show us his favor no more?
Has his love vanished for ever?
Has his promise come to an end?
Does God forget his mercy
or in anger withhold his compassion?"

I said: "This is what causes my grief;
that the way of the Most High has changed."
I remember the deeds of the Lord,
I remember your wonders of old,
I muse on all your works
and ponder your mighty deeds.

Your ways, O God, are holy.
What god is great as our God?
You are the God who works wonders.
You showed your power among the peoples.
Your strong arm redeemed your people,
the sons of Jacob and Joseph.

The waters saw you, O God,
the waters saw you and trembled;
the depths were moved with terror.
The clouds poured down rain,
the skies sent forth their voice;
your arrows flashed to and fro.

Your thunder rolled round the sky,
your flashes lighted up the world.

The earth was moved and trembled
when your way led through the sea,
your path through the mighty waters,
and no one saw your footprints.

You guided your people like a flock
by the hand of Moses and Aaron.

Psalm-prayer

Father, you established your ancient covenant by signs
and wonders, but more wondrously you confirmed the
new one through the sacrifice of your Son. Guide your
Church through the pathways of life that we may be led
to the land of promise and celebrate your name with
lasting praise.

Ant. O God, all your ways are holy; what god can
compare with our God?

Ant. 2 My heart leaps up with joy to the Lord, for he
humbles only to exalt us.

Canticle 1 Samuel 2:1-10
The humble find joy in God

*He has cast down the mighty from their thrones and has lifted
up the lowly. He has filled the hungry with good things*
(Luke 1:52-53).

My heart exults in the Lord,
my horn is exalted in my God.

I have swallowed up my enemies;
I rejoice in my victory.
There is no Holy One like the Lord;
there is no Rock like our God.

Speak boastfully no longer,
nor let arrogance issue from your mouths.
For an all-knowing God is the Lord,
a God who judges deeds.

The bows of the mighty are broken,
while the tottering gird on strength.
The well-fed hire themselves out for bread,
while the hungry batten on spoil.
The barren wife bears seven sons,
while the mother of many languishes.

The Lord puts to death and gives life;
he casts down to the nether world;
he raises up again.
The Lord makes poor and makes rich,
he humbles, he also exalts.

He raises the needy from the dust;
from the ash heap he lifts up the poor,
to seat them with nobles
and make a glorious throne their heritage.

For the pillars of the earth are the Lord's,
and he has set the world upon them.
He will guard the footsteps of his faithful ones,
but the wicked shall perish in the darkness.
For not by strength does man prevail;
the Lord's foes shall be shattered.

The Most High in heaven thunders;
the Lord judges the ends of the earth.
Now may he give strength to his king
and exalt the horn of his anointed!

Ant.   My heart leaps up with joy to the Lord, for he
        humbles only to exalt us.

Ant. 3   The Lord is king, let the earth rejoice.

Psalm 97

The glory of the Lord in his decrees for the world

*This psalm foretells a world-wide salvation and that peoples
of all nations will believe in Christ* (St. Athanasius).

The Lord is king, let earth rejoice,
let all the coastlands be glad.
Cloud and darkness are his raiment;
his throne, justice and right.

A fire prepares his path;
it burns up his foes on every side.
His lightnings light up the world,
the earth trembles at the sight.

The mountains melt like wax
before the Lord of all the earth.
The skies proclaim his justice;
all peoples see his glory.

Let those who serve idols be ashamed,
those who boast of their worthless gods.
All you spirits, worship him.

Zion hears and is glad;
the people of Judah rejoice
because of your judgments, O Lord.

For you indeed are the Lord,
most high above all the earth,
exalted far above all spirits.

The Lord loves those who hate evil:
he guards the souls of his saints;
he sets them free from the wicked.

Light shines forth for the just
and joy for the upright of heart.
Rejoice, you just, in the Lord;
give glory to his holy name.

Psalm-prayer

Father, you clothe the sky with light and the depths of
the ocean with darkness. Among the sons of men you

work wonders, and rain terror upon the enemy. Look upon your servants. Do not try us by fire but bring us rejoicing to the shelter of your home.

Ant. The Lord is king, let the earth rejoice.

Reading, responsory, antiphon for the canticle of Zechariah, intercessions and prayer, as in the Proper of Seasons.

Conclusion, as in the Ordinary.

Daytime Prayer

God, come to my assistance. Glory to the Father. As it was in the beginning. Alleluia.

HYMN, as in the Ordinary, 658.

PSALMODY

Antiphon, as in the Proper of Seasons.

Psalm 119:57-64
VIII (Heth)

My part, I have resolved, O Lord,
is to obey your word.
With all my heart I implore your favor;
show the mercy of your promise.

I have pondered over my ways
and returned to your will.
I made haste and did not delay
to obey your commands.

Though the nets of the wicked ensnared me
I remembered your law.
At midnight I will rise and thank you
for your just decrees.

I am a friend of all who revere you,
who obey your precepts.
Lord, your love fills the earth.
Teach me your commands.

Psalm-prayer

Father, may the fulfillment of your law be our aim in life, so that you yourself may be our inheritance, and we your chosen possession for ever.

Psalm 55:2-15, 17-24
Against a friend proved traitor
Jesus was seized with fear and distress (Mark 14:33).

I

O God, listen to my prayer,
do not hide from my pleading,
attend to me and reply;
with my cares, I cannot rest.

I tremble at the shouts of the foe,
at the cries of the wicked;
for they bring down evil upon me.
They assail me with fury.

My heart is stricken within me,
death's terror is on me,
trembling and fear fall upon me
and horror overwhelms me.

O that I had wings like a dove
to fly away and be at rest.
So I would escape far away
and take refuge in the desert.

I would hasten to find a shelter
from the raging wind,
from the destructive storm, O Lord,
and from their plotting tongues.

For I can see nothing but violence
and strife in the city.
Night and day they patrol
high on the city walls.

It is full of wickedness and evil;
it is full of sin.
Its streets are never free
from tyranny and deceit.

II

If this had been done by an enemy
I could bear his taunts.
If a rival had risen against me,
I could hide from him.

But it is you, my own companion,
my intimate friend!
How close was the friendship between us.
We walked together in harmony
in the house of God.

As for me, I will cry to God
and the Lord will save me.
Evening, morning and at noon
I will cry and lament.

He will deliver my soul in peace
in the attack against me:
for those who fight me are many,
but he hears my voice.

God will hear and will humble them,
the eternal judge:
for they will not amend their ways.
They have no fear of God.

The traitor has turned against his friends;
he has broken his word.
His speech is softer than butter,
but war is in his heart.
His words are smoother than oil,
but they are naked swords.

Entrust your cares to the Lord
and he will support you.
He will never allow
the just man to stumble.

But you, O God, will bring them down
to the pit of death.
Deceitful and bloodthirsty men
shall not live half their days.

O Lord, I will trust in you.

Psalm-prayer

Lord Jesus, you were rejcted by your people, betrayed
by the kiss of a friend, and deserted by your disciples.
Give us the confidence that you had in the Father, and
our salvation will be assured.

At the other hours, the complementary psalmody is used, 1191.

Reading, verse and prayer, as in the Proper of Seasons.

Conclusion, as in the Ordinary.

Evening Prayer

God, come to my assistance. Glory to the Father. As it
was in the beginning. Alleluia.

HYMN

O worship the king, all glorious above;
O gratefully sing his power and his love;
Our shield and defender, the ancient of days,
Pavilioned in splendor, and girded with praise.

O tell of his might, O sing of his grace;
Whose robe is the light, whose canopy space;
His chariots of wrath the deep thunder-clouds form,
And dark is his path on the wings of the storm.

This earth, with its store of wonders untold,
Almighty, thy power hath founded of old;

Hath 'stablished it fast by a changeless decree,
And round it has cast, like a mantle, the sea.

Thy bountiful care what tongue can recite?
It breathes in the air, it shines in the light;
It streams from the hills, it descends to the plain,
And sweetly distils in the dew and the rain.

Frail children of dust, and feeble as frail,
In thee do we trust, nor find thee to fail;
Thy mercies how tender, how firm to the end,
Our maker, defender, redeemer, and friend.

O measureless might, ineffable love,
While angels delight to hymn thee above,
Thy humbler creation, though feeble their lays,
With true adoration shall sing to thy praise.

Melody: Hanover 55.55.65.55   Music: William Croft, 1682–1727
                                 Text: Robert Grant, 1779–1838

Or:

Refrain:

For to those who love God,
Who are called in his plan,
Everything works out for good.
And God himself chose them
To bear the likeness of his Son
That he might be the first of many, many brothers.

Who is able to condemn? Only Christ who died for
     us;
Christ who rose for us, Christ who prays for us.

Refrain

In the face of all this, what is there left to say?
For if God is for us, who can be against us?

Refrain

Who can separate us from the love of Christ?
Neither trouble, nor pain, nor persecution.

Refrain

What can separate us from the love of Christ?
Not the past, the present, nor the future.

Refrain

Melody: Romans VIII

Music: Enrico Garzilli, 1970
Text: Enrico Garzilli, 1970

PSALMODY

Ant. 1   Eagerly we await the fulfillment of our hope, the glorious coming of our Savior.

Psalm 62

Peace in God

May God, the source of our hope, fill your hearts with peace as you believe in him (Romans 15:13).

In God alone is my soul at rest;
my help comes from him.
He alone is my rock, my stronghold,
my fortress: I stand firm.

How long will you all attack one man
to break him down,
as though he were a tottering wall,
or a tumbling fence?

Their plan is only to destroy:
they take pleasure in lies.
With their mouth they utter blessing
but in their heart they curse.

In God alone be at rest, my soul;
for my hope comes from him.
He alone is my rock, my stronghold,
my fortress: I stand firm.

In God is my safety and glory,
the rock of my strength.
Take refuge in God, all you people.
Trust him at all times.
Pour out your hearts before him
for God is our refuge.

Common folk are only a breath,
great men an illusion.
Placed in the scales, they rise;
they weigh less than a breath.

Do not put your trust in oppression
nor vain hopes on plunder.
Do not set your heart on riches
even when they increase.

For God has said only one thing:
only two do I know:
that to God alone belongs power
and to you, Lord, love;
and that you repay each man
according to his deeds.

Psalm-prayer

Lord God, you reward each one according to his
works. Hear us as we pour out our hearts to you seeking
your grace and secure protection. We look to you for our
stable hope in a constantly changing world.

Ant.   Eagerly we await the fulfillment of our hope, the
        glorious coming of our Savior.

Ant. 2 May God turn his radiant face toward us and fill
        us with his blessings.

When psalm 67 is the invitatory psalm, psalm 95, **648**, is used
as the second psalm of Evening Prayer.

Psalm 67

People of all nations will worship the Lord

You must know that God is offering his salvation to all the world (Acts 28:28).

O God, be gracious and bless us
and let your face shed its light upon us.
So will your ways be known upon earth
and all nations learn your saving help.

Let the peoples praise you, O God;
let all the peoples praise you.

Let the nations be glad and exult
for you rule the world with justice.
With fairness you rule the peoples,
you guide the nations on earth.

Let the peoples praise you, O God;
let all the peoples praise you.

The earth has yielded its fruit
for God, our God, has blessed us.—
May God still give us his blessing
till the ends of the earth revere him.

Psalm-prayer

Be gracious and bless us, Lord, and let your face shed its light on us, so that we can make you known with reverence and bring forth a harvest of justice.

Ant. May God turn his radiant face toward us and fill us with his blessings.

Ant. 3 Through him all things were made; he holds all creation together in himself.

Canticle   Colossians 1:12-20
Christ the first-born of all creation
and the first-born from the dead

Let us give thanks to the Father
for having made you worthy
to share the lot of the saints
in light.

He rescued us
from the power of darkness
and brought us
into the kingdom of his beloved Son.
Through him we have redemption,
the forgiveness of our sins.

He is the image of the invisible God,
the first-born of all creatures.
In him everything in heaven and on earth was
    created,
things visible and invisible.

All were created through him;
all were created for him.
He is before all else that is.
In him everything continues in being.

It is he who is head of the body, the church!
he who is the beginning,
the first-born of the dead,
so that primacy may be his in everything.

It pleased God to make absolute fulness reside in him
and, by means of him, to reconcile everything in his
    person,

both on earth and in the heavens,
making peace through the blood of his cross.

Ant. Through him all things were made; he holds all
creation together in himself.

Reading, responsory, antiphon for the canticle of Mary,
intercessions and prayer, as in the Proper of Seasons.

Conclusion, as in the Ordinary.

THURSDAY, WEEK II

Invitatory

Lord, open my lips.

Antiphon, as in the Ordinary, 647.
Invitatory psalm, 648.

Office of Readings

God, come to my assistance. Glory to the Father. As it was in the beginning. Alleluia.

This verse and response are omitted when the hour begins with the invitatory.

HYMN

O God, our help in ages past,
Our hope for years to come,
Our shelter from the stormy blast
And our eternal home.

Beneath the shadow of your throne
Your saints have dwelt secure;
Sufficient is your arm alone.
And our defense is sure.

Before the hills in order stood,
Or earth received her frame,
From everlasting you are God,
To endless years the same.

A thousand ages in your sight
Are like an evening gone,
Short as the watch that ends the night
Before the rising sun.

Time, like an ever-rolling stream,
Bears all its sons away;
They fly forgotten, as a dream
Dies at the opening day.

O God, our help in ages past,
Our hope for years to come,
Be now our guide while life shall last,
And our eternal home.

Melody: Saint Anne C.M.

Music: William Croft, 1708
Text: Isaac Watts, 1674–1748,
alt. by Rev. William Bauman

PSALMODY

Ant. 1   Lord, you are our savior; we will praise you for
ever.

Psalm 44

The misfortunes of God's people

We triumph over all these things through him who loves us
(Romans 8:37).

I

We heard with our own ears, O God,
our fathers have told us the story
of the things you did in their days,
you yourself, in days long ago.

To plant them you uprooted the nations:
to let them spread you laid peoples low.
No sword of their own won the land;
no arm of their own brought them victory.
It was your right hand, your arm
and the light of your face: for you loved them.

It is you, my king, my God,
who granted victories to Jacob.

Through you we beat down our foes;
in your name we trampled our aggressors.

For it was not in my bow that I trusted
nor yet was I saved by my sword:

it was you who saved us from our foes,
it was you who put our foes to shame.
All day long our boast was in God
and we praised your name without ceasing.

Ant.   Lord, you are our savior; we will praise you for
       ever.

Ant. 2 Spare us, O Lord; do not bring your own
        people into contempt.

II

Yet now you have rejected us, disgraced us:
you no longer go forth with our armies.
You make us retreat from the foe
and our enemies plunder us at will.

You make us like sheep for the slaughter
and scatter us among the nations.
You sell your own people for nothing
and make no profit by the sale.

You make us the taunt of our neighbors,
the laughing stock of all who are near.
Among the nations, you make us a byword,
among the peoples a thing of derision.

All day long my disgrace is before me:
my face is covered with shame
at the voice of the taunter, the scoffer,
at the sight of the foe and avenger.

Ant.   Spare us, O Lord; do not bring your own people
        into contempt.

Ant. 3 Rise up, O Lord, and save us, for you are
        merciful.

III

This befell us though we had not forgotten you;
though we had not been false to your covenant,
though we had not withdrawn our hearts;
though our feet had not strayed from your path.
Yet you have crushed us in a place of sorrows
and covered us with the shadow of death.

Had we forgotten the name of our God
or stretched out hands to another god
would not God have found this out,
he who knows the secrets of the heart?
It is for you that we face death all day long
and are counted as sheep for the slaughter.

Awake, O Lord, why do you sleep?
Arise, do not reject us for ever!
Why do you hide your face
and forget our oppression and misery?

For we are brought down low to the dust;
our body lies prostrate on the earth.
Stand up and come to our help!
Redeem us because of your love!

Psalm-prayer

Lord, rise up and come to our aid; with your strong
arm lead us to freedom, as you mightily delivered our

forefathers. Since you are the King who knows the secrets of our hearts, fill them with the light of truth.

Ant. Rise up, O Lord, and save us, for you are merciful.

Verse, reading and prayer, as in the Proper of Seasons.

Morning Prayer

God, come to my assistance. Glory to the Father. As it was in the beginning. Alleluia.

This verse and response are omitted when the hour begins with the invitatory.

HYMN

O God of light, the dawning day
Gives us new promise of your love.
Each fresh beginning is your gift,
Like gentle dew from heav'n above.

Your blessings, Father, never fail:
Your Son, who is our daily Bread,
The Holy Spirit of your love,
By whom each day your sons are led.

Make us the servants of your peace,
Renew our strength, remove all fear;
Be with us, Lord, throughout this day,
For all is joy if you are near.

To Father, Son and Spirit blest,
One only God, we humbly pray:
Show us the splendor of your light
In death, the dawn of perfect day.

Melody: Danby L.M.   Music: English Traditional Melody
Text: James Quinn, S.J.

PSALMODY

Ant. 1 **Stir up your mighty power, Lord; come to our aid.**

Psalm 80
Lord, come, take care of your vineyard

Come, Lord Jesus (Revelation 22:20).

O shepherd of Israel, hear us,
you who lead Joseph's flock,
shine forth from your cherubim throne
upon Ephraim, Benjamin, Manasseh.
O Lord, rouse up your might,
O Lord, come to our help.

God of hosts, bring us back;
let your face shine on us and we shall be saved.

Lord God of hosts, how long
will you frown on your people's plea?
You have fed them with tears for their bread,
an abundance of tears for their drink.
You have made us the taunt of our neighbors,
our enemies laugh us to scorn.

God of hosts, bring us back;
let your face shine on us and we shall be saved.

You brought a vine out of Egypt;
to plant it you drove out the nations.
Before it you cleared the ground;
it took root and spread through the land.

The mountains were covered with its shadow,
the cedars of God with its boughs.
It stretched out its branches to the sea,
to the Great River it stretched out its shoots.

Then why have you broken down its walls?
It is plucked by all who pass by.
It is ravaged by the boar of the forest,
devoured by the beasts of the field.

God of hosts, turn again, we implore,
look down from heaven and see.
Visit this vine and protect it,
the vine your right hand has planted.
Men have burnt it with fire and destroyed it.
May they perish at the frown of your face.

May your hand be on the man you have chosen,
the man you have given your strength.
And we shall never forsake you again:
give us life that we may call upon your name.

God of hosts, bring us back;
let your face shine on us and we shall be saved.

Psalm-prayer

Lord God, eternal shepherd, you so tend the vineyard
you planted that now it extends its branches even to the
farthest coast. Look down on your Church and come to
us. Help us remain in your Son as branches on the vine
that, planted firmly in your love, we may testify before
the whole world to your great power working everywhere.

Ant. Stir up your mighty power, Lord; come to our aid.

Ant. 2 The Lord has worked marvels for us; make it known to the ends of the world.

Canticle   Isaiah 12:1-6
Joy of God's ransomed people
If anyone thirsts, let him come to me and drink (John 7:37).

I give you thanks, O Lord;
though you have been angry with me,
your anger has abated, and you have consoled me.

God indeed is my savior;
I am confident and unafraid.
My strength and my courage is the Lord,
and he has been my savior.

With joy you will draw water
at the fountain of salvation, and say on that day:

Give thanks to the Lord, acclaim his name;
among the nations make known his deeds,
proclaim how exalted is his name.

Sing praise to the Lord for his glorious achievement;
let this be known throughout all the earth.

Shout with exultation, O city of Zion,
for great in your midst
is the Holy One of Israel!

Ant. The Lord has worked marvels for us; make it known to the ends of the world.

Ant. 3 Ring out your joy to God our strength.

Psalm 81

Solemn renewal of the Covenant

See that no one among you has a faithless heart (Hebrews
3:12).

Ring out your joy to God our strength,
shout in triumph to the God of Jacob.

Raise a song and sound the timbrel,
the sweet-sounding harp and the lute,
blow the trumpet at the new moon,
when the moon is full, on our feast.

For this is Israel's law,
a command of the God of Jacob.
He imposed it as a rule on Joseph,
when he went out against the land of Egypt.

A voice I did not know said to me:
"I freed your shoulder from the burden;
your hands were freed from the load.
You called in distress and I saved you.

I answered, concealed in the storm cloud,
at the waters of Meribah I tested you.
Listen, my people, to my warning,
O Israel, if only you would heed!

Let there be no foreign god among you,
no worship of an alien god.
I am the Lord your God,
who brought you from the land of Egypt.
Open wide your mouth and I will fill it.

But my people did not heed my voice
and Israel would not obey,
so I left them in their stubbornness of heart
to follow their own designs.

O that my people would heed me,
that Israel would walk in my ways!
At once I would subdue their foes,
turn my hand against their enemies.

The Lord's enemies would cringe at their feet
and their subjection would last for ever.
But Israel I would feed with finest wheat
and fill them with honey from the rock."

Psalm-prayer

Lord God, open our mouths to proclaim your glory.
Help us to leave sin behind and to rejoice in professing
your name.

Ant.   Ring out your joy to God our strength.

Reading, responsory, antiphon for the canticle of Zechariah,
intercessions and prayer, as in the Proper of Seasons.

Conclusion, as in the Ordinary.

Daytime Prayer

God, come to my assistance. Glory to the Father. As it
was in the beginning. Alleluia.

Hymn, as in the Ordinary, 658.

Psalmody

Antiphon, as in the Proper of Seasons.

Psalm 119:65-72

IX (Teth)

Lord, you have been good to your servant
according to your word.
Teach me discernment and knowledge
for I trust in your commands.

Before I was afflicted I strayed
but now I keep your word.
You are good and your deeds are good;
teach me your commandments.

Though proud men smear me with lies
yet I keep your precepts.
Their minds are closed to good
but your law is my delight.

It was good for me to be afflicted,
to learn your will.
The law from your mouth means more to me
than silver and gold.

Psalm-prayer

Lord, teach us goodness, discipline and wisdom, and
these gifts will keep us from becoming hardened by evil,
weakened by laziness or ignorant because of foolishness.

Psalm 56:2-7b, 9-14

Trust in God's word

This psalm shows Christ in his passion (Saint Jerome).

Have mercy on me, God, men crush me;
they fight me all day long and oppress me.
My foes crush me all day long,
for many fight proudly against me.

When I fear, I will trust in you,
in God whose word I praise.
In God I trust, I shall not fear:
what can mortal man do to me?

All day long they distort my words,
all their thought is to harm me.

They band together in ambush,
track me down and seek my life.

You have kept an account of my wanderings;
you have kept a record of my tears;
are they not written in your book?
Then my foes will be put to flight
on the day that I call to you.

This I know, that God is on my side.
In God, whose word I praise,
in the Lord, whose word I praise,
in God I trust; I shall not fear:
what can mortal man do to me?

I am bound by the vows I have made you.
O God, I will offer you praise
for you rescued my soul from death,
you kept my feet from stumbling
that I may walk in the presence of God
and enjoy the light of the living.

Psalm-prayer

Lord Jesus Christ, victim for our sins, you trusted in
your Father's protection and kept silent when you were
tormented. Give us that same confidence and we will
gladly suffer with you and for you, offering the Father
our sacrifice of praise and walking before him in the light
of the living.

Psalm 57

Morning prayer in affliction

This psalm tells of our Lord's passion (Saint Augustine).

Have mercy on me, God, have mercy
for in you my soul has taken refuge.
In the shadow of your wings I take refuge
till the storms of destruction pass by.

I call to God the Most High,
to God who has always been my help.
May he send from heaven and save me
and shame those who assail me.

May God send his truth and his love.

My soul lies down among lions,
who would devour the sons of men.
Their teeth are spears and arrows,
their tongue a sharpened sword.

O God, arise above the heavens;
may your glory shine on earth!

They laid a snare for my steps,
my soul was bowed down.
They dug a pit in my path
but fell in it themselves.

My heart is ready, O God,
my heart is ready.
I will sing, I will sing your praise.
Awake, my soul,
awake, lyre and harp.
I will awake the dawn.

I will thank you, Lord, among the peoples,
among the nations I will praise you
for your love reaches to the heavens
and your truth to the skies.

O God, arise above the heavens;
may your glory shine on earth!

Psalm-prayer

Lord, send your mercy and your truth to rescue us
from the snares of the devil, and we will praise you

among the peoples and proclaim you to the nations, happy to be known as companions of your Son.

At the other hours, the complementary psalmody is used, 1191.

Reading, verse and prayer, as in the Proper of Seasons.

Conclusion, as in the Ordinary.

Evening Prayer

God, come to my assistance. Glory to the Father. As it was in the beginning. Alleluia.

HYMN

Let all things now living a song of thanksgiving
To God our Creator triumphantly raise;
Who fashioned and made us, protected and stayed us,
Who guideth us on to the end of our days.
His banners are o'er us, his light goes before us,
A pillar of fire shining forth in the night:
Till shadows have vanished and darkness is banished,
As forward we travel from light into Light.

His law he enforces, the stars in their courses,
The sun in his orbit obediently shine,
The hill and the mountains, the rivers and fountains,
The depths of the ocean proclaim him divine.
We, too, should be voicing our love and rejoicing
With glad adoration, a song let us raise:
Till all things now living unite in thanksgiving,
To God in the highest, hosanna and praise.

Melody: The Ash Grove   Music: Welsh Melody
                                                      Text: Anon.

Ant. 1   I have made you the light of all nations to carry
my salvation to the ends of the earth.

Psalm 72

The Messiah's royal power

*Opening their treasures, they offered him gifts: gold,
frankincense and myrrh* (Matthew 2:11).

I

O God, give your judgment to the king,
to a king's son your justice,
that he may judge your people in justice
and your poor in right judgment.

May the mountains bring forth peace for the people
and the hills, justice.
May he defend the poor of the people
and save the children of the needy
and crush the oppressor.

He shall endure like the sun and the moon
from age to age.
He shall descend like rain on the meadow,
like raindrops on the earth.

In his days justice shall flourish
and peace till the moon fails.
He shall rule from sea to sea,
from the Great River to earth's bounds.

Before him his enemies shall fall,
his foes lick the dust.
The kings of Tarshish and the sea coasts
shall pay him tribute.

The kings of Sheba and Seba
shall bring him gifts.
Before him all kings shall fall prostrate,
all nations shall serve him.

Ant. I have made you the light of all nations to carry
my salvation to the ends of the earth.

Ant. 2 The Lord will save the children of the poor and
rescue them from slavery.

II

For he shall save the poor when they cry
and the needy who are helpless.
He will have pity on the weak
and save the lives of the poor.

From oppression he will rescue their lives,
to him their blood is dear.
Long may he live,
may the gold of Sheba be given him.
They shall pray for him without ceasing
and bless him all the day.

May corn be abundant in the land
to the peaks of the mountains.
May its fruit rustle like Lebanon;
may men flourish in the cities
like grass on the earth.

May his name be blessed for ever
and endure like the sun.
Every tribe shall be blessed in him,
all nations bless his name.

Blessed be the Lord, God of Israel,
who alone works wonders,

ever blessed his glorious name.
Let his glory fill the earth.

Amen! Amen!

Psalm-prayer

We call upon your name, Father, and pronounce it
blessed above the earth. Give your people the fullness of
peace and justice in your kingdom.

Ant. The Lord will save the children of the poor and
rescue them from slavery.

Ant. 3 Now the victorious reign of our God has begun.

Canticle   Revelation 11:17-18;12:10b-12a

The judgment of God

We praise you, the Lord God Almighty,
who is and who was.
You have assumed your great power,
you have begun your reign.

The nations have raged in anger,
but then came your day of wrath,
and the moment to judge the dead:
The time to reward your servants the prophets
and the holy ones who revere you,
the great and the small alike.

Now have salvation and power come,
the reign of our God and the authority
of his Anointed One.
For the accuser of our brothers is cast out,
who night and day accused them before God.

They defeated him by the blood of the Lamb
and by the word of their testimony;
love for life did not deter them from death.
So rejoice, you heavens,
and you that dwell therein!

Ant. Now the victorious reign of our God has begun.

Reading, responsory, antiphon for the canticle of Mary,
intercessions and prayer, as in the Proper of Seasons.

Conclusion, as in the Ordinary.

FRIDAY, WEEK II

Invitatory

Lord, open my lips.

Antiphon, as in the Ordinary, 647.

Invitatory psalm, 648.

Office of Readings

God, come to my assistance. Glory to the Father. As it was in the beginning. Alleluia.

This verse and response are omitted when the hour begins with the invitatory.

HYMN

Sing praise to our Creator,
O sons of Adam's race;
God's children by adoption,
Baptized into his grace.

Refrain:

Praise the holy Trinity,
Undivided Unity;
Holy God, Mighty God,
God Immortal, be adored.

To Jesus Christ give glory,
God's coeternal Son;
As members of his Body
We live in him as one.

Refrain

Now praise the Holy Spirit
Poured forth upon the earth;
Who sanctifies and guides us,
Confirmed in our rebirth.

Refrain

Melody: Mainz 76.76 with Refrain

Music: Mainz Melody
Text: Omer Westendorf, 1961

PSALMODY

Ant. 1   Lord, in your anger, do not punish me.

Psalm 38

A sinner in extreme danger prays earnestly to God

All his friends were standing at a distance (Luke 23:49).

I

O Lord, do not rebuke me in your anger;
do not punish me, Lord, in your rage.
Your arrows have sunk deep in me;
your hand has come down upon me.

Through your anger all my body is sick:
through my sin, there is no health in my limbs.
My guilt towers higher than my head;
it is a weight too heavy to bear.

Ant.   Lord, in your anger, do not punish me.

Ant. 2   Lord, you know all my longings.

II

My wounds are foul and festering,
the result of my own folly.
I am bowed and brought to my knees.
I go mourning all the day long.

All my frame burns with fever;
all my body is sick.
Spent and utterly crushed,
I cry aloud in anguish of heart.

O Lord, you know all my longing:
my groans are not hidden from you.

My heart throbs, my strength is spent;
the very light has gone from my eyes.

My friends avoid me like a leper;
those closest to me stand afar off.
Those who plot against my life lay snares;
those who seek my ruin speak of harm,
planning treachery all the day long.

Ant. Lord, you know all my longings.

Ant. 3 I confess my guilt to you, Lord; do not abandon
me, for you are my savior.

III

But I am like a deaf man who cannot hear,
like the dumb unable to speak.
I am like a man who hears nothing,
in whose mouth is no defense.

I count on you, O Lord:
it is you, Lord God, who will answer.
I pray: "Do not let them mock me,
those who triumph if my foot should slip."

For I am on the point of falling
and my pain is always before me.
I confess that I am guilty
and my sin fills me with dismay.

My wanton enemies are numberless
and my lying foes are many.
They repay me evil for good
and attack me for seeking what is right.

O Lord, do not forsake me!
My God, do not stay afar off!
Make haste and come to my help,
O Lord, my God, my savior!

Psalm-prayer

Do not abandon us, Lord our God; you did not forget
the broken body of your Christ, nor the mockery his love
received. We, your children, are weighed down with sin;
give us the fullness of your mercy.

Ant.   I confess my guilt to you, Lord; do not abandon
me, for you are my savior.

Verse, reading and prayer, as in the Proper of Seasons.

Morning Prayer

God, come to my assistance. Glory to the Father. As it
was in the beginning. Alleluia.

This verse and response are omitted when the hour begins with
the invitatory.

Hymn

We turn to you, O God of every nation,
Giver of life and origin of good;
Your love is at the heart of all creation,
Your hurt is people's broken brotherhood.

We turn to you that we may be forgiven
For crucifying Christ on earth again;
We know that we have never wholly striven,
Forgetting self, to love the other man.

Free every heart from pride and self-reliance,
Our ways of thought inspire with simple grace;
Break down among us barriers of defiance,
Speak to the soul of all the human race.

Teach us, good Lord, to serve the need of others,
Help us to give and not to count the cost.
Unite us all for we are born as brothers;
Defeat our Babel with your Pentecost.

Melody: Intercessor 11.10.11.10   Music: C.H.H. Parry, 1848–1918
Text: Fred Kaan, 1929–

Ant. 1 **A humble, contrite heart, O God, you will not spurn.**

Psalm 51

O God, have mercy on me

Your inmost being must be renewed, and you must put on the new man (Ephesians 4:23-24).

> Have mercy on me, God, in your kindness.
> In your compassion blot out my offense.
> O wash me more and more from my guilt
> and cleanse me from my sin.
>
> My offenses truly I know them;
> my sin is always before me.
> Against you, you alone, have I sinned;
> what is evil in your sight I have done.
>
> That you may be justified when you give sentence
> and be without reproach when you judge.
> O see, in guilt I was born,
> a sinner was I conceived.
>
> Indeed you love truth in the heart;
> then in the secret of my heart teach me wisdom
> O purify me, then I shall be clean;
> O wash me, I shall be whiter than snow.
>
> Make me hear rejoicing and gladness,
> that the bones you have crushed may revive.
> From my sins turn away your face
> and blot out all my guilt.
>
> A pure heart create for me, O God,
> put a steadfast spirit within me.
> Do not cast me away from your presence,
> nor deprive me of your holy spirit.

Give me again the joy of your help;
with a spirit of fervor sustain me,
that I may teach transgressors your ways
and sinners may return to you.

O rescue me, God, my helper,
and my tongue shall ring out your goodness.
O Lord, open my lips
and my mouth shall declare your praise.

For in sacrifice you take no delight,
a burnt offering from me you would refuse,
my sacrifice, a contrite spirit.
A humbled, contrite heart you will not spurn.

In your goodness, show favor to Zion:
rebuild the walls of Jerusalem.
Then you will be pleased with lawful sacrifice,
holocausts offered on your altar.

Psalm-prayer

Father, he who knew no sin was made sin for us, to save us and restore us to your friendship. Look upon our contrite heart and afflicted spirit and heal our troubled conscience, so that in the joy and strength of the Holy Spirit we may proclaim your praise and glory before all the nations.

Ant.   A humble, contrite heart, O God, you will not spurn.

Ant. 2   Even in your anger, Lord, you will remember compassion.

Canticle   Habakkuk 3:2-4, 13a, 15-19

God comes to judge

Lift up your heads for your redemption is at hand (Luke 21:28).

O Lord, I have heard your renown,
and feared, O Lord, your work.
In the course of the years revive it,
in the course of the years make it known;
in your wrath remember compassion!

God comes from Teman,
the Holy One from Mount Paran.
Covered are the heavens with his glory,
and with his praise the earth is filled.

His splendor spreads like the light;
rays shine forth from beside him,
where his power is concealed.
You come forth to save your people,
to save your anointed one.

You tread the sea with your steeds
amid the churning of the deep waters.
I hear, and my body trembles;
at the sound, my lips quiver.

Decay invades my bones,
my legs tremble beneath me.
I await the day of distress
that will come upon the people who attack us.

For though the fig tree blossom not
nor fruit be on the vines,
though the yield of the olive fail
and the terraces produce no nourishment,

though   the flocks disappear from the fold
and there be no herd in the stalls,
yet will I rejoice in the Lord
and exult in my saving God.

Psalm-prayer

Lord, you established peace within the borders of Jerusalem. Give the fullness of peace now to your faithful people. May peace rule us in this life and possess us in eternal life. You are about to fill us with the best of wheat; grant that what we see dimly now as in a mirror, we may come to perceive clearly in the brightness of your truth.

Ant. O praise the Lord, Jerusalem!

Reading, responsory, antiphon for the canticle of Zechariah, intercessions and prayer, as in the Proper of Seasons.

Conclusion, as in the Ordinary.

Daytime Prayer

God, come to my assistance. Glory to the Father. As it was in the beginning. Alleluia.

HYMN, as in the Ordinary, 658.

PSALMODY

Antiphon, as in the Proper of Seasons.

Psalm 119:73-80
X(Yod)

It was your hands that made me and shaped me:
help me to learn your commands.
Your faithful will see me and rejoice
for I trust in your word.

Lord, I know that your decrees are right,
that you afflicted me justly.
Let your love be ready to console me
your promise to your servant.

vour love come to me and I shall live
ur law is my delight.

Shame the proud who harm me with lies
while I ponder your precepts.

Let your faithful turn to me,
those who know your will.
Let my heart be blameless in obeying you
lest I be ashamed.

Psalm-prayer

We know that your rulings are just ones, Lord, and so
we ask for your mercy; treat us gently and we will not be
put to shame.

Psalm 59:2-5, 10-11, 17-18

Prayer for help against enemies

*These words of the Savior teach us the devotion that all
should have for the Father* (Eusebius of Caesarea).

Rescue me, God, from my foes;
protect me from those who attack me.
O rescue me from those who do evil
and save me from blood-thirsty men.

See, they lie in wait for my life;
powerful men band together against me.
For no offense, no sin of mine, Lord,
for no guilt of mine they rush to take their stand.
Awake, come to my aid and see!

O my Strength, it is you to whom I turn,
for you, O God, are my stronghold,
the God who shows me love.

O God, come to my aid
and let me look in triumph on my foes.

As for me, I will sing of your strength
and each morning acclaim your love

for you have been my stronghold,
a refuge in the day of my distress.

O my Strength, it is you to whom I turn,
for you, O God, are my stronghold,
the God who shows me love.

Psalm-prayer

Lord, God of power, you rescued your Son from the
grasp of evil men. Deliver us from evil and confirm our
trust in you, so that with our rising we may sing of your
power and exult in your mercy at dawn.

Psalm 60

Prayer after disaster

*You will suffer in the world, but have confidence: I have
overcome the world* (John 16:33).

O God, you have rejected us and broken us.
You have been angry; come back to us.

You have made the earth quake, torn it open.
Repair what is shattered for it sways.
You have inflicted hardships on your people
and made us drink a wine that dazed us.

You have given those who fear you a signal
to flee from the enemy's bow.
O come and deliver your friends,
help with your right hand and reply.

From his holy place God has made this promise:
"I will triumph and divide the land of Shechem,
I will measure out the valley of Succoth.

Gilead is mine and Manasseh,
Ephraim I take for my helmet,
Judah for my commander's staff.

he has kept my soul from death,
my eyes from tears
and my feet from stumbling.

I will walk in the presence of the Lord
in the land of the living.

Psalm-prayer

God of power and mercy, through your Son's passion
and resurrection you have freed us from the bonds of
death and the anguish of separation from you. Be ever
with us on our pilgrimage; then we shall sing rather than
weep. Keep our feet from stumbling, so that we may be
able to follow you until we come to eternal rest.

Ant.   Lord, keep my soul from death, never let me
        stumble.

Ant. 2 My help comes from the Lord, who made
        heaven and earth.

Psalm 121

Guardian of his people

*Never again will they hunger and thirst, never again know
scorching heat* (Revelation 7:16).

I lift up my eyes to the mountains:
from where shall come my help?
My help shall come from the Lord
who made heaven and earth.

May he never allow you to stumble!
Let him sleep not, your guard.
No, he sleeps not nor slumbers,
Israel's guard.

The Lord is your guard and your shade,
at your right side he stands.
By day the sun shall not smite you
nor the moon in the night.

The Lord will guard you from evil,
he will guard your soul.
The Lord will guard your going and coming
both now and for ever.

Psalm-prayer

Lord Jesus Christ, you have prepared a quiet place for
us in your Father's eternal home. Watch over our welfare
on this perilous journey, shade us from the burning heat
of day, and keep our lives free of evil until the end.

Ant.   My help comes from the Lord, who made heaven
        and earth.

Ant. 3 King of all the ages, your ways are perfect and
        true.

                        Canticle   Revelation 15:3-4
                    Hymn of adoration

Mighty and wonderful are your works,
Lord God Almighty!
Righteous and true are your ways,
O King of the nations!

Who would dare refuse you honor,
or the glory due your name, O Lord?

Since you alone are holy,
all nations shall come
and worship in your presence.
Your mighty deeds are clearly seen.

Ant.   **King of all the ages, your ways are perfect and true.**

Reading, responsory, antiphon for the canticle of Mary, intercessions and prayer as in the Proper of Seasons.

Conclusion, as in the Ordinary.

SATURDAY, WEEK II

Invitatory

Lord, open my lips.

Antiphon, as in the Ordinary, 647.

Invitatory psalm, 648.

Office of Readings

God, come to my assistance. Glory to the Father. As it was in the beginning. Alleluia.

This verse and response are omitted when the hour begins with the invitatory.

HYMN

Praise the Lord, ye heavens, adore him;
Praise him, angels in the height;
Sun and moon, rejoice before him;
Praise him, all ye stars of light.
Praise the Lord for he has spoken;
Worlds his mighty voice obeyed;
Laws which never shall be broken,
For their guidance he has made.

Praise the Lord, for he is glorious,
Never shall his promise fail;
God has made his saints victorious,
Sin and death shall not prevail.
Praise the God of our salvation;
Hosts on high his power proclaim;
Heaven and earth and all creation,
Praise and magnify his name.

Worship, honor, glory, blessing,
Lord, we offer unto thee;
Young and old, thy praise expressing,
In glad homage bend the knee.

All the saints in heaven adore thee,
We would bow before thy throne;
As thine angels serve before thee,
So on earth thy will be done.

Melody: Austria 87:87.D   Music: Franz Joseph Haydn, 1797
Text: Stanzas 1 and 2, Foundling
Hospital Collection, c. 1801;
St. 3, Edward Osler, 1836

PSALMODY

Ant. 1   Remember us, O Lord; come with your saving
help.

Psalm 106

The goodness of the Lord; the faithlessness of his people

*These things have been written for a warning for us, for we
are living at the end of the ages* (1 Corinthians 10:11).

I

O give thanks to the Lord for he is good:
for his love endures for ever.
Who can tell the Lord's mighty deeds?
Who can recount all his praise?

They are happy who do what is right,
who at all times do what is just.
O Lord, remember me
out of the love you have for your people.

Come to me, Lord, with your help
that I may see the joy of your chosen ones
and may rejoice in the gladness of your nation
and share the glory of your people.

Our sin is the sin of our fathers;
we have done wrong, our deeds have been evil.
Our fathers when they were in Egypt
paid no heed to your wonderful deeds.

They forgot the greatness of your love;
at the Red Sea defied the Most High.
Yet he saved them for the sake of his name,
in order to make known his power.

He threatened the Red Sea; it dried up
and he led them through the deep as through the
    desert.
He saved them from the hand of the foe;
he saved them from the grip of the enemy.

The waters covered their oppressors;
not one of them was left alive.
Then they believed in his words:
then they sang his praises.

But they soon forgot his deeds
and would not wait upon his will.
They yielded to their cravings in the desert
and put God to the test in the wilderness.

He granted them the favor they asked
and sent disease among them.
Then they rebelled, envious of Moses
and of Aaron, who was holy to the Lord.

The earth opened and swallowed up Dathan
and buried the clan of Abiram.
Fire blazed up against their clan
and flames devoured the rebels.

Ant. Remember us, O Lord; come with your saving
help.

Ant. 2 Keep it carefully in mind: the Lord your God
has made a covenant with you.

II

They fashioned a calf at Horeb
and worshiped an image of metal,

exchanging the God who was their glory
for the image of a bull that eats grass.

They forgot the God who was their savior,
who had done such great things in Egypt,
such portents in the land of Ham,
such marvels at the Red Sea.

For this he said he would destroy them,
but Moses, the man he had chosen,
stood in the breach before him,
to turn back his anger from destruction.

Then they scorned the land of promise:
they had no faith in his word.
They complained inside their tents
and would not listen to the voice of the Lord.

So he raised his hand to swear an oath
that he would lay them low in the desert;
would scatter their sons among the nations
and disperse them throughout the lands.

They bowed before the Baal of Peor;
ate offerings made to lifeless gods.
They roused him to anger with their deeds
and a plague broke out among them.

Then Phinehas stood up and intervened.
Thus the plague was ended
and this was counted in his favor
from age to age for ever.

They provoked him at the waters of Meribah.
Through their fault it went ill with Moses;
for they made his heart grow bitter
and he uttered words that were rash.

Ant.   Keep it carefully in mind: the Lord your God has
        made a covenant with you.

Ant. 3   Save your people, Lord; bring us together from
among the nations.

III

They failed to destroy the peoples
as the Lord had given command,
but instead they mingled with the nations
and learned to act as they did.

They worshiped the idols of the nations
and these became a snare to entrap them.
They even offered their own sons
and their daughters in sacrifice to demons.

They shed the blood of the innocent,
the blood of their sons and daughters
whom they offered to the idols of Canaan.
The land was polluted with blood.

So they defiled themselves by their deeds
and broke their marriage bond with the Lord
till his anger blazed against his people:
he was filled with horror at his chosen ones.

So he gave them into the hand of the nations
and their foes became their rulers.
Their enemies became their oppressors;
they were subdued beneath their hand.

Time after time he rescued them,
but in their malice they dared to defy him
and sank low through their guilt.
In spite of this he paid heed to their distress,
so often as he heard their cry.

For their sake he remembered his covenant.
In the greatness of his love he relented

and he let them be treated with mercy
by all who held them captive.

O Lord, our God, save us!
Bring us together from among the nations
that we may thank your holy name
and make it our glory to praise you.

Blessed be the Lord, God of Israel,
for ever, from age to age.
Let all the people cry out:
"Amen! Amen!   [Alleluia!]"

Psalm-prayer

God, our Creator, how wonderfully you made man.
You transformed dust into your own image, and gave it a
share in your own nature; yet you are more wonderful in
pardoning the man who has rebelled against you. Grant
that where sin has abounded, grace may more abound, so
that we can become holier through forgiveness and be
more grateful to you.

Ant.   Save your people, Lord; bring us together from
        among the nations.

Verse, reading and prayer, as in the Proper of Seasons.

Morning Prayer

God, come to my assistance. Glory to the Father. As it
was in the beginning. Alleluia.

This verse and response are omitted when the hour begins with
the invitatory.

Hymn

Christ is the world's Light, he and none other;
Born in our darkness, he became our brother.

If we have seen him, we have seen the Father:
   Glory to God on high.

Christ is the world's Peace, he and none other;
No man can serve him and despise his brother.
Who else unites us, one in God the Father?
   Glory to God on high.

Christ is the world's Life, he and none other;
Sold, once for silver, murdered here, our brother.
He, who redeems us, reigns with God the Father:
   Glory to God on high.

Give God the glory, God and none other;
Give God the glory, Spirit, Son and Father;
Give God the glory, God in man my brother;
   Glory to God on high.

Melody: Christe Sanctorum 11.11.11.5   Music: Paris *Antiphoner*,
                                                        1681
                                            Text: F. Pratt Green, 1903–

PSALMODY

Ant. 1 As morning breaks we sing of your mercy,
        Lord, and night will find us proclaiming your
        fidelity.

Psalm 92
Praise of God the Creator
Sing in praise of Christ's redeeming work (Saint Anthanasius).

It is good to give thanks to the Lord,
to make music to your name, O Most High,
to proclaim your love in the morning
and your truth in the watches of the night,
on the ten-stringed lyre and the lute,
with the murmuring sound of the harp.

Your deeds, O Lord, have made me glad;
for the work of your hands I shout with joy.

O Lord, how great are your works!
How deep are your designs!
The foolish man cannot know this
and the fool cannot understand.

Though the wicked spring up like grass
and all who do evil thrive:
they are doomed to be eternally destroyed.
But you, Lord, are eternally on high.
See how your enemies perish;
all doers of evil are scattered.

To me you give the wild-ox's strength;
you anoint me with the purest oil.
My eyes looked in triumph on my foes;
my ears heard gladly of their fall.
The just will flourish like the palm-tree
and grow like a Lebanon cedar.

Planted in the house of the Lord
they will flourish in the courts of our God,
still bearing fruit when they are old,
still full of sap, still green,
to proclaim that the Lord is just;
in him, my rock, there is no wrong.

Psalm-prayer

Take our shame away from us, Lord, and make us
rejoice in your saving works. May all who have been
chosen by your Son always abound in works of faith,
hope and love in your service.

Ant.   As morning breaks we sing of your mercy, Lord,
         and night will find us proclaiming your fidelity.

Ant. 2   Extol the greatness of our God.

401-15-I

Canticle Deuteronomy 32:1-12

God's kindness to his people

How often I have longed to gather your children as a hen gathers her brood under her wing (Matthew 23:37).

Give ear, O heavens, while I speak;
let the earth hearken to the words of my mouth!
May my instruction soak in like the rain,
and my discourse permeate like the dew,
like a downpour upon the grass,
like a shower upon the crops:

For I will sing the Lord's renown.
Oh, proclaim the greatness of our God!
The Rock—how faultless are his deeds,
how right all his ways!
A faithful God, without deceit,
how just and upright he is!

Yet basely has he been treated by his degenerate
children,
a perverse and crooked race!
Is the Lord to be thus repaid by you,
O stupid and foolish people?
Is he not your father who created you?
Has he not made you and established you?

Think back on the days of old,
reflect on the years of age upon age.
Ask your father and he will inform you,
ask your elders and they will tell you:

When the Most High assigned the nations their
heritage,
when he parceled out the descendants of Adam,
he set up the boundaries of the peoples
after the number of the sons of God;

While the Lord's own portion was Jacob,
his hereditary share was Israel.

He found them in a wilderness,
a wasteland of howling desert.
He shielded them and cared for them,
guarding them as the apple of his eye.

As an eagle incites its nestlings forth
by hovering over its brood,
so he spread his wings to receive them
and bore them up on his pinions.
The Lord alone was their leader,
no strange god was with him.

Ant. Extol the greatness of our God.

Ant. 3 How wonderful is your name, O Lord, in all
creation.

Psalm 8
The majesty of the Lord and man's dignity

*The Father gave Christ lordship of creation and made him
head of the Church* (Ephesians 1:22).

How great is your name, O Lord our God,
through all the earth!

Your majesty is praised above the heavens;
on the lips of children and of babes
you have found praise to foil your enemy,
to silence the foe and the rebel.

When I see the heavens, the work of your hands,
the moon and the stars which you arranged,
what is man that you should keep him in mind,
mortal man that you care for him?

Yet you have made him little less than a god;
with glory and honor you crowned him,

gave him power over the works of your hand,
put all things under his feet.

All of them, sheep and cattle,
yes, even the savage beasts,
birds of the air, and fish
that make their way through the waters.

How great is your name, O Lord our God,
through all the earth!

Psalm-prayer

Almighty Lord, how wonderful is your name. You
have made every creature subject to you; make us worthy
to give you service.

Ant. How wonderful is your name, O Lord, in all
creation.

Reading, responsory, antiphon for the canticle of Zechariah,
intercessions and prayer, as in the Proper of Seasons.

Conclusion, as in the Ordinary.

Daytime Prayer

God, come to my assistance. Glory to the Father. As it
was in the beginning. Alleluia.

HYMN, as in the Ordinary, 658.

PSALMODY

Antiphon, as in the Proper of Seasons.

Psalm 119:81-88

XI (Caph)

I yearn for your saving help;
I hope in your word.
My eyes yearn to see your promise.
When will you console me?

Though parched and exhausted with waiting
I have not forgotten your commands.
How long must your servant suffer?
When will you judge my foes?

For me the proud have dug pitfalls,
against your law.
Your commands are all true; then help me
when lies oppress me.

They almost made an end of me on earth
but I kept your precepts.
Because of your love give me life
and I will do your will.

Psalm-prayer

When evil seems to triumph, Lord, and our hope
begins to fail, give us courage and perseverance in doing
your will.

Psalm 61

Prayer of an exile

*The prayer of the just man who places his hope in the things
of heaven* (Saint Hilary).

O God, hear my cry!
Listen to my prayer!
From the end of the earth I call:
my heart is faint.

On the rock too high for me to reach
set me on high,
O you who have been my refuge,
my tower against the foe.

Let me dwell in your tent for ever
and hide in the shelter of your wings.

For you, O God, hear my prayer
and grant me the heritage of those who fear you.

May you lengthen the life of the king:
may his years cover many generations.
May he ever sit enthroned before God:
bid love and truth be his protection.

So I will always praise your name
and day after day fulfill my vows.

Psalm-prayer

Lord Jesus, love and truth of the Father, you came to
earth to relieve the pain of our exile; you took our weakness as your own. Uphold us when our hearts grow faint
until we stand with you before God and praise your
name.

Psalm 64

Prayer for help against enemies

*This psalm commemorates more than any other our Lord's
passion* (Saint Augustine).

Hear my voice, O God, as I complain,
guard my life from dread of the foe.
Hide me from the band of the wicked,
from the throng of those who do evil.

They sharpen their tongues like swords;
they aim bitter words like arrows
to shoot at the innocent from ambush,
shooting suddenly and recklessly.

They scheme their evil course;
they conspire to lay secret snares.
They say: "Who will see us?
Who can search out our crimes?"

He will search who searches the mind
and knows the depth of the heart.
God has shot them with his arrow
and dealt them sudden wounds.
Their own tongue has brought them to ruin
and all who see them mock.

Then all men will fear;
they will tell what God has done.
They will understand God's deeds.
The just will rejoice in the Lord
and fly to him for refuge.
All the upright hearts will glory.

Psalm-prayer

Father, you gave your Son victory over the men who
plotted evil against him; when he cried to you in his
agony, you delivered him from fear of his enemies. May
those who suffer with him in this life find refuge and
success in you.

At the other hours, the complementary psalmody is used, 1191.

Reading, verse and prayer, as in the Proper of Seasons.

Conclusion, as in the Ordinary.

WEEK III

SUNDAY

Evening Prayer I

God, come to my assistance. Glory to the Father. As it was in the beginning. Alleluia.

HYMN, 126 or 133.

Or:

Now thank we all our God
With heart and hands and voices,
Who wondrous things has done,
In whom his world rejoices;
Who from our mothers' arms
Has blessed us on our way
With countless gifts of love,
And still is ours today.

O may this gracious God
Through all our life be near us,
With ever joyful hearts,
And blessed peace to cheer us;
Preserve us in his grace,
And guide us in distress,
And free us from all sin,
Till heaven we possess.

All praise and thanks to God
The Father now be given,
The Son and Spirit blest,
Who reigns in highest heaven;
Eternal, Triune God,
Whom earth and heaven adore;
For thus it was, is now,
And shall be ever more.

Melody: Nun Danket
67.67.66.66

Music: Johann Crueger, 1598-1662
Text: Martin Rinkart, 1586-1649
Translator Catherine Winkworth, 1829-1878

PSALMODY

Antiphon 1

Advent: Rejoice, Jerusalem, let your joy overflow; your
Savior will come to you, alleluia.

Psalm 113
Praise the name of the Lord

He has cast down the mighty and has lifted up the lowly
(Luke 1:52).

Praise, O servants of the Lord,
praise the name of the Lord!
May the name of the Lord be blessed
both now and for evermore!
From the rising of the sun to its setting
praised be the name of the Lord!

High above all nations is the Lord,
above the heavens his glory.
Who is like the Lord, our God,
who has risen on high to his throne
yet stoops from the heights to look down,
to look down upon heaven and earth?

From the dust he lifts up the lowly,
from his misery he raises the poor
to set him in the company of princes,
yes, with the princes of his people.
To the childless wife he gives a home
and gladdens her heart with children.

Psalm-prayer

Lord Jesus, Word of God, surrendering the brightness
of your glory you became man so that we may be raised

from the dust to share your very being. May there be
innumerable children of the Church to offer homage to
your name from the rising of the sun to its setting.

Advent: Rejoice, Jerusalem, let your joy overflow; your
            Savior will come to you, alleluia.

Antiphon 2

Advent: I, the Lord, am coming to save you; already I
            am near; soon I will free you from your sins.

Psalm 116:10-19

Thanksgiving in the Temple

Through Christ let us offer God a continual sacrifice of praise
(Hebrews 13:15).

I trusted, even when I said:
"I am sorely afflicted,"
and when I said in my alarm:
"No man can be trusted."

How can I repay the Lord
for his goodness to me?
The cup of salvation I will raise;
I will call on the Lord's name.

My vows to the Lord I will fulfill
before all his people.
O precious in the eyes of the Lord
is the death of his faithful.

Your servant, Lord, your servant am I;
you have loosened my bonds.
A thanksgiving sacrifice I make:
I will call on the Lord's name.

My vows to the Lord I will fulfill
before all his people,

in the courts of the house of the Lord,
in your midst, O Jerusalem.

Psalm-prayer

Father, precious in your sight is the death of the saints,
but precious above all is the love with which Christ
suffered to redeem us. In this life we fill up in our own
flesh what is still lacking in the sufferings of Christ;
accept this as our sacrifice of praise, and we shall even
now taste the joy of the new Jerusalem.

Advent: I, the Lord, am coming to save you; already I
          am near; soon I will free you from your sins

Antiphon 3

Advent: Lord, send the Lamb, the ruler of the earth,
          from the rock in the desert to the mountain of
          the daughter of Zion.

Canticle   Philippians 2:6-11

Christ, God's holy servant

Though he was in the form of God,
Jesus did not deem equality with God
something to be grasped at.

Rather, he emptied himself
and took the form of a slave,
being born in the likeness of men.

He was known to be of human estate,
and it was thus that he humbled himself,
obediently accepting even death,
death on a cross!

Because of this,
God highly exalted him
and bestowed on him the name
above every other name,

So that at Jesus' name
every knee must bend
in the heavens, on the earth,
and under the earth,
and every tongue proclaim
to the glory of God the Father:
JESUS CHRIST IS LORD!

Advent: Lord, send the Lamb, the ruler of the earth,
from the rock in the desert to the mountain of
the daughter of Zion.

Reading, responsory, antiphon for the canticle of Mary,
intercessions and prayer, as in the Proper of Seasons.

Conclusion, as in the ordinary.

Invitatory

Lord, open my lips.

Advent:

Before December 17:

Ant. Come, let us worship the Lord, the King who is to
come.

December 17–23:

Ant. The Lord is close at hand; come, let us worship
him.

Invitatory psalm, 648.

Office of Readings

God, come to my assistance. Glory to the Father. As it
was in the beginning. Alleluia.

This verse and response are omitted when the hour begins with
the invitatory.

HYMN, 121 or 132.

Or:

Antiphon:

All you nations, sing out your joy to the Lord:
Alleluia, alleluia!

Joyfully shout, all you on earth,
give praise to the glory of God,
And with a hymn, sing out his glorious praise:
Alleluia!

Antiphon

Let all the earth kneel in his sight,
extolling his marvelous fame;
Honor his name, in highest heaven give praise:
Alleluia!

Antiphon

Come forth and see all the great works
that God has brought forth by his might;
Fall on your knees before his glorious throne:
Alleluia!

Antiphon

Glory and thanks be to the Father;
honor and praise to the Son;
And to the Spirit, source of life and of love:
Alleluia!

Antiphon

Melody: All You Nations   Music: Lucien Deiss, C.S.Sp., 1965
                                 Text: Lucien Deiss, C.S.Sp., 1965

PSALMODY

Antiphon 1

Advent: This is our heavenly king; he comes with
power and might to save the nations, alleluia.

Psalm 145

Praise of God's majesty

Lord, you are the Just One, who was and who is (Revelation 16:5).

I

I will give you glory, O God my King,
I will bless your name for ever.

I will bless you day after day
and praise your name for ever.
The Lord is great, highly to be praised,
his greatness cannot be measured.

Age to age shall proclaim your works,
shall declare your mighty deeds,
shall speak of your splendor and glory,
tell the tale of your wonderful works.

They will speak of your terrible deeds,
recount your greatness and might.
They will recall your abundant goodness;
age to age shall ring out your justice.

The Lord is kind and full of compassion,
slow to anger, abounding in love.
How good is the Lord to all,
compassionate to all his creatures.

Advent: This is our heavenly king; he comes with power and might to save the nations, alleluia.

Antiphon 2

Advent: Daughter of Jerusalem, rejoice and be glad; your King will come to you. Zion, do not fear; your Savior hastens on his way.

II

All your creatures shall thank you, O Lord,
and your friends shall repeat their blessing.
They shall speak of the glory of your reign
and declare your might, O God,

to make known to men your mighty deeds
and the glorious splendor of your reign.
Yours is an everlasting kingdom;
your rule lasts from age to age.

Advent: Daughter of Jerusalem, rejoice and be glad;
your King will come to you. Zion, do not fear;
your Savior hastens on his way.

Antiphon 3

Advent: Let us cleanse our hearts for the coming of our
great King, that we may be ready to welcome
him; he is coming and will not delay.

III

The Lord is faithful in all his words
and loving in all his deeds.
The Lord supports all who fall
and raises all who are bowed down.

The eyes of all creatures look to you
and you give them their food in due time.
You open wide your hand,
grant the desires of all who live.

The Lord is just in all his ways
and loving in all his deeds.
He is close to all who call him,
who call on him from their hearts.

He grants the desires of those who fear him,
he hears their cry and he saves them.

The Lord protects all who love him;
but the wicked he will utterly destroy.

Let me speak the praise of the Lord,
let all mankind bless his holy name
for ever, for ages unending.

Psalm-prayer

Lord, be near to all who call upon you in truth and increase the dedication of those who revere you. Hear their prayers and save them, that they may always love you and praise your holy name.

Advent: Let us cleanse our hearts for the coming of our great King, that we may be ready to welcome him; he is coming and will not delay.

Verse, reading and prayer, as in the Proper of Seasons.

Morning Prayer

God, come to my assistance. Glory to the Father. As it was in the beginning. Alleluia.

This verse and response are omitted when the hour begins with the invitatory.

HYMN

On this day, the first of days,
God the Father's name we praise;
Who, creation's Lord and Spring,
Did the world from darkness bring.

On this day the eternal Son
Over death his triumph won;
On this day the Spirit came
With his gifts of living flame.

Father, who didst fashion man
Godlike in thy loving plan,
Fill us with that love divine,
And conform our wills to thine.

Word made flesh, all hail to thee!
Thou from sin hast set us free;
And with thee we die and rise
Unto God in sacrifice.

Holy Spirit, you impart
Gifts of love to every heart;
Give us Light and Grace, we pray,
Fill our hearts this holy day.

God, the blessed Three in One,
May thy holy will be done;
In thy word our souls are free.
And we rest this day with thee.

Melody: Gott Sei Dank 77,77   Music: Freylinghausen's
                                                        Gesangbuch, 1704
                                          Text: Le Mans Breviary, 1748
                                       Translator: Henry W. Baker, 1821–1877

PSALMODY

Antiphon 1

Advent: The Lord is coming without delay. He will
           reveal things kept hidden and show himself to
           all mankind, alleluia.

Psalm 93

Splendor of God the Creator

*The Lord our mighty God now reigns supreme; let us rejoice
and be glad and give him praise* (Revelation 19:6-7).

The Lord is king, with majesty enrobed;
the Lord has robed himself with might,
he has girded himself with power.

The world you made firm, not to be moved;
your throne has stood firm from of old.
From all eternity, O Lord, you are.

The waters have lifted up, O Lord,
the waters have lifted up their voice,
the waters have lifted up their thunder.

Greater than the roar of mighty waters,
more glorious than the surgings of the sea,
the Lord is glorious on high.

Truly your decrees are to be trusted.
Holiness is fitting to your house,
O Lord, until the end of time.

Psalm-prayer

All power and all authority in heaven and on earth
have been given to you, Lord Jesus; you rule with
decrees that are firm and trustworthy. Be with us always
so that we may make disciples whose holiness will be
worthy of your house.

Advent: The Lord is coming without delay. He will
          reveal things kept hidden and show himself to
          all mankind, alleluia.

Antiphon 2

Advent: Mountains and hills shall be level, crooked
          paths straight, rough ways smooth. Come,
          Lord, do not delay, alleluia.

Canticle   Daniel 3:57-88, 56

Let all creatures praise the Lord

All you servants of the Lord, sing praise to him (Revelation
19:5).

Bless the Lord, all you works of the Lord.
Praise and exalt him above all forever.

Angels of the Lord, bless the Lord.
You heavens, bless the Lord,
All you waters above the heavens, bless the Lord.
All you hosts of the Lord, bless the Lord.
Sun and moon, bless the Lord.
Stars of heaven, bless the Lord.

Every shower and dew, bless the Lord.
All you winds, bless the Lord.
Fire and heat, bless the Lord.
Cold and chill, bless the Lord.
Dew and rain, bless the Lord.
Frost and chill, bless the Lord.
Ice and snow, bless the Lord.
Nights and days, bless the Lord.
Light and darkness, bless the Lord.
Lightnings and clouds, bless the Lord.

Let the earth bless the Lord.
Praise and exalt him above all forever.
Mountains and hills, bless the Lord.
Everything growing from the earth, bless the Lord.
You springs, bless the Lord.
Seas and rivers, bless the Lord.
You dolphins and all water creatures, bless the Lord.
All you birds of the air, bless the Lord.
All you beasts, wild and tame, bless the Lord.
You sons of men, bless the Lord.

O Israel, bless the Lord.
Praise and exalt him above all forever.
Priests of the Lord, bless the Lord.
Servants of the Lord, bless the Lord.
Spirits and souls of the just, bless the Lord.
Holy men of humble heart, bless the Lord.
Hananiah, Azariah, Mishael, bless the Lord.
Praise and exalt him above all forever.

Let us bless the Father, and the Son, and the Holy
   Spirit.
Let us praise and exalt him above all for ever.
Blessed are you, Lord, in the firmament of heaven.
Praiseworthy and glorious and exalted above all
   for ever.

Advent: Mountains and hills shall be level, crooked
          paths straight, rough ways smooth. Come,
          Lord, do not delay, alleluia.

Antiphon 3

Advent: I shall enfold Zion with my salvation and shed
           my glory around Jerusalem, alleluia.

Psalm 148

Praise to the Lord, the Creator

Praise and honor, glory and power for ever to him who sits
upon the throne and to the Lamb (Revelation 5:13).

Praise the Lord from the heavens,
   praise him in the heights.
Praise him, all his angels,
   praise him, all his host.

Praise him, sun and moon,
   praise him, shining stars.
Praise him, highest heavens
   and the waters above the heavens.

Let them praise the name of the Lord.
He commanded: they were made.
He fixed them for ever,
   gave a law which shall not pass away.

Praise the Lord from the earth,
   sea creatures and all oceans,

fire and hail, snow and mist,
stormy winds that obey his word;

all mountains and hills,
all fruit trees and cedars,
beasts, wild and tame,
reptiles and birds on the wing;

all earth's kings and peoples,
earth's princes and rulers;
young men and maidens,
old men together with children.

Let them praise the name of the Lord
for he alone is exalted.
The splendor of his name
reaches beyond heaven and earth.

He exalts the strength of his people.
He is the praise of all his saints,
of the sons of Israel,
of the people to whom he comes close.

Psalm-prayer

Lord, extolled in the heights by angelic powers, you are also praised by all earth's creatures, each in its own way. With all the splendor of heavenly worship, you still delight in such tokens of love as earth can offer. May heaven and earth together acclaim you as King; may the praise that is sung in heaven resound in the heart of every creature on earth.

Advent: I shall enfold Zion with my salvation and shed my glory around Jerusalem, alleluia.

Reading, responsory, antiphon for the canticle of Zechariah, intercessions and prayer, as in the Proper of Seasons.

Conclusion, as in the Ordinary.

Daytime Prayer

God, come to my assistance. Glory to the Father. As it
was in the beginning. Alleluia.

HYMN, as in the Ordinary, 658.

PSALMODY

Antiphon, as in the Proper of seasons.

Psalm 118
Song of joy for salvation

*This Jesus is the stone which, rejected by you builders, has
become the chief stone supporting all the rest* (Acts 4:11).

I

Give thanks to the Lord for he is good,
for his love endures for ever.

Let the sons of Israel say:
"His love endures for ever."
Let the sons of Aaron say:
"His love endures for ever."
Let those who fear the Lord say:
"His love endures for ever."

I called to the Lord in my distress;
he answered and freed me.
The Lord is at my side; I do not fear.
What can man do against me?
The Lord is at my side as my helper:
I shall look down on my foes.

It is better to take refuge in the Lord
than to trust in men:
it is better to take refuge in the Lord
than to trust in princes.

II

The nations all encompassed me;
in the Lord's name I crushed them.
They compassed me, compassed me about;
in the Lord's name I crushed them.
They compassed me about like bees;
they blazed like a fire among thorns.
In the Lord's name I crushed them.

I was hard-pressed and was falling
but the Lord came to help me.
The Lord is my strength and my song;
he was my savior.
There are shouts of joy and victory
in the tents of the just.

The Lord's right hand has triumphed;
his right hand raised me.
The Lord's right hand has triumphed;
I shall not die, I shall live
and recount his deeds.
I was punished, I was punished by the Lord,
but not doomed to die.

III

Open to me the gates of holiness:
I will enter and give thanks.
This is the Lord's own gate
where the just may enter.
I will thank you for you have answered
and you are my savior.

The stone which the builders rejected
has become the corner stone.

This is the work of the Lord,
a marvel in our eyes.
This day was made by the Lord;
we rejoice and are glad.

O Lord, grant us salvation;
O Lord, grant success.
Blessed in the name of the Lord
is he who comes.
We bless you from the house of the Lord;
the Lord God is our light.

Go forward in procession with branches
even to the altar.
You are my God, I thank you.
My God, I praise you.
Give thanks to the Lord for he is good;
for his love endures for ever.

Psalm-prayer

Lord God, you have given us the great day of rejoicing:
Jesus Christ, the stone rejected by the builders, has
become the cornerstone of the Church, our spiritual
home. Shed upon your Church the rays of your glory,
that it may be seen as the gate of salvation open to all
nations. Let cries of joy and exultation ring out from its
tents to celebrate the wonder of Christ's resurrection.

At the other hours, the complementary psalmody is used, 1191.

Reading, verse and prayer, as in the Proper of Seasons.

Conclusion, as in the Ordinary.

Evening Prayer II

God, come to my assistance. Glory to the Father. As it
was in the beginning. Alleluia.

HYMN, 126 or 133.

Or:

O Christ, you are the light and day
Which drives away the night,
The ever shining Sun of God
And pledge of future light.

As now the ev'ning shadows fall
Please grant us, Lord, we pray,
A quiet night to rest in you
Until the break of day.

Remember us, poor mortal men,
We humbly ask, O Lord,
And may your presence in our souls
Be now our great reward.

Melody: Saint Anne C.M.   Music: William Croft, 1708
                                    Text: *Christe qui Lux es et Dies*
                              Translator: Rev. M. Quinn, O.P. et al.

PSALMODY

Antiphon 1

Advent: Our Lord will come to claim his glorious
          throne in the assembly of the princes.

Psalm 110:1-5, 7

The Messiah, king and priest

Christ's reign will last until all his enemies are made subject to him (1 Corinthians 15:25).

The Lord's revelation to my Master:
"Sit on my right:
your foes I will put beneath your feet."

The Lord will wield from Zion.
your scepter of power:
rule in the midst of all your foes.

A prince from the day of your birth
on the holy mountains;
from the womb before the dawn I begot you.

The Lord has sworn an oath he will not change.
"You are a priest for ever,
a priest like Melchizedek of old."

The Master standing at your right hand
will shatter kings in the day of his great wrath.

He shall drink from the stream by the wayside
and therefore he shall lift up his head.

Psalm-prayer

Father, we ask you to give us victory and peace. In
Jesus Christ, our Lord and King, we are already seated
at your right hand. We look forward to praising you in
the fellowship of all your saints in our heavenly homeland.

Advent: Our Lord will come to claim his glorious
          throne in the assembly of the princes.

Antiphon 2

Advent: Let the mountains break out with joy and the
          hills with answering gladness, for the world's
          true light, the Lord, comes with power and
          might.

Psalm 111
God's marvelous works

*We are lost in wonder at all that you have done for us, our
Lord and mighty God* (Revelation 15:3).

I will thank the Lord with all my heart
in the meeting of the just and their assembly.
Great are the works of the Lord;
to be pondered by all who love them.

Majestic and glorious his work,
his justice stands firm for ever.
He makes us remember his wonders.
The Lord is compassion and love.

He gives food to those who fear him;
keeps his covenant ever in mind.
He has shown his might to his people
by giving them the lands of the nations.

His works are justice and truth:
his precepts are all of them sure,
standing firm for ever and ever:
they are made in uprightness and truth.

He has sent deliverance to his people
and established his covenant for ever.
Holy his name, to be feared.

To fear the Lord is the beginning of wisdom;
all who do so prove themselves wise.
His praise shall last for ever!

Psalm-prayer

Merciful and gentle Lord, you are the crowning glory
of all the saints. Give us, your children, the gift of
obedience which is the beginning of wisdom, so that we
may do what you command and be filled with your
mercy.

Advent: Let the mountains break out with joy and the
hills with answering gladness, for the world's
true light, the Lord, comes with power and
might.

Antiphon 3

Advent: Let us live in holiness and love as we patiently
await our blessed hope, the coming of our
Savior.

The following canticle is said with the **Alleluia** when Evening Prayer is sung; when the office is recited, the **Alleluia** may be said at the beginning and end of each strophe.

Canticle   See Revelation 19:1-7

The wedding of the Lamb

Alleluia.
Salvation, glory, and power to our God:
(R. Alleluia.)
his judgments are honest and true.
R. Alleluia (alleluia).

Alleluia.
Sing praise to our God, all you his servants,
(R. Alleluia.)
all who worship him reverently, great and small.
R. Alleluia (alleluia).

Alleluia.
The Lord our all-powerful God is King,
(R. Alleluia.)
let us rejoice, sing praise, and give him glory.
R. Alleluia (alleluia).

Alleluia.
The wedding feast of the Lamb has begun,
(R. Alleluia.)
and his bride is prepared to welcome him.
R. Alleluia (alleluia).

Advent: Let us live in holiness and love as we patiently
          await our blessed hope, the coming of our
          Savior.

Reading, responsory, antiphon for the canticle of Mary, intercessions and prayer, as in the Proper of Seasons.

Conclusion, as in the Ordinary.

MONDAY, WEEK III

Invitatory

Lord, open my lips.

Antiphon, as in the Ordinary, 647.

Invitatory psalm, 648.

Office of Readings

God, come to my assistance. Glory to the Father. As it was in the beginning. Alleluia.

This verse and response are omitted when the hour begins with the invitatory.

HYMN

O God of truth, prepare our minds
To hear and heed your holy word;
Fill every heart that longs for you
With your mysterious presence, Lord.

Almighty Father, with your Son
And blessed Spirit, hear our prayer;
Teach us to love eternal truth
And seek its freedom everywhere.

Melody: Warrington L.M.   Music: R. Harrison, 1748–1810
                                                Text: Stanbrook Abbey

PSALMODY

Ant. 1   Our God will be made manifest; he will not come in silence.

Psalm 50

Genuine love of God

I have come not to abolish the law but to bring it to perfection (see Matthew 5:17).

941

I

The God of gods, the Lord,
has spoken and summoned the earth,
from the rising of the sun to its setting.
Out of Zion's perfect beauty he shines.

Our God comes, he keeps silence no longer.
Before him fire devours,
around him tempest rages.
He calls on the heavens and the earth
to witness his judgment of his people.

"Summon before me my people
who made covenant with me by sacrifice."
The heavens proclaim his justice,
for God himself is the judge.

Ant.   Our God will be made manifest; he will not come
in silence.

Ant. 2   Offer to God the sacrifice of praise.

II

"Listen, my people, I will speak;
Israel, I will testify against you,
for I am God your God.
I accuse you, lay the charge before you.

I find no fault with your sacrifices,
your offerings are always before me.
I do not ask more bullocks from your farms,
nor goats from among your herds.

For I own all the beasts of the forest,
beasts in their thousands on my hills.
I know all the birds in the sky,
all that moves in the field belongs to me.

Were I hungry, I would not tell you,
for I own the world and all it holds.

Do you think I eat the flesh of bulls,
or drink the blood of goats?

Pay your sacrifice of thanksgiving to God
and render him your votive offerings.
Call on me in the day of distress.
I will free you and you shall honor me."

Ant. Offer to God the sacrifice of praise.

Ant. 3 I want a loving heart more than sacrifice,
knowledge of my ways more than holocausts.

III

But God says to the wicked:

"But how can you recite my commandments
and take my covenant on your lips,
you who despise my law
and throw my words to the winds,

you who see a thief and go with him;
who throw in your lot with adulterers,
who unbridle your mouth for evil
and whose tongue is plotting crime,

you who sit and malign your brother
and slander your own mother's son.
You do this, and should I keep silence?
Do you think that I am like you?

Mark this, you who never think of God,
lest I seize you and you cannot escape;
a sacrifice of thanksgiving honors me
and I will show God's salvation to the upright."

Psalm-prayer

Father, accept us as a sacrifice of praise, so that we
may go through life unburdened by sin, walking in the
way of salvation, and always giving thanks to you.

Ant. I want a loving heart more than sacrifice, knowledge of my ways more than holocausts.

Verse, reading and prayer, as in the Proper of Seasons.

Morning Prayer

God, come to my assistance. Glory to the Father. As it was in the beginning. Alleluia.

This verse and response are omitted when the hour begins with the invitatory.

Hymn

Brightness of the Father's glory
Springing from eternal light,
Source of light by light engendered,
Day enlightening every day,

In your everlasting radiance
Shine upon us, Christ, true sun,
Bringing life to mind and body
Through the Holy Spirit's pow'r.

Father of unfading glory
Rich in grace and strong to save,
Hear our prayers and come to save us,
Keep us far from sinful ways.

Dawn is drawing ever nearer,
Dawn that brings us all we seek,
Son who dwells within the Father,
Father uttering one Word.

Glory be to God the Father,
Glory to his Only Son,
Glory now and through all ages
To the Spirit Advocate.

Melody: Halton Holgate 87.87

Music: William Boyce, c.
1701–1779
Text: Mount Saint Bernard Abbey

PSALMODY

Antiphon 1

Blessed are they who dwell in your house, O Lord.

December 17-23:   The Lord, the ruler over the kings of
the earth, will come; blessed are they
who are ready to go and welcome
him.

Psalm 84

Longing for God's Temple

*Here we do not have a lasting city; we seek a home that is yet
to come* (Hebrews 13:14).

How lovely is your dwelling place,
Lord, God of hosts.

My soul is longing and yearning,
is yearning for the courts of the Lord.
My heart and my soul ring out their joy
to God, the living God.

The sparrow herself finds a home
and the swallow a nest for her brood;
she lays her young by your altars,
Lord of hosts, my king and my God.

They are happy, who dwell in your house,
for ever singing your praise.
They are happy, whose strength is in you,
in whose hearts are the roads to Zion.

As they go through the Bitter Valley
they make it a place of springs,
the autumn rain covers it with blessings.
They walk with ever growing strength,
they will see the God of gods in Zion.

O Lord God of hosts, hear my prayer,
give ear, O God of Jacob.
Turn your eyes, O God, our shield,
look on the face of your anointed.

One day within your courts
is better than a thousand elsewhere.
The threshold of the house of God
I prefer to the dwellings of the wicked.

For the Lord God is a rampart, a shield;
he will give us his favor and glory.
The Lord will not refuse any good
to those who walk without blame.

Lord, God of hosts,
happy the man who trusts in you!

Psalm-prayer

Bless your people, Lord. You have given us the law that we may walk from strength to strength and raise our minds to you from this valley of tears. May we receive the gifts you have gained for us.

Ant.   Blessed are they who dwell in your house, O Lord.

December 17-23:   The Lord, the ruler over the kings of the earth, will come; blessed are they who are ready to go and welcome him.

Antiphon 2

Come, let us climb the mountain of the Lord.

December 17-23:   Sing a new song to the Lord; proclaim his praises to the ends of the earth.

Canticle   Isaiah 2:2-5

The mountain of the Lord's dwelling towers above every
mountain

All peoples shall come and worship in your presence
(Revelation 15:4).

> In days to come,
> the mountain of the Lord's house
> shall be established as the highest mountain
> and raised above the hills.

> All nations shall stream toward it;
> many peoples shall come and say:
> "Come, let us climb the Lord's mountain,
> to the house of the God of Jacob,
> that he may instruct us in his ways,
> and we may walk in his paths."

> For from Zion shall go forth instruction,
> and the word of the Lord from Jerusalem.

> He shall judge between the nations,
> and impose terms on many peoples.
> They shall beat their swords into plowshares
> and their spears into pruning hooks;
> one nation shall not raise the sword against another,
> nor shall they train for war again.

> O house of Jacob, come,
> let us walk in the light of the Lord!

Ant.   Come, let us climb the mountain of the Lord.

December 17-23:   Sing a new song to the Lord,
                  proclaim his praises to the ends of
                  the earth.

Antiphon 3

Sing to the Lord and bless his name.

December 17-23: **When the Son of Man comes to earth, do you think he will find faith in men's hearts?**

Psalm 96

The Lord, king and judge of the world

A new theme now inspires their praise of God; they belong to the Lamb (see Revelation 14:3).

O sing a new song to the Lord,
sing to the Lord, all the earth.
O sing to the Lord, bless his name.

Proclaim his help day by day,
tell among the nations his glory
and his wonders among all the peoples.

The Lord is great and worthy of praise,
to be feared above all gods;
the gods of the heathens are naught.

It was the Lord who made the heavens,
his are majesty and state and power
and splendor in his holy place.

Give the Lord, you families of peoples,
give the Lord glory and power,
give the Lord the glory of his name.

Bring an offering and enter his courts,
worship the Lord in his temple.
O earth, tremble before him.

Proclaim to the nations: "God is king."
The world he made firm in its place;
he will judge the peoples in fairness.

Let the heavens rejoice and earth be glad,
let the sea and all within it thunder praise,
let the land and all it bears rejoice,
all the trees of the wood shout for joy

at the presence of the Lord for he comes,
he comes to rule the earth.
With justice he will rule the world,
he will judge the peoples with his truth.

Psalm-prayer

Lord, you have renewed the face of the earth. Your Church throughout the world sings you a new song, announcing your wonders to all. Through a virgin, you have brought forth a new birth in our world; through your miracles, a new power; through your suffering, a new patience; in your resurrection, a new hope, and in your ascension, new majesty.

Ant.   Sing to the Lord and bless his name.

December 17-23:   When the Son of Man comes to earth, do you think he will find faith in men's hearts ?

Reading, responsory, antiphon for the canticle of Zechariah, intercessions and prayer, as in the Proper of Seasons.

Conclusion, as in the Ordinary.

Daytime Prayer

God, come to my assistance. Glory to the Father. As it was in the beginning. Alleluia.

HYMN, as in the Ordinary, 658,

PSALMODY

Antiphon, as in the Proper of Seasons.

Psalm 119:89-96
XII (Lamed)
A meditation on God's law

I give you a new commandment: love one another as I have loved you (John 13:34).

Your word, O Lord, for ever
stands firm in the heavens:

your truth lasts from age to age,
like the earth you created.

By your decree it endures to this day;
for all things serve you.
Had your law not been my delight
I would have died in my affliction.

I will never forget your precepts
for with them you give me life.
Save me, for I am yours
since I seek your precepts.

Though the wicked lie in wait to destroy me
yet I ponder on your will.
I have seen that all perfection has an end
but your command is boundless.

Psalm-prayer

Lord, your Word, which stands firm for ever in heaven, dwells in your Church; may his presence bring lasting light to your temple.

Psalm 71
You have stood by me, Lord, from my youth

Let hope be your joy; be patient in trials (Romans 12:12).

I

In you, O Lord, I take refuge;
let me never be put to shame.
In your justice rescue me, free me:
pay heed to me and save me.

Be a rock where I can take refuge,
a mighty stronghold to save me;
for you are my rock, my stronghold.
Free me from the hand of the wicked,
from the grip of the unjust, of the oppressor.

It is you, O Lord, who are my hope,
my trust, O Lord, since my youth.

On you I have leaned from my birth,
from my mother's womb you have been my help.
My hope has always been in you.

My fate has filled many with awe
but you are my strong refuge.
My lips are filled with your praise,
with your glory all the day long.
Do not reject me now that I am old;
when my strength fails do not forsake me.

For my enemies are speaking about me;
those who watch me take counsel together.
They say: "God has forsaken him; follow him,
seize him; there is no one to save him."
O God, do not stay far off:
my God, make haste to help me!

Let them be put to shame and destroyed,
all those who seek my life.
Let them be covered with shame and confusion,
all those who seek to harm me.

II

But as for me, I will always hope
and praise you more and more.
My lips will tell of your justice
and day by day of your help
though I can never tell it all.

I will declare the Lord's mighty deeds
proclaiming your justice, yours alone.
O God, you have taught me from my youth
and I proclaim your wonders still.

Now that I am old and grey-headed,
do not forsake me, God.
Let me tell of your power to all ages,
praise your strength and justice to the skies,

tell of you who have worked such wonders.
O God, who is like you?

You have burdened me with bitter troubles
but you will give me back my life.
You will raise me from the depths of the earth;
you will exalt me and console me again.

So I will give you thanks on the lyre
for your faithful love, my God.
To you will I sing with the harp,
to you, the Holy One of Israel.
When I sing to you my lips shall rejoice
and my soul, which you have redeemed.
And all the day long my tongue
shall tell the tale of your justice:
for they are put to shame and disgraced,
all those who seek to harm me.

Psalm-prayer

Lord, God of the living, you give us lasting youth
through the waters of rebirth, and happiness through the
bread of life. Do not desert us when we are old but help
us to follow your will in both good times and bad, so that
we may for ever praise your faithfulness.

At the other hours the complementary psalmody from series I
and III is used, 1191.

Reading, verse and prayer, as in the Proper of Seasons.

Conclusion, as in the Ordinary.

Evening Prayer

God, come to my assistance. Glory to the Father. As it
was in the beginning. Alleluia.

HYMN

Lord Jesus Christ, abide with us,
Now that the sun has run its course;
Let hope not be obscured by night,
But may faith's darkness be as light.

Lord Jesus Christ, grant us your peace,
And when the trials of earth shall cease,
Grant us the morning light of grace,
The radiant splendor of your face.

Immortal, Holy, Threefold Light,
Yours be the kingdom, pow'r, and might;
All glory be eternally
To you, life-giving Trinity!

Melody: Old 100th L.M.   Music: Louis Bourgeois, 1551
Text: St. Joseph's Abbey, 1967, 1968

PSALMODY

Antiphon 1

Our eyes are fixed intently on the Lord, waiting for his merciful help.

December 17-23: The Lord, the ruler over the kings of the earth, will come; blessed are they who are ready to go and welcome him.

Psalm 123

The Lord, unfailing hope of his people

Two blind men cried out: "Have pity on us, Lord, Son of David" (Matthew 20:30).

To you have I lifted up my eyes,
you who dwell in the heavens:
my eyes, like the eyes of slaves
on the hand of their lords.

Like the eyes of a servant
on the hand of her mistress,
so our eyes are on the Lord our God
till he show us his mercy.

Have mercy on us, Lord, have mercy.
We are filled with contempt.

Indeed all too full is our soul
with the scorn of the rich,
with the proud man's disdain.

Psalm-prayer

Father in heaven, we lift our eyes to you and pray: confound the scorn of the proud and graciously show us your mercy.

Ant. Our eyes are fixed intently on the Lord, waiting for his merciful help.

December 17-23: The Lord, the ruler over the kings of the earth, will come; blessed are they who are ready to go and welcome him.

Antiphon 2

Our help is in the name of the Lord who made heaven and earth.

December 17-23: Sing a new song to the Lord; proclaim his praises to the ends of the earth.

Psalm 124

Our help is in the name of the Lord

The Lord said to Paul: "Fear not . . . I am with you"
(Acts 18).

"If the Lord had not been on our side,"
this is Israel's song.
"If the Lord had not been on our side
when men rose against us,
then would they have swallowed us alive
when their anger was kindled.

Then would the waters have engulfed us,
the torrent gone over us;

over our head would have swept
the raging waters."

Blessed be the Lord who did not give us
a prey to their teeth!
Our life, like a bird, has escaped
from the snare of the fowler.

Indeed the snare has been broken
and we have escaped.
Our help is in the name of the Lord,
who made heaven and earth.

Psalm-prayer

Lord Jesus, you foretold that your disciples would be despised on account of your name, but that not a hair of their heads is ever forgotten. In times of persecution, defend and revive us by the power and comfort of the Holy Spirit, so that we can be freed from our enemies and praise your saving help.

Ant.   Our help is in the name of the Lord who made heaven and earth.

December 17-23:   Sing a new song to the Lord;
                   proclaim his praises to the ends of
                   the earth.

Antiphon 3

God chose us in his Son to be his adopted children.

December 17-23:   When the Son of Man comes to
                   earth, do you think he will find faith
                   in men's hearts?

Canticle   Ephesians 1:3-10

God our Savior

Praised be the God and Father
of our Lord Jesus Christ,

who has bestowed on us in Christ
every spiritual blessing in the heavens.

God chose us in him
before the world began
to be holy
and blameless in his sight.

He predestined us
to be his adopted sons through Jesus Christ,
such was his will and pleasure,
that all might praise the glorious favor
he has bestowed on us in his beloved.

In him and through his blood, we have been
redeemed,
and our sins forgiven,
so immeasurably generous
is God's favor to us.

God has given us the wisdom
to understand fully the mystery,
the plan he was pleased
to decree in Christ.

A plan to be carried out
in Christ, in the fullness of time,
to bring all things into one in him,
in the heavens and on earth.

Ant. God chose us in his Son to be his adopted
children.

December 17-23: When the Son of Man comes to
earth, do you think he will find faith
in men's hearts?

Reading, responsory, antiphon for the canticle of Mary,
intercessions and prayer, as in the Proper of Seasons.

Conclusion, as in the Ordinary.

TUESDAY, WEEK III

Invitatory

Lord, open my lips.

Antiphon, as in the Ordinary, 647.

Invitatory psalm, 648.

Office of Readings

God, come to my assistance. Glory to the Father. As it was in the beginning. Alleluia.

This verse and response are omitted when the hour begins with the invitatory.

HYMN

> Lord, your word abiding,
> And our footsteps guiding,
> Gives us joy for ever,
> Shall desert us never.
>
> Who can tell the pleasure,
> Who recount the treasure,
> By your word imparted
> To the simplehearted?
>
> Word of mercy giving
> Succor to the living;
> Word of life supplying
> Comfort to the dying.
>
> O that we, discerning
> Its most holy learning,
> Lord, may love and fear you,
> Evermore be near you.

Melody: Ravenshaw 66.66   Music: *Ave Hierarchia*, M. Weisse,
1480–1534, adapted by W. H.
Monk, 1823–1889
Text: Henry Williams Baker, 1821–
1877, adapted by Anthony G. Petti

Or:

Lord Jesus, once you spoke to men
Upon the mountain, in the plain;
O help us listen now, as then,
And wonder at your words again.

We all have secret fears to face,
Our minds and motives to amend;
We seek your truth, we need your grace,
Our living Lord and present Friend.

The Gospel speaks, and we receive
Your light, your love, your own command.
O help us live what we believe
In daily work of heart and hand.

Melody: O Jesu, mi dulcissime L.M.   Music: Clausener
                                                 Gesangbuch, 1653
                                         Text: H. C. A. Gaunt, 1902-

PSALMODY

Ant. 1   **Let God arise, let his enemies flee before him.**

Psalm 68

The Lord's triumphant entrance into his sanctuary

Ascending on high he led captivity captive, and gave gifts to
men (Ephesians 4:10).

I

Let God arise, let his foes be scattered.
Let those who hate him flee before him.
As smoke is blown away so will they be blown away,
like wax that melts before the fire,
so the wicked shall perish at the presence of God.

But the just shall rejoice at the presence of God,
they shall exult and dance for joy.
O sing to the Lord, make music to his name;
make a highway for him who rides on the clouds.
Rejoice in the Lord, exult at his presence.

Father of the orphan, defender of the widow,
such is God in his holy place.
God gives the lonely a home to live in;
he leads the prisoners forth into freedom:
but rebels must dwell in a parched land.

When you went forth, O God, at the head of your
     people,
when you marched across the desert, the earth
     trembled:
the heavens melted at the presence of God,
at the presence of God, Israel's God.

You poured down, O God, a generous rain:
when your people were starved you gave them new
     life.
It was there that your people found a home,
prepared in your goodness, O God, for the poor.

Ant.   Let God arise, let his enemies flee before him.

Ant. 2   Our God is a saving God; he, the Lord, holds
          the keys of death.

II

The Lord gives the word to the bearers of good
     tidings:
"The Almighty has defeated a numberless army
and kings and armies are in flight, in flight
while you were at rest among the sheepfolds."

At home the women already share the spoil.
They are covered with silver as the wings of a dove,

its feathers brilliant with shining gold
and jewels flashing like snow on Mount Zalmon.

The mountains of Bashan are mighty mountains;
high-ridged mountains are the mountains of Bashan.
Why look with envy, you high-ridged mountains,
at the mountain where God has chosen to dwell?
It is there that the Lord shall dwell for ever.

The chariots of God are thousands upon thousands.
The Lord has come from Sinai to the holy place.
You have gone up on high; you have taken captives,
receiving men in tribute, O God,
even those who rebel, into your dwelling, O Lord.

May the Lord be blessed day after day.
He bears our burdens, God our savior.
This God of ours is a God who saves.
The Lord our God holds the keys of death.
And God will smite the head of his foes,
the crown of those who persist in their sins.

The Lord said: "I will bring them back from
    Bashan;
I will bring them back from the depth of the sea.
Then your feet will tread in their blood
and the tongues of your dogs take their share of the
    foe."

Ant.   Our God is a saving God; he, the Lord, holds the
        keys of death.

Ant. 3 Kingdoms of earth, sing praise to God, make
        music in honor of the Lord.

III

They see your solemn procession, O God,
the procession of my God, of my king, to the
    sanctuary:

the singers in the forefront, the musicians coming
   last,
between them, maidens sounding their timbrels.

"In festive gatherings, bless the Lord;
bless God, O you who are Israel's sons."
There is Benjamin, least of the tribes, at the head,
Judah's princes, a mighty throng,
Zebulun's princes, Naphtali's princes.

Show forth, O God, show forth your might,
your might, O God, which you have shown for us.
For the sake of your temple high in Jerusalem
may kings come to you bringing their tribute.

Threaten the wild beast that dwells in the reeds,
the bands of the mighty and lords of the peoples.
Let them bow down offering silver.
Scatter the peoples who delight in war.
Princes will make their way from Egypt:
Ethiopia will stretch out her hands to God.

Kingdoms of the earth, sing to God, praise the Lord
who rides on the heavens, the ancient heavens.
He thunders his voice, his mighty voice.
Come, acknowledge the power of God.

His glory is on Israel; his might is in the skies.
God is to be feared in his holy place.
He is the Lord, Israel's God.
He gives strength and power to his people.

Blessed be God!

Psalm-prayer

Lord Jesus Christ, King of the universe, you have
given us joy in your holy meal. Help us to understand the
significance of your death and to acknowledge you as the
conqueror of death seated at the right hand of the Father.

Ant.   Kingdoms of earth, sing praise to God, make music in honor of the Lord.

Verse, reading and prayer, as in the Proper of Seasons.

Morning Prayer

God, come to my assistance. Glory to the Father. As it was in the beginning. Alleluia.

This verse and response are omitted when the hour begins with the invitatory.

HYMN

Antiphon:

Sion, sing, break into song!
For within you is the Lord
With his saving power.

Rise and shine forth, for your light has come,
And upon you breaks the glory of the Lord;
For the darkness covers the earth,
And the thick clouds, the people.

Antiphon

But upon you the Lord shall dawn,
And in you his splendor shall be revealed;
Your light shall guide the Gentiles on their path,
And kings shall walk in your brightness.

Antiphon

Wonder and thanksgiving shall fill your heart,
As the wealth of nations enriches you;
You shall be called the City of the Lord,
Dear to the Holy One of Israel.

Antiphon

You who were desolate and alone,
A place unvisited by men,

Shall be the pride of ages untold,
And everlasting joy to the nations.

Antiphon

No more shall the sun be your light by day,
Nor the moon's beam enlighten you by night;
The Lord shall be your everlasting light,
And your God shall be your glory.

Antiphon

No more for you the setting of suns,
No more the waning of moons;
The Lord shall be your everlasting light,
And the days of your mourning shall come to an end.

Antiphon

Melody: Sion, Sing   Music: Lucien Deiss, C.S.Sp., 1965
                           Text: Lucien Deiss, C.S.Sp., 1965

PSALMODY

Antiphon 1

Lord, you have blessed your land; you have forgiven the
sins of your people.

December 17-23:   The Lord will come from his holy
                  place to save his people.

Psalm 85

Our salvation is near

God blessed the land when our Savior came to earth
(Origen).

O Lord, you once favored your land
and revived the fortunes of Jacob,
you forgave the guilt of your people
and covered all their sins.
You averted all your rage,
you calmed the heat of your anger.

Revive us now, God, our helper!
Put an end to your grievance against us.
Will you be angry with us for ever,
will your anger never cease?

Will you not restore again our life
that your people may rejoice in you?
Let us see, O Lord, your mercy
and give us your saving help.

I will hear what the Lord God has to say,
a voice that speaks of peace,
peace for his people and his friends
and those who turn to him in their hearts.
His help is near for those who fear him
and his glory will dwell in our land.

Mercy and faithfulness have met;
justice and peace have embraced.
Faithfulness shall spring from the earth
and justice look down from heaven.

The Lord will make us prosper
and our earth shall yield its fruit.
Justice shall march before him
and peace shall follow his steps.

Psalm-prayer

Show us your mercy, Lord; our misery is known to us.
May no evil desires prevail over us, for your glory and
love dwell in our hearts.

Ant. Lord, you have blessed your land; you have
forgiven the sins of your people.

December 17-23: The Lord will come from his holy
place to save his people.

Antiphon 2

My soul has yearned for you in the night, and as morning breaks I watch for your coming.

December 17-23: Zion is our mighty citadel, our saving Lord its wall and its defense; throw open the gates, for our God is here among us, alleluia.

Canticle   Isaiah 26:1-4, 7-9, 12

Hymn after the defeat of the enemy

The city wall had twelve foundation stones (see Revelation 21:14).

A strong city have we;
he sets up walls and ramparts to protect us.
Open up the gates
to let in a nation that is just,
one that keeps faith.

A nation of firm purpose you keep in peace;
in peace, for its trust in you.
Trust in the Lord forever!
For the Lord is an eternal Rock.

The way of the just is smooth;
the path of the just you make level.
Yes, for your way and your judgments, O Lord,
we look to you;
your name and your title
are the desire of our souls.

My soul yearns for you in the night,
yes, my spirit within me keeps vigil for you;
when your judgment dawns upon the earth,
the world's inhabitants learn justice.

O Lord, you mete out peace to us,
for it is you who have accomplished all we have done.

Ant. My soul has yearned for you in the night, and as morning breaks I watch for your coming.

December 17-23: Zion is our mighty citadel, our saving Lord its wall and its defense, throw open the gates, for our God is here among us, alleluia.

Antiphon 3

Lord, let the light of your face shine upon us.

December 17-23: Lord, make known your will throughout the earth; proclaim your salvation to every nation.

Psalm 67

People of all nations will worship the Lord

You must know that God is offering his salvation to all the world (Acts 28:28).

O God, be gracious and bless us
and let your face shed its light upon us.
So will your ways be known upon earth
and all nations learn your saving help.

Let the peoples praise you, O God;
let all the peoples praise you.

Let the nations be glad and exult
for you rule the world with justice.
With fairness you rule the peoples,
you guide the nations on earth.

Let the peoples praise you, O God;
let all the peoples praise you.

The earth has yielded its fruit
for God, our God, has blessed us.
May God still give us his blessing
till the ends of the earth revere him.

Let the peoples praise you, O God;
let all the peoples praise you.

Psalm-prayer

Be gracious and bless us, Lord, and let your face shed
its light on us, so that we can make you known with
reverence and bring forth a harvest of justice.

Ant. Lord, let the light of your face shine upon us.

December 17-23: Lord, make known your will
throughout the earth; proclaim your
salvation to every nation.

Reading, responsory, antiphon for the canticle of Zechariah,
intercessions and prayer, as in the Proper of Seasons.

Conclusion, as in the Ordinary.

Daytime Prayer

God, come to my assistance. Glory to the Father. As it
was in the beginning. Alleluia.

HYMN, as in the Ordinary, 658.

PSALMODY

Antiphon, as in the Proper of Seasons.

Psalm 119:97-104

XIII (Mem)

Lord, how I love your law!
It is ever in my mind.
Your command makes me wiser than my foes;
for it is mine for ever.

I have more insight than all who teach me
for I ponder your will.
I have more understanding than the old
for I keep your precepts.

I turn my feet from evil paths
to obey your word.
I have not turned away from your decrees;
you yourself have taught me.

Your promise is sweeter to my taste
than honey in the mouth.
I gain understanding from your precepts;
I hate the ways of falsehood.

Psalm-prayer

Make us so love your law, Father, as to ponder it
continually in our hearts. May it bear fruit in works
acceptable to you.

Psalm 74

Lament for the destruction of the temple

Do not fear those who can only kill the body (Matthew
10:28).

I

Why, O God, have you cast us off for ever?
Why blaze with anger against the sheep of your
    pasture?
Remember your people whom you chose long ago,
the tribe you redeemed to be your own possession,
the mountains of Zion where you made your
    dwelling.

Turn your steps to these places that are utterly
    ruined!
The enemy has laid waste the whole of the sanctuary.
Your foes have made uproar in your house of prayer:
they have set up their emblems, their foreign
    emblems,
high above the entrance to the sanctuary.

Their axes have battered the wood of its doors.
They have struck together with hatchet and pickaxe.
O God, they have set your sanctuary on fire:
they have razed and profaned the place where you
    dwell.

They said in their hearts: "Let us utterly crush
    them;
let us burn every shrine of God in the land."
There is no sign from God, nor have we a prophet,
we have no one to tell us how long it will last.

How long, O God, is the enemy to scoff?
Is the foe to insult your name for ever?
Why, O Lord, do you hold back your hand?
Why do you keep your right hand hidden?

Yet God is our king from time past,
the giver of help through all the land.

II

It was you who divided the sea by your might,
who shattered the heads of the monsters in the sea.

It was you who crushed Leviathan's heads
and gave him as food to the untamed beasts.
It was you who opened springs and torrents;
it was you who dried up ever-flowing rivers.

Yours is the day and yours is the night.
It was you who appointed the light and the sun:
it was you who fixed the bounds of the earth:
you who made both summer and winter.

Remember this, Lord, and see the enemy scoffing;
a senseless people insults your name.
Do not give Israel, your dove, to the hawk
nor forget the life of your poor servants for ever.

Remember your covenant; every cave in the land
is a place where violence makes its home.
Do not let the oppressed return disappointed;
let the poor and the needy bless your name.

Arise, O God, and defend your cause!
Remember how the senseless revile you all the day.
Do not forget the clamor of your foes,
the daily increasing uproar of your foes.

Psalm-prayer

Lord, our faithful God, you permitted the temple of
the old covenant to be destroyed and your people to be
persecuted by unbelievers. Do not forget the new
covenant sealed with the blood of your Son. Make the
Church your spiritual house and make us living stones
built upon Christ so that a full and true temple may be
founded at last.

At the other hours, the complementary psalmody from series I
and III is used, 1191.

Reading, verse and prayer, as in the Proper of Seasons.

Conclusion, as in the Ordinary.

Evening Prayer

God, come to my assistance. Glory to the Father. As it
was in the beginning. Alleluia.

Hymn

The setting sun now dies away,
And darkness comes at close of day;
Your brightest beams, dear Lord, impart,
And let them shine within our heart.

We praise your name with joy this night;
Please watch and guide us till the light;
Joining the music of the blest,
O Lord, we sing ourselves to rest.

To God the Father, God the Son,
And Holy Spirit, Three in One,
Trinity blest, whom we adore,
Be praise and glory evermore.

Melody: Angelus L.M.   Music: Georg Joseph, 1657
                              Text: *Jam sol recedit igneus*
                 Translator: Geoffrey Laycock; translation
                          based on version in *Primer*, 1706

PSALMODY

Antiphon 1

The Lord surrounds his people with his strength.

December 17-23:   The Lord will come from his holy
place to save his people.

Psalm 125

The Lord, guardian of his people

Peace to God's true Israel (Galatians 6:16).

Those who put their trust in the Lord
are like Mount Zion, that cannot be shaken,
that stands for ever.

Jerusalem! The mountains surround her,
so the Lord surrounds his people
both now and for ever.

For the scepter of the wicked shall not rest
over the land of the just
for fear that the hands of the just
should turn to evil.

Do good, Lord, to those who are good,
to the upright of heart;
but the crooked and those who do evil,
drive them away!

On Israel, peace!

Psalm-prayer

Surround your people, Lord, within the safety of your
Church, which you preserve on its rock foundation. Do
not let us stretch out our hands to evil deeds, nor be
destroyed by the insidious snares of the enemy, but bring
us to share the lot of the saints in light.

Ant. The Lord surrounds his people with his strength.

December 17-23: The Lord will come from his holy
place to save his people.

Antiphon 2

Unless you acquire the heart of a child, you cannot enter
the kingdom of God.

December 17-23: Zion is our mighty citadel, our
saving Lord its wall and its defense;
throw open the gates, for our God is
here among us, alleluia.

Psalm 131

Childlike trust in God

Learn from me, for I am gentle and humble of heart
(Matthew 11:29).

O Lord, my heart is not proud
nor haughty my eyes.

I have not gone after things too great
nor marvels beyond me.

Truly I have set my soul
in silence and peace.
As a child has rest in its mother's arms,
even so is my soul.

O Israel, hope in the Lord
both now and for ever.

Psalm-prayer

Lord Jesus, gentle and humble of heart, you declared
that whoever receives a little child in your name receives
you, and you promised your kingdom to those who are
like children. Never let pride reign in our hearts, but
may the Father's compassion reward and embrace all
who willingly bear your gentle yoke.

Ant. Unless you acquire the heart of a child, you cannot enter the kingdom of God.

December 17-23: Zion is our mighty citadel, our
saving Lord its wall and its defense;
throw open the gates, for our God is
here among us, alleluia.

Antiphon 3

Lord, you have made us a kingdom and priests for God
our Father.

December 17-23: Lord, make known your will
throughout the earth; proclaim your
salvation to every nation.

Canticle   Revelation 4:11; 5:9, 10, 12

Redemption hymn

O Lord our God, you are worthy
to receive glory and honor and power.

For you have created all things;
by your will they came to be and were made.

Worthy are you, O Lord,
to receive the scroll and break open its seals.

For you were slain;
with your blood you purchased for God
men of every race and tongue,
of every people and nation.

You made of them a kingdom,
and priests to serve our God,
and they shall reign on the earth.

Worthy is the Lamb that was slain
to receive power and riches,
wisdom and strength,
honor and glory and praise.

Ant. Lord, you have made us a kingdom and priests for
      God our Father.

December 17-23: Lord, make known your will
                 throughout the earth; proclaim your
                 salvation to every nation.

Reading, responsory, antiphon for the canticle of Mary,
intercessions and prayer, as in the Proper of Seasons.

Conclusion, as in the Ordinary.

WEDNESDAY, WEEK III

Invitatory

Lord, open my lips.

Antiphon, as in the Ordinary, 647.

Invitatory psalm, 648.

Office of Readings

God, come to my assistance. Glory to the Father. As it was in the beginning. Alleluia.

This verse and response are omitted when the hour begins with the invitatory.

HYMN

> God, whose almighty word
> Chaos and darkness heard
> And took their flight:
> Hear us, we humbly pray,
> And where the Gospel day
> Sheds not its glorious ray
> Let there be light.
>
> Savior, who came to bring
> On your redeeming wing
> Healing and sight—
> Health to the sick in mind,
> Sight to the inly blind—
> O now to all mankind
> Let there be light.
>
> Spirit of truth and love,
> Life-giving holy dove,
> Speed on your flight;
> Move on the waters' face,
> Bearing the lamp of grace,

And in earth's darkest place
Let there be light.

Holy and blessed Three,
Glorious Trinity,
Wisdom, Love, Might,
Boundless as ocean-tide
Rolling in fullest pride,
Through the world, far and wide
Let there be light.

Melody: Moscow 664.6664

Music: Felice De Giardini,
1716-1796
Text: John Marriott, 1780-1825
adapted by Anthony G. Petti

PSALMODY

Ant. 1 Wherever you are, Lord, there is mercy, there
is truth.

Psalm 89:2-38

God's favors to the house of David

*According to his promise, the Lord has raised up Jesus, a
Savior, from the family of David (Acts 13:22, 23).*

I

I will sing for ever of your love, O Lord;
through all ages my mouth will proclaim your truth.
Of this I am sure, that your love lasts for ever,
that your truth is firmly established as the heavens.

"With my chosen one I have made a covenant;
I have sworn to David my servant:
I will establish your dynasty for ever
and set up your throne through all ages."

The heavens proclaim your wonders, O Lord;
the assembly of your holy ones proclaims your truth.

For who in the skies can compare with the Lord
or who is like the Lord among the sons of God?

A God to be feared in the council of the holy ones,
great and dreadful to all around him.
O Lord God of hosts, who is your equal?
You are mighty, O Lord, and truth is your garment.

It is you who rule the sea in its pride;
it is you who still the surging of its waves.
You crushed the monster Rahab and killed it,
scattering your foes with your mighty arm.

The heavens are yours, the world is yours.
It is you who founded the earth and all it holds;
it is you who created the North and the South.
Tabor and Hermon shout with joy at your name.

Yours is a mighty arm, O Lord;
your hand is strong, your right hand ready.
Justice and right are the pillars of your throne,
love and truth walk in your presence.

Happy the people who acclaim such a king,
who walk, O Lord, in the light of your face,
who find their joy every day in your name,
who make your justice the source of their bliss.

For you, O Lord, are the glory of their strength;
by your favor it is that our might is exalted:
for our ruler is in the keeping of the Lord;
our king in the keeping of the Holy One of Israel.

Ant.   Wherever you are, Lord, there is mercy, there is
      truth.

Ant. 2   When the Son of God came into this world, he
      was born of David's line.

II

Of old you spoke in a vision.
To your friends the prophets you said:
"I have set the crown on a warrior,
I have exalted one chosen from the people.

I have found David my servant
and with my holy oil anointed him.
My hand shall always be with him
and my arm shall make him strong.

The enemy shall never outwit him
nor the evil man oppress him.
I will beat down his foes before him
and smite those who hate him.

My truth and my love shall be with him;
by my name his might shall be exalted.
I will stretch out his hand to the Sea
and his right hand as far as the River.

He will say to me: 'You are my father,
my God, the rock who saves me.'
And I will make him my first-born,
the highest of the kings of the earth.

I will keep my love for him always;
for him my covenant shall last.
I will establish his dynasty for ever,
make his throne endure as the heavens.

Ant. When the Son of God came into this world, he was
       born of David's line.

Ant. 3 Once for all I swore to my servant David: his
        dynasty shall never fail.

III

"If his sons forsake my law
and refuse to walk as I decree

and if ever they violate my statutes,
refusing to keep my commands;

then I will punish their offenses with the rod,
then I will scourge them on account of their guilt.
But I will never take back my love:
my truth will never fail.

I will never violate my covenant
nor go back on the word I have spoken.
Once for all, I have sworn by my holiness.
'I will never lie to David.

His dynasty shall last for ever.
In my sight his throne is like the sun;
like the moon, it shall endure for ever,
a faithful witness in the skies.'"

Psalm-prayer

God, you anointed your servant Jesus with holy oil and raised him higher than all kings on earth. In this you fulfilled the promise made to David's descendants and established a lasting covenant through your firstborn Son. Do not forget your holy covenant so that we who are signed with the blood of your Son through the new sacrament of faith may sing of your mercies for ever.

Ant. Once for all I swore to my servant David: his dynasty shall never fail.

Verse, reading and prayer, as in the Proper of Seasons.

Morning Prayer

God, come to my assistance. Glory to the Father. As it was in the beginning. Alleluia.

This verse and response are omitted when the hour begins with the invitatory.

Hymn

> Morning has broken
> Like the first morning,
> Blackbird has spoken
> Like the first bird.
> Praise for the singing!
> Praise for the morning!
> Praise for them, springing
> Fresh from the Word!
>
> Sweet the rains new fall
> Sunlit from heaven,
> Like the first dew fall
> On the first grass.
> Praise for the sweetness
> Of the wet garden,
> Sprung in completeness
> Where his feet pass.
>
> Mine is the sunlight!
> Mine is the morning,
> Born of the one light
> Eden saw play!
> Praise with elation,
> Praise every morning,
> God's re-creation
> Of the new day!

Melody: Bunessan 55.54.D   Music: Old Gaelic Melody
                                  Text: Eleanor Farjeon, 1881–1965

Or:

> Darkness has faded, night gives way to morning;
> Sleep has refreshed us, now we thank our Maker,
> Singing his praises, lifting up to heaven
>   Hearts, minds and voices.

Father of mercies, bless the hours before us;
While there is daylight may we work to please you,
Building a city fit to be your dwelling,
    Home for all nations.

Daystar of heaven, Dawn that ends our darkness,
Sun of salvation, Lord enthroned in splendor,
Stay with us, Jesus; let your Easter glory
    Fill all creation.

Flame of the Spirit, fire with love's devotion
Hearts love created, make us true apostles;
Give us a vision wide as heav'n's horizon,
    Bright with your promise.

Father in heaven, guide your children homewards;
Jesus, our Brother, walk beside us always;
Joy-giving Spirit, make the world one people,
    Sign of God's Kingdom.

Melody: Christe Sanctorum 11.11.11.5   Music: Paris *Antiphoner*,
    1681
Text: James Quinn, S.J.

PSALMODY

Antiphon 1

Give joy to your servant, Lord; to you I lift up my heart.

December 17-23:   The Lord, the mighty God, will
    come forth from Zion to set his
    people free.

Psalm 86

The prayer of the poor man in distress

Blessed be God who comforts us in all our trials (2
Corinthians 1:3, 4).

Turn your ear, O Lord, and give answer
for I am poor and needy.

Preserve my life, for I am faithful:
save the servant who trusts in you.

You are my God, have mercy on me, Lord,
for I cry to you all the day long.
Give joy to your servant, O Lord,
for to you I lift up my soul.

O Lord, you are good and forgiving,
full of love to all who call.
Give heed, O Lord, to my prayer
and attend to the sound of my voice.

In the day of distress I will call
and surely you will reply.
Among the gods there is none like you, O Lord;
nor work to compare with yours.

All the nations shall come to adore you
and glorify your name, O Lord:
for you are great and do marvellous deeds,
you who alone are God.

Show me, Lord, your way
so that I may walk in your truth.
Guide my heart to fear your name.

I will praise you, Lord my God, with all my heart
and glorify your name for ever;
for your love to me has been great:
you have saved me from the depths of the grave.

The proud have risen against me;
ruthless men seek my life:
to you they pay no heed.

But you, God of mercy and compassion,
slow to anger, O Lord,
abounding in love and truth,
turn and take pity on me.

O give your strength to your servant
and save your handmaid's son.
Show me a sign of your favor
that my foes may see to their shame
that you console me and give me your help.

Psalm-prayer

God of mercy and goodness, when Christ called out to
you in torment, you heard him and gave him victory over
death because of his love for you. We already know the
affection you have for us; fill us with a greater love of
your name and we will proclaim you more boldly before
men and happily lead them to celebrate your glory.

Ant. Give joy to your servant, Lord; to you I lift up my
heart.

December 17-23: The Lord, the mighty God, will
come forth from Zion to set his
people free.

Antiphon 2

Blessed is the upright man, who speaks the truth.

December 17-23: I shall not cease to plead with God
for Zion until he sends his Holy One
in all his radiant beauty.

Canticle   Isaiah 33:13-16

God's flawless judgment

*What God has promised is for you, for your children, and for
those still far away* (Acts 2:39).

Hear, you who are far off,
what I have done;
you who are near,
acknowledge my might.

On Zion sinners are in dread,
trembling grips the impious;
"Who of us can live with the consuming fire?
Who of us can live with the everlasting flames?"

He who practices virtue and speaks honestly,
who spurns what is gained by oppression,
brushing his hands
free of contact with a bribe,
stopping his ears lest he hear of bloodshed,
closing his eyes lest he look on evil.

He shall dwell on the heights,
his stronghold shall be the rocky fastness,
his food and drink
in steady supply.

Ant.   Blessed is the upright man, who speaks the truth.

December 17-23:   I shall not cease to plead with God
                  for Zion until he sends his Holy One
                  in all his radiant beauty.

Antiphon 3

Let us celebrate with joy in the presence of our Lord and
King.

December 17-23:   The Spirit of the Lord rests upon
                  me; he has sent me to preach his
                  joyful message to the poor.

Psalm 98

The Lord triumphs in his judgment

*This psalm tells of the Lord's first coming and that people of
all nations will believe in him* (Saint Athanasius).

Sing a new song to the Lord
for he has worked wonders.
His right hand and his holy arm
have brought salvation.

The Lord has made known his salvation;
has shown his justice to the nations.
He has remembered his truth and love
for the house of Israel.

All the ends of the earth have seen
the salvation of our God.
Shout to the Lord, all the earth,
ring out your joy.

Sing psalms to the Lord with the harp
with the sound of music.
With trumpets and the sound of the horn
acclaim the King, the Lord.

Let the sea and all within it thunder;
the world, and all its peoples.
Let the rivers clap their hands
and the hills ring out their joy.

Rejoice at the presence of the Lord,
for he comes to rule the earth.
He will rule the world with justice
and the peoples with fairness.

Psalm-prayer

Lord Jesus, you have revealed your justice to all
nations. We stood condemned, and you came to be
judged in our place. Send your saving power on us and,
when you come in glory, bring your mercy to those for
whom you were condemned.

Ant.   Let us celebrate with joy in the presence of our
       Lord and King.

December 17-23: The Spirit of the Lord rests upon
                 me; he has sent me to preach his
                 joyful message to the poor.

Reading, responsory, antiphon for the canticle of Zechariah, intercessions and prayer, as in the Proper of Seasons.

Conclusion, as in the Ordinary.

Daytime Prayer

God, come to my assistance. Glory to the Father. As it was in the beginning. Alleluia.

HYMN, as in the Ordinary, 658.

PSALMODY

Antiphon, as in the Proper of Seasons.

Psalm 119:105-112
XIV (Nun)

Your word is a lamp for my steps
and a light for my path.
I have sworn and have made up my mind
to obey your decrees.

Lord, I am deeply afflicted:
by your word give me life.
Accept, Lord, the homage of my lips
and teach me your decrees.

Though I carry my life in my hands,
I remember your law.
Though the wicked try to ensnare me
I do not stray from your precepts.

Your will is my heritage for ever,
the joy of my heart.
I set myself to carry out your statutes
in fullness, for ever.

Psalm-prayer

Let your Word, Father, be a lamp for our feet and a light to our path, so that we may understand what you wish to teach us and follow the path your light marks out for us.

Psalm 70

O God, come to my aid

Lord, save us, we are lost (Matthew 8:25).

O God, make haste to my rescue,
Lord, come to my aid!
Let there be shame and confusion
on those who seek my life.

O let them turn back in confusion,
who delight in my harm,
let them retreat, covered with shame,
who jeer at my lot.

Let there be rejoicing and gladness
for all who seek you.
Let them say for ever: "God is great,"
who love your saving help.

As for me, wretched and poor,
come to me, O God.
You are my rescuer, my help,
O Lord, do not delay.

Psalm-prayer

God, our help and deliverer, do not abandon us among
the many temptations of life but deliver us from evil and
turn our tears and struggles into joy.

Psalm 75

The Lord, the ruler over all

*He has cast down the mighty from their thrones and lifted up
the lowly* (Luke 1:52).

We give thanks to you, O God,
we give thanks and call upon your name.
We recount your wonderful deeds.

"When I reach the appointed time,
then I will judge with justice.
Though the earth and all who dwell in it may rock,
it is I who uphold its pillars.

To the boastful I say: 'Do not boast,'
to the wicked: 'Do not flaunt your strength,
do not flaunt your strength on high.
Do not speak with insolent pride.'"

For neither from the east nor from the west,
nor from desert or mountains comes judgment,
but God himself is the judge.
One he humbles, another he exalts.

The Lord holds a cup in his hand,
full of wine, foaming and spiced.
He pours it: they drink it to the dregs:
all the wicked on the earth must drain it.

As for me, I will rejoice for ever
and sing psalms to Jacob's God.
He shall break the power of the wicked,
while the strength of the just shall be exalted.

Psalm-prayer

Father, by the passion of your Son you proclaimed the final judgment of the world; when you raised Christ upon the cross, you deposed the prince of darkness. Strike down the pride that rules our hearts and raise us to the glory of the resurrection.

At the other hours, the complementary psalmody from series I and II is used, 1191.

Reading, verse and prayer, as in the Proper of Seasons.

Conclusion, as in the Ordinary.

Evening Prayer

God, come to my assistance. Glory to the Father. As it was in the beginning. Alleluia.

HYMN

O Father, whose creating hand.
Brings harvest from the fruitful land,
Your providence we gladly own,
And bring our hymns before your throne
To praise you for the living bread
On which our lives are daily fed.

O Lord, who in the desert fed
The hungry thousands in their need,
Where want and famine still abound
Let your relieving love be found,
And in your name may we supply
Your hungry children when they cry.

O Spirit, your revealing light
Has led our questing souls aright;
Source of our science, you have taught
The marvels human minds have wrought,
So that the barren deserts yield
The bounty by your love revealed.

Melody: Wych Cross   Music: (Wych Cross) Erik Routley, 1917-,
or Melita 88.88.88.   or (Melita) John B. Dykes, 1823-1876
                                        Text: Donald Hughes, 1911-1967

PSALMODY

Antiphon 1

Those who sow in tears will reap in joy.

December 17-23:   The Lord, the mighty God, will
                   come forth from Zion to set his
                   people free.

Psalm 126

Joyful hope in God

Just as you share in sufferings so you will share in the divine glory (2 Corinthians 1:7).

When the Lord delivered Zion from bondage,
it seemed like a dream.
Then was our mouth filled with laughter,
on our lips there were songs.

The heathens themselves said: "What marvels
the Lord worked for them!"
What marvels the Lord worked for us!
Indeed we were glad.

Deliver us, O Lord, from our bondage
as streams in dry land.
Those who are sowing in tears
will sing when they reap.

They go out, they go out, full of tears,
carrying seed for the sowing:
they come back, they come back, full of song,
carrying their sheaves.

Psalm-prayer

Lord, you have raised us from the earth; may you let the seeds of justice, which we have sown in tears, grow and increase in your sight. May we reap in joy the harvest we hope for patiently.

Ant. Those who sow in tears will reap in joy.

December 17-23: The Lord, the mighty God, will come forth from Zion to set his people free.

Antiphon 2

May the Lord build our house and guard our city.

December 17-23: I shall not cease to plead with God for Zion until he sends his Holy One in all his radiant beauty.

Psalm 127

Apart from God our labors are worthless

You are God's building (1 Corinthians 3:9)

If the Lord does not build the house,
in vain do its builders labor;
if the Lord does not watch over the city,
in vain does the watchman keep vigil.

In vain is your earlier rising,
your going later to rest,
you who toil for the bread you eat:
when he pours gifts on his beloved while they
slumber.

Truly sons are a gift from the Lord,
a blessing, the fruit of the womb.
Indeed the sons of youth
are like arrows in the hand of a warrior.

O the happiness of the man
who has filled his quiver with these arrows!
He will have no cause for shame
when he disputes with his foes in the gateways.

Psalm-prayer

You command the seed to rise, Lord God, though the farmer is unaware. Grant that those who labor for you may trust not in their own work but in your help. Remembering that the land is brought to flower not with human tears but with those of your Son, may the Church rely only upon your gifts.

Ant.   May the Lord build our house and guard our city.

December 17-23:   I shall not cease to plead with God
                  for Zion until he sends his Holy One
                  in all his radiant beauty.

                  Antiphon 3

He is the first-born of all creation; in every way the
primacy is his.

December 17-23:   The Spirit of the Lord rests upon
                  me; he has sent me to preach his
                  joyful message to the poor.

                  Canticle   Colossians 1:12-20

Christ the first-born of all creation and the first-born
                  from the dead

    Let us give thanks to the Father
    for having made you worthy
    to share the lot of the saints
    in light.

    He rescued us
    from the power of darkness
    and brought us
    into the kingdom of his beloved Son.
    Through him we have redemption
    the forgiveness of our sins.

    He is the image of the invisible God,
    the first-born of all creatures.
    In him everything in heaven and on earth was
        created,
    things visible and invisible.

    All were created through him;
    all were created for him.
    He is before all else that is.
    In him everything continues in being.

It is he who is head of the body, the church!
he who is the beginning,
the first-born of the dead,
so that primacy may be his in everything.

It pleased God to make absolute fulness reside in him
and, by means of him, to reconcile everything in his
    person,
both on earth and in the heavens,
making peace through the blood of his cross.

Ant.   He is the first-born of all creation; in every way
the primacy is his.

December 17-23:   The Spirit of the Lord rests upon
me; he has sent me to preach his
joyful message to the poor.

Reading, responsory, antiphon for the canticle of Mary,
intercessions and prayer, as in the Proper of Seasons.

Conclusion, as in the Ordinary.

THURSDAY, WEEK III

Invitatory

Lord, open my lips.

Antiphon, as in the Ordinary, 647.

Invitatory psalm, 648.

Office of Readings

God, come to my assistance. Glory to the Father. As it
was in the beginning. Alleluia.

This verse and response are omitted when the hour begins with
the invitatory.

HYMN

Eternal Father, through your Word
You gave new life to Adam's race,
Transformed them into sons of light,
New creatures by your saving grace.

To you who stooped to sinful man
We render homage and all praise:
To Father, Son and Spirit blest
Whose gift to man is endless days.

Melody: Erhalt uns, Herr L.M.　　　　Music: *Geistliche Lieder*,
　　　　　　　　　　　　　　　　　　　　Wittenberg, 1543
　　　　　　　　　　　　　　　　Text: Stanbrook Abbey

PSALMODY

Ant. 1　Look on us, Lord, and see how we are
　　　　despised.

Psalm 89:39-53

Lament for the fall of David's dynasty.

*He has raised up for us a mighty Savior born of the house of
David his servant* (Luke 1:69).

IV

And yet you have rejected and spurned
and are angry with the one you have anointed.
You have broken your covenant with your servant
and dishonored his crown in the dust.

You have broken down all his walls
and reduced his fortresses to ruins.
He is despoiled by all who pass by:
he has become the taunt of his neighbors.

You have exalted the right hand of his foes;
you have made all his enemies rejoice.
You have made his sword give way,
you have not upheld him in battle.

You have brought his glory to an end;
you have hurled his throne to the ground.
You have cut short the years of his youth;
you have heaped disgrace upon him.

Ant.   Look on us, Lord, and see how we are despised.

Ant. 2   I am the root and stock of David; I am the
morning star.

V

How long, O Lord? Will you hide yourself for ever?
How long will your anger burn like a fire?
Remember, Lord, the shortness of my life
and how frail you have made the sons of men.
What man can live and never see death?
Who can save himself from the grasp of the grave?

Where are your mercies of the past, O Lord,
which you have sworn in your faithfulness to David?
Remember, Lord, how your servant is taunted,
how I have to bear all the insults of the peoples.

Thus your enemies taunt me, O Lord,
mocking your anointed at every step.

Blessed be the Lord for ever. Amen, amen!

Psalm-prayer

Lord, God of mercy and fidelity, you made a new and
lasting pact with men and sealed it in the blood of your
Son. Forgive the folly of our disloyalty and make us keep
your commandments, so that in your new covenant we
may be witnesses and heralds of your faithfulness and
love on earth, and sharers of your glory in heaven.

Ant.   I am the root and stock of David; I am the
        morning star.

Ant. 3 Our years wither away like grass, but you, Lord
        God, are eternal.

Psalm 90
May we live in the radiance of God

*There is no time with God: a thousand years, a single day: it
is all one* (2 Peter 3:8).

O Lord, you have been our refuge
from one generation to the next.
Before the mountains were born
or the earth or the world brought forth,
you are God, without beginning or end.

You turn men back into dust
and say: "Go back, sons of men."
To your eyes a thousand years
are like yesterday, come and gone,
no more than a watch in the night.

You sweep men away like a dream,
like grass which springs up in the morning.
In the morning it springs up and flowers:
by evening it withers and fades.

So we are destroyed in your anger,
struck with terror in your fury.
Our guilt lies open before you;
our secrets in the light of your face.

All our days pass away in your anger.
Our life is over like a sigh.
Our span is seventy years
or eighty for those who are strong.

And most of these are emptiness and pain.
They pass swiftly and we are gone.
Who understands the power of your anger
and fears the strength of your fury?

Make us know the shortness of our life
that we may gain wisdom of heart.
Lord, relent! Is your anger for ever?
Show pity to your servants.

In the morning, fill us with your love;
we shall exult and rejoice all our days.
Give us joy to balance our affliction
for the years when we knew misfortune.

Show forth your work to your servants;
let your glory shine on their children.
Let the favor of the Lord be upon us:
give success to the work of our hands,
give success to the work of our hands.

Psalm-prayer

Eternal Father, you give us life despite our guilt and
even add days and years to our lives in order to bring us
wisdom. Make us love and obey you, so that the works of
our hands may always display what your hands have
done, until the day we gaze upon the beauty of your face.

Ant. Our years wither away like grass, but you, Lord
God, are eternal.

Verse, reading and prayer, as in the Proper of Seasons.

Morning Prayer

God, come to my assistance. Glory to the Father. As it
was in the beginning. Alleluia.

This verse and response are omitted when the hour begins with
the invitatory.

HYMN

When morning fills the sky,
Our hearts awaking cry:
May Jesus Christ be praised.
In all our works and prayer
His Sacrifice we share:
May Jesus Christ be praised.
The night becomes as day,
When from our hearts we say:
May Jesus Christ be praised.
The powers of darkness fear
When this glad song they hear:
May Jesus Christ be praised.

In heav'n our joy will be
To sing eternally:
May Jesus Christ be praised.
Let earth and sea and sky
From depth to height reply:
May Jesus Christ be praised.
Let all the earth now sing
To our eternal King:
May Jesus Christ be praised.
By this the eternal song,

Through ages all along:
May Jesus Christ be praised.

Melody: Old 122nd 667.667.D   Music: Louis Bourgeois,
1500–1561
Text: E. Caswall, 1814–1878, alt.

PSALMODY

Antiphon 1

Glorious things are said of you, O city of God.

December 17-23:   To you, O Lord, I lift up my soul;
come and rescue me, for you are my
refuge and my strength.

Psalm 87

Jerusalem is mother of us all

The heavenly Jerusalem is a free woman; she is our mother
(Galatians 4:26).

On the holy mountain is his city
cherished by the Lord.
The Lord prefers the gates of Zion
to all Jacob's dwellings.
Of you are told glorious things,
O city of God!

"Babylon and Egypt I will count
among those who know me;
Philistia, Tyre, Ethiopia,
these will be her children
and Zion shall be called 'Mother'
for all shall be her children."

It is he, the Lord Most High,
who gives each his place.
In his register of peoples he writes:
"These are her children,"

and while they dance they will sing:
"In you all find their home."

Psalm-prayer

Lord God, your only Son wept over ancient Jerusalem, soon to be destroyed for its lack of faith. He established the new Jerusalem firmly upon rock and made it the mother of the faithful. Make us rejoice in your Church and grant that all people may be reborn into the freedom of your Spirit.

Ant.   Glorious things are said of you, O city of God.

December 17-23:   To you, O Lord, I lift up my soul; come and rescue me, for you are my refuge and my strength.

Antiphon 2

The Lord, the mighty conqueror, will come; he will bring with him the prize of victory.

December 17-23:   Bless those, O Lord, who have waited for your coming; let your prophets be proved true.

Canticle   Isaiah 40:10–17

The Good Shepherd: God most high and most wise

See, I come quickly; I have my reward in hand (Revelation 22:12).

Here comes with power
the Lord God,
who rules by his strong arm;
here is his reward with him,
his recompense before him.

Like a shepherd he feeds his flock;
in his arms he gathers the lambs,

Carrying them in his bosom,
and leading the ewes with care.

Who has cupped in his hand the waters of the sea,
and marked off the heavens with a span?
Who has held in a measure the dust of the earth,
weighed the mountains in scales
and the hills in a balance?

Who has directed the spirit of the Lord,
or has instructed him as his counselor?
Whom did he consult to gain knowledge?
Who taught him the path of judgment,
or showed him the way of understanding?

Behold, the nations count as a drop of the bucket,
as dust on the scales;
the coastlands weigh no more than powder.

Lebanon would not suffice for fuel,
nor its animals be enough for holocausts.
Before him all the nations are as nought,
as nothing and void he accounts them.

Ant.   The Lord, the mighty conqueror, will come; he
         will bring with him the prize of victory.

December 17-23:   Bless those, O Lord, who have
                    waited for your coming; let your
                    prophets be proved true.

Antiphon 3

Give praise to the Lord our God, bow down before his
holy mountain.

December 17-23:   Turn to us, O Lord, make haste to
                    help your people.

Psalm 99
Holy is the Lord our God

Christ, higher than the Cherubim, when you took our lowly nature you transformed our sinful world (Saint Athanasius).

The Lord is king; the peoples tremble.
He is throned on the cherubim; the earth quakes.
The Lord is great in Zion.

He is supreme over all the peoples.
Let them praise his name, so terrible and great.
He is holy, full of power.

You are a king who loves what is right;
you have established equity, justice and right;
you have established them in Jacob.

Exalt the Lord our God;
bow down before Zion, his footstool.
He the Lord is holy.

Among his priests were Aaron and Moses,
among those who invoked his name was Samuel.
They invoked the Lord and he answered.

To them he spoke in the pillar of cloud.
They did his will; they kept the law,
which he, the Lord, had given.

O Lord our God, you answered them.
For them you were a God who forgives;
yet you punished all their offenses.

Exalt the Lord our God;
bow down before his holy mountain
for the Lord our God is holy.

Psalm-prayer

God, you are the source of all holiness. Though no one can see you and live, you give life most generously and in an even greater way restore it. Sanctify your priests through your life-giving Word and consecrate your people in his blood until our eyes see your face.

Ant. Give praise to the Lord our God, bow down before his holy mountain.

December 17-23: Turn to us, O Lord, make haste to help your people.

Reading, responsory, antiphon for the canticle of Zechariah, intercessions and prayer, as in the Proper of Seasons.

Conclusion, as in the Ordinary.

Daytime Prayer

God, come to my assistance. Glory to the Father. As it was in the beginning. Alleluia.

HYMN, as in the Ordinary, 658.

PSALMODY

Antiphon, as in the Proper of Seasons.

Psalm 119:113-120

XV (Samech)

I have no love for half-hearted men:
my love is for your law.
You are my shelter, my shield;
I hope in your word.

Leave me, you who do evil;
I will keep God's command.
If you uphold me by your promise I shall live;
let my hopes not be in vain.

Sustain me and I shall be saved
and ever observe your commands.
You spurn all who swerve from your statutes;
their cunning is in vain.

You throw away the wicked like dross:
  so I love your will.
I tremble before you in terror;
I fear your decrees.

Psalm-prayer

  Help us and we shall be saved, Lord God; leave us and
we are doomed. May you remain with us always so that
the fullness of life may be ours.

Psalm 79:1-5, 8-11, 13

Lament for Jerusalem

If only you had known what would bring you peace (Luke
19:42).

  O God, the nations have invaded your land,
  they have profaned your holy temple.
  They have made Jerusalem a heap of ruins.
  They have handed over the bodies of your servants
  as food to feed the birds of heaven
  and the flesh of your faithful to the beasts of the
    earth.

  They have poured out blood like water in Jerusalem,
  no one is left to bury the dead.
  We have become the taunt of our neighbors,
  the mockery and scorn of those who surround us.
  How long, O Lord? Will you be angry for ever,
  how long will your anger burn like fire?

  Do not hold the guilt of our fathers against us.
  Let your compassion hasten to meet us;
  we are left in the depths of distress.
  O God our savior, come to our help,
  come for the sake of the glory of your name.
  O Lord our God, forgive us our sins;
  rescue us for the sake of your name.

Why should the nations say: "Where is their God?"
Let us see the nations around us repaid
with vengeance for the blood of your servants that
   was shed!
Let the groans of the prisoners come before you;
let your strong arm reprieve those condemned to die.

But we, your people, the flock of your pasture,
will give you thanks for ever and ever.
We will tell your praise from age to age.

Psalm-prayer

Lord Jesus Christ, shepherd of your Church, in order
to strengthen our faith and to lead us to the kingdom,
you renewed and far surpassed the marvels of the old
law. Through the uncertainties of this earthly journey,
lead us home to the everlasting pastures.

Psalm 80

Lord, come to tend your vineyard

Come, Lord Jesus (Revelation 22:20)

O shepherd of Israel, hear us,
you who lead Joseph's flock,
shine forth from your cherubim throne
upon Ephraim, Benjamin, Manasseh.
O Lord, rouse up your might,
O Lord, come to our help.

God of hosts, bring us back;
let your face shine on us and we shall be saved.

Lord God of hosts, how long
will you frown on your people's plea?
You have fed them with tears for their bread,
an abundance of tears for their drink.

You have made us the taunt of our neighbors,
our enemies laugh us to scorn.

God of hosts, bring us back;
let your face shine on us and we shall be saved.

You brought a vine out of Egypt;
to plant it you drove out the nations.
Before it you cleared the ground;
it took root and spread through the land.

The mountains were covered with its shadow,
the cedars of God with its boughs.
It stretched out its branches to the sea,
to the Great River it stretched out its shoots.

Then why have you broken down its walls?
It is plucked by all who pass by.
It is ravaged by the boar of the forest,
devoured by the beasts of the field.

God of hosts, turn again, we implore,
look down from heaven and see.
Visit this vine and protect it,
the vine your right hand has planted.
Men have burnt it with fire and destroyed it.
May they perish at the frown of your face.

May your hand be on the man you have chosen,
the man you have given your strength.
And we shall never forsake you again:
give us life that we may call upon your name.

God of hosts, bring us back;
let your face shine on us and we shall be saved.

Psalm-prayer

Lord God, eternal shepherd, you so tend the vineyard
you planted that now it extends its branches even to the

farthest coast. Look down on your Church and come to us. Help us to remain in your Son as branches on the vine that, planted firmly in your love, we may testify before the whole world to your great power working everywhere.

At the other hours, the complementary psalmody is used, 1191.

Reading, verse and prayer, as in the Proper of Seasons.

Conclusion, as in the Ordinary.

Evening Prayer

God, come to my assistance. Glory to the Father. As it was in the beginning. Alleluia.

HYMN

> For the fruits of his creation,
>   Thanks be to God;
> For the gifts to every nation,
>   Thanks be to God;
> For the ploughing, sowing, reaping,
> Silent growth while men are sleeping,
> Future needs in earth's safe keeping,
>   Thanks be to God.
>
> In the just reward of labor,
>   God's will is done;
> In the help we give our neighbor,
>   God's will is done;
> In our world-wide task of caring
> For the hungry and despairing,
> In the harvests men are sharing,
>   God's will is done.
>
> For the harvests of his spirit,
>   Thanks be to God;
> For the good all men inherit,
>   Thanks be to God;

For the wonders that astound us,
For the truths that still confound us,
Most of all, that love has found us,
    Thanks be to God.

Melody: East Acklam 84.84.88.84

Music: Francis Jackson
Text: F. Pratt Green

PSALMODY

Antiphon 1

Let your holy people rejoice, O Lord, as they enter your
dwelling place.

December 17-23:   To you, O Lord, I lift up my soul;
                   come and rescue me, for you are my
                   refuge and my strength.

Psalm 132

God's promises to the house of David

The Lord God will give him the throne of his ancestor David
(Luke 1:32).

I

O Lord, remember David
and all the many hardships he endured,
the oath he swore to the Lord,
his vow to the Strong One of Jacob.

"I will not enter the house where I live
nor go to the bed where I rest.
I will give no sleep to my eyes,
to my eyelids I will give no slumber
till I find a place for the Lord,
a dwelling for the Strong One of Jacob."

At Ephrathah we heard of the ark;
we found it in the plains of Yearim.
"Let us go to the place of his dwelling;
let us go to kneel at his footstool."

Go up, Lord, to the place of your rest,
you and the ark of your strength.
Your priests shall be clothed with holiness:
your faithful shall ring out their joy.
For the sake of David your servant
do not reject your anointed.

Ant. Let your holy people rejoice, O Lord, as they
enter your dwelling place.

December 17-23:   To you, O Lord, I lift up my soul;
come and rescue me, for you are my
refuge and my strength.

Antiphon 2

The Lord has chosen Zion as his sanctuary.

December 17-23:   Bless those, O Lord, who have
waited for your coming; let your
prophets be proved true.

II

The Lord swore an oath to David;
he will not go back on his word;
"A son, the fruit of your body,
will I set upon your throne.

If they keep my covenant in truth
and my laws that I have taught them,
their sons also shall rule
on your throne from age to age."

For the Lord has chosen Zion;
he has desired it for his dwelling:
"This is my resting-place for ever,
here have I chosen to live.

I will greatly bless her produce,
I will fill her poor with bread.

I will clothe her priests with salvation
and her faithful shall ring out their joy.

There David's stock will flower:
I will prepare a lamp for my anointed.
I will cover his enemies with shame
but on him my crown shall shine."

Psalm-prayer

Lord Jesus Christ, you chose to suffer and be
overwhelmed by death in order to open the gates of death
in triumph. Stay with us to help us on our pilgrimage;
free us from all evil by the power of your resurrection. In
the company of your saints, and constantly remembering
your love for us, may we sing of your wonders in our
Father's house.

Ant.   The Lord has chosen Zion as his sanctuary.

December 17-23:   Bless those, O Lord, who have
                   waited for your coming; let your
                   prophets be proved true.

Antiphon 3

The Father has given Christ all power, honor and
kingship; all people will obey him.

December 17-23:   Turn to us, O Lord, make haste to
                   help your people.

Canticle   Revelation 11:17-18; 12:10b-12a

The judgment of God

We praise you, the Lord God Almighty,
who is and who was.
You have assumed your great power,
you have begun your reign.

The nations have raged in anger,
but then came your day of wrath
and the moment to judge the dead:
The time to reward your servants the prophets
and the holy ones who revere you,
the great and the small alike.

Now have salvation and power come,
the reign of our God and the authority
of his Anointed One.
For the accuser of our brothers is cast out,
who night and day accused them before God.

They defeated him by the blood of the Lamb
and by the word of their testimony;
love for life did not deter them from death.
So rejoice, you heavens,
and you that dwell therein!

Ant.   The Father has given Christ all power, honor and
       kingship; all people will obey him.

December 17-23:   Turn to us, O Lord, make haste to
                  help your people.

Reading, responsory, antiphon for the canticle of Mary,
intercessions and prayer, as in the Proper of Seasons.

Conclusion, as in the Ordinary.

FRIDAY, WEEK III

Invitatory

Lord, open my lips.

Antiphon, as in the Ordinary, 647.

Invitatory psalm, 648.

Office of Readings

God, come to my assistance. Glory to the Father. As it was in the beginning. Alleluia.

This verse and response are omitted when the hour begins with the invitatory.

HYMN

> In ancient times God spoke to man
> Through prophets, and in varied ways,
> But now he speaks through Christ his Son,
> His radiance through eternal days.
>
> To God the Father of the world,
> His Son through whom he made all things,
> And Holy Spirit, bond of love,
> All glad creation glory sings.

Melody: Herr Jesu Christ,
mein Lebens Licht L.M.

Music: *As Hymnodus Sacer,*
Leipzig, 1625
Text: Stanbrook Abbey

PSALMODY

Ant. 1   I am worn out with crying, with longing for my God.

Psalm 69:2-22, 30-37

I am consumed with zeal for your house

They offered him a mixture of wine and gall (Matthew 27:34).

I

Save me, O God,
for the waters have risen to my neck.

I have sunk into the mud of the deep
and there is no foothold.
I have entered the waters of the deep
and the waves overwhelm me.

I am wearied with all my crying,
my throat is parched.
My eyes are wasted away
from looking for my God.

More numerous than the hairs on my head
are those who hate me without cause.
Those who attack me with lies
are too much for my strength.

How can I restore
what I have never stolen?
O God, you know my sinful folly;
my sins you can see.

Let those who hope in you not be put to shame
through me, Lord of hosts:
let not those who seek you be dismayed
through me, God of Israel.

It is for you that I suffer taunts,
that shame covers my face,
that I have become a stranger to my brothers,
an alien to my own mother's sons.
I burn with zeal for your house
and taunts against you fall on me.

When I afflict my soul with fasting
they make it a taunt against me.
When I put on sackcloth in mourning

then they make me a byword,
the gossip of men at the gates,
the subject of drunkards' songs.

Ant. I am worn out with crying, with longing for my
God.

Ant. 2 I needed food and they gave me gall; I was
parched with thirst and they gave me vinegar.

II

This is my prayer to you,
my prayer for your favor.
In your great love, answer me, O God,
with your help that never fails;
rescue me from sinking in the mud;
save me from my foes.

Save me from the waters of the deep
lest the waves overwhelm me.
Do not let the deep engulf me
nor death close its mouth on me.

Lord, answer, for your love is kind;
in your compassion, turn towards me.
Do not hide your face from your servant;
answer quickly for I am in distress.
Come close to my soul and redeem me;
ransom me pressed by my foes.

You know how they taunt and deride me;
my oppressors are all before you.
Taunts have broken my heart;
I have reached the end of my strength.
I looked in vain for compassion,
for consolers; not one could I find.

For food they gave me poison;
in my thirst they gave me vinegar to drink.

Ant.   I needed food and they gave me gall; I was
parched with thirst and they gave me vinegar.

Ant. 3   Seek the Lord, and you will live.

III

As for me in my poverty and pain
let your help, O God, lift me up.

I will praise God's name with a song;
I will glorify him with thanksgiving.
A gift pleasing God more than oxen,
more than beasts prepared for sacrifice.

The poor when they see it will be glad
and God-seeking hearts will revive;
for the Lord listens to the needy
and does not spurn his servants in their chains.
Let the heavens and the earth give him praise,
the sea and all its living creatures.

For God will bring help to Zion
and rebuild the cities of Judah
and men shall dwell there in possession.
The sons of his servants shall inherit it;
those who love his name shall dwell there.

Psalm-prayer

God our Father, to show the way of salvation, you
chose that the standard of the cross should go before us,
and you fulfilled the ancient prophecies in Christ's pass-
over from death to life. Do not let us rouse your burning
indignation by sin, but rather through the contemplation
of his wounds, make us burn with zeal for the honor of
your Church and with grateful love for you.

Ant.   Seek the Lord, and you will live.

Verse, reading and prayer, as in the Proper of Seasons.

Morning Prayer

God, come to my assistance. Glory to the Father. As it was in the beginning. Alleluia.

This verse and response are omitted when the hour begins with the invitatory.

HYMN

Lord, whose love in humble service
Bore the weight of human need,
Who did on the Cross, forsaken,
Show us mercy's perfect deed:
We, your servants, bring the worship
Not of voice alone, but heart;
Consecrating to your purpose
Every gift which you impart.

As we worship, grant us vision,
Till your love's revealing light,
Till the height and depth and greatness
Dawns upon our human sight;
Making known the needs and burdens
Your compassion bids us bear,
Stirring us to faithful service
Your abundant life to share.

Called from worship into service
Forth in your great name we go,
To the child, the youth, the aged,
Love in living deeds to show.
Hope and health, goodwill and comfort,
Counsel, aid, and peace we give,
That your children, Lord, in freedom,
May your mercy know, and live.

Melody: In Babilone 87.87.D   Music: Traditional Dutch Melody
                                 Text: Albert Bayly, 1901–

PSALMODY

Antiphon 1

You alone I have grieved by my sin; have pity on me, O Lord.

December 17-23:   Our King will come from Zion; the Lord, God-is-with-us, is his mighty name.

Psalm 51

O God, have mercy on me

Your inmost being must be renewed, and you must put on the new man (Ephesians 4:23-24).

Have mercy on me, God, in your kindness.
In your compassion blot out my offense.
O wash me more and more from my guilt
and cleanse me from my sin.

My offenses truly I know them;
my sin is always before me.
Against you, you alone, have I sinned;
what is evil in your sight I have done.

That you may be justified when you give sentence
and be without reproach when you judge,
O see, in guilt I was born,
a sinner was I conceived.

Indeed you love truth in the heart;
then in the secret of my heart teach me wisdom.
O purify me, then I shall be clean;
O wash me, I shall be whiter than snow.

Make me hear rejoicing and gladness,
that the bones you have crushed may revive.
From my sins turn away your face
and blot out all my guilt.

A pure heart create for me, O God,
put a steadfast spirit within me.
Do not cast me away from your presence,
nor deprive me of your holy spirit.

Give me again the joy of your help;
with a spirit of fervor sustain me,
that I may teach transgressors your ways
and sinners may return to you.

O rescue me, God, my helper,
and my tongue shall ring out your goodness.
O Lord, open my lips
and my mouth shall declare your praise.

For in sacrifice you take no delight,
burnt offering from me you would refuse,
my sacrifice, a contrite spirit.
A humbled, contrite heart you will not spurn.

In your goodness, show favor to Zion:
rebuild the walls of Jerusalem.
Then you will be pleased with lawful sacrifice,
holocausts offered on your altar.

Psalm-prayer

Father, he who knew no sin was made sin for us, to
save us and restore us to your friendship. Look upon our
contrite heart and afflicted spirit and heal our troubled
conscience, so that in the joy and strength of the Holy
Spirit we may proclaim your praise and glory before all
the nations.

Ant. You alone I have grieved by my sin; have pity on
me, O Lord.

December 17-23: Our King will come from Zion; the
Lord, God-is-with-us, is his mighty
name.

Antiphon 2

Truly we know our offenses, Lord, for we have sinned
against you.

December 17-23:   Wait for the Lord and he will come
to you with his saving power.

Canticle   Jeremiah 14:17-21

The lament of the people in war and famine

*The kingdom of God is at hand. Repent and believe the Good
News (Mark 1:15).*

Let my eyes stream with tears
day and night, without rest,
Over the great destruction which overwhelms
the virgin daughter of my people,
over her incurable wound.

If I walk out into the field,
look! those slain by the sword;
If I enter the city,
look! those consumed by hunger.
Even the prophet and the priest
forage in a land they know not.

Have you cast Judah off completely?
Is Zion loathsome to you?
Why have you struck us a blow
that cannot be healed?

We wait for peace, to no avail;
for a time of healing, but terror comes instead.
We recognize, O Lord, our wickedness,
the guilt of our fathers;
that we have sinned against you.

For your name's sake spurn us not,
disgrace not the throne of your glory;
remember your covenant with us, and break it not.

Ant. Truly we know our offenses, Lord, for we have
sinned against you.

December 17-23: Wait for the Lord and he will come
to you with his saving power.

Antiphon 3

The Lord is God; we are his people, the flock he
shepherds.

December 17-23: Eagerly I watch for the Lord; I wait
in joyful hope for the coming of God
my Savior.

When psalm 100 is the invitatory psalm, psalm 95, 648, is used
as the third psalm at Morning Prayer.

Psalm 100
The joyful song of those entering God's temple
The Lord calls his ransomed people to sing songs of victory
(Saint Athanasius).

Cry out with joy to the Lord, all the earth.
Serve the Lord with gladness.
Come before him, singing for joy.

Know that he, the Lord, is God.
He made us, we belong to him,
we are his people, the sheep of his flock.

Go within his gates, giving thanks.
Enter his courts with songs of praise.
Give thanks to him and bless his name.

Indeed, how good is the Lord,
eternal his merciful love.
He is faithful from age to age.

Psalm-prayer

God, devoted to us as a Father, you created us as a sign of your power and elected us your people to show your goodness. Accept the thanks your children offer that all men may enter your courts praising you in song.

Ant.   The Lord is God; we are his people, the flock he shepherds.

December 17-23:   Eagerly I watch for the Lord; I wait in joyful hope for the coming of God my Savior.

Reading, responsory, antiphon for the canticle of Zechariah, intercessions and prayer, as in the Proper of Seasons.

Conclusion, as in the Ordinary.

Daytime Prayer

God, come to my assistance. Glory to the Father. As it was in the beginning. Alleluia.

HYMN, as in the Ordinary, 658.

PSALMODY

Antiphon, as in the Proper of Seasons.

Psalm 22
God hears the suffering of his Holy One

Jesus cried with a loud voice: My God, my God, why have you forsaken me? (Matthew 27:46).

I

My God, my God, why have you forsaken me?
You are far from my plea and the cry of my distress.

O my God, I call by day and you give no reply;
I call by night and I find no peace.

Yet you, O God, are holy,
enthroned on the praises of Israel.
In you our fathers put their trust;
they trusted and you set them free.
When they cried to you, they escaped.
In you they trusted and never in vain.

But I am a worm and no man,
scorned by men, despised by the people.
All who see me deride me.
They curl their lips, they toss their heads.
"He trusted in the Lord, let him save him;
let him release him if this is his friend."

Yes, it was you who took me from the womb,
entrusted me to my mother's breast.
To you I was committed from my birth,
from my mother's womb you have been my God.
Do not leave me alone in my distress;
come close, there is none else to help.

II

Many bulls have surrounded me,
fierce bulls of Bashan close me in.
Against me they open wide their jaws,
like lions, rending and roaring.

Like water I am poured out,
disjointed are all my bones.
My heart has become like wax,
it is melted within my breast.

Parched as burnt clay is my throat,
my tongue cleaves to my jaws.

Many dogs have surrounded me,
a band of the wicked beset me.
They tear holes in my hands and my feet
and lay me in the dust of death.

I can count every one of my bones.
These people stare at me and gloat;
they divide my clothing among them.
They cast lots for my robe.

O Lord, do not leave me alone,
my strength, make haste to help me!
Rescue my soul from the sword,
my life from the grip of these dogs.
Save my life from the jaws of these lions,
my poor soul from the horns of these oxen.

I will tell of your name to my brethren
and praise you where they are assembled.

III

"You who fear the Lord, give him praise;
all sons of Jacob, give him glory.
Revere him, Israel's sons.

For he has never despised
nor scorned the poverty of the poor.
From him he has not hidden his face,
but he heard the poor man when he cried."

You are my praise in the great assembly.
My vows I will pay before those who fear him.
The poor shall eat and shall have their fill.
They shall praise the Lord, those who seek him.
May their hearts live for ever and ever!

All the earth shall remember and return to the Lord,
all families of the nations worship before him
for the kingdom is the Lord's; he is ruler of the
     nations.

They shall worship him, all the mighty of the earth;
before him shall bow all who go down to the dust.

And my soul shall live for him, my children serve
     him.

They shall tell of the Lord to generations yet to
     come,
declare his faithfulness to peoples yet unborn:
"These things the Lord has done."

Psalm-prayer

Father, when your Son was handed over to torture and
seemed abandoned by you, he cried out to you from the
cross and death was destroyed, life was restored. By his
death and resurrection, may we see the day when the
poor man is saved, the downtrodden is lifted up and the
chains that bind peoples are broken. United to the thanks
that Christ gives you, your Church will sing your praises.

At the other hours, the complementary psalmody is used, 1191.

Reading, verse and prayer, as in the Proper of Seasons.

Conclusion, as in the Ordinary.

Evening Prayer

God, come to my assistance. Glory to the Father. As it
was in the beginning. Alleluia.

HYMN

     When, in his own image
     God created man,
     He included freedom
     In creation's plan.

For he loved us even
From before our birth;
By his grace he made us
Free men of this earth.

God to man entrusted
Life as gift and aim.
Sin became our prison,
Turning hope to shame.
Man against his brother
Lifted hand and sword,
And the Father's pleading
Went unseen, unheard.

Then in time, our maker
Chose to intervene,
Set his love in person
In the human scene.
Jesus broke the circle
Of repeated sin,
So that man's devotion
Newly might begin.

Choose we now in freedom
Where we should belong,
Let us turn to Jesus,
Let our choice be strong.
May the great obedience
Which in Christ we see
Perfect all our service:
Then we shall be free!

Melody: King's Weston 65.65.D   Music: R. Vaughan Williams,
                                                   1872–1958
                                         Text: Fred Kaan, 1929-

401-17-O

PSALMODY

Antiphon 1

Great is the Lord, our God, transcending all other gods.

December 17-23:　　Our King will come from Zion; the Lord, God-is-with-us, is his mighty name.

Psalm 135

Praise for the wonderful things God does for us

He has won us for himself . . . and you must proclaim what he has done for you. He has called you out of darkness into his own wonderful light (see 1 Peter 2:9)

I

Praise the name of the Lord,
praise him, servants of the Lord,
who stand in the house of the Lord
in the courts of the house of our God.

Praise the Lord for the Lord is good.
Sing a psalm to his name for he is loving.
For the Lord has chosen Jacob for himself
and Israel for his own possession.

For I know the Lord is great,
that our Lord is high above all gods.
The Lord does whatever he wills,
in heaven, on earth, in the seas.

He summons clouds from the ends of the earth;
makes lightning produce the rain;
from his treasuries he sends forth the wind.

The first-born of the Egyptians he smote,
of man and beast alike.

Signs and wonders he worked
in the midst of your land, O Egypt,
against Pharaoh and all his servants.

Nations in their greatness he struck
and kings in their splendor he slew.
Sihon, king of the Amorites,
Og, the king of Bashan,
and all the kingdoms of Canaan.
He let Israel inherit their land;
on his people their land he bestowed.

Ant.   Great is the Lord, our God, transcending all other
gods.

December 17-23:   Our King will come from Zion; the
Lord, God-is-with-us, is his mighty
name.

Antiphon 2

House of Israel, bless the Lord! Sing psalms to him, for
he is merciful.

December 17-23:   Wait for the Lord, and he will come
to you with his saving power.

II

Lord, your name stands for ever,
unforgotten from age to age:
for the Lord does justice for his people;
the Lord takes pity on his servants.

Pagan idols are silver and gold,
the work of human hands.
They have mouths but they cannot speak;
they have eyes but they cannot see.

They have ears but they cannot hear;
    there is never a breath on their lips.
Their makers will become like them
    and so will all who trust in them!

Sons of Israel, bless the Lord!
Sons of Aaron, bless the Lord!
Sons of Levi, bless the Lord!
You who fear him, bless the Lord!

From Zion may the Lord be blessed,
    he who dwells in Jerusalem!

Psalm-prayer

Father, your name and your memory last for ever. We
stand to pray in your house and praise you with psalms of
joy. We ask you in your kindness to have mercy on us in
our lowliness.

Ant.   House of Israel, bless the Lord! Sing psalms to
      him, for he is merciful.

December 17-23: Wait for the Lord, and he will come
              to you with his saving power.

Antiphon 3

All nations will come and worship before you, O Lord.

December 17-23: Eagerly I watch for the Lord; I wait
              in joyful hope for the coming of God
              my Savior.

Canticle   Revelation 15:3-4

Hymn of adoration

Mighty and wonderful are your works,
    Lord God Almighty!

Righteous and true are your ways,
O King of the nations!

Who would dare refuse you honor,
or the glory due your name, O Lord?

Since you alone are holy
all nations shall come
and worship in your presence.
Your mighty deeds are clearly seen.

Ant.   All nations will come and worship before you, O
Lord.

December 17-23:   Eagerly I watch for the Lord; I wait
in joyful hope for the coming of God
my Savior.

Reading, responsory, antiphon for the canticle of Mary,
intercessions and prayer, as in the Proper of Seasons.

Conclusion, as in the Ordinary.

SATURDAY, WEEK III

Invitatory

Lord, open my lips.

Antiphon, as in the Ordinary, 647.

Invitatory psalm, 648.

Office of Readings

God, come to my assistance. Glory to the Father. As it was in the beginning. Alleluia.

This verse and response are omitted when the hour begins with the invitatory.

HYMN

> Lord Jesus, once you spoke to men
> Upon the mountain, in the plain;
> O help us listen now, as then,
> And wonder at your words again.
>
> We all have secret fears to face,
> Our minds and motives to amend;
> We seek your truth, we need your grace,
> Our living Lord and present Friend.
>
> The Gospel speaks, and we receive
> Your light, your love, your own command.
> O help us live what we believe
> In daily work of heart and hand.

Melody: O Jesu, mi dulcissimi L.M.   Music: *Clausener Gesangbuch,*
1653
Text: H.C.A. Gaunt, 1902–

PSALMODY

Ant. 1   Let us praise the Lord for his mercy and for the
wonderful things he has done for men.

Psalm 107

Thanksgiving for deliverance

This is God's message to the sons of Israel; the good news of peace proclaimed through Jesus Christ (Acts 10:36).

I

"O give thanks to the Lord for he is good;
for his love endures for ever."

Let them say this, the Lord's redeemed,
whom he redeemed from the hand of the foe
and gathered from far-off lands,
from east and west, north and south.

Some wandered in the desert, in the wilderness,
finding no way to a city they could dwell in.
Hungry they were and thirsty;
their soul was fainting within them.

Then they cried to the Lord in their need
and he rescued them from their distress
and he led them along the right way,
to reach a city they could dwell in.

Let them thank the Lord for his love,
for the wonders he does for men.
For he satisfies the thirsty soul;
he fills the hungry with good things.

Some lay in darkness and in gloom,
prisoners in misery and chains,
having defied the words of God
and spurned the counsels of the Most High.
He crushed their spirit with toil;
they stumbled; there was no one to help.

Then they cried to the Lord in their need
and he rescued them from their distress.

He led them forth from darkness and gloom
and broke their chains to pieces.

Let them thank the Lord for his goodness,
for the wonders he does for men:
for he bursts the gates of bronze
and shatters the iron bars.

Ant.   Let us praise the Lord for his mercy and for the
        wonderful things he has done for men.

Ant. 2 Men have seen the works of God, the marvels
        he has done.

II

Some were sick on account of their sins
and afflicted on account of their guilt.
They had a loathing for every food;
they came close to the gates of death.

Then they cried to the Lord in their need
and he rescued them from their distress.
He sent forth his word to heal them
and saved their life from the grave.

Let them thank the Lord for his love,
for the wonders he does for men.
Let them offer a sacrifice of thanks
and tell of his deeds with rejoicing.

Some sailed to the sea in ships
to trade on the mighty waters.
These men have seen the Lord's deeds,
the wonders he does in the deep.

For he spoke; he summoned the gale,
raising up the waves of the sea.
Tossed up to heaven, then into the deep;
their soul melted away in their distress.

They staggered, reeled like drunken men,
for all their skill was gone.
Then they cried to the Lord in their need
and he rescued them from their distress.

He stilled the storm to a whisper:
all the waves of the sea were hushed.
They rejoiced because of the calm
and he led them to the haven they desired.

Let them thank the Lord for his love,
the wonders he does for men.
Let them exalt him in the gathering of the people
and praise him in the meeting of the elders.

Ant.   Men have seen the works of God, the marvels he
has done.

Ant. 3   Those who love the Lord will see and rejoice;
they will understand his loving kindness.

III

He changes streams into a desert,
springs of water into thirsty ground,
fruitful land into a salty waste,
for the wickedness of those who live there.

But he changes desert into streams,
thirsty ground into springs of water.
There he settles the hungry
and they build a city to dwell in.

They sow fields and plant their vines;
these yield crops for the harvest.
He blesses them; they grow in numbers.
He does not let their herds decrease.

He pours contempt upon princes,
makes them wander in trackless wastes.

They diminish, are reduced to nothing
by oppression, evil and sorrow.

But he raises the needy from distress;
makes families numerous as a flock.
The upright see it and rejoice
but all who do wrong are silenced.

Whoever is wise, let him heed these things
and consider the love of the Lord.

Psalm-prayer

You fill the hungry with good things, Lord God, and
break the sinner's chains. Hear your people who call to
you in their need and lead your Church from the shadows of death. Gather us from sunrise to sunset, that we
may grow together in faith and love and give lasting
thanks for your kindness.

Ant.   Those who love the Lord will see and rejoice; they
        will understand his loving kindness.

Verse, reading and prayer, as in the Proper of Seasons.

Morning Prayer

God, come to my assistance. Glory to the Father. As it
was in the beginning. Alleluia.

This verse and response are omitted when the hour begins with
the invitatory.

HYMN

Praise, my soul, the King of heaven;
To his feet your tribute bring;
Ransomed, healed, restored, forgiven,
Evermore his praises sing:
Alleluia! Alleluia!
Praise the everlasting King.

Praise him for his grace and favor
To his children in distress;
Praise him still the same as ever,
Slow to chide and swift to bless:
Alleluia! Alleluia!
Glorious in his faithfulness.

Father-like he tends and spares us;
Well our feeble frame he knows;
In his hand he gently bears us,
Rescues us from all our foes.
Alleluia! Alleluia!
Widely yet his mercy flows.

Angels, help us to adore him;
You behold him face to face;
Sun and moon, bow down before him,
Join the praises of our race:
Alleluia! Alleluia!
Praise with us the God of grace.

Melody: Lauda Anima 87.87.87   Music: John Goss, 1869
                                      Text: H. F. Lyte, 1834, alt.

PSALMODY

Antiphon 1

December 17-23:   Our God will come from Lebanon;
                  he shall be as brilliant as the sun.

Psalm 119:145-152

XIX (Koph)

I call with all my heart; Lord, hear me,
I will keep your commands.
I call upon you, save me
and I will do your will.

I rise before dawn and cry for help,
I hope in your word.
My eyes watch through the night
to ponder your promise.

In your love hear my voice, O Lord;
give me life by your decrees.
Those who harm me unjustly draw near:
they are far from your law.

But you, O Lord, are close:
your commands are truth.
Long have I known that your will
is established for ever.

Psalm-prayer

Save us by the power of your hand, Father, for our
enemies have ignored your words. May the fire of your
word consume our sins and its brightness illumine our
hearts.

December 17-23:   Our God will come from Lebanon;
                  he shall be as brilliant as the sun.

Antiphon 2

December 17-23:   May the Holy One from heaven
                  come down like gentle rain; may the
                  earth burst into blossom and bear
                  the tender Savior.

Canticle   Wisdom 9:1-6, 9-11

Lord, give me wisdom

*I will inspire you with wisdom which your adversaries will
be unable to resist* (Luke 21:15).

God of my fathers, Lord of mercy,
you who have made all things by your word
and in your wisdom have established man
to rule the creatures produced by you,
to govern the world in holiness and justice,
and to render judgment in integrity of heart:

Give me Wisdom, the attendant at your throne,
and reject me not from among your children:
for I am your servant, the son of your handmaid,
a man weak and short-lived
and lacking in comprehension of judgment and of
    laws.

Indeed, though one be perfect among the sons of
    men,
if Wisdom, who comes from you, be not with him,
he shall be held in no esteem.

Now with you is Wisdom who knows your works
and was present when you made the world;
who understands what is pleasing in your eyes
and what is conformable with your commands.

Send her forth from your holy heavens
and from your glorious throne dispatch her
that she may be with me and work with me,
that I may know what is your pleasure.

For she knows and understands all things,
and will guide me discreetly in my affairs
and safeguard me by her glory.

December 17-23:   May the Holy One from heaven
come down like gentle rain; may the
earth burst into blossom and bear
the tender Savior.

Antiphon 3

December 17-23:   **Israel, prepare yourself to meet the Lord, for he is coming.**

Psalm 117

Praise for God's loving compassion

I affirm that . . . the Gentile peoples are to praise God because of his mercy (Romans 15:8-9).

> O praise the Lord, all you nations,
> acclaim him all you peoples!
>
> Strong is his love for us;
> he is faithful for ever.

Psalm-prayer

God our Father, may all nations and peoples praise you. May Jesus, who is called faithful and true and who lives with you eternally, possess our hearts for ever.

December 17-23:   **Israel, prepare yourself to meet the Lord, for he is coming.**

Reading, responsory, antiphon for the canticle of Zechariah, intercessions and prayer, as in the Proper of Seasons.

Conclusion, as in the Ordinary.

Daytime Prayer

God, come to my assistance. Glory to the Father. As it was in the beginning. Alleluia.

HYMN, as in the Ordinary, 658.

PSALMODY

Antiphon, as in the Proper of Seasons.

Psalm 119:121-128

XVI (Ain)

I have done what is right and just:
let me not be oppressed.
Vouch for the welfare of your servant
lest the proud oppress me.

My eyes yearn for your saving help
and the promise of your justice.
Treat your servant with love
and teach me your commands.

I am your servant, give me knowledge;
then I shall know your will.
It is time for the Lord to act
for your law has been broken.

That is why I love your commands
more than finest gold,
why I rule my life by your precepts:
I hate the ways of falsehood.

Psalm-prayer

The light of your words, Father, gives understanding
to little ones. Prepare our hearts to receive the Advocate,
your Holy Spirit.

Psalm 34

God the savior of the just

You have tasted the sweetness of the Lord (1 Peter 2:3).

I

I will bless the Lord at all times,
his praise always on my lips;
in the Lord my soul shall make its boast.
The humble shall hear and be glad.

Glorify the Lord with me.
Together let us praise his name.
I sought the Lord and he answered me;
from all my terrors he set me free.

Look towards him and be radiant;
let your faces not be abashed.
This poor man called; the Lord heard him
and rescued him from all his distress.

The angel of the Lord is encamped
around those who revere him, to rescue them.
Taste and see that the Lord is good.
He is happy who seeks refuge in him.

Revere the Lord, you his saints.
They lack nothing, those who revere him.
Strong lions suffer want and go hungry
but those who seek the Lord lack no blessing.

II

Come, children, and hear me
that I may teach you the fear of the Lord.
Who is he who longs for life
and many days, to enjoy his prosperity?

Then keep your tongue from evil
and your lips from speaking deceit.
Turn aside from evil and do good;
seek and strive after peace.

The Lord turns his face against the wicked
to destroy their remembrance from the earth.
The Lord turns his eyes to the just
and his ears to their appeal.

They call and the Lord hears
and rescues them in all their distress.

The Lord is close to the broken-hearted;
those whose spirit is crushed he will save.

Many are the trials of the just man
but from them all the Lord will rescue him.
He will keep guard over all his bones,
not one of his bones shall be broken.

Evil brings death to the wicked;
those who hate the good are doomed.
The Lord ransoms the souls of his servants.
Those who hide in him shall not be condemned.

Psalm-prayer

Graciously hear us, Lord, for we seek only you. You
are near to those whose heart is right. Open yourself to
accept our sorrowful spirit; calm our bodies and minds
with the peace which surpasses understanding.

At the other hours, the complementary psalmody from series II
and III is used, 1193.

Reading, verse and prayer, as in the Proper of Seasons.

Conclusion, as in the Ordinary.

WEEK IV

SUNDAY

Evening Prayer I

God, come to my assistance. Glory to the Father. As it was in the beginning. Alleluia.

HYMN, 133.

Or:

At the name of Jesus
Ev'ry knee shall bow,
Ev'ry tongue confess him
King of glory now
'Tis the Father's pleasure,
We should call him Lord,
Who from the beginning
Was the mighty Word.

Humbled for a reason,
To receive a name
From the lips of sinners,
Unto whom he came,
Faithfully he bore it,
Spotless to the last,
Brought it back victorious,
When from death he passed.

Bore it up triumphant,
With its human light,
Through all ranks of creatures,
To the central height,
To the throne of Godhead,
To the Father's breast;
Filled it with the glory
Of that perfect rest.

In your hearts enthrone him;
There, let him subdue
All that is not holy
All that is not true;
May your voice entreat him
In temptation's hour;
Let his will enfold you
In its light and power.

Brothers, this Lord Jesus
Shall return again,
With his Father's glory,
O'er the earth to reign;
He is God the Savior;
He is Christ the Lord,
Ever to be worshiped,
Always blest, adored.

Melody: King's Weston 65.65D   Music: R. Vaughan Williams, d.
1958
Text: C. Noel, d. 1877, alt.

PSALMODY

Antiphon 1

Advent: He comes, the desire of all human hearts; his
dwelling place shall be resplendent with glory,
alleluia.

Psalm 122

Holy city Jerusalem

You have come to Mount Zion, to the city of the living God,
heavenly Jerusalem (Hebrews 12:22).

I rejoiced when I heard them say:
"Let us go to God's house."
And now our feet are standing
within your gates, O Jerusalem.

Jerusalem is built as a city
strongly compact.
It is there that the tribes go up,
the tribes of the Lord.

For Israel's law it is,
there to praise the Lord's name.
There were set the thrones of judgment
of the house of David.

For the peace of Jerusalem pray:
"Peace be to your homes!
May peace reign in your walls,
in your palaces, peace!"

For love of my brethren and friends
I say: "Peace upon you!"
For love of the house of the Lord
I will ask for your good.

Psalm-prayer

When you rose from the dead, Lord Jesus, you formed
the Church into your new body and made of it the new
Jerusalem, united in your Spirit. Give us peace in our
day. Make all nations come to your Church to share your
gifts in fellowship, that they may render you thanks
without end and come to your eternal city.

Advent: He comes, the desire of all human hearts; his
           dwelling place shall be resplendent with glory,
           alleluia.

Antiphon 2

Advent: Come, Lord, do not delay; free your people
           from their sinfulness.

Psalm 130

A cry from the depths

He himself will save his people from their sins (Matthew 1:21).

Out of the depths I cry to you, O Lord,
Lord, hear my voice!
O let your ears be attentive
to the voice of my pleading.

If you, O Lord, should mark our guilt,
Lord, who would survive?
But with you is found forgiveness:
for this we revere you.

My soul is waiting for the Lord,
I count on his word.
My soul is longing for the Lord
more than watchman for daybreak.
Let the watchman count on daybreak
and Israel on the Lord.

Because with the Lord there is mercy
and fullness of redemption,
Israel indeed he will redeem
from all its iniquity.

Psalm-prayer

Listen with compassion to our prayers, Lord. The forgiveness of sins is yours. Do not look on the wrong we have done, but grant us your merciful kindness.

Advent: Come, Lord, do not delay; free your people
          from their sinfulness.

Antiphon 3

Advent: The fullness of time has come upon us at last:
          God sends his Son into the world.

Canticle   Philippians 2:6-11

Christ, God's holy servant

Though he was in the form of God,
Jesus did not deem equality with God
something to be grasped at.

Rather, he emptied himself
and took the form of a slave,
being born in the likeness of men.

He was known to be of human estate,
and it was thus that he humbled himself,
obediently accepting even death,
death on a cross!

Because of this,
God highly exalted him
and bestowed on him the name
above every other name,

So that at Jesus' name
every knee must bend
in the heavens, on the earth,
and under the earth,
and every tongue proclaim
to the glory of God the Father:
JESUS CHRIST IS LORD!

Advent: The fullness of time has come upon us at last;
            God sends his Son into the world.

Reading, responsory, antiphon for the canticle of Mary,
intercessions and prayer, as in the Proper of Seasons.

Conclusion, as in the Ordinary.

Invitatory

Lord, open my lips.

December 17-23:

Ant.   **The Lord is close at hand; come, let us worship him.**

December 24:

Ant.   **Today you will know the Lord is coming, and in the morning you will see his glory.**

Invitatory psalm, 648.

Office of Readings

God, come to my assistance. Glory to the Father. As it was in the beginning. Alleluia.

This verse and response are omitted when the hour begins with the invitatory.

HYMN, 132.

Or:

> Holy, Holy, Holy! Lord God Almighty!
> Early in the morning our song shall rise to thee:
> Holy, Holy, Holy! Merciful and mighty,
> God in three persons, blessed Trinity.
>
> Holy, Holy, Holy! All the saints adore thee,
> Though the eye of sinful man thy glory may not see;
> Only thou art holy; there is none beside thee,
> Which were, and are, and ever more shall be.
>
> Holy, Holy, Holy! Lord God Almighty!
> All thy works shall praise thy name, in earth, and sky, and sea;
> Holy, holy, holy! Merciful and mighty,
> God in three persons, blessed Trinity.

Melody: Nicaea 11.12.12.10   Music: John B. Dykes, 1823-1876
                    Text: Reginald Heber, 1783-1826, alt.

PSALMODY

Antiphon 1

Advent: **This is our heavenly King; he comes with power and might to save the nations, alleluia.**

When psalm 24 is the invitatory psalm, psalm 95, **648**, is used here as the first psalm of the Office of Readings.

Psalm 24
The Lord's entry into his temple

Christ opened heaven for us in the manhood he assumed (Saint Irenaeus).

The Lord's is the earth and its fullness,
the world and all its peoples.
It is he who set it on the seas;
on the waters he made it firm.

Who shall climb the mountain of the Lord?
Who shall stand in his holy place?
The man with clean hands and pure heart,
who desires not worthless things,
who has not sworn so as to deceive his neighbor.

He shall receive blessings from the Lord
and reward from the God who saves him.
Such are the men who seek him,
seek the face of the God of Jacob.

O gates, lift high your heads;
grow higher, ancient doors.
Let him enter, the king of glory!

Who is the king of glory?
The Lord, the mighty, the valiant,
the Lord, the valiant in war.

O gates, lift high your heads;
grow higher, ancient doors.
Let him enter, the king of glory!

Who is he, the king of glory?
He, the Lord of armies,
he is the king of glory.

Psalm-prayer

When your Son was unjustly condemned, Lord God,
and surrounded by the impious, he cried to you and you
set him free. Watch over your people as the treasure of
your heart and guide their steps along safe paths that they
may see your face.

Advent: This is our heavenly King; he comes with
power and might to save the nations, alleluia.

Antiphon 2

Advent: Daughter of Jerusalem, rejoice and be glad;
your King will come to you. Zion, do not fear;
your Savior hastens on his way.

Psalm 66

Eucharistic hymn

*The Lord is risen and all people have been brought by him to
the Father* (Hesychius).

I

Cry out with joy to God, all the earth,
O sing to the glory of his name.
O render him glorious praise.
Say to God: "How tremendous your deeds!

Because of the greatness of your strength
your enemies cringe before you.
Before you all the earth shall bow;
shall sing to you, sing to your name!"

Come and see the works of God,
tremendous his deeds among men.

He turned the sea into dry land,
they passed through the river dry-shod.

Let our joy then be in him;
he rules for ever by his might.
His eyes keep watch over the nations:
let rebels not rise against him.

O peoples, bless our God,
let the voice of his praise resound,
of the God who gave life to our souls
and kept our feet from stumbling.

For you, O God, have tested us,
you have tried us as silver is tried:
you led us, God, into the snare;
you laid a heavy burden on our backs.

You let men ride over our heads;
we went through fire and through water
but then you brought us relief.

Advent: Daughter of Jerusalem, rejoice and be glad;
your King will come to you. Zion, do not fear;
your Savior hastens on his way.

Antiphon 3

Advent: Let us cleanse our hearts for the coming of our
great King, that we may be ready to welcome
him; he is coming and will not delay.

II

Burnt offering I bring to your house;
to you I will pay my vows,
the vows which my lips have uttered,
which my mouth spoke in my distress.

I will offer burnt offerings of fatlings
with the smoke of burning rams.
I will offer bullocks and goats.

Come and hear, all who fear God.
I will tell what he did for my soul:
to him I cried aloud,
with high praise ready on my tongue.

If there had been evil in my heart,
the Lord would not have listened.
But truly God has listened;
he has heeded the voice of my prayer.

Blessed be God who did not reject my prayer
nor withhold his love from me.

Psalm-prayer

Almighty Father, in the death and resurrection of your
own Son you brought us through the waters of baptism to
the shores of new life. By those waters and the fire of the
Holy Spirit you have given each of us consolation. Accept
our sacrifice of praise; may our lives be a total offering to
you, and may we deserve to enter your house and there
with Christ praise your unfailing power.

Advent: Let us cleanse our hearts for the coming of our
           great King, that we may be ready to welcome
           him; he is coming and will not delay.

Verse, reading and prayer, as in the Proper of Seasons.

Morning Prayer

God, come to my assistance. Glory to the Father. As it
was in the beginning. Alleluia.

This verse and response are omitted when the hour begins with
the invitatory.

HYMN, 132.

Or:

    Sing with all the sons of glory,
    Sing the resurrection song!

Death and sorrow, earth's dark story,
To the former days belong.
All around the clouds are breaking,
Soon the storms of time shall cease;
In God's likeness, man awaking,
Knows the everlasting peace.

O what glory, far exceeding
All that eye has yet perceived!
Holiest hearts for ages pleading,
Never that full joy conceived.
God has promised, Christ prepares it,
There on high our welcome waits;
Every humble spirit shares it,
Christ has passed the eternal gates.

Life eternal! heaven rejoices:
Jesus lives who once was dead;
Join, O man, the deathless voices;
Child of God, lift up thy head!
Patriarchs from the distant ages,
Saints all longing for their heaven,
Prophets, psalmists, seers, and sages,
All await the glory given.

Life eternal! O what wonders
Crowd on faith; what joy unknown,
When, amidst earth's closing thunders,
Saints shall stand before the throne!
O to enter that bright portal,
See that glowing firmament,
Know, with thee, O God immortal,
"Jesus Christ whom thou hast sent!"

Melody: Hymn to Joy 87.87.D Music: Arr. from Ludwig van
Beethoven, 1770–1827,
by Edward Hodges 1796–1867
Text: William J. Irons, 1812–1883

PSALMODY

Antiphon 1

Advent: Sound the trumpet in Zion; the day of the
          Lord is near; he comes to save us, alleluia.

If this Sunday occurs on December 24, the antiphons are said as
above, 381.

Psalm 118

Song of joy for salvation

*This Jesus is the stone which, rejected by you builders, has
become the chief stone supporting all the rest* (Acts 4:11).

Give thanks to the Lord for he is good,
for his love endures for ever.

Let the sons of Israel say:
"His love endures for ever."
Let the sons of Aaron say:
"His love endures for ever."
Let those who fear the Lord say:
"His love endures for ever."

I called to the Lord in my distress;
he answered and freed me.
The Lord is at my side; I do not fear.
What can man do against me ?
The Lord is at my side as my helper:
I shall look down on my foes.

It is better to take refuge in the Lord
than to trust in men:
it is better to take refuge in the Lord
than to trust in princes.

The nations all encompassed me;
in the Lord's name I crushed them.
They compassed me, compassed me about;
in the Lord's name I crushed them.

They compassed me about like bees;
they blazed like a fire among thorns.
In the Lord's name I crushed them.

I was hard-pressed and was falling
but the Lord came to help me.
The Lord is my strength and my song;
he is my savior.
There are shouts of joy and victory
in the tents of the just.

The Lord's right hand has triumphed;
his right hand raised me.
The Lord's right hand has triumphed;
I shall not die, I shall live
and recount his deeds.
I was punished, I was punished by the Lord,
but not doomed to die.

Open to me the gates of holiness:
I will enter and give thanks.
This is the Lord's own gate
where the just may enter.
I will thank you for you have answered
and you are my savior.

The stone which the builders rejected
has become the corner stone.
This is the work of the Lord,
a marvel in our eyes.
This day was made by the Lord;
we rejoice and are glad.

O Lord, grant us salvation;
O Lord, grant success.
Blessed in the name of the Lord
is he who comes.

We bless you from the house of the Lord;
the Lord God is our light.

Go forward in procession with branches
even to the altar.
You are my God, I thank you.
My God, I praise you.
Give thanks to the Lord for he is good;
for his love endures for ever.

Psalm-prayer

Lord God, you have given us the great day of rejoicing:
Jesus Christ, the stone rejected by the builders, has
become the cornerstone of the Church, our spiritual
home. Shed upon your Church the rays of your glory,
that it may be seen as the gate of salvation open to all
nations. Let cries of joy and exultation ring out from its
tents, to celebrate the wonder of Christ's resurrection.

Advent: Sound the trumpet in Zion; the day of the
Lord is near; he comes to save us, alleluia.

Antiphon 2

Advent: The Lord is here; go out to meet him, saying:
Great his birth, eternal his kingdom: Strong
God, Ruler of all, Prince of Peace, alleluia.

Canticle   Daniel 3:52-57

Let all creatures praise the Lord

The Creator . . . is blessed for ever (Romans 1:25).

Blessed are you, O Lord, the God of our fathers,
praiseworthy and exalted above all forever.

And blessed is your holy and glorious name,
praiseworthy and exalted above all for all ages.

Blessed are you in the temple of your holy glory,
praiseworthy and glorious above all forever.

Blessed are you on the throne of your kingdom,
praiseworthy and exalted above all forever.

Blessed are you who look into the depths
from your throne upon the cherubim,
praiseworthy and exalted above all forever.

Blessed are you in the firmament of heaven,
praiseworthy and glorious forever.

Bless the Lord, all you works of the Lord,
praise and exalt him above all forever.

Advent: The Lord is here; go out to meet him, saying:
Great his birth, eternal his kingdom: Strong
God, Ruler of all, Prince of Peace, alleluia.

Antiphon 3

Advent: Your all-powerful Word, O Lord will come to
earth from his throne of glory, alleluia.

Psalm 150

Praise the Lord

*Let mind and heart be in your song: this is to glorify God
with your whole self* (Hesychius).

Praise God in his holy place,
praise him in his mighty heavens.
Praise him for his powerful deeds,
praise his surpassing greatness.

O praise him with sound of trumpet,
praise him with lute and harp.
Praise him with timbrel and dance,
praise him with strings and pipes.

O praise him with resounding cymbals,
praise him with clashing of cymbals.
Let everything that lives and that breathes
give praise to the Lord.

Psalm-prayer

Lord God, maker of heaven and earth and of all
created things, you make your just ones holy and you
justify sinners who confess your name. Hear us as we
humbly pray to you: give us eternal joy with your saints.

Advent: Your all-powerful Word, O Lord will come to
           earth from his throne of glory, alleluia.

Reading, responsory, antiphon for the canticle of Zechariah,
intercessions and prayer, as in the Proper of Seasons.

Conclusion, as in the Ordinary.

Daytime Prayer

God, come to my assistance. Glory to the Father. As it
was in the beginning. Alleluia.

HYMN, as in the Ordinary, 658.

PSALMODY

Antiphon, as in the Proper of Seasons.

Psalm 23

The Good Shepherd

*The Lamb himself will be their shepherd and will lead them
to the springs of living waters* (Revelation 7:17).

The Lord is my shepherd;
there is nothing I shall want.
Fresh and green are the pastures
where he gives me repose.

Near restful waters he leads me,
to revive my drooping spirit.

He guides me along the right path;
he is true to his name.
If I should walk in the valley of darkness
no evil would I fear.
You are there with your crook and your staff;
with these you give me comfort.

You have prepared a banquet for me
in the sight of my foes.
My head you have anointed with oil;
my cup is overflowing.

Surely goodness and kindness shall follow me
all the days of my life.
In the Lord's own house shall I dwell
for ever and ever.

Psalm-prayer

Lord Jesus Christ, shepherd of your Church, you give
us new birth in the waters of baptism, you anoint us with
saving oil, and you call us to salvation at your table.
Dispel the terrors of death and the darkness of error.
Lead your people along safe paths that they may rest
securely in you and live for ever in your Father's house.

Psalm 76
Thanksgiving for victory

They will see the Son of Man coming on the clouds of heaven
(Matthew 24:30).

I

God is made known in Judah;
in Israel his name is great.
He set up his tent in Jerusalem
and his dwelling place in Zion.

It was there he broke the flashing arrows,
the shield, the sword, the armor.

You, Lord, are resplendent,
more majestic than the everlasting mountains.
The warriors, despoiled, slept in death;
the hands of the soldiers were powerless.
At your threat, O God of Jacob,
horse and rider lay stunned.

II

You, you alone, strike terror.
Who shall stand when your anger is roused?
You uttered your sentence from the heavens;
the earth in terror was still
when God arose to judge,
to save the humble of the earth.

Men's anger will serve to praise you;
its survivors surround you in joy.
Make vows to your God and fulfill them.
Let all pay tribute to him who strikes terror,
who cuts short the breath of princes,
who strikes terror in the kings of the earth.

Psalm-prayer

Your power is awesome, Father, and wonderful is your
holiness. In your presence the earth both trembles and
stands still, for you shattered death's power by the cross.
Rise to help your people: give your light, and grant
salvation to the meek of the earth, that they may praise
your name in heaven.

At the other hours, the complementary psalmody is used, 1191.

Reading, verse and prayer, as in the Proper of Seasons.

Conclusion, as in the Ordinary.

Evening Prayer II

God, come to my assistance. Glory to the Father. As it was in the beginning. Alleluia.

HYMN, 133.

Or:

Love divine, all loves excelling,
Joy of heaven to earth come down,
And impart to us, here dwelling,
Grace and mercy all around.
Jesus, source of all compassion,
Pure, unbounded love you share;
Grant us many choicest blessings,
Keep us in your loving care.

Come, oh source of inspiration,
Pure and spotless let us be:
Let us see your true salvation,
Perfect in accord with thee.
Praising Father for all glory
With the Spirit and the Son;
Everlasting thanks we give thee,
Undivided, love, in one.

Melody: Hyfrydol 87.87.D   Music: Rowland H. Prichard,
                                        1811–1887
                        Text: Charles Wesley, 1707-1788, adapted by
PSALMODY   C.T. Andrews, 1968

Antiphon 1

Advent: See how glorious he is, coming forth as Savior
           of all peoples!

Psalm 110:1-5, 7

The Messiah, king and priest

Christ's reign will last until all his enemies are made subject to him (1 Corinthians 15:25).

The Lord's revelation to my Master:
"Sit on my right:
your foes I will put beneath your feet."

The Lord will wield from Zion
your scepter of power:
rule in the midst of all your foes.

A prince from the day of your birth
on the holy mountains;
from the womb before the dawn I begot you.

The Lord has sworn an oath he will not change.
"You are a priest for ever,
a priest like Melchizedek of old."

The Master standing at your right hand
will shatter kings in the day of his great wrath.

He shall drink from the stream by the wayside
and therefore he shall lift up his head.

Psalm-prayer

Father, we ask you to give us victory and peace. In
Jesus Christ, our Lord and King, we are already seated at
your right hand. We look forward to praising you in the
fellowship of all your saints in our heavenly homeland.

Advent: See how glorious he is, coming forth as Savior
of all peoples!

Antiphon 2

Advent: Crooked paths will be straightened and rough
ways made smooth. Come, O Lord, do not
delay, alleluia.

Psalm 112

The happiness of the just man

*Live as children born of the light. Light produces every kind
of goodness and justice and truth* (Ephesians 5:8-9) .

Happy the man who fears the Lord,
who takes delight in his commands.
His sons will be powerful on earth;
the children of the upright are blessed.

Riches and wealth are in his house;
his justice stands firm for ever
He is a light in the darkness for the upright:
he is generous, merciful and just.

The good man takes pity and lends,
he conducts his affairs with honor.
The just man will never waver:
he will be remembered for ever.

He has no fear of evil news;
with a firm heart he trusts in the Lord.
With a steadfast heart he will not fear;
he will see the downfall of his foes.

Open-handed, he gives to the poor;
his justice stands firm for ever.
His head will be raised in glory.

The wicked man sees and is angry,
grinds his teeth and fades away;
the desire of the wicked leads to doom.

Psalm-prayer

Lord God, you are the eternal light which illumines
the hearts of good people. Help us to love you, to rejoice
in your glory, and so to live in this world as to avoid
harsh judgment in the next. May we come to see the light
of your countenance.

Advent: Crooked paths will be straightened and rough
           ways made smooth. Come, O Lord, do not
           delay, alleluia.

Antiphon 3

Advent: **Ever wider will his kingdom spread, eternally at peace, alleluia.**

The following canticle is said with the **Alleluia** when Evening Prayer is sung; when the office is recited, the **Alleluia** may be said at the beginning and end of each strophe.

Canticle   See Revelation 19:1-7

The wedding of the Lamb

Alleluia.
Salvation, glory, and power to our God:
(R. Alleluia.)
his judgments are honest and true.
R. Alleluia (alleluia).

Alleluia.
Sing praise to our God, all you his servants,
(R. Alleluia.)
all who worship him reverently, great and small.
R. Alleluia (alleluia).

Alleluia.
The Lord our all-powerful God is King,
(R. Alleluia.)
let us rejoice, sing praise, and give him glory.
R. Alleluia (alleluia).

Alleluia.
The wedding feast of the Lamb has begun,
(R. Alleluia.)
and his bride is prepared to welcome him.
R. Alleluia (alleluia).

Advent: **Ever wider will his kingdom spread, eternally at peace, alleluia.**

Reading, responsory, antiphon for the canticle of Mary, intercessions and prayer, as in the Proper of Seasons.

Conclusion, as in the Ordinary.

MONDAY, WEEK IV

Invitatory

Lord, open my lips,

Antiphon, as in the Ordinary, 647.
Invitatory psalm, 648.

Office of Readings

God, come to my assistance. Glory to the Father. As it was in the beginning. Alleluia.

This verse and response are omitted when the hour begins with the invitatory.

HYMN

> Sing praise to God who reigns above,
> The God of all creation,
> The God of power, the God of love,
> The God of our salvation;
> With healing balm my soul he fills,
> And every faithless murmur stills:
> To God all praise and glory.
>
> What God's almighty power hath made,
> His gracious mercy keepeth;
> By morning glow or evening shade
> His watchful eye never sleepeth;
> Within the kingdom of his might,
> Lo! all is just and all is right:
> To God all praise and glory.
>
> Then all my gladsome way along,
> I sing aloud thy praises,
> That men may hear the grateful song
> My voice unwearied raises;

Be joyful in the Lord, my heart,
Both soul and body, bear your part:
To God all praise and glory.

O ye who name Christ's holy name,
Give God all praise and glory;
All ye who own his power, proclaim
Aloud the wondrous story!
Cast each false idol from his throne.
The Lord is God, and he alone:
To God all praise and glory.

Melody: Mit Freuden Zart 87.87.887   Music: *Bohemian Brethren's*
Hymnbook, 1566
Text: Johann J. Schutz, 1640–1690
Translator: Frances E. Cox, 1812–1897

PSALMODY

Ant. 1   How good is the God of Israel to the pure of
heart!

Psalm 73

Why is it that the good have many troubles?

Blessed is the man who does not lose faith in me (Matthew
11:16).

I

How good God is to Israel,
to those who are pure of heart.
Yet my feet came close to stumbling,
my steps had almost slipped
for I was filled with envy of the proud
when I saw how the wicked prosper.

For them there are no pains;
their bodies are sound and sleek.
They have no share in men's sorrows;
they are not stricken like others.

So they wear their pride like a necklace,
they clothe themselves with violence.
Their hearts overflow with malice,
their minds seethe with plots.

They scoff; they speak with malice;
from on high they plan oppression.
They have set their mouths in the heavens
and their tongues dictate to the earth.

So the people turn to follow them
and drink in all their words.
They say:"How can God know?
Does the Most High take any notice?"
Look at them, such are the wicked,
but untroubled, they grow in wealth.

Ant.   How good is the God of Israel to the pure of heart!

Ant. 2   Their laughter will turn to weeping, their
merriment to grief.

II

How useless to keep my heart pure
and wash my hands in innocence,
when I was stricken all day long,
suffered punishment day after day.

Then I said: "If I should speak like that,
I should abandon the faith of your people."
I strove to fathom this problem,
too hard for my mind to understand,
until I pierced the mysteries of God
and understood what becomes of the wicked.

How slippery the paths on which you set them;
you make them slide to destruction.
How suddenly they come to their ruin,
wiped out, destroyed by terrors.

Like a dream one wakes from, O Lord,
when you wake you dismiss them as phantoms.

Ant. Their laughter will turn to weeping, their
merriment to grief.

Ant. 3 Those who depart from you will perish; my joy
is to remain with you, my God.

III

And so when my heart grew embittered
and when I was cut to the quick,
I was stupid and did not understand,
no better than a beast in your sight.

Yet I was always in your presence;
you were holding me by my right hand.
You will guide me by your counsel
and so you will lead me to glory.

What else have I in heaven but you?
Apart from you I want nothing on earth.
My body and my heart faint for joy;
God is my possession for ever.

All those who abandon you shall perish;
you will destroy all those who are faithless.
To be near God is my happiness.
I have made the Lord God my refuge.
I will tell of all your works
at the gates of the city of Zion.

Psalm-prayer

It is good to be with you, Father; in you is fullness of
life for your faithful people; in you all hope resides. May
you lead us to everlasting happiness.

Ant. Those who depart from you will perish; my joy is
to remain with you, my God.

Verse, reading and prayer, as in the Proper of Seasons.

Morning Prayer

God, come to my assistance. Glory to the Father. As it was in the beginning. Alleluia.

This verse and response are omitted when the hour begins with the invitatory.

HYMN

Antiphon:

All you nations, sing out your joy to the Lord:
Alleluia, alleluia!

Joyfully shout, all you on earth,
give praise to the glory of God;
And with a hymn, sing out his glorious praise:
Alleluia!

Antiphon

Let all the earth kneel in his sight,
extolling his marvelous fame;
Honor his name, in highest heaven give praise:
Alleluia!

Antiphon

Come forth and see all the great works
that God has brought forth by his might;
Fall on your knees before his glorious throne:
Alleluia!

Antiphon

Glory and thanks be to the Father;
honor and praise to the Son;
And to the Spirit, source of life and of love:
Alleluia!

Antiphon

Melody: All You Nations   Music: Lucien Deiss, C.S.Sp., 1965
                               Text: Lucien Deiss, C.S.Sp., 1965

Or:

I sing the mighty power of God,
That made the mountains rise;
That spread the flowing seas abroad,
And built the lofty skies.
I sing the wisdom that ordained
The sun to rule the day;
The moon shines full at his command,
And all the stars obey.

I sing the goodness of the Lord,
That filled the earth with food;
He formed the creatures with his word,
And then pronounced them good.
Lord, how your wonders are displayed,
Where e'er I turn my eye:
If I survey the ground I tread,
Or gaze upon the sky!

There's not a plant or flower below,
But makes your glories known;
And clouds arise, and tempests blow,
By order from your throne;
While all that borrows life from you
Is ever in your care,
And everywhere that man can be,
Thou, God, art present there.

Melody: 86.86.D   Music: *Our Parish Prays and Sings*, 1968
                                    Text: Isaac Watts, 1715

PSALMODY

Antiphon 1

December 17-23:   The Lord, the ruler over the kings of
                   the earth, will come; blessed are they
                   who are ready to go and welcome
                   him.

Psalm 90
May we live in the radiance of God

There is no time with God: a thousand years, a single day: it is all one (2 Peter 3:8).

O Lord, you have been our refuge
from one generation to the next.
Before the mountains were born
or the earth or the world brought forth,
you are God, without beginning or end.

You turn men back into dust
and say: "Go back, sons of men."
To your eyes a thousand years
are like yesterday, come and gone,
no more than a watch in the night.

You sweep men away like a dream,
like grass which springs up in the morning.
In the morning it springs up and flowers:
by evening it withers and fades.

So we are destroyed in your anger,
struck with terror in your fury.
Our guilt lies open before you;
our secrets in the light of your face.

All our days pass away in your anger.
Our life is over like a sigh.
Our span is seventy years
or eighty for those who are strong.

And most of these are emptiness and pain.
They pass swiftly and we are gone.
Who understands the power of your anger
and fears the strength of your fury?

Make us know the shortness of our life
that we may gain wisdom of heart.

Lord, relent! Is your anger for ever?
Show pity to your servants.

In the morning, fill us with your love;
we shall exult and rejoice all our days.
Give us joy to balance our affliction
for the years when we knew misfortune.

Show forth your work to your servants;
let your glory shine on their children.
Let the favor of the Lord be upon us:
give success to the work of our hands,
give success to the work of our hands.

Psalm-prayer

Lord, send your mercy and your truth to rescue us
from the snares of the devil, and we will praise you
among the peoples and proclaim you to the nations,
happy to be known as companions of your Son.

December 17-23: The Lord, the ruler over the kings of
the earth, will come; blessed are they
who are ready to go and welcome
him.

Antiphon 2

December 17-23: Sing a new song to the Lord,
proclaim his praises to the ends of
the earth.

Canticle   Isaiah 42:10-16

God, victor and savior

They were singing a new hymn before the throne of God
(Revelation 14:3).

Sing to the Lord a new song,
his praise from the end of the earth:

Let the sea and what fills it resound,
the coastlands, and those who dwell in them.
Let the steppe and its cities cry out,
the villages where Kedar dwells;

Let the inhabitants of Sela exult,
and shout from the top of the mountains.
Let them give glory to the Lord,
and utter his praise in the coastlands.

The Lord goes forth like a hero,
like a warrior he stirs up his ardor;
he shouts out his battle cry,
against his enemies he shows his might:

I have looked away, and kept silence,
I have said nothing, holding myself in;
but now, I cry out as a woman in labor,
gasping and panting.

I will lay waste mountains and hills,
all their herbage I will dry up;
I will turn the rivers into marshes,
and the marshes I will dry up.

I will lead the blind on their journey;
by paths unknown I will guide them.
I will turn darkness into light before them,
and make crooked ways straight.

December 17-23: Sing a new song to the Lord, proclaim
his praises to the ends of the earth.

Antiphon 3

December 17-23: **When the Son of Man comes to
earth, do you think he will find faith
in men's hearts?**

Psalm 135:1-12

Praise for the wonderful things God does for us

He has won you for himself . . . and you must proclaim
what he has done for you: he has called you out of darkness
into his own wonderful light (1 Peter 2:9).

Praise the name of the Lord,
praise him, servants of the Lord,
who stand in the house of the Lord,
in the courts of the house of our God.

Praise the Lord for the Lord is good.
Sing a psalm to his name for he is loving.
For the Lord has chosen Jacob for himself
and Israel for his own possession.

For I know the Lord is great,
that our Lord is high above all gods.
The Lord does whatever he wills,
in heaven, on earth, in the seas.

He summons clouds from the ends of the earth;
makes lightning produce the rain;
from his treasuries he sends forth the wind.

The first-born of the Egyptians he smote,
of man and beast alike.
Signs and wonders he worked
in the midst of your land, O Egypt,
against Pharaoh and all his servants.

Nations in their greatness he struck
and kings in their splendor he slew.
Sihon, king of the Amorites,
Og, the king of Bashan,
and all the kingdoms of Canaan.
He let Israel inherit their land;
on his people their land he bestowed.

Psalm-prayer

Where two or three gather in your name, Lord, you promised to be with them and share their fellowship. Look down upon your family gathered here in your name, and graciously pour out your blessing upon us.

December 17-23: When the Son of Man comes to earth, do you think he will find faith in men's hearts?

Reading, responsory, antiphon for the canticle of Zechariah, intercessions and prayer, as in the Proper of Seasons.

Conclusion, as in the Ordinary.

Daytime Prayer

God, come to my assistance. Glory to the Father. As it was in the beginning. Alleluia.

HYMN, as in the Ordinary, 658.

PSALMODY

Antiphon, as in the Proper of Seasons.

Psalm 119:129-136

XVII (Pe)

A meditation on God's law

The whole law is summed up in love (Romans 13:10).

Your will is wonderful indeed;
therefore I obey it.
The unfolding of your word gives light
and teaches the simple.

I open my mouth and I sigh
as I yearn for your commands.
Turn and show me your mercy;
show justice to your friends.

Let my steps be guided by your promise;
let no evil rule me.
Redeem me from man's oppression
and I will keep your precepts.

Let your face shine on your servant
and teach me your decrees.
Tears stream from my eyes
because your law is disobeyed.

Psalm-prayer

You are just, Lord God, and righteous are your
judgments. Deliver those who cry to you in their
affliction; give them peace and calm to reflect on your
commands.

Psalm 82

Denunciation of evil judges

*Do not attempt to judge another now; the Lord's coming will
reveal all* (1 Corinthians 4:5).

God stands in the divine assembly.
In the midst of the gods he gives judgment.

"How long will you judge unjustly
and favor the cause of the wicked?
Do justice for the weak and the orphan,
defend the afflicted and the needy.
Rescue the weak and the poor;
set them free from the hand of the wicked.

Unperceiving, they grope in the darkness
and the order of the world is shaken.
I have said to you: 'You are gods,
and all of you, sons of the Most High.'
And yet, you shall die like men,
you shall fall like any of the princes.''

Arise, O God, judge the earth,
for you rule all the nations.

Psalm-prayer

You are always true to your word, Father. Look down
from heaven and put an end to our foolishness. Save us
from groundless fears and help us to please you with
undivided heart.

Psalm 120

Longing for peace

Be patient in suffering; persevere in prayer (Romans 12:12)

To the Lord in the hour of my distress
I call and he answers me.
"O Lord, save my soul from lying lips,
from the tongue of the deceitful."

What shall he pay you in return,
O treacherous tongue?
The warrior's arrows sharpened
and coals, red-hot, blazing.

Alas, that I abide a stranger in Meshech,
dwell among the tents of Kedar!

Long enough have I been dwelling
with those who hate peace.
I am for peace, but when I speak,
they are for fighting.

Psalm-prayer

You declared peacemakers happy, Lord Jesus, since
they will be called sons of God. Give us that peace which
the world cannot give so that your Church may be freed
from the schemes of arrogant men, and, devoted to
works of peace, go forward joyfully to meet you, the
King of Peace.

At the other hours, the complementary psalmody from series II and III is used, 1193.

Reading, verse and prayer, as in the Proper of Seasons.

Conclusion, as in the Ordinary.

Evening Prayer

God, come to my assistance. Glory to the Father. As it was in the beginning. Alleluia.

HYMN

> Now fades all earthly splendor,
> The shades of night descend;
> The dying of the daylight
> Foretells creation's end.
> Though noon gives place to sunset,
> Yet dark gives place to light:
> The promise of tomorrow
> With dawn's new hope is bright.
>
> The silver notes of morning
> Will greet the rising sun,
> As once the Easter glory
> Shone round the Risen One.
> So will the night of dying
> Give place to heaven's day,
> And hope of heaven's vision
> Will light our pilgrim way.
>
> So will the new creation
> Rise from the old reborn
> To splendor in Christ's glory
> And everlasting morn.
> All darkness will be ended
> As faith gives place to sight

Of Father, Son and Spirit,
One God, in heaven's light.

Melody: Ewing 76.76.D   Music: Alexander Ewing, 1830–1895
Text: James Quinn, S.J., 1968

PSALMODY

Antiphon 1

December 17-23:   The Lord, the ruler over the kings of
the earth, will come; blessed are they
who are ready to go and welcome
him.

Psalm 136

Easter hymn

We praise God by recalling his marvelous deeds (Cassiodorus).

I

O give thanks to the Lord for he is good,
for his love endures for ever.
Give thanks to the God of gods,
for his love endures for ever.
Give thanks to the Lord of lords,
for his love endures for ever;

who alone has wrought marvellous works,
for his love endures for ever;
whose wisdom it was made the skies,
for his love endures for ever;
who fixed the earth firmly on the seas,
for his love endures for ever.

It was he who made the great lights,
for his love endures for ever,
the sun to rule in the day,
for his love endures for ever,
the moon and stars in the night,
for his love endures for ever.

December 17-23: The Lord, the ruler over the kings of the earth will come; blessed are they who are ready to go and welcome him.

Antiphon 2

December 17-23: Sing a new song to the Lord, proclaim his praises to the ends of the earth.

II

The first-born of the Egyptians he smote,
for his love endures for ever.
He brought Israel out from their midst,
for his love endures for ever;
arm outstretched, with power in his hand,
for his love endures for ever.

He divided the Red Sea in two,
for his love endures for ever;
he made Israel pass through the midst,
for his love endures for ever;
he flung Pharaoh and his force in the sea,
for his love endures for ever.

Through the desert his people he led,
for his love endures for ever.
Nations in their greatness he struck,
for his love endures for ever.
Kings in their splendor he slew,
for his love endures for ever.

Sihon, king of the Amorites,
for his love endures for ever;
and Og, the king of Bashan,
for his love endures for ever.

He let Israel inherit their land,
  for his love endures for ever.
On his servant their land he bestowed,
  for his love endures for ever.
He remembered us in our distress,
  for his love endures for ever.

And he snatched us away from our foes,
  for his love endures for ever.
He gives food to all living things,
  for his love endures for ever.
To the God of heaven give thanks,
  for his love endures for ever.

Psalm-prayer

Almighty God, remember our lowliness and have
mercy. Once you gave our fathers a foreign land to
inherit. Free us today from sin and give us a share in your
inheritance.

December 17-23:   Sing a new song to the Lord,
                   proclaim his praises to the ends of
                   the earth.

Antiphon 3

December 17-23:   When the Son of Man comes to
                   earth, do you think he will find faith
                   in men's hearts?

                   Canticle   Ephesians 1:3-10

                   God our Savior

Praised be the God and Father
of our Lord Jesus Christ,
who has bestowed on us in Christ
every spiritual blessing in the heavens.

God chose us in him
before the world began
to be holy
and blameless in his sight.

He predestined us
to be his adopted sons through Jesus Christ,
such was his will and pleasure,
that all might praise the glorious favor
he has bestowed on us in his beloved.

In him and through his blood, we have been
    redeemed,
and our sins forgiven,
so immeasurably generous
is God's favor to us.

God has given us the wisdom
to understand fully the mystery,
the plan he was pleased
to decree in Christ.

A plan to be carried out
in Christ, in the fullness of time,
to bring all things into one in him,
in the heavens and on earth.

December 17-23:   **When the Son of Man comes to
earth, do you think he will find faith
in men's hearts?**

Reading, responsory, antiphon for the canticle of Mary,
intercessions and prayer, as in the Proper of Seasons.

Conclusion, as in the Ordinary.

TUESDAY, WEEK IV

Invitatory

Lord, open my lips.

Antiphon, as in the Ordinary, 647.

Invitatory psalm, 648.

Office of Readings

God, come to my assistance. Glory to the Father. As it was in the beginning. Alleluia.

This verse and response are omitted when the hour begins with the invitatory.

HYMN

With hearts renewed by living faith,
We lift our thoughts in grateful prayer
To God our gracious Father,
Whose plan it was to make us sons
Through his own Son's redemptive death,
That rescued us from darkness.
Lord, God, Savior,
Give us strength to mold our hearts in your true
    likeness.
Sons and servants of our Father.

So rich God's grace in Jesus Christ,
That we are called as sons of light
To bear the pledge of glory.
Through him in whom all fullness dwells,
We offer God our gift of self
In union with the Spirit.
Lord, God, Savior,

Give us strength to mold our hearts in your true
likeness.
Sons and servants of our Father.

Melody: Frankfort 887.887.48.48   Music: Philip Nicolai, 1599,
arr. by J.S. Bach, 1730
Text: Jack May, S.J.

PSALMODY

Ant. 1   Lord, let my cry come to you; do not hide your
face from me.

Psalm 102

The longings and prayers of an exile

God comforts us in all our troubles (2 Corinthians 1:4).

I

O Lord, listen to my prayer
and let my cry for help reach you.
Do not hide your face from me
in the day of my distress.
Turn your ear towards me
and answer me quickly when I call.

For my days are vanishing like smoke,
my bones burn away like a fire.
My heart is withered like the grass.
I forget to eat my bread.
I cry with all my strength
and my skin clings to my bones.

I have become like a pelican in the wilderness,
like an owl in desolate places.
I lie awake and I moan
like some lonely bird on a roof.
All day long my foes revile me;
those who hate me use my name as a curse.

The bread I eat is ashes;
my drink is mingled with tears.
In your anger, Lord, and your fury
you have lifted me up and thrown me down.
My days are like a passing shadow
and I wither away like the grass.

Ant.   Lord, let my cry come to you; do not hide your
face from me.

Ant. 2 Be attentive, Lord, to the prayer of the
helpless.

II

But you, O Lord, will endure for ever
and your name from age to age.
You will arise and have mercy on Zion:
for this is the time to have mercy;
yes, the time appointed has come
for your servants love her very stones,
are moved with pity even for her dust.

The nations shall fear the name of the Lord
and all the earth's kings your glory,
when the Lord shall build up Zion again
and appear in all his glory.
Then he will turn to the prayers of the helpless;
he will not despise their prayers.

Let this be written for ages to come
that a people yet unborn may praise the Lord;
for the Lord leaned down from his sanctuary on
high.
He looked down from heaven to the earth
that he might hear the groans of the prisoners
and free those condemned to die.

The sons of your servants shall dwell untroubled
and their race shall endure before you

that the name of the Lord may be proclaimed in Zion
and his praise in the heart of Jerusalem,
when peoples and kingdoms are gathered together
to pay their homage to the Lord.

Ant.   Be attentive, Lord, to the prayer of the helpless.

Ant. 3   You, O Lord, established the earth, and the
heavens are the work of your hands.

III

He has broken my strength in mid-course;
he has shortened the days of my life.
I say to God: "Do not take me away
before my days are complete,
you, whose days last from age to age.

Long ago you founded the earth
and the heavens are the work of your hands.
They will perish but you will remain.
They will all wear out like a garment.
You will change them like clothes that are changed.
But you neither change, nor have an end."

Psalm-prayer

Lord, you live in the hearts of your saints, and so have
built up Zion. May you always show your greatness
through their good works.

Ant.   You, O Lord, established the earth, and the
heavens are the work of your hands.

Verse, reading and prayer, as in the Proper of Seasons.

Morning Prayer

God, come to my assistance. Glory to the Father. As it
was in the beginning. Alleluia.

This verse and response are omitted when the hour begins with
the invitatory.

Hymn

God Father, praise and glory
your children come to sing.
Good will and peace to mankind,
the gifts your kingdom brings.

Refrain:

O most Holy Trinity,
Undivided Unity;
Holy God, Mighty God,
God Immortal, be adored.

And you, Lord Coeternal,
God's sole begotten Son;
O Jesus, King anointed,
You have redemption won.

Refrain

O Holy Ghost, Creator,
The Gift of God most high;
Life, love and holy wisdom,
Our weakness now supply.

Refrain

Melody: Mainz 76.76 with Refrain　　　Music: Mainz Melody
Text: Anon.
Translator: John Rathensteiner, 1936, alt.

Or:

This day God gives me
Strength of high heaven,
Sun and moon shining,
    Flame in my hearth,
Flashing of lightning,
Wind in its swiftness,
Deeps of the ocean,
    Firmness of earth.

This day God sends me
Strength as my steersman,
Might to uphold me,
    Wisdom as guide.
Your eyes are watchful,
Your ears are listening,
Your lips are speaking,
    Friend at my side.

God's way is my way,
God's shield is round me,
God's host defends me,
    Saving from ill.
Angels of heaven,
Drive from me always
All that would harm me,
    Stand by me still.

Rising, I thank you,
Mighty and strong one,
King of creation,
    Giver of rest,
Firmly confessing
Threeness of persons,
Oneness of Godhead,
    Trinity blest.

Melody: Bunessan 55.54.D

Music: Old Gaelic Melody
Text: James Quinn, S.J.

PSALMODY

Antiphon 1

December 17-23:   The Lord will come from his holy
place to save his people.

Psalm 101
Avowal of a good ruler

If you love me, keep my commandments (John 14:15).

My song is of mercy and justice;
I sing to you, O Lord.
I will walk in the way of perfection.
O when, Lord, will you come?

I will walk with blameless heart
within my house;
I will not set before my eyes
whatever is base.

I will hate the ways of the crooked;
they shall not be my friends.
The false-hearted must keep far away;
the wicked I disown.

The man who slanders his neighbor in secret
I will bring to silence.
The man of proud looks and haughty heart
I will never endure.

I look to the faithful in the land
that they may dwell with me.
He who walks in the way of perfection
shall be my friend.

No man who practices deceit
shall live within my house.
No man who utters lies shall stand
before my eyes.

Morning by morning I will silence
all the wicked in the land,
uprooting from the Lord's city
all who do evil

Psalm-prayer

So that your people may walk in innocence, you came
to us, Lord Jesus, and told us to be holy as your Father is
holy. Help your children to love what is truly perfect, so

that we may neither speak what is evil nor do what is wrong. Let us stand in your sight and celebrate with you the Father's love and justice.

December 17-23:　The Lord will come from his holy place to save his people.

Antiphon 2

December 17-23:　Zion is our mighty citadel, our saving Lord its wall and its defense; throw open the gates, for our God is here among us, alleluia.

Canticle　　　　　　　　　　　Daniel 3:26, 27, 29, 34-41

Azariah's prayer in the furnace

With your whole hearts turn to God and he will blot out all your sins (Acts 3:19).

Blessed are you, and praiseworthy,
O Lord, the God of our fathers,
and glorious forever is your name.

For you are just in all you have done;
all your deeds are faultless, all your ways right,
and all your judgments proper.

For we have sinned and transgressed
by departing from you,
and we have done every kind of evil.

For your name's sake, do not deliver us up forever,
or make void your covenant.

Do not take away your mercy from us,
for the sake of Abraham, your beloved,
Isaac your servant, and Israel your holy one,

to whom you promised to multiply their offspring
like the stars of heaven,
or the sand on the shore of the sea.

For we are reduced, O Lord, beyond any other
    nation,
brought low everywhere in the world this day
because of our sins.

We have in our day no prince, prophet, or leader,
no holocaust, sacrifice, oblation, or incense,
no place to offer first fruits, to find favor with you.

But with contrite heart and humble spirit
let us be received;
as though it were holocausts of rams and bullocks,
or thousands of fat lambs,
so let our sacrifice be in your presence today
as we follow you unreservedly;
for those who trust in you cannot be put to shame.

And now we follow you with our whole heart,
we fear you and we pray to you.

December 17-23:   Zion is our mighty citadel, our
                   saving Lord its wall and its defense;
                   throw open the gates, for our God is
                   here among us, alleluia.

Antiphon 3

December 17-23:   Lord, make known your will
                   throughout the earth; proclaim your
                   salvation to every nation.

Psalm 144:1-10
Prayer for victory and peace

I can do all things in him who strengthens me (Philippians
4:13).

Blessed be the Lord, my rock,
who trains my arms for battle,
who prepares my hands for war.

He is my love, my fortress;
he is my stronghold, my savior,
my shield, my place of refuge.
He brings peoples under my rule.

Lord, what is man that you care for him,
mortal man, that you keep him in mind;
man, who is merely a breath,
whose life fades like a passing shadow?

Lower your heavens and come down;
touch the mountains; wreathe them in smoke.
Flash your lightnings; rout the foe,
shoot your arrows and put them to flight.

Reach down from heaven and save me;
draw me out from the mighty waters,
from the hands of alien foes
whose mouths are filled with lies,
whose hands are raised in perjury.

To you, O God, will I sing a new song;
I will play on the ten-stringed harp
to you who give kings their victory,
who set David your servant free.

Psalm-prayer

Lord, God of strength, you gave your Son victory over
death. Direct your Church's fight against evil in the
world. Clothe us with the weapons of light and unite us
under the one banner of love, that we may receive our
eternal reward after the battle of earthly life.

December 17-23:   Lord, make known your will
                  throughout the earth; proclaim your
                  salvation to every nation.

Reading, responsory, antiphon for the canticle of Zechariah,
intercessions and prayer, as in the Proper of Seasons.

Conclusion, as in the Ordinary.

Daytime Prayer

God, come to my assistance. Glory to the Father. As it
was in the beginning. Alleluia.

HYMN, as in the Ordinary, 658.

PSALMODY

Antiphon, as in the Proper of Seasons.

Psalm 119:137-144

XVIII (Sade)

Lord, you are just indeed;
  your decrees are right.
You have imposed your will with justice
  and with absolute truth.

I am carried away by anger
  for my foes forget your word.
Your promise is tried in the fire,
  the delight of your servant.

Although I am weak and despised
  I remember your precepts.
Your justice is eternal justice
  and your law is truth.

Though anguish and distress have seized me,
  I delight in your commands.
The justice of your will is eternal:
  if you teach me, I shall live.

Psalm-prayer

You are just indeed, Lord, and your commandments
are eternal. Teach us to love you with all our hearts and
to love our neighbor as ourselves.

Psalm 88
Prayer of a person who is gravely ill

This is your moment—when darkness reigns (Luke 22:53).

I

Lord my God, I call for help by day;
I cry at night before you.
Let my prayer come into your presence.
O turn your ear to my cry.

For my soul is filled with evils;
my life is on the brink of the grave.
I am reckoned as one in the tomb:
I have reached the end of my strength,

like one alone among the dead;
like the slain lying in their graves;
like those you remember no more,
cut off, as they are, from your hand.

You have laid me in the depths of the tomb,
in places that are dark, in the depths.
Your anger weighs down upon me:
I am drowned beneath your waves.

II

You have taken away my friends
and made me hateful in their sight.
Imprisoned, I cannot escape;
my eyes are sunken with grief.

I call to you, Lord, all the day long;
to you I stretch out my hands.
Will you work your wonders for the dead?
Will the shades stand and praise you?

Will your love be told in the grave
or your faithfulness among the dead?
Will your wonders be known in the dark
or your justice in the land of oblivion?

As for me, Lord, I call to you for help:
in the morning my prayer comes before you.

Lord, why do you reject me?
Why do you hide your face?

Wretched, close to death from my youth,
I have borne your trials; I am numb.
Your fury has swept down upon me;
your terrors have utterly destroyed me.

They surround me all the day like a flood,
they assail me all together.
Friend and neighbor you have taken away:
my one companion is darkness.

Psalm-prayer

Lord Jesus, redeemer of all and author of our
salvation, for us you went down to the realm of death and
became free of death. Hear the prayers of your family
and lift us from our slavery to evil, that we may be
redeemed by you and see your Father's glory.

At the other hours, the complementary psalmody is used, 1191.

Reading, verse and prayer, as in the Proper of Seasons.

Conclusion, as in the Ordinary.

Evening Prayer

God, come to my assistance. Glory to the Father. As it
was in the beginning. Alleluia.

HYMN
Day is done, but love unfailing
    Dwells ever here;
Shadows fall, but hope, prevailing,
    Calms every fear.
Loving Father, none forsaking,
Take our hearts, of Love's own making,
Watch our sleeping, guard our waking,
    Be always near.

Dark descends, but Light unending
    Shines through our night;
You are with us, ever lending
    New strength to sight;
One in love, your truth confessing,
One in hope of heaven's blessing,
May we see, in love's possession,
    Love's endless light!

Eyes will close, but you, unsleeping,
    Watch by our side;
Death may come: in Love's safe keeping
    Still we abide.
God of love, all evil quelling,
Sin forgiving, fear dispelling,
Stay with us, our hearts indwelling,
    This eventide.

Melody: Ar Hyd Y Nos
84.84.88.84

Music: *Welsh Traditional Melody*
Text: James Quinn, S.J., 1968

PSALMODY

Antiphon 1

December 17-23:   The Lord will come from his holy
place to save his people.

Psalm 137:1-6

By the rivers of Babylon

The Babylonian captivity is a type of our spiritual captivity
(Saint Hilary).

By the rivers of Babylon
there we sat and wept,
remembering Zion;
on the poplars that grew there
we hung up our harps.

For it was there that they asked us,
our captors, for songs,
our oppressors, for joy.
"Sing to us," they said,
"one of Zion's songs."

O how could we sing
the song of the Lord
on alien soil?
If I forget you, Jerusalem,
let my right hand wither!

O let my tongue
cleave to my mouth
if I remember you not,
if I prize not Jerusalem
above all my joys!

Psalm-prayer

Lord, remember your pilgrim Church. We sit weeping at the streams of Babylon. Do not let us be drawn into the current of the passing world, but free us from every evil and raise our thoughts to the heavenly Jerusalem.

December 17-23: The Lord will come from his holy place to save his people.

Antiphon 2

December 17-23: Zion is our mighty citadel, our saving Lord its wall and its defense; throw open the gates, for our God is here among us, alleluia.

Psalm 138

Thanksgiving

The kings of the earth will bring glory and honor into the holy city (see Revelation 21:24).

I thank you, Lord, with all my heart,
you have heard the words of my mouth.
In the presence of the angels I will bless you.
I will adore before your holy temple.

I thank you for your faithfulness and love
which excel all we ever knew of you.
On the day I called, you answered;
you increased the strength of my soul.

All earth's kings shall thank you
when they hear the words of your mouth.
They shall sing of the Lord's ways:
"How great is the glory of the Lord!"

The Lord is high yet he looks on the lowly
and the haughty he knows from afar.
Though I walk in the midst of affliction
you give me life and frustrate my foes.

You stretch out your hand and save me,
your hand will do all things for me.
Your love, O Lord, is eternal,
discard not the work of your hands.

Psalm-prayer

Listen to the prayers of your Church, Lord God; in the
presence of the angels we praise your name. You keep the
proud at a distance and look upon the lowly with favor.
Stretch out your hand to us in our suffering, perfect in us
the work of your love and bring us to life.

December 17-23:   Zion is our mighty citadel, our
saving Lord its wall and its defense;
throw open the gates, for our God is
here among us, alleluia.

Antiphon 3

December 17-23:   Lord, make known your will
                  throughout the earth; proclaim your
                  salvation to every nation.

Canticle   Revelation 4:11; 5:9, 10, 12
                  Redemption hymn

O Lord our God, you are worthy
to receive glory and honor and power.

For you have created all things;
by your will they came to be and were made.

Worthy are you, O Lord,
to receive the scroll and break open its seals.

For you were slain;
with your blood you purchased for God
men of every race and tongue,
of every people and nation.

You made of them a kingdom,
and priests to serve our God,
and they shall reign on the earth.

Worthy is the Lamb that was slain
to receive power and riches,
wisdom and strength,
honor and glory and praise.

December 17-23:   Lord, make known your will
                  throughout the earth; proclaim your
                  salvation to every nation.

Reading, responsory, antiphon for the canticle of Mary,
intercessions and prayer, as in the Proper of Seasons.

Conclusion, as in the Ordinary.

WEDNESDAY, WEEK IV

Invitatory

Lord, open my lips.

Antiphon, as in the Ordinary, 647.

Invitatory psalm, 648.

Office of Readings

God, come to my assistance. Glory to the Father. As it was in the beginning. Alleluia.

This verse and response are omitted when the hour begins with the invitatory.

HYMN

Lord Jesus Christ, be present now,
And let your Holy Spirit bow
All hearts in love and truth today
To hear your word and keep your way.

Give us the grace to grasp your word,
That we may do what we have heard.
Instruct us thru the scriptures, Lord,
As we draw near, O God adored.

May your glad tidings always bring
Good news to men, that they may sing
Of how you came to save all men.
Instruct us till you come again.

To God the Father and the Son
And Holy Spirit, three in one;
To you, O blessed Trinity,
Be praise thruout eternity.

Melody: Herr Jesu
Christ Dich L.M.

Music: *Cantionale Germanicum,*
Dresden, 1628.
Text: Herr Jesu Christ Dich, Anon.
Translator: Catherine Winkworth, 1863, alt.
Stanza 2, Dennis Fitzpatrick

Or:

>Praise to the Lord, the Almighty, the King of
>   creation:
>O my soul, praise him, for he is thy health and
>   salvation.
>All ye who hear,
>Now to his altar draw near,
>Joining in glad adoration.
>
>Praise to the Lord who doth prosper thy work and
>   defend thee;
>Surely his goodness and mercy shall daily attend
>   thee.
>Ponder anew
>What the Almighty can do,
>Who with his love doth befriend thee.
>
>Praise to the Lord, O let all that is in me adore him!
>All that has life and breath come now in praises
>   before him!
>Let the Amen
>Sound from his people again:
>Now as we worship before him.

Melody: Lobe Den Herren 14.14.478   Music: *Stralsund*
                                    Gesangbuch, 1665
                        Text: J. Neander, 1650-1680
                   Translator: Catherine Winkworth, 1829-1878

PSALMODY

Ant. 1   Bless the Lord, my soul; never forget all he has
          done for you.

Psalm 103

Praise for God's tender compassion

*In the tender compassion of our God, the dawn from on high
shall break upon us* (see Luke 1:78).

I

My soul, give thanks to the Lord,
all my being, bless his holy name.
My soul, give thanks to the Lord
and never forget all his blessings.

It is he who forgives all your guilt,
who heals every one of your ills,
who redeems your life from the grave,
who crowns you with love and compassion,
who fills your life with good things,
renewing your youth like an eagle's.

The Lord does deeds of justice,
gives judgment for all who are oppressed.
He made known his ways to Moses
and his deeds to Israel's sons.

Ant.   Bless the Lord, my soul; never forget all he has
done for you.

Ant. 2   As a father is gentle with his children, so is the
Lord with those who revere him.

II

The Lord is compassion and love,
slow to anger and rich in mercy.
His wrath will come to an end;
he will not be angry for ever.
He does not treat us according to our sins
nor repay us according to our faults.

For as the heavens are high above the earth
so strong is his love for those who fear him.
As far as the east is from the west
so far does he remove our sins.

As a father has compassion on his sons,
the Lord has pity on those who fear him;

for he knows of what we are made,
he remembers that we are dust.

As for man, his days are like grass;
he flowers like the flower of the field;
the wind blows and he is gone
and his place never sees him again.

Ant. As a father is gentle with his children, so is the
Lord with those who revere him.

Ant. 3 Bless the Lord, all you his works!

III

But the love of the Lord is everlasting
upon those who hold him in fear;
his justice reaches out to children's children
when they keep his covenant in truth,
when they keep his will in their mind.

The Lord has set his sway in heaven
and his kingdom is ruling over all.
Give thanks to the Lord, all his angels,
mighty in power, fulfilling his word,
who heed the voice of his word.

Give thanks to the Lord, all his hosts,
his servants who do his will.
Give thanks to the Lord, all his works,
in every place where he rules.
My soul, give thanks to the Lord!

Psalm-prayer

You have compassion for the sinner, Lord, as a father
has compassion for his children. Heal the weakness of
your people and save us from lasting death that we may
praise and glorify you for ever.

Ant.   Bless the Lord, all you his works!

Verse, readings and prayer, as in the Proper of Seasons.

Morning Prayer

God, come to my assistance. Glory to the Father. As it was in the beginning. Alleluia.

This verse and response are omitted when the hour begins with the invitatory.

HYMN

> All creatures of our God and King,
> Lift up your voice and with us sing
>   Alleluia, alleluia!
> Thou burning sun with golden beam,
> Thou silver moon with softer gleam:

Refrain:

> O praise him, O praise him, alleluia, alleluia, alleluia!

> Thou rushing winds that are so strong,
> Ye clouds that sail in heaven along,
>   O praise him, alleluia!
> Thou rising morn, in praise rejoice,
> Ye lights of evening, find a voice:

Refrain

Melody: Vigiles et Sancti   Music: *Cologne Gesangbuch*, 1623
88.44.88.44.44.444   Text: St. Francis of Assisi, 1182–1226
                   Translator: William H. Draper, 1855–1933, alt.

Or:

> We plough the fields and scatter
> The good seed on the land,
> But it is fed and watered
> By God's almighty hand;
> He sends the snow in winter,

The warmth to swell the grain,
The breezes and the sunshine,
And soft refreshing rain:

Refrain:
All good gifts around us
Are sent from heav'n above.
Then thank the Lord,
O thank the Lord for all his love.

He only is the maker
Of all things near and far;
He paints the wayside flower,
He lights the ev'ning star.
The winds and waves obey him,
By him the birds are fed:
Much more to us his children,
He gives our daily bread:

Refrain

We thank you then, dear Father,
For all things bright and good:
The seedtime and the harvest,
Our life, our health, our food.
And all that we can offer
Your boundless love imparts,
The gifts to you most pleasing
Are humble, thankful hearts:

Refrain

Melody: Wir Pflugen 76.76.D
with Refrain

Music: Johann A.P. Schultz,
1747–1800

Text: *Wir pflügen und wir streuen*,
M. Claudius, 1740–1815

Translator: Jane N. Campbell

PSALMODY

Antiphon 1

December 17-23:   The Lord, the mighty God, will
come forth from Zion to set his
people free.

Psalm 108

Praise of God and a plea for help

Since the Son of God has been exalted above the heavens, his glory is proclaimed through all the earth (Arnobius).

My heart is ready, O God;
I will sing, sing your praise.
Awake, my soul;
awake, lyre and harp.
I will awake the dawn.

I will thank you, Lord, among the peoples,
among the nations I will praise you,
for your love reaches to the heavens
and your truth to the skies.
O God, arise above the heavens;
may your glory shine on earth!

O come and deliver your friends;
help with your right hand and reply.
From his holy place God has made this promise:
"I will triumph and divide the land of Shechem;
I will measure out the valley of Succoth.

Gilead is mine and Manasseh.
Ephraim I take for my helmet,
Judah for my commander's staff.
Moab I will use for my washbowl,
on Edom I will plant my shoe.
Over the Philistines I will shout in triumph."

But who will lead me to conquer the fortress?
Who will bring me face to face with Edom?
Will you utterly reject us, O God,
and no longer march with our armies?

Give us help against the foe:
for the help of man is vain.

With God we shall do bravely
and he will trample down our foes.

Psalm-prayer

Accept the prayers of your servants, Lord, and prepare
our hearts to praise your holy name. Come to our aid in
times of trouble and make us worthy to sing you songs of
thanksgiving.

December 17-23: The Lord, the mighty God, will
come forth from Zion to set his
people free.

Antiphon 2

December 17-23: I shall not cease to plead with God
for Zion until he sends his Holy One
in all his radiant beauty.

Canticle   Isaiah 61:10—62:5
The prophet's joy in the vision of a new Jerusalem

*I saw the holy city, new Jerusalem, with the beauty of a bride
adorned for her husband* (Revelation 21:2).

I rejoice heartily in the Lord,
in my God is the joy of my soul;
for he has clothed me with a robe of salvation,
and wrapped me in a mantle of justice,
like a bridegroom adorned with a diadem,
like a bride bedecked with her jewels.

As the earth brings forth its plants,
and a garden makes its growth spring up,
so will the Lord God make justice and praise
spring up before all the nations.

For Zion's sake I will not be silent,
for Jerusalem's sake I will not be quiet,

until her vindication shines forth like the dawn
and her victory like a burning torch.

Nations shall behold your vindication,
and all kings your glory;
you shall be called by a new name
pronounced by the mouth of the Lord.
You shall be a glorious crown in the hand of the
    Lord,
a royal diadem held by your God.

No more shall men call you "Forsaken,"
or your land "Desolate,"
but you shall be called "My Delight,"
and your land "Espoused."
For the Lord delights in you,
and makes your land his spouse.

As a young man married a virgin,
your Builder shall marry you;
and as a bridegroom rejoices in his bride
so shall your God rejoice in you.

December 17-23:   I shall not cease to plead with God
for Zion until he sends his Holy One
in all his radiant beauty.

Antiphon 3

December 17-23:   The Spirit of the Lord rests upon
me; he has sent me to preach his
joyful message to the poor.

Psalm 146

Those who trust in God know what it is to be happy

To praise God in our lives means all we do must be for his glory (Arnobius).

My soul, give praise to the Lord;
I will praise the Lord all my days,
make music to my God while I live.

Put no trust in princes,
in mortal men in whom there is no help.
Take their breath, they return to clay
and their plans that day come to nothing.

He is happy who is helped by Jacob's God,
whose hope is in the Lord his God,
who alone made heaven and earth,
the seas and all they contain.

It is he who keeps faith for ever,
who is just to those who are oppressed.
It is he who gives bread to the hungry,
the Lord, who sets prisoners free,

the Lord who gives sight to the blind,
who raises up those who are bowed down,
the Lord, who protects the stranger
and upholds the widow and orphan.

It is the Lord who loves the just
but thwarts the path of the wicked.
The Lord will reign for ever,
Zion's God, from age to age.

Psalm-prayer

God of glory and power, those who have put all their
trust in you are happy indeed. Shine the brightness of
your light on us, that we may love you always with a pure
heart.

December 17-23:   The Spirit of the Lord rests upon
                   me; he has sent me to preach his
                   joyful message to the poor.

Reading, responsory, antiphon for the canticle of Zechariah, intercessions and prayer, as in the Proper of Seasons.

Conclusion, as in the Ordinary.

Daytime Prayer

God, come to my assistance. Glory to the Father. As it was in the beginning. Alleluia.

HYMN, as in the Ordinary, 658.

PSALMODY

Antiphon, as in the Proper of Seasons.

Psalm 119:145-152

XIX (Koph)

I call with all my heart; Lord, hear me,
I will keep your commands.
I call upon you, save me
and I will do your will.

I rise before dawn and cry for help,
I hope in your word.
My eyes watch through the night
to ponder your promise.

In your love hear my voice, O Lord;
give me life by your decrees.
Those who harm me unjustly draw near:
they are far from your law.

But you, O Lord, are close:
your commands are truth.
Long have I known that your will
is established for ever.

Psalm-prayer

Save us by the power of your hand, Father, for our enemies have ignored your words. May the fire of your

word consume our sins and its brightness illumine our
hearts.

Psalm 94

The Lord will avenge the just

*God punishes wicked conduct; he has called you to share his
holiness. You must have nothing to do with impurity* (1
Thessalonians 4:6-7).

I

O Lord, avenging God,
avenging God, appear!
Judge of the earth, arise,
give the proud what they deserve!

How long, O Lord, shall the wicked,
how long shall the wicked triumph?
They bluster with arrogant speech;
the evil-doers boast to each other.

They crush your people, Lord,
they afflict the ones you have chosen.
They kill the widow and the stranger
and murder the fatherless child.

And they say: "The Lord does not see;
the God of Jacob pays no heed."
Mark this, most senseless of people;
fools, when will you understand?

Can he who made the ear, not hear?
Can he who formed the eye, not see?
Will he who trains nations, not punish?
Will he who teaches men, not have knowledge?

The Lord knows the thoughts of men.
He knows they are no more than a breath.

II

Happy the man whom you teach, O Lord,
whom you train by means of your law:
to him you give peace in evil days
while the pit is being dug for the wicked.

The Lord will not abandon his people
nor forsake those who are his own:
for judgment shall again be just
and all true hearts shall uphold it.

Who will stand up for me against the wicked?
Who will defend me against those who do evil?
If the Lord were not to help me,
I would soon go down into the silence.

When I think: "I have lost my foothold",
your mercy, Lord, holds me up.
When cares increase in my heart
your consolation calms my soul.

Can judges who do evil be your friends?
They do injustice under cover of law;
they attack the life of the just
and condemn innocent blood.

As for me, the Lord will be a stronghold;
my God will be the rock where I take refuge.
He will repay them for their wickedness,
destroy them for their evil deeds.
The Lord, our God, will destroy them.

Psalm-prayer

Lord Jesus, you taught your disciples not to fear the
world. Do not abandon your inheritance to sinners, nor
ignore the power of the enemy against the Church. Grant
us always to seek the wisdom of the cross and the blessing

of those who suffer for the sake of justice. May we always be filled with your happiness.

At the other hours, the complementary psalmody is used, 1191.

Reading, verse and prayer, as in the Proper of Seasons.

Conclusion, as in the Ordinary.

Evening Prayer

God, come to my assistance. Glory to the Father. As it was in the beginning. Alleluia.

HYMN

O worship the king, all glorious above;
O gratefully sing his power and his love;
Our shield and defender, the ancient of days,
Pavilioned in splendor, and girded with praise.

O tell of his might, O sing of his grace;
Whose robe is the light, whose canopy space;
His chariots of wrath the deep thunder clouds form,
And dark is his path on the wings of the storm.

This earth, with its store of wonders untold,
Almighty, thy power hath founded of old;
Hath 'stablished it fast by a changeless decree,
And round it has cast, like a mantle, the sea.

Thy bountiful care what tongue can recite?
It breathes in the air, it shines in the light;
It streams from the hills, it descends to the plain,
And sweetly distils in the dew and the rain.

Frail children of dust, and feeble as frail,
In thee do we trust, nor find thee to fail;
Thy mercies how tender, how firm to the end,
Our maker, defender, redeemer, and friend.

O measureless might, ineffable love,
While angels delight to hymn thee above,
Thy humbler creation, though feeble their lays,
With true adoration shall sing to thy praise.

Melody: Hanover 55.55.65.55   Music: William Croft, 1682–1727
                               Text: Robert Grant, 1779–1838

Or:

Refrain:

For to those who love God,
Who are called in his plan,
Everything works out for good.
And God himself chose them
To bear the likeness of his Son
That he might be the first of many, many brothers.

Who is able to condemn? Only Christ who died for
    us;
Christ who rose for us, Christ who prays for us.

Refrain

In the face of all this, what is there left to say?
For if God is for us, who can be against us?

Refrain

Who can separate us from the love of Christ?
Neither trouble, nor pain, nor persecution.

Refrain

What can separate us from the love of Christ?
Not the past, the present, nor the future.

Refrain

Melody: Romans VIII   Music: Enrico Garzilli, 1970
                       Text: Enrico Garzilli, 1970

Antiphon 1

December 17-23: The Lord, the mighty God, will
come forth from Zion to set his
people free.

Psalm 139:1-18, 23-24

God sees all that is

Who has known the mind of God, who has been his
counselor? (Romans 11:34).

I

O Lord, you search me and you know me,
you know my resting and my rising,
you discern my purpose from afar.
You mark when I walk or lie down,
all my ways lie open to you.

Before ever a word is on my tongue
you know it, O Lord, through and through.
Behind and before you besiege me,
your hand ever laid upon me.
Too wonderful for me, this knowledge,
too high, beyond my reach.

O where can I go from your spirit,
or where can I flee from your face?
If I climb the heavens, you are there.
If I lie in the grave, you are there.

If I take the wings of the dawn
and dwell at the sea's furthest end,
even there your hand would lead me,
your right hand would hold me fast.

If I say: "Let the darkness hide me
and the light around me be night,"
even darkness is not dark for you
and the night is as clear as the day.

December 17-23: The Lord, the mighty God, will
come forth from Zion to set his
people free.

Antiphon 2

December 17-23: I shall not cease to plead with God
for Zion until he sends his Holy One
in all his radiant beauty.

II

For it was you who created my being,
knit me together in my mother's womb.
I thank you for the wonder of my being,
for the wonders of all your creation.

Already you knew my soul,
my body held no secret from you
when I was being fashioned in secret
and molded in the depths of the earth.

Your eyes saw all my actions,
they were all of them written in your book,
every one of my days was decreed
before one of them came into being.

To me, how mysterious your thoughts,
the sum of them not to be numbered!
If I count them, they are more than the sand;
to finish, I must be eternal, like you.

O search me, God, and know my heart.
O test me and know my thoughts.
See that I follow not the wrong path
and lead me in the path of life eternal.

Psalm-prayer

You watch over heaven and earth, Lord Jesus. Your
death brought light to the dead; your resurrection gave
joy to the saints; your ascension made the angels rejoice.
Your power exceeds all power. Lead us to life eternal,
and watch over us with your love. May your friends be
filled with honor and join you in heaven.

December 17-23:   I shall not cease to plead with God
                   for Zion until he sends his Holy One
                   in all his radiant beauty.

                   Antiphon 3

December 17-23:   The Spirit of the Lord rests upon
                   me; he has sent me to preach his
                   joyful message to the poor.

                   Canticle   Colossians 1:12-20
Christ the first-born of all creation and the first-born
                  from the dead

    Let us give thanks to the Father
    for having made you worthy
    to share the lot of the saints
    in light.

    He rescued us
    from the power of darkness
    and brought us
    into the kingdom of his beloved Son.
    Through him we have redemption,
    the forgiveness of our sins.

    He is the image of the invisible God,
    the first-born of all creatures.
    In him everything in heaven and on earth was
        created,
    things visible and invisible.

All were created through him;
all were created for him.
He is before all else that is.
In him everything continues in being.

It is he who is head of the body, the church!
he who is the beginning,
the first-born of the dead,
so that primacy may be his in everything.

It pleased God to make absolute fullness reside in him
and, by means of him, to reconcile everything in his
     person,
both on earth and in the heavens,
making peace through the blood of his cross.

December 17-23:   The Spirit of the Lord rests upon
                  me; he has sent me to preach his
                  joyful message to the poor.

Reading, responsory, antiphon for the canticle of Mary,
intercessions and prayer, as in the Proper of Seasons.

Conclusion, as in the Ordinary.

THURSDAY, WEEK IV

Invitatory

Lord, open my lips.

Antiphon, as in the Ordinary, 647.

Invitatory psalm, 648.

Office of Readings

God, come to my assistance. Glory to the Father. As it was in the beginning. Alleluia.

This verse and response are omitted when the hour begins with the invitatory.

HYMN

O God, our help in ages past,
Our hope for years to come,
Our shelter from the stormy blast
And our eternal home;

Beneath the shadow of your throne
Your saints have dwelt secure;
Sufficient is your arm alone,
And our defense is sure.

Before the hills in order stood,
Or earth received her frame,
From everlasting you are God,
To endless years the same.

A thousand ages in your sight
Are like an evening gone,
Short as the watch that ends the night
Before the rising sun.

Time, like an ever-rolling stream,
Bears all its sons away;
They fly forgotten, as a dream
Dies at the opening day.

O God, our help in ages past,
Our hope for years to come,
Be now our guide while life shall last,
And our eternal home.

Melody: Saint Anne C.M.

Music: William Croft, 1708
Text: Isaac Watts, 1674–1748
altered by Rev. William Bauman

PSALMODY

Ant. 1   Their own strength could not save them; it was
your strength and the light of your face.

Psalm 44

The misfortunes of God's people

We triumph over all these things through him who loved us
(Romans 8:35).

I

We heard with our own ears, O God,
our fathers have told us the story
of the things you did in their days,
you yourself, in days long ago.

To plant them you uprooted the nations:
to let them spread you laid peoples low.
No sword of their own won the land;
no arm of their own brought them victory.
It was your right hand, your arm
and the light of your face: for you loved them.

It is you, my king, my God,
who granted victories to Jacob.
Through you we beat down our foes;
in your name we trampled our aggressors.

For it was not in my bow that I trusted
nor yet was I saved by my sword:
it was you who saved us from our foes,
it was you who put our foes to shame.
All day long our boast was in God
and we praised your name without ceasing.

Ant.   Their own strength could not save them; it was
        your strength and the light of your face.

Ant. 2 Turn back to the Lord; he will not hide his
        face.

II

Yet now you have rejected us, disgraced us:
you no longer go forth with our armies.
You make us retreat from the foe
and our enemies plunder us at will.

You make us like sheep for the slaughter
and scatter us among the nations.
You sell your own people for nothing
and make no profit by the sale.

You make us the taunt of our neighbors,
the laughing stock of all who are near.
Among the nations, you make us a byword,
among the peoples a thing of derision.

All day long my disgrace is before me;
my face is covered with shame
at the voice of the taunter, the scoffer,
at the sight of the foe and avenger.

Ant.   Turn back to the Lord; he will not hide his face.

Ant. 3   Arise, Lord, do not abandon us for ever.

III

This befell us though we had not forgotten you;
though we had not been false to your covenant,
though we had not withdrawn our hearts;
though our feet had not strayed from your path.
Yet you have crushed us in a place of sorrows
and covered us with the shadow of death.

Had we forgotten the name of our God
or stretched out our hands to another god
would not God have found this out,
he who knows the secrets of the heart?
It is for you we face death all day long
and are counted as sheep for the slaughter.

Awake, O Lord, why do you sleep?
Arise, do not reject us for ever!
Why do you hide your face
and forget our oppression and misery?

For we are brought down low to the dust;
our body lies prostrate on the earth.
Stand up and come to our help!
Redeem us because of your love!

Psalm-prayer

Lord Jesus, you foretold that we would share in the
persecutions that brought you to a violent death. The
Church formed at the cost of your precious blood is even
now conformed to your Passion; may it be transformed,
now and eternally, by the power of your resurrection.

Ant.   Arise, Lord, do not abandon us for ever.

Reading, verse and prayer, as in the Proper of Seasons.

Morning Prayer

God, come to my assistance. Glory to the Father. As it was in the beginning. Alleluia.

This verse and response are omitted when the hour begins with the invitatory.

HYMN

> O God of light, the dawning day
> Gives us new promise of your love.
> Each fresh beginning is your gift,
> Like gentle dew from heav'n above.
>
> Your blessings, Father, never fail:
> Your Son, who is our daily Bread,
> The Holy Spirit of your love,
> By whom each day your sons are led.
>
> Make us the servants of your peace,
> Renew our strength, remove all fear;
> Be with us, Lord, throughout this day,
> For all is joy if you are near.
>
> To Father, Son and Spirit blest,
> One only God, we humbly pray:
> Show us the splendor of your light
> In death, the dawn of perfect day.

Melody: Danby L.M.   Music: English Traditional Melody
                           Text: James Quinn, S.J.

PSALMODY

Antiphon 1

December 17-23: To you, O Lord, I lift up my soul;
                 come and rescue me, for you are my
                 refuge and my strength.

Psalm 143:1-11

Prayer in distress

A man is not justified by observance of the law but only
through faith in Jesus Christ (Galatians 2:16).

Lord, listen to my prayer;
turn your ear to my appeal.
You are faithful, you are just; give answer.
Do not call your servant to judgment
for no one is just in your sight.

The enemy pursues my soul;
he has crushed my life to the ground;
he has made me dwell in darkness
like the dead, long forgotten.
Therefore my spirit fails;
my heart is numb within me.

I remember the days that are past:
I ponder all your works.
I muse on what your hand has wrought
and to you I stretch out my hands.
Like a parched land my soul thirsts for you.

Lord, make haste and answer;
for my spirit fails within me.
Do not hide your face
lest I become like those in the grave.

In the morning let me know your love
for I put my trust in you.
Make me know the way I should walk:
to you I lift up my soul.

Rescue me, Lord, from my enemies;
I have fled to you for refuge.

Teach me to do your will
for you, O Lord, are my God.
Let your good spirit guide me
in ways that are level and smooth.

For your name's sake, Lord, save my life;
in your justice save my soul from distress.

Psalm-prayer

Lord Jesus, early in the morning of your resurrection,
you made your love known and brought the first light of
dawn to those who dwell in darkness. Your death has
opened a path for us. Do not enter into judgment with
your servants; let your good Spirit guide us together into
the land of justice.

December 17-23:   To you, O Lord, I lift up my soul;
                   come and rescue me, for you are my
                   refuge and my strength.

               Antiphon 2

December 17-23:   Bless those, O Lord, who have
                   waited for your coming; let your
                   prophets be proved true.

               Canticle   Isaiah 66:10-14a
               Joys of heaven

The heavenly Jerusalem is a free woman and our mother
(Galatians 4:26).

Rejoice with Jerusalem and be glad because of her,
all you who love her;
exult, exult with her,
all you who were mourning over her!

Oh, that you may suck fully
of the milk of her comfort,
that you may nurse with delight
at her abundant breasts!

For thus says the Lord:
Lo, I will spread prosperity over her like a river,
and the wealth of the nations like an overflowing
  torrent.
As nurslings, you shall be carried in her arms,
and fondled in her lap;

As a mother comforts her son,
so will I comfort you;
in Jerusalem you shall find your comfort.
When you see this, your heart shall rejoice,
and your bodies flourish like the grass.

December 17-23:   Bless those, O Lord, who have
waited for your coming; let your
prophets be proved true.

Antiphon 3

December 17-23:   Turn to us, O Lord, make haste to
help your people.

Psalm 147:1-11
The loving kindness of God who can do all he wills

*You are God: we praise you; you are the Lord: we acclaim
you.*

Praise the Lord for he is good;
sing to our God for he is loving:
to him our praise is due.

The Lord builds up Jerusalem
and brings back Israel's exiles,
he heals the broken-hearted,
he binds up all their wounds.
He fixes the number of the stars;
he calls each one by its name.

Our Lord is great and almighty;
his wisdom can never be measured.
The Lord raises the lowly;
he humbles the wicked to the dust.
O sing to the Lord, giving thanks;
sing psalms to our God with the harp.

He covers the heavens with clouds;
he prepares the rain for the earth,
making mountains sprout with grass
and with plants to serve man's needs.
He provides the beasts with their food
and young ravens that call upon him.

His delight is not in horses
nor his pleasure in warriors' strength.
The Lord delights in those who revere him,
in those who wait for his love.

Psalm-prayer

God our Father, great builder of the heavenly
Jerusalem, you know the number of the stars and call
each of them by name. Heal hearts that are broken,
gather together those who have been scattered, and
enrich us all from the plenitude of your eternal wisdom.

December 17-23:   Turn to us, O Lord, make haste to
                              help your people.

Reading, responsory, antiphon for the canticle of Zechariah, intercessions and prayer, as in the Proper of Seasons.

Conclusion, as in the Ordinary.

Daytime Prayer

God, come to my assistance. Glory to the Father. As it was in the beginning. Alleluia.

HYMN, as in the Ordinary, 658.

PSALMODY

Antiphon, as in the Proper of Seasons.

Psalm 119:153-160

XX (Resh)

See my affliction and save me
for I remember your law.
Uphold my cause and defend me;
by your promise give me life.

Salvation is far from the wicked
who are heedless of your commands.
Numberless, Lord, are your mercies;
with your decrees give me life.

Though my foes and oppressors are countless
I have not swerved from your will.
I look at the faithless with disgust;
they ignore your promise.

See how I love your precepts;
in your mercy give me life.
Your word is founded on truth:
your decrees are eternal.

Psalm-prayer

Help us always to rejoice in your promise, Father, and to praise the glory of your deeds. Keep us united in the love of your peace; then we shall have little to fear from the threats of the mighty.

Psalm 128

Happiness of family life rooted in God

"May the Lord bless you from Zion" refers to the Church (Arnobius).

O blessed are those who fear the Lord
and walk in his ways!

By the labor of your hands you shall eat.
You will be happy and prosper;
your wife like a fruitful vine
in the heart of your house;
your children like shoots of the olive,
around your table.

Indeed thus shall be blessed
the man who fears the Lord.
May the Lord bless you from Zion
all the days of your life!
May you see your children's children
in a happy Jerusalem!

On Israel, peace!

Psalm-prayer

Give lasting happiness, Lord, to those who reverence your name, so that our life and work may be such as to deserve your commendation and bring us, laden with good fruit, to our everlasting home.

Psalm 129

God's people reaffirm their trust in time of affliction

The voice of the Church lamenting its suffering is heard in this psalm (Saint Augustine).

"They have pressed me hard from my youth,"
this is Israel's song.
"They have pressed me hard from my youth
but could never destroy me.

They ploughed my back like ploughmen,
drawing long furrows.
But the Lord, who is just, has destroyed
the yoke of the wicked."

Let them be shamed and routed,
those who hate Zion!
Let them be like grass on the roof
that withers before it flowers.

With that no reaper fills his arms,
no binder makes his sheaves
and those passing by will not say:
"On you the Lord's blessing!"

"We bless you in the name of the Lord."

Psalm-prayer

Lord Jesus, living in glory as the Son of Man, remember that when our sins had ploughed long furrows on your back, your death broke the bonds of sin and Satan for ever. Bless your Church, wounded in its members, and strengthen it by your invincible power and grace.

At the other hours, the complementary psalmody from series I and II is used, **1191**.

Reading, verse and prayer, as in the Proper of Seasons.

Conclusion, as in the Ordinary.

Evening Prayer

God, come to my assistance. Glory to the Father. As it was in the beginning. Alleluia.

HYMN

Let all things now living a song of thanksgiving
To God our Creator triumphantly raise;
Who fashioned and made us, protected and stayed
    us,
Who guideth us on to the end of our days.
His banners are o'er us, his light goes before us,
A pillar of fire shining forth in the night:
Till shadows have vanished and darkness is
    banished,
As forward we travel from light into Light.

His law he enforces, the stars in their courses,
The sun in his orbit obediently shine,
The hills and the mountains, the rivers and
    fountains,
The depths of the ocean proclaim him divine.
We, too, should be voicing our love and rejoicing.
With glad adoration, a song let us raise:
Till all things now living unite in thanksgiving,
To God in the highest, Hosanna and praise.

Melody: The Ash Grove   Music: Welsh Melody
                                        Text: Anon.

Antiphon 1

December 17-23: **To you, O Lord, I lift up my soul;
come and rescue me, for you are my
refuge and my strength.**

Psalm 144

Prayer for victory and peace

*Christ learned the art of warfare when he overcame the
world, as he said: "I have overcome the world"* (Saint
Hilary).   I

Blessed be the Lord, my rock
who trains my arms for battle,
who prepares my hands for war.

He is my love, my fortress;
he is my stronghold, my savior,
my shield, my place of refuge.
He brings peoples under my rule.

Lord, what is man that you care for him,
mortal man, that you keep him in mind;
man, who is merely a breath
whose life fades like a shadow?

Lower your heavens and come down;
touch the mountains; wreathe them in smoke.
Flash your lightnings; rout the foe,
shoot your arrows and put them to flight.

Reach down from heaven and save me;
draw me out from the mighty waters,
from the hands of alien foes
whose mouths are filled with lies,
whose hands are raised in perjury.

December 17-23: To you, O Lord, I lift up my soul;
come and rescue me, for you are my
refuge and my strength.

Antiphon 2

December 17-23: Bless those, O Lord, who have
waited for your coming; let your
prophets be proved true.

II

To you, O God, will I sing a new song;
I will play on the ten-stringed harp
to you who give kings their victory,
who set David your servant free.

You set him free from the evil sword;
you rescued him from alien foes
whose mouths were filled with lies,
whose hands were raised in perjury.

Let our sons then flourish like saplings
grown tall and strong from their youth:
our daughters graceful as columns,
adorned as though for a palace.

Let our barns be filled to overflowing
with crops of every kind;
our sheep increasing by thousands,
myriads of sheep in our fields,
our cattle heavy with young,

no ruined wall, no exile,
no sound of weeping in our streets.
Happy the people with such blessings;
happy the people whose God is the Lord.

Psalm - prayer

Lord, God of strength, you gave your Son victory over death. Direct your Church's fight against evil in the world. Clothe us with the weapons of light and unite us under the one banner of love that we may receive our eternal reward after the battle of earthly life.

December 17-23:   Bless those, O Lord, who have waited for your coming; let your prophets be proved true.

Antiphon 3

December 17-23:   Turn to us, O Lord, make haste to help your people.

Canticle   Revelation 11:17-18; 12:10b-12a

The judgment of God

We praise you, the Lord God Almighty,
who is and who was.
You have assumed your great power,
you have begun your reign.

The nations have raged in anger,
but then came your day of wrath
and the moment to judge the dead:
The time to reward your servants the prophets
and the holy ones who revere you,
the great and the small alike.

Now have salvation and power come,
the reign of our God and the authority
of his Anointed One.
For the accuser of our brothers is cast out,
who night and day accused them before God.

They defeated him by the blood of the Lamb
and by the word of their testimony;
love for life did not deter them from death.
So rejoice, you heavens,
and you that dwell therein!

December 17-23: **Turn to us, O Lord, make haste to help your people.**

Reading, responsory, antiphon for the canticle of Mary, intercessions and prayer, as in the Proper of Seasons.

Conclusion, as in the Ordinary.

FRIDAY, WEEK IV

Invitatory

Lord, open my lips.

Antiphon, as in the Ordinary, 647.

Invitatory psalm, 648.

Office of Readings

God, come to my assistance. Glory to the Father. As it was in the beginning. Alleluia.

This verse and response are omitted when the hour begins with the invitatory.

HYMN

> Sing praise to our Creator,
> O sons of Adam's race;
> God's children by adoption,
> Baptized into his grace.

Refrain:

> Praise the holy Trinity,
> Undivided Unity;
> Holy God, Mighty God,
> God Immortal, be adored.

> To Jesus Christ give glory,
> God's coeternal Son;
> As members of his Body
> We live in him as one.

Refrain

> Now praise the Holy Spirit
> Poured forth upon the earth;

Who sanctifies and guides us,
Confirmed in our rebirth.

Refrain

Melody: Mainz 76.76 with Refrain   Music: Mainz Melody
Text: Omer Westendorf, 1961

PSALMODY

Ant. 1   Our fathers have told us of the Lord's power;
they have recounted for us his marvelous deeds.

Psalm 78:1-39

Salvation history reveals the goodness
of God and the faithlessness of his people

These events are recalled as a warning to us (1 Corinthians
10:6).

I

Give heed, my people, to my teaching;
turn your ear to the words of my mouth.
I will open my mouth in a parable
and reveal hidden lessons of the past.

The things we have heard and understood,
the things our fathers have told us,
these we will not hide from their children
but will tell them to the next generation:

the glories of the Lord and his might
and the marvellous deeds he has done,
the witness he gave to Jacob,
the law he established in Israel.

He gave a command to our fathers
to make it known to their children
that the next generation might know it,
the children yet to be born.

They too should arise and tell their sons
that they too should set their hope in God

and never forget God's deeds
but keep every one of his commands:

so that they might not be like their fathers,
a defiant and rebellious race,
a race whose heart was fickle,
whose spirit was unfaithful to God.

The sons of Ephraim, armed with the bow,
turned back in the day of battle.
They failed to keep God's covenant
and would not walk according to his law.

They forgot the things he had done,
the marvellous deeds he had shown them.
He did wonders in the sight of their fathers,
in Egypt, in the plains of Zoan.

He divided the sea and led them through
and made the waters stand up like a wall.
By day he led them with a cloud:
by night, with a light of fire.

He split the rocks in the desert.
He gave them plentiful drink as from the deep.
He made streams flow out from the rock
and made waters run down like rivers.

Ant.   Our fathers have told us of the Lord's power; they
        have recounted for us his marvelous deeds.

Ant. 2 The children of Israel ate the manna and drank
        from the spiritual rock which followed after
        them.

II

Yet still they sinned against him;
they defied the Most High in the desert.
In their heart they put God to the test
by demanding the food they craved.

They even spoke against God.
They said: "Is it possible for God
to prepare a table in the desert?

It was he who struck the rock,
water flowed and swept down in torrents.
But can he also give us bread?
Can he provide meat for his people?"

When he heard this the Lord was angry.
A fire was kindled against Jacob,
his anger rose against Israel
for having no faith in God;
for refusing to trust in his help.

Yet he commanded the clouds above
and opened the gates of heaven.
He rained down manna for their food,
and gave them bread from heaven.

Mere men ate the bread of angels.
He sent them abundance of food:
he made the east wind blow from heaven
and roused the south wind by his might.

He rained food on them like dust,
winged fowl like the sands of the sea.
He let it fall in the midst of their camp
and all around their tents.

So they ate and had their fill;
for he gave them all they craved.
But before they had sated their craving,
while the food was still in their mouths,

God's anger rose against them.
He slew the strongest among them,
struck down the flower of Israel.

Ant. The children of Israel ate the manna and drank
from the spiritual rock which followed after them.

Ant. 3　They remembered that God was their helper
　　　　and redeemer.

III

Despite this they went on sinning;
they had no faith in his wonders:
so he ended their days like a breath
and their years in sudden ruin.

When he slew them then they would seek him,
return and seek him in earnest.
They would remember that God was their rock,
God the Most High their redeemer.

But the words they spoke were mere flattery;
they lied to him with their lips.
For their hearts were not truly with him;
they were not faithful to his covenant.

Yet he who is full of compassion
forgave their sin and spared them.
So often he held back his anger
when he might have stirred up his rage.

He remembered they were only men,
a breath that passes never to return.

Psalm-prayer

Lord Jesus Christ, Shepherd of your Church, in order
to strengthen our faith and to lead us to the kingdom,
you renewed and far surpassed the marvels of the old
law. Through the uncertainties of this earthly journey,
lead us home to the everlasting pastures.

Ant.　They remembered that God was their helper and
　　　redeemer.

Verse, reading and prayer, as in the Proper of Seasons.

Morning Prayer

God, come to my assistance. Glory to the Father. As it
was in the beginning. Alleluia.

This verse and response are omitted when the hour begins with
the invitatory.

HYMN

> We turn to you, O God of every nation,
> Giver of life and origin of good;
> Your love is at the heart of all creation,
> Your hurt is people's broken brotherhood.

> We turn to you that we may be forgiven
> For crucifying Christ on earth again;
> We know that we have never wholly striven,
> Forgetting self, to love the other man.

> Free every heart from pride and self-reliance,
> Our ways of thought inspire with simple grace;
> Break down among us barriers of defiance,
> Speak to the soul of all the human race.

> Teach us, good Lord, to serve the need of others,
> Help us to give and not to count the cost.
> Unite us all for we are born as brothers;
> Defeat our Babel with your Pentecost.

Melody: Intercessor 11.10.11.10　　Music: C.H.H. Parry, 1848-1918
Text: Fred Kaan, 1929-

PSALMODY

Antiphon 1

December 17-23:　　Our King will come from Zion; the
Lord, God-is-with-us, is his mighty
name.

Psalm 51

O God, have mercy on me

Your inmost being must be renewed, and you must put on the new man (Ephesians 4:23-24).

Have mercy on me, God, in your kindness.
In your compassion blot out my offense.
O wash me more and more from my guilt
and cleanse me from my sin.

My offenses truly I know them;
my sin is always before me.
Against you, you alone, have I sinned;
what is evil in your sight I have done.

That you may be justified when you give sentence
and be without reproach when you judge,
O see, in guilt I was born,
a sinner was I conceived.

Indeed you love truth in the heart;
then in the secret of my heart teach me wisdom.
O purify me, then I shall be clean;
O wash me, I shall be whiter than snow.

Make me hear rejoicing and gladness,
that the bones you have crushed may revive.
From my sins turn away your face
and blot out all my guilt.

A pure heart create for me, O God,
put a steadfast spirit within me.
Do not cast me away from your presence,
nor deprive me of your holy spirit.

Give me again the joy of your help;
with a spirit of fervor sustain me,

that I may teach transgressors your ways
and sinners may return to you.

O rescue me, God, my helper,
and my tongue shall ring out your goodness.
O Lord, open my lips
and my mouth shall declare your praise.

For in sacrifice you take no delight,
burnt offering from me you would refuse,
my sacrifice, a contrite spirit.
A humbled, contrite heart you will not spurn.

In your goodness, show favor to Zion:
rebuild the walls of Jerusalem.
Then you will be pleased with lawful sacrifice,
holocausts offered on your altar.

Psalm-prayer

Father, he who knew no sin was made sin for us, to
save us and restore us to your friendship. Look upon our
contrite heart and afflicted spirit and heal our troubled
conscience, so that in the joy and strength of the Holy
Spirit we may proclaim your praise and glory before all
the nations.

December 17-23: Our King will come from Zion; the
Lord, God-is-with-us, is his mighty
name.

Antiphon 2

December 17-23: Wait for the Lord and he will come
to you with his saving power.

Canticle   Tobit 13: 8-11, 13-15

Thanksgiving for the people's deliverance

He showed me the holy city Jerusalem which shone with the
glory of God (Revelation 21:10-11).

Let all men speak of his majesty
and sing his praises in Jerusalem.

O Jerusalem, holy city,
he scourged you for the works of your hands,
but will again pity the children of the righteous.

Praise the Lord for his goodness,
and bless the King of the ages,
so that his tent may be rebuilt in you with joy.

May he gladden within you all who were captives;
all who were ravaged may he cherish within you
for all generations to come.

A bright light will shine to all parts of the earth;
many nations shall come to you from afar,
and the inhabitants of all the limits of the earth,
drawn to you by the name of the Lord God,
bearing in their hands their gifts for the King of
    heaven.

Every generation shall give joyful praise in you,
and shall call you the chosen one,
through all ages forever.

Go, then, rejoice over the children of the righteous,
who shall all be gathered together
and shall bless the Lord of the ages.

Happy are those who love you,
and happy those who rejoice in your prosperity.

Happy are all the men who shall grieve over you,
over all your chastisements,

for they shall rejoice in you
as they behold all your joy forever.

My spirit blesses the Lord, the great King.

December 17-23:   Wait for the Lord and he will come
to you with his saving power.

Antiphon 3

December 17-23:   Eagerly I watch for the Lord; I wait
in joyful hope for the coming of God
my Savior.

Psalm 147:12-20
The restoration of Jerusalem

Come, I will show you the bride of the Lamb (Revelation
21:9).

O praise the Lord, Jerusalem!
Zion, praise your God!

He has strengthened the bars of your gates,
he has blessed the children within you.
He established peace on your borders,
he feeds you with finest wheat.

He sends out his word to the earth
and swiftly runs his command.
He showers down snow white as wool,
he scatters hoar-frost like ashes.

He hurls down hailstones like crumbs.
The waters are frozen at his touch;
he sends forth his word and it melts them:
at the breath of his mouth the waters flow.

He makes his word known to Jacob,
to Israel his laws and decrees.
He has not dealt thus with other nations;
he has not taught them his decrees.

Psalm-prayer

All-powerful God, it is through your Church, generously endowed with gifts of grace and fortified by the Holy Spirit, that you send out your word to all nations. Strengthen your Church with the best of all food and make it dauntless in faith. Multiply its children to celebrate with one accord the mysteries of your love at the altar on high.

December 17-23:   Eagerly I watch for the Lord; I wait in joyful hope for the coming of God my Savior.

Reading, responsory, antiphon for the canticle of Zechariah, intercessions and prayer, as in the Proper of Seasons.

Conclusion, as in the Ordinary.

Daytime Prayer

God, come to my assistance. Glory to the Father. As it was in the beginning. Alleluia.

HYMN, as in the Ordinary, 658.

PSALMODY

Antiphon, as in the Proper of Seasons.

Psalm 119:161-168

XXI (Shin)

Though princes oppress me without cause
I stand in awe of your word.
I take delight in your promise
like one who finds a treasure.

Lies I hate and detest
but your law is my love.
Seven times a day I praise you
for your just decrees.

The lovers of your law have great peace;
they never stumble.
I await your saving help, O Lord,
I fulfill your commands.

My soul obeys your will
and loves it dearly.
I obey your precepts and your will;
all that I do is before you.

Psalm-prayer

There is great peace, Lord, for those who love your
law; they never stumble. Grant that those who love you
above all else may be undisturbed by thoughts of evil.

Psalm 133

Joy when hearts are united in love

Let us love one another, for love is of God (1 John 4:7).

How good and how pleasant it is,
when brothers live in unity!

It is like precious oil upon the head
running down upon the beard,
running down upon Aaron's beard,
upon the collar of his robes.

It is like the dew of Hermon which falls
on the heights of Zion.
For there the Lord gives his blessing,
life for ever.

Psalm-prayer

Pour out over your Church, Lord, the spirit of
brotherly love and a longing for your peace. May this
precious oil of the Holy Spirit flow over us to fill us with
your gracious benediction.

Psalm 140:1-9, 13-14

Lord, you are my refuge

The Son of Man will be handed over to wicked men
(Matthew 26:45).

Rescue me, Lord, from evil men;
from the violent keep me safe,
from those who plan evil in their hearts
and stir up strife every day;
who sharpen their tongue like an adder's,
with the poison of viper on their lips.

Lord, guard me from the hands of the wicked;
from the violent keep me safe;
they plan to make me stumble.
The proud have hidden a trap,
have spread out lines in a net,
set snares across my path.

I have said to the Lord: "You are my God."
Lord, hear the cry of my appeal!
Lord my God, my mighty help,
you shield my head in the battle.
Do not grant the wicked their desire
nor let their plots succeed.

I know that the Lord will avenge the poor,
that he will do justice for the needy.
Yes, the just will praise your name:
the upright shall live in your presence.

Psalm-prayer

Lord, you keep constant guard over your faithful
people. Protect us from hidden snares and make us holy,
that we may praise and bless your name and live in
righteousness before you.

At the other hours, the complementary psalmody is used, 1191.

Reading, verse and prayer, as in the Proper of Seasons.

Conclusion, as in the Ordinary.

Evening Prayer

God, come to my assistance. Glory to the Father. As it was in the beginning. Alleluia.

HYMN

> Father, we thank thee who hast planted
> Thy holy Name within our hearts.
> Knowledge and faith and life immortal
> Jesus, thy Son, to us imparts.
> Thou, Lord, didst make all for thy pleasure,
> Didst give man food for all his days,
> Giving in Christ the Bread eternal;
> Thine is the power, be thine the praise.
>
> Watch o'er thy Church, O Lord, in mercy,
> Save it from evil, guard it still;
> Perfect it in thy love, unite it,
> Cleansed and conformed unto thy will.
> As grain, once scattered on the hill sides,
> Was in this broken bread made one,
> So from all lands thy Church be gathered
> Into thy kingdom by thy Son.

Melody: Rendez à Dieu 98.98.D   Music: Louis Bourgeois, 1543
                                          Text: *Didache*, ca. 110
                             Translator: F. Bland Tucker, 1941

PSALMODY

Antiphon 1

December 17-23:   Our King will come from Zion; the
                  Lord, God-is-with-us, is his mighty
                  name.

Psalm 145

Praise of God's majesty

Lord, you are the Just One, who was and who is (Revelation 16:5).

I

I will give you glory, O God my King,
I will bless your name for ever.

I will bless you day after day
and praise your name for ever.
The Lord is great, highly to be praised,
his greatness cannot be measured.

Age to age shall proclaim your works,
shall declare your mighty deeds,
shall speak of your splendor and glory,
tell the tale of your wonderful works.

They will speak of your terrible deeds,
recount your greatness and might.
They will recall your abundant goodness;
age to age shall ring out your justice.

The Lord is kind and full of compassion,
slow to anger, abounding in love.
How good is the Lord to all,
compassionate to all his creatures.

All your creatures shall thank you, O Lord,
and your friends shall repeat their blessing.
They shall speak of the glory of your reign
and declare your might, O God,

to make known to men your mighty deeds
and the glorious splendor of your reign.
Yours is an everlasting kingdom;
your rule lasts from age to age.

December 17-23:   **Our King will come from Zion; the Lord, God-is-with-us, is his mighty name.**

Antiphon 2

December 17-23:   **Wait for the Lord and he will come to you with his saving power.**

II

The Lord is faithful in all his words
and loving in all his deeds.
The Lord supports all who fall
and raises all who are bowed down.

The eyes of all creatures look to you
and you give them their food in due time.
You open wide your hand,
grant the desires of all who live.

The Lord is just in all his ways
and loving in all his deeds.
He is close to all who call him,
who call on him from their hearts.

He grants the desires of those who fear him,
he hears their cry and he saves them.
The Lord protects all who love him;
but the wicked he will utterly destroy.

Let me speak the praise of the Lord,
let all mankind bless his holy name
for ever, for ages unending.

Psalm-prayer

Lord, be near to all who call upon you in truth and increase the dedication of those who revere you. Hear their prayers and save them, that they may always love you and praise your holy name.

Young and old, thy praise expressing,
In glad homage bend the knee,
All the saints in heaven adore thee,
We would bow before thy throne;
As thine angels serve before thee,
So on earth thy will be done.

Melody: Austria 87.87.D   Music: Franz Joseph Haydn, 1797
                                 Text: Stanzas 1 and 2, Foundling
          Hospital Collection, c. 1801; St. 3, Edward Osler, 1836

PSALMODY

Ant. 1   The Lord delivered his people from the
         oppressor.

Psalm 78:40-72

Salvation history reveals the goodness
of God and the faithlessness of his people

These events are recalled as a warning to us (1 Corinthians
10:6).

IV

How often they defied him in the wilderness
and caused him pain in the desert!

Yet again they put God to the test
and grieved the Holy One of Israel.
They did not remember his deeds
nor the day he saved them from the foe;

when he worked his miracles in Egypt,
his wonders in the plains of Zoan:
when he turned their rivers into blood,
made their streams impossible to drink.

He sent dog-flies against them to devour them
and swarms of frogs to molest them.
He gave their crops to the grub,
the fruit of their labor to the locust.

He destroyed their vines with hail,
their sycamore trees with frost.
He gave up their cattle to plague,
their flocks and herds to pestilence.

He turned on them the heat of his anger,
fury, rage and havoc,
a troop of destroying angels.
He gave free course to his anger.

He did not spare them from death
but gave their lives to the plague.
He struck all the first-born in Egypt,
the finest flower in the dwellings of Ham.

Ant.   The Lord delivered his people from the oppressor.

Ant. 2   The Lord led his people to his holy mountain.

V

Then he brought forth his people like sheep;
he guided his flock in the desert.
He led them safely with nothing to fear,
while the sea engulfed their foes.

So he brought them to his holy land,
to the mountain which his right hand had won.
He drove out the nations before them,
and divided the land for their heritage.

Their tents he gave as a dwelling
to each one of Israel's tribes.
Still they put God to the proof and defied him;
they refused to obey the Most High.

They strayed, as faithless as their fathers,
like a bow on which the archer cannot count.
With their mountain shrines they angered him;
made him jealous with the idols they served.

God saw and was filled with fury:
he utterly rejected Israel.
He forsook his dwelling place in Shiloh,
the tent where he lived among men.

He gave his ark into captivity,
his glorious ark into the hands of the foe.
He gave up his people to the sword,
in his anger against his chosen ones.

So war devoured their young men,
their maidens had no wedding songs;
their priests fell by the sword
and their widows made no lament.

Ant. The Lord led his people to his holy mountain.

Ant. 3 The Lord chose the tribe of Judah and David,
his servant, to shepherd Israel, his chosen
people.

VI

Then the Lord awoke as if from sleep,
like a warrior overcome with wine.
He struck his foes from behind
and put them to everlasting shame.

He rejected the tent of Joseph;
he did not choose the tribe of Ephraim
but he chose the tribe of Judah,
the hill of Zion which he loves.

He built his shrine like the heavens,
or like the earth which he made firm for ever.
And he chose David his servant
and took him away from the sheepfolds.

From the care of the ewes he called him
to be shepherd of Jacob his people,
of Israel his own possession.

He tended them with blameless heart,
with discerning mind he led them.

Psalm-prayer

For your people, Lord Jesus, you bring water from
the rock and rain bread from heaven; you forgive sins
with limitless generosity. Do not let us be marked by un-
faithfulness, as in days of old, but grant that the covenant
you sealed with your blood may merit us a place with
you in your kingdom.

Ant.   The Lord chose the tribe of Judah and David,
his servant, to shepherd Israel, his chosen one.

Verse, reading and prayer, as in the Proper of Seasons.

Morning Prayer

God, come to my assistance. Glory to the Father. As it
was in the beginning. Alleluia.

This verse and response are omitted when the hour begins with
the invitatory.

HYMN

Christ is the world's Light, he and none other;
Born in our darkness, he became our brother.
If we have seen him, we have seen the Father:
    Glory to God on high.

Christ is the world's Peace, he and none other;
No man can serve him and despise his brother.
Who else unites us, one in God the Father?
    Glory to God on high.

Christ is the world's Life, he and none other;
Sold, once for silver, murdered here, our brother.
He, who redeems us, reigns with God the Father:
    Glory to God on high.

Give God the glory, God and none other;
Give God the glory, Spirit, Son, and Father;
Give God the glory, God in man my brother;
    Glory to God on high.

Melody: Christe Sanctorum   Music: Paris *Antiphoner*, 1681
11.11.11.5   Text: F. Pratt Green, 1903–

PSALMODY

Antiphon 1

December 24: Bethlehem in Judah's land, how glori-
              ous your future! The king who will rule
              my people comes from you.

Psalm 92

Praise of God the creator

Sing in praise of Christ's redeeming work (Saint Athanasius).

It is good to give thanks to the Lord,
  to make music to your name, O Most High,
to proclaim your love in the morning
  and your truth in the watches of the night,
on the ten-stringed lyre and the lute,
  with the murmuring sound of the harp.

Your deeds, O Lord, have made me glad;
  for the work of your hands I shout with joy.
O Lord, how great are your works!
How deep are your designs!
The foolish man cannot know this
  and the fool cannot understand.

Though the wicked spring up like grass
  and all who do evil thrive:
they are doomed to be eternally destroyed.
But you, Lord, are eternally on high.
See how your enemies perish;
  all doers of evil are scattered.

To me you give the wild-ox's strength;
you anoint me with the purest oil.
My eyes looked in triumph on my foes;
my ears heard gladly of their fall.
The just will flourish like the palm-tree
and grow like a Lebanon cedar.

Planted in the house of the Lord
they will flourish in the courts of our God,
still bearing fruit when they are old,
still full of sap, still green,
to proclaim that the Lord is just.
In him, my rock, there is no wrong.

Psalm-prayer

Take our shame away from us, Lord, and make us
rejoice in your saving works. May all who have been
chosen by your Son always abound in works of faith,
hope and love in your service.

December 24:   Bethlehem in Judah's land, how glorious your future! The king who will rule
my people comes from you.

Antiphon 2

December 24:   Lift up your heads and see; your
redemption is now at hand.

Canticle   Ezekiel 36:24-28

The Lord will renew his people

*They will be his own people, and God himself will be with
them, their own God (Revelation 21:3).*

I will take you away from among the nations,
gather you from all the foreign lands,
and bring you back to your own land.

I will sprinkle clean water upon you
to cleanse you from all your impurities,
and from all your idols I will cleanse you.

I will give you a new heart
and place a new spirit within you,
taking from your bodies your stony hearts
and giving you natural hearts.

I will put my spirit within you
and make you live by my statutes,
careful to observe my decrees.

You shall live in the land I gave your fathers;
you shall be my people,
and I will be your God.

December 24: Lift up your heads and see; your
redemption is now at hand.

Antiphon 3

December 24: The day has come at last when Mary
will bring forth her firstborn Son.

Psalm 8
The majesty of the Lord and man's dignity

The Father gave Christ lordship of creation and made him head of the Church (Ephesians 1:22).

How great is your name, O Lord our God,
through all the earth!

Your majesty is praised above the heavens;
on the lips of children and of babes
you have found praise to foil your enemy,
to silence the foe and the rebel.

When I see the heavens, the work of your hands,
the moon and the stars which you arranged,

what is man that you should keep him in mind,
mortal man that you care for him?

Yet you have made him little less than a god;
with glory and honor you crowned him,
gave him power over the works of your hand,
put all things under his feet.

All of them, sheep and cattle,
yes, even the savage beasts,
birds of the air, and fish
that make their way through the waters.

How great is your name, O Lord our God,
through all the earth!

Psalm-prayer

Almighty Lord, how wonderful is your name. You
have made every creature subject to you; make us worthy
to give you service.

December 24:　The day has come at last when Mary
　　　　　　　　will bring forth her firstborn Son.

Reading, responsory, antiphon for the canticle of Zechariah,
intercessions and prayer, as in the Proper of Seasons.

Conclusion, as in the Ordinary.

Daytime Prayer

God, come to my assistance. Glory to the Father. As it
was in the beginning. Alleluia.

Hymn, as in the Ordinary, 658.

Psalmody

Antiphon, as in the Proper of Seasons.

Psalm 119:169-176

XXII (Tau)

Lord, let my cry come before you:
teach me by your word.
Let my pleading come before you;
save me by your promise.

Let my lips proclaim your praise
because you teach me your commands.
Let my tongue sing your promise
for your commands are just.

Let your hand be ready to help me,
since I have chosen your precepts.
Lord, I long for your saving help
and your law is my delight.

Give life to my soul that I may praise you.
Let your decrees give me help.
I am lost like a sheep; seek your servant
for I remember your commands.

Psalm-prayer

Lord, grant that we should always offer you the hymns
you have made; then we will live to praise you and never
forget your commands.

Psalm 45

The marriage of the king

The Bridegroom is here; go out and welcome him (Matthew
25:6).

I

My heart overflows with noble words.
To the king I must speak the song I have made;
my tongue as nimble as the pen of a scribe.

You are the fairest of the children of men
and graciousness is poured upon your lips:
because God has blessed you for evermore.

O mighty one, gird your sword upon your thigh;
in splendor and state, ride on in triumph
for the cause of truth and goodness and right.

Take aim with your bow in your dread right hand.
Your arrows are sharp: peoples fall beneath you.
The foes of the king fall down and lose heart.

Your throne, O God, shall endure for ever.
A scepter of justice is the scepter of your kingdom.
Your love is for justice; your hatred for evil.

Therefore God, your God, has anointed you
with the oil of gladness above other kings:
your robes are fragrant with aloes and myrrh.

From the ivory palace you are greeted with music.
The daughters of kings are among your loved ones.
On your right stands the queen in gold of Ophir.

II

Listen, O daughter, give ear to my words:
forget your own people and your father's house.
So will the king desire your beauty:
he is your lord, pay homage to him.

And the people of Tyre shall come with gifts,
the richest of the people shall seek your favor.
The daughter of the king is clothed with splendor,
her robes embroidered with pearls set in gold.

She is led to the king with her maiden companions.
They are escorted amid gladness and joy;
they pass within the palace of the king.

Sons shall be yours in place of your fathers:
you will make them princes over all the earth.
May this song make your name for ever remembered.
May the peoples praise you from age to age.

Psalm-prayer

When you took on flesh, Lord Jesus, you made a marriage of mankind with God. Help us to be faithful to your word and endure our exile bravely, until we are called to the heavenly marriage feast, to which the Virgin Mary, exemplar of your Church, has preceded us.

At the other Hours, the complementary psalmody is used, 1191.

Reading, verse and prayer, as in the Proper of Seasons.

Conclusion, as in the Ordinary.

AFTER EVENING PRAYER I
ON SUNDAYS AND SOLEMNITIES

All as in the Ordinary, 671, except the following:

HYMNS

> We praise you, Father, for your gifts
> Of dusk and nightfall over earth,
> Foreshadowing the mystery
> Of death that leads to endless day.
>
> Within your hands we rest secure;
> In quiet sleep our strength renew;
> Yet give your people hearts that wake
> In love to you, unsleeping Lord.
>
> Your glory may we ever seek
> In rest, as in activity,
> Until its fullness is revealed,
> O source of life, O Trinity.

Melody: Te lucis ante terminum (plainchant)   Music: Anon.,
                                                      Gregorian
                                          Text: West Malling Abbey

Or:

> Holy God, we praise thy Name!
> Lord of all, we bow before thee!
> All on earth thy scepter claim,
> All in heaven above adore thee!
> Infinite thy vast domain,
> Everlasting is thy reign.
>
> Hark the loud celestial hymn
> Angel choirs above are raising;
> Cherubim and Seraphim,
> In unceasing chorus praising,

Fill the heavens with sweet accord:
Holy, Holy, Holy Lord!

Holy Father, Holy Son,
Holy Spirit, Three we name thee,
While in essence only One,
Undivided God we claim thee;
And adoring bend the knee,
While we own the mystery.

Melody: Grosser Gott 78.78.77   Music: *Katholisches Gesang-*
buch, Vienna, c. 1774
Text: Ignaz Franz, 1719-1790
Or: Translator: Clarence Walworth, 1820-1900

This world, my God, is held within your hand,
Though we forget your love and steadfast might
And in the changing day uncertain stand,
Disturbed by morning, and afraid of night.

From youthful confidence to careful age,
Help us each one to be your loving friend,
Rewarded by the faithful servant's wage,
God in three persons, reigning without end.

Melody: In Manus Tuas 10.10.10.10.   Music: Herbert Howells
Text: Hamish Swanston

Or:

Now at the daylight's ending
We turn, O God, to you:
Send forth your Holy Spirit,
Our spirit now renew.

To you in adoration,
In thankfulness and praise,
In faith and hope and gladness,
Our loving hearts we raise.

The gift you gave at daylight
This night you take away,

To leave within our keeping
The blessings of this day.

Take all its joy and sorrow,
Take all that love can give,
But all that needs forgiveness,
Dear Father, now forgive.

With watchful eyes, O Shepherd,
Look down upon your sheep;
Stretch forth your hands in healing
And close our eyes in sleep.

Come down, O Holy Spirit,
To be our loving Guest;
Be near us, holy angels,
And guard us as we rest.

We praise you, heav'nly Father:
From you all light descends;
You give us heaven's glory
When life's brief daylight ends.

We praise you, Jesus, Savior,
The light of heav'n above;
We praise you, Holy Spirit,
The living flame of love.

Melody: Christus Der Ist
Mein Leben

Music: Melchior Vulpius, 1609
Text: James Quinn, S.J.

Or:

O Christ, you are the light and day
Which drives away the night,
The ever shining Sun of God
And pledge of future light.

As now the evening shadows fall
Please grant us, Lord, we pray,
A quiet night to rest in you
Until the break of day.

Remember us, poor mortal men,
We humbly ask, O Lord,
And may your presence in our souls
Be now our great reward.

Melody: Saint Anne C.M.   Music: William Croft, 1708
Text: *Christe qui Lux es et Dies,* c. 800
Translator: Rev. M. Quinn, O.P. et al.

Or:

All praise to you, O God, this night
For all the blessings of the light;
Keep us, we pray, O King of kings,
Beneath your own almighty wings.

Forgive us, Lord, through Christ your Son,
Whatever wrong this day we've done;
Your peace give to the world, O Lord,
That man might live in one accord.

Enlighten us, O blessed Light,
And give us rest throughout this night.
O strengthen us, that for your sake,
We all may serve you when we wake.

Melody: Illsley L.M.   Music: J. Bishop, 1665–1737
Text: Thomas Ken, 1709, alt.

Or:

The Master came to bring good news,
The news of love and freedom,
To heal the sick and seek the poor,
To build the peaceful kingdom.

Refrain:

Father, forgive us! Through Jesus, hear us!
As we forgive one another.

Through Jesus Christ the Law's fulfilled,
The man who lived for others.
The law of Christ is love alone,
To serve now all our brothers.

Refrain

To seek the sinners Jesus came,
To live among the friendless,
To show them love that they might share
The kingdom that is endless.

Refrain

Forgive us, Lord, as we forgive
And seek to help each other.
Forgive us, Lord, and we shall live
To pray and work together.

Refrain

Melody: Mainz 87.87 with Refrain — Music: Mainz, 1900
Text: Gabriel Huck, 1965

Or:

Te lucis ante terminum,
rerum creator, poscimus,
ut solita clementia
sis praesul ad custodiam.

Te corda nostra somnient,
te per soporem sentiant,
tuamque semper gloriam
vicina luce concinant.

Vitam salubrem tribue,
nostrum calorem refice,
taetram noctis caliginem
tua collustret claritas.

Praesta, Pater omnipotens,
per Iesum Christum Dominum,
qui tecum in perpetuum
regnat cum Sancto Spiritu. Amen.

Or:

Christe, qui, splendor et dies,
noctis tenebras detegis,
lucisque lumen crederis,
lumen beatis praedicans.

Precamur, sancte Domine,
hac nocte nos custodias;
sit nobis in te requies,
quietas horas tribue.

Somno si dantur oculi,
cor semper ad te vigilet;
tuaque dextra protegas
fideles, qui te diligunt.

Defensor noster, aspice,
insidiantes reprime,
guberna tuos famulos,
quos sanguine mercatus es.

Sit, Christe, rex piissime,
tibi Patrique gloria,
cum Spiritu Paraclito,
in sempiterna saecula. Amen.

PSALMODY

Ant. 1   Have mercy, Lord, and hear my prayer.

Psalm 4

Thanksgiving

The resurrection of Christ was God's supreme and wholly marvelous work (Saint Augustine).

When I call, answer me, O God of justice;
from anguish you released me; have mercy and
hear me!

O men, how long will your hearts be closed,
will you love what is futile and seek what is false?

It is the Lord who grants favors to those whom he
loves;
the Lord hears me whenever I call him.

Fear him; do not sin: ponder on your bed and be
   still.
Make justice your sacrifice and trust in the Lord.

"What can bring us happiness?" many say.
Let the light of your face shine on us, O Lord.

You have put into my heart a greater joy
than they have from abundance of corn and new
   wine.

I will lie down in peace and sleep comes at once
for you alone, Lord, make me dwell in safety.

Ant.   Have mercy, Lord, and hear my prayer.

Ant. 2   In the silent hours of night, bless the Lord.

Psalm 134
Evening prayer in the temple

*Praise our God, all you his servants, you who fear him, small
and great* (Revelation 19:5).

O come, bless the Lord,
all you who serve the Lord,
who stand in the house of the Lord,
in the courts of the house of our God.

Lift up your hands to the holy place
and bless the Lord through the night.

May the Lord bless you from Zion,
he who made both heaven and earth.

Ant.   In the silent hours of night, bless the Lord.

READING   Deuteronomy 6:4-7

Hear, O Israel! The Lord is our God, the Lord alone!
Therefore, you shall love the Lord, your God, with all
your heart, and with all your soul, and with all your
strength. Take to heart these words which I enjoin on

you today. Drill them into your children. Speak of them at home and abroad, whether you are busy or at rest.

RESPONSORY

Into your hands, Lord, I commend my spirit.
—Into your hands, Lord, I commend my spirit.

You have redeemed us, Lord God of truth.
—I commend my spirit.

Glory to the Father . . .
—Into your hands . . .

Ant.   Protect us, Lord, as we stay awake; watch over us as we sleep, that awake, we may keep watch with Christ, and asleep, rest in his peace.

GOSPEL CANTICLE   Luke 2:29-32

Christ is the light of the nations and the glory of Israel

Lord, now you let your servant go in peace;
your word has been fulfilled:

my own eyes have seen the salvation
which you have prepared in the sight of every people:

a light to reveal you to the nations
and the glory of your people Israel.

Ant.   Protect us, Lord, as we stay awake; watch over us as we sleep, that awake, we may keep watch with Christ, and asleep, rest in his peace.

Prayer

Lord,
be with us throughout this night.
When day comes may we rise from sleep
to rejoice in the resurrection of your Christ,
who lives and reigns for ever and ever.

Or: on solemnities that do not occur on Sunday:

Lord,
we beg you to visit this house
and banish from it
all the deadly power of the enemy.
May your holy angels dwell here
to keep us in peace,
and may your blessing be upon us always.
We ask this through Christ our Lord.

Conclusion and antiphon of the Blessed Virgin Mary, as on 1188.

AFTER EVENING PRAYER II
ON SUNDAYS AND SOLEMNITIES

All as in the Ordinary, 671, except the following:

PSALMODY

Ant.   Night holds no terrors for me sleeping under God's wings.

Psalm 91

Safe in God's sheltering care

I have given you the power to tread upon serpents and scorpions (Luke 10:19).

He who dwells in the shelter of the Most High
and abides in the shade of the Almighty
says to the Lord: "My refuge,
my stronghold, my God in whom I trust!"

It is he who will free you from the snare
of the fowler who seeks to destroy you;
he will conceal you with his pinions
and under his wings you will find refuge.

You will not fear the terror of the night
nor the arrow that flies by day,
nor the plague that prowls in the darkness
nor the scourge that lays waste at noon.

A thousand may fall at your side,
ten thousand fall at your right,
you, it will never approach;
his faithfulness is buckler and shield.

Your eyes have only to look
to see how the wicked are repaid,
you who have said: "Lord, my refuge!"
and have made the Most High your dwelling.

Upon you no evil shall fall,
no plague approach where you dwell.
For you has he commanded his angels,
to keep you in all your ways.

They shall bear you upon their hands
lest you strike your foot against a stone.
On the lion and the viper you will tread
and trample the young lion and the dragon.

Since he clings to me in love, I will free him;
protect him for he knows my name.
When he calls I shall answer: "I am with you."
I will save him in distress and give him glory.

With length of life I will content him;
I shall let him see my saving power.

Ant.   Night holds no terrors for me sleeping under
       God's wings.

READING   Revelation 22:4-5

They shall see him face to face and bear his name on
their foreheads. The night shall be no more. They will

need no light from lamps or the sun, for the Lord God shall give them light, and they shall reign forever.

RESPONSORY

Into your hands, Lord, I commend my spirit.
—Into your hands, Lord, I commend my spirit.

You have redeemed us, Lord God of truth.
—I commend my spirit.

Glory to the Father . . .
—Into your hands . . .

Ant. Protect us, Lord, as we stay awake; watch over us as we sleep, that awake, we may keep watch with Christ, and asleep, rest in his peace.

GOSPEL CANTICLE   Luke 2:29-32

Christ is the light of the nations and the glory of Israel

Lord, now you let your servant go in peace;
your word has been fulfilled:

my own eyes have seen the salvation
which you have prepared in the sight of every
    people:

a light to reveal you to the nations
and the glory of your people Israel.

Ant. Protect us, Lord, as we stay awake; watch over us as we sleep, that awake, we may keep watch with Christ, and asleep, rest in his peace.

Prayer

Lord,
we have celebrated today
the mystery of the rising of Christ to new life.
May we now rest in your peace,
safe from all that could harm us,

and rise again refreshed and joyful,
to praise you throughout another day.
We ask this through Christ our Lord.

Or: on solemnities that do not occur on Sunday:

Lord,
we beg you to visit this house
and banish from it
all the deadly power of the enemy.
May your holy angels dwell here
to keep us in peace,
and may your blessing be upon us always.
We ask this through Christ our Lord.

Conclusion and antiphon of the Blessed Virgin Mary, as on
1188.

MONDAY

All as in the Ordinary, 671, except the following:

PSALMODY

Ant.   O Lord, our God, unwearied is your love for us.

Psalm 86

Poor man's prayer in trouble

Blessed be God who comforts us in all our trials (2
Corinthians 1:3, 4).

Turn your ear, O Lord, and give answer
for I am poor and needy.
Preserve my life, for I am faithful:
save the servant who trusts in you.

You are my God; have mercy on me, Lord,
for I cry to you all the day long.
Give joy to your servant, O Lord,
for to you I lift up my soul.

O Lord, you are good and forgiving,
full of love to all who call.
Give heed, O Lord, to my prayer
and attend to the sound of my voice..

In the day of distress I will call
and surely you will reply.
Among the gods there is none like you, O Lord;
nor work to compare with yours.

All the nations shall come to adore you
and glorify your name, O Lord:
for you are great and do marvellous deeds,
you who alone are God.

Show me, Lord, your way
so that I may walk in your truth.
Guide my heart to fear your name.

I will praise you, Lord my God, with all my heart
and glorify your name for ever;
for your love to me has been great:
you have saved me from the depths of the grave.

The proud have risen against me;
ruthless men seek my life:
to you they pay no heed.

But you, God of mercy and compassion,
slow to anger, O Lord,
abounding in love and truth,
turn and take pity on me.

O give your strength to your servant
and save your handmaid's son.
Show me a sign of your favor
that my foes may see to their shame
that you console me and give me your help.

Ant.   O Lord, our God, unwearied is your love for us.

READING   1 Thessalonians 5:9-10

God has destined us for acquiring salvation through our Lord Jesus Christ. He died for us, that all of us, whether awake or asleep, together might live with him.

RESPONSORY

Into your hands, Lord, I commend my spirit.
—Into your hands, Lord, I commend my spirit.

You have redeemed us, Lord God of truth.
—I commend my spirit.

Glory to the Father . . .
—Into your hands . . .

Ant.   Protect us, Lord, as we stay awake; watch over us
        as we sleep, that awake, we may keep watch with
        Christ, and asleep, rest in his peace.

GOSPEL CANTICLE   Luke 2:29-32

Christ is the light of the nations and the glory of Israel

Lord, now you let your servant go in peace;
your word has been fulfilled:

my own eyes have seen the salvation
which you have prepared in the sight of every
people:

a light to reveal you to the nations
and the glory of your people Israel.

Ant.   Protect us, Lord, as we stay awake; watch over us
        as we sleep, that awake, we may keep watch with
        Christ, and asleep, rest in his peace.

Prayer

Lord,
give our bodies restful sleep
and let the work we have done today

bear fruit in eternal life.
We ask this through Christ our Lord.

Conclusion and antiphon of the Blessed Virgin Mary, as on
1188.

TUESDAY

All as in the Ordinary, 671, except the following:

PSALMODY

Ant.   Do not hide your face from me; in you I put my
        trust.

Psalm 143:1-11

Prayer in distress

*Only by faith in Jesus Christ is a man made holy in God's
sight. No observance of the law can achieve this* (Galatians
2:16).

Lord, listen to my prayer:
turn your ear to my appeal.
You are faithful, you are just; give answer.
Do not call your servant to judgment
for no one is just in your sight.

The enemy pursues my soul;
he has crushed my life to the ground;
he has made me dwell in darkness
like the dead, long forgotten.
Therefore my spirit fails;
my heart is numb within me.

I remember the days that are past:
I ponder all your works.
I muse on what your hand has wrought
and to you I stretch out my hands.
Like a parched land my soul thirsts for you.

Lord, make haste and answer;
for my spirit fails within me.
Do not hide your face
lest I become like those in the grave.

In the morning let me know your love
for I put my trust in you.
Make me know the way I should walk:
to you I lift up my soul.

Rescue me, Lord, from my enemies;
I have fled to you for refuge.
Teach me to do your will
for you, O Lord, are my God.
Let your good spirit guide me
in ways that are level and smooth.

For your name's sake, Lord, save my life;
in your justice save my soul from distress.

Ant. Do not hide your face from me; in you I put my trust.

READING   1 Peter 5:8-9a

Stay sober and alert. Your opponent the devil is prowling like a roaring lion looking for someone to devour. Resist him, solid in your faith.

RESPONSORY

Into your hands, Lord, I commend my spirit.
—Into your hands, Lord, I commend my spirit.

You have redeemed us, Lord God of truth.
—I commend my spirit.

Glory to the Father . . .
—Into your hands . . .

Ant. Protect us, Lord, as we stay awake; watch over us as we sleep, that awake, we may keep watch with Christ, and asleep, rest in his peace.

Christ is the light of the nations and the glory of Israel

> Lord, now you let your servant go in peace;
> your word has been fulfilled:
>
> my own eyes have seen the salvation
> which you have prepared in the sight of every
> people:
>
> a light to reveal you to the nations
> and the glory of your people Israel.

Ant. Protect us, Lord, as we stay awake; watch over us
as we sleep, that awake, we may keep watch with
Christ, and asleep, rest in his peace.

Prayer

Lord,
fill this night with your radiance.
May we sleep in peace and rise with joy
to welcome the light of a new day in your name.
We ask this through Christ our Lord.

Conclusion and antiphon of the Blessed Virgin Mary, as on
1188.

WEDNESDAY

All as in the Ordinary, 671, except the following:

PSALMODY

Ant. 1 Lord God, be my refuge and my strength.

Psalm 31:1-6
Trustful prayer in adversity

Father, into your hands I commend my spirit (Luke 23:46).

> In you, O Lord, I take refuge.
> Let me never be put to shame.

In your justice, set me free,
hear me and speedily rescue me.

Be a rock of refuge for me,
a mighty stronghold to save me,
for you are my rock, my stronghold.
For your name's sake, lead me and guide me.

Release me from the snares they have hidden
for you are my refuge, Lord.
Into your hands I commend my spirit.
It is you who will redeem me, Lord.

Ant. Lord God, be my refuge and my strength.

Ant. 2 Out of the depths I cry to you, Lord.

Psalm 130

A cry from the depths

He will save his people from their sins (Matthew 1:21).

Out of the depths I cry to you, O Lord,
Lord, hear my voice!
O let your ears be attentive
to the voice of my pleading.

If you, O Lord, should mark our guilt,
Lord, who would survive?
But with you is found forgiveness:
for this we revere you.

My soul is waiting for the Lord,
I count on his word.
My soul is longing for the Lord
more than watchman for daybreak.
Let the watchman count on daybreak
and Israel on the Lord.

Because with the Lord there is mercy
and fullness of redemption,

Israel indeed he will redeem
from all its iniquity.

Ant.   Out of the depths I cry to you, Lord.

READING   Ephesians 4:26-27

If you are angry, let it be without sin. The sun must
not go down on your wrath; do not give the devil a
chance to work on you.

RESPONSORY

Into your hands, Lord, I commend my spirit.
—Into your hands, Lord, I commend my spirit.

You have redeemed us, Lord God of truth.
—I commend my spirit.

Glory to the Father . . .
—Into your hands . . .

Ant.   Protect us, Lord, as we stay awake; watch over us
as we sleep, that awake, we may keep watch with
Christ, and asleep, rest in his peace.

GOSPEL CANTICLE   Luke 2:29-32

Christ is the light of the nations and the glory of Israel

Lord, now you let your servant go in peace;
your word has been fulfilled:

my own eyes have seen the salvation
which you have prepared in the sight of every
people:

a light to reveal you to the nations
and the glory of your people Israel.

Ant.   Protect us, Lord, as we stay awake; watch over us
as we sleep, that awake, we may keep watch with
Christ, and asleep, rest in his peace.

Prayer

Lord Jesus Christ,
you have given your followers
an example of gentleness and humility,
a task that is easy, a burden that is light.
Accept the prayers and work of this day,
and give us the rest that will strengthen us
to render more faithful service to you
who live and reign for ever and ever.

Conclusion and antiphon of the Blessed Virgin Mary, as on
1188.

THURSDAY

All as in the Ordinary, 671, except the following:

PSALMODY

Ant.   In you, my God, my body will rest in hope.

Psalm 16

God is my portion, my inheritance

*The Father raised up Jesus from the dead and broke the
bonds of death* (Acts 2:24).

Preserve me, God, I take refuge in you.
I say to the Lord: "You are my God.
My happiness lies in you alone."

He has put into my heart a marvellous love
for the faithful ones who dwell in his land.
Those who choose other gods increase their sorrows.
Never will I offer their offerings of blood.
Never will I take their name upon my lips.

O Lord, it is you who are my portion and cup;
it is you yourself who are my prize.
The lot marked out for me is my delight:
welcome indeed the heritage that falls to me!

I will bless the Lord who gives me counsel,
who even at night directs my heart.
I keep the Lord ever in my sight:
since he is at my right hand, I shall stand firm.

And so my heart rejoices, my soul is glad;
even my body shall rest in safety.
For you will not leave my soul among the dead,
nor let your beloved know decay.

You will show me the path of life,
the fullness of joy in your presence,
at your right hand happiness for ever.

Ant.   In you, my God, my body will rest in hope.

READING   1 Thessalonians 5:23

May the God of peace make you perfect in holiness.
May he preserve you whole and entire, spirit, soul, and
body, irreproachable at the coming of our Lord Jesus
Christ.

RESPONSORY

Into your hands, Lord, I commend my spirit.
—Into your hands, Lord, I commend my spirit.

You have redeemed us, Lord God of truth.
—I commend my spirit.

Glory to the Father . . .
—Into your hands . . .

Ant.   Protect us, Lord, as we stay awake; watch over us
as we sleep, that awake, we may keep watch with
Christ, and asleep, rest in his peace.

GOSPEL CANTICLE   Luke 2:29-32

Christ is the light of the nations and the glory of Israel

Lord, now you let your servant go in peace;
your word has been fulfilled:

my own eyes have seen the salvation
which you have prepared in the sight of every
people:

a light to reveal you to the nations
and the glory of your people Israel.

Ant.   Protect us, Lord, as we stay awake; watch over us
        as we sleep, that awake, we may keep watch with
        Christ, and asleep, rest in his peace.

Prayer

Lord God,
send peaceful sleep
to refresh our tired bodies.
May your help always renew us
and keep us strong in your service.
We ask this through Christ our Lord.

Conclusion and antiphon of the Blessed Virgin Mary, as on 1188.

FRIDAY

All as in the Ordinary, 671, except the following:

PSALMODY

Ant.   Day and night I cry to you, my God.

Psalm 88
Prayer of a very sick person

This is your hour when darkness reigns (Luke 22:53).

Lord my God, I call for help by day;
I cry at night before you.
Let my prayer come into your presence.
O turn your ear to my cry.

For my soul is filled with evils;
my life is on the brink of the grave.
I am reckoned as one in the tomb:
I have reached the end of my strength,

like one alone among the dead;
like the slain lying in their graves;
like those you remember no more,
cut off, as they are, from your hand.

You have laid me in the depths of the tomb,
in places that are dark, in the depths.
Your anger weighs down upon me:
I am drowned beneath your waves.

You have taken away my friends
and made me hateful in their sight.
Imprisoned, I cannot escape;
my eyes are sunken with grief.

I call to you, Lord, all the day long;
to you I stretch out my hands.
Will you work your wonders for the dead?
Will the shades stand and praise you?

Will your love be told in the grave
or your faithfulness among the dead?
Will your wonders be known in the dark
or your justice in the land of oblivion?

As for me, Lord, I call to you for help:
in the morning my prayer comes before you.
Lord, why do you reject me?
Why do you hide your face!

Wretched, close to death from my youth,
I have borne your trials; I am numb.
Your fury has swept down upon me;
your terrors have utterly destroyed me.

They surround me all the day like a flood,
they assail me all together.
Friend and neighbor you have taken away:
my one companion is darkness.

Ant.   Day and night I cry to you, my God.

READING   Jeremiah 14:9a

You are in our midst, O Lord,
   your name we bear:
   do not forsake us, O Lord, our God!

RESPONSORY

Into your hands, Lord, I commend my spirit.
—Into your hands, Lord, I commend my spirit.

You have redeemed us, Lord God of truth.
—I commend my spirit.

Glory to the Father . . .
—Into your hands . . .

Ant.   Protect us, Lord, as we stay awake; watch over us
       as we sleep, that awake, we may keep watch with
       Christ, and asleep, rest in his peace.

GOSPEL CANTICLE   Luke 2:29-32

   Christ is the light of the nations and the glory of Israel

   Lord, now you let your servant go in peace;
   your word has been fulfilled:

   my own eyes have seen the salvation
   which you have prepared in the sight of every
      people:

   a light to reveal you to the nations
   and the glory of your people Israel.

Ant.   Protect us, Lord, as we stay awake; watch over us as we sleep, that awake, we may keep watch with Christ, and asleep, rest in his peace.

Prayer

All-powerful God
keep us united with your Son
in his death and burial
so that we may rise to new life with him,
who lives and reigns for ever and ever.

Conclusion

The blessing is said, even in individual recitation:

May the all-powerful Lord grant us a restful night and a peaceful death.
—Amen.

Antiphons in Honor of the Blessed Virgin

Then one of the antiphons in honor of Mary is said. Other hymns approved by the conference of bishops may be used.

Hail, holy Queen, mother of mercy,
our life, our sweetness, and our hope.
To you do we cry,
poor banished children of Eve.
To you do we send up our sighs,
mourning and weeping in this vale of tears.
Turn then, most gracious advocate,
your eyes of mercy toward us,
and after this exile
show to us the blessed fruit of your womb, Jesus.
O clement, O loving,
O sweet Virgin Mary.

Or:

Loving mother of the Redeemer,
gate of heaven, star of the sea,
assist your people who have fallen yet strive to rise
    again.
To the wonderment of nature you bore your Creator,
yet remained a virgin after as before.
You who received Gabriel's joyful greeting,
have pity on us poor sinners.

Or:

Hail Mary, full of grace,
the Lord is with you!
Blessed are you among women,
and blessed is the fruit of your womb, Jesus.
Holy Mary, Mother of God,
pray for us sinners,
now and at the hour of our death.

Or:

Alma Redemptoris Mater, quae pervia caeli
porta manes, et stella maris, succurre cadenti,
surgere qui curat, populo: tu quae genuisti,
natura mirante, tuum sanctum Genitorem,
Virgo prius ac posterius, Gabrielis ab ore
sumens illud Ave, peccatorum miserere.

Or:

Ave, Regina caelorum,
ave, Domina angelorum,
salve, radix, salve, porta,
ex qua mundo lux est orta.

Gaude, Virgo gloriosa,
super omnes speciosa;
vale, o valde decora,
et pro nobis Christum exora.

Or:

Salve, Regina, mater misericordiae;
vita, dulcedo et spes nostra, salve.
Ad te clamamus, exsules filii Evae.
Ad te suspiramus, gementes et flentes
in hac lacrimarum valle.

Eia ergo, advocata nostra,
illos tuos misericordes oculos
ad nos converte.
Et Iesum, benedictum fructum ventris tui,
nobis post hoc exsilium ostende.
O clemens, o pia, o dulcis Virgo Maria.

COMPLEMENTARY PSALMODY
FOR MIDMORNING, MIDDAY AND
MIDAFTERNOON

After the verse **God, come to my assistance** and the hymn, the gradual psalms, which follow, are said, with their antiphon as in the Proper.

Series I (Midmorning)

Psalm 120

Longing for peace

Be patient in suffering, be constant in prayer (Romans 12:12).

> To the Lord in the hour of my distress
> I call and he answers me.
> "O Lord, save my soul from lying lips,
> from the tongue of the deceitful."
>
> What shall he pay you in return,
> O treacherous tongue?
> The warrior's arrows sharpened
> and coals, red-hot, blazing.
>
> Alas, that I abide a stranger in Meshech,
> dwell among the tents of Kedar!
>
> Long enough have I been dwelling
> with those who hate peace.
> I am for peace, but when I speak,
> they are for fighting.

Psalm 121

Guardian of his people

Never again will they hunger and thirst, never again know scorching heat (Revelation 7:16).

I lift up my eyes to the mountains:
from where shall come my help?
My help shall come from the Lord
who made heaven and earth.

May he never allow you to stumble!
Let him sleep not, your guard.
No, he sleeps not nor slumbers,
Israel's guard.

The Lord is your guard and your shade;
at your right side he stands.
By day the sun shall not smite you
nor the moon in the night.

The Lord will guard you from evil,
he will guard your soul.
The Lord will guard your going and coming
both now and for ever.

Psalm 122

The holy city, Jerusalem

*You have come to Mount Zion, to the city of the living God,
the heavenly Jerusalem* (Hebrews 12:22).

I rejoiced when I heard them say:
"Let us go to God's house."
And now our feet are standing
within your gates, O Jerusalem.

Jerusalem is built as a city
strongly compact.
It is there that the tribes go up,
the tribes of the Lord.

For Israel's law it is,
there to praise the Lord's name.
There were set the thrones of judgment
of the house of David.

For the peace of Jerusalem pray:
"Peace be to your homes!
May peace reign in your walls,
in your palaces, peace!"

For love of my brethren and friends
I say: "Peace upon you!"
For love of the house of the Lord
I will ask for your good.

Series II (Midday)

Psalm 123

The Lord is the hope of his people

Two blind men cried out: "Lord, Son of David, have mercy on us" (Matthew 20:30).

To you have I lifted up my eyes,
you who dwell in the heavens:
my eyes, like the eyes of slaves
on the hand of their lords.

Like the eyes of a servant
on the hand of her mistress,
so our eyes are on the Lord our God
till he show us his mercy.

Have mercy on us, Lord, have mercy.
We are filled with contempt.
Indeed all too full is our soul
with the scorn of the rich,
with the proud man's disdain.

Psalm 124

Our help is in the name of the Lord

The Lord said to Paul: "Fear not. . . . I am with you" (Acts 18:9-10).

"If the Lord had not been on our side,
this is Israel's song.
"If the Lord had not been on our side
when men rose against us,
then would they have swallowed us alive
when their anger was kindled.

Then would the waters have engulfed us,
the torrent gone over us;
over our head would have swept
the raging waters."

Blessed be the Lord who did not give us
a prey to their teeth!
Our life, like a bird, has escaped
from the snare of the fowler.

Indeed the snare has been broken
and we have escaped.
Our help is in the name of the Lord,
who made heaven and earth.

Psalm 125

The Lord, the guardian of his people

Peace to God's true Israel (Galatians 6:16).

Those who put their trust in the Lord
are like Mount Zion, that cannot be shaken,
that stands for ever.

Jerusalem! The mountains surround her,
so the Lord surrounds his people
both now and for ever.

For the scepter of the wicked shall not rest
over the land of the just
for fear that the hands of the just
should turn to evil.

Do good Lord, to those who are good,
to the upright of heart;
but the crooked and those who do evil,
drive them away!

On Israel, peace!

Series III (Midafternoon)

Psalm 126

Joyful hope in God

Companions with him in suffering, you will share his
overflowing happiness (2 Corinthians 1:7).

When the Lord delivered Zion from bondage,
it seemed like a dream.
Then was our mouth filled with laughter,
on our lips there were songs.

The heathens themselves said: "What marvels
the Lord worked for them!"
What marvels the Lord worked for us!
Indeed we were glad.

Deliver us, O Lord, from our bondage
as streams in dry land.
Those who are sowing in tears
will sing when they reap.

They go out, they go out, full of tears,
carrying seed for the sowing:
they come back, they come back, full of song,
carrying their sheaves.

Psalm 127

Apart from God our labors are worthless

You are God's building (1 Corinthians 3:9).

If the Lord does not build the house,
in vain do its builders labor;
if the Lord does not watch over the city,
in vain does the watchman keep vigil.

In vain is your earlier rising,
your going later to rest,
you who toil for the bread you eat:
when he pours gifts on his beloved while they
    slumber.

Truly sons are a gift from the Lord,
a blessing, the fruit of the womb.
Indeed the sons of youth
are like arrows in the hand of a warrior.

O the happiness of the man
who has filled his quiver with these arrows!
He will have no cause for shame
when he disputes with his foes in the gateways.

Psalm 128

Happiness of family life rooted in God

"May the Lord bless you from Zion," that is, from the Church (Arnobius).

O blessed are those who fear the Lord
and walk in his ways!

By the labor of your hands you shall eat.
You will be happy and prosper;
your wife like a fruitful vine
in the heart of your house;
your children like shoots of the olive,
around your table.

Indeed thus shall be blessed
the man who fears the Lord.

May the Lord bless you from Zion
all the days of your life!
May you see your children's children
in a happy Jerusalem!

On Israel, peace!

PROPER OF SAINTS

NOVEMBER

November 30

ANDREW, APOSTLE

Feast

Andrew, born at Bethsaida, was a disciple of John the Baptist before he became a follower of Christ, to whom he also brought his brother Peter. With Philip he presented the Gentiles to Christ and, before the miracle in the desert, it was Andrew who pointed out to Christ the boy carrying the loaves and fishes. After Pentecost he preached the Gospel in many lands and was put to death by crucifixion at Achaia.

From the common of apostles, 1354, except for the following:

Office of Readings

FIRST READING

From the first letter of the apostle Paul
to the Corinthians   1:18—2:5

The apostles proclaim the message of the cross

The message of the cross is complete absurdity to those who are headed for ruin, but to us who are experiencing salvation it is the power of God. Scripture says,

"I will destroy the wisdom of the wise,
and thwart the cleverness of the clever."

Where is the wise man to be found? Where the scribe? Where is the master of worldly argument? Has not God turned the wisdom of this world into folly?

Since in God's wisdom the world did not come to know him through "wisdom," it pleased God to save those who believe through the absurdity of the preaching of the gospel. Yes, Jews demand "signs" and Greeks look for "wisdom," but we preach Christ crucified—a stumbling block to Jews, and an absurdity to Gentiles; but to those who are called, Jews and Greeks alike, Christ the power of God and the wisdom of God. For God's folly is wiser than men, and his weakness more powerful than men.

Brothers, you are among those called. Consider your situation. Not many of you are wise, as men account wisdom; not many are influential; and surely not many are well-born. God chose those whom the world considers absurd to shame the wise; he singled out the weak of this world to shame the strong. He chose the world's lowborn and despised, those who count for nothing, to reduce to nothing those who were something, so that mankind can do no boasting before God. God it is who has given you life in Christ Jesus. He has made him our wisdom and also our justice, our sanctification, and our redemption. This is just as you find it written, "Let him who would boast, boast in the Lord."

As for myself, brothers, when I came to you I did not come proclaiming God's testimony with any particular eloquence or "wisdom." No, I determined that while I was with you I would speak of nothing but Jesus Christ and him crucified. When I came among you it was in weakness and fear, and with much trepidation. My message and my preaching had none of the persuasive force of "wise" argumentation, but the convincing power of the Spirit. As a consequence, your faith rests not on the wisdom of men but on the power of God.

RESPONSORY   See Matthew 4:18, 19

As the Lord was walking by the Sea of Galilee,
he saw Peter and Andrew casting their nets into the sea;
he called out to them, saying:
— Come, follow me, I will make you fishers of men.

They were fishermen, so he said to them:
— Come, follow me . . .

SECOND READING

From a homily on the Gospel of John by Saint John
Chrysostom, bishop

(Hom. 19,1: PG 59, 120-121)

We have found the Messiah

After Andrew had stayed with Jesus and had learned
much from him, he did not keep this treasure to himself,
but hastened to share it with his brother. Notice what
Andrew said to him: *We have found the Messiah, that is to
say, the Christ.* Notice how his words reveal what he has
learned in so short a time. They show the power of the
master who has convinced them of this truth. They
reveal the zeal and concern of men preoccupied with this
question from the very beginning. Andrew's words
reveal a soul waiting with the utmost longing for the
coming of the Messiah, looking forward to his appearing
from heaven, rejoicing when he does appear, and
hastening to announce so great an event to others. To
support one another in the things of the spirit is the true
sign of good will between brothers, of loving kinship and
sincere affection.

Notice, too, how, even from the beginning, Peter is
docile and receptive in spirit. He hastens to Jesus,
without delay. *He brought him to Jesus,* says the
evangelist. But Peter must not be condemned for his
readiness to accept Andrew's word without much
weighing of it. It is probable that his brother had given
him, and many others, a careful account of the event; the
evangelists, in the interest of brevity, regularly summa-
rize a lengthy narrative. Saint John does not say that
Peter believed immediately, but that *he brought him to
Jesus.* Andrew was to hand him over to Jesus, to learn
everything for himself. There was also another disciple

present, and he hastened with them for the same
purpose.

When John the Baptist said, *This is the Lamb,* and *he
baptizes in the Spirit,* he left the deeper understanding of
these things to be received from Christ. All the more so
would Andrew act in the same way, since he did not
think himself able to give a complete explanation. He
brought his brother to the very source of light, and Peter
was so joyful and eager that he would not delay even for a
moment.

RESPONSORY

As soon as Andrew heard the Lord preaching,
he left the nets which were his livelihood and way of life,
—and followed the Lord who gives eternal life.

This is the man who endured suffering for the love of
    Christ and for his law,
—And followed the · · ·

HYMN, Te Deum, 651.

Prayer, as in Morning Prayer.

Morning Prayer

HYMN

Great Saint Andrew, friend of Jesus,
Lover of his glorious cross,
Quickly, at the Master's bidding,
Called from ease to pain and loss;
Strong Saint Andrew, Simon's brother,
Like him started life anew,
Gladly spread the holy gospel
Which from Word of God he drew.

Blest Saint Andrew, noble herald,
True apostle, martyr bold,

Who by deeds his words confirming
Sealed with blood the truth he told.
Never was a crown more glorious,
Never prize to heart so dear,
As to him the cross of Jesus
When its promised joys drew near.

Melody: Contemplation 87.87 D   Music: Felix Mendelssohn,
                                                      1809–1847
                                   Text: Frederick Oakeley, 1802–1880,
                                        adapted by Anthony G. Petti

Ant. 1   Two men followed the Lord from the begin-
          ning; one of these was Andrew, the brother of
          Simon Peter.

Psalms and canticle from Sunday, Week I, 688.

Ant. 2   The Lord loved Andrew and cherished his
          friendship

Ant. 3   Andrew said to his brother Simon: We have
          found the Messiah, and he brought him to
          Jesus.

READING   Ephesians 2:19-22

   You are strangers and aliens no longer. No, you are
fellow citizens of the saints and members of the
household of God. You form a building which rises on
the foundation of the apostles and prophets, with Christ
Jesus himself as the capstone. Through him the whole
structure is fitted together and takes shape as a holy
temple in the Lord; in him you are being built into this
temple, to become a dwelling place for God in the Spirit.

RESPONSORY

You have made them rulers over all the earth.
—You have made them rulers over all the earth.

They will always remember your name, O Lord,
—over all the earth.

Glory to the Father . . .
—You have made them rulers over all the earth.

CANTICLE OF ZECHARIAH

Ant.   I bow before the cross made precious by Christ,
        my Master. I embrace it as his disciple.

INTERCESSIONS

Beloved friends, we have inherited heaven along with the
    apostles. Let us voice our thanks to the Father for all
    his gifts:
    The company of apostles praises you, O Lord.
Praise be to you, Lord, for the banquet of Christ's body
    and blood given us through the apostles,
—which refreshes us and gives us life.
    The company of apostles praises you, O Lord.
Praise be to you, Lord, for the feast of your word
    prepared for us by the apostles,
—giving us light and joy.
    The company of apostles praises you, O Lord.
Praise be to you, Lord, for your holy Church, founded
    on the apostles,
—where we are gathered together into your community.
    The company of apostles praises you, O Lord.
Praise be to you, Lord, for the cleansing power of
    baptism and penance that you have entrusted to your
    apostles,
—through which we are cleansed of our sins.
    The company of apostles praises you, O Lord.

Our Father . . .

Prayer

Lord,
in your kindness hear our petitions.
You called Andrew the apostle
to preach the Gospel and guide your Church in faith.
May he always be our friend in your presence
to help us with his prayers.

We ask this through our Lord Jesus Christ, your Son,
who lives and reigns with you and the Holy Spirit,
one God, for ever and ever.

Daytime Prayer

Psalms from the weekday with the antiphon from the Proper of
Seasons. Reading from the common of apostles, 1363. Prayer as
above.

Evening Prayer

HYMN from the common of apostles, 1364.

Ant. 1   The Lord saw Peter and Andrew; he called
them to follow him.

Psalms and canticle from the common of apostles, 1365.

Ant. 2   Come, follow me, said the Lord. I will make
you fishers of men.

Ant. 3   They left their nets to follow Christ, their Lord
and Redeemer.

READING   Ephesians 4:11-13

Christ gave apostles, prophets, evangelists, pastors and
teachers in roles of service for the faithful to build up the
body of Christ, till we become one in faith and in the
knowledge of God's Son, and form that perfect man who
is Christ come to full stature.

RESPONSORY

Tell all the nations how glorious God is.
—Tell all the nations how glorious God is.

Make known his wonders to every people.
—How glorious God is.

Glory to the Father . . .
—Tell all the . . .

CANTICLE OF MARY

Ant.   Andrew served Christ and loyally preached the
        Gospel; with his brother Peter, he laid down his
        life for God.

INTERCESSIONS

My brothers, we build on the foundation of the apostles.
    Let us pray to our almighty Father for his holy people
    and say:
    Be mindful of your Church, O Lord.
Father, you wanted your Son to be seen first by the
    apostles after the resurrection from the dead,
—we ask you to make us his witnesses to the farthest
    corners of the world.
You sent your Son to preach the good news to the poor,
—help us to preach this Gospel to every creature.
You sent your Son to sow the seed of unending life,
—grant that we who work at sowing the seed may share
    the joy of the harvest.
You sent your Son to reconcile all men to you through his
    blood,
—help us all to work toward achieving this reconcilia-
    tion.
Your Son sits at your right hand in heaven,
—let the dead enter your kingdom of joy.

Our Father . . .

Prayer

Lord,
in your kindness hear our petitions.
You called Andrew the apostle
to preach the Gospel and guide your Church in faith.
May he always be our friend in your presence
to help us with his prayers.
We ask this through our Lord Jesus Christ, your Son,
who lives and reigns with you and the Holy Spirit,
one God, for ever and ever.

December 3
FRANCIS XAVIER, PRIEST

Memorial

Francis Xavier was born in Spain in 1506. While studying the liberal arts at Paris, he became a follower of Ignatius Loyola. In 1537 he was ordained at Rome and there devoted himself to works of charity. Francis went to the Orient in 1541 where for ten years he tirelessly proclaimed the Gospel in India and Japan, and through his preaching brought many to believe. He died in 1552 near the China coast on the island of Sancian.

From the common of pastors, 1428.

Office of Readings

SECOND READING

From the letters to Saint Ignatius by Saint Francis Xavier, priest

(E Vita Francisci Xaverii, auctore H. Tursellini, Romae, 1956, Lib. 4, epist. 4 [1542] et 5 [1544])

Woe to me if I do not preach the Gospel

We have visited the villages of the new converts who accepted the Christian religion a few years ago. No Portuguese live here—the country is so utterly barren and poor. The native Christians have no priests. They know only that they *are* Christians. There is nobody to say Mass for them; nobody to teach them the Creed, the Our Father, the Hail Mary and the Commandments of God's Law.

I have not stopped since the day I arrived. I conscientiously made the rounds of the villages. I bathed in the sacred waters all the children who had not yet been baptized. This means that I have purified a very large number of children so young that, as the saying goes, they could not tell their right hand from their left. The older children would not let me say my Office or eat or sleep until I taught them one prayer or another. Then I began to understand: "The kingdom of heaven belongs to such as these."

I could not refuse so devout a request without failing in devotion myself. I taught them, first the confession of faith in the Father, the Son and the Holy Spirit; then the Apostles' Creed, the Our Father and Hail Mary. I noticed among them persons of great intelligence. If only someone could educate them in the Christian way of life, I have no doubt that they would make excellent Christians.

Many, many people hereabouts are not becoming Christians for one reason only: there is nobody to make them Christians. Again and again I have thought of going round the universities of Europe, especially Paris, and everywhere crying out like a madman, riveting the attention of those with more learning than charity: "What a tragedy: how many souls are being shut out of heaven and falling into hell, thanks to you!"

I wish they would work as hard at this as they do at their books, and so settle their account with God for their learning and the talents entrusted to them.

This thought would certainly stir most of them to meditate on spiritual realities, to listen actively to what God is saying to them. They would forget their own desires, their human affairs, and give themselves over entirely to God's will and his choice. They would cry out with all their heart: *Lord, I am here! What do you want me to do?* Send me anywhere you like—even to India!

RESPONSORY   Luke 10:2; Acts 1:8

So great a harvest, and so few to gather it in;
—pray to the Lord of the harvest,
beg him to send out laborers for his harvest.

You will receive power when the Holy Spirit comes upon
    you,
and you will be my witnesses to the ends of the earth.
    —Pray to the . . .

Prayer

God our Father,
by the preaching of Francis Xavier
you brought many nations to yourself.
Give his zeal for the faith to all who believe in you,
that your Church may rejoice in continued growth
throughout the world.

Grant this through our Lord Jesus Christ, your Son,
who lives and reigns with you and the Holy Spirit,
one God, for ever and ever.

December 4

JOHN DAMASCENE, PRIEST AND DOCTOR

John Damascene was born of a Christian family in Damascus
in the latter part of the seventh century. Learned in philosophy,
he became a monk in the monastery of Saint Sabbas near
Jerusalem and was then ordained a priest. He wrote many
doctrinal works, particularly against iconoclasts. He died in the
middle of the eighth century.

From the common of doctors, 1458.

Office of Readings

SECOND READING

From The Statement of Faith by Saint John Damascene,
priest

(Cap. 1: PG 95, 417–419)

You have called me, Lord, to minister to your people

O Lord, you led me from my father's loins and formed me in my mother's womb. You brought me, a naked babe, into the light of day, for nature's laws always obey your commands.

By the blessing of the Holy Spirit, you prepared my creation and my existence, not because man willed it or flesh desired it, but by your ineffable grace. The birth you prepared for me was such that it surpassed the laws of our nature. You sent me forth into the light by adopting me as your son and you enrolled me among the children of your holy and spotless Church.

You nursed me with the spiritual milk of your divine utterances. You kept me alive with the solid food of the body of Jesus Christ, your only-begotten Son and our God, and you let me drink from the chalice of his life-giving blood, poured out to save the whole world.

You loved us, O Lord, and gave up your only-begotten Son for our redemption. And he undertook the task willingly and did not shrink from it. Indeed, he applied himself to it as though destined for sacrifice, like an innocent lamb. Although he was God, he became man, and in his human will, became obedient to you, God his Father, *unto death, even death on a cross.*

In this way you have humbled yourself, Christ my God, so that you might carry me, your stray sheep, on your shoulders. You let me graze in green pastures, refreshing me with the waters of orthodox teaching at the hands of your shepherds. You pastured these shepherds, and now they in turn tend your chosen and special flock. Now you have called me, Lord, by the hand of your bishop to minister to your people. I do not know why you have done so, for you alone know that. Lord, lighten the heavy burden of the sins through which I have seriously transgressed. Purify my mind and heart. Like a shining lamp, lead me along the straight path. When I open my mouth, tell me what I should say. By the fiery tongue of your Spirit make my own tongue ready. Stay with me always and keep me in your sight.

Lead me to pastures, Lord, and graze there with me. Do not let my heart lean either to the right or to the left, but let your good Spirit guide me along the straight path. Whatever I do, let it be in accordance with your will, now until the end.

And you, O Church, are a most excellent assembly, the noble summit of perfect purity, whose assistance comes from God. You in whom God lives, receive from us an exposition of the faith that is free from error, to strengthen the Church, just as our Fathers handed it down to us.

RESPONSORY   Malachi 2:6; Psalm 89:22

True teaching was in his mouth;
no evil was ever found on his lips.
—He walked with me in goodness and in peace.

My hand will be a steady help to him,
my arm will give him strength.
—He walked with . . .

Prayer

Lord,
may the prayers of Saint John Damascene help us,
and may the true faith he taught so well
always be our light and our strength.

We ask this through our Lord Jesus Christ, your Son,
who lives and reigns with you and the Holy Spirit,
one God, for ever and ever.

December 6

NICHOLAS, BISHOP

Nicholas was the bishop of Myra in Lycia (now part of Turkey). He died in the middle of the fourth century and, particularly since the tenth century, has been honored by the whole Church.

From the Common of Pastors, 1428.

Office of Readings

SECOND READING

From a treatise on John by Saint Augustine, bishop

(Tract. 123, 5: CCL 36, 678–680)

The strength of love ought to overcome the fear of death

When the Lord asks Peter if he loves him, he is asking something he already knows. Yet he does not ask only once, but a second and third time. Each time Peter's answer is the same: *You know I love you.* Each time the Lord gives him the same command: *Tend my sheep.*

Peter had denied Christ three times, and to counter this he must profess his faith three times. Otherwise his tongue would seem quicker to serve fear than love, and the threat of death would seem to have made him more eloquent than did the presence of life. If denying the shepherd was proof of fear, then the task of love is to tend his flock.

When those who are tending Christ's flock wish that the sheep were theirs rather than his, they stand convicted of loving themselves, not Christ. And the Lord's words are a repeated admonition to them and to all who, as Paul writes sadly, are seeking their own ends, not Christ's.

Do you love me? Tend my sheep. Surely this means: "If you love me, your thoughts must focus on taking care of my sheep, not taking care of yourself. You must tend them as mine, not as yours; seek in them my glory, not yours; my sovereign rights, not yours; my gain, not yours. Otherwise you will find yourself among those who belong to the 'times of peril,' those who are guilty of self-love and the other sins that go with that beginning of evils."

So the shepherds of Christ's flock must never indulge in self-love; if they do they will be tending the sheep not as Christ's but as their own. And of all vices this is the one that the shepherds must guard against most earnestly: seeking their own purposes instead of Christ's, furthering their own desires by means of those persons for whom Christ shed his blood.

The love of Christ ought to reach such a spiritual pitch in his shepherds that it overcomes the natural fear of death which makes us shrink from the thought of dying even though we desire to live with Christ. However distressful death may be, the strength of love ought to master the distress. I mean the love we have for Christ who, although he is our life, consented to suffer death for our sake.

Consider this: if death held little or no distress for us, the glory of martyrdom would be less. But if the Good Shepherd, who laid down his life for his sheep, has made so many of those same sheep martyrs and witnesses for him, then how much more ought Christ's shepherds to fight for the truth even to death and to shed their blood in opposing sin? After all, the Lord has entrusted them with tending his flock and with teaching and guiding his lambs.

With his passion for their example, Christ's shepherds are most certainly bound to cling to the pattern of his suffering, since even the lambs have so often followed that pattern of the chief shepherd in whose one flock the shepherds themselves are lambs. For the Good Shepherd who suffered for all mankind has made all mankind his lambs, since in order to suffer for them all he made himself a lamb.

<small>RESPONSORY</small>   Sirach 45:3; Psalm 78:70, 71

The Lord glorified him in the sight of kings,
and gave him commandments for his people.
—God revealed to him his glory.

The Lord chose him to be his servant,
a shepherd of his own Israel.
—God revealed to . . .

Prayer

Father,
hear our prayers for mercy,
and by the help of Saint Nicholas
keep us safe from all danger,
and guide us on the way of salvation.

Grant this through our Lord Jesus Christ, your Son,
who lives and reigns with you and the Holy Spirit,
one God, for ever and ever.

December 7

AMBROSE, BISHOP AND DOCTOR

Memorial

Ambrose was born of a Roman family at Trier about the year 340. He studied at Rome and served in the imperial government at Sirmium. In 374, while living in Milan, he was elected bishop of the city by popular acclaim and ordained on December 7. He devotedly carried out his duties and especially distinguished himself by his service to the poor and as an effective pastor and teacher of the faithful. He strenuously guarded the laws of the Church and defended orthodox

401-20-O

teaching by writings and actions against the Arians. He died on Holy Saturday, April 4, 397.

From the Common of Doctors, 1458.

Office of Readings

SECOND READING

From a letter by Saint Ambrose, bishop

(Epist. 2, 1-2. 4-5. 7: PL [edit. 1845,] 879,881)

By the grace of your words win over your people

You have entered upon the office of bishop. Sitting at the helm of the Church, you pilot the ship against the waves. Take firm hold of the rudder of faith so that the severe storms of this world cannot disturb you. The sea is mighty and vast, but do not be afraid, for as Scripture says: *he has founded it upon the seas, and established it upon the waters.*

The Church of the Lord is built upon the rock of the apostles among so many dangers in the world; it therefore remains unmoved. The Church's foundation is unshakable and firm against the assaults of the raging sea. Waves lash at the Church but do not shatter it. Although the elements of this world constantly beat upon the Church with crashing sounds, the Church possesses the safest harbor of salvation for all in distress. Although the Church is tossed about on the sea, it rides easily on rivers, especially those rivers that Scripture speaks of: *The rivers have lifted up their voice.* These are the rivers flowing from the heart of the man who is given drink by Christ and who receives from the Spirit of God. When these rivers overflow with the grace of the Spirit, they lift up their voice.

There is also a stream which flows down on God's saints like a torrent. There is also a rushing river giving joy to the heart that is at peace and makes for peace. Whoever has received from the fullness of this river, like John the Evangelist, like Peter and Paul, lifts up his voice. Just as the apostles lifted up their voices and preached the Gospel throughout the world, so those who drink these waters begin to preach the good news of the Lord Jesus.

Drink, then, from Christ, so that your voice may also be heard. Store up in your mind the water that is Christ, the water that praises the Lord. Store up water from many sources, the water that rains down from the clouds of prophecy.

Whoever gathers water from the mountains and leads it to himself or draws it from springs, is himself a source of dew like the clouds. Fill your soul, then, with this water, so that your land may not be dry, but watered by your own springs.

He who reads much and understands much, receives his fill. He who is full, refreshes others. So Scripture says: *If the clouds are full, they will pour rain upon the earth.*

Therefore, let your words be rivers, clean and limpid, so that in your exhortations you may charm the ears of your people. And by the grace of your words win them over to follow your leadership. Let your sermons be full of understanding. Solomon says: *The weapons of the understanding are the lips of the wise;* and in another place he says: *Let your lips be bound with wisdom.* That is, let the meaning of your words shine forth, let understanding blaze out. See that your addresses and expositions do not need to invoke the authority of others, but let your words be their own defense. Let no word escape your lips in vain or be uttered without depth of meaning.

RESPONSORY   2 Timothy 4:2; Sirach 48:4, 8

Proclaim the message, in season and out of season;
—refute falsehood, correct error, call to obedience.

Who is able to boast as you can?
You have anointed kings as champions of righteousness.
—Refute falsehood, correct . . .

Prayer, as in Morning Prayer.

Morning Prayer

HYMN, as in the common of doctors, 1464.

Prayer

Lord,
you made Saint Ambrose
an outstanding teacher of the Catholic faith
and gave him the courage of an apostle.
Raise up in your Church more leaders after your own
    heart,
to guide us with courage and wisdom.
We ask this through our Lord Jesus Christ, your Son,
who lives and reigns with you and the Holy Spirit,
one God, for ever and ever.

December 8
IMMACULATE CONCEPTION

Solemnity

Evening Prayer I

HYMN

Mary, crowned with living light,
Temple of the Lord,
Place of peace and holiness,
Shelter of the Word.

Mystery of sinless life
In our fallen race,
Free from shadow, you reflect
Plenitude of grace.

Virgin-Mother of our God,
Lift us when we fall,
Who were named upon the Cross
Mother of us all.

Father, Son and Holy Ghost,
Heaven sings your praise;
Mary magnifies your name
Through eternal days.

Melody: Glorification . Music: Gossner's *Choralbuch*, Leipzig, 1832
75.75.D   Text: Stanbrook Abbey

Or:

Salve, Regina, mater misericordiae;
vita, dulcedo et spes nostra, salve.
Ad te clamamus, exsules filii Evae.
Ad te suspiramus, gementes et flentes
in hac lacrimarum valle.

Eia ergo, advocata nostra,
illos tuos misericordes oculos
ad nos converte.
Et Iesum, benedictum fructum ventris tui,
nobis post hoc exsilium ostende.
O clemens, o pia, o dulcis Virgo Maria.

Melody: Salve Regina

Music: Paris, 1634
Text: 11th century

Ant. 1 I will make you enemies, you and the woman, your offspring and hers.

Psalms and canticle from the common of the Blessed Virgin Mary, 1321.

Ant. 2 The Lord has clothed me with garments of salvation; he has covered me with a robe of justice.

Ant. 3 Hail Mary, full of grace; the Lord is with you.

READING Romans 8:29-30

Those whom God foreknew he predestined to share the image of his Son. Those he predestined he likewise called; those he called he also justified.

RESPONSORY

I shall glorify you, Lord, for you have rescued me.
—I shall glorify you, Lord, for you have rescued me.

You have not let my enemies rejoice over me.
—For you have rescued me.

Glory to the Father . . .
—I shall glorify . . .

CANTICLE OF MARY

Ant. All generations will call me blessed: the Almighty has done great things for me.

INTERCESSIONS

Let us praise God our almighty Father, who wished that Mary, his Son's mother, be celebrated by each generation. Now in need we ask:

Mary, full of grace, intercede for us.

O God, worker of miracles, you made the immaculate Virgin Mary share, body and soul, in your Son's glory in heaven,

—direct the hearts of your children to that same glory.

You made Mary our mother. Through her intercession grant strength to the weak, comfort to the sorrowing, pardon to sinners,

—salvation and peace to all.

You made Mary the mother of mercy,

—may all who are faced with trials feel her motherly love.

You wished Mary to be the mother of the family in the home of Jesus and Joseph,

—may all mothers of families foster love and holiness through her intercession.

You crowned Mary queen of heaven,

—may all the dead rejoice in your kingdom with the saints for ever.

Our Father . . .

Prayer

Father,
you prepared the Virgin Mary
to be the worthy mother of your Son.
You let her share beforehand
in the salvation Christ would bring by his death,
and kept her sinless from the first moment of her conception.
Help us by her prayers
to live in your presence without sin.

We ask this through our Lord Jesus Christ, your Son,
who lives and reigns with you and the Holy Spirit,
one God, for ever and ever.

Alternative Prayer

Father,
the image of the Virgin is found in the Church.
Mary had a faith that your Spirit prepared
and a love that never knew sin,
for you kept her sinless from the first moment of her
   conception.
Trace in our actions the lines of her love,
in our hearts her readiness of faith.
Prepare once again a world for your Son
who lives and reigns with you and the Holy Spirit,
one God, for ever and ever.

Invitatory

Ant.   Come, let us celebrate the Immaculate Conception
          of the Virgin Mary; let us worship her Son, Christ
          the Lord.

Invitatory psalm as in the Ordinary, 648.

Office of Readings

HYMN

> To one that is so fair and bright
> Velut maris stella,
> Brighter than the day is light,
> Parens et puella,
> I cry to thee to turn to me:
> Lady, pray thy Son for me,
> Tam pia,
> That I may come to thee,
> Maria.

In sorrow, counsel thou art best,
Felix fecundata:
For all the weary thou art rest,
Mater honorata:
Beseech him in thy mildest mood,
Who for us did shed his blood
In cruce,
That we may come to him
In luce.

All this world was forlorn,
Eva peccatrice,
Till our Savior Lord was born
De te genetrice;
With thy Ave sin went away,
Dark night went and in came day
Salutis.
The well of healing sprang from thee
Virtutis.

Lady, flower of every thing,
Rosa sine spina,
Thou bore Jesu, heaven's King,
Gratia divina.
Of all I say thou bore the prize,
Lady, Queen of paradise,
Electa;
Maiden mild, Mother
Es effecta.

Melody: Trochrague

Music: Francis Duffy
Text: Anon. medieval

Or: Antiphon:

You are the honor, you are the glory of our people,
Holy Virgin Mary.

You are the glory of Jerusalem, Holy Virgin Mary.

Antiphon

You are the greatest joy of Israel, Holy Virgin Mary.

Antiphon

You are the highest honor of our race, Holy Virgin Mary.

Antiphon

May you be blessed by the Lord most high, Holy Virgin Mary.

Antiphon

Now, and for all ages without end, Holy Virgin Mary.

Antiphon

Give praise to God in the Church, and Christ, Holy Virgin Mary.

Antiphon

Melody: You are   Music: Lucien Deiss, C.S.Sp., 1965
The Honor   Text: Lucien Deiss, C.S.Sp., 1965

Ant. 1   At her conception Mary received a blessing from the Lord and loving kindness from God her savior.

Psalms from the common of the Blessed Virgin Mary, 1328.

Ant. 2   God gave her his help from the dawning of her days; the Most High has made his dwelling place a holy temple.

Ant. 3   Glorious things are said of you, O city of God, established on his holy mountain.

The God of power has given me his strength.
—He has kept me in the way of holiness.

FIRST READING

From the letter of the apostle Paul
to the Romans   5:12-21

Where sin abounds, there is an abundance of grace

Just as through one man sin entered the world and with sin death, death thus coming to all men inasmuch as all sinned—before the law there was sin in the world, even though sin is not imputed when there is no law—I say, from Adam to Moses death reigned, even over those who had not sinned by breaking a precept as did Adam, that type of the man to come.

But the gift is not like the offense. For if by the offense of the one man all died, much more did the grace of God and the gracious gift of the one man, Jesus Christ, abound for all. The gift is entirely different from the sin committed by the one man. In the first case, sentence followed upon one offense and brought condemnation, but in the second, the gift came after many offenses and brought acquittal. If death began its reign through one man because of his offense, much more shall those who receive the overflowing grace and gift of justice live and reign through the one man, Jesus Christ.

To sum up, then: just as a single offense brought condemnation to all men, a single righteous act brought all men acquittal and life. Just as through one man's disobedience all became sinners, so through one man's obedience all shall become just.

The law came in order to increase offenses; but despite the increase of sin, grace has far surpassed it, so that, as sin reigned through death, grace may reign by way of justice leading to eternal life, through Jesus Christ our Lord.

RESPONSORY   Romans 5:12; Luke 1:30;
                              see Psalm 115:8; 17:19

Through one man sin came into the world;
in him all men have sinned.

—Do not be afraid, Mary, you have found favor with
  God.

The Lord has rescued you from death
and sheltered you from all harm.

—Do not be . . .

From a sermon by Saint Anselm, bishop

(Oratio 52: PL 158, 955-956)

Virgin Mary, all nature is blessed in you.

Blessed Lady, sky and stars, earth and rivers, day and
night—everything that is subject to the power or use of
man—rejoice that through you they are in some sense
restored to their lost beauty and are endowed with
inexpressible new grace. All creatures were dead, as it
were, useless for men or for the praise of God, who made
them. The world, contrary to its true destiny, was
corrupted and tainted by the acts of men who served
idols. Now all creation has been restored to life and
rejoices that it is controlled and given splendor by men
who believe in God.

The universe rejoices with new and indefinable
loveliness. Not only does it feel the unseen presence of
God himself, its Creator, it sees him openly, working and
making it holy. These great blessings spring from the
blessed fruit of Mary's womb.

Through the fullness of the grace that was given you,
dead things rejoice in their freedom, and those in heaven
are glad to be made new. Through the Son who was the
glorious fruit of your virgin womb, just souls who died
before his life-giving death rejoice as they are freed from
captivity, and the angels are glad at the restoration of
their shattered domain.

Lady, full and overflowing with grace, all creation receives new life from your abundance. Virgin, blessed above all creatures, through your blessing all creation is blessed, not only creation from its Creator, but the Creator himself has been blessed by creation.

To Mary God gave his only-begotten Son, whom he loved as himself. Through Mary God made himself a Son, not different but the same, by nature Son of God and Son of Mary. The whole universe was created by God, and God was born of Mary. God created all things, and Mary gave birth to God. The God who made all things gave himself form through Mary, and thus he made his own creation. He who could create all things from nothing would not remake his ruined creation without Mary.

God, then, is the Father of the created world and Mary the mother of the re-created world. God is the Father by whom all things were given life, and Mary the mother through whom all things were given new life. For God begot the Son, through whom all things were made, and Mary gave birth to him as the Savior of the world. Without God's Son, nothing could exist; without Mary's Son, nothing could be redeemed.

Truly the Lord is with you, to whom the Lord granted that all nature should owe as much to you as to himself.

RESPONSORY   Psalm 34:4; 86:13; Luke 1:48

Proclaim with me the glory of the Lord,
—for great is his merciful love for me.

From this day all generations will call me blessed.
— For great is . . .

HYMN, Te Deum, 651.

Prayer, as in Morning Prayer

Morning Prayer

HYMN

Mary immaculate, star of the morning,
Chosen before the creation began,
Chosen to bring, for thy bridal adorning,
Woe to the serpent and rescue to man.

Here, in an orbit of shadow and sadness,
Veiling thy splendor, thy course thou hast run;
Now thou art throned in all glory and gladness,
Crowned by the hand of the savior and Son.

Sinners, we worship thy sinless perfection;
Fallen and weak, for thy pity we plead;
Grant us the shield of thy sovereign protection,
Measure thine aid by the depth of our need.

Bend from thy throne at the voice of our crying,
Bend to this earth which thy footsteps have trod;
Stretch out thine arms to us, living and dying,
Mary immaculate, Mother of God.

Melody: Liebster
Immanuel 11.10.11.10

Music: Melody from Himmels-Lust,
1679, adapted and harmonized
by J. S. Bach
Text: F. W. Weatherell

Or:

Refrain:

Holy Mary, now we crown you
Honored Queen of all our race:
Noble Virgin, may our tribute
Win you love and gain us grace.

On this day we sing your praises,
Purest Maid of all the earth:
While the beauty of the springtime
Tells your joy at Jesus' birth.

Refrain

Glorious Queen, look down in kindness
While before your throne we stand:
Bring God's blessing to your children;
Watch our homes and guard our land.

Refrain

Gate of Heaven, you were Mother
To the King of heav'n and earth:
Now be Mother to your subjects,
In our souls give Jesus birth.

Refrain

Queen of Mankind, while creation
Speaks the grandeur of God's love,
Mold our hearts to seek his glory
Till we reach our home above.

Refrain

Melody: Holy Mary, Now We Crown You   Music: J. L. Steiner,
1735
Text: Melvin Farrell, S. S.

Ant. 1   O Mother, how pure you are, you are
untouched by sin; yours was the privilege to
carry God within you.

Psalms and canticle from Sunday, Week I, 688.

Ant. 2   The Lord God Most High has blessed you,
Virgin Mary, above all the women of the earth.

Ant. 3   Sinless Virgin, let us follow joyfully in your
footsteps; draw us after you in the fragrance of
your holiness.

READING   Isaiah 43:1

But now, thus says the Lord,
who created you, O Jacob,
and formed you, O Israel:
Fear not, for I have redeemed you;
I have called you by name: you are mine.

RESPONSORY

The God of power has given me his strength.
—The God of power has given me his strength.

He has kept me in the way of holiness.
—And has given me his strength.

Glory to the Father . . .
—The God of . . .

CANTICLE OF ZECHARIAH

Ant.　The Lord God said to the serpent: I will make you
enemies, you and the woman, your offspring and
her offspring; she will crush your head, alleluia.

INTERCESSIONS

Let us glorify our Savior, who chose the Virgin Mary for
his mother. Let us ask him:
　May your mother intercede for us, Lord.
Sun of Justice, the Immaculate Virgin was the white
dawn announcing your rising,
—grant that we may always live in the light of your
coming.
Savior of the world, by your redeeming might you
preserved your mother beforehand from all stain of
sin,
—keep watch over us, lest we sin.
You are our redeemer, who made the Immaculate Virgin
Mary your purest home and the sanctuary of the Holy
Spirit,
—make us temples of your Spirit for ever.
King of kings, you lifted up your mother, body and soul,
into heaven;
—help us to fix our thoughts on things above.

Our Father . . .

Prayer

Father,
you prepared the Virgin Mary
to be the worthy mother of your Son.
You let her share beforehand
in the salvation Christ would bring by his death,
and kept her sinless from the first moment of her
    conception.
Help us by her prayers
to live in your presence without sin.

We ask this through our Lord Jesus Christ, your Son,
who lives and reigns with you and the Holy Spirit,
one God, for ever and ever.

Alternative Prayer

Father,
the image of the Virgin is found in the Church.
Mary had a faith that your Spirit prepared
and a love that never knew sin,
for you kept her sinless from the first moment of her
    conception.
Trace in our actions the lines of her love,
in our hearts her readiness of faith.
Prepare once again a world for your Son
who lives and reigns with you and the Holy Spirit,
one God, for ever and ever.

Daytime Prayer

Complementary psalmody, 1191; in place of psalm 122, 129 is
said, 1129, and in place of 127, psalm 131 may be said, 972.

Midmorning

Ant. Praise the Lord of life, for he has lavished his
      mercy upon me.

READING — Ephesians 1:4

God chose us in Christ before the world began, to be holy and blameless in his sight, to be full of love.

Today we celebrate the Immaculate Conception of the Blessed Virgin Mary.
—She has crushed the serpent's head with her foot.

Midday

Ant. The Lord will take great delight in you; your God will look on you with endless joy.

READING — Ephesians 1:11-12

In Christ we were chosen; for in the decree of God, who administers everything according to his will and counsel, we were predestined to praise his glory.

My heart and my flesh.
—Rejoice in the living God.

Midafternoon

Ant. God created me in holiness; he took my hand and kept me safe.

READING — Ephesians 5:25-27

Christ loved the church. He gave himself up for her to make her holy, to present to himself a glorious church, holy and immaculate, without stain or wrinkle or anything of that sort.

Your Immaculate Conception, Virgin Mother of God.
—Fills the whole world with joy.

Evening Prayer II

Hymn, as at Evening Prayer I, 1221.

Ant. 1   You are all beautiful, O Mary; in you there is no trace of original sin.

Psalms and canticle from the common of the Blessed Virgin Mary, 1345.

Ant. 2   You are the glory of Jerusalem, the joy of Israel; you are the fairest honor of our race.

Ant. 3   The robe you wear is white as spotless snow; your face is radiant like the sun.

READING   Romans 5:20-21

Despite the increase of sin, grace has far surpassed it, so that, as sin reigned through death, grace may reign by way of justice leading to eternal life, through Jesus Christ our Lord.

RESPONSORY

By this I know you have chosen me.
—By this I know you have chosen me.

You have not let my enemy triumph over me.
—You have chosen me.

Glory to the Father . . .
—By this I . . .

CANTICLE OF MARY

Ant.   Hail Mary, full of grace; the Lord is with you; blessed are you among women, and blessed is the fruit of your womb, alleluia.

INTERCESSIONS

Let us praise God our almighty Father, who wished that Mary, his Son's mother, be celebrated by each generation. Now in need we ask:
Mary, full of grace, intercede for us.

O God, worker of miracles, you made the immaculate Virgin Mary share, body and soul, in your Son's glory in heaven,
—direct the hearts of your children to that same glory.

You made Mary our mother. Through her intercession grant strength to the weak, comfort to the sorrowing, pardon to sinners,
—salvation and peace to all.

You made Mary the mother of mercy,
—may all who are faced with trials feel her motherly love.

You wished Mary to be the mother of the family in the home of Jesus and Joseph,
—may all mothers of families foster love and holiness through her intercession.

You crowned Mary queen of heaven,
—may all the dead rejoice in your kingdom with the saints for ever.

Our Father . . .

Prayer

Father,
you prepared the Virgin Mary
to be the worthy mother of your Son.
You let her share beforehand
in the salvation Christ would bring by his death,
and kept her sinless from the first moment of her conception.

Help us by her prayers
to live in your presence without sin.

We ask this through our Lord Jesus Christ, your Son,
who lives and reigns with you and the Holy Spirit,
one God, for ever and ever.

Alternative Prayer

Father,
the image of the Virgin is found in the Church.
Mary had a faith that your Spirit prepared
and a love that never knew sin,
for you kept her sinless from the first moment of her
    conception.
Trace in our actions the lines of her love,
in our hearts her readiness of faith.
Prepare once again a world for your Son
who lives and reigns with you and the Holy Spirit,
one God, for ever and ever.

December 11

DAMASUS I, POPE

Damasus was born in Spain around the year 305. He was
admitted to the Roman clergy and in 366, during a period of
upheaval in the Church, was ordained bishop of Rome. He
summoned synods to work against schismatics and heretics and
widely promoted the cult of martyrs whose burial places he
adorned with sacred verse. He died in 384.

From the common of pastors, 1428.

Office of Readings

SECOND READING

From a treatise against Faustus by Saint Augustine, bishop

(Lib. 20, 21: CSEL 25, 562-563)

We celebrate the martyrs with the veneration of love and
fellowship

We, the Christian community, assemble to celebrate the memory of the martyrs with ritual solemnity because we want to be inspired to follow their example, share in their merits, and be helped by their prayers. Yet we erect no altars to any of the martyrs, even in the martyrs' burial chapels themselves.

No bishop, when celebrating at an altar where these holy bodies rest, has ever said, "Peter, we make this offering to you," or "Paul, to you," or "Cyprian, to you." No, what is offered is offered always to God, who crowned the martyrs. We offer in the chapels where the bodies of those he crowned rest, so the memories that cling to those places will stir our emotions and encourage us to greater love both for the martyrs whom we can imitate and for God whose grace enables us to do so.

So we venerate the martyrs with the same veneration of love and fellowship that we give to the holy men of God still with us. We sense that the hearts of these latter are just as ready to suffer death for the sake of the Gospel, and yet we feel more devotion toward those who have already emerged victorious from the struggle. We honor those who are fighting on the battlefield of this life here below, but we honor more confidently those who have already achieved the victor's crown and live in heaven.

But the veneration strictly called "worship," or *latria*, that is, the special homage belonging only to the divinity, is something we give and teach others to give to God alone. The offering of a sacrifice belongs to worship in this sense (that is why those who sacrifice to idols are called idol-worshipers), and we neither make nor tell others to make any such offering to any martyr, any holy soul, or any angel. If anyone among us falls into this error, he is corrected with words of sound doctrine and must then either mend his ways or else be shunned.

The saints themselves forbid anyone to offer them the worship they know is reserved for God, as is clear from the case of Paul and Barnabas. When the Lycaonians were so amazed by their miracles that they wanted to sacrifice to them as gods, the apostles tore their garments, declared that they were not gods, urged the people to believe them, and forbade them to worship them.

Yet the truths we teach are one thing, the abuses thrust upon us are another. There are commandments that we are bound to give; there are breaches of them that we are commanded to correct, but until we correct them we must of necessity put up with them.

RESPONSORY   Psalm 116:15; 34:21; see Judith 10:3

Precious in the sight of the Lord is the death of his
    faithful ones;
—their very bones are dear to him,
not one of them shall be broken.

The Lord clothes them with gladness.
—Their very bones . . .

Prayer

Father,
as Saint Damasus loved and honored your martyrs,
so may we continue to celebrate their witness for Christ,
who lives and reigns with you and the Holy Spirit,
one God, for ever and ever.

December 12

JANE FRANCES DE CHANTAL, RELIGIOUS

Jane Frances was born in Dijon, France, in 1572. She was married to the nobleman de Chantal, and had six sons to whom she carefully taught the Christian faith. When her husband died, she wholeheartedly embraced the religious life under the guidance of Saint Francis de Sales and performed works of charity especially for the poor and sick. She founded the Visitation Order which she directly wisely until her death in 1641.

From the common of holy women: religious, 1554.

Office of Readings

SECOND READING

From The Memoirs by the secretary of Saint Jane Frances de Chantal.

(Francoise-Madeleine de Chaugy, Memoires sur la vie et les vertus de Sainte J.-F. de Chantal, III, 3: 3e edit., Paris 1853, pp. 306-307)

Love is as strong as death

One day Saint Jane spoke the following eloquent words, which listeners took down exactly as spoken:

"My dear daughters, many of our holy fathers in the faith, men who were pillars of the Church, did not die martyrs. Why do you think this was?" Each one present offered an answer; then their mother continued. "Well, I myself think it was because there is another martyrdom: the martyrdom of love. Here God keeps his servants and handmaids in this present life so that they may labor for him, and he makes of them both martyrs and confessors. I know," she added, "that the Daughters of the Visitation are meant to be martyrs of this kind and that, by the favor of God, some of them, more fortunate than others in that their desire has been granted, will actually suffer such a martyrdom."

One sister asked what form this martyrdom took. The saint answered: "Yield yourself fully to God, and you will find out! Divine love takes its sword to the hidden recesses of our inmost soul and divides us from ourselves. I know one person whom love cut off from all that was dearest to her, just as completely and effectively as if a tyrant's blade had severed spirit from body."

We realized that she was speaking of herself. When another sister asked how long the martyrdom would continue, the Saint replied: "From the moment when we commit ourselves unreservedly to God, until our last breath. I am speaking, of course, of great-souled individuals who keep nothing back for themselves, but instead are faithful in love. Our Lord does not intend this martyrdom for those who are weak in love and perseverance. Such people he lets continue on their mediocre way, so that they will not be lost to him; he never does violence to our free will."

Finally, the saint was asked whether this martyrdom of love could be put on the same level as martyrdom of the body. She answered: "We should not worry about equality. I do think, however, that the martyrdom of love cannot be relegated to a second place, for *love is as strong as death*. For the martyrs of love suffer infinitely more in remaining in this life so as to serve God, than if they died a thousand times over in testimony to their faith and love and fidelity."

RESPONSORY   See Philippians 4:8-9

There are many things that are true, honorable and just, many that are pure, worthy of love and deserving of
   praise:
these you must do.
—And the God of peace will be with you.

If there is anything virtuous, anything worthy of
   admiration,
think of these things above all else.
—And the God . . .

Prayer

Lord,
you chose Saint Jane Frances to serve you
both in marriage and in religious life.
By her prayers
help us to be faithful in our vocation
and always to be the light of the world.
We ask this through our Lord Jesus Christ, your Son,
who lives and reigns with you and the Holy Spirit,
one God, for ever and ever.

December 13
LUCY, VIRGIN AND MARTYR

Memorial

Lucy died at Syracuse, probably during the persecution of
Diocletian. From antiquity her cult spread throughout the
Church, and her name was therefore introduced into the Ro-
man Canon.

From the common of martyrs, 1401, or virgins, 1473.

Office of Readings

SECOND READING

From the book On Virginity by Saint Ambrose, bishop

(Cap. 12, 68. 74–75; 13,77–78: PL 16 [edit. 1845], 281. 283. 285–286)

You light up your grace of body
with your splendor of soul

You are one of God's people, of God's family, a virgin
among virgins; you light up your grace of body with your

splendor of soul. More than others you can be compared to the Church. When you are in your room, then, at night, think always on Christ, and wait for his coming at every moment.

This is the person Christ has loved in loving you, the person he has chosen in choosing you. He enters by the open door; he has promised to come in, and he cannot deceive. Embrace him, the one you have sought; turn to him, and be enlightened; hold him fast, ask him not to go in haste, beg him not to leave you. The Word of God moves swiftly; he is not won by the lukewarm, nor held fast by the negligent. Let your soul be attentive to his word; follow carefully the path God tells you to take, for he is swift in his passing.

What does his bride say? *I sought him, and did not find him; I called him, and he did not hear me.* Do not imagine that you are displeasing to him although you have called him, asked him, opened the door to him, and that this is the reason why he has gone so quickly; no, for he allows us to be constantly tested. When the crowds press him to stay, what does he say in the Gospel? *I must preach the word of God to other cities, because I have been sent for that.* But even if it seems to you that he has left you, go out and seek him once more.

Who but holy Church is to teach you how to hold Christ fast? Indeed, she has already taught you, if you only understood her words in Scripture: *How short a time it was when I left them before I found him whom my soul has loved. I held him fast, and I will not let him go.*

How do we hold him fast? Not by restraining chains or knotted ropes but by bonds of love, by spiritual reins, by the longing of the soul.

If you also, like the bride, wish to hold him fast, seek him and be fearless of suffering. It is often easier to find him in the midst of bodily torments, in the very hands of persecutors.

His bride says: *How short a time it was after I left them.* In a little space, after a brief moment, when you have escaped from the hands of your persecutors without yielding to the powers of this world, Christ will come to you, and he will not allow you to be tested for long.

Whoever seeks Christ in this way, and finds him, can say: *I held him fast, and I will not let him go before I bring him into my mother's house, into the room of her who conceived me.* What is this "house," this "room," but the deep and secret places of your heart?

Maintain this house, sweep out its secret recesses until it becomes immaculate and rises as a spiritual temple for a holy priesthood, firmly secured by Christ, the cornerstone, so that the Holy Spirit may dwell in it.

Whoever seeks Christ in this way, whoever prays to Christ in this way, is not abandoned by him; on the contrary, Christ comes again and again to visit such a person, for he is with us until the end of the world.

RESPONSORY

The grace of the Lord gave her strength in the battle,
and she was glorified before God and man.
In the presence of the prince she spoke with wisdom,
—and therefore the Lord of heaven and earth has loved her.

She is the virgin
who prepared a joyful home for God in her heart.
—And therefore the . . .

Prayer, as in Morning Prayer.

Morning Prayer

CANTICLE OF ZECHARIAH

Ant.   I am the Lord's poor servant; to him alone, the
       living God, I have offered all in sacrifice; I have
       nothing else to give; I offer him myself.

Prayer

Lord,
give us courage through the prayers of Saint Lucy.
As we celebrate her entrance into eternal glory,
we ask to share her happiness in the life to come.

Grant this through our Lord Jesus Christ, your Son,
who lives and reigns with you and the Holy Spirit,
one God, for ever and ever.

Evening Prayer

CANTICLE OF MARY

Ant.   Lucy, bride of Christ, by your suffering you have
       gained the mastery of your soul. You have
       despised worldly values and now you are glorious
       among the angels. With your own blood you have
       triumphed over the enemy.

December 14

JOHN OF THE CROSS, PRIEST AND DOCTOR

Memorial

John of the Cross was born at Fontiveros in Spain around
1542. After a number of years as a Carmelite, he was
persuaded by Saint Teresa of Avila in 1568 to lead a reform
movement among the brothers which brought a new energy to
the Carmelite Order. Renowned for his wisdom and sanctity,
he died at Ubeda in 1591. His spiritual writings remain a fitting
testimony to his life.

From the common of doctors, 1458.

Office of Readings

SECOND READING

From a spiritual Canticle by Saint John of the Cross, priest

(Red. B, str. 36–37)

The knowledge of the mystery hidden in Christ Jesus

Though holy doctors have uncovered many mysteries and wonders, and devout souls have understood them in this earthly condition of ours, yet the greater part still remains to be unfolded by them, and even to be understood by them.

We must then dig deeply in Christ. He is like a rich mine with many pockets containing treasures: however deep we dig we will never find their end or their limit. Indeed, in every pocket new seams of fresh riches are discovered on all sides.

For this reason the apostle Paul said of Christ: *In him are hidden all the treasures of the wisdom and knowledge of God.* The soul cannot enter into these treasures, nor attain them, unless it first crosses into and enters the thicket of suffering, enduring interior and exterior labors, and unless it first receives from God very many blessings in the intellect and in the senses, and has undergone long spiritual training.

All these are lesser things, disposing the soul for the lofty sanctuary of the knowledge of the mysteries of Christ: this is the highest wisdom attainable in this life.

Would that men might come at last to see that it is quite impossible to reach the thicket of the riches and wisdom of God except by first entering the thicket of much suffering, in such a way that the soul finds there its consolation and desire. The soul that longs for divine wisdom chooses first, and in truth, to enter the thicket of the cross.

Saint Paul therefore urges the Ephesians *not to grow weary in the midst of tribulations,* but to be *rooted and grounded in love, so that they may know with all the saints the breadth, the length, the height and the depth—to know what is beyond knowledge, the love of Christ, so as to be filled with all the fullness of God.*

The gate that gives entry into these riches of his wisdom is the cross; because it is a narrow gate, while many seek the joys that can be gained through it, it is given to few to desire to pass through it.

RESPONSORY   1 Corinthians 2:9-10

No eye can see, no ear can hear, no heart can imagine
—the marvels that God has prepared for those who love him.

Yet God has revealed them to us through his Spirit.
—The marvels that . . .

Prayer

Father,
you endowed John of the Cross with a spirit of self-denial
and a love of the cross.
By following his example,
may we come to the eternal vision of your glory.
We ask this through our Lord Jesus Christ, your Son,
who lives and reigns with you and the Holy Spirit,
one God, for ever and ever.

December 21

PETER CANISIUS, PRIEST AND DOCTOR

Commemoration

Peter Canisius was born in Nijmegen, Holland, in 1521. He studied at Cologne, entered the Society of Jesus, and was ordained a priest in 1546. Sent to Germany, he worked strenuously for many years by his writings and teachings to safeguard and confirm the Catholic faith. Of his numerous books, the *Catechism* is most renowned. Saint Peter died at Fribourg, Switzerland in 1597.

Office of Readings

READING

From the writings by Saint Peter Canisius, priest

(Edit. O. Brunsberger, Petri Canisii Epistulae et Acta, I, Friburgi Brisgoviae, 1896, pp. 53–55)

A spiritual experience

Before he set out for Germany—he is rightly called the second apostle of that country—Saint Peter Canisius received the apostolic blessing, and underwent a profound spiritual experience. He describes it in these words.

"Eternal High Priest, you allowed me in your boundless goodness to commend the fruit and confirmation of that blessing to your apostles, to whom men go on pilgrimage to the Vatican and who there work wonders under your guidance. It was there that I experienced great consolation and the presence of your grace, offered to me through these great intercessors. They too gave their blessings, and confirmed the mission to Germany; they seemed to promise their good will to me as an apostle of that country. You know, Lord, how strongly and how often you committed Germany to my care on that very day: I was to continue to be solicitous for it thereafter, I was to desire to live and die for it.

"At length, it was as if you opened to me the heart in your most sacred body: I seemed to see it directly before my eyes. You told me to drink from this fountain, inviting me, that is, to draw the waters of my salvation from your wellsprings, my Savior. I was most eager that streams of faith, hope and love should flow into me from that source. I was thirsting for poverty, chastity, obedience. I asked to be made wholly clean by you, to be clothed by you, to be made resplendent by you.

"So, after daring to approach your most loving heart and to plunge my thirst in it, I received a promise from you of a garment made of three parts: these were to cover my soul in its nakedness, and to belong especially to my religious profession. They were peace, love and perseverance. Protected by this garment of salvation, I was confident that I would lack nothing but all would succeed and give you glory."

RESPONSORY   Matthew 13:52; see Proverbs 14:33

When a teacher of the law becomes a disciple of the
     kingdom of heaven,
—he is like the head of a household
who is able to take from his storeroom treasures new and
     old.
Wisdom makes its home in a discerning heart,
and it can even teach those who are foolish.
—He is like . . .

Morning Prayer

CANTICLE OF ZECHARIAH

Ant.   Those who are learned will be as radiant as the sky
         in all its beauty; those who instruct the people in
         goodness will shine like the stars for all eternity.

Prayer

Lord,
you gave Saint Peter Canisius
wisdom and courage to defend the Catholic faith.
By the help of his prayers
may all who seek the truth rejoice in finding you

and may all who believe in you
be loyal in professing their faith.
Grant this through our Lord Jesus Christ, your Son,
who lives and reigns with you and the Holy Spirit,
one God, for ever and ever.

Evening Prayer

CANTICLE OF MARY

Ant.   O blessed doctor, Saint Peter, light of holy
        Church and lover of God's law, pray to the Son of
        God for us.

December 23
JOHN OF KANTY, PRIEST

Commemoration

John was born at Kanty in the diocese of Cracow in 1390.
After his ordination to the priesthood, he taught for many years
at the academy in Krakow and then became pastor of the parish
at Olkusz. He distinguished himself as an orthodox teacher of
the faith, and by his piety and love of neighbor gave Christian
example to his colleagues and students. He died in 1473.

Office of Readings

READING

From a letter by Pope Clement XIII

(2 Febr. 1767: Bullarii romani continuatio, IV, pars II, Pratis 1843, pp.
1314–1316)

In heart and speech he was attuned to God

Saint John of Kanty deserves a high place among the
great saints and scholars who practice what they preach
and defend the true faith against those who attack it.
When heresy and schism were gaining ground in
neighboring territories, his teaching at the University of

Krakow was untainted by any error. At the pulpit he fought to raise the standard of holiness among the faithful, and his preaching was reinforced by his humility, his chastity, his compassion, his bodily penance and the other qualities of a dedicated priest and apostle.

He was a unique contribution to the reputation and credit of the professors of the university; he also bequeathed a wonderful example to those of his profession, an inspiration of complete dedication to duty and to their teaching—in theology and other sciences—for the honor and glory of the one God.

With the sense of worship that he brought to his teaching of the sacred sciences he combined humility. He never put himself above another, but treated himself as of no account, even though he was acknowledged by all as their master. So far was he from pretenses that he even wished to be an object of contempt in the eyes of all who underestimated his worth. He could take their insults and cutting remarks in stride.

With his humility went a rare and childlike simplicity: the thoughts of his heart were revealed in his words and actions. If he suspected that someone had taken offense at speaking the truth, before going to the altar he would ask forgiveness for what was not so much his own sin as the other person's misunderstanding. Every day after his round of duties he would go straight from the lecture room to church. There he would spend long hours in contemplation and prayer before the hidden Christ of the eucharist. The God in his heart and the God on his lips were one and the same God.

RESPONSORY   Isaiah 58:7-8

Share your bread with the hungry,
and take the poor and homeless into your own house.

—Then your light will break forth like the dawn,
and your holiness will go before you.

When you see a man who is naked, clothe him,
and do not scorn your brother.
—Then your light . . .

Prayer, as in Morning Prayer.

Morning Prayer

CANTICLE OF ZECHARIAH

Ant.   All the world will recognize you as my disciples
when they see the love you have one for another.

Prayer

Almighty Father,
through the example of John of Kanty
may we grow in the wisdom of the saints.
As we show understanding and kindness to others,
may we receive your forgiveness.

We ask this through our Lord Jesus Christ, your Son,
who lives and reigns with you and the Holy Spirit,
one God, for ever and ever.

Evening Prayer

CANTICLE OF MARY

Ant.   I tell you most solemnly, what you did for the
least of men you did for me. Come, my Father
delights in you; receive the kingdom prepared for
you from the foundation of the world.

December 26
STEPHEN, FIRST MARTYR
Feast

Invitatory

Ant.   Come, let us worship the newborn Christ who
        has given the glorious crown to Saint Stephen.

Invitatory psalm as in the Ordinary, 648.

Office of Readings

HYMN as in the common of one martyr, 1401.

Ant. 1   Stephen, filled with the Holy Spirit, looked to
          heaven and saw the glory of God, and Jesus
          standing at the right hand of the Father.

Psalms from the common of one martyr, 1402.

Ant. 2   Stephen fell to his knees and cried out in a loud
          voice: Lord Jesus, do not hold this sin against
          them.

Ant. 3   No one was able to resist the wisdom of blessed
          Stephen, for the Holy Spirit spoke through
          him.

Affliction and distress surround me.
—Yet your law is my delight.

FIRST READING

From the Acts of the Apostles   6:8—7, 2a, 44-59

The martyrdom of Stephen

Stephen was a man filled with grace and power, who
worked great wonders and signs among the people.
Certain members of the so-called "Synagogue of Roman

Freedmen" (that is, the Jews from Cyrene, Alexandria, Cilicia and Asia) would undertake to engage Stephen in debate, but they proved no match for the wisdom and spirit with which he spoke.

They persuaded some men to make the charge that they had heard him speaking blasphemies against Moses and God, and in this way they incited the people, the elders, and the scribes. All together they confronted him, seized him, and led him off to the Sanhedrin. There they brought in false witnesses, who said: "This man never stops making statements against the holy place and the law. We have heard him claim that Jesus the Nazorean will destroy this place and change the customs which Moses handed down to us." The members of the Sanhedrin who sat there stared at him intently. Throughout, Stephen's face seemed like that of an angel.

The high priest asked whether the charges were true. To this Stephen replied: "My brothers! Fathers! Listen to me. Our fathers in the desert had the meeting tent as God prescribed it when he spoke to Moses, ordering him to make it according to the pattern he had seen. The next generation of our fathers inherited it. Under Joshua, they brought it into the land during the conquest of those peoples whom God drove out to make room for our fathers. So it was until the time of David, who found favor with God and begged that he might find a dwelling place for the house of Jacob. It was Solomon, however, who constructed the building for that house. Yet the Most High does not dwell in buildings made by human hands, for as the prophet says:

'The heavens are my throne,
    the earth is my footstool;
What kind of house can you build me?
    asks the Lord.

What is my resting-place to be like?
   Did not my hand make all these things?'

"You stiff-necked people, uncircumcised in heart and ears, you are always opposing the Holy Spirit just as your fathers did before you. Was there ever any prophet whom your fathers did not persecute? In their day, they put to death those who foretold the coming of the Just One; now you in your turn have become his betrayers and murderers. You who received the law through the ministry of angels have not observed it."

Those who listened to his words were stung to the heart; they ground their teeth in anger at him. Stephen meanwhile, filled with the Holy Spirit, looked to the sky above and saw the glory of God, and Jesus standing at God's right hand. "Look!" he exclaimed, "I see an opening in the sky, and the Son of Man standing at God's right hand." The onlookers were shouting aloud, holding their hands over their ears as they did so. Then they rushed at him as one man, dragged him out of the city, and began to stone him. The witnesses meanwhile were piling their cloaks at the feet of a young man named Saul.

As Stephen was being stoned he could be heard praying, "Lord Jesus, receive my spirit." He fell to his knees and cried out in a loud voice, "Lord, do not hold this sin against them." And with that he died. Saul, for his part, concurred in the act of killing.

RESPONSORY

While the Jews were stoning Stephen, God's servant,
the heavens opened before him;
he saw, he entered in.

—Happy the man to whom the heavens opened.

As the stones crashed upon him,
from the depths of heaven the living splendor shone on
  him.
—Happy the man to whom the heavens opened.

SECOND READING

From a sermon by Saint Fulgentius of Ruspe, bishop
(Sermo 3, 1–3. 5–6: CCL 91A, 905–909)

The armament of love

Yesterday we celebrated the birth in time of our
eternal King. Today we celebrate the triumphant
suffering of his soldier. Yesterday our king, clothed in his
robe of flesh, left his place in the virgin's womb and
graciously visited the world. Today his soldier leaves the
tabernacle of his body and goes triumphantly to heaven.

Our king, despite his exalted majesty, came in
humility for our sake; yet he did not come empty-hand-
ed. He brought his soldiers a great gift that not only
enriched them but also made them unconquerable in
battle, for it was the gift of love, which was to bring men
to share in his divinity. He gave of his bounty, yet
without any loss to himself. In a marvelous way he
changed into wealth the poverty of his faithful followers
while remaining in full possession of his own inexhaustible riches.

And so the love that brought Christ from heaven to
earth raised Stephen from earth to heaven; shown first in
the king, it later shone forth in his soldier. Love was
Stephen's weapon by which he gained every battle, and
so won the crown signified by his name. His love of God
kept him from yielding to the ferocious mob; his love for
his neighbor made him pray for those who were stoning

him. Love inspired him to reprove those who erred, to make them amend; love led him to pray for those who stoned him, to save them from punishment. Strengthened by the power of his love, he overcame the raging cruelty of Saul and won his persecutor on earth as his companion in heaven. In his holy and tireless love he longed to gain by prayer those whom he could not convert by admonition.

Now at last, Paul rejoices with Stephen, with Stephen he delights in the glory of Christ, with Stephen he exults, with Stephen he reigns. Stephen went first, slain by the stones thrown by Paul, but Paul followed after, helped by the prayer of Stephen. This, surely, is the true life, my brothers, a life in which Paul feels no shame because of Stephen's death, and Stephen delights in Paul's companionship, for love fills them both with joy. It was Stephen's love that prevailed over the cruelty of the mob, and it was Paul's love that covered the multitude of his sins; it was love that won for both of them the kingdom of heaven.

Love, indeed, is the source of all good things; it is an impregnable defense, and the way that leads to heaven. He who walks in love can neither go astray nor be afraid: love guides him, protects him, and brings him to his journey's end.

My brothers, Christ made love the stairway that would enable all Christians to climb to heaven. Hold fast to it, therefore, in all sincerity, give one another practical proof of it, and by your progress in it, make your ascent together.

RESPONSORY

Yesterday the Lord was born on earth that Stephen might be born in heaven;

—the Lord entered into our world that Stephen might enter into heaven.

Yesterday our King, clothed in our flesh,
came forth from the virgin's womb to dwell among us.
—The Lord entered . . .

HYMN, Te Deum, 651.

Prayer, as in Morning Prayer.

Morning Prayer

HYMN as in the common of one martyr, 1409.

Ant. 1   My soul has held fast to you, my God; for your sake I suffered death by stoning.

Psalms and canticle from Sunday, Week I, 688.

Ant. 2   Stephen saw the heavens open; he saw and entered in. Happy the man to whom the heavens opened.

Ant. 3   Behold I see the heavens open, and Jesus standing at the right hand of the almighty God.

READING   Acts 6:2b-5a

"It is not right for us to neglect the word of God in order to wait on tables. Look around your own number, brothers, for seven men acknowledged to be deeply spiritual and prudent, and we shall appoint them to this task. This will permit us to concentrate on prayer and the ministry of the word." The proposal was unanimously accepted by the community.

RESPONSORY

The Lord is my strength, and I shall sing his praise.
—The Lord is my strength, and I shall sing his praise.

The Lord is my savior,
—and I shall sing his praise.

Glory to the Father . . .
—The Lord is . . .

CANTICLE OF ZECHARIAH

Ant.   The gates of heaven opened out to blessed
        Stephen, and he was crowned first of martyrs.

INTERCESSIONS

Our Savior's faithfulness is mirrored in the fidelity of his
    witnesses who shed their blood for the word of God.
    Let us praise him in remembrance of them:
    You redeemed us by your blood.
Your martyrs freely embraced death in bearing witness to
    the faith,
—give us the true freedom of the Spirit, O Lord.
Your martyrs professed their faith by shedding their
    blood,
—give us a faith, O Lord, that is constant and pure.
Your martyrs followed in your footsteps by carrying the
    cross,
—help us to endure courageously the misfortunes of life.
Your martyrs washed their garments in the blood of the
    Lamb,
—help us to avoid the weaknesses of the flesh and
    worldly allurements.

Our Father . . .

Prayer

Lord,
today we celebrate the entrance of Saint Stephen
into eternal glory.
He died praying for those who killed him.

Help us to imitate his goodness
and to love our enemies.

We ask this through our Lord Jesus Christ, your Son,
who lives and reigns with you and the Holy Spirit,
one God, for ever and ever.

Daytime Prayer

Psalms and antiphon from the current weekday.

Midmorning

Ant.   Mary, the mother of Jesus, and Joseph were filled
        with wonder at all that was said of the child.

READING   1 Peter 5:10–11

The God of all grace, who called us to his everlasting
glory in Christ, will himself restore, confirm, strengthen,
and establish those who have suffered a little while.
Dominion be his throughout the ages! Amen.

God clothed him in gladness.
—And placed a crown of glory on his head.

Midday

Ant.   Mary treasured all these words and pondered
        them in her heart.

READING   James 1:12

Happy the man who holds out to the end through trial!
Once he has been proved, he will receive the crown of life
the Lord has promised to those who love him.

I have put my hope in God.
—I have no fear of man.

Midafternoon

Ant. My own eyes have seen the salvation which you
have prepared in the sight of every people.

READING   Wisdom 3:1-2a, 3b

The souls of the just are in the hand of God,
  and no torment shall touch them.
They seemed, in the view of the foolish, to be dead.
But they are in peace.

They come, see they come singing for joy.
—Homeward bound, laden with sheaves.

Prayer, as in Morning Prayer.

Evening Prayer

Everything is taken from the octave of Christmas as on December 26, 436.

If the feast of Saint Stephen is observed as a solemnity: the hymn, antiphons, reading and responsory are taken from Morning Prayer, 1258; psalms, canticle and intercessions from the common of martyrs, 1416.

December 27
JOHN, APOSTLE AND EVANGELIST

Feast

Invitatory

Ant. Come, let us worship the Lord, the King of
apostles.

Invitatory psalm, as in the Ordinary, 648.

Office of Readings

HYMN as in the common of apostles, 1354.

PSALMODY

Ant. 1 **John gave testimony to the Word of God; he gave witness to Jesus Christ whom he had seen.**

Psalm 19A

The heavens proclaim the glory of God
and the firmament shows forth the work of his
    hands.
Day unto day takes up the story
and night unto night makes known the message.

No speech, no word, no voice is heard
yet their span extends through all the earth,
their words to the utmost bounds of the world.

There he has placed a tent for the sun;
it comes forth like a bridegroom coming from his
    tent,
rejoices like a champion to run its course.

At the end of the sky is the rising of the sun;
to the furthest end of the sky is its course.
There is nothing concealed from its burning heat.

Ant. John gave testimony to the Word of God; he gave witness to Jesus Christ whom he had seen.

Ant. 2 This is the disciple whom Jesus loved.

Psalm 64

Hear my voice, O God, as I complain,
guard my life from dread of the foe.
Hide me from the band of the wicked,
from the throng of those who do evil.

They sharpen their tongues like swords;
they aim bitter words like arrows
to shoot at the innocent from ambush,
shooting suddenly and recklessly.

They scheme their evil course;
they conspire to lay secret snares.
They say: "Who will see us?
Who can search out our crimes?"

He will search who searches the mind
and knows the depths of the heart.
God has shot them with his arrow
and dealt them sudden wounds.
Their own tongue has brought them to ruin
and all who see them mock.

Then all men will fear;
they will tell what God has done.
They will understand God's deeds.
The just will rejoice in the Lord
and fly to him for refuge.
All the upright hearts will glory.

Ant.   This is the disciple whom Jesus loved.

Ant. 3   At the last supper John reclined close to the
Lord; blessed that apostle to whom the
mysteries of heaven were revealed.

Psalm 99

The Lord is king; the peoples tremble.
He is throned on the cherubim; the earth quakes.
The Lord is great in Zion.

He is supreme over all the peoples.
Let them praise his name, so terrible and great.
He is holy, full of power.

You are a king who loves what is right;
you have established equity, justice and right;
you have established them in Jacob.

Exalt the Lord our God;
bow down before Zion, his footstool.
He the Lord is holy.

Among his priests were Aaron and Moses,
among those who invoked his name was Samuel.
They invoked the Lord and he answered.

To them he spoke in the pillar of cloud.
They did his will; they kept the law,
which he, the Lord, had given.

O Lord our God, you answered them.
For them you were a God who forgives;
yet you punished all their offenses.

Exalt the Lord our God;
bow down before his holy mountain
for the Lord our God is holy.

Ant. At the last supper John reclined close to the Lord;
blessed that apostle to whom the mysteries of
heaven were revealed.

They proclaimed the Lord's praises, told of his power to
save.
—And of the wonders he had worked.

FIRST READING

From the first letter of the apostle John   1:1–2:3

Word of life and light of God

This is what we proclaim to you:
what was from the beginning,
what we have heard,
what we have seen with our eyes,
what we have looked upon
and our hands have touched—
we speak of the word of life.

(This life became visible;
we have seen and bear witness to it,
and we proclaim to you the eternal life
that was present to the Father
and became visible to us.)
What we have seen and heard
we proclaim in turn to you
so that you may share life with us.
This fellowship of ours is with the Father
and with his Son, Jesus Christ.
Indeed, our purpose in writing you this
is that our joy may be complete.

Here, then, is the message
we have heard from him
and announce to you:
that God is light;
in him there is no darkness.
If we say, "We have fellowship with him,"
while continuing to walk in darkness,
we are liars and do not act in truth.
But if we walk in light,
as he is in the light, ·
we have fellowship with one another,
and the blood of his Son Jesus cleanses us from all sin.

If we say, "We are free of the guilt of sin,"
we deceive ourselves; the truth is not to be found in us.
But if we acknowledge our sins,
he who is just can be trusted
to forgive our sins
and cleanse us from every wrong.
If we say, "We have never sinned,"
we make him a liar
and his word finds no place in us.

My little ones,
I am writing this to keep you from sin.
But if anyone should sin,
we have, in the presence of the Father,
Jesus Christ, an intercessor who is just.
He is an offering for our sins,
and not for our sins only,
but for those of the whole world.

The way we can be sure of our knowledge of him
is to keep his commandments.

RESPONSORY   1 John 1:2, 4; John 20:31

We proclaim to you the eternal life
which was with the Father and has been revealed to us.
We write of this that you may rejoice,
—and that your joy may be full.

These things have been written,
that you may believe that Jesus is the Christ, the Son of
    God,
and believing you may have life in his name.
—And that your . . .

SECOND READING

From the tractates on the first letter of John by Saint Augustine, bishop

(Tract 1, 1.3: PL 35, 1978. 1980)

Life itself was revealed in the flesh

Our message is the Word of life. We announce what existed from the beginning, what we have heard, what we have seen with our own eyes, what we have touched with our own hands. Who could touch the Word with his hands unless *the Word was made flesh and lived among us?*

Now this Word, whose flesh was so real tht he could be touched by human hands, began to be flesh in the Virgin Mary's womb; but he did not begin to exist at that moment. We know this from what John says: *What existed from the beginning.* Notice how John's letter bears witness to his Gospel, which you just heard a moment ago: *In the beginning was the Word, and the Word was with God.*

Someone might interpret the phrase *the Word of life* to mean a word about Christ, rather than Christ's body itself which was touched by human hands. But consider what comes next: *and life itself was revealed.* Christ therefore is himself the Word of life.

And how was this life revealed? It existed from the beginning, but was not revealed to men, only to angels, who looked upon it and feasted upon it as their own spiritual bread. But what does Scripture say? *Mankind ate the bread of angels.*

Life itself was therefore revealed in the flesh. In this way what was visible to the heart alone could become visible also to the eye, and so heal men's hearts. For the Word is visible to the heart alone, while flesh is visible to bodily eyes as well. We already possessed the means to see the flesh, but we had no means of seeing the Word. The Word was made flesh so that we could see it, to heal the part of us by which we could see the Word.

John continues: *And we are witnesses and we proclaim to you that eternal life which was with the Father and has been revealed among us*—one might say more simply, "revealed *to* us."

We proclaim to you what we have heard and seen. Make sure that you grasp the meaning of these words. The disciples saw our Lord in the flesh, face to face; they heard the words he spoke, and in turn they proclaimed the message to us. So we also have heard, although we have not seen.

Are we then less favored than those who both saw and heard? If that were so, why should John add: *so that you too may have fellowship with us?* They saw, and we have not seen; yet we have fellowship with them, because we and they share the same faith.

And our fellowship is with God the Father and Jesus Christ his Son. And we write this to you to make your joy complete—complete in that fellowship, in that love and in that unity.

RESPONSORY

At the last supper John reclined close to the Lord;
—blessed that apostle to whom the mysteries of heaven
　　were revealed.

He drank from the streams of living water
which flowed from the heart of the Lord.
—Blessed that apostle . . .

HYMN, Te Deum, 651.

Prayer, as in Morning Prayer.

Morning Prayer

HYMN, as in the common of apostles, 1361.

Ant. 1　John, the apostle and evangelist, a virgin
　　　　chosen by the Lord, was loved by the Lord
　　　　above the others.

Psalms and canticle from Sunday, Week I, 688.

Ant. 2　To the virgin John, Christ, dying on the cross,
　　　　entrusted his virgin mother.

Ant. 3　The disciple whom Jesus loved cried out: It is
　　　　the Lord, alleluia.

READING   Acts 4:19-20

Peter and John answered, "Judge for yourselves
whether it is right in God's sight for us to obey you rather
than God. Surely we cannot help speaking of what we
have heard and seen."

RESPONSORY

You have made them rulers over all the earth.
—You have made them rulers over all the earth.

They will always remember your name, O Lord,
—over all the earth.

Glory to the Father . . .
—You have made . . .

CANTICLE OF ZECHARIAH

Ant. The Word was made flesh and lived among us,
      and we have seen his glory.

INTERCESSIONS

My brothers, we build on the foundation of the apostles.
    Let us pray to our almighty Father for his holy people
    and say:
    Be mindful of your Church, O Lord.
Father, you wanted your Son to be seen first by the
    apostles after the resurrection from the dead,
—we ask you to make us his witnesses to the farthest
    corners of the world.
You sent your Son to preach the good news to the poor,
—help us to preach this Gospel to every creature.
You sent your Son to sow the seed of unending life,
—grant that we who work at sowing the seed may share
    the joy of the harvest.
You sent your Son to reconcile all men to you through his
    blood,

—help us all to work toward achieving this reconciliation.

Our Father . . .

Prayer

God our Father,
you have revealed the mysteries of your Word
through John the apostle.
By prayer and reflection
may we come to understand the wisdom he taught.

Grant this through our Lord Jesus Christ, your Son,
who lives and reigns with you and the Holy Spirit,
one God, for ever and ever.

Daytime Prayer

Psalms from the current weekday.

Midmorning

Ant.   Mary, the mother of Jesus, and Joseph were filled
with wonder at all that was said of the child.

READING   2 Corinthians 5:19b–20

God has entrusted the message of reconciliation to us.
This makes us ambassadors for Christ, God as it were appealing through us. We implore you, in Christ's name:
be reconciled to God!

Their voice has gone out to the limits of the earth.
—Their words to the ends of the world.

Midday

Ant.   Mary treasured all these words and pondered
them in her heart.

Through the hands of the apostles, many signs and wonders occurred among the people. And more and more believers, men and women in great numbers, were continually added to the Lord.

I have held fast to Christ's message.
—I have kept the precepts he gave me.

Midafternoon

Ant.   My own eyes have seen the salvation which you have prepared in the sight of every people.

The apostles left the Sanhedrin full of joy that they had been judged worthy of ill-treatment for the sake of the Name. Day after day, both in the temple and at home, they never stopped teaching and proclaiming the good news of Jesus the Messiah.

Rejoice and be glad, says the Lord.
—For your names are written in heaven.

Prayer, as in Morning Prayer.

Evening Prayer

Everything is taken from the octave of Christmas as on December 27, **438**.

If the feast of Saint John is observed as a solemnity, the hymn, antiphons, reading and responsory are taken from Morning Prayer, **1268**; psalms, canticle and intercessions from the common of the apostles, **1365**.

December 28
HOLY INNOCENTS, MARTYRS
Feast

Invitatory

Ant. Come, let us worship the newborn Christ who crowns with joy these children who died for him.

Invitatory psalm as in the Ordinary, 648.

Office of Readings

HYMN, as in the common of martyrs, 1375.

Ant. 1 Lord, these little ones praise you and skip with joy like lambs, for you have set them free.

Psalms from the common of martyrs, 1376.

Ant. 2 These are the first of mankind to be won for God and the Lamb; innocent, they stand before the throne of God.

Ant. 3 Joy and everlasting gladness will be their lot. They will never again know sorrow and pain.

These holy ones sang a new song before the throne of God and the Lamb.
—Earth resounds with the echo of their song.

FIRST READING

From the book of Exodus   1:8-16, 22

Slaughter of the Hebrew children in Egypt

A new king, who knew nothing of Joseph, came to power in Egypt. He said to his subjects, "Look how numerous and powerful the Israelite people are growing, more so than we ourselves! Come, let us deal shrewdly with them to stop their increase; otherwise, in time of war they too may join our enemies to fight against us, and so leave our country."

Accordingly, taskmasters were set over the Israelites to oppress them with forced labor. Thus they had to build for Pharaoh the supply cities of Pithom and Raamses. Yet the more they were oppressed, the more they multiplied and spread. The Egyptians, then, dreaded the Israelites and reduced them to cruel slavery, making life bitter for them with hard work in mortar and brick and all kinds of field work—the whole cruel fate of slaves.

The king of Egypt told the Hebrew midwives, one of whom was called Shiphrah and the other Puah, "When you act as midwives for the Hebrew women and see them giving birth, if it is a boy kill him; but if it is a girl, she may live."

Pharaoh then commanded all his subjects, "Throw into the river every boy that is born to the Hebrews, but you may let all the girls live."

RESPONSORY   Isaiah 65:19; Revelation 21:4,5

I will take delight in my people.
—Never again will weeping and crying be heard among
  them.

Death shall be no more;
grief, tears and sorrow will be forgotten,
for behold I make all things new.
—Never again will . . .

SECOND READING

From a sermon by Saint Quodvultdeus, bishop

(Sermo 2 de Symbolo: PL 40, 655)

They cannot speak, yet they bear witness to Christ

A tiny child is born, who is a great king. Wise men are led to him from afar. They come to adore one who lies in a manger and yet reigns in heaven and on earth. When they tell of one who is born a king, Herod is disturbed. To save his kingdom he resolves to kill him, though if he would have faith in the child, he himself would reign in peace in this life and for ever in the life to come.

Why are you afraid, Herod, when you hear of the birth of a king? He does not come to drive you out, but to conquer the devil. But because you do not understand this you are disturbed and in a rage, and to destroy one child whom you seek, you show your cruelty in the death of so many children.

You are not restrained by the love of weeping mothers or fathers mourning the deaths of their sons, nor by the cries and sobs of the children. You destroy those who are tiny in body because fear is destroying your heart. You imagine that if you accomplish your desire you can prolong your own life, though you are seeking to kill Life himself.

Yet your throne is threatened by the source of grace—so small, yet so great—who is lying in the manger. He is using you, all unaware of it, to work out his own purposes freeing souls from captivity to the devil. He has taken up the sons of the enemy into the ranks of God's adopted children.

The children die for Christ, though they do not know it. The parents mourn for the death of martyrs. The child makes of those as yet unable to speak fit witnesses to himself. See the kind of kingdom that is his, coming as he did in order to be this kind of king. See how the deliverer is already working deliverance, the savior already working salvation.

But you, Herod, do not know this and are disturbed and furious. While you vent your fury against the child, you are already paying him homage, and do not know it.

How great a gift of grace is here! To what merits of their own do the children owe this kind of victory? They cannot speak, yet they bear witness to Christ. They cannot use their limbs to engage in battle, yet already they bear off the palm of victory.

RESPONSORY   Revelation 5:14; 4:10; 7:11

They worshiped him who lives for ever and ever;
—they laid their crowns before the throne of the Lord
    their God

They fell on their faces before his throne,
and gave praise to him who lives for ever and ever.
—They laid their . . .

HYMN, Te Deum, 651.

Prayer, as in Morning Prayer.

Morning Prayer

HYMN as in the common of martyrs, 1383.

Ant. 1   Clothed in white robes, they will walk with me,
         says the Lord, for they are worthy.

Psalms and canticle from Sunday, Week I, 688.

Ant. 2   These children cry out their praises to the
         Lord; by their death they have proclaimed what
         they could not preach with their infant voices.

Ant. 3   From the mouths of children and babies at the
         breast you have found praise to foil your
         enemies.

Jeremiah 31:15

In Ramah is heard the sound of moaning,
   of bitter weeping!
Rachel mourns her children,
   she refuses to be consoled
   because her children are no more.

RESPONSORY

The just are the friends of God.
They live with him for ever.
— The just are the friends of God.
They live with him for ever.

God himself is their reward.
— They live with him for ever.

Glory to the Father . . .
— The just are. . .

CANTICLE OF ZECHARIAH

Ant.   At the king's command these innocent babies and
little children were put to death; they died for
Christ, and now in the glory of heaven as they
follow him, the sinless Lamb, they sing for ever:
Glory to you, O Lord.

INTERCESSIONS

We rejoice in the glory of Jesus Christ, who conquered
   the enemy not by force of arms but with a white-robed
   army of children, and we cry out:
   The white-robed army of martyrs praise you.
The Holy Innocents gave witness not by words but by
   their life's blood,
— give us strength to be your witnesses before men, both
   by words and actions.

They were not ready for battle but you made them fit to
win the palm of victory,
—now that we are prepared for victory, do not let us
despair.

You washed the robes of the Innocents in your blood;
—cleanse us from all sin.

You rewarded the child martyrs with the first share in
your kingdom,
—do not let us be cast out from the unending heavenly
banquet.

You knew persecution and exile as a child,
—protect all children whose lives are in danger from
famine, war and disasters.

Our Father . . .

Prayer

Father,
the Holy Innocents offered you praise
by the death they suffered for Christ.
May our lives bear witness
to the faith we profess with our lips.

We ask this through our Lord Jesus Christ, your Son,
who lives and reigns with you and the Holy Spirit,
one God, for ever and ever.

Daytime Prayer

Psalms from the current weekday.

Midmorning

Ant.   Mary, the mother of Jesus, and Joseph were filled
with wonder at all that was said of the child.

READING   Lamentations 1:16

At this I weep,
my eyes run with tears;

My sons were reduced to silence
　when the enemy prevailed.

God clothed them in gladness.
—And crowned them with glory.

Midday

Ant.　Mary treasured all these words and pondered
　　　them in her heart.

READING　　　　　　　　　　　　　　Lamentations 2:11

Worn out from weeping are my eyes,
　within me all is in ferment,
As child and infant faint away
　in the open spaces of the town.

The just will live for ever.
—To live in God is their reward.

Midafternoon

Ant.　My own eyes have seen the salvation which you
　　　have prepared in the sight of every people.

READING　　　　　　　　　　　　　Jeremiah 31:16, 17a

Cease your cries of mourning,
　wipe the tears from your eyes.
The sorrow you have shown
　shall have its reward.
There is hope for your future,
　says the Lord.

The saints will exult in glory.
—They will sing for joy as they bow down before the
　Lord.

Prayer, as in Morning Prayer.

Roman Pontiff. Under him the ministers of Mother
Church exercise the powers committed to them, each in
his own sphere of responsibility.

Remember then how our fathers worked out their
salvation; remember the sufferings through which the
Church has grown, and the storms the ship of Peter has
weathered because it has Christ on board. Remember
how the crown was attained by those whose sufferings
gave new radiance to their faith. The whole company of
saints bears witness to the unfailing truth that without
real effort no one wins the crown.

RESPONSORY

The Lord crowned you with holiness;
—he clothed you in glory.
God, the Holy One of Israel, dwells in you.

You have fought the good fight,
you have run the race to the finish;
now a crown of holiness awaits you.
—He clothed you . . .

HYMN, Te Deum, 651.

Prayer, as in Morning Prayer.

Morning Prayer

CANTICLE OF ZECHARIAH

Ant.   Whoever hates his life in this world keeps it safe
         for life everlasting.

Prayer

Almighty God,
you granted the martyr Thomas
the grace to give his life for the cause of justice.
By his prayers
make us willing to renounce for Christ

our life in this world
so that we may find it in heaven.
We ask this through our Lord Jesus Christ, your Son,
who lives and reigns with you and the Holy Spirit,
one God, for ever and ever.

Evening Prayer

CANTICLE OF MARY

Ant.   The saints find their home in the kingdom of
heaven; their life is eternal peace.

December 31
SYLVESTER I, POPE
Commemoration

Sylvester was ordained bishop of Rome in 314. He ruled the
Church during the reign of Constantine the Great when the
Arian heresy and the Donatist schism had provoked great
discord. He died in 335 and is buried in the cemetery of
Priscilla on the Salarian Way.

Office of Readings

READING

From the Ecclesiastical History by Eusebius of Caesarea,
bishop

(Lib 10, 1–3: PG 20, 842–847)

The peace of Constantine

Glory to God the almighty, the King of the universe,
for all his gifts, and gratitude to Jesus Christ, the Savior
and Redeemer of our souls, through whom we pray that
this peace may be preserved for us stable and unshaken
for ever: a peace that will keep us safe from troubles

outside as well as from all anxieties and disturbances of soul. When this bright and radiant day, darkened by no cloud, shone with heavenly light on the churches of Christ throughout the world, even those outside our community, though they had not the same cause for rejoicing, shared at least some of the blessings that God had bestowed on us. For us above all, who had placed our hopes in Christ, there was inexpressible joy and a heavenly happiness shone on every face. Every place that a short time before had been laid waste by the tyrants' wickedness we now saw restored to life, recovering, as it seemed, from a long and deadly disease. Churches were once again rising from the ground high into the air, far surpassing in splendor and magnificence the ones that had previously been stormed and destroyed.

Then came the spectacle that we had prayed and hoped for: dedication festivals throughout the cities, and the consecration of the newly erected houses of worship. For this there were convocations of bishops, gatherings of pilgrims from far distant lands, warm and loving contact between the different communities, as the members of Christ's body united in complete harmony. The mysterious prophecy: *There came together bone to bone and joint to joint* was thus fulfilled, as were all the other prophecies which had been unerringly proclaimed by type and symbol. All the members were filled with the grace of the one divine Spirit, all were of one mind, with the same enthusiasm for the faith, and on the lips of all there was one hymn of praise.

Yes, and our bishops performed religious rites with full ceremonial, priests officiated at the liturgy, the solemn ritual of the Church, chanting psalms, proclaiming the other parts of our God-given Scriptures, and celebrating the divine mysteries. Baptism was also administered, the sacred symbol of our Savior's passion.

Without the slightest distraction, men and women of all ages united in prayer and thanksgiving, their minds and hearts full of joy as they gave glory to God the giver of all good gifts.

RESPONSORY   Col. 3:15; Gal. 3:28; Ps. 149:1

Let the peace of Christ reign in your hearts;
as members of one body you have been called to that peace;
be thankful.
—All of you are one in Christ Jesus.

Sing to the Lord a new song,
let the assembly of the faithful sing his praise.
—All of you . . .

HYMN, Te Deum, 651.

Prayer, as in Morning Prayer.

Morning Prayer

CANTICLE OF ZECHARIAH

Ant.   What you say of me does not come from
        yourselves; it is the Spirit of my Father speaking
        in you.

Prayer

Lord,
help and sustain your people
by the prayers of Pope Sylvester.
Guide us always in this present life
and bring us to the joy that never ends.

We ask this through our Lord Jesus Christ, your Son,
who lives and reigns with you and the Holy Spirit.
one God, for ever and ever.

January 2

BASIL THE GREAT AND GREGORY NAZIANZEN, BISHOPS AND DOCTORS

Memorial

Basil was born of a Christian family at Caesarea in Cappadocia in 330. Conspicuous for his learning and virtue, for a time he led the life of a hermit but in 370 was made bishop of Caesarea. He fought against the Arians and wrote many admirable works, especially his monastic rule which many Eastern monks still follow. Saint Basil died on January 1, 379.

Gregory Nazianzen was also born in 330. Traveling as a youth in the pursuit of learning, he first joined his friend Basil as a hermit and was later ordained priest and bishop. In the year 381 he was elected bishop of Constantinople; however, because of factions dividing the Church, he returned to Nazianzen where he died on January 25, 389 or 390. He was called *theologus* because of his outstanding teaching and eloquence.

From the common of pastors: for several pastors, 1428, or from the common of doctors, 1458.

Office of Readings

SECOND READING

From a sermon by Saint Gregory Nazianzen, bishop
(Oratio 43, in laudem Basilii Magni, 15. 16–17. 19–21; PG 36, 514–423)

Two bodies, but a single spirit

Basil and I were both in Athens. We had come, like streams of a river, from the same source in our native land, had separated from each other in pursuit of learning, and were now united again as if by plan, for God so arranged it.

I was not alone at that time in my regard for my friend, the great Basil. I knew his irreproachable conduct, and the maturity and wisdom of his conversation. I sought to persuade others, to whom he was less well known, to have the same regard for him. Many fell immediately under his spell, for they had already heard of him by reputation and hearsay.

What was the outcome? Almost alone of those who had come to Athens to study he was exempted from the customary ceremonies of initiation for he was held in higher honor than his status as a first-year student seemed to warrant.

Such was the prelude to our friendship, the kindling of that flame that was to bind us together. In this way we began to feel affection for each other. When, in the course of time, we acknowledged our friendship and recognized that our ambition was a life of true wisdom, we became everything to each other: we shared the same lodging, the same table, the same desires, the same goal. Our love for each other grew daily warmer and deeper.

The same hope inspired us: the pursuit of learning. This is an ambition especially subject to envy. Yet between us there was no envy. On the contrary, we made capital out of our rivalry. Our rivalry consisted, not in seeking the first place for oneself but in yielding it to the other, for we each looked on the other's success as his own.

We seemed to be two bodies with a single spirit. Though we cannot believe those who claim that "everything is contained in everything," yet you must believe that in our case each of us was in the other and with the other.

Our single object and ambition was virtue, and a life of hope in the blessings that are to come; we wanted to withdraw from this world before we departed from it. With this end in view we ordered our lives and all our actions. We followed the guidance of God's law and spurred each other on to virtue. If it is not too boastful to say, we found in each other a standard and rule for discerning right from wrong.

Different men have different names, which they owe to their parents or to themselves, that is, to their own pursuits and achievements. But our great pursuit, the great name we wanted, was to be Christians, to be called Christians.

RESPONSORY   Daniel 2:21-22; 1 Corinthians 12:11

The Lord gives wisdom to the wise
and knowledge to those who have understanding.
—He reveals what is deep and hidden;
all light has its source in him.

One and the same Spirit is at work in all,
and he gives to each as he wills.
—He reveals what . . .

Prayer, as in Morning Prayer.

Morning Prayer

CANTICLE OF ZECHARIAH

Ant.   Those who are learned will be as radiant as the sky in all its beauty; those who instruct the people in goodness will shine like the stars for all eternity.

Prayer

God our Father,
you inspired the Church
with the example and teaching of your saints Basil and
    Gregory.
In humility may we come to know your truth
and put it into action with faith and love.

Grant this through our Lord Jesus Christ, your Son,
who lives and reigns with you and the Holy Spirit,
one God, for ever and ever.

Evening Prayer

CANTICLE OF MARY

Ant. The man who not only teaches but does what is
right will be counted great in the kingdom of
God.

January 7

RAYMOND OF PENYAFORT, PRIEST

Raymond of Penyafort was born near Barcelona around
1175. He became a canon of the diocese of Barcelona and
afterward joined the Order of Preachers. At the command of
Pope Gregory IX, he produced a collection of canon law. He
was elected general of his order and directed it wisely. The
Summa casuum, which treats of the correct and fruitful
administration of the sacrament of penance, is the most notable
of his works. He died in 1275.

From the common of pastors, 1428.

Office of Readings

SECOND READING

From a letter by Saint Raymond, priest
(Monumenta Ord. Praed. Hist. 6, 2, Romae 1901, pp. 84–85)

May the God of love and peace set your hearts at rest

The preacher of God's truth has told us that all who
want to live righteously in Christ will suffer persecution.
If he spoke the truth and did not lie, the only exception
to this general statement is, I think, the person who

either neglects, or does not know how, *to live temperately, justly and righteously in this world.*

May you never be numbered among those whose house is peaceful, quiet and free from care; those on whom the Lord's chastisement does not descend; those who live out their days in prosperity, and in the twinkling of an eye will go down to hell.

Your purity of life, your devotion, deserve and call for a reward; because you are acceptable and pleasing to God your purity of life must be made purer still, by frequent buffetings, until you attain perfect sincerity of heart. If from time to time you feel the sword falling on you with double or treble force, this also should be seen as sheer joy and the mark of love.

The two-edged sword consists in conflict without, fears within. It falls with double or treble force within, when the cunning spirit troubles the depths of your heart with guile and enticements. You have learned enough already about these kinds of warfare, or you would not have been able to enjoy peace and interior tranquillity in all its beauty.

The sword falls with double and treble force externally when, without cause being given, there breaks out from within the Church persecution in spiritual matters, where wounds are more serious, especially when inflicted by friends.

This is that enviable and blessed cross of Christ, which Andrew, that manly saint, received with joyful heart: the cross in which alone we must make our boast, as Paul, God's chosen instrument, has told us.

Look then on Jesus, the author and preserver of faith: in complete sinlessness he suffered, and at the hands of those who were his own, and was numbered among the wicked. As you drink the cup of the Lord Jesus (how glorious it is!), give thanks to the Lord, the giver of all blessings.

May the God of love and peace set your hearts at rest and speed you on your journey; may he meanwhile shelter you from disturbance by others in the hidden recesses of his love, until he brings you at last into that place of complete plenitude where you will repose for ever in the vision of peace, in the security of trust and in the restful enjoyment of his riches.

RESPONSORY

The light of his teaching has shone on those who dwelt in
  darkness.
—By the strength of his love he has delivered the poor
  and freed captives from their chains.

He led out those who wandered in the paths of sin,
and freed the poor man from the grasp of his oppressors.
—By the strength . . .

Prayer

Lord,
you gave Saint Raymond the gift of compassion
in his ministry to sinners.
May his prayers free us from the slavery of sin
and help us to love and serve you in liberty.

We ask this through our Lord Jesus Christ, your Son,
who lives and reigns with you and the Holy Spirit,
one God, for ever and ever.

COMMONS

The antiphons for the Canticle of Mary which are given in Evening Prayer I may also be used at Evening Prayer on the memorials of saints.

COMMON OF THE DEDICATION OF A CHURCH

Evening Prayer I

HYMN, as in Evening Prayer II, 1312.

PSALMODY

Ant. The streets of Jerusalem will ring with rejoicing;
they will resound with the song of praise: Alleluia.

Psalm 147:1-11

Praise the Lord for he is good;
sing to our God for he is loving:
to him our praise is due.

The Lord builds up Jerusalem
and brings back Israel's exiles,
he heals the broken-hearted,
he binds up all their wounds.
He fixes the number of the stars;
he calls each one by its name.

Our Lord is great and almighty;
his wisdom can never be measured.
The Lord raises the lowly;
he humbles the wicked to the dust.
O sing to the Lord, giving thanks;
sing psalms to our God with the harp.

He covers the heavens with clouds;
he prepares the rain for the earth,
making mountains sprout with grass
and with plants to serve man's needs.
He provides the beasts with their food
and young ravens that call upon him.

His delight is not in horses
nor his pleasure in warriors' strength.
The Lord delights in those who revere him,
in those who wait for his love.

Ant.   The streets of Jerusalem will ring with rejoicing;
they will resound with the song of praise: Alleluia.

Ant. 2   How safe a dwelling the Lord has made you;
how blessed the children within your walls.

Psalm 147:12-20

O praise the Lord, Jerusalem!
Zion, praise your God!

He has strengthened the bars of your gates,
he has blessed the children within you.
He established peace on your borders,
he feeds you with finest wheat.

He sends out his word to the earth
and swiftly runs his command.
He showers down snow white as wool,
he scatters hoar-frost like ashes.

He hurls down hailstones like crumbs.
The waters are frozen at his touch;
he sends forth his word and it melts them:
at the breath of his mouth the waters flow.

He makes his word known to Jacob,
to Israel his laws and decrees.
He has not dealt thus with other nations;
he has not taught them his decrees.

Ant.   How safe a dwelling the Lord has made you; how
blessed the children within your walls.

Ant. 3   In the holy city, throngs of saints make jubilee;
angels pour out their songs of praise before the
throne of God, alleluia.

The following canticle is sung with the **Alleluia** when Evening Prayer is sung; when the office is recited, the **Alleluia** may be said at the beginning and end of each strophe.

Canticle   See Revelation 19:1-7
The wedding feast of the Lamb

Alleluia.
Salvation, glory, and power to our God:
(R. Alleluia.)
his judgments are honest and true.
R. Alleluia (alleluia).

Alleluia.
Sing praise to our God, all you his servants,
(R. Alleluia.)
all who worship him reverently, great and small.
R. Alleluia (alleluia).

Alleluia.
The Lord our all-powerful God is King;
(R. Alleluia.)
let us rejoice, sing praise, and give him glory.
R. Alleluia (alleluia).

Alleluia.
The wedding feast of the Lamb has begun,
(R. Alleluia.)
and his bride is prepared to welcome him.
R. Alleluia (alleluia).

Ant.   In the holy city, throngs of saints make jubilee;
angels pour out their songs of praise before the
throne of God, alleluia.

READING   Ephesians 2:19-22
You are strangers and aliens no longer. No, you are fellow citizens of the saints and members of the household
of God. You form a building which rises on the founda-

tion of the apostles and prophets, with Christ Jesus himself as the capstone. Through him the whole structure is fitted together and takes shape as a holy temple in the Lord; in him you are being built into this temple, to become a dwelling place for God in the Spirit.

RESPONSORY

Your house, O Lord, must always be a holy place.
—Your house, O Lord, must always be a holy place.

For ever and ever.
—A holy place

Glory to the Father . . .
—Your house, O Lord . . .

CANTICLE OF MARY

Ant.   All you who love Jerusalem, rejoice with her for ever.

INTERCESSIONS

Our Savior laid down his life so that all God's scattered children might be gathered together. In our need let us cry out:
    Remember your Church, Lord.
Lord Jesus, you built your house upon a rock,
—strengthen your Church with solid and lasting faith.
Lord Jesus, blood and water flowed from your side,
—give new life to your Church through the sacraments of your new and unending covenant.
Lord Jesus, you are in the midst of those who gather in your name,
—hear the prayers of your universal Church.
Lord Jesus, you prepare a dwelling place in your Father's house for all who love you,
—help your Church to grow in divine love.

Lord Jesus, you never cast out anyone who comes to you,
—open your Father's house to all those who have died.

Our Father . . .

Prayer

In the dedicated church:

Father,
each year we recall the dedication of this church to your
    service.
Let our worship always be sincere
and help us to find your saving love in this church.

Grant this through our Lord Jesus Christ, your Son,
who lives and reigns with you and the Holy Spirit,
one God, for ever and ever.

Outside the dedicated church:

God our Father,
from living stones, your chosen people,
you built an eternal temple to your glory.
Increase the spiritual gifts you have given to your Church
that your faithful people may continue to grow
into the new and eternal Jerusalem.

We ask this through our Lord Jesus Christ, your Son,
who lives and reigns with you and the Holy Spirit,
one God, for ever and ever.

Or:

Father,
you called your people to be your Church.
As we gather together in your name,
may we love, honor, and follow you
to eternal life in the kingdom you promise.

Grant this through our Lord Jesus Christ, your Son,
who lives and reigns with you and the Holy Spirit,
one God, for ever and ever.

Invitatory

Ant.   Come, let us worship Christ, the Bridegroom of his Church.

Or: Come, let us worship Christ, who has shown his love for the Church.

Invitatory psalm, as in the Ordinary, 648.

Office of Readings

HYMN

Antiphon:

I saw the new city, Jerusalem, descending from God,
   the source of all love.
Comely, clothed like a bride who waits, adorned, as
   for her spouse.

I saw the city of God, the new holy Jerusalem,
descending from God, who dwells on high.

Antiphon

She was adorned as would be a bride who was
   waiting for her spouse.
Then I heard a voice from the throne which proclaimed:

Antiphon

"Behold the dwelling of God among this people,
for among them he shall make his abode."

Antiphon

"They shall be his people. And he shall be their Lord
   and God.
He shall have mercy and wipe the tears from their
   eyes."

Antiphon

"No more sorrow or tears, no more death or pain
   shall there be:
for the old order has passed away."

Antiphon

Melody: I Saw the New Jerusalem   Music: Lucien Deiss,
                                                        C.S.Sp., 1965
                                     Text: Lucien Deiss, C.S.Sp., 1965

PSALMODY

Ant. 1   Open wide the doors and gates. Lift high the
         ancient portals.

When psalm 24 is the invitatory psalm, psalm 95, **648**, is used
as the first psalm of the Office of Readings.

Psalm 24

The Lord's is the earth and its fullness,
the world and all its peoples.
It is he who set it on the seas;
on the waters he made it firm.

Who shall climb the mountain of the Lord?
Who shall stand in his holy place?
The man with clean hands and pure heart,
who desires not worthless things,
who has not sworn so as to deceive his neighbor.

He shall receive blessings from the Lord
and reward from the God who saves him.
Such are the men who seek him,
seek the face of the God of Jacob.

O gates, lift high your heads;
grow higher, ancient doors.
Let him enter, the king of glory!

Who is the king of glory?
The Lord, the mighty, the valiant,
the Lord, the valiant in war.

O gates, lift high your heads;
grow higher, ancient doors.
Let him enter, the king of glory!

Who is he, the king of glory?
He, the Lord of armies,
he is the king of glory.

Ant.   Open wide the doors and gates. Lift high the ancient portals.

Ant. 2   How lovely is your dwelling place, O Lord of
power and might.

Psalm 84

How lovely is your dwelling place,
Lord, God of hosts.

My soul is longing and yearning,
is yearning for the courts of the Lord.
My heart and my soul ring out their joy
to God, the living God.

The sparrow herself finds a home
and the swallow a nest for her brood;
she lays her young by your altars,
Lord of hosts, my king and my God.

They are happy, who dwell in your house,
for ever singing your praise.
They are happy, whose strength is in you,
in whose hearts are the roads to Zion.

As they go through the Bitter Valley
they make it a place of springs,
the autumn rain covers it with blessings.
They walk with ever growing strength,
they will see the God of gods in Zion.

O Lord God of hosts, hear my prayer,
give ear, O God of Jacob.
Turn your eyes, O God, our shield,
look on the face of your anointed.

One day within your courts
is better than a thousand elsewhere.
The threshold of the house of God
I prefer to the dwellings of the wicked.

For the Lord God is a rampart, a shield;
he will give us his favor and glory.
The Lord will not refuse any good
to those who walk without blame.

Lord, God of hosts,
happy the man who trusts in you!

Ant.   How lovely is your dwelling place, O Lord of
power and might.

Ant. 3   Glorious things are said of you, O city of God.

Psalm 87

On the holy mountain is his city
cherished by the Lord.
The Lord prefers the gates of Zion
to all Jacob's dwellings.
Of you are told glorious things,
O city of God!

"Babylon and Egypt I will count
among those who know me;
Philistia, Tyre, Ethiopia,
these will be her children
and Zion shall be called 'Mother'
for all shall be her children."

It is he, the Lord Most High,
who gives each his place.
In his register of peoples he writes:
"These are her children,"
and while they dance they will sing:
"In you all find their home."

Ant.   Glorious things are said of you, O city of God.

I will worship at your holy temple.
—And I will extol your name, O Lord.

FIRST READING

From the book of Revelation
of the apostle John   21:9-27

Vision of the Heavenly Jerusalem

One of the seven angels who held the seven bowls filled
with the seven last plagues came and said to me, "Come,
I will show you the woman who is the bride of the
Lamb,"

He carried me away in spirit to the top of a very high
mountain and showed me the holy city Jerusalem coming
down out of heaven from God. It gleamed with the splendor of God. The city had the radiance of a precious jewel
that sparkled like a diamond. Its wall, massive and high,
had twelve gates at which twelve angels were stationed.
Twelve names were written on the gates, the names of
the twelve tribes of Israel. There were three gates facing
east, three north, three south, and three west. The wall
of the city had twelve courses of stones as its foundation,
on which were written the names of the twelve apostles of
the Lamb.

The one who spoke to me held a rod of gold for mea-
suring the city, its gates, and its wall. The city is perfectly square, its length and its width being the same. He

measured the city with the rod and found it twelve thousand furlongs in length, in width, and in height.

Its wall measured a hundred and forty-four cubits in height by the unit of measurement the angel used. The wall was constructed of jasper; the city was of pure gold, crystal-clear.

The foundation of the city wall was ornate with precious stones of every sort: the first course of stones was jasper, the second sapphire, the third chalcedony, the fourth emerald, the fifth sardonyx, the sixth carnelian, the seventh chrysolite, the eighth beryl, the ninth topaz, the tenth chrysoprase, the eleventh hyacinth, and the twelfth amethyst.

The twelve gates were twelve pearls, each made of a single pearl; and the streets of the city were of pure gold, transparent as glass.

I saw no temple in the city. The Lord, God the Almighty, is its temple—he and the Lamb. The city had no need of sun or moon, for the glory of God gave it light, and its lamp was the Lamb. The nations shall walk by its light; to it the kings of the earth shall bring their treasures. During the day its gates shall never be shut, and there shall be no night.

The treasures and wealth of the nations shall be brought there, but nothing profane shall enter it, nor anyone who is a liar or has done a detestable act. Only those shall enter whose names are inscribed in the book of the living kept by the Lamb.

RESPONSORY   See Revelation 21:21; Tobit 13:21, 22, 13

Your streets of gold, Jerusalem, will ring with happy song,
—throughout your length and breadth one great cry from the lips of all:
Alleluia.

You will shine in splendor like the sun; all men on earth
  will pay you homage.
—Throughout your length and breadth one great cry
  from the lips of all:
Alleluia.

SECOND READING

From a homily on Joshua, son of Nun, by Origen, priest
(Homilia 9, 1–2; SC 71, 244–246)

*As living stones we are built into the house and the altar of
                    God*

All of us who believe in Christ Jesus are said to be living stones, according to the words of Scripture: *But you
are living stones, built as a spiritual house in a holy priesthood, that you may offer spiritual sacrifices acceptable to God
through Jesus Christ.*

When we look at an earthly building, we can see that
the larger and stronger stones are the first to be set in
place as the foundation, so that the weight of the whole
structure may rest on them securely. In the same way understand that some of the living stones become the foundation of the spiritual building. What are these living
stones placed in the foundation? They are the apostles
and prophets. That is what Paul says when he teaches:
*We have been built upon the foundation of the apostles and
prophets, with our Lord Jesus Christ himself as the
cornerstone.*

You, my hearers, must learn that Christ himself is also
the foundation of the building we are now describing, so
that you may prepare yourselves more eagerly for the
construction of this building and become stones that lie
closer to the foundation. As the apostle Paul says: *No
foundation can be laid other than the one that has been laid
already; I mean Christ Jesus.* Blessed are those, therefore,

who build a religious and holy structure upon such a noble foundation.

In this building of the Church, there must also be an altar. I think that if those of you, disposed and eager for prayer, offer petitions and prayers of supplication to God day and night, you will become the living stones for the altar which Jesus is building.

Consider what praise is ascribed to these stones which make up the altar. *The lawgiver Moses said that the altar was to be made of stones, uncovered by iron.* What are those stones? Perhaps those uncut and undefiled stones are the holy apostles, all making a single altar, because of their unity of mind and heart. For it was known that with one accord they all opened their lips to pray: *You, Lord, know the hearts of all.*

Therefore, these who were able to pray with one mind, one voice and one spirit, are perhaps worthy to form together one altar, where Jesus may offer his sacrifice to the Father.

Let us strive to agree among ourselves and to have one mind and voice. May we never quarrel or act from vainglory. But may we remain united in belief and purpose. Then even we may hope to become stones fit for the altar.

RESPONSORY   See Isaiah 2:2,3; Psalm 126:6

The Lord's house is built on the mountain summit;
it is high above the hills.
—From the ends of the earth men come running to it,
    crying out;
Glory to you, Lord.

They come, see, they come,
laughing for joy, laden with sheaves.
—From the ends of the earth . . .

Alternative:

From a sermon by Saint Augustine, bishop
(Sermo 336, 1. 6: PL 38 [edit. 1861], 1471. 1475)

The building and dedication of God's house within us

We are gathered together to celebrate the dedication of a house of prayer. This is our house of prayer, but we too are a house of God. If we are a house of God, its construction goes on in time so that it may be dedicated at the end of time. The house, in its construction, involves hard work, while its dedication is an occasion for rejoicing.

What was done when this church was being built is similar to what is done when believers are built up into Christ. When they first come to believe they are like timber and stone taken from woods and mountains. In their instruction, baptism and formation they are, so to speak, shaped, leveled and smoothed by the hands of carpenters and craftsmen.

But Christians do not make a house of God until they are one in charity. The timber and stone must fit together in an orderly plan, must be joined in perfect harmony, must give each other the support as it were of love, or no one would enter the building. When you see the stones and beams of a building holding together securely, you enter the building with an easy mind; you are not afraid of its falling down in ruins.

Christ the Lord wants to come in to us and dwell in us. Like a good builder he says: *A new commandment I give you: love one another.* He says: *I give you a commandment.* He means: Before, you were not engaged in building a house for me, but you lay in ruins. Therefore, to be raised up from your former state of ruin you must love one another.

Dear brethren, remember that this house is still in process of being built in the whole world: this is the promise of prohpecy. When God's house was being built after the Exile, it was prophesied, in the words of a psalm: *Sing a new song to the Lord; sing to the Lord, all the earth.* For *a new song* our Lord speaks of *a new commandment.* A new song implies a new inspiration of love. To sing is a sign of love. The singer of this new song is full of the warmth of God's love.

The work we see complete in this building is physical; it should find its spiritual counterpart in your hearts. We see here the finished product of stone and wood; so too your lives should reveal the handiwork of God's grace.

Let us then offer our thanksgiving above all to the Lord our God, from whom every best and perfect gift comes. Let us praise his goodness with our whole hearts. He it was who inspired in his faithful people the will to build this house of prayer; he stirred up their desire and gave them his help. He awakened enthusiasm among those who were at first unconvinced, and guided to a successful conclusion the efforts of men of good will. So God, *who gives to those of good will both the desire and the accomplishment* of the things that belong to him, is the one who began this work, the one who has brought it to completion.

RESPONSORY   Psalm 84:2-3, 5

How I long, O mighty Lord,
for the holy temple where you dwell!
—My soul yearns for the courts of the Lord.

Those who live in your house, O Lord, will praise you
  endlessly.
—My soul yearns . . .

HYMN, Te Deum, 651.

Prayer, as in Morning Prayer.

Morning Prayer

HYMN

The Church's one foundation
Is Jesus Christ her Lord;
She is his new creation
By water and the word:
From heav'n he came and sought her
To be his holy bride;
With his own blood he bought her,
And for her life he died.

Elect from ev'ry nation,
Yet one o'er all the earth,
Her charter of salvation,
One Lord, one faith, one birth;
One holy Name she blesses,
Partakes one holy food,
And to one hope she presses,
With ev'ry grace endued.

Though with a scornful wonder
Men see her sore opprest,
By schisms rent asunder,
By heresies distrest;
Yet saints their watch are keeping,
Their cry goes up, "How long?"
And soon the night of weeping
Shall be the morn of song. Amen.

Melody: Aurelia 76.76 D   Music: Samuel Sebastian Wesley, 1864
Text: Samuel John Stone, 1866

Ant. 1   My house will be called a house of prayer.

Psalms and canticle from Sunday, Week I, 688.

Ant. 2   Blessed are you, O Lord, in your holy temple.

Ant. 3   Praise the Lord in the assembly of his holy people.

READING Isaiah 56:7

Them I will bring to my holy mountain
   and make joyful in my house of prayer;
Their holocausts and sacrifices
   will be acceptable on my altar,
For my house shall be called
   a house of prayer for all peoples.

RESPONSORY

The Lord is great beyond all telling, he exceeds all
   praise.
— The Lord is great beyond all telling, he exceeds all
   praise.

In the city of our God and on his holy mountain.
— He exceeds all praise.

Glory to the Father . . .
— The Lord is . . .

CANTICLE OF ZECHARIAH

Ant.   Zacchaeus, hurry down, I mean to stay with you
       today. He hurried down and welcomed Christ
       with joy, for this day salvation had come to his
       house.

INTERCESSIONS

We are the living stones, laid upon the cornerstone that is
   Christ. Let us pray to our all-powerful Father for his
   Son's beloved Church, professing our faith in her as
   we say:
   This is the house of God and the gate of heaven.
Father, like the farmer, prune your vineyard, protect it
   and increase its yield,
— until it extends before you throughout the world.

Eternal shepherd, protect and increase your flock,
—that all the sheep may be gathered into one flock under
   your Son, the one shepherd.
All-powerful sower, plant the word in your field,
—that it may yield a hundredfold for your eternal harvest.
Wise builder, sanctify your home and your family,
—that the heavenly city, the new Jerusalem, your
   spouse, may appear before all as your glorious bride.

Our Father . . .

Prayer

In the dedicated church:

Father,
each year we recall the dedication of this church to your
   service.
Let our worship always be sincere
and help us to find your saving love in this church.

Grant this through our Lord Jesus Christ, your Son,
who lives and reigns with you and the Holy Spirit,
one God, for ever and ever.

Outside the dedicated church:

God our Father,
from living stones, your chosen people,
you built an eternal temple to your glory.
Increase the spiritual gifts you have given to your Church
that your faithful people may continue to grow
into the new and eternal Jerusalem.

We ask this through our Lord Jesus Christ, your Son,
who lives and reigns with you and the Holy Spirit,
one God, for ever and ever.

Or:

Father,
you called your people to be your Church.
As we gather together in your name,
may we love, honor, and follow you
to eternal life in the kingdom you promise.
Grant this through our Lord Jesus Christ, your Son,
who lives and reigns with you and the Holy Spirit,
one God, for ever and ever.

Daytime Prayer

Midmorning

For the gradual psalms, psalm 129, 1129, may be said in place
of psalm 122.

Ant. This is God's holy temple. He lavished care on it;
he built it stone by stone.

READING   1 Corinthians 3:16-17

Are you not aware that you are the temple of God, and
that the Spirit of God dwells in you? If anyone destroys
God's temple, God will destroy him. For the temple of
God is holy, and you are that temple.

Lord, I love the beauty of your house.
—The place where your glory dwells.

Midday

Ant. Your house, O Lord, must be a holy place for ever
and ever.

READING   2 Corinthians 6:16

You are the temple of the living God, just as God has
said:
"I will dwell with them and walk among them.

I will be their God
and they shall be my people."

Pray for the peace of Jerusalem.
—May those who love you prosper.

Midafternoon

Ant.   This is the house of the Lord; it is firmly built on
solid rock.

READING   Jeremiah 7:2b, 4-5a, 7a

Hear the word of the Lord, all you of Judah who enter
these gates to worship the Lord. Put not your trust in the
deceitful words: "This is the temple of the Lord! The
temple of the Lord! The temple of the Lord!" Only if
you thoroughly reform your ways and your deeds, will I
remain with you in this place.

Go within his gates giving thanks.
—Enter his courts with songs of praise.

Prayer, as in Morning Prayer.

Evening Prayer II

HYMN

Christ is made our sure foundation,
Christ is head and Cornerstone;
Chosen of the Lord and precious,
Binding all the Church in one,
Holy Zion's help for ever,
And her confidence alone.

To this temple, we implore you,
Come, great Lord of hosts, today;
Come with all your loving kindness,
Hear your servants as they pray,
And your fullest benediction
Shed in all its brightest ray.

Grant, we pray, to all your people,
All the grace they ask to gain;
What they gain from you for ever
With the blessed to retain,
And hereafter in your glory
Evermore with you to reign.

Praise and honor to the Father,
Praise and honor to the Son,
Praise and honor to the Spirit,
Ever Three and ever One:
Unified in power and glory,
While unending ages run.

Melody: Belville (Westminster Abbey) 87.87.87
Music: Adapted by Ernest Hawkins 1802–1868
from an anthem by Henry Purcell, 1659–1695
Text: *Urbs beata Jerusalem.* ca. 7th century
Translator: John mason Neale, 1816–1866
alt. by Anthony G. Petti

PSALMODY

Ant. 1 This is God's dwelling place and he has made it
holy; it will stand for ever firm.

Psalm 46

God is for us a refuge and strength,
a helper close at hand, in time of distress:
so we shall not fear though the earth should rock,
though the mountains fall into the depths of the sea,
even though its waters rage and foam,
even though the mountains be shaken by its waves.

The Lord of hosts is with us:
the God of Jacob is our stronghold.

The waters of a river give joy to God's city,
the holy place where the Most High dwells.
God is within, it cannot be shaken;
God will help it at the dawning of the day.

Nations are in tumult, kingdoms are shaken:
he lifts his voice, the earth shrinks away.

The Lord of hosts is with us:
the God of Jacob is our stronghold.

Come, consider the works of the Lord,
the redoubtable deeds he has done on the earth.
He puts an end to wars over all the earth;
the bow he breaks, the spear he snaps.
He burns the shields with fire.
"Be still and know that I am God,
supreme among the nations, supreme on the earth!"

The Lord of hosts is with us:
the God of Jacob is our stronghold.

Ant.   This is God's dwelling place and he has made it
holy; it will stand for ever firm.

Ant. 2   Let us go up with rejoicing to the house of the
Lord.

Psalm 122

I rejoiced when I heard them say:
"Let us go to God's house."
And now our feet are standing
within your gates, O Jerusalem.

Jerusalem is built as a city
strongly compact.
It is there that the tribes go up,
the tribes of the Lord.

For Israel's law it is,
there to praise the Lord's name.
There were set the thrones of judgment
of the house of David.

For the peace of Jerusalem pray:
"Peace be to your homes!
May peace reign in your walls,
in your palaces, peace!"

For love of my brethren and friends
I say: "Peace upon you!"
For love of the house of the Lord
I will ask for your good.

Ant. Let us go up with rejoicing to the house of the
      Lord.

Ant. 3 All you his saints, sing out the praises of our
       God.

The following canticle is sung with the **Alleluia** when Evening
Prayer is sung; when the office is recited, the **Alleluia** may be
said at the beginning and end of each strophe.

Canticle   See Revelation 19:1-7

The wedding feast of the Lamb

Alleluia.
Salvation, glory, and power to our God:
(R. Alleluia.)
his judgments are honest and true.
R. Alleluia (alleluia).

Alleluia.
Sing praise to our God, all you his servants,
(R. Alleluia.)
all who worship him reverently, great and small.
R. Alleluia (alleluia).

Alleluia.
The Lord our all-powerful God is King;
(R. Alleluia.)

let us rejoice, sing praise, and give him glory.
R. Alleluia (alleluia).

Alleluia.
The wedding feast of the Lamb has begun,
(R. Alleluia.)
and his bride is prepared to welcome him.
R. Alleluia (alleluia).

Ant.   All you his saints, sing out the praises of our God.

READING   Revelation 21:2-3, 22, 27

I saw a new Jerusalem, the holy city, coming down out of heaven from God, beautiful as a bride prepared to meet her husband. I heard a loud voice from the throne cry out: "This is God's dwelling among men. He shall dwell with them and they shall be his people and he shall be their God who is always with them." I saw no temple in the city. The Lord, God the Almighty, is its temple—he and the Lamb. But nothing profane shall enter it, nor anyone who is a liar or has done a detestable act. Only those shall enter whose names are inscribed in the book of the living kept by the Lamb.

RESPONSORY

Blessed are they who dwell in your house, O Lord.
—Blessed are they who dwell in your house, O Lord.

They will praise you for ever.
—In your house, O Lord.

Glory to the Father . . .
—Blessed are they . . .

CANTICLE OF MARY

Ant.   This is God's dwelling place and he has made it holy; here we call on his name, for Scripture says: There you will find me.

INTERCESSIONS

Our Savior laid down his life so that all God's scattered
   children might be gathered together. In our need we
   cry out:
   Remember your Church, Lord.
Lord Jesus, you built your house upon a rock,
—strengthen your Church with solid and lasting faith.
Lord Jesus, blood and water flowed from your side,
—give new life to your Church through the sacraments of
   your new and unending covenant.
Lord Jesus, you are in the midst of those who gather in
   your name,
—hear the prayers of your universal Church.
Lord Jesus, you prepare a dwelling place in your Father's
   house for all who love you,
—help your Church to grow in divine love.
Lord Jesus, you never cast out anyone who comes to you,
—open your Father's house to all those who have died.

Our Father . . .

Prayer

Inside the dedicated church:

Father,
each year we recall the dedication of this church to your
   service.
Let our worship always be sincere
and help us to find your saving love in this church.

Grant this through our Lord Jesus Christ, your Son,
who lives and reigns with you and the Holy Spirit,
one God, for ever and ever:

Outside the dedicated church:

God our Father,
from living stones, your chosen people,

you built an eternal temple to your glory.
Increase the spiritual gifts you have given to your Church
that your faithful people may continue to grow
into the new and eternal Jerusalem.

We ask this through our Lord Jesus Christ, your Son,
who lives and reigns with you and the Holy Spirit,
one God, for ever and ever.

Or:

Father,
you called your people to be your Church.
As we gather together in your name,
may we love, honor, and follow you
to eternal life in the kingdom you promise.

Grant this through our Lord Jesus Christ, your Son,
who lives and reigns with you and the Holy Spirit,
one God, for ever and ever.

COMMON OF THE BLESSED VIRGIN MARY

Evening Prayer I

Hymn

Antiphon:

Joy to you, O Virgin Mary, Mother of the Lord!

Humble maiden of Nazareth town,
Betrothed to the carpenter Joseph,
You became the mother of God.

Antiphon

You are the handmaid of God;
You found favor with him;
Full of grace, the Lord is with you.

Antiphon

Lovely Mother of Abraham's Son,
Praised Mother of David's Son,
Holy Mother of Jesus, the Lord:

Antiphon

You are blessed among all women;
Blessed is the fruit of your womb;
You are praised by all generations.

Antiphon

God's Spirit came upon you,
In you the Word became flesh,
Through your grace, he dwells among us.

Antiphon

Your Son you bore in a manger,
Angels sang: "Glory to God,
On earth, peace to men of good will!"

Antiphon

Your child was sung by the angels,
Was acclaimed in joy by the shepherds;
And you marveled at your wondrous child.

Antiphon

You showed your child to the wise men,
You brought him up to the temple,
You brought joy to Simeon's old age.

Antiphon

Chosen Mother of the Messiah,
Virgin and daughter of Zion,
Joy and glory of God's holy people;

Antiphon

Suffering Mother under the cross,
Glorious Mother of the Apostles,
Queen and mother of all generations;

Antiphon

Glorious woman clothed with the sun,
With the moon under your feet,
On your head a crown of twelve stars.

Antiphon

Melody: Joy to You   Music: Lucien Deiss, C.S.Sp., 1970
                            Text: Lucien Deiss, C.S.Sp., 1970

Or:

Ave Maria, gratia plena, Dominus tecum,
benedicta tu in mulieribus,
et benedictus fructus ventris tui, Jesus.
Sancta Maria, Mater Dei,
ora pro nobis peccatoribus,
nunc et in hora mortis nostrae. Amen.

Melody: Ave Maria   Music: Traditional, Gregorian
Gregorian Mode I   Text: Traditional

PSALMODY

Ant. 1   Blessed are you, O Virgin Mary, for you carried
          the Creator of the world in your womb.

Psalm 113

Praise, O servants of the Lord,
praise the name of the Lord!
May the name of the Lord be blessed
both now and for evermore!
From the rising of the sun to its setting
praised be the name of the Lord!

High above all nations is the Lord,
above the heavens his glory.
Who is like the Lord, our God,
who has risen on high to his throne
yet stoops from the heights to look down,
to look down upon heaven and earth?

From the dust he lifts up the lowly,
from his misery he raises the poor
to set him in the company of princes,
yes, with the princes of his people.
To the childless wife he gives a home
and gladdens her heart with children.

Ant.   Blessed are you, O Virgin Mary, for you carried
          the Creator of the world in your womb.

Ant. 2   You are the mother of your Maker, yet you re-
          main a virgin for ever.

Psalm 147:12-20

O praise the Lord, Jerusalem!
Zion, praise your God!

He has strengthened the bars of your gates,
he has blessed the children within you.

He established peace on your borders,
he feeds you with finest wheat.

He sends out his word to the earth
and swiftly runs his command.
He showers down snow white as wool,
he scatters hoar-frost like ashes.

He hurls down hailstones like crumbs.
The waters are frozen at his touch;
he sends forth his word and it melts them:
at the breath of his mouth the waters flow.

He makes his word known to Jacob,
to Israel his laws and decrees.
He has not dealt thus with other nations;
he has not taught them his decrees.

Ant.   You are the mother of your Maker, yet you re-
        main a virgin for ever.

Ant. 3 We share the fruit of life through you, O daugh-
        ter blessed by the Lord.

                    Canticle   Ephesians 1:3-10

Praised be the God and Father
of our Lord Jesus Christ,
who bestowed on us in Christ
every spiritual blessing in the heavens.

God chose us in him
before the world began,
to be holy
and blameless in his sight.

He predestined us
to be his adopted sons through Jesus Christ,
such was his will and pleasure,
that all might praise the glorious favor
he has bestowed on us in his beloved.

In him and through his blood, we have been redeemed,
and our sins forgiven,
so immeasurably generous
is God's favor to us.

God has given us the wisdom
to understand fully the mystery,
the plan he was pleased
to decree in Christ.

A plan to be carried out
in Christ, in the fullness of time,
to bring all things into one in him,
in the heavens and on the earth.

Ant.   We share the fruit of life through you, O daughter
       blessed by the Lord.

READING   Galatians 4:4-5

   When the designated time had come, God sent forth
his Son born of a woman, born under the law, to deliver
from the law those who were subjected to it, so that we
might receive our status as adopted sons.

RESPONSORY

After the birth of your son, you remained a virgin.
—After the birth of your son, you remained a virgin.

Mother of God, intercede for us;
—you remained a virgin.

Glory to the Father . . .
—After the birth . . .

CANTICLE OF MARY

Ant.   The Lord has looked with favor on his lowly serv-
       ant; the Almighty has done great things for me.

Or: All generations will call me blessed: the Lord has
       looked with favor on his lowly servant.

INTERCESSIONS

Let us praise God our almighty Father, who wished that
    Mary, his Son's mother, be celebrated by each genera-
    tion. Now in need we ask:
    Mary, full of grace, intercede for us.
O God, worker of miracles, you made the Immaculate
    Virgin Mary share, body and soul, in your Son's glory
    in heaven,
—direct the hearts of your children to that same glory.
You made Mary our mother. Through her intercession
    grant strength to the weak, comfort to the sorrowing,
    pardon to sinners,
—salvation and peace to all.
You made Mary full of grace,
—grant all men the joyful abundance of your grace.
Make your Church of one mind and one heart in love,
—and help all those who believe to be one in prayer with
    Mary, the mother of Jesus.
You crowned Mary queen of heaven,
—may all the dead rejoice in your kingdom with the
    saints for ever.

Or:

Let us praise God our almighty Father, who wished that
    Mary, his Son's mother, be celebrated by each genera-
    tion. Now in need we ask:
    Mary, full of grace, intercede for us.
You made Mary the mother of mercy,
—may all who are faced with trials feel her motherly
    love.
You wished Mary to be the mother of the family in the
    home of Jesus and Joseph,

—may all mothers of families foster love and holiness
through her intercession.

You gave Mary strength at the foot of the cross and filled
her with joy at the resurrection of your Son,

—lighten the hardships of those who are burdened and
deepen their sense of hope.

You make Mary open to your word and faithful as your
servant,

—through her intercession make us servants and true followers of your Son.

You crowned Mary queen of heaven,

—may all the dead rejoice in your kingdom with the
saints for ever.

Our Father . . .

Prayer

If there is no proper prayer, one of the following is said;
Advent:

Father,
in your plan for our salvation
your Word became man,
announced by an angel and born of the Virgin Mary.
May we who believe that she is the Mother of God
receive the help of her prayers.

We ask this through our Lord Jesus Christ, your Son,
who lives and reigns with you and the Holy Spirit,
one God, for ever and ever.

Christmas Season:

Father,
you gave the human race eternal salvation
through the motherhood of the Virgin Mary.
May we experience the help of her prayers in our lives,

for through her we received the very source of life,
your Son, our Lord Jesus Christ,
who lives and reigns with you and the Holy Spirit,
one God, for ever and ever.

Invitatory

Ant.   Come, let us worship Christ, the Son of Mary.

Or: Come, let us sing to the Lord as we celebrate this
feast of the Blessed Virgin Mary.

Invitatory Psalm, as in the Ordinary, 648.

Office of Readings

HYMN

The God whom earth and sea and sky
Adore and laud and magnify,
Whose might they own, whose praise they tell,
In Mary's body deigned to dwell.

O Mother blest! the chosen shrine
Wherein the Architect divine,
Whose hand contains the earth and sky,
Vouchsafed in hidden guise to lie:

Blest in the message Gabriel brought;
Blest in the work the Spirit wrought;
Most blest, to bring to human birth
The long desired of all the earth.

O Lord, the Virgin born, to thee
Eternal praise and glory be,
Whom with the Father we adore
And Holy Ghost for ever more.

Melody: Eisenach L.M.   Music: Johann H. Schein, 1586–1630
Text: Venantius Fortunatus, 530–609
Translator: J. M. Neale, 1818–1866

Or:

Ye who own the faith of Jesus
Sing the wonders that were done,
When the love of God the Father
O'er our sin the victory won,
When he made the Virgin Mary
Mother of his only Son.
Hail, Mary, full of grace.

Blessed were the chosen people
Out of whom the Lord did come,
Blessed was the land of promise
Fashioned for his earthly home;
But more blessed far the mother
She who bore him in her womb.
Hail, Mary, full of grace.

Wherefore let all faithful people
Tell the honor of her name,
Let the Church in her foreshadowed
Part in her thanksgiving claim;
What Christ's mother sang in gladness
Let Christ's people sing the same.
Hail, Mary, full of grace.

Praise, O Mary, praise the Father,
Praise thy Savior and thy Son,
Praise the everlasting Spirit,
Who hath made thee ark and throne.
O'er all creatures high exalted,
Lowly praise the three in one.
Hail, Mary, full of grace.

Melody: Den das Vaters Sinn geboren   Music: J.A. Freylinghausen
87.87.876   1670–1739
                              Text: V.S.S. Coles, 1845–1929

PSALMODY

Ant. 1 **Mary received a blessing from the Lord and loving kindness from God her savior.**

When psalm 24 is the invitatory psalm, psalm 95, **648,** is used as the first psalm of the Office of Readings.

Psalm 24

The Lord's is the earth and its fullness,
the world and all its peoples.
It is he who set it on the seas;
on the waters he made it firm.

Who shall climb the mountain of the Lord?
Who shall stand in his holy place?
The man with clean hands and pure heart,
who desires not worthless things,
who has not sworn so as to deceive his neighbor.

He shall receive blessings from the Lord
and reward from the God who saves him.
Such are the men who seek him,
seek the face of the God of Jacob.

O gates, lift high your heads;
grow higher, ancient doors.
Let him enter, the king of glory!

Who is the king of glory?
The Lord, the mighty, the valiant,
the Lord, the valiant in war.

O gates, lift high your heads;
grow higher, ancient doors.
Let him enter, the king of glory!

Who is he, the king of glory?
He, the Lord of armies,
he is the king of glory.

Ant. Mary received a blessing from the Lord and loving kindness from God her savior.

Ant. 2 The Most High has made his dwelling place a holy temple.

Psalm 46

God is for us a refuge and strength,
a helper close at hand, in time of distress:
so we shall not fear though the earth should rock,
though the mountains fall into the depths of the sea,
even though its waters rage and foam,
even though the mountains be shaken by its waves.

The Lord of hosts is with us:
the God of Jacob is our stronghold.

The waters of a river give joy to God's city,
the holy place where the Most High dwells.
God is within, it cannot be shaken;
God will help it at the dawning of the day.
Nations are in tumult, kingdoms are shaken:
he lifts his voice, the earth shrinks away.

The Lord of hosts is with us:
the God of Jacob is our stronghold.

Come, consider the works of the Lord,
the redoubtable deeds he has done on the earth.
He puts an end to wars over all the earth;
the bow he breaks, the spear he snaps.
He burns the shields with fire.
"Be still and know that I am God,
supreme among the nations, supreme on the earth!"

The Lord of hosts is with us:
the God of Jacob is our stronghold.

Ant. The Most High has made his dwelling place a holy
temple.

Ant. 3 Glorious things are said of you, O Virgin Mary.

Psalm 87

On the holy mountain is his city
cherished by the Lord.
The Lord prefers the gates of Zion
to all Jacob's dwellings.
Of you are told glorious things,
O city of God!

"Babylon and Egypt I will count
among those who know me;
Philistia, Tyre, Ethiopia,
these will be her children
and Zion shall be called 'Mother'
for all shall be her children."

It is he, the Lord Most High,
who gives each his place.
In his register of peoples he writes:
"These are her children,"
and while they dance they will sing:
"In you all find their home."

Ant. Glorious things are said of you, O Virgin Mary.

Blessed are those who hear the word of God.
—And cherish it in their hearts.

First Reading

From the first book of Chronicles   17:1-15

A prophecy concerning David's son

After David had taken up residence in his house, he
said to Nathan the prophet, "See, I am living in a house

of cedar, but the ark of the covenant of the Lord dwells under tentcloth." Nathan replied to David, "Do, therefore, whatever you desire, for God is with you."

But that same night the word of God came to Nathan: "Go and tell my servant David, Thus says the Lord: It is not you who are to build a house for me to dwell in. For I have never dwelt in a house, from the time when I led Israel onward, even to this day, but I have been lodging in tent or pavilion as long as I have wandered about with all of Israel. Did I ever say a word to any of the judges of Israel whom I commmanded to guide my people, such as, 'Why have you not built me a house of cedar?'

"Therefore, tell my servant David, Thus says the Lord of hosts: I took you from the pasture, from following the sheep, that you might become ruler over my people Israel. I was with you wherever you went, and I cut down all your enemies before you. I will make your name great like that of the greatest on the earth. I will assign a place for my people Israel and I will plant them in it to dwell there henceforth undisturbed; nor shall wicked men ever again oppress them, as they did at first, and during all the time when I appointed judges over my people Israel. And I will subdue all your enemies.

"Moreover, I declare to you that I, the Lord, will build you a house; so that when your days have been completed and you must join your fathers, I will raise up your offspring after you who will be one of your own sons, and I will establish his kingdom. He it is who shall build me a house, and I will establish his throne forever. I will be a father to him, and he shall be a son to me, and I will not withdraw my favor from him as I withdrew it from him who preceded you; but I will maintain him in my house and in my kingdom forever, and his throne shall be firmly established forever."

All these words and this whole vision Nathan related exactly to David.

RESPONSORY

How blessed are you, Virgin Mary,
for you carried within you the Lord, the Creator of the
    world.
—Mother of your Maker, you remain a virgin for ever.

Hail Mary, full of grace, the Lord is with you.
—Mother of your . . .

SECOND READING

From a sermon by Saint Sophronius, bishop

(Oratio 2, in sanctissimae Deiparae annuntiatione, 21–22. 26: PG 87, 3, 3242. 3250)

Through Mary the Father's blessing has shone forth on mankind

Hail, full of grace, the Lord is with you. What joy could surpass this, O Virgin Mother? What grace can excel that which God has granted to you alone? What could be imagined more dazzling or more delightful? Before the miracle we witness in you, all else pales; all else is inferior when compared with the grace you have been given. All else, even what is most desirable, must take second place and enjoy a lesser importance.

The Lord is with you. Who would dare challenge you? You are God's mother; who would not immediately defer to you and be glad to accord you a greater primacy and honor? For this reason, when I look upon the privilege you have above all creatures, I extol you with the highest praise: *Hail, full of grace, the Lord is with you.* On your account joy has not only graced men, but is also granted to the powers of heaven.

Truly, *you are blessed among women.* For you have changed Eve's curse into a blessing; and Adam, who hitherto lay under a curse, has been blessed because of you.

Truly, you are blessed among women. Through you the Father's blessing has shone forth on mankind, setting them free of their ancient curse.

Truly, you are blessed among women, because through you your forebears have found salvation. For you were to give birth to the Savior who was to win them salvation.

Truly, you are blessed among women, for without seed you have borne, as your fruit, him who bestows blessings on the whole world and redeems it from that curse that made it sprout thorns.

Truly, you are blessed among women, because, though a woman by nature, you will become, in reality, God's mother. If he whom you are to bear is truly God made flesh, then rightly do we call you God's mother. For you have truly given birth to God.

Enclosed within your womb is God himself. He makes his abode in you and comes forth from you like a bridegroom, winning joy for all and bestowing God's light on all.

You, O Virgin, are like a clear and shining sky, in which God *has set his tent.* From you *he comes forth like a bridegroom leaving his chamber.* Like a giant running his course, he will run the course of his life which will bring salvation for all who will ever live, and extending from the highest heavens to the end of them, it will fill all things with divine warmth and with life-giving brightness.

RESPONSORY

Truly you are the most favored of women,
where Eve brought a curse, you have brought a blessing.
—Through you the Father's Gift has been bestowed on
    us.

Through you, your ancestors have found salvation.
—Through you the Father's Gift has been bestowed on
us.

Alternative:

From a sermon by Saint Aelred, abbot

(Sermo 20, In Nativitate beatae Mariae: PL 195, 322-324)

Mary our mother

Let us come to his bride, his mother, his perfect handmaid, for the blessed Mary is all of this.

But what are we to do for her? What kind of gifts shall
we offer her? Would that we could at least return what we
are in duty bound to do, for we owe her honor and service, we owe her love and praise. We owe her honor, for
she is the mother of our Lord. He who fails to honor the
mother clearly dishonors the son. Also, Scripture says:
Honor your father and your mother.

What then, my brothers, shall we say? Is she not our
mother? Yes, my brothers, she is indeed our mother, for
through her we have been born, not for the world but for
God.

Once we all lay in death, as you know and believe, in
sin, in darkness, in misery. In death, because we had lost
the Lord; in sin, because of our corruption; in darkness,
for we were without the light of wisdom, and thus had
perished utterly.

But then we were born, far better than through Eve,
through Mary the blessed, because Christ was born of
her. We have recovered new life in place of sin, immortality instead of mortality, light in place of darkness.

She is our mother—the mother of our life, the mother
of our incarnation, the mother of our light. As the apostle
says of our Lord: *He became for us by God's power our wisdom and justice, and holiness and redemption.*

She then, as mother of Christ, is the mother of our wisdom and justice, of our holiness and redemption. She is more our mother than the mother of our flesh. Our birth from her is better, for from her is born our holiness, our wisdom, our justice, our sanctification, our redemption.

Praise the Lord in his holy ones, say the Scriptures. If our Lord is to be praised in those holy ones through whom he brings to being deeds of power and miracles, how much more is he to be praised in her in whom he fashioned himself, who is wonderful beyond all wonders.

RESPONSORY

Happy are you, holy Virgin Mary, and most worthy of all praise;
—from your womb Christ the Sun of Justice has risen.
Through him we have salvation and deliverance.

Let us celebrate with joy this feast in honor of the Blessed Virgin Mary.
—From your womb . . .

Alternative:

From the dogmatic constitution on the Church of the Second Vatican Council

(Lumen gentium, nn. 61–62)

Mary's motherhood in the order of grace

The Blessed Virgin was predestined to be the Mother of God in the eternal plan for the incarnation of God's Word. By decree of God's providence she was, here on earth, the loving mother of the divine Redeemer, the noblest of all his companions, and the humble servant of the Lord. In conceiving Christ, in bearing him, in nursing him, in presenting him to the Father in the temple, in sharing her Son's passion, as he was dying on the cross, by her obedience, her faith, her hope and burning love, she cooperated, in a way that was quite unique, in the work of the Savior in restoring supernatural life to souls. She is therefore a mother to us in the order of grace.

This motherhood of Mary in the order of grace—from the consent which she gave in faith at the annunciation, and which she continued to give unhesitatingly at the foot of the cross—lasts without interruption until all the elect enter into eternal fulfillment. When she was taken up into heaven, she did not lay aside this saving role but she continues by her intercession for all to gain for us the gifts of eternal salvation.

In her maternal love she cares for the brothers and sisters of her Son as they journey on earth in the midst of dangers and hardships, until they are brought safely home to the happiness of heaven.

The Blessed Virgin is thus invoked in the Church under the titles of Advocate, Auxiliatrix, Adjutrix and Mediatrix. These titles must not, however, be understood as in any way detracting from, or adding to, the dignity and effectiveness of Christ, the one Mediator.

No creature can ever be classed as an equal with the incarnate Word, the Redeemer. But just as the priesthood of Christ is shared in various ways by his ministers and his faithful people, and as the goodness of God, one though it is, is, in different ways, really shared with creatures, so also the unique mediation of Christ does not exclude but brings about a variety of shared cooperation, deriving from the one unique source.

The Church does not hesitate to acknowledge this kind of subordinate role in the person of Mary. The Church has continuous experience of its effects, and commends it to the hearts of the faithful, so that as they lean on her motherly protection they may be brought into closer union with the Mediator, our Savior.

O pure and holy Virgin, how can I find words to praise
   your beauty?
—The highest heavens cannot contain God whom you
   carried in your womb.

Blessed are you among women, and blessed is the fruit of
   your womb.
—The highest heavens . . .

On solemnities and feasts, Te Deum, 651

Prayer, as in Morning Prayer.

Morning Prayer

HYMN

O Mary, of all women
Thou art the chosen one,
Who ancient prophets promised
Would bear God's only Son;
All Hebrew generations
Prepared the way to thee,
That in your womb the God-man
Might come to set man free.

O Mary, you embody
All God taught to our race,
For you are first and foremost
In fullness of his grace;
We praise this wondrous honor
That you gave birth to him
Who from you took his manhood
And saved us from our sin.

Melody: Au fort de ma detresse 76.76.D   Music: 17th century
                                                Flemish Melody
                                         Text: Michael Gannon

Or:

Mary the dawn, Christ the Perfect Day;
Mary the gate, Christ the Heavenly Way!

Mary the root, Christ the Mystic Vine;
Mary the grape, Christ the Sacred Wine!

Mary the wheat, Christ the Living Bread;
Mary the stem, Christ the Rose blood-red!

Mary the font, Christ the Cleansing Flood;
Mary the cup, Christ the Saving Blood!

Mary the temple, Christ the temple's Lord;
Mary the shrine, Christ the God adored!

Mary the beacon, Christ the Haven's Rest;
Mary the mirror, Christ the Vision Blest!

Mary the mother, Christ the mother's Son
By all things blest while endless ages run. Amen.

Melody: Mary the Dawn   Music: Anon.
                      Test: Anon., alt. by the Dominican Sisters
                                              of Summit, 1972

Or:

Praise to Mary, Heaven's Gate,
Guiding Star of Christians' way,
Mother of our Lord and King,
Light and hope to souls astray.

When you heard the call of God
Choosing to fulfill his plan,
By your perfect act of love
Hope was born in fallen man.

Help us to amend our ways,
Halt the devil's strong attack,
Walk with us the narrow path,
Beg for us the grace we lack.

Mary, show your motherhood,
Bring your children's prayers to Christ,
Christ, your son, who ransomed man,
Who, for us, was sacrificed.

Virgin chosen, singly blest,
Ever faithful to God's call,
Guide us in this earthy life,
Guard us lest, deceived, we fall.

Mary, help us live our faith
So that we may see your son;
Join our humble prayers to yours,
Till life's ceaseless war is won.

Praise the Father, praise the Son,
Praise the holy Paraclete;
Offer all through Mary's hands,
Let her make our prayers complete.

Melody: Gott sei dank 77.77   Music: Freylinghausen's *Gesangbuch,*
1704
Text: *Ave Maris Stella,* 9th century
Translator: Rev. M. Quinn, O.P. et al., alt.

Ant. 1   Blessed are you, O Mary, for the world's salvation came forth from you; now in glory, you rejoice for ever with the Lord. Intercede for us
with your Son.

Psalms and canticle from Sunday, Week I, **688.**

Ant. 2   You are the glory of Jerusalem, the joy of Israel;
you are the fairest honor of our race.

Ant. 3   O Virgin Mary, how great your cause for joy;
God found you worthy to bear Christ our Savior.

READING   See Isaiah 61:10

I rejoice heartily in the Lord,
    in my God is the joy of my soul;
For he has clothed me with a robe of salvation,
    and wrapped me in a mantle of justice,
    like a bride bedecked with her jewels.

RESPONSORY

The Lord has chosen her,
his loved one from the beginning.
—The Lord has chosen her,
his loved one from the beginning.

He has taken her to live with him,
—his loved one from the beginning.

Glory to the Father . . .
—The Lord has . . .

CANTICLE OF ZECHARIAH

Ant.   Eve shut all her children out of Paradise; the Vir-
        gin Mary opened wide its gates.

INTERCESSIONS

Let us glorify our Savior, who chose the Virgin Mary for
    his mother. Let us ask him:
        May your mother intercede for us, Lord.
Sun of Justice, the immaculate Virgin was the white
    dawn announcing your rising,
—grant that we may always live in the light of your com-
    ing.
Eternal Word, you chose Mary as the uncorrupted ark of
    your dwelling place,

—free us from the corruption of sin.

Savior of mankind, your mother stood at the foot of your cross,

—grant, through her intercession, that we might rejoice to share in your passion.

With ultimate generosity and love, you gave Mary as a mother to your beloved disciple,

—help us to live as worthy sons of so noble a mother.

Or:

Let us glorify our Savior, who chose the Virgin Mary for his mother. Let us ask him:
May your mother intercede for us, Lord.

Savior of the world, by your redeeming might you preserved your mother beforehand from all stain of sin,

—keep watch over us, lest we sin.

You are our redeemer, who made the immaculate Virgin Mary your purest home and the sanctuary of the Holy Spirit,

—make us temples of your Spirit for ever.

Eternal Word, you taught your mother to choose the better part,

—grant that in imitating her we might seek the food that brings life everlasting.

King of kings, you lifted up your mother, body and soul, into heaven;

—help us to fix our thoughts on things above.

Lord of heaven and earth, you crowned Mary and set her at your right hand as queen,

—make us worthy to share this glory.

Our Father . . .

Prayer

If there is no proper prayer, one of the following is said:

Advent:

Father,
in your plan for our salvation
your Word became man,
announced by an angel and born of the Virgin Mary.
May we who believe that she is the Mother of God
receive the help of her prayers.

We ask this through our Lord Jesus Christ, your Son,
who lives and reigns with you and the Holy Spirit,
one God, for ever and ever.

Christmas Season:

Father,
you gave the human race eternal salvation
through the motherhood of the Virgin Mary.
May we experience the help of her prayers in our lives,
for through her we received the very source of life,
your Son, our Lord Jesus Christ,
who lives and reigns with you and the Holy Spirit,
one God, for ever and ever.

Daytime Prayer

For the gradual psalms, in place of psalm 122, psalm 129, 1129, may be said, and in place of psalm 127, psalm 131, 972, may be said.

Midmorning

Ant.   All of them, united in heart, continued in prayer,
with Mary the mother of Jesus.

In him and through his blood, we have been redeemed,
and our sins forgiven,
so immeasurably generous
is God's favor to us.

God has given us the wisdom
to understand fully the mystery,
the plan he was pleased
to decree in Christ.

A plan to be carried out
in Christ, in the fullness of time,
to bring all things into one in him,
in the heavens and on the earth.

Ant.   Blessed are you among women, and blessed is the
       fruit of your womb.

READING   Galatians 4:4-5

When the designated time had come, God sent forth
his Son born of a woman, born under the law, to deliver
from the law those who were subjected to it, so that we
might receive our status as adopted sons.

RESPONSORY

Hail Mary, full of grace, the Lord is with you.
—Hail Mary, full of grace, the Lord is with you.

Blessed are you among women, and blessed is the fruit of
   your womb.
—The Lord is with you.

Glory to the Father . . .
—Hail Mary, full . . .

<small>CANTICLE OF MARY</small>

Ant.   Blessed are you, O Virgin Mary, for your great
       faith; all that the Lord promised you will come to
       pass through you.

<small>INTERCESSIONS</small>

Let us praise God our almighty Father, who wished that
     Mary, his Son's mother, be celebrated by each genera-
     tion. Now in need we ask:
     Mary, full of grace, intercede for us.
O God, worker of miracles, you made the immaculate
     Virgin Mary share body and soul in your Son's glory
     in heaven,
—direct the hearts of your children to that same glory.
You made Mary our mother. Through her intercession
     grant strength to the weak, comfort to the sorrowing,
     pardon to sinners,
—salvation and peace to all.
You made Mary full of grace,
—grant all men the joyful abundance of your grace.
Make your Church of one mind and one heart in love,
—and help all those who believe to be one in prayer with
     Mary, the mother of Jesus.
You crowned Mary queen of heaven,
—may all the dead rejoice in your kingdom with the
     saints for ever.

Or:

Let us praise God our almighty Father, who wished that
     Mary, his Son's mother, be celebrated by each genera-
     tion. Now in need we ask:
     Mary, full of grace, intercede for us.

You made Mary the mother of mercy,
—may all who are faced with trials feel her motherly
  love.
You wished Mary to be the mother of the family in the
  home of Jesus and Joseph,
—may all mothers of families foster love and holiness
  through her intercession.
You gave Mary strength at the foot of the cross and filled
  her with joy at the resurrection of your Son,
—lighten the hardships of those who are burdened and
  deepen their sense of hope.
You made Mary open to your word and faithful as your
  servant,
—through her intercession make us servants and true followers of your Son.
You crowned Mary queen of heaven,
—may all the dead rejoice in your kingdom with the
  saints for ever.

Our Father . . .

Prayer

If there is no proper prayer, one of the following is said:

Advent:

Father,
in your plan for our salvation
your Word became man,
announced by an angel and born of the Virgin Mary.
May we who believe that she is the Mother of God
receive the help of her prayers.

We ask this through our Lord Jesus Christ, your Son,
who lives and reigns with you and the Holy Spirit,
one God, for ever and ever.

Christmas Season:

Father,
you gave the human race eternal salvation
through the motherhood of the Virgin Mary.
May we experience the help of her prayers in our lives,
for through her we received the very source of life,
your Son, our Lord Jesus Christ,
who lives and reigns with you and the Holy Spirit,
one God, for ever and ever.

COMMON OF APOSTLES

Evening Prayer I

Hymn, as in Evening Prayer II, 1364.

Psalmody

Ant. 1   Of those whom he called to follow him, Jesus chose out twelve, and made them his apostles.

Psalm 117

O praise the Lord, all you nations,
acclaim him, all you peoples!

Strong is his love for us;
he is faithful for ever.

Ant.   Of those whom he called to follow him, Jesus chose out twelve, and made them his apostles.

Ant. 2   They left their nets to follow the Lord and Redeemer.

Psalm 147:12-20

O praise the Lord, Jerusalem!
Zion, praise your God!

He has strengthened the bars of your gates,
he has blessed the children within you.
He established peace on your borders,
he feeds you with finest wheat.

He sends out his word to the earth
and swiftly runs his command.
He showers down snow white as wool,
he scatters hoar-frost like ashes.

He hurls down hailstones like crumbs.
The waters are frozen at his touch;

he sends forth his word and it melts them:
at the breath of his mouth the waters flow.

He makes his word known to Jacob,
to Israel his laws and decrees.
He has not dealt thus with other nations;
he has not taught them his decrees.

Ant.   They left their nets to follow the Lord and Re-
        deemer.

Ant. 3 You are my friends, for you have remained
        steadfast in my love.

                        Canticle   Ephesians 1:3-10

Praised be the God and Father
of our Lord Jesus Christ,
who bestowed on us in Christ
every spiritual blessing in the heavens.

God chose us in him
before the world began,
to be holy
and blameless in his sight.

He predestined us
to be his adopted sons through Jesus Christ,
such was his will and pleasure,
that all might praise the glorious favor
he has bestowed on us in his beloved.

In him and through his blood, we have been   redeemed,
and our sins forgiven,
so immeasurably generous
is God's favor to us.

God has given us the wisdom
to understand fully the mystery,

the plan he was pleased
to decree in Christ.

A plan to be carried out
in Christ, in the fullness of time,
to bring all things into one in him,
in the heavens and on the earth.

Ant.   You are my friends, for you have remained steadfast in my love.

READING   Acts 2:42-45

They devoted themselves to the apostles' instruction
and the communal life, to the breaking of bread and the
prayers. A reverent fear overtook them all, for many
wonders and signs were performed by the apostles.
Those who believed shared all things in common; they
would sell their property and goods, dividing everything
on the basis of each one's need.

RESPONSORY

All the world will know, you are living as I taught you.
—All the world will know, you are living as I taught you.

If you love one another.
—You are living as I taught you.

Glory to the Father . . .
—All the world . . .

CANTICLE OF MARY

Ant.   You did not choose me, but I chose you to go
forth and bear fruit that will last for ever.

INTERCESSIONS

My brothers, we build on the foundation of the apostles.
    Let us pray to our almighty Father for his holy people
    and say:

Be mindful of your Church, O Lord.

Father, you wanted your Son to be seen first by the apostles after the resurrection from the dead,

—we ask you to make us his witnesses to the farthest corners of the world.

You sent your Son to preach the good news to the poor,

—help us to preach this Gospel to every creature.

You sent your Son to sow the seed of unending life,

—grant that we who work at sowing the seed may share the joy of the harvest.

You sent your Son to reconcile all men to you through his blood,

—help us all to work toward achieving this reconcilation.

Your Son sits at your right hand in heaven,

—let the dead enter your kingdom of joy.

Our Father . . .

Prayer, as in the Proper of Saints.

Invitatory

Ant.   Come, let us worship the Lord, the King of apostles.

Invitatory psalm, as in the Ordinary, 648.

Office of Readings

HYMN

> Your hand, O Lord, has guided
> Your church from age to age;
> The wondrous tale is written
> So clearly on each page;
> Our fathers praised your goodness,
> And we their deeds record;
> And both to this bear witness:
> One Church, one Faith, one Lord.

Your heralds brought glad tidings
To greatest and to least;
They told all men to hasten
To share the great King's feast;
And this was all their teaching
In every deed and word,
To all alike proclaiming:
One Church, one Faith, one Lord.

Through many days of darkness,
Through many scenes of strife,
The faithful few fought bravely
To guard the Christian life;
Their gospel of redemption,
Sin pardoned, man restored,
Was all in this enfolded:
One Church, one Faith, one Lord.

Your mercy will not fail us,
Nor leave your work undone;
With all your strength to help us,
The vict'ry shall be won;
And then by men and angels
Your name shall be adored,
And this shall be their anthem:
One Church, one Faith, one Lord.

Melody: Thornbury 76.76.D   Music: Basil Harwood, 1859–1949
                              Text: Edward H. Plumptre, 1821–1891,
                                   alt. by anthony G. Petti

Or:

Antiphon:

This I ask: that you love each other
as I have loved you.
I look on you as friends, as friends.

Don't be distressed;
let your hearts be free,
for I leave with you my peace, my word.

Antiphon

If you really love me,
be glad, have hope,
for I leave with you my Spirit to guide you.

Antiphon

Too much blood has been wasted,
too many deaths;
so remember what I have told you, have love.

Antiphon

When the end is near
I still am with you
for I will never leave you alone.

Antiphon

Melody: John 15   Music: Enrico Garzilli, 1970
                                    Text: Enrico Garzilli, 1970

PSALMODY

Ant. 1   Their voice has gone out to the limits of the
earth, their words to the ends of the world.

Psalm 19A

The heavens proclaim the glory of God
and the firmament shows forth the work of his
    hands.
Day unto day takes up the story
and night unto night makes known the message.

No speech, no word, no voice is heard
yet their span extends through all the earth,
their words to the utmost bounds of the world.

There he has placed a tent for the sun;
it comes forth like a bridegroom coming from his
    tent,
rejoices like a champion to run its course.

At the end of the sky is the rising of the sun;
to the furthest end of the sky is its course.
There is nothing concealed from its burning heat.

Ant.   Their voice has gone out to the limits of the earth,
    their words to the ends of the world.

Ant. 2   They proclaimed what God has done for us;
    they grasped the meaning of his deeds.

Psalm 64

Hear my voice, O God, as I complain,
guard my life from dread of the foe.
Hide me from the band of the wicked,
from the throng of those who do evil.

They sharpen their tongues like swords;
they aim bitter words like arrows
to shoot at the innocent from ambush,
shooting suddenly and recklessly.

They scheme their evil course;
they conspire to lay secret snares.
They say: "Who will see us?
Who can search out our crimes?"

He will search who searches the mind
and knows the depths of the heart.
God has shot them with his arrow
and dealt them sudden wounds.
Their own tongue has brought them to ruin
and all who see them mock.

Then will all men fear;
they will tell what God has done.
They will understand God's deeds.
The just will rejoice in the Lord
and fly to him for refuge.
All the upright hearts will glory.

Ant.   They proclaimed what God has done for us; they
       grasped the meaning of his deeds.

Ant. 3   God's holiness was revealed by them; all nations
         saw God's glory.

Psalm 97

The Lord is king, let earth rejoice,
the many coastlands be glad.
Cloud and darkness are his raiment;
his throne, justice and right.

A fire prepares his path;
it burns up his foes on every side.
His lightnings light up the world,
the earth trembles at the sight.

The mountains melt like wax
before the Lord of all the earth.
The skies proclaim his justice;
all peoples see his glory.

Let those who serve idols be ashamed,
those who boast of their worthless gods.
All you spirits, worship him.

Zion hears and is glad;
the people of Judah rejoice
because of your judgments, O Lord.

For you indeed are the Lord,
most high above all the earth,
exalted far above all spirits.

The Lord loves those who hate evil:
he guards the souls of his saints;
he sets them free from the wicked.

Light shines forth for the just
and joy for the upright of heart.
Rejoice, you just, in the Lord;
give glory to his holy name.

Ant.   God's holiness was revealed by them; all nations
       saw God's glory.

They proclaimed the Lord's praises, told of his power to
save.
—And of the wonders he had worked.

FIRST READING

From the first letter of the apostle Paul
to the Corinthians   1:18—2:5

The apostles preach the cross

The message of the cross is complete absurdity to those
who are headed for ruin, but to us who are experiencing
salvation it is the power of God. Scripture says,

"I will destroy the wisdom of the wise,
and thwart the cleverness of the clever."

Where is the wise man to be found? Where the scribe?
Where is the master of worldly argument? Has not God
turned the wisdom of this world into folly?

Since in God's wisdom the world did not come to know
him through "wisdom," it pleased God to save those who
believe through the absurdity of the preaching of the gospel. Yes, Jews demand "signs" and Greeks look for "wisdom," but we preach Christ crucified—a stumbling
block to Jews, and an absurdity to Gentiles; but to those
who are called, Jews and Greeks alike, Christ the power

of God and the wisdom of God. For God's folly is wiser than men, and his weakness more powerful than men.

Brothers, you are among those called. Consider your situation. Not many of you are wise, as men account wisdom; not many are influential; and surely not many are well-born. God chose those whom the world considers absurd to shame the wise; he singled out the weak of this world to shame the strong. He chose the world's lowborn and despised, those who count for nothing, to reduce to nothing those who were something; so that mankind can do no boasting before God. God it is who has given you life in Christ Jesus. He has made him our wisdom and also our justice, our sanctification, and our redemption. This is just as you find it written, "Let him who would boast, boast in the Lord."

As for myself, brothers, when I came to you I did not come proclaiming God's testimony with any particular eloquence or "wisdom." No, I determined that while I was with you I would speak of nothing but Jesus Christ and him crucified. When I came among you it was in weakness and fear, and with much trepidation. My message and my preaching had none of the persuasive force of "wise" argumentation, but the convincing power of the Spirit. As a consequence, your faith rests not on the wisdom of men but on the power of God.

RESPONSORY   Matthew 10:18; 19:20

When you are arraigned before the rulers of this world,
do not plan beforehand what you will say;
—when the time comes, words will be given you.

Then what you say will not come from you;
the Spirit of your Father will speak through you.
—When the time . . .

SECOND READING is taken from the Proper of Saints.

On solemnities and feasts, Te Deum, 651.

Prayer, as in the Proper of Saints.

Morning Prayer

HYMN

> Let all on earth their voices raise,
> Resounding heaven's praise,
> To him who gave apostles grace
> To run their glorious race.
>
> Of Gospel truth they bore the light
> To brighten earthly night;
> May we that heav'nly light impart
> To ev'ry mind and heart.
>
> Praise God the Father and the Son
> And Spirit Three in One,
> Who sent these men with holy fire
> All mankind to inspire. Amen.

Melody: Saint Peter C.M.   Music: A.R. Reingale, 1799–1877
Text: *Exultet Orbis Gaudiis*,
10th century; Stanza 3
Roger Nachtwey, 1965
Translator: Roger Nachtwey, 1965

Ant. 1   My commandment is this: love one another as I
have loved you.

Psalms and canticle from Sunday, Week I, 688.

Ant. 2   There is no greater love than to lay down your
life for your friends.

Ant. 3   You are my friends, says the Lord, if you do
what I command you.

READING   Ephesians 2:19-20

You are strangers and aliens no longer. No, you are fellow citizens of the saints and members of the household of God. You form a building which rises on the foundation of the apostles and prophets, with Christ Jesus himself as the capstone. Through him the whole structure is fitted together and takes shape as a holy temple in the Lord; in him you are being built into this temple, to become a dwelling place for God in the Spirit.

RESPONSORY

You have made them rulers over all the earth.
—You have made them rulers over all the earth.

They will always remember your name, O Lord.
—Over all the earth.

Glory to the Father . . .
—You have made . . .

CANTICLE OF ZECHARIAH

Ant. On the foundation stones of the heavenly Jerusalem, the names of the twelve apostles of the Lamb are written; the Lamb of God is the light of that holy city.

INTERCESSIONS

Beloved friends, we have inherited heaven along with the apostles. Let us give thanks to the Father for all his gifts:
   The company of apostles praises you, O Lord.
Praise be to you, Lord, for the banquet of Christ's body and blood given us through the apostles,
—which refreshes us and gives us life.
   The company of apostles praises you, O Lord.

Praise be to you, Lord, for the feast of your word prepared for us by the apostles,
—giving us light and joy.
The company of apostles praises you, O Lord.
Praise be to you, Lord, for your holy Church, founded on the apostles,
—where we are gathered together into your community.
The company of apostles praises you, O Lord.
Praise be to you, Lord, for the cleansing power of baptism and penance that you have entrusted to your apostles,
—through which we are cleansed of our sins.
The company of apostles praises you, O Lord.

Our Father . . .

Prayer, as in the Proper of Saints,

Daytime Prayer

Midmorning

Ant.   Go forth and proclaim the good news of the kingdom; and freely share with others what God has given you.

READING   2 Corinthians 5:19b-20

God has entrusted the message of reconciliation to us. This makes us ambassadors for Christ, God as it were appealing through us. We implore you, in Christ's name: be reconciled to God!

Their voice has gone out to the limits of the earth.
—Their words to the ends of the world.

Midday

Ant.   Know that I am with you always, even until the end of the world.

READING   Acts 5:12a, 14

Through the hands of the apostles, many signs and wonders occurred among the people. Nevertheless more and more believers, men and women in great numbers, were continually added to the Lord.

The apostles held fast to Christ's message.
—They kept the precepts he gave them.

Midafternoon

Ant.   By your trusting acceptance of trials, you will gain true life.

For the gradual psalms, in place of psalm 126, psalm 129, 1129, may be said.

READING   Acts 5:41-42

The apostles for their part left the Sanhedrin full of joy that they had been judged worthy of ill-treatment for the sake of the Name. Day after day, both in the temple and at home, they never stopped preaching and proclaiming the good news of Jesus the Messiah.

Rejoice and be glad, says the Lord.
—For your names are written in heaven.

Prayer, as in the Proper of Saints.

Evening Prayer II

HYMN

The eternal gifts of Christ the King,
The apostles' glory, let us sing,
And all with hearts of gladness, raise
Due hymns of thankful love and praise.

Their faith in Christ, the Lord, prevailed;
Their hope, a light that never failed;

Their love ablaze o'er pathways trod
To lead them to the eternal God.

In them the Father's glory shone,
In them the will of God the Son,
In them exults the Holy Ghost,
Through them rejoice the heav'nly host.

To thee, Redeemer, now we cry,
That thou wouldst join to them on high
Thy servants, who this grace implore,
For ever and for ever more.

Melody: King's Majesty L.M.   Music: Graham George, 1941
Text: Saint Ambrose, d. 397
Translator: J. M. Neale, d. 1866

PSALMODY

Ant. 1   You are the men who have stood by me in my
time of trial.

Psalm 116:10-19

I trusted, even when I said:
"I am sorely afflicted,"
and when I said in my alarm:
"No man can be trusted."

How can I repay the Lord
for his goodness to me?
The cup of salvation I will raise;
I will call on the Lord's name.

My vows to the Lord I will fulfill
before all his people.
O precious in the eyes of the Lord
is the death of his faithful.

Your servant, Lord, your servant am I;
you have loosened my bonds.
A thanksgiving sacrifice I make:
I will call on the Lord's name.

My vows to the Lord I will fulfill
before all his people,
in the courts of the house of the Lord,
in your midst, O Jerusalem.

Ant. You are the men who have stood by me in my time
of trial.

Ant. 2 I have lived among you as one who ministers to
others.

Psalm 126

When the Lord delivered Zion from bondage,
it seemed like a dream.
Then was our mouth filled with laughter,
on our lips there were songs.

The heathens themselves said: "What marvels
the Lord worked for them!"
What marvels the Lord worked for us!
Indeed we were glad.

Deliver us, O Lord, from our bondage
as streams in dry land.
Those who are sowing in tears
will sing when they reap.

They go out, they go out, full of tears,
carrying seed for the sowing:
they come back, they come back, full of song,
carrying their sheaves.

Ant. I have lived among you as one who ministers to
others.

Ant. 3 I no longer call you servants, but my friends,
for I have shared with you everything I have
heard from my Father.

Canticle   Ephesians 1:3-10

Praised be the God and Father
of our Lord Jesus Christ,
who bestowed on us in Christ
every spiritual blessing in the heavens.

God chose us in him
before the world began,
to be holy
and blameless in his sight.

He predestined us
to be his adopted sons through Jesus Christ,
such was his will and pleasure,
that all might praise the glorious favor
he has bestowed on us in his beloved.

In him and through his blood, we have been re-
     deemed,
and our sins forgiven,
so immeasurably generous
is God's favor to us.

God has given us the wisdom
to understand fully the mystery,
the plan he was pleased
to decree in Christ.

A plan to be carried out
in Christ, in the fullness of time,
to bring all things into one in him,
in the heavens and on the earth.

Ant.   I no longer call you servants, but my friends, for I
       have shared with you everything I have heard
       from my Father.

READING   Ephesians 4:11-13

It is he who gave apostles, prophets, evangelists, pastors and teachers in roles of service for the faithful to build up the body of Christ, till we become one in faith and in the knowledge of God's Son, and form that perfect man who is Christ come to full stature.

RESPONSORY

Tell all the nations how glorious God is.
—Tell all the nations how glorious God is.

Make known his wonders to every people.
—How glorious God is.

Glory to the Father . . .
—Tell all the . . .

CANTICLE OF MARY

Ant.   When all things are made new, and the Son of Man is enthroned in majesty, you will sit in judgment over the twelve tribes of Israel.

INTERCESSIONS

My brothers, we build on the foundation of the apostles.
     Let us pray to our almighty Father for his holy people
     and say:
     Be mindful of your Church, O Lord.
Father, you wanted your Son to be seen first by the apostles after the resurrection from the dead,
—we ask you to make us his witnesses to the farthest corners of the world.
You sent your Son to preach the good news to the poor,
—help us to preach this Gospel to every creature.
You sent your Son to sow the seed of unending life,
—grant that we who work at sowing the seed may share the joy of the harvest.

You sent your Son to reconcile all men to you through his
    blood,
—help us all to work toward achieving this reconcilia-
    tion.
Your Son sits at your right hand in heaven,
—let the dead enter your kingdom of joy.

Our Father . . .

Prayer, as in the Proper of Saints.

COMMON OF MARTYRS

FOR SEVERAL MARTYRS

Evening Prayer I

HYMN, as in Evening Prayer II, 1389.

PSALMODY

Ant. 1   The saints endured many torments to gain the martyr's crown.

Psalm 118

I

Give thanks to the Lord for he is good,
for his love endures for ever.

Let the sons of Israel say:
"His love endures for ever."
Let the sons of Aaron say:
"His love endures for ever."
Let those who fear the Lord say:
"His love endures for ever."

I called to the Lord in my distress;
he answered and freed me.
The Lord is at my side; I do not fear.
What can man do against me?
The Lord is at my side as my helper:
I shall look down on my foes.

It is better to take refuge in the Lord
than to trust in men:
it is better to take refuge in the Lord
than to trust in princes.

The nations all encompassed me;
in the Lord's name I crushed them.

They compassed me, compassed me about;
in the Lord's name I crushed them.
They compassed me about like bees;
they blazed like a fire among thorns.
In the Lord's name I crushed them.

I was hard-pressed and was falling
but the Lord came to help me.
The Lord is my strength and my song;
he is my savior.
There are shouts of joy and victory
in the tents of the just.

The Lord's right hand has triumphed;
his right hand raised me.
The Lord's right hand has triumphed;
I shall not die, I shall live
and recount his deeds.
I was punished, I was punished by the Lord,
but not doomed to die.

Ant.   The saints endured many torments to gain the
       martyr's crown.

Ant. 2   Triumphant, the saints reach the kingdom, to be
         wreathed in splendor by the hand of God.

II

Open to me the gates of holiness:
I will enter and give thanks.
This is the Lord's own gate
where the just may enter.
I will thank you for you have answered
and you are my savior.

The stone which the builders rejected
has become the corner stone.
This is the work of the Lord,

a marvel in our eyes.
This day was made by the Lord;
we rejoice and are glad.

O Lord, grant us salvation;
O Lord, grant success.
Blessed in the name of the Lord
is he who comes.
We bless you from the house of the Lord;
the Lord God is our light.

Go forward in procession with branches
even to the altar.
You are my God, I thank you.
My God, I praise you.
Give thanks to the Lord for he is good;
for his love endures for ever.

Ant.   Triumphant, the saints reach the kingdom, to be
        wreathed in splendor by the hand of God.

Ant. 3 The martyrs died for Christ and received the
        gift of eternal life.

Canticle   1 Peter 2:21-24

Christ suffered for you,
and left you an example
to have you follow in his footsteps.

He did no wrong;
no deceit was found in his mouth.
When he was insulted
he returned no insult.

When he was made to suffer,
he did not counter with threats.
Instead he delivered himself up
to the One who judges justly.

In his own body
he brought your sins to the cross,
so that all of us, dead to sin,
could live in accord with God's will.

By his wounds you were healed.

Ant.   The martyrs died for Christ and received the gift
of eternal life.

READING   Romans 8:35, 37-39

Who will separate us from the love of Christ? Trial, or
distress, or persecution, or hunger, or nakedness, or danger, or the sword? Yet in all this we are more than con-
querors because of him who has loved us. For I am certain that neither death nor life, neither angels nor principalities, neither the present nor the future, nor powers,
neither height nor depth nor any other creature, will be
able to separate us from the love of God that comes to us
in Christ Jesus, our Lord.

RESPONSORY

These are the friends of God; they lie safe in his hands.
—These are the friends of God; they lie safe in his hands.

Nothing can harm them now.
—They lie safe in his hands.

Glory to the Father . . .
—These are the . . .

CANTICLE OF MARY

Ant.   Renouncing all this world could offer, these martyrs are now in God's kingdom; with their robes
washed clean in the blood of the Lamb, they share
his joy for ever.

INTERCESSIONS

This is the hour when the King of martyrs offered his life in the upper room and laid it down on the cross. Let us thank him and say:
We praise you, O Lord.

We praise you, O Lord, our Savior, inspiration and example for every martyr, for loving us to the end:
We praise you, O Lord.

For calling all repentant sinners to the rewards of life:
We praise you, O Lord.

For entrusting to your Church the blood of the new and everlasting covenant poured out for the remission of sin:
We praise you, O Lord.

For our perseverance in your grace today:
We praise you, O Lord.

For incorporating our dead brothers and sisters into your own death today:
We praise you, O Lord.

Our Father . . .

Prayer

If there is no proper prayer, one of the following is said:

All-powerful, ever-living God,
turn our weakness into strength.
As you gave your martyrs N. and N.
the courage to suffer death for Christ,
give us the courage to live in faithful witness to you.
Grant this through our Lord Jesus Christ, your Son,
who lives and reigns with you and the Holy Spirit,
one God, for ever and ever.

Or:

Lord,
hear the prayers of the martyrs N. and N.

and give us courage to bear witness to your truth.

Grant this through our Lord Jesus Christ, your Son,
who lives and reigns with you and the Holy Spirit,
one God, for ever and ever.

For virgin martyrs:

God our Father,
you give us joy each year
in honoring the memory of Saints N. and N.
May their prayers be a source of help for us,
and may their example of courage and chastity be our
   inspiration.

Grant this through our Lord Jesus Christ, your Son,
who lives and reigns with you and the Holy Spirit,
one God, for ever and ever.

For holy women:

Father,
in our weakness your power reaches perfection.
You gave Saints N. and N. the strength
to defeat the power of sin and evil.
May we who celebrate their glory share in their triumph.

We ask this through our Lord Jesus Christ, your Son,
who lives and reigns with you and the Holy Spirit,
one God, for ever and ever.

Invitatory

Ant.   Come, let us worship Christ, the King of martyrs.

Invitatory psalm, as in the Ordinary, 648.

Office of Readings

HYMN

    Faith of our fathers! faith and prayer
    Shall win all nations unto thee;

And through the truth that comes from God,
Mankind shall then indeed be free.

Refrain:

Faith of our fathers, holy faith!
We will be true to thee till death.

Faith of our fathers! we will love
Both friend and foe in all our strife:
And preach thee too, as love knows how,
By kindly deeds and virtuous life.

Refrain

Melody: Saint Catherine L.M.   Music: Henri F. Hemy 1818–1888
with Refrain   and James G. Walton, 1821–1905
                          Text: Frederick W. Faber, 1814–1863

PSALMODY

Ant. 1   The holy martyrs died for Christ; with their
           blood they enriched the earth. Their gift is
           crowned with everlasting life.

Psalm 2

Why this tumult among nations,
among peoples this useless murmuring?
They arise, the kings of the earth,
princes plot against the Lord and his Anointed.
"Come, let us break their fetters,
come, let us cast off their yoke."

He who sits in the heavens laughs;
the Lord is laughing them to scorn.
Then he will speak in his anger,
his rage will strike them with terror.
"It is I who have set up my king
on Zion, my holy mountain."

I will announce the decree of the Lord:

The Lord said to me: "You are my Son.
It is I who have begotten you this day.

Ask and I shall bequeath you the nations,
put the ends of the earth in your possession.
With a rod of iron you will break them,
shatter them like a potter's jar."

Now, O kings, understand,
take warning, rulers of the earth;
serve the Lord with awe
and trembling, pay him your homage
lest he be angry and you perish;
for suddenly his anger will blaze.

Blessed are they who put their trust in God.

Ant.   The holy martyrs died for Christ; with their blood
they enriched the earth. Their gift is crowned
with everlasting life.

Ant. 2   The just will live for ever; to live in God is their
reward.

Psalm 33

I

Ring out your joy to the Lord, O you just;
for praise is fitting for loyal hearts.

Give thanks to the Lord upon the lyre,
with a ten-stringed harp sing him songs.
O sing him a song that is new,
play loudly, with all your skill.

For the word of the Lord is faithful
and all his works to be trusted.
The Lord loves justice and right
and fills the earth with his love.

By his word the heavens were made,
by the breath of his mouth all the stars.
He collects the waves of the ocean;
he stores up the depths of the sea.

Let all the earth fear the Lord,
all who live in the world revere him.
He spoke; and it came to be.
He commanded; it sprang into being.

He frustrates the designs of the nations,
he defeats the plans of the peoples.
His own designs shall stand for ever,
the plans of his heart from age to age.

Ant.   The just will live for ever; to live in God is their
       reward.

Ant. 3   My saints, you fought the good fight in this
         world; I will give you the reward of your labors.

II

They are happy, whose God is the Lord,
the people he has chosen as his own.
From the heavens the Lord looks forth,
he sees all the children of men.

From the place where he dwells he gazes
on all the dwellers on the earth,
he who shapes the hearts of them all
and considers all their deeds.

A king is not saved by his army,
nor a warrior preserved by his strength.
A vain hope for safety is the horse;
despite its power it cannot save.

The Lord looks on those who revere him,
on those who hope in his love,
to rescue their souls from death,
to keep them alive in famine.

Our soul is waiting for the Lord.
The Lord is our help and our shield.

In him do our hearts find joy.
We trust in his holy name.

May your love be upon us, O Lord,
as we place all our hope in you.

Ant.   My saints, you fought the good fight in this world;
I will give you the reward of your labors.

Our spirits yearn for the Lord.
—He is our help and our protector.

FIRST READING

If the vigil is extended, in place of the following reading the reading from the book of **Wisdom 5:1-16**, p. 1503, with its responsory **These holy men**, p. 1380, may be used.

From the book of Wisdom   3:1-15

The friends of God lie safe in his hands

The souls of the just are in the hand of God,
    and no torment shall touch them.
They seemed, in the view of the foolish, to be dead;
    and their passing away was thought an affliction
    and their going forth from us, utter destruction.
But they are in peace.
For if before men, indeed, they be punished,
    yet is their hope full of immortality;
Chastised a little, they shall be greatly blessed,
    because God tried them
    and found them worthy of himself.
As gold in the furnace, he proved them,
    and as sacrificial offerings he took them to himself.

In the time of their visitation they shall shine,
    and shall dart about as sparks through stubble;
They shall judge nations and rule over peoples,
    and the Lord shall be their King forever.

Those who trust in him shall understand truth,
  and the faithful shall abide with him in love:
Because grace and mercy are with his holy ones,
  and his care is with his elect.

But the wicked shall receive a punishment to match their
      thoughts,
  since they neglected justice and forsook the Lord.
For he who despises wisdom and instruction is doomed.
Vain is their hope, fruitless are their labors,
  and worthless are their works.
Their wives are foolish and their children wicked;
  accursed is their brood.

Yes, blessed is she who, childless and undefiled,
  knew not transgression of the marriage bed;
  she shall bear fruit at the visitation of souls.
So also the eunuch whose hand wrought no misdeed,
  who held no wicked thoughts against the Lord—
For he shall be given fidelity's choice reward
  and a more gratifying heritage in the Lord's temple.
For the fruit of noble struggles is a glorious one;
  and unfailing is the root of understanding.

RESPONSORY   See Ephesians 4:4-5

These holy men poured out their blood for the Lord;
they loved Christ in life; they followed him in his death.
—They have won the glorious crown.

They shared the one Spirit;
they held fast to one faith.
—They have won . . .

SECOND READING

From a letter of Saint Cyprian, bishop and martyr
(Ep. 6, 1–2; CSEL 3, 480–482)

We desire to gain the Lord's promises; we must
then imitate him in all things

I greet you, dearest brothers, and would like also to enjoy your company face to face, if only the conditions in
which I find myself did not prevent my coming to see
you. What could be more desirable or more joyful for me
than to embrace you now, to be encircled by those pure
and sinless hands that have kept the faith of the Lord and
refused to offer sacrilegious worship?

What could be more pleasant, more sublime, than to
kiss at this moment those lips of yours, which have given
such glorious utterance in praise of the Lord; to be seen
also by those eyes of yours, which have despised the
world and proved themselves worthy of seeing God?

But, because there is no opportunity for my sharing
this joy, I send this letter as my representative for your
ears and eyes to hear and see. Through it I congratulate
you, and at the same time urge you to persevere courageously and steadfastly in your witness to heavenly glory,
and to continue with spiritual courage, now that you have
entered on the way that the Lord has graciously opened
up for you, until you receive the crown of victory. You
have the Lord as your protector and guide, for he has
said: *Behold, I am with you always, even to the end of the
world.*

How blessed is the prison honored by your presence,
how blessed the prison that sends men of God to heaven!
Darkness brighter than the sun itself, more resplendent
than this light of the world, for it is here that God's temples are now established, and your limbs made holy by
your praise of God.

Let nothing else be now in your hearts and minds except God's commandments and the precepts of heaven:
by their means the Holy Spirit has always inspired you to
bear your sufferings. Let no one think of death, but only

of immortality; let no one think of suffering that is for a time, but only of glory that is for eternity. It is written: *Precious in the sight of God is the death of his holy ones.* And again: *A sacrifice to God is an afflicted spirit; a broken and humbled heart God does not despise.*

Holy Scripture speaks also of the sufferings which consecrate God's martyrs and sanctify them by the very testing of pain: *Though in the eyes of men they suffered torments, their hope is full of immortality. They will judge nations, and rule over peoples, and the Lord will reign over them for ever.*

When, therefore, you recall that you will be judges and rulers with Christ the Lord, you must rejoice, despising present suffering for joy at what is to come. You know that from the beginning of the world it was so; justice is here oppressed in its conflict with the world, for at the very outset Abel the just is killed, and after him the just, and those sent as prophets and apostles.

The Lord himself is an example of all this in his own person. He teaches us that only those who have followed him along his way arrive at his kingdom: *He who loves his life in this world, will lose it. And he who hates his life in this world, will save it for eternal life.* And again he says: *Do not fear those who kill the body, but cannot kill the soul; fear rather him who can kill both body and soul and send them to hell.*

Paul too admonishes us, that as we desire to gain the Lord's promises we must imitate the Lord in all things. *We are God's children,* he tells us. *If children, we are also heirs of God, and coheirs with Christ, if only we suffer with him, that we may also be glorified with him.*

RESPONSORY

We are warriors now, fighting on the battlefield of faith, and God sees all we do;

the angels watch and so does Christ.

—What honor and glory and joy, to do battle in the presence of God,

and to have Christ approve our victory.

Let us arm ourselves in full strength
and prepare ourselves for the ultimate struggle
with blameless hearts, true faith, and unyielding courage.

—What honor and . . .

On solemnities and feasts, **Te Deum, 651.**

Prayer, as in Morning Prayer.

Morning Prayer

HYMN

Christ, in whose passion once was sown
All virtue of all saints to be,
For the white field of these thy own
We praise the seed and sower, thee.

Thine was the first and holiest grain
To die and quicken and increase;
And then came these, and died again,
That spring and harvest should not cease.

From thee the martyrs, we from those,
Each in thy grace's measure, spring;
Their strength upon our weakness flows
And guides us to the goal we sing.

These were thy great ones: we, thy least,
One in desire and faith with them,
Called by the Lord to keep one feast,
Journey to one Jerusalem.

Melody: Mein' Seel'. O Gott,   Music: M. Praetorius, 1571–1621
muss Loben Dich L.M.   Text: Walter Shewring

Or:

> A mighty fortress is our God,
> A bulwark never failing;
> Our helper he amid the flood
> Of mortal ills prevailing:
> For still our ancient foe
> Does seek to work us woe;
> His craft and power are great
> And, armed with cruel hate,
> On earth is not his equal.

> Did we in our own strength confide,
> Our striving would be losing;
> Were not the right man on our side,
> The man of God's own choosing:
> You ask who that may be?
> Christ Jesus, it is he;
> Lord Sabaoth his Name,
> From age to age the same,
> And he must win the battle.

> And tho' this world, with devils filled,
> Should threaten to undo us;
> We will not fear, for God has willed
> His truth to triumph through us:
> The prince of darkness grim,
> We tremble not for him;
> His rage we can endure,
> For lo! his doom is sure,
> One little word shall fell him.

Melody: Ein' Feste Burg   Music: Martin Luther, 1529
87.87.66.667   Text: Martin Luther, 1529
                    Translator: Frederick Henry Hedge, 1852, alt.

Or:

Refrain:

> For to those who love God,
> Who are called in his plan,

Everything works out for good.
And God himself chose them
To bear the likeness of his Son
That he might be the first of many, many brothers.

Who is able to condemn? Only Christ who died for
    us;
Christ who rose for us, Christ who prays for us.

Refrain

In the face of all this, what is there left to say?
For if God is for us, who can be against us?

Refrain

Who can separate us from the love of Christ?
Neither trouble, nor pain, nor persecution.

Refrain

What can separate us from the love of Christ?
Not the past, the present, nor the future.

Refrain

Melody: Romans VIII   Music: Enrico Garzilli, 1970
                              Text: Enrico Garzilli, 1970

Ant. 1   The martyrs fixed their eyes on heaven, and
         cried out in their torments: Come, Lord, be
         with us in this hour.

Psalms and canticle from Sunday, Week I, 688.

Ant. 2   Blessed spirits and souls of the just, pour out
         your songs of praise to the Lord, alleluia.

Ant. 3   You throng of martyrs, praise God with endless
         praise.

READING   2 Corinthians 1:3-5

Praised be God, the Father of our Lord Jesus Christ,
the Father of mercies, and the God of all consolation! He
comforts us in all our afflictions and thus enables us to

comfort those who are in trouble, with the same consolation we have received from him. As we have shared much in the suffering of Christ, so through Christ do we share abundantly in his consolation.

RESPONSORY

The just are the friends of God.
They live with him for ever.
—The just are the friends of God.
They live with him for ever.

God himself is their reward.
—They live with him for ever.

Glory to the Father . . .
—The just are . . .

CANTICLE OF ZECHARIAH

Ant.   Blessed are those who suffer persecution for the sake of justice; the kingdom of heaven is theirs.

INTERCESSIONS

Our Savior's faithfulness is mirrored in the fidelity of his witnesses who shed their blood for the word of God.
   Let us praise him in remembrance of them:
   You redeemed us by your blood.
Your martyrs freely embraced death in bearing witness to the faith,
—give us the true freedom of the Spirit, O Lord.
Your martyrs professed their faith by shedding their blood,
—give us a faith, O Lord, that is constant and pure.
Your martyrs followed in your footsteps by carrying the cross,
—help us to endure courageously the misfortunes of life.
Your martyrs washed their garments in the blood of the Lamb,

—help us to avoid the weaknesses of the flesh and worldly allurements.

Our Father . . .

Prayer

If there is no proper prayer, one of the following is said:

All-powerful, ever-living God,
turn our weakness into strength.
As you gave your martyrs N. and N.
the courage to suffer death for Christ,
give us the courage to live in faithful witness to you.

Grant this through our Lord Jesus Christ, your Son,
who lives and reigns with you and the Holy Spirit,
one God, for ever and ever.

Or:

Lord,
hear the prayers of the martyrs N. and N.
and give us courage to bear witness to your truth.

Grant this through our Lord Jesus Christ, your Son,
who lives and reigns with you and the Holy Spirit,
one God, for ever and ever.

For virgin martyrs:

God our Father,
you give us joy each year
in honoring the memory of Saints N. and N.
May their prayers be a source of help for us,
and may their example of courage and chastity be our inspiration.

Grant this through our Lord Jesus Christ, your Son,
who lives and reigns with you and the Holy Spirit,
one God, for ever and ever.

For holy women:

Father,
in our weakness your power reaches perfection.
You gave Saints N. and N. the strength
to defeat the power of sin and evil.
May we who celebrate their glory share in their triumph.

We ask this through our Lord Jesus Christ, your Son,
who lives and reigns with you and the Holy Spirit,
one God, for ever and ever.

Daytime Prayer

Midmorning

Ant.   The Lord gave them victory after a bitter contest,
         for no power can conquer the wisdom of God.

READING   1 Peter 5:10-11

The God of all grace, who called us to his everlasting
glory in Christ, will himself restore, confirm, strengthen,
and establish those who have suffered a little while. Dominion be his throughout the ages. Amen.

The friends of God have put their hope in him.
— They will be clothed in his unfailing strength.

Midday

Ant.   The Lord crowned them with a crown of holiness
         and gave them a glorious name.

READING   See Hebrews 11:33

The saints by faith conquered kingdoms, did what was
just, obtained the promises in Christ Jesus our Lord.

You will know sorrow.
   But your sorrow will be turned into joy.

Midafternoon

Ant.   They went out weeping and crying, and bitter was
        the sowing.

READING   Wisdom 3:1-2a, 3b

The souls of the just are in the hand of God,
    and no torment shall touch them.
They seemed, in the view of the foolish, to be dead.
    But they are in peace.

They come, see, they come singing for joy.
—Homeward bound, laden with sheaves.

Prayer, as in Morning Prayer.

Evening Prayer II

HYMN

For all the saints who from their labors rest,
Who thee by faith before the world confessed,
Thy name, O Jesus, be for ever blest:
    Alleluia, alleluia!

Thou wast their rock, their fortress and their might;
Thou, Lord, their captain in the well-fought fight;
Thou in the darkness drear their one true light:
    Alleluia, alleluia!

O blest communion, fellowship divine!
We feebly struggle, they in glory shine;
Yet all are one in thee, for all are thine:
    Alleluia, alleluia!

But, lo, there breaks a yet more glorious day;
The saints triumphant rise in bright array :
The King of glory passes on his way:
    Alleluia, alleluia!

Melody: Sine Nomine 10.10.10   Music: R. Vaughan Williams,
with alleluias   1872–1958
                        Text: William W. How, 1823–1897

PSALMODY

Ant. 1 The mortal bodies of God's saints lie buried in peace, but they themselves live with God for ever.

Psalm 116:1-9

I love the Lord for he has heard
the cry of my appeal;
for he turned his ear to me
in the day when I called him.

They surrounded me, the snares of death,
with the anguish of the tomb;
they caught me, sorrow and distress.
I called on the Lord's name.

O Lord my God, deliver me!

How gracious is the Lord, and just;
our God has compassion.
The Lord protects the simple hearts;
I was helpless so he saved me.

Turn back, my soul, to your rest
for the Lord has been good;
he has kept my soul from death,
my eyes from tears
and my feet from stumbling.

I will walk in the presence of the Lord
in the land of the living.

Ant. The mortal bodies of God's saints lie buried in peace, but they themselves live with God for ever.

Ant. 2 I saw the souls of those put to death for the word of God and for their faithful witness.

Psalm 116: 10-19

I trusted, even when I said:
"I am sorely afflicted,"
and when I said in my alarm:
"No man can be trusted."

How can I repay the Lord
for his goodness to me?
The cup of salvation I will raise;
I will call on the Lord's name.

My vows to the Lord I will fulfill
before all his people.
O precious in the eyes of the Lord
is the death of his faithful.

Your servant, Lord, your servant am I;
you have loosened my bonds.
A thanksgiving sacrifice I make:
I will call on the Lord's name.

My vows to the Lord I will fulfill
before all his people,
in the courts of the house of the Lord,
in your midst, O Jerusalem.

Ant.   I saw the souls of those put to death for the word
of God and for their faithful witness.

Ant. 3   These are the saints who surrendered their bodies in witness to God's covenant; they have
washed their robes in the blood of the Lamb.

Canticle   Revelation 4:11; 5:9, 10, 12

O Lord, our God, you are worthy
to receive glory and honor and power.
For you have created all things;
by your will they came to be and were made.

Worthy are you, O Lord,
to receive the scroll and break open its seals.

For you were slain.
With your blood you purchased for God
men of every race and tongue,
of every people and nation.

You made of them a kingdom,
and priests to serve our God,
and they shall reign on the earth.

Worthy is the Lamb that was slain
to receive power and riches,
wisdom and strength,
honor and glory and praise.

Ant.   These are the saints who surrendered their bodies
in witness to God's covenant; they have washed
their robes in the blood of the Lamb.

READING   1 Peter 4:13-14

Dearly beloved: Rejoice in the measure that you share
Christ's sufferings. When his glory is revealed, you will
rejoice exultantly. Happy are you when you are insulted
for the sake of Christ, for then God's Spirit in its glory
has come to rest on you.

RESPONSORY

Let the just rejoice and sing for joy in the Lord.
—Let the just rejoice and sing for joy in the Lord.

Delight in his love, you pure of heart.
— And sing for joy in the Lord.

Glory to the Father . . . . . .
—Let the just . . . . . .

CANTICLE OF MARY

Ant.   The holy friends of Christ rejoice in heaven; they
followed in his footsteps to the end. They have
shed their blood for love of him and will reign
with him for ever.

INTERCESSIONS

This is the hour when the King of martyrs offered his life
in the upper room and laid it down on the cross. Let us
thank him and say:
We praise you, O Lord.

We praise you, O Lord, our Savior, inspiration and example for every martyr, for loving us to the end:
We praise you, O Lord.

For calling all repentant sinners to the rewards of life:
We praise you, O Lord.

For entrusting to your Church the blood of the new and
everlasting convenant poured out for the remission of
sin:
We praise you, O Lord.

For our perseverance in your grace today:
We praise you, O Lord.

For incorporating our dead brothers and sisters into your
own death today:
We praise you, O Lord.

Our Father . . .

Prayer

If there is no proper prayer, one of the following is said:

All-powerful, ever-living God,
turn our weakness into strength.
As you gave your martyrs N. and N.
the courage to suffer death for Christ,
give us the courage to live in faithful witness to you.
Grant this through our Lord Jesus Christ, your Son,

who lives and reigns with you and the Holy Spirit,
one God, for ever and ever.

Or:

Lord,
hear the prayers of the martyrs N. and N.
and give us courage to bear witness to your truth.

Grant this through our Lord Jesus Christ, your Son,
who lives and reigns with you and the Holy Spirit,
one God, for ever and ever.

For virgin martyrs:

God our Father,
you give us joy each year
in honoring the memory of Saints N. and N.
May their prayers be a source of help for us,
and may their example of courage and chastity be our in-
    spiration.

Grant this through our Lord Jesus Christ, your Son,
who lives and reigns with you and the Holy Spirit,
one God, for ever and ever.

For holy women:

Father,
in our weakness your power reaches perfection.
You gave Saints N. and N. the strength
to defeat the power of sin and evil.
May we who celebrate their glory share in their triumph.

We ask this through our Lord Jesus Christ, your Son,
who lives and reigns with you and the Holy Spirit,
one God, for ever and ever.

FOR ONE MARTYR

Evening Prayer I

Hymn, as in Evening Prayer II, 1415.

Psalmody

Ant. 1 If anyone declares himself for me before men, I
will declare myself for him before my Father.

Psalm 118

I

Give thanks to the Lord for he is good,
for his love endures for ever.

Let the sons of Israel say:
"His love endures for ever."
Let the sons of Aaron say:
"His love endures for ever."
Let those who fear the Lord say:
"His love endures for ever."

I called to the Lord in my distress;
he answered and freed me.
The Lord is at my side; I do not fear.
What can man do against me?
The Lord is at my side as my helper:
I shall look down on my foes.

It is better to take refuge in the Lord
than to trust in men:
it is better to take refuge in the Lord
than to trust in princes.

The nations all encompassed me;
in the Lord's name I crushed them.
They compassed me, compassed me about;
in the Lord's name I crushed them.

They compassed me about like bees;
they blazed like a fire among thorns.
In the Lord's name I crushed them.

I was hard-pressed and was falling
but the Lord came to help me.
The Lord is my strength and my song;
he is my savior.
There are shouts of joy and victory
in the tents of the just.

The Lord's right hand has triumphed;
his right hand raised me.
The Lord's right hand has triumphed;
I shall not die, I shall live
and recount his deeds.
I was punished, I was punished by the Lord,
but not doomed to die.

Ant.   If anyone declares himself for me before men, I
will declare myself for him before my Father.

Ant. 2   Whoever follows me does not walk in the dark;
he will have the light of life.

II

Open to me the gates of holiness:
I will enter and give thanks.
This is the Lord's own gate
where the just may enter.
I will thank you for you have answered
and you are my savior.

The stone which the builders rejected
has become the corner stone.
This is the work of the Lord,
a marvel in our eyes.
This day was made by the Lord;
we rejoice and are glad.

O Lord, grant us salvation;
O Lord, grant success.
Blessed in the name of the Lord
is he who comes.
We bless you from the house of the Lord;
the Lord God is our light.

Go forward in procession with branches
even to the altar.
You are my God, I thank you.
My God, I praise you.
Give thanks to the Lord for he is good;
for his love endures for ever.

Ant.   Whoever follows me does not walk in the dark; he
        will have the light of life.

Ant. 3 If we share fully in the sufferings of Christ,
        through Christ we shall know the fullness of his
        consolation.

                      Canticle   1 Peter 2:21-24

Christ suffered for you,
and left you an example
to have you follow in his footsteps.

He did no wrong;
no deceit was found in his mouth.
When he was insulted
he returned no insult.

When he was made to suffer,
he did not counter with threats.
Instead he delivered himself up
to the One who judges justly.

In his own body
he brought your sins to the cross,
so that all of us, dead to sin,
could live in accord with God's will.

By his wounds you were healed.

Ant. If we share fully in the sufferings of Christ,
      through Christ we shall know the fullness of his
      consolation.

READING   Romans 8:35, 37-39

Who will separate us from the love of Christ? Trial, or
distress, or persecution, or hunger, or nakedness, or danger, or the sword? Yet in all this we are more than con-
querors because of him who has loved us. For I am certain that neither death nor life, neither angels nor principalities, neither the present nor the future, nor powers,
neither height nor depth nor any other creature, will be
able to separate us from the love of God that comes to us
in Christ Jesus, our Lord.

RESPONSORY

For a man:

With glory and honor, Lord, you have crowned him.
—With glory and honor, Lord, you have crowned him.

You set him over the works of your hands.
—Lord, you have crowned him.

Glory to the Father . . .
—With glory and . . .

For a woman:

The Lord has chosen her, his loved one from the beginning.
— The Lord has chosen her, his loved one from the beginning.

He has taken her to live with him.
—His loved one from the beginning.

Glory to the Father . . .
—The Lord has . . .

CANTICLE OF MARY

For a man:

Ant.   For the law of God this holy man engaged in com-
        bat to the death. His faith was founded on solid
        rock; he feared no wicked threats.

For a woman:

Ant.   She has girded herself with strength and made her
        arms sturdy. The light she has kindled will never
        go out.

INTERCESSIONS

This is the hour when the King of martyrs offered his life
    in the upper room and laid it down on the cross. Let us
    thank him and say:
        We praise you, O Lord.
We praise you, O Lord, our Savior, inspiration and ex-
    ample for every martyr, for loving us to the end:
        We praise you, O Lord.
For calling all repentant sinners to the rewards of life:
        We praise you, O Lord.
For entrusting to your Church the blood of the new and
    everlasting covenant poured out for the remission of
    sin:
        We praise you, O Lord.
For our perseverance in your grace today:
        We praise you, O Lord.
For incorporating our dead brothers and sisters into your
    own death today:
        We praise you, O Lord.

Our Father . . .

Prayer

If there is no proper prayer, one of the following is said:

God of power and mercy,

you gave N., your martyr, victory over pain and suffering.

Strengthen us who celebrate this day of his triumph

and help us to be victorious over the evils that threaten us.

Grant this through our Lord Jesus Christ, your Son,

who lives and reigns with you and the Holy Spirit,

one God, for ever and ever.

Or:

All-powerful, ever-living God,

you gave Saint N. the courage to witness to the gospel of Christ

even to the point of giving his life for it.

By his prayers help us to endure all suffering for love of you

and to seek you with all our hearts,

for you alone are the source of life.

Grant this through our Lord Jesus Christ, your Son,

who lives and reigns with you and the Holy Spirit,

one God, for ever and ever.

For a virgin martyr:

God our Father,

you give us joy each year

in honoring the memory of Saint N.

May her prayers be a source of help for us,

and may her example of courage and chastity be our inspiration.

Grant this through our Lord Jesus Christ, your Son,

who lives and reigns with you and the Holy Spirit,

one God, for ever and ever.

For a holy woman:

Father,
in our weakness your power reaches perfection.
You gave Saint N. the strength
to defeat the power of sin and evil.
May we who celebrate her glory share in her triumph.

We ask this through our Lord Jesus Christ, your Son,
who lives and reigns with you and the Holy Spirit,
one God, for ever and ever.

Invitatory

Ant.   Come, let us worship Christ, the King of martyrs.

Invitatory psalm, as in the Ordinary, 648.

Office of Readings

HYMN

Faith of our fathers! faith and prayer
Shall win all nations unto thee;
And through the truth that comes from God,
Mankind shall then indeed be free.

Refrain:

Faith of our fathers, holy faith!
We will be true to thee till death.

Faith of our fathers! we will love
Both friend and foe in all our strife:
And preach thee too, as love knows how,
By kindly deeds and virtuous life.

Refrain

Melody: St. Catherine L.M.   Music: Henri F. Hemy, 1818–1888
with Refrain   and James G. Walton, 1821–1905
                                      Text: Frederick W. Faber, 1814–1863

PSALMODY

Ant. 1   Men will hate you because you are mine, but he
         who perseveres will be saved.

Psalm 2

Why this tumult among nations,
among peoples this useless murmuring?
They arise, the kings of the earth,
princes plot against the Lord and his Anointed.
"Come, let us break their fetters,
come, let us cast off their yoke."

He who sits in the heavens laughs;
the Lord is laughing them to scorn.
Then he will speak in his anger,
his rage will strike them with terror.
"It is I who have set up my king
on Zion, my holy mountain."

I will announce the decree of the Lord:

The Lord said to me: "You are my Son.
It is I who have begotten you this day.
Ask and I shall bequeath you the nations,
put the ends of the earth in your possession.
With a rod of iron you will break them,
shatter them like a potter's jar."

Now, O kings, understand,
take warning, rulers of the earth;
serve the Lord with awe
and trembling, pay him your homage
lest he be angry and you perish;
for suddenly his anger will blaze.

Blessed are they who put their trust in God.

Ant.   Men will hate you because you are mine, but he
       who perseveres will be saved.

Ant. 2 The sufferings of this life cannot be compared
        to the glory that will be revealed in us in the life
        to come.

Psalm 11

In the Lord I have taken my refuge.
How can you say to my soul:
"Fly like a bird to its mountain.

See the wicked bracing their bow;
they are fixing their arrows on the string
to shoot upright men in the dark.
Foundations once destroyed, what can the just do?"

The Lord is in his holy temple,
the Lord, whose throne is in heaven.
His eyes look down on the world;
his gaze tests mortal men.

The Lord tests the just and the wicked:
the lover of violence he hates.
He sends fire and brimstone on the wicked;
he sends a scorching wind as their lot.

The Lord is just and loves justice:
the upright shall see his face.

Ant. The sufferings of this life cannot be compared to
      the glory that will be revealed in us in the life to
      come.

Ant. 3 The Lord tested his chosen ones as gold tested
        by fire; he has received them for ever as a sac-
        rificial offering.

Psalm 17

Lord, hear a cause that is just,
pay heed to my cry.
Turn your ear to my prayer:
no deceit is on my lips.

From you may my judgment come forth.
Your eyes discern the truth.

You search my heart, you visit me by night.
You test me and you find in me no wrong.
My words are not sinful as are men's words.

I kept from violence because of your word,
I kept my feet firmly in your paths;
there was no faltering in my steps.

I am here and I call, you will hear me, O God.
Turn your ear to me; hear my words.
Display your great love, you whose right hand saves
your friends from those who rebel against them.

Guard me as the apple of your eye.
Hide me in the shadow of your wings
from the violent attack of the wicked.

My foes encircle me with deadly intent.
Their hearts tight shut, their mouths speak proudly.
They advance against me, and now they surround
    me.

Their eyes are watching to strike me to the ground
as though they were lions ready to claw
or like some young lion crouched in hiding.

Lord, arise, confront them, strike them down!
Let your sword rescue my soul from the wicked;
let your hand, O Lord, rescue me from men,
from men whose reward is in this present life.

You give them their fill of your treasures;
they rejoice in abundance of offspring
and leave their wealth to their children.

As for me, in my justice I shall see your face
and be filled, when I awake, with the sight of your
    glory.

Ant.   The Lord tested his chosen ones as gold tested by
       fire; he has received them for ever as a sacrificial
       offering.

I have known tribulation and distress.
—But in your commands I have found consolation.

FIRST READING

From the book of Sirach   51:1-12

Thanksgiving to God who delivers his people from their trials

I give you thanks, O God of my father;
    I praise you, O God my savior!

I will make known your name, refuge of my life;
    you have been my helper against my adversaries.
You have saved me from death,
    and kept back my body from the pit,
From the clutches of the nether world you have
    snatched my feet;
    you have delivered me, in your great mercy,
From the scourge of a slanderous tongue,
    and from lips that went over to falsehood;
From the snare of those who watched for my downfall,
    and from the power of those who sought my life;
From many a danger you have saved me,
    from flames that hemmed me in on every side;
From the midst of unremitting fire,
    from the deep belly of the nether world;
From deceiving lips and painters of lies,
    from the arrows of dishonest tongues.

I was at the point of death,
    my soul was nearing the depths of the nether world;
I turned every way, but there was no one to help me,
    I looked for one to sustain me, but could find no one.

But then I remembered the mercies of the Lord,
   his kindness through ages past;
For he saves those who take refuge in him,
   and rescues them from every evil.
So I raised my voice from the very earth,
   from the gates of the nether world, my cry.
I called out: O Lord, you are my father,
   you are my champion and my savior;
Do not abandon me in time of trouble,
   in the midst of storms and dangers.

I will ever praise your name
   and be constant in my prayers to you.
Thereupon the Lord heard my voice,
   he listened to my appeal;
He saved me from evil of every kind
   and preserved me in time of trouble.
For this reason I thank him and I praise him;
   I bless the name of the Lord.

RESPONSORY   Sirach 51:2; Psalm 31:8

I will praise your name, O Lord,
—for you have been my protector and my strength.

I will rejoice and be glad, because you, O Lord,
have shown mercy to me.
—For you have . . .

SECOND READING

From a sermon by Saint Augustine, bishop

(Sermo 329, in natali martyrum: PL 38, 1454-1456)

The death of martyrs is precious, bought at the cost of
Christ's death

   The Church everywhere flourishes through the glorious deeds of the holy martyrs. With our own eyes we can

judge the truth of our song, that *the death of his saints is precious in the sight of the Lord.* It is precious in our sight and in the sight of the Lord as well, for in his name they died.

But the price of these deaths is the death of one man. See how many deaths he paid for by dying himself! For if he had not died, would the grain of wheat have been multiplied? You have heard what he said on his way to his passion, which was our redemption: *Unless the grain of wheat falls to the ground and dies, it remains alone; but if it dies, it bears much fruit.*

On the cross he made the great exchange. There the purse which held our price was opened, for when the soldier's spear opened his side, the price of the whole world flowed forth. Thus he purchased the faithful and the martyrs. But the faith of the martyrs has been tested; their blood is the proof. They paid back the price Christ paid for them, thus fulfilling the words of Saint John: *Just as Christ laid down his life for us, we too must lay down our lives for our brothers.*

Elsewhere it is said: *You are seated at a great table. Observe carefully all that is set before you, for you also must prepare such a banquet.* The table is large, for the banquet is none other than the Lord of the table himself. No one has his guests feed upon himself, and yet this is precisely what Christ our Lord does; though host, he himself is both food and drink. The martyrs recognized the food and drink they were given, in order to make repayment in kind.

But how can they make repayment, unless he first spends his riches on them and gives them the means to repay? And what does the psalm we have sung recommend when it says: *The death of the saints is precious in the sight of the Lord?*

In this psalm man ponders the great things he has received from God, the great gifts of grace from the almighty: God created man, sought him when he was lost, pardoned him when he was found, supported him when he struggled in weakness, did not abandon him when he was in danger, crowned him in victory, and gave himself as the prize. Reflecting on all this man cries out, saying: *What shall I give the Lord for all he has given me? I shall take up the cup of salvation.*

What is this cup? It is the cup of suffering, bitter yet healthful: the cup which, if the physician did not first drink it, the sick man would fear to touch. Yes, it is the cup of suffering, and of it Christ is speaking when he says: *Father, if it is possible let this cup pass from me.*

Of this cup the martyrs said: *I shall take the cup of salvation and call upon the name of the Lord.* But are you not afraid you will weaken? No, they reply. And why? Because *I shall call upon the name of the Lord.* Do you think martyrs could have been victorious, unless he was victorious in the martyrs who said: *Rejoice, for I have overcome the world?* The Lord of the heavens directed their minds and tongues; through them he overcame the devil on earth and crowned them as martyrs in heaven. Blessed are those who have drunk of this cup! Their torments are at an end, and they have taken their place of honor. And so, my dear ones, consider: although you cannot see with your eyes, do so with your mind and soul, and see that *the death of the saints is precious in the sight of the Lord.*

RESPONSORY   2 Timothy 4:7-8; Philippians 3:8-10

I have fought the good fight,
I have run the race to the finish,
I have kept the faith;
—now a crown of holiness awaits me.

Nothing has seemed worthwhile to me except to know
   Christ,
to be one with him in his sufferings,
to bear his death in my body.
—Now a crown . . .

On solemnities and feasts, **Te Deum**, 651.

Prayer, as in Morning Prayer.

Morning Prayer

HYMN

Christ, in whose passion once was sown
All virtue of all saints to be,
For the white field of these thy own
We praise the seed and sower, thee.

Thine was the first and holiest grain
To die and quicken and increase;
And then came these, and died again,
That spring and harvest should not cease.

From thee the martyrs, we from those,
Each in thy grace's measure, spring;
Their strength upon our weakness flows
And guides us to the goal we sing.

These were thy great ones: we, thy least,
One in desire and faith with them,
Called by the Lord to keep one feast,
Journey to one Jerusalem.

Melody: Mein' Seel'. O Gott,   Music: M. Praetorius, 1571–1621
muss Loben Dich L.M.   Text: Walter Shewring

Or:

A mighty fortress is our God,
A bulwark never failing;
Our helper he amid the flood

Of mortal ills prevailing:
For still our ancient foe
Does seek to work us woe;
His craft and power are great
And, armed with cruel hate,
On earth is not his equal.

Did we in our own strength confide,
Our striving would be losing;
Were not the right man on our side,
The man of God's own choosing:
You ask who that may be?
Christ Jesus, it is he;
Lord Sabaoth his Name,
From age to age the same,
And he must win the battle.

And tho' this world, with devils filled,
Should threaten to undo us;
We will not fear, for God has willed
His truth to triumph through us:
The prince of darkness grim,
We tremble not for him;
His rage we can endure,
For lo! his doom is sure,
One little word shall fell him.

Melody: Ein' Feste Burg 87.87.66.667 Music: Martin Luther, 1529
Text: Martin Luther, 1529
Translator: Frederick Henry Hedge, 1852, alt.

Or:

Refrain:

For to those who love God,
Who are called in his plan,
Everything works out for good.
And God himself chose them
To bear the likeness of his Son
That he might be the first of many, many brothers.

Who is able to condemn? Only Christ who died for
  us;
Christ who rose for us, Christ who prays for us.

Refrain

In the face of all this, what is there left to say?
For if God is for us, who can be against us?

Refrain

Who can separate us from the love of Christ?
Neither trouble, nor pain, nor persecution.

Refrain

What can separate us from the love of Christ?
Not the past, the present, nor the future.

Refrain

Melody: Romans VIII   Music: Enrico Garzilli, 1970
                             Text: Enrico Garzilli, 1970

Ant. 1 My lips will praise you, Lord, for sweeter than
        life is your merciful love.

Psalms and canticle from Sunday, Week I, **688**.

Ant. 2 Martyrs of the Lord, bless the Lord for ever.

Ant. 3 I will make the man who is victorious a pillar in
        my temple, says the Lord.

READING   2 Corinthians 1:3-5

Praised be God, the Father of our Lord Jesus Christ,
the Father of mercies, and the God of all consolation!
He comforts us in all our afflictions and thus enables us to
comfort those who are in trouble, with the same consolation we have received from him. As we have shared much
in the suffering of Christ, so through Christ do we share
abundantly in his consolation.

RESPONSORY

The Lord is my strength, and I shall sing his praise.
—The Lord is my strength, and I shall sing his praise.

The Lord is my savior.
—And I shall sing his praise.

Glory to the Father . . .
—The Lord is . . .

CANTICLE OF ZECHARIAH

Ant.   Whoever hates his life in this world keeps it safe
        for life everlasting.

INTERCESSIONS

Our Savior's faithfulness is mirrored in the fidelity of his
    witnesses who shed their blood for the word of God.
    Let us praise him in remembrance of them:
    You redeemed us by your blood.

Your martyrs freely embraced death in bearing witness to
    the faith,
—give us the true freedom of the Spirit, O Lord.

Your martyrs professed their faith by shedding their
    blood,
—give us a faith, O Lord, that is constant and pure.

Your martyrs followed in your footsteps by carrying the
    cross,
—help us to endure courageously the misfortunes of life.

Your martyrs washed their garments in the blood of the
    Lamb,
—help us to avoid the weaknesses of the flesh and world-
    ly allurements.

Our Father . . .

                          Prayer

If there is no proper prayer, one of the following is said:

God of power and mercy,
you gave N., your martyr, victory over pain and suffer-
     ing.
Strengthen us who celebrate this day of his triumph
and help us to be victorious over the evils that threaten us

Grant this through our Lord Jesus Christ, your Son,
who lives and reigns with you and the Holy Spirit,
one God, for ever and ever.

Or:

All-powerful, ever-living God,
you gave Saint N. the courage to witness to the gospel of
     Christ
even to the point of giving his life for it.
By his prayers help us to endure all suffering for love of
     you
and to seek you with all our hearts,
for you alone are the source of life.
Grant this through our Lord Jesus Christ, your Son,
who lives and reigns with you and the Holy Spirit,
one God, for ever and ever.

For a virgin martyr:

God our Father,
you give us joy each year
in honoring the memory of Saint N.
May her prayers be a source of help for us,
and may her example of courage and chastity be our in-
     spiration.
Grant this through our Lord Jesus Christ, your Son, who
lives and reigns with you and the Holy Spirit, one God,
for ever and ever.

For a holy woman:

Father,
in our weakness your power reaches perfection.
You gave Saint N. the strength
to defeat the power of sin and evil.
May we who celebrate her glory share in her triumph.

We ask this through our Lord Jesus Christ, your Son,
who lives and reigns with you and the Holy Spirit,
one God, for ever and ever.

Daytime Prayer

Midmorning

Ant.   The Lord gave them victory after a bitter contest,
for no power can conquer the wisdom of God.

READING   1 Peter 5:10-11

The God of all grace, who called you to his everlasting
glory in Christ, will himself restore, confirm, strengthen,
and establish those who have suffered a little while. Dominion be his throughout the ages! Amen.

God clothed him (her) in gladness.
—And placed a crown of glory on his (her) head.

Midday

Ant.   The Lord crowned him (her) with the crown of
holiness and gave him (her) a glorious name.

READING   James 1:12

Happy the man who holds out to the end through trial!
Once he has been proved, he will receive the crown of life
the Lord has promised to those who love him

I have put my hope in God.
—I have no fear of man.

Midafternoon

Ant.   They went out weeping and crying, and bitter was
        the sowing.

READING   Wisdom 3:1-2a, 3b

The souls of the just are in the hand of God,
    and no torment shall touch them.
They seemed, in the view of the foolish, to be dead.
    But they are in peace.

They come, see, they come singing for joy.
—Homeward bound, laden with sheaves.

Prayer, as in Morning Prayer

Evening Prayer II

HYMN

Amazing grace! how sweet the sound,
That saved a wretch like me!
I once was lost, but now am found,
Was blind, but now I see.

'Twas grace that taught my heart to fear,
And grace my fears relieved;
How precious did that grace appear
The hour I first believed!

Through many dangers, toils, and snares,
I have already come;
'Tis grace hath brought me safe thus far,
And grace will lead me home.

Amazing Grace 86.86   Music: Early American Melody
                               Text: John Newton, 1725–1807
Or:

For all the saints who from their labors rest,
Who thee by faith before the world confessed,
Thy name, O Jesus, be for ever blest:
    Alleluia, alleluia!

Thou wast their rock, their fortress and their might;
Thou, Lord, their captain in the well-fought fight;
Thou in the darkness drear their one true light:
    Alleluia, alleluia!

O blest communion, fellowship divine!
We feebly struggle, they in glory shine;
Yet all are one in thee, for all are thine:
    Alleluia, alleluia!

But, lo, there breaks a yet more glorious day;
We feebly struggle, they in glory shine;
Yet all are one in thee, for all are thine:
    Alleluia, alleluia!

But, lo, there breaks a yet more glorious day;
The saints triumphant rise in bright array:
The King of glory passes on his way:
    Alleluia, alleluia!

Melody: Sine Nomine 10.10.10   Music: R. Vaughan Williams,
with alleluias   1872–1958
                           Text: William W. How, 1823–1897

PSALMODY

Ant. 1   If anyone wishes to come after me, he must
           deny himself, take up his cross, and follow me.

Psalm 116:1-9

I love the Lord for he has heard
    the cry of my appeal;
for he turned his ear to me
    in the day when I called him.

They surrounded me, the snares of death,
    with the anguish of the tomb;
they caught me, sorrow and distress.
    I called on the Lord's name.

O Lord my God, deliver me!

How gracious is the Lord, and just;
our God has compassion.
The Lord protects the simple hearts;
I was helpless so he saved me.

Turn back, my soul, to your rest
for the Lord has been good;
he has kept my soul from death,
my eyes from tears
and my feet from stumbling.

I will walk in the presence of the Lord
in the land of the living.

Ant.   If anyone wishes to come after me, he must deny
himself, take up his cross, and follow me.

Ant. 2   Whoever serves me will be honored by my Father in heaven.

Psalm 116:10-19

I trusted, even when I said:
"I am sorely afflicted,"
and when I said in my alarm:
"No man can be trusted."

How can I repay the Lord
for his goodness to me?
The cup of salvation I will raise;
I will call on the Lord's name.

My vows to the Lord I will fulfill
before all his people.
O precious in the eyes of the Lord
is the death of his faithful.

Your servant, Lord, your servant am I;
you have loosened my bonds.
A thanksgiving sacrifice I make:
I will call on the Lord's name.

My vows to the Lord I will fulfill
before all his people,
in the courts of the house of the Lord,
in your midst, O Jerusalem.

Ant.   Whoever serves me will be honored by my Father
in heaven.

Ant. 3   He who loses his life because of me will find it
for ever.

Canticle   Revelation 4:11; 5:9, 10, 12

O Lord, our God, you are worthy,
to receive glory and honor and power.
For you have created all things;
by your will they came to be and were made.

Worthy are you, O Lord,
to receive the scroll and break open its seals.

For you were slain.
With your blood you purchased for God
men of every race and tongue,
of every people and nation.

You made of them a kingdom,
and priests to serve our God,
and they shall reign on the earth.

Worthy is the Lamb that was slain
to receive power and riches,
wisdom and strength,
honor and glory and praise.

Ant.   He who loses his life because of me will find it for
ever.

READING   1 Peter 4:13-14

Rejoice in the measure that you share Christ's sufferings. When his glory is revealed, you will rejoice exultantly. Happy are you when you are insulted for the sake
of Christ, for then God's Spirit in its glory has come to
rest on you.

RESPONSORY

You have tried us by fire, O God,
then led us to a place of refreshment.
—You have tried us by fire, O God,
then led us to a place of refreshment.

You refined us as silver in the furnace,
—then led us to a place of refreshment.

Glory to the Father . . .
—You have tried . . .

CANTICLE OF MARY

Ant.   The saints find their home in the kingdom of
         heaven; their life is eternal peace.

INTERCESSIONS

This is the hour when the King of martyrs offered his life
     in the upper room and laid it down on the cross. Let us
     thank him and say:
     We praise you, O Lord.
We praise you, O Lord, our Savior, inspiration and ex-
     ample for every martyr, for loving us to the end:
     We praise you, O Lord.
For calling all repentant sinners to the rewards of life:
     We praise you, O Lord.
For entrusting to your Church the blood of the new and
     everlasting covenant poured out for the remission of
     sin:

We praise you, O Lord.
For our perseverance in your grace today:
   We praise you, O Lord.
For incorporating our dead brothers and sisters into your
   own death today:
   We praise you, O Lord.

Our Father . . .

Prayer

If there is no proper prayer, one of the following is said:

God of power and mercy,
you gave N., your martyr, victory over pain and suffering.
Strengthen us who celebrate this day of his triumph
and help us to be victorious over the evils that threaten
   us.

Grant this through our Lord Jesus Christ, your Son,
who lives and reigns with you and the Holy Spirit,
one God, for ever and ever.

Or:

All-powerful, ever-living God,
you gave Saint N. the courage to witness to the gospel of
   Christ
even to the point of giving his life for it.
By his prayers help us to endure all suffering for love of
   you
and to seek you with all our hearts,
for you alone are the source of life.

Grant this through our Lord Jesus Christ, your Son,
who lives and reigns with you and the Holy Spirit,
one God, for ever and ever.

For a virgin martyr:

God our Father,
you give us joy each year
in honoring the memory of Saint N.
May her prayers be a source of help for us,
and may her example of courage and chastity be our in-
    spiration.
Grant this through our Lord Jesus Christ, your Son,
who lives and reigns with you and the Holy Spirit,
one God, for ever and ever.

For a holy woman:

Father,
in our weakness your power reaches perfection.
You gave Saint N. the strength
to defeat the power of sin and evil.
May we who celebrate her glory share in her triumph.
We ask this through our Lord Jesus Christ, your Son,
who lives and reigns with you and the Holy Spirit,
one God, for ever and ever.

COMMON OF PASTORS

Evening Prayer I

HYMN, as in Evening Prayer II, **1449**.

PSALMODY

Ant. 1 I will give you shepherds after my own heart;
they will nourish you with knowledge and
sound teaching.

Psalm 113

Praise, O servants of the Lord,
praise the name of the Lord!
May the name of the Lord be blessed
both now and for evermore!
From the rising of the sun to its setting
praised be the name of the Lord!

High above all nations is the Lord,
above the heavens his glory.
Who is like the Lord, our God,
who has risen on high to his throne
yet stoops from the heights to look down,
to look down upon heaven and earth?

From the dust he lifts up the lowly,
from his misery he raises the poor
to set him in the company of princes,
yes, with the princes of his people.
To the childless wife he gives a home
and gladdens her heart with children.

Ant. I will give you shepherds after my own heart; they
will nourish you with knowledge and sound teaching.

Ant. 2 I shall feed my flock; I shall search for the lost
and lead back those who have strayed.

Psalm 146

My soul, give praise to the Lord;
I will praise the Lord all my days,
make music to my God while I live.

Put no trust in princes,
in mortal men in whom there is no help.
Take their breath, they return to clay
and their plans that day come to nothing.

He is happy who is helped by Jacob's God,
whose hope is in the Lord his God,
who alone made heaven and earth,
the seas and all they contain.

It is he who keeps faith for ever,
who is just to those who are oppressed.
It is he who gives bread to the hungry,
the Lord, who sets prisoners free,

the Lord who gives sight to the blind,
who raises up those who are bowed down,
the Lord, who protects the stranger
and upholds the widow and orphan.

It is the Lord who loves the just
but thwarts the path of the wicked.
The Lord will reign for ever,
Zion's God, from age to age.

Ant.   I shall feed my flock; I shall search for the lost and
lead back those who have strayed.

Ant. 3   The Good Shepherd laid down his life for his
sheep.

Canticle   Ephesians 1:3-10

Praised be the God and Father
of our Lord Jesus Christ,

who bestowed on us in Christ
every spiritual blessing in the heavens.

God chose us in him
before the world began,
to be holy
and blameless in his sight.

He predestined us
to be his adopted sons through Jesus Christ,
such was his will and pleasure,
that all might praise the glorious favor
he has bestowed on us in his beloved.

In him and through his blood, we have been redeemed,
and our sins forgiven,
so immeasurably generous
is God's favor to us.

God has given us the wisdom
to understand fully the mystery,
the plan he was pleased
to decree in Christ.

A plan to be carried out
in Christ, in the fullness of time,
to bring all things into one in him,
in the heavens and on the earth.

Ant.   The Good Shepherd laid down his life for his
       sheep.

READING   1 Peter 5:1-4

   To the elders among you I, a fellow elder, a witness of
Christ's sufferings and sharer in the glory that is to be revealed, make this appeal. God's flock is in your midst;
give it a shepherd's care. Watch over it willingly as God
would have you do, not under constraint; and not for

shameful profit either, but generously. Be examples to
the flock, not lording it over those assigned to you, so
that when the chief Shepherd appears you will win for
yourselves the unfading crown of glory.

RESPONSORY

Priests of the Lord, give thanks and praise to the Lord.
—Priests of the Lord, give thanks and praise to the Lord.

You of holy and humble heart, acclaim your Lord.
—Give thanks and praise to the Lord.

Glory to the Father . . .
—Priests of the . . .

CANTICLE OF MARY

For a pope or bishop:

Ant.   Priest of the Most High God and mirror of good-
        ness, you were a good shepherd to your people
        and pleasing to the Lord.

For a priest:

Ant.   I became all things to all men, that all might find
        salvation.

INTERCESSIONS

Jesus Christ is worthy of all praise, for he was appointed
    high priest among men and their representative before
    God. We honor him and in our weakness we pray:
    Bring salvation to your people, Lord.
You marvelously illuminated your Church through dis-
    tinguished leaders and holy men and women,
—let Christians rejoice always in such splendor.
You forgave the sins of your people when their holy lead-
    ers like Moses sought your compassion,
—through their intercession continue to purify and sanc-
    tify your holy people.

In the midst of their brothers and sisters you anointed
    your holy ones and filled them with the Holy Spirit,
—fill all the leaders of your people with the same Spirit.
You yourself are the only visible possession of our holy
    pastors,
—let none of them, won at the price of your blood, re-
    main far from you.
The shepherds of your Church keep your flock from be-
    ing snatched out of your hand. Through them you
    give your flock eternal life,
—save those who have died, those for whom you gave up
    your life.

Our Father . . .

Prayer

If there is no proper prayer, one of the following is said:

For a pope:

All-powerful and ever-living God,
you called Saint N. to guide your people
by his word and example.
With him we pray to you:
watch over the pastors of your Church
with the people entrusted to their care,
and lead them to salvation.

We ask this through our Lord Jesus Christ, your Son,
who lives and reigns with you and the Holy Spirit,
one God, for ever and ever.

For a bishop:

Lord God,
you counted Saint N. among your holy pastors,
renowned for faith and love which conquered evil in this
    world.
By the help of his prayers

keep us strong in faith and love
and let us come to share his glory.

Grant this through our Lord Jesus Christ, your Son,
who lives and reigns with you and the Holy Spirit,
one God, for ever and ever.

For the founder of a church:

Lord,
you called our fathers to the light of the gospel
by the preaching of Saint N.
By his prayers help us to grow in the love and knowledge
of your Son, our Lord Jesus Christ,
who lives and reigns with you and the Holy Spirit,
one God, for ever and ever.

For a pastor:

God our Father,
in Saint N. you gave
a light to your faithful people.
You made him a pastor of the Church
to feed your sheep with his word
and to teach them by his example.
Help us by his prayers to keep the faith he taught
and follow the way of life he showed us.

Grant this through our Lord Jesus Christ, your Son,
who lives and reigns with you and the Holy Spirit,
one God, for ever and ever.

Or:

Lord God,
you gave your Saint N.
the spirit of truth and love
to shepherd your people.
May we who honor him on this feast
learn from his example

and be helped by his prayers.
We ask this through our Lord Jesus Christ, your Son,
who lives and reigns with you and the Holy Spirit,
one God, for ever and ever.

For a missionary:

God of mercy,
you gave us Saint N. to proclaim the riches of Christ.
By the help of his prayers
may we grow in knowledge of you,
be eager to do good,
and learn to walk before you
by living the truth of the gospel.
Grant this through our Lord Jesus Christ, your Son,
who lives and reigns with you and the Holy Spirit,
one God, for ever and ever.

Invitatory

Ant.   Come, let us worship Christ, chief shepherd of the
       flock.

Invitatory psalm, as in the Ordinary, 648.

Office of Readings

HYMN

The earth is full of the goodness of Christ,
He feeds his lambs and guards his sheep,
He walks abroad as the Shepherd of souls,
And gathers all into his keep.

We know the voice of our Pastor, the Lord,
He calls our names eternally,
Our hearts rejoice at the words that he speaks:
"And I know mine and mine know me."

When danger comes all the hirelings will flee,
But Christ remains to guard our sleep,
When evil comes the Good Shepherd of souls
Lays down his life to save his sheep.

We shall not want, for our Pastor is Christ,
He makes us lie in fields of grace,
Where, shorn of sin and refreshed by his love,
We gaze in prayer upon his face.

Melody: The Earth Is Full of the   Music: Hendrik Andriessen
Goodness of Christ 10.8.10.8   Text: Michael Gannon

PSALMODY

Ant. 1   If anyone wishes to be first, he must become the
          last and the servant of all.

Psalm 21:2-8, 14

O Lord, your strength gives joy to the king;
how your saving help makes him glad!
You have granted him his heart's desire;
you have not refused the prayer of his lips.

You came to meet him with the blessings of success,
you have set on his head a crown of pure gold.
He asked you for life and this you have given,
days that will last from age to age.

Your saving help has given him glory.
You have laid upon him majesty and splendor,
you have granted your blessings to him for ever.
You have made him rejoice with the joy of your
    presence.

The king has put his trust in the Lord:
through the mercy of the Most High he shall stand
    firm.

O Lord, arise in your strength;
we shall sing and praise your power.

Ant.   If anyone wishes to be first, he must become the last and the servant of all.

Ant. 2   **When the prince of pastors comes again, you will receive from him an unfading crown of glory.**

Psalm 92

I

It is good to give thanks to the Lord
to make music to your name, O Most High,
to proclaim your love in the morning
and your truth in the watches of the night,
on the ten-stringed lyre and the lute,
with the murmuring sound of the harp.

Your deeds, O Lord, have made me glad;
for the work of your hands I shout with joy.
O Lord, how great are your works!
How deep are your designs!
The foolish man cannot know this
and the fool cannot understand.

Though the wicked spring up like grass
and all who do evil thrive:
they are doomed to be eternally destroyed.
But you, Lord, are eternally on high.

Ant.   When the prince of pastors comes again, you will receive from him an unfading crown of glory.

Ant. 3   **My good and faithful servant, come and share your master's joy.**

II

See how your enemies perish;
all doers of evil are scattered.

To me you give the wild-ox's strength;
you anoint me with the purest oil.
My eyes looked in triumph on my foes;
my ears heard gladly of their fall.
The just will flourish like the palm-tree
and grow like a Lebanon cedar.

Planted in the house of the Lord
they will flourish in the courts of our God,
still bearing fruit when they are old,
still full of sap, still green,
to proclaim that the Lord is just;
in him, my rock, there is no wrong.

Ant.   My good and faithful servant, come and share
your master's joy.

You will hear the word from my mouth.
—You will tell others what I have said.

First Reading

For a pope or bishop:

From the first letter of the apostle Paul
to the Thessalonians   2:1-13, 19-20

Remember our labors for you

You know well enough, brothers, that our coming
among you was not without effect.

Fresh from the humiliation we had suffered at Philippi—about which you know—we drew courage from our
God to preach his good tidings to you in the face of great
opposition. The exhortation we deliver does not spring
from deceit or impure motives or any sort of trickery;
rather, having met the test imposed on us by God, as men
entrusted with the good tidings, we speak like those who
strive to please God, "the tester of our hearts," rather
than men.

We were not guilty, as you well know, of flattering words or greed under any pretext, as God is our witness! Neither did we seek glory from men, you or any others, even though we could have insisted on our own importance as apostles of Christ.

On the contrary, while we were among you we were as gentle as any nursing mother fondling her little ones. So well disposed were we to you, in fact, that we wanted to share with you not only God's tidings but our very lives, so dear had you become to us.

You must recall, brothers, our efforts and our toil: how we worked day and night all the time we preached God's good tidings to you in order not to impose on you in any way. You are witnesses, as is God himself, of how upright, just, and irreproachable our conduct was toward you who are believers. You likewise know how we exhorted every one of you, as a father does his children— how we encouraged and pleaded with you to make your lives worthy of the God who calls you to his kingship and glory.

That is why we thank God constantly that in receiving his message from us you took it, not as the word of men, but as it truly is, the word of God at work within you who believe.

Who, after all, if not you, will be our hope or joy, or the crown we exult in, before our Lord Jesus Christ at his coming? You are our boast and our delight.

RESPONSORY   See Acts 20:28; 1 Corinthians 4:2

You must have at heart every member of the flock,
for the Holy Spirit has made you their shepherds.
—You must rule over the Church of God
which he made his own through the blood of his Son.

The great quality of a steward is to be faithful to his duty.
—You must rule . . .

For a priest:

From the first letter of the apostle Paul to Timothy   5:17-22; 6:10-14
The good fight of priests and men of God

Presbyters who do well as leaders deserve to be paid double, especially those whose work is preaching and teaching. The Scripture says, "You shall not put a muzzle on an ox when he is threshing the grain," and also, "The worker deserves his wages."

Pay no attention to an accusation against a presbyter unless it is supported by two or three witnesses. The ones who do commit sin, however, are to be publicly reprimanded, so that the rest may fear to offend.

I charge you before God, Christ Jesus, and the chosen angels: apply these rules without prejudice, act with complete impartiality! Never lay hands hastily on anyone, or you may be sharing in the misdeeds of others. Keep yourself pure.

The love of money is the root of all evil. Some men in their passion for it have strayed from the faith, and have come to grief amid great pain.

Man of God that you are, flee from all this. Instead, seek after integrity, piety, faith, love, steadfastness, and a gentle spirit. Fight the good fight of faith. Take firm hold on the everlasting life to which you were called when, in the presence of many witnesses, you made your noble profession of faith.

Before God, who gives life to all, and before Christ Jesus, who in bearing witness made his noble profession before Pontius Pilate, I charge you to keep God's command without blame or reproach until our Lord Jesus Christ shall appear.

RESPONSORY   1 Corinthians 4:1-2; Proverbs 20:6

It should be clear to men that we are Christ's servants,
    stewards of the mysteries of God;
—the great quality of a steward is to be faithful to his
    duty.

Many men are said to be merciful,
but how often do we find one who is faithful to his duty?
    The great quality . . .

SECOND READING

For a pope:

From a sermon by Saint Leo the Great, pope
(Sermo 3 de natali ipsius, 2-3: PL 54, 145-146)

Christ's foundation on Peter abides

Beloved, I am both weak and lazy in fulfilling the obligations of my office; whenever I try to act with vigor and devotedness, the frailty of our human condition slows me down. Yet I share in the ever-present atoning work of that almighty and eternal high priest, who is like us and yet equal to the Father; he brought the godhead down to our human level and raised our humanity to the godhead. Rightly, then, do we rejoice in what he established; for, though he delegated to many shepherds the care of his sheep, he has not ceased to watch over in person the flock that is dear to him.

It is from this ultimate inexhaustible source of security that we have received strength in our apostolic task; for his activity is never relaxed. The powerful foundation upon which the whole structure of the Church rests is never shaken by the weight of the temple that presses upon it.

That faith which Christ commended in the prince of the apostles remains for ever unshaken. And, just as Peter's faith in Christ endures, so does Christ's foundation upon Peter. The structure of truth persists; blessed Peter retains his rock-like strength and has not abandoned the helm of the Church which he took over.

Peter is called the rock; he is declared to be the foundation; he is made doorkeeper of the heavenly kingdom; he is made judge of what is to be bound or loosed, and his judgments remain valid even in heaven; in these various ways, he is assigned a rank above the others. By reflecting on the hidden meaning of these titles of his, we can come to appreciate how close he is to Christ.

In our day he carries out his trust over a wider field and with greater power; he attends to every department of his duties and responsibilities in and along with him who gave him that dignity.

And so, if I do anything well, if my judgment is sound, if I obtain anything from God's mercy by my daily prayer, all this is due to the achievement and the deserts of Peter; it is his power that lives on in his See, it is his prestige that reigns.

This, beloved, is the outcome of that profession of faith which God the Father inspired in the apostle's heart. That declaration rose above the doubts of all merely human opinion, and took on the solidity of a rock unshaken by any outside pressure.

For, in the world-wide Church, every day Peter declares: *You are the Christ, the Son of the living God,* and every man who acknowledges the Lord is enabled to proclaim what those words mean.

RESPONSORY   Matthew 16:18; Psalm 48:9

Jesus said to Simon: I tell you most solemnly that you are Peter,
and I will build my Church upon this rock foundation.
—And the powers of hell will never overcome it.

For all eternity, God's Church stands firm.
—And the powers . . .

For the founder of a church:

From a treatise on Psalm 126 by Saint Hilary, bishop
(Nn. 7-10: PL 9, 696-697)

God builds and protects his city

Unless the Lord builds a house, the builders labor in vain. You are the temple of God. The Spirit of God dwells in you. This is the house and temple of God, full of his doctrine and his power, a dwelling-place holy enough to house the heart of God. It is of this that the same inspired author is speaking, in the words: *Your temple is holy, marvelous in its goodness.* Man's holiness, justice and self-restraint constitute God's temple.

Such a temple must be built by God; if it were constructed by human effort, it would not last; it is not held together by resting on merely worldly teachings, nor will it be protected by our own vain efforts or anxious concern. We must build it and protect it in a different way. It must not have its foundations on earth or on sand that is unstable and treacherous. Its foundations must be rooted in the prophets and apostles.

It must be built up from living stones, held together by a cornerstone; an ever-increasing unity will make it grow into a perfect humanity, to the scale of Christ's body; its beauty and its charm are the adornment given to it by supernatural grace.

A house so built by God, that is, by God's guidance, will not collapse. Through the efforts of the individual faithful this house will grow into many houses, and thus will arise the blessed and spacious city of God.

For many years now God has been watching over this city, ever on the alert. He cared for Abraham in his wanderings; he rescued Isaac when he was about to be sacrificed; Jacob he enriched in his time of servitude; it is he who set Joseph over Egypt, after he had been sold into slavery; who supported Moses against Pharaoh; chose Joshua to lead his nation in war; rescued David from every peril and endowed Solomon with wisdom. He came to the aid of the prophets, he took Elijah up to heaven, chose Elisha; fed Daniel, and stood by and refreshed the three young men in the fiery furnace. He told Joseph, through an angel, of his virginal conception, he strengthened Mary, and sent John ahead to prepare the way. He chose the apostles and prayed for them, saying to his Father: *Father most holy, protect them. While I was with them, I kept them safe by the power of your name.* Finally after his passion, he promised us his eternal, watchful protection, in the words: *Behold I am with you always until the end of the world.*

Such is the never-failing protection given to this blessed and holy city, a city built for God, fashioned by the coming together of many, yet seen in each one of us. It is therefore the Lord who must build this city if it is to grow to its appointed size. A building just begun is not the perfect work; final perfection is brought about only in the very process of building.

RESPONSORY   1 Peter 2:4-5, Psalm 118:21

Come near to Christ, the living stone;
—you too must be living stones, built up in him to form a
    spiritual temple,
a holy priesthood to offer through Christ Jesus
the spiritual sacrifice acceptable to God.

Jesus is the stone which has become the cornerstone.
—You too must . . .

Alternative, particularly for a bishop:

From a sermon by Saint Fulgentius of Ruspe, bishop

(Sermo 1, 2-3: CCL 91A, 889-890)

The faithful and wise steward

The Lord, in his desire to explain the special function of those servants whom he placed over his people, said: *Who do you think is the faithful and wise steward whom his master has set over his household to give them their portion of food at the proper time? That servant is blessed if he is found doing this when his master comes.*

And who is the master? None other than Christ, who said to his disciples: *You call me teacher and master, and you are right, for so I am.* And who is the master's household? Surely, it is the Church which the Lord redeemed from the power of the adversary, and which he purchased for himself, thereby becoming its master. This household is the holy Catholic Church which is so fruitfully extended far and wide over the world, rejoicing that it has been redeemed by the precious blood of the Lord. As the Lord himself says: *The Son of Man came not to be served but to serve, and to give his life as a ransom for many.* Furthermore, he is the Good Shepherd who has laid down his life for his sheep; the Good Shepherd's flock is this household of the Redeemer.

But who is the steward who must be both faithful and wise? The apostle Paul tells us when he says of himself and his companions: *This is how one should regard us, as servants of Christ and stewards of the mysteries of God. Moreover, it is required of stewards that they be found faithful.*

But this does not mean that the apostles alone have been appointed our stewards, nor that any of us may give up our duty of spiritual combat and, as lazy servants, sleep our time away, and be neither faithful nor wise. For the blessed Apostle tells us that the bishops too are stewards. *A bishop*, he says, *must be blameless because he is God's steward.*

We bishops, then, are the servants of the householder, the stewards of the Master, and we have received the portion of food to dispense to you. If we should wonder what that portion of food is, the blessed Apostle Paul tells us when he says: *To each according to the measure of faith which God has assigned to him.* Hence what Christ calls the portion of food, Paul calls the measure of faith. We may therefore take this spiritual food to mean the venerable mystery of the Christian faith. And we give you this portion of food in the Lord's name as often as we, enlightened by the gift of grace, teach you in accordance with the rule of the true faith. In turn, you daily receive the portion of food at the hands of the Lord's stewards when you hear the word of truth from the servants of God.

RESPONSORY   Matthew 25:21, 20

Well done, my good and faithful servant;
you have been faithful in the little tasks I gave you;
now I will entrust you with greater ones.
—Come and share my joy.

Lord, you gave me five coins,
and see, I bring you back double.
—Come and share my joy.

For a priest:

From the decree on the ministry and life of priests of the Second Vatican Council
(Presbyterorum ordinis, Cap. 3, 12)

The priestly vocation to perfection

By the sacrament of Orders priests are formed in the image of Christ the Priest, to be ministers of Christ the Head in constructing and building up his whole Body, the Church, as fellow-workers with the order of bishops. In the consecration of baptism they have already received, in common with all Christians, the sign and gift of so great a vocation and grace that, even in their human weakness, they have the power, and the duty, to seek perfection, in accordance with our Lord's words: *Be perfect, then, as your Father in heaven is also perfect.*

Priests are obliged in a special way to acquire this perfection. By receiving holy Orders they have been consecrated in a new way, and made living instruments of Christ the eternal Priest, so as to be able to continue through the years Christ's wonderful work which, by divine power, has restored to wholeness the entire family of man.

Since each priest acts, as far as he may, in the person of Christ himself, he is given special grace to help him grow toward the perfection of the one whose role he plays, as he ministers to his flock and the whole people of God. He receives grace for the healing of human weakness from the holiness of Christ, who became for us a high priest, *holy, innocent, undefiled, separated from sinners.*

Christ, whom the Father sanctified, that is, consecrated, and sent into the world, *gave himself for us, to redeem us from all sin, and to purify for himself an acceptable people, zealous for good works.* So, through his passion he entered into his glory. In the same way, priests, consecrated as they are by the anointing of the Holy Spirit and sent by Christ, put an end in their lives to the sins of our selfish nature, and give themselves wholly to the service of mankind, and so are enabled to grow to perfect manhood in the holiness with which they are enriched in Christ.

As they exercise the ministry of the Spirit and of holiness, they are strengthened in the spiritual life, provided that they are docile to Christ's Spirit, who gives them life and is their guide. By the sacred actions they perform

daily, and by their entire ministry in communion with their bishop and fellow-priests, they are set on
the way that leads to perfection.

The holiness of priests is itself an important contribution to the fruitfulness of their ministry. It is true that
God's grace can effect the work of salvation even through
unworthy ministers, but God ordinarily prefers to show
his wonders by means of those who are more submissive
to the inspiration and guidance of the Holy Spirit, and,
who through close union with Christ and holiness of life,
are able to say with Saint Paul: *I live, but no longer is it I
who live, it is Christ who lives within me.*

RESPONSORY   1 Thessalonians 2:8; Galatians 4:19

I have longed to give you the Gospel,
and more than that, to give you my very life;
—you have become very dear to me.

My little children, I am like a mother giving birth to you,
until Christ is formed in you.
—You have become . . .

For a missionary:
From the decree on the missionary activity of the Church
of the Second Vatican Council.

(Ad gentes, nn. 4-5)

Go and teach all nations

The Lord Jesus, before giving his life freely for the
world, made his arrangements for the apostolic ministry,
and gave his promise that the Holy Spirit was to be sent.
He did this in such a way that both the Spirit and ministry might be partners in carrying into effect the work of
salvation in every age and place.

The Holy Spirit gives to the whole Church at all times
unity in communion and ministry. He endows it with a

diversity of gifts, hierarchical and charismatic; he gives life to its institutions, becoming as it were their soul, and instills into the hearts of the faithful the very missionary spirit that was the driving force in Christ himself. At times he is seen preparing the way for apostolic activity, just as in different ways he always accompanies it and directs it.

The Lord Jesus, from the very beginning, *called to himself those whom he wanted; he arranged for twelve to be with him, and to be sent by him to preach.* Thus the apostles were the first beginnings of the new Israel, and at the same time the origin of the sacred hierarchy.

Afterward, when he had once for all, by his death and resurrection, brought to completion in his own person the mysteries of our salvation and of the renewal of all things, the Lord, having received all power in heaven and on earth, before he was taken up into heaven, founded his Church as the sacrament of salvation, and sent the apostles into the whole world, just as he himself had been sent by the Father. He commanded them: *Go then and teach all nations, baptizing them in the name of the Father and of the Son and of the Holy Spirit, teaching them to observe all things that I have commanded you.*

From then onward there is a duty laid on the Church of spreading the faith and the salvation that come from Christ. This duty is in virtue of the express command inherited from the apostles by the college of bishops, assisted by the priests, in communion with Peter's successor, the chief shepherd of the Church; it is in virtue also of the life that Christ causes to flow into his members.

The mission of the Church is therefore fulfilled by that activity by which the Church, in obedience to Christ's command and under the impulse of the grace and love of the Holy Spirit, becomes fully and actively present to all men and to all peoples, to lead them by the example of its life, by its preaching, by the sacraments and other means of grace, to the faith, freedom and peace of Christ, so that there lies open before them a free and firm path to a full sharing in the mystery of Christ.

RESPONSORY   Mark 16:15-16; John 3:5

Go out to the ends of the earth,
and tell every living creature the good news of Christ.
—Everyone who believes and is baptized will be saved.

Unless a man is born again of water and the Holy Spirit,
he cannot enter the kingdom of God.
—Everyone who believes . . .

On solemnities and feasts, **Te Deum**, 651.

Prayer, as in Morning Prayer.

Morning Prayer

HYMN

Loving shepherd of the sheep,
Keep thy lamb, in safety keep;
Nothing can thy power withstand,
None can pluck me from thy hand.

I would bless thee every day,
Gladly all thy will obey,
Like thy blessed ones above,
Happy in thy precious love.

Loving Shepherd, ever near,
Teach thy lamb thy voice to hear;
Suffer not my steps to stray
From the straight and narrow way.

Where thou leadest I would go,
Walking in thy steps below,

Till before my Father's throne
I shall know as I am known.

Melody: Buchland 77.77   Music: Leighton Hayne, 1836-1883
Text: Jane E. Leeson, 1807-1882

Or:

The King of love my shepherd is,
Whose goodness fails me never;
I nothing lack if I am his
And he is mine for ever.

Where streams of living water flow,
To rest my soul he leads me;
Where fresh and fertile pastures grow,
With heav'nly food he feeds me.

Perverse and foolish I have strayed,
But he with love has sought me,
And on his shoulder gently laid,
And home, rejoicing, brought me.

In death's dark vale I fear no ill,
With you, dear Lord, beside me;
Your rod and staff my comfort still,
Your cross will ever guide me.

You spread a banquet in my sight,
My head with oil anointing,
And let me taste the sweet delight
From your pure chalice flowing.

And so through all my length of days
Your goodness fails me never;
Good Shepherd, may I sing your praise
Within your house for ever.

Melody: Saint Columba 87.87   Music: Traditional Irish Melody
Text: Psalm 23 paraphrased by
Henry Williams Baker
1821-1877, alt. by Anthony G. Petti

Ant. 1 You are the light of the world; a city set on a hill cannot be hidden.

Psalms and canticle from Sunday, Week I, **688**.

Ant. 2 Let your light shine before men, that they may see your good works and give glory to your Father.

Ant. 3 God's word is alive; it strikes to the heart. It pierces more surely than a two-edged sword.

READING   Hebrews 13:7-9a

Remember your leaders who spoke the word of God to you; consider how their lives ended, and imitate their faith. Jesus Christ is the same yesterday, today, and forever. Do not be carried away by all kinds of strange teaching.

RESPONSORY

On your walls, Jerusalem, I have set my watchmen to guard you.
—On your walls, Jerusalem, I have set my watchmen to guard you.

Day or night, they will not cease to proclaim the name of the Lord.
—I have set my watchmen to guard you.

Glory to the Father . . .
—On your walls . . .

CANTICLE OF ZECHARIAH

Ant. What you say of me does not come from yourselves; it is the Spirit of my Father speaking in you.

INTERCESSIONS

Christ is the Good Shepherd who laid down his life for
his sheep. Let us praise and thank him as we pray:
Nourish your people, Lord.
Christ, you decided to show your merciful love through
your holy shepherds,
—let your mercy always reach us through them.
Through your vicars you continue to perform the ministry of shepherd of souls,
—direct us always through our leaders.
Through your holy ones, the leaders of your people, you
served as physician of our bodies and our spirits,
—continue to fulfill your ministry of life and holiness in
us.
You taught your flock through the prudence and love of
your saints,
—grant us continual growth in holiness under the direction of our pastors.

Our Father . . .

Prayer

If there is no proper prayer, one of the following is said:

For a pope:

All-powerful and ever-living God,
you called Saint N. to guide your people
by his word and example.
With him we pray to you:
watch over the pastors of your Church
with the people entrusted to their care,
and lead them to salvation.

We ask this through our Lord Jesus Christ, your Son,
who lives and reigns with you and the Holy Spirit,
one God, for ever and ever.

For a bishop:

Lord God,
you counted Saint N. among your holy pastors,
renowned for faith and love which conquered evil in this
    world.
By the help of his prayers
keep us strong in faith and love
and let us come to share his glory.

Grant this through our Lord Jesus Christ, your Son,
who lives and reigns with you and the Holy Spirit,
one God, for ever and ever.

For the founder of a church:

Lord,
you called our fathers to the light of the gospel
by the preaching of Saint N.
By his prayers help us to grow in the love and knowledge
of your Son, our Lord Jesus Christ,
who lives and reigns with you and the Holy Spirit,
one God, for ever and ever.

For a pastor:

God our Father,
in Saint N. you gave
a light to your faithful people.
You made him a pastor of the Church
to feed your sheep with his word
and to teach them by his example.
Help us by his prayers to keep the faith he taught
and follow the way of life he showed us.

Grant this through our Lord Jesus Christ, your Son,
who lives and reigns with you and the Holy Spirit,
one God, for ever and ever.

Or:

Lord God,
you gave your Saint N.
the spirit of truth and love
to shepherd your people.
May we who honor him on this feast
learn from his example
and be helped by his prayers.

We ask this through our Lord Jesus Christ, your Son,
who lives and reigns with you and the Holy Spirit,
one God, for ever and ever.

For a missionary:

God of mercy,
you gave us Saint N. to proclaim the riches of Christ.
By the help of his prayers
may we grow in knowledge of you,
be eager to do good,
and learn to walk before you
by living the truth of the gospel.

Grant this through our Lord Jesus Christ, your Son,
who lives and reigns with you and the Holy Spirit,
one God, for ever and ever.

Daytime Prayer

Midmorning

Ant.   My Father, as you sent me into the world so I
send my disciples.

READING   1 Timothy 4:16

Watch yourself and watch your teaching. Persevere at
both tasks. By doing so you will bring to salvation yourself and all who hear you.

This is the man the Lord has chosen as his servant.
—He has called him to shepherd his inheritance Jacob.

Midday

Ant.   Whoever welcomes you welcomes me, and the man who welcomes me welcomes him who sent me.

I thank Christ Jesus our Lord, who has strengthened me, that he has made me his servant and judged me faithful.

I am not ashamed to proclaim the Gospel.
—It is the saving power of God at work.

Midafternoon

Ant.   We are fellow-workers with God; you are his harvest field, you are the temple he builds.

Those who serve well as deacons gain a worthy place for themselves and much assurance in their faith in Christ Jesus.

Unless the Lord builds the house.
—Those who build it labor in vain.

Prayer, as in Morning Prayer.

Evening Prayer II

HYMN

Shepherd of souls, in love come, feed us,
Life-giving Bread for hungry hearts!
To those refreshing waters lead us
Where dwells that peace your grace imparts.

May we, the wayward in your fold,
By your forgiveness rest consoled.

Life-giving vine, come, feed and nourish,
Strengthen each branch with life divine;
Ever in you O may we flourish,
Fruitful the branches on the vine.
Lord, may our souls be purified
So that in Christ may we abide.

Sinful is man who kneels before you,
Worthy of you are you alone;
Yet in your name do we implore you,
Rich are the mercies you have shown.
Say but the word, O Lord divine,
Then are our hearts made pure like thine.

Melody: Du Meiner Seelen   Music: Hungarian chorale
98.98.88   Melody, 16th cent.
PSALMODY   Text: Omer Westendorf

Ant. 1   My life is at the service of the Gospel; God has
given me this gift of his grace.

Psalm 15

Lord, who shall be admitted to your tent
and dwell on your holy mountain?

He who walks without fault;
he who acts with justice
and speaks the truth from his heart;
he who does not slander with his tongue;

he who does no wrong to his brother,
who casts no slur on his neighbor,
who holds the godless in disdain,
but honors those who fear the Lord;

he who keeps his pledge, come what may;
who takes no interest on a loan

and accepts no bribes against the innocent.
Such a man will stand firm for ever.

Ant.   My life is at the service of the Gospel; God has giv-
en me this gift of his grace.

Ant. 2   This servant proved himself faithful and wise;
the Lord entrusted the care of his household to
him.

Psalm 112

Happy the man who fears the Lord,
who takes delight in all his commands.
His sons will be powerful on earth;
the children of the upright are blessed.

Riches and wealth are in his house;
his justice stands firm for ever.
He is a light in the darkness for the upright:
he is generous, merciful and just.

The good man takes pity and lends,
he conducts his affairs with honor.
The just man will never waver:
he will be remembered for ever.

He has no fear of evil news;
with a firm heart he trusts in the Lord.
With a steadfast heart he will not fear;
he will see the downfall of his foes.

Open-handed, he gives to the poor;
his justice stands firm for ever.
His head will be raised in glory.

The wicked man sees and is angry,
grinds his teeth and fades away;
the desire of the wicked leads to doom.

Ant.   This servant proved himself faithful and wise; the
Lord entrusted the care of his household to him.

Ant. 3   My sheep will hear my voice; and there shall be
          one fold and one shepherd.

Canticle   Revelation 15:3b-4

Mighty and wonderful are your works,
    Lord God Almighty!
Righteous and true are your ways,
    O King of the nations!

Who would dare refuse you honor,
    or the glory due your name, O Lord!

Since you alone are holy,
    all nations shall come and worship in your presence.
    Your mighty deeds are clearly seen.

Ant.   My sheep will hear my voice; and there shall be
         one fold and one shepherd.

READING   1 Peter 5:1-4

To the elders among you I, a fellow elder, a witness of
Christ's sufferings and sharer in the glory that is to be revealed, make this appeal. God's flock is in your midst;
give it a shepherd's care. Watch over it willingly as God
would have you do, not under constraint; and not for
shameful profit either, but generously. Be examples to
the flock, not lording it over those assigned to you, so
that when the chief Shepherd appears you will win for
yourselves the unfading crown of glory.

RESPONSORY

This is a man who loved his brethren and ever prayed for
    them.
—This is a man who loved his brethren and ever prayed
    for them.

He spent himself in their service,
—and ever prayed for them.

Glory to the Father . . .
—This is a . . .

CANTICLE OF MARY

Ant.   This is a faithful and wise steward: the Lord en-
       trusted the care of his household to him, so that he
       might give them their portion of food at the pro-
       per season.

Or: O Christ, Good Shepherd, I thank you for leading
       me to glory; I pray that the flock you have entrust-
       ed to my care will share with me in your glory for
       ever.

INTERCESSIONS

Jesus Christ is worthy of all praise, for he was appointed
    high priest among men and their representative before
    God. We honor him and in our weakness we pray:
    Bring salvation to your people, Lord.
You marvelously illuminated your Church through dis-
    tinguished leaders and holy men and women,
—let Christians rejoice always in such splendor.
You forgave the sins of your people when their holy lead-
    ers like Moses sought your compassion,
—through their intercession continue to purify and sanc-
    tify your holy people.
In the midst of their brothers and sisters you anointed
    your holy ones and filled them with the Holy Spirit,
—fill all the leaders of your people with the same Spirit.

You yourself are the only visible possession of our holy
    pastors,

—let none of them, won at the price of your blood, remain far from you.
The shepherds of your Church keep your flock from being snatched out of your hand. Through them you
give your flock eternal life,
—save those who have died, those for whom you gave up
your life.

Our Father . . .

Prayer

If there is no proper prayer, one of the following is said

For a pope:

All-powerful and ever-living God,
you called Saint N. to guide your people
by his word and example.
With him we pray to you:
watch over the pastors of your Church
with the people entrusted to their care,
and lead them to salvation.
We ask this through our Lord Jesus Christ, your Son,
who lives and reigns with you and the Holy Spirit,
one God, for ever and ever.

For a bishop:

Lord God,
you counted Saint N. among your holy pastors,
renowned for faith and love which conquered evil in this
world.
By the help of his prayers
keep us strong in faith and love
and let us come to share his glory.
Grant this through our Lord Jesus Christ, your Son,
who lives and reigns with you and the Holy Spirit,
one God, for ever and ever.

For the founder of a church:

Lord,
you called our fathers to the light of the gospel
by the preaching of Saint N.
By his prayers help us to grow in the love and knowledge
of your Son, our Lord Jesus Christ,
who lives and reigns with you and the Holy Spirit,
one God, for ever and ever.

For a pastor:

God our Father,
in Saint N. you gave
a light to your faithful people.
You made him a pastor of the Church
to feed your sheep with his word
and to teach them by his example.
Help us by his prayers to keep the faith he taught
and follow the way of life he showed us.

Grant this through our Lord Jesus Christ, your Son,
who lives and reigns with you and the Holy Spirit,
one God, for ever and ever.

Or:

Lord God,
you gave your Saint N.
the spirit of truth and love
to shepherd your people.
May we who honor him on this feast
learn from his example
and be helped by his prayers.

We ask this through our Lord Jesus Christ, your Son,
who lives and reigns with you and the Holy Spirit,
one God, for ever and ever.

For a missionary:

God of mercy,
you gave us Saint N. to proclaim the riches of Christ.
By the help of his prayers
may we grow in knowledge of you,
be eager to do good,
and learn to walk before you
by living the truth of the gospel.
Grant this through our Lord Jesus Christ, your Son,
who lives and reigns with you and the Holy Spirit,
one God, for ever and ever.

COMMON OF DOCTORS OF THE CHURCH

Everything is taken from the common of pastors, 1422, except
the following:

Evening Prayer I

HYMN, as in Evening Prayer II, 1466.

READING   James 3:17-18

Wisdom from above is first of all innocent. It is also
peaceable, lenient, docile, rich in sympathy and the kindly deeds that are its fruits, impartial and sincere. The
harvest of justice is sown in peace for those who cultivate
peace.

RESPONSORY

The just man will speak the wisdom he has pondered in
     his heart.
—The just man will speak the wisdom he has pondered
     in his heart.

Truth will come from his lips,
—the wisdom he has pondered in his heart.

Glory to the Father . . .
—The just man . . .

CANTICLE OF MARY

Ant.   The man who not only teaches but does what is
         right will be counted great in the kingdom of God.

Prayer

If there is no proper prayer, the following is said:

Lord God,
you filled Saint N. with heavenly wisdom.
By his help may we remain true to his teaching
and put it into practice.

1442

We ask this through our Lord Jesus Christ, your Son,
who lives and reigns with you and the Holy Spirit,
one God, for ever and ever.

Invitatory

Ant.   Come, let us worship the Lord, fount of all wisdom.

Invitatory psalm, as in the Ordinary, 648.

Office of Readings

HYMN, as in Evening Prayer II, 1466.

FIRST READING

From the book of Wisdom   7:7-16, 22-30

The joy of the just united with God

I prayed, and prudence was given me;
    I pleaded, and the spirit of Wisdom came to me.
I preferred her to scepter and throne,
And deemed riches nothing in comparison with her,
    nor did I liken any priceless gem to her;
Because all gold, in view of her, is a little sand,
    and before her, silver is to be accounted mire.
Beyond health and comeliness I loved her,
And I chose to have her rather than the light,
    because the splendor of her never yields to sleep.

Yet all good things together came to me in her company,
    and countless riches at her hands;
And I rejoiced in them all, because Wisdom is their leader,
    though I had not known that she is the mother of
    these.
Simply I learned about her, and ungrudgingly do I
    share—
    her riches I do not hide away;

For to men she is an unfailing treasure;
  those who gain this treasure win the friendship of God,
  to whom the gifts they have from discipline commend
    them.

Now God grant I speak suitably
  and value these endowments at their worth:
For he is the guide of Wisdom
  and the director of the wise.
For both we and our words are in his hand,
  as well as all prudence and knowledge of crafts.
For in her is a spirit
  intelligent, holy, unique,
Manifold, subtle, agile,
  clear, unstained, certain,
Not baneful, loving the good, keen,
  unhampered, beneficent, kindly,
Firm, secure, tranquil,
  all-powerful, all-seeing,
And pervading all spirits,
  though they be intelligent, pure and very subtle.
For Wisdom is mobile beyond all motion,
  and she penetrates and pervades all things by reason of
    her purity.

For she is an aura of the might of God
  and a pure effusion of the glory of the Almighty;
  therefore nought that is sullied enters into her.
For she is the refulgence of eternal light,
  the spotless mirror of the power of God,
  the image of his goodness.

And she, who is one, can do all things,
  and renews everything while herself perduring;
And passing into holy souls from age to age,
  she produces friends of God and prophets.

For there is nought God loves,
  be it not one who dwells with Wisdom.
For she is fairer than the sun
  and surpasses every constellation of the stars.
Compared to light, she takes precedence;
  for that, indeed, night supplants,
  but wickedness prevails not over Wisdom.

RESPONSORY   Wisdom 7:7-8; James 1:5

I prayed for understanding, and it was given to me;
—I pleaded for wisdom, and the spirit of wisdom came to
  me.
I valued her more than all earthly power and glory.

If anyone of you lacks wisdom, he has only to turn to God
  in prayer,
and it will be given to him;
for God gives generously to all and turns no one away.
—I pleaded for . . .

SECOND READING

From The Mirror of Faith by William of Thierry, abbot
(PL 180, 384)

Seek the understanding of faith from the Holy Spirit

When in your life of faith you are confronted with the
deeper mysteries it is natural to become a little frightened. When this happens, take heart, faithful Christian.
Do not raise objections, but ask with loving submission,
"How can these things be?" Let your question be a prayer, an expression of love and self-surrender to God. Let it
be an expression of your humble desire not to penetrate
his sublime majesty, but to find salvation through the
saving deeds of God our Savior.

Then the angel of good counsel will reply: *When the
Paraclete comes, whom I shall send you from the Father, he*

will remind you of everything and teach you all truth. Even
as no one *knows a man's secret thoughts except his own spirit
within him, so no one comprehends the mysteries of God except the Spirit of God.*

Hasten therefore to receive the Holy Spirit. He is with
you when you call upon him; you can call upon him only
because he is already present. But when he comes in answer to your prayer, he comes with an abundance of divine blessing; he is the river whose streams give joy to the
city of God.

If when he comes he finds you humble, silent and
trembling at the words of God, he will rest upon you and
reveal what God the Father has hidden from the wise and
the prudent of this world. You will then begin to understand the things holy Wisdom could have told his disciples on earth, but which they were unable to bear until
the Spirit of truth came who was to teach them all truth.
For this reason we cannot hope to learn from the lips of
any man truths that Truth himself could not convey. As
he himself has told us: *God is Spirit.* As those who worship him must worship in spirit and truth, so those who
wish to know him must seek understanding of their faith
and perception of its pure and simple truth only in the
Holy Spirit.

In the darkness and ignorance of this life the Holy
Spirit enlightens the poor in spirit. He is the love that
draws them on, the sweetness that attracts them, the way
in which a man approaches God. He is the love of the lover. He is devotion. He is piety. From one degree of faith
to the next he is ever revealing to believers the justice of
God, so that grace follows grace, and the faith that comes
from hearing yields to a faith enlightened by understanding.

Matthew 13:52; Proverbs 14:33

When a teacher of the law becomes a disciple of the king-
    dom of heaven,
—he is like the head of a household
who is able to take from his storeroom treasures new and
    old.

Wisdom makes its home in a discerning heart,
and it can even teach those who are foolish.
—He is like . . .

_____

Alternative:

From the dogmatic constitution on Divine Revelation of
the Second Vatican Council

(Dei Verbum, nn. 7–8)

How God's revelation is handed on

Christ the Lord, in whom the whole revelation of the
most high God is brought to completion, commanded the
apostles to preach the Gospel to all mankind. The Gospel, promised through the prophets, was fulfilled in his
own person and promulgated by his own lips. The apostles were to proclaim it as the source of all saving truth
and all moral discipline, and in so doing to communicate
the gifts of God to men.

This command was faithfully carried out. First, by the
apostles, who in their preaching by word of mouth, their
example and their instructions handed on what they had
received from Christ's lips, from his life among them and
from his actions, or had learnt from the prompting of the
Holy Spirit; then, by those apostles and apostolic men
who committed the message of salvation to writing, under the inspiration of the same Holy Spirit.

To ensure that the Gospel might remain always alive and whole within the Church, the apostles left bishops as their successors, and made over to them their own position of responsibility as teachers. What was handed on by the apostles comprises all that makes for holy living among God's people and the increase of their faith. So, in its teaching, life and worship the Church perpetuates and transmits to every generation all that it is, and all that it believes.

This tradition received from the apostles develops within the Church under the guiding presence of the Holy Spirit. Understanding of the realities and the words handed down grows through contemplation and study by the faithful as they ponder them in their hearts, through the deep insight into spiritual things that they come to experience, and through the preaching of those who, with succession in the episcopate, have received the sure charism of truth. Thus the Church throughout the ages is always advancing toward the fullness of divine truth, until the words of God are brought to completion within it.

The writings of the holy Fathers of the Church testify to the life-giving presence of this tradition, as its riches flow into the life and practice of the Church, in its belief and in its prayer.

Through the same tradition the complete canon of the sacred books is made known, and Holy Scripture itself is understood in greater depth and becomes continuously alive and active. In this way God, who spoke in times past, continues to converse for ever with the bride of his beloved Son; and the Holy Spirit, through whom the living voice of the Gospel reechoes in the Church, and through the Church in the world also, guides the faithful into all truth, and causes the word of Christ to dwell among them in all its abundance.

RESPONSORY   1 Peter 1:25; Luke 1:2

The word of the Lord endures for ever.

—This same word, the Gospel, has been proclaimed to
  you.

The message has been handed on to us
by those who were with the Lord from the beginning.
As the ministers of his word, they gave witness
to all they had seen.

—This same word . . .

On solemnities and feasts, Te Deum, 651.

Prayer, as in Morning Prayer.

Morning Prayer

HYMN

Rise up, O men of God!
Have done with lesser things,
Give heart, and soul, and mind, and strength
To serve the King of kings.

Rise up, O men of God!
His kingdom tarries long:
Bring in the day of brotherhood
And end the night of wrong.

Rise up, O men of God!
The Church for you does wait:
Sent forth to serve the needs of men;
In Christ our strength is great!

Lift high the cross of Christ!
Tread where his feet have trod.
As brothers of the Son of man,
Rise up, O men of God!

Melody: Festal Song S.M.   Music: William H. Walter, 1894
                              Text: William Pierson Merrill, 1911

Wisdom 7:13-14

Simply I learned about Wisdom, and ungrudgingly do I
    share—
her riches I do not hide away;
For to men she is an unfailing treasure;
    those who gain this treasure win the friendship of God,
    to whom the gifts they have from discipline commend
    them.

RESPONSORY

Let the peoples proclaim the wisdom of the saints.
—Let the peoples proclaim the wisdom of the saints.

With joyful praise let the Church tell forth
—the wisdom of the saints.

Glory to the Father . . .
—Let the peoples . . .

CANTICLE OF ZECHARIAH

Ant.   Those who are learned will be as radiant as the sky
      in all its beauty; those who instruct the people in
      goodness will shine like the stars for all eternity.

Prayer

If there is no proper prayer, the following is said:

Lord God,
you filled Saint N. with heavenly wisdom.
By his help may we remain true to his teaching
and put it into practice.
We ask this through our Lord Jesus Christ, your Son,
who lives and reigns with you and the Holy Spirit,
one God, for ever and ever.

Evening Prayer II

HYMN

This is the feast day of the Lord's true witness,
Whom thru the ages all have held in honor;
Now let us praise him and his deeds of glory
With exultation.

So now in chorus, giving God the glory,
We sing his praises and his mighty triumph,
That in his glory we may all be sharers
Here and hereafter.

Praise to the Father and the Son most holy,
Praise to the Spirit, with them coeternal,
Who give examples in the lives of all saints,
That we may follow.

Melody: Herr Deinen Zorn 11.11.11.5   Music: Johann Crueger,
1653
Text: *Iste Confessor*, 8th century
Translator: Composite

Or:

Faith of our fathers! faith and prayer
Shall win all nations unto thee;
And through the truth that comes from God,
Mankind shall then indeed be free.

Refrain:

Faith of our fathers, holy faith!
We will be true to thee till death.

Faith of our fathers! we will love
Both friend and foe in all our strife:
And preach thee too, as love knows how,
By kindly deeds and virtuous life.

Refrain

Melody: Saint Catherine   Music: Henri F. Hemy, 1818-1888
L.M. with Refrain   and James G. Walton, 1821-1905
Text: Frederick W. Faber, 1814-1863

READING   James 3:17-18

Wisdom from above is first of all innocent. It is also peaceable, lenient, docile, rich in sympathy and the kindly deeds that are its fruits, impartial and sincere. The harvest of justice is sown in peace for those who cultivate peace.

RESPONSORY

In the midst of the Church he spoke with eloquence.
—In the midst of the Church he spoke with eloquence.

The Lord filled him with the spirit of wisdom and understanding.
—He spoke with eloquence.

Glory to the Father . . .
—In the midst . . .

CANTICLE OF MARY

Ant.   O blessed doctor, Saint N., light of holy Church and lover of God's law, pray to the Son of God for us.

Prayer

If there is no proper prayer, the following is said:

Lord God,
you filled Saint N. with heavenly wisdom.
By his help may we remain true to his teaching
and put it into practice.

We ask this through our Lord Jesus Christ, your Son,
who lives and reigns with you and the Holy Spirit,
one God, for ever and ever.

COMMON OF VIRGINS

Evening Prayer I

Hymn, as in Evening Prayer II, 1487.

Psalmody

Ant. 1   Come, daughters, draw close to the Lord, and
           share the splendor of his light.

Psalm 113

Praise, O servants of the Lord,
praise the name of the Lord!
May the name of the Lord be blessed
both now and for evermore!
From the rising of the sun to its setting
praised be the name of the Lord!

High above all nations is the Lord,
above the heavens his glory.
Who is like the Lord, our God,
who has risen on high to his throne
yet stoops from the heights to look down,
to look down upon heaven and earth?

From the dust he lifts up the lowly,
from his misery he raises the poor
to set him in the company of princes,
yes, with the princes of his people.
To the childless wife he gives a home
and gladdens her heart with children.

Ant.   Come, daughters, draw close to the Lord, and
           share the splendor of his light.

Ant. 2   With all our heart we follow you in awe; we
           long to see you face to face. Lord, do not disap-
           point our hope.

Psalm 147:12-20

O praise the Lord, Jerusalem!
Zion, praise your God!

He has strengthened the bars of your gates,
he has blessed the children within you.
He established peace on your borders,
he feeds you with finest wheat.

He sends out his word to the earth
and swiftly runs his command.
He showers down snow white as wool,
he scatters hoar-frost like ashes.

He hurls down hailstones like crumbs.
The waters are frozen at his touch;
he sends forth his word and it melts them:
at the breath of his mouth the waters flow.

He makes his word known to Jacob,
to Israel his laws and decrees.
He has not dealt thus with other nations;
he has not taught them his decrees.

Ant.   With all our heart we follow you in awe; we long
        to see you face to face. Lord, do not disappoint
        our hope.

Ant. 3   Sing for joy, virgins of Christ; he is your spouse
        for all eternity.

Canticle   Ephesians 1:3-10

Praised be the God and Father
of our Lord Jesus Christ,
who bestowed on us in Christ
every spiritual blessing in the heavens.

God chose us in him
before the world began,

to be holy
and blameless in his sight.

He predestined us
to be his adopted sons through Jesus Christ,
such was his will and pleasure,
that all might praise the glorious favor
he has bestowed on us in his beloved.

In him and through his blood, we have been re-
    deemed,
and our sins forgiven,
so immeasurably generous
is God's favor to us.

God has given us the wisdom
to understand fully the mystery,
the plan he was pleased
to decree in Christ.

A plan to be carried out
in Christ, in the fullness of time,
to bring all things into one in him,
in the heavens and on the earth

Ant. Sing for joy, virgins of Christ; he is your spouse
    for all eternity.

READING   1 Corinthians 7:32b, 34a

The unmarried man is busy with the Lord's affairs,
concerned with pleasing the Lord. The virgin—indeed,
any unmarried woman—is concerned with things of the
Lord, in pursuit of holiness in body and spirit.

RESPONSORY

The Lord is my inheritance; this I know in my heart.
—The Lord is my inheritance; this I know in my heart.

The Lord is good to those who seek him;
—this I know in my heart.

Glory to the Father . . .
—The Lord is . . .

CANTICLE OF MARY

For a virgin and martyr:

Ant. With courageous heart she followed the Lamb,
who was crucified for love of us; she offered herself as a chaste and spotless victim.

For a virgin:

Ant. When the Bridegroom came, he found the wise
virgin ready to enter the wedding feast with him.

For several virgins:

Ant. Keep watch with love, wise virgins, with your
lamps alight. See, the Bridegroom comes; go out
to welcome him.

INTERCESSIONS

Christ extolled those who practiced virginity for the sake
of the kingdom. Let us praise him joyfully and pray to
him:

Jesus, example of virgins, hear us.

Christ, you presented the Church to yourself as a chaste
virgin to her spouse,
—keep her holy and inviolate.

Christ, the holy virgins went out to meet you with their
lamps alight,
—keep the fidelity of your consecrated handmaids burning brightly.

Lord, your virgin Church has always kept its faith whole
and untarnished,
—grant all Christians a whole and untarnished faith.

You have given your people joy in celebrating the feast of
    your holy virgin N.,
—give us constant joy through her intercession.

You have admitted the holy virgins to your marriage ban-
    quet,
—in your mercy lead the dead to your heavenly feast.

Our Father . . .

Prayer

If there is no proper prayer, one of the following is said:

Lord,
you have told us that you live for ever
in the hearts of the chaste.
By the prayers of the virgin N.,
help us to live by your grace
and remain a temple of your Spirit.

Grant this through our Lord Jesus Christ, your Son,
who lives and reigns with you and the Holy Spirit,
one God, for ever and ever.

Or:

Lord,
hear the prayers of those who recall the devoted life of the
    virgin N.
Guide us on our way and help us to grow
in love and devotion as long as we live.

We ask this through our Lord Jesus Christ, your Son,
who lives and reigns with you and the Holy Spirit,
one God, for ever and ever.

    For several virgins:

Lord,
increase in us your gifts of mercy and forgiveness.
May we who rejoice at this celebration
in honor of the virgins N. and N.

receive the joy of sharing eternal life with them.

We ask this through our Lord Jesus Christ, your Son,
who lives and reigns with you and the Holy Spirit,
one God, for ever and ever.

Invitatory

Ant.   The holy virgins praise their Lord and King;
come, let us join in their worship.

Or: Come, let us worship the Lamb with the virgins
who followed him.

Invitatory psalm, as in the Ordinary, **648**.

Office of Readings

HYMN

Let us with joy our voices raise
In that heroic woman's praise,
Whose courage, strength and holy fame
Have given her an honored name.

O Strength of all the strong, God's Son,
Thru whom alone great deeds are done,
By your great strength and thru her prayer
May we bear witness ev'rywhere.

Praise God the Father and the Son
And Holy Spirit, Three in One,
Who gave this noble woman grace
A life of virtue to embrace.

Melody: Eisenach L.M.   Music: Johan Herman Schein, 1628
                                Text: *Fortem Virile Pectore,*
                                Silvio Antoniano, 1540–1603;
                                Stanza 3, Roger Nachtwey, 1964
                                Translator: Roger Nachtwey, 1964

Or:

Blessed are the poor of heart,
Blessed are the merciful,

For they will be blessed upon the earth.
Blessed are the poor!

Blessed are they who suffer,
Blessed are they who are persecuted,
For they shall be the rulers of the world.
Blessed are the poor!

Blessed are they who hunger and thirst
For justice and the rights of all,
For they shall eat the meal of the Lord.
Blessed are the poor!

Blessed are they whose hearts are clean
And blessed are they who keep his word,
For they have inherited the land.
Blessed are the poor!

Blessed are they who labor for peace,
Blessed are they who suffer in war,
For they shall meet the Prince of Peace.
Blessed are the poor!

Melody: The Beatitudes   Music: Enrico Garzilli, 1970
                              Text: Enrico Garzilli, 1970

PSALMODY

Ant. 1   Radiant virgin, prudent and wise, you are the
         spouse of the holy Word of God.

Psalm 19A

The heavens proclaim the glory of God
and the firmament shows forth the work of his
   hands.
Day unto day takes up the story
and night unto night makes known the message.

No speech, no word, no voice is heard
yet their span extends through all the earth,
their words to the utmost bounds of the world.

Christian chastity

With respect to virgins, I have not received any commandment from the Lord, but I give my opinion as one who is trustworthy, thanks to the Lord's mercy. It is this: In the present time of stress it seems good to me for a person to continue as he is.

Are you bound to a wife? Then do not seek your freedom. Are you free of a wife? If so, do not go in search of one. Should you marry, however, you will not be committing sin. Neither does a virgin commit a sin if she marries. But such people will have trials in this life, and these I should like to spare you.

I tell you, brothers, the time is short. From now on those with wives should live as though they had none; those who weep should live as though they were not weeping, and those who rejoice as though they were not rejoicing; buyers should conduct themselves as though they owned nothing, and those who make use of the world as though they were not using it, for the world as we know it is passing away.

I should like you to be free of all worries. The unmarried man is busy with the Lord's affairs, concerned with pleasing the Lord; but the married man is busy with this world's demands and occupied with pleasing his wife. This means he is divided. The virgin—indeed, any unmarried woman—is concerned with things of the Lord, in pursuit of holiness in body and spirit. The married woman, on the other hand, has the cares of this world to absorb her and is concerned with pleasing her husband. I am going into this with you for your own good. I have no desire to place restrictions on you, but I do want to promote what is good, what will help you to devote yourselves entirely to the Lord.

If anyone thinks he is behaving dishonorably toward his virgin because a critical moment has come and it seems that something should be done, let him do as he wishes. He commits no sin if there is a marriage. The man, however, who stands firm in his resolve, who while without constraint and free to carry out his will makes up his mind to keep his virgin, also acts rightly. To sum up: the man who marries his virgin acts fittingly; the one who does not, will do better.

A wife is bound to her husband as long as he lives. If her husband dies she is free to marry, but on one condition, that it be in the Lord. She will be happier, though, in my opinion, if she stays unmarried. I am persuaded that in this I have the Spirit of God.

RESPONSORY

The King has desired your beauty,
which he himself has given you;
—your God and King has become your spouse.

He has provided for you and adorned you;
he has redeemed you and made you holy.
Now you are wedded to your King and your God.
—Your God and . . .

SECOND READING

From a sermon On the Dress of Virgins by Saint Cyprian, bishop and martyr

(Nn. 3-4, 22. 23: CSEL 3, 189-190. 202-204)

The more numerous her virgins, the greater the joy of mother Church

Now I wish to address the order of virgins. Because their way of life is more exalted, our concern for them must be greater. If we compare the Church to a tree, then they are its blossom. Virgins show forth the beauty of God's grace; they are the image of God that reflects the holiness of the Lord; they are the more illustrious members of Christ's flock. They are the glory of mother Church and manifest her fruitfulness. The more numerous her virgins are, the greater is her joy.

To these virgins then I speak and address my exhortation, out of love rather than any sense of authority; and I do this without claiming the right to censure them, for I am among the last and the least and fully aware of my lowliness; I do it rather because the more anxious and concerned I am about them, the more I fear the devil's attack. For it is no idle concern nor vain fear that takes thought of the path to salvation and keeps the Lord's life-giving commandments.

They have dedicated themselves to Christ, and, renouncing the pleasures of the flesh, have consecrated themselves body and soul to God, in order to finish a task that is destined to win a great prize; they should not strive to adorn themselves or give pleasure to anyone but the Lord, from whom they hope to receive the reward for their chastity.

Virgins, persevere in the way of life you have begun, persevere in what you are to be. For you will receive a glorious prize for your virtue, a most excellent reward for your chastity. You have already begun to be now what we shall all be in the future. You already possess, here in this world, the glory of the resurrection. You pass through this world without the world's infection. If you persevere in chastity and virginity, you are equal to God's angels. Only keep your profession of virginity strong and inviolate. You began your way of life courageously, now persevere without faltering. Seek right conduct as your adornment, not jewelry or attractive clothing.

Listen to the voice of the Apostle Paul, God's chosen vessel, sent to announce the commands of heaven. Paul said: *The first man was made of the dust of the earth; the second is from heaven. Those who are made from earth are like him who was on the earth. Those who are of heaven are like him who is from heaven. As we have borne the image of the man who is of the earth, so let us bear the image of the man who is from heaven.* This image is shown forth in virginity, purity, holiness and truth.

RESPONSORY   1 Corinthians 7:34; Psalm 73:26

The thoughts of the virgin are always upon God.
—Her desire is to be holy both in body and soul.

The God of my heart is my portion for ever.
—Her desire is . . .

Alternative:

From the decree on the renewal of religious life of the Second Vatican Council

(Perfectae Caritatis, nn. 1. 5. 6. 12. 25)

The Church follows Christ, its only spouse

From the beginning of the Church there have been men and women who have sought to follow Christ with greater freedom, and to imitate him with closer fidelity through the practice of the evangelical counsels. They have led lives dedicated to God, each in his or her own way. Many of them, under the inspiration of the Holy Spirit, have lived in solitude or have founded religious communities, which the Church willingly recognized and approved by its authority.

As a result, in accordance with God's plan, there has grown up a wonderful variety of religious families. These have been of great service to the Church in equipping it *for every good work* and preparing it *for the work of the ministry for the building up of the Body of Christ,* and also in adorning it with the different gifts of its children, so that the Church may appear in beauty *as a bride adorned for her husband, and show forth the many-faceted wisdom of God.*

Surrounded by this rich profusion of gifts, all who are called by God to the practice of the evangelical counsels, and profess them with fidelity, dedicate themselves to the Lord in a special way. They follow Christ, who in virginity and poverty redeemed and sanctified mankind through obedience, *even to death upon a cross.*

Driven thus by the love that the Holy Spirit pours into their hearts, they live more and more for Christ and for *his Body which is the Church.* The more fervent their union with Christ through this gift of self throughout their lives, the richer is the life of the Church, and the more vigorous and fruitful its apostolate.

The members of each institute should remember above all that in professing the evangelical counsels they have given their response to the call of God in such a way that they are to live for God alone, not only by dying to sin but also by renouncing the world. They have surrendered to his service the whole of their lives: this constitutes a special consecration, deeply rooted in the consecration of baptism, to which it gives fuller expression.

Those who profess the evangelical counsels should seek and love above all things the God who has first loved us. In every circumstance of life they should strive to foster a life hidden with Christ in God; such a life is a source of, and a stimulus to, the love of one's neighbor for the salvation of the world and the building up of the Church. This love is the animating and guiding principle for the practice of the evangelical counsels.

Chastity for the sake of the kingdom of heaven, professed by religious, is to be valued as an outstanding gift of grace. In a unique way it sets free man's heart, so that it may be the more inflamed with love for God and for all mankind. It is therefore a special sign of the blessings of heaven, and a most fitting means by which religious dedicate themselves eagerly to the service of God and the works of the apostolate. In this way they bring to the minds of all the faithful that wonderful marriage between the Church and Christ, its only spouse: a marriage that has been established by God, and will be fully revealed in the world to come.

RESPONSORY

How beautiful you are, virgin of Christ;
—the Lord has given you the gift of perpetual virginity.

Nothing can rob you of your reward
or separate you from the love of the Son of God.
—The Lord has . . .

On solemnities and feasts, Te Deum, 651.

Prayer, as in Morning Prayer

Morning Prayer

HYMN

Now, from the heav'ns descending,
Is seen a glorious light,
The Bride of Christ in splendor,
Arrayed in purest white.
She is the holy City,
Whose radiance is the grace
Of all the saints in glory,
From every time and place.

This is the hour of gladness
For Bridegroom and for Bride,
The Lamb's great feast is ready,
His Bride is at his side.
How bless'd are those invited
To share his wedding feast:
The least become the greatest,
The greatest are the least.

He who is throned in heaven
Takes up his dwelling-place
Among his chosen people,
Who see him face to face.
No sound is heard of weeping,
For pain and sorrow cease,
And sin shall reign no longer,
But love and joy and peace.

See how a new creation
Is brought at last to birth,
A new and glorious heaven,
A new and glorious earth.
Death's power for ever broken,
Its empire swept away,
The promised dawn of glory
Begins its endless day.

Melody: Moville 76.76.D   Music: Traditional Irish Melody
                                 Text: James Quinn, S.J. 1968

Ant. 1   With my whole being I worship Christ; I long
          for him and desire to be with him for ever.

Psalms and canticle from Sunday, Week I, **688.**

Ant. 2   O virgins, praise the Lord with all your heart.
          He sowed the seeds of your virtue; he crowned
          the fruits of your life with his gifts.

Ant. 3   The saints will sing for joy in heaven's glory; ra-
          diant is their victory over human frailties.

READING   Song of Songs 8:7

Deep waters cannot quench love,
   nor floods sweep it away.
Were one to offer all he owns to purchase love,
   he would be roundly mocked.

RESPONSORY

My heart is ever pleading, show me your face.
—My heart is ever pleading, show me your face.

I long to gaze upon you, Lord.
—Show me your face.

Glory to the Father . . .
—My heart is . . .

CANTICLE OF ZECHARIAH

For a virgin and martyr:

Ant.   Happy the virgin who denied herself and took up
        her cross. She imitated the Lord, the spouse of
        virgins and prince of martyrs.

For a virgin:

Ant.   Now this wise virgin has gone to Christ. Among
        the choirs of virgins she is radiant as the sun in the
        heavens.

For several virgins:

Ant.   Virgins of the Lord, bless the Lord for ever.

INTERCESSIONS

Christ is the spouse and crowning glory of virgins. Let us
   praise him with joy in our voices and pray to him with
   sincerity in our hearts:

Jesus, crown of virgins, hear us.

Christ, the holy virgins loved you as their one true
    spouse,
—grant that nothing may separate us from your love.

You crowned Mary, your mother, queen of virgins,
—through her intercession, let us continually serve you
    with pure hearts.

Your handmaids were always careful to love you with
    whole and undivided attention, that they might be
    holy in body and spirit,
—through their intercession grant that the lure of this
    passing world may not distract our attention from you.

Lord Jesus, you are the spouse whose coming was an-
    ticipated by the wise virgins,
—grant that we may wait for you in hope and expecta-
    tion.

Through the intercession of Saint N., who was one of the
    wise and prudent virgins,
—grant us wisdom and innocence of life.

Our Father . . .

Prayer

If there is no proper prayer, one of the following is said:

Lord,
you have told us that you live for ever
in the hearts of the chaste.
By the prayers of the virgin N.,
help us to live by your grace
and remain a temple of your Spirit.

Grant this through our Lord Jesus Christ, your Son,
who lives and reigns with you and the Holy Spirit,
one God, for ever and ever.

Or:

Lord,
hear the prayers of those who recall the devoted life of the
    virgin N.
Guide us on our way and help us to grow
in love and devotion as long as we live.
We ask this through our Lord Jesus Christ, your Son,
who lives and reigns with you and the Holy Spirit,
one God, for ever and ever.

For several virgins:

Lord,
increase in us your gift of mercy and forgiveness.
May we who rejoice at this celebration
    in honor of the virgins N. and N.
receive the joy of sharing eternal life with them.
We ask this through our Lord Jesus Christ, your Son,
who lives and reigns with you and the Holy Spirit,
one God, for ever and ever.

Daytime Prayer

For the gradual psalms, in place of psalm 122, psalm 129, **1129**,
may be said, and in place of psalm 127, psalm 131 may be said,
972.

Midmorning

Ant.   What joy to be near to my God, to place all my
             trust in the Lord.

READING   Wisdom 8:21a

I knew that I could not otherwise possess her except God
    gave it—
    and this, too, was prudence, to know whose is the gift.

This is the wise virgin.
—The Lord found her ready for the marriage feast.

Midday

Ant.   Uphold me, Lord, according to your promise, and
        I shall live; let my hope in you not be in vain.

READING   1 Corinthians 7:25

With respect to virgins, I have not received any commandment from the Lord, but I give my opinion as one
who is trustworthy, thanks to the Lord's mercy.

This is a wise virgin.
—She was among those prepared for the Lord's coming.

Midafternoon

Ant.   How beautiful are they whose purity of life is ac-
        claimed.

READING   Revelation 19:6, 7

The Lord is king,
    our God, the Almighty!
Let us rejoice and be glad,
    and give him glory!
For this is the wedding day of the Lamb;
    his bride has prepared herself for the wedding.

I found him whom I love.
—I held him fast; I would not leave him.

Prayer, as in Morning Prayer.

Evening Prayer II

HYMN

You holy angels bright,
Who wait at God's right hand,
Or through the realms of light
Fly at your Lord's command,
Assist our song,

For else the theme
Too high will seem
For mortal tongue.

You blessed souls at rest,
Who ran this earthly race,
And now, from sin released,
Behold the Savior's face;
His praises sound,
As in his sight
With sweet delight
You all abound.

Let us who toil below
Adore our heav'nly King,
And onward as we go
Our joyful anthem sing;
With one accord,
Through good or ill,
We praise him still,
Eternal Lord.

My soul, now take your part,
Acclaiming God above:
And with a well-tuned heart
Sing out the songs of love.
Let all your days
Till life shall end,
What e'er he send,
Be filled with praise.

Melody: Darwall's 148th

Music: John Darwall, 1731–1789
Text: Richard Baxter, 1615–1691, et al
adapted by Anthony G. Petti, 1971

PSALMODY

Ant. 1 I have kept myself for you alone, and now with
　　　　lamp alight I run to meet my Spouse.

Psalm 122

I rejoiced when I heard them say:
"Let us go to God's house."
And now our feet are standing
within your gates, O Jerusalem.

Jerusalem is built as a city
strongly compact.
It is there that the tribes go up,
the tribes of the Lord.

For Israel's law it is,
there to praise the Lord's name.
There were set the thrones of judgment
of the house of David.

For the peace of Jerusalem pray:
"Peace be to your homes!
May peace reign in your walls,
in your palaces, peace!"

For love of my brethren and friends
I say: "Peace upon you!"
For love of the house of the Lord
I will ask for your good.

Ant.   I have kept myself for you alone, and now with
       lamp alight I run to meet my Spouse.

Ant. 2   Blessed are the pure of heart, for they shall see
         God.

Psalm 127

If the Lord does not build the house,
in vain do its builders labor;
if the Lord does not watch over the city,
in vain does the watchman keep vigil.

In vain is your earlier rising,
your going later to rest,

you who toil for the bread you eat:
when he pours gifts on his beloved while they
  slumber.

Truly sons are a gift from the Lord,
a blessing, the fruit of the womb.
Indeed the sons of youth
are like arrows in the hand of a warrior.

O the happiness of the man
who has filled his quiver with these arrows!
He will have no cause for shame
when he disputes with his foes in the gateways.

Ant.   Blessed are the pure of heart, for they shall see
       God.

Ant. 3   My faith is firmly established, for I have built
         my life on Christ.

Canticle   Ephesians 1:3-10

Praised be the God and Father
of our Lord Jesus Christ,
who bestowed on us in Christ
every spiritual blessing in the heavens.

God chose us in him
before the world began,
to be holy
and blameless in his sight.

He predestined us
to be his adopted sons through Jesus Christ,
such was his will and pleasure,
that all might praise the glorious favor
he has bestowed on us in his beloved.

In him and through his blood, we have been redeemed,

and our sins forgiven,
so immeasurably generous
is God's favor to us.

God has given us the wisdom
to understand fully the mystery,
the plan he was pleased
to decree in Christ.

A plan to be carried out
in Christ, in the fullness of time,
to bring all things into one in him,
in the heavens and on the earth.

Ant.   My faith is firmly established, for I have built my
life on Christ.

READING   1 Corinthians 7:32, 34

The unmarried man is busy with the Lord's affairs,
concerned with pleasing the Lord. The virgin—indeed,
any unmarried woman—is concerned with things of the
Lord, in pursuit of holiness in body and spirit.

RESPONSORY

The virgins are led into the presence of the King, amid
gladness and joy.
—The virgins are led into the presence of the King, amid
gladness and joy.

They are brought into the King's dwelling-place,
—amid gladness and joy.

Glory to the Father . . .
—The virgins are . . .

CANTICLE OF MARY

For a virgin martyr:

Ant.   In this one victim we hail the double crown of purity and devotion; hers the glory of virginity, hers the palm of martyrdom.

For a virgin:

Ant.   Come, spouse of Christ, receive the crown the Lord has prepared for you from all eternity.

For several virgins:

Ant.   These holy ones seek the Lord; they long to see him face to face.

INTERCESSIONS

Christ extolled those who practiced virginity for the sake of the kingdom. Let us praise him joyfully and pray to him:

Jesus, example of virgins, hear us.

Christ, you presented the Church to yourself as a chaste virgin to her spouse,

—keep her holy and inviolate.

Christ, the holy virgins went out to meet you with their lamps alight,

—keep the fidelity of your consecrated handmaids burning brightly.

Lord, your virgin Church has always kept its faith whole and untarnished,

—grant all Christians a whole and untarnished faith.

You have given your people joy in celebrating the feast of your holy virgin N.,

—give us constant joy through her intercession.

You have admitted the holy virgins to your marriage banquet,

—in your mercy lead the dead to your heavenly feast.

Our Father . . .

Prayer

If there is no proper prayer, one of the following is said:

Lord,
you have told us that you live for ever
in the hearts of the chaste.
By the prayers of the virgin N.,
help us to live by your grace
and remain a temple of your Spirit.

Grant this through our Lord Jesus Christ, your Son,
who lives and reigns with you and the Holy Spirit,
one God, for ever and ever.

Or:

Lord,
hear the prayers of those who recall the devoted life of the
    virgin N.
Guide us on our way and help us to grow
in love and devotion as long as we live.

We ask this through our Lord Jesus Christ, your Son,
who lives and reigns with you and the Holy Spirit,
one God for ever and ever.

For several virgins:

Lord,
increase in us your gifts of mercy and forgiveness.
May we who rejoice at this celebration
in honor of the virgins N. and N.
receive the joy of sharing eternal life with them.

We ask this through our Lord Jesus Christ, your Son,
who lives and reigns with you and the Holy Spirit,
one God, for ever and ever.

COMMON OF HOLY MEN

Evening Prayer I

Hymn, as in Evening Prayer II, 1519.

Psalmody

Ant. 1   All you saints, sing praise to our God.

Psalm 113

Praise, O servants of the Lord,
praise the name of the Lord!
May the name of the Lord be blessed
both now and for evermore!
From the rising of the sun to its setting
praised be the name of the Lord!

High above all nations is the Lord,
above the heavens his glory.
Who is like the Lord, our God,
who has risen on high to his throne
yet stoops from the heights to look down,
to look down upon heaven and earth?

From the dust he lifts up the lowly,
from his misery he raises the poor
to set him in the company of princes,
yes, with the princes of his people.
To the childless wife he gives a home
and gladdens her heart with children.

Ant.   All you saints, sing praise to our God.

Ant. 2   Blessed are they who hunger and thirst for holiness; they will be satisfied.

Psalm 146

My soul, give praise to the Lord;
I will praise the Lord all my days,
make music to my God while I live.

Put no trust in princes,
in mortal men in whom there is no help.
Take their breath, they return to clay
and their plans that day come to nothing.

He is happy who is helped by Jacob's God,
whose hope is in the Lord his God,
who alone made heaven and earth,
the seas and all they contain.

It is he who keeps faith for ever,
who is just to those who are oppressed.
It is he who gives bread to the hungry,
the Lord, who sets prisoners free,

the Lord who gives sight to the blind,
who raises up those who are bowed down,
the Lord, who protects the stranger
and upholds the widow and orphan.

It is the Lord who loves the just
but thwarts the path of the wicked.
The Lord will reign for ever,
Zion's God, from age to age.

Ant.   Blessed are they who hunger and thirst for holiness; they will be satisfied.

Ant. 3   Blessed be God! He has chosen us to live in
love, holy and without blemish in his sight.

Canticle   Ephesians 1:3–10

Praised be the God and Father
of our Lord Jesus Christ,

who bestowed on us in Christ
every spiritual blessing in the heavens.

God chose us in him
before the world began,
to be holy
and blameless in his sight.

He predestined us
to be his adopted sons through Jesus Christ,
such was his will and pleasure,
that all might praise the glorious favor
he has bestowed on us in his beloved.

In him and through his blood, we have been re-
    deemed,
and our sins forgiven,
so immeasurably generous
is God's favor to us.

God has given us the wisdom
to understand fully the mystery,
the plan he was pleased
to decree in Christ.

A plan to be carried out
in Christ, in the fullness of time,
to bring all things into one in him,
in the heavens and on the earth.

Ant.   Blessed be God! He has chosen us to live in love,
        holy and without blemish in his sight.

READING   Philippians 3:7–8

Those things I used to consider gain I have now reap-
praised as loss in the light of Christ. I have come to rate
all as loss in the light of the surpassing knowledge of my
Lord Jesus Christ. For his sake I have forfeited every-

thing; I have accounted all else rubbish so that Christ may be my wealth.

RESPONSORY

The Lord loved him, and shared with him his glory.
—The Lord loved him, and shared with him his glory.

He wrapped him in a splendid robe,
—and shared with him his glory.

Glory to the Father . . .
—The Lord loved . . .

CANTICLE OF MARY

Ant.   He is like the wise man who built his house upon rock.

For several holy men:

Ant.   The eyes of the Lord are on those who fear him, on those who hope in his mercy.

INTERCESSIONS

Let us pray to the Father, the source of all holiness, and ask him to lead us to holiness of life through the example and intercession of his saints:
    May we be holy as you are holy.
Holy Father, you want us to be called your sons and truly to be such,
—grant that your holy Church may proclaim you throughout the world.
Holy Father, you want us to walk worthily and please you in all we do,
—let us abound in doing good works.
Holy Father, you have reconciled us to yourself through Christ,
—preserve us in your name so that all may be one.

Holy Father, you have called us to a heavenly banquet,
—through the bread that came down from from heaven
   make us worthy to grow in perfect love.
Holy Father, forgive the offenses of every sinner,
—let the dead perceive the light of your countenance.

Our Father . . .

Prayer

If there is no proper prayer, one of the following is said:

God our Father,
you alone are holy;
without you nothing is good.
Trusting in the prayers of Saint N.
we ask you to help us
to become the holy people you call us to be.
Never let us be found undeserving
of the glory you have prepared for us.

We ask this through our Lord Jesus Christ, your Son,
who lives and reigns with you and the Holy Spirit,
one God, for ever and ever.

Or:

All-powerful God,
help us who celebrate the memory of Saint N.
to imitate his way of life.
May the example of your saints
be our challenge to live holier lives.

Grant this through our Lord Jesus Christ, your Son,
who lives and reigns with you and the Holy Spirit,
one God, for ever and ever.

For several holy men:

Ever-living God,
the signs of your love are manifest

in the honor you give your saints.
May their prayers and their example encourage us
to follow your Son more faithfully.

We ask this through our Lord Jesus Christ, your Son,
who lives and reigns with you and the Holy Spirit,
one God, for ever and ever.

For a religious:
Lord God,
you kept Saint N. faithful to Christ's pattern of poverty
    and humility.
May his prayers help us to live in fidelity to our calling
and bring us to the perfection you have shown us in your
    Son,
who lives and reigns with you and the Holy Spirit,
one God, forever and ever.

For one who worked for the underprivileged:
Lord God,
you teach us that the commandments of heaven
are summarized in love of you and love of our neighbor.
By following the example of Saint N.
in practicing works of charity
may we be counted among the blessed in your kingdom.

Grant this through our Lord Jesus Christ, your Son,
who lives and reigns with you and the Holy Spirit,
one God, for ever and ever.

For a teacher:
Lord God,
you called Saint N. to serve you in the Church
by teaching his fellow man the way of salvation.
Inspire us by his example:
help us to follow Christ our teacher,
and lead us to our brothers and sisters in heaven.

We ask this through our Lord Jesus Christ, your Son,
who lives and reigns with you and the Holy Spirit,
one God, for ever and ever.

Invitatory

Ant.   Come, let us worship God, wonderful in his
saints.

Or: Let us sing praise to God, as we acclaim Saint

Invitatory psalm, as in the Ordinary, 648.

Office of Readings

Hymn

This is the feast day of the Lord's true witness,
Whom thru the ages all have held in honor;
Now let us praise him and his deeds of glory
With exultation.

So now in chorus, giving God the glory,
We sing his praises and his mighty triumph,
That in his glory we may all be sharers
Here and hereafter.

Praise to the Father and the Son most holy,
Praise to the Spirit, with them coeternal,
Who give examples in the lives of all saints,
That we may follow.

Melody: Herr, Deinen Zorn 11.11.11.5   Music: Johann Crueger,
1653
Text: *Iste Confessor*, 8th century
Translator: Composite

Or:

Blest are the pure in heart,
For they shall see our God:
The secret of the Lord is theirs,
Their soul is Christ's abode.

The Lord, who left the heavens
Our life and peace to bring,
To dwell in lowliness with men,
Their pattern and their King:

Still to the lowly soul
He doth himself impart,
And for his dwelling and his throne
Chooseth the pure in heart.

Lord, we thy presence seek;
may ours this blessing be;
Give us a pure and lowly heart,
A temple fit for thee.

Melody: Franconia S. M.   Music: W. H. Havergal, 1793–1870
                                  Text: J. Keble, 1792–1866 et al.

PSALMODY

Ant. 1   He asked to share your life, O Lord, and you
         have heard his prayer; you have clothed him
         with glory and great beauty.

Psalm 21:2–8, 14

O Lord, your strength gives joy to the king;
how your saving help makes him glad!
You have granted him his heart's desire;
you have not refused the prayer of his lips.

You came to meet him with the blessings of success,
you have set on his head a crown of pure gold.
He asked you for life and this you have given,
days that will last from age to age.

Your saving help has given him glory.
You have laid upon him majesty and splendor,
you have granted your blessings to him for ever.
You have made him rejoice with the joy of your pres-
    ence.

The king has put his trust in the Lord:
through the mercy of the Most High he shall stand
   firm.
O Lord, arise in your strength;
we shall sing and praise your power.

Ant.   He asked to share your life, O Lord, and you have
heard his prayer; you have clothed him with glory
and great beauty.

Ant. 2   The path of the just is like the passage of the
dawn; it grows from first light to the full splendor of day.

Psalm 92
I

It is good to give thanks to the Lord,
to make music to your name, O Most High,
to proclaim your love in the morning
and your truth in the watches of the night,
on the ten-stringed lyre and the lute,
with the murmuring sound of the harp.

Your deeds, O Lord, have made me glad;
for the work of your hands I shout with joy.
O Lord, how great are your works!
How deep are your designs!
The foolish man cannot know this
and the fool cannot understand.

Though the wicked spring up like grass
and all who do evil thrive:
they are doomed to be eternally destroyed.
But you, Lord, are eternally on high.

Ant.   The path of the just is like the passage of the
dawn; it grows from first light to the full splendor
of day.

Ant. 3   The just man will flourish like the palm tree; he
         will grow like a cedar of Lebanon.

II

See how your enemies perish;
all doers of evil are scattered.

To me you give the wild-ox's strength;
you anoint me with the purest oil.
My eyes looked in triumph on my foes;
my ears heard gladly of their fall.
The just will flourish like the palm-tree
and grow like a Lebanon cedar.

Planted in the house of the Lord
they will flourish in the courts of our God,
still bearing fruit when they are old,
still full of sap, still green,
to proclaim that the Lord is just.
In him, my rock, there is no wrong.

Ant.   The just man will flourish like the palm tree; he
       will grow like a cedar of Lebanon.

The Lord led this holy man along a sure path.
—He showed him the kingdom of God.

FIRST READING

From the book of Wisdom   5:1–16

The righteous are indeed the sons of God

Then shall the just one with great assurance confront
   his oppressors who set at nought his labors.
Seeing this, they shall be shaken with dreadful fear,
   and amazed at the unlooked-for salvation.
They shall say among themselves, rueful
   and groaning through anguish of spirit:

"This is he whom once we held as a laughingstock
   and as a type for mockery, fools that we were!
His life we accounted madness,
   and his death dishonored.
See how he is accounted among the sons of God;
   how his lot is with the saints!

We, then, have strayed from the way of truth,
   and the light of justice did not shine for us,
   and the sun did not rise for us.
We had our fill of the ways of mischief and of ruin;
   we journeyed through impassable deserts,
   but the way of the Lord we knew not.

What did our pride avail us?
   What have wealth and its boastfulness afforded us?
All of them passed like a shadow
   and like a fleeting rumor;
Like a ship traversing the heaving water,
   of which, when it has passed, no trace can be found,
   no path of its keel in the waves.

Or like a bird flying through the air;
   no evidence of its course is to be found—
But the fluid air, lashed by the beat of pinions,
   and cleft by the rushing force
Of speeding wings, is traversed:
   and afterward no mark of passage can be found in it.

Or as, when an arrow has been shot at a mark,
   the parted air straightway flows together again
   so that none discerns the way it went through—
Even so we, once born, abruptly came to nought
   and held no sign of virtue to display,
   but were consumed in our wickedness."

Yes, the hope of the wicked is like thistledown borne on
    the wind,
  and like fine, tempest-driven foam;
Like smoke scattered by the wind,
  and like the passing memory of the nomad camping for
    a single day.
But the just live forever,
  and in the Lord is their recompense,
  and the thought of them is with the Most High.

RESPONSORY   1 John 3:7, 8, 10

Let no one deceive you:
the just man is the one who does what is right;
—the man who sins belongs to the devil,
for the devil has sinned from the beginning.

In this way we see who are the children of God and the
    children of the devil.
—The man who . . .

Alternative:

From the letter of the apostle Paul
to the Philippians   1:29—2:16

Let this mind be in you which was also in Christ Jesus

It is your special privilege to take Christ's part—not
only to believe in him but also to suffer for him. Yours is
the same struggle as mine, the one in which you formerly
saw me engaged and now hear that I am caught up.

In the name of the encouragement you owe me in
Christ, in the name of the solace that love can give, of fellowship in spirit, compassion, and pity, I beg you: make
my joy complete by your unanimity, possessing the one
love, united in spirit and ideals. Never act out of rivalry
or conceit; rather, let all parties think humbly of others

as superior to themselves, each of you looking to others' interests rather than his own.

Your attitude must be that of Christ:

Though he was in the form of God
   he did not deem equality with God
   something to be grasped at.

Rather, he emptied himself
   and took the form of a slave,
   being born in the likeness of men.

He was known to be of human estate,
   and it was thus that he humbled himself,
   obediently accepting even death,
   death on a cross!

Because of this,
   God highly exalted him
   and bestowed on him the name
   above every other name,

So that at Jesus' name
   every knee must bend
   in the heavens, on the earth,
   and under the earth,
   and every tongue proclaim
   to the glory of God the Father:
JESUS CHRIST IS LORD!

So then, my dearly beloved, obedient as always to my urging, work with anxious concern to achieve your salvation, not only when I happen to be with you but all the more now that I am absent. It is God who, in his good will toward you, begets in you any measure of desire or achievement.

In everything you do, act without grumbling or arguing; prove yourselves innocent and straightforward, children of God beyond reproach in the midst of a twisted and depraved generation—among whom you shine like the stars in the sky while holding fast to the word of life. As I look to the Day of Christ, you give me cause to boast that I did not run the race in vain or work to no purpose.

RESPONSORY   Philippians 2:12–13; John 15:5

In fear and trembling work out your salvation;
—it is God who is working in you
so that you both will and do
according to his own good purpose.

The Lord says: Without me you can do nothing.
—It is God . . .

For a married man:

From the first letter of the apostle Peter   3:7–17
Worship the Lord in your hearts

You husbands, too, must show consideration for those who share your lives. Treat women with respect as the weaker sex, heirs just as much as you to the gracious gift of life. If you do so, nothing will keep your prayers from being answered.

In summary, then, all of you should be like-minded, sympathetic, loving toward one another, kindly disposed, and humble. Do not return evil for evil or insult for insult. Return a blessing instead. This you have been called to do, that you may receive a blessing as your inheritance.

"He who cares for life
and wants to see prosperous days
must keep his tongue from evil
and his lips from uttering deceit.

He must turn from evil and do good,
seek peace and follow after it,
because the Lord has eyes for the just
and ears for their cry;
but against evildoers the Lord sets his face."

Who indeed can harm you if you are committed deeply to doing what is right? Even if you should have to suffer for justice' sake, happy will you be. "Fear not and do not stand in awe of what this people fears." Venerate the Lord, that is, Christ, in your hearts. Should anyone ask you the reason for this hope of yours, be ever ready to reply, but speak gently and respectfully. Keep your conscience clear, so that, whenever you are defamed, those who libel your way of life in Christ may be shamed. If it should be God's will that you suffer, it is better to do so for good deeds than for evil ones.

RESPONSORY   1 Peter 1:13, 15; Leviticus 11:44

Be pure and intent of heart, bent on him, the holy One, who has called you;
—be holy in all you do.

I am your own God, your Lord;
be holy for I am holy.
—Be holy in . . .

SECOND READING

From a homily on the Acts of the Apostles by Saint John Chrysostom, bishop

(Homilia 20, 4: PG 60, 162–164)

The light of a Christian cannot escape notice

There is nothing colder than a Christian who does not seek to save others.

You cannot plead poverty here; the widow putting in her two small coins will be your accuser. Peter said: *Silver and gold I have not.* Paul was so poor that he was often hungry and went without necessary food.

You cannot plead humble birth, for they were humbly born, of humble stock. You cannot offer the excuse of lack of education, for they were uneducated. You cannot plead ill-health, for Timothy also had poor health, with frequent illnesses.

Each one can help his neighbor if only he is willing to do what is in his power. Look at the trees that do not bear fruit: have you not noticed how strong and fine they are, upstanding, smooth and tall? If we had a garden, we would much prefer trees with fruit—pomegranates and olives—to trees that are for pleasure, not for utility, and any utility these have is small.

Such are those men who think only of their own concerns. In fact, they are even worse: the trees are at least useful for building or for protection, whereas the selfish are fit only for punishment. Such were those foolish virgins who were chaste, comely and self-controlled, but did nothing for anyone. So they are consumed in the fire. Such are those men who refuse to give Christ food.

Notice that none of them is accused of personal sins. They are not accused of committing fornication or perjury or any such sin at all: only of not helping anybody else. The man who buried the talent was like this. His life was blameless, but he was of no service to others.

How can such a person be a Christian? Tell me, if yeast did not make the whole mass like itself, is it really yeast? Again, if perfume failed to pervade all around it with its fragrance, would we call it perfume?

Do not say: it is impossible for me to influence others. If you are a Christian, it is impossible for this not to happen. Things found in nature cannot be denied; so here, for it is a question of the nature of the Christian.

Do not insult God. If you say that the sun cannot shine, you have insulted him. If you say that a Christian cannot help others, you have insulted God and called him a liar. It is easier for the sun not to give warmth or shine than for the Christian not to shed his light. It is easier for light to be darkness than for this to happen.

Do not say then that it is impossible. The opposite is impossible. Do not insult God. If we have put our affairs in order, these things will certainly come to be, and will follow as a natural consequence. The light of a Christian cannot escape notice. So bright a lamp cannot be hidden.

RESPONSORY　　　　　Ephesians 5:8–9; Matthew 5:14, 16

Now you are light in the Lord;
live as men native to the light;
— light makes you gentle, loving and true.

I have given you to the world as its light,
and you must shine for all to see.
— Light makes you . . .

Alternative:

From a sermon by Saint Augustine, bishop

(Sermo 96, 1. 4. 9: PL 38, 584. 586. 588)

All men are called to holiness

If anyone wishes to come after me, let him deny himself, take up his cross and follow me. The Lord's command seems difficult and painful: that anyone who wishes to follow him must deny himself. But his command is not really difficult or painful, since he himself helps us to do what he commands. For the verse of the psalm addressed to him was truly spoken: *Because of the words of your lips I have abided by hard ways.* True also are his own words: *My yoke is mild and my burden is light.* For love makes easy whatever is difficult in his commands.

What does it mean, *let him take up his own cross?* It means he must endure many things that are painful; that is the way he must follow me. When he begins to follow me in my life and my teachings, many will contradict him, try to stop him, or dissuade him, even those who call themselves Christ's disciples. It was they who walked with Christ that tried to stop the blind men from calling out to him. So if you wish to follow Christ, you will take these threats or flattery or any kind of obstacle and fashion them into the cross; you must endure it, carry it, and not give way under it. And so in this world that is the Church, a world of the good, the reconciled, and the saved—or rather, those destined for salvation, but already saved by hope, as it is written, *by hope we are saved*—in this world of the Church, which completely follows Christ, he has said to everyone: *If anyone wishes to follow me, let him deny himself.*

This is not a command for virgins to obey and brides to ignore, for widows and not for married women, for monks and not for married men, or for the clergy and not for the laity. No, the whole Church, the entire body, all the members in their distinct and varied functions, must follow Christ. She who is totally unique, the dove, the spouse who was redeemed and dowered by the blood of her bridegroom, is to follow him. There is a place in the Church for the chastity of the virgin, for the continence of the widow, and for the modesty of the married. Indeed, all her members have their place, and this is where they are to follow Christ, in their function and in their way of life. They must deny themselves, that is, they must not presume on their own strength. They must take up their cross by enduring in the world for Christ's sake whatever pain the world brings.

Let them love him who alone can neither deceive nor be deceived, who alone will not fail them. Let them love him because his promises are true. Faith sometimes falters because he does not reward us immediately. But hold out, be steadfast, endure, bear the delay, and you have carried the cross.

RESPONSORY

This holy man worked wonders in the sight of God;
he praised the Lord with his whole heart.
— May he intercede for sinful mankind.

He was a man without bitterness,
his life a living praise to God.
He avoided all evil deeds and kept himself sinless to the
   end.
—May he intercede . . .

On solemnities and feasts, **Te Deum**, 651.

Prayer, as in Morning Prayer.

Morning Prayer

HYMN

    Rise up, O men of God!
    Have done with lesser things,
    Give heart, and soul, and mind, and strength
    To serve the King of kings.

    Rise up, O men of God!
    His kingdom tarries long:
    Bring in the day of brotherhood
    And end the night of wrong.

    Rise up, O men of God!
    The Church for you does wait:
    Sent forth to serve the needs of men,
    In Christ our strength is great!

    Lift high the cross of Christ!
    Tread where his feet have trod.
    As brothers of the Son of man,
    Rise up, O men of God!

Melody: Festal Song S.M.   Music: William H. Walter, 1894
                          Text: William Pierson Merrill, 1911

Or:

O God, our help in ages past,
Our hope for years to come,
Our shelter from the stormy blast
And our eternal home;

Beneath the shadow of your throne
Your saints have dwelt secure;
Sufficient is your arm alone,
And our defense is sure.

Before the hills in order stood,
Or earth received her frame,
From everlasting you are God,
To endless years the same.

A thousand ages in your sight
Are like an evening gone,
Short as the watch that ends the night
Before the rising sun.

Time, like an ever-rolling stream,
Bears all its sons away;
They fly forgotten, as a dream
Dies at the opening day.

O God, our help in ages past,
Our hope for years to come,
Be now our guide while life shall last,
And our eternal home.

Melody: Saint Anne C.M.

Music: William Croft, 1708
Text: Isaac Watts, 1674–1748,
alt. by Rev. William Bauman

Or:

Who would true valor see,
   Let him come hither;
One here will constant be
   Come wind, come weather;
There's no discouragement

Shall make him once relent
His first avowed intent
   To be a pilgrim.

Whoso beset him round
   With dismal stories,
Do but themselves confound;
   His strength the more is.
No lion can him fright,
He'll with a giant fight,
But he will have a right
   To be a pilgrim.

No power of evil field
   Can daunt his spirit;
He knows he at the end
   Shall life inherit.
Then fancies fly away,
He'll fear not what men say;
He'll labor night and day
   To be a pilgrim.

Melody: Monks Gate 65.65.66.65   Music: R. Vaughan Williams,
1872–1958
Text: John Bunyan, 1628–1688, alt.

Ant. 1   The Lord has given them unending glory; their
name shall be in everlasting remembrance.

Psalms and canticle from Sunday, Week I, 688.

Ant. 2   Servants of the Lord, bless the Lord for ever.

Ant. 3   The saints will exult in glory; they will sing for
joy as they bow down before the Lord.

READING   Romans 12:1–2

Brothers, I beg you through the mercy of God to offer
your bodies as a living sacrifice holy and acceptable to
God, your spiritual worship. Do not conform yourselves

to this age but be transformed by the renewal of your
mind, so that you may judge what is God's will, what is
good, pleasing and perfect.

RESPONSORY
In the depths of his heart, the law of God is his guide.
__In the depths of his heart, the law of God is his guide.

He will never lose his way;
__the law of God is his guide.

Glory to the Father . . .
__In the depths . . .

For several holy men:
Let the just rejoice in the presence of God.
__Let the just rejoice in the presence of God.

Let them be filled with gladness,
__in the presence of God.

Glory to the Father . . .
__Let the just . . .

CANTICLE OF ZECHARIAH
Ant.   The man of God welcomes the light that searches
his deeds and finds them true.

For several holy men:
Ant.   Blessed are the peacemakers, and blessed are the
pure of heart; they shall see God.

INTERCESSIONS
My brothers, let us praise Christ, asking to serve him and
to be holy and righteous in his sight all the days of our
life. Let us acclaim him:
Lord, you alone are the holy one.
You desired to experience everything we experience but
sin,

—have mercy on us, Lord Jesus.

You called us to love perfectly,

—make us holy, Lord Jesus.

You commissioned us to be the salt of the earth and the
    light of the world,

—let your light shine on us, Lord Jesus.

You desired to serve, not to be served.

—help us, Lord Jesus, to give humble service to you and
    to our neighbors.

You are in the form of God sharing in the splendor of the
    Father,

—Lord Jesus, let us see the glory of your face.

    Our Father . . .

Prayer

If there is no proper prayer, one of the following is said:

God our Father,
you alone are holy;
without you nothing is good.
Trusting in the prayers of Saint N.
we ask you to help us
to become the holy people you call us to be.
Never let us be found undeserving
of the glory you have prepared for us.

We ask this through our Lord Jesus Christ, your Son,
who lives and reigns with you and the Holy Spirit,
one God, for ever and ever.

Or:

All-powerful God,
help us who celebrate the memory of Saint N.
to imitate his way of life.
May the example of your saints
be our challenge to live holier lives.

Grant this through our Lord Jesus Christ, your Son,
who lives and reigns with you and the Holy Spirit,
one God, for ever and ever.

For several holy men:

Ever-living God,
the signs of your love are manifest
in the honor you give your saints.
May their prayers and their example encourage us
to follow your Son more faithfully.
We ask this through our Lord Jesus Christ, your Son,
who lives and reigns with you and the Holy Spirit,
one God, for ever and ever.

For a religious:

Lord God,
you kept Saint N. faithful to Christ's pattern of poverty
and humility.
May his prayers help us to live in fidelity to our calling
and bring us to the perfection you have shown us in your
Son,
who lives and reigns with you and the Holy Spirit,
one God, for ever and ever.

For one who worked for the underprivileged:

Lord God,
you teach us that the commandments of heaven
are summarized in love of you and love of our neighbor.
By following the example of Saint N.
in practicing works of charity
may we be counted among the blessed in your kingdom.

Grant this through our Lord Jesus Christ, your Son,
who lives and reigns with you and the Holy Spirit,
one God, for ever and ever.

For a teacher:

Lord God,
you called Saint N. to serve you in the Church
by teaching his fellow man the way of salvation.
Inspire us by his example:
help us to follow Christ our teacher,
and lead us to our brothers and sisters in heaven.

We ask this through our Lord Jesus Christ, your Son,
who lives and reigns with you and the Holy Spirit,
one God, for ever and ever.

Daytime Prayer

Midmorning

Ant.   If anyone takes to heart what Christ has said, he
will know perfect love.

READING   Galatians 6:7b–8

A man will reap only what he sows. If he sows in the
field of the flesh, he will reap a harvest of corruption; but
if his seed-ground is the spirit, he will reap everlasting
life.

The Lord teaches the humble his way.
—He guides the gentle-hearted along the right path.

Midday

Ant.   The man who does the will of my heavenly Father
will enter the kingdom of heaven.

READING   1 Corinthians 9:26–27a

I do not run like a man who loses sight of the finish
line. I do not fight as if I were shadowboxing. What I do
is discipline my own body and master it.

Lord, blessed is the man whom you instruct.
—You guide him by your law.

Midafternoon

Ant.   No eye has seen what you have prepared, O God,
for those who wait for you.

READING   Philippians 4:8, 9

My brothers, your thoughts should be wholly directed
to all that is true, all that deserves respect, all that is honest, pure, admirable, decent, virtuous, or worthy of
praise. Then will the God of peace be with you.

Let all who hope in you rejoice.
—Eternal gladness will be theirs, and you will dwell with
them.

Prayer, as in Morning Prayer.

Evening Prayer II

HYMN

For all the saints who from their labors rest,
Who thee by faith before the world confessed,
Thy name, O Jesus, be for ever blest:
    Alleluia, alleluia!

Thou wast their rock, their fortress and their might;
Thou, Lord, their captain in the well-fought fight;
Thou in the darkness drear their one true light:
    Alleluia, alleluia!

O blest communion, fellowship divine!
We feebly struggle, they in glory shine;
Yet all are one in thee, for all are thine:
    Alleluia, alleluia!

But, lo, there breaks a yet more glorious day;
The saints triumphant rise in bright array:
The King of glory passes on his way:
    Alleluia, alleluia!

Melody: Sine Nomine 10.10.10
with alleluias

Music: R. Vaughan Williams,
1872–1958
Text: William W. How, 1823–1897

Or:

Faith of our fathers! faith and prayer
Shall win all nations unto thee;
And through the truth that comes from God,
Mankind shall then indeed be free.

Refrain:

Faith of our fathers, holy faith!
We will be true to thee till death.

Faith of our fathers! we will love
Both friend and foe in all our strife:
And preach thee too, as love knows how,
By kindly deeds and virtuous life.

Refrain

Melody: Saint Catherine L. M.
with Refrain

Music Henri F. Hemy,
1818–1888
and James G. Walton, 1821–1905
Text: Frederick W. Faber, 1814–1863

PSALMODY

Ant. 1   God found him pure and strong; he will have
    everlasting glory.

Psalm 15

Lord, who shall be admitted to your tent
and dwell on your holy mountain?

He who walks without fault;
he who acts with justice

and speaks the truth from his heart;
he who does not slander with his tongue;

he who does no wrong to his brother,
who casts no slur on his neighbor,
who holds the godless in disdain,
but honors those who fear the Lord;

he who keeps his pledge, come what may;
who takes no interest on a loan
and accepts no bribes against the innocent.
Such a man will stand firm for ever.

Ant.   God found him pure and strong; he will have everlasting glory.

Ant. 2   God's saints will be filled with his love and mercy; he watches over his chosen ones.

Psalm 112

Happy the man who fears the Lord,
who takes delight in all his commands.
His sons will be powerful on earth;
the children of the upright are blessed.

Riches and wealth are in his house;
his justice stands firm for ever.
He is a light in the darkness for the upright:
he is generous, merciful and just.

The good man takes pity and lends,
he conducts his affairs with honor.
The just man will never waver:
he will be remembered for ever.

He has no fear of evil news;
with a firm heart he trusts in the Lord.
With a steadfast heart he will not fear;
he will see the downfall of his foes.

Open-handed, he gives to the poor;
his justice stands firm for ever.
His head will be raised in glory.

The wicked man sees and is angry,
grinds his teeth and fades away;
the desire of the wicked leads to doom.

Ant.   God's saints will be filled with his love and mercy;
he watches over his chosen ones.

Ant. 3   The whole earth echoes with the melody of
heaven where the saints are singing before the
throne of God and the Lamb.

Canticle   Revelation 15:3–4

Mighty and wonderful are your works,
Lord God Almighty!
Righteous and true are your ways,
O King of the nations!

Who would dare refuse you honor,
or the glory due your name, O Lord?

Since you alone are holy,
all nations shall come
and worship in your presence.
Your mighty deeds are clearly seen.

Ant.   The whole earth echoes with the melody of heaven
where the saints are singing before the throne of
God and the Lamb.

READING   Romans 8:28–30

We know that God makes all things work together for
the good of those who have been called according to his
decree. Those whom he foreknew he predestined to share
the image of his Son, that the Son might be the first-born
of many brothers. Those he predestined he likewise

called; those he called he also justified; and those he justified he in turn glorified.

Just is the Lord, in justice he delights.
— Just is the Lord, in justice he delights.

He looks with favor on the upright man;
— in justice he delights.

Glory to the Father . . .
— Just is the . . .

CANTICLE OF MARY

Ant. Good and faithful servant, enter into the joy of
      your Lord.

For several holy men:

Ant. These holy ones persevered even unto death; the
      Lord has bestowed on them the crown of life.

INTERCESSIONS

Let us pray to the Father, the source of all holiness, and
    ask him to lead us to holiness of life through the exam-
    ple and intercession of his saints:
    May we be holy as you are holy.
Holy Father, you want us to be called your sons and truly
    to be such,
— grant that your holy Church may proclaim you
    throughout the world.
Holy Father, you want us to walk worthily and please
    you in all we do,
— let us abound in doing good works.
Holy Father, you have reconciled us to yourself through
    Christ,
— preserve us in your name so that all may be one.

Holy Father, you have called us to a heavenly banquet,
—through the bread that came down from heaven make
   us worthy to grow in perfect love.
Holy Father, forgive the offenses of every sinner,
—let the dead perceive the light of your countenance.

Our Father . . .

Prayer

If there is no proper prayer, one of the following is said:

God our Father,
you alone are holy;
without you nothing is good.
Trusting in the prayers of Saint N.
we ask you to help us
to become the holy people you call us to be.
Never let us be found undeserving
of the glory you have prepared for us.

We ask this through our Lord Jesus Christ, your Son,
who lives and reigns with you and the Holy Spirit,
one God, for ever and ever.

Or:

All-powerful God,
help us who celebrate the memory of Saint N.
to imitate his way of life.
May the example of your saints
be our challenge to live holier lives.

Grant this through our Lord Jesus Christ, your Son,
who lives and reigns with you and the Holy Spirit,
one God, for ever and ever.

For several holy men:

Ever-living God,
the signs of your love are manifest
in the honor you give your saints.
May their prayers and their example encourage us
to follow your Son more faithfully.

We ask this through our Lord Jesus Christ, your Son,
who lives and reigns with you and the Holy Spirit,
one God, for ever and ever.

For a religious:

Lord God,
you kept Saint N. faithful to Christ's pattern of poverty
    and humility.
May his prayers help us to live in fidelity to our calling
and bring us to the perfection you have shown us in your
    Son,
who lives and reigns with you and the Holy Spirit,
one God, for ever and ever.

For one who worked for the underprivileged:

Lord God,
you teach us that the commandments of heaven
are summarized in love of you and love of our neighbor.
By following the example of Saint N.
in practicing works of charity
may we be counted among the blessed in your kingdom.

Grant this through our Lord Jesus Christ, your Son,
who lives and reigns with you and the Holy Spirit,
one God, for ever and ever.

For a teacher:

Lord God,
you called Saint N. to serve you in the Church
by teaching his fellow man the way of salvation.
Inspire us by his example:
help us to follow Christ our teacher,
and lead us to our brothers and sisters in heaven.

We ask this through our Lord Jesus Christ, your Son,
who lives and reigns with you and the Holy Spirit,
one God, for ever and ever.

COMMON OF HOLY WOMEN

Evening Prayer I

HYMN, as in Evening Prayer II, **1546.**

PSALMODY

Ant. 1 Blessed be the Lord; he has filled his handmaid
with his mercy.

Psalm 113

Praise, O servants of the Lord,
praise the name of the Lord!
May the name of the Lord be blessed
both now and for evermore!
From the rising of the sun to its setting
praised be the name of the Lord!

High above all nations is the Lord,
above the heavens his glory.
Who is like the Lord, our God,
who has risen on high to his throne
yet stoops from the heights to look down,
to look down upon heaven and earth?

From the dust he lifts up the lowly,
from his misery he raises the poor
to set him in the company of princes,
yes, with the princes of his people.
To the childless wife he gives a home
and gladdens her heart with children.

Ant. Blessed be the Lord; he has filled his handmaid
with his mercy.

Ant. 2 Give glory to the Lord, Jerusalem; he has
blessed every child within you.

Psalm 147:12-20

O praise the Lord, Jerusalem!
Zion, praise your God!

He has strengthened the bars of your gates,
he has blessed the children within you.
He established peace on your borders,
he feeds you with finest wheat.

He sends out his word to the earth
and swiftly runs his command.
He showers down snow white as wool,
he scatters hoar-frost like ashes.

He hurls down hailstones like crumbs.
The waters are frozen at his touch;
he sends forth his word and it melts them:
at the breath of his mouth the waters flow.

He makes his word known to Jacob,
to Israel his laws and decrees.
He has not dealt thus with other nations;
he has not taught them his decrees.

Ant.   Give glory to the Lord, Jerusalem; he has blessed
every child within you.

Ant. 3   The Lord delights in you; you are the joy of his
heart.

Canticle   Ephesians 1:3-10

Praised be the God and Father
of our Lord Jesus Christ,
who bestowed on us in Christ
every spiritual blessing in the heavens.

God chose us in him
before the world began,
to be holy
and blameless in his sight.

He predestined us
to be his adopted sons through Jesus Christ,
such was his will and pleasure,
that all might praise the glorious favor
he has bestowed on us in his beloved.

In him and through his blood, we have been re-
    deemed,
and our sins forgiven,
so immeasurably generous
is God's favor to us.

God has given us the wisdom
to understand fully the mystery,
the plan he was pleased
to decree in Christ.

A plan to be carried out
in Christ, in the fullness of time,
to bring all things into one in him,
in the heavens and on the earth.

Ant.   The Lord delights in you; you are the joy of his
      heart.

READING   Philippians 3:7–8

Those things I used to consider gain I have now reap-
praised as loss in the light of Christ. I have come to rate
all as loss in the light of the surpassing knowledge of my
Lord Jesus Christ. For his sake I have forfeited everything; I have accounted all else rubbish so that Christ
may be my wealth.

RESPONSORY

Joy and gladness fill my heart; the Lord has been merci-
    ful to me.
—Joy and gladness fill my heart; the Lord has been mer-
    ciful to me.

He has looked with favor on his lowly servant.
—The Lord has been merciful to me.

Glory to the Father . . .
—Joy and gladness . . .

CANTICLE OF MARY

Ant.   Give her the reward of her deeds; they will proclaim her as she enters the gates.

For several holy women:

Ant.   Praise the holy name of the Lord; the heart that
seeks him will rejoice.

INTERCESSIONS

Through the intercession of holy women, let us pray for
the Church in these words:
Be mindful of your Church, Lord.
Through all the women martyrs who conquered bodily
death by their courage,
—strengthen your Church in the hour of trial.
Through married women who have advanced in grace by
holy matrimony,
—make the apostolic mission of your Church fruitful.
Through widows who eased their loneliness and sanctified it by prayer and hospitality,
—help your Church reveal the mystery of your love to
the world.
Through mothers who have borne children for the kingdom of God and the human community,
—help your Church bring all men to a rebirth in life and
salvation.
Through all your holy women who have been worthy to
contemplate the light of your countenance,
—let the deceased members of your Church exult in that
same vision for ever.

Our Father . . .

Prayer

If there is no proper prayer, one of the following is said;

God our Father,
every year you give us joy on this feast of Saint N.
As we honor her memory by this celebration,
may we follow the example of her holy life.
We ask this through our Lord Jesus Christ, your Son,
who lives and reigns with you and the Holy Spirit,
one God, for ever and ever.

Or:

Lord,
pour upon us the spirit of wisdom and love
with which you filled your servant Saint N.
By serving you as she did,
may we please you with our faith and our actions.
Grant this through our Lord Jesus Christ, your Son,
who lives and reigns with you and the Holy Spirit,
one God, for ever and ever.

For several holy women:

All-powerful God,
may the prayers of Saints N. and N. bring us help from
   heaven
as their lives have already given us
an example of holiness.
We ask this through our Lord Jesus Christ, your Son,
who lives and reigns with you and the Holy Spirit,
one God, for ever and ever.

For a religious:

Lord God,
you kept Saint N. faithful to Christ's pattern of poverty
   and humility.

May her prayers help us to live in fidelity to our calling
and bring us to the perfection you have shown us in your
    Son,
who lives and reigns with you and the Holy Spirit,
one God, for ever and ever.

For one who worked for the underprivileged:

Lord God,
you teach us that the commandments of heaven
are summarized in love of you and love of our neighbor.
By following the example of Saint N.
in practicing works of charity
may we be counted among the blessed in your kingdom.
Grant this through our Lord Jesus Christ, your Son,
who lives and reigns with you and the Holy Spirit,
one God, for ever and ever.

For a teacher:

Lord God,
you called Saint N. to serve you in the Church
by teaching her fellow man the way of salvation.
Inspire us by her example:
help us to follow Christ our teacher,
and lead us to our brothers and sisters in heaven.
We ask this through our Lord Jesus Christ, your Son,
who lives and reigns with you and the Holy Spirit,
one God, for ever and ever.

Invitatory

Ant.   Come, let us worship God, wonderful in his
        saints.

Or: Let us sing praise to God, as we acclaim Saint N.

Invitatory psalm, as in the Ordinary, **648**.

Office of Readings

HYMN

Let us with joy our voices raise
In that heroic woman's praise,
Whose courage, strength and holy fame
Have given her an honored name.

O Strength of all the strong, God's Son,
Thru whom alone great deeds are done,
By your great strength and thru her prayer
May we bear witness ev'rywhere.

Praise God the Father and the Son
And Holy Spirit, Three in One,
Who gave this noble woman grace
A life of virtue to embrace.

Melody: Eisenach L.M.   Music: Johan Herman Schein, 1628
Text: *Fortem Virili Pectore*,
Silvio Antoniano, 1540–1603;
Stanza 3, Roger Nachtwey, 1964
Translator: Roger Nachtwey, 1964

Or:

Blessed are the poor of heart,
Blessed are the merciful,
For they will be blessed upon the earth.
Blessed are the poor!

Blessed are they who suffer,
Blessed are they who are persecuted,
For they shall be the rulers of the world.
Blessed are the poor!

Blessed are they who hunger and thirst
For justice and the rights of all,
For they shall eat the meal of the Lord.
Blessed are the poor!

Blessed are they whose hearts are clean
And blessed are they who keep his word,

For they have inherited the land.
Blessed are the poor!

Blessed are they who labor for peace,
Blessed are they who suffer in war,
For they shall meet the Prince of Peace.
Blessed are the poor!

Melody: The Beatitudes   Music: Enrico Garzilli, 1970
Text: Enrico Garzilli, 1970

PSALMODY

Ant. 1 Her mouth uttered words of wisdom; her
    tongue spoke words of compassion.

Psalm 19A

The heavens proclaim the glory of God
and the firmament shows forth the work of his
  hands.
Day unto day takes up the story
and night unto night makes known the message.

No speech, no word, no voice is heard
yet their span extends through all the earth,
their words to the utmost bounds of the world.

There he has placed a tent for the sun;
it comes forth like a bridegroom coming from his
  tent,
rejoices like a champion to run its course.

At the end of the sky is the rising of the sun;
to the furthest end of the sky is its course.
There is nothing concealed from its burning heat.

Ant. Her mouth uttered words of wisdom; her tongue
    spoke words of compassion.

Ant. 2 Trusting themselves to God, these holy women
    sang his praises with heartfelt love.

Psalm 45

I

My heart overflows with noble words.
To the king I must speak the song I have made;
my tongue as nimble as the pen of a scribe.

You are the fairest of the chldren of men
and graciousness is poured upon your lips:
because God has blessed you for evermore.

O mighty one, gird your sword upon your thigh;
in splendor and state, ride on in triumph
for the cause of truth and goodness and right.

Take aim with your bow in your dread right hand.
Your arrows are sharp: peoples fall beneath you.
The foes of the king fall down and lose heart.

Your throne, O God, shall endure for ever.
A scepter of justice is the scepter of your kingdom.
Your love is for justice; your hatred for evil.

Therefore God, your God, has anointed you
with the oil of gladness above other kings:
your robes are fragrant with aloes and myrrh.

From the ivory palace you are greeted with music.
The daughters of kings are among your loved ones.
On your right stands the queen in gold of Ophir.

Ant.　Trusting themselves to God, these holy women
　　　sang his praises with heartfelt love.

Ant. 3　Singing for joy, they are brought into the
　　　King's presence.

II

Listen, O daughter, give ear to my words:
forget your own people and your father's house.

So will the king desire your beauty:
He is your lord, pay homage to him.

And the people of Tyre shall come with gifts,
the richest of the people shall seek your favor.
The daughter of the king is clothed with splendor,
her robes embroidered with pearls set in gold.

She is led to the king with her maiden companions.
They are escorted amid gladness and joy;
they pass within the palace of the king.

Sons shall be yours in place of your fathers:
you will make them princes over all the earth.
May this song make your name for ever remembered.
May the peoples praise you from age to age.

Ant.   Singing for joy, they are brought into the King's
presence.

The thoughts of my heart are always before you, O Lord.
—You are my help and my redeemer.

FIRST READING

Appropriate texts may be taken from the common of holy men,
1503-1507.

Alternative reading, for a married woman:

From the book of Proverbs   31:10–31

A woman who reveres the Lord

When one finds a worthy wife,
    her value is far beyond pearls.
Her husband, entrusting his heart to her,
    has an unfailing prize.
She brings him good, and not evil,
    all the days of her life.

She obtains wool and flax
   and makes cloth with skillful hands.
Like merchant ships,
   she secures her provisions from afar.
She rises while it is still night,
   and distributes food to her household.

She picks out a field to purchase;
   out of her earnings she plants a vineyard.
She is girt about with strength,
   and sturdy are her arms.
She enjoys the success of her dealings;
   at night her lamp is undimmed.

She puts her hands to the distaff,
   and her fingers ply the spindle.
She reaches out her hands to the poor,
   and extends her arms to the needy.
She fears not the snow for her household;
   all her charges are doubly clothed.

She makes her own coverlets;
   fine linen and purple are her clothing.
Her husband is prominent at the city gates
   as he sits with the elders of the land.
She makes garments and sells them,
   and stocks the merchants with belts.

She is clothed with strength and dignity,
   and she laughs at the days to come.
She opens her mouth in wisdom,
   and on her tongue is kindly counsel.
She watches the conduct of her household,
   and eats not her food in idleness.

Her children rise up and praise her;
   her husband, too, extols her:

"Many are the women of proven worth,
    but you have excelled them all."

Charm is deceptive and beauty fleeting;
    the woman who fears the Lord is to be praised.
Give her a reward of her labors,
    and let her works praise her at the city gates.

RESPONSORY   See Proverbs 31:17, 18; see Psalm 46:6

She set herself to work with courage,
she put forth all her strength;
—therefore her lamp will never go out.

The Lord will help her;
his loving presence will be with her.
He dwells in her; she will not falter.
—Therefore her lamp . . .

Additional alternative, for a married woman:

From the first letter of the apostle Peter   3:1-6, 8–17
Praise Christ in your hearts

You married women must obey your husbands, so that
any of them who do not believe in the word of the gospel
may be won over apart from preaching, through their
wives' conduct. They have only to observe the reverent
purity of your way of life. The affection of an elaborate
hairdress, the wearing of golden jewelry, or the donning
of rich robes is not for you. Your adornment is rather the
hidden character of the heart, expressed in the unfading
beauty of a calm and gentle disposition. This is precious
in God's eyes. The holy women of past ages used to adorn
themselves in this way, reliant on God and obedient to
their husbands—for example, Sarah, who was subject to
Abraham and called him her master. You are her children when you do what is right and let no fears alarm
you.

In summary, then, all of you should be like-minded, sympathetic, loving toward one another, kindly disposed, and humble. Do not return evil for evil or insult for insult. Return a blessing instead. This you have been called to do, that you may receive a blessing as your inheritance.

"He who cares for life
and wants to see prosperous days
must keep his tongue from evil
and his lips from uttering deceit.
He must turn from evil and do good,
seek peace and follow after it,
because the Lord has eyes for the just
and ears for their cry;
but against evildoers the Lord sets his face."

Who indeed can harm you if you are committed deeply to doing what is right? Even if you should have to suffer for justice' sake, happy will you be. "Fear not and do not stand in awe of what this people fears." Venerate the Lord, that is, Christ, in your hearts. Should anyone ask you the reason for this hope of yours, be ever ready to reply, but speak gently and respectfully. Keep your conscience clear, so that, whenever you are defamed, those who libel your way of life in Christ may be shamed. If it should be God's will that you suffer, it is better to do so for good deeds than for evil ones.

RESPONSORY   Phil. 2:2, 3, 4; 1 Thes. 5:14–15

Love one another; humbly consider others to be better than yourselves;
— do not think of your own interests alone, but look to the interests of others.

Support the weak, be patient with all;

seek to do what is good for each other and for all men.
  —Do not think . . .

SECOND READING

Appropriate texts may be taken from the common of holy men, 1508-1511

On solemnities and feasts, **Te Deum, 651.**

Prayer, as in Morning Prayer.

Morning Prayer

HYMN

> Now, from the heav'ns descending,
> Is seen a glorious light,
> The Bride of Christ in splendor,
> Arrayed in purest white.
> She is the holy City,
> Whose radiance is the grace
> Of all the saints in glory,
> From every time and place.
>
> This is the hour of gladness
> For Bridegroom and for Bride,
> The Lamb's great feast is ready,
> His Bride is at his side.
> How bless'd are those invited
> To share his wedding-feast:
> The least become the greatest,
> The greatest are the least.
>
> He who is throned in heaven
> Takes up his dwelling-place
> Among his chosen people,
> Who see him face to face.
> No sound is heard of weeping,
> For pain and sorrow cease,

And sin shall reign no longer,
But love and joy and peace.

See how a new creation
Is brought at last to birth,
A new and glorious heaven,
A new and glorious earth.
Death's power for ever broken,
Its empire swept away,
The promised dawn of glory
Begins its endless day.

Melody: Moville 76.76.D   Music: Traditional Irish Melody
                                    Text: James Quinn, S.J., 1968

Or:

O God, our help in ages past,
Our hope for years to come,
Our shelter from the stormy blast
And our eternal home;

Beneath the shadow of your throne
Your saints have dwelt secure;
Sufficient is your arm alone,
And our defense is sure.

Before the hills in order stood,
Or earth received her frame,
From everlasting you are God,
To endless years the same.

A thousand ages in your sight
Are like an evening gone,
Short as the watch that ends the night
Before the rising sun.

Time, like an ever-rolling stream,
Bears all its sons away;
They fly forgotten, as a dream
Dies at the opening day.

O God, our help in ages past,
Our hope for years to come,
Be now our guide while life shall last,
And our eternal home.

Melody: Saint Anne C.M.

Music: William Croft, 1708
Text: Isaac Watts, 1674–1748,
alt. by Rev. William Bauman

Ant. 1   My soul clings to you; with your right hand you
have raised me up.

Psalms and canticle from Sunday, Week I, 688.

Ant. 2   The hand of the Lord has given you strength;
you will be praised for ever.

Ant. 3   Lord, I shall rejoice and be glad, for you have
been merciful to me.

READING   Romans 12:1–2
Brothers, I beg you through the mercy of God to offer
your bodies as a living sacrifice holy and acceptable to
God, your spiritual worship. Do not conform yourselves
to this age but be transformed by the renewal of your
mind, so that you may judge what is God's will, what is
good, pleasing and perfect.

RESPONSORY

The Lord will help her; his loving presence will be with
her.
—The Lord will help her; his loving presence will be
with her.

He dwells in her; she will not falter.
—His loving presence will be with her.

Glory to the Father . . .
—The Lord will . . .

For several holy women:

Let the just rejoice in the presence of God.
—Let the just rejoice in the presence of God.

Let them be filled with gladness,
— in the presence of God.

Glory to the Father . . .
—Let the just . . .

CANTICLE OF ZECHARIAH

Ant.   The kingdom of heaven is like a merchant seeking
       fine pearls; he finds one of great value and gives all
       that he has to possess it.

INTERCESSIONS

My brothers, with all the holy women, let us profess our
       faith in our Savior and call upon him:
       Come, Lord Jesus.
Lord Jesus, you forgave the sinful woman because she
       loved much,
—forgive us who have sinned much.
Lord Jesus, the holy women ministered to your needs
       during your journeys,
—help us to follow your footsteps.
Lord Jesus, master, Mary listened to your words while
       Martha served your needs,
—help us to serve you with love and devotion.
Lord Jesus, you call everyone who does your will your
       brother, sister and mother,
—help us to do what is pleasing to you in word and ac-
       tion.

Our Father . . .

Prayer

If there is no proper prayer, one of the following is said:

God our Father,
every year you give us joy on this feast of Saint N.
As we honor her memory by this celebration,
may we follow the example of her holy life.

We ask this through our Lord Jesus Christ, your Son,
who lives and reigns with you and the Holy Spirit,
one God, for ever and ever.

Or:

Lord,
pour upon us the spirit of wisdom and love
with which you filled your servant Saint N.
By serving you as she did,
may we please you with our faith and our actions.

Grant this through our Lord Jesus Christ, your Son,
who lives and reigns with you and the Holy Spirit,
one God, for ever and ever.

For several holy women:

All-powerful God,
may the prayers of Saints N. and N. bring us help from
    heaven
as their lives have already given us
an example of holiness.

We ask this through our Lord Jesus Christ, your Son,
who lives and reigns with you and the Holy Spirit,
one God, for ever and ever.

For a religious:

Lord God,
you kept Saint N. faithful to Christ's pattern of poverty
    and humility.

May her prayers help us to live in fidelity to our calling
and bring us to the perfection you have shown us in your
    Son,
who lives and reigns with you and the Holy Spirit,
one God, for ever and ever.

For one who worked for the underprivileged:

Lord God,
you teach us that the commandments of heaven
are summarized in love of you and love of our neighbor.
By following the example of Saint N.
in practicing works of charity
may we be counted among the blessed in your kingdom.

Grant this through our Lord Jesus Christ, your Son,
who lives and reigns with you and the Holy Spirit,
one God, for ever and ever.

For a teacher:

Lord God,
you called Saint N. to serve you in the Church
by teaching her fellow man the way of salvation.
Inspire us by her example:
help us to follow Christ our teacher,
and lead us to our brothers and sisters in heaven.

We ask this through our Lord Jesus Christ, your Son,
who lives and reigns with you and the Holy Spirit,
one God, for ever and ever.

Daytime Prayer

For the gradual psalms, in place of psalm 122, psalm 129, 1129,
may be said, and in place of psalm 127, psalm 131, 972, may be
said.

Midmorning

Ant.   Upon all who do my will, I shall pour my spirit.

READING   Galatians 6:7b–8

A man will reap only what he sows. If he sows in the field of the flesh, he will reap a harvest of corruption; but if his seed-ground is the spirit, he will reap everlasting life.

Blessed are they whose way is blameless.
—Who walk according to the law of the Lord.

Midday

Ant.   My heart and my flesh rejoice in the living God.

READING   1 Corinthians 9:26, 27a

I do not run like a man who loses sight of the finish line. I do not fight as if I were shadowboxing. What I do is discipline my own body and master it.

I found him whom I love.
—I held him fast; I would not leave him.

Midafternoon

Ant.   My beloved belongs to me; I to him.

READING   Philippians 4:8, 9

My brothers, your thoughts should be wholly directed to all that is true, all that deserves respect, all that is honest, pure, admirable, decent, virtuous, or worthy of praise. Then will the God of peace be with you.

I will sing to you, Lord.
—I will rejoice and I will follow your blameless way.

Prayer, as in Morning Prayer.

Evening Prayer II

HYMN

You holy angels bright,
Who wait at God's right hand,
Or through the realms of light
Fly at your Lord's command,
Assist our song,
For else the theme
Too high will seem
For mortal tongue.

You blessed souls at rest,
Who ran this earthly race,
And now, from sin released,
Behold the Savior's face;
His praises sound,
As in his sight
With sweet delight
You all abound.

Let us who toil below
Adore our heav'nly King,
And onward as we go
Our joyful anthem sing;
With one accord,
Through good or ill,
We praise him still,
Eternal Lord

My soul, now take your part,
Acclaiming God above:
And with a well-tuned heart
Sing out the songs of love.
Let all your days
Till life shall end,

What e'er he send,
Be filled with praise.

Melody: Darwall's 148th   Music: John Darwall, 1731–1789
Text: Richard Baxter, 1615–1691, et al.,
adapted by Anthony G. Petti, 1971

PSALMODY

Ant. 1   Now your servant rejoices, Lord, for you have
saved her.

Psalm 122

I rejoiced when I heard them say:
"Let us go to God's house."
And now our feet are standing
within your gates, O Jerusalem.

Jerusalem is built as a city
strongly compact.
It is there that the tribes go up,
the tribes of the Lord.

For Israel's law it is,
there to praise the Lord's name.
There were set the thrones of judgment
of the house of David.

For the peace of Jerusalem pray:
"Peace be to your homes!
May peace reign in your walls,
in your palaces, peace!"

For love of my brethren and friends
I say: "Peace upon you!"
For love of the house of the Lord
I will ask for your good.

Ant.   Now your servant rejoices, Lord, for you have
saved her.

Ant. 2 Like a house built on enduring rock, so the
commandments of God will remain firm in the
heart of a holy woman.

Psalm 127

If the Lord does not build the house,
in vain do its builders labor;
if the Lord does not watch over the city,
in vain does the watchman keep vigil.

In vain is your earlier rising,
your going later to rest,
you who toil for the bread you eat:
when he pours gifts on his beloved while they slumber.

Truly sons are a gift from the Lord,
a blessing, the fruit of the womb.
Indeed the sons of youth
are like arrows in the hand of a warrior.

O the happiness of the man
who has filled his quiver with these arrows!
He will have no cause for shame
when he disputes with his foes in the gateways.

Ant. Like a house built on enduring rock, so the commandments of God will remain firm in the heart of
a holy woman.

Ant. 3 The hand of the Lord has given her strength;
she will be praised for ever.

Canticle   Ephesians 1:3–10

Praised be the God and Father
of our Lord Jesus Christ,
who bestowed on us in Christ
every spiritual blessing in the heavens.

God chose us in him
before the world began,
to be holy
and blameless in his sight.

He predestined us
to be his adopted sons through Jesus Christ,
such was his will and pleasure,
that all might praise the glorious favor
he has bestowed on us in his beloved.

In him and through his blood, we have been redeemed,
and our sins forgiven,
so immeasurably generous
is God's favor to us.

God has given us the wisdom
to understand fully the mystery,
the plan he was pleased
to decree in Christ.

A plan to be carried out
in Christ, in the fullness of time,
to bring all things into one in him,
in the heavens and on the earth.

Ant. The hand of the Lord has given her strength; she
will be praised for ever.

READING   Romans 8:28-30

We know that God makes all things work together for
the good of those who have been called according to his
decree. Those whom he foreknew he predestined to share
the image of his Son, that the Son might be the first-born
of many brothers. Those he predestined he likewise
called; those he called he also justified; and those he justified he in turn glorified.

RESPONSORY

The Lord has chosen her, his loved one from the beginning.
—The Lord has chosen her, his loved one from the beginning.

He has taken her to live with him,
—his loved one from the beginning.

Glory to the Father . . .
—The Lord has . . .

CANTICLE OF MARY

Ant.   My heart sings for joy and overflows with gladness, for the Lord is my savior.

INTERCESSIONS

Through the intercession of holy women let us pray for
the Church in these words:
Be mindful of your Church, Lord.

Through all the women martyrs who conquered bodily
death by their courage,
—strengthen your Church in the hour of trial.

Through married women who have advanced in grace by
holy matrimony,
—make the apostolic mission of your Church fruitful.

Through widows who eased their loneliness and sanctified it by prayer and hospitality,
—help your Church reveal the mystery of your love to
the world.

Through mothers who have borne children for the kingdom of God and the human community,
—help your Church bring all men to a rebirth in life and
salvation.

Through all your holy women who have been worthy to
contemplate the light of your countenance,

—let the deceased members of your Church exult in that
    same vision for ever.

Our Father . . .

Prayer

If there is no proper prayer, one of the following is said:

God our Father,
every year you give us joy on this feast of Saint N.
As we honor her memory by this celebration,
may we follow the example of her holy life.

We ask this through our Lord Jesus Christ, your Son,
who lives and reigns with you and the Holy Spirit,
one God, for ever and ever.

Or:

Lord,
pour upon us the spirit of wisdom and love
with which you filled your servant Saint N.
By serving you as she did,
may we please you with our faith and our actions.

Grant this through our Lord Jesus Christ, your Son,
who lives and reigns with you and the Holy Spirit,
one God, for ever and ever.

For several holy women:

All-powerful God,
may the prayers of Saints N. and N. bring us help from
    heaven
as their lives have already given us
an example of holiness.

We ask this through our Lord Jesus Christ, your Son,
who lives and reigns with you and the Holy Spirit,
one God, for ever and ever.

For a religious:

Lord God,
you kept Saint N. faithful to Christ's pattern of poverty
    and humility.
May her prayers help us to live in fidelity to our calling
and bring us to the perfection you have shown us in your
    Son,
who lives and reigns with you and the Holy Spirit,
one God, for ever and ever.

For one who worked for the underprivileged:

Lord God,
you teach us that the commandments of heaven
are summarized in love of you and love of our neighbor.
By following the example of Saint N.
in practicing works of charity
may we be counted among the blessed in your kingdom.

Grant this through our Lord Jesus Christ, your Son,
who lives and reigns with you and the Holy Spirit,
one God, for ever and ever.

For a teacher

Lord God,
you called Saint N. to serve you in the Church
by teaching her fellow man the way of salvation.
Inspire us by her example:
help us to follow Christ our teacher,
and lead us to our brothers and sisters in heaven.

We ask this through our Lord Jesus Christ, your Son,
who lives and reigns with you and the Holy Spirit,
one God, for ever and ever.

FOR RELIGIOUS

Everything is taken from the common of holy men, **1494**, or of holy women, **1526**, except the following:

Evening Prayer I

Hymn, as in Evening Prayer II, **1560**.

Canticle of Mary

Ant. Unless you give up all you possess, you cannot be my disciple, says the Lord.

Or, for a man:

Ant. This man will receive blessings and compassion from the Lord God, his Savior, for this is the reward of those who seek the Lord.

Or, for a woman:

Ant. The Lord chose her for his spouse with a loyal, compassionate love that will last for ever.

Prayer

If there is no proper prayer, one of the following is said:

Lord God,
you kept Saint N. faithful to Christ's pattern of poverty and humility.
May his (her) prayers help us to live in fidelity to our calling
and bring us to the perfection you have shown us in your Son,
who lives and reigns with you and the Holy Spirit,
one God, for ever and ever.

For an abbot:

Lord,
in your abbot N.

you give an example of the gospel lived to perfection.
Help us to follow him
by keeping before us the things of heaven
amid all the changes of this world.

Grant this through our Lord Jesus Christ, your Son,
who lives and reigns with you and the Holy Spirit,
one God, for ever and ever.

Invitatory

Ant. Come, let us worship God, wonderful in his saints.

Or: Let us sing praise to God, as we acclaim Saint N.

Invitatory psalm, as in the Ordinary, 648.

Office of Readings

HYMN, as in Evening Prayer II, 1560.

FIRST READING

From the letter of the apostle Paul
to the Ephesians   4:1–24

Grace has been given to each one for the building up of the
body of Christ

I plead with you, then, as a prisoner for the Lord, to
live a life worthy of the calling you have received, with
perfect humility, meekness, and patience, bearing with
one another lovingly. Make every effort to preserve the
unity which has the Spirit as its origin and peace as its
binding force. There is but one body and one Spirit, just
as there is but one hope given all of you by your call.
There is one Lord, one faith, one baptism; one God and
Father of all, who is over all, and works through all, and
is in all.

Each of us has received God's favor in the measure in which Christ bestows it. Thus you find Scripture saying:

"When he ascended on high, he took a host of captives and gave gifts to men."

"He ascended"—what does this mean but that he had first descended into the lower regions of the earth? He who descended is the very one who ascended high above the heavens, that he might fill all men with his gifts.

It is he who gave apostles, prophets, evangelists, pastors and teachers in roles of service for the faithful to build up the body of Christ, till we become one in faith and in the knowledge of God's Son, and form that perfect man who is Christ come to full stature.

Let us, then, be children no longer, tossed here and there, carried about by every wind of doctrine that originates in human trickery and skill in proposing error. Rather, let us profess the truth in love and grow to the full maturity of Christ the head. Through him the whole body grows, and with the proper functioning of the members joined firmly together by each supporting ligament, builds itself up in love.

I declare and solemnly attest in the Lord that you must no longer live as the pagans do—their minds empty, their understanding darkened. They are estranged from a life in God because of their ignorance and their resistance; without remorse they have abandoned themselves to lust and the indulgence of every sort of lewd conduct.

That is not what you learned when you learned Christ! I am supposing, of course, that he has been preached and taught to you in accord with the truth that is in Jesus: namely, that you must lay aside your former way of life and the old self which deteriorates through illusion and desire, and acquire a fresh, spiritual way of thinking.

You must put on that new man created in God's image,
whose justice and holiness are born of truth.

RESPONSORY   Matthew 19:29, 27

If you leave your home, your brothers or sisters, father or
    mother,
wife or children, or lands for love of me,
—you will have it all returned a hundredfold
and will inherit eternal life.

Lord, we have left everything to follow you;
what will become of us!
—You will have . . .

Or, for a woman:

RESPONSORY   See Luke 10:42, 39

There is only one thing necessary:
—this, the best part of all,
is what she has chosen
and it will not be taken from her.

She sat at the Lord's feet listening to his words.
—This, the best . . .

SECOND READING

From a homily on the Gospels by Saint Gregory the
Great, pope

(Lib. 2, hom. 36, 11–13: PL 76, 1272–1274)

In the world, yet not of it

I would like to urge you to forsake everything, but that
I do not presume to do. Yet, if you cannot give up everything of this world, at least keep what belongs to the
world in such a way that you yourself are not kept prisoner by the world. Whatever you possess must not possess
you; whatever you own must be under the power of your

soul; for if your soul is overpowered by the love of this world's goods, it will be totally at the mercy of its possessions.

In other words, we make use of temporal things, but our hearts are set on what is eternal. Temporal goods help us on our way, but our desire must be for those eternal realities which are our goal. We should give no more than a side glance at all that happens in the world, but the eyes of our soul are to be focused right ahead; for our whole attention must be fixed on those realities which constitute our goal.

Whatever is vicious must be utterly eradicated, wrenched away not merely from being put into act but even from being so much as thought of. No carnal pleasure, no worldly curiosity, no surge of ambition must keep us from the Lord's Supper. But further, our minds should merely skirt even the good deeds we perform in this life; in this way, the physical things which give us pleasure will serve our bodily needs without hindering the soul's progress. You see, my brothers, I dare not say to you, give up everything. Yet, if you will, you can give everything up even while keeping it, provided you handle temporal things in such a way that your whole mind is directed toward what is eternal. A man can use the world as if he were not using it, if he makes all external needs minister to the support of his life without allowing them to dominate his soul. They remain external to him and under his control, serving him without halting the soul's drive to higher things. For such men, everything in this world is there for their use, not to be desired. Nothing should interfere with your soul's longing; no created pleasure in the world should ensnare you.

If the object of love is what is good, then the soul should take its delight in the higher good, the things of heaven. If the object of fear is what is evil, then we should keep before ourselves the things that are eternally evil. In this way, if the soul sees that we should have a greater love and a greater fear about what concerns the next life, it will never cling to this life.

To help us to achieve all this we have the help of the mediator between God and man. Through him we shall obtain all this the more quickly, the more we burn with a great love for him, who lives and reigns with the Father and the Holy Spirit, for ever and ever. Amen.

RESPONSORY   1 Corinthians 7:29, 30, 31; 2:12

The time is growing short,
so we must rejoice as though we were not rejoicing;
we must work in the world yet without becoming im-
    mersed in it,
—for the world as we know it is passing away.

We have not adopted the spirit of the world.
—For the world . . .

On solemnities and feasts, Te Deum, 651.

Prayer, as in Morning Prayer.

Morning Prayer

HYMN

> O God, our help in ages past,
> Our hope for years to come,
> Our shelter from the stormy blast
> And our eternal home;
>
> Beneath the shadow of your throne
> Your saints have dwelt secure;
> Sufficient is your arm alone,
> And our defense is sure.

Before the hills in order stood,
Or earth received her frame,
From everlasting you are God,
To endless years the same.

A thousand ages in your sight
Are like an evening gone,
Short as the watch that ends the night
Before the rising sun.

Time, like an ever-rolling stream,
Bears all its sons away;
They fly forgotten, as a dream
Dies at the opening day.

O God, our help in ages past,
Our hope for years to come,
Be now our guide while life shall last,
And our eternal home.

Melody: Saint Anne C.M.

Music: William Croft, 1708
Text: Isaac Watts, 1674–1748,
alt. by Rev. William Bauman

CANTICLE OF ZECHARIAH

Ant.   Whoever does my Father's will, says the Lord, he
is my brother, my sister and my mother.

Or: The Lord is my inheritance; he is good to those
who seek him.

Prayer

If there is no proper prayer, one of the following is said:

Lord God,
you kept Saint N. faithful to Christ's pattern of poverty
and humility.
May his (her) prayers help us to live in fidelity to our
calling
and bring us to the perfection you have shown us in your
Son,

who lives and reigns with you and the Holy Spirit,
one God, for ever and ever.

For an abbot:

Lord,
in your abbot N.
you give an example of the gospel lived to perfection.
Help us to follow him
by keeping before us the things of heaven
amid all the changes of this world.

Grant this through our Lord Jesus Christ, your Son,
who lives and reigns with you and the Holy Spirit,
one God, for ever and ever.

Evening Prayer II

HYMN

For all the saints who from their labors rest,
Who thee by faith before the world confessed,
Thy name, O Jesus, be for ever blest:
   Alleluia, alleluia!

Thou wast their rock, their fortress and their might;
Thou, Lord, their captain in the well-fought fight;
Thou in the darkness drear their one true light:
   Alleluia, alleluia!

O blest communion, fellowship divine!
We feebly struggle, they in glory shine;
Yet all are one in thee, for all are thine:
   Alleluia, alleluia!

But, lo, there breaks a yet more glorious day;
The saints triumphant rise in bright array:
The King of glory passes on his way:
   Alleluia, alleluia!

Melody: Sine Nomine 10.10.10   Music: R. Vaughan Williams,
with alleluias   1872–1958
                                  Text: William W. How, 1823–1897

Or:

> Faith of our fathers! faith and prayer
> Shall win all nations unto thee;
> And through the truth that comes from God,
> Mankind shall then indeed be free.

Refrain:

> Faith of our father, holy faith!
> We will be true to thee till death.

> Faith of our fathers! we will love
> Both friend and foe in all our strife:
> And preach thee too, as love knows how,
> By kindly deeds and virtuous life.

Refrain

Melody Saint Catherine L.M.
with Refrain

Music: Henri F. Hemy, 1818–1888
and James G. Walton, 1821–1905
Text: Frederick W. Faber, 1814–1863

CANTICLE OF MARY

Ant.   You have left everything to follow me; you will
have it all returned a hundredfold and will inherit
eternal life.

Or: Where brothers praise God together, there the
Lord will shower his graces.

Prayer, as in Morning Prayer.

FOR THOSE WHO WORKED FOR
THE UNDERPRIVILEGED

Everything is taken from the common of holy men, 1494, or of
holy women, 1526, except the following:

Evening Prayer I

CANTICLE OF MARY

Ant. How blessed the man whose heart goes out to the
poor; those who trust in the Lord delight in showing mercy.

Prayer, as in Morning Prayer.

Office of Readings

FIRST READING

From the first letter of the apostle John   4:7–21

Let us care for each other, because love is from God

Beloved,
let us love one another
because love is of God;
everyone who loves is begotten of God
and has knowledge of God.
The man without love has known nothing of God,
for God is love.
God's love was revealed in our midst in this way:
he sent his only Son to the world
that we might have life through him.
Love, then, consists in this:
not that we have loved God
but that he has loved us
and has sent his Son as an offering for our sins.

Beloved,
if God has loved us so,

we must have the same love for one another.
No one has ever seen God.
Yet if we love one another
God dwells in us,
and his love is brought to perfection in us.
The way we know we remain in him
and he in us
is that he has given us of his Spirit.

We have seen for ourselves, and can testify,
that the Father has sent the Son as savior of the world.
When anyone acknowledges that Jesus is the Son of God,
God dwells in him
and he in God.
We have come to know and to believe
in the love God has for us.
God is love,
and he who abides in love
abides in God,
and God in him.

Our love is brought to perfection in this,
that we should have confidence on the day of judgment;
for our relation to this world is just like his.
Love has no room for fear;
rather, perfect love casts out all fear.
And since fear has to do with punishment,
love is not yet perfect in one who is afraid.
We, for our part, love
because he first loved us.

If anyone says, "My love is fixed on God,"
yet hates his brother,
he is a liar.
One who has no love for the brother he has seen
cannot love the God he has not seen.

The commandment we have from him is this:
whoever loves God must also love his brother.

RESPONSORY 1 John 5:3; Sirach 23:37

Loving God means keeping his commands,
—and his commands are not burdensome.

There is nothing sweeter than obeying the Lord's commands.
—And his commands . . .

SECOND READING

From a homily on the Letter to the Romans by Saint
John Chrysostom, bishop

(Homilia 15, 6: PG 60, 547–548)

Compassion is Christ's command

God gave us his own Son; but you will not even share
your bread with him who was given us and put to death
for your sake.

On account of you the Father did not spare him
though he was indeed his Son; you disregard him when
he is wasting away with starvation, even though you
would be spending on him what is really his, spending it
moreover for your own good. What can be worse than
such injustice? He was given up for you, put to death for
you, went about hungry for you; you would be giving
only what is his, giving moreover for your own benefit;
even so, you refuse to give.

What stone could be more insensitive than such men,
for despite so many inducements they persist in this sa-
tanic cold-heartedness. He was not satisfied only to endure death on a cross; he chose to become poor and
homeless, a beggar and naked, to be thrown into prison
and suffer sickness, so that in this way too he might invite
you to join him.

"If you will make me no return for having suffered for you, at least have pity on my poverty. If not that, be moved at least by my sickness and imprisonment. If none of these elicit your compassion, at least grant me this, because it is so small a request. I want nothing expensive, just a little bread, shelter, a few kind words. If all this leaves you unmoved, at least improve your conduct for the kingdom of heaven's sake, for all the rewards I have promised. Or is this too of no account in your eyes? Well, at least out of natural pity you might feel upset when you see me naked; and remember how I was naked on the cross, which I suffered for your sake; or, if not this, then recall the poverty and nakedness I endure today in the poor. Once I was in fetters for you; I am still in fetters for you, so that whether by those earlier bonds or by these present ones, you might be moved to show some feeling for me. I fasted for you and I go hungry again, still for your sake; I thirsted as I hung upon the cross, and I am thirsty again in the poor of today. In one way or another, I would draw you to myself; for your soul's sake, I would have you compassionate.

"You are bound to me by innumerable favors, and now I ask you to make some return. Not that I demand it as my due. I reward you as though you were acting out generosity; for your trifling gestures, I am giving you a kingdom.

"I do not say: 'Put an end to my poverty,' or 'Make over to me your wealth, although it was for you that I became poor.' All I ask for is a little bread, clothing and a little comfort in my hunger.

"If I am in prison, I do not ask you to set me free of my chains and release me; all I ask is that, for my sake, you should visit someone in prison. This will be favor enough; in return I bestow upon you heaven. I released you from the heaviest chains; it will be enough for me if you visit me in prison.

"I could, of course, reward you without any of this; but I want to be in your debt, so that, along with your reward, you may have confidence in yourself."

RESPONSORY   Matthew 25:35, 40

I was hungry and you gave me food;
I was thirsty and you gave me drink;
I was homeless and you took me in.
—Now I tell you this:
When you did these things for the most neglected of my brothers,
you did them for me.

The man who is merciful to the poor lends to the Lord.
—Now I tell . . .

On solemnities and feasts, Te Deum, 651.

Prayer, as in Morning Prayer.

Morning Prayer

CANTICLE OF ZECHARIAH

Ant. All the world will recognize you as my disciples when they see the love you have one for another.

Prayer

If there is no proper prayer, the following is said:

Lord God,
you teach us that the commandments of heaven
are summarized in love of you and love of our neighbor.
By following the example of Saint N.
in practicing works of charity
may we be counted among the blessed in your kingdom.
Grant this through our Lord Jesus Christ, your Son,

who lives and reigns with you and the Holy Spirit,
one God, for ever and ever.

Evening Prayer II

CANTICLE OF MARY

Ant.   I tell you most solemnly, what you did for the
least of men you did for me. Come, my Father delights in you; receive the kingdom prepared for
you from the foundation of the world.

FOR TEACHERS

Everything is taken from the common of holy men, 1494, or of holy women, 1526, except the following:

Evening Prayer I

CANTICLE OF MARY

Ant. My son, observe your father's commands and do not reject your mother's precepts; keep them close to your heart.

Prayer, as in Morning Prayer.

Office of Readings

SECOND READING

From a homily on the Gospel of Matthew by Saint John Chrysostom, bishop

(Hom. 59: PG 58, 580. 584)

We must be concerned for the children's good

By the words: *Their angels see my Father's face* and *for this purpose have I come,* and *this is my Father's will,* the Lord is calling for greater care from those who are in charge of children.

Do you not see what a protective wall he has built round them? Appalling punishments are threatened for those who cause their downfall; great blessings are promised to those who protect and care for them; and all this is confirmed by the example both he and his Father give. Let us too imitate him and refuse no task, however humble and arduous it may seem, on behalf of those who are our brothers. We may have to serve someone who is small and unimportant, if we undertake this work; the job may be very taxing; mountains and precipices may lie in our way; for the sake of our brothers' salvation everything must be endured. God, after all, cares so much for the soul of man that *he did not spare even his Son.* So, I beg you, from the very moment we leave our homes in the morning, let us have but one aim in view, let this be our chief concern, to rescue anyone who is in danger.

Nothing is as precious as a human soul. *For what does it profit a man if he gains the whole world but suffers the loss of his soul?* Yet the love of money has perverted and destroyed all our values; it has driven out the fear of God and holds our souls in its power, as a tyrant holds a citadel. In consequence we neglect the spiritual welfare of our children and of ourselves in our desire to become richer and leave our wealth to others, who will in their turn leave it to yet others, and they again to their descendants. We are not really owners of our money and other possessions; we merely hand them on. The folly of it! Our children become lower than our slaves. We punish slaves, not for their own good, but for our own advantage; but our children do not profit from our forethought, and in effect are regarded as less valuable than our slaves.

But why talk about slaves? We take less care of our children than our cattle; we worry more about our horses and donkeys than about our sons. If a man owns a mule he takes good care to find the best driver for it, not some scoundrel who is dishonest, drunken and inexperienced. Whereas if our son needs a teacher, we take on the first man who comes along, quite haphazardly and without any selection. Yet no profession is more important than that of teaching.

For what could equal an art which aims at directing the soul and forming the mind and character of a young man? One with these gifts should be more conscientious than any painter or sculptor. Yet we completely neglect all this. The one thing that matters to us is that our son should learn to speak well. And even this we are keen on simply for the sake of making money. He does not study a language primarily to enable him to speak well, but only to enable him to get rich. In fact, if man could become wealthy without being able to speak at all, we would not bother about such lessons.

What a tyranny money exercises! It invades the whole of life forcing men to go where it chooses, like slaves in chains. But what good is our invective? We make a verbal attack on this tyranny; it defeats us by the sheer force of events. Nonetheless, I shall not stop lashing it with my tongue; if my words achieve anything, you and I will both be the gainers; if, however, you remain of the same mind, at least I shall have done my duty.

Still, may God cure you of this disease, and grant me the satisfaction of being able to take pride in you. To him be glory and power for ever and ever. Amen.

RESPONSORY   Proverbs 23:26; 1:9; 5:1

My son, surrender your heart to me
and keep your eyes on my footsteps,
—then I will place a crown of grace on your head.

My son, open your heart to my wisdom,
listen to what I say.
—Then I will . . .

On solemnities and feasts, Te Deum, 651.

Prayer, as in Morning Prayer.

Morning Prayer

CANTICLE OF ZECHARIAH

Ant.   The man of compassion guides and teaches his brothers with the gentle care of the good shepherd for his sheep.

Prayer

If there is no proper prayer, the following is said:

Lord God,
you called Saint N. to serve you in the Church
by teaching his (her) fellow man the way of salvation.
Inspire us by his (her) example:
help us to follow Christ our teacher,
and lead us to our brothers and sisters in heaven.

We ask this through our Lord Jesus Christ, your Son,
who lives and reigns with you and the Holy Spirit,
one God, for ever and ever.

Evening Prayer II

CANTICLE OF MARY

Ant.   Let the little children come to me, for they are at
home in my Father's kingdom.

OFFICE FOR THE DEAD

The prayers are to be adapted in gender and number according to circumstances.

OFFICE FOR THE DEAD

Invitatory

Ant. Come, let us worship the Lord, all things live for
      him.

Invitatory psalm, as in the Ordinary, 648.

Office of Readings

HYMN

Antiphon:

Keep in mind that Jesus Christ has died for us
and is risen from the dead.
He is our saving Lord,
he is joy for all ages.

If we die with the Lord,
we shall live with the Lord.

Antiphon

If we endure with the Lord,
we shall reign with the Lord.

Antiphon

In him all our sorrow,
in him all our joy.

Antiphon

In him hope of glory,
in him all our love.

Antiphon

In him our redemption,
in him all our grace.

Antiphon

In him our salvation,
in him all our peace.

Antiphon

Melody: Keep in Mind   Music: Lucien Deiss, C.S.Sp., 1965
                               Text: Lucien Deiss, C.S.Sp., 1965

Ant.   From the earth you formed me, with flesh you
clothed me; Lord, my Redeemer, raise me up
again at the last day.

Psalm 40:2-14, 17-18

I

I waited, I waited for the Lord
and he stooped down to me;
he heard my cry.

He drew me from the deadly pit,
from the miry clay.
He set my feet upon a rock
and made my footsteps firm.

He put a new song into my mouth,
praise of our God.
Many shall see and fear
and shall trust in the Lord.

Happy the man who has placed
his trust in the Lord
and has not gone over to the rebels
who follow false gods.

How many, O Lord my God,
are the wonders and designs
that you have worked for us;
you have no equal.
Should I proclaim and speak of them,
they are more than I can tell!

You do not ask for sacrifice and offerings,
but an open ear.
You do not ask for holocaust and victim.
Instead, here am I.

In the scroll of the book it stands written
that I should do your will.
My God, I delight in your law
in the depth of my heart.

Glory to the Father . . .

The verse **Glory to the Father** is said at the end of all the psalms
and canticles.

Ant.   From the earth you formed me, with flesh you
clothed me; Lord, my Redeemer, raise me up
again at the last day.

Ant. 2   Lord, may it please you to rescue me; look
upon me and help me.

II

Your justice I have proclaimed
in the great assembly.
My lips I have not sealed;
you know it, O Lord.

I have not hidden your justice in my heart
but declared your faithful help.
I have not hidden your love and your truth
from the great assembly.

O Lord, you will not withhold
your compassion from me.
Your merciful love and your truth
will always guard me.

For I am beset with evils
too many to be counted.
My sins have fallen upon me
and my sight fails me.
They are more than the hairs of my head
and my heart sinks.

O Lord, come to my rescue,
Lord, come to my aid.

O let there be rejoicing and gladness
for all who seek you.
Let them ever say: "The Lord is great,"
who love your saving help.

As for me, wretched and poor,
the Lord thinks of me.
You are my rescuer, my help,
O God, do not delay.

Ant.   Lord, may it please you to rescue me; look upon
        me and help me.

Ant. 3   My soul is thirsting for the living God; when
          shall I see him face to face?

Psalm 42

Like the deer that yearns
for running streams,
so my soul is yearning
for you, my God.

My soul is thirsting for God,
the God of my life;
when can I enter and see
the face of God?

My tears have become my bread,
by night, by day,
as I hear it said all the day long:
"Where is your God?"

These things will I remember
as I pour out my soul:
how I would lead the rejoicing crowd
into the house of God,

amid cries of gladness and thanksgiving,
the throng wild with joy.

Why are you cast down, my soul,
why groan within me?
Hope in God; I will praise him still,
my savior and my God.

My soul is cast down within me
as I think of you,
from the country of Jordan and Mount Hermon,
from the Hill of Mizar.

Deep is calling on deep,
in the roar of waters:
your torrents and all your waves
swept over me.

By day the Lord will send
his loving kindness;
by night I will sing to him,
praise the God of my life.

I will say to God, my rock:
"Why have you forgotten me?
Why do I go mourning
oppressed by the foe?"

With cries that pierce me to the heart,
my enemies revile me,
saying to me all the day long:
"Where is your God?"

Why are you cast down, my soul,
why groan within me?
Hope in God; I will praise him still,
my savior and my God.

Ant.	My soul is thirsting for the living God; when shall
I see him face to face?

Lord, countless are your mercies.
—Give me life according to your word.

First Reading

From the first letter of the apostle Paul
to the Corinthians   15:12-34

The resurrection of Christ is the hope of the faithful

Tell me, if Christ is preached as raised from the dead,
how is it that some of you say there is no resurrection of
the dead? If there is no resurrection of the dead, Christ
himself has not been raised. And if Christ has not been
raised, our preaching is void of content and your faith is
empty too. Indeed, we should then be exposed as false
witnesses of God, for we have borne witness before him
that he raised up Christ; but he certainly did not raise
him up if the dead are not raised. Why? Because if the
dead are not raised, then Christ was not raised; and if
Christ was not raised, your faith is worthless. You are
still in your sins, and those who have fallen asleep in
Christ are the deadest of the dead. If our hopes in Christ
are limited to this life only, we are the most pitiable of
men.

But as it is, Christ is now raised from the dead, the first
fruits of those who have fallen asleep. Death came
through a man; hence the resurrection of the dead comes
through a man also. Just as in Adam all die, so in Christ
all will come to life again, but each one in proper order:
Christ the first fruits and then, at his coming, all those
who belong to him. After that will come the end, when,
after having destroyed every sovereignty, authority, and
power, he will hand over the kingdom to God the Father.

Christ must reign until God has put all enemies under
his feet, and the last enemy to be destroyed is death.
Scripture reads that God "has placed all things under his

feet." But when it says that everything has been made subject, it is clear that he who has made everything subject to Christ is excluded. When, finally, all has been subjected to the Son, he will then subject himself to the One who made all things subject to him, so that God may be all in all.

If the dead are not raised, what about those who have themselves baptized on behalf of the dead? If the raising of the dead is not a reality, why be baptized on their behalf? And why are we continually putting ourselves in danger? I swear to you, brothers, by the very pride you take in me, which I cherish in Christ Jesus our Lord, that I face death every day. If I fought those beasts at Ephesus for purely human motives, what profit was there for me? If the dead are not raised, "Let us eat and drink, for tomorrow we die!" Do not be led astray any longer. "Bad company corrupts good morals." Return to reason, as you ought, and stop sinning. Some of you are quite ignorant of God; I say it to your shame.

RESPONSORY   1 Cor. 15:25-26; see Rv. 20:13, 14

Christ must reign until God has brought all enemies under his feet.
—And the last enemy to be destroyed is death.

Then death and Sheol will give up their dead,
death and Sheol will be cast into the fiery lake.
—And the last . . .

Alternative:

From the first letter of the apostle Paul
to the Corinthians   15:35-57

The resurrection of the dead and the coming of Lord

Perhaps someone will say, "How are the dead to be raised up? What kind of body will they have?" A nonsensical question! The seed you sow does not germinate unless it dies. When you sow, you do not sow the full-blown plant, but a kernel of wheat or some other grain. God gives body to it as he pleases—to each seed its own fruition. Not all bodily nature is the same. Men have one kind of body, animals another. Birds are of their kind, fish are of theirs. There are heavenly bodies and there are earthly bodies. The splendor of the heavenly bodies is one thing, that of the earthly another. The sun has a splendor of its own, so has the moon, and the stars have theirs. Even among the stars, one differs from another in brightness.

So is it with the resurrection of the dead. What is sown in the earth is subject to decay, what rises is incorruptible. What is sown is ignoble, what rises is glorious. Weakness is sown, strength rises up. A natural body is put down and a spiritual body comes up.

If there is a natural body, be sure there is also a spiritual body. Scripture has it that Adam, the first man, became a living soul; the last Adam has become a life-giving spirit. Take note, the spiritual was not first; first came the natural and after that the spiritual.

The first man was of earth, formed from dust, the second is from heaven. Earthly men are like the man of earth, heavenly men are like the man of heaven.

Just as we resemble the man from earth, so shall we bear the likeness of the man from heaven. This is what I mean, brothers: flesh and blood cannot inherit the kingdom of God; no more can corruption inherit incorruption.

Now I am going to tell you a mystery. Not all of us shall fall asleep, but all of us are to be changed—in an instant, in the twinkling of an eye, at the sound of the last trumpet. The trumpet will sound and the dead will be raised incorruptible, and we shall be changed. This corruptible body must be clothed with incorruptibility, this mortal body with immortality. When the corruptible frame takes on incorruptibility and the mortal immortality, then will the saying of Scripture be fulfilled: "Death is swallowed up in victory." "O death, where is your victory? O death, where is your sting?" The sting of death is sin, and sin gets its power from the law. But thanks be to God who has given us the victory through our Lord Jesus Christ.

RESPONSORY   See Job 19:25, 26, 27

I know that my Redeemer lives and on the last day I shall rise again.
—In my body I shall look on God, my Savior.

I myself shall see him; my own eyes will gaze on him.
—In my body . . .

Alternative:

From the second letter of the apostle Paul
to the Corinthians   4:16—5:10

*When the body of our earthly dwelling place lies in death,
we gain an everlasting dwelling place in heaven*

We do not lose heart, because our inner being is renewed each day even though our body is being destroyed at the same time. The present burden of our trial is light enough, and earns for us an eternal weight of glory beyond all comparison. We do not fix our gaze on what is seen but on what is unseen. What is seen is transitory; what is unseen lasts forever.

Indeed, we know that when the earthly tent in which we dwell is destroyed we have a dwelling provided for us by God, a dwelling in the heavens, not made by hands but to last forever. We groan while we are here, even as we yearn to have our heavenly habitation envelop us. This it will, provided we are found clothed and not naked. While we live in our present tent we groan; we are weighed down because we do not wish to be stripped naked but rather to have the heavenly dwelling envelop us, so that what is mortal may be absorbed by life. God has fashioned us for this very thing and has given us the Spirit as a pledge of it.

Therefore we continue to be confident. We know that while we dwell in the body we are away from the Lord. We walk by faith, not by sight. I repeat, we are full of confidence and would much rather be away from the body and at home with the Lord. This being so we make it our aim to please him whether we are with him or away from him. The lives of all of us are to be revealed before the tribunal of Christ so that each one may receive his recompense, good or bad, according to his life in the body.

RESPONSORY

Lord, do not judge me according to my deeds:
I have done nothing worthy in your sight:
therefore I implore you, God of majesty,
—blot out all my guilt.

Lord, wash away my iniquities, and cleanse me from my sins.
—Blot out all my guilt.

SECOND READING

From a sermon by Saint Anastasius of Antioch, bishop

(Oratio 5, de Resurrectione Christi, 6-7. 9: PG 89, 1358-1359. 1361-1362)

Christ will change our lowly body

To this end Christ died and rose to life that he might be Lord both of the dead and of the living. But God is not God of the dead, but of the living. That is why the dead, now under the dominion of one who has risen to life, are no longer dead but alive. Therefore life has dominion over them and, just as *Christ, having been raised from the dead, will never die again,* so too they will live and never fear death again. When they have been thus raised from the dead and freed from decay, they shall never again see death, for they will share in Christ's resurrection just as he himself shared in their death.

This is why Christ descended into the underworld, with its imperishable prison-bars: *to shatter the doors of bronze and break the bars of iron* and, from decay, to raise our life to himself by giving us freedom in place of servitude.

But if this plan does not yet appear to be perfectly realized—for men still die and bodies still decay in death—this should not occasion any loss of faith. For, in receiving the first fruits, we have already received the pledge of all the blessings we have mentioned; with them we have reached the heights of heaven, and we have taken our place beside him who has raised us up with himself, as Paul says: *In Christ God has raised us up with him, and has made us sit with him in the heavenly places.*

And the fulfillment will be ours on the day predetermined by the Father, when we shall put off our childish ways and come to *perfect manhood.* For this is the decree of the Father of the ages: the gift, once given, is to be secure and no more to be rejected by a return to childish attitudes.

There is no need to recall that the Lord rose from the dead with a spiritual body, since Paul in speaking of our bodies bears witness that they are *sown as animal bodies* and *raised as spiritual bodies:* that is, they are transformed in accordance with the glorious transfiguration of Christ who goes before us as our leader.

The Apostle, affirming something he clearly knew, also said that this would happen to all mankind through Christ, *who will change our lowly body to make it like his glorious body.*

If this transformation is a change into a spiritual body and one, furthermore, like the glorious body of Christ, then Christ rose with a spiritual body, a body that *was sown in dishonor,* but the very body that was transformed in glory.

Having brought this body to the Father as the first-fruits of our nature, he will also bring the whole body to fulfillment. For he promised this when he said: *I, when I am lifted up, will draw all men to myself.*

RESPONSORY John 5:28-29; 1 Corinthians 15:52

All who are in their graves shall hear the voice of the Son of God;
—those who have done good deeds will go forth to the resurrection of life;
those who have done evil will go forth to the resurrection of judgment.

In an instant, in the twinkling of an eye, at the final trumpet blast,
the dead shall rise.
—Those who have . . .

Alternative:

From a letter by Saint Braulio, bishop of Saragossa
(Epist. 19: PL 80, 665-666)

The risen Christ is the hope of all Christians

Lazarus our friend is sleeping. In saying this, Christ who is the hope of all believers refers to the departed as those who are asleep. By no means does he regard them as dead.

Paul the apostle does not want us to grieve about those who have fallen asleep. Our faith tells us that all who believe in Christ will never die; indeed faith assures us that Christ is not dead, nor shall we die.

The Lord himself will come down from heaven and there will be the command of the archangel's voice and the sound of the trumpet; then those who were united with Christ in death will rise.

Let the hope of resurrection encourage us, then, because we shall see again those whom we lose here below. Of course, we must continue to believe firmly in Christ; we must continue to obey his commandments. His power is so great that it is easier for him to raise the dead to life than it is for us to arouse those who are sleeping As we are saying all these things some unknown feeling causes us to burst into tears; some hidden feeling discourages the mind which tries to trust and to hope. Such is the sad human condition; without Christ all of life is utter emptiness.

O death! You separate those who are joined to each other in marriage. You harshly and cruelly divide those whom friendship unites. But your power is broken. Your heinous yoke has been destroyed by the One who sternly threatened you when Hosea cried out: *O Death! I shall be your death.* And with the words of the Apostle we, too, deride you: *O death! Where is your victory? O death! Where is your sting!*

Your conqueror redeemed us. He handed himself over to wicked men so that he could transform the wicked into persons who were truly dear to him. It would take too long to narrate all the consolations intended for our benefit in the Scriptures. But by focusing our attention upon the glory of our Redeemer there is sufficient hope for our resurrection. Through faith we know that we are already risen from the dead. The Apostle writes: *If we have died with Christ, we believe that we are at the same time living with him.*

We do not really belong to ourselves; we belong to the One who redeemed us. Our will should always depend on his. For this reason we say in the Lord's Prayer: *Your will be done.* Confronted with death, the sentiments of Job should be our own: *The Lord gave and the Lord took away. May his name be blessed!* Let us repeat here and now what Job said, lest we turn out to be unlike him, when our time comes.

RESPONSORY   1 Thessalonians 4:13-14; Jeremiah 22:10

Concerning those who are asleep, do not be sad like men
  who have no hope;
— for if we believe that Jesus died and rose again,
God will bring forth with Jesus all who have fallen asleep
  believing in him.

Do not weep for the dead,
do not mourn them with tears.
— For if we . . . .

Prayer

Lord, hear our prayers.
By raising your Son from the dead, you have given us
  faith.
Strengthen our hope that N., our brother (sister),
will share in his resurrection.
We ask this through our Lord Jesus Christ, your Son,
who lives and reigns with you and the Holy Spirit,
one God, for ever and ever.

Or:

Lord God,
you are the glory of believers

and the life of the just.
Your Son redeemed us
by dying and rising to life again.
Our brother (sister) N. was faithful
and believed in our own resurrection.
Give to him (her) the joys and blessings
of the life to come.
We ask this through our Lord Jesus Christ, your Son,
who lives and reigns with you and the Holy Spirit,
one God, for ever and ever.

Or:

Lord of mercy,
hear our prayer.
May our brother (sister) N.,
whom you called your son (daughter) on earth,
enter the kingdom of peace and light,
where your saints live in glory.
We ask this through our Lord Jesus Christ, your Son,
who lives and reigns with you and the Holy Spirit,
one God, for ever and ever.

For several people:

God, our creator and redeemer,
by your power Christ conquered death
and returned to you in glory.
May all your people (N. and N.) who have gone before us
   in faith
share his victory
and enjoy the vision of your glory for ever,
where Christ lives and reigns with you and the
   Holy Spirit,
one God, for ever and ever.

For relatives, friends, and benefactors :
Father,
source of forgiveness and salvation for all mankind,
hear our prayer.
By the prayers of the ever-virgin Mary,
may our friends, relatives, and benefactors
who have gone from this world
come to share eternal happiness with all your saints.

We ask this through our Lord Jesus Christ, your Son,
who lives and reigns with you and the Holy Spirit,
one God, for ever and ever.

Morning Prayer

HYMN

Christ the Lord is risen today, Alleluia!
Sons of men and angels say: Alleluia!
Raise your joys and triumphs high; Alleluia!
Sing, ye heavens, and earth reply, Alleluia!

Vain the stone, the watch, the seal; Alleluia!
Christ hath burst the gates of hell: Alleluia!
Death in vain forbids his rise; Alleluia!
Christ hath opened paradise, Alleluia!

Hail, the Lord our earth and heaven! Alleluia!
Praise to thee by both be given; Alleluia!
Thee we greet triumphant now; Alleluia!
Hail, the resurrection Thou! Alleluia! Amen.

Melody: Llanfair 7.7.7.7 with Alleluias   Music: Robert Williams,
1781-1821
Text: Charles Wesley, 1707-1788

Or:

O radiant Light, O sun divine
Of God the Father's deathless face,
O image of the light sublime
That fills the heav'nly dwelling place.

Lord Jesus Christ, as daylight fades,
As shine the lights of eventide,
We praise the Father with the Son,
The Spirit blest and with them one.

O Son of God, the source of life,
Praise is your due by night and day;
Unsullied lips must raise the strain
Of your proclaimed and splendid name.

Melody: Jesu, dulcis memoria,   Music: Traditional Gregorian
Plain Song, L.M.   Melody
                                  Text: *Phos Hilaron*, Greek 3rd cent.
                                  Translator: William G. Storey, 1973.

PSALMODY

Ant. 1   The bones that were crushed shall leap for joy
         before the Lord.

Psalm 51

Have mercy on me, God, in your kindness.
In your compassion blot out my offense.
O wash me more and more from my guilt
and cleanse me from my sin.

My offenses truly I know them;
my sin is always before me.
Against you, you alone, have I sinned;
what is evil in your sight I have done.

That you may be justified when you give sentence
and be without reproach when you judge,
O see, in guilt I was born,
a sinner was I conceived.

Indeed you love truth in the heart;
then in the secret of my heart teach me wisdom.
O purify me, then I shall be clean;
O wash me, I shall be whiter than snow.

Make me hear rejoicing and gladness,
that the bones you have crushed may revive.
From my sins turn away your face
and blot out all my guilt.

A pure heart create for me, O God,
put a steadfast spirit within me.
Do not cast me away from your presence,
nor deprive me of your holy spirit.

Give me again the joy of your help;
with a spirit of fervor sustain me,
that I may teach transgressors your ways
and sinners may return to you.

O rescue me, God, my helper,
and my tongue shall ring out your goodness.
O Lord, open my lips
and my mouth shall declare your praise.

For in sacrifice you take no delight,
burnt offering from me you would refuse,
my sacrifice, a contrite spirit.
A humbled, contrite heart you will not spurn.

In your goodness, show favor to Zion:
rebuild the walls of Jerusalem.
Then you will be pleased with lawful sacrifice,
holocausts offered on your altar.

Ant.   The bones that were crushed shall leap for joy before the Lord.

Ant. 2   At the very threshold of death, rescue me, Lord.

Canticle   Isaiah 38:10-14, 17-20

Once I said,
"In the noontime of life I must depart!

To the gates of the nether world I shall be consigned
for the rest of my years."

I said, "I shall see the Lord no more
in the land of the living.
No longer shall I behold my fellow men
among those who dwell in the world."

My dwelling, like a shepherd's tent,
is struck down and borne away from me;
you have folded up my life, like a weaver
who severs the last thread.

Day and night you give me over to torment;
I cry out until the dawn.
Like a lion he breaks all my bones;
day and night you give me over to torment.

Like a swallow I utter shrill cries;
I moan like a dove.
My eyes grow weak, gazing heaven-ward:
O Lord, I am in straits; be my surety!

You have preserved my life
from the pit of destruction,
when you cast behind your back
all my sins.

For it is not the nether world that gives you thanks,
nor death that praises you;
neither do those who go down into the pit
await your kindness.

The living, the living give you thanks,
as I do today.
Fathers declare to their sons,
O God, your faithfulness.

The Lord is our savior;
we shall sing to stringed instruments

in the house of the Lord
all the days of our life.

Ant.   At the very threshold of death, rescue me, Lord.

Ant. 3   I will praise my God all the days of my life.

Psalm 146

My soul, give praise to the Lord;
I will praise the Lord all my days,
make music to my God while I live.

Put no trust in princes,
in mortal men in whom there is no help.
Take their breath, they return to clay
and their plans that day come to nothing.

He is happy who is helped by Jacob's God,
whose hope is in the Lord his God,
who alone made heaven and earth,
the seas and all they contain.

It is he who keeps faith for ever,
who is just to those who are oppressed.
It is he who gives bread to the hungry,
the Lord, who sets prisoners free,

the Lord, who gives sight to the blind,
who raises up those who are bowed down,
the Lord, who protects the stranger
and upholds the widow and orphan.

It is the Lord who loves the just
but thwarts the path of the wicked.
The Lord will reign for ever,
Zion's God, from age to age.

Ant.   I will praise my God all the days of my life.

Or:

Ant. 3   Let everything that breathes give praise to the
          Lord.

Psalm 150

Praise God in his holy place,
   praise him in his mighty heavens.
Praise him for his powerful deeds,
   praise his surpassing greatness.

O praise him with sound of trumpet,
   praise him with lute and harp.
Praise him with timbrel and dance,
   praise him with strings and pipes.

O praise him with resounding cymbals,
   praise him with clashing of cymbals.
Let everything that lives and that breathes
   give praise to the Lord.

Ant.   Let everything that breathes give praise to the
         Lord.

READING   1 Thessalonians 4:14

If we believe that Jesus died and rose, God will bring
forth with him from the dead those also who have fallen
asleep believing in him.

RESPONSORY

I will praise you, Lord, for you have rescued me.
—I will praise you, Lord, for you have rescued me.

You turned my sorrow into joy,
—for you have rescued me.

Glory to the Father . . .
—I will praise . . .

Canticle of Zechariah

Ant.   I am the Resurrection, I am the Life; to believe in me means life, in spite of death, and all who believe and live in me shall never die.

Intercessions

Let us pray to the all-powerful Father who raised Jesus from the dead and gives new life to our mortal bodies, and say to him:

Lord, give us new life in Christ.

Father, through baptism we have been buried with your Son and have risen with him in his resurrection,

—grant that we may walk in newness of life so that when we die, we may live with Christ for ever.

Provident Father, you have given us the living bread that has come down from heaven and which should always be eaten worthily,

—grant that we may eat this bread worthily and be raised up to eternal life on the last day.

Lord, you sent an angel to comfort your Son in his agony,

—give us the hope of your consolation when death draws near.

You delivered the three youths from the fiery furnace,

—free your faithful ones from the punishment they suffer for their sins.

God of the living and the dead, you raised Jesus from the dead,

—raise up those who have died and grant that we may share eternal glory with them.

Our Father . . .

Prayer

Lord, hear our prayers.
By raising your Son from the dead, you have given us faith.

Strengthen our hope that N., our brother (sister),
will share in his resurrection.

We ask this through our Lord Jesus Christ, your Son,
who lives and reigns with you and the Holy Spirit,
one God, for ever and ever.

Or:

Lord God,
you are the glory of believers
and the life of the just.
Your Son redeemed us
by dying and rising to life again.
Our brother (sister) N. was faithful
and believed in our own resurrection.
Give to him (her) the joy and blessings
of the life to come.

We ask this through our Lord Jesus Christ, your Son,
who lives and reigns with you and the Holy Spirit,
one God, for ever and ever.

Or:

Lord of mercy,
hear our prayer.
May our brother (sister) N.,
whom you called your son (daughter) on earth,
enter the kingdom of peace and light,
where your saints live in glory.

We ask this through our Lord Jesus Christ, your Son,
who lives and reigns with you and the Holy Spirit,
one God, for ever and ever.

For several people:

God, our creator and redeemer,
by your power Christ conquered death
and returned to you in glory.

May all your people (N. and N.), who have gone before
  us in faith,
share his victory
and enjoy the vision of your glory for ever,
where Christ lives and reigns with you and the Holy
  Spirit,
one God, for ever and ever.

For relatives, friends, and benefactors:

Father,
source of forgiveness and salvation for all mankind,
hear our prayer.
By the prayers of the ever-virgin Mary,
may our friends, relatives, and benefactors
who have gone from this world
come to share eternal happiness with all your saints.

We ask this through our Lord Jesus Christ, your Son,
who lives and reigns with you and the Holy Spirit,
one God, for ever and ever.

Daytime Prayer

HYMN

Antiphon:

This I ask: that you love each other
as I have loved you.
I look on you as friends, as friends.

Don't be distressed;
let your hearts be free,
for I leave with you my peace, my word.

Antiphon

If you really love me,
be glad, have hope,
for I leave with you my Spirit to guide you.

Antiphon

Midafternoon

Ant.   Be my salvation, Lord, true to your name, and by
       your mighty power set me free.

READING   Isaiah 25:8

God will destroy death forever;
   the Lord will wipe away
   the tears from all faces;
The reproach of his people he will remove
   from the whole earth;
   for the Lord has spoken.

O God, hear my prayer.
—To you all flesh must come.

Prayer, as in Morning Prayer, 1596-1598.

Evening Prayer

HYMN

   For all the saints who from their labors rest,
   Who thee by faith before the world confessed,
   Thy name, O Jesus, be for ever blest:
      Alleluia, alleluia!

   Thou wast their rock, their fortress and their might;
   Thou, Lord, their captain in the well-fought fight;
   Thou in the darkness drear their one true light:
      Alleluia, alleluia!

   O blest communion, fellowship divine!
   We feebly struggle, they in glory shine;
   Yet all are one in thee, for all are thine:
      Alleluia, alleluia!

   But, lo, there breaks a yet more glorious day
   The saints triumphant rise in bright array:

The King of glory passes on his way:
   Alleluia, alleluia!

Melody: 10.10.10 with Alleluias   Music: R. Vaughan Williams,
                                               1872-1958
                                    Text: William W. How, 1823-1897

Or:

May flights of angels lead you on your way
To paradise, and heav'n's eternal day!
May martyrs greet you after death's dark night,
And bid you enter into Zion's light!
May choirs of angels sing you to your rest
With once poor Laz'rus, now for ever blest!

Melody: Unde et memores   Music: William H. Monk, 1875
10.10.10.10.10.10   Text: James Quinn, S.J., 1969

Or:

I am the bread of Life, he who comes to me shall not
   hunger;
He who believes in me shall not thirst.
No one can come to me unless the Father draw him.

Refrain:

And I will raise him up.
And I will raise him up,
And I will raise him up on the last day.

I am the resurrection, I am the life.
He who believes in me
Even if he die, he shall live for ever.

                        Refrain

Yes, Lord, I believe that you are the Christ,
The Son of God,
The Son of God, who has come into the world.

                        Refrain

I am the way and the truth; I am the life.
No one comes to the Father,

Except he come through me, except he come
through me.

Refrain

Melody: I Am the Bread of Life   Music: S. Suzanne Toolan
Text: S. Suzanne Toolan

PSALMODY

Ant. 1   The Lord will keep you from all evil. He will
guard your soul.

Psalm 121

I lift up my eyes to the mountains:
from where shall come my help?
My help shall come from the Lord
who made heaven and earth.

May he never allow you to stumble!
Let him sleep not, your guard.
No, he sleeps not nor slumbers,
Israel's guard.

The Lord is your guard and your shade;
at your right side he stands.
By day the sun shall not smite you
nor the moon in the night.

The Lord will guard you from evil,
he will guard your soul.
The Lord will guard your going and coming
both now and for ever.

Ant.   The Lord will keep you from all evil. He will
guard your soul.

Ant. 2   If you kept a record of our sins, Lord, who
could escape condemnation?

Psalm 130

Out of the depths I cry to you, O Lord,
Lord, hear my voice!

O let your ears be attentive
to the voice of my pleading.

If you, O Lord, should mark our guilt,
Lord, who would survive?
But with you is found forgiveness:
for this we revere you.

My soul is waiting for the Lord,
I count on his word.
My soul is longing for the Lord
more than watchman for daybreak.
Let the watchman count on daybreak
and Israel on the Lord.

Because with the Lord there is mercy
and fullness of redemption,
Israel indeed he will redeem
from all its iniquity.

Ant.   If you kept a record of our sins, Lord, who could
       escape condemnation?

Ant. 3   As the Father raises the dead and gives them
        life, so the Son gives life to whom he wills.

                   Canticle   Philippians 2:6-11

Though he was in the form of God,
Jesus did not deem equality with God
something to be grasped at.

Rather, he emptied himself
and took the form of a slave,
being born in the likeness of men.

He was known to be of human estate,
and it was thus that he humbled himself,
obediently accepting even death,
death on a cross!

Because of this,
God highly exalted him
and bestowed on him the name
above every other name,

so that at Jesus' name
every knee must bend
in the heavens, on the earth,
and under the earth,
and every tongue proclaim
to the glory of God the Father:
JESUS CHRIST IS LORD!

Ant.   As the Father raises the dead and gives them life,
so the Son gives life to whom he wills.

READING   1 Corinthians 15:55-57

O death, where is your victory? O death, where is your
sting? But thanks be to God who has given us the victory
through our Lord Jesus Christ.

RESPONSORY

In you, Lord, is our hope. We shall never hope in vain.
—In you, Lord, is our hope. We shall never hope in vain.

We shall dance and rejoice in your mercy.
—We shall never hope in vain.

Glory to the Father . . .
—In you, Lord . . .

Or:

Lord, in your steadfast love, give them eternal rest.
—Lord, in your steadfast love, give them eternal rest.

You will come to judge the living and the dead.
—Give them eternal rest.

Glory to the Father . . .
—Lord, in your . . .

CANTICLE OF MARY

Ant. All that the Father gives me will come to me, and whoever comes to me I shall not turn away.

INTERCESSIONS

We acknowledge Christ the Lord through whom we hope that our lowly bodies will be made like his in glory, and we say:

Lord, you are our life and resurrection.

Christ, Son of the living God, who raised up Lazarus, your friend, from the dead,

—raise up to life and glory the dead whom you have redeemed by your precious blood.

Christ, consoler of those who mourn, you dried the tears of the family of Lazarus, of the widow's son, and the daughter of Jairus,

—comfort those who mourn for the dead.

Christ, Savior, destroy the reign of sin in our earthly bodies, so that just as through sin we deserved punishment,

—so through you we may gain eternal life.

Christ, Redeemer, look on those who have no hope because they do not know you,

—may they receive faith in the resurrection and in the life of the world to come.

You revealed yourself to the blind man who begged for the light of his eyes,

—show your face to the dead who are still deprived of your light.

When at last our earthly home is dissolved,

—give us a home, not of earthly making, but built of eternity in heaven.

Our Father . . .

Prayer

Lord, hear our prayers.
By raising your Son from the dead, you have given us
    faith.
Strengthen our hope that N., our brother (sister),
will share in his resurrection.

We ask this through our Lord Jesus Christ, your Son,
who lives and reigns with you and the Holy Spirit,
one God, for ever and ever.

Or:

Lord God,
you are the glory of believers
and the life of the just.
Your Son redeemed us
by dying and rising to life again.
Our brother (sister) N. was faithful
and believed in our own resurrection.
Give to him (her) the joys and blessings
of the life to come.

We ask this through our Lord Jesus Christ, your Son,
who lives and reigns with you and the Holy Spirit,
one God, for ever and ever.

Or:

Lord of mercy,
hear our prayer.
May our brother (sister) N.,
whom you called your son (daughter) on earth,
enter the kingdom of peace and light,
where your saints live in glory.

We ask this through our Lord Jesus Christ, your Son,
who lives and reigns with you and the Holy Spirit,
one God, for ever and ever.

For several people:

God, our creator and redeemer,
by your power Christ conquered death
and returned to you in glory.
May all your people (N. and N.), who have gone before
  us in faith
share his victory
and enjoy the vision of your glory for ever,
where Christ lives and reigns with you and the Holy
  Spirit,
one God, for ever and ever.

For relatives, friends, and benefactors:

Father,
source of forgiveness and salvation for all mankind,
hear our prayer.
By the prayers of the ever-virgin Mary,
may our friends, relatives, and benefactors
who have gone from this world
come to share eternal happiness with all your saints.

We ask this through our Lord Jesus Christ, your Son,
who lives and reigns with you and the Holy Spirit,
one God, for ever and ever.

Night Prayer

All as on Sunday, 1172

APPENDICES

APPENDICES

APPENDIX I

CANTICLES AND GOSPEL READINGS FOR VIGILS

Those who wish to extend the celebration of the vigils of Sundays, solemnities and feasts, according to tradition, first celebrate the Office of Readings. After both readings and before the **Te Deum,** they may add canticles and a gospel reading as indicated below. When a feast of the Lord falls on Sunday, the gospel may be taken either from the current Sunday, as below, or from the feast, in which case the reading is taken from the Lectionary for Mass.

A homily on the gospel may be given. Afterward the **Te Deum** is sung, the prayer is said, and the hour is concluded as in the Ordinary.

PROPER OF SEASONS

Advent Season

CANTICLES

Ant.   Rejoice and sing for joy, daughter of Zion, for I come to live in your midst, says the Lord.

Canticle I   Isaiah 40:10–17

The Good Shepherd: God most high and most wise

See, I come quickly; I have my reward in hand (Revelation 22:12).

> Here comes with power
> the Lord God,
> who rules by his strong arm;
> here is his reward with him,
> his recompense before him.
>
> Like a shepherd he feeds his flock;
> in his arms he gathers the lambs,
> carrying them in his bosom,
> and leading the ewes with care.

1613

Who has cupped in his hand the waters of the sea,
and marked off the heavens with a span?
Who has held in a measure the dust of the earth,
weighed the mountains in scales
and the hills in a balance?

Who has directed the spirit of the Lord,
or has instructed him as his counselor?
Whom did he consult to gain knowledge?
Who taught him the path of judgment,
or showed him the way of understanding?

Behold, the nations count as a drop of the bucket,
as dust on the scales;
the coastlands weigh no more than powder.

Lebanon would not suffice for fuel,
nor its animals be enough for holocausts.
Before him all the nations are as nought,
as nothing and void he accounts them.

Canticle II   Isaiah 42:10–16

God victor and savior

They were singing a new hymn before the throne of God (Revelation 14:3).

Sing to the Lord a new song,
his praise from the end of the earth:

Let the sea and what fills it resound,
the coastlands, and those who dwell in them.
Let the steppe and its cities cry out,
the villages where Kedar dwells;

Let the inhabitants of Sela exult,
and shout from the top of the mountains.
Let them give glory to the Lord,
and utter his praise in the coastlands.

The Lord goes forth like a hero,
like a warrior he stirs up his ardor;
he shouts out his battle cry,
against his enemies he shows his might:

I have looked away, and kept silence,
I have said nothing, holding myself in;
but now, I cry out as a woman in labor,
gasping and panting.

I will lay waste mountains and hills,
all their herbage I will dry up;
I will turn the rivers into marshes,
and the marshes I will dry up.

I will lead the blind on their journey;
by paths unknown I will guide them.
I will turn darkness into light before them,
and make crooked ways straight.

Canticle III   Isaiah 49:7–13
God redeems the people through his Servant

God has sent his only-begotten Son into the world that we might have life through him (1 John 4:9).

Thus says the Lord,
the redeemer and the Holy One of Israel,
to the one despised, whom the nations abhor,
the slave of rulers:

When kings see you, they shall stand up,
and princes shall prostrate themselves
because of the Lord who is faithful,
the Holy One of Israel who has chosen you.

Thus says the Lord:
In a time of favor I answer you,
on the day of salvation I help you,

to restore the land
and allot the desolate heritages,
saying to the prisoners: Come out!
to those in darkness: Show yourselves!

Along the ways they shall find pasture,
on every bare height shall their pastures be.
They shall not hunger or thirst,
nor shall the scorching wind or the sun strike them;
for he who pities them leads them
and guides them beside springs of water.

I will cut a road through all my mountains,
and make my highways level.
See, some shall come from afar,
others from the north and the west,
and some from the land of Syene.

Sing out, O heavens, and rejoice, O earth,
break forth into song, you mountains.
For the Lord comforts his people
and shows mercy to his afflicted.

Ant.   Rejoice and sing for joy, daughter of Zion, for I
come to live in your midst, says the Lord.

Then the gospel of the Resurrection is read.

GOSPEL

First Sunday of Advent

A reading from the holy gospel according to Luke

24:1–12

Why do you seek the living among the dead?

On the first day of the week, at dawn, the women came
to the tomb bringing the spices they had prepared. They
found the stone rolled back from the tomb; but when
they entered the tomb, they did not find the body of the

Lord Jesus. While they were still at a loss over what to think of this, two men in dazzling garments stood beside them.

Terrified, the women bowed to the ground. The men said to them: "Why do you search for the Living One among the dead? He is not here; he has been raised up. Remember what he said to you while he was still in Galilee—that the Son of Man must be delivered into the hands of sinful men, and be crucified, and on the third day rise again." With this reminder, his words came back to them.

On their return from the tomb, they told all these things to the Eleven and the others. The women were Mary of Magadala, Joanna, and Mary the mother of James. The other women with them also told the apostles, but the story seemed like nonsense and they refused to believe them.

Peter, however, got up and ran to the tomb. He stooped down but could see nothing but the wrappings. So he went away full of amazement at what had occurred.

HYMN, Te Deum, 651.

Prayer, as in the Proper, 138.

Conclusion, as in the Ordinary.

Second Sunday of Advent

A reading from the holy gospel according to Luke

24:13–35

Stay with us, for evening is near

Two disciples of Jesus that same day [the first day of the sabbath] were making their way to a village named Emmaus seven miles distant from Jerusalem, discussing as they went all that had happened. In the course of their lively exchange, Jesus approached and began to walk along with them. However, they were restrained from recognizing him.

He said to them, "What are you discussing as you go your way?" They halted, in distress, and one of them, Cleopas by name, asked him, "Are you the only resident of Jerusalem who does not know the things that went on there these past few days?" He said to them, "What things?"

They said: "All those that had to do with Jesus of Nazareth, a prophet powerful in word and deed in the eyes of God and all the people; how our chief priests and leaders delivered him up to be condemned to death, and crucified him. We were hoping that he was the one who would set Israel free. Besides all this, today, the third day since these things happened, some women of our group have just brought us some astonishing news. They were at the tomb before dawn and failed to find his body, but returned with the tale that they had seen a vision of angels who declared he was alive. Some of our number went to the tomb and found it to be just as the women said, but him they did not see."

Then he said to them, "What little sense you have! How slow you are to believe all that the prophets have announced! Did not the Messiah have to undergo all this so as to enter into his glory?" Beginning, then, with Moses and all the prophets, he interpreted for them every passage of Scripture which referred to him.

By now they were near the village to which they were going, and he acted as if he were going farther. But they pressed him: "Stay with us. It is nearly evening—the day is practically over." So he went in to stay with them.

When he had seated himself with them to eat, he took bread, pronounced the blessing, then broke the bread and began to distribute it to them. With that their eyes were opened and they recognized him; whereupon he vanished from their sight. They said to one another, "Were not our hearts burning inside us as he talked to us on the road and explained the Scriptures to us?"

They got up immediately and returned to Jerusalem, where they found the Eleven and the rest of the company assembled. They were greeted with, "The Lord has been raised! It is true! He has appeared to Simon." Then they recounted what had happened on the road and how they had come to know him in the breaking of bread.

HYMN, Te Deum, 651.

Prayer, as in the Proper, 198.

Conclusion, as in the Ordinary.

Third Sunday of Advent

A reading from the holy gospel according to Luke
24:35–53

Was it not right for Christ to suffer in this way and rise from the dead?

The disciples recounted what had happened on the road to Emmaus and how they had come to know Jesus in the breaking of bread.

While they were still speaking about all this, he himself stood in their midst [and said to them, "Peace to you"]. In their panic they thought they were seeing a ghost. He said to them, "Why are you disturbed? Why do such ideas cross your mind? Look at my hands and my feet; it is really I. Touch me, and see that a ghost does not have flesh and bones as I do." As he said this he showed them his hands and feet. They were still incredulous for sheer joy and wonder, so he said to them, "Have you anything here to eat?" They gave him a piece of cooked fish, which he ate in their presence. Then he said to them, "Recall those words I spoke to you when I was still with you: everything written about me in the law of Moses and the prophets and psalms had to be fulfilled." Then he opened their minds to the understanding of the Scriptures.

He said to them: "Thus it is written that the Messiah must suffer and rise from the dead on the third day. In his name, penance for the remission of sins is to be preached to all the nations, beginning at Jerusalem. You are witnesses of this. See, I send down upon you the promise of my Father. Remain here in the city until you are clothed with power from on high."

Then he led them out near Bethany, and with hands upraised, blessed them. As he blessed, he left them, and was taken up to heaven. They fell down to do him reverence, then returned to Jerusalem filled with joy. There they were to be found in the temple constantly, speaking the praises of God.

HYMN, Te Deum, 651.

Prayer, as in the Proper, 257.

Conclusion, as in the Ordinary.

Fourth Sunday of Advent

A reading from the holy gospel according to John

20:1–18

It is right that he should rise from the dead

Early in the morning on the first day of the week, while it was still dark, Mary Magdalene came to the tomb. She saw that the stone had been moved away, so she ran off to Simon Peter and the other disciple (the one Jesus loved) and told them, "The Lord has been taken from the tomb! We don't know where they have put him!"

At that, Peter and the other disciple started out on their way toward the tomb. They were running side by side, but then the other disciple outran Peter and reached the tomb first. He did not enter but bent down to peer in, and saw the wrappings lying on the ground. Presently, Simon Peter came along behind him and entered the tomb. He observed the wrappings on the ground and saw the piece of cloth which had covered the head not lying with the wrappings, but rolled up in a place by itself.

Then the disciple who had arrived first at the tomb went in. He saw and believed. (Remember, as yet they did not understand the Scripture that Jesus had to rise from the dead.) With this, the disciples went back home.

Meanwhile, Mary stood weeping beside the tomb. Even as she wept, she stooped to peer inside, and there she saw two angels in dazzling robes. One was seated at the head and the other at the foot of the place where Jesus' body had lain. "Woman," they asked her, "why are you weeping?" She answered them, "Because the Lord has been taken away, and I do not know where they have put him." She had no sooner said this than she turned around and caught sight of Jesus standing there. But she did not know him.

"Woman," he asked her, "why are you weeping? Who is it you are looking for?" She supposed he was the gardener, so she said, "Sir, if you are the one who carried him off, tell me where you have laid him and I will take him away." Jesus said to her, "Mary!" She turned to him and said [in Hebrew], *"Rabbouni!"* (meaning "Teacher"). Jesus then said: "Do not cling to me, for I have not yet ascended to the Father. Rather, go to my brothers and tell them, 'I am ascending to my Father and your Father, to my God and your God!'"

Mary Magdalene went to the disciples. "I have seen the Lord!" she announced. Then she reported what he had said to her.

HYMN, Te Deum, 651.

Prayer, as in the Proper, 310.

Conclusion, as in the Ordinary.

Christmas Season

CANTICLES

Antiphons

Christmas and Second Sunday after Christmas:

His name will be Emmanuel, which means God-is-with-us.

Holy Family:

Truly you are a hidden God, the God of Israel, the Savior.

Mary, Mother of God:

O how sinless is this Mother, the blessed Virgin Mary: without harm to her virginity she became the Mother of God; without pain she gave birth to Christ Jesus our Savior.

Epiphany:

Today for us the Virgin gave birth to the God of heaven, wise men from the East worship him with their gifts, and all kneel before him in reverence, for he has set us free.

Baptism of the Lord:

The Jordan River trembled as the Lord Jesus entered; from the water rose a new creation to bring light to all the world.

Canticle I   Isaiah 26:1–4, 7–9, 12
      Hymn after the defeat of the enemy

*Jerusalem the Holy City has a great, high wall and twelve
gates* (See Revelation 21:12).

> A strong city have we;
> he sets up walls and ramparts to protect us.
> Open up the gates
> to let in a nation that is just,
> one that keeps faith.

> A nation of firm purpose you keep in peace;
> in peace, for its trust in you.
> Trust in the Lord forever!
> For the Lord is an eternal Rock.

> The way of the just is smooth;
> the path of the just you make level.
> Yes, for your way and your judgments, O Lord,
> we look to you;
> your name and your title
> are the desire of our souls.

> My soul yearns for you in the night,
> yes, my spirit within me keeps vigil for you;
> when your judgment dawns upon the earth,
> the world's inhabitants learn justice.

> O Lord, you mete out peace to us,
> for it is you who have accomplished all we have done.

Canticle II   Isaiah 40:1–8

The coming of the Lord

*The word of the Lord endures for ever. This word has in-
deed been proclaimed to you* (1 Peter 1:25).

> Comfort, give comfort to my people,
> says your God.

Speak tenderly to Jerusalem, and proclaim to her
that her service is at an end,
her guilt is expiated;
indeed, she has received from the hand of the Lord
double for all her sins.

A voice cries out:
In the desert prepare the way of the Lord!
Make straight in the wasteland a highway for our God!
Every valley shall be filled in,
every mountain and hill shall be made low;
the rugged land shall be made a plain,
the rough country, a broad valley.
Then the glory of the Lord shall be revealed,
and all mankind shall see it together;
for the mouth of the Lord has spoken.

A voice says, "Cry out!"
I answer, "What shall I cry out?"
"All mankind is grass,
and all their glory like the flower of the field.
The grass withers, the flower wilts,
when the breath of the Lord blows upon it.
[So then, the people is the grass.]
Though the grass withers and the flower wilts,
the word of our God stands forever."

Canticle III   Isaiah 66:10–14a
Joys of heaven

The heavenly Jerusalem is a free woman and our mother
(Galatians 4:26).

Rejoice with Jerusalem and be glad because of her,
all you who love her;
exult, exult with her,
all you who were mourning over her!

Oh, that you may suck fully
of the milk of her comfort,
that you may nurse with delight
at her abundant breasts!

For thus says the Lord:
Lo, I will spread prosperity over her like a river,
and the wealth of the nations like an overflowing torrent.

As nurslings, you shall be carried in her arms,
and fondled in her lap;
as a mother comforts her son,
so will I comfort you;
in Jerusalem you shall find your comfort.

When you see this, your heart shall rejoice,
and your bodies flourish like the grass.

Christmas and Second Sunday after Christmas:

His name will be Emmanuel, which means God-is-
with-us.

Holy Family:

Truly you are a hidden God, the God of Israel, the Savior.

Mary, Mother of God:

O how sinless is this Mother, the blessed Virgin Mary:
without harm to her virginity she became the Mother of
God; without pain she gave birth to Christ Jesus our Savior.

Epiphany:

Today for us the Virgin gave birth to the God of heaven,
wise men from the East worship him with their gifts, and
all kneel before him in reverence, for he has set us free.

Baptism of the Lord:

The Jordan River trembled as the Lord Jesus entered; from the water rose a new creation, to bring light to all the world.

Then the gospel of the Resurrection is read.

Christmas

Gospel as in the Mass of the Vigil, either the long form: **Matthew 1:1-25**, or the short form: **Matthew 1:18-25.**

Sunday in the Octave of Christmas
Holy Family
Feast

A reading from the holy gospel according to John 20:19-31

The appearance of Jesus after eight days

On the evening of that first day of the week, even though the disciples had locked the doors of the place where they were for fear of the Jews, Jesus came and stood before them. "Peace be wtih you," he said. When he had said this, he showed them his hands and his side. At the sight of the Lord the disciples rejoiced. "Peace be with you," he said again.

"As the Father has sent me,
so I send you."

Then he breathed on them and said:

"Receive the Holy Spirit.
If you forgive men's sins,
they are forgiven them;
if you hold them bound,
they are held bound."

It happened that one of the Twelve, Thomas (the name means "Twin"), was absent when Jesus came. The other disciples kept telling him: "We have seen the Lord!" His answer was, "I will never believe it without probing the nailprints in his hands, without putting my finger in the nailmarks and my hand into his side."

A week later, the disciples were once more in the room, and this time Thomas was with them. Despite the locked doors, Jesus came and stood before them. "Peace be with you," he said; then, to Thomas: "Take your finger and examine my hands. Put your hand into my side. Do not persist in your unbelief, but believe!" Thomas said in response, "My Lord and my God!" Jesus then said to him:

"You became a believer because you saw me.
Blest are they who have not seen and have believed."

Jesus performed many other signs as well—signs not recorded here—in the presence of his disciples. But these have been recorded to help you believe that Jesus is the Messiah, the Son of God, so that through this faith you may have life in his name.

Or one of the gospel readings from the feast which is not read at Mass this year.

HYMN, **Te Deum**, 651.

Prayer, as in the Proper, **423**.

Conclusion, as in the Ordinary.

January 1
Mary, Mother of God.
Solemnity

Gospel from the Common of the Blessed Virgin.

HYMN, **Te Deum**, 651.

Prayer, as in the Proper, **478**.

Conclusion, as in the Ordinary.

Second Sunday after Christmas

A reading from the holy gospel according to John 21:1–14

Jesus appeared and gave them the bread and fish

At the Sea of Tiberias, Jesus showed himself to the disciples [once again]. This is how the appearance took place Assembled were Simon Peter, Thomas ("the Twin"), Nathanael (from Cana in Galilee), Zebedee's sons, and two other disciples. Simon Peter said to them, "I am going out to fish." "We will join you," they replied, and went off to get into their boat. All through the night they caught nothing.

Just after daybreak Jesus was standing on the shore, though none of the disciples knew it was Jesus. He said to them, "Children, have you caught anything to eat?" "Not a thing," they answered. "Cast your net off to the starboard side," he suggested, "and you will find something." So they made a cast, and took so many fish they could not haul the net in.

Then the disciple Jesus loved cried out to Peter, "It is the Lord!" On hearing it was the Lord, Simon Peter threw on some clothes—he was stripped—and jumped into the water. Meanwhile the other disciples came in the boat, towing the net full of fish. Actually they were not far from land—no more than a hundred yards.

When they landed, they saw a charcoal fire there with a fish laid on it and some bread. "Bring some of the fish you just caught," Jesus told them. Simon Peter went aboard and hauled ashore the net loaded with sizable fish—one hundred fifty-three of them! In spite of the great number, the net was not torn.

"Come and eat your meal," Jesus told them. Not one of the disciples presumed to inquire, "Who are you?" for they knew it was the Lord. Jesus came over, took the bread and gave it to them, and did the same with the fish. This marked the third time that Jesus appeared to the disciples after being raised from the dead.

HYMN, Te Deum, 651.

Prayer, as in the Proper, 495.

Conclusion, as in the Ordinary.

January 6

Epiphany

Gospel, as in the Mass of Christmas, John 1:1–18, or from the Mass of the Second Sunday in Ordinary Time, cycle C, John 2:1–12.

HYMN, Te Deum, 651.

Prayer, as in the Proper, 551.

Conclusion, as in the Ordinary.

Sunday after January 6

Baptism of the Lord

A reading from the holy gospel according to Matthew
28:1–10, 16–20

He has risen from the dead and is going before you to Galilee

After the sabbath, as the first day of the week was dawning, Mary Magdalene came with the other Mary to inspect the tomb. Suddenly there was a mighty earthquake, as the angel of the Lord descended from heaven. He came to the stone, rolled it back, and sat on it. In appearance he resembled a flash of lightning while his garments were as dazzling as snow. The guards grew paralyzed with fear of him and fell down like dead men.

Then the angel spoke, addressing the women: "Do not be frightened. I know you are looking for Jesus the crucified, but he is not here. He has been raised, exactly as he promised. Come and see the place where he was laid. Then go quickly and tell his disciples: 'He has been raised from the dead and now goes ahead of you to Galilee, where you will see him.' That is the message I have for you."

They hurried away from the tomb half-overjoyed, half-fearful, and ran to carry the good news to his disciples. Suddenly, without warning, Jesus stood before them and said, "Peace!" The women came up and embraced his feet and did him homage. At this Jesus said to them, "Do not be afraid! Go and carry the news to my brothers that they are to go to Galilee, where they will see me."

The eleven disciples made their way to Galilee, to the mountain to which Jesus had summoned them. At the sight of him, those who had entertained doubts fell down in homage.

Jesus came forward and addressed them in these words:

"Full authority has been given to me
both in heaven and on earth;
go, therefore, and make disciples of all the nations.
Baptize them in the name
'of the Father,
and of the Son, and of the Holy Spirit.'
Teach them to carry out everything I have commanded you.
And know that I am with you always, until the end of the world!"

Or one of the gospel readings from the feast which is not read at Mass this year.

HYMN, **Te Deum, 651.**

Prayer, as in the Proper, **627.**

Conclusion, as in the Ordinary.

PROPER OF SAINTS

December 8
Immaculate Conception

Ant. Hail, rose of paradise, brought to blossom in the enduring love of the Lord our God; hail, bride of the Spirit, adorned in costly gold; hail, virgin Mother, more pleasing to God than all the radiant choirs of angels.

Canticles from the Common of the Blessed Virgin, 1634.

Gospel from the Common of the Blessed Virgin from the Lectionary for Mass.

Hymn, Te Deum, 651.

Prayer, as in the Proper, 1233.

Conclusion, as in the Ordinary.

COMMONS

For the dedication of a church and in the commons for the saints, the gospel is taken from one of the readings which is not read at Mass this year.

Common of the Dedication of a Church

Ant. Blessed are you, Lord, in the holy temple of your glory, a holy place built to the honor and glory of your name, alleluia.

Canticle I   Tobit 13:8–11, 13–15

The future glory of Jerusalem

You have come to Mount Zion, to the city of the living God (Hebrews 12:22).

Let all men speak of the Lord's majesty.
and sing his praises in Jerusalem.

O Jerusalem, holy city,
he scourged you for the works of your hands.
but will again pity the children of the righteous.

Praise the Lord for his goodness,
and bless the King of the ages,
so that his tent may be rebuilt in you with joy.

May he gladden within you all who were captives;
all who were ravaged may he cherish within you
for all generations to come.

A bright light will shine to all parts of the earth;
many nations shall come to your from afar,
and the inhabitants of all the limits of the earth,
drawn to you by the name of the Lord God,
bearing in their hands their gifts for the King of
heaven.

Every generation shall give joyful praise in you,
and shall call you the chosen one,
through all ages forever.

Go, then, rejoice over the children of the righteous,
who shall all be gathered together
and shall bless the Lord of the ages.

Happy are those who love you,
and happy those who rejoice in your prosperity.

Happy are all the men who shall grieve over you,
over all your chastisements,

for they shall rejoice in you
as they behold all your joy forever.

My spirit blesses the Lord, the great King.

Canticle II   Isaiah 2:2–3

All the nations shall come to the house of the Lord

*The kings of the earth will bring glory and honor to Jerusa-
lem, the holy city* (Revelation 21:24).

> In days to come,
> the mountain of the Lord's house
> shall be established as the highest mountain
> and raised above the hills.
> All nations shall stream toward it.

> Many peoples shall come and say:
> "Come, let us climb the Lord's mountain,
> to the house of the God of Jacob,
> that he may instruct us in his ways,
> and we may walk in his paths."

> For from Zion shall go forth instruction,
> and the word of the Lord from Jerusalem.

Canticle III   Jeremiah 7:2–7

Walk along the upright paths and I shall dwell with you

*Go first to be reconciled with your brother, and then come and
offer your gift* (Matthew 5:24).

> Hear the word of the Lord,
> all you of Judah
> who enter these gates to worship the Lord.

> Thus says the Lord of hosts, the God of Israel:
> Reform your ways and your deeds,
> so that I may remain with you in this place.

> Put not your trust in the deceitful words:
> "This is the temple of the Lord!
> The temple of the Lord! The temple of the Lord!"

> Only if you thoroughly reform your ways and your
>   deeds;

if each of you deals justly with his neighbor;
if you no longer oppress the resident alien, the orphan and the widow;

if you no longer shed innocent blood in this place,
or follow strange gods to your own harm,
will I remain with you in this place,
in the land which I gave your fathers
long ago and forever.

Ant. Blessed are you, Lord, in the holy temple of your
glory, a holy place built to the honor and glory of
your name, alleluia.

Gospel from the common of the dedication of a church from the
Lectionary for Mass.

HYMN, **Te Deum, 651.**

Prayer, as in the Commons, **1310.**

Conclusion, as in the Ordinary.

Common of the Blessed Virgin Mary

Ant. Be glad, Virgin Mary, for you have deserved to
bear the Christ, the creator of heaven and earth;
you have brought forth the Savior of the world.

Canticle I   Isaiah 61:10—62:3

The prophet rejoices over the new Jerusalem

*I saw the new Jerusalem, the holy city, prepared as a bride
adorned for her bridegroom (Revelation 21:2).*

I rejoice heartily in the Lord,
in my God is the joy of my soul;
for he has clothed me with a robe of salvation,
and wrapped me in a mantle of justice,
like a bridegroom adorned with a diadem,
like a bride bedecked with her jewels.

As the earth brings forth its plants,
and a garden makes its growth spring up,
so will the Lord God make justice and praise
spring up before all the nations.

For Zion's sake I will not be silent,
for Jerusalem's sake I will not be quiet,
until her vindication shines forth like the dawn
and her victory like a burning torch.

Nations shall behold your vindication,
and all kings your glory;
you shall be called by a new name
pronounced by the mouth of the Lord.

You shall be a glorious crown in the hand of the
Lord,
a royal diadem held by your God.

Canticle II   Isaiah 62:4–7
The glory of the new Jerusalem

*Here God lives among men. He will make his home among
them* (Revelation 21:3).

No more shall men call you "Forsaken,"
or your land "Desolate,"
but you shall be called "My Delight,"
and your land "Espoused."
For the Lord delights in you,
and makes your land his spouse.

As a young man marries a virgin,
your Builder shall marry you;
and as a bridegroom rejoices in his bride
so shall your God rejoice in you.

Upon your walls, O Jerusalem,
I have stationed watchmen;

never, by day or by night,
shall they be silent.

O you who are to remind the Lord,
take no rest
and give no rest to him,
until he re-establishes Jerusalem
and makes of it
the pride of the earth.

Canticle III   Sirach 39:13–16a

How praiseworthy are the works of the Lord!

*Thanks to be God who through us is spreading the knowledge
of himself like a pleasant fragrance* (2 Corinthians 2:14).

Listen, my faithful children: open up your petals,
like roses planted near running waters;
send up the sweet odor of incense,
break forth in blossoms like the lily.

Send up the sweet odor of your hymn of praise;
bless the Lord for all he has done!

Proclaim the greatness of his name,
loudly sing his praises,
with music on the harp and all stringed instruments;
sing out with joy as you proclaim:
The works of God are all of them good.

Ant.   Be glad, Virgin Mary, for you have deserved to
        bear the Christ, the creator of heaven and earth;
        you have brought forth the Savior of the world.

Gospel from the common of the Blessed Virgin Mary from the
Lectionary for Mass.

HYMN, Te Deum, 651.

Prayer, as in the Proper.

Conclusion, as in the Ordinary.

Common of Apostles

Ant.   Rejoice and be glad, says the Lord, for your
       names are written in heaven.

Canticle I   Isaiah 61:6–9

The covenant of the Lord with his ministers

God has made us suitable ministers of a new covenant (2 Corinthians 3:6).

> You shall be named priests of the Lord,
> ministers of our God you shall be called.
> You shall eat the wealth of the nations
> and boast of riches from them.
>
> Since their shame was double
> and disgrace and spittle were their portion,
> they shall have a double inheritance in their land,
> everlasting joy shall be theirs.
>
> For I, the Lord, love what is right,
> I hate robbery and injustice;
> I will give them their recompense faithfully,
> a lasting covenant I will make with them.
>
> Their descendants shall be renowned among the na-
>   tions,
> and their offspring among the peoples;
> all who see them shall acknowledge them
> as a race the Lord has blessed.

Canticle II   Wisdom 3:7–9

The future glory of the just

*The just shall shine forth as the sun in the kingdom of their
Father* (Matthew 13:43).

> In the time of their visitation the just shall shine,
> and shall dart about as sparks through stubble;

they shall judge nations and rule over peoples,
and the Lord shall be their King forever.

Those who trust in him shall understand truth,
and the faithful shall abide with him in love:
beccause grace and mercy are with his holy ones,
and his care is with his elect.

Canticle III   Wisdom 10:17–21

God led his people to deliverance

Those who had overcome the beast sang the song of Moses,
the servant of God, and the song of the Lamb (Revelation
15:2, 3).

God gave the holy ones the recompense of their labors,
conducted them by a wondrous road,
and became a shelter for them by day
and a starry flame by night.

He took them across the Red Sea
and brought them through the deep waters—
but their enemies he overwhelmed,
and cast them up from the bottom of the depths.

Therefore the just despoiled the wicked;
and they sang, O Lord, your holy name
and praised in unison your conquering hand—
because Wisdom opened the mouths of the dumb,
and gave ready speech to infants.

Ant.   Rejoice and be glad, says the Lord, for your
names are written in heaven.

Gospel from the common of pastors, or from the Mass of Friday, Week II in Ordinary Time: **Mark 3:13–19.**

HYMN, **Te Deum**, 651.
Prayer, as in the Proper.
Conclusion, as in the Ordinary.

Common of Martyrs

I. FOR SEVERAL MARTYRS

Ant. The Lord shall wipe away every tear from the eyes
of his saints and there shall no longer be mourning, nor crying, nor pain; for all that used to be
has passed away.

Canticle I   Wisdom 3:1–6

The souls of the just are in the hands of God

Blessed are the dead who die in the Lord. Now . . . let
them rest from their labors (Revelation 14:13).

The souls of the just are in the hand of God,
and no torment shall touch them.

They seemed, in the view of the foolish, to be dead;
and their passing away was thought an affliction
and their going forth from us, utter destruction.
But they are in peace.

For if before men, indeed, they be punished,
yet is their hope full of immortality;
chastised a little, they shall be greatly blessed,
because God tried them
and found them worthy of himself.

As gold in the furnace, he proved them,
and as sacrificial offerings he took them to himself.

Canticle II   Wisdom 3:7–9

The future glory of the just

The just shall shine forth as the sun in the kingdom of their
Father (Matthew 13:43).

In the time of their visitation the just shall shine,
and shall dart about as sparks through stubble;

they shall judge nations and rule over peoples,
and the Lord shall be their King forever.

Those who trust in him shall understand truth,
and the faithful shall abide with him in love:
because grace and mercy are with his holy ones,
and his care is with his elect.

Canticle III   Wisdom 10:17–21

God leads his people to deliverance

*Those who had overcome the beast sang the canticle of
Moses, the servant of God, and the canticle of the Lamb*
(Revelation 15:2, 3).

God gave the holy ones the recompense of their labors,
conducted them by a wondrous road,
and became a shelter for them by day
and a starry flame by night.

He took them across the Red Sea
and brought them through the deep waters—
but their enemies he overwhelmed,
and cast them up from the bottom of the depths.

Therefore the just despoiled the wicked;
and they sang, O Lord, your holy name
and praised in unison your conquering hand—
because Wisdom opened the mouths of the dumb,
and gave ready speech to infants.

Ant.   The Lord shall wipe away every tear from the eyes
of his saints and there shall no longer be mourning, nor crying, nor pain; for all that used to be
has passed away.

Gospel from the common, from the Lectionary for Mass.

HYMN, **Te Deum,** 651.

Prayer, as in the Proper.

Conclusion, as in the Ordinary.

II. FOR ONE MARTYR

Ant.   I shall fill up in my body what is lacking from the
sufferings of Christ for his body, the Church.

Canticles from the common of holy men and women, as below.

Gospel from the common, from the Lectionary for Mass.

Hymn, **Te Deum, 651.**

Prayer, as in the Proper.

Conclusion, as in the Ordinary.

Common of Holy Men and Women

For a man, a woman, or for several saints:

Ant.   Let your belts be fastened round your waists, and
have your lamps burning ready.

For a virgin:

Ant.   At midnight a cry was made: Behold, the Bridegroom comes; go out to meet him.

Canticle I   Jeremiah 17:7–8

Blessed are those who hope in the Lord

Blessed are they who hear the word of God and keep it (Luke
11:28).

Blessed is the man who trusts in the Lord,
whose hope is the Lord.

He is like a tree planted beside the waters
that stretches out its roots to the stream:

It fears not the heat when it comes,
its leaves stay green;

in the year of drought it shows no distress,
but still bears fruit.

Canticle II   Sirach 14:20; 15:3–5a, 6b

The happiness of the wise man

Wisdom is justified by her children (Luke 7:35).

Happy the man who meditates on wisdom,
and reflects on knowledge.

She will nourish him with the bread of understanding,
and give him the water of learning to drink.

He will lean upon her and not fall,
he will trust in her and not be put to shame.

She will exalt him above his fellows;
and he will inherit an everlasting name.

Canticle III   Sirach 31:8–11

Blessed are those who do not seek after gold

Make for yourselves a never-failing treasure in heaven
(Luke 12:33).

Happy the rich man found without fault,
who turns not aside after gain!

Who is he, that we may praise him?
he, of all his kindred, has done wonders,
for he has been tested by gold and come off safe,
and this remains his glory.

He could have sinned but did not,
could have done evil but would not,
so that his possessions are secure,
and the assembly recounts his praises.

For a man, a woman, or for several saints:

Ant.   Let your belts be fastened round your waists, and
        have your lamps burning ready.

For a virgin:

Ant.   At midnight a cry was made: Behold, the Bride-
        groom comes; go out to meet him.

Gospel from the common of holy men and women, from the
Lectionary for Mass.

HYMN, Te Deum, 651.

Prayer, as in the Proper.

Conclusion, as in the Ordinary.

APPENDIX II

SHORTER FORMS OF THE INTERCESSIONS TO BE USED AT EVENING PRAYER

These very brief intercessory prayers may be used at Evening Prayer in the place of the longer form. If one chooses, the names of particular persons may be joined to the appropriate petitions.

Sunday

Let us pray to God who cares for all, and with earnest humility say:

Have mercy on your people, Lord.

Guard the Church,
Protect Pope N.
Aid our bishop N.
Save your people.
Preserve us in peace.
Enlighten those who do not believe.
Guide the rulers of nations.
Bring assistance to those in want.
Comfort those who are troubled.
Be compassionate toward orphans.
Grant consolation to the dead.

Monday

Let us pray to God who cares for all, and with earnest humility say:

Come to your people, Lord.

Assist your Church.
Preserve N. our Pope.
Protect our bishop N.
Direct those who preach the Gospel.

Clothe your priests with holiness.
Strengthen religious men and women in their pursuit of
    holiness.
Bring an end to strife and hatred.
Nourish children by your loving care.
Enable young people to grow in wisdom.
Support and give solace to the aged.
Grant blessings to those we love.
Admit those who have died into the company of the saints.

Tuesday

Let us pray to God who cares for all, and with earnest
humility say:

Hear us, Lord.

Be mindful of your Church.
Defend our Holy Father Pope N.
Aid our bishop N.
Assist our nation.
Reward those who have been good to us.
Keep married couples one in love.
Guide parents in the fulfillment of their responsibilities.
Give work to the unemployed.
Grant assistance to those in need.
Be a helper to the poor.
Shield those who endure persecution.
Bring home those who have wandered.
Give unending glory to those who have died.

Wednesday

Let us pray to God who cares for all, and with earnest
humility say:

Lord, save your people.

Make the Church for ever new.
Grant your gifts to N. our Pope.
Aid our bishop N.
Preserve peace among the nations.
Fill every home with your presence.
Be mindful of this community (congregation).
Further justice.
Give full harvests to farmers.
Be a companion to those who are traveling.
Assist workers by your presence.
Aid widows.
Grant eternal life to those who have gone before us.

Thursday

Let us pray to God who cares for all, and with earnest humility say:

Lord, in you we place our trust.

Preserve the unity of your Church.
Be a source of vibrant life to N. our Pope.
Enlighten N. our bishop.
Call new workers to gather the harvest.
Fill our families with blessings.
Grant health to the sick.
Be present to those who are dying.
Bring exiles back to their homeland.
Guard us from natural disasters.
Give us clean air.
Give us rain as we need it.
Give unfailing life to those who have died.

Friday

Let us pray to God who cares for all, and with earnest humility say:

Lord, in you we place our trust.

Bring your Church to perfection.
Watch over N. our Pope.
Aid N. our bishop.
Guide the college of bishops.
Give shelter to the homeless.
Give food to the hungry.
Enlighten those who go in darkness.
Be a source of consoling support to the aged.
Strengthen those consecrated to a life of virginity.
Call your chosen people to the new Covenant.
Give wisdom to those who make our laws.
Strengthen those who are tempted.
Give unfailing light to those who have died.

Saturday

Let us pray to God who cares for all, and with earnest humility say:

Come to the aid of your people, Lord.

Gather all men into your Church.
Preserve N. our Pope.
Protect and bless N. our bishop.
Guide priests with your hand.
Further holiness among the laity.
Assist workers.
Help those who have gifts to use them in your service.
Be a strong helper to the defenseless.
Grant deliverance to captives.
Guard us from earthquakes.
Save us from a sudden death.
Bring those who have died into the light of your presence.

APPENDIX III

ADDITIONAL PRAYERS FOR USE AT THE LITURGY OF THE HOURS

The following prayers may be said on the weekdays in Ordinary Time and in votive offices.

1

God our Father,
in your care and wisdom
you extend the kingdom of Christ to embrace the world
to give all men redemption.
May the Catholic Church be the sign of your salvation,
may it reveal for us the mystery of your love,
and may that love become effective in our lives.
Grant this through our Lord Jesus Christ, your Son,
who lives and reigns with you and the Holy Spirit,
one God, for ever and ever.

2

God our Father,
by the promise you made
in the life, death, and resurrection of Christ your Son,
you bring together in your Spirit, from all the nations,
a people to be your own.
Keep the Church faithful to its mission:
may it be a leaven in the world
renewing us in Christ,
and transforming us into your family.
We ask this through our Lord Jesus Christ, your Son,
who lives and reigns with you and the Holy Spirit,
one God, for ever and ever.

3

God our Father,
may your Church always be your holy people,

united as you are one with the Son and the Holy Spirit.
May it be for all the world a sign of your unity and holi-
    ness,
as it grows to perfection in your love.

We ask this through our Lord Jesus Christ, your Son,
who lives and reigns with you and the Holy Spirit,
one God, for ever and ever.

4

Almighty and eternal God,
in Christ your Son
you have shown your glory to the world.
Guide the work of your Church:
help it to proclaim your name,
to persevere in faith
and to bring your salvation to people everywhere.

We ask this through our Lord Jesus Christ, your Son,
who lives and reigns with you and the Holy Spirit,
one God, for ever and ever.

5

God our Father,
in all the churches scattered throughout the world
you show forth the one, holy, catholic and apostolic
    Church.
Through the gospel and the eucharist
bring your people together in the Holy Spirit
and guide us in your love.
Make us a sign of your love for all people,
and help us to show forth
the living presence of Christ in the world,
who lives and reigns with you and the Holy Spirit,
one God, for ever and ever.

6

God our Father,
you send the power of the gospel into the world
as a life-giving leaven.
Fill with the Spirit of Christ
those whom you call to live in the midst of the world
and its concerns;
help them by their work on earth
to build up your eternal kingdom.

We ask this through our Lord Jesus Christ, your Son,
who lives and reigns with you and the Holy Spirit,
one God, for ever and ever.

7

Almighty and eternal God,
you keep together those you have united.
Look kindly on all who follow Jesus your Son.
We are all consecrated to you by our common baptism;
make us one in the fullness of faith
and keep us one in the fellowship of love.

We ask this through our Lord Jesus Christ, your Son,
who lives and reigns with you and the Holy Spirit,
one God, for ever and ever.

8

Lord,
lover of mankind,
fill us with the love your Spirit gives.
May we live in a manner worthy of our calling;
make us witnesses of your truth to all men
and help us work to bring all believers together
in the unity of faith and the fellowship of peace.

Grant this through our Lord Jesus Christ, your Son,
who lives and reigns with you and the Holy Spirit,
one God, for ever and ever.

9

God our Father,
you bring many nations together
to unite in praising your name.
Make us able and willing to do what you ask.
May the people you call to your kingdom
be one in faith and love.

We ask this through our Lord Jesus Christ, your Son,
who lives and reigns with you and the Holy Spirit,
one God, for ever and ever.

10

Lord,
hear the prayers of your people
and bring the hearts of believers together in your praise
and in common sorrow for their sins.
Heal all divisions among Christians
that we may rejoice in the perfect unity of your Church
and move together as one
to eternal life in your kingdom.

Grant this through our Lord Jesus Christ, your Son,
who lives and reigns with you and the Holy Spirit,
one God, for ever and ever.

11

Father,
look with love on your people
and pour out upon them the gifts of your Spirit.
May they constantly grow in the love of truth.
May they study and work together
for perfect unity among Christians.

We ask this through our Lord Jesus Christ, your Son,
who lives and reigns with you and the Holy Spirit,
one God, for ever and ever.

12

Lord,
pour out upon us the fullness of your mercy
and by the power of your Spirit
remove divisions among Christians.
Let your Church rise more clearly as a sign for all the
    nations
that the world may be filled with the light of your Spirit
and believe in Jesus Christ whom you have sent,
who lives and reigns with you and the Holy Spirit,
one God, for ever and ever.

13

God our Father,
you will all men to be saved
and come to the knowledge of your truth.
Send workers into your great harvest
that the gospel may be preached to every creature
and your people, gathered together by the word of life
and strengthened by the power of the sacraments,
may advance in the way of salvation and love.

We ask this through our Lord Jesus Christ, your Son,
who lives and reigns with you and the Holy Spirit,
one God, for ever and ever.

14

God our Father,
you sent your Son into the world to be its true light.
Pour out the Spirit he promised us
to sow the truth in men's hearts
and awaken in them obedience to the faith.
May all men be born again to new life in baptism
and enter the fellowship of your one holy people.

Grant this through our Lord Jesus Christ, your Son,
who lives and reigns with you and the Holy Spirit,
one God, for ever and ever.

15

Father,
you will your Church to be the sacrament of salvation for
    all peoples.
Make us feel more urgently
the call to work for the salvation of all men,
until you have made us all one people.
Inspire the hearts of all your people
to continue the saving work of Christ everywhere
until the end of the world.

Grant this through our Lord Jesus Christ, your Son,
who lives and reigns with you and the Holy Spirit,
one God, for ever and ever.

16

Lord,
pour out on us the spirit of understanding, truth, and
    peace.
Help us to strive with all our hearts
to know what is pleasing to you,
and when we know your will
make us determined to do it.

We ask this through our Lord Jesus Christ, your Son,
who lives and reigns with you and the Holy Spirit,
one God, for ever and ever.

17

God our Father,
your Son promised to be with all who gather in his name.
Make us aware of his presence among us
and fill us with his grace, mercy, and peace,
so that we may live in truth and love.

Grant this through our Lord Jesus Christ, your Son,
who lives and reigns with you and the Holy Spirit,
one God, for ever and ever.

18

Father,
you have given all peoples one common origin,
and your will is to gather them as one family in yourself.
Fill the hearts of all men with the fire of your love
and the desire to ensure justice for all their brothers and
    sisters.
By sharing the good things you give us
may we secure justice and equality for every human
    being,
an end to all division,
and a human society built on love and peace.
We ask this through our Lord Jesus Christ, your Son,
who lives and reigns with you and the Holy Spirit,
one God, for ever and ever.

19

God our Father,
you reveal that those who work for peace
will be called your sons.
Help us to work without ceasing
for that justice
which brings true and lasting peace.
We ask this through our Lord Jesus Christ, your Son,
who lives and reigns with you and the Holy Spirit,
one God, for ever and ever.

20

Lord,
you guide all creation with fatherly care.
As you have given all men one common origin,
bring them together peacefully into one family
and keep them united in brotherly love.
We ask this through our Lord Jesus Christ, your Son,
who lives and reigns with you and the Holy Spirit,
one God, for ever and ever.

21

God our Father,
creator of the world,
you establish the order which governs all the ages.
Hear our prayer and give us peace in our time
that we may rejoice in your mercy
and praise you without end.

We ask this through our Lord Jesus Christ, your Son,
who lives and reigns with you and the Holy Spirit,
one God, for ever and ever.

22

God of perfect peace,
violence and cruelty can have no part with you.
May those who are at peace with one another
hold fast to the good will that unites them;
may those who are enemies forget their hatred
and be healed.

We ask this through our Lord Jesus Christ, your Son,
who lives and reigns with you and the Holy Spirit,
one God, for ever and ever.

23

God our Creator,
it is your will that man accept the duty of work.
In your kindness may the work we begin
bring us growth in this life
and help to extend the kingdom of Christ.

We ask this through our Lord Jesus Christ, your Son,
who lives and reigns with you and the Holy Spirit,
one God, for ever and ever.

24

God our Father,
by the labor of man you govern

and guide to perfection
the work of creation.
Hear the prayers of your people
and give all men work that enhances their human dignity
and draws them closer to each other in the service of their
  brothers.

We ask this through our Lord Jesus Christ, your Son,
who lives and reigns with you and the Holy Spirit,
one God, for ever and ever.

25

God our Father,
you have placed all the powers of nature
under the control of man and his work.
May we bring the spirit of Christ to all our efforts
and work with our brothers and sisters at our common
  task,
establishing true love and guiding your creation to perfect
  fulfillment.

We ask this through our Lord Jesus Christ, your Son,
who lives and reigns with you and the Holy Spirit,
one God, for ever and ever.

26

God our Father,
our strength in adversity,
our health in weakness,
our comfort in sorrow,
be merciful to your people.
As you have given us the punishment we deserve,
give us also new life and hope as we rest in your kindness.

We ask this through our Lord Jesus Christ, your Son,
who lives and reigns with you and the Holy Spirit,
one God, for ever and ever.

27

All-powerful Father,
God of mercy,
look kindly on us in our suffering.
Ease our burden and make our faith strong
that we may always have confidence and trust
in your fatherly care.

Grant this through our Lord Jesus Christ, your Son,
who lives and reigns with you and the Holy Spirit,
one God, for ever and ever.

28

Father of mercy,
you always answer your people in their sufferings.
We thank you for your kindness
and ask you to free us from all evil,
that we may serve you in happiness all our days.

We ask this through our Lord Jesus Christ, your Son,
who lives and reigns with you and the Holy Spirit,
one God, for ever and ever.

29

God and Father of all gifts,
we praise you, the source of all we have and are.
Teach us to acknowledge always
the many good things your infinite love has given us.
Help us to love you with all our heart and all our strength.

We ask this through our Lord Jesus Christ, your Son,
who lives and reigns with you and the Holy Spirit,
one God, for ever and ever.

30

Lord,
hear the prayers of those who call on you,

forgive the sins of those who confess to you,
and in your merciful love
give us your pardon and your peace.

We ask this through our Lord Jesus Christ, your Son,
who lives and reigns with you and the Holy Spirit,
one God, for ever and ever.

31

Lord,
be merciful to your people
and free us from our sins.
May your loving forgiveness keep us safe
from the punishment we deserve.

We ask this through our Lord Jesus Christ, your Son,
who lives and reigns with you and the Holy Spirit,
one God, for ever and ever.

32

Lord,
fill our hearts with the spirit of your charity,
that we may please you by our thoughts,
and love you in our brothers and sisters.

We ask this through our Lord Jesus Christ, your Son,
who lives and reigns with you and the Holy Spirit,
one God, for ever and ever.

33

God our Father,
source of unity and love,
make your faithful people one in heart and mind
that your Church may live in harmony,
be steadfast in its profession of faith,
and secure in unity.

We ask this through our Lord Jesus Christ, your Son,
who lives and reigns with you and the Holy Spirit,
one God, for ever and ever.

POETRY

I Sing of a Maiden

I sing of a maiden
That is matchless;
King of all kings,
For her son she chose.

He came all so still
Where his mother was,
As dew in April
That falleth on the grass.

He came all so still
To his mother's bowr,
As dew in April
That falleth on the flower.

He came all so still
Where his mother lay,
As dew in April
That falleth on the spray.

Mother and maiden
Was never none but she;
Well may such a lady
Godes mother be.

Anonymous

The Bellman's Good-Morrow

From sluggish sleep and slumber
  good Christians all arise

for Christ his sake I pray you
  lift up your drowsy eyes
The night of shame and sorrow
  is parting clean away
God give you all good morrow
  and send you happy day

from all the rage of wickedness
  look that you strip you quite
in garments of true godliness
  see that your selves be dight
Shake off all shame and sorrow
  which doth your souls destroy
God give you all good morrow:
  and send you happy day

And being thus attired
  you may in peace proceed
Unto the heavenly table
  of Christ our lord indeed
Where neither shame nor sorrow
  shall you in aught annoy
God give you all good morrow
  and send you happy day

Then looke your lamps be ready
  and that with oil of store
to wait upon the bridegroom
  even at his Chamber door
Where neither shame nor sorrow
  shall you in aught annoy
God give you all good morrow:
  and send you happy day

Then shall you rest in blessedness
  which never shall have end

enjoying Christ his presence
   our sweet and surest friend
where neither shame nor sorrow
   shall you in aught annoy
God give you all good morrow:
   and send you happy day

Thus with my bell, and lantern
   I bid you all farewell
and keep in your remembrance
   the sounding of my bell
lest that with sin and sorrow
   you do your selves destroy
God give you all good morrow
   & send you happy joy.

Anonymous, 16th Century

The Incarnation

Then He summoned an archangel,
Saint Gabriel: and when he came,
Sent him forth to find a maiden,
   Mary was her name.

Only through her consenting love
Could the mystery be preferred
That the Trinity in human
   Flesh might clothe the Word.

Though the three Persons worked the wonder
It only happened in the One.
So was the Word made incarnation
   In Mary's womb, a son.

So He who only had a Father
Now had a Mother undefiled,
Though not as ordinary maids
    Had she conceived the Child.

By Mary, and with her own flesh
He was clothed in His own frame:
Both Son of God and Son of Man
    Together had one name.

Saint John of the Cross
Translator: Roy Campbell

The Nativity of Christ

Behold the father is his daughter's son,
The bird that built the nest is hatched therein,
The old of years an hour hath not outrun,
Eternal life to live doth now begin,
The Word is dumb, the mirth of heaven doth weep,
Might feeble is, and force doth faintly creep.

O dying souls, behold your living spring;
O dazzled eyes, behold your sun of grace;
Dull ears, attend what word this Word doth bring;
Up, heavy hearts, with joy your joy embrace.
From death, from dark, from deafness, from despair:
This life, this light, this Word, this joy repairs.

Gift better than himself God doth not know;
Gift better than his God no man can see.
This gift doth here the giver given bestow;
Gift to this gift let each receiver be.
God is my gift, himself he freely gave me;
God's gift am I, and none but God shall have me.

Man altered was by sin from man to beast;
Beast's food is hay, hay is all mortal flesh.
Now God is flesh and lies in manger pressed
As hay, the brutest sinner to refresh.
O happy field wherein this fodder grew,
Whose taste doth us from beasts to men renew.

Robert Southwell

The Divine Image

To Mercy, Pity, Peace, and Love
All pray in their distress;
And to these virtues of delight
Return their thankfulness.

For Mercy, Pity, Peace, and Love
Is God, our Father dear,
And Mercy, Pity, Peace, and Love
Is man, His child and care.

For Mercy has a human heart,
Pity a human face.
And Love, the human form divine,
And Peace, the human dress.

Then every man, of every clime,
That prays in his distress,
Prays to the human form divine,
Love, Mercy, Pity, Peace.

And all must love the human form,
In heathen, Turk, or Jew:
Where Mercy, Love, and Pity dwell
There God is dwelling too.

William Blake

The Virgin

Mother! whose virgin bosom was uncrost
With the least shade of thought to sin allied;
Woman! above all women glorified,
Our tainted nature's solitary boast;
Purer than foam on central ocean tost
Brighten than eastern skies at daybreak strewn
With fancied roses, than the unblemished moon
Before her wane begins on heaven's blue coast;
Thy Image falls to earth. Yet some, I ween,
Not unforgiven the suppliant knee might bend
As to a visible Power, in which did blend
All that was mixed and reconciled in thee
Of mother's love with maiden purity,
Of high with low, celestial with terrene!

William Wordsworth

In the Bleak Mid-Winter

In the bleak mid-winter
  Frosty wind made moan,
Each stood hard as iron,
  Water like a stone;
Snow had fallen, snow on snow,
  Snow on snow,
In the bleak mid-winter
  Long ago.

Our God, Heaven cannot hold him,
  Nor earth sustain;
Heaven and earth shall flee away
  When he comes to reign:

In the bleak mid-winter
  A stable-place sufficed
The Lord God Almighty
  Jesus Christ.

Enough for him, whom cherubim
  Worship night and day,
A breastful of milk
  And a mangerful of hay;
Enough for him, whom angels
  Fall down before,
The ox and ass and camel
  Which adore.

Angels and archangels
  May have gathered there,
Cherubim and Seraphim
  Thronged the air;
But only His mother
  In her maiden bliss
Worshipped the beloved
  With a kiss.

What can I give him,
  Poor as I am?
If I were a shepherd
  I would bring a lamb,
If I were a Wise Man
  I would do my part,
Yet what I can I give Him,
  Give my heart.

Christi

The Pilgrim Way has led to the Abyss.
Was it to meet such grinning evidence
We left our richly odoured ignorance?
Was the triumphant answer to be this?
The Pilgrim Way has led to the Abyss.

We who must die demand a miracle.
How could the Eternal do a temporal act,
The Infinite become a finite fact?
Nothing can save us that is possible:
We who must die demand a miracle.

W. H. Auden

The Flight in the Desert

The last settlement scraggled out with a barbed wire fence
And fell from sight. They crossed coyote country:
Mesquite, sage, the bunchgrass knotted in patches;
And there the prairie dog yapped in the valley;
And on the high plateau the short-armed badger
Delved his clay. But beyond that the desert,
Raw, unslakable, its perjured dominion wholly contained
In the sun's remorseless mandate, where the dim trail
Died ahead in the watery horizon: God knows where.

And there the failures: skull of the ox,
Where the animal terror trembled on in the hollowed eyes;
The catastrophic wheel, split, sandbedded;
And the sad jawbone of a horse. These the denials
Of the retributive tribes, fiercer than pestilence,
Whose scrupulous realm this was.

Only the burro took no notice: the forefoot
Placed with the nice particularity of one

To whom the evil of the day is wholly sufficient.
Even the jocular ears marked time.
But they, the man and the anxious woman,
Who stared pinch-eyed into the settling sun,
They went forward into its denseness
All apprehensive, and would many a time have turned
But for what they carried. That brought them on.
In the gritty blanket they bore the world's great risk,
And knew it; and kept it covered, near to the blind heart,
That hugs in a bad hour its sweetest need,
Possessed against the drawn night
That comes now, over the dead arroyos,
Cold and acrid and black.

This was the first of his goings forth into the wilderness
of the world.
There was much to follow: much of portent, much of
dread.
But what was so meek then and so mere, so slight and
strengthless,
(Too tender, almost, to be touched)—what they ner-
vously guarded
Guarded them. As we, each day, from the lifted chalice,
That strengthless Bread the mildest tongue subsumes,
To be taken out in the blatant kingdom,
Where Herod sweats, and his deft henchmen
Riffle the tabloids—that keeps us.

Over the campfire the desert moon
Slivers the west, too chaste and cleanly
To mean hard luck. The man rattles the skillet
To take the raw edge off the silence;
The woman lifts up her heart; the Infant
Knuckles the generous breast, and feeds.

                                        Brother Antoninus

The Beauty of Creation Bears Witness to God

Question the beauty of the earth,
the beauty of the sea,
the beauty of the wide air around you,
the beauty of the sky;
question the order of the stars,
the sun whose brightness lights the days,
the moon whose splendor softens the gloom of night;
question the living creatures that move in the waters,
that roam upon the earth,
that fly through the air;
the spirit that lies hidden,
the matter that is manifest;
the visible things that are ruled,
the invisible things that rule them;
question all these.
They will answer you:
"Behold and see, we are beautiful."
Their beauty is their confession of God.
Who made these beautiful changing things,
if not one who is beautiful and changeth not?

Saint Augustine

Saint Patrick's Breastplate

I arise to-day
Through a mighty strength, the invocation of the Trinity,
Through belief in the threeness,
Through confession of the oneness
Of the Creator of Creation.

I arise to-day
Through the strength of Christ's birth with His baptism,
Through the strength of His crucifixion with His burial,

Through the strength of His resurrection with His ascen-
    sion,
Through the strength of His descent for the judgment of
    Doom.

I arise to-day
Through the strength of the love of Cherubim,
In obedience of angels,
In the service of archangels,
In hope of resurrection to meet with reward.
In prayers of patriarchs,
In predictions of prophets,
In preachings of apostles,
In faiths of confessors,
In innocence of holy virgins,
In deeds of righteous men.

I arise to-day
Through the strength of heaven:
Light of sun
Radiance of moon,
Splendour of fire,
Speed of lightning,
Swiftness of wind,
Depth of sea,
Stability of earth,
Firmness of rock.

I arise to-day
Through God's strength to pilot me:
God's might to uphold me,
God's wisdom to guide me,
God's eye to look before me,
God's ear to hear me,
God's word to speak for me,

God's hand to guard me,
God's way to lie before me,
God's shield to protect me,
God's host to save me
From snares of devils,
From temptations of vices,
From every one who shall wish me ill,
Afar and anear,
Alone and in a multitude.

I summon to-day all these powers between me and those
    evils,
Against every cruel merciless power that may oppose my
    body and soul,
Against incantations of false prophets,
Against black laws of pagandom,
Against false laws of heretics,
Against craft of idolatry,
Against spells of women and smiths and wizards,
Against every knowledge that corrupts man's body and
    soul.

Christ to shield me to-day
Against poison, against burning,
Against drowning, against wounding,
So that there may come to me abundance of reward.
Christ with me, Christ before me, Christ behind me,
Christ in me, Christ beneath me, Christ above me,
Christ on my right, Christ on my left,
Christ when I lie down, Christ when I sit down, Christ
    when I arise,
Christ in the heart of every man who thinks of me,
Christ in the mouth of every one who speaks of me,
Christ in every eye that sees me,
Christ in every ear that hears me.

I arise to-day
Through a mighty strength, the invocation of the Trinity,
Through belief in the threeness,
Through confession of the oneness
Of the Creator of Creation.

Ascribed to Saint Patrick
Translator: Kuno Meyer

Canticle of the Sun

Oh, Most High, Almighty, Good Lord God, to Thee belong praise, glory, honor and all blessing.

Praised be my Lord God, with all His creatures, and especially our brother the Sun, who brings us the day and who brings us the light: fair is he, and he shines with a very great splendor.

O Lord, he signifies us to thee!

Praised be my Lord for our sister the Moon, and for the stars, the which He has set clear and lovely in the heaven.

Praised be my Lord for our brother the wind, and for air and clouds, calms and all weather, by which Thou upholdest life and all creatures.

Praised be my Lord for our sister water, who is very serviceable to us, and humble and precious and clean.

Praised be my Lord for our brother fire, through whom Thou givest us light in the darkness; and he is bright and pleasant and very might and strong.

Praised be my Lord for our mother the earth, the which doth sustain us and keep us, and bringeth forth divers fruits and flowers of many colors, and grass.

Praised be my Lord for all those who pardon one another
   for love's sake, and who endure weakness and tribulation: blessed are they who peacefully shall endure, for
   Thou, O Most High, wilt give them a crown.

Praised be my Lord for our sister, the death of the body,
   from which no man escapeth. Woe to him who dieth
   in mortal sin. Blessed are those who die in Thy most
   holy will, for the second death shall have no power to
   do them harm.

Praise ye and bless the Lord, and give thanks to Him and
   serve Him with great humility.

Saint Francis of Assisi

Saint Bernard's Prayer to the Virgin Mary
from The Divine Comedy

Maiden and Mother, daughter of thine own Son,
   Beyond all creatures lowly and lifted high,
   Of the Eternal Design the corner-stone!
Thou art she who did man's substance glorify
   So that its own Maker did not eschew
   Even to be made of its mortality.
Within thy womb the Love was kindled new
   By generation of whose warmth supreme
   This flower to bloom in peace eternal grew.
Here thou to us art the full noonday beam
   Of love revealed: below, to mortal sight,
   Hope, that for ever springs in living stream.
Lady, thou art so great and hast such might
   That whoso crave grace, nor to thee repair,
   Their longing even without wing seeketh flight.

Thy charity doth not only him up-bear
　　Who prays, but in thy bounty's large excess
　　Thou oftentimes dost even forerun the prayer.
In thee is pity, in thee tenderness,
　　In thee magnificence, in thee the sum
　　Of all that in creation most can bless.

Dante
Translator: Laurence Binyon

The Measure of Love

If love be strong, hot, mighty and fervent,
There may no trouble, grief or sorrow fall,
But that the lover would be well content
All to endure and think it eke too small,
Though it were death, so might therewithal
The joyful presence of that person get
On whom he hath his heart and love y-set

Thus should of God the lover be content
Any distress or sorrow to endure,
Rather than to be from God absent,
And glad to die, so that he may be sure
By his departing hence for to procure,
After this valley dark, the heavenly light,
And of his love the glorious sight.

Not only a lover content in his heart
But coveteth eke and longeth to sustain
Some labour, incommodity, or smart,
Loss, adversity, trouble or pain:
And of his sorrow, joyful is and fain,
And happy thinketh himself that he may take
Some misadventure for his lovers' sake.

Thus shouldest thou, that lovest God also,
In thine heart wish covet, and be glad
For him to suffer trouble, pain and woe:
For whom if thou be never so woe bestead,
Yet thou ne shalt sustain (be not adread)
Half the dolour, grief and adversity
That he already suffered hath for thee.

Saint Thomas More
after Pico della Mirandola

Lines Written in Her Breviary

Let nothing disturb thee,
Nothing affright thee;
All things are passing;
God never changeth;
Patient endurance
Attaineth to all things;
Who God possesseth
In nothing is wanting;
Alone God sufficeth.

Saint Teresa
Translator: Arthur Symons

A Hymn to God the Father

Wilt Thou forgive that sin where I begun
  Which was my sin, though it were done before?
Wilt Thou forgive that sin through which I run,
  And do run still, though still I do deplore?
    When Thou hast done, Thou hast not done,
      For I have more.

Wilt Thou forgive that sin which I have won
  Others to sin? and made my sin their door?
Wilt Thou forgive that sin which I did shun
  A year or two, but wallowed in a score?
    When Thou hast done, Thou hast not done,
      For I have more.

I have a sin of fear, that when I have spun
  My last thread, I shall perish on the shore;
But swear by Thy self, that at my death Thy Son
  Shall shine as he shines now and heretofore;
    And, having done that, Thou hast done,
      I fear no more.

John Donne

Love

Love bade me welcome; yet my soul drew back,
  Guilty of dust and sin.
But quick-eyed Love, observing me grow slack
  From my first entrance in,
Drew nearer to me, sweetly questioning,
  If I lacked anything.

"A guest," I answered, "worthy to be here."
  Love said, "You shall be he."
"I, the unkind, ungrateful? Ah, my dear,
  I cannot look on thee."
Love took my hand, and smiling did reply,
  "Who made the eyes but I?"

"Truth, Lord, but I have marred them; let my shame
  Go where it doth deserve."

"And know you not," says Love, "who bore the blame?"
　　"My dear, then I will serve."
"You must sit down," says Love, "and taste my meat."
　　So I did sit and eat.

George Herbert

Redemption

Having been tenant long to a rich lord,
　　Not thriving, I resolved to be bold,
　　And make a suit unto him, to afford
A new small-rented lease, and cancel the old.
In heaven at his manor I him sought:
　　They told me there that he was lately gone
　　About some land, which he had dearly bought
Long since on earth, to take possession.
I straight returned, and knowing his great birth,
　　Sought him accordingly in great resorts:
　　In cities, theatres, gardens, parks, and courts.
At length I heard a ragged noise and mirth
　　Of thieves and murderers: there I him espied,
　　Who straight, "Your suit is granted," said, and died.

George Herbert

The Collar

I struck the board, and cry'd, No more;
　　I will abroad.
What? shall I ever sigh and pine?
My lines and life are free, free as the road,
　　Loose as the wind, as large as store.
　　　Shall I be still in suit?

Have I no harvest but a thorn
To let me blood, and not restore
What I have lost with cordial fruit?
      Sure there was wine
Before my sighs did dry it; there was corn
      Before my tears did drown it;
   Is the year only lost to me?
     Have I no bays to crown it?
No flowers, no garlands gay? all blasted,
      All wasted?

Not so, my heart: but there is fruit,
      And thou hast hands.
Recover all thy sigh-blown age
On double pleasures: Leave thy cold dispute
Of what is fit, and not. Forsake thy cage,
      Thy rope of sands,
Which petty thoughts have made, and made to thee
    Good cable, to enforce and draw,
      And be thy law,

While thou didst wink and wouldst not see.
      Away! take heed:
     I will abroad.
Call in thy death's-head there: tie up thy fears.
      He that forbears
  To suit and serve his need,
     Deserves his load.
But as I rav'd and grew more fierce and wild
     At every word,
  Methought I heard one calling, "Child";
    And I reply'd, "My Lord."

George Herbert

The Pulley

When God at first made man,
Having a glass of blessings standing by,
Let us (said he) pour on him all we can:
Let the world's riches, which dispersed lie,
    Contract into a span.

So strength first made a way;
Then beauty flow'd, then wisdom, honour, pleasure:
When almost all was out, God made a stay,
Perceiving that, alone of all his treasure,
    Rest in the bottom lay.

For if I should (said he)
Bestow this jewel also on my creature,
He would adore my gifts instead of me,
And rest in Nature, not the God of Nature:
    So both should losers be.

Yet let him keep the rest,
But keep them with repining restlessness;
Let him be rich and weary, that at least,
If goodness lead him not, yet weariness
    May toss him to my breast.

George Herbert

Peace

My soul, there is a country
    Far beyond the stars,
Where stands a wingéd sentry
    All skilful in the wars:

There above noise and danger
 Sweet Peace sits crowned with smiles,
And One born in a manger
 Commands the beauteous files.
He is thy gracious friend
 And—O my soul, awake!—
Did in pure love descend
 To die here for thy sake.
If thou canst get but thither,
 There grows the flower of Peace,
The Rose that cannot wither,
 Thy fortress, and thy ease.
Leave then thy foolish ranges,
 For none can thee secure,
But one who never changes,
 Thy God, thy life, thy cure.

Henry Vaughan

Lead, Kindly Light

Lead, kindly Light, amid the encircling gloom,
 Lead thou me on;
The night is dark, and I am far from home,
 Lead thou me on.
Keep thou my feet; I do not ask to see
The distant scene; one step enough for me.

I was not ever thus, nor prayed that thou
 Shouldst lead me on;
I loved to choose and see my path; but now
 Lead thou me on.

I loved the garish day, and, spite of fears,
Pride ruled my will: remember not past years.

So long thy power hath blest me, sure it still
Will lead me on
O'er moor and fen, o'er crag and torrent, till
The night is gone,
And with the morn those Angel faces smile,
Which I have loved long since, and lost awhile.

J. H. Newman

God's Grandeur

The world is charged with the grandeur of God.
  It will flame out, like shining from shook foil;
  It gathers to a greatness, like the ooze of oil
Crushed. Why do men then now not reck his rod?
Generations have trod, have trod, have trod;
  And all is seared with trade, bleared, smeared with toil;
  And wears man's smudge and shares man's smell; the
    soil
Is bare now, nor can foot feel, being shod.

And for all this, nature is never spent;
  There lives the dearest freshness deep down things;
And though the last lights off the black West went
  Oh, morning, and the brown brink eastward, springs—
Because the Holy Ghost over the bent
  World broods with warm breast and with ah! bright
    wings.

Gerard Manley Hopkins

I Wake and Feel the Fell of Dark

I wake and feel the fell of dark, not day.
What hours, O what black hours we have spent
This night! what sights you, heart, saw; ways you went!
And more must, in yet longer light's delay.
   With witness I speak this. But where I say
Hours I mean years, mean life. And my lament
Is cries countless, cries like dead letters sent
To dearest him that lives alas! away.

   I am gall, I am heartburn. God's most deep decree
Bitter would have me taste: my taste was me;
Bones built in me, flesh filled, blood brimmed the curse.
   Selfyeast of spirit a dull dough sours. I see
The lost are like this, and their scourge to be
As I am mine, their sweating selves; but worse.

Gerard Manley Hopkins

My Own Heart Let Me More Have Pity On

My own heart let me more have pity on; let
Me live to my sad self hereafter kind,
Charitable; not live this tormented mind
With this tormented mind tormenting yet.
   I cast for comfort I can no more get
By groping round my comfortless, than blind
Eyes in their dark can day or thirst can find
Thirst's all-in-all in all a world of wet.

Soul, self; come, poor Jackself, I do advise
You, jaded, let be; call off thoughts awhile
Elsewhere; leave comfort root-room; let joy size

At God knows when to God knows what; whose smile
's not wrung, see you; unforeseen times rather—as skies
Betweenpie mountains—lights a lovely mile.

Gerard Manley Hopkins

Thou Art Indeed Just, Lord

*Justus quidem tu es, Domine, si disputem tecum:
verumtamen justa loquar ad te: Quare via impiorum
prosperatur? &c.* [Jeremiah xii.i]

Thou are indeed just, Lord, if I contend
With thee; but, sir, so what I plead is just.
Why do sinners' ways prosper? and why must
Disappointment all I endeavour end?
    Wert thou my enemy, O thou my friend,
How wouldst thou worse, I wonder, than thou dost
Defeat, thwart me? Oh, the sots and thralls of lust
Do in spare hours more thrive than I that spend,
Sir, life upon thy cause. See, banks and brakes
Now, leaved how thick! laced they are again
With fretty chervil, look, and fresh wind shakes
Them; birds build—but not I build; no, but strain,
Time's eunuch, and not breed one work that wakes.
Mine, O thou lord of life, send my roots rain.

Gerard Manley Hopkins

St. Malachy

In November, in the days to remember the dead
When air smells cold as earth,
St. Malachy, who is very old, gets up,
Parts the thin curtains of trees and dawns upon our land.

His coat is filled with drops of rain, and he is bearded
With all the seas of Poseidon.
(Is it a crozier, or a trident in his hand?)
He weeps against the gothic window, and the empty
    cloister
Mourns like an ocean shell.

Two bells in the steeple
Talk faintly to the old stranger
And the tower considers his waters.
"I have been sent to see my festival," (his cavern speaks!)
"For I am the saint of the day.
Shall I shake the drops from my locks and stand in your
    transept,
Or, leaving you, rest in the silence of my history?"

So the bells rang and we opened the antiphoners
And the wrens and larks flew up out of the pages.
Our thoughts became lambs. Our hearts swam like seas.
One monk believed that we should sing to him
Some stone-age hymn
Or something in the giant language.
So we played to him in the plainsong of the giant Gregory:
Oceans of Scripture sang upon bony Eire.

Then the last salvage of flowers
(Fostered under glass after the gardens foundered)
Held up their little lamps on Malachy's altar
To peer into his wooden eyes before the Mass began.

Rain sighed down the sides of the stone church.
Storms sailed by all day in battle fleets.
At five o'clock, when we tried to see the sun, the speech-
    less visitor
Sighed and arose and shook the humus from his feet
And with his trident stirred our trees
And left down-wood, shaking some drops upon the
    ground.

Thus copper flames fall, tongues of fire fall,
The leaves in hundreds fall upon his passing
While night sends down her dreadnought darkness
Upon this spurious Pentecost.

And the Melchisedec of our year's end
Who came without a parent, leaves without a trace,
And rain comes rattling down upon our forest
Like the doors of a country jail.

                                        Thomas Merton

Northumbrian Sequence IV

Let in the wind,
Let in the rain,
Let in the moors tonight,

The storm beats on my window-pane,
Night stands at my bed-foot,
Let in the fear,
Let in the pain,
Let in the trees that toss and groan,
Let in the north tonight.

Let in the nameless formless power
That beats upon my door,
Let in the ice, let in the snow,
The banshee howling on the moor,
The bracken-bush on the bleak hillside,
Let in the dead tonight.

The whistling ghost behind the dyke,
The dead that rot in mire,
Let in the thronging ancestors
The unfulfilled desire,
Let in the wraith of the dead earl,
Let in the dead tonight.

Let in the cold,
Let in the wet,
Let in the loneliness,
Let in the quick,
Let in the dead,
Let in the unpeopled skies.

Oh how can virgin fingers weave
A covering for the void,
How can my fearful heart conceive
Gigantic solitude?
How can a house so small contain
A company so great?
Let in the dark,
Let in the dead,
Let in your love tonight.

Let in the snow that numbs the grave,
Let in the acorn-tree,
The mountain stream and mountain stone,
Let in the bitter sea.

Fearful is my virgin heart
And frail my virgin form,
And must I then take pity on
The raging of the storm
That rose up from the great abyss
Before the earth was made,
That pours the stars in cataracts
And shakes this violent world?

Let in the fire,
Let in the power,
Let in the invading might.

Gentle must my fingers be
And pitiful my heart
Since I must bind in human form
A living power so great,
A living impulse great and wild
That cries about my house
With all the violence of desire
Desiring this my peace.

Pitiful my heart must hold
The lonely stars at rest,
Have pity on the raven's cry,
The torrent and the eagle's wing,
The icy water of the tarn
And on the biting blast.

Let in the wound,
Let in the pain,
Let in your child tonight.

                          Kathleen Raine

APPENDIX V

December 12

OUR LADY OF GUADALUPE

Memorial

The shrine of Our Lady of Guadalupe, near Mexico City, is one of the most celebrated places of pilgrimages in North America. On December 9, 1531, the Blessed Virgin Mary appeared to an Indian convert, Juan Diego, and left with him a picture of herself impressed upon his cloak. Devotion to Mary under this title has continually increased, and today she is the Patroness of the Americas. Because of the close link between the Church in Mexico and the Church in the United States this feast was also celebrated in the United States and then placed on the calendar for the dioceses of the United States.

From the common of the Blessed Virgin Mary, 1326, except for the following:

Prayer

God of power and mercy,
you blessed the Americas at Tepeyac
with the presence of the Virgin Mary at Guadalupe.
May her prayers help all men and women
to accept each other as brothers and sisters.
Through your justice present in our hearts
may your peace reign in the world.

We ask this through our Lord Jesus Christ, your Son,
who lives and reigns with you and the Holy Spirit,
one God, for ever and ever.

January 4
ELIZABETH ANN SETON

Memorial

Elizabeth Seton was born on August 28, 1774, of a wealthy and distinguished Episcopalian family. She was baptized in the Episcopal faith and was a faithful adherent of the Episcopal Church until her conversion to Catholicism. In 1794, Elizabeth married William Seton and they reared five children amid suffering and sickness. Elizabeth and her sick husband traveled to Leghorn, Italy, and there William died. While in Italy Elizabeth became acquainted with Catholicism and in 1805 she made her profession of faith in the Catholic Church. She established her first Catholic school in Baltimore in 1808; in 1809, she established a religious community in Emmitsburg, Maryland. After seeing the expansion of her small community of teaching sisters to New York and as far as St. Louis, she died on January 4, 1821 and was declared a saint by Pope Paul VI on September 14, 1975.

From the common of holy women: religious, 1554, except for the following:

Office of Readings

Second Reading

From a conference to her spiritual daughters

Our daily work is to do the will of God

I will tell you what is my own great help. I once read or heard that an interior life means but the continuation of our Savior's life in us; that the great object of all his mysteries is to merit for us the grace of his interior life and communicate it to us, it being the end of his mission to lead us into the sweet land of promise, a life of constant union with himself. And what was the first rule of our

dear Savior's life? You know it was to do his Father's will.
Well, then, the first end I propose in our daily work is to
do the will of God; secondly, to do it in the manner he
wills; and thirdly, to do it because it is his will.

I know what his will is by those who direct me; whatever they bid me do, if it is ever so small in itself, is the
will of God for me. Then do it in the manner he wills it,
not sewing an old thing as if it were new, or a new thing as
if it were old; not fretting because the oven is too hot, or
in a fuss because it is too cold. You understand—not flying and driving because you are hurried, not creeping like
a snail because no one pushes you. Our dear Savior was
never in extremes. The third object is to do his will *because* God wills it, that is, to be ready to quit at any moment and to do anything else to which you may be called. . . .

You think it very hard to lead a life of such restraint unless you keep your eye of faith always open. Perseverance
is a great grace. To go on gaining and advancing every
day, we must be resolute, and bear and suffer as our blessed forerunners did. Which of them gained heaven without
a struggle? . . .

What are our real trials? By what name shall we call
them? One cuts herself out a cross of pride; another, one
of causeless discontent; another, one of restless impatience or peevish fretfulness. But is the whole any better
than children's play if looked at with the common eye of
faith? Yet we know certainly that our God calls us to a
holy life, that he gives us every grace, every abundant
grace; and though we are so weak of ourselves, this grace
is able to carry us through every obstacle and difficulty.

But we lack courage to keep a continual watch over
nature, and therefore, year after year, with our thousand
graces, multiplied resolutions, and fair promises, we run

around in a circle of misery and imperfections. After a long time in the service of God, we come nearly to the point from whence we set out, and perhaps with even less ardor for penance and mortification than when we began our consecration to him.

You are now in your first setout. Be above the vain fears of nature and efforts of your enemy. You are children of eternity. Your immortal crown awaits you, and the best of Fathers waits there to reward your duty and love. You may indeed sow here in tears, but you may be sure there to reap in joy.

RESPONSORY   1 Corinthians 7:29, 30, 31; 2:12

The time is growing short,
so we must rejoice as though we were not rejoicing;
we must work in the world yet without becoming immersed in it,
—for the world as we know it is passing away.
We have not adopted the spirit of the world.
—For the world . . .

Prayer

Lord God,
you blessed Elizabeth Seton with gifts of grace
as wife and mother, educator and foundress,
so that she might spend her life in service to your people.
Through her example and prayers
may we learn to express our love for you
in love for our fellow men and women.
We ask this through our Lord Jesus Christ, your Son,
who lives and reigns with you and the Holy Spirit,
one God, for ever and ever.

January 5

BLESSED JOHN NEUMANN, bishop

Memorial

John Neumann was born in Bohemia on March 20, 1811. Since he had a great desire to dedicate himself to the American missions, he came to the United States as a cleric and was ordained in New York in 1836 by Bishop Dubois. In 1840, he entered the Congregation of the Most Holy Redeemer (Redemptorists). He labored in Ohio, Pennsylvania and Maryland. In 1852, he was consecrated bishop of Philadelphia. There he worked hard for the establishment of parish schools and for the erection of many parishes for the numerous immigrants. Bishop Neumann died on January 5, 1860; he was beatified in 1963.

From the common of pastors, 1428, except for the following:

Office of Readings

SECOND READING

From a letter to Cardinal Barnabo by John Neumann, bishop

(Archives of Propaganda Fide, America Centrale, 1858-1860, Vol. XVIII, fol. 386 v, Neumann to Barnabo, October 1858, as quoted in Michael J. Curley, Venerable John Neumann [Washington, D.C.: Catholic University of America Press, 1950, pp. 325-326]).

I have labored with all my powers to fulfill the duties of my office

Indeed, I have apparently delayed too long in writing to the Holy See the letter promised by the Archbishop of Baltimore in the name of the council. However, this delay was not without reason. For the council was scarcely finished and I was discussing the division of Diocese of Philadelphia and my translation to a new see with one of the Fathers of the council, when the Father intimated to me [that he did not know] whether that could more probably be hoped for, since the Holy See thought that I would resign from the episcopate, or wished to resign. In the same way when the Archbishop of Baltimore informed me of the designation of a coadjutor, he added that in the event that I should persevere in the desire to resign, the Holy See would permit me to give the title of the ecclesiastical property to the same coadjutor.

I was no little disturbed by the fear that I had done something that so displeased the Holy Father that my resignation would appear desirable to him. If this be the case, I am prepared without any hesitation to leave the episcopacy. I have taken this burden out of obedience, and I have labored with all my powers to fulfill the duties of my office, and with God's help, as I hope, not without fruit.

When the care of temporal things weighed upon my mind and it seemed to me that my character was little suited for the very cultured world of Philadelphia, I made known to my fellow bishops during the Baltimore council of 1858 that it seemed opportune to me to request my translation to one or the other see that was to be erected (namely in the City of Pottsville or in Wilmington, North Carolina). But to give up the episcopal career never entered my mind, although I was conscious of my unworthiness and ineptitude; for things had not come to such a pass that I had one or the other reason out of the six for which a bishop could safely ask the Holy Father permission to resign. For a long time I have doubted what should be done. . . .

Although my coadjutor has proposed to me that he would take the new see if it is erected, I have thought it much more opportune and I have asked the Fathers that he be appointed to the See of Philadelphia, since he is much more highly endowed with facility and alacrity concerning the administration of temporal things. Indeed, I am much more accustomed to the country, and will be able to care for the people and faithful living in the mountains, in the coal mines and on the farms, since I would be among them.

If, however, it should be displeasing to His Holiness to divide the diocese, I am, indeed, prepared either to remain in the same condition in which I am at present, or if God so inspires His Holiness to give the whole administration of the diocese to the Most Reverend James Wood, I am equally prepared to resign from the episcopate and to go where I may more securely prepare myself for death and for the account which must be rendered to the Divine Justice.

I desire nothing but to fulfill the wish of the Holy Father whatever it may be.

RESPONSORY   Matthew 25:21, 20

Well done, my good and faithful servant;
you have been faithful in the little tasks I gave you;
now I will entrust you with greater ones.
—Come and share my joy.

Lord, you gave me five coins,
and see, I bring you back double.
—Come and share my joy.

Prayer

Father,
you called blessed John Neumann to labor for the gospel
among the people of the new world.
His ministry strengthened many others in the Christian
    faith:
through his prayers may faith grow strong in this land.

Grant this through our Lord Jesus Christ, your Son,
who lives and reigns with you and the Holy Spirit,
one God, for ever and ever.

Father,
you called blessed John Neumann to labor for the gospel
among the people of the new world.
His ministry strengthened many others in the Christian
faith;
through his prayers may faith grow strong in this land.
Grant this through our Lord Jesus Christ, your Son,
who lives and reigns with you and the Holy Spirit,
one God, for ever and ever.

INDICES

INDEX OF PSALMS

INDEX OF CANTICLES

INDEX OF BIBLICAL READINGS

INDEX OF NON-BIBLICAL READINGS

INDEX OF HYMNS

Antiphons in honor of the Blessed Virgin Mary

ALPHABETICAL INDEX OF CELEBRATIONS

ACKNOWLEDGMENTS

The International Committee on English in the Liturgy, Inc. is grateful to the following for permission to reproduce copyright material:

HYMNS

Acta Foundation, © copyright 1967, for the Rev. Willard F. Jabusch, "The King of glory."

Ampleforth Abbey Trustees, for Ralph Wright O.S.B., "Almighty ruler, God of truth."

Benedictine Nuns of Saint Mary's Abbey, West Malling, Sussex, for "We praise you, Father, for your gift."

Benedictine Nuns of Stanbrook Abbey, from *Stanbrook Abbey Hymnal*, "Eternal Father, through your Word," "In ancient times God spoke to man," "Lord God and Maker of all things," "O God of truth, prepare our minds," "Unto us a child is given," "When Jesus comes to be baptized."

Geoffrey Chapman Publishers, for James Quinn, S. J., "Darkness has faded, night gives way to morning," "Day is done but love unfailing," "Father, Lord of earth and heaven," "May flights of angels lead you on your way," "Now at the daylight's ending," "Now fades all earthly splendor," "Now from the heav'ns descending," "O God of light, the dawning day," "This day God gives me."

J. Curwen & Sons Ltd., Roberton Publications used by permission of G. Schmirer, Inc., for "All creatures of our God and King."

Faber Music Ltd., London, from *New Catholic Hymnal,* © 1971 copyright by Faber Music Ltd., "Breathe on me breath of God" (adapted by Anthony G. Petti), "Christ is made our sure foundation" (adapted by Anthony G. Petti), "Firmly I believe and truly" (adapted by Anthony G. Petti), "God, whose almighty word" (adapted by Anthony G. Petti), "Great Saint Andrew" (adapted by Anthony G. Petti), "Hear the herald voice resounding" (adapted by Anthony G. Petti), "Lord of all being, throned afar" (adapted by Anthony G. Petti), "Lord, your word abiding" (adapted by Anthony G. Petti), "Most ancient of all mysteries" (adapted by Geoffrey Laycock), "Songs of praise the angels sang" (adapted by Anthony G. Petti), "The King of love my shepherd is" (adapted by Anthony G. Petti), "The setting sun now dies away" (translated by Geoffrey Laycock), "This world, my God, is held within your hand" (text by Hamish Swanston), "You holy angels bright" (adapted by Anthony G. Petti), "Your hand, O Lord, has guided" (adapted by Anthony G. Petti).

B. Feldman & Company, London, for Fred Kaan, "We turn to you, O God."

F.E.L. Publications Ltd., 1925 Pontius Avenue, Los Angeles, Cal. 90025, from *The F.E.L. Hymnal,* Third Printing, 1972: No. 120 "Let all on earth their voices raise" © copyright 1965 by F.E.L. Publications, Ltd.; No. 123 "Let us with joy our voices raise" © copyright 1965 by F.E.L. Publications, Ltd.; No. 34 "Lord Jesus Christ, be present now" © copyright 1965 by F.E.L. Publications, Ltd.; No. 73 "The coming of our God" © copyright 1965 by F.E.L. Publications, Ltd.; No. 122 "This is the feast day of the Lord's true witness" © copyright 1965 by F.E.L. Publications, Ltd. Performance clearance through A.S.C.A.P. Copying only permitted by F.E.L. through its "Annual Copy License."

Fides Publishers, Inc., Notre Dame, Indiana, from *Morning Praise and Evensong* © 1973 copyright by Fides Publishers, Inc., "All praise to you, O God, this night," "O radiant Light, O Sun divine."

Brian Foley, "Holy Spirit, come, confirm us."

F.T.T.W.L., Box No. 3672, Rolfe Street, Cranston, Rhode Island, from *For to Those Who Love God* © 1970 copyright by F.T.T.W.L. and Rev. Enrico Garzilli, "Blessed are the poor of heart," "For to those who love God," "This I ask."

H.C.A. Gaunt, "Lord Jesus, once you spoke to men."

G.I.A. Publications, Inc., Chicago, Illinois, from *Worship* © 1971 copyright by G.I.A. Publications, "Love divine, all loves excelling," for S. Suzanne Toolan, "I am the bread of life."

Monsignor Martin B. Hellriegel, for "To Jesus Christ, Our Sovereign King."

David Higham Associates, Ltd., London, from *The Children's Bells,* © copyright by Oxford University Press, for Eleanor Farjeon "Morning has broken," © copyright by David Higham Associates, Ltd.

J. R. Hughes, "O Father, whose creating hand."

Hymn Society of America, New York, N.Y., for W. W. Reid, "Help us, O Lord, to learn," from *Fifteen Christian Education Hymns,* by William W. Reid, Jr. © 1959 copyright by the Hymn Society of America; used by permission.

Jerome Leamon, "Lord Jesus Christ, abide with us."

The Liturgical Conference, Washington D.C., for Gabriel Huck, "The Master came to bring good news."

McLaughlin & Reilly Company, for Jack May, S.J., "With hearts renewed by living faith" and for John Rathensteiner, "God Father, praise and glory."

Earnest Merril, "Rise up, O men of God."

Methodist Publishing House, London, for Albert Bayly, "Lord, whose love in humble service."

Mount Saint Bernard Abbey, Coalville, Leicester, England, "Brightness of the Father's glory."

North America Liturgy Resources, for Huub Oosterhuis, "Song of Salvation."

Oxford University Press, London, for "Ye who own the faith of Jesus," © V.S.S. Coles 1845-1929, from *The English Hymnal;* "Christ is the world's Light, he and none other," and "For the fruits of his creation," © F. Pratt Green 1903- ; "Lord of all hopefulness" and "When Mary brought her treasure," © Jan Struther 1901-1955, from *Enlarged Songs of Praise.*

Search Press, London, for hymn text from *Westminster Hymnal:* for Walter Shewring, "Christ, in whose passion once was sown."

Stainer & Bell Ltd., London, from *Pilgrim Praise* © 1972 copyright by Stainer & Bell Ltd., for Fred Kaan, "When in his own image."

World Library Publications, Inc., 2145 Central Parkway, Cincinnati, Ohio, from *Biblical Hymns and Psalms, Volume I,* © 1965 copyright by World Library Publications, by Rev. Lucien Deiss C.S.Sp., "All you nations," "I saw the new city, Jerusalem," "Keep in mind," "Maranatha! Come O Christ the Lord," "Mother of Holy

Hope," "Sion, sing," "Unto us a child is born," "You are the honor"; from *Biblical Hymns and Psalms, Volume II,* © 1970 copyright by World Library Publications, by Lucien Deiss C.S.Sp., "Joy to you"; for the Rev. M. Quinn, O.P., "O Christ, you are the light and day," "Praise to Mary, heaven's gate"; from *Peoples Mass Book,* © copyright 1965 by World Library Publications, "O Mary of all women," "The earth is full of the goodness of Christ," "You heavens, open from above"; from *Peoples Mass Book* © 1971 copyright, "Behold a Virgin bearing him," "Holy Mary, now we crown you," "Shepherd of souls, in love come, feed us," "Sing Praise to our Creator"; © 1968 copyright by World Library Publications, "Be consoled, my people," by Tom Parker.

RELIGIOUS POETRY

The Clarendon Press, Oxford, for William Wordsworth, "The Virgin" from the *Poetical Works of William Wordsworth* ed. E. de Selincourt and Helen Darbishire, 2nd ed. 1954, Vol. III, p. 373.

Collins Publishers, for Teilhard de Chardin, "Fire in the Earth," from *Hymn of the Universe.*

University of Detroit Press, for Brother Antoninus, "The Flight in the Desert."

Faber and Faber Ltd. and Random House Inc. for W. H. Auden "We Demand a Miracle," from Chorus from "For the Time Being," in *Collected Longer Poems,* copyright by Faber and Faber Ltd. and Random House Inc.

Hamish Hamilton, London, for Kathleen Raine, "Northumbrian Sequent IV," from *Collected Poems of Kathleen Raine,* © 1965 Kathleen Raine.

William Heinemann Ltd., London, for Arthur Symons, "Lines Written in Her Breviary: Let Nothing Disturb Thee," from the *Poems of Arthur Symons.*

Hughes Massie Ltd., for Roy Campbell, "The Incarnation."

Thomas Merton, "St. Malachy," from *Selected Poems.* Copyright 1949 by Our Lady of Gethsemani Monastery. Reprinted by permission of New Directions Publishing Corporation, New York.

Oxford University Press, London for Gerard Manley Hopkins, S.J., "God's Grandeur," "I Wake and Feel the Fell of Dark," "My Own Heart Let Me More Have Pity On," "Thou Art Indeed Just, Lord," taken from the *Oxford Book of English Mystical Verse.*

The Society of Authors and Mrs. Nicolete Gray, for Laurence Binyon, from translations from Dante, "Saint Bernard's Prayer to the Virgin Mary from the Divine Comedy," copyright by Mrs. Nicolete Gray and the Society of Authors, on behalf of the Laurence Binyon Estate.

PSALMS

The complete psalms first published in 1963 by and available through Wm. Collins, Sons & Co., Ltd. In North America through the Paulist Press, Inc. and Collins † World.